THE OXFORD HA

INTERNATIONAL HUMAN RIGHTS LAW

THE OXFORD HANDBOOK OF

INTERNATIONAL HUMAN RIGHTS LAW

Edited by

DINAH SHELTON

OXFORD
UNIVERSITY PRESS

OXFORD
UNIVERSITY PRESS

Great Clarendon Street, Oxford, OX2 6DP,
United Kingdom

Oxford University Press is a department of the University of Oxford.
It furthers the University's objective of excellence in research, scholarship,
and education by publishing worldwide. Oxford is a registered trade mark of
Oxford University Press in the UK and in certain other countries

First published 2013
First published in paperback 2015

Published in the United States of America by Oxford University Press
198 Madison Avenue, New York, NY 10016, United States of America

British Library Cataloguing in Publication Data
Data available

Library of Congress Cataloging in Publication Data
Data available

ISBN 978-0-19-964013-3 (Hbk.)
ISBN 978-0-19-874829-8 (Pbk.)

Table of Contents

PART II HISTORICAL AND LEGAL SOURCES

PART III STRUCTURAL PRINCIPLES

PART IV NORMATIVE EVOLUTION

PART V INSTITUTIONS AND ACTORS

PART VI HUMAN RIGHTS AND GENERAL INTERNATIONAL LAW

PART VII ASSESSMENTS

Table of National Cases

Country Cases

Algeria

Australia

Belgium

Canada

Chile

France

Germany

Greece

India

Ireland

Italy

Kenya

The Netherlands

New Zealand

South Africa

Switzerland

United Kingdom

United States

Zimbabwe

International Cases

African Commission on Human and Peoples' Rights

Claims Commissions (RIAA)

European Court of Human Rights

European Court of Justice

Human Rights Committee

Inter-American Commission of Human Rights

Inter-American Court of Human Rights

International Court of Justice

International Criminal Court

Committee Decisions

Permanent Court of International Justice

World Trade Organization Decisions

Other Tribunals

Other Cases

Table of Treaties, Declarations, and Other International Instruments

Table of Abbreviations

ACP countries	African, Caribbean, and Pacific Group of States
AfChHPR	African Charter on Human and Peoples' Rights
AfCHPR	African Commission on Human and Peoples' Rights
APRM	African Peer Review Mechanism
AU	African Union
AoA	Agreement on Agriculture
TRIPS	Agreement on Trade Related Aspects of Intellectual Property
AAA	American Anthropological Association
ACLU	American Civil Liberties Union
ACHR	American Convention on Human Rights
AFL	American Federation of Labor
AICHR	ASEAN Intergovernmental Commission on Human Rights
ASEAN	Association of South-East Asian Nations
BJP	Bharatiya Janata Party
BIT	Bilateral Investment Treaty
CELS	Center for Legal and Social Studies
CSVR	Centre for the Study of Violence and Reconciliation
CAP	Collective Action Problem
CVR	Comisión de la Verdad y Reconciliación
COI	Commission of Inquiry
CSW	Commission on the Status of Women
CAT	Committee Against Torture
CM	Committee of Ministers
CESCR	Committee on Economic, Social and Cultural Rights
CED	Committee on Enforced Disappearances
CMW	Committee on Migrant Workers
CEDAW	Convention on the Elimination of All Forms of Discrimination against Women
CERD Committee	Committee on the Elimination of Racial Discrimination
CRPD	Convention on the Rights of Persons with Disabilities

CoE	Council of Europe
CTC	Counter-Terrorism Committee
CFI	Court of First Instance
CJEU	Court of Justice of the European Union
DRC	Democratic Republic of the Congo
ECOSOC	Economic and Social Council
ECOWAS	Economic Community of West African States
ESC or ESCR	Economic, Social and Cultural Rights
ECHR	European Convention on Human Rights
ECtHR	European Court of Human Rights
ECJ	European Court of Justice
EU	European Union
FAO	Food and Agricultural Organization
GATT	General Agreement on Tariffs and Trade
GATS	General Agreement on Trade in Services
GA	General Assembly
GDP	Gross Domestic Product
HDI	Human Development Index
IP	Intellectual Property
IACHR	Inter-American Commission on Human Rights
IACtHR	Inter-American Court of Human Rights
IIHR	Inter-American Institute of Human Rights
IGO	Intergovernmental Organization
IAASTD	International Assessment of Agricultural Knowledge, Science and Technology for Development
IALL	International Association for Labor Legislation
ICISS	International Commission on Intervention and State Sovereignty
ICRC	International Committee of the Red Cross
ICFTU	International Confederation of Trade Unions
ICJ	International Court of Justice
ICCPR	International Covenant on Civil and Political Rights
ICESCR	International Covenant on Economic, Social and Cultural Rights
CPED	International Convention for the Protection of All Persons from Enforced Disappearances
CERD	International Convention on the Elimination of All Forms of Racial Discrimination
ICRMW	International Convention on the Protection of the Rights of All Migrant Workers and Members of Their Families

CRPD	International Convention on the Rights of Persons with Disabilities
ICC	International Criminal Court
ICTY	International Criminal Tribunal for the Former Yugoslavia
IFRCRCS	International Federation of Red Cross and Red Crescent Societies
IHRL	International Human Rights Law
IHL	International Humanitarian Law
ILO	International Labour Organization
IMF	International Monetary Fund
LDC	Least Developed Country
LOI	List of Issues
LOIPR	List of Issues Prior to Reporting
MERCOSUR	Mercado Común del Sur
MFN	Most Favored Nation
NAACP	National Association for the Advancement of Colored Peoples
PNC	National Civil Police Force
NHRC	National Human Rights Commission
NHRI	National Human Rights Institutions
NRC	National Research Center
UNITA	National Union for Total Independence of Angola
NGO	Non-Governmental Organization
NAFTA	North American Free Trade Agreement
NATO	North Atlantic Treaty Organization
OLA	Office of Legal Affairs
OPCAT	Optional Protocol to UNCAT
OHCHR	Office of the High Commissioner for Human Rights
OECD	Organization for Economic Co-operation and Development
OSCE	Organization for Security and Co-operation in Europe
OAU	Organization of African Unity
OAS	Organization of American States
OIC	Organization of Islamic Cooperation
PACE	Parliamentary Assembly of the Council of Europe
PCIJ	Permanent Court of International Justice
PoC	Protection of Civilians
RIAA	Reports of International Arbitral Awards
RUDs	Reservations, Understandings, and Declarations
R2P	Responsibility to Protect
SAARC	South Asian Association for Regional Cooperation

SADC	Southern African Development Community
SCSL	Special Court for Sierra Leone
SP	Special Procedure
SPT	Sub-Committee on Prevention of Torture
TOR	Terms of Reference
UNDG	UN Development Group
UK	United Kingdom
UN	United Nations
UNCHR	United Nations Commission on Human Rights
UNCESCR	United Nations Committee on Economic, Social and Cultural Rights
UNCTAD	United Nations Conference on Trade and Development
UNCAT	United Nations Convention against Torture and Other Cruel, Inhuman or Degrading Treatment or Punishment
CRC	United Nations Convention on the Rights of the Child
UNDP	United Nations Development Program
UNESCO	United Nations Educational, Scientific, and Cultural Organization
UNGA	United Nation General Assembly
HRC	United Nations Human Rights Committee
HRCouncil	United Nations Human Rights Council
ILC	United Nations International Law Commission
UNOCI	United Nations Operation in Côte d'Ivoire
UNRISD	United Nations Research Institute for Social Development
UNSC	United Nations Security Council
US	United States
USD	United States Dollar
SCOTUS	United States Supreme Court
UDHR	Universal Declaration of Human Rights
UPR	Universal Periodic Review
VCLT	Vienna Convention on the Law of Treaties
WGHR	Working Group on Human Rights
WB	World Bank
WHA	World Health Assembly
WHO	World Health Organization
WTO	World Trade Organization
WWI	World War I

Notes on the Contributors

Nisuke Ando is Director, Kyoto Human Rights Research Institute (2001–present); Professor Emeritus, Kyoto University, Kyoto, Japan; member, Permanent Court of Arbitration (2001–present); member, Institut de Droit International (1999–present); member, Human Rights Committee under the ICCPR (1987–2006, Chair 1993–94).

Yutaka Arai-Takahashi LLB (Gakui-Juyo Kiko), LLM (Keio), and PhD (Cambridge), is a Reader in International Law and International Human Rights Law at the University of Kent at Brussels (UKB) and the University of Kent at Canterbury (UKC). He specializes in the areas of international human rights law, international humanitarian law, and international criminal law, and his major publications include *The Law of Occupation—the Continuity and Change of International Humanitarian Law, and its Interaction with International Humanitarian Law* (Martinus Nijhoff 2009); '"Scrupulous but Dynamic"—The Freedom of Expression and the Principle of Proportionality under European Community Law' (2005) 24 *Yearbook of European Law* 27–80 (OUP 2006); and 'Preoccupied with Occupation—Critical Examinations of the Historical Development of the Law of Occupation' (2012) 94 *International Review of the Red Cross* 885, 1–30.

Paolo G Carozza is Professor of Law and Director of the Kellogg Institute for International Studies at the University of Notre Dame, where he also directs the Center for Civil and Human Rights and the Law School's JSD programme in international human rights law. From 2006–10, he was a member of the Inter-American Commission on Human Rights and served as its President in 2008–09. His extensive research and writing covers areas in human rights, comparative constitutional law, European and Latin American legal traditions, public international law, and law and human development.

Jarlath Clifford works for Irwin Mitchell LLP in London. Prior to this he was a Legal Officer, and later a consultant, at the Equal Rights Trust where he worked on national and international equality law reform initiatives. He has worked as an Investigator and a Policy Officer for the former British Commission for Racial Equality. He has carried out legal and human rights research for a number of academic institutions and NGOs including the University College London, the British Institute of International and Comparative Law, Amnesty International, and the Center for Policy Alternatives. He has also previously served as Assistant Editor of the *Equal*

Rights Review. He would like to thank Amal de Chickera for his helpful comments on the chapter.

Catherine Cone is a 2013 JD candidate at American University Washington College of Law who served as research assistant to Juan E Méndez. She has worked for the International Center for Transitional Justice in Bogotá, Colombia, and the American Bar Association's Rule of Law Initiative in Washington DC. At her law school, she serves on the *American University Law Review* and founded a mentoring programme for first generation law students.

Janelle M Diller was appointed Deputy Legal Adviser of the International Labour Organization in 2008. Since she joined the ILO in 1998, she has held various positions, including Legal Officer, Principal Legal Officer, and Chief ad interim of the Multinational Enterprises Programme. She also provided advice on international law as a member of the Technical Secretariat of the World Commission on the Social Dimension of Globalization. Prior to joining the ILO, she worked as Legal Director of the International Human Rights Law Group in Washington DC (1990–95) and as Associate to a private multinational law firm in San Francisco (1986–88), and she was appointed to a Federal judicial clerkship in Puerto Rico (1984–86). She has held various teaching positions in international and human rights law, including at Georgetown University Law Center and the University of Virginia School of Law (1993–97), and served as a legal consultant to the United Nations, Inter-American, and other organizations (1988–90, 1995–97).

Siegfried van Duffel is Assistant Professor at Nazarbayev University. He was trained as a philosopher, but completed his PhD in Law at Ghent University Law School. After spending three years as an Assistant Professor at Groningen University, where he taught Ethics and Political Theory, he became a post-doctoral fellow in the National University of Singapore's Department of Philosophy. In 2010, he worked on a research project with the Center of Excellence in Philosophical Psychology, Morality and Politics at the University of Helsinki. He later taught three semesters at the University of Hong Kong and one semester at the National Taiwan University in Taipei. He is widely published, with articles appearing in the *European Journal of Philosophy*, *The Encyclopedia of Political Thought*, and *The Pacific Philosophical Quarterly*, among others. Currently, his main project is to complete a book on human rights and cultural differences, that aims to describe human rights theories as an aspect of the culture in which they were developed.

Malgosia Fitzmaurice is Chair in Public International Law, at the University of London. She is an expert on the law of treaties, international environmental law, and indigenous rights. She has published extensively on all these subjects. She frequently lectures abroad. She is a regular lecturer at the International Maritime Law Institute at Malta and recently completed a series of lectures at Sorbonne Pantheon.

Mark Goodale is an anthropologist, sociolegal scholar, and social theorist. He is currently Associate Professor of Conflict Analysis and Anthropology at George Mason University and Series Editor of Stanford Studies in Human Rights. Before coming to George Mason, he was the first Marjorie Shostak Distinguished Lecturer in Anthropology at Emory University. He is the author or editor of seven books, including, most recently, *Human Rights at the Crossroads* (OUP 2012), *Mirrors of Justice* (with Kamari Maxine Clarke, CUP 2010), *Surrendering to Utopia* (Stanford UP 2009), *Human Rights: An Anthropological Reader* (Blackwell 2009), *Dilemmas of Modernity* (Stanford UP 2008), and *The Practice of Human Rights* (with Sally Engle Merry, CUP 2007). His writings have appeared in *Law & Society Review*, *Law & Social Inquiry*, *Social & Legal Studies*, *Current Anthropology*, *American Anthropologist*, and *American Ethnologist*, among others. He is currently working on a number of new projects, including a study of the constitutional revolution in Bolivia based on several years of research funded by the National Science Foundation and the Wenner-Gren Foundation.

Gisella Gori is currently Senior Political Adviser in the Political, Security, and Development Section of the Delegation of the European Union to the United States, in Washington DC, working on human rights and democracy, UN and multilateralism, international humanitarian law and Guantanamo, and legal issues in general. Since 2002, she has been a lawyer at the Council of Europe's Directorate General of Human Rights and Legal Affairs, Department for the Execution of the Judgments of the European Court of Human Rights, in Strasbourg (currently on sabbatical). She is specialized in European Union (EU) law and in international human rights law and is the author of articles on EU law, economic and social rights, and education law. She previously taught EU law at George Washington University Law School and the University of Strasbourg. She holds a PhD in Law (JD) from the European University Institute.

Ariel Gould is a graduate student in a joint degree programme at the George Washington University Law School and the Elliott School of International Affairs. She received a JD in Law and an MA in Latin American and Hemispheric Studies in May 2014. She received a BA in International Studies and a BA in Spanish from the University of North Carolina at Chapel Hill in 2010. Her main area of focus is the protection of human rights in the Americas.

M Christian Green JD/PhD, holds degrees from Georgetown University in History and Government, Emory University in Law and Theology, and the University of Chicago in Religious Ethics. She has taught at DePaul University, Harvard Divinity School, and the Candler School of Theology at Emory University. She has managed research projects at the Religion, Culture, and Family Project at the University of Chicago, the Park Ridge Center for the Study of Health, Faith, and Ethics. During the 2010–11 academic year, she was a Visiting Research Fellow at the Kroc Institute for International Peace Studies at the University of Notre Dame. She is currently a nonresident Senior Fellow at the Center for the Study of Law and Religion and serves as book review editor for the *Journal of Law and Religion*. Her research interests include law and religion, human rights, gender and family, bioethics, comparative religious ethics, and religion and world affairs. Her research focuses mostly on law, religion, and human rights in Sub-Saharan Africa.

Christof Heyns was appointed United Nations Special Rapporteur on extrajudicial, summary, or arbitrary executions in August 2010. He is Professor of Human Rights Law at the University of Pretoria, and Co-Director of the Institute for International and Comparative Law in Africa. He is an Adjunct Professor at the Washington College of Law of the American University, and teaches in the human rights master's programme at Oxford University, where he is a Visiting Fellow. He has served as a consultant of the UN Office of the High Commissioner for Human Rights, the Organization of African Unity/African Union, and the South African Human Rights Commission. He has published widely in the field of international human rights law and is a founding Co-Editor-in-Chief of the *African Human Rights Law Reports*, and was a founding Co-Editor of the *African Human Rights Law Journal*.

Sarah Joseph is Professor of Human Rights Law at Monash University and is the Director of its Castan Centre for Human Rights Law. Her latest book is on trade law and human rights, entitled *Blame it on the WTO: a Human Rights Critique* (OUP 2011). Other books and articles relate to the International Covenant on Civil and Political Rights, as well as linkages between human rights and multinational corporations, social media, and terrorism. She has also written on the right of self-determination, extraterritorial human rights obligations, as well as Australian constitutional law.

Robin Bradley Kar is Professor of Law and Philosophy at the University of Illinois College of Law. He earned his bachelor of arts magna cum laude from Harvard University, his JD from Yale Law School, and his PhD from the University of Michigan, where he was a Rackham Merit Fellow, Rackham Predoctoral Fellow, and Charlotte Newcombe Fellow. He is also a former law clerk to the Honorable Sonia Sotomayor, now an Associate Justice for the US Supreme Court. One of his primary research interests is in moral psychology, where he has focused on identifying and describing special psychological attitudes that animate moral and legal systems. To that end, he has developed a general account of the human sense of moral and legal obligation, which draws on recent advances in a number of cognate fields (including evolutionary game theory, sociology, psychology, anthropology, animal behavioural studies, and philosophy), and which provides a more fundamental challenge to economic assumptions about human action than is present in the behavioural economics literature. More recently, he has been studying the conditions under which legal systems (including international legal systems) can emerge and remain stable as independent institutions, beginning from the simpler forms of social complexity that typically precede law. He also has broad research interests in jurisprudence and moral and political philosophy, and in those areas of the law that appear to reflect moral imperatives. His work in these areas proceeds from the conviction that many longstanding jurisprudential and normative questions can only be adequately addressed with a better understanding of moral psychology.

Chimène I Keitner is Professor of Law at the University of California, Hastings College of the Law, where her research focuses on cutting-edge issues at the intersection of international law and domestic litigation. She is the author of the book, *The Paradoxes of Nationalism* (SUNY 2007), and over twenty articles, essays, and book chapters on questions surrounding the relationship among law, communities, and borders. She holds a bachelor's degree in History and Literature from Harvard, a JD from Yale, and a doctorate in International Relations from Oxford, where she was a Rhodes Scholar. After law school, she clerked for the Chief Justice of the Supreme Court of Canada. She served as Co-Chair for the American Society of International Law's 105th annual meeting in Washington DC, and serves as Co-Chair of the ASIL International Law in Domestic Courts Interest Group. She is a member of the American Law Institute.

Magnus Killander is Senior Lecturer and Head of Research at the Center for Human Rights, Faculty of Law, University of Pretoria. He currently serves as Editor-in-Chief for the *African Human Rights Law Reports*; the Africa Editor for *International Human Rights Law, Oxford Reports on International Law*; Associate Editor (Africa) for *International Law in Domestic Courts, Oxford Reports on International Law*; and Co-Editor for *African Human Rights Law Journal*. He has widely published in books and academic journals, with his research largely focusing on African human rights law, African regional integration law, international human rights monitoring mechanisms, relationship between domestic law and international law.

Miloon Kothari is a leading voice on human rights, especially economic, social, and cultural rights. An architect by training, he has extensive experience in the area of housing and land rights and graduated from the Pratt Institute and Columbia University, and the Maharaja Sayajirao University. He had been Guest Professor at many universities and institutions. He is the coordinator of the South Asian Regional Programme of the Habitat International Coalition's Housing and Land Rights Network, and is a founding member of the International NGO Committee on Human Rights in Trade and Investment. He is also a member of the Leadership Council of the Global Women and AIDS Coalition, UNAIDS. In September 2000, the UN Commission on Human Rights appointed him as the Special Rapporteur on Adequate Housing. In his work as Rapporteur, he focused on strategies to ensure respect for human rights in post-conflict and post-disaster situations. He actively contributed to the standard-setting process as part of his Rapporteur work, including the preparation of Principles and Guidelines on Development-Based Evictions and Displacement, in his 2007 report to the UN Human Rights Council. In recent years, he has been particularly active on issues such as women's rights to land, inheritance, property, housing and globalization, and trade liberalization and their impacts on the right to adequate housing, and other related rights. He currently serves as Convener of the Working Group on Human Rights in India and the UN.

Péter Kovács PhD (1987), dr habil (1997), DSc (2011), studied at the University of Szeged (1978–83) and the Centre européen universitaire—Université de Nancy II, and International Institute of Human Rights of Strasbourg (1983–84). He is Professor of International Law at the Péter Pázmány Catholic University of Budapest (since 1997) and has consulted with the Hungarian Ministry of Foreign Affairs (1990–94, 1998–99). He participated as governmental expert in the drafting of the European Charter for Regional or Minority Languages and of the Framework Convention for the Protection of National Minorities (Strasbourg, Council of Europe, 1990–92 and 1993–94). Since 2005, he has served as Judge of the Constitutional Court of Hungary. He has been a Visiting Professor at French universities including Montpellier (March 2000), Paris XI (March 2002), Paris II (February 2003, March 2009), Nantes (March 2003), and also in Germany: Regensburg (August 2011). He was a Fulbright Visiting Professor at Denver University, College of Law in 2002.

Michelle Lafferty is a legal secretary/référendaire with the Registry of the European Court of Human Rights. She graduated from the University of Glasgow and was admitted as a solicitor in Scotland in 2003 (currently non-practising). She holds masters degrees from the European University Institute, and Birkbeck College. Before joining the Registry, she worked as a legal adviser to the House of Lords' European Union committees and, formerly, in private practice.

Paul Gordon Lauren is Regents Professor at the University of Montana, where he previously served as the founding Director of the Maureen and Mike Mansfield Center, and as the Mansfield Professor of Ethics and Public Affairs. He earned his PhD from Stanford University and has received many fellowships and awards for his teaching, research, administrative leadership, and public service. He has published many articles, chapters, and thirteen books, including the award-winning *Power and Prejudice* and the widely acclaimed *Evolution of International Human Rights: Visions Seen*, nominated for a Pulitzer Prize. His work is internationally known in the fields of history, international law, political science, and philosophy, and has been translated in whole or in part into seven languages. Lauren has lectured widely to a variety of audiences around the world, including students and professors, activists, analysts, judges, attorneys, diplomats, military and intelligence officers, legislators, and policymakers. He also has delivered invited addresses to the Nobel Institute, the Smithsonian Institution, and before the United Nations, where he has been described as possibly the world's leading authority on the history of international human rights.

George A Lopez holds the Reverend Theodore M Hesburgh, CSC Chair in Peace Studies at the Joan B Kroc Institute for International Peace Studies at the University of Notre Dame. He has advised various UN agencies and member states regarding the humanitarian and human rights impacts of sanctions since 1990. In 2010–11, he served on the UN Panel of Experts for sanctions on North Korea. Working often with David Cortright he has been Co-Editor/Author of six books and dozens of articles on economic sanctions. Their academic and policy work is available at <http://www.sanctionsandsecurity.org>.

Francisco López-Bermúdez is a scholar-practitioner with multidisciplinary experience in human rights, democracy, and civil society. He holds a JD from the Pontifical Catholic University of Ecuador (PUCE) and an MA in Public Opinion and Polling from the Department of Government at the University of Essex. He also studied for a Doctorate in Human Rights at the Carlos III University of Madrid (Spain) and is currently working towards his PhD in Political Science at the University of Nebraska. He founded and directed the Human Rights and Democracy Program at PUCE, where he also taught public international law, international organizations, and human rights. As an active member of civil society in the global South, he fostered the creation of a number of institutions and initiatives dealing with human rights and democracy. He co-founded and directed Auditoría Democrática Andina, and was the architect and first consultant of Ecuador's National Human Rights Plan. In recognition of his work, he was awarded the inaugural UNESCO Chair in Education for Peace, Human Rights, and Democracy at Utrecht University, for the academic year 2007.

Jenny S Martinez is Professor of Law, and Warren Christopher Professor in the Practice of International Law and Diplomacy at Stanford Law School. Previously, she clerked for Justice Stephen Breyer of the US Supreme Court, and Judge Guido Calabresi of the US Court of Appeals for the Second Circuit; she was also an Associate Legal Officer for Judge Patricia Wald of the United Nations International Criminal Tribunal for the former Yugoslavia in the Hague, where she worked on trials involving genocide, crimes against humanity, and war crimes. She is a leading expert on international courts and tribunals, international human rights, national security, constitutional law, and the laws of war. Her research focuses on the role of courts and tribunals in advancing and protecting human rights, ranging from the nineteenth-century international tribunals involved in the suppression of the trans-Atlantic slave trade to contemporary institutions, and the role of courts in policing human rights abuses in connection with anti-terrorism policies. She is the author of *The Slave Trade and the Origins of International Human Rights Law* (OUP 2012) and numerous articles in leading academic journals. She serves on the board of directors for the Open Society Justice Initiative, which promotes human rights, and builds legal capacity for open societies around the world. Previously, she has served as a consultant on international human rights issues for both Human Rights First and the International Center for Transitional Justice. She is also a member of the US State Department's Advisory Committee on International Law. She is a faculty affiliate of Stanford's Center on International Security and Cooperation, and Stanford's Center on Democracy Development and the Rule of Law.

Fiona McKay is a British lawyer who has been the Chief of the Victims Participation and Reparations Section within the Registry of the International Criminal Court, since August 2004. Previously she worked in several capacities providing legal services to victims of human rights violations, including serving as Director of a legal aid centre in the Occupied Palestinian Territories, and Deputy Director of the Kurdish Human Rights Project which litigates before the European Court of Human Rights. She has specialized in the right of victims of gross violations of human rights or international humanitarian law to reparation, and international justice in general: she worked at the NGO Redress in London and directed the International Justice Program at Human Rights First in New York.

Cecilia Medina currently serves as Professor of International Human Rights Law at the University of Chile and the Director of its Human Rights Center. She previously served for eight years as a member of the UN Human Rights Committee, of which she served as Chair Person from 1999–2000. In 2004, she was elected to the International Commission of Jurists and the Inter-American Court of Human Rights, serving as its President from 2008–09. She has taught at various universities and institutions, including the University of Lund, the International Institute of Human Rights, the University of Toronto, the UN Institute for Peace, Harvard University, and the University of Utrecht. She has widely published on topics such as the Inter-American human rights system, the American Convention, and, women's and human rights. She has also been recognized through various awards, such as the Chilean Women's Leadership Award, the Gruber Foundation's Women's Prize, and Award of Equality Now, and has been decorated as a Ridder of the Oranje-Nassau. She received a licence in Social and Juridical Sciences from the University of Chile and a doctorate in Law from the University of Utrecht.

Juan E Méndez holds an Abogado degree (JD equivalent) from the Stella Maris Catholic University, and a certificate from the Washington College of Law of the American University (1980). He is admitted to the Bar of the District of Columbia, and of Buenos Aires and Mar del Plata. He teaches at the Washington College of Law and is currently the United Nations Special Rapporteur on Torture. He is the author, with Marjory Wentworth, of *Taking a Stand: The Evolution of Human Rights* (Palgrave MacMillan 2011). He was President of the International Center for Transitional Justice between 2004 and 2009. He is a Visiting Fellow, Kellogg

College, Oxford, and, in 2009 and 2010, he was an Adviser to the Prosecutor, International Criminal Court, on Crime Prevention. In the summer of 2009 he was a Scholar-in-Residence at the Ford Foundation. He is also former Special Adviser to the Secretary General (UN) on Prevention of Genocide. At Human Rights, Watch he directed the Americas division (1982–93) and was later General Counsel (1994–96). He was Executive Director of the Inter-American Institute of Human Rights in Costa Rica (1996–99). From 2000 to 2003, he was a member—and in 2002, the President—of the Inter-American Commission on Human Rights, Organization of American States. He has taught at the University of Notre Dame, Georgetown Law School, and Johns Hopkins School of Advanced International Studies (SAIS), and he teaches regularly at the Oxford Masters Programme in International Human Rights Law.

Gerald L Neuman is J Sinclair Armstrong Professor of International, Foreign, and Comparative Law at Harvard Law School, where he teaches human rights, constitutional law, and immigration and nationality law, and Co-Director of the school's Human Rights Program. His current research focuses on international human rights bodies, transnational dimensions of constitutionalism, and rights of foreign nationals. He is the author of *Strangers to the Constitution: Immigrants, Borders, and Fundamental Law* (Princeton 1996), and co-author of Louis Henkin et al., *Human Rights* (2nd edn, Foundation Press 2009). Since January 2011, he has been a member of the Human Rights Committee, which monitors compliance with the International Covenant on Civil and Political Rights.

Gerd Oberleitner is Lecturer at the Institute of International Law and International Relations at the University of Graz. From 1998 to 1999, he served in the Human Rights Department of the Austrian Federal Ministry for Foreign Affairs. From 1999 to 2002, he was Executive Director of the European Training and Research Centre for Human Rights and Democracy (ETC) in Graz and is presently on the Centre's Executive Board. From 2002 to 2004, he was Lecturer in Human Rights at the London School of Economics and Political Science (LSE) and from 2004 to 2007, Visiting Fellow at the LSE's Centre for the Study of Human Rights. He was also a Visiting Scholar at the European Inter-University Centre in Venice (2009) and the Université du Quebéc à Montréal, the University of Prishtina (2010). He is course instructor in human rights distance learning programmes of Human Rights Education Associates (HREA) and teaches in the European Regional Master Programme in Democracy and Human Rights in South-East Europe, and the European Master's Programme in Human Rights and Democratisation. His publications include *Global Human Rights Institutions: Between Remedy and Ritual* (Polity 2007).

Michael O'Boyle was elected Deputy Registrar of the European Court of Human Rights in 2006 and was re-elected in 2011. He has worked extensively as a lawyer with the former European Commission and Court of Human Rights as well as the present

Court. He graduated in law from Queens University, Belfast, and was called to the Bar in Northern Ireland. He was a Kennedy Scholar at the Harvard Law School where he obtained his LLM and holds a Diploma from the Cassin Institute for Human Rights in Strasbourg. He is the co-author (with Professors Harris, Warbrick, E Bates, and C Buckley) of *The Law of the European Convention on Human Rights* (OUP 2009).

Bertrand G Ramcharan LLM, PhD, (LSE), Barrister-at-Law; Diploma of the Hague Academy of International Law. Previously he worked as Professor (First Swiss Chair of Human Rights) at the Graduate Institute of International and Development Studies; Deputy and then Acting UN High Commissioner for Human Rights; Chancellor of the University of Guyana; Commissioner of the International Commission of Jurists; Member of the Permanent Court of Arbitration.

Chris A. Robinson is Professor at Bronx Community College of the City University of New York. He holds a BA from the University of California, in Integrative Biology, and an MA and a PhD in Anthropology from New York University. He has recently published research papers in the *Journal of Human Evolution* and *The Anatomical Record*, exploring methods of identifying species in the human fossil record using analyses of variation in the three-dimensional shape of the teeth and jaws of extant humans and apes, and fossil humans. He has also written a book chapter on fossil giraffes based on research at the early human site of Laetoli, Tanzania, from which the earliest human footprints were recovered. He contributed a chapter on evidence for genocide in the fossil record for the award-winning *Encyclopedia of Genocide and Crimes against Humanity*.

Nigel S Rodley is an international lawyer who specializes in human rights. He is currently Professor of Law at the University of Essex, and has served as a member of the UN Human Rights Committee since 2001 and as its Vice-Chair since 2003. Since 2003, he has also served on the International Commission of Jurists. He previously worked as an Assistant Professor of Law at Dalhousie University and was appointed as a Reader in Law at the University of Essex in 1990. He assumed his current position as a Professor of Law in 1994 and served as Dean of Law from 1992 to 1995. From 1993 to 2001, he also worked as the Special Rapporteur on Torture of the UN Commission on Human Rights. He received an LLB from the University of Leeds, an LLM from Columbia University, an LLM from New York University, and a PhD from the University of Essex. He was knighted in 1998 in the Queen's New Years Honours list for services to Human Rights and International Law, and received an honorary LLD from Dalhousie University in 2000. In 2005, he was a joint recipient of the American Society of International Law's 2005 Goler T Butcher Medal, for distinguished work in human rights. In 2008, he was appointed as an Honorary Fellow of the Faculty of Forensic and Legal Medicine of the Royal College of Physicians.

Martin Scheinin has been Professor of Public International Law and Human Rights at the European University Institute, since 2008, after serving fifteen years as professor in Finland. From 1993 to 1998, he was Professor of Constitutional Law at the University of Helsinki where he also got his doctorate in Law in 1991. In 1998–2008, he was Professor of Constitutional and International Law and Director of the Institute for Human Rights at Åbo Akademi University in Turku, Finland. He was the founder of the Finnish Graduate School in Human Rights Research as well as the Nordic School in Human Rights Research. From 1997 to 2004, he was a member of the United Nations Human Rights Committee, the treaty body acting under the Covenant on Civil and Political Rights. In 2005 he was appointed as the first United Nations Special Rapporteur on human rights and counter-terrorism, a position of trust he held until July 2011. He was one of the senior legal experts in the FRALEX network, providing advice and producing reports to the EU Fundamental Rights Agency. Within the International Law Association, he has served on the Committee on Human Rights Law and Practice as well as the Committee on the Rights of Indigenous Peoples. Since 2010, he has been the President of the International Association of Constitutional Law. He has published extensively in the fields of human rights law and comparative, and Finnish constitutional law.

Dinah Shelton is the Manatt/Ahn Professor Emeritus at the George Washington University Law School. She previously taught International Law and was Director of the doctoral programme in International Human Rights Law at the University of Notre Dame Law School (1996–2004). She served as a member of the Inter-American Human Rights Commission (2010–2014), and in 2010, she was President of the Commission. She is the author of three prize-winning books, *Protecting Human Rights in the Americas* (Engel 1982) (co-authored with Thomas Buergenthal), *Remedies in International Human Rights Law* (2nd edn, OUP 2006), and the three-volume *Encyclopedia of Genocide and Crimes against Humanity* (Macmillan 2004). She has also authored other articles and books on international law, human rights law, and international environmental law. She is a member of the board of editors of the *American Journal of International Law* (Macmillan 2004). She has served as a legal consultant to international organizations and is on the board of numerous human rights and environmental organizations. In 2006, she was awarded the Elisabeth Haub Prize for Environmental Law, and in 2013, she received the Goler Butcher Prize in Human Rights; she was conferred the degree of doctor honoris causa at the University of Stockholm in 2012.

Ramesh Thakur is Professor of International Relations in the Crawford School of Public Policy, Australian National University and Adjunct Professor in the Institute for Ethics, Governance and Law, Griffith University. He was formerly Senior Vice Rector of the United Nations University and UN Assistant Secretary-General, Commissioner and one of the principal authors of *The Responsibility to Protect*, and

Senior Adviser on *Reforms*, and Principal Writer of Secretary-General Kofi Annan's second reform report. He was educated in India and Canada, he has held full-time professorships in Canada and New Zealand, and serves on the international advisory boards of institutes in Africa, Asia, Europe, and North America.

Christian Tomuschat is Professor of International and Constitutional Law at Humboldt University Berlin. He was a member of the Human Rights Committee under the International Covenant on Civil and Political Rights from 1977 to 1986 and Chairman of the International Law Commission from 1985 to 1996.

Bryan S Turner is the Presidential Professor of Sociology and the Director of the Committee on Religion at the Graduate Center at the City University of New York. He was the Alona Evans Distinguished Visiting Professor of Sociology at Wellesley College (2009–10) and Professor of Sociology at Cambridge University England (1998–2005). He was awarded Doctor of letters by the University of Cambridge in 2009. His publications in the field of citizenship and human rights include *Vulnerability and Human Rights* (2006), *Rights and Virtues. Political Essays on Citizenship and Social Justice* (2008), and *Religion and Modern Society. Citizenship, Secularization, and the State* (2011). He is the Editor of *The Cambridge Dictionary of Sociology* (2006), and the founding Editor of the journal *Citizenship Studies*. He was recently appointed as General Editor of the *Blackwell Encyclopaedia of Social Theory*.

Johan D van der Vyver is IT Cohen Professor of International Law and Human Rights in the School of Law of Emory University. His current teaching obligations include Public International Law, International Human Rights, International Criminal Law, International Humanitarian Law, and Comparative Constitutional Law. He is also an extraordinary Professor in the Department of Private Law at the University of Pretoria. Before joining the Faculty of Law at Emory in 1995, he was Professor of Law in the University of the Witwatersrand. His academic qualifications include a Doctor of Laws (PhD) degree of the University of Pretoria (1974), a Doctor of Laws degree (honoris causa) of the University of Zululand (1993), and one of the Potchefstroom University for Christian Higher Education (2003) in South Africa, as well as the Diploma in International and Comparative Law of the International Institute of Human Rights in Strasbourg (1986). He is the author of eight books and in excess of 200 law review articles, chapters in books, and book reviews.

Annemarieke Vermeer-Künzli is Assistant Professor at the Amsterdam Center for International Law, University of Amsterdam. Her main areas of research concern state responsibility in general, and diplomatic protection and non-recognition of illegality in particular. She has published widely on diplomatic protection, the topic on which she also wrote her doctoral thesis. In this context, she also assisted Prof John Dugard in his work for the UN International Law Commission. She is a member of the ILA-Committee on recognition/non-recognition. At the University of Amsterdam, she teaches International Law and the Law of State Responsibility.

David Weissbrodt is the Regents Professor and Fredrikson & Byron Professor of Law at the University of Minnesota Law School. He has written twenty books and over 200 articles. His writing focuses principally on international human rights law and he teaches International Human Rights Law, Administrative Law, Immigration Law, and Torts. He has established the University of Minnesota Human Rights Center and helped to launch the University of Minnesota Human Rights Library on the Internet. He also helped to establish the Center for Victims of Torture, the Advocates for Human Rights, and the International Human Rights Internship Program. He served as a member (1996–2003) and Chairperson (2001) of the UN Sub-Commission on the Promotion and Protection of Human Rights; he also served as a member (2005–10) and Chairperson (2008–10) of the Board of Trustees of the UN Trust Fund on Contemporary Forms of Slavery; he further was the United Nations Special Rapporteur on the Rights of Non-Citizens (2001–03).

Erika de Wet is Co-Director of the Institute for International and Comparative Law in Africa and Professor of International Law in the Faculty of Law of the University of Pretoria. Between 2004 and 2010 she was tenured Professor of International and Constitutional Law at the Amsterdam Center for International Law, University of Amsterdam, a position which she still holds part-time. She lectures on international law at the University of Zurich and the University of Bonn on a regular basis. Between 2007 and 2010 she served as a member of the Advisory Committee of the Netherlands on Issues of Public International Law. Her most recent book (with Jure Vidmar) is *Hierarchy in International Law: The Place of Human Rights* (OUP 2012). Together with Professor André Nollkaemper, she is Editor-in-Chief of the Oxford Reports on International Law in Domestic Courts (ILDC) Online; she is also one of the General Editors of the Oxford Constitutions Online, with Professors Rüdiger Wolfrum and Rainer Grote of the Max Planck Institute for Comparative Public Law and International Law in Heidelberg.

John Witte, Jr is Jonas Robitscher Professor of Law, Alonzo L McDonald Distinguished Professor, and Director of the Center for the Study of Law and Religion Center at Emory University. A specialist in legal history, marriage law, and religious liberty, he has published 220 articles, thirteen journal symposia, and twenty-six books. Recent book titles include: *Sex, Marriage and Family Life in John Calvin's Geneva*, 2 vols (2005, 2012); *Modern Christian Teachings on Law, Politics, and Human Nature*, 3 vols (2006); *God's Joust, God's Justice: Law and Religion in the Western Tradition* (2006); *The Reformation of Rights: Law, Religion, and Human Rights in Early Modern Calvinism* (2007); *Christianity and Law: An Introduction* (2008); *The Sins of the Fathers: The Law and Theology of Illegitimacy Reconsidered* (2009); *Christianity and Human Rights: An Introduction* (2010); *Religion and the American Constitutional Experiment* (3rd edn, 2011); and *Religion and Human Rights: An Introduction* (2012). He edits two major book series, 'Studies in Law and Religion,' and 'Religion, Marriage and Family'. He has been selected eleven times by the Emory law students as the Most Outstanding Professor and has won dozens of other awards and prizes for his teaching and research.

Rüdiger Wolfrum has been a Judge of the International Tribunal for the Law of the Sea since 1996 and is a Professor of International Law at the University of Heidelberg and an Emeritus Professor of the Max Planck Institute for Comparative Public Law and International Law. He has been a member of numerous committees, including the International Law Association and the UN Committee on the Elimination of Racial Discrimination, and is a Founding Member of the Humanities Section of the German Academy of Natural Sciences (Leopoldina). He is the general editor of the ten-volume Max Planck Encyclopedia for Public International Law (OUP 2013) as well as the author of numerous other publications. He was educated at the University of Bonn.

INTRODUCTION

DINAH SHELTON

INTERNATIONAL human rights law has become a major branch of international law in a relatively short period of time. Most of the normative instruments, institutions, and procedures that exist in the field of human rights have emerged only since the late 1940s. Since that time, human rights standard-setting has brought forth a mutually reinforcing network of global and regional treaties and other instruments that guarantee the enumerated human rights and set forth the corresponding obligations of states, state agents and, in some instances non-state actors. Nearly all human rights instruments derive their inspiration from and include reference to the Universal Declaration of Human Rights, adopted without dissent by the United Nations General Assembly on 10 December 1948. Implementation of such instruments by states is monitored by treaty bodies, regional courts and commissions, and some of the United Nations specialized agencies. Perhaps most significantly, billions of persons throughout the world now have access to some form of international review procedure when their domestic governing bodies fail to comply with the applicable international guarantees and afford no redress for the violations that occur.

This world of international law appears very different from the one that existed a century ago, when the dominant legal doctrine was that public international law concerned interstate relations only.[1] Some scholars continued to assert until

[1] *Oppenheim's Treatise on International Law*, written at the beginning of the twentieth century, opined that 'the so-called rights of man' cannot enjoy protection under international law because that law is concerned solely with the relations between states and cannot confer rights on individuals. L Oppenheim, 1 *International Law: A Treatise* § 212 (2nd edn, 1912).

recently that the individual is an object but not a subject of international law.[2] Yet, the traditional view no longer adequately describes or explains the changes wrought by and the prominent place of human rights in international law today. Looking at the emergence and current status of human rights law, the evolutionary theory of punctuated equilibrium[3] seems particularly apt. That is, the emergence of human rights law has taken place through an evolution in human history characterized by long periods of stability, during which particular events brought some incremental changes, without modifying the general power structure or theory of sovereignty and domestic jurisdiction, but then, in the second half of the twentieth century, a short period of rapid change punctuated the equilibrium and ushered in entirely new doctrines, laws, and governing institutions, fundamentally changing the international legal system. The punctuation that shattered the equilibrium came with the Second World War. The wall separating individuals and groups from international law was breached and human rights became a matter of international concern. In the millennia before this shattering event, international law—such as existed at the time—responded ad hoc to particular problems, such as the European religious wars of the seventeenth century,[4] the slave trade,[5] and the need to protect the sick and wounded during armed conflict.[6] These incremental responses to particular problems did not affect the dominant theory that in general how nations treated those within their boundaries and jurisdiction remained exclusively a matter of domestic concern.

The somewhat sudden emergence and rapid evolution of human rights law has given rise to many unanswered questions. The main objective of this volume is to address some of the most significant questions that repeatedly and perhaps inevitably demand attention in the field of human rights, presenting in some instances a variety of answers developed within different disciplines: Why do humans have rights? What is the source of the rights that humans have? What are the historical and cultural origins of human rights? Are human rights universal? Are there underlying structural principles that bind together the catalogue of internationally guaranteed rights and provide criteria for the emergence of new rights? What institutions and procedures seem best adapted to ensure compliance and enforcement of rights? Has international human rights law made a difference in the lives and well-being of individuals and groups? How can such differences be known and measured?

[2] See eg P Weil, 'Le droit international en quête de son identité' *General Course of Public International Law*, 237 RCADI 9-370 at 122.

[3] N Eldredge and SJ Gould, 'Punctuated Equilibria: An Alternative to Phyletic Gradualism' in TJM Schopf (ed), *Models in Paleobiology* (Freeman, Cooper and Company 1972) 82–115. See also, SJ Gould, *Punctuated Equilibrium* (Belknap Press of Harvard UP 2007).

[4] See Arts 2 and 28 of the Treaties of Peace, signed at Munster and Osnabruck, known as the Treaties of Westphalia, 1648, in *Major Peace Treaties of Modern History* 7 (Fred L Israel, ed, 1967).

[5] See Chapter 9 by Jenny Martinez.

[6] See Chapter 11 by Gerd Oberleitner.

The chapters in this volume are designed to address these questions, with the aim of providing thought-provoking analysis for use by those being introduced to human rights for the first time, as well as for those who are experienced scholars and practitioners. The book is not a casebook, a treatise, or an encyclopedia, all of which exist in many valuable editions. Instead, the *Handbook* tackles significant and perennial theoretical, historical, and structural issues in human rights law. As such, it is hoped and intended that the contents will prove to have value over the long term. Each chapter is written by an expert in the field and the names will likely be very well-known to many readers. The editor was extremely fortunate that the first choice author accepted the invitation to contribute in all instances. Four chapters originally intended for the book are not included because the authors withdrew too late in the process to obtain substitutes or, in one instance, simply never communicated after accepting to contribute. For this reason, chapters discussing challenges to the existence of human rights, state responsibility for human rights violations, and a general conclusion are not included in the text.

The *Handbook* starts with the fundamental question of why humans have rights. In relation to the drafting of the Universal Declaration of Human Rights Jacques Maritain famously commented that 'it is doubtless not easy but it is possible to establish a common formulation of... rights possessed by man' but impossible to find a 'common rational justification of these... rights'.[7] In the light of that comment, the *Handbook* begins with several justifications for the existence of human rights, as understood from different disciplines: theology, philosophy, biology, psychology, anthropology, and sociology. These provocative chapters ultimately are all concerned with the issue of what it means to be human and how the attributes of humanness may or may not lead to human rights.

The next part of the *Handbook* turns to historical antecedents for modern human rights law. The lineage is not necessarily direct in the sense of having influenced the emergence of current norms and institutions, but some of the premises, ideas, and normative framework can be seen to parallel existing human rights law. As Paul Gordon Lauren demonstrates in his opening chapter, the idea of rights is as old as civilization, albeit in constant tension with ideas of hierarchy, power, and subordination. From these sometimes ancient legal texts from around the world, the idea of universality of human rights emerges, challenging the idea of an exclusively Western origin for concepts of justice and rights. The important role of civil society appears to have developed early, as is evident in the chapters on the slave trade and humanitarian law. Legal doctrines such as abuse of rights and petition procedures to international bodies also find their origins in earlier efforts to protect (some) human rights, revealed in the chapters on diplomatic protection and League of Nations precedents. Finally, this section includes a chapter on the early efforts

[7] J Maritain, *Man and the State* (1951, reprinted by Catholic University of America, 1998) ch 4.

to enshrine economic, social, and cultural rights in international law, through the work of the International Labor Organization, making this set of rights more accurately described as the first generation of rights in international law.

Part III of the Handbook shifts from the past to the present, as each chapter examines one of the principles that is overarching and fundamental to human rights law. These principles also may be seen to emerge from the theoretical foundations of Part I and the historical traditions of Part II. Paolo Carozza presents the principle of human dignity, a term that appears in many human rights instruments and is sometimes taken itself as a foundation for all human rights. Another foundational principle is that of equality, discussed by Jarlath Clifford. In contrast to dignity and equality, other structural principles are more directed at issues of governance and role of international human rights law in relation to states in the international community. Subsidiarity, sovereignty, and proportionality are all terms that international tribunals use in determining their own competence, the degree of deference they should afford to government decisions, and the limits of international scrutiny of state (mis)conduct. Increasingly, human rights law is also being examined in the context of democratic governance and the rule of law. Christian Tomuschat addresses this issue. Finally, this section takes up one of the principles discussed more widely in recent times, that of solidarity. This chapter links closely with that of Ramesh Thakur on the responsibility to protect, appearing later in the book.

The process of human rights law-making and some of the main concepts now widely accepted form the heart of Part IV. Bertram Ramcharan, a long-time major figure in the development of human rights law at the United Nations, examines the law-making process in general, as it has unfolded over the past nearly seventy years. This chapter leads into the discussions by Martin Scheinin and Erika de Wet of some of the outcomes of the process, in the development of normative concepts like 'core rights' and '*erga omnes*' obligations, as well as the increasing invocation of *jus cogens* in the field of human rights.

In Part V, the *Handbook* turns to implementation and compliance, examining the role of various actors, institutions, and procedures: national and international, state and non-state. Miloon Kothari brings his experience as a UN special rapporteur to the discussion of UN Charter bodies and special procedures, while Sir Nigel Rodley does the same for UN treaty bodies, on which he has served with great distinction. Cecilia Medina has likewise served on a UN treaty body, but in addition was a judge on the Inter-American Court of Human Rights. She is thus well-placed to discuss the role of the international judge and members of quasi-judicial human rights bodies. From these first chapters on global institutions, the section turns to the regional level, where Christof Heyns and Magnus Killander ably present the invaluable contributions of regional institutions to the international law of human rights. Finally, Nisuke Ando describes the complexities of national implementation across the wide variety of existing national legal systems and David Weissbrodt expertly reviews the many roles of non-state actors, not only in respect to their contributions to human rights, but also with regard to their potential responsibility for human rights violations.

Part VI of the *Handbook* reflects some of the recent debates about 'fragmentation' in international law, debates that began in part due to some of the claims about the specificity of human rights law.[8] Clearly, human rights law does have some differences from other areas of international law: it is not governed, in general, by a principle of reciprocity, but is more 'unilateral' in character; it protects individuals and groups rather than states; it is 'objective' and survives changes in sovereignty.[9] At the same time, human rights law is a part of general international law rather than a fully self-contained and autonomous normative system. The chapters in Part VI examine several of the main topics in which discussion has emerged about a special regime for human rights law. Malgosia Fitzmaurice looks at treaty interpretation, where human rights bodies give strong emphasis to the 'object and purpose' of the agreements, the principle of effectiveness, and the notion of 'living instruments' much more than the original intent of the drafters. Chimene Keitner examines another area of general international law, that of state and diplomatic immunities, where human rights law has pressed for change. George Lopez and Ramesh Thakur take up the issue of enforcement, the former looking at the issue of economic sanctions, while the latter tackles the law on use of force and development of the doctrine of responsibility to protect. Finally, Sarah Joseph considers what is often referred to as 'regime conflict' in analysing the relationship between the different bodies of international law relating to trade, investment, and human rights.

The final section of the book attempts to provide some evaluation of the human rights project and whether it has made a difference to the lives of people throughout the world. The first two chapters in the section attempt to evaluate what we know and how we know it. Francisco Lopez-Bermudez critically examines the development and use of human rights indicators as a means to assess whether or not states comply with their human rights obligations. Gisella Gori then looks at the issue from the perspective of institutions that review and evaluate compliance. Fiona McKay takes up the critical question of outcome for the victims: what redress can and do they receive and how the international system can be improved in this regard. The book then concludes with a moving chapter by Juan Mendez and Catherine Cone on the impact of human rights law in one region of the world over the past few decades in which the law and institutions have matured.

The care and attention of each author to the contributed chapter is evident in the quality of the product. The editor must thank each author for the timely and

[8] In particular the law of reservations became a matter of controversy. See eg I Ziemele (ed), *Reservations to Human Rights Treaties and the Vienna Convention Regime: Conflict, Harmony or Reconciliation* (Martinus Nijhoff 2004).

[9] See Linos-Alexander Sicilianos, 'The Human Face of International Law—Interactions between General International Law and Human Rights: An Overview' (2012) 22 HRLJ 1.

excellent submissions and the generous acceptance of edits that were made. Reading each chapter was a joy that I hope will be shared by many readers. I would also like to thank John Louth and Merel Alstein at Oxford University Press for entrusting me with this work and for their assistance in contacting authors and concluding the project. Finally, enormous thanks are due to Ariel Gould, JD George Washington University Law School 2013, who not only assisted with the editing, but undertook the laborious and sometimes difficult task of tracking down sources, formatting footnotes, and preparing the tables. Her work has been exemplary and deserving of considerable credit.

PART I

THEORETICAL FOUNDATIONS

CHAPTER 1

RELIGION

M CHRISTIAN GREEN
JOHN WITTE, JR

RIGHTS talk has become a dominant mode of political, legal, and moral discourse, especially since the second half of the twentieth century. Today, human rights protections and violations are increasingly important issues in international relations and diplomacy. Often overlooked is the fact that most rights and liberties have millennia-long roots in legal systems shaped by religious and philosophical tenets. Indeed, religious beliefs provide perhaps the most widely accepted foundations on which human rights law has been built. Some religions ground the origins of humanity in a creation that imbues all persons with a divine spark, entitling each individual to equal respect. Many religions and moral philosophies address fundamental ethical and moral questions of justice and the 'right' life, inevitably considering questions of how power should be exercised and what duties individuals owe to each other. As Paul Gordon Lauren has observed: 'All of the major religions of the world seek in one way or another to speak to the issue of human responsibility to others... [A]ll of the great religious traditions share a universal interest in addressing the integrity, worth, and dignity of all persons and, consequently, the duty toward other people who suffer without distinction.'[1] By developing their values, ideals, and concepts of responsibility to common humanity, religious traditions provided an inherent beginning for the evolution of rights discourse.

[1] Paul Gordon Lauren, *The Evolution of International Human Rights: Visions Seen* (University of Pennsylvania Press 1998) 5.

This chapter focuses on the comparative development of human rights beliefs and norms in Hinduism, Confucianism, Buddhism, Judaism, Islam, and Christianity. Although the focus is on the religious sources of and contributions to human rights, the chapter also attends to the ambivalences and tensions around religion and human rights that remain the subject of ongoing debate. The concluding section argues both that human rights need the resources of all religious traditions to survive and flourish, and that religions themselves must attend to human rights in order to do justice and affirm human dignity.[2]

1. Religion and Human Rights in the East

1.1 Hinduism

Inquiry into the sources and development of human rights in Eastern religions must begin with Hinduism, which emerged out of the cultures and practices of the peoples of the Indus Valley prior to 2000 BCE. Unlike most other world religions, Hinduism has neither origins in a particular leader or historical event, nor a set of determinate doctrines. Over time and across the Indian subcontinent, it has embraced a diversity of religious practices, texts, and rituals. The tradition's mystical quality and spiritual objective of each person attaining freedom from material existence has sometimes caused it to seem otherworldly and unconcerned with such tangible matters as the realization of human rights.[3] The modern association of Hinduism with the caste system, the widow-sacrifice known as *sati* and other forms of gender inequality, and the ongoing tensions with non-Hindu inhabitants of the subcontinent have all been cited against the Hindu record of human rights. Yet, Hinduism's traditional respect for tolerance, diversity, and harmony, and the timeless example of Mahatma Gandhi's ethic of nonviolence, also suggest important sources and resources for human rights in the Hindu tradition.

[2] This chapter draws and distils the following books that also include detailed citations to the literature: John Witte, Jr, *The Reformation of Rights: Law, Religion, and Human Rights in Early Modern Calvinism* (CUP 2007); John Witte, Jr and M Christian Green (eds), *Religion and Human Rights: An Introduction* (OUP 2011); John Witte, Jr and Frank S Alexander (eds), *Christianity and Human Rights* (CUP 2010); John Witte, Jr, and Johan D van der Vyver (eds), *Religious Human Rights in Global Perspective*, 2 vols (Martinus Nijhoff 1996).

[3] Exemplary of this stereotype is Max Weber, *The Religion of India: The Sociology of Hinduism and Buddhism*, trans and ed Hans H Gerth and Don Martindale (Free Press 1958).

The Hindu concern for harmony amid the diversity of its forms is captured in the early texts known as the Vedas, particularly in the emphasis on *Brahman*, a concept of a transcendent, eternal, and absolute reality beyond the plurality, diversity, and contingency of the material world. The subset of Vedas known as the Upanishads contain the elements of what would come to be identified as Hindu philosophy. In light of the diversity of its deities, practices, and beliefs, Hinduism has often been considered to be more philosophical than theological in its conception. Key Hindu ideas include the concept of reincarnation through which believers eventually escape the cycle of death and rebirth (*samsara*), and the moral force of causation and consequence (*karma*) flowing from their actions within those cycles. Various schools of Indian philosophy and practice focus on the cultivation of physical, spiritual, and intellectual discipline for attaining liberation (*moksha*) from these cycles of earthly existence. This goal of transcendence does not take away from the joy and reverence for life (*ahimsa*) apparent in colourful and ornate Hindu rituals and practices. This reverence extends famously not only to human life, but also the lives of animals, some of which are designated sacred, and more generally to life in all its forms.

The divinity that Hindus see as resting in every human being is inseparable from the divinity manifest throughout creation. This expansive sense of the divine includes a number of deities, alongside a more over-arching sense of the divine, identified with the concept of *Brahman*. This theistic diversity is accompanied by understanding of history as recurring cycles of activity rather than a simply linear progression. Within the Hindu tradition, the human self (*atman*) is conceived in a certain sense as transcending historical time and space, existing as an eternal soul without beginning or end. These multiple and diverse senses of divinity and temporality, along with the plurality of rituals and beliefs that make up the Hindu tradition are suggestive of a profound concern for both universality and particularity, two concepts that are central, but often in tension, in human rights today.

The emphasis on individual spiritual development in Hinduism can seem purely individualistic, with no obvious connection to broader notions of human rights or social justice, but the fundamentals of a Hindu social ethic are encapsulated in the notion of duty (*dharma*) as a principle of social organization, particularly as outlined in the *dharma-shastra* manuals of rules and right conduct practised in the Vedic schools. The framing of many of these *dharma* discussions in terms of the Hindu concept of the needs of different stages of life (*ashramas*) (studenthood, householdership, retirement, and renunciation) connects *dharma* duties to specific rights to material sustenance (*kama*), adequate legal, political, and economic structures (*artha*), the pursuit of law and justice (*dharma*), and the quest for liberation (*moksha*).[4] These protections of social, economic, and cultural rights to *kama* and

[4] See Arvind Sharma, *Hinduism and Human Rights: A Conceptual Approach* (OUP 2004).

artha, and of civil and political rights, including religious rights, to *dharma* and *moksha*, have resonance with modern conventions guaranteeing human rights in international law.

In light of India's extensive interaction with the West through the presence of British and other colonial authorities, it is not surprising that ongoing tensions around human rights in Hinduism have roots in how the tradition was constructed in the minds of missionaries and colonizers. As Werner Menski, a scholar of Hindu law and religion, has observed:

> Well before the Christian era, Vedic Hindus, Buddhists, and Jains battled over the right way to lead a good life for all humans, and even other creatures. It is here that the literate Brahmin elite of ancient India allegedly first began to assert its privileged position and built an elaborate empire of ritual precision, higher consciousness and ultimately right knowledge and action, to claim privilege and power to the exclusion, potentially, of all other humans. This led many analysts to claim that the Brahmins did not develop human rights, but elaborated only their own caste-based interests.[5]

In Menski's analysis, the missionaries of yore may, in some respects, have held a more positive view of Hinduism and human rights than today's human rights scholars and advocates. The missionaries 'turned themselves into social workers and virtual anthropologists', Menski maintains, in a way that 'led them to acknowledge a common humanity with Hindus, and even more positive attitudes towards Hinduism'. This attitude is in stark contrast to the many human rights activists who today 'myopically treat anything Hindu as incapable of addressing human rights concepts',[6] pointing to 'backward customs such as *sati* (the burning of widows on the husband's funeral pyre), forced marriages, dowry demands, frantic killings of non-believers in communal riots, and, of course, multiple caste-based discriminations'.[7] Such concerns about matters of caste and gender are far from resolved, as evidenced by the recent extensive debate about a proposal to include a question about caste in the Indian Census of 2011.[8] The rates of sex-selective abortion, female infanticide, child marriage, and dowry murders continue to raise concerns about the status of women in Hindu culture, especially in India.[9] In addition, the rise of the Hindu nationalist Bharatiya Janata Party (BJP) in the 1990s drew international

[5] Werner Menski, 'Hinduism and Human Rights' in *Religion and Human Rights*, 77. For a more expansive discussion of the relationship between traditional and modern interpretations of Hinduism in the law, see Werner Menski, *Hindu Law: Beyond Tradition and Modernity* (OUP 2009).

[6] Menski (n 5) 79. [7] Menski (n 5) 79.

[8] See 'Census 2011 to Include Caste' *The Hindustan Times* (New Delhi) 7 May 2010; Jason Overdorf, 'Don't Ask, Don't Tell, Don't Count' *Global Post* (Boston), 5 June 2010; D'Vera Cohn 'India's Census and the Caste Question', Pew Research Center, 9 June 2010; 'India Approves Caste-Based Census', BBC News, 10 August 2010.

[9] For further analysis of the status of women in India and the Hindu tradition, see Martha C Nussbaum, *Women and Human Development: The Capabilities Approach* (CUP 2000).

attention to the implications of religious nationalism for tolerance and pluralism. The BJP challenged both India's constitutional secularism and what the party perceived as negative depictions of Hinduism at home and abroad. Incidents of communal violence with BJP connections have drawn international attention,[10] raising concerns about the capacity of the recent nationalist and political iterations of Hinduism to engage in the toleration and religious pluralism that many see as necessary supports for human rights.

Scholars and practitioners of non-Western religions are right to point out, as Menski has, that the human rights community, reflecting a strong Western presumption of separation of religion from law and politics, often overlooks the more subtle relationships among religion, culture, and society—including the potential for religion to be a positive source of support for human rights. The Hindu tolerance of a multiplicity and diversity of beliefs, deities, practices, and rituals—along with the over-arching ethical principle of *dharma*—is suggestive of a concern for both universality and harmony of rights and duties that can be the basis for Hindu understanding of human rights. As leading Hindu scholar Arvind Sharma has explained, 'Hinduism is conscious of its universalism because it considers consciousness to be the most universal dimension of existence'.[11] What this means, Sharma adds, is that 'Hinduism's raison d'être should continue to be tolerance... the acceptance of all the religions of the world by all human beings as the inalienable religious heritage of every human being'.[12] In other words, as Gandhi put it: 'Christ can save, and Hindus can still be Hindus.'[13]

1.2 Buddhism

Buddhism, like Hinduism and for some of the same reasons, has also often suffered from misunderstanding and mischaracterization in the West when it comes to human rights and social ethics. Buddhism emerged as an alternative offshoot from Hinduism in the sixth century BCE, when Prince Siddhartha Gautama, the son of a powerful ruler of a small Indian kingdom defied his father, left his wife and children behind, and set out to experience the world in his twenty-ninth year. A sage had foretold that the prince would become either an ascetic or a monarch. His father had sought

[10] In 2002, Muslim mobs in the Indian state of Gujarat attacked a train carrying Hindu activists returning from a Hindu religious site at Ayodhya, previously the site of the 500-year-old Babri mosque that was demolished by a Hindu mob in 1992. In a tenth-anniversary attack, the Muslim mobs set two train cars on fire, sending fifty-eight passengers to horrific deaths. In response, Hindu mobs destroyed Muslim businesses, reportedly raped Muslim women, and killed nearly a thousand Indian Muslims. For analysis of these and other aspects of Hindu nationalism, see Martha C Nussbaum, *The Clash Within: Democracy, Religious Violence, and India's Future* (Belknap Press of Harvard University 2007).

[11] Arvind Sharma, *Are Human Rights Western?: A Contribution to the Dialogue of Civilizations* (OUP 2006) 62

[12] Sharma (n 11) 94.

[13] Sharma (n 11) 113.

to prevent asceticism from flourishing by raising his son in a life of royal luxury. Having never experienced human suffering, Gautama found the hardships of the world to be a rude awakening. On his journey, he encountered a holy man who appeared to embody perfect happiness and serenity as a result of attaining complete liberation through enlightenment (*nirvana*) from worldly suffering. The experience would eventually lead to Gautama's awakening to compassion and benevolence, such that he would come to be known as Gautama Buddha, or more simply the Buddha, meaning the 'enlightened one'. The aim of Buddhist practice is for each person, in the manner of the Buddha, to realize through enlightenment the Buddha nature that exists within all sentient beings, but is concealed by the distortions of desire, anger, and ignorance.

Buddhism shares with Hinduism the notions of *dharma*, *karma*, and liberation from the material world, but with a somewhat more unified doctrinal sense of how to manage these along a path toward enlightenment. Central among these principles are the Four Noble Truths, namely that: (1) life is suffering, (2) suffering is caused by craving and attachment, (3) craving and attachment can be overcome, (4) and that the road to this overcoming is the Eightfold Path. The Eightfold Path includes: (1) right understanding, (2) right purpose, (3) right speech, (4) right conduct, (5) right livelihood, (6) right effort, (7) right alertness, and (8) right concentration. There are important correlations between certain of these 'rights'—for example, speech and livelihood—and the rights that have been protected in international human rights texts. The concern for alertness and concentration might be the basis of educational and labour rights, or political rights of thought, conscience, and belief. The ability to act in accordance with right understanding, purpose, conduct, and effort might be seen as the basis of political rights or broader rights of development. Indeed, there are important resonances between the Buddhist Eightfold Path and human rights philosopher Martha Nussbaum's list of human capabilities as a basis for human rights and development.[14]

The mystical qualities of Buddhist enlightenment and emphasis on individual practice have caused Buddhism, like Hinduism, often to be perceived as disengaged from the worldly realm of human rights. This perception of disengagement, however, has changed in recent decades, largely through the efforts of the contemporary social and political activist movements known as 'Engaged Buddhism'. Sallie B King, a leading scholar of Engaged Buddhism, describes these movements as having 'deeply incorporated the language of human rights into their campaigns to bring about fundamental political changes in their home countries'.[15] Indeed, King maintains: 'While there is debate among Buddhist intellectuals about the extent to which the concept of human rights is compatible with Buddhist culture, Buddhist activists

[14] See Martha C Nussbaum, *Creating Capabilities: The Human Development Approach* (Belknap Press of Harvard University 2011) 33–34.

[15] Sallie B King, *Socially Engaged Buddhism* (University of Hawaii Press 2009). See also; Sallie B King, *Being Benevolence: Social Ethics of Engaged Buddhism* (University of Hawaii Press 2006); Christopher S Queen, *Engaged Buddhism in the West* (Wisdom Publications 2000); Christopher S Queen, *Engaged Buddhism: Buddhist Liberation Movements in Asia* (SUNY, 1996).

continue to rely heavily upon the language of human rights as an integral part of their work.'[16] Admitting that 'working out a properly Buddhist framework for understanding and justifying the use of human rights language is a complex business', King maintains that 'Buddhist intellectuals who embrace the notion of human rights have given thoughtful explanations of how they are able to ground this embrace of human rights in properly Buddhist concepts, principles, and values'.[17]

The pursuit of this Buddhist foundation is complicated, King observes, by Buddhism's formal lack of a concept of 'rights'. Nonetheless, she argues, 'Buddhism does assign a high value to human beings, proclaims the inherent equality of human beings, and advocates for moral behavior, nonviolence, and human freedom. These traditional values form the foundation of Buddhist justifications for embracing human rights.'[18] King identifies five sources of Buddhist justification of human rights.[19] First, Buddhism recognizes the inherent dignity of the human being in the teachings on the 'preciousness of human birth' and innate and universal capacity for 'human enlightenability' in all sentient beings. All human beings possess this Buddha Nature. Second, the Five Lay Precepts of Buddhism against killing, theft, lies, sexual misconduct, and the ingestion of intoxicants set forth a moral code that gives 'negative claim-rights' to those who might be harmed by these practices. Third, the Buddhist tradition has a strong commitment to human equality, as manifest in the Buddha's willingness to teach all who would listen and his principled rejection of the caste system. Fourth, Buddhism is strongly committed to an ethic of nonviolence and, more positively, to benevolence and compassion toward others. Finally, Buddhism is committed to human freedom, particularly by individuals in their decisions about their own spiritual path as determined by their own experience, rather than external sources. The Buddha's dying words about this matter—with apologies to the later John Donne—are reported to have included the recommendation: 'Be islands unto yourselves.... Be a refuge to yourselves.'[20] This freedom principle, according to King, constitutes 'one of the most thoroughly Buddhist of all potential Buddhist justifications for human rights: the freedom to pursue Buddhahood, or self-perfection, is our innate right as human beings, based upon the deepest level of our identity as human beings'.[21] The principle of freedom could give rise to a 'full list of human rights', King maintains, on the basis of the recognition that they are important supports for 'the pursuit of spiritual self-development'.[22] Extrapolating from self-development to social development, there is again resonance with Nussbaum's basic human capabilities and related international human rights. The Buddhist tradition, through

[16] King, *Socially Engaged Buddhism* (note 15) 103.
[17] King, *Socially Engaged Buddhism* (note 15) 106.
[18] King, *Socially Engaged Buddhism* (note 15) 107.
[19] King, *Socially Engaged Buddhism* (note 15) 106–109.
[20] King, *Socially Engaged Buddhism* (note 15) 108.
[21] King, *Socially Engaged Buddhism* (note 15) 109.
[22] King, *Socially Engaged Buddhism* (note 15).

its core principles, the contemporary Engaged Buddhist movement, and such recent engagement as the 'Saffron Revolution' uprising of Burmese monks against the authoritarian Myanmar government, is a repository of human rights wisdom and practice.

1.3 Confucianism

In China, roughly contemporary with the development of Buddhism in India in the sixth century BCE, a new ethical and philosophical system emerged in connection with the philosopher Confucius. After Confucius' death, the tradition was further developed in the fourth century BCE by the philosophers Mencius and Xunzi. More of a moral and ethical philosophy than a religion, Confucianism sought to elaborate principles of ethical and humane administration of government as a means of political and social reform. It emphasized personal moral development along with obedience to forms of proper conduct (*li*) dictated by different social relationships. The six relationships that are the focus of Confucianism are: (1) parent and child, (2) ruler and minister, (3) government officials, (4) husband and wife, (5) older and younger siblings, and (6) friend to friend. All of these relationships are understood to be founded upon a profound principle of benevolence, compassion, and love (*jen*). The profound emphasis on filial piety of children toward parents is a distinctive feature of Confucianism that has sometimes been grafted onto other relationships, particularly the political relationships between rulers and the ruled. Family structures and virtues have, thus, been extended to other realms.[23] But right relations in each of the six realms are thought to conduce to a general social harmony.

Confucianism shares with Hinduism, Buddhism, and other Eastern religions an emphasis on humaneness, compassion, tolerance, harmony, and duty—all of which can contribute to a culture of human rights. The notion of love (*jen*) that is properly manifest in relational conduct (*li*) incorporates an understanding of reciprocity that is often described as the Confucian 'Golden Rule'—translated as 'do not impose on others what you yourself do not desire'.[24] Joseph Chan, a scholar of Confucian political thought, notes that this reciprocal aspect of the tradition extends beyond the conventional relationships in observing:

> To be sure, Confucianism does place significant ethical constraints upon human action and a good number of these have to do with social roles. But it would be a mistake to think

[23] For more on Confucian understandings of the family and society, see Patricia Buckley Ebrey, 'Confucianism' in Don S Browning, M Christian Green, and John Witte, Jr (eds), *Sex, Marriage, and World Religions* (Columbia UP 2006).

[24] Joseph CW Chan, 'Confucianism and Human Rights' in *Religion and Human Rights: An Invitation* (OUP 2011) 92.

that Confucianism sees all duties, or rights if any, as arising solely from social relationships... Although Confucianism does place great emphasis on relationships, it is not a purely role-based or relation-based ethics. Confucian ethics of benevolence is ultimately based upon a common humanity rather than differentiated social roles—it carries ethical implications beyond these roles... Confucianism can accept non-role-based moral claims.[25]

In a related observation, Chan also debunks the stereotype of Confucianism as having an inescapably collectivist ethic. 'I think it is fair to say that Confucianism does not give importance to the idea of individuals freely choosing their own ends, whatever these ends may be', Chan argues. 'The emphasis is more on acting rightly than freely, and to act rightly is to act in accordance with one's best understanding of the requirement of Confucian morality. But Confucianism never denounces or belittles individual interests understood as the needs and legitimate desires of individuals.'[26] As for the implications for international human rights, Chan maintains:

In light of this understanding, we may conclude not only that Confucian thought would not oppose basic individual interests as constituting the common good, but rather that it would take them as a basis for a legitimate social and political order. So Confucianism would not reject human rights on the ground that they protect fundamental individual interests... Social order and harmony can only be affirming and protecting people's interests in security, material goods, social relationships, and fair treatment. On these issues, at least, there is no incompatibility between Confucianism and the concept of human rights.[27]

The main incompatibility that Chan sees between the Confucian tradition and human rights has to do with the difference between an instrumental function of human rights as an 'important device to protect people's fundamental interests' and a non-instrumental function as 'necessary expressions of human dignity or worth'.[28] Confucianism, Chan argues would agree with the former, but not the latter, accepting human rights in a 'fallback-instrumental role', rather than as an 'abstract ideal' of human dignity, and resisting 'any view that tightly links human dignity with rights as the capacity to make rights claims'.[29] Thus, in Chan's view:

Confucians would regard human rights as... important when virtuous relationships break down and mediation fails to reconcile conflicts. However, human rights are not necessary for human dignity or constitutive of human virtues. To avoid the rise of rights talk, Confucians would prefer to keep the list of human rights short. They would restrict it to civil and political rights, not because social and economic needs are less important, but because these rights are more suitable for legal implementation.[30]

[25] Chan (n 24) 91–92. [26] Chan (n 24) 92. [27] Chan (n 24) 93. [28] Chan (n 24) 94.
[29] Chan (n 24) 97, 94. [30] Chan (n 24) 99.

2. Religion and Human Rights in the West

2.1 Judaism

Parallel to these developments in religion and human rights in the East, new understandings of rights were emerging in the deserts of the Middle East that would inform later rights understandings in the West. The first of these, chronologically, was Judaism, which grew out of the Noahide Covenant with the Jews as the chosen people after the great flood and was reinforced with the Mosaic Covenant that included the Decalogue, or Ten Commandments. For David Novak, a scholar of Jewish religion and philosophy, the Jewish tradition raises the question 'of whether a "human" right can only be exercised by an individual or whether a human collective can exercise a right too', particularly when it comes to 'specifically Jewish duties', that 'only members of the covenant between God and Israel can exercise because they alone are the people obligated by the full Torah'.[31] There are three kinds of rights in Judaism, Novak points out: '(1) those rights that God justifiably claims for himself, (2) natural rights that all humans justifiably claim for themselves, individually or collectively, and (3) Torah rights that Jews justifiably claim for themselves, individually or collectively.'[32] Along with this third set of rights flowing from the covenant (*ha-berit*), the Jewish understanding of rights emphasizes normative commandments (*mitsvot*) as required by the covenant and by normative law (*halakhah*) as interpreted by Jewish rabbinical and legal authorities. The Jewish understanding of duty (*mitsvah*) is one in which 'a right engenders a duty instead of a duty engendering a right'.[33]

These rights and duties are manifest in relations between humans and God and between humans and other humans, including the relationship between the individual and the community. That humans are created in the image of God (*be-tselem elohim*) is the basis for both the dignity of the human being in which 'humans share with God the personal attributes of intellect and will' and the basis for rights, including the specific right of religious freedom by which humans are 'capable of being addressed by God' and possessed of the 'capacity freely to accept or reject what God has commanded one to do'.[34] In this way, religious freedom in Judaism is construed less as freedom of choice, than as freedom to assent to the invitation and command of God. In relations between humans, Jews are to observe the biblical commandment 'you shall love your neighbor as yourself' (Leviticus 19:18). This rendering of

[31] David Novak, 'Jewish Theory of Human Rights' in John Witte, Jr and M Christian Green (eds), *Religion and Human Rights: An Invitation* (OUP 2011) 27.

[32] Novak (n 31) 28. [33] Novak (n 31) 30. [34] Novak (n 31) 31.

the Golden Rule in the Jewish tradition is the foundation of the moral law, sometimes also encountered in the negative formulation of Rabbi Hillel the Elder: 'What is hateful to you, do not do to your fellow.'[35] Relations with fellow Jews are lived out under the understanding that they are both created in the image of God and fellow members of a covenant community. Relations with non-Jews are governed by the principle pertaining to 'resident sojourners' (*ger toshav*) under which non-Jews who accept the basic moral law can 'enjoy the same civil rights and be obligated by the same duties as a full-fledged Jewish citizen of that polity'.[36] Jews living in foreign lands, as many have done in the course of various Jewish diasporas, are expected to adhere to the principle of *dina d'malkhuta dina*—'the law of the land is the law'—a principle of political obedience to the law, except where it conflicts with *halakhah*. Orthodox Jewish communities around the world retain rabbinical courts (*bet din*) charged with adjudicating matters of ritual law and personal status, including the issuance of bills of divorce.

2.2 Islam

A second Middle Eastern religion, developing millennia later in the seventh century CE, was Islam. Muslim understandings of human rights have been a major topic of debate since the inception of the modern human rights regime that began with the adoption of the Universal Declaration of Human Rights (UDHR) in 1948, but tensions have re-emerged in recent decades in the form of vocal challenges to Western human rights norms by some Islamist schools.[37] Islam today is an extremely diverse and fast-growing religion, extending through large swaths of Africa and Asia, from Morocco to Indonesia, with sizeable immigrant communities in Europe and North America. Abdullahi An-Na'im, an Islamic law scholar, argues that the framing of the discussion in terms of the compatibility of human rights with Islam is both problematic and counterproductive. The compatibility argument 'assumes that there is a verifiably identifiable monolithic "Islam" to be contrasted with a definitively settled preconceived notion of "human rights"', when in light of the diversity and decentralized leadership structure of Islam, the 'most anyone can legitimately speak of is his or her view of Islam, never Islam as such, and of human rights as they are accepted around the world, including by Muslims'.[38]

[35] Novak (n 31) 35. [36] Novak (n 31) 36.

[37] See Universal Islamic Declaration of Human Rights (Paris and London, 19 September 1981), accessible at: <http://www1.umn.edu/humanrts/instree/islamic_declaration_HR.html>; Cairo Declaration on Human Rights in Islam (Cairo, 1990) UN Doc A/CONF. 157/PC/62/Add. 18 (June 9, 1993); Arab Charter on Human Rights (Cairo: League of Arab States, 1994), accessible at: <http://www.unhcr.org/refworld/docid/3ae6b38540.html>.

[38] Abdullahi Ahmed An-Na'im, 'Islam and Human Rights' in John Witte and M Christian Green (eds), *Religion and Human Rights: An Invitation* (OUP 2011) 56.

Granting the necessary caveats about Muslim diversity and human rights universality, there are principles within Islam that can be seen as providing certain core commitments to human rights analogous to those of other world religions. As Islamic legal scholars Azizah Y Al-Hibri and Raja M El Habti have pointed out:

> The Qur'an states that God created all humanity from a single *nafs* (soul or spirit), created from like nature its mate, and from the two made humanity into nations and tribes so that they may get to know each other, that is, to enjoy and learn from each other's diversity. (Q. 4:1, 49:13) The only proper criterion for preference among people is that of piety, a quality achievable by anyone (Q. 49:13).[39]

This principle has been interpreted as both an affirmation of Muslim diversity and a basis for gender equality.[40] In interpreting these Qur'anic passages on diversity, they further note that 'Muslim scholars permitted Muslims in various countries to import into their laws cultural norms that do not contradict Muslim law'.[41] This principle allowed such practices as polygamy to exist in the Muslim world, though with limits on the number of wives and normative expectations of regarding equality that also reflect Muslim ambivalence about the justice of the marital relationships that may result, particularly for women.

Other practices, such as 'honour killings' for the crime of extramarital sex (*zina*) have been more widely proscribed under Islamic law. Other passages in the Qur'an suggest a basis for educational (Q. 39:9) and economic (Q. 4:32) rights for both men and women,[42] a reflection of the concern for intellectual and social development in Islam that sustained centuries of Islamic scholarship and exchange of ideas with the West, along with economic development through the interest-free system of Islamic finance under Sharia. Islam also contains a principle of religious freedom in the Qur'anic injunction that there can be 'no compulsion in religion' (Q. 2:256), as well as principles protecting the religious rights of non-Muslims (*dhimmis*) residing in Muslim lands.[43]

The question of Sharia has been a prominent one in international human rights debates, particularly around the common practice of Muslim nations inserting reservations into international human rights agreements, pledging adherence only insofar as the content does not contradict Sharia. Sharia is both a system of religious law and a moral code, including criminal and economic law and political and civil liberties, as well as areas of personal law dealing with sexuality, marriage, and family, and ritual laws

[39] Azizah Y Al-Hibri and Raja M El Habti, 'Islam' in *Sex, Marriage, and Family in World Religions* (n 23) 151.

[40] For more on the status of women in Islam, see Riffat Hassan, 'Rights of Women in Islamic Communities' in *Religious Human Rights in Global Perspective* (n 2) 361–86.

[41] Al-Hibri and El Habti (n 39) 156.

[42] See Al-Hibri and El Habti (n 39) 218–22.

[43] For a discussion of this principle against religious compulsion and related themes of tolerance and democracy in Islam, see Irene Oh, *The Rights of God: Islam, Human Rights, and Comparative Ethics* (Georgetown UP 2007), esp ch 4. For discussion of the religious rights of dissidents and non-Muslims in Islam, see Donna E Arzt, 'The Treatment of Religious Dissidents Under Classical and Contemporary Islamic Law' in *Religious Human Rights in Global Perspective* (n 2) 387–454.

addressing procedures for religious observance. The comprehensiveness with which Sharia governs Muslim life, sometimes to the severe qualification—and sometimes abrogation—of human rights is a topic of particular concern. As the Islamic scholar Hisham Hellyer has observed: 'Religion in the Islamic sense "does not concede the dichotomy of the sacred and the profane"; it includes both the temporal and material world (*al-dunya*), and the world beyond (*al-akhirah*)... A rights discourse sustainable within Islam flows from metaphysical and spiritual considerations that at the very least do not contradict religion, and ideally derive from it.'[44] Thus, he maintains: 'If religion is not relevant for all spheres of activity, it is simply not religion, as far as believers are concerned.'[45]

Hellyer further observes that, in contradistinction to Islam:

> Rights discourse has different points of departure and remains a secular discourse at least in its origins. Rights accorded to the individual in Islam do not find their authenticity or authority by claiming interpretations of rationality or reason, even though reason and the rational may indeed be brought to bear on the issue in deeply influential ways.[46]

The heart of the human being in Islam is thought to contain the divine, Hellyer notes, in a way that makes the individual human being a 'representative of God Himself on earth (*khalifat-l-Allah fi-l'ard*)'[47] and demands a purity and comprehensiveness of submission in most, if not all, areas of life in a way that is challenging for secular conceptions of human rights. Yet, that very notion of a divine element in each human being provides perhaps a stronger foundation for human rights than other claimed rationales.

2.3 Christianity

The development of human rights in the Western Christian[48] tradition that has been so influential in the modern development of human rights has its origins both in Jewish law and in classical Roman understandings of rights and liberties, particularly as elaborated in the medieval and early modern period. These Roman understandings form an intricate latticework of arguments about individual and group rights and liberties which were eventually informed and transformed by Stoic and Christian ideas. Both before and after the Christianization of Rome in the fourth

[44] Hisham A Hellyer, 'Worldviews and Universalisms: Islam and the West' in Wes Williams (ed), *Religion and Rights: The Oxford Amnesty Lectures* (Manchester UP 2011) 88.

[45] Hellyer (n 44) 89. [46] Hellyer (n 44) 90. [47] Hellyer (n 44) 90.

[48] For reasons of space we omit here a discussion of human rights principles in the smaller, but very diverse, tradition of the Orthodox Churches of Eastern Christianity. For this see John McGuckin, 'The Issue of Human Rights in Byzantium and the Orthodox Tradition' in *Christianity and Human Rights* (n 2) 173–89; John Witte, Jr and Michael Bourdeaux (eds), *Proselytism and Orthodoxy in Russia: The New War for Souls* (Wipf & Stock 2009).

century CE, classical Roman jurists sometimes used the Latin term *jus* to identify a subjective 'right' in the sense of a person, a subject, 'having a right' against another that could be defended and vindicated. These ideas would later be developed by medieval Catholic canonists and moralists and expanded by later neo-scholastic writers.

The rediscovery of the ancient texts of Roman law in the late eleventh and twelfth centuries–made available to Western Christian scholars in Latin translations from the Arabic versions in use by Muslim scholars in the Middle East and in such polyglot and interreligious centres as Cordoba in the Andalusia region of Spain[49]—helped to trigger a renaissance of subjective rights talk in the West. Medieval jurists differentiated all manner of rights and liberties. They grounded these rights and liberties in the law of nature (*lex naturae*) or natural law (*jus naturale*), and associated them variously with a power (*facultas*) inhering in rational human nature and with the property (*dominium*) of a person or the power (*potestas*) of an office of authority (*officium*).

Medieval jurists repeated and glossed many of the subjective rights and liberties set out in Roman law–especially the public rights and powers of rulers, the private rights and liberties of property. They also set out what they called the 'rights of liberty' (*jura libertatis*), which comprised a whole series of freedoms, powers, immunities, protections, and capacities for different groups and persons.[50] Among the most important of these were the rights protecting the 'freedom of the church' from secular authorities. These early formulations of religious group rights against secular authorities would become axiomatic for the later Western tradition—and now figure prominently in modern concepts of religious autonomy, corporate free exercise rights, and the rights of legal personality for religious groups. In the twelfth and thirteenth centuries, canon law jurists refined the rights further, promulgating rules and rights that are still at the heart of the modern *Code of Canon Law* that governs Catholicism worldwide.

These rights set out at medieval Catholic canon law were, in practice, often narrowly defined in scope and limited in application. Medieval Christendom was no liberal democracy—as the blood of too many martyrs can attest. But a great number of the basic public, private, penal, and procedural rights that are recognized by state and international political authorities today were prototypically formed in this medieval period. These basic rights formulations came to be seen as 'natural rights'—rights inhering in a person's human nature—regardless of that person's status within church, state, or society. This natural rights theory was greatly expanded

[49] See Maria Rosa Menocal, *The Ornament of the World: How Muslims, Jews, and Christians Created a Culture of Tolerance in Medieval Spain* (Little, Brown, and Company 2002); Richard Rubenstein, *Aristotle's Children: How Christians, Muslims, and Jews Rediscovered Ancient Wisdom and Illuminated the Dark Ages* (Houghton Mifflin 2003).

[50] Quoted in Brian Tierney, *The Idea of Natural Rights* (Eerdmans 1997) 57.

in the later Middle Ages and early modern periods through the work of such scholars as William of Ockham, Bartolomé de las Casas, Francisco de Vitoria, Fernando Vázquez, Francisco Suarez, and others. Vitoria was especially prescient in pressing for the rights of indigenous peoples as well as the rights of soldiers and prisoners of war—both critical topics in the budding international law of the day.

This development of human rights within the medieval and early modern Catholic tradition gave way in subsequent centuries to contestation around the notion of human rights in general, and of religious human rights in particular. Much of this was reaction to the rise of a modernity in which principles of Enlightenment liberalism seemed to be winning the day in ways that threatened Church authority and autonomy and which seemed inadequate buffers against the rise of forces of communism, fascism, and revolution. As Catholic theologian Charles Curran has observed, the Church 'staunchly opposed human rights in the eighteenth and nineteenth centuries and well into the twentieth century', resisting both 'modern liberties and the human rights associated with them'.[51] Pope Leo XIII, author of the papal social encyclicals that laid the groundwork for the tradition of Catholic social thought that subsequently led the articulation of all manner of rights and duties in the name of social justice and the common good, was also opposed to religious liberty and the freedom of worship as contraventions of 'the chiefest and holiest human duty'[52] to the one true God in the one true religion. It would be seventy-five years before Pope John XXIII would support the concept of human rights in the encyclical *Pacem in terris* and two more years before the Second Vatican Council in 1965, under the influence of the American Jesuit theologian John Courtney Murray, would embrace the right to religious freedom for all human beings. In recounting these developments, Curran argues that the more recent teachings of Pope John Paul II and Pope Benedict XVI have returned in ways, to the earlier privileging of truth over freedom when it comes to religion and human rights.[53]

While 'freedom of the church' was the initial manifesto of the twelfth-century Papal Revolution, 'freedom of the Christian' was the initial manifesto of the sixteenth-century Protestant Reformation. Martin Luther, Thomas Cranmer, Menno Simons, John Calvin, and other leading sixteenth-century Protestant reformers all turned to Biblical texts to press for rights. They were particularly drawn to the many New Testament aphorisms on freedom. They were also drawn to the Bible's radical calls to equality.[54] These and other biblical passages inspired Luther and his colleagues to demand freedom of the individual conscience from intrusive canon laws and clerical controls, freedom of political officials from ecclesiastical power and

[51] Charles E Curran, 'Human Rights in the Roman Catholic Tradition' in Wes Williams (ed), *Religion and Rights: The Oxford Amnesty Lectures* (Manchester UP 2011) 73.

[52] Curran (n 51) 73, quoting Pope Leo XIII, *Libertas praestantissimum* (1888).

[53] See Curran (n 51) 78–81.

[54] Galatians 3:28, 5:1,13; 2 Corinthians 3:17; John 8:32,36; Romans 8:21 (Revised Standard Version).

privileges, and freedom of the local clergy from central papal rule and oppressive princely controls.

One important Protestant contribution to Western rights talk was to link human rights with biblical duties. Early Protestants believed that God had given each human the freedom needed to choose to follow the commandments of the faith. Freedoms and commandments, rights and duties belonged together in their view. To speak of one without the other was ultimately destructive. Rights without duties to guide them quickly became claims of self-indulgence. Duties without rights to exercise them quickly became sources of deep guilt. Protestants thus translated the moral duties set out in the Bible into reciprocal rights.

Protestants focused first on the duties set out in the Decalogue, or Ten Commandments, which they took to be the most pristine summary of the natural law. The First Table of the Decalogue, they noted, prescribes duties of love that each person owes to God—to honour God and God's name, to observe the Sabbath day of rest and holy worship, to avoid false gods and false swearing. The Second Table prescribes duties of love that each person owes to neighbours—to honour one's parents and other authorities, not to kill, not to commit adultery, not to steal, not to bear false witness, not to covet. A person's duties toward God can be cast as the rights of religion. Each person's duties towards a neighbour, in turn, can be cast as a neighbour's right to have that duty discharged. Starting with this biblical logic, Protestant writers spun out endless elaborations of rights based on other biblical duties toward the poor and needy, widows and orphans, slaves and sojourners, the persecuted and imprisoned, the sick and the grieving, and other vulnerable parties to food, shelter, support, nurture, comfort, education, housing, and more.

Another major Protestant contribution to the religious foundation of rights was its emphasis on the role of the individual believer in the economy of salvation. The Protestant Reformation did not invent the individual or individual rights. But sixteenth-century Protestant reformers gave new emphasis to the (religious) rights and liberties of individuals at both religious law and civil law. The Anabaptist doctrine of adult baptism, in particular, built on a voluntarist understanding of religion in which believers were called to make a conscientious choice to accept the faith—metaphorically, to scale the wall of separation between the fallen world and the perfection of Christ in the realm of religion. Later Free Church followers converted this cardinal image into a powerful platform of liberty of conscience, free exercise of religion, and separation of church and state—not only for Christians, but eventually for all peaceable believers. Their views had a great influence on the formation of protections of religious liberty in the American Constitution. They would later come to expression in international human rights instruments that guaranteed the right freely to choose and change one's religion.

An important contribution to Western rights talk was the Protestant logic of revolution against tyrants who persistently and pervasively violated the people's 'fundamental rights'. Protestant jurists and theologians developed a theory of political revolution that was based effectively on a Christian government contract or covenant theory. Every political government, they argued, is formed by a tacit or explicit covenant or contract sworn between the rulers and their subjects before God. If any of the people violate the terms of this political covenant and become criminals, God empowers the rulers to prosecute and punish them, up to and including the death penalty in extreme cases. In turn, if any of the rulers violate the terms of the political covenant and become tyrants, God empowers the people to resist and to remove them from office, through lethal force if necessary.

The issue that remained for early modern Protestant political theorists was how to determine which rights were so 'fundamental', so 'inalienable', that, if chronically and pervasively breached by a tyrant, triggered the foundational right to organized resistance and revolt against the tyrant. The first and most important rights, they reasoned, had to be the people's religious rights. Christians, after all, are first and foremost the subjects of God and called to honour and worship God above all else. If the magistrate breaches these religious rights, then nothing can be sacred and secure any longer. By 1650, Protestants had used this logic to develop and defend almost every one of the 'fundamental rights and liberties' that would appear, a century and a half later, in the United States Bill of Rights of 1791. They set out these fundamental rights in detailed constitutions and bills of rights written for the Netherlands, Scotland, England, and the American colonies in the seventeenth century.

A third major Protestant contribution to Western rights talk was its development of new understandings of the relationship of church and state, and new ways of constructing the rights of the church. The Protestant Reformation permanently broke the unity of Western Christendom under central papal rule, and thereby laid the foundations for the modern constitutional system of confessional pluralism. Particularly prescient was the Anabaptist Reformation idea of building a *Scheidingsmaurer*, a 'wall of separation' between the redeemed realm of religion and the fallen realm of the world. Anabaptist religious communities were ascetically withdrawn from the world into small, self-sufficient, intensely democratic communities, governed internally by biblical principles of discipleship, simplicity, charity, and Christian obedience.

Also influential was the Calvinist model of governing the church as a democratically elected consistory of pastors, elders, and deacons. These consistories featured separation among the offices of preaching, discipline, and charity, and a fluid, dialogical form of religious polity and policing centred around collective worship, the congregational meeting, and the democratic election of religious officials with term limits. Later Calvinists in Europe and North America would use these democratic church polities as prototypes for democratic state polities with separation of powers, democratic election, term limits, and town hall meetings with the right of all members to petition the political authorities. Both Calvinists and Anabaptists were critical in the development of the logic of separation of religion and the state that dominates modern Western constitutionalism.

3. Religion and the Modern International Human Rights Framework

The rights and liberties guaranteed in contemporary international and national legal systems, although having roots developed over millennia in various religious, philosophical, and cultural traditions, owe their definitive modern formulation to the promulgation of the UDHR (1948). Subsequent international instruments have refined these and elaborated additional protections, including for religious rights and liberties: (1) the International Covenant on Civil and Political Rights (ICCPR) (1966);[55] (2) the United Nations Declaration on the Elimination of All Forms of Intolerance and Discrimination Based on Religion or Belief ('the Declaration on Religion or Belief') (1981);[56] (3) the Concluding Document of the Vienna Follow-up Meeting of Representatives of the Participating States of the Conference on Security and Cooperation in Europe ('the Vienna Concluding Document') (1989);[57] and (4) the Declaration on the Rights of Persons Belonging to National or Ethnic, Religious, and Linguistic Minorities ('the Minorities Declaration') (1992).[58]

The ICCPR distinguishes between the right to freedom of religion or belief and the freedom to manifest one's religion or belief. The right to freedom of religion (the freedom to have, to alter, or to adopt a religion of one's choice) is an absolute right from which no derogation may be made and which may not be restricted or impaired in any manner. This is a contested issue today among some Muslim groups who recognize the right to enter Islam, but not to exit it; those who choose to leave the Muslim faith are apostates who deserve death. Freedom to manifest or exercise one's religion (individually or collectively, publicly or privately) may be subject only to such limitations as are prescribed by law and are necessary to protect public

[55] International Covenant on Civil and Political Rights, GA Res 2200A (XXI), 21 UN GAOR Supp (No 16) at 52, UN Doc A/6316, 999 UNTS (16 Dec 1966), Arts 18, 20/2, 2, 26.

[56] Declaration on the Elimination of All Forms of Intolerance and Discrimination Based on Religion or Belief, GA Res 36/55, UN GAOR Supp (No 151), UN Doc A/RES/36/55 (25 Nov 1981).

[57] Concluding Document of the Vienna Follow-up Meeting of Representatives of the Participating States of the Conference on Security and Cooperation in Europe, 28 ILM 527 (17 January 1989).

[58] Declaration on the Rights of Persons Belonging to National or Ethnic, Religious, and Linguistic Minorities, GA Res 47/135, Annex, UN Doc A/Res/47/135/Annex (18 Dec 1992).

safety, order, health, or morals or the fundamental rights and freedoms of others. The requirement of necessity implies that any such limitation on the manifestation of religion must be proportionate to its aim to protect any of the listed state interests.[59] The ICCPR also calls for state parties to prohibit 'any advocacy of national, racial, or religious hatred that constitutes incitement to discrimination, hostility, or violence' and provides that the principles of equal treatment and nondiscrimination should apply to religion or belief.

The Declaration on Religion or Belief elaborates the religious liberty provisions adumbrated in the ICCPR. Like the ICCPR, the Declaration on its face applies to believers both 'individually or in community', and 'in public or in private'. The Declaration catalogues a number of specific rights to 'freedom of thought, conscience, and religion', including the rights to worship or assemble and to establish and maintain places for these purposes; to establish and maintain appropriate charitable or humanitarian institutions; to make, acquire, and use articles and materials related to religious rites or customs; to write, issue, and disseminate relevant publications in these areas; to teach a religion or belief in suitable places; to solicit and receive voluntary financial and other contributions; to train, appoint, elect, and designate appropriate leaders; to observe days of rest and celebrate holy days; and to establish and maintain communications with individuals and communities, both nationally and internationally, on matters of religion and belief.[60] Additional provisions detail the religious rights of parents and children. The Declaration also includes more elaborate prohibitions than the ICCPR on religious discrimination and intolerance, barring religious 'discrimination by any State, institution, group of persons, or person'. Accordingly, the Declaration calls on all states parties 'to take effective measures to prevent and eliminate' such discrimination 'in all fields of civil, economic, political, social, and cultural life'. The Vienna Concluding Document expands the religious liberty norms of the 1981 Declaration. It provides an elaborate catalogue of the rights of religious groups to govern their own polity, property, and personnel; to establish charities, schools, and seminaries; and to have access to literature, media, and religious worship items.

The refinement and articulation of these religious group rights coincides with the development in international human rights law of the 'right to self-determination' of religious, cultural, or linguistic communities. The 1992 Minorities Declaration

[59] See Symposium, 'The Permissible Scope of Legal Limitations on the Freedom of Religion and Belief'(2005) 19 *Emory International Law Review* 465–1320.

[60] The 1990 Copenhagen Document adds to the 1981 Declaration 'the right of everyone to have conscientious objection to military service' and calls for 'various forms of alternative service... in combatant or civilian service' 'which are compatible with the reasons for conscientious objections to military service'. Document of the Copenhagen Meeting of Representatives of the Participating States of the Conference on the Human Dimension of the Conference on Security and Co-operation in Europe (1990), Principle 18, reprinted in OSCE/ODIHR, *Guidelines for Review of Legislation Pertaining to Religion or Belief* (June, 2004), 45.

clearly spells out the government's obligation to each of these groups to protect and encourage conditions for the promotion of the concerned group identities of minorities, afford to minorities the special competence to participate effectively in decisions pertinent to the group to which they belong, not discriminate in any way against any person on the basis of his or her group identity, and take actions to secure their equal treatment at law. The Minorities Declaration further provides that: 'States shall take measures to create favorable conditions to enable persons belonging to minorities to express their characteristics and to develop their culture, language, religion, traditions and customs, except where specific practices are in violation of national law and contrary to international standards.'[61] The recent 2007 United Nations Declaration on the Rights of Indigenous Peoples elaborates these rights of self-determination even further for indigenous, aboriginal, or first peoples and their distinctive sites and rites of religious identity and practice.[62]

These international instruments highlight the issues about religion that now regularly confront national and international tribunals. How to protect religious and cultural minorities within a majoritarian religious culture—particularly controversial groups sometimes pejoratively referred to as 'sects' or 'cults' who often bring charges of religious and cultural discrimination. How to define the limits of religious and anti-religious exercises and expressions that cause offence or harm to others or elicit charges of blasphemy, defamation, or sacrilege. How to adjudicate challenges that a state's proscriptions or prescriptions run directly counter to core claims of conscience or cardinal commandments of the faith. How to balance private and public exercises of religion, including the right to proselytize. How to balance conflicts between the rights of parents to bring up their children in the faith and the duties of the state to protect the best interest of the child. How to protect the distinct religious needs of prisoners, soldiers, refugees, and others who don't enjoy ready access to traditional forms and forums of religious worship and expression. These issues all highlight important dimensions of the right to religious freedom in a religiously pluralistic and globalized world.

Many religion and human rights issues involve religious groups whose right to govern themselves free from unwarranted state intrusion is itself often a critical issue. How to negotiate the complex needs and norms of religious groups without according them too much sovereignty over their members or their members too little relief from secular courts. How to balance the rights of religious groups to self-governance with the guarantees to individuals of freedom from discrimination based on religion, gender, culture, and sexual orientation. How to balance

[61] 1992 Minorities Declaration, Art 4.2.

[62] United Nations Declaration on the Rights of Indigenous Peoples, UN GAOR, A/61/L.67/Annex (2007). For a discussion of the challenges that consideration of indigenous religion poses to contemporary human rights discourse, see Ronald Niezen, 'Indigenous Religion and Human Rights' in *Religion and Human Rights*, 119–34.

the rights of competing religious groups who each claim access to a common holy site, or a single religious or cultural group whose sacred site is threatened with desecration, development, or disaster. How to protect the relations between local religious communities and their foreign co-religionists. How to adjudicate intra- or interreligious disputes that come before secular tribunals for resolution. How to determine the proper levels of state cooperation with and support of religious officials and institutions in the delivery of vital social services—child care, education, charity, medical services, disaster relief, among others. These concerns typically arise in the context of the official registration process that many states require religion to undertake in order to be allowed to compete, in cases of interreligious competition and prestige, and in cases in which believers invoke the protection of the state from human rights abuses perpetrated by other members and institutions of their faith.

4. The Place of Religion in Human Rights Today

A number of distinguished commentators have argued that religion should have no place in a modern regime of human rights. Religions may well have been the sources of human rights in earlier eras, and may even have helped to inspire the modern human rights revolution. Nonetheless, these sceptics argue, religion has now outlived its utility. Religion is, by its nature, too expansionistic and monopolistic, too patriarchal and hierarchical, too antithetical to the very ideals of pluralism, toleration, and equality inherent in a human rights regime. Religion is also too dangerous, divisive, and diverse in its demands to be accorded special protection. Religion is better viewed as just another category of liberty and expression and given no more preference than its secular counterparts. Indeed, to accord religion special human rights treatment is in effect to establish it and to discriminate against non-religious parties in the same position. Purge religion entirely from special consideration, this argument concludes, and the human rights paradigm will thrive.

It is undeniable that religion has been, and still is, a formidable force for both political good and political evil, and that it has fostered benevolence and belligerence, peace and pathos of untold dimensions. The proper response to religious belligerence and pathos, however, cannot be to deny that religion exists or to dismiss it to the private sphere and sanctuary. The proper response is to castigate the vices and to cultivate the virtues of religion, to confirm those religious teachings and practices that are most conducive to human rights, democracy, and rule of law.

First, without religion, many rights are cut from their roots. Contrary to conventional wisdom, the theory and law of human rights are neither new nor secular in origin. Human rights are, in no small part, the modern political fruits of ancient religious beliefs and practices. Religious communities must be open to a new human rights hermeneutic—fresh methods of interpreting their sacred texts and traditions that will allow them to reclaim their essential roots and roles in the cultivation of human rights. Religious traditions will not allow secular human rights norms to be imposed on them from without; they must (re)discover them from within.

Second, without religion, the regime of human rights becomes infinitely expandable. Many religious communities adopt and advocate human rights in order to protect religious duties. Religious rights provide the best example of the organic linkage between rights and duties. Without the link, rights become abstract, with no obvious limit on their exercise or their expansion, with no ontological grounding that keeps them from becoming a simple wish list of individual preferences.

Third, many religious traditions cannot conceive of, nor accept, a system of rights that excludes, deprecates, or privatizes religion. For these traditions, religion is inextricably integrated into every facet of life. Religious rights are thus an inherent part of rights of speech, press, assembly, and other individual rights as well as ethnic, cultural, linguistic, and similar associational rights. No system of rights that ignores or deprecates this cardinal place of religion can be respected or adopted.

Fourth, the simple state versus individual dialectic of many modern human rights theories leaves it to the state alone to protect and provide rights. In reality, the state is not, and cannot be, so omni-competent. Numerous 'mediating structures' stand between the state and the individual, religious institutions prominently among them. They play a vital role in the cultivation and realization of rights. They can create the conditions (sometimes the prototypes) for the realization of civil and political rights. They can provide a critical (sometimes the principal) means to meet rights of education, health-care, child care, labour organizations, employment, artistic opportunities, among others. They can offer some of the deepest insights into norms of stewardship, solidarity, and servanthood that lie at the heart of rights concerned with the environment.

Finally, without religion, human rights norms have no enduring narratives to ground them. There is, of course, some value in simply declaring human rights norms of 'liberty, equality, and fraternity' or 'life, liberty, and property'—if for no other reason than to pose an ideal against which a person or community might measure itself, to preserve a normative totem for later generations to make real. But, ultimately, these abstract human rights ideals of the good life and the good society depend on the visions and values of human communities and institutions to give them content and coherence—to provide what Jacques Maritain once called 'the scale of values governing [their] exercise and concrete manifestation'.[63] It is here that religion must play a vital role. Religion is an ineradicable condition of human lives and human communities.

Further Reading

An-Na'im A et al (eds), *Human Rights and Religious Values: An Uneasy Relationship* (Eerdmans 2005)

de Bary Wt and Tu W, *Confucianism and Human Rights* (Columbia UP 1998)

Durham Wc Jr and Scharffs BG, *Law and Religion: National, International, and Comparative Perspectives* (Aspen 2010)

Keown D Prebish CS, and Husted WR, *Buddhism and Human Rights* (Curzon 1998)

Lerner N, *Religion, Secular Beliefs and Human Rights: 25 Years After the Human Rights Declaration* (Martinus Nijhoff 2006)

Lindholm T, Durham WC Jr, and Tahzib-Lie BG, *Facilitating Freedom of Religion or Belief: A Deskbook* (Martinus Nijhoff 2004)

Novak D, *Jewish Social Ethics* (OUP 1992)

Nurser J, *For All Peoples and All Nations: Christian Churches and Human Rights* (WCC Press 2005)

Perry MJ, *Toward a Theory of Human Rights: Religion, Law, Courts* (CUP 2007)

Runzo J, Martin NM, and Sharma A (eds), *Human Rights and Responsibilities in the World Religions* (Oneworld 2003)

Sachedina A, *Islam and the Challenge of Human Rights* (OUP 2009)

Sharma A, *Hinduism and Human Rights: A Conceptual Approach* (OUP 2004)

Stahnke T and Martin JP (eds), *Religion and Human Rights: Basic Documents* (Center for the Study of Human Rights, Columbia University 1998)

Van ver Venn JA, Dreyer JS, and Pieterse HJC, *Is There a God in Human Rights? The Complex Relationship Between Human Rights and Religion* (Brill 2004)

Witte J Jr, *The Reformation of Rights: Law, Religion and Human Rights in Early Modern Calvinism* (CUP 2007)

——, and Alexander FS (eds), *Christianity and Human Rights* (CUP 2010)

——, and van der Vyver JD (eds), *Religious Human Rights in Global Perspective,* 2 vols (The Hague: Martinus Nijhoff Publishers 1996)

——, and Christian Green M (eds), *Religion and Human Rights: An Introduction* (OUP 2011)

[63] Jacques Maritain, 'Introduction' to UNESCO, *Human Rights: Comments and Interpretations* (Columbia UP 1949) 1.

CHAPTER 2

MORAL PHILOSOPHY

SIEGFRIED VAN DUFFEL

THE twentieth century saw a remarkable shift in the attitudes and preconceptions of moral philosophers. In the first half of the century, few philosophers showed any interest in the analysis and theory of human rights. It seemed as if philosophers had discarded the idea of human rights as a confused or incoherent remnant of the past. Yet, a dramatic change in the fate of human rights theory appeared in the second half of the twentieth century. Discussions about the nature of rights, the place of rights in moral theories, and the value and justification of human rights, took centre stage in academic philosophy journals. This literature has become so vast and wide-ranging that it is impossible to provide a comprehensive overview of it. This chapter, therefore, will focus on a number of long-standing debates in moral philosophy, indicating the interrelations between these debates, as they bear on the foundations of human rights. Before doing so, the chapter will begin by considering a recent challenge to the topic as such, one which asks whether moral philosophy has anything useful to say about the idea of human rights.

1. The Political Conception of Human Rights

The orthodox view of human rights is that they are inherent and derive simply from the fact of being human. This view distinguishes human rights from legal and conventional rights, as well as from moral rights that arise due to special relationships, like the right to fulfilment of a promise made. Orthodoxy further has it that ordinary moral reasoning suffices to determine, for example, which rights inhere in human beings. This stands to reason, because if rights exist independently of any convention or institutional arrangement, it is hard to conceive of another method through which to grasp them, apart from ordinary moral reasoning.

Little more than a decade ago, most philosophers would have been surprised if someone asked whether moral philosophy were relevant to the topic of human rights. The orthodoxy has been challenged, however, by what are now generally known as 'political conceptions' of human rights, as John Rawls first set forth in *The Law of Peoples.*[1] More recently, Joseph Raz,[2] Bernard Williams,[3] Joshua Cohen,[4] and Charles Beitz[5] have presented alternative versions. Political conceptions of human rights reject the idea that human rights are rights that inhere to people simply by virtue of them sharing a common humanity, asserting that this approach disregards the distinctively political role of human rights. Rawls, for example, while he does not deny that human rights belong to all human beings, characterizes them by the role they play in regulating relations between societies. Human rights limit toleration among peoples. They are 'the necessary conditions of any…cooperation',[6] and they are distinguished from other moral rights, according to Rawls, in that their widespread violation can generate a pro tanto justification for forceful intervention by another (well-ordered) society.[7] The immunity of any society from intervention, therefore, is conditioned on its respect for the rights to life, to liberty, to property, and to formal equality. This is a notoriously truncated list, which probably explains the unease that even Rawls's admirers have displayed towards his account of human rights.

Rawls also challenged another tenet of the orthodoxy on human rights. While noting that 'comprehensive doctrines, religious or non-religious, might base the idea of human rights on a theological, philosophical, or moral conception of the nature of the human person',[8] he specifically rejected the possibility of such a grounding for the purpose of constructing a law of peoples. He reasons that peoples from different religious, philosophical, and moral backgrounds should be able to

[1] John Rawls, *The Law of Peoples* (Harvard UP 1999).

[2] Joseph Raz, 'Human Rights without Foundations' in Samantha Besson and John Tasioulas (eds), *The Philosophy of International Law* (OUP 2010).

[3] Bernard Williams, *In the Beginning Was the Deed: Realism and Moralism in Political Argument* (Geoffrey Hawthorn (ed), Princeton UP 2005).

[4] Joshua Cohen, 'Is there a Human Right to Democracy?' in Christine Sypnowich (ed), *The Egalitarian Conscience: Essays in Honour of GA Cohen* (OUP 2006).

[5] Charles R Beitz, *The Idea of Human Rights* (OUP 2009).

[6] Rawls (n 1) 68.

[7] John Tasioulas, 'Are Human Rights Essentially Triggers for Intervention?' (2009) 4 *Philosophy Compass* 938, 940.

[8] Rawls (n 1) 81.

agree freely on the set of principles and norms of which human rights are a part (ie on the law of peoples). If human rights were to be grounded in a particular comprehensive religious or philosophical doctrine of human nature, many peoples might reject them 'as in some way distinctive of Western political tradition and prejudicial to other cultures'.[9]

This quote highlights one of the main motivating reasons for developing a political conception of human rights, and—specifically—for separating human rights theory from moral philosophy. But Rawls's conception has failed to convince even many of his devoted pupils, in part because of the very short list of rights that it generates. Rawls appears to be applying the label 'human rights' to only a sub-set of human rights proper. He does recognize a larger category of rights—liberal constitutional rights—which seems co-extensive with what are commonly identified as human rights, but his theory would come down to a proposal for enforcing only *some* (say, basic) human rights in international law, and hence it would not count as a conception of human rights.[10]

Charles Beitz's recent work, *The Idea of Human Rights*,[11] has taken the political conception of human rights in a very different direction—one that is particularly relevant to the question of whether moral philosophy has something to contribute. '[H]uman rights', Beitz writes, 'names not so much an abstract normative idea as an emergent political practice'.[12] This is perplexing, inviting the question of how to distinguish the doings that constitute this practice, other than by saying that they are related to the idea of human rights. How something can be a practice and simultaneously an idea that plays a role *in* the same practice is rather puzzling. The claim that human rights *is* a practice might be charitably re-interpreted to mean a claim that there is a practice which consists of actions, institutions, etc that are in some way related to the idea of human rights. So when Beitz uses phrases like 'the doctrine of human rights', 'the idea of human rights', and 'the concept of human rights' one may suppose that he is referring to something like 'the doctrine/idea/concept inherent in the practice'.

Beitz grants that there exist other conceptions and doctrines than the ones he identifies as inherent in the practice, but he thinks these are misguided insofar as they conceive of human rights 'as if they had an existence in the moral order that can be grasped independently of their embodiment in international doctrine and practice'.[13] The view that human rights 'express and derive their authority from some such deeper order of values' is also mistaken, according to Beitz.[14] The familiar conceptions beg questions 'in presuming to understand and criticize an existing normative practice on the basis of one or another governing conception that does not,

[9] Rawls (n 1) 68.

[10] Tasioulas (n 7) 943. See further S Matthew Liao and Adam Etinson, 'Political and Naturalistic Conceptions of Human Rights: A False Polemic?' (2012) 9 *J Moral Philosophy* 327.

[11] Beitz (n 5). [12] Beitz (n 5) xii. [13] Beitz (n 5) 7. [14] Beitz (n 5) 7.

itself, take account of the functions that the idea of a human right is meant to play, and actually does play, in the practice'.[15] This is unlikely to impress the proponents of the familiar theories, because their aim was not to explicate some existing practice (only Beitz claims that human rights *is* a practice), but rather the idea of human rights. The approach does, however, highlight an important question. What does it mean for some doctrine or conception to be inherent in a practice? How does one identify the role that the idea of human rights plays in the practice? If conceptions of human rights are at work in real life, they are those of the people who participate in the practice. Beitz would probably agree that many of these participants hold beliefs that natural rights theories aptly describe. People do talk about human rights as if they express and derive their authority from a deeper order of values, and they do—sometimes—criticize existing human rights practice on the basis of such moral beliefs. Moreover, Beitz does not give a good reason to think that it is impossible to characterize the idea of human rights as its practitioners hold it to be and to do so independently of the practice in which it is said to play a role. This is, of course, exactly what many moral philosophers understand themselves to be doing.

Obviously, explicating the idea of human rights that practitioners hold is not the same as describing the practice itself, although Beitz sometimes seems to insist that human rights really *is* the latter. It may still be the case that the conceptions of human rights that ordinary people have do not adequately describe the practice in which they are participating. If naturalistic conceptions distort our perception of human rights, as Beitz claims, this would presumably put into question the relevance of moral philosophy for the topic. One way of vindicating the recent contributions of moral philosophers, then, is to explain how these challenges can be met. The next section will focus in particular on four challenges: (1) the ground of human rights, (2) the scope of human rights, (3) the way human rights ground action, and (4) universality from the perspective of the (supposed) rights holders.

2. Four Challenges to Moral Philosophy

The first challenge is this: the people who drafted the Universal Declaration and subsequent treaties were convinced that no particular religious tradition or particular comprehensive doctrine (or morality) grounded human rights.[16] Christians may

[15] Beitz (n 5) 8.

[16] See eg Johannes Morsink, *The Universal Declaration of Human Rights: Origins, Drafting & Intent* (University of Pennsylvania Press 2000).

well believe that faith in Christ and a commitment to obey His commandments also requires respect for human rights, just as a Muslim may believe that Islam requires her to respect other people's human rights, but allegiance to human rights does not require one to become a Christian or Muslim, nor does it require one to renounce one's religion or to become a liberal. The problem with developing a normative theory of human rights, then, is that it seems to deny this stance; the idea of such a theory seems to suggest that accepting human rights entails endorsing the theory, and this threatens the possibility of a universal acceptance of human rights. This issue is too complex to fully address in this chapter, which will limit itself to attempting to demonstrate that moral philosophy is able to generate far more interesting and rich (better) answers to questions that political theories cannot address. For that reason alone, it deserves the close attention of anyone concerned with the topic.

The second challenge is the contention that natural rights theories end up misrepresenting and narrowing the scope of human rights, for example, by claiming that only political and civil rights can be accorded the status of genuine human rights. This critique certainly applies to certain natural rights theories, although it would be too simplistic to dismiss such theories on the assumption that their subject is too narrow compared to our ordinary judgements. Moreover, the challenge does not apply to all theories. Nevertheless, there is good reason to take the challenge seriously, because it will reveal something important about the subject. But once again, the insight can only be gained by paying serious attention to moral theories.

Thirdly, some people think that human rights are rights that citizens have against their respective government, at least in the first instance, and that natural rights theories cannot but deny this. Natural rights theorists should be worried about this challenge, even though it is mistaken, because it points to a significant problem in human rights theory—a problem that has been the subject of considerable debate among philosophers. It is a challenge not just to the natural rights approach but to anyone who takes human rights seriously.

Finally, it is often said that rights protect interests. Universal human rights, then, protect universal human interests. The fourth challenge is to determine whether there are indeed interests that every human shares, and whether these rights can somehow be derived from human nature. In particular, one might worry that anything that *can* be derived from human nature must be something much more modest than what constitutes a comprehensive list of human rights. The picture that emerges from contemporary theories, however, is somewhat more complex, and again contains the seed of a better understanding of the dynamics of contemporary human rights discourse.

The thrust of this chapter, therefore, is that natural or human rights theories are a rich source of insights that those concerned with the issue should contemplate. Before delving into the normative theories themselves, it will be useful to start with a topic that has generated much heat in the last half century; ie the question 'What are Rights?'.

3. The Nature of Rights Debate

It may seem obvious that in order to know what human rights are, we have to know what 'rights' are. Yet, in writings about human rights, one seldom finds that any attention is paid to the nature of rights. More often than not, texts simply include a definition of 'rights' before the author swiftly moves ahead to address other questions. Many seem convinced that readers have a firm enough grasp of the nature of the concept. This is true enough if it means that persons are generally able, without hesitation, to distinguish normative incidences that are instantiations of 'right' (in the subjective sense) from those incidences that are not. However, seeking an answer to what makes something into a right, or what is common to (all) subjective rights, reveals that the matter has been highly contested and that there is still no widely accepted answer. Philosophers writing on the topic can be generally grouped into two camps. The first is composed of proponents of the 'Interest Theory' of the nature of rights, who hold that whenever someone has a right, this means that an interest of the right-holder is being normatively protected. In other words, rights protect people's well-being. Proponents of the 'Will Theory' of rights disagree, positing that central to the concept of a right is the idea that the holder of the right has some kind of freedom, autonomy, or sovereignty, which is not necessarily the case when someone's interest is being normatively protected.[17]

The obvious way to decide in favour of one theory or the other would be to consider, on the one hand, whether the normative incidences normally recognized as 'rights' are also captured by the theory, and, on the other hand, whether all normative incidences that are described by the theory as 'rights' are normally recognized as 'rights' as well. This 'extensional' test thus seeks to know whether the extension of the theory differs in any way from common-sense judgment (or, if we are considering legal rights, the judgment of lawyers and jurists). Most of the debate between proponents of both theories has, in fact, been a back and forth on the shortcomings of either theory in this respect.

Bentham, one of the early proponents of the Interest Theory, had held that someone has a right if she 'stands to benefit' from the performance of a duty.[18] Certainly, in many cases, when people have rights they stand to benefit from someone else's duty in some way. A citizen would not have a (legal) right to political participation unless others (including the government) had duties that protect this citizen's ability to exercise her right. These duties would include a duty not to interfere with the citizen's attempt at exercising her right, and perhaps also duties to enable her

[17] A good introduction to the debate is Matthew H Kramer, NE Simmonds, and Hillel Steiner (eds), *A Debate over Rights: Philosophical Enquiries* (OUP 1998).

[18] For analysis, see David Lyons, *Rights, Welfare and Mill's Moral Theory* (OUP 1994) 27–30.

to exercise the right in some way. So it seems as if standing to benefit from someone's performance of a duty is (often, at least) a necessary condition for recognizing someone as a right-holder. But is it also a sufficient condition? Consider the following example. Everyone has a duty not to murder my friend. Clearly I stand to benefit from the performance of this duty. But we wouldn't say that *I* therefore have a right that my friend not be murdered. My friend's right not to be murdered correlates with duties that are owed to her, not to me. So standing to benefit from someone's performance of a duty is not a sufficient condition for being a right-holder. Even if right-holders stand to benefit from someone's fulfilment of a duty, not everyone who stands to benefit from other people's fulfilment of a duty is a right-holder.

Interest Theorists, from the twentieth century until recently, have geared much of their work towards solving problems such as these. Some of the famous attempts refer in some way to the intentions of the lawgiver or to the reasons that the lawgiver might have. Thus it has been suggested that a person has a right when the lawgiver imposes a duty *in order to* protect some interest of hers (or an aspect of her interest), or when an interest of hers *is a reason to* impose duties.[19] Yet this approach raises problems of unearthing the intentions of the lawgiver, or the reason for the imposition of a duty. What were the intentions of the lawgiver when murder was outlawed, and how will we know the reason for imposing a duty (on government officials) to provide basic education for children? Perhaps safeguarding a continuous supply of qualified labour for enterprises concerned the lawgiver more than the interests of children. It seems doubtful that any perception of an intention of the lawgiver can guide the identification of rights.[20] There is, moreover, a more serious problem that follows from speculation about the intentions of the lawgiver; it may lead to a conclusion that some rights are not intended to protect the interests of the right-holders, but are directed at the interests of others. Take the right of a journalist to withhold information on her sources from the police. This right clearly serves to protect the ability of the journalist to carry out her job, and thus it protects an interest of hers. However, it seems at least as plausible that the right to withhold information regarding sources arose in order to protect the interest(s) of the public at large (in a free press), rather than the interests of journalists in the ability to carry out their profession (even though the latter is of course a necessary condition for the former).[21]

The example just given seems to show that protecting a right-holder's interest is not always the reason for the existence of the right, and this presents a serious challenge to attempts to provide a definition that consists of necessary and sufficient conditions for the existence of a right, based on the reasons for protecting an interest. To be sure, not all versions of Interest Theory are of this kind; for example,

19 See Joseph Raz, 'Legal Rights' (1984) 4 *OJLS* 1; Lyons (n 18) 23–46.

20 See Kramer, "Rights Without Trimmings." In Kramer, Simmonds and Steiner (eds), supra n. 16 at p. 85.

21 For discussion and references, see Gopal Sreenivasan, 'A Hybrid Theory of Claim-Rights' (2005) 25 *OJLS* 257, 265–66.

Matthew Kramer has recently developed a quite different version. But, no existing version seems to capture adequately the intuitive judgements regarding the identification of rights.

The most distinguished proponent of Will Theory was Herbert Hart. He thought that the characteristic feature of rights is that they provide the holder with some kind of control over another person's duty 'so that in the area of conduct covered by that duty the individual who has the right is a small-scale sovereign to whom the duty is owed'.[22] Take the right of a patient to be treated by her doctor. The doctor has a duty to treat the patient to the best of her ability, but the patient controls this duty in the sense that the doctor cannot do anything without the patient's consent. The patient also may waive or extinguish the doctor's duty. Moreover, if the doctor breaches her duty, the patient may choose whether to sue or not and may waive or extinguish the duty to pay compensation. Having some of these powers over someone else's duty makes one a small-scale sovereign and thus a right-holder. This definition seems to capture something of the reason why the patient is considered a genuine right-holder and not a mere beneficiary of the doctor's duty. It also captures the idea that we can *exercise* rights. However, the definition has consequences that many find disconcerting. Hart himself recognized that, according to his definition, criminal law did not confer rights on people. Thus, to claim a (legal) right not to be killed or not to be harassed on the street would at best be to use the term 'right' in a loose, imprecise way.

The problems do not stop there. Because rights, according to Will Theory, involve some kind of control over someone's duty, it would seem sensible to ascribe rights only to beings that are capable of exercising such control. Consequently, it seems that human infants and the mentally infirm, for example, do not have rights. For many critics, this consequence amounts to a *reductio ad absurdum* of Will Theory; if a theory of the nature of rights denies rights to children, this can only be an indication that something has gone awfully wrong. Another troubling consequence of Will Theory is that it may entail in some cases that a right is lost when the law strengthens protection of an interest. The classic example is that of a minimum wage. Should the law require employers to pay employees a certain minimum wage, the right of employees can be strengthened—so it seems—by making workers unable to contract to work for a salary less than the minimum wage (simply by declaring any such contract invalid). For the Will Theory, however, it seems that such a law, by taking away the control of a worker, divests the worker of a right. Conversely, most of us would rather consider the rule that eliminates the worker's ability to contract for a lower salary as strengthening the right to a minimum wage.

The debate between Interest Theorists and Will Theorists has raged for many decades. Although new contributions to the debate continue to appear, one can discern

[22] HLA Hart, *Essays on Bentham: Studies in Jurisprudence and Political Theory* (Clarendon Press 1982) 183.

a sense of exasperation with the seemingly endless nature of the debate. One scholar concluded that the debate has ended in a stand-off,[23] and others have thought that a solution to the problem must be found in some combination or hybrid of the two theories. Before turning to that possibility, it is useful to consider what exactly philosophers have been doing when attempting to give an account of the nature of rights. There are two rather crude candidates for an answer to this question, both of which turn out to be unsatisfactory. This suggests that there exists a real problem here, deserving of a better response. A third alternative requires consideration of the historical roots of the contemporary debate on the nature of rights.

The first answer seems to impose itself when considering the kind of objections that proponents of either account have raised against the competing account. Typically they have tried to show that the competing account diverges from linguistic intuitions on the topic of human rights—that it identifies normative incidences as rights that are not recognized as rights or, conversely, that it fails to classify certain normative incidences as rights that are commonly characterized as rights. This cannot be correct. If one could decide the disagreement by gauging the extensional adequacy of each account, the debate would have ended decades ago, for it must be obvious to any observer that Interest Theory does considerably better than Will Theory in this respect. So why has the debate continued? One reason is that not merely intuitions about the proper *extension* of the domain of rights, but also what one could call the *intension* of the concept, motivate it. This would explain why Will Theorists tend to be relatively untroubled by the awareness that their conception of rights effectively rules out many common-sense intuitions regarding the word 'right'. It also provides an explanation of why the debate seems interminable; different kinds of intuitions are pulling in different directions, with no obvious way to establish the weight of these different intuitions, making it hard to see how either side in the debate might come up with an argument that would convince the other side.

The second answer considers that if some intuitions regarding 'rights' are indeed incompatible with others, then it would seem necessary for the purpose of scholarly debate to narrow down the use of the term, perhaps so that it refers to the largest consistent subset of those intuitions. This would involve more or less consciously ruling out some intuitions as improper, thus stipulating away some of the intuitions (preferably as few as possible) in order to distil a vocabulary suitable for academic discourse. This suggestion may make sense of the continued existence of different definitions of 'rights', but it generates a huge problem of intelligibility. How is it possible for intelligent individuals to debate stipulative definitions for decades? Of course, some stipulative definitions may be closer to the usage of a word in ordinary language (or in legal discourse), but such observations could not obtain the status they have acquired in the nature of rights debate, namely that of casting doubt on

[23] Leif Wenar, 'The Nature of Rights' (2005) 33 *Phil & Pub Aff* 223, 223.

the acceptability of the definition. At the least, semblance to linguistic intuitions could only be one of a set of criteria among other criteria, such as coherence and clarity, by which to judge the usefulness of a definition of rights. The most effective defence of a stipulative definition would be to show that it is (or could be) part of a powerful theory, but proponents of either account have not tried to make this argument. Instead of using their respective definition to build a theory on the topic, they have baptized their definitions with the label 'theory' and have argued that it corresponds better to intuitions in comparison with other definitions.

If neither response makes sense of the debate, other options must be considered. There is good reason to think that the debate is misguided; Interest Theory and Will Theory are better seen as attempting to capture different kinds of rights.[24] If that is correct, neither Interest Theory nor Will Theory is a genuine account of 'rights' and therefore to ask which of the two definitions of rights is the correct one is to ask a pseudo-question. This raises two important questions: first, if two different kinds of rights ('Interest Theory rights' and 'Will Theory rights') exist, is it more than linguistic coincidence that we call them both rights? Or, to put the question differently, what makes both kinds of rights, rights? The first is a question for a better conceptual analysis. Second, why has the debate taken this particular shape? This is a question about the historical roots of the debate. I would like to suggest that both kinds of rights are the basis of two very different theories of natural rights, and this accounts for some of the assumptions which have sustained the contemporary debate.

4. New Analyses of Rights

An increasing number of scholars, exasperated with the seemingly interminable debate between Interest Theory and Will Theory, have started searching for alternatives that would combine the virtues of both. These alternatives have taken several forms: multi-function theories, normative constraint views, capacious versions of either theory, and hybrid theories.[25] This author's own theory will be used as a starting point for the rest of the chapter. This analysis of rights connects the two kinds of rights in a non-ad hoc manner. In addition, there is a fit between the best analysis of the concept of rights and the best contemporary theories of human rights. Further, the twofold structure of the concept of rights parallels two very

[24] Siegfried Van Duffel, 'The Nature of Rights Debate Rests on a Mistake' (2012) 93 *Pac Phil Q* 104.

[25] See eg Rowan Cruft, 'Rights: Beyond Interest Theory and Will Theory?' (2004) 23 *L &Phil* 347; Sreenivasan (n 21); Wenar (n 23); George W Rainbolt, *The Concept of Rights* (Springer 2006); Gopal Sreenivasan, 'Duties and their Direction' (2010) 120 *Ethics* 465.

different theories of human rights and, historically, two traditions (or theories) of natural rights. These traditions have shaped not only intuitions about the proper reference of the word 'right', but also a broader framework of assumptions taken for granted when talking about rights. Consequently, it will become clear how seemingly unsolvable problems in contemporary human rights theories are the product of an evolution which can only be genuinely understood in light of the historical antecedents from which contemporary human rights theories have emerged. The upshot is that moral philosophy, if analysis and more than a mere superficial knowledge of the historical development of natural rights theories properly inform it, is indispensable in order to understand the problems that plague contemporary human rights thinking.

A new analysis of the concept of rights, in order to be an acceptable replacement of existing analyses, should do better than these existing analyses in capturing intuitions about rights. Given the current state of the debate, and the suggestion that there are two different kinds of rights, a new analyses (1) should be extensionally at least as adequate as the best versions of Interest Theory; (2) should make sense of the twofold nature of the domain of rights; and (3) should do so in a non-ad hoc manner (ie it should explain what 'Will Theory rights' and 'Interest Theory rights' have in common). An analysis of rights that does this and more posits that rights enable agency and that they do so in two different ways. Rights ('Interest Theory rights') enable agency by removing normative impediments to action and by normatively protecting the interests of the agent. They also enable agency by granting agents normative power and, hence, by making it possible to act normatively—ie to generate normative changes ('Will Theory rights'). If this analysis of rights indeed solves the problems that plague Interest Theory and Will Theory, it serves to establish an intimate connection between rights and agency. And, as it happens, this link between rights and agency is also an enduring feature of the best theories of human rights.

If we trace the historical roots of the contemporary debate over the nature of rights, it should become clear why the debate has taken this particular shape. This should not be understood as a mere historical claim. In the following section, it will become clear that no single natural rights theory can accommodate 'Will Theory rights' and 'Interest Theory rights'—even though both are normative incidences that enable agency—at least not in respect to fundamental rights. When they are considered as natural rights, both kinds of rights give rise to normatively incompatible theories. This is why the history of natural rights theories can be seen as a history of two theories, despite the fact that historically many authors have tried to combine both kinds of rights. In the next section, right-libertarianism is presented as the theory which takes 'Will-Theory rights' as basic. It will show that some versions of the theory fail to establish the conclusions they purport to establish, precisely because they have interpreted the rights fundamental to their theory as interest-based. For the sake of convenience, in looking at natural rights theories in which 'Will Theory rights' and 'Interest Theory rights' are embedded, the remaining sections will refer to natural property rights and natural rights to welfare.

5. Human Rights as Natural Property Rights

The contemporary version of the theory that takes fundamental human rights to be 'Will Theory rights' is libertarianism (or certain versions thereof), although not all libertarians have thought of libertarianism as a natural rights theory. The theories here share the claim that there are only negative, and not positive, moral rights.[26] Negative rights are rights against interference. So there may be a negative right not to be harassed on the street, or a negative right not to have one's car stolen or to be prevented from entering one's home. The characteristic feature of negative rights is that they correlate with duties that people can discharge without actually doing anything—they are obligations of abstention. To enjoy the right, it suffices that everyone abstains from doing anything. This is what distinguishes negative rights from positive rights, for the latter sometimes requires other people to do something in order to discharge their duty toward the right-holder. The human right to affordable healthcare seems incomplete unless someone has a duty to provide affordable healthcare to me; and this would obviously be a positive duty, because that person or agent may have to do something in order to discharge it.

It will be clear that libertarianism's claim that there are no positive, but only negative rights, has radical consequences for human rights doctrine, because it entails, for example, that there is no right to adequate nutrition, basic healthcare, or education.[27] For most persons, such consequences are counter-intuitive, and libertarians have not usually relied exclusively on an appeal to intuition to defend their position. One alternative way to defend libertarianism—particularly apt, of course, to a natural rights theory—is by appealing to human nature. Human beings, philosophers often say, are different from animals in the human ability to make genuine decisions. Genuine human action is not instinctive or impulsive, but rather based on evaluation. Reflection may lead to a decision not to satisfy some desires, while others are deemed worth pursuing. Developing projects or deciding to pursue certain complex goals may in turn generate particular new needs. The importance of this for a theory of natural rights is that genuine human action can be seen to require such real choices, and—crucially—that each individual can only make such a choice for

[26] Eg Jan Narveson, *The Libertarian Idea* (Temple UP 1988) 58.
[27] Loren E Lomasky, *Persons, Rights, and the Moral Community* (OUP 1987) 96.

herself (because nobody can determine another person's values or pursuits). Hence it is central to living a truly human life that one is allowed to make such choices and, presumably, to act on them. Thus 'Freedom of Choice', in many libertarian writings, is supposed to ground libertarian conclusions, but there is at least one line of argument from this idea that clearly does not deliver the desired conclusion, and it is important to examine why it does not.

All persons presumably have an interest in leading a life appropriate to human beings. If making choices and acting on them is what is critical to being human, then surely there is an interest in being able to do so. And since these interests are weighty enough to deserve protection, they (at least prima facie) provide the foundation for 'Interest Theory rights' not to be interfered with in the exercise of one's choices.[28] For the libertarian, only the negative duty not to interfere with the freedom of another limits this right—or freedom—to do what one chooses to do. Grounding human rights in interests, however, does not deliver libertarian conclusions for three incontrovertible reasons. First, even if it is agreed that humans have an interest not to suffer interference when pursuing their aims, this is clearly not their only interest. In fact, it is arguably not even their most urgent interest. Before seeking to be free from other people's interference, individuals need to be functional human beings, which requires that one have access, among other things, to basic nutrition and health. If an interest in freedom grounds rights, it is hard to see why an interest in survival should not ground rights as well. These survival rights cannot be merely negative. While abstention from interference will ensure individual freedom of action, protection of the interest in sustenance requires assistance from other people in those instances when persons are unable to provide for themselves. This in itself is enough to dismiss those versions of libertarianism which aim to ground rights in interests.

The libertarian may attempt to defend the interest theory by saying that: 'Even if we have interests other than the interest in no one interfering with our actions, the latter still is more fundamental to a genuine human existence, and it therefore grounds human rights that trump other rights in case of conflict. But enforcing positive duties *always* conflicts with free choice, and this in effect makes positive rights irrelevant.' This leads to the second reason why the libertarian argument fails; the interest in freedom does not require that choices are *never* restricted. Freedom in a society cannot be absolute; individuals can still be free in most of what they do, even if governments collect income tax to provide for the needy.

The third reason for the failure of the libertarian case for negative rights based on an interest in freedom is that this interest *would* ground positive duties. This is especially the case if this interest is thought to ground property rights. Libertarianism

[28] See eg Murray N Rothbard, *For a New Liberty: The Libertarian Manifesto* (rev edn, Collier Books 1978) 17. The first part of Hegel's *Philosophy of Right* contains the classical defence of property along these lines, but Hegel was of course not a libertarian.

does not guarantee property, but if there is an interest in being able to control property, then there must also be an interest in *having* some property. More generally, an interest in freedom exists because there is an interest in being able to pursue things, and the protection of this ability requires positive duties, as well as negative ones.

As may be obvious by now, attempts to ground libertarianism in human interests fail because the intuitions which underlie the theory are of a different kind. Libertarianism is not a theory of rights based on interests, but a theory of fundamental property rights. To fully understand this idea, it is helpful to see how it developed historically. By the early fourteenth century, the Franciscan religious order had been embroiled for decades in a dispute over the spiritual foundation of their order. The Franciscans distinguished themselves from other religious orders in that they claimed not to own anything, either individually or in common. They even claimed not to have any (legally enforceable) right to the things they used. In the language of the period, the Franciscans sought to live a life without any *dominium* (lordship). Pope John XXII strongly attacked this doctrine, and in one of his writings, he claimed that Adam, the first human being, already had exclusive *dominium* of temporal things.[29] A Dominican cleric, John of Paris, had suggested some two decades earlier that true *dominium* is not dependent on human law, because it is the result of labour.[30] Two decades later, German theologian Konrad von Megenberg would make a very similar claim.[31] It seems that the core of the labour theory of property, now associated with John Locke, was already emerging three-and-a-half centuries earlier.

In Roman law, *dominium* referred to the actual control of a landlord (a *dominus*) over his property. However, in the later Middle Ages, the meaning of *dominium* expanded in at least two ways. First, it came to mean any form of normative control, so that anyone having a legal right could be said to have a kind of *dominium*. Second, it came to refer to the control of a human being over her faculties. Aquinas, for example, held that the *dominium* of man over his own will makes him capable of *dominium* over other things.[32] In the sixteenth century, these ideas were further developed into a full-fledged theory of fundamental property rights (allowing for

[29] Virpi Mäkinen, *Property Rights in the Late Medieval Discussion on Franciscan Poverty* (Peeters 2001).

[30] See John of Paris, *On Royal and Papal Power* (JA Watt (tr), Pontifical Institute of Medieval Studies 1971) 103. On John of Paris, see especially Janet Coleman, 'Medieval Discussions of Property: Ratio and Dominium According to John of Paris and Marsilius of Padua' (1983) 4 *Hist Pol Thought* 209. See also Janet Coleman, 'Dominium in Thirteenth and Fourteenth-Century Political Thought and its Seventeenth-Century Heirs: John of Paris and Locke' (1985) 33 *Pol Stud* 73.

[31] On Konrad von Megenberg, see Gisela Drossbach, *Die 'Yconomica' des Konrad von Megenberg: Das 'Haus' als Norm für Politische und Soziale Strukturen* (Böhlau 1997) 185–87; Karl Ubl and Lars Vinx, 'Kirche, Arbeit und Eigentum bei Johannes Quidort von Paris' in Christoph Egger and Herwig Weigl (eds), *Text-Schrift-Codex* (Mitteilungen des Instituts für Österreichische Geschichtsforschung 2000).

[32] Aquinas, *De Perfectione Spiritualis Vitae*, ch XI, quoted in Annabel S Brett, *Liberty, Right and Nature: Individual Rights in Later Scholastic Thought* (CUP 1997) 14.

a very wide sense of 'property', so that it encompassed the fundamental right of a people to its own jurisdiction) during the fierce dispute over the rights of the American 'Indians'. The Spanish theologian Francisco de Vitoria argued that even a sinner 'does not lose dominion (*dominium*) over his own acts and his body'.[33] For Vitoria this was demonstrably true, because many observers had agreed that the 'Indians' had built cities and ordered their affairs; the 'Indians' were not simply running around like brutes. This was enough for Vitoria to conclude that the Spanish conquistadors were not entitled to appropriate any indigenous property or to subject them forcefully to the Spanish king. In sum, for Vitoria, the mere fact of having control (*dominium*) over one's will seemed to entail having *dominium*, in the sense of normative control (rights) over one's possessions, and *dominium*, in the sense of the normative control of a community over itself, entailing immunity from being subjected to a ruler that one has not chosen oneself.[34]

Contemporary intuitions regarding fundamental property rights are the descendants of the idea that human beings have *dominium* over their will and actions, and therefore over parts of the outside world. The best support for this claim is that the idea generates a theory of fundamental property rights that is more adequate than its contenders. Two ideas (both of which Locke used) have been at the forefront in recent debates over the justification for fundamental property rights: one is the labour theory of property acquisition, and the other is the idea that one can acquire property if one leaves 'enough and as good'. The latter has been the subject of intense debate.[35] The problem with the 'Lockean proviso' is that no one has up to now been able to give it specific content that will allow it to function as a criterion of just appropriation in the state of nature.[36] However, the proviso—even if one were to develop a workable version—only restricts legitimate acquisition; it does little or nothing to justify property acquisition. References to labour usually play this role, and the mixing-labour argument for property acquisition is notoriously problematic.

One problem with the labour theory is that in many cases it fails to provide an adequate reference to what is acquired: how much labour is required, and what exactly has an individual mixed with her labour when she has built a fence around a piece of land?[37] More importantly, it remains unclear how the mixing argument justifies appropriation at all. How could it, for example, justify acquisition of land? Moreover, the argument from labour mixing seems to presuppose self-ownership. A theory of fundamental property rights should first try to make sense of the intuition that human beings are self-owners and owners of things they have made, as

[33] Anthony Pagden and Jeremy Lawrence, *Vitoria: Political Writings* (CUP 1991) 242.

[34] Francisco de Vitoria, 'De Indis' in Pagden and Lawrance (n 33) esp 250–51.

[35] For an overview, see Helga Varden, 'The Lockean 'Enough-and-as-Good' Proviso: An Internal Critique' (2012) 9 *J Moral Phil* 410.

[36] Varden (n 35) 442.

[37] See Robert Nozick, *Anarchy, State, and Utopia* (Basic Books 1974) 174–75.

well as the intuition that individuals can appropriate external goods, including natural resources and parts of land. All this can be done by assuming that the underlying notion is that human beings incorporate things into plans. The medieval theory discussed above connects the ability to have *dominium* to free will and hence to intentional behaviour. This approach makes sense even of such difficult questions as why humans own themselves (they use their own body purposively) and how they can acquire property in resources and land (both can play an essential part in human projects). The crucial idea here is that of creation.[38] In other words, the idea that human beings are sovereigns secularizes the idea that God has *dominium* over the universe because he has created it. This in turn suggests questioning whether these ideas have any place in a secular world. Similar doubts emerge when examining the basis of natural rights to welfare.

6. Natural Rights to Welfare

Authors of current human rights texts often lament the proliferation of human rights claims, apparently fearing that too many claims will erode the special status of human rights. In common discourse, a human rights violation is perceived as particularly grave, associated with genocide and war crimes, rather than, for example, the lack of a smoke-free environment. If all that people desire to claim from their government is called a human right, then the sense of urgency normally attached to human rights will surely dissipate. More dangerously, if human rights claims cannot be distinguished from other human desires, this may foment scepticism towards the language of human rights as such. The responses of moral philosophers to this situation can be divided into three categories. A minority does not see proliferation as problematic. A second group consists mostly of libertarians who think that the only sensible conception of human rights is that of natural property rights discussed above. Many of them view proliferation as the result of misconceiving rights as anything other than civil and political rights.[39] A third group consists of philosophers who share a broader view of human rights, but who think that philosophy has a role to fulfil in distinguishing rights claims from other claims.

One way to evaluate these responses is by bringing in the second challenge to natural rights theories—the claim that these theories end up misrepresenting the

[38] For discussion, see Siegfried Van Duffel, 'Libertarian Natural Rights' (2004) 16 *Critical Review* 353.

[39] Maurice Cranston, *What Are Human Rights?* (Basic Books 1962) 36–38; Maurice Cranston, 'Human Rights: Real and Supposed' in DD Raphael (ed), *Political Theory and the Rights of Man* (Macmillan 1967) 52.

scope of human rights. This claim has some initial plausibility when levelled against the theories of fundamental property rights discussed in the previous section, but it is much less obviously true with regard to theories that construe natural rights as protecting interests of human beings. These theories are often critical of the more extravagant rights-claims and hence do not aim to merely describe actual human rights discourse. However, in light of the widespread belief that the domain of human rights is becoming overstretched, it seems too rash to rule them out as serious attempts to describe the phenomenon of human rights on this basis alone. To do so would be to deny that the belief is as much part of contemporary human rights discourse as the more extravagant right claims. When looking carefully at theories of natural rights to welfare, however, it becomes apparent that they do not succeed in stopping the proliferation of human rights.

Theories of 'natural rights to welfare' come in many different varieties. One theory that has attracted considerable attention recently is the 'capabilities approach' to human rights. Martha Nussbaum, for example, has argued that humans need certain capabilities in order to lead a fully human life.[40] However, it is far from clear how this criterion might lead to a more or less determinate list of capabilities that deserve to be protected as human rights. The most promising versions of the theory start from the idea that the fact that human beings are agents distinguishes them from other beings. Thus, the starting point of these theories is very similar to that of the theory of natural property rights: human beings are distinct from other beings, because humans can evaluate their desires and urges and choose the projects they want to pursue. Since leading a fully human life is leading the life of an agent, these theories posit, human rights entitle each person to the things needed in order to be functioning agents. This suggestion grounds rights to adequate nutrition, to health-care, to (basic) education, to freedom, etc.

Theories of welfare rights that base these rights on the notion of agency face the obvious objection that not all human beings are agents. Most significantly, infants are not agents in the relevant sense. In response to this objection, some theorists have simply bitten the bullet and maintained that not all human beings, only agents, have rights.[41] If this result is hard to accept, one can extend the theory by arguing that human rights protect not only existing agency but also the coming into being of human agents.[42] Unfortunately, that addition doesn't solve the problem; some human beings

[40] See eg Martha C Nussbaum, 'Human Functioning and Social Justice: In Defense of Aristotelian Essentialism' (1992) 20 *Pol Theory* 202. Literature on the capabilities approach is vast. A recent critique along these lines is Rutger Claassen and Marcus Düwell, 'The Foundations of Capability Theory: Comparing Nussbaum and Gewirth' [April 2012] *Ethical Theory and Moral Practice*.

[41] Most recently James Griffin, *On Human Rights* (OUP 2008) 34, 83–95. CS Nino, *The Ethics of Human Rights* (OUP 1991) 35–37. Dereck Beyleveld, *The Dialectical Necessity of Morality: An Analysis and Defense of Alan Gewirth's Argument to the Principle of Generic Consistency* (University of Chicago Press 1991) 446–48.

[42] This argument is problematic in its own right. A good discussion is Roy W Perret, 'Taking Life and the Argument from Potentiality' (2000) 24 *Midwest Studies in Philosophy* 186–97.

never have been or never will be agents. Conversely, some animals may possess the capacities associated with agency. Intuitions regarding human rights, however, are that *all* and *only* human beings have human rights, a conclusion not captured by a theory that grants rights to agents and potential agents.

Another problem with these theories—one that has given rise to an extensive literature—is that they give rise to positive rights (ie rights that entail positive duties). The right to medical healthcare implies that someone has a duty to provide it. Now it may well be possible, in the twenty-first century, to provide adequate nutrition and perhaps even basic healthcare for everyone, but this has not always been the case, and it is not something that can be taken for granted even for the future. Most philosophers agree that there is no duty to do something if it cannot be performed. Therefore, if people living in the third quarter of the twentieth century were unable to feed the world population, they could not have had a duty to do so.[43] Consequently, if they did not have this duty, then no one had a right to adequate nutrition. This result does not sit squarely with the idea that human rights are universal in both time and space, and libertarians have used it to argue that human rights must therefore be negative rights only. Friends of welfare rights have taken different approaches to avert this conclusion. First, some have tried to blur the distinction between positive and negative rights, arguing that the protection of negative rights also entails positive duties.[44] Second, others have argued that positive rights do not require everyone to act; they merely require support for institutions that provide the things that people have a right to.[45] Third, some have held that humans only have duties to do what is in their power to provide the things to which people have rights.[46] Fourth, it has been suggested that humans only have rights to those things that are effectively enforceable.[47] None of these responses solve the problem, however, leaving a seemingly incoherent conception of human rights.

[43] See eg Carl Wellman, *Welfare Rights* (Rowman and Allanheld 1982) 35–39, 159–63; Allan Buchanan, *Justice, Legitimacy, and Self-Determination: Moral Foundations for International Law* (OUP 2004) 181–86; Katherine Eddy, 'Welfare Rights and Conflicts of Rights' (2006) 12 *Res Pub* 337, 351; Danny Frederick, 'Why Universal Welfare Rights Are Impossible and What It Means' (2010) 9 *Politics, Philosophy & Economics* 428.

[44] See eg Henry Shue, *Basic Rights: Subsistence, Affluence, and US Foreign Policy* (Princeton UP 1980) ch 2; Raymond Plant, 'Citizenship, Rights, Welfare' in Jane Franklin (ed), *Social Policy and Social Justice* (Polity Press 1998); Stephen Holmes and Cass R Sunstein, *The Cost of Rights: Why Liberty Depends on Taxes* (WW Norton 2000); Thomas W Pogge, *World Poverty and Human Rights* (Polity Press 2002) ch 2; Raymond Plant, 'Social and Economic Rights Revisited' (2003) 14 *King's College Law Journal* 1, 11.

[45] See Jan Narveson, *Morality and Utility* (Johns Hopkins UP 1967) 235–36; Elizabeth Ashford, 'The Duties Imposed by the Human Right to Basic Necessities' in Thomas Pogge (ed), *Freedom from Poverty as a Human Right: Who Owes What to the Very Poor?* (OUP 2007) 216–17.

[46] Eg Amartya Sen, 'Elements of a Theory of Human Rights' (2004) 32 *Phil & Pub Aff* 315, 339. See also Eddy (n 43) 354.

[47] See Raymond Geuss, *History and Illusion in Politics* (CUP 2001) 146; Susan James, 'Rights and Enforceable Claims' (2003) 103 *Proceedings of the Aristotelian Society* 133. Much of this is inspired by Onora O'Neill's famous critique of 'manifesto rights'. See eg 'Women's Rights, Whose Obligations?' in Onora O'Neill, *Bounds of Justice* (CUP 2000) 99. Although her writings sometimes seem to imply this much (eg Onora O'Neill, *Towards Justice and Virtue: A Constructive Account of Practical Reasoning*

The third problem is the most serious. Surely, if a theory of human rights is to be of any use at all, it should provide a solid basis on which to distinguish real from 'supposed' human rights. At first sight, this is exactly what these theories do. They claim that humans have a right only to the things necessary to be an agent, ie to the things needed to be able to develop and pursue a conception of the good.[48] This requires autonomy (the ability to develop a conception of the good), some amount of welfare (enough to protect the ability to pursue each person's conception of the good), and freedom. The crucial question, however, is: how much of each is required? It is clear that autonomy comes in many different degrees, and it is far from clear how reference to the idea of human agency can provide anything close to a precise limit to the level of education to which human rights entitle each individual.[49] Similarly, it is unclear how rights to welfare can be derived with any amount of precision from the requirement that individuals must be able to function as agents. In one sense of 'agency', it seems that neither education nor welfare is necessary, except in extreme circumstances. After all, most human beings, no matter how uneducated or poor they happen to be, are still functioning agents. The same goes even more for freedom. Someone who is unjustly imprisoned does not lose agency in the process. If this sense of agency is taken as a guideline, the result will be a list of human rights that is even thinner than Rawls's. In fact, it would be unrecognizable as a list of human rights. However, contrary to what might be expected, these theorists actually generate very extensive lists of human rights. Griffin, recognizing the difficulty, writes that his account of rights has an 'ampler' conception of agency at its heart, which includes both having certain capacities and exercising them. He recognizes that this provides a highly indeterminate list of human rights, and so he suggests considering 'practicalities' in order to make it more determinate. The same is true for Gewirth. He requires that the means of acquiring wealth and income be distributed equally so far as possible. Thus it turns out that these theories, rather than constraining the proliferation of human rights, provide either highly indeterminate or sheer limitless accounts of the things individuals are entitled to as human rights.[50]

The persistence of these problems would suggest that they are inherent to any theory of welfare rights. However, there is a religious version of the theory that is

(CUP 1996) 134), O'Neill has not gone so far as to deny that rights may exist, even if they are not 'realized' or 'matched' by a set of distributed obligations.

[48] Griffin (n 41) 34; Alan Gewirth, *Reason and Morality* (U Chicago Press 1978) 64; Raymond Plant, 'The Moral Basis of Welfare Provision' in Raymond Plant, Harry Lesser, and Peter Taylor-Gooby, *Political Philosophy and Social Welfare: Essays on the Normative Basis of Welfare Provision* (Routledge and Kegan Paul 1980) 61; Alan Gewirth, 'The Basis and Content of Human Rights' in Alan Gewirth, *Human Rights: Essays on Justification and Application* (U Chicago Press 1982) 53; Raymond Plant, 'Needs, Agency, and Welfare Rights' in J Donald Moon (ed), *Responsibility, Rights, and Welfare: The Theory of the Welfare State* (Westview Press 1988) 60.

[49] Most authors do not even raise the question. Gewirth does raise it, but never answers it. See Alan Gewirth, *The Community of Rights* (U Chicago Press 1998) 105.

[50] Griffin (n 41) 37–39; Gewirth, *Reason and Morality* (n 48) 246–47. In a highly illuminating analysis, Donald Regan has argued Gewirth's case requires that agents value the freedom to pursue their

not troubled by them. Brian Tierney is one of several historians who have suggested that throughout the early history of natural rights theories, rights were persistently linked not with the ability to develop projects, but with the idea of conscience.[51] The importance of this difference can hardly be over-emphasized. A sense of obligation to obey God's commandments, as well as an idea that human beings have a role to fulfil in God's plan for the world, pervaded Medieval European culture. It was natural for Christians to assume that God had given each and every individual the talents needed to carry out their duties. It was also commonly assumed that God had given the earth and its produce so that humans may be nourished. Under these conditions, rights to subsistence could be construed as negative rights—ie the right that others not take more than what they need, in case doing so would prevent another from surviving. In fact, from the thirteenth century onwards, there was a stable consensus among canon lawyers, theologians, and Roman lawyers, to the effect that, in times of necessity, every human being had a right to take whatever was needed in order to survive. Since this was a negative right, it did not suffer from the problems associated with positive human rights. Also, Christians did not need to tie this right to any human capacity; nobody doubted that all human beings, and only human beings, had this special role in God's plan. The stable consensus (from the thirteenth century on to at least the second half of the seventeenth century) to the effect that this right only applied to cases of extreme necessity is only natural given these assumptions. The idea was not—as in modern, secular theories—that humans have these rights in order to carry out their own plans. Rather, the idea was that individuals should be able to perform their role in God's plan. Thus, the problems that seem so incontrovertible in the context of modern theories did not plague this religious version of natural rights to welfare. This suggests—again—that the problems are due to the secularization of the original theories.

7. Conclusion

This chapter aimed to show the importance of the work of moral philosophers to the understanding of contemporary human rights. The underlying conviction guiding the story is that the traditions of natural rights theories, as they have developed

future projects *whatever they turn out to be*. Donald Regan, 'Gewirth on Necessary Goods: What is the Agent Committed to Valuing?' in Michael Boylan (ed), *Gewirth: Critical Essays on Action, Rationality and Community* (Rowman and Littlefield 1999). Similarly agents must also value the ability to pursue their future projects whatever they turn out to be.

[51] Brian Tierney, *The Idea of Natural Rights: Studies on Natural Rights, Natural Law and Church Law 1150–1625* (Wm B Eerdmans 1997).

since the thirteenth century, still influence contemporary human rights language in profound ways. These traditions continue to shape debates from that of the nature of rights to attempts to answer questions like 'Which rights do we have?' or 'Who is responsible for delivering the things to which we are entitled?'. Failure to recognize this theoretical foundation results in an impoverished understanding of the current condition and (theoretical) problems.

The answer to the first challenge against the relevance of moral philosophy has been the article as a whole. It may well be that those who prepared the Universal Declaration of 1948 shared a strong conviction that they were creating a new language, but that does not preclude unearthing the ways in which traditions found in the abundant work of moral philosophers have moulded both the concept and theory of human rights.

The second challenge—that moral philosophy ends up misrepresenting the scope of human rights—requires a qualified response. Certain theories certainly generate lists that diverge significantly from the rights ordinarily identified as human rights.[52] Other theories, however, expose almost exactly the same indeterminacy as can be found in contemporary human rights discourse. The stance of this chapter has been that studying these theories is rewarding in that it can expose the dynamics that drive the discourse.

The third challenge—that natural rights theories misrepresent the distinctly political character of human rights—can be answered by contending that this character has been exaggerated. It is true that governments are the most common violators of human rights and that special responsibilities are assigned to governments to protect human rights. To some extent this reflects the fact that governments are among the most powerful actors in today's world. Yet, locating the primary responsibility for protecting human rights with political institutions does not solve the immense problem with the conception of human rights as positive. An intuitive understanding of rights is at odds with the idea that the only genuine human rights are those that governments can in fact protect. Hence there remains a problem understanding how there can be positive human rights without correlative duties.

A fully adequate response to the fourth challenge is beyond the scope of this chapter. If the historical development of the natural rights tradition influences human rights language and theory in profound ways, it would be surprising indeed if there were no significant differences in the ways in which human rights are understood and conceptualized in non-Western cultures. Such differences may have been of marginal political importance until now, but they may well become increasingly potent as the geopolitical power of many non-Western nations continues to grow. China, for example, has been very active in developing its own conception of human rights. Despite the extensive literature on 'non-Western conceptions of

[52] Not many moral philosophers would regard this as a flaw. Their self-assumed task is not to catalogue human rights.

human rights', there is only rudimentary understanding of these issues in the West. Scholars and activists may continue for a long time to debate whether the idea of human rights is distinctly Western or not. This chapter has suggested that the search for an answer to that question should start with a thorough study of the works of moral philosophers.

Further Reading

Beitz CR, *The Idea of Human Rights* (OUP 2009)
Griffin J, *On Human Rights* (OUP 2008)
Gewirth A, *Reason and Morality* (U Chicago Press 1978)
Kramer MH, Simmonds NE, and Steiner H, *A Debate Over Rights: Philosophical Enquiries* (OUP 1998)
Nozick R, *Anarchy, State, and Utopia* (Basic Books 1974)
Tuck R, *Natural Rights Theories: Their Origin and Development* (CUP 1979)

CHAPTER 3

BIOLOGICAL FOUNDATIONS OF HUMAN RIGHTS

CHRIS A ROBINSON

> There can be no doubt that a tribe including many members who . . . were always ready to give aid to each other and to sacrifice themselves for the common good, would be victorious over most other tribes.[1]

1. Introduction

CHARLES Darwin and Alfred Wallace[2] developed the theory of evolution by natural selection independently of each other, but the idea is popularly ascribed to Darwin alone—due in large part to his seminal work *On the Origin of Species*.[3] The theory

[1] Charles Darwin, *The Descent of Man, and Selection in Relation to Sex* (John Murray 1871).

[2] Charles Darwin and Alfred Wallace, 'On the Tendency of Species to Form Varieties; And on the Perpetuation of Varieties and Species by Natural Means of Selection' (1858) 3 *Journal of the Proceedings of the Linnean Society (Zoology)* 45.

[3] Charles Darwin, *On the Origin of Species by Means of Natural Selection, or the Preservation of Favoured Races in the Struggle for Life* (John Murray 1859).

argues that individuals compete with one another for limited resources in their environment; those with traits providing them greater ability to obtain necessary resources and respond to threats in that environment will be more likely to survive and reproduce. The alleles for the specific traits enabling one individual to survive and out-compete others reproductively will then be more likely to be passed down and become more common in future generations. Thus, competition with other individuals in one's own group is essential to this fundamental biological theory. Competition leads to individuals striving for dominance over other individuals in a given species (including the human species), to gain greater access to resources, such as food, sleeping sites, and mates. While popular views on evolution focus on competition among individuals, animals that live in social groups also need to cooperate with one another for many aspects of their survival, including finding sources of food and defending their territory against other groups. This necessitates helping fellow group members and sometimes providing assistance and protection to the most vulnerable members of the group, so that the group is as large and strong as possible when it attempts to find resources and confront other groups. Thus, the group must suppress extreme individualistic tendencies towards competition and the repression of others in order to be able to survive. This tension, between inter-individual competition to maximize individual success and cooperation among individuals within groups to maximize group success, is part of the evolutionary history of humans. It has resulted in humans possessing biological predispositions towards both selfish/dominant and altruistic behaviours.

While many animals can and do come to the aid of others in their group, the biological capacity to develop laws that provide protection for basic human rights depends on an aptitude that may be uniquely human: the ability to be altruistic towards individuals outside of one's family or immediate group. While some reserve the term altruism for intentional, selfless behaviours requiring self-awareness,[4] most biologists define altruistic behaviours as those in which an individual performs an act that benefits another at some cost to himself.[5]

Some have suggested that altruism is one of the defining characteristics of humanity.[6] While other animals appear to be able to provide such benefits for their relatives, and while some may reciprocate altruistic acts with others in their group, it may be that only humans have the capacity to be altruistic towards strangers.

[4] C Robert Cloninger and Sita Kedia, 'The Phylogenesis of Human Personality: Identifying the Precursors of Cooperation, Altruism, and Well-Being' in Robert W Sussman and C Robert Cloninger (eds), *Origins of Altruism and Cooperation* (Springer 2011).

[5] Eg Edward O Wilson, 'Some Central Problems of Sociobiology' (1975) 14 *Social Science Information* 5; Robert Trivers, *Social Evolution* (Benjamin/Cummings Publishing Co 1985); Katherine C MacKinnon and Agustín Fuentes, 'Primates, Niche Construction, and Social Complexity: The Roles of Social Cooperation and Altruism' in Sussman and Cloninger, *Origins of Altruism* (n 4).

[6] Robert W Sussman and C Robert Cloninger, 'Introduction: Cooperation and Altruism' in Sussman and Cloninger, *Origins of Altruism* (n 4).

Clearly there is no biological mandate for all humans to be altruistic in every situation, and there is variation in the capacity of individuals to perform these actions, but most humans are likely born with the potential to express such prosocial behaviours (among many others). The biological predispositions of humans that provide sufficient capacity to care about others outside of their group have allowed, and possibly encouraged, the development of laws that protect their rights.

While some evolutionary biologists have argued in the past that true altruism does not exist in nature, that it is actually a 'sophisticated kind of selfishness',[7] most researchers today agree that altruistic behaviours have evolved in many species. Debates remain, primarily over how and when human capacity for this behaviour evolved. Are human altruistic abilities something that arose only with the evolution of *Homo sapiens*, or did modern humans build upon the behavioural capacities of earlier ancestral species? Also, how did altruism initially evolve and persist, given that it is costly to the individual and, thus, will make it less likely that an individual acting in an altruistic manner will survive and reproduce? Genes that predispose an individual towards altruism should be selected against, since they will be less likely to be passed on to the next generation. For the potential to behave altruistically to have evolved via natural selection, there must have been greater benefits or fewer costs for those who were altruistic than for those who were not.

Altruistic acts have been documented in many non-human animal species, including some that are life-threatening to the individual, and they are common among humanity's closest living relatives, the non-human primates. In many instances, kin selection, mutualism, or possibly reciprocity can drive these acts, as discussed below in Sections 3 to 5. These behaviours potentially represent a first step towards the development of true altruism, in which one individual, without expectation of reciprocity, provides a benefit to an unrelated individual at some detriment to themselves. True altruistic behaviours are likely to have been restricted to one's immediate group initially. However, at some stage during evolution, the human lineage built on these abilities to evolve an extraordinary capacity to care about the welfare of those outside of their groups, enabling humans to come to the aid of any fellow species-member (and even members of other species) and eventually to develop laws providing human rights protections for all.

The following discussion examines the theories and evidence in the science of biology about the evolution of human traits that are relevant for the development of human rights law. This review involves a discussion of the emergence of a biological capacity for altruism, which provides an explanation for the origin of the concern for human rights. The chapter begins by making note of the human potential for violent, aggressive acts that is shared with one of the closest living relatives

[7] Telmo Pievani, 'Born to Cooperate? Altruism as Exaptation and the Evolution of Human Sociality' in Sussman and Cloninger, *Origins of Altruism* (n 4) 45. See also Lee Alan Dugatkin, *The Altruism Equation: Seven Scientists Search for the Origins of Goodness* (Princeton UP 2006).

of humans, the chimpanzee, but which exceeds even their capacity, producing a need for social controls that include international human rights law. It continues by discussing various biological hypotheses as to why humans and other animals perform altruistic acts and how the capacity for such behaviour may have evolved. The chapter then explores hypotheses as to how groups of animals, including humans, maintain cooperative and altruistic behaviours, given the conflicting need to compete with others in the group for resources. In particular, how do groups combat the potential for individual success by gaining the benefits of the group's cooperative behaviours, but not by providing any effort towards helping others in the group? Following this the selective advantages for the group of having more individuals acting in a cooperative, altruistic manner than other groups are examined. The final section discusses some of the biological adaptations that have enabled humans, and a few other cognitively advanced species, to engage regularly in altruistic behaviours towards those outside of their family and immediate group.

2. The Need for Rights: Violence and Altruism

Some researchers have argued that humans and our closest living relatives, particularly chimpanzees, have a greater capacity for violent behaviour than most other species.[8] Most studies of chimpanzees have observed 'border patrols' of the males that attack individuals from neighbouring communities.[9] Goodall[10] observed one instance of chimpanzees from Gombe systematically killing all males in a neighbouring group in a phenomenon that some have likened to warfare (*Pan*ocide?). Humans, too, have the capacity to be irrationally harmful towards others (genocide). In addition, while humans have a tendency to reciprocate kind acts, they also respond in kind to harmful acts. Some researchers contend that violent behaviours manifest themselves in chimpanzees only under certain conditions, which anthropogenic changes to their environment primarily cause.[11] Similarly, some have argued, based on cross-cultural

[8] Richard W Wrangham, Michael L Wilson, and Martin N Muller, 'Comparative Rates of Violence in Chimpanzees and Humans' (2006) 47 *Primates* 14; Christophe Boesch and others, 'Intergroup Conflicts among Chimpanzees in Taï National Park: Lethal Violence and the Female Perspective' (2008) 70 *American Journal of Primatology* 519; Richard W Wrangham, 'Chimpanzee Violence is a Serious Topic: A Response to Sussman and Marshack's Critique of Demonic Males: Apes and the Origins of Human Violence' (2010) 1 *Global Nonkilling Working Papers* 29.

[9] MacKinnon and Fuentes (n 5).

[10] Jane Goodall, *The Chimpanzees of Gombe: Patterns of Behavior* (Harvard UP 1986).

[11] Robert W Sussman, 'The Myth of Man the Hunter, Man the Killer and the Evolution of Human Morality' (1999) 34 *Zygon* 453; Donna Hart and Robert W Sussman, *Man the Hunted: Primates,*

studies, that human warfare is limited to specific cultural and environmental contexts that include stress, abuse, or neglect;[12] and that the more 'natural' human behaviour is peaceful coexistence, with conflict resolution avoiding outbreaks of physical violence.[13] In support of this hypothesis, it has been noted that the vast majority of the individuals on this planet do not have regular violent interactions with one another.[14] In addition, evidence that cultural anthropologies have gathered from studies of traditionally foraging groups indicates that cooperative and altruistic societies are more common than warlike, combative societies[15] (although the evidence from Bowles, discussed in Section 7.2, suggests that this may not have been true in the past).

Even if high levels of violence in human and chimpanzees occur only under certain conditions, it does not necessarily follow that violent behaviours have no underlying genetic basis. While it is well established that extreme violence does occur in humans and chimpanzees, such behaviour has not been documented in most other species living under similar environmental conditions. The presence of this capacity in our two species makes it plausible to hypothesize that the capacity also existed in our common ancestor.

Modern humans possess the capacity for substantially greater levels of violence and aggressive behaviour, including warfare and genocide, than is found in chimpanzees or any other animal species, leading to the need for humans to adopt formalized social restraints (including legal restraints) on individuals. How humans evolved the capacity to care enough about others to have developed these formalized rules, particularly those governing the behaviour of those outside of their group, is the subject of the rest of this chapter.

3. Kin Selection

Altruistic behaviours that related individuals perform in various animal species are typically thought to have evolved as a result of kin selection, in which individuals

Predators, and Human Evolution (Westview Press 2009); RW Sussman and Donna Hart, 'Gentle Savage or Bloodthirsty Brute?' in Joám Evans Pim (ed), *Nonkilling Societies* (Center for Global Nonkilling 2010).

[12] Cloninger and Kedia (n 4).

[13] Raymond C Kelly, *Warless Societies and the Origin of War* (U Michigan Press 2000); Douglas P Fry, *The Human Potential for Peace: An Anthropological Challenge to Assumptions about War and Violence* (OUP 2006); Marc Bekoff and Jessica Pierce, *Wild Justice: The Moral Lives of Animals* (U Chicago Press 2009); Cloninger and Kedia (n 4); Douglas P Fry, 'Human Nature: The Nomadic Forager Model' in Sussman and Cloninger, *Origin of Altruism* (n 4); Sussman and Cloninger, 'Introduction' (n 6).

[14] Donna Hart and Robert W Sussman, 'The Influence of Predation on Primate and Early Human Evolution: Impetus for Cooperation' in Sussman and Cloninger, *Origins of Altruism* (n 4).

[15] Fry, 'Human Nature' (n 13).

perform altruistic acts for those to whom they are closely related.[16] In general, animals are more likely to assist their relatives (and less likely to compete with them) than to assist other members of their species. Eusocial insects, in which non-reproductive individuals raise the offspring of close relatives and are highly dependent on one another to survive and reproduce, such as is the case with bees and ants, are one of the most widely cited examples of kin selection.[17] They perform many altruistic acts other than alloparenting;[18] some even sting hive invaders, dying in the process. These selfless behaviours are among the most widely cited examples of kin selection,

Kin selection is based on the theory of inclusive fitness, which Haldane originally described,[19] but which Hamilton formalized as an equation.[20] The principle behind the theory is that, because kin share many of the same genes, aiding one another serves to perpetuate one's own genes, including those that predispose an individual towards altruistic acts. According to this theory, the more closely related two individuals are, the more likely it should be that they will come to each other's aid. In the words of Haldane, 'I will jump into the river and save two brothers or eight cousins'.[21] Studies support the inclusive fitness theory, finding that altruistic behaviours are more common in groups in which members are closely related.[22] The explanation for these behaviours is that these individuals are closely related to their infants and, in many cases, to fellow group members that they help in defending resources.

One could envision an evolutionary model in which an allele for altruism towards one's relatives arose via mutation and then became more common as individuals assisted relatives who also had that allele. Over generations, kin selection could cause the altruistic behaviour to become widespread in a population. Some researchers have argued that the likelihood of an allele for altruism spreading through a population depends on how closely related individuals in that population are to one another,[23] with only weak selection pressure needed for altruism to evolve in a population of closely related individuals.[24] For most researchers, kin selection

[16] But see recent challenge in the case of eusocial insects by Martin A Nowak, Corina E Tarnita, and Edward O Wilson, 'The Evolution of Eusociality' (2010) 466 *Nature* 1057, and responses by Patrick Abbot and others, 'Inclusive Fitness Theory and Eusociality' (2011) 471 *Nature* E1.

[17] John Maynard Smith, 'Group Selection and Kin Selection' (1964) 201 *Nature* 1145.

[18] Alloparenting involves helping to care for the offspring of others.

[19] JBS Haldane, 'Population Genetics' (1955) 18 *New Biology* 34.

[20] WD Hamilton, 'The Genetical Evolution of Social Behavior, Part I' (1964) 7 *Journal of Theoretical Biology* 1.

[21] This is because he shares, on average, half of his genes with his brothers and one-eighth of them with his cousins.

[22] See Tim Clutton-Brock, 'Breeding Together: Kin Selection and Mutualism in Cooperative Vertebrates' (2002) 296 *Science* 69; Tim Clutton-Brock, 'Cooperation between Non-Kin in Animal Societies' (2009) 462 *Nature* 51.

[23] Regis Ferriere and Richard E Michod, 'Inclusive Fitness in Evolution' (2011) 471 *Nature* E6.

[24] Sébastien Lion and Minus van Baalen, 'From Infanticide to Parental Care: Why Spatial Structure Can Help Adults Be Good Parents' (2007) 170(2) *The American Naturalist* E26.

provides a reasonable explanation as to why relatives of many species provide aid to one another, which could be seen as a first step towards the evolution of true altruism in humans.

4. Mutualism and Group Augmentation

Though, for most scholars, kin selection can reasonably explain acting altruistically towards one's relatives, providing aid to unrelated individuals seems to be contrary to natural selection. At times, though, even unrelated animals may benefit from cooperating with fellow group members, rather than competing against them for resources. Mutualism refers to altruistic acts among non-kin, in which both individuals immediately benefit or are assured of benefitting in the future from the interaction. Mutualism typically involves behaviour that individuals would engage in even in the absence of a partner, but which will be more successful with the assistance of another individual. In many species, mutualism enables animals to work together to find food or defend their territory, providing immediate (food) or future (keeping others away from shared resources) benefits to all members of the group. This behaviour has been suggested as a contributing factor, allowing non-human primates to live in large and relatively stable social groups.[25] Such groups are likely the foundation upon which the extremely cooperative and altruistic human social groups were built.

5. Reciprocity

5.1 Direct reciprocity

Many examples are cited of aid provided by one animal to an unrelated individual where it does not appear that any immediate benefit is given in return, nor a future benefit assured. Biologists strongly debate how populations evolve and maintain these altruistic behaviours.[26] In some cases, help may be repaid in the future,

[25] Hart and Sussman, 'The Influence of Predation' (n 14).
[26] See Clutton-Brock, 'Cooperation between Non-Kin' (n 22).

via what has traditionally been referred to as reciprocal altruism[27]—the primary hypothesis proposed to explain non-mutualistic altruism among unrelated individuals. Most researchers now refer to this phenomenon as direct or cost-cutting reciprocity;[28] one individual will incur a temporary cost that is less than the benefit provided to another, and in turn, at a later time, the receiving individual will suffer a temporary cost while reciprocating a greater benefit to the first individual.[29] Over time, such reciprocally-provided aid to others will lead to greater overall benefits for all involved than independent individual actions would. As one possible example, a meerkat will often stand sentinel, watching for predators, while others in its group feed and engage in social activities. The meerkat may be trusting that others in its group will reciprocate in the future by providing services that are beneficial to that individual. The trust that direct reciprocity requires of non-kin, that they will repay acts of kindness (ie 'overcom[ing] the fear of betrayal')[30] can be seen as another stepping stone towards the evolution of true altruism, whereby individuals have the capacity to assist anyone in need, partly due to trusting that someone else will act similarly towards them in the future.

To engage in direct reciprocity, an animal needs to have the cognitive capacity to predict the future behaviour of others. According to some researchers, many species (including some that lack highly developed cognitive skills) have this ability,[31] while other scientists have argued that this behaviour is rare among animals and have questioned whether any non-human animal has the brain power necessary to engage in direct reciprocity.[32] Various behaviours among non-human animal species have been proposed as examples of direct reciprocity:[33] social mongooses have been known to mob predators that have trapped fellow group members,[34] and dolphins have lifted injured dolphins to the surface to breathe.[35] In more explicit examples of direct reciprocity, male chimpanzees have been observed to provide meat to females in exchange

[27] Robert L Trivers, 'The Evolution of Reciprocal Altruism' (1971) 46 *The Quarterly Review of Biology* 35.

[28] See Clutton-Brock, 'Breeding Together' (n 22); Martin A Nowak, 'Five Rules for the Evolution of Cooperation' (2006) 314 *Science* 1560; Clutton-Brock, 'Cooperation between Non-Kin' (n 22).

[29] See Martin A Nowak and Karl Sigmund, 'Evolution of Indirect Reciprocity' (2005) 437 *Nature* 1291; Nowak, 'Five Rules' (n 28).

[30] James K Rilling, 'The Neurobiology of Cooperation and Altruism' in Sussman and Cloninger, *Origins of Altruism* (n 4) 297.

[31] Thomas Pfeiffer, Claudia Rutte, Timothy Killingback, Michael Taborsky, Sebastian Bonhoeffer, 'Evolution of Cooperation by Generalized Reciprocity' (2005) 272 *Proceedings of the Royal Society B* 1115; Bekoff and Pierce (n 13).

[32] Clutton-Brock, 'Breeding together' (n 22); Dorothy L Cheney, 'Extent and Limits of Cooperation in Animals' (2011) 108 *PNAS* 10902.

[33] See Lee A Dugatkin, *Cooperation among Animals: An Evolutionary Perspective* (OUP 1997); Clutton-Brock, 'Cooperation between Non-Kin' (n 22).

[34] Jon P Rood, 'Banded Mongoose Rescues Pack Member from Eagle' (1983) 31 *Animal Behaviour* 1261.

[35] Richard C Connor and Kenneth S Norris, 'Are Dolphins Reciprocal Altruists?' (1982) 119(3) *The American Naturalist* 358.

for later reproductive access; they have also reciprocated the sharing of meat with one another.[36]

Some scientists dispute the evidence for direct reciprocity, because in many cases it is unknown whether reciprocation occurred between the same individuals or whether the partners were close relatives.[37] In addition, there is little documented evidence that providing aid temporarily costs the assisting individual in terms of their reproductive fitness; some of the most frequently documented cases of reciprocity (eg non-human primate males working together to gain reproductive access to a female, or vampire bats sharing blood) may not meet the criteria for direct reciprocity.[38]

The above critiques of the evidence for direct reciprocity have led some to argue that this behaviour may only occur in animals via 'pseudo-reciprocity'[39] or the 'tit-for-tat' strategy,[40] in which individuals trade benefits with one another over a short period of time and in which there are few opportunities not to reciprocate (eg during grooming bouts in non-human primates[41]).[42] Monkeys and apes provide reciprocal assistance in other ways, however, in response to grooming, including lending support during intragroup conflicts.[43] Recent studies have made a more complex assessment of the link between grooming and reciprocating benefits, by showing benefits in the form of reduced stress hormone levels for both the groomer and the one being groomed during this action.[44]

[36] John C Mitani and David P Watts, 'Demographic Influences on the Hunting Behavior of Chimpanzees' (1999) 109(4) *American Journal of Physical Anthropology* 439; John C Mitani and David P Watts, 'Why Do Chimpanzees Hunt and Share Meat?' (2001) 61 *Animal Behaviour* 915; John C Mitani, 'Reciprocal Exchange in Chimpanzees and Other Primates' in PM Kappeler and CP van Schaik (eds), *Cooperation in Primates and Humans: Mechanisms and Evolution* (Springer 2006).

[37] Clutton-Brock, 'Breeding Together' (n 22); Peter Hammerstein, 'Why is Reciprocity So Rare in Social Animals? A Protestant Appeal' in Peter Hammerstein (ed), *Genetic and Cultural Evolution of Cooperation* (MIT Press 2003); SA West, AS Griffin, and A Gardner, 'Social Semantics: Altruism, Cooperation, Mutualism, Strong Reciprocity and Group Selection' (2007) 20 *Journal of Evolutionary Biology* 415; Clutton-Brock, 'Cooperation between Non-Kin' (n 22).

[38] See Clutton-Brock, 'Cooperation between Non-Kin' (n 22).

[39] Richard C Connor, 'Altruism among Non-Relatives: Alternatives to the "Prisoner's Dilemma"' (1995) 10(2) *Trends in Ecology & Evolution* 84.

[40] Robert L Trivers, 'Reciprocal Altruism: 30 Years Later' in Kappeler and van Schaik, *Cooperation in Primates* (n 36).

[41] Louise Barrett, S Peter Henzi, Tony Weingrill, John E Lycett, and RA Hill, 'Market Forces Predict Grooming Reciprocity in Female Baboons' (1999) 266 *Proceedings of the Royal Society B* 665; Louise Barrett and S Peter Henzi, 'Monkeys, Markets and Minds: Biological Markets and Primate Sociality' in Kappeler and van Schaik, *Cooperation in Primates* (n 36).

[42] Clutton-Brock, 'Breeding Together' (n 22); Clutton-Brock, 'Cooperation between Non-Kin' (n 22).

[43] Robert M Seyfarth and Dorothy L Cheney, 'Grooming, Alliances and Reciprocal Altruism in Vervet Monkeys' (1984) 308 *Nature* 541; Frans BM de Waal, 'The Chimpanzee's Service Economy: Food for Grooming' (1997) 18(6) *Evolution and Human Behavior* 375.

[44] Kathryn Shutt, Ann MacLarnon, Michael Heistermann, and Stuart Semple, 'Grooming in Barbary Macaques: Better to Give than to Receive?' (2007) 3(3) *Biology Letters* 231; Charles T Snowdon, 'Behavioral and Neuroendocrine Interactions in Affiliation' in Sussman and Cloninger, *Origins of Altruism* (n 4).

Whether or not other animals exhibit direct reciprocity, it is clear that this behaviour is common among humans, with some listing it as one of the 'human universals'.[45] It appears that the human capacity for direct reciprocity may have an evolutionary basis, as reports of this behaviour are especially common among the non-human primates.[46] In addition, chimpanzees and bonobos, the closest living relatives of humans, are cited as having higher levels of direct reciprocity (eg meat sharing) than other mammals.[47] Nonetheless, some critics argue that the instances of meat sharing, for example, do not represent reciprocity, but instead constitute 'tolerated theft', as chimpanzees harass those with meat until they are given a share.[48]

5.2 Indirect reciprocity

Theoretically, direct reciprocity should become progressively more difficult as group size increases, dispersal between groups increases, and lifespan decreases,[49] primarily because individuals will not interact frequently enough with one another in their lifetime to ensure that a partner repays the 'debt' in a symmetrical fashion. Helping those who have consistently helped the group (those with a good reputation), or providing aid to the kin of their partners or to individuals with whom the latter are closely bonded, are other possible means by which individuals can 'pay back' one another. This is known as indirect reciprocity.[50] It has been suggested that humans may have needed these more complex means of reciprocating cooperation with one another due to the greater numbers of individuals in populations during the later stages of human evolution,[51] although simulations have suggested that as group sizes become very large, it may be difficult to maintain even indirect reciprocity.[52]

The pervasiveness of indirect reciprocity among human populations has been suggested to be related to the dietary behaviour of early modern hunter-gatherer groups, in which meat was an important but rarely obtained food item. It has been hypothesized that these groups had to have the ability to share meat via indirect reciprocity in order to survive, because animals were typically caught by one individual or a small group of individuals, and if they did not share this rare resource,

[45] Donald E Brown, *Human Universals* (McGraw Hill 1991).

[46] Clutton-Brock, 'Cooperation between Non-Kin' (n 22).

[47] Mitani, 'Reciprocal Exchange' (n 36); Kevin E Langergraber, John C Mitani, and Linda Vigilant, 'The Limited Impact of Kinship on Cooperation in Wild Chimpanzees' (2007) 104 *PNAS* 7786.

[48] Ian C Gilby, 'Meat Sharing among the Gombe Chimpanzees: Harassment and Reciprocal Exchange' (2006) 71 *Animal Behaviour* 953, 954.

[49] MacKinnon and Fuentes (n 5).

[50] Richard D Alexander, *The Biology of Moral Systems* (2nd edn, Aldine Transaction 1987).

[51] Cloninger and Kedia (n 4).

[52] Shinsuke Suzuki and Eizo Akiyama, 'Evolution of Indirect Reciprocity in Groups of Various Sizes and Comparison with Direct Reciprocity' (2007) 245 *Journal of Theoretical Biology* 539.

hunter-gatherer groups would not have survived.[53] Reciprocity would likely have been indirect, because not all individuals would be able to reciprocate directly with the individual obtaining the meat.

It is thought that indirect reciprocity requires a 'theory of mind', the ability to attribute mental states to both oneself and others,[54] to be able to judge interactions between two individuals as positive or negative and to recall those judgments when interacting with third parties.[55] It also requires triadic awareness,[56] an understanding of the social bonds of others. While humans clearly have this ability, there is debate over whether or not non-human primates possess it.[57]

Researchers have suggested that while animals seem able to engage in simpler forms of indirect reciprocity, only humans can fully exhibit this behaviour, likely due to the complex cognitive mechanisms needed to keep track of who is providing interpersonal assistance in a group.[58] In much of today's industrialized world, indirect reciprocity is a regular feature of life; many interactions are with strangers, requiring an individual frequently to trust others based on their reputations. Taking into account reputation when deciding whether or not to assist a fellow group member is thought to be necessary for indirect reciprocity to develop, so that if an individual does not consistently cooperate with others in the group, members of the group will be cognizant of the fact and can withhold help in the future.[59] Otherwise it would be too easy for someone to cheat by obtaining 'work free' assistance, and the system of reciprocity would break down, as discussed further below.

It is also necessary for individuals to pass information about reputations amongst each other for indirect reciprocity to be maintained, particularly in large groups. Humans have a unique ability to rapidly transmit large amounts of social information to members of the group. Humans constantly judge the behaviours of others and can discuss those judgments, including through gossip. Gossip, in fact, has been viewed as an important mechanism for maintaining a cooperative social network, by passing on to others information on what an individual has done (or has not done), thereby ensuring that those with poor reputations are not provided aid.[60] This makes reputation important, and it typically influences actions by inducing individuals to act

[53] Rilling, 'The Neurobiology of Cooperation' (n 30).

[54] Andrew Whiten and Richard W Byrne, *Machiavellian Intelligence II: Extensions and Evaluations* (2nd edn, CUP 1997).

[55] Nowak and Sigmund (n 29).

[56] F de Waal, *Chimpanzee Politics: Power and Sex amongst the Apes* (Harper & Row 1982).

[57] Dorothy L Cheney, Robert M Seyfarth, and Joan B Silk, 'The Responses of Female Baboons (*Papio Cynocephalus Ursinus*) to Anomalous Social Interactions: Evidence for Causal Reasoning?' (1995) 109(2) *Journal of Comparative Psychology* 134; Joan B Silk, 'Male Bonnet Macaques Use Information about Third-Party Rank Relationships to Recruit Allies' (1999) 58 *Animal Behaviour* 45.

[58] Nowak, 'Five Rules' (n 28).

[59] Nowak and Sigmund (n 29).

[60] Robin Dunbar, *Grooming, Gossip, and the Evolution of Language* (Harvard UP 1996); Nowak and Sigmund (n 29).

only after thinking about the consequences of their action, or inaction, on reputation. Experiments finding that people are more generous when they know that their reputation will be passed along to others have supported this theory.[61]

Discussing the reputations of group members via gossip was likely important and may have been selected for in the fission/fusion social systems that seemingly characterized earlier human species. In a fission/fusion system, individuals in a large population frequently split into smaller subgroups, such as when foraging for food, and then reassemble at some later time. It has been suggested that to be successful in these groups, individuals need to attend to the social relationships of their fellow group members, including by knowing who has a good reputation for helping others.[62] It would have been an advantage for an early human to pass along information about what happened in their subgroup (including information that was relevant to another's reputation) to their kin and social partners. In this manner, those individuals close to the first group would be aware of events that occurred when they were not present, and they could therefore act on that information when deciding with whom to cooperate.

The group must agree upon expected behaviours, the social norms, in order for reputation to be important for maintaining cooperation via indirect reciprocity. Some have argued that the development of human cultural norms[63] and morality[64] are related to the evolution of indirect reciprocity involving reputation. One can envision a feedback loop wherein increased monitoring of the reputation of others to ensure their continued assistance to third parties leads to more social rules governing one's behaviour, which in turn leads to further reliance on reputation for individual success in the social group. The capacity to develop these culturally based norms of behaviour, such as in the form of international human rights laws, is posited as a human universal not found in other species,[65] although one could say that all animals have their norms of behaviour (and possibly their own morality).[66] Non-human animals know not to violate these norms, including through such acts as exhibiting threatening behaviour towards the dominant male or attempting to feed where there is a dominant female already feeding. Play behaviour among canids

[61] Nowak and Sigmund (n 29); Ingrid Seinen and Arthur Schram, 'Social Status and Group Norms: Indirect Reciprocity in a Repeated Helping Experiment' (2006) 50 *Eur Ec Rev* 581.

[62] Mary SM Pavelka, 'Mechanisms of Cohesion in Black Howler Monkeys' in Sussman and Cloninger, *Origins of Altruism* (n 4).

[63] Hannelore Brandt and Karl Sigmund, 'The Logic of Reprobation: Assessment and Action Rules for Indirect Reciprocation' (2004) 231 *Journal of Theoretical Biology* 475; Hisashi Ohtsuki and Yoh Iwasa, 'How Should We Define Goodness?—Reputation Dynamics in Indirect Reciprocity' (2004) 231 *Journal of Theoretical Biology* 107.

[64] Alexander (n 50).

[65] See Nowak and Sigmund (n 29).

[66] Marc Bekoff, 'Cooperation and the Evolution of Social Living: Moving beyond the Constraints and Implications of Misleading Dogma: Introduction Part II' in Sussman and Cloninger, *Origins of Altruism* (n 4).

has rules of fairness that the canids must follow, or the play stops and individuals can be punished for breaking the rules (including through ostracism), similar to what happens in games among human children.[67] Nonetheless, while behavioural rules have been documented in other animals, culturally defined normative behaviours are most well-developed in humans, and enforcement through monitoring reputation may be unique to our species.[68] This remains relevant today at every level of interaction; 'naming and shaming' is one of the most important ways of promoting and protecting human rights.

6. True Altruism

Humans, and possibly a few other species, have the capacity for true altruism, in which aid is provided to non-kin without the expectation of reciprocity. Humans often show concern for the welfare of complete strangers, and there are numerous cases of people providing benefits to unrelated individuals at personal cost, sometimes even dying as a result. The biological potential for such action is necessary for the human species to have developed the concept of universal human rights. Even now, although many individuals need never invoke human rights law during their lifetimes, these individuals accept that human rights law is important for protecting the basic human rights of all peoples, even if providing that protection may be costly.

It is unclear whether the capacity for true altruism is present in other species and, thus, biologists are unsure of how far back this ability goes in our evolutionary history. Some have suggested that it is possible that perceived observations of true altruism in other species are merely a function of anthropomorphizing the behaviours of animals by imagining that they are consciously deciding to help one another.[69] In support of this, researchers have found that the parts of the brain activated when humans are performing altruistic acts have no homologous region in monkeys.[70] However, there is some evidence to support the contention that true altruism is possible for the closest living relatives of humans, especially chimpanzees and bonobos.[71] Male and female adult chimpanzees have been documented as

[67] Bekoff, 'Cooperation and the Evolution of Social Living' (n 66).

[68] Nowak and Sigmund (n 29), although the evidence Bekoff presented in 2011 in his studies of canid play might suggest otherwise.

[69] Cloninger and Kedia (n 4); Ian Tattersall, 'Cooperation, Altruism, and Human Evolution: Introduction Part I' in Sussman and Cloninger, *Origins of Altruism* (n 4).

[70] D Öngür and JL Price, 'The Organization of Networks within the Orbital and Medial Prefrontal Cortex of Rats, Monkeys and Humans' (2000) 10(3) *Cerebral Cortex* 206.

[71] Frans BM de Waal, 'With a Little Help from a Friend' (2007) 5(7) *PLoS Biology* e190; Felix Warneken, Brian Hare, Alicia P Melis, Daniel Hanus, and Michael Tomasello, 'Spontaneous Altruism

caring for unrelated infants whose mothers had died and using substantial amounts of their time and resources to do so.[72] Chimpanzees in experimental settings have been found to help an unrelated chimpanzee obtain a reward by moving an instrument to aid that individual, even when their efforts provided them no reward,[73] and similar behaviours have been observed in some monkey species.[74]

Some of the most convincing examples of true altruism among non-human animals come from interspecies interactions, in which a member of one species provides aid to a member of a different species; clearly, this is unlikely to improve their reproductive fitness in any way. Anecdotal accounts of altruistic acts have been documented in domesticated cats and dogs, elephants, and cetaceans, in particular.[75] In 2012, two humpback whales intervened when a pod of orcas attempted to separate a gray whale calf from its mother.[76] While their attempts to save the baby were unsuccessful, they did put themselves in harm's way to aid a baby of another species. This seems difficult to categorize as anything other than true altruism. Elephants have been observed opening gates to allow captive antelopes to escape.[77] There are also numerous examples of dogs caring for infant animals of other species, including, recently, a one-year-old human child.

It is generally assumed that those behaviours shared by humans and our closest relatives, species of the genus *Pan* (chimpanzees and bonobos), were also likely to have been present in our earliest human ancestors.[78] Therefore, understanding to what extent *Pan* species are able to perform altruistic actions tells us much about our evolutionary history. There are clearly substantial differences between humans and *Pan* (and all other species) in their capacities for altruistic behaviour, however.

Given that behaviours do not fossilize one must attempt to infer by other means when the exceptional modern human ability to be altruistic towards those not in the

by Chimpanzees and Young Children' (2007) 5(7) *PLoS Biology* e184; Felix Warneken and Michael Tomasello, 'Varieties of Altruism in Children and Chimpanzees' (2009) 13(9) *Trends in Cognitive Sciences* 397.

[72] Christophe Boesch, Camille Bolé, Nadin Eckhardt, and Hedwige Boesch, 'Altruism in Forest Chimpanzees: The Case of Adoption' (2010) 5 *PLoS ONE* e8901.

[73] Warneken and others, 'Spontaneous Altruism by Chimpanzees and Young Children' (n 71); Julia R Greenberg, Katharina Hamann, Felix Warneken, and Michael Tomasello, 'Chimpanzee Helping in Collaborative and Noncollaborative Contexts' (2010) 80 *Animal Behaviour* 873; Alicia P Melis, Felix Warneken, and Brian Hare, 'Collaboration and Helping in Chimpanzees' in Elizabeth V Lonsdorf, Stephen R Ross, and Tetsuro Matsuzawa (eds), *The Mind of the Chimpanzee: Ecological and Experimental Perspectives* (U Chicago Press 2010).

[74] Bekoff and Pierce (n 13).

[75] Bekoff and Pierce (n 13); Candace Calloway Whiting, 'Humpback Whales Intervene in Orca Attack on Gray Whale Calf' *Digital Journal* (8 May 2012).

[76] Whiting (n 75). [77] Bekoff and Pierce (n 13).

[78] This assumption is based on the theory of parsimony, which suggests that the most likely explanation for the facts (ie that if *Homo sapiens* and *Pan* share particular features, so did their common ancestor) is probably the correct one.

immediate group evolved in the human lineage. It has been suggested that early human species in Africa, during the Pliocene era,[79] had to live in large, socially complex groups, in which there were high levels of cooperation and reciprocity, for protection from the diverse array of predators living at that time.[80] If so, the social interactions of the individuals in these groups could have been the precursor for the substantial amounts of cooperative, altruistic behaviour seen in modern humans. There is indirect evidence of food sharing and extensive cooperation among group members at Middle Pleistocene sites,[81] including evidence of home bases, where pregnant women, children, and other injured or sick individuals could remain and stay safe, while others obtained food for them.[82] Also, Middle and Late Pleistocene[83] deposits contain specimens, including a number of Neanderthals, with injuries that would have made it quite difficult for them to forage for themselves, suggesting that the group was caring for them.[84] These examples may imply modern human-like capabilities for altruism in the later stages of human evolution, although others have argued that the extensive abilities of modern humans to be altruistic and cooperative are probably only possible with the evolution of symbolic cognition and reasoning.[85]

7. Competition and Cooperation

7.1 Collective action problems

Humans and other animals not only cooperate with one another, they also compete. In general, individuals are more successful in groups when they outcompete

79 Approximately 5.0–2.5 million years ago.

80 Hart and Sussman (n 11); Adrian Treves and Paul Palmqvist, 'Reconstructing Hominin Interactions with Mammalian Carnivores (6.0–1.8 Ma)' in Sharon Gursky and K Nekaris (eds), *Primate Anti-Predator Strategies* (Springer 2007); Hart and Sussman, *Man the Hunted* (n 11); Hart and Sussman, 'The Influence of Predation' (n 14).

81 Specifically at Gesher Benot Ya'Aqov, Israel, dated to approximately 800,000 years ago. Rivka Rabinovich, Sabine Gaudzinski-Windheuser, and Naama Goren-Inbar, 'Systematic Butchering of Fallow Deer (Dama) at the Early Middle Pleistocene Acheulian Site of Gesher Benot Ya'Aqov (Israel)' (2008) 54 *Journal of Human Evolution* 134.

82 Cloninger and Kedia (n 4).

83 The Middle and Late Pleistocene are dated to between 780 and 126 ka, and 120 and 10 ka, respectively.

84 Jean-Jacques Hublin, 'The Prehistory of Compassion' (2009) 106(16) *PNAS* 6429.

85 Ian Tattersall, 'What Happened in the Origin of Human Consciousness?' (2004) 267B *Anatomical Record* 19; Ian Tattersall, 'An Evolutionary Framework for the Acquisition of Symbolic Cognition by *Homo Sapiens*' (2008) 3 *Comparative Cognition and Behavior Reviews* 99; Tattersall, 'Cooperation, Altruism, and Human Evolution' (n 69).

fellow group members. Intragroup competition is relevant to one of the most frequently discussed problems in explaining how altruism evolved. Theoretically, it should be possible for an individual to 'cheat the system' and become a free-rider, benefitting from the altruistic behaviours of others in the group and failing to reciprocate in kind—for example, by not helping to find food or not contributing to group defence. When the maximization of individual interests overrides concern for the community, the result can be 'the tragedy of the commons'.[86] The 'collective action problem' (CAP)[87] recognizes that there is an incentive for competitive individuals to refrain from aiding others in the group, while still benefiting from their altruistic behaviours. If there is no countervailing selective pressure, the genes of individuals that behave in this manner are more likely to be transmitted to the next generation, because these competitive individuals will gain all of the benefits of, for example, access to food and safety, while expending less energy and taking none of the risks that would result in harm. Consequently, the cooperative system would break down, and the population would eventually lose the alleles for altruistic behaviours. Some suggest that the CAP is the reason why reciprocity is much less common than mutualism in non-human animals.[88]

If altruism is based on mutualism, the CAP is easy to overcome, because either there are immediate benefits to both individuals, or benefits are assured to both parties in the future. Thus, it would be difficult for an individual to cheat by not reciprocating after aid is provided, because there is little or no gap between the giving and receiving of cooperative assistance. The benefits of free-riding are also reduced in groups of closely related individuals, because there are advantages to helping kin due to inclusive fitness, in addition to the potential benefits of having those behaviours reciprocated. The potential for cheating the system is also reduced in smaller groups. Game theory, based on Prisoner's Dilemma models,[89] suggests that in small groups where individuals are likely to encounter one another frequently, direct reciprocity of altruistic acts could readily evolve, because one could not avoid those persons that provided previous aid.[90]

For reciprocity to evolve in a larger group of less closely related individuals, it is necessary to keep track of whether or not individuals reciprocate assistance in kind, either through direct reciprocation or by providing group benefits. In other words, the group must be able to identify the 'cheaters'. It has been suggested that forming long-term social bonds, and thereby creating greater confidence in future paybacks, aids in other animal species' ability to overcome the CAP and provide consistent

[86] Garrett Hardin, Garrett (1968) 'The Tragedy of the Commons' (1968) 162 *Science* 1243–48.

[87] Charles L Nunn, 'Collective Benefits, Free-Riders, and Male Extra-Group Conflict' in Peter M Kappeler, *Primate Males: Causes and Consequences of Variation in Group Composition* (CUP 2000).

[88] Rilling, 'The Neurobiology of Cooperation' (n 30).

[89] Robert Axelrod and William D Hamilton, 'The Evolution of Cooperation' (1981) 211 *Science* 1390.

[90] Nowak, 'Five Rules' (n 28).

reciprocal benefits to non-kin.[91] Long-term social bonds between non-kin are especially well documented in non-human primates.

Humans also typically help those with whom they have established strong bonds, without the expectation or need for immediate reciprocity, confident that those individuals will be willing to provide reciprocal benefits in the future, if needed. These two behavioural phenomena, providing assistance and forming long-term bonds, may reinforce one another, with evidence that providing mutualistic benefits may help in maintaining long-term bonds.[92] It has been suggested that, as in humans, the strength of a social bond and the likelihood that two animals will reciprocate altruism, is based on a sort of 'book-keeping' mechanism of past interactions.[93] In other words, an individual will be more likely to provide aid if, over the long term, their partner has provided assistance to them consistently. This behaviour has been referred to as attitudinal reciprocity.[94] If non-human primates (in particular apes and monkeys) can do this, the ability to overcome the CAP and develop the capacity for reciprocal altruism may have evolved early in the prehistory of anthropoids.[95] Some have countered that altruism among non-kin in non-human primate species is a biological markets principle that is more akin to mutualism, based on calculations about the current social situation not on long-term book keeping.[96] Under this model, individuals trade social benefits with one another, choosing their partners based on who will provide the greatest benefits to them at that moment.[97]

For altruism based on reciprocity to evolve and persist in a population, the group must have mechanisms for responding to those who cheat, to prevent them from benefiting from their actions (or inaction). One means by which the group can respond to cheating is by providing rewards to individuals who behave altruistically. This could increase the evolutionary fitness of individuals who behave

[91] Joan B Silk, 'The Adaptive Value of Sociality in Mammalian Groups' (2007) 362 *Philosophical Transactions of the Royal Society B* 539; Robin IM Dunbar and Susanne Shultz, 'Bondedness and Sociality' (2010) 147 *Behaviour* 775; David P Watts, 'Dominance, Power, and Politics in Non-Human and Human Primates' in Peter M Kappeler and Joan B Silk (eds), *Mind the Gap: Tracing the Origins of Human Universals* (Springer 2010); Robert M Seyfarth and Dorothy L Cheney, 'The Evolutionary Origins of Friendship' (2012) 63 *Annual Review of Psychology* 153.

[92] de Waal, *Chimpanzee Politics* (n 56); Barbara B Smuts, *Sex and Friendship among Baboons* (Aldine 1985). Clutton-Brock, 'Cooperation between Non-Kin' (n 22).

[93] G Schino and F Aureli, 'The Relative Roles of Kinship and Reciprocity in Explaining Primate Altruism' (2010) 13 *Ecological Letters* 45.

[94] Susan F Brosnan and Frans BM de Waal, 'A Proximate Perspective on Reciprocal Altruism' (2002) 13 *Human Nature* 129; Frans BM de Waal and Sarah F Brosnan, 'Simple and Complex Reciprocity in Primates' in Kappeler and van Schaik, *Cooperation in Primates* (n 36).

[95] The Superfamily Anthropoidea is a taxonomic group that includes monkeys, apes, and humans.

[96] Barrett and others, 'Market Forces' (n 41); L Barrett and SP Henzi, 'Constraints of Relationship Formation among Female Primates' (2002) 139 *Behaviour* 263; Louise Barrett, Peter Henzi, and Drew Rendall, 'Social Brains, Simple Minds: Does Social Complexity Really Require Cognitive Complexity?' (2007) 362 *Philosophical Transactions of the Royal Society B* 561.

[97] MacKinnon and Fuentes (n 5).

altruistically, making it more likely that the alleles predisposing them to altruism pass on to future generations. Being altruistic could potentially attract members of the opposite sex, which would increase the reproductive output of altruistic individuals. There is some evidence that this may occur among some non-human species, especially those with greater cognitive abilities. Female capuchins, one of the more cognitively advanced monkey species, appear to reward males that participate more frequently in intergroup conflicts to protect the group's territory, by providing additional mating opportunities and grooming.[98] Many human cultures use prizes, medals, and honours to reward those that assist others, and there is evidence from game theory experiments that people who consistently help others are more likely to be helped themselves.[99]

The use of social sanctions is another response to those who fail to help others in the group. It is thus another possible means by which altruism could have been selected for and the CAP overcome. Applying the stick rather than the carrot, those who do not assist fellow group members may be excluded from accessing certain resources, or social support may be withheld from those individuals during conflicts. It has been suggested that capuchin monkeys have the ability to identify and react against inequalities in exchanges between individuals,[100] and both wild and captive chimpanzees have been observed punishing those who, through their selfish behaviours, threaten the success of the group in some way.[101] Similarly, canids avoid those who did not interact fairly with other members of the group, typically forcing those individuals to leave the group and face a greater mortality risk.[102]

If the non-performance of expected behaviours leads to the identification and exclusion of non-cooperators from the benefits of group living, as with the canid species, then altruism could be an evolutionarily stable strategy, since then only those individuals that behave in an altruistic manner would benefit from public goods. Game theory predicts that ceasing assistance to consistent cheaters is necessary for cooperation to persist among individuals in large populations.[103] However, while some argue that punishing those who do not cooperate is necessary for reciprocity to evolve,[104] others contend that punishment is not a mechanism by which

[98] Susan Perry, 'Intergroup Encounters in Wild White-Faced Capuchins (*Cebus Capuchinus*)' (1996) 17 *International Journal of Primatology* 309.

[99] See Nowak and Sigmund (n 29); Nowak, 'Five Rules' (n 28).

[100] Sarah F Brosnan and Frans BM de Waal, 'Monkeys Reject Unequal Pay' (2003) 425 *Nature* 297.

[101] Frans de Waal, *Good Natured: The Origins of Right and Wrong in Humans and Other Animals* (Harvard UP 1996); Bekoff and Pierce (n 13).

[102] Bekoff and Pierce (n 13); Bekoff, 'Cooperation and the Evolution of Social Living' (n 66).

[103] Robert Axelrod, *The Evolution of Cooperation* (Basic Books 1984); Ernst Fehr and Urs Fischbacher, 'The Nature of Human Altruism: Proximate Patterns and Evolutionary Origins' (2003) 425 *Nature* 78; Joseph Henrich and Natalie Henrich, 'Culture, Evolution and the Puzzle of Human Cooperation' (2006) 7 *Cognitive Systems Research* 220; Nowak, 'Five Rules' (n 28); Clutton-Brock, 'Cooperation between Non-Kin' (n 22).

[104] Pievani (n 7).

reciprocity and altruism could initially evolve (although it could help to promote these behaviours once they emerge), because the act of punishing cheaters is itself an altruistic act—meaning that altruism must have evolved initially via some other mechanism.[105]

Humans frequently sanction those who act in a manner that in some fashion threatens the group or individuals in the group, sometimes even using costly forms of punishment. In hunter-gatherer groups, a violation of egalitarian ethics can lead to serious consequences, including ostracism.[106] This may have been true of earlier hominin species, as well.[107] While the studies cited above suggest that other animals punish those that do not cooperate with the group, some contend that there is little evidence that non-human primates in particular use social sanctions to punish those who do not act altruistically, and even argue that they may lack the cognitive abilities to do so.[108] If so, it may be that social sanctions evolved only in earlier human species.

One possibility is that humans developed social sanctions as a means to ensure cooperation and altruistic behaviour in the larger and more complex social groups that formed later in human evolution. In modern societies, we have codified these social sanctions by creating laws that coerce us to act in particular ways, overriding our personal interest for the good of others. Modern human groups also depend on reputation much more than other animals to determine whether and how we interact with one another. We frequently make reputations public knowledge, in an effort to identify those who have not followed normative behaviours and to ensure future cooperative behaviour from others. At times, individuals have been made to wear particular items of clothing (scarlet letters) or have been subjected to physical interventions (eg shaved heads or amputations), to signal their poor conduct and reputation to others.

The loss of important social bonds is another potential consequence of a failure to cooperate with others, which could reinforce altruistic behaviours among group members. In many social species, animals compete with one another to establish and maintain social bonds with particular individuals, using many different altruistic behaviours to do so, including grooming, consolation, and support during agonistic encounters. Chimpanzees use various tactics, including coercion and cooperation, to establish relationships and to break apart the alliances of potential rivals, just like humans do. Social bonds are important to many animals, especially gregarious primates, because they depend on others for their success and, sometimes, their survival. Social status in anthropoids depends substantially on one's

[105] Nowak, 'Five Rules' (n 28).

[106] Christopher Boehm, 'The Natural Selection of Altruistic Traits' (1999) 10(3) *Human Nature* 205.

[107] Robin B Kar, 'The Deep Structure of Law and Morality' (2006) 84 *Tex L Rev* 877.

[108] Jeffrey R Stevens and Marc D Hauser, 'Why Be Nice? Psychological Constraints on the Evolution of Cooperation' (2004) 8(2) *Trends in Cognitive Sciences* 60.

social bonds, and individuals performing actions that result in the loss of those bonds will be less likely to receive support in intragroup conflicts and may have reduced access to the best resources. Being in positive social relationships with others also has been found to reduce stress levels in non-human primates,[109] which may help explain the results from long-term studies that relationship quality with fellow adults can influence reproductive success in female baboons.[110] In human societies, the most socially adept individuals with the best reputations benefit from their social connections through reduced stress levels, increased reproductive rates, higher infant survival, and greater longevity.[111] Therefore, in a social group in which individuals rely on strong bonds with others for support and aid, selection for altruistic behaviours would likely occur to maintain those bonds. Acknowledging these consequences, human societies have long considered exile and shunning as particularly harsh sanctions.

7.2 Group benefits of altruism

Among most anthropoid primates, the success of individuals is not only dependent on their own ability to survive and reproduce, but also on how their group succeeds relative to other groups and their species relative to other species. The emergence of altruistic behaviours would have provided a number of advantages to individuals in those groups and species exhibiting such behaviours, because they would obtain greater support from one another. Both biological theory and experimental simulations support the hypothesis that a group made up of individuals who cooperate with one another will be at a selective advantage over groups of selfish individuals,[112] as Darwin predicted.[113] Strong social bonds among members of a group, facilitated by altruistic aid to one another, provide benefits—including more resources and mating opportunities, and a reduction in infant mortality and predation risk. It has been suggested that some early hominin groups may have had a selective advantage over others, because of their more extensive cooperation by sharing parenting responsibilities[114] and/or

[109] Hart and Sussman, 'The Influence of Predation' (n 14).

[110] Joan B Silk, Susan C Alberts, and Jeanne Altmann, 'Social Bonds of Female Baboons Enhance Infant Survival' (2003) 302 *Science* 1231.

[111] Silk, Alberts, and Altmann (n 110); Joan B Silk, Jacinta C Beehner, Thore J Bergman, Catherine Crockford, Anne L Engh, Liza R Moscovice, Roman M Wittig, Robert M Seyfarth, and Dorothy L Cheney, 'The Benefits of Social Capital: Close Social Bonds among Female Baboons Enhance Offspring Survival' (2009) 276 *Proceedings of the Royal Society B* 3099.

[112] Nowak, 'Five Rules' (n 28); Paul A Garber and Martin K Kowalewski, 'Collective Action and Male Affiliation in Howler Monkeys (*Alouatta Caraya*)' in Sussman and Cloninger, *Origins of Altruism* (n 4); Pievani (n 7).

[113] Darwin, *The Descent of Man* (n 1).

[114] Sarah Blaffer Hrdy, *Mothers and Others: The Evolutionary Origins of Mutual Understanding* (Harvard UP 2009).

exhibiting greater cooperation in group defence.[115] Increased intergroup competition during human evolution may have led to substantial advantages for those groups that were the most cooperative and altruistic. There is evidence that selection pressure from intergroup conflict was substantial; archeological and ethnographic evidence suggest that it accounted for 14 per cent of deaths among prehistoric hunter-gatherer groups.[116]

Group selection is one of the oldest hypotheses proposed to explain the evolution of altruism.[117] This hypothesis posits that individuals in cooperative, altruistic groups are more likely to survive and reproduce than individuals in groups where aggressive, intragroup competition dominates, leading to more individuals with a predisposition towards altruism. As noted above, there is evidence that groups with more altruistic members would be at an advantage over those groups with more selfish individuals. However, because of the CAP, most biologists argue that it would be difficult for group selection, in and of itself, to lead to altruism; that altruism evolved via other mechanisms, such as kin selection and reciprocity, among individuals within the group; and that groups with more altruistic members were at an advantage over other groups, which further selected for altruistic behaviours.

Bowles identified a problem with the group selection model (and most other models) for the evolution of true altruism, noting that '[g]enerosity and solidarity towards one's own may have emerged only in combination with hostility towards outsiders'.[118] Studies suggest that the same hormone that leads to feelings of trust within a group (oxytocin) also leads to feelings of antagonism towards non-group members.[119]

How did humans overcome this, to have at least the potential to be altruistic towards complete strangers? One potential solution could be found in what is referred to as an 'exaptation',[120] a biological trait that was selected for one reason and which now performs a different function; for example, the dexterous human hands that human ancestors once used to grasp tree limbs are now used for writing and creating tools. Pievani[121] makes a convincing argument for exaptations being

[115] Kappeler and van Schaik (n 36).

[116] Samuel Bowles, 'Did Warfare among Ancestral Hunter-Gatherers Affect the Evolution of Human Social Behaviors?' (2009) 324 *Science* 1293.

[117] Darwin, *The Descent of Man* (n 1); Petr Alekseevich Kropotkin, *Modern Science and Anarchism* (Mother Earth Publishing Association 1908); VC Wynne-Edwards, 'Intergroup Selection in the Evolution of Social Systems' (1963) 200 *Nature* 623; David Sloan Wilson, 'A Theory of Group Selection' (1975) 72 *PNAS* 143; VC Wynne-Edwards, *Evolution Through Group Selection* (Blackwell Science Inc 1986).

[118] Samuel Bowles, 'Being Human: Conflict: Altruism's Midwife' (2008) 456 *Nature* 326, 326.

[119] Carsten KW De Dreu, Lindred L Greer, Michel JJ Handgraaf, Shaul Shalvi, Gerben A van Kleef, Matthijs Baas, Femke S ten Velden, Eric van Dijk, and Sander WW Feith, 'The Neuropeptide Oxytocin Regulates Parochial Altruism in Intergroup Conflict among Humans' (2010) 328 *Science* 1408.

[120] Stephen Jay Gould and Elisabeth S Vrba, 'Exaptation—A Missing Term in the Science of Form' (1982) 8 *Paleobiology* 4–15.

[121] Pievani (n 7).

critically important in the evolution of prosocial behaviours in humans, with the roots of these behaviours, as suggested here, grounded in the provision of aid to kin and the reciprocation of cooperation and aid to fellow group members. He suggests that pleasurable feelings resulting from altruistic acts towards strangers are an extension of the positive hormonal responses human ancestors (and other animals) received from helping their children or close relatives. This could explain the evolution of the ability to care about, and be kind to, those outside the group, though the ability to be altruistic towards non-group members is clearly an ongoing evolutionary struggle. Many persons are still either genetically or environmentally predisposed to be parochial in their altruistic behaviours, while others are more able to extend altruism to strangers. Unfortunately for the cause of universal human rights, it seems that that more inward-looking, group-first individuals are ascending in many societies today.

8. Biological Adaptations for Altruism in Humans and Other Animals

It has been suggested that the extraordinary human capacity to exchange altruistic aid via direct and indirect reciprocity is due to advanced cognitive and language abilities.[122] It is well established that the substantially expanded and more complex frontal lobe in humans enables future planning and that humans have the ability to discuss those plans and detail expectations for future exchanges of assistance with others through language. Other animals lack this linguistic capacity, so it may not be possible for them to cooperate extensively via direct reciprocity. Language and advanced cognitive abilities could also help with the development of complex forms of indirect reciprocity involving reputation, as it is necessary to remember the other individuals' interactions and whether or not they assisted fellow group members. In addition, in large groups like the typical human population, every individual will not observe all interactions. Therefore, to spread information about the reputation of an individual through the group, language appears to be necessary. The development of the ability to understand the importance of, and spread information about,

[122] Eric A Smith, 'Human Cooperation: Perspectives from Behavioral Ecology' in Peter Hammerstein, *Genetic and Cultural Evolution* (n 37); Stevens and Hauser (n 109); Clutton-Brock, 'Cooperation between Non-Kin' (n 22).

reputation may have been one of the key factors influencing the evolution of human cognitive abilities.[123]

How and when language first evolved during human evolution has been extensively debated. Some have argued that expressive speech could have been present in the earliest members of the human genus.[124] The syntactical language of modern humans, however, has been related to the evolution of self-awareness and perspective-taking, which are both important factors for the capacity to perform acts of true altruism.[125]

Empathy towards strangers is a necessary precursor to true altruism, and, thus, to the ability to develop laws that provide for the protection of others. A number of social animal species are thought to have the ability to empathize, which requires that an individual have the cognitive capacity to take another's perspective.[126] Some argue that this is a uniquely human ability,[127] but African great apes, especially chimpanzees and bonobos, have convincingly demonstrated consolation between one conflict partner and a third party not involved in the conflict, which requires this capacity for empathy.[128]

Cetaceans, humans, African great apes, and elephants have specialized neurons in their brains, known as spindle or von Economo neurons, which allow for the rapid transmission of communication around the relatively large brains of these taxa. These structures are found in the areas of the human brain that deal with, among other things, empathy, speech, and intuitions about the feelings of others. Their presence

[123] Nowak and Sigmund (n 29).

[124] MC Corballis, 'From Mouth to Hand: Gesture, Speech, and the Evolution of Righthandedness' (2003) 26 *Behavioral and Brain Sciences* 199.

[125] Ian Tattersall, 'Human Origins: Out of Africa' (2009) 106 *PNAS* 16,018; Cloninger and Kedia (n 4).

[126] Frans BM de Waal, 'Putting the Altruism Back into Altruism: The Evolution of Empathy' (2008) 59 *Annual Review of Psychology* 279; Bekoff and Pierce (n 14); Bekoff, 'Cooperation and the Evolution of Social Living' (n 66); MacKinnon and Fuentes (n 5).

[127] Cloninger and Kedia (n 4).

[128] Frans BM de Waal and Angeline van Roosmalen, 'Reconciliation and Consolation among Chimpanzees' (1979) 5 *Behavioral Ecology and Sociobiology* 55; Frans BM de Waal and Filippo Aureli, 'Consolation, Reconciliation, and a Possible Cognitive Difference between Macaque and Chimpanzee' in Anne E Russon, Kim A Bard, and Sue Taylor Parker (eds), *Reaching into Thought: The Minds of the Great Apes* (CUP 1996); Roman M Wittig and Christophe Boesch, 'The Choice of Post-Conflict Interactions in Wild Chimpanzees (Pan Troglodytes)' (2003) 140 *Behaviour* 1527; Nobuyuki Kutsukake and Duncan L Castles, 'Reconciliation and Post-Conflict Third-Party Affiliation among Wild Chimpanzees in the Mahale Mountains, Tanzania' (2004) 45 *Primates* 157; Elisabetta Palagi, Tomasso Paoli, and Silvana Borgognini Tarli, 'Reconciliation and Consolation in Captive Bonobos (*Pan Paniscus*)' (2004) 62(1) *American Journal of Primatology* 15; Elisabetta Palagi, Giada Cordoni, and Silvana Borgognini Tarli, 'Possible Roles of Consolation in Captive Chimpanzees (*Pan Troglodytes*)' (2006) 129 *American Journal of Physical Anthropology* 105; Giada Cordoni, Elisabetta Palagi, and Silvana Borgognini Tarli, 'Reconciliation and Consolation in Captive Western Gorillas' (2006) 27 *International Journal of Primatology* 1365; Sonja E Koski and Elisabeth HM Sterck, 'Triadic Post-Conflict Affiliation in Captive Chimpanzees: Does Consolation Console?' (2007) 73 *Animal Behavior* 133.

may relate to the evolution of complex social behaviours,[129] including empathy and altruism, in these groups. Cetaceans and elephants, as noted above, seem to have the ability to empathize, even with members of other species. Marino[130] argues that cetaceans may be able to generalize the need for help from one species to another. It is intriguing that all of these species live in large groups, which suggests that negotiating constantly shifting social groupings may select for increased brain complexity. It seems plausible that it was beneficial for members of the group to be altruistic, in order both to maintain important social partners and for the group to be cohesive when competing against other groups. These behaviours could then have been extended to those outside of one's own group, even to members of different species, via the hormonal mechanisms described above.

Studies have found evidence that the human brain is well adapted to detect cheating in social interactions and that humans can quite effectively recall those individuals who have been least trustworthy in their interactions with them.[131] Humans typically react negatively towards selfishness and generally avoid interacting with those they perceive to be cheaters. Human brains appear to contain hormonal mechanisms for discouraging cooperation with those who do not reciprocate assistance[132] and provide rewards for punishing cheaters.[133]

There is also evidence that the threat of punishment motivates individuals to be less selfish and more altruistic,[134] although some have argued that even without the threat of punishment, humans would still continue to act altruistically, because human brains have evolved a predisposition to act towards others in such a fashion.[135] Other studies, though, suggest an intermediate position, concluding that this

[129] Camilla Butti, Chet C Sherwood, Atiya Y Hakeem, John M Allman, and Patrick R Hof, 'Total Number and Volume of Von Economo Neurons in the Cerebral Cortex of Cetaceans' (2009) 515 *Journal of Comparative Neurology* 243.

[130] Whiting (n 75).

[131] Linda Mealey, Christopher Daood, and Michael Krage, 'Enhanced Memory for Faces of Cheaters' (1996) 17 *Ethology and Sociobiology* 119; Leda Cosmides and John Tooby, 'The Cognitive Neuroscience of Social Reasoning' in Michael S Gazzaniga (ed), *The New Cognitive Neurosciences* (2nd edn, MIT Press 2000); Seth D Pollak, 'Early Social Experience and the Ontogenesis of Emotion Regulatory Behavior in Children' in Sussman and Cloninger, *Origins of Altruism* (n 4).

[132] James K Rilling, David A Gutman, Thorsten R Zeh, Giuseppe Pagnoni, Gregory S Berns, and Clinton D Kilts, 'A Neural Basis for Social Cooperation' (2002) 35 *Neuron* 395; James K Rilling, Alan G Sanfey, Jessica A Aronson, Leigh E Nystrom, and Jonathan D Cohen, 'Opposing BOLD Responses to Reciprocated and Unreciprocated Altruism in Putative Reward Pathways' (2004) 15 *Neuroreport* 2539; Rilling, 'The Neurobiology of Cooperation' (n 30).

[133] Dominique JF de Quervain, Urs Fischbacher, Valerie Treyer, Melanie Schellhammer, Ulrich Schnyder, Alfred Buck, and Ernst Fehr, 'The Neural Basis of Altruistic Punishment' (2004) 305 *Science* 1254; Tania Singer, Ben Seymour, John P O'Doherty, Klaas E Stephan, Raymond J Dolan, and Chris D Frith, 'Empathic Neural Responses Are Modulated by the Perceived Fairness of Others' (2006) 439 *Nature* 466.

[134] Rilling, 'The Neurobiology of Cooperation' (n 30).

[135] Patricia S Churchland, *Braintrust: What Neuroscience Tells Us about Morality* (Princeton UP 2011).

behaviour varies among humans, with some individuals cooperating with others only when threatened with punishment, while others cooperate readily.[136]

The finding that most children by age five will think that harming others is wrong, whether or not an authority figure has taught them that, supports the hypothesis that humans have altruistic predispositions.[137] Some suggest that human emotions, such as guilt, may have evolved to reinforce these altruistic tendencies.[138] In addition, studies suggest that non-psychopathic subjects have to use extra cognitive effort to cheat, by overriding their emotional tendency to cooperate with one another.[139] This would seem to imply that cooperation with others is the more typical human behaviour. Kar terms these evolved tendencies 'obligata',[140] which he says cause us to act in ways that benefit others. Laws regarding diminished mental capacity recognize that there is a biological potential for moral behaviour in most humans and that some are born without that capacity.

There is evidence, as well, that the human nervous and endocrine systems have evolved to provide positive feedback when humans behave altruistically. Researchers studying brain images have noted that the human nervous system is adapted in such a way as to generate feelings of reward when individuals are cooperating with and assisting others (including when donating to charities), and that those neurological rewards increase the more humans cooperate with one another.[141] The positive stimuli received when providing assistance to others apparently cause the release of dopamine, which leads to pleasurable feelings,[142] suggesting that altruistic behaviours can be reinforced hormonally. This may help humans to overcome the desire for immediate rewards at the expense of others. Beyond merely providing pleasurable sensations, this may bring evolutionary benefits by reducing stress hormones and, as a result, reducing morbidity and mortality in those individuals who act altruistically. This could lead to those with genes that predispose them to engage

[136] Ernst Fehr and Simon Gächter, 'Altruistic Punishment in Humans' (2002) 415 *Nature* 137.

[137] Elliot Turiel, *The Culture of Morality: Social Development, Context, and Conflict* (CUP 2002).

[138] Trivers, 'The Evolution of Reciprocal Altruism' (n 27); Daniel MT Fessler and Kevin J Haley, 'The Strategy of Affect: Emotions in Human Cooperation' in Hammerstein, *Genetic and Cultural Evolution* (n 37).

[139] James K Rilling, Andrea L Glenn, Meeta R Jairam, Giuseppe Pagnoni, David R Goldsmith, Hanie A Elfenbein, and Scott O Lilienfeld, 'Neural Correlates of Social Cooperation and Non-Cooperation as a Function of Psychopathy' (2007) 61 *Biological Psychiatry* 1260; Rilling, 'The Neurobiology of Cooperation' (n 30).

[140] Kar (n 107).

[141] Rilling and others, 'A Neural Basis for Social Cooperation' (n 132); Rilling and others, 'Opposing Bold Responses' (n 132); MR Delgado, RH Frank, and EA Phelps, 'Perceptions of Moral Character Modulate the Neural Systems of Reward During the Trust Game' (2005) 8 *Nature Neuroscience* 1611; Jorge Moll, Frank Krueger, Roland Zahn, Matteo Pardini, Ricardo de Oliveira-Souza, and Jordan Grafman, 'Human Fronto–Mesolimbic Networks Guide Decisions about Charitable Donation' (2006) 103 *PNAS* 15623; Rilling, 'The Neurobiology of Cooperation' (n 30).

[142] Rilling and others, 'A Neural Basis for Social Cooperation' (n 132); Rilling, 'The Neurobiology of Cooperation' (n 30).

in altruistic behaviour being at a selective advantage and provide another means by which those genes would become more common in humans.

9. Conclusion

It appears that human solidarity, the ability to care about the rights of those outside the kinship or immediate social group, likely has its roots in evolutionary history, with *Homo sapiens* building upon the behavioural capacities of earlier species. Initially altruism evolved via kin selection as a means of perpetuating an individual's genes by helping those related to the individual. Then, in smaller groups, some species evolved the ability to extend this aid to unrelated individuals, as long as they reciprocated that aid at some point in the near or distant future. As groups increased in size, individuals were no longer able to ensure that they would interact with all others with sufficient frequency to ensure direct reciprocity. They thus began to keep track of who was consistently helping out those in the group in ways that were deemed important for the group, and who was not. Consequently, one's reputation for behaving in ways that followed the social and moral norms of the group became important for one's success. The advantages conferred on an individual who could keep track of the reputation of others led to selection for increases in brain size and complexity. This helped lead to the evolution of self-awareness and the human ability to perform selfless acts for strangers, with a positive hormonal feedback serving as a proximate mechanism that encouraged these behaviours. Finally, the social norms of human populations became codified through laws, including international human rights laws.

Humans are typically born with the biological potential of exhibiting, to a greater or lesser extent, both extreme cruelty and extraordinary acts of altruism, as part of what some would call a 'continuum of potential human behaviours'.[143] Social experiences modifying genetic predispositions then determine where on the spectrum between these extremes an individual member of the species of 'bipolar apes'[144] may fall. As Wilson recently noted, in modern humans, the capacity for self-serving behaviour that helps individuals outcompete others within their group is combined with the capacity for providing aid to fellow group members, which in turn helps the group outcompete other groups.

Some individuals or groups of individuals may have greater genetic and/or environmental predispositions towards competing against others, as opposed to

[143] See Tattersall, 'Cooperation, Altruism, and Human Evolution' (n 69).
[144] Sussman and Cloninger, 'Introduction' (n 6) ix.

cooperating with those in their group, while others have a greater tendency towards altruistic, cooperative behaviours. Similarly, if reciprocity evolved through competition with other groups, humans may also have predispositions for hostility towards those outside of their group, combined with affiliative feelings towards those in their group,[145] possibly as a result of the same hormonal mechanism. In many cases, humans have a difficult time overcoming these tendencies, as seen in religious wars and wars between nation-states. Without the genes that provide humans with the cognitive abilities to engage in these complex affiliative and agonistic behaviours, the species would not have developed, nor had the need to develop, the concept of universal human rights. While other animals provide assistance to relatives due to kin selection, and though they may possess the potential to reciprocate the aid that another gives to them, humans have built on these altruistic abilities and evolved the capacity for true altruism, which only a few, if any, other species possess. True altruism includes the ability to conceive of and, in most people, hope for human rights for all.

Social Darwinists, and many conservatives, have argued that social services impede evolution, because in states providing such benefits, resources are used on those who would normally be selected against, and individuals are not free to fully compete with one another. Thus, individuals with the most beneficial alleles will not be selected for. However, our predisposition for altruistic behaviours is a product of natural selection (as is a predisposition towards being selfish, cruel, and violent), and research suggests that groups with greater numbers of altruistic individuals will outperform those whose members behave in a manner following Social Darwinist theories, as Darwin himself proposed.[146] Thus, it is ironic that populations relying on 'every man for himself' to encourage competition will typically find themselves outcompeted by those in which there is greater cooperation and altruism among individuals.

Further Reading

Alexander RD, *The Biology of Moral Systems* (2nd edn, Aldine Transaction 1987)
Axelrod R, *The Evolution of Cooperation* (Basic Books 1984)
Bekoff M and Pierce J, *Wild Justice: The Moral Lives of Animals* (U Chicago Press 2009)
Boehm C, 'The Natural Selection of Altruistic Traits' (1999) 10(3) *Human Nature* 205
Churchland PS, *Braintrust: What Neuroscience Tells Us about Morality* (Princeton UP 2011)
Connor RC, 'Altruism among Non-Relatives: Alternatives to the "Prisoner's Dilemma"' (1995) 10(2) *Trends in Ecology & Evolution* 84

[145] See Kar, Chapter 5, in this *Handbook*.
[146] Darwin, *The Descent of Man* (n 1).

Darwin C, *On the Origin of Species by Means of Natural Selection, or the Preservation of Favoured Races in the Struggle for Life* (John Murray 1859)
—— *The Descent of Man, and Selection in Relation to Sex* (John Murray 1871)
—— and Wallace A, 'On the Tendency of Species to form Varieties; and on the Perpetuation of Varieties and Species by Natural Means of Selection' (1858) 3 *Journal of the Proceedings of the Linnean Society (Zoology)* 45
de Waal F, *Good Natured: The Origins of Right and Wrong in Humans and Other Animals* (Harvard UP 1996)
Dugatkin LA, *Cooperation among Animals: An Evolutionary Perspective* (OUP 1997)
—— *The Altruism Equation: Seven Scientists Search for the Origins of Goodness* (Princeton UP 2006)
Dunbar R, *Grooming, Gossip, and the Evolution of Language* (Harvard UP 1996)
Fry DP, *The Human Potential for Peace: An Anthropological Challenge to Assumptions about War and Violence* (OUP 2006)
Hammerstein P (ed), *The Genetic and Cultural Origins of Cooperation* (MIT Press 2003)
Hart D and Sussman RW, *Man the Hunted: Primates, Predators, and Human Evolution* (Westview Press 2005)
Kappeler PM and van Schaik CP (eds), *Cooperation in Primates and Humans: Mechanisms and Evolution* (Springer 2006)
Kar RB, 'The Deep Structure of Law and Morality' (2006) 84 *Tex L Rev* 877
Kitcher D, 'The Evolution of Human Altruism' (1993) 90(10) *Journal of Philosophy* 497
Sussman RW and Cloninger CR (eds), *Origins of Altruism and Cooperation* (Springer 2011)
Trivers R, *Social Evolution* (Benjamin/Cummings Publishing Co 1985)
Wilson EO, *The Social Conquest of Earth* (Norton 2012)

CHAPTER 4

SOCIOLOGY OF HUMAN RIGHTS

BRYAN S TURNER

1. Introduction: The Missing Sociology of Human Rights

Unsurprisingly, lawyers, philosophers, and historians have dominated the academic study of human rights. Any discussion of rights tends to evoke questions that are the routine business of political philosophy and legal theory—justice, entitlement, dignity, and legality (the rule of law). Sociologists, to the contrary, have been generally absent from the study of human rights, partly because professional sociology has difficulty addressing overtly normative issues. In classical sociology, this absence is closely associated with the legacy of Max Weber (1864–1920). It is important, therefore, to start with a consideration of Weber, who made substantial contributions to and has cast a long shadow over the development of the sociology of law.

Weber's epistemological arguments partly explain the historical reluctance of sociologists to discuss natural law, human rights, and issues around justice. Weber is inevitably associated with the idea of 'value neutrality' and hence the exclusion of any normative evaluation of social conditions.[1] Furthermore, he believed that class struggle, characteristic of industrial capitalism, was reshaping the legal order

[1] Max Weber, *Economy and Society: An Outline of Interpretive Sociology*, vols 1–2 (Guenther Roth and Claus Wittich (eds), U California P 1978).

through the emergence of what he called 'the social law' about which he was dismissive, noting that it was based on 'such emotionally coloured ethical postulates as "justice" or "human dignity" '.[2] For example, the notion of 'economic duress' is, according to Weber, merely 'amorphous'. These critical comments were connected with his dismissal of natural law as a foundation of modern law. Although he recognized that it would be difficult to eradicate entirely the natural-law legacy from legal practice, he claimed that, as a consequence of modern rationalism and enlightened scepticism, natural law had 'lost all capacity to provide the fundamental basis of a legal system'.[3] Consequently, the forward march of legal positivism was all but 'irresistible'.

While he remained critical of 'meta-juristic axioms', he was genuinely influenced by his friend and colleague, Georg Jellinek. In *The Declaration of the Rights of Man and of Citizens*,[4] Jellinek had traced the origins of the doctrine of universal and inalienable rights, not to the French Revolution or Roman law, or to English common law, but to the Puritans in colonial New England, who had asserted the absolute freedom of conscience for all religions, including Turks and heathens. Weber had intended to look more closely into legal developments in the time of Oliver Cromwell, and we can assume that Weber welcomed Jellinek's ideas as compatible with his own treatment of Protestantism in 1905–06.[5] However, Weber's overriding notion of secularity ruled out the possibility that religion could continue to influence the evolution of rights in the modern societies that legal rationalism dominated.

Weber did follow Jellinek's general theory of law in his classification of law. He recognized two distinct historical origins of rights, namely those tied to social status and those associated with economic markets. A right of inheritance might illustrate the first set, and contracts to regulate exchange, the second. He recognized the difference between a 'claim norm' against another person, a privilege (or immunity), and an obligation. This scheme in *Economy and Society* resembles the more elaborate account of rights and duties with which we are now familiar.[6] For Weber, a right is simply a claim that has the empirical probability of being recognized in law, where law is a set of commands that have the ultimate backing of the state. These claims are empirically measurable as 'facts' in a system of rules that determine rights and duties. From Weber's perspective, the rights that people *ought* to enjoy cannot be answered from the standpoint of the science of law. Evidently, Weber wanted to avoid any suggestion that in a secular society rights could have a moral force relating to religion, natural law, or similar traditions. Similarly Weber's theory of the

[2] Weber, *Economy and Society* (n 1) vol 2, 874.

[3] Weber, *Economy and Society* (n 1) vol 2, 874.

[4] Georg Jellinek, *The Declaration of the Rights of Man and of Citizens* (World Library Classics 2009).

[5] Max Weber, *The Protestant Ethic and the Spirit of Capitalism and Other Writings* (Peter Baehr and Gordon C Wells (eds), Penguin 2002).

[6] See Wesley Hohfeld, *Fundamental Legal Conceptions* (WW Cook (ed), Yale UP 1919).

state had a noticeable Machiavellian flavour, his primary interest being 'the rule of man over man'.[7]

Thus, sociologists, and even more so anthropologists, in embracing radical versions of cultural relativism, have been averse to any universalistic claims about 'human rights'. Rejecting the idea of a shared humanity and a universal rationality, sociologists concluded that the only thing social groups have in common is that they are all different. In theories of human rights, it is conventional, with respect to the question of a common humanity, to make a distinction between political and practical perspectives, and humanistic and naturalistic approaches. In the former, individuals claim rights 'against certain institutional structures, in particular the modern states, in virtue of interests they have in contexts that include them', and in the latter 'human rights are pre-institutional claims that individuals have against other individuals in virtue of interests characteristic of their common humanity'.[8] It is difficult, in fact, to distinguish sharply between 'rights against certain institutional structures' and social citizenship; in turning their back on humanistic approaches, sociological theories of human rights are predominantly political and practical.

This absence or underdevelopment of the sociology of human rights may be further attributed to the influence of 'methodological nationalism', which underpins much of the research within the discipline, in which adherents implicitly equate 'the social' or 'society' with the 'national society'.[9] Consequently, sociologists have been more comfortable conducting research on the social rights of citizenship, which are bounded by the nation-state, than investigating universal human rights. The classic example is the prominent work of TH Marshall.[10] He traced the evolution of juridical, political, and social rights in the United Kingdom over a period of three centuries, showing how citizenship rights mitigated the harsh negative effects of capitalism on the working class, thereby offering ordinary people a 'modicum' of civilized life.

Globalization has more recently challenged these (often implicit) assumptions about the study of national societies, and hence sociologists can no longer continue to ignore human rights, because the spread of international law and human-rights institutions are important illustrations of late twentieth-century juridical globalization. Sociological interest in globalization, evolving out of so-called 'civilizational analysis', world-systems theory, and comparative sociology of religion in the 1970s and 1980s, was in full swing by the early 1990s.[11] As a consequence, there are signs of an emerging sociology of human rights in recent handbooks and textbooks.[12] The emergence of

[7] Peter Lassman, 'The Rule of Man over Man: Politics, Power and Legitimation' in Stephen Turner (ed), *The Cambridge Companion to Weber* (CUP 2000) 83–98.

[8] Pablo Gilabert, 'Humanist and Political Perspectives on Human Rights' (2011) 39 *Pol Theory* 439, 440.

[9] Anthony Elliott and Bryan S Turner, *On Society* (Polity Press 1992).

[10] Thomas Humphrey Marshall, *Citizenship and Social Class and Other Essays* (CUP 1950).

[11] See Roland Robertson, *Globalization: Social Theory and Global Culture* (Sage 1992).

[12] Rhiannon Morgan and Bryan S Turner (eds), *Interpreting Human Rights: Social Science Perspectives* (Routledge 2009); Judith Blau and Mark Frezzo (eds), *Sociology and Human Rights: A Bill*

sociology of human rights as a consequence of taking globalization seriously opens up the possibility of combining forces with international law theory around the concept of 'community necessity'.

2. Human Rights or Citizenship Rights?

In order to grapple with the sociology of rights, it is important to examine in more depth the distinction between the social rights of citizens and the human rights of human beings. Sociologists might reasonably ask the question: if all citizens in their various nation-states enjoyed comprehensive social rights, why would they need human rights at all? This position might draw on the legacy of Edmund Burke (1729–97), who famously railed against the Enlightenment philosophers of revolution, claiming that the 'pretended rights of these theorists are all extremes; and in proportion as they are metaphysically true, they are morally and politically false'.[13] The traditional rights of Englishmen, built up over centuries, were more valuable than the abstract concoctions of the Rights of Man.

To begin with simple definitions, 'citizenship' herein means a set of entitlements that the members of a political community or nation-state enjoy. Modern citizenship can be defined as a bundle of social rights and duties that defines citizens' legal status and identity and at the same time significantly determines their access to and enjoyment of resources. Whether or not people have such entitlements will depend on how their membership is defined, that is, on the nature of their social inclusion within a political community, typically a state. Citizenship depends on the possession of certain legal documents—crucially, a birth certificate, a social security or national identity number, and/or a passport. The peculiarity of citizenship is that, while it is said to have universalistic features being independent of race and gender, for example, the majority of people acquire it through the accident of birth.[14] Citizenship rights are exclusionary, and the enforcement of state boundaries closely protects their existence. With a few notable exceptions, visas and work permits are issued on a limited basis with restricted rights, and naturalization for foreigners is typically a complex and difficult process.

of Rights for the Twenty-First Century (Sage 2011); Thomas Cushman (ed), *The Handbook of Human Rights* (Routledge 2011); David L Brunsma, Keri E Iyall Smith, and Brian K Gran (eds), *Handbook of Sociology and Human Rights* (Paradigm 2012).

[13] Edmund Burke, *Reflections on the Revolution in France* (first published 1790, Apollo Press 1814) 63.

[14] Ayelet Shachar and Ran Hirschl, 'Citizenship as Inherited Property' (2007) 35 *Pol Theory* 253.

By contrast, human rights are the rights (essentially claims and immunities) that people enjoy by virtue of being human. Human rights may be defined as the entitlements of individuals qua human beings to life, security, and well-being. They are said to be universal, incontrovertible and subjective—that is, individuals possess them because of their capacity for rationality, agency, and autonomy. Human rights legislation assumes that individuals have certain fundamental powers ('inalienable rights') that no political order can expunge. Humans have, according to the 1948 Universal Declaration of Human Rights (UDHR), a wide range of 'copper-bottom' entitlements that guarantee security of life and protection from coercion, exploitation, and discrimination. Jurisprudential reasoning often claims that human rights have no 'correlativity' because there are no corresponding duties, but leading human rights instruments—including the UDHR, the American Declaration of the Rights and Duties of Man, and the African Charter on Human and Peoples' Rights—contain catalogues of duties as well as rights.

One critical issue for the sociology of rights is the debate over whether social and human rights reinforce or, rather, contradict each other. States can enforce rights and expect duties, but it is not clear who enforces human rights apart from nation-states. The confusion between citizenship and human rights was already evident in the French Declaration of 1789, which referred both to the Rights of Man and Citizen. In any discussion of this problem, the jurisprudential literature commonly refers to a position that Hannah Arendt espoused in her analysis of totalitarianism.[15] She argued that without the power to enforce rights claims, universal rights are empty words. The European Jews were the tragic example of a people who, once deprived of citizenship, no other country could easily accept; the absence of any documentation of Jews' social membership effectively expunged their 'right to rights'. This formulation of the problem is well known, and it has clearly influenced the scepticism of sociologists towards the idea of inalienable rights.

Sociologists have generally been interested not simply in citizenship, but in active citizenship—that is, in the idea of citizens involved in collective action to protect or extend rights. By contrast, human rights are often invoked on behalf of individuals or groups who are the victims of some crisis—a civil war, state repression, drought, or other natural disaster. John Rawls[16] treats human rights as rights of last resort, or as a special class of 'urgent rights', such as freedom from slavery and serfdom. Claims with respect to human rights often come into play when everything else has failed. In the absence of effective global or regional governance, nation-states typically enforce human rights. Yet the agents of nation-states, especially failed states, are the main perpetrators of human rights abuses. Consequently, jurisprudential criticisms of human rights declarations have argued that such rights are not 'justiciable', because they cannot be effectively enforced without the cooperation and involvement of states.

[15] Hannah Arendt, *The Origins of Totalitarianism* (Harcourt Brace 1951).

[16] John Rawls, *The Law of Peoples with 'The Idea of Public Reason Revisited'* (Harvard UP 1999) 79.

As discussed herein, this argument is now somewhat out of date, because there is a wide range of international and national organizations that seek and may succeed in enforcing human rights, often against the interests of national governments.

The historical origins of citizenship and human rights are also different. While Jellinek traced human rights back to the Puritan struggle for demands for religious freedom, international human rights are typically regarded as the product of twentieth-century demands for greater security in response to the destruction of the European Jews in the Holocaust, the bombing of Japanese and German cities, the destruction of civilians as a consequence of the industrialization of warfare, and the Cold War conflicts. Human rights emerge out of direct threats to human beings who are vulnerable. The social rights of modern citizenship emerged out of social struggles for resources and representation that were characteristic of the working-class movements, or out of strategies to improve the efficiency of the working class by social insurance schemes in nineteenth-century capitalism. More recently, the women's movement (for equal pay and equal treatment), as well as gay and lesbian activists claiming rights that come under the umbrella of 'sexual citizenship', have enhanced citizenship rights. Whereas citizenship often involves exclusionary processes of nation-building, human rights are fashioned to guarantee inclusion in the human community.

In summary, the sociology of citizenship is a well-developed area of inquiry.[17] Citizens have social rights, because in principle they make contributions to support society, and so there is a correlation between rights and duties. The sociology of human rights is problematic, however, because we have rights as humans (regardless of whether we belong to a state or society). While sociologists have been sceptical about normative claims that *individuals* have rights, some social philosophers have been equally sceptical about claims involving any reference to *society*. Mabbot for example, in viewing all references to collective entities, wanted to 'banish [the term] "society" in the interests of clear thinking', but also went on to dismiss natural rights as 'indeterminate and capricious'.[18]

3. Human Vulnerability and Recognition

The overriding issues for sociology, then, have been a reluctance to enter into normative debate about 'rights'; a scepticism about their transnational relevance,

[17] Engin F Isin and Bryan S Turner, *Handbook of Citizenship Studies* (Sage 2002).

[18] JD Mabbot, *The State and the Citizen: An Introduction to Political Philosophy* (Grey Arrow 1958).

despite the recent globalization of rights discourse and procedures; and an implicit commitment to 'methodological nationalism', thereby constraining any understanding of an international society. At a deeper level, there has been scepticism about the relevance of ontology in understanding social relations. What is it that humans share in common that might allow us to talk about a common world? The notion of human rights assumes that we can define 'human' with some degree of cross-cultural and trans-historical certainty. If we do not share a common culture or a common language, can we find an argument from human ontology to secure an underpinning for human rights? Of course, some human rights theorists claim we do not need a well-developed (thick) ontology (of human nature) in order to support human rights claims that can be justified by a (thin) theory of human dignity and agency. Michael Ignatieff[19] provides an important defence of the notion that debates about ontology are unhelpful and possibly unnecessary. It is sufficient simply to recognize human suffering and to take steps to alleviate misery.

Nonetheless, the notion of human vulnerability might resolve some of the long-standing problems in the debate between natural law, utilitarianism, and legal positivism.[20] This notion connects the idea of human embodiment to that of mutual dependency, based on four basic assumptions: the inescapable vulnerability of human beings as embodied agents; the resulting dependency of humans on each other, especially during childhood and old age; the general reciprocity and social interconnectedness of the live world; and finally, the inevitable precariousness and fragility of social institutions. The idea of a shared ontology can function to overcome some of the traditional objections from cultural relativism and provide a clear justification for claims to life, health, a clean environment, and freedom from torture.

'Vulnerability' is from the Latin *vulnus*, or 'wound', from which it may be understood that humans, equipped with consciousness and subjectivity, are wounded animals. This basic idea of incomplete and wounded animals is from the work of Peter L. Berger and Thomas Luckmann,[21] which in turn helped develop Arnold Gehlen's (1904–76) idea that human beings are instinctually poor (*Instinktarmut*). Human beings are ontologically vulnerable and insecure, and their social and natural environments are fragile. In order to protect themselves from the contingencies of the everyday world, humans must create and sustain social institutions that collectively constitute what we call 'society'. Humans depend on institutions rather than instincts. The family, kinship groups, tribes, and wider communities are all means of mutual support. In more complex societies, these protective institutions come to include a wide range of institutions, most obviously the law. According to

[19] Michael Ignatieff, *Human Rights as Politics and Idolatry* (Princeton UP 2001).

[20] Bryan S Turner, *Vulnerability and Human Rights* (Pa St UP 2006).

[21] Peter L Berger and Thomas Luckmann, *The Social Construction of Reality: A Treatise in the Sociology of Knowledge* (Doubleday 1967).

Heraclitus, the laws of the ancient city—the *nomoi*—were the walls that protected the citizens from the animals and barbarians who lived outside the city gates.[22] These walls could never fully guarantee our security and hence, in modern societies, sociologists have analysed the threat of a social breakdown, or *anomie*, in a world without secure norms.

Humans are biologically vulnerable and thus need to build legal and political institutions (such as human rights regimes) to provide for collective security. Most commonly and most notably these have included the state. Institutions, however, are themselves precarious and cannot be easily designed or fabricated, but rather require time and tradition to become legitimate and effective. Institutions cannot work effectively without wise leadership and good fortune to provide an enduring and reliable social environment. Traditions do not last forever, social norms offer no enduring blue-print for action, and the moral guardians of social order—priests, academics, lawyers, and others—are all too often open to corruption, mendacity, and naked self-interest. These afflictions and perturbations of everyday life also generate inter-societal patterns of dependency and connectedness; and in this shared world of risk and uncertainty, such dependence may give rise to sympathy, empathy, and trust, without which all social life would crumble. The social world, as the Greek tragedies so clearly revealed, is an inherently contradictory and unstable balance between fate (*Fortuna*) and virtue (*virtu*), or between luck and ethics, and hence we can interpret the existence of an order of rights as a response to this foundational contingency.[23]

This socio-ontological argument can be further developed via a theory of recognition that WGF Hegel (1770–1831) first outlined. Interdependency in a community of risk presupposes the basic act of mutual recognition. Such an act of recognition is required if people are to be mutually recognizable as moral agents, and thereby to recognize the rights claims of others. Contemporary Hegelian philosophers, such as Charles Taylor,[24] have appealed to recognition ethics as the baseline for the enjoyment of rights in a multicultural society of strangers. Without recognition of minority rights, no liberal democratic society can function. Rights also presuppose (relatively) free, autonomous, and self-conscious agents, capable of rational choice and moral deliberation, and thus capable of being held responsible for their actions. No blame attaches to animals for their rapacious and aggressive behaviour simply because they have no capacity for moral agency. Human psychotic killers may also be thought to have no capacity for rationality and moral judgement. The argument that moral agents must be free and autonomous raises another problem for any

[22] Arlene W Saxonhouse, *Fear of Diversity: The Birth of Political Science in Ancient Greek Thought* (U Chicago Press 1992) 21.

[23] Martha Nussbaum, *The Fragility of Goodness: Luck and Ethics in Greek Tragedy and Philosophy* (CUP 1986).

[24] Charles Taylor, *Multiculturalism and the Politics of Recognition* (Princeton UP 1992).

sociology that aspires to discover the causal laws that shape and determine human behaviour. While modern sociology has largely abandoned this nineteenth-century quest for Social Laws that govern society, there is a remaining tension between explaining human *behaviour* by reference to causes and understanding social *actions* in terms of reasons.

In a human community, this basic act of recognition requires some degree of equality. Hegel's master-slave analysis takes account of the fact that neither slave nor master can achieve mutual recognition, because the master perceives the slave as property, while the slave is too lowly to see the master. Hence, without some degree of social equality, there can be no ethical community, and a system of rights and obligations cannot function. Material scarcity undercuts the roots of social solidarity without which conscious, rational agency is compromised. Taking their cue from Karl Marx's (1818–83) critique of liberal theories of rights, sociologists have remained sceptical about human rights traditions that have no corresponding social policies to secure some minimum level of equality through strategies of redistribution, such as progressive taxation.[25] Rights to individual freedoms without democratic egalitarianism are thought to be merely symbolic claims for recognition.

In addition to some degree of equality, there must be open channels of communication between dominant host society (master) and subordinate minority (slave) groups in order for mutual recognition to emerge. Recognition of minorities must be the first step towards establishing a framework of human rights. This notion is modelled on Jürgen Habermas's (1929–) communicative theory of democracy and normative order, which in turn is derived from sociological studies of 'speech situations' involving exchange through mutual recognition of the norms of communication, such as forming queues in question-answer sequences. An ideal speech situation must already be in place for dialogic recognition to occur, and an ideal context for recognition requires a set of procedural rules: ideology does not severely distort communication; speakers have roughly equal opportunities to participate; there is no arbitrary closure of conversations; and so forth.[26] Applying these notions to actual social encounters in multicultural societies, cultural rights require an open-ended opportunity for dialogue between host and minority groups, in which agreed-upon procedural norms enforced by the law restrain power relations. This model of critical recognition pays attention to the fact that identities in modern societies are typically contested (given migration, multiculturalism, and globalization). In actual social encounters, one might include additional criteria. First, mutual recognition has to be able to incorporate and work with mutual criticism. Second, productive dialogue has to have an opt-out clause through which members

[25] Jeremy Waldron (ed), *'Nonsense upon Stilts': Bentham, Burke and Marx on the Rights of Man* (Methuen 1987).

[26] Jürgen Habermas, *The Theory of Communicative Action: Lifeworld and System: A Critique of Functionalist Reason* (Thomas McCarthy (tr), Beacon Press 1985) vol 2.

of minority groups are not compelled to remain within their own local customs and can opt out (for example, reject forced marriage or infibulation), just as members of host societies can also opt out of their own group by emigration. In a democratic context, social groups have to remain relatively open in terms of entry and exit.

This Habermasian communication model has enjoyed widespread acceptance in sociology, precisely because his early work relied heavily on a sociological tradition that is now referred to as 'conversational analysis'. However, there are problems with Habermas's approach to democratic communicative encounters. His theory appears to presuppose the social consensus it sets out to explain. Furthermore, his approach has been labelled a 'yes-saying' philosophy, thereby excluding the phenomenon of 'no-saying' in civil disobedience.[27] Moreover, his model, especially in his work on post-secularism, does not allow for the fact that religious fundamentalists may not wish to communicate with secular liberals. Refusal to engage in a conversation is an important example of no-saying. These analytical difficulties raise serious questions about the actual substance of rational consensus. Human rights require a wide social consensus or 'an overlapping consensus of comprehensive doctrines',[28] as expressed, for example, in the rule of law. Can this social consensus be grounded in recognition of our common vulnerability and corresponding need for effective social institutions to compensate for our shared ontological insecurity? Is human vulnerability variable?

Stephen K White has argued in favour of a weak ontology, by which he means a collection of 'figures', including 'language, finitude, natality, and the articulation of our deepest "sources of the self"'.[29] These ontological figures only command weak, rather than absolute, commitment. He suggests that 'economic conditions and the level of health care render Turner's shared experiential ground far more variable than he thinks'.[30] Medical intervention suggests that human ontology is in fact not static and stationary, but moulded by social and technological changes. Modern technologies, especially medical technology, can significantly transform the balance between vulnerability, dependency, reciprocity, and precariousness. Bio-gerontological sciences which promise to extend life significantly have important implications for our vulnerability. If our embodiment is the real source of our common sociability, then changes to embodiment must have implications for vulnerability and interconnectedness. Given the rate of scientific and technological innovation, many writers are exploring the possibility of a 'post-human society' or a 'trans-human society' in which we no longer share a common ontology. Therefore, post-humans might not share a common set of human rights. Francis Fukuyama[31]

[27] Stephen K White and Evan Robert Farr, '"No-Saying" in Habermas' (2012) 40 *Pol Theory* 32.

[28] John Rawls, *The Law of Peoples* (Harvard UP 1999) 16.

[29] Stephen K White, *The Ethos of a Late-Modern Citizen* (Harvard UP 2009) 4.

[30] White (n 29) 70.

[31] Francis Fukuyama, 'Transhumanism' (2004) Foreign Pol'y <http://www.foreignpolicy.com/articles/2004/09/01/transhumanism> accessed 1 September 2012.

(1952–) has claimed that the idea of trans-humanism is a threat to democracy, which depends on a shared biological and cultural foundation as the ultimate grounding of human equality. Other philosophers of trans-humanism argue that it is possible to manage the existential risks arising from technological and medical advances without undermining shared rights.[32] However, one troublesome, if ironic, outcome of a post-human society is that it would also require a system of post-human rights. This debate raises the obvious question: Is human nature changing for the better, permitting a more optimistic view of the progress of human rights?

4. Human Rights and The Civilizing Process

Human beings are essentially vulnerable, but societies change and evolve. As a result of social change, including the institutionalization of rights, are humans living in a less violent world with more protection from law and the state? Steven Pinker[33] (1954–) has marshalled a wealth of statistical information to show that violence has indeed declined significantly in modern societies. An important aspect of his argument, especially when he considers the decline in homicide rates, depends overtly on the historical sociology of Norbert Elias (1897–1990). In *The Civilizing Process*,[34] Elias developed a theory of self-control and self-restraint against the background of the rise of the modern state. Describing the transition of the man-on-horseback in warrior societies, through feudalism, to the rise of court society and the bourgeoisie household, Elias argued that norms of self-restraint meant that society could depend less on external violence to achieve social order and more on inner psycho-social mechanisms. In order to understand these emergent behavioural patterns, he studied etiquette books; manuals describing correct knightly behaviour, especially towards women; and guides to courtesy and refined table manners[35] to demonstrate the decline of interpersonal violence.

Unfortunately, interpretations of Elias concentrated on these norms, often neglecting his theory of the state. Interpersonal forms of violence—such as the duel—declined because the state, to use Weber's terminology, had acquired a

[32] Nick Bostrom, 'Human Genetic Enhancements: A Transhumanist Perspective' (2003) 37 *Journal of Value Inquiry* 493.

[33] Steven Pinker, *The Better Angels of Our Nature: Why Violence Has Declined* (Viking 2011).

[34] Norbert Elias, *The Civilizing Process: Sociogenetic and Psychogenetic Investigations* (Blackwell 2000).

[35] Domestic changes, such as the adoption of the fork, which allowed people to avoid using their hands to pick up meat at table, often illustrated these civilized manners.

monopoly of violence. In England, the aristocracy was de-militarized at an early period and, because Great Britain is an archipelago of islands, the royal navy played an important role in the decline of civil violence. The absence of a large standing army in England is often associated with this gradual transition to a more pacific society. English aristocrats abandoned their swords and shields in public encounters at court, and etiquette required them to abandon the spittoon and embrace the handkerchief. As they left the battlefield for the City to become gentleman capitalists, they accepted norms of good conduct which they learnt on the cricket field. As the aristocracy declined, a new bourgeois class became dominant, bringing with it new gentlemanly values about domesticity, care of children, and suburban stability.

Elias's work is widely respected, but it has also been widely criticized. His parents died in German concentration camps and, against the background of the destruction of the Jews of Europe, his critics have asked how he could ever believe that Europeans had become more civilized. One possible answer is that, if one considers the Norse epics in the *Prose Edda*, one encounters warriors who killed with enthusiastic gusto. Similarly, accounts of the war-like exploits of Plains Indians, such as the Cheyenne, also illustrate the different emotional structure of violence in traditional societies. One group of Cheyenne warriors, called 'dog rope men', denied themselves the possibility of escaping from the enemy by fixing themselves to the ground with a rope tied to a wooden stake. Fighting from this ground position, they sang their death songs, while inviting the enemy to kill them.[36] This type of killing contrasts with modern wars of the twentieth century, in which men kill at a distance; in the war in Afghanistan, the aerial manipulation of drones through distant computers occurs outside the battlefield. Rampage by intoxicated warriors is now the exception, not the rule. The modern state relies on specialized training and military discipline to produce professional soldiers who are able to carry out their tasks with emotional neutrality. The calling of the modern soldier does not include any of the enjoyment of killing that was characteristic in earlier periods.

The debate around Elias's legacy raises a question that is also relevant to Pinker's historical account: does the discourse concern the nature of men or the social relationships and the normative structure of interaction that result in less violence? Have social conditions improved (for example, through laws and policing that aim to protect women from rape in and out of marriage), or has there been an actual change in human nature, in our ontology? Is it the better angels of our nature that provide the answer or more civilized societies, or both? Pinker's work is often characterized as depending on explanations that involve biological reductionism in which the social is simply an emanation of some feature of the human brain. On closer inspection, his explanations of change towards more peaceful times are typically sociological and political. For example, one cause of the reduction in violence

[36] JH Moore, *The Cheyenne* (Blackwell 1999).

appears to be the Matthew effect. The decline in violence against women is connected to a set of 'wholesome factors'—'democracy, prosperity, economic freedom, education, technology, decent government'.[37] Obviously, these factors cannot be the whole story, because some developed societies, such as South Korea and Japan, have relatively high rates of domestic violence. The difference may be explained by societies in which women have greater representation in democratic government and the professions, and by individualistic cultures that promote women's rights to empower them to function equally alongside men in the public domain. The decline of violence against women in the West is 'pushed along by a humanist mindset that elevates the rights of individual people over the traditions of the community'.[38]

This is not exactly 'our better angels' trumping culture and social structure. Perhaps the explanation is both nature (mindset) and social arrangements (filial piety). The argument can be examined by other illustrations in his study, such as the decline of rape, lynching, and homicide. Definitions of rape are inevitably contentious, and hence the measurement of the incidence of rape can never be precise, but Pinker makes a good case for its recent decline.[39] Certainly there has been a quantifiable shift in attitudes and values. He argues that the publication of Susan Brownmiller's *Against Our Will*[40] in 1975 was an important turning point in bringing the debate about rape onto the public agenda. The Violence against Women Act of 1994[41] is further evidence that sexual violence against women is being taken seriously by the law.

As regards lynching in the United States, the incidence of this crime against African Americans declined rapidly between 1890 and 1940; hate-crime murders also declined in a similar fashion. In terms of homicide rates, the United States has a history of violence that has no parallel in other parts of the developed world. Frontier violence explains part of this violent history. The homicide rate in the eastern colonies was 100 per 100,000 adults, which declined after 1637, when state control over the frontier was consolidated. Those states that remained backwaters beyond the reach of state control continued to experience high homicide rates. In the South, where self-help justice prevailed alongside a culture of honour, there was a distinctive pattern of violence unlike that in the North. Young men between fifteen and thirty years of age are primarily responsible for committing violent crime in society, and hence frontier violence began to decline as women arrived in greater numbers, and aggressive young men settled down to become responsible husbands and fathers.

37 Pinker (n 33) 413.

38 Pinker (n 33) 414.

39 In the United States, the annual rate of rape has fallen from 250 per 100,000 women over the age of twelve in 1973, to 50 per 100,000 in 2008. The earlier figure should probably have been higher due to under-reporting caused by the stigma surrounding rape that existed until recently. There has been a similar decline in reported cases of domestic violence, and recognition of rape in marriage signals the fact that women are no longer regarded as merely the property of their husbands.

40 Susan Brownmiller, *Against Our Will: Men, Women, and Rape* (Bantam Books 1975).

41 42 USC § 13981 *et seq.*

In these examples, state regulation plays a critical role in reducing violence and creating a social environment with some degree of security. In this respect, the United States and Europe are divergent in terms of the history of state building. In Europe, the state disarmed the people, created a monopoly of violence, and established itself as a sovereign power. In America, with independence from the British monarchy, the people took over the state and, as the Second Amendment affirms, they retained a right to bear arms. Violence declined as state power became more systematically established, and hence the 'civilizing process' required the state and marriage to bring violent men into peaceful and stable domesticity. The emergence of human rights institutions and values is simply one component of a longer sociological process of civilizing human behaviour.

5. Globalization and Community Necessity

One problem with the sociological perspectives so far presented is that none of them offers a convincing account of the origin and nature of international societies. These sociological studies of citizenship, social rights, social movements, and human violence are basically national, rather than international, studies. Human rights, which are prime examples of the growth of international regulation and cooperation, have only recently become important in the curriculum of sociology departments in the modern university. The current interest among sociologists in human rights is closely bound up with their research into globalization. The work of Anthony Woodiwiss is an obvious example. His research on international labour[42] became a point of entry into the study of the globalization of human rights, with special reference to Asian societies. In recent years, there have been serious attempts to rethink the conceptual basis of rights by sociologists such as Cushman,[43] Morris,[44] Nash,[45] and Beck and Sznaider.[46] These developments in sociology are driven by recognition of the contradictory nature of globalization, which in its economic and

[42] Anthony Woodiwiss, *Globalisation, Human Rights and Labour Law in Pacific Asia* (CUP 1998); Anthony Woodiwiss, *Making Human Rights Work Globally* (The GlassHouse Press 2003).

[43] Thomas Cushman, 'The Globalization of Human Rights' in Bryan S Turner (ed), *The Routledge Handbook of Globalization Studies* (Routledge 2010).

[44] Lydia Morris (ed), *Rights: Sociological Perspectives* (Routledge 2006).

[45] Kate Nash, *The Cultural Politics of Human Rights: Comparing the US and UK* (CUP 2009).

[46] Ulrich Beck and Natan Sznaider, 'New Cosmopolitanism in the Social Sciences' in Bryan S Turner (ed), *The Routledge Handbook of Globalization Studies* (Routledge 2010).

military forms is often 'predatory',[47] but which simultaneously creates new opportunities for cooperation and mutuality, as indicated in an emerging cosmopolitan consciousness.[48]

In their approach to the globalization of human rights, sociologists have been interested first in the possibility of a global civil society, looking specifically at the growth of non-governmental organizations, social movements, and activists. Second, they have paid special attention to the role of new communication systems, such as the internet, in creating awareness of human rights issues relating to civil wars, 'new wars', ethnic conflict, and ethnic cleansing. Third, they have become concerned with understanding the impact of human rights issues on marginal populations, especially aboriginal communities. Fourth, they have more recently become interested in environmental rights under the broad heading of rights to health. Among these diverse research foci, sociological approaches are perhaps best characterized as concentrating on empirical studies of how the institutional structure of the delivery of human rights actually functions at both the local and the global level.

The 'juridical revolution' of the twentieth century, involving the international recognition of human rights as formulated in the 1948 UDHR, is the principal illustration of the general process of legal globalization. Human rights are contained in legal instruments which may oblige the state to make reparations to those whose rights are violated. In some instances, moreover, the despotic leaders of government can be held criminally responsible under international law and prosecuted in the courts of justice for the ways in which they mistreat their own citizens. Human rights were initially twentieth-century legal responses to atrocities committed against civilian populations in war-time, as a consequence of the industrialization of military combat. Technological changes in warfare have made civilians increasingly the targets of military conflict. The bombing of civilians in the Basque town of Guernica in 1937 during the Spanish Civil War (1936–39) has become a potent symbol of such atrocities. The carnage of the Second World War and the genocide committed against Jews, gypsies, homosexuals, the disabled, Armenians, and the mentally ill, were important causes of twentieth-century human rights legislation. The UDHR has been followed by the creation of many international institutions that defend human rights, bring war criminals to trial, and enforce social rights through such agencies as the International Labour Organization (ILO).

Both sociologists and legal theorists argue that with globalization there has been some erosion of state sovereignty and a corresponding growth of legal pluralism.[49] With economic and financial globalization, there has been a corresponding growth of commercial law, which is not specific to state boundaries.[50] The human rights

[47] Richard Falk, *Predatory Globalization: A Critique* (Polity Press 1999).
[48] Beck and Sznaider (n 46).
[49] Gunter Teubner (ed), *Global Law without a State* (Aldershot 1997).
[50] William Twining, *Globalisation and Legal Theory* (Butterworths 2000).

movement has therefore accompanied the erosion of the strong doctrine of state sovereignty originally created by the Treaty of Westphalia, in 1648, and the ascending status of the individual as the victim of war, between and within states. In the aftermath of the First World War, the Allies remained committed to the traditional legal view that only states were the legitimate subjects of international law. The greater emphasis on victim status has been the underpinning of the rise of reparations—of making good again (*Wiedergutmachung*). Dual citizenship, international marriages, international adoption of children, labour migration, and multiculturalism, which are further markers of these global social changes, raise complex legal questions about the rights of citizens who are no longer living in their homelands.

There is another aspect of the globalization of human rights, namely the emergence of a global civil society that is concerned with the protection, security, development, and representation of local communities. There are thousands of civil society organizations that the United Nations recognizes. A proliferation of human rights groups, like Charter 77, emerged after the signing of the Helsinki Accords in 1975; and a similar expansion of local activist groups came after the 1992 Global Forum and Earth Summit in Rio de Janeiro, after the population conferences in Beijing and Cairo, and after the Vienna Conference on Human Rights in 1993.

Many civil society organizations have direct links, through Article 71 of the Charter, with various parts of the United Nations system, a network of inter-governmental organizations (specialized agencies) that includes the World Health Organization and the United Nations Educational, Scientific and Cultural Organization (UNESCO). Inter-governmental organizations such as UNESCO have been important in fostering local activism in relation to environmental lobby groups. States can work as partners of both non-governmental organizations (NGOs) and inter-governmental organizations, but they can also be in an antagonistic relationship with those critical of government. Organizations such as *Médecins Sans Frontières* (Doctors without Borders), Oxfam, and Greenpeace function through a mixture of self-reliance and dependency on governments and international organizations. Many agencies now work on programmes to defend the human rights of aboriginal communities, particularly over issues relating to land rights.[51] One characteristic of the sociology of human rights in the field of land claims is the study of how rights claims are articulated in the interaction between local organizations and international agencies.[52] Although the heterogeneity of values and organizational structures prevents a unified political programme, global civil society now acts as a distinctive

[51] Rachel Sieder, 'Recognising Indigenous Law and the Politics of State Formation in Mesoamerica' in Rachel Sieder (ed), *Multiculturalism in Latin America: Indigenous Rights, Diversity and Democracy* (Palgrave Macmillan 2002); Rhiannon Morgan, *Transforming Law and Institution: Indigenous Peoples, the United Nations and Human Rights* (Ashgate 2011).

[52] Carlos Gigoux and Colin Samson, 'Globalization and Indigenous Peoples: New Old Patterns' in Bryan S Turner (ed), *The Routledge Handbook of Globalization Studies* (Routledge 2010).

constraint on the activities of national governments and is an important site of sociological investigation.[53]

Despite the political difficulties that surrounded UN involvement in Rwanda (1994), Kosovo (1999), and Darfur (2004), there is evidence of a global concern to intervene against despotic governments and to support humanitarian intervention to protect civilians. International intervention in Libya in 2011 is one obvious, if complex, example. What has changed historically to make human rights a prominent feature of global attempts to regulate violence? The globalization of communications has created opportunities for criticism of government actions, and governments cannot easily regulate or scrutinize these channels. Twitter and Facebook both played an important role in coordinating social protest against the authoritarianism of the Mubarak regime in Egypt during the Arab Spring of 2011.[54] The development of photography has facilitated the rapid communication, through dramatic images, of war crimes and military violence. Media coverage of the Vietnam War (1965–73) was an important turning point in the creation of global audiences of war; and news agencies, such as Al-Jazeera, and countless websites offered alternative views of the wars in Iraq and Afghanistan. When a worldwide audience has witnessed contemporary atrocities, including genocide and ethnic cleansing, with the spread of global communication systems, the ethical aspiration is that people begin to think and act as responsible global citizens.

Developments in the social sciences have found their parallel in the field of international law, in the works of Jonathan Charney (1943–2002), Louis Henkin (1917–2010), and Christian Tomuschat (1936–). Indeed, it is possible to argue that human rights issues did not become a prominent feature in public affairs until the 1970s, when international lawyers made human rights a basic component of their scholarly research, and law schools introduced human rights courses into the curriculum.[55] The human rights provisions of the UDHR were overshadowed in the 1950s and 1960s by the international emphasis on self-determination, creating new states in the Third World where nationalist politicians were inclined to regard human rights as part of the legacy of Western imperialism. Prior to the engagement of international legal scholars, human rights were often either ignored or regarded as hopelessly utopian. In his monumental work *Between Facts and Norms*,[56] Habermas, who regularly sets the agenda for sociology in Europe, has embraced international law arguments in his reflections on the limitations of the 'constitutional state'. Following Immanuel Kant's (1724–1804) idea of a 'cosmopolitan society', he has cautioned that for actionable rights to emerge from the Declaration, international courts 'will first be able to function adequately only when the age of individual sovereign states

[53] John Keane, *Global Civil Society?* (CUP 2003).

[54] Jeffrey C Alexander, *Performative Revolution in Egypt: An Essay in Cultural Power* (Bloomsbury Academic 2011).

[55] Samuel Moyn, *The Last Utopia: Human Rights in History* (Harvard UP 2010).

[56] Jürgen Habermas, *Between Facts and Norms: Contributions to a Discourse Theory of Law and Democracy* (Polity Press 1996).

has come to an end through a United Nations that can not only pass but also act upon and enforce its resolutions'.[57] He went on to observe that the slow development of the recognition of rights and obligations across the European community by political elites resulted, not only from claims of national sovereignty, but because the democratic process operated 'only inside national boundaries'.[58] International law has been more positive in detecting an emerging arena of mutual interest with respect to fundamental issues that require collective responses.

In this field of legal studies, attention is drawn to the emergence of a network of legal provisions that bind nation-states to agreements that enforce and regulate behaviour with respect to key issues, where there is a mutuality of interests in response to slavery, serfdom, genocide, and scarce resources (such as water). Modern international human rights laws can be said to arise from three recognized sources: treaties, customary law, and the 'general principles of law'.[59] The Statute of the International Court of Justice has recognized these. Perhaps the most significant features of this global juridical framework are so-called *erga omnes* obligations, which are of concern to all states. These shared obligations are created by a common recognition of a set of fundamental human rights relating, for example, to war, genocide, and slavery.

Historically, legal relationships between autonomous nation-states were couched in treaties and had only a limited provenance. International lawyers now recognize that the autonomy of nation-states is often limited by an assembly of multilateral treaties that address issues of common concern. Early examples of the legal regulation of common interests would include laws to regulate access to the sea, international trade, and the treatment of prisoners. Medieval trade was regulated by *lex mercatoria*, and in recent history, exploration rights for oil and gas, where state borders in coastal areas are contentious, require legal intervention. The United Nations Convention on the Law of the Sea in 1982 was significant in this regard.[60] The development of legally binding relations within the European community has also been seen as an important example of legal internationalism. For example, in 1951 the Treaty Establishing the European Coal and Steel Community made provision for an independent court, the Court of Justice, to interpret and enforce the treaty's provisions. Another example is the creation of the European Court of Human Rights pursuant to the 1950 European Convention on Human Rights. These international legal relations have multiplied with juridical globalization, in clear recognition of the need to develop a set of universal norms to address global concerns relating to major issues, especially the environment.

[57] Habermas (n 56) 456. [58] Habermas (n 56) 502.

[59] Brian D Lepard, *Customary International Law: A New Theory with Practical Applications* (CUP 2010).

[60] Jonathan Charney (ed), *International Maritime Boundaries* (vols 1–2, Springer 2002).

Many of these important legal developments were summarized in Charney's article on 'Universal International Law',[61] in which he argued that we now have an international legal system that constrains and regulates the behaviour of nation-states through consensual multilateral forums. Many of these legal arrangements concern a mutual interest in protecting the environment, and they have serious implications for the autonomy of the nation-state. Charney notes 'the enormous destructive potential of some activities and the precarious condition of some objects of international concern make full autonomy undesirable, if not potentially catastrophic'.[62] Where there is recognition that a common good is threatened, then there are compelling reasons for legally enforced cooperation between states.

Of special interest is the role of *jus cogens*, or 'compelling law', namely a peremptory legal principle that is regarded as binding on states, irrespective of their consent. Where there is an obvious need for common action over a shared problem (such as pollution or the dumping of nuclear waste), it is possible to argue that there exists a 'community necessity' over which there should be binding agreements. These notions, especially around 'customary law', have been much disputed, but there is some agreement that, where a majority of states supports a legal norm, there is a threshold in which a customary norm is binding on states, including those (such as the 'persistent objector') that actively oppose the norm. The implication of these legal developments that recognize community necessity is that, in the absence of legitimate global governance, there is already in place a legal framework for the enforcement of human rights.

6. Conclusion: Critical Observations

The development of globalization studies has been characterized by either extreme pessimism or naive optimism. With the final collapse of the Soviet system between 1989 and 1992, many political scientists welcomed the potential development of a peace dividend, the conclusion of the Cold War, and the prospect of global cooperation over trade, security, and cultural exchange. Globalization was welcomed as the flowering of human rights and global peace, and political philosophers looked back towards the Enlightenment and Kant's aspirations for world government and perpetual peace as a model of a future global civil society. The globalization of the

[61] Jonathan Charney, 'Universal International Law' (1993) 87 *AJIL* 529.

[62] Charney (n 61) 530.

human rights regime was believed to offer the prospect of a more just and stable world.[63]

However, an alternative voice has also become influential in international relations theory with the growth of international terrorism and the need for greater security. Samuel Huntington's 'clash of cultures' sparked off a controversy about the possibility of new conflicts around ethnicity and religion.[64] After 11 September 2001, the bombings in London, Madrid, and Bali, and subsequent terrorist attacks on Mumbai in 2008, globalization studies took a more critical and pessimistic turn, with greater emphasis on the state, political borders, and security. It is recognized that globalization also brings with it the globalization of violence, low-intensity conflicts, international crime, and trafficking in drugs and people. While optimistic visions of globalization had talked about mobility across borders as a key feature of a global world, the porous nature of societies, the possible decline of the nation-state, and the security crisis of the twenty-first century, produced a renewed interest in state activities in controlling migration and patrolling borders. There is also recognition of the extent of global slavery in the modern world economy.[65] It was clear that globalization could also result in less mobility and greater restrictions on labour movements, through work permits and visas, and enhanced internal security measures. The result of securitization will not be an open liberal society, but rather an enclave society.

This discussion of the sociology of rights opened with Max Weber and will conclude with reference to the same author. For Weber, all social relations are relations of power, namely the potential of individuals or social groups to achieve their ends and impose their will, without the consent and against the interests of other individuals or groups. Definitions of power have been much disputed in sociology and political science.[66] The point is that a critical sociology is inclined to question the legal view that there exists a 'community necessity' and is more inclined to accept a realist view of international politics as a competitive field of nation-states operating in terms of their geo-political interests. Despite a shared interest in the security of seaways within the region, China's attempt to impose its exclusionary claims to the South China Sea against its neighbours in Vietnam, Philippines, and Thailand, is a case in point.

There are a number of obvious and distinct objections to the idea of a globally effective human rights regime. First, international reluctance to define civil conflict as 'genocide' has permitted intentional and extensive killing of civilians with a view to remove or destroy communities in the Sudan and elsewhere. Second, the Security

[63] Jeffrey N Wasserstrom, Lynn Hunt, and Marilyn B Young (eds), *Human Rights and Revolutions* (Rowman & Littlefield 2000).

[64] Samuel P Huntington, 'The Clash of Civilizations' (1993) 72 *Foreign Affairs* 22; Samuel P Huntington, *The Clash of Civilizations and the Remaking of World Order* (Simon & Schuster 1996).

[65] Keith Bales, *Disposable People: New Slavery in the Global Economy* (U California P 1999).

[66] Steven Lukes, *Power: A Radical View* (Macmillan 1974).

Council has been either reluctant or unable to intervene in major human rights crises, such as the violent conflict in Syria in 2012, where there has been no agreement between the major powers. Third, while there is obviously a 'community necessity' with respect to the prevention of nuclear arms proliferation, the international community has been unable to limit the spread of such weapons, or attempts to build such devices, in Iran and North Korea. Fourth, there is an argument that human rights have actually promoted international conflicts, giving rise to 'human rights wars' in Iran and Afghanistan during the administration of George W Bush. Fifth, there are serious problems in defining and then controlling the use of torture, as exemplified by the United States' employment of water-boarding in the interrogation of terrorist suspects. Finally, the creation of Guantanamo as an extra-legal zone for holding terror suspects without trial is an example of what Carl Schmitt meant by 'sovereignty', namely the capacity to declare a situation of emergency.[67] In these zones of 'bare life', human rights can be ignored with a large degree of impunity.[68] There are therefore substantial gaps in the system of international regulation that raise fundamental questions about the role of 'community necessity' in structuring the relations between states.

In conclusion, most of these macro political, social, and economic issues have not been tackled by sociologists as much as by historians and political philosophers. Contemporary empirical sociological research is largely conducted at the meso- or micro-level. Consequently, sociologists have, to some extent, turned away from the long-standing philosophical problems surrounding human rights, regarding them as abstract meta-theoretical difficulties. There remain, therefore, a number of legitimate sociological areas of inquiry. These include research on (1) the social and political conditions that have produced the entitlements or juridical revolutions; (2) the nature of the institutions (such as NGOs) that promote and advocate rights at the national and local levels; and (3) the social movements (such as indigenous people's or women's movements) that have fostered human rights developments. Sociologists consider the complex problem of the intersection between social rights (supported by sovereign states and their agencies) and human rights (supported by emerging global agencies such as the UN, the International Court of Justice, the ILO, and various courts of justice). In these terms, the field of the sociology of rights can be identified as the intersection between global institutions, national agencies, and social movements that are the social vehicles of political advocacy. Because the sociology of human rights has become closely associated with advocacy groups, an empirical sociology of rights cannot wholly avoid addressing the normative issues that cling to the idea of a right. In this respect, Weber's view that a right is simply the probability that a rights claim will be respected does not offer an adequate basis for advocacy on the part of activist sociologists who want to exercise a role as public

[67] Carl Schmitt, *The Concept of the Political* (U Chicago Press 1996).

[68] Georgio Agamben, *Homo Sacer: Sovereign Power and Bare Life* (Stanford UP 1998).

intellectuals. Sociology still requires a solution to the fact-value dichotomy that is present in the division between a political and a humanistic perspective if it is to engage effectively with the urgent debate about human rights, international law, and the quest for global justice. In this respect, the Weber legacy is both a blessing and a curse.

Further Reading

Alexander JC, *Performative Revolution in Egypt: An Essay in Cultural Power* (Bloomsbury Academic 2011)

Arendt H, *The Origins of Totalitarianism* (Harcourt Brace 1951)

Beck U and Sznaider N, 'New Cosmopolitanism in the Social Sciences' in Bryan S Turner (ed), *The Routledge Handbook of Globalization Studies* (Routledge 2010) 635–52

Berger PL and Luckmann T, *The Social Construction of Reality: A Treatise in the Sociology of Knowledge* (Doubleday 1967)

Brownmiller S, *Against Our Will: Men, Women and Rape* (Penguin 1975)

Brysk A (ed), *Globalization and Human Rights* (U California P 2002)

Fukuyama F 'Transhumanism' (2004) Foreign Pol'y <http://www.foreignpolicy.com/articles/2004/09/01/transhumanism> accessed 1 September 2012

Habermas J and Ratzinger J, *Dialectics of Secularization: On Reason and Religion* (Ignatius Press 2006)

Jellinek G, *The Declaration of the Rights of Man and of Citizens* (World Library Classics 2009)

Lepard BD, *Customary International Law: A New Theory with Practical Applications* (CUP 2010)

Marshall TH, *Citizenship and Social Class and Other Essays* (CUP 1950)

Moyn S, *The Last Utopia: Human Rights in History* (Harvard UP 2010)

Robertson R, *Globalization: Social Theory and Global Culture* (Sage 1992)

Saxonhouse AW, *Fear of Diversity: The Birth of Political Science in Ancient Greek Thought* (U Chicago Press 1992)

Schmitt C, *The Concept of the Political* (U Chicago Press 1996)

Shachar A and Hirschl R, 'Citizenship as Inherited Property' (2007) 35 *Pol Theory* 253

Taylor C, *Multiculturalism and the Politics of Recognition* (Princeton UP 1992)

Turner BS 'Outline of a General Theory of Human Rights' (1993) 27 *Sociology* 489

—— 'Weber and Elias on Religion and Violence: Warrior Charisma and the Civilizing Process' in Loyal S and Quilley S (eds), *The Sociology of Norbert Elias* (CUP 2004)

—— *Vulnerability and Human Rights* (Pa St UP 2006)

—— 'The Enclave Society: Towards a Sociology of Immobility' (2007) 10 *EJ Social Theory* 287

Weber M, *The Methodology of the Social Sciences* (Shils EA and Finch HA (trs), The Free Press 1949)

—— *Economy and Society: An Outline of Interpretive Sociology*, vols 1–2 (Roth G and Wittich C (eds), U California P 1978)

Williams RR, *Hegel's Ethics of Recognition* (U California P 1997)

CHAPTER 5

THE PSYCHOLOGICAL FOUNDATIONS OF HUMAN RIGHTS

ROBIN BRADLEY KAR

1. Introduction

THAT all human beings have certain inalienable rights that arise simply by virtue of their status as human beings is a relatively new idea in human affairs. It is much newer than the idea, already found in early Buddhist and Christian thought, that universal compassion is a virtue to be promoted. Of course, both of these ideas promote a form of moral concern that is universalized and hence non-parochial, but the idea that *rights* should be distributed equally to all human beings is one that—apart from some early limited exceptions[1]—only began to gain real traction during the Western Enlightenment. A brief comparison of the two ideas reveals that they reference very different psychological capacities. For most human beings, the ideal of universal compassion is difficult enough to achieve in practice that perceived instances of it (met typically only in story or legend) can inspire awe and admiration. Respect for human rights, on the other hand, is something that many ordinary people from many parts of the world have begun increasingly

[1] See Paul Gordon Lauren, Chapter 7 in this *Handbook*.

to exhibit and expect of one another. Although universal compassion may well be the more noble ideal, it would be futile, even madness, to mandate it by law because very few could consistently comply, even if the law could define an objective way to measure compassion or identify it as a motive for specific acts. In contrast, within the last sixty or so years, legal regimes that require a minimal respect for human rights have begun to proliferate, and empirical grounds now exist for cautious optimism about the general direction in which the world has been heading in this regard.[2]

Despite these facts, a great deal of research on the causes and conditions of human rights violations has proceeded without a clear enough understanding of the distinctive ways in which the psychological capacity to identify and respond to rights functions. The most important psychological research has focused on processes of so-called 'dehumanization', which have been shown to correlate with increased human rights violations.[3] Dehumanization appears to do this because it involves a failure to attribute mental states to others, which can cause failures of empathy (or compassion) and disinhibit aggression.[4] These are important psychological findings, but they do not reference any specific capacity to identify and respond to rights, and hence are not always sensitive to its distinctive features. This is especially true when these features are best exposed by contemporary work in non-psychological fields. Hence the current psychological understanding of the causes and conditions of human rights violations does not yet reflect a range of important insights that might be gleaned from a broader approach.

The purpose of this chapter is to cure this deficiency by developing a clearer account of the psychological capacities that humans use to identify and respond to rights. Understanding how these capacities function will require integrating contemporary insights from social and cognitive psychology with findings from a broader range of fields, including philosophy and evolutionary theory. Section 2 builds on contemporary philosophical insights into the meaning of terms like 'right' and 'obligation' to highlight some of the special features that these capacities possess and to offer an initial characterization of them.[5] Emphasis is placed on the distinctive ways that humans reason about rights; the distinctive relations that thoughts about rights have to a more primary set of thoughts about interpersonal obligation; and the distinctive forms of human social life and interaction that these combined thoughts about rights and obligation animate. The psychological capacities that animate these forms of life are critical both to law and to those

[2] Steven Pinker, *The Better Angels of Our Nature: Why Violence Has Declined* (Viking Press 2001).

[3] For a review of the literature, see Nick Haslam, 'Dehumanization: an Integrative Review' (2006) 10 *Personality and Social Psychology Review* 252.

[4] Adam Waytz, Kurt Gray, Nicholas Epley, and Daniel M Wegner, 'Causes and Consequences of Mind Perception' (2010) 14 *Trends in Cognitive Sciences* 383.

[5] See also Siegfried van Duffel, Chapter 2 in this *Handbook*.

dimensions of moral thought and practice that focus on perceptions of interpersonal obligation.

Section 3 then builds upon this initial characterization by offering an evolutionary account of the origin and function of these special psychological capacities, arguing that they have a range of innate features that are best understood from an evolutionary perspective. The capacities in fact have a surprising number of features, which appear functionally well-designed to enable humans to resolve certain recurrent problems of cooperation, often referred to as 'social contract problems', in a flexible manner. Evolutionary considerations will help isolate these features and clarify the complex ways they interrelate, thereby providing a more detailed description of the special psychological capacities needed to produce respect for human rights. Section 2 thereby contributes to a growing literature, which suggests that humans have some innate moral psychological capacities, just as they have some innate capacities for language.[6]

The conclusion, finally, acknowledges that even if humans have an innate capacity to identify and respond to rights, which naturally generates the perception that some other humans (typically other in-group members) have the authority to make claims on their conduct, the more specific phenomenon of respect for human rights is at least in part a culturally emergent phenomenon. It thus returns to the question of the causes and conditions of human rights violations and suggests a number of ways in which further progress on this question might be made. Most importantly, further research should seek to identify those factors that directly engage the human capacity to identify and respond to rights and help orient it to produce more stable and universally shared perceptions of human rights.

[6] See eg Richard Joyce, *The Evolution of Morality* (MIT Press 2006); Robin Kar, 'The Deep Structure of Law and Morality' (2006) 106 *Tex L Rev* 877; John Mikhail, 'Universal Moral Grammar: Theory, Evidence and the Future' (2007) 11 *Trends in Cognitive Science* 143; Marc D Hauser, Liane Young, and Fiery Cushman, 'Reviving Rawls's Linguistic Analogy: Operative Principles and the Causal Structure of Moral Actions' in Walter Sinnott-Armstrong (ed), *Moral Psychology: The Cognitive Science of Morality: Intuition and Diversity*, vol 2 (MIT Press 2008); Walter Sinnott-Armstrong, *Moral Psychology: The Evolution of Morality: Adaptations and Innateness*, vol I (MIT Press 2008); John Mikhail, *Elements of Moral Cognition: Rawls's Linguistic Analogy and the Cognitive Science of Moral and Legal Judgment* (CUP 2011); Robin Kar, 'The Two Faces of Morality: How Evolutionary Theory Can Both Vindicate and Debunk Morality' in James E Fleming and Sanford Levinson (eds), *NOMOS: Evolution and Morality* (NYU Press 2012); Michael Tomasello and Amrisha Vaish, 'Origins of Human Cooperation and Morality' (2013) 64 *Annual Review of Psychology* 231. In ways that are broadly consistent with the main claims of this chapter, John Mikhail has recently extended his work in moral psychology to the topic of human rights as well. See John Mikhail, 'Moral Grammar and Human Rights: Some Reflections on Cognitive Science and Enlightenment Rationalism' in Ryan Goodman, Derek Jinks, and Andrew K Woods (eds), *Understanding Social Action: Promoting Human Rights* (OUP 2012).

2. Human Rights and the Basic Psychology of Rights and Obligation

The empirical study of moral psychology has been developing rapidly over the last several decades, leading to greatly improved understandings of human capacities for moral thought, emotion, development, and behaviour. This research suggests that humans exhibit not one capacity for moral thought and action but rather a bundle of distinct capacities, which can often interact with one another in complex ways but plausibly serve somewhat different functions. Some form of moral motivation is, for example, a near universal in human life, but different humans exhibit moral motivations that can be linked in different ways not only to perceptions of harm and fairness but also to perceptions of spiritual purity, in-group loyalty and/or deference to hierarchical authority (often rooted in religious authority or tradition).[7] Different cultural dynamics can also support the emergence and stability of different mixtures of these different moral capacities and orientations in different populations.[8] A recent study of the United States found, for example, that: 'Political liberals construct their moral systems primarily upon two psychological foundations—Harm/care and Fairness/reciprocity—whereas political conservatives construct moral systems more evenly upon five psychological foundations—the same ones as liberals, plus Ingroup/loyalty, Authority/respect, and Purity/sanctity.'[9]

Empirical research like this is extremely useful, but it tends to investigate a very broad range of psychological phenomena and sometimes conflates different classes of moral phenomena. The literature on the psychological causes and conditions of human rights violations does not, for example, always distinguish between violations caused by aggression or lack of compassion and violations caused by failures to engage the more specific human capacity to identify and respond to rights. It will therefore help to seek conceptual clarity over the specific types of psychological capacities referred to in speaking of the human capacity to identify and respond to rights.

[7] Jonathan Haidt, 'The New Synthesis in Moral Psychology' (2007) 316 *Science* 998.

[8] Dov Cohen, 'Cultural Variation: Considerations and Implications' (2001) 127(4) *Psychological Bulletin* 451; Angela KY Leung and Dov Cohen, 'Within and Between Culture Variation: Individual Differences and the Cultural Logics of Honor, Face, and Dignity Cultures' (2012) 100(3) *Journal of Personality and Social Psychology* 507.

[9] J Graham, J Haidt, and B Nosek, 'Liberals and Conservatives Rely on Different Sets of Moral Foundations' (2009) 96(5) *Journal of Social Psychology* 1029, 1029. Other researchers have traced differences like these to the distinctive cultural dynamics that predominate in different regions of the United States. Cohen, 'Cultural Variation' (n 8); Leung and Cohen, 'Within and Between' (n 8).

This section builds on several prominent lines of philosophical thought to produce the needed clarity. Although philosophical work is often glossed over in the psychological literature, philosophers have done some of the best work to date clarifying distinctions between a range of different moral judgments and expressions. Philosophers have also done some of the best work to date articulating the implications that are typically taken to follow from different classes of moral judgment. Distinctions like these have important psychological correlates. If, for example, a philosopher can identify concrete distinctions between the meanings or perceived implications of two different classes of moral expression, then people who use these different expressions sincerely, and with full knowledge of their meaning, will typically be expressing distinguishable psychological attitudes. The distinctions that philosophers have identified can therefore help generate an initial characterization of the psychological attitudes. In addition, a number of prominent philosophers have proposed so-called 'expressivist'[10] (or 'non-cognitivist') accounts of the meanings of various moral terms, including terms like 'good', 'right', and 'obligation'—the last two of which will prove especially important for present purposes. Because expressivist accounts often seek to characterize the special psychological states that are expressed with different moral terms, work of this kind can also help clarify important aspects of human moral psychology.

Section 2.1 discusses philosophical work on the logic of rights. Although thoughts about rights exhibit a number of important complexities and ambiguities, this section argues that this entire range of thoughts can be understood in terms of the effects that these thoughts have—either directly, indirectly, or recursively—on a more basic set of thoughts about interpersonal obligation. Section 2.2 then offers an expressivist account of 'obligation,' which builds upon HLA Hart's influential work on the topic.[11] The account suggests that thoughts about interpersonal obligation are best understood as expressive of a special kind of psychological attitude, which animates a highly distinctive and deeply structured form of human social life and interaction. Together, these sections thus produce an initial characterization of the special psychological capacities needed to support a more stable and universally shared form of respect for human rights in the modern world.

[10] An 'expressivist' account of a moral term is one that accounts for its meaning in various propositions as expressive of a specific type of motivational attitude, rather than as a belief about the natural world. Expressivists go to great lengths to distinguish expressions of these special motivational attitudes from expressions of beliefs that one has these special motivational attitudes. Expressivists thus believe that moral expressions are different in kind from all expressions of beliefs about the natural world—including purely descriptive statements about moral psychology.

[11] HLA Hart, *The Concept of Law* (2nd edn, OUP 1961).

2.1 On the logic of rights as it relates to interpersonal obligations

Although human rights are a distinctive class of rights, they are first and foremost a class of rights. To understand the special psychological capacities that humans use to identify and respond to them, it therefore helps to begin with the capacities humans use to identify and respond to rights more generally. Wesley Newcomb Hohfeld's seminal work on the logic of rights serves as a useful starting point for these purposes.[12]

One of Hohfeld's most lasting insights was that the language of rights is often ambiguous among four distinct classes of phenomena, which can be defined in terms of the systematically describable relationships that they bear to one another. Hohfeld called these four phenomena 'claims', 'privileges' (or 'freedoms' or 'liberties'), 'powers', and 'immunities'.[13] Figure 1 depicts these four classes of rights, along with the relations they bear to one another. The remainder of this section describes these relations, then draws upon Hohfeld's work to show that this entire range of thoughts about rights can be understood in terms of the effects they have—either directly, indirectly or recursively—on a more primary set of thoughts about interpersonal obligation.

The most straightforward relationship between thoughts about rights and thoughts about interpersonal obligations arises in the case of claim rights (item (1)). As shown in the top left corner of Figure 1, a person is said to have a claim right against another to perform a particular action just in case the second person has an obligation[14] to the first to perform the action. The right to healthcare, which appears in the Universal Declaration of Human Rights, illustrates this phenomenon because this right is typically taken to entail a primary obligation on the part of the state (or some other delegated entity) to ensure a minimal level of healthcare to each of its inhabitants. As noted above, facts like these have important psychological correlates. In the present case, these facts establish that any broad psychological consensus within a community that each of its members has a claim right against the state to healthcare will tend to involve a similar consensus over the proposition that the state has a primary obligation to each of its citizens to ensure this minimal level of healthcare. Further psychological correlates like these can be easily identified once the remaining logical properties of rights talk have been clarified.

[12] Wesley Newcomb Hohfeld, 'Some Fundamental Legal Conceptions as Applied in Judicial Reasoning' (1913) 23 *Yale LJ* 16; Wesley Newcomb Hohfeld, *Fundamental Legal Conceptions as Applied in Judicial Reasoning and Other Legal Essays* (Walter Wheeler Cook (ed), Yale UP 1919).

[13] Hohfeld, 'Some Fundamental Legal Conceptions' (n 12) 30.

[14] Hohfeld often uses the term 'duty', but 'duty' can sometimes be used to refer to requirements that are owed to no one, and it is clear that Hohfeld means to reference only those phenomena that are more commonly referred to as interpersonal obligations.

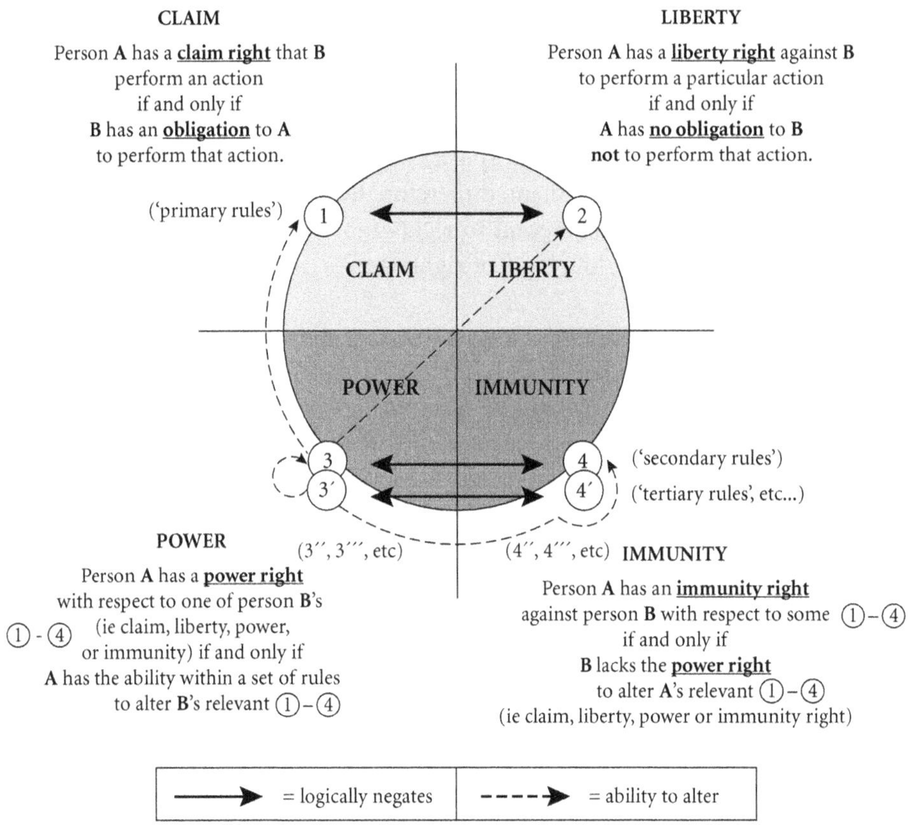

FIGURE 1 Hohfeld on the Logic of Rights

Liberty rights are, in turn, defined in terms of the absence of claim rights (item (2)). As shown in the top right corner of Figure 1, a person is therefore said to have a liberty right (or privilege or freedom) against another to perform a particular action just in case the first person has *no obligation* to the second *not* to perform the action. The right to freedom of religion, which also appears in the Universal Declaration of Human Rights, illustrates this second phenomenon, because it is typically taken to involve the absence of any claim rights on the part of the state against its inhabitants for them to join or participate in any particular religion. This liberty right thus entails that there is no primary obligation on the part of anyone to the state to join or participate in any particular religion; and thoughts about liberty rights can similarly be understood in terms of their perceived implications for a more basic set of thoughts about interpersonal obligation.

Because both claim rights and liberty rights have direct implications for human conduct, they operate on instances of what HLA Hart calls 'primary rules' of conduct. This term refers to any rule that requires humans 'to do or abstain from certain actions, whether they wish to or not'.[15] If thoughts about rights were limited to thoughts like these, then their cognitive dimension would reflect a fairly simple psychological capacity. As Hohfeld correctly observed, however, thoughts about rights are not always this simple because 'rights' sometimes refers to certain abilities that a person has to *change* these primary rules of conduct.[16]

Consider, for example, the right to contract, which cannot be understood as a claim right because it does not make any direct claims on conduct. Neither can it be reduced to a mere liberty right, because the right to contract is more than the absence of an obligation not to contract. The right to contract is best construed as involving the further ability, or *power*, to grant other people new claim rights (against oneself) to perform various new actions by voluntarily committing oneself to those performances in the appropriate circumstances. The valid exercise of the right to contract can thus change the primary rules of conduct that apply to the person who exercises this right.

In order to clarify this distinction, HLA Hart uses the term 'secondary rule' to refer to any rule like the one under discussion, which either gives or withdraws a person's ability to change a primary rule.[17] These rules 'are in a sense parasitic upon or secondary to the first; for they provide that human beings may by doing or saying certain things introduce new rules of the primary type, extinguish or modify old ones, or in various ways determine their incidence or control their operations'.[18] The ability to operate with secondary rules adds a further layer of complexity to the cognitive capacities that humans use to think about rights.

In fact, Hohfeld defines two distinct types of rights that reflect secondary rules. As shown in item (3) of Figure 1, Hohfeld uses the term 'power' right to refer to any right, like the right to contract, which consists in an ability, within a given set of rules, to alter some claim or liberty right.[19] Hohfeld then defines an 'immunity' right (item (4)) as the absence of a power right. The prohibition of slavery, which appears in the Universal Declaration of Human Rights, provides an example of this last phenomenon, because it in effect renders each person immune from others' power to demand any particular form of labour without consent. Like the power rights discussed thus far, immunity rights thus reflect secondary rules, which affect peoples' ability to change various primary rules of conduct without themselves laying any direct claims on anyone's conduct.

As so far described, both power and immunity rights can thus be understood as reflecting rules that either allow or disallow people to change a more basic set

[15] HLA Hart, *The Concept of Law* (n 11) 78–79.

[16] Hohfeld, 'Some Fundamental Legal Conceptions' (n 12).

[17] Hart, *The Concept of Law* (n 11).

[18] Hart, *The Concept of Law* (n 11) 79.

[19] The ability to alter these two classes of rights is depicted with dotted arrow lines leading from (3) to (1) and (2). As discussed further below, Hohfeld's definition of a 'power' right also includes abilities, within a set of rules, to alter some power or immunity right.

of claim or liberty rights. Because claim and liberty rights have themselves been defined in terms of the (direct) implications they are taken to have on a more primary set of interpersonal obligations, these thoughts about power and immunity rights can now be understood in terms of the (indirect) effects that they either allow or disallow individuals' actions to have on this more primary set of interpersonal obligations. Figure 1 provides visual verification of this fact: it shows that one can always find a pathway from any simple power or immunity right to some claim or liberty right.

A careful look at Figure 1 shows, however, that powers and immunities can sometimes reflect an additional layer of complexity needing comment. All of the examples discussed thus far involve powers or immunities that confer the ability (or inability) to alter either claims or liberties, but as Figure 1 shows, powers and immunities can also sometimes confer the ability (or inability) to alter other powers and immunities. This fact does not render the definition of powers or immunities circular, but rather demonstrates that the human capacity to understand rights has recursive[20] potential: higher order powers and immunities can, in other words, sometimes be defined in terms of lower order powers or immunities, so long as all of these more complex definitions lead by a chain of recursive definition to effects on some simple claim or liberty right. Once again, Figure 1 provides visual verification of this fact: it shows that one can always find a pathway from any higher order power or immunity right (labelled 3′′, 3′′′ etc., and 4′′, 4′′′ etc.) through an iterated set of lower order ones that leads to a simple claim or liberty right.

Consider the constitutional right to contract as an example. This right is easy enough for most people to understand, and so it might be surprising to learn that it in effect gives each member of a state a (fourth order) immunity right to be free from the (third order) power right of the state to limit his or her (second order) power right to contract—which, when exercised, could be used to create new (first order) claim rights against the original holder of the right to contract. Recursive complexities like these are rarely consciously articulated or perceived, but they can operate quite effectively in human unconscious life.

It should be clear now that all of the different types of rights judgments that Hohfeld has carefully distinguished can be analysed—either directly, indirectly, or recursively—in terms of their perceived implications for a more primary set of perceived interpersonal obligations. These four classes of rights exhaust the core concept of a right, as it appears in human life. Hence, the entire range of human thoughts about this core concept can now be understood to engage a distinctive cognitive capacity, which displays a number of characteristic patterns of logic and

[20] 'Recursion…is commonly defined as the looping back into a set of rules of its own output, so as to produce a potentially infinite set of outputs.' N Evans and SC Levinson, 'The Myth of Language Universals: Language Diversity and its Importance for Cognitive Science' (2009) 32 *Behavioral and Brain Sciences* 429, 442.

reasoning and operates through its effects on a more primary sense of interpersonal obligation.

The next subsection will explore this underlying psychology of interpersonal obligation in more detail, but before that several facts about the human capacity to operate with recursion deserve comment. In his well-known work on natural language, Noam Chomsky has suggested that the human capacity for language employs a fundamental set of rules, which he calls the 'universal grammar' of language.[21] These rules have recursive properties,[22] which are critical to the rich flexibility that human language displays because they allow simple thoughts to be embedded in increasingly complex syntactic structures, thereby giving humans the ability to generate an indefinitely complex range of linguistic thoughts.[23] In both natural language and thoughts about rights, the relevant recursive operations can appear complex once articulated, and they are rarely explicitly taught or consciously perceived. In both instances, the vast majority of people nevertheless exhibit a basic fluency with the underlying mental operations.[24] Facts like these suggest that not only the capacity for language but also the capacity to cognize rights have important innate components.[25]

In addition, Chomsky and others have suggested that it is just these innate properties of recursion that distinguish human language from most animal forms of communication,[26] and the capacity to define rights recursively would also appear to be distinctively human. It is therefore worth noting that a number of anthropologists, archaeologists and linguists have suggested that the recursive features of human language may have first emerged during the Upper Paleolithic transition (which began as early as 55,000 BP (before present) and was complete in many regions by about 40,000 BP), a time when the archaeological record suggests that humans underwent not only a great burst in technological and symbolic capacities but also in their capacities to sustain more flexible forms of social complexity and culture, and more highly differentiated traditions of tool usage.[27] The possibility that these more complex linguistic and social

[21] Noam Chomsky, 'Three Factors in Language Design' (2005) 36 *Linguistic Inquiry* 1.

[22] Although some have challenged Chomsky's claim that these recursive properties of human language are literally universal (as opposed to nearly universal), the major debate at this stage seems to be about the source (not the existence) of these recursive properties in most human languages. As two of Chomsky's most recent and eminent critics have put the point: 'No one doubts that humans have the ability to create utterances of indefinite complexity, but there can be serious doubt about where exactly this recursive property resides, in the syntax or elsewhere' Evans and Levinson (n 20). Others have argued that these recursive properties distinguish human language from most—if not all—other forms of animal communication. See MD Hauser, N Chomsky, and WT Fitch, 'The Faculty of Language: What is It, Who has It, and How Did it Evolve?' (2002) 298 *Science* 1569.

[23] Hauser, Chomsky, and Fitch (n 22).

[24] Indeed, although Hohfeld was struck by the rampant ambiguity in human talk about rights, and he therefore became an eloquent champion for greater clarity, one should be equally struck by how rarely these ambiguities lead to miscommunication in practice.

[25] Kar, 'The Deep Structure' (n 6); Mikhail, 'Moral Grammar and Human Rights' (n 6).

[26] Hauser, Chomsky, and Fitch (n 22).

[27] Richard G Klein, 'Archaeology and the Evolution of Human Behavior' (2000) 9 *Evolutionary Anthropology* 17; Quentin D Atkinson, Russell D Gray, and Alexei J Drummond, 'mtDNA Variation

capacities may have evolved together at a crucial turning point in the natural history of humans, which involved the development or novel deployment of a special capacity to operate with recursion in several different psychological domains, is thus an important one that merits further investigation.[28]

2.2 Examining the basic psychology of obligation

Building on Hohfeld's work on the logic of rights, this chapter suggests that all cognitive functions involving the core concept of a right can ultimately be understood as operating—either directly, indirectly, or recursively—on a more primary set of judgements about interpersonal obligation. This section now turns to these more primary judgements of interpersonal obligation, and argues that they express a special complex of psychological phenomena, which animate a highly distinctive and deeply structured form of human social life and interaction. A better understanding of this special dimension of human life is critical for a contemporary understanding of the psychological foundations of human rights.

One way to introduce this next topic is to highlight an important feature of sincere moral judgements: these judgements appear to have an especially tight link, the precise nature of which is debated, to some kind of *motivation*.[29] When people sincerely believe that something is good or right, for example, they will typically perceive themselves to have reasons that arise from these judgements and will typically have some motivation to respond to these perceived reasons—at least so long as their capacities to respond to reasons remain intact.

In the more specific case of judgements about interpersonal obligation, the relevant motivation can also be distinguished from a range of other putatively moral and non-moral motives. The motivations that go into the perceptions of interpersonal obligation are special in that obligations are typically taken to depend not on any of an obligee's antecedent desires, inclinations or interests for any particular outcome or state of affairs, or even on any feelings of compassion that he or she might have

Predicts Population Size in Humans and Reveals a Major Southern Asian Chapter in Human Prehistory' (2008) 25(2) *Molecular Biology and Evolution* 468.

[28] It should be noted that some have attributed recursion to certain other basic human capacities, including theory of mind and the ability to make tools. Evans and Levinson (n 20); Patricia M Greenfield, 'Language, Tools and Brain: The Ontogeny and Phylogeny of Hierarchically Organized Sequential Behavior' (1991) 14 *Brain and Behavioral Sciences* 531. Some of these capacities plausibly expanded during the Upper Paleolithic transition, but another possibility is that certain basic capacities for recursive thought predated the Upper Paleolithic transition and were later amplified and/or redeployed in the service of more complex linguistic and moral capacities.

[29] For a recent review of the literature that supports this claim, see Fredrik Björklund, Gunnar Björnsson, John Erikkson, Ragnar Francén Olinder, and Caj Strandberg, 'Recent Work on Motivational Internalism' (2011) 72 *Analysis* 124. It should be noted that the precise nature of this link is often disputed. See ibid.

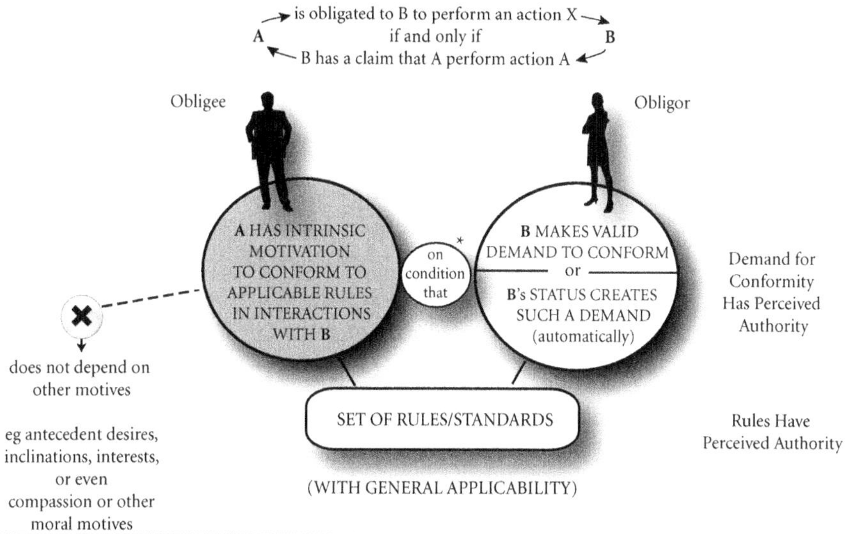

* For a person who sincerely accepts the authority of an interpersonal obligation, and is motivated by this acceptance, the motivation to conform to the relevant demand is thus **authority-dependent**: it depends on perceptions of the authority of (1) the person who is making the demand and (2) the underlying rules. Hence, these special motives do not depend on an obligee's antecedent desires, inclinations, or interests for states of affairs. Nor do these special motives depend upon compassion or many other moral motives.

FIGURE 2 The Primary (Authority-Dependent) Motives of Interpersonal Obligation

for another person, but rather on certain facts about the perceived *authority* of, first, the rule that gives rise to the obligation and, second, the person who demands conformity to it. This authority to demand conformity can come in two basic forms. On the one hand, another person may be perceived to have the authority within a given set of rules either to demand conformity or not. In this first situation, the special motivation to conform to the underlying rule will therefore be taken to be conditioned on certain properties of this other person's will. In other instances, however, certain rights, along with the obligations they entail, are deemed inalienable, and the demand for conformity is thus perceived to arise from some feature of this other person's status, independently of their will. In this second scenario, the special motivation to conform to the underlying rule should therefore be conditioned on perceptions about this other person's normative status, which will be perceived to create an automatic demand for conformity. These special features of the motivations that go into sincere beliefs about interpersonal obligation are shown in Figure 2.

As Figure 2 suggests, perceptions of interpersonal obligation can provide motivations that are independent of an obligee's antecedent desires, interests, or inclinations in at least two senses. First, perceptions of obligations typically involve the perception of *reasons* that can motivate an obligee to action independently of the obligee's antecedent desires, inclinations or interests to perform the action that is owed.[30] Second, obligations are typically taken to arise from rules that have some generality of application, and can thus apply regardless of an obligee's antecedent desires, inclinations or interests in having them apply in his or her particular case.[31] Perceptions of obligation thus have two of the central properties that Immanuel Kant famously observed when he said that common sense moral obligations purport to give rise to imperatives that are *categorical*—or that have a form of authority that operates independently of a person's antecedent desires, inclinations, and interests.[32]

Kant's famous notion of a 'categorical' imperative contains a further commitment, however, which is reflected in the important distinction between reasons and requirements. To say that an imperative is 'categorical' is to say not just that it gives rise to reasons, which arise from rules that have some generality of application (all independently of an obligee's antecedent desires, interests, and inclinations), but also that these reasons have the authority to *override* some other reasons that arise from an obligee's antecedent desires, interests, and inclinations.[33] Interpersonal obligations purport to have this special form of authority as well, and it is thus important to ask how this further perception of authority shows up in human moral psychology.

HLA Hart's influential work on the concept of obligation will serve as a useful starting point for these purposes. Although Hart's account of obligation underwent a number of subtle transformations over the course of his career, his core idea throughout was to approach the question by psychologizing it and then describing the special psychological attitudes that people express when they make sincere statements about interpersonal obligation. According to Hart's views in *The Concept of Law*,[34] when one sincerely believes that one is under an obligation that arises from a given rule, one takes the rule not only as (1) a guide to action but also as (2-a) grounds for criticism and for (2-b) allowing certain serious forms of social pressure, such as coercion or punishment for non-compliance.[35] Hart's reference to the special psychology that goes into taking an obligation as a (1) 'guide to action' can now be refined by taking the relevant source of motivation to be authority-dependent in the specific senses discussed above and depicted in Figure 2. The other parts of Hart's account (namely, parts (2-a) and (2-b)) can then be used with some modifications to specify the further sense in which obligations are perceived to be overriding.

[30] David Brink, 'Kantian Rationalism: Inescapability, Authority and Supremacy' in Garrett Cullity and Berys Gaut (eds), *Ethics and Practical Reason* (OUP 1997) 255–67, 280–87.

[31] Brink (n 30).

[32] Brink (n 30); Immanuel Kant, 'Groundwork for the Metaphysics of Morals' in Mary J Gregor (ed), *Practical Philosophy* (first published 1785, CUP 1997).

[33] Brink puts this point in terms of the purported 'supremacy' of moral requirements. See Brink (n 30).

[34] Hart, *The Concept of Law* (n 11).

[35] Hart, *The Concept of Law* (n 11) 83–84.

Hart's reference to both grounds for criticism and for allowing certain serious forms of social pressure such as coercion or punishment for non-compliance bring a critical interpersonal dimension into his early account of obligation. In order to account for the difference between social obligations and a range of other phenomena, such as habits, rules and non-obligatory reasons, Hart essentially brought the psychological attitudes of the larger community toward the obligee into his account. When a person fails to conform to an ordinary reason or rule, this larger community might take the person's actions to be a ground for criticism (ie that the person is acting contrary to reason or is deviating from a rule), but the community does not typically take the deviation to warrant more serious reactions like punishment or coercion, and this distinction is part of what makes obligations special in Hart's early account.[36] Reactions like punishment and coercion are also special in that they are typically perceived to be impermissible absent a breach. Figure 3 thus depicts the situation in which an entire community can be said to share the belief that one person has an obligation to another, based on a synthesis of Hart's early account of obligation and the discussions of motivation set forth in this chapter. Note that Figure 3 draws upon Figure 2 to characterize the primary authority-dependent motivations that go into a person's sense that he or she is under an obligation to another, as shown in the top half of the diagram, but then adds Hart's idea that failures to meet a perceived obligation will typically be taken by the rest of the community to warrant certain serious forms of social pressure, which would otherwise be impermissible, such as punishment or coercion for non-compliance. These latter phenomena are depicted in the bottom half of Figure 3.

In Figure 3, the shared belief among the members of a hypothetical community that one person has an obligation to another is thus reflected not only in the primary psychological phenomena discussed in prior sections, but also in certain secondary psychological phenomena that are depicted in the bottom half of the diagram. These secondary phenomena include shared expectations (shown in the leftmost circle) on the part of the larger community that an obligee will conform to the relevant rules in the same conditions of perceived authority that should intrinsically motivate the obligee. These secondary phenomena also include shared perceptions that the relevant conditions obtain for these shared expectations of conformity to

[36] Hart mentions three features that distinguish obligations from rules in his early view. First, '[r]ules are conceived and spoken of as imposing obligations when the general demand for conformity is insistent and the social pressure brought to bear on upon those who deviate or threaten to deviate is great'. Hart, *The Concept of Law* (n 11) 84. Second, '[t]he rules supported by this serious pressure are thought important because they are believed to be necessary to the maintenance of social life or some highly prized feature of it'. Hart, *The Concept of Law* (n 11) 85. And third, 'it is generally recognized that the conduct required by these rules may, while benefiting others, conflict with what the person who owes the duty may wish to do'. He mentions physical sanctioning as one form of social pressure that meets the first criterion, but suggests that the use of physical sanctions (or punishment and coercion) is characteristic of legal obligations, whereas dependence on emotions, like guilt, shame, and remorse, is more characteristic of moral obligation.

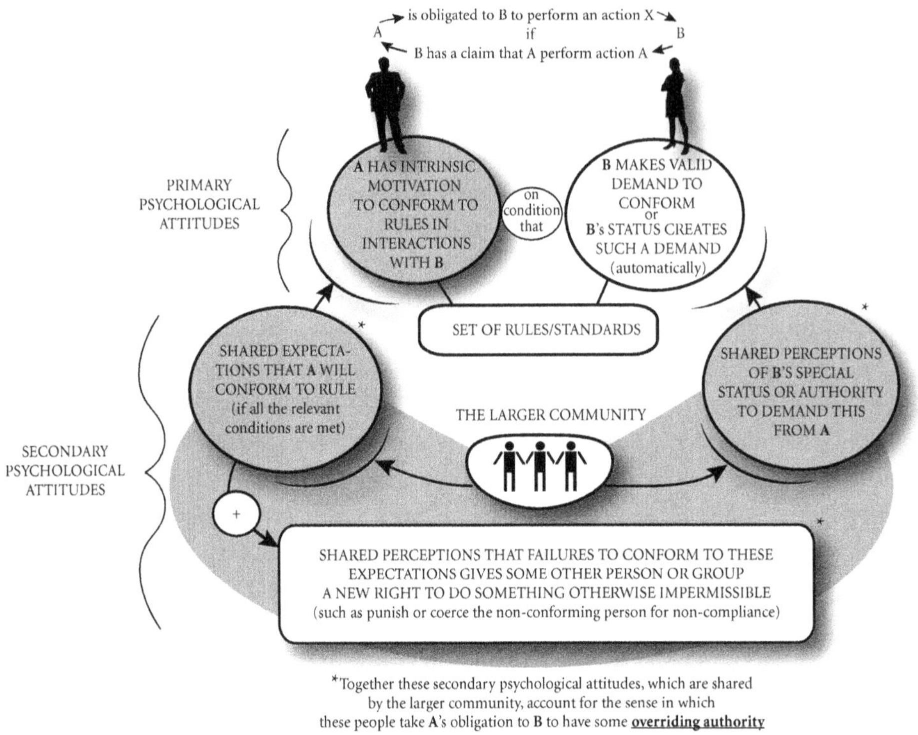

FIGURE 3 The Psychology of Obligation: Primary Motives With Secondary Attitudes of Community

arise (shown in the rightmost circle), either because the community takes the obligor to have made a demand with authority or because the obligor is perceived to have a special normative status that automatically creates a demand for the obligee to conform. In Hart's early version of the idea, any breaches of the community's shared expectations are also taken to permit certain social reactions that would otherwise be impermissible, such as punishment or coercion for non-compliance (shown in the bottom box). Secondary phenomena like these can now be understood to characterize a more complex situation, in which the members of a larger community take a set of rules to give rise not only to reasons for action but also to requirements that are overriding.

The present goal is, however, to articulate a general and purely descriptive account of the psychology of interpersonal obligation, and, for that purpose, the account described thus far has two important shortcomings. The first is that it seeks to define the overriding force of obligations in terms of the equally puzzling notion of a 'permission' that is warranted by the failure to conform to a rule. The second is that the account defines the relevant permissions very narrowly, in terms of serious social pressure such as punishment or coercion, and thus fails to capture important features of a broader set of interpersonal obligations. The remainder of this section addresses each of these objections and responds to them with suggested modifications to the basic account.

Beginning with the first objection, the notion of a permission is just as potentially mysterious from a naturalistic perspective as the notion of an obligation, and so one might wonder what it means to believe that the breach of an obligation gives rise to a new permission. Hart's use of terms like 'punishment' and 'coercion' in this context are similarly problematic, because they imply the *legitimate* use of physical force, and therefore contain implicit reference to a similar conception of permission. Fortunately, there is at least one class of obligations for which objections of this first kind can be circumvented. Let the term 'self-referential' obligation refer to any obligation the overriding force of which is defined solely in terms of permissions to engage in the very same acts that would otherwise be prohibited by the obligation itself. If, for example, a group were to perceive there to be an obligation on the part of each member of the community not to harm any other member physically, then, for reasons already discussed, these people could be understood as perceiving each member of the community to have a claim right against all others not to be physically harmed. For these people, the further belief that breach of this obligation warrants a new 'permission' to 'coerce' or 'punish' the breaching party could then be understood in terms of a shared belief that failure to conform *simply negates* the breaching party's initial claim rights not to be physically harmed. So construed, this obligation not to harm others physically would be self-referential, and the reference it makes to permissions in the case of breach could be understood in terms of the simpler concept of logical negation as applied recursively to the original obligation. These facts suggest that the capacity to operate with self-referential obligations depends on a form of recursive thinking itself.

The possibility of self-referential obligations is a very important one in human life, because it provides a critical starting point against which a community can define a much broader set of obligations. Once a community has accepted the self-referential obligation not to harm other members physically, the community can, for example, begin to accept other obligations the overriding force of which is understood in terms of permissions to punish or coerce in cases of breach. In some circumstances, a very broad set of obligations (which might include the perceived obligation to keep one's promises, to be honest, to respect certain sexual taboos, and so on) can thus be defined in part by reference to their implications for other obligations, which are either self-referential themselves or lead by a chain of recursive definition to a self-referential obligation.

In his recent discussions of so-called 'primitive law', or the law of pre-state societies, Christoph Kletzer[37] has recently come to a similar set of conclusions, suggesting that primitive law operates essentially in this way. In his view, the perceived

[37] See Christopher Kletzer, 'Primitive Law' (unpublished manuscript, on file with author, 2013).

authority to demand conformity with a particular set of rules against physical harm is tied to a person's perceived status as a member of a particular band or tribe in many pre-state societies. Failure to conform to the rule is then taken to warrant negation of that in-group status, which thereby in effect 'permits' a range of retributive acts that can include physical violence or even the murder of a nonconforming person. Consistent with the views developed here, Kletzer believes that modern law differs from primitive law in being more complex and exhibiting a more centralized monopoly over coercion, but he suggests that modern law still rests on a deeper foundation of obligations that operate in these simpler ways. The first objection to the present account can thus be met by recognizing the potential for self-referential obligations in human life and seeing how they can be used to support a much more complex set of perceived obligations within a community.

The second problem with the present account of the psychology of obligation is that it is insufficiently general to capture the broad range of perceived obligations that appear in moral and legal practice. Although Hart sometimes tried to account for the distinctive nature of obligations by reference to permissions to engage in serious social pressure for non-compliance, a look at the broader set of obligations that arise in moral and legal practice suggests that breaches are often taken to warrant other types of reactions.[38] Sometimes, for example, the breach of a perceived obligation is taken to give rise not to a new permission (essentially a new privilege or liberty right) but rather to a new claim right on the part of the victim of the breach. The breach of certain rules of tort law along with their moral analogues are, for example, commonly taken to give the victims of these breaches new claim rights for compensation from the breaching party. At other times, the breach of an obligation gives rise to a new permission, but it is one that is unrelated to serious social pressure, as, for example, when the breach of contract releases the victim of the breach from any remaining performance obligations to the breaching party.[39] At still other times, the breach of an obligation creates a new power, such as when the breach of certain professional obligations gives professional organizations the power to revoke a professional licence. And, finally, sometimes the breach of obligations creates new immunities, as, for example, when the breach of certain parental obligations to a child are taken to warrant the child's emancipation from the parent's custody and care (thereby rendering the child immune from a range of power rights that the parent would otherwise have over the child) along with the creation of a new custodial arrangement. These further possibilities are depicted in Figure 4.

[38] Hart was aware of complexities like these and even made reference to some of them when he distinguished between 'primary' and 'secondary' rules. His focus on serious social pressure in his early account of obligation nevertheless sits in tension with this awareness.

[39] As this last example shows, self-referential obligations need not even be limited to the obligation not to harm; they can include other obligations, including the obligation to perform one's contracts.

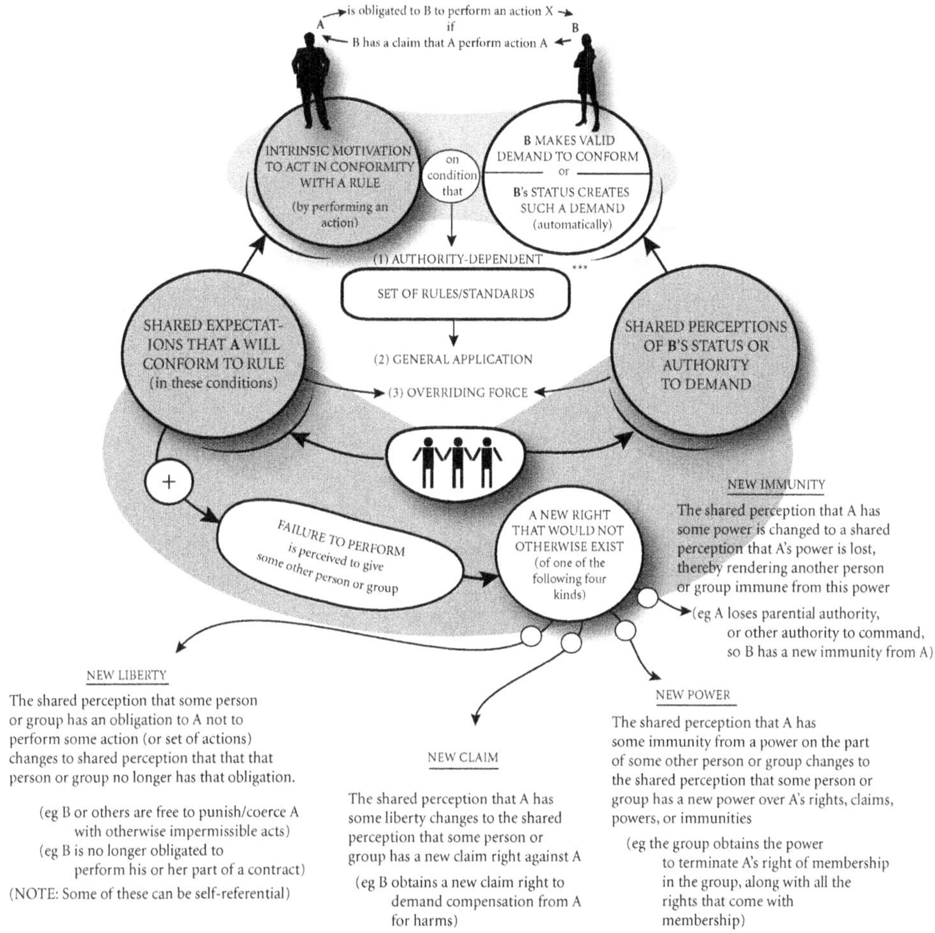

*** NOTE: The underlying set of rules depicted here can in principle represent a complex blend of primary, secondary, and higher order rules, as described in Section 1(A) and depicted in Figure 1 above. The fact that these rules have properties (1)–(3) means that they are also perceived as giving rise to interpersonal obligations that are *categorical*

FIGURE 4 The Complete Psychology of Interpersonal Obligation

The fact that the overriding force of an interpersonal obligation can be defined not just self-referentially but also in terms of the perceived warrant (in the case of breach) of a much broader range of new claim rights, liberty rights, power rights, and immunity rights is an important one. This broader class of rights must, of course, still be definable—either directly, indirectly, or recursively—in terms of effects on a more basic set of self-referential obligations. Still, the fact that some obligations can be made overriding by reference to others suggests that there is yet another recursive dimension to the human capacity to identify and respond to rights, which augments its potential complexity and flexibility.

It should nevertheless be clear now that all human thoughts about the core concepts of rights and interpersonal obligations are ultimately bound up with a special complex of psychological attitudes, which can be described at a higher level of abstraction. This complex includes perceptions of obligation, special authority-dependent motives on the part of (most) obligees within a community to conform to these obligations, shared expectations of conformity in the community at large, and shared dispositions to react to deviations in certain regular and predictable ways. The next section will add a number of other phenomena to this list, such as practices of claim-making, shared dispositions to credit certain standard excuses and justifications, a tendency to focus on the intentionality of many perceived wrongs, and much more. The psychological capacity to identify and respond to rights will thus be shown to animate a highly familiar and deeply structured form of human social life and interaction.

It should also be clear that these psychological capacities need to be engaged directly to support a more stable and universally shared form of respect for human rights in the modern world. These capacities are, however, clearly distinct from a broad range of other putatively moral and non-moral psychological phenomena, including the capacity for compassion, the capacity to attribute mental states to others, the capacity to engage in instrumental (or purely goal-oriented) practical reasoning, and a range of other character traits that one might think necessary for virtue. Even if all of these psychological phenomena can interact in complex ways, a better understanding of the distinctive ways the psychological capacity to identify and respond to rights functions is therefore needed for the advancement of human rights.

3. Placing the Psychology of Rights and Obligation into a Contemporary Evolutionary Framework

The last section developed several lines of philosophical inquiry to produce an initial description of the psychological capacities that humans use to identify and respond to rights. This section turns to contemporary insights from evolutionary theory to enhance the description. It argues that the human capacity to identify and respond to rights is best understood as having an identifiable evolutionary history, which endows it with a specific natural function: to allow humans to resolve social contract problems flexibly and thereby engage in a form of social cooperation that has proven absolutely critical for human life.

Sections 3.1 and 3.2 clarify the meaning and importance of the terms 'natural function' and 'social contract problem', as they appear in this claim. Sections 3.3 and 3.4 then present evidence for the claim. In the process, systematic links are established between the distinctive form of human social life and interaction that was described in the last section and a much broader range of social and psychological phenomena.[40]

The evolutionary arguments in this section will also lend support to the claim, first broached in the last section, that the psychological capacity to identify and respond to rights is innate. Nothing about this innateness claim should be taken to mean that the capacity must be present at birth. Nor does the claim imply that the capacity should be expected to develop normally without certain species-typical social and environmental cues, or even that it must develop in the exact same way in response to different social influences. To say that these capacities are innate is to say two things. First, ordinary humans have a special psychological capacity to identify and respond to rights, which develops in certain regular and predictable ways in response to species-typical social interactions that arise in almost all human communities. Second, this capacity can be described at a certain level of abstraction as being universal (in the sense of being deeply species-typical) and by reference to universal principles that govern its ordinary development and operation. To qualify as universal in the relevant sense, these principles should govern in all (or nearly all) forms that the capacity takes, even if the capacity develops in slightly different ways in different social circumstances, and even if it attaches people with different cultural or life histories to different senses of moral, legal, and/or other obligation.

In all of these respects, the claim that humans have an innate capacity to identify and respond to rights should thus be understood as paralleling the more familiar claim that humans have an innate capacity for language.[41] As is well known, children only acquire their ability to speak their first language in response to certain species-typical patterns of socialization during a critical period of development after birth.[42] Different patterns of socialization also cause different children to learn different native languages. These facts are nevertheless consistent with the claim that the human capacity for language is governed by a special set of principles, which can be described at a higher level of abstraction and are exhibited in all (or nearly all) human languages.[43]

[40] Figure 7 depicts this broader range of features in one place.

[41] See eg Noam Chomsky, *On Nature and Language* (CUP 2002).

[42] Kuniyoshi L Sakai, 'Language Acquisition and Brain Development' (2005) 310 *Science* 815; Maria Teresa Guasti, *Language Acquisition: The Growth of Grammar* (MIT Press 2002).

[43] For formal proof, see Martin A Nowak and Natalia L Komarova Partha Niyogi, 'Computational and Evolutionary Aspects of Language' (2002) 417 *Nature* 611.

3.1 The concept 'natural function' and why it matters

The central claim of this section is that the human capacity to identify and respond to rights should be understood as innate and as having a specific natural function: to allow humans to resolve social contract problems flexibly. The term 'natural function' is a technical one, which makes inelimanable reference to the correct evolutionary explanation of a trait. Some initial discussion of the meaning and importance of this term is therefore needed.

Of course, not every human trait has an evolutionary explanation, but some do, and so the first question is how one might identify the natural function of a trait when such an explanation is available. To answer this question, it may help to consider the case of the human heart. For reasons to be discussed, the human heart can be plausibly understood as having the (or at least *a*) 'natural function' of pumping blood to and from the human body. But what exactly is the relationship between this claim about natural function and the correct evolutionary explanation of the human heart?

Evolutionary theorists who seek to explain a given trait typically focus on some set of heritable phenotypes[44] within a population, and then ask whether their change in frequency over time can be explained in part by reference to any known evolutionary process. Natural selection is the most important such process for present purposes, because traits can only be said to have a natural function if they are produced by natural selection. To say that natural selection has produced a trait is to say that one can explain its proliferation through ancestral populations by reference to the relative reproductive advantages that it gave its ancestral bearers.

The key to understanding the concept of a natural function is then to make a further distinction: viz between the ultimate evolutionary explanation of a trait, which is framed in terms of reproductive benefits, and the more specific proximate effects of the trait that explain *why* it produced these relative reproductive benefits in ancestral populations. The natural function of a trait is, in fact, defined as the set of its regular proximate consequences that explain why it was naturally selected for in ancestral populations.

To illustrate, Figure 5 depicts a hypothetical population with genetic makeups that make the development of two different types of heart more or less likely. The first type of heart (the 'good' heart, shown in grey) pumps blood more reliably to and from the human body relative to the second type of heart (the 'bad' heart, shown in white). These two types of heart should be assumed to function at equal caloric and other cost to their bearers, so that the only relevant difference between them lies in how reliably they pump blood to and from the human body.

Given these assumptions, 'good' hearts should tend to conduce to the reproductive success of their bearers better than 'bad' hearts. 'Good' hearts should do this by

[44] Phenotypes are any observable traits or characteristics.

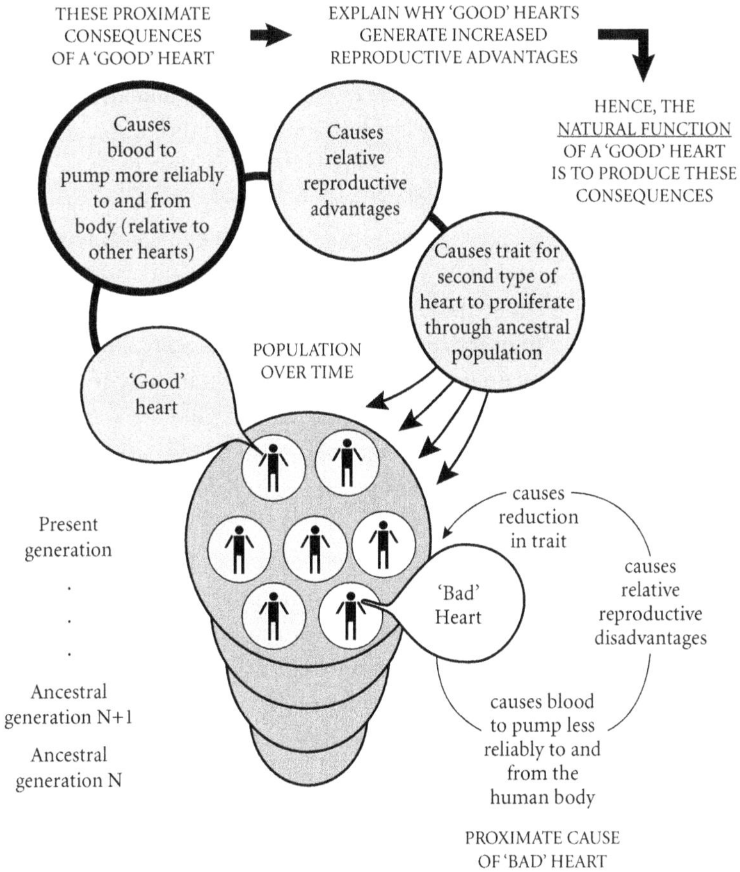

FIGURE 5 What it Means to Say that the 'Natural Function' of the Human Heart is to Pump Blood

virtue of their proximate capacities to pump blood more reliably to and from the human body (as shown in the circle in the top left with the thick lines) than 'bad' hearts. To the extent that these traits are heritable, natural selection should therefore cause 'good' hearts to increase in representation and 'bad' hearts to decrease over succeeding generations. The processes depicted in Figure 5 are, of course, highly simplified and schematic, but they plausibly characterize at least *part* of the correct evolutionary explanation for why humans have the hearts that they do. To the extent that this is so, it is thus appropriate to say that the 'natural function' (or at least *a* natural function) of the human heart is to pump blood reliably to and from the human body. Evolutionary biologists will also sometimes say that hearts are 'adaptations' *for* the production of these specific proximate consequences: viz for pumping blood reliably to and from the human body.

Later sections will argue that the natural function of the human capacity to identify and respond to rights is to allow humans to resolve social contract problems flexibly, but before that three points about the scope and usefulness of natural function claims should be addressed. First, although claims about natural functions make ineliminable reference to the correct evolutionary explanation of a trait, they do not thereby preclude a range of other possible explanations. A complete answer to why a particular human heart functions in the way that it does will typically require a much broader range of explanations. Culture will also play an important explanatory role if, for example, it causes different people to eat different foods that are more or less likely to cause a hardening of the arteries. Individual decisions can also have important effects if, for example, different people have made different choices about how much to exercise or what to eat. In at least some cases, instances of physical trauma will play an especially important explanatory role and it is even possible for a single trait to have more than one natural function—in which case the trait will show some evidence of design for more than one function. Facts like these should hold equally true for claims about the natural function of a psychological capacity.

Still, and second, the correct identification of the natural function of a trait can generate insights that are not easily derivable from other sources. Once it is understood that the natural function (or at least a natural function) of the human heart is to pump blood to and from the human body, it will, for example, begin to make sense why the human heart has its normal musculature; why it is connected to neural circuitry that helps govern its rhythmic pulse; why it is connected up to arteries and veins, which carry blood from the human heart to the human body and back again; and why the human heart appears so well designed, in these and other ways, to pump blood reliably to and from the human body. The identification of a natural function can also help to explain why hearts tend to develop many of these properties during embryonic development, and why they tend to do so regularly, even if they also sometimes fail. These are important features of the human heart, which cannot be understood as the product of culture, individual choice, or even the simple operation of physical laws. Identifying the natural function of a trait can thus produce valuable insights into the trait, including insights into the nature and function of its component parts and the complex ways they interrelate. Once again, facts like these should hold equally true if one can identify the natural function of a psychological capacity.[45]

[45] 'When one is trying to discover the structure of an information-processing system as complex as the human brain, knowing what its components were "designed" to do is like being given an aerial map of a territory one is about to explore by foot. If one knows what adaptive functions the human mind was designed to accomplish, one can make many educated guesses about what design features it should have, and can then design experiments to test for them. This can allow one to discover new, previously unsuspected, psychological mechanisms.' Leda Cosmides, John Tooby, and Jerome H Barkow, 'Introduction: Evolutionary Psychology and Conceptual Integration' in Jerome H Barkow, Leda Cosmides, and John Tooby (eds), *The Adapted Mind: Evolutionary Psychology and the Generation of Culture* (OUP 1992) 10.

Third, and finally, the natural function of a trait can be identified independently of how well any particular version of the trait serves this natural function. Because of this fact, natural selection can work through a cyclical process, whereby a series of traits that build upon earlier successes but are better and better suited to a single natural function begin to proliferate through ancestral populations in a series of selective waves. Over time, evolution can thus produce versions of a trait that appear better and better designed for a single natural purpose, in which case the traits should be expected to show increased evidence of complexity and design. Although some sub-optimality should always be expected, evolutionary insights can also help identify special circumstances in which a trait is most likely to serve its natural function well.

3.2 The concept 'social contract problem' and why it matters

Having clarified the concept of a 'natural function', this section explains what it means to claim that the natural function of the human capacity to identify and respond to rights is to allow humans to resolve 'social contract problems'. The term 'social contract problem' is used here to refer to any situation in which each member of a group could do better (as measured by an appropriate standard of personal welfare) if all were to follow a particular rule of conduct in their relations with all other members of the group than if none were, but in which each could do better still if all other members of the group were to follow this rule while allowing a single exception for him or herself. Many rules of common-sense morality and law have this property, as do most (indeed arguably all) of the rules in Universal Declaration of Human Rights.

To illustrate with the well-known situation referred to as a 'Tragedy of the Commons',[46] imagine a group of ancestral human sheep herders who are purely self-interested and inhabit a common pasture, where they engage in a purely pastoralist and nomadic form of subsistence. These sheep herders rely on their flocks to produce a range of meat and wool products needed for survival, but they also live near certain agriculturalist groups, who provide them with an open market for surplus goods. In any given year, each sheep herder thus has personal incentives to allow his or her sheep to graze as much as possible, so as to yield the largest possible surplus of meat and wool products. This particular pasture will, however, become wholly unusable for grazing in five years' time if each sheep herder allows unbridled grazing, whereas the pasture will remain usable in perpetuity by all, with only minor decreases in annual surplus, if all limit their use to 90 per cent maximal

[46] For classic exposition, see Garrett Hardin, 'The Tragedy of the Commons' (1968) 162 *Science* 1243.

grazing. If, on the other hand, only one herder limits his or her grazing, the pasture will still become unusable in five years' time. These herders clearly have a problem, which they may or may not have the psychological capacities to resolve.

One way for these herders to resolve this problem would be for them to enter into an explicit and effective social contract, which gives them each a separate private property right to a distinct parcel of land. In these circumstances, each sheep herder would then have private incentives to limit his or her pasturing activities on his or her private plot to 90 per cent so as to ensure its perpetual private use. At the same time, however, each could do better still if all others were to respect these rules of private property while making a single exception for oneself.[47] And if no one else were to follow the rules, then each would still do better to break them, so as to avoid being the single person with a reduced surplus for the final five years of the pasture's life.

In these circumstances, each sheep herder would thus do better if all were to follow the rules of the social contract than if none were, but each also has personal incentives to break the rules regardless of what others are doing. These sheep herders face a classic social contract problem.[48]

So what are these sheep herders to do? They might be able to resolve this problem if they had an effective sense of obligation that was capable of overriding their self-interested motives and felt obligated by a rule that requires promise keeping. In these circumstances, an explicit social contract might just work. But absent such a sense, these sheep herders will face a number of well-known difficulties. They will not be able to make credible promises or trust one another's promises without the further threat of sanction, and so an explicit social contract standing alone will no longer work. Nor can these sheep herders simply form a state to impose sanctions because states are themselves large-scale cooperative enterprises, and creating one would therefore require these herders to resolve a social contract problem that has the exact same form as the problem they are seeking to resolve. Reputational consequences can help, but they are not always effective, especially as groups become larger and more anonymous.[49] Threats of private punishment, finally, tend to work

[47] Any single person for whom an exception was made could profit even more by restricting the grazing of his or her own herd to 90 per cent on his or her own personal plot of land, while breaking the social contract and letting his or her herd engage in additional grazing on others' plots.

[48] For those with a more formalistic bent, their problem can also be modelled as having the underlying game-theoretic structure of an n-person prisoners' dilemma. For further elaboration, see Kar, 'The Deep Structure' (n 6).

[49] Patterns of in-group favouritism have also been shown to interfere with reputational effects in larger social settings. Naoki Masuda, 'Ingroup Favoritism and Intergroup Cooperation Under Indirect Reciprocity Based on Group Reputation' (2012) 311 *Journal of Theoretical Biology* 8. Reputational effects can, on the other hand, have very strong effects when they work in tandem with an underlying sense of reciprocity that extends to larger group settings. See Ernst Fehr, Martin Brown, and Christian Zehnder, 'On Reputation: A Microfoundation of Contract Enforcement and Price Rigidity' (2009) 119 *The Economic Journal* 333.

best when they involve threats of *costly* punishment, whereas these sheep herders have only self-interested forms of motivation and so cannot make credible threats to perform costly retributive acts.

If, on the other hand, these sheep herders were to have an effective sense of obligation, which was capable of overriding some of their self-interested motives and attaching them to a broad and flexible set of rules (which might include rules of private property), then these sheep herders might be able to resolve this social contract problem *and many others like it*, all without the need for an explicit agreement. The next sections argue that humans do in fact have a special capacity to resolve social contract problems flexibly, which operates through perceptions of rights and interpersonal obligations.

3.3 Obligata and the natural function of the human sense of obligation

The sheep herders of the last section would clearly profit from an innate capacity with the natural function of allowing them to resolve social contract problems flexibly. It is, however, one thing to recognize this fact and quite another to suggest that humans are endowed with such a capacity. This section and the next argue that humans have such a capacity: it is the psychological capacity to identify and respond to rights, which operates on a more primary sense of interpersonal obligation.

Claims about the natural function of a trait can be supported by three main sources of evidence: first, by evidence that the environment of evolutionary adaptation for the trait did in fact present ancestral populations with selection pressures for a trait with the proposed natural function; second, by tests of empirical predictions that flow from the functional claim against a broader body of evidence; and, third, by evidence of special design (ie that the trait itself appears specially designed, and/or is made up of a complex set of components that appear specially designed to work together, to serve the proposed natural function).[50] This chapter draws on all three types of evidence to support its central functional claim.

Beginning with the first class of evidence, there can be little doubt that humans (and even their pre-human ancestors) faced recurrent social contract problems throughout their natural history. Social contract problems have been defined

[50] 'Adaptations are recognizable by "evidence of special design"; that is, by recognizing certain features of the evolves species-typical design of an organism as "components of some special problem-solving machinery".' Leda Cosmides and John Tooby, 'The Psychological Foundations of Culture' in Barkow, Cosmides, and Tooby, *The Adapted Mind* (n 45) 62. See also Cosmides, Tooby, and Barkow, 'Introduction' (n 45) 10 ('If one knows what adaptive functions the human mind was designed to accomplish, one can make many educated guesses about what design features it should have, and can then design experiments to test for them').

in a highly abstract manner, and they arise whenever shared rules that require self-sacrifice could in principle generate cooperative benefits for the members of a group. So defined, social contract problems arise daily in the life of almost all organisms that live in groups—even though not all organisms have the capacities to resolve them.

In any event, humans spent the greater part of their natural history in small hunter-gatherer bands, and studies of hunter-gatherers suggest that they tend to be intensely cooperative and share a broad range of moral rules that help them sustain this cooperation.[51] It is only at the tail end of this natural history that these small band formations began to yield increasingly to larger-scale forms of social structure, including, according to one influential taxonomy, tribes,[52] chiefdoms, and then states.[53] More recently, the emergence of numerous international institutions suggests that yet another form of social complexity should be added to this list. Developments like these present humans with ever expanding problems of cooperation, but have done little to undermine the importance of cooperation in smaller groups. Throughout their entire natural history, humans have thus faced many different and often shifting social contract problems. The level of sociality that humans engage in and depend on for their lives is, moreover, almost unparalleled in the animal world, and these distinctively human forms of sociality are a large part of what explains the incredible recent success of the human species.[54]

Turning to the second class of evidence, there are two initial predictions that flow from the claim that the natural function of the capacity to identify and respond to rights is to allow humans to resolve social contract problems flexibly. The first is that this capacity must have provided ancestral humans with a source of motivation to follow rules that in fact resolved social contract problems in their interactions

[51] See eg Christopher Boehm, *Hierarchy in the Forest: The Evolution of Egalitarian Behavior* (Harvard UP 2001); Andrew Whiten and David Erdal, 'The Human Socio-Cognitive Niche and Its Evolutionary Origins' (2012) 367 *Philosophical Transactions of the Royal Society B* 2119. Robert Layton, Sean O'Hara, and Alan Bilsborough, 'Antiquity and Social Functions of Multilevel Social Organization Among Human Hunter-Gatherers' (2012) 33 *International Journal of Primatology* 1215.

[52] Tribal structures are likely to have emerged fairly early in human prehistory.

[53] The taxonomy of bands, tribes, chiefdoms, and states, which has proven influential, was first introduced by Elman Rogers Service. See Elman Rogers Service, *Primitive Social Organization: An Evolutionary Perspective* (2nd edn, Random House 1971). While this taxonomy is useful, it should be remembered that no particular developments toward social complexity are likely to have proceeded in as simple or unilateral a manner as this taxonomy would suggest. Many societies have exhibited reversals and have only developed toward larger-scale forms of social complexity in fits and starts. Many societies have also exhibited features that make them hard to classify as falling only into one of these four types. Still, the taxonomy is helpful for identifying large-scale trends in the development of human social complexity.

[54] Kesebir and others have analogized the level of sociality that humans exhibit to that of the most social insects, which are sometimes said to form cooperative 'superorganisms'. S Kesebir, 'The Superorganism Account of Human Sociality: How and When Human Groups Are Like Beehives' (2012) 16 *Personality and Social Psychology Review* 233. As Kesebir notes, '[s]uperorganismic species are rare emergences in the history of life, yet when they emerge they are extremely successful' (233).

with one another. Rules that resolve social contract problems tend to require some self-sacrifice, however, and so this source of motivation must have been capable of overriding some of these peoples' more instrumental and self-interested motives. The motives that go into the human sense of interpersonal obligation fit this bill perfectly, because they depend on the perceived authority of rules and persons rather than an obligee's antecedent desires, inclinations or interests.[55] These motives can also override those of self-interest.[56] Hence, the existence, structure and method of operation of these special motives are all consistent with the current prediction, and these facts provide some preliminary support for this chapter's central functional claim.

The second basic prediction that flows from this functional claim can be introduced by examining an evolutionary puzzle that it appears to generate. In most circumstances, motives to engage in self-sacrifice toward non-kin should cause their bearers to suffer decreased reproductive success in comparison to those who lack the motives.[57] Standing alone, authority-dependent motives to follow the rules of a social contract should therefore be selected against. Fortunately, there are now a number of well-developed models to explain the general conditions under which natural selection might produce motives like these.[58] Call those members of a population who have authority-dependent motives to follow a social contract 'cooperators' and those who lack them 'non-cooperators'. Natural selection could produce the relevant authority-dependent motives if they were bound up with a more complex set of (secondary) psychological attitudes the natural function of which is to identify and exclude non-cooperators from the benefits of these cooperative enterprises.[59] These secondary psychological phenomena would provide the evolutionary stability conditions for the cooperative motives, by ensuring that the benefits of cooperation flow primarily to other cooperators.

Figure 6 depicts the precise way in which natural selection could favour this highly distinctive bundle of (primary) authority-dependent motivation and (secondary) reactive attitude, in much the same way that it can favour hearts that are better adapted to pump blood. Following the pattern of earlier discussions,[60] Figure 6 distinguishes between two types of traits, which in this instance are psychological. The first, analogous to 'good' hearts, are referred to as 'obligata', singular 'obligatum', and the second, analogous to 'bad' hearts, are labelled 'no obligata'. 'Obligata' are defined as any psychological complex the natural function of which is to resolve social contract problems. As the present discussion shows, obligata can only plausibly serve this function if they include *both* the kinds of authority-dependent motives that go into the human sense of obligation *and* certain secondary psychological reactions the natural function of which is to identify and exclude non-cooperators from the

[55] See Section 2.2, Figure 2. [56] See Section 2.2, Figures 3, 4.

[57] See Chris Robinson, Chapter 3 in this *Handbook*. [58] Kar, 'The Deep Structure' (n 6) 913.

[59] Kar, 'The Deep Structure' (n 6) 910–14. [60] See Figure 5 and Section 3.1 in this chapter.

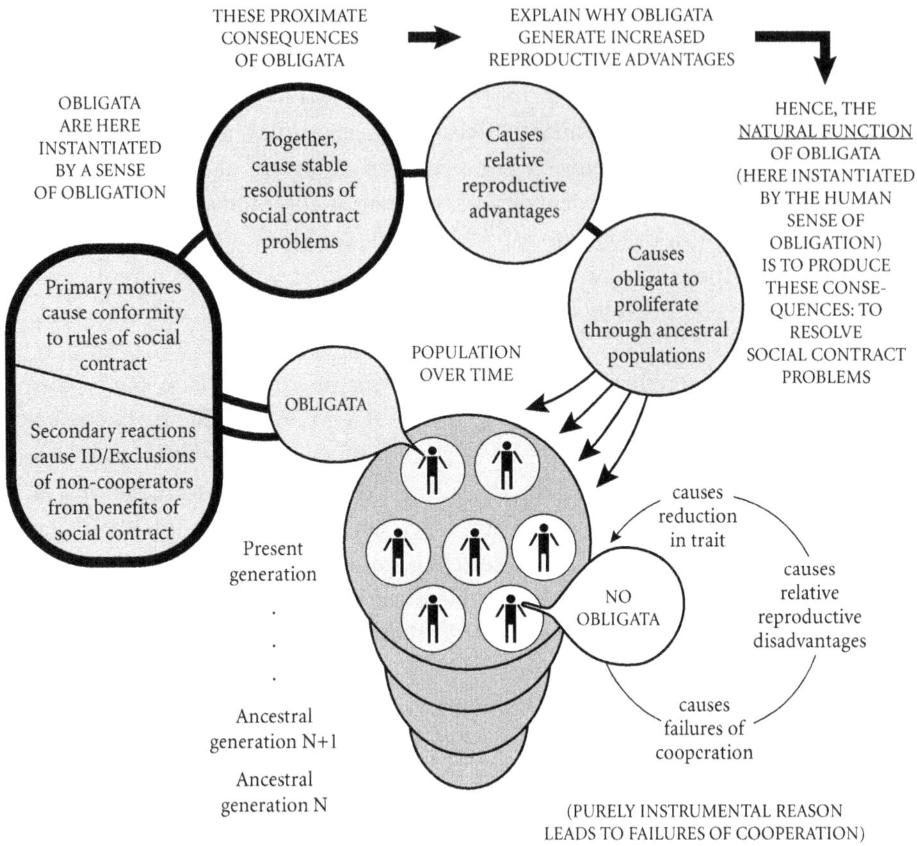

FIGURE 6 The Natural Function of Obligata is to Resolve Social Contract Problems

benefits of a social contract. This special combination of psychological phenomena is therefore depicted as instantiating obligata in Figure 6. People who lack obligata should be understood, finally, as lacking this special complex of psychological phenomena. These people are non-cooperators, who are motivated solely by instrumental reason.

In the special circumstances depicted in Figure 6, having a sense of obligation that inclines one to follow rules that confer benefits on others while requiring some seeming self-sacrifice could, in fact, provide one with relative reproductive advantages. These advantages would be caused by a more specific proximate mechanism: by the tendency of this sense of obligation to cause its bearers to resolve social contract problems with one another flexibly. If this is indeed part of the correct evolutionary explanation for the human sense of obligation, then it would therefore be correct to say that the (or at least a) natural function of the human sense of obligation is to allow humans to resolve social contract problems flexibly. The human sense of obligation would therefore be an instance of an 'obligatum', which serves its natural function through the complex interactions and specialized functions of its component parts. For reasons already discussed, these component parts would be systematically bound up with a special cognitive capacity that allows humans to understand and identify an indefinitely complex set of perceived rights.[61] Hence, the human capacity to identify and respond to rights, which operates through its effects on a more primary sense of interpersonal obligation, would also be an 'obligatum'.

The second prediction that flows from this chapter's central functional claim is thus that the authority-dependent motivations that go into thoughts about rights and obligations should be systematically bound up with certain second order psychological phenomena that function naturally to identify and exclude non-cooperators from the benefits of these cooperative enterprises. Evidence from the larger ethnographic record suggests that these predicted phenomena do in fact exist: moralistic aggression in response to norm violations is a cross-cultural feature of human life (even in hunter gatherer bands, which tend to display a highly egalitarian ethos) and violations of group norms can generate reactions of ridicule, ostracism, physical sanctioning, exile, and sometimes even group killings of norm violators.[62] Domestic law similarly sets forth a complex set of sanctions and other reactions that are deemed warranted by the breach of a legal obligation. As Oona Hathaway and Scott Shapiro have recently shown, even international law, which has a status and efficacy that some have questioned, is now supported by robust practices of 'outcasting'.[63] 'Outcasting' is defined as the denial of the benefits of international cooperation and membership to disobedient states.[64]

Although reactions like these are often complex and varied on the surface,[65] the current prediction is they should be united by a common thread: they should exhibit some tendency, despite this surface variation, to function within the context of a broader set of perceived obligations to help identify and exclude non-cooperators from the cooperative benefits that are made possible by these different systems of obligation. Many of these seemingly diverse reactions do, in fact, function this way. The fact that they exist and accompany perceptions of interpersonal obligation so

[61] See Section 1 in this chapter.

[62] See Boehm (n 51) 30–63, 214–15.

[63] Oona Hathaway and Scott Shapiro, 'Outcasting: Enforcement in Domestic and International Law' (2011) 121 *Yale LJ Online* 252.

[64] Hathaway and Shapiro (n 63) 252.

[65] Earlier discussions showed that these reactions can, for example, sometimes be defined self-referentially and sometimes by reference to other obligations that lead, by a chain of recursive definition, to a self-referential obligation. See Section 2.2 and Figure 4. These reactions can also include new claim rights, liberty rights, power rights, and immunity rights.

systematically thus provides an additional layer of support to this chapter's central functional claim.

3.4 Further evidence for obligata and the natural function of obligation

Additional support for this chapter's central functional claim can now be derived from a broader survey of predictions that flow from it. The discussion thus far has focused on explaining how various aspects of the human sense of obligation that were already described in prior sections can be understood as operating together to serve a single natural function. Figure 7 now combines all of these prior features with an additional set of features discussed in this section. For ease of exposition, all of the features discussed in prior sections are framed by dotted lines and listed under heading (1), whereas the additional features to be introduced below appear against a grey background and are numbered (2)–(4).

Figure 7 can appear complex at first. It should therefore be remembered that part of the case for thinking that the natural function of the human sense of obligation is to allow humans to resolve social contract problems flexibly is that the claim has incredible explanatory power. For reasons to be discussed, the claim can be used to explain coherently a surprisingly broad range of facts, which tend to accompany human thoughts about rights and interpersonal obligations.

The first set of new predictions depicted in Figure 7 appear under heading (2), which lists 'claim-making' 'intentions', 'excuses', and 'justifications'. To understand what these labels refer to, it should be remembered that the human sense of obligation can only plausibly serve the natural function of allowing humans to resolve social contract problems flexibly if it includes secondary psychological mechanisms that function to identify and exclude non-cooperators from the benefits of the relevant cooperative enterprises.[66] Hence, if this chapter's central functional claim is true, then humans should have epistemic capacities that naturally function to produce the relevant identification. There is, in fact, now evidence to suggest that humans have special psychological capacities that are specifically designed for generalized 'cheat-detection'.[67]

In the more specific case of rules that resolve social contract problems, these cheat-detection mechanisms appear to operate by inclining individuals to take actions that are inconsistent with the facial mandates of a social contract as prima facie evidence of non-cooperative motivation. Evidence of this kind tends to generate an initial claim of breach or wrongdoing by the victim of the breach. As a

[66] See Section 3.3 in this chapter.

[67] See Leda Cosmides and John Tooby, 'Cognitive Adaptations for Social Exchange' in Barkow, Cosmides, and Tooby, *The Adapted Mind* (n 45) 178–206.

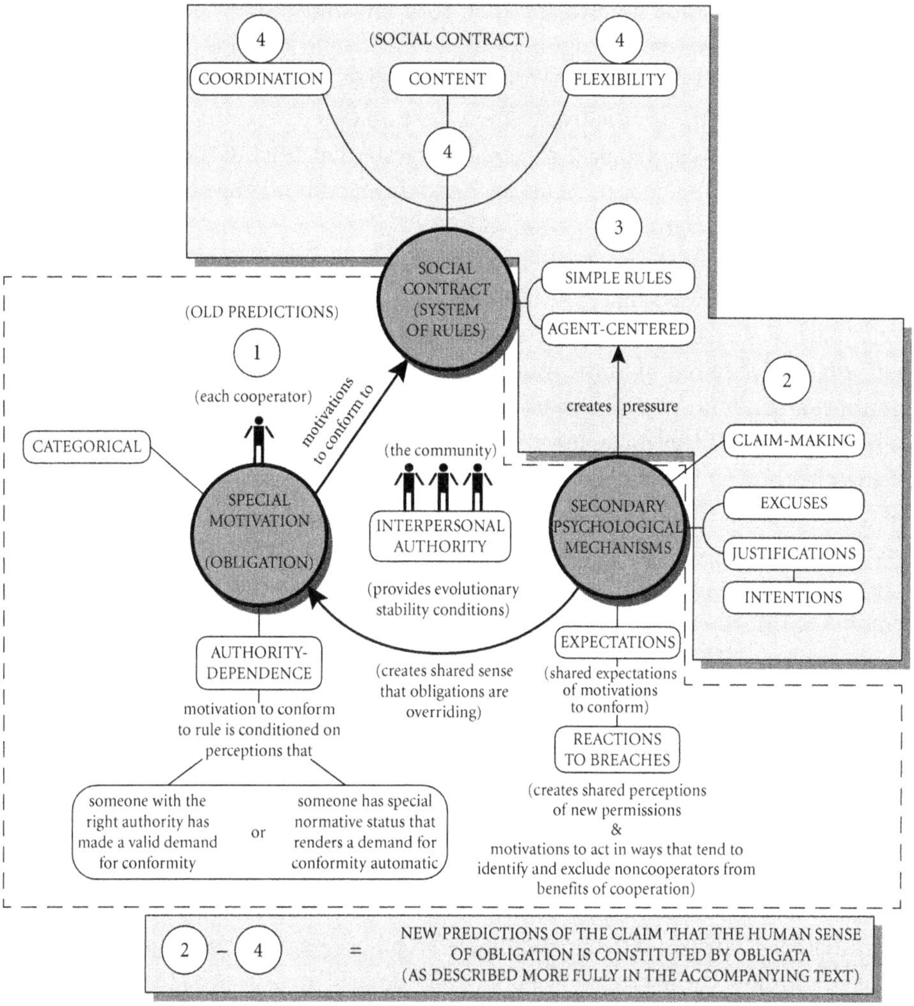

FIGURE 7 Complex Predictions of Claim that Obligata Constitute the Human Sense of the Obligation

moment's reflection will show, however, there are also a number of regular and predictable situations in which even people who are cooperatively motivated will sometimes act in ways that are inconsistent with the facial mandates of a code. These situations include ones where the facial breach is caused by a mistake of fact, an accident, impossibility, duress, and the like. It is therefore noteworthy that humans exhibit strong tendencies in both morality and law to respond to claims of wrongdoing by citing facts like these as *excuses*, and that all of these circumstances serve as standard excusing conditions in morality and law.

In fact, the standard excuses typically operate by undermining the perception (or defeating the claim) that actions inconsistent with a code were performed intentionally. It is thus noteworthy that both law and morality tend to focus on intentional wrongs when assigning culpability.[68] One further prediction is that humans should be especially attentive to the intentionality of perceived wrongdoings but need not be as sensitive to the intentionality of acts that are perceived as permissible. The psychological research suggests that this asymmetry in attributions of intentionality does in fact exist,[69] and this fact should be puzzling absent the present functional claim.

Another set of situations in which a person who is cooperatively motivated may nevertheless act in ways that appear inconsistent with a code is when the act violates some part of the code but can be shown, upon further examination, to be either permitted or required by some other part. It is therefore noteworthy that in these circumstances, both common-sense morality and the law recognize the possibility of *justification* as a legitimate means of answering claims of wrongdoing. Hence, all of the phenomena listed under heading (2)—ie practices of 'claim making', a focus on 'intentions', and the use and crediting of 'excuses' and 'justifications'—would be predicted by the present functional claim. The fact that these phenomena accompany perceptions of rights and obligations so persistently thus provides additional support to this functional claim.

The next predictions listed in Figure 7 appear under heading (3), which mentions 'simple rules' that are 'agent-centred'. Like the last set of predictions, these are ultimately traceable in part to the more basic need for humans to be able to identify and exclude non-cooperators if they are to have a special capacity to resolve social contract problems. The critical fact to recognize is that the *content* of a code can sometimes affect the ease with which breaches are identified. It will, for example, generally be much easier to identify breaches of rules that are stated in relatively simple terms (such as 'Keep your promises!' or 'Do not harm others physically!') than standards that are stated in extremely broad or open-ended terms (such as 'Act so as to promote the impartial welfare of all humans!' or 'Act so as to resolve social contract problems!'). The obligations of common-sense morality and law do, in fact, have this quality to them: they tend to reflect collections of relatively simple rules, which can be easily applied to many concrete and recurrent circumstances, rather than single broad standards that are more amorphous in application. These facts thus lend some further support to this chapter's central functional claim.

For similar reasons, it is typically much easier to determine whether a person has complied personally with a simple rule than to determine whether that person has

[68] See eg Y Ohtsubo, 'Perceiver Intentionality Intensifies Blameworthiness of Negative Behaviors: Blame-Praise Asymmetry in Intensification Effect' (2007) 49 *J Psych Res* 100–10; Fiery Cushman, 'Crime and Punishment: Distinguishing the Roles of Causal and Intentional Analyses in Moral Judgment' (2008) 108 *Cognition* 353.

[69] Carey K Morewedge, 'Negativity Bias in Attribution of External Agency' (2009) 138 *J Experimental Psychology: General* 535.

acted so as to promote the most number of compliances by all people in a group. If the natural function of the human sense of obligation is to allow humans to resolve social contract problems flexibly, then one should therefore predict that many of the obligations in morality and law will tend to have an 'agent-centred' rather than an 'agent-neutral' form:[70] they should tell each person to conform to his or her own personal obligations rather than promote the most instances of conformity in others. As is well known, the vast majority of obligations that arise in common-sense morality and in law do, in fact, have this agent-centred form, and John Mikhail has recently produced empirical evidence to suggest that some agent-centred moral intuitions appear cross-culturally.[71] Hence, both of the features listed under heading (3) in Figure 7—ie tendencies to focus on 'simple rules' that arise in an 'agent-centred' form—are predicted by this chapter's functional claim, and their persistence lends it further support.

Heading (4), finally, lists three more interrelated predictions, which are labelled 'content (social contract)', 'flexibility', and 'coordination'. Beginning with the first, the claim that the natural function of the human sense of obligation is to allow humans to resolve social contract problems flexibly has further implications for the content of perceived moral and legal obligations. Most obviously, these perceptions should exhibit some discernable tendency to reflect rules that in fact resolve social contract problems. This tendency should be discernable even if the people who perceive a given set of interpersonal obligations neither know what a social contract problem is nor reason with one another about the content these obligations and associated rights in terms of the concept of a social contract. At the same time, however, this chapter's central functional claim is perfectly compatible with the possibility that these psychological capacities serve some other functions (whether natural or artificial) as well. The tendency that is being proposed may thus co-exist with other, less cooperative tendencies, which can affect the perceived content of interpersonal obligations in other ways.[72] The present prediction is also consistent

[70] An 'agent-centred' requirement is defined as any requirement that can give different persons different fundamental aims, whereas an 'agent-neutral' requirement is defined as one that gives all agents the same fundamental aim. Many requirements can be framed in either agent-centred or agent-neutral terms. Consider, for example, the requirement that promises be kept—as discussed in the main text. If we construe this requirement to give all persons the single aim of minimizing the overall number of broken promises in the world (regardless of who is breaking them), then we will be construing it as agent-neutral. If, on the other hand, we construe this requirement as giving each person the separate aim of making sure he or she does not break his or her own promises, then we will be construing it as agent-centred. It should therefore be clear that the obligation to keep one's promises, as it typically appears in our perceptions of common-sense morality, is agent-centred.

[71] This arises in his evidence that humans cross-culturally respond to so-called 'trolley problems' in ways that show they have agent-centred moral intuitions. See Mikhail, *Elements of Moral Cognition* (n 6).

[72] This capacity does in fact appear to serve some other natural functions and to exhibit some antisocial tendencies. See Kar, 'The Two Faces of Morality' (n 6).

with the possibility—indeed probability—that this proposed tendency (ie to generate content that tracks the correct resolutions to social contract problems) is less than perfectly adapted to this function, especially in some modern circumstances that differ from the most common patterns of hunter-gatherer life.

It is therefore noteworthy that, despite these facts and despite the great amount of cultural variation that is often found in the moral and legal codes of different groups, a great number of rules that humans have taken to be obligatory in almost every society resolve social contract problems. Some obvious examples would include rules that prohibit lying, promise breaking, stealing, and the wanton infliction of physical harm. The present view would also explain why many philosophers who have tried to discern the deep principles that govern the perceived content of moral and political obligations in their respective societies have tended to arrive at social contract principles—which is precisely how the work of philosophers like Immanuel Kant, John Rawls, and Tim Scanlon can be read.[73] The fact that the human sense of obligation shows a discernible tendency to reflect the correct resolutions to social contract problems in so many different circumstances and incarnations, and often without any conscious understanding of the concept of a social contract problem, thus lends additional support to this chapter's central functional claim.

The prediction of 'flexibility', which refers to the claim that the content of perceived obligations is innately fixed, is in one sense already part of the definition of the natural function that is being claimed. This feature has been included to make room for the fact that different human groups exhibit different views about the legitimate content of morality and law. The present view is perfectly consistent with this fact for two basic reasons. First, social problems tend to *underdetermine* their correct resolutions, in the sense that more than one rule can often resolve a singe social contract problem. The social contract problem of the sheep herders discussed above can be resolved, for example, not only with a private property rule but also with a rule that prohibits overgrazing. Second, social contract problems are defined in such general terms that different human groups will tend to face many different and often changing social contract problems over time. Different human societies with different social histories should therefore transmit different portfolios of solutions to the specific cooperative problems they have faced. A psychological capacity that functions to allow humans to resolve social contract problems flexibly should therefore produce many of the patterns of cultural variation that are found in the larger ethnographic record.

The only other prediction listed under heading (4) is labelled 'coordination'. This last prediction can be explained by examining a problem that a flexible capacity

[73] The present view would also explain why competing utilitarian theories often produce recommendations that are psychologically counterintuitive

to resolve social contract problems might create. Earlier discussions have suggested that a capacity to resolve social contract problems can only remain evolutionarily stable if it includes second order psychological mechanisms that function to identify and exclude non-cooperators from the benefits of the social contract. This capacity must also include an epistemic capacity that generates inferences of non-cooperative motive from actions that are facially inconsistent with a code; and tendencies to take intentional breaches to warrant actions that would otherwise be impermissible. If different members of a group were to maintain highly uncoordinated senses of obligation, then the same psychological capacities that allow humans to identify and respond to rights, and might otherwise tend to produce critical forms of cooperation, will thus tend to generate escalating cycles of conflict. This is because the capacities would dispose the members of this group to perceive some others' actions as wrong, which these others perceive as innocent, and thus to engage in reactions that would otherwise be impermissible, and are in fact deemed impermissible by these others' lights. These reactions would thus tend to provoke counter-reactions, which have the very same properties, and would tend to provoke further rounds of counter-reaction—and so on down the line.

If the human capacity to identify and respond to rights is to function naturally to allow humans to resolve social contract problems flexibly, then it should therefore include special psychological mechanisms that allow groups to modify the content of their moral and legal codes while maintaining a sufficient modicum of interpersonal coordination over their codes' content. There is, in fact, evidence to suggest that practices of face-to-face normative discussion and disagreement with perceived insiders functions to coordinate the moral views of people who engage in it, and that these processes thus allow for both flexibility and coordination of moral content—even if the people who engage in these forms of discussion view moral truths to be timeless and fixed.[74] Coordination mechanisms like these appear particularly well adapted to the kinds of hunter-gatherer social structures that characterize the vast majority of the natural history of the human species. In these circumstances, face-to-face discussion would have allowed hunter-gatherer bands to adapt their moral codes to the different patterns of social contract problem that they faced while maintaining a sufficient modicum of interpersonal coordination over moral content.

The law, on the other hand, is a much more recent human creation, which tends to coordinate content in a very different way. The law depends first and foremost upon a division of psychological labour between most ordinary citizens and a much smaller group of officials, who are given lengthy training in how to

[74] See eg Haidt (n 7) 819–25; Allan Gibbard, *Wise Choices, Apt Feelings: A Theory of Normative Judgment* (Harvard UP 1992) 64–80.

identify the law. This training tends to produce coordinated perceptions among officials about how legal content is produced and changed, and the law contains further appellate mechanisms to settle any remaining disagreements among officials with jurisdiction in particular cases. Officials can thus produce a form of legal judgment that is sufficiently coordinated for present purposes, and most citizens in a well-functioning legal system exhibit attitudes of deference both to the law and to the final judgements of officials about its application in particular cases. The law thus offers a coordination mechanism that appears better adapted to resolving social contract problems in larger groups, where it is impossible for all members to engage in face-to-face discussion and where normative discussion often tends to create a plurality of uncoordinated moral views rather than consensus. The fact that coordination mechanisms of these kinds are found in both morality and law provides additional support for the claim that the natural function of the human sense of obligation is to resolve social contract problems flexibly.

For all of the foregoing reasons, the human capacity to identify and respond to rights, which operates through its effects on a more primary sense of obligation, appears to have the natural function of allowing humans to resolve social contract problems. It serves this function through the complex interaction of its many component parts, which together animate a deeply structured form of human social life and interaction. This form of life includes many familiar phenomena, such as: perceptions of obligation; special authority-dependent motives on the part of (most) obligees within a community to conform to these obligations; shared expectations of conformity in the community at large; shared dispositions to react to deviations in certain regular and predictable ways; epistemic capacities that function to identify people who are insufficiently motivated to follow the rules of a social contract; dispositions to base initial claims of wrongdoing on actions inconsistent with a code; dispositions to focus on the intentionality of perceived wrongs, and to answer these claims with a set of standard excuses and justifications that are in fact credited when available; tendencies to focus on obligations that reflect a large collection of relatively simple rules, rather than a single broad mandate; tendencies to perceive obligations as having an agent-centred form; some tendencies for perceived obligations to reflect real solutions to changing social contract problems; and a larger set of psychosocial mechanisms that tend to produce coordinated and flexible content. This form of life also includes certain cognitive capacities, which allow humans to understand and identify an indefinitely complex set of perceived rights, all of which operate—either directly, indirectly, or recursively—on this more primary sense of interpersonal obligation. The capacities that animate this distinctive form of human life are critical for the promotion of a more universal form of respect for human rights, and it is therefore *these* capacities that needs to be better understood within the human rights literature.

4. Conclusion: From Rights to Human Rights

This chapter has argued that humans have an innate psychological capacity to identify and respond to rights, which is bound up in certain systematic ways with a more primary sense of interpersonal obligation. This portfolio of psychological phenomena animates a deeply structured and highly familiar form of human social life and interaction, which cannot be understood as the product of a broad range of other moral and non-moral motives. This portfolio also has a specific natural function: to allow humans to resolve social contract problems flexibly. It is therefore an instance of an 'obligatum', which has been defined as any psychological phenomenon the natural function of which is to resolve social contract problems, and many of the structural features that one would predict for obligata have been shown to infuse the human sense of rights and obligation.

Human rights are nevertheless a distinctive class of rights and respect for them is at least in part a culturally emergent phenomenon. Before concluding, it will therefore help to suggest two ways in which a better understanding of the psychological capacity to identify and respond to rights might generate valuable insights into the psychological causes and conditions of human rights violations.

First, the discussions in this chapter suggest that much more attention needs to be paid to identifying the special factors that might engage the human capacity to identify and respond to rights and orient it to produce a more stable and universally shared respect for human rights in the modern world. This capacity may be innate, but it appears to have evolved in circumstances where its primary function was to resolve social contract problems in relatively small hunter-gatherer bands. This would explain why so many people over the course of world history have been inclined to treat other members of their primary groups as having some authority to make claims on their conduct but have not always been inclined to extend this form of respect further.

It is, however, not very plausible that this kind of lack of respect always arises from affirmative processes of 'dehumanization', at least if that process is construed as involving the purely cognitive failure to attribute mental states to others. The ethnographic record is too chocked full of cases where human groups view their enemies as formidable opponents, with a broad range of mental states, but do not view them as having the standing to make any claims on their conduct. It has, in other words, been quite common for people to view other people as having mental states and all of the other physical and psychological traits that make them part of the human species, without seeing their humanity as a status that automatically creates certain inalienable rights.[75]

[75] If, on the other hand, one sees another as having the standing to make claims on one's conduct, and hence as someone to whom one must be capable of justifying one's actions, it is hard to imagine how one could fail to attribute mental states to this other person.

Given these facts, the most critical question to ask is: what factors, or social conditions, might engage the innate human capacity to identify and respond to rights in ways that will incline more people, in more parts of the world, to extend a form of treatment that they readily give to in-group members to all of humanity?

Second, when trying to answer this question, one should remember that obligata have been defined functionally and can therefore be multiply instantiated. This means that humans might, in principle, have more than one set of obligata, which animate more than one sense of obligation. This is more than just an abstract possibility: humans appear fully capable of developing distinctive senses of obligation (eg moral, religious, legal, international), and these different senses appear better or worse suited to resolving different classes of social contract problems.

If one wants to know how to create the social and psychological conditions needed to support a more stable and universal sense of respect for human rights in the modern world, then one will therefore need to ask a number of important questions. Does the human sense of moral obligation, standing alone, exhibit tendencies toward pluralism, parochialism and in-group favouritism, due in part to its evolutionary origins in hunter-gatherer bands and its tendencies to coordinate content through face-to-face normative discussion? If so, then can the stable emergence of a separate sense of international legal obligation respond to these problems by supporting a more unified and coordinated conception of human rights for use throughout the modern world? What, then, are the social and psychological conditions needed for the emergence of a more robust sense of respect for international law in the modern world?[76] And how, finally, should international law interact with moral and domestic legal codes?

These are the types of questions that further research into the psychological causes and conditions of human rights violations will need to answer. When investigating them, researchers should remain sensitive to the role that dehumanization can play in generating human rights violations. They must, however, also discard the prevailing assumption that dehumanization as traditionally construed is the main culprit.

Further Reading

Haslam N, 'Dehumanization: an Integrative Review' (2006) 10 *Personality and Social Psychology Review* 252

Kar RB, 'The Deep Structure of Law and Morality' (2006) 84 *Tex L Rev* 877

——'The Two Faces of Morality: How Evolutionary Theory Can Both Vindicate *and* Debunk Morality' in James E Fleming and Sanford Levinson (eds), *NOMOS: Evolution and Morality* (vol II, NYU Press 2012) 31–99

[76] On this question, see Robin B Kar, 'Outcasting, Globalization, and the Emergence of International Law' (2012) 121 *Yale LJ* 411.

——'Outcasting, Globalization, and the Emergence of International Law' (2012) 121 *Yale LJ Online* 411
McFarland S, 'The Slow Creation of Humanity' (2011) 32 *Political Psychology* 1
Mikhail J, 'Universal Moral Grammar: Theory, Evidence and the Future' (2007) 11 *Trends in Cognitive Science* 143
——*Elements of Moral Cognition: Rawls' Linguistic Analogy and the Cognitive Science of Moral and Legal Judgment* (CUP 2011)
——'Moral Grammar and Human Rights: Some Reflections on Cognitive Science and Enlightenment Rationalism' in Ryan Goodman, Derek Jinks, and Andrew K Woods (eds), *Understanding Social Action, Promoting Human Rights* (OUP 2012) 160–202

CHAPTER 6

ANTHROPOLOGY AND THE GROUNDS OF HUMAN RIGHTS

MARK GOODALE

One should necessarily examine the curious history of anthropology's ambivalent relationship to human rights for at least two reasons. First, this history illuminates certain basic dilemmas associated with the emergence of the post-war human rights project and the ways in which particular political and philosophical approaches to human rights became more powerful than other alternatives. Indeed, there is a distinct irony in the fact that subtle forms of power came to define a legal and ethical regime that was conceived in order to prevent or redress the violent assertion of illegitimate power within international relations. The study of anthropology's exile from the early and formative development of human rights reveals how this shift in function was possible. Although not widely appreciated, either within the wider human rights community or in academia, the exclusion of anthropology from the critical moments in the emergence of the postwar human rights system would have lasting consequences.[1]

By the mid-twentieth century, anthropology had established itself as the pre-eminent source of scientific expertise on many empirical facets of culture and society, from law to kinship and from religion to morality. Yet it was at precisely

[1] An earlier version of this chapter appeared in Mark Goodale, *Surrendering to Utopia: An Anthropology of Human Rights* (Stanford UP 2009).

this moment, when anthropology as a discipline was reaching the peak of its legitimacy and self-confidence, that it was blocked from contributing in any meaningful way to the development of understanding about what was—and still is—the most important putative cross-cultural fact: that human beings are essentially the same and that this essential sameness entails a specific normative framework. It was as if everything society knew or thought about the evolution of *Homo sapiens* included contributions from every discipline except biological anthropology, which, despite its exclusion, nevertheless continued to produce knowledge that spoke directly to the problem. The history of anthropology's relationship to human rights, therefore, enables a better understanding of how and why human rights developed as they did and, by extension, the ways in which they might have developed had the insights of anthropology played a role.

The examination of this intellectual and political history is not only, or even most importantly, retrospective. Anthropological forms of knowledge and practical engagement can and should be used as part of a wider project of reconceptualizing the meaning and potential of human rights. Both the historical absence of anthropology from the development of contemporary human rights and the more recent attempts by individual anthropologists and the discipline's largest professional association to re-engage with human rights as both an object of study and a vehicle for emancipatory political practice contain justifications for this assertion.

If the wider engagement of anthropology is a necessary precondition for the transformation of contemporary human rights, it is in part because anthropology as a discipline is committed to the systematic and comparative investigation of social practices, including normative practices. The examination of human rights in terms of anthropology's troubled history is meant to reveal both profound potential and basic limitations—not within anthropology, but within a reconfigured human rights.

1. A Curious History

In 1947, the United Nations (UN) Commission on Human Rights, which Eleanor Roosevelt chaired, sought statements on the draft version of what would become the 1948 Universal Declaration of Human Rights. It solicited these statements in a variety of ways and through a variety of institutional channels, perhaps most importantly through the efforts of the United Nations Educational, Scientific, and Cultural Organization (UNESCO). UNESCO sought statements on the proposed declaration from academic, cultural, and artistic institutions and individuals. Although the colonialist milieu within which the United Nations emerged after the Second World War made any attempt to achieve universal consensus through its organs essentially utopian, UNESCO intended its outreach efforts to gauge the diversity of world opinion about what Johannes Morsink describes as the 'aggressive' push to forge an 'international consensus about human rights'.[2]

Within anthropology, conventional wisdom says that UNESCO asked the American Anthropological Association (AAA) to write an advisory opinion on human rights, which it (through one or more of its members) did in 1947, after which *American Anthropologist*, the flagship journal of the AAA, published this official AAA 'Statement on Human Rights', simultaneous with the AAA Executive Board's submission of it to the Commission for Human Rights on behalf of its membership. The journal did publish the 'Statement on Human Rights' in 1947 as the lead article in its October–December issue,[3] prefaced by a note that indicated that the Executive Board of the AAA had submitted it to the UN Commission on Human Rights.

It would not be surprising if UNESCO had turned to the AAA for an advisory opinion from the field of anthropology on a proposed declaration of universal human rights.[4] By the mid-twentieth century, all three major anthropological traditions—'schools' is perhaps too strong a description—had together established themselves as an important source of scientific knowledge about the range of both diversity and unity in human culture and society. The evidence indicates, however, that most of the conventional wisdom about the Statement on Human Rights is wrong.

Documents in the US National Anthropological Archives[5] show no record of UNESCO making a request to the AAA for an advisory opinion on a declaration of human rights. Instead, it appears that UNESCO approached one anthropologist, Melville Herskovits, in his capacity as chairman of the Committee for International Cooperation in Anthropology of the National Research Council (NRC), a post which he assumed in 1945.[6] Herskovits had been a student of Franz Boas at Columbia University, where he earned his PhD in anthropology in 1923. Although his research and writings present a more complicated theoretical and political picture than has been supposed, there is no question that Herskovits's orientation to culture and society was shaped by his training in what is known as American historical particularism, an anthropological approach that Boas developed, which emphasized studying the evolution of particular cultural traditions within their historical contexts.[7]

[2] Johannes Morsink, *The Universal Declaration of Human Rights: Origins, Drafting, Intent* (U Pennsylvania Press 1999) 12.

[3] American Anthropological Association, 'Statement on Human Rights' (1947) 49 *Amer Anthrop* 539.

[4] The Statement on Human Rights was published almost exactly one year before the UN Third General Assembly adopted the Universal Declaration of Human Rights on 10 December 1948.

[5] A Smithsonian Museum Support Center in Suitland, Maryland, currently houses these archives. I thank the administrator of the National Anthropological Archives for (NAA) allowing me to conduct research in the archives and for guiding me through the documentary sources of the AAA.

[6] Herskovits, a prominent American anthropologist, was a member of the AAA's Executive Board during this time and chairman of the Department of Anthropology at Northwestern University.

[7] George W Stocking (ed), *A Franz Boas Reader: The Shaping of American Anthropology, 1883–1911* (U Chicago Press 1989).

In focusing so intensely and ethnographically on particular cultures within what was believed to be their unique historical trajectories, American cultural anthropologists like Herskovits became associated with a distinct outlook toward social phenomena. Two aspects of this outlook are relevant to the history of anthropology's relationship with human rights. First, the detailed study of cultures within history revealed the ways in which particular dimensions of culture—law, politics, religion, morality—resulted from a process of situated evolution, one that could not be understood in general terms or through the use of universal analytical categories. There might be 'patterns of culture', as Ruth Benedict, another Boasian, described them; but these patterns were only rough outlines, ways of describing the fact that all cultures are in fact patterned in their own terms. The content of these patterns, however—the features that made a particular culture 'Japanese', say, and not 'Norwegian'—was the result of the entire range of historical contingencies that could never be reproduced or predicted for other places and times. It was only a short step from this essentially empirical approach to culture, to something more normative; if each culture was unique, the result of a particular and contingent history, then it was not possible to evaluate or measure cultures in terms of some set of standards that could be justified in a way that was not, itself, part of a particular cultural tradition or of interplay between cultural traditions. This normative implication of American historical particularism is usually labelled as 'cultural relativism'.

Second, there was a political dimension to American historical particularism and the kind of anthropology the Boasians pursued. Although Boas believed anthropology to be the 'science of mankind', he also believed that it provided a valuable social function by documenting the richness of cultures that were under threat of destruction, tragically misunderstood, or both. American cultural anthropology at mid-century—less so British and French social anthropology—was concerned with the condition of what today would be described as marginalized or subaltern populations, and this concern was the result of both epistemological and political imperatives within American anthropology and of individual anthropologists. So when UNESCO approached Melville Herskovits through the National Research Council's Committee on International Cooperation in Anthropology, he considered the ways in which a declaration of universal human rights would affect the cultural traditions and political standing of those populations that seemed to stand apart from the confluence of legal, political, and social forces behind the 'aggressive' drive for an international human rights system.

Although UNESCO contacted Herskovits by virtue of his position as head of an influential NRC committee dedicated to fostering international collaboration between anthropologists and other scientists, and to the development of what today would be called 'public anthropology' (ie the use of anthropological knowledge within consequential public debates), it is important to acknowledge that this NRC committee acted as a de facto committee of the AAA, or at least coordinated its activities with the AAA Executive Board. Most of the members of the NRC committee during the mid-1940s were also members of the AAA. In 1946, the year before Herskovits drafted the Statement on Human Rights, this included one past and one future president of the AAA.[8]

Nevertheless, the documentary record shows that UNESCO did *not* first contact the AAA; rather, UNESCO solicited Melville Herskovits's committee at the NRC for a representative anthropological opinion on a declaration of human rights.[9] Herskovits worked on his Statement on Human Rights in early 1947 and began communicating with the AAA leadership about their intentions regarding it. By June 1947, Herskovits had already sent the Statement to UNESCO, on behalf of himself and the NRC anthropology committee. At the same time, Ralph Beals, an AAA Executive Board member, was writing to Clyde Kluckhohn, the AAA president, with a recommendation that Herskovits's 'rights of man' statement be adopted by the Executive Board and published as the lead article in the forthcoming *American Anthropologist*.[10] To underscore the importance the Executive Board gave to the Statement, Beals recommended that the AAA order 1000 reprints (with special covers) of the Statement for public relations purposes.

Although, in late 1947, *American Anthropologist* published the Statement with a note indicating that the Statement was forwarded to UNESCO, this must be seen as a post hoc ratification of what Herskovits had already done some four to six months earlier. There is very little evidence that the Commission for Human Rights considered the Statement during its deliberations. Further, despite the fact that the AAA was a much smaller and less representative organization at mid-century, it still functioned as a democratic association, in which the membership voted on the major initiatives. With the Statement on Human Rights, however, no such vote took place, and, except for correspondence between several high-ranking AAA members, there is no indication that association members had any knowledge of the Statement until its publication in *American Anthropologist*.

The relationship of American anthropology to human rights has been fundamentally misconstrued in a second manner. In Morsink's otherwise excellent history of the 'origins, drafting, and intent' of the Universal Declaration of Human Rights (UDHR), his foregrounding of the 1947 AAA Statement on Human Rights gives a distorted impression of it and, by extension, anthropology's impact on the emergence of human rights after the Second World War. In fact, he begins his history with a detailed discussion of the Statement's content and suggests that the Commission on Human Rights proceeded *despite* the objections and criticisms made in the Statement. He mentions that in '1947 the UN Human Rights

[8] Robert Lowie, 1935, and Frederica de Laguna, 1967. NAA, 'General File' (1930–49) Box 23.

[9] No evidence has surfaced that other professional anthropological associations were solicited by UNESCO during this time.

[10] NAA, 'AAA Executive Board Minutes' (March 1946–May 1954) Box 192.

Commission that wrote the Declaration received a long memorandum from the American Anthropological Association'.[11] Then later, after reviewing parts of the Statement, he observes that the 'drafters of the Declaration... went ahead in spite of these warnings'.[12] As Morsink's own comprehensive account of the drafting process makes clear, however, it is likely that even if the Statement on Human Rights was technically received from the NRC or, later, the AAA Executive Board, it played almost no role in the drafting of the UDHR.

The status of the Statement on Human Rights among anthropologists has also at times been misconstrued. With the exception of two recent articles on the relationship between anthropology and human rights,[13] two earlier extended publications attempted to characterize this history, one by an anthropologist[14] and the other by a law professor.[15] Both attempts leave the wrong impression about the events surrounding the production of the Statement on Human Rights, and, more importantly, the impact of the Statement on anthropologists who might have participated more actively in the development of human rights theory and practice in the early post-UDHR period.

Messer and Engle both tend to read the early history of anthropology's relationship to human rights in terms of its much more recent history. Engle says that anthropologists 'have been embarrassed ever since' the publication of the Statement in 1947[16] and even more directly characterizes the impact of the Statement on the AAA itself. As she writes, '[f]or the past fifty years, the Statement has caused the AAA great shame. Indeed, the term "embarrassment" is continually used in reference to the Statement'.[17] The problem is that, with the exception of three brief comments on the Statement published in 1947 and 1948,[18] both the Statement and human rights vanish from the anthropological radar for almost forty years. It is difficult, therefore, to demonstrate that that Statement on Human Rights caused widespread shame or embarrassment after its publication, because there was very little reaction at all, either in the period immediately after its publication or during the decades in which the international, and eventually transnational, human rights regimes emerged. Why and how this happened is described in more detail below, but the fact remains that American anthropology, not to mention the wider

[11] Morsink (n 2) ix. [12] Morsink (n 2) x.

[13] See eg Mark Goodale, 'Introduction to "Anthropology and Human Rights in a New Key"' (2006) 108 *Amer Anthrop* 1; Mark Goodale, 'Toward a Critical Anthropology of Human Rights' (2006) 47 *Current Anthropology* 485.

[14] Ellen Messer, 'Anthropology and Human Rights' (1993) 22 *Annual Review of Anthropology* 221.

[15] Karen Engle, 'From Skepticism to Embrace: Human Rights and the American Anthropological Association from 1947–1999' (2001) 23 *Hum Rts Q* 536.

[16] Engle (n 15) 536. [17] Engle (n 15) 541.

[18] HG Barnett, 'On Science and Human Rights' (1948) 50 *Amer Anthrop* 352; Julian Steward, 'Comment on the Statement on Human Rights' (1948) 50 *Amer Anthrop* 351; John W Bennett, 'Science and Human Rights: Reason and Action' (1949) 51 *Amer Anthrop* 329.

discipline, played almost no role in the formal development of human rights theory or institutional practice in the important first decades of the postwar period.

1.1 Melville Herskovits's Statement on Human Rights

The Statement on Human Rights has been poorly understood, most commonly construed—especially by scholars who have rewritten the early history of anthropology's relationship to human rights in order to make a clean break—as an example of cultural relativism run amok, something made all the more unpardonable by the events that led to the founding of the United Nations and the push to create an international political and legal order based on universal human rights.

In several of his essays on the nineteenth-century Russian intelligentsia, the intellectual historian Isaiah Berlin has written that that which characterized the group of disaffected young people who would eventually become revolutionaries, was their proclivity to borrow ideas from Western Europe and then to take them to their logical, absurd, and violent extreme. Herskovits's Statement on Human Rights is usually characterized in this way: yes, he was well-meaning; yes, cultural relativism was developed as an intellectual buffer against colonialism, racism, and all other universal systems that had the effect of oppressing some human populations while elevating others; yes, the principles of the Universal Declaration cannot be understood apart from the political and economic interests associated with its creation; *nevertheless*, what about the Nazis? How could anthropologists employ their services against the Nazis during the war (as they did in considerable numbers, in different capacities), yet lack a legitimate moral basis for doing so? Shouldn't the contrarian Statement on Human Rights be simply dismissed as either the misapplication of certain ideas about cultural diversity, or as a piece of bad logic, or both?

Herskovits's and then the AAA's Statement on Human Rights is much more complicated, and thus revealing, than its caricature would suggest. The Statement makes three distinct critiques of a proposed declaration of universal human rights. These can be divided into the epistemological, the empirical, and the ethical. First, Herskovits made the observation that because the Commission on Human Rights was interested in gathering opinions on human rights from different perspectives and approaches to knowledge, he was required to consider the idea of universal human rights *as a scientist*. And because the 'sciences that deal[t] with the study of human culture'[19] had not developed methods for evaluating a proposed list of human rights in relation to the many other moral and legal systems that exist in the world, many of which would appear to conflict with the set of human rights

[19] AAA, 'Statement on Human Rights' (n 3) 539.

emerging from the Commission, anthropology was unable to provide the tools necessary for proving—or disproving—their scientific validity.

Herskovits also played both sides of the problem, assuming, for the sake of argument, that the anthropological evidence *could* be used to make claims about the validity (or not) of a proposed declaration of human rights. As he quite sensibly explained:

Over the past fifty years, the many ways in which man resolves the problems of subsistence, of social living, of political regulation of group life, of reaching accord with the Universe and satisfying his aesthetic drives has been widely documented by the researches of anthropologists among peoples living in all parts of the world. All peoples do achieve these ends. No two of them, however, do so in exactly the same way, and some of them employ means that differ, often strikingly, from one another.[20]

This has been taken as a rigid and dogmatic expression of cultural relativism, which all but guaranteed that Herskovits would reject the idea of universal human rights. But what is ignored is what comes soon after. The real problem, he argues, is not with the idea of human rights itself; rather, the problem is that for political and economic reasons, proposals for human rights (so far) have always been conceived for the wrong purposes and based on the wrong set of assumptions. As he says:

Definitions of freedom, concepts of the nature of human rights, and the like, have . . . been narrowly drawn. Alternatives have been decried, and suppressed where controls have been established over non-European peoples. The hard core of *similarities* between cultures has consistently been overlooked.[21]

In other words, he seems to be suggesting here that the empirical question is still open; a declaration of universal human rights that is legitimate across cultures *might* be drafted—one that codifies and expresses this 'hard core of similarities'. But the Anglo-European proposals of 1947, which became the UDHR, did not speak to this 'hard core of similarities', and so they should be rejected.

Finally, and arguably most importantly, Herskovits raised a number of ethical objections to the proposal for a declaration of human rights by the United Nations. This critique, more than any other, has been ignored in the subsequent rush to condemn Herskovits. The substance of the ethical critiques in the Statement on Human Rights, taken together, underscore the basic fact, rarely acknowledged, that it was, above all else, an act of moral and intellectual courage, given the context; the horrors of the Holocaust and the violence of the Second World War were being fully exposed through the ongoing Nuremberg Trials, among other sources; there was broad consensus among the major powers around an international legal and political order based on some version of human rights; and, behind all of this, scholars, experts, political leaders, and influential public figures across the range were

[20] AAA, 'Statement on Human Rights' (n 3) 540.
[21] AAA, 'Statement on Human Rights' (n 3) 540 (emphasis in original).

hurrying to lend their services in order to bring this new legal and political order to fruition.

Herskovits, followed by the Executive Board of the AAA, forcefully dissented. Eventually, in his view, a declaration of human rights, instead of serving as a bulwark against fascism and the oppression of the weak, would become a doctrine 'employed to implement economic exploitation and... deny the right to control their own affairs to millions of people over the world, where the expansion of Europe and America has not [already] meant the literal extermination of whole populations'.[22] This concern was not only prospective; Herskovits drew on history in making the argument that declarations of human rights were often legal smokescreens for the oppression of one group of humans by another. For example, the 'American Declaration of Independence, or the American Bill of Rights, could be written by men who themselves were slave-owners', and the revolutionary French embrace of the rights of man only became legitimate when extended 'to the French slave-owning colonies'.[23] Regardless of the growing international consensus, regardless of the stated intentions of what claimed to be a diverse and representative Commission on Human Rights (and, more generally, United Nations), and regardless of the democratic nature of the UN Charter, Herskovits refused to see the proposed declaration of human rights as anything other than a set of aspirations 'circumscribed by the standards of [a] single culture'.[24] Such a 'limited Declaration',[25] Herskovits argued, would exclude more people than it would include, *because of*—not despite—its claims of universality.

1.2 The wilderness years

After 1948, the international human rights system emerged only haltingly, in part because the imperatives of the bipolar Cold War world imposed a series of political, ideological, and cultural constraints on the realization of what were clearly competing visions for international affairs. Even though Eleanor Roosevelt had hoped that the idea of human rights would be carried along what she called a 'curious grapevine' behind the walls of repressive states and ideologies, to reach those most in need of its protections, her dream had to be deferred.[26]

In the meantime, anthropologists *were* participating in the development of postwar institutions and knowledge regimes, but not those that were framed in terms of human rights. A good example of public anthropology during the 1950s and early

22 AAA, 'Statement on Human Rights' (n 3) 540.

23 AAA, 'Statement on Human Rights' (n 3) 542.

24 AAA, 'Statement on Human Rights' (n 3) 543.

25 AAA, 'Statement on Human Rights' (n 3) 543.

26 William Korey, *NGOs and the Universal Declaration on Human Rights: 'A Curious Grapevine'* (St Martin's Press 1998).

1960s was the formative role that anthropologists, in particular Alfred Métraux, Ashley Montagu, and Claude Lévi-Strauss, played in the series of UNESCO statements on race, which called into question the biological concept of race and described in some detail the ways in which race should instead be seen as a social construct. This provocative and progressive reframing of the race issue came at a time when, in the United States and South Africa for example, the traditional biological understanding of racial differences was still codified in law and reflected in patterns of political and social inequality. Yet human rights did not frame this work on race, despite the basic idea of human rights that assumes that human beings are essentially the same, both biologically and morally.

Anthropologists, including Melville Herskovits himself,[27] were active in the civil rights movement in the United States throughout this period, but civil rights were understood differently from human rights, within a different system of political and legal legitimacy, and anchored in a different set of assumptions about human nature and the foundations of citizenship.

While anthropologists during the 1950s and 1960s did not frame their different *political* interventions in terms of human rights, the anthropological voice was equally absent from developments in the *philosophy* of human rights, especially to the extent that such evolving ideas influenced the content of the important instruments that followed the UDHR. For anthropology, then, these were the wilderness years, the period in which the international human rights system was established as a set of ideas, practices, and documents, despite the fact that the actual protection or enforcement of human rights by nation-states and international institutions was often minimal throughout much of the world. The emergence and eventual transnationalization of human rights discourse, after the end of the Cold War, would not have been possible without these preexisting institutional and philosophical foundations, which were laid without contributions from anthropological forms of knowledge and methods of studying social practices.

1.3 Social justice and other Universalist projects

The political and cultural climates changed dramatically during the mid- to late-1960s, and anthropologists were active participants in these changes. A major difference between the mid-1950s to early-1960s, and the late-1960s through the 1970s, was the fact that the anthropological contributions to the political and cultural movements of the latter period were fuelled, in part, by correspondingly dramatic intellectual shifts within the wider discipline. Anthropologists still did not use the idea of human rights in their writings to justify their participation in these

[27] Jerry Gershenhorn, *Melville J Herskovits and the Racial Politics of Knowledge* (U Nebraska Press 2004).

political and cultural movements; rather, the most common intellectual (and political) rationale for the anthropological participation in anti-colonialism, or protests against the war in Vietnam, was some version of Marxism or neo-Marxism. What is important herein about the incorporation of the Marxist critique in anthropological writings on social justice issues, is that it offered an alternative universalizing framework for addressing pressing political and social problems, one that, at least theoretically, was as hostile to the cultural relativism of the 1947 Statement on Human Rights as the competing claims of the UDHR itself.

In sum, during the 1960s and 1970s anthropology underwent a profound shift, one mirrored in other academic disciplines, in the United States and elsewhere, that had the effect of creating formal *epistemological* links between scholarship and political activism. The Marxist (or neo-Marxist) emphasis on the inevitability of conflict, the role of intellectuals in political movements, and the importance of understanding structures of inequality within broad historical contexts, made it an ideal source of inspiration for anthropologists desperately seeking a way out of the box that enclosed the dominant theoretical approaches of earlier generations, which either ignored the dynamic interplay between cultures (American historical particularism); downplayed the wider historical, economic, and political forces that shaped particular cultures and societies (British functionalism and structural-functionalism); or denied the influence of history altogether (French structuralism). So, although human rights did not figure into the profound shift in the way many anthropologists justified their participation in movements for social justice, the influence of Marxism inadvertently created an opening through which another (and essentially liberal) universalizing project could pass. By the end of the 1970s, anthropology was ready for human rights. But were human rights ready for anthropology?

1.4 The prodigal son returns

It was not until the 1980s that anthropology as a discipline took a sustained interest in human rights, but there was an earlier event that foreshadowed the shape of this new interest. In 1972, the anthropologist David Maybury-Lewis and his wife, Pia Maybury-Lewis, co-founded Cultural Survival, Inc. They did not establish Cultural Survival as a research institution, but rather as a non-governmental organization dedicated to the survival of indigenous cultures through political advocacy, education, and public awareness programmes. There is some question, however, about the extent to which Cultural Survival was founded initially as a human rights organization or an indigenous cultures organization that only later made indigenous rights a centrepiece for education and advocacy. Although Cultural Survival now makes 'indigenous peoples' rights' the basic framework through which it works to ensure the survival of indigenous cultures in different parts of the world, this focus apparently did not emerge within the organization until the 1980s. Nevertheless, the plight of indigenous peoples eventually became *the* issue on which anthropology staked a claim within human rights; it was a small claim at the beginning, to be sure, but as indigenous rights discourse took on greater importance in the 1980s, anthropology's involvement became more noticeable and politically consequential.

The 1980s were turbulent times for anthropology. Especially in the United States, the epistemological shifts of the 1960s and 1970s[28] came home to roost in the form of a period of intense disciplinary self-critique and eventual fragmentation. By the mid-1980s, anthropology as a discipline was in a state of crisis, with clear lines forming between anthropologists who wanted to reaffirm the scientific foundations of the discipline and those who saw these same foundations as a symbol of a longer history of Western colonialism, orientalism, and the assertion of technocratic power against vulnerable populations. The critics of scientific anthropology[29] came close to dismantling American cultural anthropology, in particular; at the very least, they made a series of arguments about research methods, ethnographic writing, and the nature of anthropology as a neo-colonial encounter that had the effect of painting anthropology into a corner.

There were two major ways out of this corner, one theoretical and the other political. For some anthropologists, the period of intense critique was both revelatory and liberating. Finally, here was a public debate within anthropology about the basic questions of scientific legitimacy, the relationship between science and economic and political exploitation, and, even more abstractly, the questionable assumptions about the nature of social reality on which the 'science of mankind' depended. But if this public debate was a revelation for many anthropologists, the path toward liberation quickly became highly theoretical and disconnected from the concerns with social practice that figured, at least symbolically, in some of the field's earlier critical writings. Instead, the earlier discussion of the problematic nature of the great object/subject divide within social science evolved into an extended debate about subjectivity itself;[30] the critique of ethnographic writing transformed into a debate over the politics of writing genres;[31] and concerns over the way anthropologists chose places in which to conduct fieldwork evolved into an excursus into the definitions and implications of 'space', 'place', and 'the field'.[32]

[28] During this time, scholarship and political action were connected within one of several variations of Marxist/neo-Marxist social theory.

[29] Richard G Fox (ed), *Recapturing Anthropology: Working in the Present* (SAR Press 1991); James Clifford and George E Marcus (eds), *Writing Culture: The Poetics and Politics of Ethnography* (U California Press 1986).

[30] Melford E Spiro, 'Cultural Relativism and the Future of Anthropology' (1986) 1 *Cultural Anthropology* 259.

[31] Roger Sanjek (ed), *Fieldnotes: The Makings of Anthropology* (Cornell UP 1990).

[32] Vered Amit (ed), *Constructing the Field: Ethnographic Fieldwork in the Contemporary World* (Routledge 1999).

Another response to the disciplinary crisis within anthropology emerged in the 1980s and early 1990s. Since much of the critique of anthropology focused on the ways in which anthropologists were unwitting actors in larger political and economic projects, some anthropologists reacted not by trying to eliminate the political from anthropology, but by making anthropology *more* political. The idea was to put anthropological knowledge to work at the service of specific groups of people struggling against specific forms of systematic oppression and violence. For anthropologists working with indigenous peoples, this was an obvious move, since many indigenous groups found themselves suffering under a range of new or intensified constraints, as the era of neoliberalism took root in places like Latin America. Parallel to the politicization of anthropology and the increase in violence against indigenous peoples as a result of neoliberal political and economic restructuring during the mid- to late-1980s, another development made the anthropological embrace of human rights possible: the advent of 'indigenous rights' as a distinct and recognized category within the broader human rights system.

For some anthropologists, indigenous rights discourse provided a means through which they could put their understanding of an essentially political anthropology into practice. What eventually became a transnational indigenous rights movement provided a way out of the human rights wilderness for anthropology. The discipline that embodied the most promise as a source of knowledge about the meanings and potential of human rights in 1948, but which had spent the intervening decades in exile as the idea of human rights was refined conceptually and elaborated institutionally, could now return home. The problem for anthropology was that this way home, while creating new openings for political and institutional action, had the effect of obscuring other possible ways in which anthropology might contribute to human rights theory and practice. In the end, this narrowness in anthropology's (re-)engagement with human rights would prove to be only temporary.

Major shifts within the AAA can symbolize the new orientation of anthropology toward human rights. In 1990, the AAA established a Special Commission, which Terence Turner chaired, to investigate encroachments on traditional Yanomami territory by the Brazilian state.[33] The creation of this commission and its subsequent report (1991) led AAA Executive Board to establish a Commission on Human Rights (1992), which it charged with:

> develop[ing] a human rights conceptual framework and identify[ing] relevant human rights issues...develop[ing] human rights education and networking, and...develop[ing] and implement[ing] mechanisms for organizational action on issues affecting the AAA, its members and the discipline.[34]

[33] The following is drawn from: Barbara Rose Johnston, Committee for Human Rights, '1995–2000 Cumulative 5-Year Report' (*American Anthropological Association*, 30 January 2001) <http://www.aaanet.org/committees/cfhr/ar95-00.htm> accessed 20 January 2008.

[34] Johnston, 'Cumulative 5-Year Report' (n 33).

In 1995, the Commission on Human Rights was converted into a permanent standing committee of the Association—the Committee for Human Rights. Among other activities, the members of the Committee for Human Rights began working on a new statement of principles that would have the effect of definitively repudiating the 1947 Statement on Human Rights. These efforts culminated in the 1999 'Declaration on Anthropology and Human Rights'.[35] Unlike in the case of the Statement on Human Rights, a majority vote of the general AAA membership *did* formally adopt this Declaration.

The Declaration's most important assertion is that '[p]eople and groups have a generic right to realize their capacity for culture'.[36] Far from expressing any doubts about the cross-cultural validity of human rights instruments like the Universal Declaration, the 1999 Declaration locates a putative human right to realize a capacity for culture within a set of as-yet-to-be-articulated human rights that actually go well beyond the current rights that international law recognizes. As the Declaration states, its new position 'reflects a commitment to human rights consistent with international principles but not limited by them'.[37] The Declaration thus clearly reversed the AAA's earlier position on human rights, but it also signalled the conversion of (at least a subset of) the world's largest association of professional anthropologists into a human rights advocacy non-governmental organization focused on vulnerable populations and emerging rights categories.

Finally, in 2000, the Committee for Human Rights augmented its original set of guidelines and objectives into a set of operating principles for the Committee: (1) to promote and protect human rights; (2) to expand the definition of human rights within an anthropological perspective; (3) to work internally with the membership of the AAA to educate anthropologists and to mobilize their support for human rights; (4) to work externally with foreign colleagues, the people and groups with whom anthropologists work, and other human rights organizations to develop an anthropological perspective on human rights and to consult with them on human rights violations and the appropriate actions to be taken; (5) to influence and educate the media, policymakers, non-governmental organizations, and decision-makers in the private sector; and (6) to encourage research on all aspects of human rights from the conceptual to the applied.[38]

[35] Committee on Human Rights, 'Declaration on Anthropology and Human Rights' (AAA, June 1999) <http://www.aaanet.org/about/Policies/statements/Declaration-on-Anthropology-and-Human-Rights.cfm> accessed 28 May 2013.

[36] Committee on Human Rights, 'Declaration on Anthropology and Human Rights' (n 35).

[37] Committee on Human Rights, 'Declaration on Anthropology and Human Rights' (n 35).

[38] Johnston, 'Cumulative 5-Year Report' (n 33).

1.5 Toward an ecumenical anthropology of human rights

After the AAA ratified the 1999 Declaration, the Association continued to transform its orientation toward human rights. The Committee for Human Rights became one of the most visible and active of the Association's working bodies, through a series of high-profile investigations and interventions, a website dedicated to human rights activism and education, and its collaboration with other human rights bodies within other professional associations.

After 1995, the work of the Committee for Human Rights was not simply political. Apart from the 1993 review essay by Ellen Messer already mentioned—which was as much a programmatic call to action as a review of anthropology and human rights—several founding members of the Committee brought together their arguments for a robust engagement with human rights in a special issue of the *Journal of Anthropological Research*.[39] One of these articles, by Terence Turner,[40] encapsulated both the importance and tone of this period in anthropology's relationship with human rights. Turner, whose own activist scholarship on behalf of the Kayapo has come to embody anthropology's rediscovery of human rights and its repudiation of what are understood to be the mistakes of the 1947 generation, argued that anthropologists should contribute to an 'emancipatory cultural politics'.[41] By this, he meant that much of the emerging cultural rights discourse has been, and should continue to be, supported through a kind of anthropological research that is conducted *in terms of* specific projects for social change. And because human rights—for example, the 'right to culture' that the 1999 Declaration (which Turner played a major role in drafting) described—had become essential to these projects, especially those involving indigenous people, anthropological knowledge could prove useful in making legal and political claims in the increasingly dominant language of rights. This emancipatory cultural politics approach to human rights through anthropology remains the primary orientation for anthropologists interested in human rights, including those who work outside academia in high-profile roles within the non-governmental and activist communities.

Beginning about 1995, another anthropological approach to human rights emerged. Here, anthropologists converted the practice of human rights into a topic for ethnographic research and analysis. They reconceptualized human rights, in part as a transnational discourse linked to the spread of neoliberal logics of legal and political control after the end of the Cold War. As such, anthropologists working in this analytical mode remained ambivalent, or even sceptical, about social

[39] (1997) 53 *Journal of Anthropological Research*.

[40] Terence Turner, 'Human Rights, Human Difference: Anthropology's Contribution to an Emancipatory Cultural Politics' (1997) 53 *Journal of Anthropological Research* 273.

[41] Turner (n 40).

actors' use of human rights discourse in the course of their struggles for social change. This research and analysis, made possible by the rapid rise in human rights talk and institutional development since the early 1990s, both documented the contradictions and contingencies that surround the practice of human rights and led to the creation of a cross-cultural database on the meanings of human rights.[42]

Finally, even more recently, yet a third approach to human rights through anthropology can be distinguished. To a certain extent, a critical anthropology of human rights synthesizes both the emancipatory cultural politics and ethnographic approaches; it is committed, at some level, to the idea of human rights (though in some cases a radically reconfigured idea), and it makes information derived from the practice of human rights the basis for analysis, critique, policymaking, and political action.[43] There are profound implications to making the practice of human rights both the conceptual source for understanding what human rights *are* (and can be) and the source of legitimacy for claims based on human rights, not the least of which is the fact that it calls into question many of the basic assumptions of postwar human rights theory and practice. Moreover, to the extent that the international human rights system is a reflection of these assumptions, then it too must be reconsidered.

There can be no doubt about the important contributions by the range of legal scholars, philosophers, ethicists, and others who were instrumental in creating the modern human rights system (and the ideas that supported and then flowed from it). Nevertheless, the critical ethnography of human rights suggests both a different human rights ontology and the grounds on which a potentially global, normative project like human rights can be justified. In other words, there is still a tremendous reservoir of untapped potential in the idea of human rights, even if there are also certain basic limitations that must be acknowledged and institutionalized.

[42] See eg Jane K Cowan, Marie-Bénédicte Dembour, and Richard A Wilson (eds), *Culture and Rights: Anthropological Perspectives* (CUP 2001); Richard A Wilson, *The Politics of Truth and Reconciliation in South Africa: Legitimizing the Post-Apartheid State* (CUP 2001); Susan Slyomovics, *The Performance of Human Rights in Morocco* (U Pennsylvania Press 2005); Harri Englund, *Prisoners of Freedom: Human Rights and the African Poor* (U California Press 2006); Sally Engle Merry, *Human Rights and Gender Violence: Translating International Law into Local Justice* (U Chicago Press 2006); Mark Goodale, *Dilemmas of Modernity: Bolivian Encounters with Law and Liberalism* (Stanford UP 2008); Mark Goodale and Sally Engle Merry (eds), *The Practice of Human Rights: Tracking Law Between the Global and the Local* (CUP 2007); Winfred Tate, *Counting the Dead: The Culture and Politics of Human Rights Activism in Colombia* (U California Press 2007); Shannon Speed, *Rights in Rebellion: Indigenous Struggle and Human Rights in Chiapas* (Stanford UP 2008).

[43] See eg Thomas Hylland Eriksen, 'Between Universalism and Relativism: A Critique of the UNESCO Concept of Culture' in Cowan, Dembour, and Wilson, *Culture and Rights* (n 42); Jane Cowan, 'Culture and Rights after Culture and Rights' (2006) 108 *Amer Anthrop* 9; Kamari Maxine Clarke, *Fictions of Justice: The International Criminal Court and the Challenge of Legal Pluralism in Sub-Saharan Africa* (CUP 2009).

Further Reading

Goodale M (ed), *Human Rights: An Anthropological Reader* (Wiley-Blackwell 2009)
——*Surrendering to Utopia: An Anthropology of Human Rights* (Stanford UP 2009)
Hernández-Truyol BE (ed), *Moral Imperialism: A Critical Anthology* (NYU Press 2002)
Riles A, *The Network Inside Out* (U Michigan Press 2000)
United Nations Educational, Scientific and Cultural Organization, *Four Statements on the Race Question* (UNESCO 1969)
Wilson RA and Mitchell JP (eds), *Human Rights in Global Perspective: Anthropological Studies of Rights, Claims, and Entitlements* (Routledge 2003)

PART II

HISTORICAL AND LEGAL SOURCES

CHAPTER 7

THE FOUNDATIONS OF JUSTICE AND HUMAN RIGHTS IN EARLY LEGAL TEXTS AND THOUGHT

PAUL GORDON LAUREN

1. Introduction

IDEAS of justice and human rights possess a long and rich history. They did not originate exclusively in any single geographical region of the world, any single country, any single century, any single manner, or even any single political form of government or legal system. They emerged instead in many ways from many places, societies, religious and secular traditions, cultures, and different means of expression, over thousands of years. Indeed, they took millennia to evolve, since they always depended upon their specific historical context and what was possible in the face of established tradition and often determined resistance, at the time. Sometimes these ideas came from solemn reflection and quiet contemplation, based upon religious belief or philosophical opinion. On other occasions, they emerged from outrage over a sense of injustice or the pain of violent abuse, brutal atrocities, or war and revolution. Sometimes they took the form of visions or thoughts about the future and how human dignity might be protected. Other times, these ideas were transformed into actual legal texts, designed in some measure to serve justice and to guarantee rights.[1]

Although it is necessary to guard against the shallow and unhistorical view that all societies somehow have always subscribed to the same basic beliefs, it is also essential to recognize that justice and the moral worth of human beings are values that no single civilization, or location, or people, or nation, or time, can claim as uniquely its own. The reason for this is that these subjects raise age-old and universal questions about the meaning of justice and the purpose of the rule of law, the relationship between duties and rights, and what it means to be truly human. Indeed, as one authoritative study insightfully concludes: 'The struggle for human rights is as old as [world] history itself, because it concerns the need to protect the individual against the abuse of power by the monarch, the tyrant, or the state.'[2]

2. Ancient Near and Middle East

The long-standing and widespread interest in justice is evident from the very beginnings of civilization itself. Once nomadic tribal peoples began to settle in permanent organized societies, they began to create rules to regulate and govern their behaviour that might enable them to avoid complete anarchy and the arbitrary abuse of power. The development of writing permitted such rules to be written down and recorded as laws. Archeologists have discovered fragments of the earliest legal documents and collections from ancient Egypt and Mesopotamia. These include the Sumerian Code of Ur-Nammu (c 2100–2050 BCE), the codex of Lipit-Ishtar (c 1930 BCE), and the Akkadian Laws of Eshnunna (c 1770 BCE).[3]

Among these early codes, one of the most significant and remarkable contributions to the historical evolution of law came from King Hammurabi (c 1792–1750 BCE), who ruled ancient Babylon. His famous Code of Hammurabi is the oldest set of complete laws known to exist in the world. Some laws are written in cuneiform script impressed on baked clay tablets, while the most famous ones are carved on solid stone steles designed for public display. One copy introduces the text with an image depicting Hammurabi receiving these laws directly from the sun god, a

[1] For a comprehensive discussion, see Paul Gordon Lauren (ed), *The Evolution of International Human Rights: Visions Seen* (3rd edn, U Pennsylvania Press 2011).

[2] AH Robertson and JG Merrills, *Human Rights in the World: An Introduction to the Study of the International Protection of Human Rights* (Manchester UP 1996) 9.

[3] The most detailed treatment of these legal codes can be found in Raymond Westbrook (ed), *A History of Ancient Near Eastern Law* (Brill 2003).

deity of the time that was most often associated with justice. In fact, Hammurabi himself described his code as representing 'the laws of Justice'. 'Let the oppressed', he announced, 'come into the presence of my statute'.[4] The text itself explicitly speaks of his desire 'to further the well-being of mankind' by creating protections 'so that the strong should not harm the weak'.[5]

The Code of Hammurabi, written in orderly groups of columns and paragraphs, contains nearly 300 separate provisions of commercial, criminal, and civil law. These provisions cover contracts, judicial procedures, penalties, or punishments, progressively scaled to the nature of crimes, family relationships, inheritance, and certain aspects of what we today call human rights. To illustrate, the code presents some of the earliest examples of the right to freedom of speech, the presumption of innocence, the right to present evidence, and the right to a fair trial by judges. To reinforce the rule of law and maintain the integrity of the judiciary, judges were held accountable according to a strict code of justice:

> If a judge renders a judgment, gives a verdict, or deposits a sealed opinion, after which he reverses his judgment, they shall charge and convict that judge…and he shall give twelve-fold the claim of that judgment; moreover, they shall unseat him from his judgment in the assembly, and he shall never again sit in judgment with the judges.[6]

The Code of Hammurabi also provides certain protections for all classes in Babylonian society, including women, widows, orphans, the poor, and even slaves. Perhaps its most significant contribution can be found in its establishment of one particularly critical principle of the rule of law: some laws are so fundamental that they apply to everyone, even the king.

The requirement that all persons obey the law raised a foundational and enduring issue for human rights. That is, it revealed the existence of a direct connection between duties and rights. Early texts were initially less interested in the claims of individuals against governments or others than in the ways to order life within a society so as to protect the worth of its members. Everyone therefore had duties to others; however, if these remained unperformed, then others had a right to claim them.

The form and function of the 'Law of Moses', or Mosaic Law, in the kingdoms of ancient Israel and Judah enhanced these evolving ancient Near and Middle East legal requirements about duties and responsibilities. This law reflected experiences in Egypt and Mesopotamia, and it displayed many similarities with developments

[4] Quoted in Roger Normand and Sarah Zaidi, *Human Rights at the UN: The Political History of Universal Justice* (UN Intellectual History Project 2008) 12.

[5] 'Laws of Hammurabi', as cited in Martha Roth, *Law Collections from Mesopotamia and Asia Minor* (2nd edn, Scholars Press 1997) 76. See also LW King (tr), 'Code of Hammurabi' (*The Avalon Project*) <http://avalon.law.yale.edu/ancient/hamframe.asp> accessed 14 February 2013; and GR Driver and John C Miles (eds), *The Babylonian Laws* (Wipf & Stock 2007).

[6] Roth (n 5) 82.

among those neighbours, with whom they shared many customs, antecedents, and conditions. The singular exception, of course, is that Mosaic Law referred to a monotheistic deity, rather than just a secular ruler or society, as the Torah (which the Greeks translated as *nomos* or 'Law') recorded throughout the books of Exodus, Leviticus, Numbers, and Deuteronomy. Although disputes exist over precisely how this body of law and its set of teachings and instructions evolved, as well as over when it was composed or compiled, most modern scholars believe that Mosaic Law took its final, canonical form sometime between the Babylonian Exile (c 600 BCE) and the early Persian period (c 400 BCE). The law contains provisions regarding relationships to God and relationships to other people that range over many subjects, from moral and social issues to ceremonial details about Jewish feasts, offerings, and purity.[7]

Provisions in Mosaic Law that address what we would now describe as early conceptions of human rights are explicit about the necessity of fulfilling responsibilities toward others under the law (including six of the Ten Commandments) and of applying rules of justice to individuals both friend and stranger, free and slave, man and woman, young and old, rich and poor, and healthy and disabled.[8] They speak of reciprocal duties and rights, the sanctity of life, compassion for those who suffer, mercy, economic and social justice, release from bondage, the rights of employers and employees, protection for widows and children, and the rights of foreigners in one's own land. The injunctions are clear: 'You shall not oppress… You shall do no injustice… You shall love your neighbor as yourself.'[9] These written laws, along with their subsequent interpretations (which took the form of oral laws), came to be considered supreme over all other sources of authority, including the king and his officials, with instructions to disregard government decrees if they were contrary to the letter and the spirit of the law. Thus, when abuses occurred, prophets spoke out and challenged their own leaders—as Isaiah forcefully did with his charge 'to loose the bonds of wickedness, to undo the tongs of the yoke, to let the oppressed go free… to share your bread with the hungry, and to bring the homeless poor into your house', and thereby 'bring justice to the nations'.[10]

Other developments occurred to the east. Cyrus the Great (c 580–529 BCE), the founder of the vast Persian Empire that spread from the shores of the Mediterranean

[7] See and Raymond Westbrook, 'Biblical and Cuneiform Law Codes' (1985) 92 *Revue Biblique* 247; Joseph Blenkinsopp, *The Pentateuch: An Introduction to the First Five Books of the Bible* (Yale UP 2000); Gideon Libson, *Jewish and Islamic Law: A Comparative Study of Custom during the Geonic Period* (Harvard Law School 2003); Douglas A Knight, *Law, Power, and Justice in Ancient Israel* (Westminster John Knox Press 2011); Bernard M Levinson, *'The Right Chorale': Studies in Biblical Law and Interpretation* (Eisenbrauns 2011).

[8] See Milton R Konvitz (ed), *Judaism and Human Rights* (2nd edn, Transaction 2001); Rabbis for Human Rights, 'Home' <http://rhr.org.il/eng/> accessed 14 February 2013.

[9] Leviticus 9:13, 15, 18.

[10] Isaiah 58:6–7; 42:1. See also the books of Amos and Micah.

Sea to the Indus River, earned his title as 'The Lawgiver' by promulgating what is known as the Charter of Cyrus. The Charter of Cyrus is written in Akkadian cuneiform script, inscribed on two fragments of a small, barrel-shaped clay cylinder found in the ruins of ancient Babylon. The incomplete text begins by describing how Cyrus entered the city not as a conqueror, but as a liberator, replacing a ruling tyrant who had imposed 'a yoke without relief' upon his subjects.[11] In keeping with a long-standing Mesopotamian tradition whereby new rulers began their reigns by announcing changes, it goes on to explain that he instituted reforms, granted certain rights, released captives, abolished forced labour, and 'shepherded in justice'.[12] Biblical accounts credit Cyrus with freeing Jews from their exile in Babylon and allowing them to return to their homeland, though the precise translation and meaning of portions of the text remain in dispute.[13] Nevertheless, there are those who interpret particular passages as providing early support for religious toleration, freedom of movement, racial and linguistic equality, and several economic and social rights. Indeed, some have even described it as 'the first human rights charter in history'.[14]

The laws described thus far all relied on the power of the ruler not only to promulgate them, but also to enforce them; but power has different sources of legitimacy. In some instances, especially in religious communities, commandments or instructions often are considered to have the force of law when governing behaviour.[15] Jesus of Nazareth (c 6 BCE–30 CE), for example, told his followers to live lives of love, justice, peace, and compassion. He commanded those who would follow him to be responsible for the well-being of others, to clothe the naked, to heal the sick, to feed the hungry, to welcome the stranger, to provide hope to the hopeless, and to care for the poor and the oppressed of the world. In this regard, Jesus stressed

[11] Quoted in Lawrence H Schiffman, *Texts and Traditions: A Source Reader for the Study of Second Temple and Rabbinic Judaism* (KTAV Publishing 1998) 71.

[12] Irving Finkel (tr), 'Translation of the Text on the Cyrus Cylinder' (*The British Museum*) <http://www.britishmuseum.org/explore/highlights/articles/c/cyrus_cylinder_-_translation.aspx> accessed 15 February 2013.

[13] See Bill T Arnold and Piotr Michalowski, 'Achaemenid Period Historical Texts Concerning Mesopotamia' in Mark W Chavalas (ed), *The Ancient Near East: Historical Sources in Translation* (Wiley-Blackwell 2006) 426–30; Jona Lendering, 'Cyrus Cylinder' (*Livius*, 28 January 2007) <http://www.livius.org/ct-cz/cyrus_I/cyrus_cylinder.html> accessed 14 February 2013.

[14] See Kaveh Farrokh, *Shadows in the Desert: Ancient Persia at War* (Osprey Publishers 2007) 44; Robertson and Merrills (n 2) 7; Network of Iranian American Society, 'Cyrus Cylinder' <http://www.niasnet.org/iran-history/artifacts-historical-places-of-iran/cyruscylinder> accessed 14 February 2013; FarsiNet, 'Cyrus Charter of Human Rights Cylinder' <http://www.farsinet.com/cyrus> accessed 14 February 2013; Shirin Ebadi, 'In the Name of the God of Creation and Wisdom' (Nobel Lecture, Oslo, 10 December 2003) <http://www.nobelprize.org/nobel_prizes/peace/laureates/2003/ebadi-lecture-e.html> accessed 15 February 2013.

[15] See the chapter on the religious foundations of human rights by John Witte and M Christian Green in this *Handbook*; Micheline R Ishay, *The History of Human Rights: From Ancient Times to the Globalization Era* (U California Press 2008).

the critical importance of loving one's neighbour as one's self and centred what is perhaps his most famous and profound parable about the Good Samaritan around this principle. His disciples and those who followed him took this message to heart, as the apostle Paul's admonition to break down ethnic, class, and gender divisions by recognizing that 'there is neither Jew nor Greek, nor slave nor free, nor man or woman, but we are all one'[16] reveals. He concluded directly: 'For the entire law is fulfilled in keeping this one command: "Love your neighbor as yourself".'[17] At the time and long thereafter, these tenets generally remained expressions of ideals, rather than descriptions of reality, but many of them would join with those tenets of other religious faiths and inspire many human rights activists, while eventually finding their way into provisions of international human rights law.

The tenets of Islam, pronounced 500 years later and revealed in the writings of the prophet Muhammad (c 570–632 CE), also stress the responsibility or duty (*fard*) to care for the well-being of others. There is a command to protect the weakest members of society and to practise charity. The Qur'an speaks to social justice, the sanctity of life, personal safety, mercy, compassion, and respect for all human beings, rooted in the obligations that believers owe to Allah, or God. Moreover, since the Prophet Muhammad also possessed secular power as a government administrator, judge, and statesman, Islam quickly recognized a connection between religious belief and the law of a political community. In a society riven with class and tribal distinctions and the tyranny of vested interests, the Constitution of Medina, written to govern the first Islamic state, addressed matters of freedom and injustices born of special privilege, created a judicial system, and provided certain protections for individuals—including provisions respecting religious toleration. The text establishes that, 'Jews [and later Christians] who attach themselves to our commonwealth shall be protected... [T]hey shall have an equal right with our own people... and shall practice their religion as freely as the Muslims', thereby convincing some observers to describe it as 'the first charter of freedom of conscience in human history'.[18] These early beginnings, in turn, set the stage for the gradual evolution of Islamic jurisprudence and what is known as Sharia law, governing aspects of religious, civil, political, constitutional, and procedural law, based not upon formally codified statutes but upon certain Muslim legal scholars' various, and often differing, interpretations of the Qur'an and Muhammad's life and teachings.[19]

16 Galatians 3:28.   17 Galatians 5:14.

18 Huston Smith, *The Religions of Man* (Harper & Row 1958) 249. See Mahmood Monshipouri, 'Islamic Thinking and the Internationalization of Human Rights' (1994) 84 *Muslim World* 217; Ann Elizabeth Mayer, *Islam and Human Rights* (Westview 2012).

19 See Wael B Hallaq, *The Origins and Evolution of Islamic Law* (CUP 2005).

3. Ancient China

Contributions to ideas about justice and what would become human rights discourse also came from Asia, where the emphasis was placed on the broader ethical principles of protecting others by means of practising duty and virtue, rather than on formal laws, legal codes, or judicial procedures. At approximately the same time as the emergence of Buddhism, for example, the ancient Chinese philosopher and sage Kong Qiu (551–479 BCE), known as Confucius, stressed the importance of responsible behaviour, based not on fear of legal punishments, but rather on a desire to behave toward others to the best of human capacity, in the form of goodness, benevolence, and what he called human-heartedness. Toward this end, he emphasized the duty of doing no harm, respecting the intrinsic worth and 'moral force' of all people, practising tolerance, having laws that service justice, and acknowledging a common humanity throughout the world and the fact that 'within the four seas, all men are brothers'.[20] He spoke out strongly against oppressive governments that maintained power by exploitation and by the coercion of armed force. When he was asked whether there existed a single saying or principle that one could act on all day and every day, he famously answered: 'What you do not want others to do to you, do not do to others.'[21]

Other Chinese philosophers further developed many of these ideas. One of them, Mo Tzu (c 470–391 BCE), founded the Mohist school of moral philosophy. Writing at a time of incessant warfare, violence, and widespread abuse, he condemned acts that were harmful to others, rigid divisions in society that treated people differently, and any situation in which 'the strong oppressed the weak'. In contrast, he urged self-sacrifice, the establishment of uniform moral standards, fulfillment of responsibilities for the well-being of others, and respect for all—not only those confined to one's own family or clan, but, in his words, 'universally throughout the world'.[22] The Confucius sage Meng Zi (372–289 BCE), known as Mencius, went on to insist that 'all human beings' naturally share a common humanity, moral worth, inherent dignity and goodness, and compassionate mind capable of empathy 'that cannot bear to see the suffering of others'.[23] It is the responsibility of governments, he argued, to nurture these natural qualities. Rulers who engaged in oppression and persecution lost what he called the Mandate of Heaven, and they thereby forfeited the legitimacy needed to govern. In this regard—centuries before John Locke and

[20] Confucius, as cited in HG Creel, *Confucius: The Man and the Myth* (Day 1949) 150.

[21] Confucius, *The Analects of Confucius* (Burton Watson (tr), Columbia UP 2009) 80.

[22] Mo Tzu, *Basic Writings* (Burton Watson (tr), Columbia UP 1963) 39–49.

[23] As cited in Irene Bloom, 'Fundamental Institutions and Consensus Statements: Mencius Confucianism and Human Rights' in Wm Theodore de Bary and Tu Weiming (eds), *Confucianism and Human Rights* (Columbia UP 1998) 101–102.

the Enlightenment in Europe—he argued that people possessed the right to overthrow a tyrant. In language that Chinese human rights activists have recalled with considerable pride ever since, Mencius declared: 'The individual is of infinite value, institutions and conventions come next, and the person of the ruler is of least significance.'[24] The ancient philosopher Xunzi (c 312–230 BCE) went on to assert the same principle even more emphatically when he wrote: 'In order to relieve anxiety and eradicate strife, nothing is as effective as the institution of corporate life based on a clear recognition of individual rights.'[25]

4. Ancient India

Significant early contributions emerged from ancient India as well. Between the end of the fourth and early-third century BCE, the beginnings of the classic Sanskrit treatise entitled *The Arthashastra* appeared. Although a number of authors eventually contributed to it over a period of time, it is largely attributed to Kautilya (c 370–283 BCE), also known as Chanakya, the Indian philosopher, economist, prime minister, and royal counsellor.[26] Based upon his own experiences helping to create and then sustain the Mauryan Empire that ruled over most of the Indian subcontinent, he sought to write about the theories, principles, and practices regarding actually governing a state. The book combines a discussion of some of the very pragmatic issues of exercising power in the face of adversity, with some of the moral teachings of the Hindu scriptures known as the Vedas. Parts of the text reflect brutal scheming and shocking ruthlessness, while other parts convey a deep concern for the well-being of the kingdom's people, as well as compassion for those who suffer from abuse. Like Hammurabi, Kautilya argued that kings needed to be just and wise and that they had an obligation to rule their subjects fairly and benevolently, by promoting justice, guaranteeing property rights, and protecting certain kinds of rights for the poor, for women, for workers and servants, and for slaves. He devoted a large portion of his book to the subject of 'Law and Justice'. It deals with civil and criminal law, stressing

[24] As cited in 'The Evolution of Human Rights' *United Nations Weekly Bulletin* (12 August 1946). Chinese students recited this statement in Tiananmen Square in 1989.

[25] As cited in UNESCO, *The Birthright of Man* (UNESCO 1969) 303. See also Zhuangzi, *Basic Writings* (Burton Watson (tr), Columbia UP 2003).

[26] For treatments of Kautilya, see Roger Boesche, *The First Great Political Realist: Kautilya and His Arthashastra* (Lexington Books 2003); VN Jha (ed), *Kautilya's Arthaśātra and Social Welfare* (Sahitya Akademi 2006); TN Ramaswamy, *Essentials of Indian Statecraft: Kautilya's Arthasastra for Contemporary Readers* (Munshiram Manoharlal 2007); Patrick Olivelle, *King, Government, and Law in Ancient India: Kautilya's Arthaśātra* (OUP 2013).

the necessity of creating a 'just and deserved' penal system, establishing clear procedures for the use of evidence, and managing a transparent judiciary composed of qualified judges administering justice with integrity and impartiality. 'Rule of Law [alone]', he concluded, 'can guarantee security of life and the welfare of the people'.[27]

These thoughts very likely influenced Asoka (304–232 BCE), the third king of the Mauryan dynasty who governed a vast, powerful, and multi-ethnic Indian subcontinent for nearly forty years. He came to be known as Asoka the Great, and scholars and other observers often regard him as one of the exemplary rulers in world history. Brutal ruthlessness and military conquest for purposes of expanding the empire characterized his early career, but after viewing the widespread carnage and suffering that one particularly devastating war of his had caused, he expressed overwhelming remorse for what he had done and the injustice that he had caused. This profound experience led to a deep and dramatic conversion to Buddhism, with its emphasis on the sanctity of life 'for all beings', nonviolence, and compassion. The transformation was so powerful that it convinced him to change both his personal and public life by renouncing war and devoting himself to the well-being of his subjects.[28]

Over the course of his reign, Asoka launched many innovations and instituted many reforms to the existing administrative, judicial, and legal systems by issuing his famous Edicts of Asoka. Like Hammurabi, he wanted these laws to be widely known and given prominence. He thus inscribed them on highly visible boulders and especially on a series of huge, free-standing stone pillars averaging between forty and fifty feet in height. These are found at numerous locations throughout what are now modern India, Nepal, Pakistan, Afghanistan, and Bangladesh. The texts of the inscriptions focus on social and moral precepts, and convey the Buddhist concept of *dharma*, or duty and proper behaviour towards others. They also explicitly stress the necessity of being 'completely law-abiding'.

The Edicts of Asoka address wide-ranging issues related to concepts of justice and human rights. They speak directly about compassion, social welfare, equal protection under the law regardless of political belief or caste, respect for all life, environmental protection, humanitarian assistance for those who suffer, humane treatment of employees and servants, 'the hearing of petitions and the administration of justice', the banning of slavery, the right to be free from 'harsh or cruel' punishment, and the possibility of amnesty from the death penalty. One reads: 'This edict has been inscribed here to remind the judicial officers in this city to try at all times to avoid unjust imprisonment or unjust torture.'[29] Despite Asoka's deep personal commitment to Buddhism, the Edicts establish religious toleration for all sects and the

[27] Kautilya, *The Arthashastra* (LN Rangarajan (tr), Penguin 1987) 119.

[28] For studies of his life and contributions, see DC Ahir, *Asoka the Great* (BR Publishing 1995); Charles Allen, *Ashoka: The Search for India's Lost Emperor* (Little Brown 2012). See also Harry Falk, *Aśokan Sites and Artefacts* (von Zabern 2006).

[29] Kalinga Edict I, 'Public Administration: The Promulgation of Morality and the Administration of Justice' in NA Nikam and Richard McKeon (eds), *The Edicts of Asoka* (U Chicago Press 1978) 62.

right to freely practise one's own beliefs. In one well-known Edict, Asoka observes that he greatly values 'growth in the qualities essential to religion in men of all faiths'.[30] 'This growth', he continues,

> may take many forms, but its root is in guarding one's speech to avoid extolling one's own faith and disparaging the faith of others improperly or, when the occasion is appropriate, immoderately. The faiths of others all deserve to be honored... By honoring them, one exalts one's own faith and at the same time performs a service to the faith of others.[31]

Asoka also proclaimed the critical importance of 'impartiality' in legal procedures and in punishments to implement the rule of law.[32]

5. Classical Greece and Rome

Writing at approximately the same time as Mencius in China, some Greek philosophers began to consider the broader origins and meanings of law itself. They knew of the practical contributions that Cyrus the Great and others had made before them. But, their interest focused on the existence of an all-encompassing law of nature that they believed pervaded the entire world. This law, they argued, was eternal and universal and thus placed well above and beyond the specific context or needs of a particular state, the customs or rules of a specific society, or the will of a single law-maker. It governed every aspect of the universe and provided a framework for rights. Human conduct thus needed to be brought into harmony with this law of nature and to be judged according to it.[33]

Plato (427–347 BCE), for example, wrote frequently about that which is 'natural', 'according to nature', and 'naturally just'. In his longest book, *The Laws*,[34] he argued that nature establishes normative standards for human behaviour and that universal legal and moral issues are so intertwined that they cannot be separated. The purpose of all law, he asserted, is to make it possible for people to act with reason, virtue, and justice

[30] Quoted in Micheline R Ishay, *The Human Rights Reader: Major Political Essays, Speeches, and Documents from Ancient Times to the Present* (Routledge 2007) 29.

[31] Rock Edict XII, 'Against Religious Intolerance and Discrimination within the Community' in Nikam and McKeon (n 29) 51–52.

[32] Pillar Edict 4 in Nikam and McKeon (n 29) 60–61.

[33] Alan S Rosenbaum (ed), *The Philosophy of Human Rights: International Perspectives* (Greenwood Press 1980) 9–10.

[34] Plato, *The Laws* (Benjamin Jowett (tr), DigiReads 2009).

toward others.[35] Toward this end, and while serving as the voice of his teacher Socrates (469–399 BCE) in his political treatise *The Republic*, Plato championed just actions by the state and by individuals, to advance the common good and protect rights. In one well-known dialogue he asked: 'don't just actions produce justice, and unjust actions injustice?'[36] When discussing rights, in what would eventually become known as humanitarian law during times of warfare and armed conflict, Plato spoke out against enslaving enemies and killing innocents. To further protect civilians, he wrote, 'Then let us lay it down as a law for our Guardians that they are neither to ravage land nor burn houses'.[37] Moreover, and highly unusual at the time, Plato supported the idea of certain rights for women, arguing that 'the natures of men and women are akin', that they possess similar abilities, that they should receive the same kind of education, and that they should be entrusted with similar offices.[38]

In his works entitled *Politics* and *Nicomachean Ethics*, Aristotle (384–322 BCE) insisted that the rule of law is necessary for good government and to safeguard the interests of individuals. He maintained that an intimate connection exists between justice and law. 'Natural justice' and 'natural right', according to Aristotle, came from 'natural law'. Manmade positive laws thus must conform to this law of nature, rather than contravene or subvert it. If the laws did not, and if what was just by the laws of men was not just by the law of nature, the higher authority of the latter could be appropriately invoked to disobey the former.[39] This position is perhaps best represented by the fictional character of Antigone, who, after being reproached by her king for refusing his specific command not to bury her slain brother, boldly asserts: 'Nor did I deem thine edicts of such force [t]hat they, a mortal's bidding, should o'erride [u]nwritten laws, eternal in the heavens. Not of today or yesterday are these, [b]ut live from everlasting, and from whence [t]hey sprang, none knoweth.'[40]

Stoic philosophers from ancient Greece and Rome extended these ideas by contending that the laws of nature provided rational, purposeful, and egalitarian principles governing the entire universe. They entailed not only physical rules, such as the succession of the seasons or the alternation between day and night, but also ethical rules, such as the obligation of individuals to respect one another as moral equals. Zeno of Citium (c 334–262 BCE), one of the founders of Stoicism, insisted

[35] See Huntington Cairns, 'Plato's Theory of Law' (1942) 56 *Harv L Rev* 359; V Bradley Lewis, '"Reason Striving to Become Law": Nature and Law in Plato's *Laws*' (2009) 54 *Am J Juris* 67; Christopher Bobonich, *Plato's Laws: A Critical Guide* (CUP 2010).

[36] Plato, *The Republic* (Desmond Lee (tr), 2nd edn, Penguin 1987) 154.

[37] Plato, *The Republic* (n 36) 188.

[38] Plato, *The Republic* (n 36) 163–66.

[39] See Fred D Miller, *Nature, Justice, and Rights in Aristotle's Politics* (OUP 1995); Richard Tuck, *Natural Rights Theories: Their Origin and Development* (CUP 1998); Richard O Brooks and James Bernard Murphy (eds), *Aristotle and Modern Law* (Ashgate 2003).

[40] Sophocles, *Antigone* (Robert Whitelaw (tr), Clarendon Press 1906) lns 453–58.

on the worth and dignity of each human life. His teachings stressed the relationship between natural law, virtue, and reason.

The great Roman statesman, orator, philosopher, and legal scholar Marcus Tullius Cicero (106–43 BCE) also focused his attention on natural law, which he believed imposed responsibilities for the well-being of others and had been founded 'ages before any written law existed or any state had been established'.[41] As he described in a frequently quoted passage from *The Republic*:

> [True] law in the proper sense is right reason in harmony with nature. It is spread through the whole human community, unchanging and eternal, calling people to their duty by its commands and deterring them from wrong-doing by its prohibitions... This law cannot be countermanded, nor can it be in any way amended, nor can it be totally rescinded. We cannot be exempted from this law by any decree of the Senate or the people... There will not be one such law in Rome and another in Athens, one now and another in the future, but all peoples at all times will be embraced by a single and eternal and unchangeable law.[42]

The critical element in this law, he insisted, was a sense of justice based 'in nature'. He famously and insightfully wrote in *The Laws*:

> Most foolish of all is the belief that everything decreed by the institutions or laws of a particular country is just. *What if the laws are the laws of tyrants?* If the notorious Thirty [a group who abolished the law courts and instituted a reign of terror and murder] had wished to impose their laws on Athens... should those laws on that account be considered just? No more, in my opinion, should that law be considered just which our interrex passed [a bill creating unlimited powers], allowing the Dictator to execute with impunity any citizen he wished, even without trial. There is one, single, justice. It binds together human society and has been established by one, single law... Justice is completely non-existent if it is not derived from nature... [V]irtues are rooted in the fact that we are inclined by nature to have a regard for others; and that is the basis of justice.[43]

Cicero returned to this theme in his last treatise, *On Duties*, concluding that natural law creates both responsibilities and rights for all people, as they seek justice and virtue in their relationships with each other.

Many of these theories in philosophy found their way into practice in Roman legal texts, including a remarkable body of law known as the *jus gentium*, or 'law of peoples' or 'law of nations', sometimes described as Rome's greatest contribution to history. Based on the principles of natural law, it recognized certain universal duties and rights that extended to all human beings as members of the world community as a whole. Further developments occurred when the Emperor Justinian (c 482–565 CE) ordered the collection, compilation, and codification of the fundamental works

[41] Quoted in Fernando Llano Alonso, 'Natural Law: Autonomous or Heteronomous? The Thomistic Perspective' in Francisco José Contreras (ed), *The Threads of Natural Law: Unravelling a Philosophical Tradition* (Springer 2013) 30.

[42] Marcus Tullius Cicero, *The Republic and The Laws* (Niall Rudd (tr), OUP 1998) 68–69.

[43] Cicero, *The Republic and The Laws* (n 42) 111–12 [my emphasis]. See also Richard O Brooks (ed), *Cicero and Modern Law* (Ashgate 2009).

of laws, codes, decrees, case law, writings of the celebrated Roman jurist Gaius,[44] and other opinions and interpretations, as they had evolved up to that point. The result, known as the *Corpus Juris Civilis*, articulated principles and created an ordered system that still serve as the basis of civil law in many modern states, of canon law, and of the continued use of Latin in jurisprudence and legal procedures today. Indeed, one of its components, *The Institutes*, has been described as 'the most influential law book ever written'.[45] One of its more notable provisions reads: 'Justice is an unswerving and perpetual determination to acknowledge all men's rights.'[46]

6. The Medieval Period

The long-standing and constant struggle to find ways of using law to administer justice and protect those unable to protect themselves became even more critical after the fall of the Western Roman Empire. Once centralized authority that enforced a unified legal system collapsed, other legal systems and judicial procedures necessarily emerged to prevent arbitrary behaviour and abuse, creating a wide variety of written forms of law in various locations during the Early Medieval Period.[47] In the West, these include canon law, post-Roman Vulgar law, Frankish law, Norse (or Scandinavian) law, Anglo-Saxon common law, early Norman law, 'Feudal' law, Visigothic codes, Germanic law, as well as local laws from a variety of indigenous legal systems known as *Volksrecht*. Designed to protect the weak against the strong, these often contained provisions for kinship or family rights, property rights, women's rights, the right to compensation for personal injury, and the right to a process of public litigation, among others.[48] A number of town charters, created at the urging of mercantile groups, also established areas known as 'islands

[44] See WM Gordon and OF Robinson (trs), *The Institutes of Gaius* (Duckworth 1997), especially his commentary on civil law and natural law.

[45] 'Introduction' in Peter Birks and Grant McLeod (trs), *Justinian's Institutes* (Cornell UP 1987) 18.

[46] Birks and MacLeod (n 45) 37. See also Andrew M Riggsby, *Roman Law and the Legal World of the Romans* (CUP 2010).

[47] Some sense of the richness of this law can be found at: Fordham University, 'Medieval Legal History' (*Internet Medieval Sourcebook*, 27 March 2007) <http://www.fordham.edu/halsall/sbook-law.asp> accessed 15 February 2013; 'Medieval Documents: 400–1399' (*The Avalon Project*) <http://avalon.law.yale.edu/subject_menus/medieval.asp> accessed 15 February 2013.

[48] See eg Mary P Richards and B Jane Stanfield, 'Concepts of Anglo-Saxon Women in the Laws' in Helen Damico and Alexandra Hennessey Olsen (eds), *New Readings on Women in Old English Literature* (Indiana UP 1990); Lisi Oliver, *The Body Legal in Barbarian Law* (U Toronto Press 2011).

of freedom', using the phrase '*Stadtluft Macht Frei*', which had some measure of self-determination from feudal lords.[49]

In Constantinople, poised between Europe and Asia, the Eastern Roman Empire prospered, especially after Emperor Leo III (c 685–741 CE) issued the *Ecloga*, a concise but systematic compilation of Byzantine law. Although drawing heavily upon Justinian's legal texts, as well as regional customary law, he revised his legal code to be comprehensible and specifically to address the practical needs of daily life, all in the spirit 'of greater humanity' and justice and with the justification of spreading Christian principles. These new laws went further than previous efforts to establish the principle of equality before the law. The criminal law, for example, prescribed equal punishment for all individuals, regardless of their social class, and reduced the use of the death penalty. In civil law, the rights of women and children were enhanced and given much greater protection. Other provisions liberated serfs and elevated them to the status of free tenants. Moreover, in order to strengthen the rule of law by reducing corruption, the laws provided salaries for judicial officials and forbade them from accepting bribes.[50]

A growing sophistication in ideas about the nature, meaning, and application of law began to visibly emerge in the late eleventh and early twelfth centuries, with the founding of European universities. They began to teach law for the first time as a distinct and systematized body of knowledge, described as 'legal science' or the 'science of law'. Secular and ecclesiastical legal decisions, rules, procedures, concepts, and enactments were objectively studied, systematically analysed, and carefully explained in terms of larger concepts and universal principles. Great attention was given to the study of many of the ancient legal texts discussed above, especially after the rediscovery in about 1080 of Justinian's compilation of Roman law. Knowledge and interpretation merged with understanding and then with practical application. Trained in the new legal science, successive generations of graduating students were employed in the chanceries and other governmental offices to serve as counsellors, judges, advocates, administrators, and legislative draftsmen. Universities thus increasingly accelerated the role of the scholar in shaping and developing law by creating and developing a legal profession that utilized education in order to conceptualize and give coherence and structure to the accumulating mass of legal norms and systems relating to justice and rights.[51]

A monumental development in this evolution occurred during the early thirteenth century in England. Feudal barons claimed King John and his oppressive regime had failed to meet his obligations to protect the rights and property of his

[49] I am indebted to William Farr for bringing this to my attention.

[50] See George Ostrogorsky, *History of the Byzantine State* (Rutgers UP 1969); Edwin Hanson Freshfield (tr), *A Manual of Later Roman Law: The Ecloga as Procheiron Mutata* (CUP 1927).

[51] Harold J Berman, *Law and Revolution: The Formation of the Western Legal Tradition* (Harvard UP 1983) provides the most authoritative study on this subject.

subjects under natural law. They rebelled and demanded that he accept restraints upon his abusive exercise of power by acknowledging the supremacy of the rule of law in the land, as the Magna Carta articulated in 1215. This 'Great Charter' remains one of the most renowned legal texts in history. In the original version and in several modified versions that followed, it recognized the principle that even royal government had limits, and certain liberties must be guaranteed. These liberties included the right to own and inherit property, the right to be free from excessive taxes, and the right of widows who owned property to opt not to remarry. The text also famously proclaimed: 'No free-man shall be seized, or imprisoned, or dispossessed, or outlawed, or in any way destroyed; nor we will we condemn him, nor will we commit him to prison, excepting by the legal judgment of his peers, or by *the laws of the land*.'[52] This clause has been widely viewed as providing an early guarantee of the legal concepts of the right to a trial by jury and the right to due process. More expansively, the text reads: '[T]o none will we deny... [or] delay right [or] justice.'[53]

Shortly thereafter, and in a very similar way, the nobles of Hungary forced their king, Andrew II Arpad, to accept the Golden Bull (*Aranybulla*) of 1222. This document, so named for the hanging golden seal attached to royal pronouncements, was, and still is, frequently likened to the Magna Carta, in that it placed limits on the powers of the monarch. It codified certain rights for members of the nobility, including the inviolability of person and property. The text also established the right to disobey the king if he acted contrary to the law (*jus resistendi*).[54] Its significance in legal history is such that it has been called 'the first written constitution of Hungary'.[55] Further to the north, the king of Norway, Magnus Haakonsson, earned the epithet of the 'Law-Mender' by issuing his famous Magnus Lagaboters Landslov between 1274 and 1276. Drawing upon customary laws and a variety of provincial codes, he created a comprehensive legal text that defined the power of the government and protected the individual person by providing a certain measure of equality before the law and guaranteeing due process.[56]

During the course of the same century, the highly influential Christian theologian and philosopher Thomas Aquinas (c 1225–74) wrote his magisterial *Summa Theologie*. A significant portion of this work is called 'Treatise on Law'. His attention focused on natural law, which he believed was divinely created by God and designed to be just and to make it possible for all individuals to realize their dignity and reach full development. He believed that when human beings act in accord with moral

[52] Magna Carta, as cited in Boyd C Barrington, *The Magna Charta and Other Great Charters of England* (Campbell 1900) 239 [my emphasis].

[53] Barrington (n 52) 239.

[54] Elemér Hantos, *The Magna Carta of the English and of the Hungarian Constitution: A Comparative View of the Law and Institutions of the Early Middle Ages* (Lawbook Exchange 2005).

[55] See 'The Constitutional Court of Hungary' <http://www.mkab.hu/constitional-court> accessed 15 February 2013.

[56] See Rory McTurk (ed), *A Companion to Old Norse-Icelandic Literature* (Wiley-Blackwell 2007).

behaviour and justice toward others, they live out of the love and the design of the divine for themselves and for others in a broader community. This brought Aquinas to postulate that a critical relationship existed between natural law and positive law. All human or positive laws, he insisted, must be judged by their conformity to the standards of natural law. 'Laws', he wrote, 'have binding force insofar as they have justice'.[57] Their purpose is 'to restrain the ability of the wicked to inflict harm'.[58] The fact that a manmade law existed, in other words, did not mean that it was necessarily just. An unjust law might have the 'appearance' of law in the way that it was created and enforced, but it might actually be a 'perversion of law and no longer a law' if it did not meet these standards.[59] Very much like Mencius in ancient China and philosophers in classical Greece and Rome, Aquinas reinforced the radical idea that if laws were not just, then people had the right to disobey them. This concept would lay a foundation for the subsequent development of theories of natural rights, and those who eventually campaigned on behalf of human rights against tyranny and oppression would seize upon it.

7. The Renaissance, Reformation, and Age of Exploration

Concepts about justice and rights, and laws that seek to transform them into practice, have always been tied to political, economic, social, scientific, religious, and intellectual developments throughout history. In this regard, as already demonstrated, widely diverse forces that unfolded in a variety of different places over the course of many centuries shaped the evolution of ideas about justice and the importance of individual autonomy and personal rights. As such, it can hardly be claimed that early ideas and even legal texts concerning human rights were somehow part of a Western monopoly. What the West did provide through time, however, were greater opportunities for these rights to receive much fuller consideration, articulation, public discussion, and eventual implementation. In Europe, the decline of feudalism, with its rigid hierarchy and monopolistic economy, for example, gradually made way for the rise of the free markets of capitalism and a middle class, thereby

57 Aquinas, *A Summary of Philosophy* (Richard J Regan (ed), Hackett 2003) 191.

58 Aquinas, *On Law, Morality, and Politics* (William P Baumgarth and Richard J Regan (eds), 2nd edn, Hackett 2002) 52.

59 Aquinas, *Treatise on Law* (Richard Regan (tr), Hackett 2000) 44–47. See also John Goyette, Mark S Latkovic, and Richard S Myers (eds), *St. Thomas Aquinas & the Natural Law Tradition: Contemporary Perspectives* (Catholic University of America Press 2004).

strengthening the concept of an individual's right to own private property. This, in turn, led to the desire to transform personal economic rights into broader political and civil rights.

Such forces of movement in Europe could be seen during the fourteenth and fifteenth centuries, with the emergence of the Renaissance. A remarkable flourishing of literature, science, education, political and diplomatic innovations, the study and practice of law, and artistic expression, opened up new paths for self-awareness, personal expression, and freedom.

This can be seen in the art of Leonardo da Vinci (1452–1519), as well as the sculptures of Michelangelo (1475–1564). The latter's *David* powerfully conveys individuality, and *The Prisoners* visually demonstrates a passion to break away the marble encasing the figures in order to set them free to realize their potential as individual human beings. The courageous and pioneering writings of Christine de Pizan (c 1363–1434), the poet and author of *Book of the City of Ladies*, challenged the misogyny and gender stereotypes of her day, insisting that any discussion of natural law must include the rights of women as well as the rights of men.[60] Further articulation emerged from Giovanni Pico della Mirandola (c 1463–94), whose *Oration on the Dignity of Man* is frequently described as the 'Manifesto of the Renaissance', due to its forceful argument insisting on the worth of each person and the universal human capacity for self-transformation.[61]

Such thinking, which the invention of the printing press increasingly spread, was also reflected in ideas about individual belief and the right to freedom of religion. One of the early path breakers was John Wycliffe (c 1328–84), the English theologian, professor, and careful student of law, who challenged existing religious authorities and led the effort to translate the Bible into the vernacular language, in order that it might be more widely read. He went on to heavily influence the Czech priest, philosopher, and professor, Jan Hus (c 1372–1415), who became an outspoken martyr on behalf of religious freedom. 'I would ask you to love one another', he said just before being burned at the stake for heresy, 'not to let the good be suppressed by force and to give every person his rights'.[62]

These challenges inspired others, and by the sixteenth century, the movement was known as the Reformation. Protestants protested (hence their name) existing and entrenched clerical authorities and their practices. They rejected the exclusive power that the institutional Church and the Pope (as its leader) claimed. Instead, they emphasized personal spiritual emancipation, individual conscience and responsibility, greater tolerance, and freedom of religious belief and opinion.

[60] Christine de Pizan, *The Book of the City of Ladies* (Rosalind Brown-Grant (tr), Penguin 2000).

[61] Pico della Mirandola, *Oration on the Dignity of Man* (Francesco Borghesi, Michael Papio, and Massimo Riva (eds), CUP 2012).

[62] As cited in H Gordon Skilling, *Charter 77 and Human Rights in Czechoslovakia* (Allen & Unwin 1981) epigraph.

Importantly, they engaged in serious political dissent in order to realize their objectives. Humanistic philosophers, such as Erasmus of Rotterdam (c 1466–1536) further stressed the relationship between this kind of faith and the political, economic, and social reform that promoted individual human dignity. 'The doctrine of Christ', he wrote, 'casts aside no age, no sex, no fortune, or position in life. It keeps no one at a distance'.[63] All these thoughts contributed to a considerable expansion of discourse about justice, equality, freedom, individual rights, and the use of law to protect them.

One of the particularly significant developments in this expansion of the rule of law, and one that eventually had long-term implications for international human rights, was visible in the efforts to apply legal principles of protection beyond the confines of domestic jurisdiction, to a broader world. The fact that it was precisely during the late-fifteenth and early-sixteenth centuries that the 'Age of Exploration' began greatly enhanced this process. New technological inventions, including navigational instruments and the caravel sailing ship, made it possible for Europeans to explore Africa, the Americas, Asia, and Oceania as never before in history. In these areas, they encountered a vast array of peoples different from themselves and discovered a much larger world than they had ever imagined. Yet, discovery quickly turned to conquest. Seeking to build their overseas empires, Europeans engaged in ruthless massacres and exploitation. The massive suffering of indigenous peoples that resulted became so horrifying that it provoked outrage. Such abuses raised deeply troubling questions about the meaning of 'humanity' as a whole and whether justice, rights, and the rule of law ought to be universally applied to non-white and non-Christian peoples who lived continents and oceans away. This prompted the noted Dominican theologian and law professor of the sixteenth century, Francisco de Vitoria (c 1483–1546), to go beyond mere abstraction to focus his attention on very specific abuses and very real victims, by rejecting notions of subhuman 'backward' and 'inferior' races and speaking out against the Spanish government's brutal treatment of the Aztecs and the Incas. He argued on behalf of what he called a 'republic of the whole world' (*res publica totius orbis*) and of the necessity of developing a universal *jus gentium*, or 'law of nations', to protect the rights of all peoples.[64]

These efforts to develop and apply the law to concrete issues internationally encouraged other legal experts to do the same, including those who turned their attention to a particularly controversial subject of state policy not known for restraint: warfare. Building on the writings of Aquinas and Vitoria, a number of

[63] Cited in Mark Kishlansky, Patrick Geary, and Patricia O'Brien, *Civilization in the West* (2nd edn, HarperCollins 1995) 392.

[64] James Brown Scott, *The Spanish Origin of International Law: Francisco de Vitoria and His Law of Nations* (Lawbook Exchange 2000). On the historic problem of race, see Paul Gordon Lauren, *Power and Prejudice: The Politics and Diplomacy of Racial Discrimination* (2nd edn, Westview Press 1996). See also John M Headley, *The Europeanization of the World: On the Origins of Human Rights and Democracy* (Princeton UP 2008).

leading jurists insisted that humans must apply standards of justice to all activity, including war. Alberico Gentili (1552–1608), the regius professor of civil law at Oxford University, was one of these. His contemporary, Francisco Suárez (1548–1617), the Spanish jurist, Jesuit priest, and prominent Scholastic philosopher who lay some of the first foundations of international law, was another. The teachings and writings of Suárez stressed that all human promulgation of positive law must be based on the natural law that governs all creation. Since all men are created equal, he argued, this precluded any patriarchal theories of government or any exaggerated claims by kings of divine rights that gave them unlimited power to do whatever they wished, including how they launched or fought wars. To restrain such behaviour, and to protect the rights of innocents in the midst of death and devastation, Suárez stressed the necessity of establishing international legal norms for justice, both in and of warfare. Each of these ideas contributed to an emerging body of thought that would become known as just war theory, entailing the justice of war (*jus ad bellum*) and justice in war (*jus in bello*).[65]

8. The Enlightenment and its Three Revolutions

The concept of natural law and its relationship to natural rights and manmade law received enormous attention during the course of the broad and transforming movement known as the Enlightenment, or Age of Reason. By the middle of the seventeenth century, revolutionary discoveries in the sciences expanded knowledge to unimagined levels, dramatically changing ways of thinking which tradition, superstition, dogma, and ignorance had previously circumscribed. This created a secular intellectual milieu which believed that human reason could discover rational and universal laws. If laws of physics, mathematics, biology, and medicine could be discovered in nature, it was asked, then why not laws of government and human behaviour that might help reform politics, society, and law as well?

Such thinking is clearly seen in the writings of Hugo de Groot (Grotius) (1583–1645), the brilliant Dutch legal scholar and diplomat who often is credited as being the 'Father of Modern International Law'. In his seminal book, *On the Law of War and Peace*, he declared that natural law—both physical and moral—exists independently

[65] For more discussion, see Paul Gordon Lauren, Gordon A Craig, and Alexander L George, *Force and Statecraft: Diplomatic Challenges of Our Time* (5th edn, OUP 2014) ch 12. See also David Kennedy, 'Primitive Legal Scholarship' (1986) 27 *Harvard International Law Journal* 1–98.

of any political authority. This law, he wrote, stands above all human-created governments and institutions and serves as a measuring rod against which to judge any regime. It also provides all people with certain natural rights of protection and just and equal treatment, which they ought to be free to enjoy without regard to any religious or civil status.[66] Interestingly, Huang Zongxi (1610–95) was expressing similar ideas during exactly the same century in China. Huang Zongxi was a reformist political theorist and Confucian philosopher, sometimes described as the 'Father of Chinese Enlightenment', who wrote that attention needed to shift from the exclusive rights of rulers to the rights of people and that the rule of law should protect these individuals.[67]

Grotius insisted that states had the responsibility to protect these rights in times of war. The international application of these principles became particularly pressing as emerging sovereign nation-states become recklessly powerful and willing to engage in unrestrained violence during the exhausting religious wars of his time. As Grotius looked at the world of anarchy around him, he saw:

> a license in making war of which even barbarous nations would have been ashamed; recourse being had to arms for slight reasons or no reason; and when arms were once taken up, all reverence for divine and human law was thrown away, just as if men were thenceforth authorized to commit all crimes without restraint.[68]

The only way to break this vicious pattern, Grotius declared, was to create a broader order, or system, based on legal norms that respected the 'laws of nations', established specific criteria for 'just war', and honoured the 'natural rights' of individual human beings.[69] Samuel Pufendorf (1632–94), the famous German jurist and historian, endorsed and amplified Grotius's thoughts on just war. Of particular importance, in *On the Law of Nature and of Nations* and in *On the Duty of Man and Citizen According to Natural Law*, which served as basic texts in universities throughout the Enlightenment, Pufendorf emphasized that natural law and natural rights, and their protection in international law (especially in times of war), must not be confined to the West or to Christendom, but seen as a common bond between all nations and peoples, as a part of a larger and universal humanity.[70] Such ideas helped to establish the foundation on which international humanitarian law eventually would be built.

[66] See Tuck (n 39); Knud Haakonssen, *Natural Law and Moral Philosophy: From Grotius to the Scottish Enlightenment* (CUP 1996).

[67] Lynn Struve, 'Huang Zongxi in Context: A Reappraisal of His Major Writings' (1988) 47 *J Asian Stud* 474; Peter Zarrow, 'Citizenship and Human Rights in Early Twentieth Century Chinese Thought' in de Bary and Weiming (n 28).

[68] As quoted in William Cullen Dennis, 'The Diplomatic Correspondence Leading Up to the War: Part I' (1915) 9 *AJIL* 402, 476.

[69] Dennis (n 68) 476.

[70] Samuel Pufendorf, *On the Duty of Man and Citizen According to Natural Law* (James Tully (ed), CUP 1991).

Throughout history, laws and legal thought have profoundly influenced the course of human events, and, reciprocally at other times, human events have acted to profoundly shape laws and legal thought. These dynamics and the interactions between them were revealed with striking clarity during the seventeenth century, with the dramatic upheavals surrounding the English Revolution. In 1628, Parliament passed the Petition of Right, subsequently described as 'one of England's most famous constitutional documents'.[71] It spoke of 'diverse Rights and Liberties', reaffirmed due process and the rule of law, and enacted prohibitions against seizing private property, imprisoning without cause, quartering troops on citizens, and imposing martial law in peacetime. With such direct challenges to the absolutist claims and practices of the monarch, deep divisions exploded into violence. Civil war began in 1642, pitting the supporters of Parliament against those of the Crown, and launching a period of more than forty years of warfare and turmoil, including the trial for treason and beheading of a king, assassination attempts, the emergence of a military dictatorship, several changes of government, and popular uprisings. One radical group, known as the 'Levellers', called for guarantees of the 'native rights' to life, property, equal protection under the law, the election of representatives, and freedom of religion. In 1679, Parliament passed the Habeas Corpus Act, providing protection against arbitrary arrest by strengthening the right of a prisoner under detention to be brought before a court of law in person, in order that the court might examine the legality of his case. This milestone in English constitutional history remains on the statute books to this day.

Then, another monumental landmark in the rule of law and the history of civil and political rights occurred when Parliamentary leaders passed the 1689 Bill of Rights. This act fundamentally transformed the nature of the English, Scottish, and Irish government into that of a constitutional monarchy, by rejecting claims about the divine right of kings, elevating Parliament above the Crown, and subjecting royal power to strict limits under the law. Each of these elements stood in marked contrast to the 'absolute' monarchs who dominated the rest of Europe. The bill was clearly founded on the conviction that individuals possessed certain natural rights and the rule of law needed to protect these rights. The bill's provisions thus addressed the right to own property, the right to petition the monarch without fear of retribution, the right to be free from royal interference with the law and the courts, the right to free elections for representative government, the right of freedom of speech in Parliament, the right to a trial by jury, and the right to be free from excessive bail or 'cruel and unusual' punishment, among others—all in the name of 'ancient' and 'undoubted' natural rights, and all designed to protect individuals

[71] Jess Stoddart Flemion, 'The Struggle for the Petition of Right in the House of Lords: The Study of an Opposition Party Victory' (1973) 45 *J Mod Hist* 193, 193. See also John Hostettler, *Sir Edward Coke: A Force for Freedom* (Universal Law Publishing 2006).

'from the violation of their rights'.[72] The Bill of Rights would go on to have global influence. It is still in effect today.

The momentous events of the English Revolution, in turn, influenced ideas about law, natural law, and natural rights—particularly those of the most influential philosopher, John Locke (1632–1704). First through his *A Letter Concerning Toleration* of 1689, with its forceful argument for freedom of religion and conscience, and then through his seminal *Second Treatise of Government* of 1690, Locke stressed that all humans possessed certain natural rights prior to the existence of any organized societies. Importantly, this concept applied not just to those in Europe, but also to 'common humanity' and 'governments all through the world'.[73] Every individual, he wrote, irrespective of the particular political, socioeconomic, or cultural conditions under which he lives, possesses:

> a title to perfect freedom and uncontrolled enjoyment of all the rights and privileges of the law of nature equally with every other man or number of men in the world and has by nature a power not only to preserve his property—that is his life, liberty, and estate—against the injuries and attempts of other men, but to judge and punish the breaches of that law in others.[74]

From this premise, it followed that people had formed societies and established governments in order to protect these rights—not to surrender them. Governments thus derived their authority and legitimacy from the consent of the governed. If government leaders failed in fulfilling this responsibility and broke their side of the contract, said Locke (while sounding very much like Mencius in ancient China, Aristotle in ancient Greece, Cicero in ancient Rome, and Aquinas in the Medieval period), the government leaders thereby absolved people from further obedience and gave them the right to resist. Such a vision possessed enormous power, and Locke's ideas, along with those developed throughout the earlier centuries, influenced many of the ideas of those that followed him. They still inspire those who challenge entrenched privilege and abuse and struggle on behalf of human rights.

During the eighteenth century, leading Enlightenment intellectuals, known as the *philosophes*, were inspired by these ideas and encouraged by the dynamic temper of the time, and therefore sought to promote even further the connection between rights and the rule of law. In this regard, the fact that in French the word *droit* covers both meanings, *law* and *right*, assisted them. These luminaries included Charles de Secondat, Baron de Montesquieu (1689–1755), who wrote in his *Spirit of Laws* that political freedom and basic human rights cannot be protected, unless the power of government is divided among separate branches; Voltaire (1694–1778),

[72] English Bill of Rights 1689. See also Bernard Schwartz, *The Roots of Freedom: A Constitutional History of England* (Hill & Wang 1967); Tim Harris, *Revolution: The Great Crisis of the British Monarchy, 1685–1720* (Penguin 2008); Steven Pincus, *1688: The First Modern Revolution* (Yale UP 2011).

[73] John Locke, *Two Treatises of Government* (Hafner Library of Classics 1947) 124, 128.

[74] John Locke, *Two Treatises* (n 73) 163.

who insisted in his *Treatise on Toleration* that natural law established the right of all people to freely practise their religion, without fear of persecution; and Jean-Jacques Rousseau (1712–78), who argued in his *Social Contract: Principles of Political Right* for the necessity of people joining together in civil society to create laws and legal institutions that promoted justice and protected individual rights. They were joined by Denis Diderot (1713–84), who stressed that natural rights are universal and exist for all human beings at all times and in all places, in the entry on 'Natural Law' in his *Encyclopedia*;[75] and Immanuel Kant (1724–1804), who emphasized the ethical responsibility to defend the dignity and worth of all people and declared in one of his most celebrated statements: 'Because a... community widely prevails among the Earth's peoples, a transgression of rights in *one* place in the world is felt *everywhere*.'[76] In his hard-hitting *On Crimes and Punishments*, Cesare Beccaria (1738–94) defended the right of all to be free from the then-common practices of prisoner abuse, brutal torture, and the death penalty. Many other notable writers of the period could be mentioned, as well.[77] What these individuals had in common was a desire to expand liberty, the right to enjoy freedom of religion and expression, limited constitutional government, the right to be free from torture, the right to be free from slavery and exploitation, the right to life and to property, the right to justice, and the right to be protected by the rule of law.

The thoughts of these great philosophers of the Enlightenment began to create visions of a future that would influence the growth of civil society and shape the course of events. They had taken ideas about law, natural law, and natural rights that had evolved over the course of many centuries and from different places, built upon them, and then crafted them so that they addressed particular problems. Those who believed that their rights were being denied or flagrantly abused, and who sought protection against the arbitrary exercise of power as well as justification for resistance to oppression, now came to readily invoke these ideas. In fact, these challenges emerged in the first place in reaction to the abject failure of European monarchs and the hereditary elite to modify the political despotism, privileged class positions, economic exploitation, social suppression, torture, bigotry, intolerance, and absence of the rule of the law that characterized the era, and therefore their failure to respect the principles of freedom and equality inherent in natural law and natural rights philosophy. As one scholar has aptly described it: 'Absolutism prompted man to claim rights precisely because it denied them.'[78]

[75] Denis Diderot, *Encyclopédie ou Dictionnaire Raissonné des Sciences, des Arts et des métiers* (Sociétés Typographiques 1781).

[76] Immanuel Kant, *Perpetual Peace and Other Essays* (Ted Humphrey (tr), Hackett 1983) 121.

[77] See Lynn Hunt, *Inventing Human Rights: A History* (WW Norton 2008).

[78] Maurice Cranston, as cited in Burns Weston, 'Human Rights' in Richard Pierre Claude and Burns H Weston (eds), *Human Rights in the World Community: Issues and Action* (2nd edn, U Pennsylvania Press 1992) 16.

Such claims reached a deafening crescendo among the leaders of the American Revolution, many of whom had received careful schooling in the philosophy and political theory of the Enlightenment. Even prior to the outbreak of violence, the First Continental Congress, meeting in Philadelphia in 1774, enacted its own Declaration of Rights, invoking entitlement to 'life, liberty, and property' for all men.[79] Lest these rights be restricted, and the expression 'men' be considered exclusive, Abigail Adams (1744–1818) warned her husband that, when drafting a 'new code of laws', he should:

> [R]emember the ladies and be more generous to them than your ancestors. Do not put such unlimited power in the hands of the husbands. Remember, all men would be tyrants if they could. If particular care and attention is not paid to the ladies, we are determined to foment a rebellion, and will not hold ourselves bound by any laws in which we have no voice or representation.[80]

Explosions of discontent, and the outbreak of actual war between the colonists and British forces in 1775, produced further discourse and articulations of law, natural law, and natural rights. The Virginia Declaration of Rights, for example, announced that 'all men are by nature equally free and independent, and have certain inherent rights'.[81] Thomas Jefferson (1743–1826) followed this Declaration within days by giving eloquent expression to the philosophy of the time; the Declaration of Independence of 4 July 1776, referred to 'the laws of Nature and Nature's God'. He stated his case with these dramatic words:

> We hold these truths to be self-evident, that all men are created equal, that they are endowed by their Creator with certain unalienable rights, that among these are life, liberty, and the pursuit of happiness. That to secure these rights, Governments are instituted among Men, deriving their just powers from the consent of the governed. That whenever any Form of Government becomes destructive of those ends, it is the right of the people to alter or abolish it, and to institute new Government.[82]

Despite the eloquence and inspiration of this language, it took several years of struggle in warfare, the loss of life, bitter sacrifices, and foreign military assistance, before the colonists secured victory against the British and thus gained their independence. But the ability to fight and to destroy with the force of arms is not the same as the ability to create a new government with the force of argument and ideas. It took years of intense debate to resolve differences of opinion and interests. The

[79] 'Declarations and Resolves of the First Continental Congress' (*The Avalon Project*) <http://avalon.law.yale.edu/18th_century/resolves.asp> accessed 15 February 2013.

[80] '31 March 1776: Abigail Adams to John Adams' (*The Liz Library*) <http://www.thelizlibrary.org/suffrage/abigail.htm> accessed 15 February 2013.

[81] 'Virginia Bill of Rights: June 1776' in Benjamin Poore, *Federal and State Constitutions, Colonial Charters, and Other Organic Laws of the United States*, vol 2 (Franklin 1972) 1908–09.

[82] 'Declaration of Independence, 4 July 1776' (*The Avalon Project*) <http://avalon.law.yale.edu/18th_century/declare.asp> accessed 15 February 2013.

desire 'to form a more perfect Union'[83] eventually resulted in the US Constitution of 1787, which became the supreme law of the land. It established the world's first modern democratic republic, based upon the consent of the governed, the federal separation of powers coupled with a system of checks and balances, the placement of judicial authority in the hands of the Supreme Court and in such lesser courts as Congress might establish, and the legal recognition of the civil right to a trial by jury and the political rights to vote and to hold public office.

The Constitution marked a monumental achievement for the new United States, but for many the text did not guarantee enough legal protection of the 'natural rights' for which they had fought in the American Revolution. They thus devoted considerable efforts to changing this situation as soon as possible by amending the Constitution itself. The result took the form of the first ten amendments, collectively known as the Bill of Rights, which offered guarantees under law of the rights of individual citizens against threats from the two most likely sources of abuse: the excessive power of a strong national government, and (importantly and uniquely for the time) the tyranny of the majority—or, as James Madison (1751–1817), who drafted the amendments, so aptly described it, the 'impulse of passion, or of interest, adverse to the rights of other citizens'.[84] These rights included freedom of religion, of speech, and of the press; the right to petition and to peacefully assemble; freedom from unreasonable searches and seizures and from cruel and unusual punishments; due process and equal protection under the rule of law; and the right to a speedy and public trial by jury, among others. This legal text, written and ratified in the eighteenth century, would remain at the core of the most critical and controversial issues to be raised in the nation's subsequent history. To this day, it remains the greatest foundation, bulwark, and symbol of rights in the United States.[85]

The final upheaval of this period to contribute fundamentally to the foundations of justice and human rights came with the French Revolution. The successes of the American Revolution in challenging a monarch, in overthrowing the established order, and in creating a new government with legal protections for certain rights, offered encouragement, but internal pressures and abuses suffered under a despotic king and the hereditary elite of privilege and power within France provided the immediate causes of the outbreak of violence. Within mere weeks of the beginning of the revolution in 1789, deputies in the National Assembly adopted the landmark Declaration of the Rights of Man and Citizen. Drawing upon the ideas of the Enlightenment, their own *philosophes*, and the US Declaration of Independence,

[83] 'Constitution of the United States: Preamble' (*The Avalon Project*) <http://avalon.law.yale.edu/18th_century/preamble.asp> accessed 15 February 2013.

[84] James Madison, 'Federalist Paper No 10' in Alexander Hamilton, James Madison, and John Jay, *The Federalist Papers* (New American Library 1961) 78.

[85] See Jack Rakove, *Declaring Rights: A Brief History with Documents* (Bedford/St. Martins 1997); Leonard W Levy, *Origins of the Bill of Rights* (Yale UP 2001).

the deputies forcefully asserted that '[m]en are born and remain free and equal in rights'; that these rights are universal, valid for all times and places, and 'natural and imprescriptible'; and that they include 'liberty, property, security, and resistance to oppression'.[86] They wrote the text in such a way as to give more precise definition to these broad concepts, by specifically delineating the political right to vote and the civil rights of equality before the law, protection against arbitrary arrest and punishment, the presumption of innocence until proven guilty, freedom of personal opinions and religious beliefs, freedom of expression, and the right to possess property. By making this declaration an integral part of their new constitution, the deputies transformed their vision of natural law and natural rights into the positive law of the land. They thereby established that the legitimacy of their government no longer derived from the will of the monarch and the traditional order of the *ancien régime*, based upon inherited privilege and hierarchy, but instead from the guarantee of individual rights. The eventual impact of this sweeping foundational document on France and on other countries and peoples in the world struggling against abuse and oppression was profound. The historian Lord Acton described it as 'a single confused page... that outweighed libraries and was stronger than all of the armies of Napoleon'.[87] Indeed, a more recent authority concludes that this particular legal text 'remains to this day the classic formulation of the inviolable rights of the individual vis-à-vis the state'.[88]

The Declaration of the Rights of Man and Citizen immediately began to inspire other visions and efforts. New articles were added to the French constitution, for example, specifying legal guarantees for political and civil rights, including ones for freedom of thought and worship that protected Protestants and Jews who previously had been persecuted. Others abolished slavery within the borders of France. Still other provisions mandated public relief for the poor and free public education—items completely unknown in any other constitution of the time, and ones that would inspire the development of economic and social rights. The Declaration additionally inspired a self-educated playwright and political activist, Olympe de Gouges (1748–93) to issue her own Declaration of the Rights of Woman and Citizen, a pioneering document in the history of the struggle for women's rights. In that document, she called for legal reforms, insisting that 'woman is born free and lives equal to man in her rights'.[89] She added, passionately:

[86] 'Declaration of the Rights of Man—1789' (*The Avalon Project*) <http://avalon.law.yale.edu/18th_century/rightsof.asp> accessed 15 February 2013. See also Stéphane Rials (ed), *La Déclaration des Droits de l'Homme et du Citoyen* (Hachette 1988); Lynn Hunt (ed), *The French Revolution and Human Rights: A Brief Documentary History* (Bedford/St. Martins 1996).

[87] Lord Acton, as cited in Robertson and Merrills (n 2) 4.

[88] Frede Castberg, 'Natural Law and Human Rights: An Idea-Historical Survey' in Asbjørn Eide and August Schou (eds), *International Protection of Human Rights* (Almquist & Wiksell 1968) 19. See also Stephen Marks, 'From the "Single Confused Page"' (1998) 20 *Hum Rts Q* 459.

[89] Olympe de Gouges, 'Declaration of the Rights of Woman, 1791' <http://www.library.csi.cuny.edu/dept/americanstudies/lavender/decwom2.html> accessed 15 February 2013.

Women, wake up; the tocsin of reason sounds throughout the universe; recognize your rights...! Women, when will you cease to be blind? Whatever the barriers set up against you, it is in your power to overcome them; you only have to want it![90]

These voices and developments on behalf of justice and rights struck powerful chords. They challenged past thinking and practices, ignited passion, and generated the commitment to push even further among others. Mary Wollstonecraft (1759–97), to illustrate, became determined to advocate for gender equity in her book, *A Vindication of the Rights of Woman*.[91] Thomas Spence (1750–1814) followed with his *The Rights of Infants*.[92] Many others forcefully spoke out on behalf of the victims that racial slavery and the slave trade were utterly abusing. As one group of Quakers poignantly wrote:

We conjure you, as you love Liberty, to extend its influence, and investigate its import; examine your Declaration of Rights, and see if you can find in it a *term* which conveys the idea of *human* merchandise; examine your hearts, and see if you can find a spark of brotherhood for men who *deal* in men. To defend your own liberties is noble, but to befriend the friendless is Godlike; complete then your Revolution by demanding Commerce to be just, that Africa may bless you as well as Europe.[93]

Unwilling to wait for gradual reform on this matter, black slaves in Saint Domingue (now Haiti) launched a violent revolt against their white masters in order to obtain their rights.

The impassioned and visionary pamphleteer, Thomas Paine (1737–1809), published the first part of his sensational and provocative *Rights of Man* in 1791.[94] Here, he drew upon the theories of natural law and natural rights, as well as his own personal involvement with both the American and the French Revolutions, and spoke boldly about political, civil, and economic rights. This brought him to the critical point of recognizing the inextricable connection between rights on the one hand, and the responsibility to create and uphold just law on the other. 'A Declaration of Rights is', he wrote, 'by reciprocity, a Declaration of Duties also. Whatever is my right as a man is also the right of another; and it becomes my duty to guarantee as well as to possess'.[95]

[90] 'Déclaration des Droits de la Femme et de la Citoyenne, 1791' in Olympe de Gouges, Œuvres (Mercure de France 1986) 99–112. See also Françoise Thébaud, 'La Première Féministe Milite' [2000] *Historia* 62.

[91] Mary Wollstonecraft, *A Vindication of the Rights of Woman* (first published 1792).

[92] Thomas Spence, *The Rights of Infants* (first published 1796).

[93] London Revolution Society (2 September 1792), as cited in George Mellor, *British Imperial Trusteeship: 1783–1850* (Faber & Faber 1951) 22 (emphasis in original).

[94] Thomas Paine, *Rights of Man* (Penguin 1984).

[95] Paine (n 94) 114.

9. Perspectives and Assessments

By the end of the eighteenth century, an impressive array of early legal texts and thoughts, evolving from a long and rich history, thus addressed a wide range of fundamental issues of justice and human rights. To appreciate the significance of this development, one must remember that almost all of them emerged out of traditional, hierarchical, patriarchal, and pre-industrial societies ruled by imperial or authoritarian regimes. Up to this point in history, abuse had largely characterized the long-standing pattern. Here, the few ruled the many, and stark stratification separated the strong from the weak. Men dominated women and expected them 'to know their proper place'. Human bondage and exploitation in slavery and serfdom were widely practised. Discrimination and persecution on the basis of race, of class or caste, of belief, or of ethnicity, were common. Existing authorities expected obedience rather than claims to individual rights. Moreover, virtually all governments regarded how they treated those under their control as a matter exclusively within their own sovereign, domestic jurisdiction. In these settings, advocacy for justice and rights was more often than not regarded as synonymous with subversion and thus as something that could be expected to provoke determined resistance.

The fact that laws and ideas of justice and human rights would emerge out of such fiercely constrained settings provides an indication of the extraordinarily widespread appeal and the power to transform ways of thinking and acting that characterized them.[96] In the face of oppression, abuse, and resistance, outspoken and courageous men and women were able to incorporate elements of justice and rights into legal texts and a variety of published writings, from books and pamphlets to declarations and collections of letters. By the end of the eighteenth century, they had contributed the specific expressions of 'natural law', 'natural rights', 'natural justice', 'the law of nations', 'the rights of man', 'the law of peoples', 'the rights of mankind', 'the laws of justice', 'humanity's laws', 'moral laws', 'the rights of humanity', and 'human rights', among others. Although closely connected, these phrases, and the concepts they represented, were not always equivalent or defined in exactly the same way as we might today. Instead, they marked beginning efforts, impulses, habits of the heart, and embryonic attempts to express ideas about justice and rights and, if possible, to incorporate them into legal texts close to home whenever they could. They were not fully developed doctrines, precisely articulated definitions, or carefully crafted international laws. At this early stage in their evolution, they hardly could be expected to do otherwise. They would evolve, expand, and become more sophisticated only through time and within their own historical contexts.

[96] This theme is developed throughout Lauren, *The Evolution of International Human Rights* (n 1).

Nevertheless, and despite their limitations, they taught significant lessons and laid essential foundations for developments that eventually would result in international human rights law. One of these was an appreciation for the absolutely critical importance of the rule of law itself. Those who spoke out early in history on behalf of justice and human rights came to understand, often through frustrating experience and painful persecution, that whatever visions they held would likely remain dreams and never become reality, unless they created legal guarantees. Only in this way, they reasoned, could they check the arbitrary exercise of power. Only in this way, they concluded, could victims of abuse be transformed from objects of pity into actual subjects of law. This explains why so much effort was expended in drafting, negotiating, promulgating, legislating, or otherwise enacting legal texts.

But those who championed justice and human rights in the past also came to realize that the existence of written guarantees in legal texts alone is never sufficient to protect the rights of the abused. As Confucius and Cicero pointed out centuries ago, the mere existence of laws does not necessarily mean that they serve justice. There are just laws, and there are unjust laws. This fact requires that great care be taken to ensure that the norms they enshrine are of the former. In addition, laws in and of themselves hold little practical value, unless they are actually enforced. The 'force of law' possesses meaning only if there is genuine enforcement. Centuries of historical experience has demonstrated that there are always those unwilling to share power, those with vested interests in special privileges, and those with prejudices against others, as well as leaders claiming that they can act entirely as they wish, without restraint. These individuals will strongly resist, will challenge the law, or will seek to subvert it in order to exclude, deny, and prevent others from legal protection of their rights. The struggles in implementing the Bill of Rights in the US Constitution itself, in the face of slavery, segregation, lynching, gender discrimination, and limits on the freedom of speech, to name only a few, provide more than enough evidence to demonstrate the magnitude of this kind of challenge.

The realization of the responsibility for enforcing just laws provided yet another major contribution to the evolution of justice and human rights, by revealing the clear connection between duties and rights. Law establishes responsibilities owed to others in society. As Thomas Paine noted so well in his *Rights of Man*, in order to enjoy the rule of law's protection of one's rights, one must enforce the rule of that law on behalf of others. But if those duties remain unperformed or unfilled, then others have a right to claim them. It is for this reason that the ideas about human duties, or what one is due to do, lead quite naturally to ideas of human rights, or what is due to one. This explains why, after looking back across historical time and place, Mahatma Gandhi, in a more recent century, concluded: 'The true source of rights is duty.'[97]

[97] Mohandas Gandhi, as cited in UNESCO, *The Birthright of Man* (n 30) 24.

Finally, the early ideas of natural law and natural rights provided a necessary foundation for the whole development of subsequent international human rights law. If one accepts that all human beings can claim certain rights simply as a result of being human, then it does not matter where, when, or under what form of government these individuals live. This is precisely the foundational concept, taken from legal texts and thoughts, which had evolved up to the end of the eighteenth century, and seized upon by those delegates who wrote the monumental Universal Declaration of Human Rights (UDHR)—a document that virtually every international human rights treaty that would follow cites. Indeed, they consciously chose the very language of natural law and natural rights from the different historical times, cultures, and places around the world that this chapter has discussed. This led the drafters to declare in the preface that the provisions are designed 'for all peoples and all nations' and in the first article that, 'All human beings are born free and equal in dignity and rights'.[98] To emphasize the point, they began a number of provisions with exactly the same simple—but extremely powerful—word: 'Everyone'. They selected many specific provisions directly from earlier historical legal texts. Moreover, the authors drew upon a particularly important lesson they had learned from history, by declaring in the text 'that human rights should be protected by the rule of law'.[99] It is for this reason that the declaration explicitly states: 'All are equal before the law and are entitled without any discrimination to equal protection of the law.'[100]

Together, these critical contributions from the past lay the foundation for the evolution of international human rights law that would follow. They established an essential beginning. Those who worked on behalf of justice and human rights in previous centuries understood that they needed to take the first step, by developing ideas and principles and then applying them in the only place they could: in law and practice close to home. But, they held a vision that, when the opportunity arose, the broader rule of law and the protection of human rights should be extended beyond their own immediate circumstances and applied to the world at large. How they worked to achieve this goal will be seen in the many cases discussed throughout this volume.

Further Reading

Cicero MT, *The Republic and The Laws* (Niall Rudd (tr), OUP 1998)
de Bary WT and Weiming T (eds), *Confucianism and Human Rights* (Columbia UP 1998)

[98] UDHR, preamble, Art 1. [99] UDHR, preamble. [100] UDHR, Art 7.

The Avalon Project, 'Documents in Law, History, and Diplomacy' <http://avalon.law.yale.edu/> accessed 16 February 2013.
Lauren PG, *The Evolution of International Human Rights: Visions Seen* (3rd edn, U Pennsylvania Press 2011)
Nikam NA and McKeon R (eds), *The Edicts of Asoka* (U Chicago Press 1978)
Paine T, *Rights of Man* (first published 1791, Penguin 1984)
Westbrook R (ed), *A History of Ancient Near Eastern Law* (Brill 2003)

CHAPTER 8

GENERAL PRINCIPLES AND CONSTITUTIONS AS SOURCES OF HUMAN RIGHTS LAW

MICHAEL O'BOYLE

MICHELLE LAFFERTY[1]

1. Introduction

ALTHOUGH the term 'human rights' is often understood as a Western concept, many of the basic values underlying human rights—reason, justice, the inherent dignity of human beings, and the need to secure their welfare—have long been current in other civilizations and cultures, as well. Important historic texts, some of which are discussed below and elsewhere in this volume, include the Code of Hammurabi, the Charter of Cyrus (Persia), the Hungarian Golden Bull, and the Magna Carta. Acceptance of the need for enforceable human rights guarantees is, however, of

[1] The views and opinions expressed are those of the authors and do not necessarily reflect the position of the Court.

more recent vintage. The first real breakthrough occurred with the adoption of human rights declarations in the late eighteenth century and their subsequent inclusion in the constitutions of France and the United States. A number of developments in international law, including the concept of diplomatic protection, the emergence of humanitarian law, and a growing awareness of the need for protection of minorities, further promoted human rights ideals. The progress made in human rights protection prior to the end of the Second World War, however, is dwarfed by the explosion in human rights instruments and jurisprudence which has occurred since the creation of the United Nations in 1945. The adoption of the Universal Declaration of Human Rights (UDHR) in 1948 marked a turning point in international human rights protection due to its comprehensive content and wide geographic remit, and it has since been at the root of the development of human rights at international, regional, and national levels.

This chapter will examine the role general principles and constitutions played both in the formulation of human rights standards, principally in the UDHR, and in their interpretation and application by international courts.

2. Preliminary Comments on General Principles and Constitutions

The term 'general principles' is a familiar, though elusive, concept. Article 38 § 1(c) of the Statute of the International Court of Justice (ICJ) refers to 'the general principles of law recognized by civilized nations' as one of the four sources of international law to be applied by the court.[2] However, two immediate complications arise.

The first concerns the meaning of the phrase 'general principles of law' in this context. As Lammers commented in 1980: 'Few things have in the past given rise to so much diversity of opinion as precisely the nature and function of these principles.'[3] The thirty years which have passed since this comment have done little to bring clarity to this area.[4] General principles of law identified in the case law

[2] The provision replicates Art 38(c) of the Statute of the Permanent Court of International Justice. More recently, the term 'general principles' has also appeared in Art 21 § 1(c) of the 1998 Rome Statute of the International Criminal Court, which instructs the court to apply 'general principles of law derived by the Court from national laws of legal systems of the world'.

[3] JG Lammers, 'General Principles of Law Recognized by Civilised Nations' in Frits Kalshoven, Pieter J Kuyper, and Johann G Lammers (eds), *Essays on the Development of the International Legal Order: In Memory of Haro F van Panhuys* (Martinus Nijhoff 1980) 53.

[4] A vast amount of literature exists on the interpretation of 'general principles of law', and it is outside the scope of this chapter to explore in any detail the different views that literature expresses. See, among many other scholarly works, LC Green, 'General Principles of Law and Human Rights'

of international courts and arbitral tribunals, derived from commonly accepted domestic rules, include, inter alia, the principle of good faith, the obligation to make reparation for international wrongs, the principle of *res judicata*, the principle of estoppel, the principle of *jus novit curia*, equality of the parties to a dispute, the rights of the defence, and respect for fundamental rights.[5] They have served to fill the gaps resulting from the absence of any treaty or customary obligation. A basic distinction is often drawn between principles which arise from domestic or 'municipal' law (*foro domestico*) and principles proper to international law itself.[6] While the inclusion of the former in the 'general principles of law' to which Article 38 refers is widely accepted, the extent to which the latter are encompassed by that provision is the subject of doctrinal controversy. Alston and Simma argue that the development of international human rights law has had a significant impact on our understanding of the notion of 'general principles', and certain human rights principles have been progressively 'accepted and recognized' as binding, even peremptory, by the international community of states as a whole. Such a process does not necessarily lead to the formation of customary law—although this is also possible—but to the formulation of general principles within the meaning of Article 38 § 1(c) of the ICJ Statute.

The second difficulty arises from the fact that those drawing on 'general principles' as a source of human rights law do not always define them as such or distinguish them from principles of customary law. In the *Mavrommatis Palestine Concessions* case, for example, the Permanent Court of International Justice spoke of 'an elementary principle' of international law,[7] while the International Court of Justice in the *Corfu Channel* case referred to 'general and well-recognized principles' of international law.[8] The European Court of Human Rights, for its part, has invoked 'fundamental principles of law'[9] and 'generally recognised international standards' in some of its judgments.[10] These references may relate to the concept of general principles of law, but the ambiguity that the use of different terminology

(1955–56) 8 *CLP* 162; Sir Arnold McNair, 'The General Principles of Law Recognised by Civilised Nations' (1957) *British YBIL* 1; Lammers (n 3); Maria Panezi, 'Sources of Law in Transition: Re-visiting General Principles of International Law' (2007) 2 *Ancilla Iuris* 66; Giorgio Gaja, 'General Principles of Law' in *The Max Planck Encyclopedia of Public International Law* (OUP 2008) online edition: <http://www.mpepil.com> accessed 22 April 2012.

[5] For a comprehensive list, see Patrick Dallier, Mathias Forteau, and Alain Pellet, *Droit International Public* (8th edn, LGDJ 2009) 380–86. International human rights courts have recognized many of these principles in their adjudication of disputes—see, in this context, the judgments of the European Court of Human Rights, referred to below in the section examining the Court's case law, and the judgments of the Inter-American Court of Human Rights, which Judge Cançado Trindade referred to in his concurring opinion in the Advisory Opinion of 17 September 2003 on the *Juridical Condition and Rights of the Undocumented Migrants* para 55.

[6] See Green (n 4) 176–218; Lammers (n 3) 56–59; Gaja (n 4).

[7] *The Mavrommatis Palestine Concessions Case* para 21.

[8] *Corfu Channel Case* para 22.

[9] *Golder v UK*, para 35.

[10] *John Murray v UK*, para 45.

causes leaves a certain doubt and is probably meant to do so. Notably, the European Court of Human Rights has so far refrained from elucidating the content of the reference to 'general principles' in Article 7(2) of the ECHR, even when the nature of the case invites it to do so—perhaps to steer clear of the difficulties under discussion.[11] This chapter, in contrast, explores the extent to which general principles of law that neither originate in nor derive their validity from treaty or customary law can be said to have contributed to the elaboration of human rights standards.

It is clear that some overlap exists between general principles and constitutions in this context. If at least some of the general principles are said to derive from municipal law, then in the human rights context such law may well be of a constitutional nature. An examination of the constitutions of democratic states today reveals that the vast majority of them, if not all of them, contain human rights provisions. This is unsurprising given the significant developments in human rights protection which began with the adoption of the UDHR in 1948, followed by the formulation of other human rights standards, which both inspired and obliged states to mirror these provisions in their domestic constitutions. However, the presence of provisions guaranteeing respect for human rights in constitutions around the world cannot solely be attributed to the influence of international human rights instruments adopted, and obligations imposed, in the wake of the UDHR. Long before the Nazi atrocities of the Second World War had created the political impetus to put in place international human rights guarantees, human rights standards were present in constitutional documents across the globe. Some of these constitutional provisions remain in force today.

In the United Kingdom, the Magna Carta, adopted in 1215 by King John and the nobility, was intended to curb the excesses of monarchical power.[12] It stipulated, inter alia, that no one's rights or justice would be refused or withheld, nor would he be dispossessed of his property rights without the legal judgment of his peers. These provisions have been described as the precursors of the rights against arbitrary detention and unfair trials that many modern human rights instruments contain.[13] They also lay the foundation for the development of the rule of law and influenced constitution makers throughout the common law world and beyond. The subsequent English Bill of Rights of 1689 included a right to free elections and guaranteed freedom of speech in Parliament. It also prohibited cruel and unusual punishment. Much of the Bill of Rights remains in force today.[14]

France proclaimed the Declaration of the Rights of Man and of the Citizen in 1789. The text of its preamble refers to the natural, inalienable, and sacred rights of man,

[11] See *Streletz, Kessler and Krenz v Germany*, discussed later.

[12] Parliament has since confirmed the Magna Carta on a number of occasions, and some of its provisions are still in force today.

[13] AW Bradley and KD Ewing, *Constitutional and Administrative Law* (12th edn, Longman 1998) 15.

[14] The Scottish Parliament enacted a Claim of Rights, in similar terms, in 1689.

and stipulates, in its Article 1, that men are born and remain free and equal in rights. It also contains provisions prohibiting unlawful arrest and retroactive criminal law, as well as protecting freedom of expression and opinion and property rights. The Declaration was included in the 1791 French Constitution and, with one limited exception, all subsequent constitutions have protected the rights it contains. The current 1958 Constitution establishing the Fifth Republic refers to the Declaration in its preamble.

In the United States, the 1776 Declaration of Independence proclaimed that all men were created equal, that they were endowed with certain unalienable rights, and that among these rights were life, liberty, and the pursuit of happiness. The Bill of Rights of the United States, in the form of amendments to the federal Constitution, was ratified in 1791 and protects citizens from, inter alia, unreasonable search and seizure, double jeopardy, self-incrimination, and deprivation of property, liberty, or life without due process of law. It also contains fair trial guarantees and prohibits cruel and unusual punishment. State constitutions, some containing more extensive guarantees than those of the federal Constitution, both preceded and followed the federal amendments.

The emergence of independent states in Latin American in the nineteenth century saw the enactment of further constitutional guarantees. In the first half of the twentieth century, an increasing number of states in other parts of the world began to include human rights provisions in their constitutions. As will be seen, the inclusion of human rights guarantees in constitutions had a significant impact on the content of the rights which were ultimately included in the UDHR.

3. The Universal Declaration of Human Rights

The adoption of the Universal Declaration of Human Rights constituted a landmark moment in human rights law. Its thirty articles cover civil, political, economic, social, and cultural rights. Two international covenants, under discussion at the same time and which together with the UDHR constitute the international bill of rights, further developed these rights. The drafting of the UDHR was heavily influenced by the provisions of national constitutions and the general principles of law derived from them, both of which formed the raw material out of which the rights were fashioned during the drafting process.[15]

[15] See, among many others works, Nehemiah Robinson, *The Universal Declaration of Human Rights: Its Origin, Significance, Application, and Interpretation* (Institute of Jewish Affairs and World

The UN Commission on Human Rights designated a drafting committee to be responsible for drafting a human rights instrument. At its first meeting, the drafting committee charged three of its members with responsibility for drafting a human rights instrument. The three members were Eleanor Roosevelt, the US member and chairman of the committee; Peng-Chun Chang, the member representing the Republic of China; and Charles Malik, the member for Lebanon. They were charged with preparing a preliminary draft of the Declaration with the assistance of the secretariat.[16]

The then Director of the United Nations Division of Human Rights, John Humphrey, prepared the initial text of the declaration, containing forty-eight articles.[17] In putting together his draft outline of the declaration, Humphrey drew on material from a number of sources. He had at his disposal, and made extensive use of, draft declarations submitted by governments and by non-governmental organizations.[18] Alongside the draft outline, the Secretariat also compiled a 408-page 'documented outline'[19] linking each of the rights in the Humphrey draft to provisions contained in the constitutions of the then fifty-five member states of the United Nations.[20] This document clearly underlines the important role constitutions played as sources of the rights contained in the Declaration. Each of the forty-eight articles in the original Humphrey draft was linked in the documented outline to a corresponding constitutional guarantee which existed, in some form, in world constitutions at that time. However, national constitutions played a greater role in the elaboration of some standards than others.

Jewish Congress 1958); Asbjørn Eide, Gudmundur Alfredsson, Göran Melander, Lars Adam Rehof, Allan Rosas, and Theresa Swineheart (eds), *The Universal Declaration of Human Rights: A Commentary* (Scandinavian UP 1993); Johannes Morsink, *The Universal Declaration of Human Rights: Origin, Drafting & Intent* (U Pennsylvania Press 1999).

16 See UNCHR 'Memorandum on Historical Background of the Committee' (29 May 1947) UN Doc E/CN.4/AC.1/2.

17 UNCHR 'Draft Outline of International Bill of Rights' (4 June 1947) UN Doc E/CN.4/AC.1/3.

18 See Morsink (n 15) generally, and more specifically at 6, 131. The governments of Chile, Cuba, and Panama each submitted draft declarations, and the governments of India and the United States of America submitted proposals.

19 UNCHR 'International Bill of Rights Documented Outline' (11 June 1947) UN Doc E/CN.4/AC.1/3/Add.1.

20 UNCHR, 'International Bill of Rights Documented Outline' (n 20). The fifty-five member states were Afghanistan, Argentina, Australia, Belgium, Bolivia, Brazil, the Byelorussian Soviet Socialist Republic, Canada, Chile, China, Colombia, Costa Rica, Cuba, Czechoslovakia, Denmark, the Dominican Republic, Ecuador, Egypt, El Salvador, Ethiopia, France, Greece, Guatemala, Haiti, Honduras, Iceland, India, Iran, Iraq, Lebanon, Liberia, Luxembourg, Mexico, the Netherlands, New Zealand, Nicaragua, Norway, Panama, Paraguay, Peru, the Philippine Republic, Poland, Saudi Arabia, Siam, Sweden, Syria, Turkey, the Ukrainian Soviet Socialist Republic, the Union of South Africa, the Union of Soviet Socialist Republics, the United Kingdom, the United States, Uruguay, Venezuela, Yugoslavia.

The inclusion of civil and political rights in the UDHR was hardly surprising. As observed above, such rights were already well-established in eighteenth-century human rights texts, and these provisions had inspired similar constitutional texts in many of the member states.[21] As Morsink explains, most delegations had 'little difficulty' voting for many of the rights contained in the draft Declaration, because similar guarantees appeared in their own national constitutions.[22]

The inclusion of economic, social, and cultural rights in the UDHR was a more significant development, however.[23] These rights appeared in a large number of the constitutions, from Latin American and Communist states in particular, and the draft declarations submitted by Chile, Panama, and Cuba included the socialist rights guaranteed by their constitutions. Although other member states of the UN did not have corresponding constitutional provisions, Humphrey decided to include them in his first draft, based on the draft declarations he had received and supported by the constitutional provisions of a large number of Latin American states. This was the first step towards ensuring their inclusion in the final text of the UDHR.[24]

After Humphrey had prepared his draft, the drafting committee met and agreed to set up a temporary working group composed inter alios of René Cassin (France), Geoffrey Wilson (the United Kingdom), and Mr Malik (Lebanon).[25] Its mandate was largely to suggest a 'logical rearrangement' of the articles of the draft outline the Secretariat supplied and to suggest a redraft of the various articles in the light of the discussions of the drafting committee.[26] The working group requested that René Cassin undertake the writing of a draft declaration based on the Secretariat draft outline. He prepared a draft with a preamble and forty-four articles, a draft discussed and revised in the working group before being presented to the drafting committee. The texts prepared at the various stages of the procedure were submitted to the Commission on Human Rights and formed the basis of negotiations for the final text.[27]

The fate of some of the economic rights first included in the draft outline by John Humphrey is instructive. The draft contained five work-related rights—the

[21] See Lauri Hannikainen and Kristian Myntti, 'Article 19' and Allan Rosas, 'Article 21' in Eide (n 15) 275, 300.

[22] Morsink (n 15) 72.

[23] Asbjørn Eide comments that Roosevelt's 'freedom from want' was the most innovative in the new international humanitarian order envisaged after the Second World War. Asbjørn Eide, 'Article 25' in Eide (n 15) 385.

[24] See Morsink (n 15) 89, 130–33, 157, 191.

[25] UNCHR 'Summary Record of the Sixth Meeting' (16 June 1947) UN Doc E/CN.4/AC.1/SR.6.

[26] UNCHR 'Draft Report of the Drafting Committee to the Commission on Human Rights' (23 June 1947) UN Doc E/CN.4/AC.1/14.

[27] UNCHR 'Report of the Drafting Committee to the Commission on Human Rights' (1 July 1947) UN Doc E/CN.4/21.

right of equal access to vocations and professions (draft Article 24); the right and duty to perform socially useful work (draft Article 37); the right to good working conditions (draft Article 38); the right to an equitable share of the national income as justified by a person's work (draft Article 39); and the right to the public help necessary to support a family (draft Article 40). As the documented outline indicates, a right of equal access to professions and vocations appeared in the Chilean draft declaration. Similar or related provisions could also be found in the constitutions of fifteen Latin American states, three Scandinavian countries, two Communist countries, Afghanistan, and Siam. The provisions subsequently appeared as Article 16 of the Cassin redraft. A right to work appeared in the three draft declarations Chile, Cuba, and Panama submitted and was guaranteed in the constitutions of ten Latin American states and five Communist states. Aside from these fifteen states, only China, France, and Turkey guaranteed a right to employment. The right and duty to work duly appeared in the Humphrey draft and in Article 29 of the Cassin revised text. The right to good working conditions also appeared in the three draft declarations submitted to the Secretariat by the Latin American states. In the documented outline, it is linked to constitutional provisions in fourteen Latin American states, as well as China, France, the Philippines, Poland, and Yugoslavia. It appears in a revised form in Cassin's Article 31. Humphrey's Article 39 originated exclusively in Latin American and Communist traditions; the documented outline links this article to provisions in two of the three Latin American drafts, as well as the constitutions of six Latin American and four Communist states. Article 40 had its roots in provisions contained in two of the drafts that the committee submitted. Related provisions appeared in a large number of constitutions: fifteen Latin American states, three Communist states, China, France, and the Netherlands. The same idea appeared in Article 31 of Cassin's redraft.

It can be seen that the five work-related rights that appeared in the original Humphrey draft, inspired largely by the Latin American tradition as manifested in the constitutional provisions of those states, are the foundation of the final provision which appears today in the UDHR. In large part as a result of their common constitutional traditions, Latin American states were in broad agreement as to the inclusion of these rights in the UDHR throughout the drafting process. Their general consensus was separately manifested in their adoption, together with the United States, of the American Declaration of the Rights and Duties of Man in April 1948, while the UDHR was still under negotiation. With the support of the Communist bloc, most of the economic, social, and cultural rights survived the drafting process in some form.[28] Article 23 of the Declaration is one of the lengthier articles in the Declaration and proclaims a number of work-related rights, including the right to

[28] For a detailed discussion of the drafting of the 'work-related' rights contained in the UDHR, see Morsink (n 15) ch 5.

work, to free choice of employment, to just and favourable work conditions, and to protection against unemployment; the right to equal pay for equal work; the right to just and favourable remuneration supplemented, if necessary, by other means of social protection; and the right to form and to join trade unions for the protection of one's interests. While it is important not to overstate the role that Latin American, and to a lesser extent Communist, state constitutions played in the final inclusion of a detailed right to work in the UDHR, it is clear from the above analysis that the protection of a variety of rights in the constitutions of a large number of Latin American states strongly influenced both their inclusion and content in the Humphrey draft, as well as their eventual position in the final text.[29]

The influence of constitutions is all the more striking if one examines the drafting history of Article 24 of the Declaration, which guarantees the right to rest and leisure, including reasonable limitations on working hours and periodic holidays with pay. Such a provision did not appear in any of the draft declarations to which Humphrey referred in preparing his draft outline. However, the right to rest-days or to paid annual leave appeared in the constitutions of thirteen of the states surveyed: nine Latin American states and four Communist states. From these constitutional provisions, Humphrey accordingly drafted a provision on the right to rest and leisure, which was preserved in Article 36 of the Cassin draft and finally adopted in the Declaration text itself (Article 24).

More generally, the human rights instruments of the eighteenth century mark the overall tenor and language of the UDHR.[30] One of the principal similarities can be seen in the underlying rationale behind the UDHR, set out in the first recital of its preamble, namely the 'inherent dignity' and the 'equal and inalienable rights of all members of the human family', which reflect the provisions of the French Declaration, as well as the US Declaration of Independence. The inspiration these texts provided is also seen in the UDHR's first article, which stipulates that all men are born free and equal in dignity and rights.[31]

The Humphrey draft did not include a draft preamble, but merely made reference to what such a preamble should contain. There was no reference to human dignity or equality, nor did any article of the Humphrey draft contain language of the nature

[29] Morsink explains that the united voice of the Latin American delegations, together with the support of the Communist states, ensured that the substance of the original work-related provisions remained in Art 23 as finally adopted. Morsink (n 15) 130, ch 5 generally. However, a number of other organizations also played a role, especially in the development of the trade union rights in the Declaration, including the International Labour Organization, the World Federation of Trade Unions, and the American Federation of Labor. See Morsink (n 15) 168–81.

[30] See Morsink (n 15) 281.

[31] The similarities are noted by Tore Lindholm, 'Article 1: A New Beginning' in Eide (n 15) and discussed by Morsink (n 15) ch 8.

found in Article 1 of the UDHR. The inclusion of Article 1 in the text occurred during Cassin's re-working of the Humphrey draft. It is clear that in carrying out this task, Cassin drew inspiration from the provisions of the 1789 French Declaration, and in particular its preamble and first article. Indeed, Morsink describes the first sentence of Article 1 of the UDHR as 'a virtual rewrite' of Article 1 of the French Declaration.[32]

The drafting history of the UDHR demonstrates that a number of sources inspired its thirty articles. That the principal motivation for the declaration stemmed from the atrocities of the Second World War is indisputable; frequent reference was made during the deliberations to the human rights violations committed in Nazi Germany prior to and during the War.[33] However, the rights that national constitutions across the globe had already secured inspired the formulation and content of the rights. For certain topics, some of which have been discussed above, the influence of constitutional rights was considerable. If one accepts, as is often claimed,[34] that the first draft of the Declaration was prepared by John Humphrey, then the influence of constitutions on the rights it contains is indisputable. In any case, it can be concluded that constitutions were treated as a source of human rights in the drafting process of the UDHR and that their contribution was significant.

As noted above, the Universal Declaration has in turn inspired a wide range of human rights texts at the international level, as well as human rights provisions in national constitutions.[35] As such, the UDHR has been described as the constitution of the entire human rights movement,[36] a description which is arguably no exaggeration. Indeed, it has been suggested that the UDHR may well constitute an expression of the 'general principles of law recognised by civilised nations',[37] and many of its provisions are now considered to form part of customary international law.[38]

[32] Morsink (n 15) 281. [33] For an overview, see generally Morsink (n 15).

[34] See eg Morsink (n 15) 6.

[35] See Jan Mårtenson, 'The Preamble of the Universal Declaration of Human Rights and the UN Human Rights Programme' in Eide (n 15); Morsink (n 15) 20. The 2002 issue of the United Nations' compilation of international human rights instruments covered almost 100 human rights instruments. UN High Commissioner for Human Rights, *Human Rights: A Compilation of International Instruments* (UN 2002).

[36] Henry J Steiner, Philip Alston, and Ryan Goodman, *International Human Rights in Context: Law, Politics, Morals: Text and Materials* (3rd edn, OUP 2008) 136.

[37] See Green (n 4) 174–75; and Gunnar G Schram, 'Article 15' in Eide (n 15).

[38] Simma and Alston (n 4) 84, 90–96; Steiner, Alston, and Goodman (n 36) 137.

4. The Application and Interpretation of Human Rights by International Courts

The adoption of human rights instruments is only one part of the story of the development of human rights to date. Human rights treaties by their nature often focus on broad principles; even when drafters provide some details regarding particular rights, their specific content and scope is generally left to national courts or international treaty bodies to develop. Aside from judicial bodies created with the specific role of ensuring the effective implementation of a particular human rights treaty, international courts more generally may be called upon to develop human rights standards in the context of their activities in other areas of international law.

The following section examines the practice of the Permanent Court of International Justice (PCIJ) and International Court of Justice (ICJ), as well as the European Court of Human Rights (ECtHR) and the Court of Justice of the European Union (CJEU), in order to explore the extent to which general principles and constitutions play a role in the application and development of human rights standards today.

4.1 The Permanent Court of International Justice and the International Court of Justice

The PCIJ and, in its later incarnation, the ICJ are unique among the courts examined here, in that from the outset their respective statutes conferred on them a mandate to apply general principles of law recognized by civilized nations.[39] As noted above, despite the inclusion of the phrase in the statutes of the two courts, there was no agreement as to what it envisaged. Even the drafters of the PCIJ Statute were not united in their understanding of the meaning of the term.[40] Despite this uncertain origin, the courts have made regular reference to general principles in deciding the cases before them. Bearing in mind, however, that they are courts of public international law and not human rights courts, an examination of their jurisprudence

[39] See above. The European Convention on Human Rights (ECHR), the basis of the activities of the ECtHR, does refer to general principles of law in the context of Art 7 (which reflects the principle of legality). However, the ECHR does not contain any general provision indicating that principles are a source of law relevant to interpreting its provisions and are to be applied by the ECtHR. The founding treaties of the European Communities contained no reference to general principles.

[40] See Gaja (n 4) para 3.

paints a more nuanced picture of the extent to which the general principles they have invoked have contributed to the development of human rights law.

One early example arose in the case of the *Minority Schools in Albania*.[41] Following the conclusion of the First World War and the redrawing of national boundaries in Europe, various states concluded a number of minority treaties to protect the newly created national minorities. Albania, home to a large Greek-speaking minority, had made a declaration before the Council of the League of Nations in 1921 to the effect that its racial, religious, and linguistic minorities would have the same rights as other Albanian nationals. The Council subsequently requested that the PCIJ express an opinion on whether the abolition of private schools in Albania, which included Greek schools, conformed to the letter and spirit of the 1921 Declaration. The PCIJ observed that the 1921 Declaration was intended to apply to Albania the general principles of the minority treaties, and it therefore approached the question before it from this perspective. It explained that the idea underlying the minority treaties was to secure for racial, linguistic, or religious minorities the possibility of living peaceably alongside the majority population, while at the same time preserving their distinctive characteristics and satisfying the special needs which resulted therefrom. The PCIJ found that in order to achieve this, two aspects were particularly necessary: first, a prohibition on discrimination; and second, putting in place measures permitting the minority group to preserve its minority culture and traditions.[42] Against this background, and after careful examination of the text of the 1921 Declaration, the PCIJ concluded that the general abolition of private schools, although a universal measure, failed to conform to the Declaration's letter and spirit.

This was not, strictly speaking, a case in which general principles lay at the heart of the court's reasoning. Nonetheless, its decision to situate the dispute within the general context of the minorities regime then in place, and to examine the idea underlying the minorities regime, before considering Albania's obligations arising from the 1921 Declaration was an important signal that the court was willing to look beyond treaty law and custom and to take into account more general considerations arising in respect of minority rights in deciding the case before it.

The ICJ first referred to general principles in its judgment in the *Corfu Channel* case.[43] The United Kingdom brought the case against Albania as a claim for compensation following the death of naval personnel and damage to naval vessels resulting from hitting a minefield in Albanian waters in 1946. The court found that the laying of the minefield could not have been accomplished without the knowledge of the Albanian authorities. As a consequence, the Albanian authorities had a duty to warn of the imminent danger the British warships faced. The court found

[41] *Minority Schools in Albania Case.*
[42] *Minority Schools in Albania Case* (n 41) 17.
[43] *Corfu Channel Case* (n 8).

that this obligation arose not under the Hague Convention of 1907, which applied in times of war, but under 'certain general and well-recognized principles', which included 'elementary considerations of humanity, even more exacting in peace than in war'.[44] The principles to which the court was referring here appeared to be of the nature of fundamental principles of international law itself, which imposed a duty, independent of treaty or customary international law, to take steps to avert a serious threat to life and to property.

Subsequently, in its Advisory Opinion on the *Reservations to the Genocide Convention*, the court found that the principles underlying the Genocide Convention were principles which civilized nations recognized as binding on states, even without any conventional obligation.[45] In the formulation used, the court left open whether it was referring to general principles or to customary international law. In its 1973 Advisory Opinion on the *Application for Review of Judgment No 158 of the United Nations Administrative Tribunal*, the ICJ referred to the content of the general principles of law as regards procedural rights and equality of arms, concluding that there did not appear to be any principle which required an opportunity to make oral representations in review proceedings, provided that both parties had an equal opportunity to present their cases in written submissions.[46]

In its judgment in the *United States Diplomatic and Consular Staff in Tehran* case, having concluded that Iran had breached its obligations towards the United States in respect of the seizure and occupation of the US embassy in Tehran, the court went on to say that:

> wrongfully to deprive human beings of their freedom and to subject them to physical constraint in conditions of hardship is in itself manifestly incompatible with the principles of the Charter of the United Nations, as well as with the fundamental principles enunciated in the Universal Declaration of Human Rights.[47]

It is regrettable that this statement appeared in the judgment almost as a kind of postscript; the court had already concluded on the basis of a detailed examination in the earlier pages of its judgment that Iran had breached its international obligations.[48] However, the court's statement is nonetheless a welcome suggestion that the principles set out in the UDHR and the 'human rights' and 'fundamental freedoms'

[44] *Corfu Channel Case* (n 8) 22.

[45] *Reservations to the Genocide Convention Case* 23. The ICJ subsequently held that the prohibition of genocide constitutes an *erga omnes* obligation and is *jus cogens*. See *Application of the Convention on the Prevention and Punishment of the Crime of Genocide* 616; *Armed Activities on the Territory of the Congo* 32.

[46] *Application for Review of Judgment No 158* 181.

[47] *US Diplomatic and Consular Staff in Tehran Case* 42.

[48] *US Diplomatic and Consular Staff Case* (n 47) 42.

to which the Charter refers, are principles which may be capable of being invoked in future cases.[49]

More recently, in its 1996 Advisory Opinion in the *Legality of the Threat or Use of Nuclear Weapons* case, the ICJ indicated that states had to take environmental considerations into account when assessing necessity and proportionality in the pursuit of legitimate military objectives.[50] In support of its approach, it referred to provisions of the Rio Declaration[51] and to a General Assembly resolution on the protection of the environment in times of armed conflict.[52] In formulating this requirement to consider environmental considerations, the court based its approach on provisions of 'soft law', rather than on any legally binding instruments. Such soft law, constituting neither treaty law nor customary international law, is arguably one of the most significant sources of the general principles to which Article 38 § 1(c) refers. The ICJ's reference to the Rio Declaration and the General Assembly resolution allowed it to develop its case law regarding environmental rights.

Notwithstanding these precedents, there is a remarkable absence of discussion of human rights principles in the case law of the ICJ. In recent cases in which human rights issues have, at least from a general perspective, been firmly in the foreground, the court has eschewed any reference to, or development of, general principles as an important element of its reasoning or as the foundation for its decisions.[53] The reluctance of the ICJ to develop general principles in the context of human rights has been the subject of comment in two weighty separate opinions.

In the *South-West Africa Cases*,[54] Liberia and Ethiopia commenced proceedings against South Africa, contending that the latter had, by its policy of apartheid, violated international law in the discharge of its obligations as mandatory in respect of what is now Namibia. The court ultimately rejected the claims on the grounds that Liberia and Ethiopia had no legal right or interest in the subject matter. Judge Tanaka dissented and set out his reasons in full in a 150-page opinion.[55] In his view, the cases essentially concerned the question of whether there existed a legal norm regarding equality or non-discrimination, which he explained was intimately related to the essence and nature of fundamental human rights, the promotion and encouragement of which was

[49] Rodley takes a different view of the significance of the case. See Nigel S Rodley, 'Human Rights and Humanitarian Intervention: The Case Law of the World Court' (1989) 38 *ICLQ* 321, 324–27.

[50] *Legality of the Threat or Use of Nuclear Weapons Case* 242.

[51] Principle 24 of the 1992 Rio Declaration on Environment and Development provides that states should respect international law by providing protection for the environment in times of armed conflict.

[52] Protection of the Environment in Times of Armed Conflict, UNGA Res 47/37 (25 November 1992) UN Doc A/47/49.

[53] See, for example, *South-West Africa Cases*, discussed later; *US States Diplomatic and Consular Staff Case* (n 47).

[54] *South-West Africa Cases (Second Phase) Judgment* [1966] ICJ Rep 6.

[55] *South-West Africa Cases* (n 54) 250, dissenting Opinion of Judge Tanaka.

one of the purposes of the UN according to its Charter.[56] He considered that such an obligation arguably arose from the terms of the UN Charter and was a norm of customary international law. He then turned to examine whether it formed part of the general principles of law.[57] Drawing on the reasoning of the court in the *Reservations to the Genocide Convention* advisory opinion, he concluded that human rights are not created, but merely declared by treaties; they exist independently of the will of states. As a consequence, he considered that the general principles mentioned in Article 38 § 1(c) included the concept of human rights and of their protection. The principle of equality and non-discrimination, he noted, were stipulated in the list of human rights that the domestic systems of virtually every state recognized and had become an integral part of the constitutions of most of the world's civilized countries. As such, it constituted, in his view, one of the specific general principles to which Article 38 referred.[58] The Inter-American Court of Human Rights has developed the point further. In its Advisory Opinion on the *Juridical Condition and Rights of the Undocumented Migrants*, it considered the 'fundamental principles of equality and non-discrimination' to have entered the domain of *jus cogens* and to entail obligations *erga omnes* that bind all states and generate effects with regard to third parties, including individuals.[59]

In the *Pulp Mills* case,[60] the ICJ was asked to rule on a dispute between Argentina and Uruguay in respect of pulp mills constructed on the Uruguay River which forms the border between the two countries. Both parties contended that the 1975 Statute of the River Uruguay had to be interpreted in the light of principles governing the law of international watercourses and principles of international law ensuring protection of the environment, although they disagreed as to the content of those principles. The ICJ made a brief reference to the 'principle of prevention' and to a precautionary approach, but it did not afford either any particular attention in its judgment. In his separate opinion,[61] Judge Cançado Trindade lamented the fact that the ICJ had overlooked the general principles of law in deciding the case, despite the fact that they were invoked by both parties. He considered that in taking the approach it did, the ICJ had missed 'a unique occasion to give a remarkable contribution to our discipline'.[62] He discussed the use made of general principles by both the PCIJ and the ICJ in some depth, observing that considerably more

[56] *South-West Africa Cases* (n 54) 287.

[57] *South-West Africa Cases* (n 54) from 294.

[58] *South-West Africa Cases* (n 54) 299–300.

[59] See also Judge Cançado Trindade's concurring opinion in the same context, discussing the interrelationship between general principles and international human rights norms. The United Nations Human Rights Committee has been more cautious, but in its General Comment No 18, it finds that 'equality before the law and equal protection of the law without any discrimination, constitute a basic and general principle relating to the protection of human rights'. UNHRC 'General Comment No 18: Non-Discrimination' (10 November 1989) UN Doc HRI/GEN/1/Rev.9.

[60] *Pulp Mills on the River Uruguay*.

[61] *Pulp Mills* (n 60) para 135 (separate opinion of Judge Cançado Trindade).

[62] *Pulp Mills* (n 60) para 5.

attention was devoted to the principles of international law decades ago (including the times of the PCIJ) than at present.[63] As to the issues arising in the *Pulp Mills case*, he considered the applicable law to be composed of the 1975 Statute, together with the relevant principles of law. The latter encompassed, in his view, principles of international environmental law, which included the principles of prevention, precaution, and sustainable development.[64]

It seems clear, particularly in light of the opinions of Judges Tanaka and Cançado Trindade, that the ICJ has displayed a certain reluctance to invoke general principles of law in cases in which human rights issues arise. There is no doubt that the vast and complex network of international legal instruments provides, in many instances, a highly regulated framework within which to decide disputes, but there remain nonetheless areas in which general principles have a role to play. This is particularly so in cases, such as those touching upon issues of environmental law, where the rights in question have not been the subject of any detailed treaty obligations.[65] Referring to general principles, rather than treaty obligations, as a source of human rights obligations may also be particularly important in cases where the respondent state has not ratified any relevant treaty, or simply to make the point that the rights in question are fundamental. In this respect it is worth mentioning the court's case law attesting to the existence of *jus cogens*, which are peremptory norms of international law and are generally agreed to include a number of human rights principles.[66] Courts often refer to the prohibition of torture and genocide, the principles of equality and non-discrimination, the prohibition of racial discrimination and apartheid, the prohibition of slavery and the slave trade, the prohibition of massive pollution of the atmosphere or of the seas, and the right of self-determination as falling into this elevated category of human rights norms.[67] However, given the uncertain and evolving nature of *jus cogens* rules, claims in

[63] *Pulp Mills* (n 60) para 37.

[64] *Pulp Mills* (n 60) para 220. See also his concurring opinion in the Advisory Opinion of the Inter-American Court of Human Rights on the *Juridical Condition and Rights of Undocumented Migrants* (n 5).

[65] This is likely to be the case in respect of most of the 'third generation' rights.

[66] The Court alluded to the existence of such norms in *Barcelona Traction, Light and Power Company, Limited* 32 (rights giving rise to duties *erga omnes*). The ICJ cited protection from slavery and racial discrimination as examples of *erga omnes* norms. See also *East Timor* 102 (right to self-determination); *Application of the Convention on the Prevention and Punishment of the Crime of Genocide* (n 45) 616 (prohibition of genocide). The ICJ has, on occasion, expressly referred to *jus cogens* in its judgments and advisory opinions. See eg *Legality of the Threat or Use of Nuclear Weapons* (n 50) 258 (not necessary to pronounce on whether principles and rules of humanitarian law are part of *jus cogens*); *Armed Activities on the Territory of the Congo* (n 45) 32 (prohibition of genocide is *jus cogens*). The International Criminal Tribunal for the Former Yugoslavia has also invoked the principle of *jus cogens*. See *Prosecutor v Furundžija* 55, 58–61 (prohibition of torture is *jus cogens*).

[67] See Chapter 24 in this *Handbook* and, generally Alexander Orakhelashvili, *Peremptory Norms in International Law* (OUP 2008); Jochen A Frowein, '*Ius Cogens*', *The Max Planck Encyclopaedia of Public International Law* (OUP 2008) online edition: <http://www.mpepil.com> accessed 22 April 2012.

this area are to be treated with circumspection, and generally international human rights tribunals, with the notable exception of the Inter-American Court, have been cautious in their pronouncements. The UN Human Rights Committee in its General Comment on States of Emergency lists a series of principles, beyond the list of non-derogable provisions set out in Article 4(2) of the International Covenant on Civil and Political Rights, from which there can be no derogation under Article 4 because, in the Committee's view, they have become absolute norms of general international law.[68]

By finding the source of such obligations outside treaty law, the possibility of their universal application is ensured and their potential for contributing to the development of the ICJ's human rights case law enhanced. It would appear, therefore, that whatever the view held as to the contribution of general principles to the development of human rights by the ICJ to date, there remains much scope for such principles to be employed to greater effect in the future.

4.2 The European Court of Human Rights

In the European Convention on Human Rights, reference is made to 'general principles' in Article 7, which encapsulates the principle of *nullum crimen nulla poena sine lege*. Concerned with ensuring that the article did not impugn the validity of the Nuremberg judgments, the article reproduces the text of the corresponding article of the International Covenant on Civil and Political Rights, clarifying that: 'This article shall not prejudice the trial and punishment of any person for any act or omission which, at the time when it was committed, was criminal according to the general principles of law recognised by civilised nations.'[69] In its case law, the Court has not sought to develop the meaning of general principles in this context. In *Streletz, Kessler and Krenz v Germany*, which concerned the legal basis under

[68] See UNHRC, 'General Comment No 29: States of Emergency (article 4)' (31 August 2001), UN Doc No CCPR/C/21/Rev.1/Add.11 paras 11–13. While this would appear to be, at least in part, a reference to *jus cogens* norms, the Committee took care not to characterize them as such. The list includes the following (a) all persons deprived of their liberty shall be treated with humanity and with respect for the inherent dignity of the human person; (b) prohibitions against the taking of hostages, abductions, or unacknowledged detention; (c) the international protection of the rights of persons belonging to minorities includes elements that must be respected in all circumstances (as reflected in the prohibition against genocide, the inclusion of a non-discrimination clause in Art 4 § 1, as well as the non-derogable nature of Art 18); (d) deportation or forcible transfers of populations that amount to a crime against humanity as set out in the Rome Statute of the International Criminal Court.

[69] Article 7 § 2 of the Convention. See Art 15 § 2 of the ICCPR. There are two other references in the ECHR. Article 35 § 1 requires that all domestic remedies be exhausted 'according to the generally recognised rules of international law'. Article 1 of Protocol No 1 protecting the right to property provides that: 'No one shall be deprived of his possessions except in the public interest and subject to the conditions provided for by law and by the general principles of international law.' In the field of

German law for the convictions of senior officials held responsible for the policy of killing those seeking to escape from the GDR, the court found that the acts in question also constituted offences that the rules of international law on the protection of human rights defined with sufficient accessibility and foreseeability. It was thus not necessary to consider Article 7 § 2. Several judges concurring in the result considered, however, that the acts amounted to a crime against humanity which was a general principle of international law at the material time.[70] The United Nations Human Rights Committee, dealing with a similar case, noted that 'the disproportionate use of lethal force was criminal according to the general principles of law recognized by the community of nations already at the time when the author committed his acts'.[71]

Despite this limited reference to general principles in the text of the ECHR, the court has, from an early stage, drawn on the concept of general principles in order to interpret and apply the rights guaranteed by the Convention. For example, it regularly relies on the general principle of estoppel in rejecting preliminary objections relating to admissibility.[72] The court also applies the principle of *res judicata* as an element of legal certainty, itself inherent in the rule of law. In *Brumarescu v Romania* it found a violation of Article 6 (right to a fair trial) on the grounds that the Supreme Court of Justice had set aside a judicial decision that was irreversible under Romanian law.[73] It is tempting to consider the principle of proportionality as a general principle that runs throughout the Convention, but the principle has no operation in cases concerning Article 3 (prohibition of torture, inhuman, and degrading treatment). The court has asserted the principle of 'fair balance' between the rights of the individual and the interests of the community in the *Soering* judgment,[74] but it is more a principle of interpretation rather than a general principle of law. In *Vilho Eskelinen and Others v Finland*, on the other hand, the court attached weight to the general principle of judicial control of administrative action—a principle of law underlying the constitutional traditions common to member states and reflected in Articles 6 and 13 (right to an effective remedy) of the ECHR—in finding that civil servants (in this case police officials) should be able to submit their disputes to a court. The right of access to a court has long been considered to be a general principle.

In the case of *Golder v United Kingdom*, the applicant, a serving prisoner, complained to the court under Article 6 § 1 that the UK authorities had refused to permit him to consult a solicitor with a view to bringing a civil action for libel against

expropriation these principles have been held not to apply to the taking of the property of nationals (*James v UK*, paras 60–66).

[70] *Streletz, Kessler and Krenz v Germany* (n 11) paras 105–106. See also the concurring opinions of Judges Loucaides and Levits.

[71] *Baumgarten v Germany* para 9.4.

[72] For example, *Markin v Russia*, para 96.

[73] Paragraph 62.

[74] *Soering v UK*.

a prison officer. The applicant argued that the right to a fair trial that the ECHR guaranteed encompassed a right of access to court. Citing Article 31 § 3(c) of the Vienna Convention on the Law of Treaties (although not yet in force at the time), the court referred to the need to take into account any relevant rules of international law applicable between the parties, which in its view included general principles of law. Indeed, the court observed that during the negotiations on the drafting of the Convention, the Committee on Legal and Administrative Questions had foreseen in August 1950 that the court 'must necessarily apply such principles' in the execution of its duties and thus considered it unnecessary to insert a specific clause to this effect in the Convention.[75] The court found that the principle whereby a civil claim must be capable of being submitted to a judge ranked as one of the 'universally "recognised" fundamental principles of law'. It considered the same to be true of the principle of international law which forbade the denial of justice. It concluded that Article 6 § 1 had to be read in light of these principles, and on that basis concluded that it did include a right of access to a court.[76] Other notable examples can be given.

In *Marckx v Belgium* the court relied on the principle of legal certainty to dispense the Belgian state from reopening legal acts or situations that antedated the delivery of judgment finding inter alia that distinctions in succession law between 'legitimate' and 'illegitimate' children were discriminatory and in breach of Article 14 (prohibition of discrimination).

In *John Murray v United Kingdom*, the court, when asked by an applicant to interpret the right to a fair trial as including the right to remain silent and the privilege against self-incrimination, found that these were 'generally recognised international standards which [lay] at the heart of the notion of a fair procedure under Article 6'.[77] Also in *Scoppola (No 2) v Italy*, the court was influenced by the identification of the *lex mitior* as a fundamental principle of criminal law. Remarkably, it found that where the penalty for a crime had been lowered since the commission of the offence, Article 7 § 1 of the Convention required that the convicted person be given the benefit of the more lenient penalty. The court's interpretation is notable since the language of Article 7 § 1 is confined textually to the principle that penalties should not be greater than that existing at the time of the offence.[78] Nothing is said about lesser penalties. The court has thus relied on a general principle to implicitly amend a Convention provision, undoubtedly influenced by a similar provision in the EU Charter on Fundamental Rights.[79]

[75] Consultative Assembly, 'Working Paper No 93' (1950) vol III, 982.

[76] *Golder* (n 9) paras 35–36.

[77] *John Murray* (n 10) para 45.

[78] See, in this respect, *Scoppola (No 2) v Italy*; the partly dissenting opinions of Judges Nicolau, Bratza, Lorenzen, Jociene, Villiger, and Sajó; and Art 49 § 1 of the Charter.

[79] See below for a discussion of the Charter. In the area of criminal law, see also *AP, MP and TP v Switzerland*, where the court considered that criminal liability does not survive the person who has committed the criminal act. This was considered to be a fundamental rule of criminal law linked to the presumption of innocence. Inheritance of the guilt of the dead was not considered to be compatible with the standards of criminal justice in a society governed by the rule of law.

It should also be mentioned that the court will interpret the ECHR against the background of international law (including general principles) and will seek to harmonize its interpretation of the ECHR with such principles.[80] It also operates a rebuttable presumption that Security Council resolutions do not impose a requirement to breach fundamental rights.[81] In *Al-Adsani v United Kingdom*, the court further recognized the prohibition of torture to be a peremptory norm of international law (*jus cogens*), but it also held that it did not trump the principle of the sovereign immunity of states.[82]

It appears that even more significant in the development of the court's case law is its practice of reviewing the national laws and constitutions of member states when examining the scope and content of Convention rights. This practice is particularly evident in its assessment of the qualified rights contained principally in Articles 8 to 11 of the Convention, which expressly permit restrictions on rights, provided that these restrictions are in accordance with a legitimate aim and are necessary in a democratic society. In such areas, the court has developed the concept of the margin of appreciation, which essentially permits member states a certain degree of discretion in deciding how best to secure the rights set out in the Convention. The width of the margin depends on various factors, and one such factor is the presence or absence of a European consensus on the matter in question.[83] Aside from having regard to member states' constitutional provisions, the court also has regard to other international norms concluded in the relevant field in assessing the extent of any margin of appreciation which arises and the content of the obligations that a particular Convention provision imposes.

Examples of both practices can be seen in the court's 2008 judgment in *Demir and Baykara v Turkey*, a case in which the court was asked to examine the extent to which Article 11 (freedom of association) guaranteed rights of association to civil servants, including the right to join trade unions and the right to collective bargaining. The court reiterated its approach to interpreting the provisions of the Convention and referred to its practice of taking into account the relevant rules and principles of international law, quoting with approval its finding in the *Golder* case that the relevant rules of international law included 'general principles of law

[80] *Al-Saadoon and Mufdhi v UK*, para 126. See also *Mamatkulov and Askarov v Turkey*, where the dissenters (Judges Caflisch, Turmen, and Kovler) considered that there was no general principle of law recognizing the interim measure that an international court issues as obligatory. The majority found that such a measure, under the Convention, was binding on the state, but reached this conclusion on the basis of an interpretation of the ECHR, without making a finding concerning the existence of a general principle.

[81] *Al-Jedda v UK*, para 102.

[82] Paragraph 61. The ICJ vindicated the Court's view on state immunity in the *Jurisdictional Immunities of the State* case, 37–39.

[83] See Kanstantsin Dzehtsiarou, 'Does Consensus Matter? Legitimacy of European Consensus in the Case Law of the European Court of Human Rights' [2011] *PL* 534.

recognised by civilised nations'.[84] In this connection, it found that the common international or domestic law standards of European states, composed as they were of rules and principles accepted by the vast majority of states, reflected a reality which the court could not disregard when called upon to clarify the scope of a Convention provision.[85] Importantly, the court emphasized that the level of consensus established by the existence of norms of international law was not dependent on the respondent state in the case having ratified the international norm in question.[86] The court summarized its approach as follows:

> The Court, in defining the meaning of terms and notions in the text of the Convention, can and must take into account elements of international law other than the Convention, the interpretation of such elements by competent organs, and the practice of European States reflecting their common values. The consensus emerging from specialised international instruments and from the practice of Contracting States may constitute a relevant consideration for the Court when it interprets the provisions of the Convention in specific cases.
>
> ...In this context, it is not necessary for the respondent State to have ratified the entire collection of instruments that are applicable in respect of the precise subject matter of the case concerned. It will be sufficient for the Court that the relevant international instruments denote a continuous evolution in the norms and principles applied in international law or in the domestic law of the majority of member States of the Council of Europe and show, in a precise area, that there is common ground in modern societies.[87]

In concluding that civil servants were entitled to the guarantees of Article 11, the court drew support from the practice of European states, observing that all member states of the Council of Europe recognized the right of such employees to join trade unions.[88] As to whether civil servants enjoyed the right to bargain collectively, the Court noted that such a right had been recognized as applicable to civil servants in the 'vast majority' of the member states, albeit subject to certain restrictions.[89] This was one of the factors which led the court to conclude, in a landmark judgment, that its previous case law to the effect that the right to bargain collectively did not constitute an inherent element of Article 11 should be reconsidered.[90] In short the court found that such a right had become 'one of the essential elements' of the right to form and join trade unions that Article 11 guaranteed.[91]

The case law of the court is rich in examples of its practice of referring to member states' constitutions in order to determine the width of the margin of appreciation in a given case. Thus in *Ünal Tekeli v Turkey*,[92] the court considered the emergence of a consensus among the member states of the Council of Europe, which favoured allowing parties to a marriage to choose the family name, to be

[84] *Demir and Baykara v Turkey*, paras 67, 71.
[85] *Demir and Baykara* (n 84) para 76.
[86] *Demir and Baykara* (n 84) para 79.
[87] *Demir and Baykara* (n 84) paras 85–86.
[88] *Demir and Baykara* (n 84) para 106.
[89] *Demir and Baykara* (n 84) para 151.
[90] *Demir and Baykara* (n 84) para 152.
[91] *Demir and Baykara* (n 84) para 155.
[92] Paragraph 61.

relevant to the applicant's complaint that the refusal of the Turkish courts to allow her to bear her maiden name after her marriage constituted a violation of Article 8 of the Convention (the right to respect for private life), read alone and in conjunction with Article 14. In *Evans v United Kingdom*,[93] a case involving the destruction of embryos, the court held that the issue of when the right to life began fell within the margin of appreciation of the respondent state (which did not recognize any independent rights or interests enjoyed by embryos), in light of the absence of any European consensus on the scientific and legal definition of the beginning of life. In its judgment in *Lautsi and Others v Italy*,[94] the court considered that the decision whether crucifixes should be present in state-school classrooms was a matter falling within the margin of appreciation of the respondent state, in the absence of any European consensus on the question of the presence of religious symbols in state schools. A very recent application of the court's approach can be seen in *Stübing v Germany*,[95] which involved a criminal conviction for incest, where the court considered that the data before it were demonstrative of a broad consensus that sexual relations between siblings were accepted by neither the legal order nor society as a whole. It concluded that there was insufficient empirical support for the assumption of a general trend towards decriminalization of such acts, and as a result, no violation of the Convention had occurred.

There is similarly a wealth of developing case law on the court's use of obligations set out in international instruments to assess the compatibility of states' acts or omissions with provisions of the Convention. In *Rantsev v Cyprus and Russia*,[96] the court borrowed heavily from the Palermo Protocol to the United Nations Convention against Transnational Organised Crime and the Council of Europe's Convention on Action against Trafficking in Human Beings in order to identify the positive obligations which arose under Article 4 (prohibition of slavery and servitude) in the context of human trafficking. In *Tănase v Moldova*,[97] which concerned the right of dual nationals to stand for election, the court reiterated that it was for it to decide which international instruments and reports it considered relevant and how much weight to attribute to them. In the case before it, such relevant instruments and reports included the European Convention on Nationality, the conclusions and reports of European Commission against Racism and Intolerance and the European Commission for Democracy through Law, as well as the resolutions of the Parliamentary Assembly of the Council of Europe.

The above examples show that the European Court of Human Rights consistently looks to both national constitutions and international instruments in order to identify general principles or common approaches when applying the provisions of the ECHR. Through its dynamic interpretation of the Convention, the court has

[93] Paragraphs 54–56. [94] Paragraphs 26–28, 70. [95] Paragraphs 60–61.
[96] Paragraphs 285–89. [97] Paragraph 176.

made a significant contribution to the protection of human rights across Europe. As domestic legislatures review and modernize their approaches to human rights within the national arena, so too can the court continue to evolve by drawing on those standards in order to ensure the effective and practical protection of human rights across Europe and beyond.

5. The Court of Justice of the European Union

The founding treaties of the European Communities[98] contained no general provisions on the protection of human rights.[99] The Communities were conceived as essentially economic organizations, and as such their founders appear to have considered that there was no need for such provisions in the Community legal order.[100] In the absence of any treaty provision, the European Court of Justice,[101] the judicial body of the European Communities, was initially reluctant to accept that fundamental rights its member states' constitutions guaranteed could form part of any general principles that it was required to apply in its adjudication of cases brought before it.[102]

The court's approach raised a number of concerns in Germany, where a system of constitutional review existed in order to examine the constitutionality of legislation passed, about the absence of any human rights protection under Community law.[103] These concerns led to a decision of the German Constitutional Court in October 1967 that provisions of Community law had to be assessed at the national level in order to review their compliance with the German constitution. The decision had

98 European Coal and Steel Community Treaty, concluded in 1951, and the 1957 Treaties of Rome, which created the European Economic Community and the European Atomic Energy Community.

99 The only human rights guarantee appeared in Art 4 of the Treaty of Rome which prohibited, within the scope of application of the Treaty, discrimination on the grounds of nationality, a prohibition reflected in other more specific articles of the Treaty (see, for example, Art 40(3)).

100 See Ulrich Scheuner, 'Fundamental rights in European community law and in national constitutional law' (1975) 12 *CML Rev* 171; GF Mancini, 'The Making of a Constitution for Europe' (1989) 26 *CML Rev* 595, 608–609; Bruno De Witte, 'The Past and Future Role of the European Court of Justice in the Protection of Human Rights' in Philip Alston (ed), *The EU and Human Rights* (OUP 1999) 864.

101 It was renamed the Court of Justice of the European Union following the treaty changes the Treaty of Lisbon introduced in 2007.

102 See *Stork v High Authority*; *Geitling and Others v High Authority*; *Sgarlata and Others v Commission*.

103 See Mancini (n 100) 609; and Scheuner (n 100) 172–73, 177–80 for more detailed discussion.

significant implications, as the European Court of Justice had only recently adopted its judgment establishing the primacy of Community law.[104] If national courts subjected Community law to internal scrutiny, and reserved to themselves the power to strike down provisions which they considered did not apply, the very foundations of the Community legal order could have been thrown into doubt.

Accordingly, in a series of rulings beginning in the late 1960s, the court was forced to review its approach to the question of the extent to which general principles, including considerations of human rights, formed part of Community law. The real turning point came with the Court's judgment in *Internationale Handelgesellschaft*. The Frankfurt Administrative Court referred the case to the court for a ruling on the validity of a system of deposits for issuing export licences for cereals, established by an EEC Regulation, under which the deposit was forfeited if exportation was not effected during the period of validity of the export licence. In its referral order, the Frankfurt Administrative Court emphasized that although Community Regulations were not German national laws, they had to respect the elementary fundamental rights guaranteed by the German constitution and the essential structural principles of national law. It further emphasized that in the event of an incompatibility with those principles, the primacy of supranational law conflicted with the principles of the German Basic Law.

The Court began by observing that the validity of a Community measure could not be challenged as being contrary to fundamental rights set out in national constitutions, because the Treaty of Rome was an independent source of law which could not be overridden by provisions of national law without the legal basis of the Community itself being called into question. However, it explained that it was necessary to examine whether any 'analogous guarantee inherent in Community law' had been disregarded.[105] It found:

> In fact, respect for fundamental rights forms an integral part of the general principles of law protected by the Court of Justice. The protection of such rights, whilst inspired by the constitutional traditions common to the Member States, must be ensured within the framework of the structure and objectives of the Community.[106]

Over the ensuing years, the Court of Justice continued to develop its case law on fundamental rights, adding to the catalogue of rights to be guaranteed as fundamental principles of Community law. In *Nold v Commission*, the applicant alleged a violation of his fundamental rights, invoking inter alia the right to property and the right to free pursuit of business activity guaranteed by the German Basic Law, by the constitutions of other member states, and by various international treaties, including the ECHR. The court reiterated that fundamental rights formed an integral part of the general principles of law, the observance of which the court ensured.

[104] *Costa v ENEL*. [105] *Internationale Handelsgesellschaft*, para 4.
[106] *Internationale Handelsgesellschaft* (n 105) para 4.

It explained that in safeguarding these rights, it was 'bound to draw inspiration from constitutional traditions common to the member States', and that it could not uphold measures which were incompatible with fundamental rights that member states' constitutions recognized and protected.[107] It further indicated that international human rights treaties, such as the ECHR, could supply 'guidelines' which should be followed within the framework of Community law. As to the extent of the rights in question, it noted that the rights invoked, as guaranteed by national constitutions, were subject to limitations in the public interest, and that such limitations were also legitimate within the Community legal order.

In 1977, the Commission, the Council, and the Parliament adopted a Joint Declaration of Fundamental Rights. In the preamble to the declaration, the three institutions noted that the Court of Justice had recognized that the law applicable to the activities of the European Community included the general principles of law and, in particular, the fundamental rights on which the constitutional law of the member states was based. The institutions accordingly stressed the prime importance they attached to the protection of fundamental rights, as derived in particular from the constitutions of the member states and the ECHR.[108]

In *AM & S v Commission*, the applicants argued, in the context of a challenge to a Commission decision regarding a competition investigation, that the principle of legal privilege applied and that a provision of the decision requiring full disclosure of confidential documents should be annulled. The court heard extensive evidence as to the practice of the member states in this field. It concluded that Community law had to take into account the principles and concepts common to the laws of the member states concerning the observance of lawyer–client confidentiality.

The Court of Justice's approach to human rights was finally enshrined in the Maastricht Treaty in 1992, which established the European Union and provided that the Union would respect fundamental rights, as guaranteed by the ECHR and as they resulted from the constitutional traditions common to the member states, as general principles of Community law.[109] Thus was the court's approach to protection of fundamental rights via general principles derived from the constitutional traditions of the member states confirmed and firmly entrenched in the legal order of the European Union. The court's continued application of this approach over the subsequent years has seen the confirmation of a number of human rights as applicable in the Community legal order.

The continued efforts of the court in the course of the 1990s went hand in hand with moves at a political level to place human rights protection in the European Community and the European Union on a more secure legal footing. These

[107] *Nold v Commission*, para 13.

[108] For consideration of the Declaration in the context of the right to property, see *Hauer v Land Rheinland-Pfalz*.

[109] Article 6(2).

developments culminated in the December 2000 proclamation of a Charter of Fundamental Rights, which although without binding legal effect, was nonetheless of significant political importance. The Charter did not create new rights; instead, it drew together for the first time in a single document, existing rights which were to be protected within the EU legal order. It states in its preamble that it reaffirms the rights contained in the Charter as they result, in particular, from the constitutional traditions and international obligations common to the member states, the ECHR, the Social Charters that the Union and the Council of Europe adopted, and the case law of the Court of Justice and of the European Court of Human Rights. Article 52 § 4 of the Charter provides that, in so far as the Charter recognizes fundamental rights as they result from the constitutional traditions common to the member states, such rights are to be interpreted in harmony with those traditions.

The significance of the Charter was that it essentially codified the various fundamental rights which the Court of Justice had developed in its extensive case law. In the context of the institutional changes which occurred with the conclusion of the Treaty of Lisbon in December 2007, the Charter acquired legally binding force. At the time, the Bureau of the Convention prepared informal explanations to provide information on the source of each of the rights contained in the Charter,[110] and these were updated and published following the conclusion of the Lisbon Treaty.[111] These explanations illustrate clearly the pivotal role of the Court of Justice in developing a number of the Charter rights, as well as the importance of general principles deriving from the member states' constitutional traditions. Thus, they reveal, freedom to choose an occupation enshrined in Article 15(1) of the Charter was a right originally developed by the Court of Justice in the early cases of *Nold* and *Hauer v Land Rheinland-Pfalz*, both mentioned earlier. Article 20 of the Charter, which guarantees equality before the law, 'corresponds to a general principle of law which is included in all European constitutions'.[112] It was also recognized as a basic principle of Community law in the court's judgments in *Racke* and *Karlsson*. Article 47 of the Charter guarantees the right to an effective remedy before a tribunal, a right the Court of Justice originally elaborated as a general principle of Union law in *Johnston*.[113] The origin of the *ne bis in idem* rule in Article 50 also lies in the extensive case law of the Court of Justice and the Court of First Instance.[114] The Charter is now regularly invoked before and by the Court of Justice in cases which raise

[110] 'Draft Charter of Fundamental Rights of the European Union' (11 October 2000) CHARTE 4473/00.

[111] Explanations Relating to the Charter of Fundamental Rights [2007] OJ C303/17.

[112] Explanations Relating to the Charter of Fundamental Rights [2007] OJ C303/17.

[113] *Johnston v Chief Constable of the Royal Ulster Constabulary.*

[114] See eg *Gutmann v Commission*; *Limburgse Vinyl Maatschappij NV and Others v Commission*; *Gözütok and Brugge.*

human rights issues.[115] In a process of cross fertilization, the ECJ today interprets the Charter with regard to case law developed by the Strasbourg court—indeed it is mandated to do so by Article 52 § 3 of the Charter—and the broader wording of provisions of the Charter and their interpretation by the Court of Justice in turn influence that court.

Thus it can be seen that general principles and constitutional traditions common to the member states lay at the very heart of the development of a system for human rights protection in the European Union. Through its judgments, the Court of Justice essentially read an 'unwritten bill of rights' into Community law, in a remarkable development.[116] In due course, the case law of the court formed the basis of a written charter of human rights which now has legally binding force in the field of the activities of the European Union and the implementation of EU legislation.[117]

6. Conclusion

There can be no doubt as to the central role that general principles and constitutions played as sources of human rights law. The eighteenth-century human rights declarations, which formed part of the constitutions of France and the United States, were influential in the general approach taken to the underlying philosophy of the UDHR. The nature and content of the rights guaranteed was heavily inspired by the constitutional traditions of the fifty-five member states of the United Nations. It is arguable that given their relative novelty at the time of the UDHR negotiations, the economic and social rights the UDHR guaranteed may never have seen the light of day without reference to the constitutions of the Latin American and Communist states. The vast majority of human rights instruments and provisions subsequently adopted at the national and international levels have built upon the guarantees elaborated in that timeless instrument.

Clearly, the role of constitutions and general principles as sources of human rights guarantees did not cease with the conclusion of the UDHR. An examination of the approach international courts have taken to questions of interpretation of human rights standards demonstrates the central role that the concept of general principles

[115] The first case in which the Court of Justice referred to the Charter in its reasoning was *European Parliament v Council*.

[116] Mancini (n 100) 611.

[117] See Allan Rosas and Heidi Kaila, 'L'Application de la Charte des Droits Fondamentaux de l'Union Européenne par la Cour de Justice: Un Premier Bilan' [2011] *Il Diritto dell'Unione Europa* 9.

and the content of national constitutions retain. The ICJ has indicated that the provisions of the UDHR are relevant principles to be taken into account in its judgments, although there is potential for greater use of general principles by the ICJ judges. General principles and constitutions are solely responsible for the importation of human rights standards into the activities of the European Community and the later European Union, now enshrined in a legally binding Charter of Fundamental Rights, applicable in the EU's legal space and radiating an influence on how the Court in Strasbourg interprets provisions of the ECHR. Finally, general principles and constitutions regularly influence the approach of regional tribunals, such as the European Court of Human Rights and the Inter-American Court of Human Rights, to the interpretation of the respective Conventions, ensuring that the guarantees they contain remain relevant to the threats posed today. The Inter-American Court stands out, in particular, through its development of *jus cogens*.[118]

In 1955, Green wrote:

> There is not sufficient in common among the nations of the world, nor in their historical development, to allow human rights, even though they may be generally recognised in the various systems of law, to be considered as general principles of law recognised by civilised nations and, as such, rules of international law.[119]

The practice of the International Court of Justice, the European and Inter-American Courts of Human Rights, and the Court of Justice of the European Union, suggests the contrary is true today.

Further Reading

Hersch J (ed), *Birthright of Man* (UNESCO 1968)

Lammers JG, 'General Principles of Law Recognized by Civilised Nations' in Frits Kalshoven, Pieter J Kuyper, and Johann G Lammers (eds), *Essays on the Development of the International Legal Order: In Memory of Haro F van Panhuys* (Martinus Nijhoff 1980) 53

Leuprecht P, *Reason, Justice and Dignity: A Journey to Some Unexplored Sources of Human Rights* (Martinus Nijhoff 2012)

Simma B and Alston P, 'The Sources of Human Rights Law: Custom, *Jus Cogens*, and General Principles' (1988–89) 12 *Aust YBIL* 82

[118] See Judge Cançado Trindade, 'The Expansion of the Material Context of *Jus Cogens*: The Contribution of the Inter-American Court of Human Rights' in Dean Spielmann, Marialena Tsirli and Panayotis Voyatzis (eds), *The European Convention on Human Rights, a Living Instrument; Essays in Honour of Christos L Rozakis* (Bruylant 2011) 27–46.

[119] See Green (n 4) 183.

CHAPTER 9

THE ANTI-SLAVERY MOVEMENT AND THE RISE OF INTERNATIONAL NON-GOVERNMENTAL ORGANIZATIONS

JENNY S MARTINEZ

TODAY, non-governmental organizations (NGOs) play a central role in international human rights law and practice. As of 2012, more than 3,500 NGOs have been granted consultative status with the United Nations;[1] countless other organizations work on a local level in particular countries or regions. Not only has the number of such organizations grown exponentially in the past few decades, but the reach of these organizations has grown, as well.

The term 'non-governmental organization' is said to have come into common usage with the founding of the United Nations in 1945. Article 71 of the UN Charter provides that '[t]he Economic and Social Council may make suitable arrangements for consultation with non-governmental organizations which are concerned with

[1] United Nations Department of Economic and Social Affairs, NGO Branch, 'Consultative Status with ECOSOC and Other Accreditations' <http://esango.un.org/civilsociety/displayConsultativeStatusSearch.do?method=search&sessionCheck=false> accessed 13 August 2012.

matters within its competence'. At the founding convention of the United Nations in San Francisco in 1945, representatives of NGOs were pivotal in pushing for the inclusion of references to human rights in the UN Charter. The great powers that had crafted the charter had not included any mention of human rights in the original draft; Britain feared this might add fuel to the independence movements in its colonies, and the Soviet Union did not want interference in its growing sphere of influence.[2] Because of pressure from civil society and smaller countries, references to human rights were included in the final version of the Charter.

In the following decades, an increasing number of NGOs received consultative status before various parts of the UN; some of these NGOs worked to promote policy agendas that encompassed the advancement of various rights enumerated in the Universal Declaration of Human Rights (UDHR).[3] Nevertheless, it was not until the late 1970s and early 1980s that use of the term NGO, along with the number and influence of such organizations, began to flood the international scene.[4] Popular usage of the term 'human rights' also increased sharply in this same time period.[5]

A recent historian has asserted that the international human rights movement of today (including the central role played by human rights NGOs) is really only a product of the 1970s or later.[6] Yet another scholar suggests that even the 1970s is too early, asserting that 'if one must find a recent starting point, a more appropriate

[2] Dorothy B Robins, *Experiment in the Democracy: The Story of U.S. Citizen Organizations in Forging the Charter of the United Nations* (Parkside Press 1971) 129–32; Clark M Eichelberger, *Organizing for Peace: A Personal History of the United Nations* (Harper and Row 1977) 268–72; Lynn Hunt, *Inventing Human Rights: A History* (WW Norton, New York 2007) 203 (citing Jan Herman Burgers, 'The Road to San Francisco: The Revival of the Human Rights Idea in the Twentieth Century' (1992) 14 *Hum Rts Q* 447).

[3] United Nations Department of Economic and Social Affairs, 'NGO Branch' <http://esa.un.org/coordination/ngo/new/index.asp?page=table2007> accessed 13 August 2012 (noting that forty NGOs had consultative status before the UN Economic and Social Council by 1948 and 180 in 1968). See also eg United Nations Department of Economic and Social Affairs, 'Civil Society Participation' <http://esango.un.org/civilsociety/displayConsultativeStatusSearch.do> accessed 13 August 2012 (International League for Human Rights accredited in 1946; Women's International League for Peace and Freedom accredited in 1948; Anti-Slavery International accredited in 1950; Amnesty International accredited in 1964). Until 1996, only international NGOs were allowed consultative status, but a resolution in that year allowed regional and national NGOs to apply as well. See ECOSOC 'Consultative Relationship between the United Nations and Non-Governmental Organizations' Res 1996/31 (25 July 1996).

[4] Google, 'Ngram Viewer' <http://books.google.com/ngrams/graph?content=nongovernmental+organization&year_start=1800&year_end=2000&corpus=0&smoothing=0> accessed 13 August 2012 (histogram on usage of term 'nongovernmental organization' in books, showing a slow increase in usage from 1940 through the 1960s, and a sharp increase in the 1980s to the present); Google, 'Ngram Viewer' <http://books.google.com/ngrams/graph?content=NGO&year_start=1800&year_end=2000&corpus=0&smoothing=3> accessed 13 August 2012 (similar for term 'NGO').

[5] Google, 'NGram Viewer' <http://books.google.com/ngrams/graph?content=human+rights&year_start=1800&year_end=2000&corpus=0&smoothing=3> accessed 13 August 2012 (histogram on usage of term 'human rights' in books).

[6] Samuel Moyn, *The Last Utopia: Human Rights in History* (Harvard UP 2010) 7.

decade would be the 1990s, when human rights organizations truly flourished and international criminal tribunals became reality' in the geopolitical space that opened up as a result of the end of the Cold War.[7] Still other commentators contend that the euphoric, post-Berlin Wall 1990s were a blip in history and that 11 September 2001, is the proper date from which to evaluate the impact, if any, of the concept of international human rights and the role of NGOs.[8]

A larger group of scholars, however, has taken a broader view, in which they treat earlier episodes in history (though distinguishable on a variety of grounds) as having relevance to those seeking to understand international human rights law and advocacy today. Many have emphasized connections with the post-Second World War period,[9] including the Nuremberg trials,[10] the drafting of the UDHR,[11] and the Genocide Convention.[12] Still others have reached further back. For example, as one scholar has written:

> If you think of 'human rights activism' in another way—as efforts to make claims across borders in the name of basic rights—this activism has been intermittently strong but not sustained. The international campaign against slavery, scattered attempts in the 1880s and 1890s to regulate the Ottoman Empire's treatment of Christians, the birth of the international women's rights movement are all examples.[13]

As one scholar has noted in relation to activism on behalf of women's rights:

> [long before the past few decades,] women were engaged in collective action to restructure civil society. Such groups were nongovernmental not by choice but by necessity. Until all too recently, women could not vote, run for office, become lawyers, serve in the military or as jurors, or, if married, contract or hold property in their own names. Yet, lacking juridical voice, women nevertheless voiced their views through the means then available, often inventing organizations that had small numbers but grand aspirations.[14]

[7] Belinda Cooper, 'New Birth of Freedom' *The New York Times* (New York, 24 September 2010) BR16.

[8] Michael Ignatieff, 'Is the Human Rights Era Ending?' *The New York Times* (New York, 5 February 2002) <http://www.nytimes.com/2002/02/05/opinion/is-the-human-rights-era-ending.html> accessed 13 August 2012; Jordan Michael Smith, 'The Birth and Death of Human Rights Doctrine: The Last Utopia Traces the History of Human Rights Policy' (*Slate*, 3 January 2010) <http://www.slate.com/articles/arts/books/2011/01/the_birth_and_death_of_human_rights_doctrine.html> accessed 13 August 2012.

[9] Paul Gordon Lauren, *Evolution of International Human Rights: Visions Seen* (University of Pennsylvania Press 2003).

[10] Philippe Sands (ed), *From Nuremberg to the Hague: The Future of International Criminal Justice* (CUP 2003).

[11] Mary Ann Glendon, *A World Made New: Eleanor Roosevelt and the Universal Declaration of Human Rights* (Random House 2001).

[12] Samantha Power, *'A Problem From Hell': American in the Age of Genocide* (3rd edn, Harper Perennial 2003).

[13] Kenneth J Cmiel, 'The Recent History of Human Rights' in Akike Iriye, Petra Goedde, and William I Hitchcock, *The Human Rights Revolution: An International History* (OUP 2012) 37.

[14] Judith Resnik, 'Sisterhood, Slavery, and Sovereignty: Transnational Antislavery Work and Women's Rights Movements in the United States During the Twentieth Century' in Kathryn Kish

This chapter, focused on the antislavery and women's movements of the nineteenth and early twentieth century, clearly falls into this latter camp in the historiography of human rights. That is, it asserts that there is some relationship between these movements, the organizations and legal frameworks they inspired, and the international human rights law of today. But the disagreement among scholars suggests that a word of caution is necessary at the outset. The nineteenth-century abolitionists and crusaders for women's rights were not quite the same as those involved with Save Darfur,[15] the Coalition for the International Criminal Court,[16] or Human Rights First,[17] and not just because they lacked cell phones and Twitter accounts. It would be foolish to assume similarities that do not exist between the social, intellectual, economic, and political milieu of an entirely different time and place in history; it would be more foolish still to assume that history led inexorably towards the present state of things. The world is far more contingent than that, and the past is always distinguishable from today.

And yet, the nascent international activism of nineteenth-century civil society organizations reveals some of the key developments that undergird twentieth-century international human rights law. For example, it was in the context of the campaign against the international slave trade that '[t]he idea that nations should use international lawmaking to protect the rights of individuals outside their own territory was first put into practice'.[18] The widespread adoption of treaties against the slave trade:

> introduced into modern international legal discourse the idea that violations of human rights were offenses of concern to humankind generally, and not just matters between a people and their sovereign. This is the key conceptual step that separates the contemporary world of international human rights law from the ideals of natural and universal rights that arose during the Enlightenment and took national legal form in documents like the Declaration of Independence, the U.S. Constitution, and the French Declaration of the Rights of Man (which focus on the relationship between individuals and the sovereign states where they reside).[19]

Moreover, 'attempts to subject the slave trade to universal jurisdiction by declaring it piracy' also foreshadowed the later idea that 'national sovereignty is not an impenetrable barrier to international law action in the case of human rights violations'.[20]

Sklar and James Brewer Stewart (eds), *Women's Rights and Transatlantic Antislavery in the Era of Emancipation* (Yale UP 2007) 23.

[15] Save Darfur Coalition, 'Save Darfur' <http://www.savedarfur.org> accessed 13 August 2012.

[16] Coalition of the International Criminal Court, 'Together for Justice' <http://www.iccnow.org> accessed 13 August 2012.

[17] Human Rights First, 'Human Rights First' <http://www.humanrightsfirst.org> accessed 18 August 2012.

[18] Jenny S Martinez, *The Slave Trade and the Origins of International Human Rights Law* (OUP 2012) 138.

[19] Martinez (n 18) 149. [20] Martinez (n 18) 138.

Like modern human rights movements, the movement for the abolition of slavery and the slave trade involved transborder activism by privately organized individuals and included, as one goal, the strengthening of international treaty regimes concerning the slave trade. Later campaigns for reform in other areas—for example, the movement for women's suffrage—grew out of the abolition effort, as activists who had learned organizing techniques in the context of abolitionism turned to other issues. As scholars have explained:

> T[t]he transnational antislavery campaign provided a 'language of politics' and organizational and tactical recipes for other transnational campaigns as well. The women's suffrage campaign initially drew many of its activists and tactics from the antislavery movement.[21]

This chapter addresses the emergence in the nineteenth century of NGOs, with particular attention to those organized around slavery and women's rights and suffrage.[22] While not every aspect of these campaigns mirrors modern human rights activism, the ties between these historical campaigns and the present, underscore the ways in which contemporary international human rights law is deeply rooted in the past.

1. The Rise of Abolitionism: Religion, Natural Rights, and Civil Society

From the 1500s to the 1800s, chattel slavery was a central feature of the social and economic landscape of the Atlantic world.[23] In the year 1800, the system was flourishing; in the first decade of the nineteenth century, slave ships carried some 600,000 slaves from Africa to the Americas. The slave population of the Western Hemisphere numbered in the millions. But cracks in the facade were beginning to emerge. In 1807, Britain and the United States each passed domestic legislation

[21] Margaret Keck and Kathryn Sikkink, 'Historical Precursors to Modern Transnational Social Movements and Networks' in John A Guidrie, Michael D Kennedy, and Mayer N Zald (eds), *Globalizations and Social Movements: Culture, Power, and the Transnational Public Sphere* (University of Michigan Press 2000) 37–38.

[22] Bill Seary, 'The Early History: From the Congress of Vienna to the San Francisco Conference' in Peter Willetts (ed), *'The Conscience of the World': The Influence of Non-Governmental Organisations in the U.N. System* (Brookings 1996) 16 ('These new organisations covered a wide range of topics, such as the treatment of offenders, the slave trade, the traffic in women and children, organised labour, the opium trade, peace and humanitarian assistance').

[23] Portions of this chapter draw on my earlier work, including Martinez (n 18) and 'Antislavery Courts and the Dawn of International Human Rights Law' (2008) 117 *Yale LJ* 550.

banning participation in the African slave trade. Newly independent Latin American countries, including Mexico, Argentina, and Chile, took steps towards ending slavery itself within their territories.[24] Slavery was abolished in British West Indian colonies in 1834. By the 1840s, more than twenty nations—including all the major Atlantic maritime powers—had joined international treaties committed to the abolition of the slave trade. By the late 1860s, only a few hundred slaves per year were illegally transported across the Atlantic. And by 1900, every country in the Western Hemisphere had outlawed slavery itself.

Seeking to explain this dramatic change, historians, economists, political scientists, and others have debated the causes and origins of abolition. The abolition movement spanned the Atlantic world and grew from early efforts to suppress the slave trade, in the late eighteenth century, to the eventual extinction of slavery itself, in the nineteenth century. Abolitionism took earlier and deeper root in some countries than others, and the ties between abolitionists in different countries varied. Britain was a leader, and there were particularly strong personal and organizational ties between British and North American abolitionists, but anti-slavery organizations in other European and Latin American countries were intermittently active and in contact with one another, as well. Early writers emphasized the idealistic motives of those individuals, organizations, and nations who led the abolition campaign,[25] though it quickly became apparent that this was too simplistic. Later, more sceptical writers suggested that, far from being a selfless endeavour, abolitionism served the economic self-interest of influential factions of society made wealthy by the rise of industrial capitalism.[26] In addition, some have argued that putting a spotlight on the evils of the slave trade and slavery deflected attention from other problematic issues, such as European colonization of Africa and the Indian subcontinent, the so-called 'wage slavery' that factory workers experienced, and efforts by countries such as Britain to gain dominance over the oceans for commercial reasons.[27] Anti-slavery thus reinforced some problematic social structures

[24] The last New World countries to abolish slavery were Brazil and Cuba, which did so after the United States. See generally Christopher Schmidt-Nowara, *Slavery, Freedom, and Abolition in Latin America and the Atlantic World* (University of New Mexico Press 2011).

[25] William Edward and Hartpole Lecky, *History of European Morals: From Augustus to Charlemagne* (vol 1, 3rd edn, D Appleton and Company 1897) 153, quoted in Christoph Lloyd, *The Navy and the Slave Trade: The Suppression of the African Slave Trade in the Nineteenth Century* (2nd edn, Routledge 1968) xiii ('[t]he unweary, unostentatious and inglorious crusade of England against slavery may probably be regarded as among the three or four perfectly virtuous pages comprised in the history of nations').

[26] See eg Eric Williams, *Capitalism and Slavery* (Russell & Russell 1944) (arguing that anti-slavery efforts resulted not from humanitarian and religious impulses, but because of relations among different social classes and components of the British empire). For a discussion of the historiography, see eg David Turley, 'Complicating the Story: Religion and Gender in the Historical Representation of British and American Anti-Slavery' in Elizabeth J Clapp and Julie Roy Jeffrey (eds), *Women, Dissent and Anti-Slavery in Britain and America, 1790–1865* (OUP 2011) 25–27.

[27] Laurie Benton, 'Legal Spaces of Empire: Piracy and the Origins of Ocean Regionalism' (2005) 47 *Comp Stud Soc'y & Hist* 700.

and hierarchies, even as it dismantled others. More recent scholarship has landed somewhere in the middle, suggesting that a fortuitous convergence of both idealistic and self-interested motives was involved. Factors including the spread of Enlightenment ideas about natural rights, the attention given to such rights in the American and French revolutions, changes in the structure of the economy, and the spread of religious revival movements that provided both a motive and an organizational structure for reform campaigns, all played a part.[28] Some scholars have challenged the degree to which antislavery campaigns did deflect attention from other labour issues and have suggested, instead, that capitalism's key contribution to the antislavery movement was a subtler one: an awareness of cause and effect across the marketplace led ordinary people to understand that their purchase of consumer goods, such as sugar, led to demand for slave labour on plantations, which in turn led to a demand for slaves and the perpetuation of the slave trade.[29] Other scholars have argued more generally that 'social movements emerged in the eighteenth century from "structural changes that were associated with capitalism" such as "new forms of association, regular communication linking center and periphery, and the spread of print and literacy"',[30] and that abolition was linked to broader humanitarian movements in many countries that addressed issues such as poor laws, labour standards, and prison conditions.[31] Still others have emphasized the ways in which literature—eighteenth-century novels in particular—encouraged the development of empathy for the inner lives of others and emphasized personal autonomy.[32] Historians have also countered the emphasis on elite interests by underscoring the genuine importance of widespread, popular support for the abolitionist cause, which the hundreds of thousands of individuals who signed petitions in support of

[28] For the evolution of views on the causes of abolitionism over time, see eg WE Burghardt DuBois, *The Suppression of the African Slave Trade to the United States of America: 1638–1870* (Longmans, Green, and Co 1896); David Brion Davis, *The Problem of Slavery in Western Culture* (OUP 1966); Roger Anstey, *The Atlantic Slave Trade and British Abolition 1760–1810* (Humanities Press 1975); Seymour Drescher, *Econocide: British Slavery in the Era of Abolition* (University of Pittsburgh Press 1977); Seymour Drescher, *Capitalism and Antislavery: British Mobilization in Comparative Perspective* (OUP 1986); David Eltis, *Economic Growth and the Ending of the Transatlantic Slave Trade* (OUP 1987); Eric Williams, *Capitalism and Slavery* (University of North Carolina Press 1994); Seymour Drescher, *From Slavery to Freedom: Comparative Studies in the Rise and Fall of Atlantic Slavery* (NYU Press 1999); David Brion Davis, *The Problem of Slavery in the Age of Revolution, 1770–1823* (OUP 1999); Christopher Leslie Brown, *Moral Capital: Foundations of British Abolitionism* (2006); Robin Blackburn, *The American Crucible: Slavery, Emancipation and Human Rights* (2011).

[29] Thomas L Haskell, 'Capitalism and Origins of the Humanitarian Sensibility, Part 1' in Thomas Bender (ed), *The Antislavery Debate: Capitalism and Abolitionism as a Problem in Historical Interpretation* (University of California Press 1992).

[30] Keck and Sikkink, 'Historical Precursors to Modern Transnational Social Movements and Networks' (n 21) 37 (quoting Sidney G Tarrow, *Power in Movement: Social Movements and Contentious Politics* (CUP 1994) 48).

[31] Thomas W Laqueur, 'Bodies, Details, and the Humanitarian Narrative' in Lynn Hunt (ed), *The New Cultural History* (University of California Press 1987) 176.

[32] Hunt, *Inventing Human Rights* (n 2) 38–67; Laqueur (n 31) 176.

antislavery efforts, attended mass rallies, and participated in consumer boycotts of sugar from slave plantations, demonstrated.[33] As one commentator has argued in the context of US history:

> If anti-slavery promoted the hegemony of middle class values, it also provided a language of politics, a training in organization, for critics of the emerging order. The anti-slavery crusade was a central terminus, from which tracks ran leading to every significant attempt to transform American society after the Civil War.[34]

Antislavery was at 'the vanguard of a new mode of collective action', in which organizers deployed 'a new repertoire of public meetings, demonstrations, and special interest associations', while 'using newspapers to project their demands and presence onto a national and international stage'.[35] Scholars have identified the abolition movement as a product of the space opened up by the development of 'civil society' in Western Europe and North America from the mid-eighteenth through the mid-nineteenth centuries.[36] As one scholar has noted, '[o]ccupying the broad swath of social life that unfolded between the formal authority of the state and the economic domain of the marketplace, civil society steadily expanded in the Atlantic world between 1750 and 1850'.[37] Moreover, '[w]ithin civil society antislavery ideas and social movements steadily acquired the power to challenge the alliance between state and marketplace that legitimized slavery'.[38] As discussed in great depth below, women were an important part of this movement. For them, civil society took form

> as gatherings of private citizens meeting together, and explicitly engaging in the formation of public opinion. This might take the form of elite salons and tea tables, or voluntary associations of various descriptions, but for many... it also meant their churches and chapels.[39]

The development of civil society was particularly pronounced in both the United States and Britain. Alexis de Tocqueville observed the proliferation of civil associations in the United States for not just political or commercial enterprises, but for all manner of purposes.[40] Across the Atlantic, '[r]apid economic development,

[33] Seymour Drescher, 'Whose Abolition? Popular Pressure and the Ending of the British Slave Trade' (1994) 143 *Past and Present* 136. For an account of British abolitionism written for a general audience, see Adam Hochschild, *Bury the Chains: Prophets and Rebels in the Fight to Free an Empire's Slaves* (Mariner Books 2005).

[34] Eric Foner, *Politics and Ideology in the Age of the Civil War* (OUP 1980) 76.

[35] Seymour Drescher, 'Women's Mobilization in the Era of Slave Emancipation: Some Anglo-French Comparisons' in Sklar and Stewart, *Women's Rights and Transatlantic Antislavery* (n 14) 112.

[36] Elizabeth J Clapp, 'Introduction' in Clapp and Jeffrey (n 26) 16–17.

[37] Kathryn Kish Sklar and James Brewer Stewart, 'Introduction' in Sklar and Stewart, *Women's Rights and Transatlantic Antislavery* (n 14) xii.

[38] Sklar and Stewart, 'Introduction' (n 37) xii.

[39] Clapp, 'Introduction' (n 36) 17. See Drescher, 'Women's Mobilization in the Era of Slave Emancipation' (n 35) 112–13.

[40] Drescher, 'Women's Mobilization in the Era of Slave Emancipation' (n 35) 112; Alexis de Tocqueville, *Democracy in America* (Harvey C Mansfield and Delba Winthrop trs, University of Chicago Press 2000) 184, 489, 492.

combined with a reduction or governmental authority and the decline of governmental censorship in Britain', led to a proliferation of newspapers and voluntary associations.[41]

Opponents of slavery and the slave trade conceptualized the issue at least partially in terms of individual rights (described as 'the rights of man', 'natural rights', or occasionally even 'human rights'), as well as of religious and moral obligations to end a practice that was increasingly understood to be barbaric and cruel. In 1776, one member of the British Parliament argued, for example, that the '[s]lave-trade was contrary to the laws of God, and the rights of men'.[42] Another speaker before Parliament in 1806, Lord Grenville, described slavery as contrary to the 'rights of nature' whereby 'every human being is entitled to the fruit of his own labour'.[43] That same year, President Thomas Jefferson wrote that he supported legislation banning the slave trade because it would 'withdraw the citizens of the United States from all further participation in those violations of human rights which have been so long continued on the unoffending inhabitants of Africa'.[44]

Arguments against slavery and the slave trade were deeply intertwined with ideas of natural law and natural rights, and also with international law (then called the 'law of nations'). Slavery was a particularly complicated case, because although some philosophers going back to Aristotle had characterized slavery as a natural part of the order of the world (and perhaps even mandated by God), over time other philosophers had concluded that slavery was contrary to natural law (or *jus naturale*, to use the older terminology). At the same time, *jus gentium*, the Roman predecessor of the law of nations, sanctioned slavery as a lawful consequence of warfare. Indeed, texts on Roman law pointed to slavery as the sole example of a conflict between

[41] Drescher, 'Women's Mobilization in the Era of Slave Emancipation' (n 35) 112.

[42] Thomas Clarkson, *The History of the Rise, Progress, and Accomplishment of the Abolition of the African Slave Trade by the British Parliament* (vol 1, Longman, Hurst, Reed, and Orme 1808) 84 (quoting David Hartley).

[43] *Substance of the Debates on a Resolution for Abolishing the Slave Trade* (Philips and Fardon 1806) 99 (statement of Lord Grenville).

[44] Thomas Jefferson, Statement to Congress, 2 December 1806, in James D Richardson (ed), *A Compilation of the Messages and Papers of the Presidents*, (vol 1, Bureau of National Literature and Art 1908) 408. See also DuBois (n 28) 80 (quoting petitions for the abolition of the slave trade to the United States that describe the trade as 'an outrageous violation of one of the most essential rights of human nature' and 'degrading to the rights of man'); Executive Committee of the American Antislavery Society, *Slavery and the Internal Slave Trade in the United States of North America* (photo repr, Thomas Ward and Co 1841) 162 (referring to 'the cause of human rights'). This view of the slave trade as a human rights issue was carried on through the later part of the nineteenth century, as when Yale college president Theodore Dwight Woolsey's 1860 edition of *Introduction to the Study of International Law* explained that under the 'correct views of human rights', slavery was a status unprotected by the law of nations and that 'new views of men's rights' had led to the prohibition of the slave trade in international law. Theodore D Woolsey, *Introduction to the Study of International Law* (James Munroe 1860) 316–17.

the *jus naturale* and the *jus gentium*.[45] Slavery and the slave trade were tolerated by the law of nations into the seventeenth and eighteenth centuries, and usually justified on grounds that prisoners captured in war could be enslaved instead of killed. While it was no longer the custom for Europeans to enslave one another, this was described as a custom based on shared religion and not an obligation that either natural law or the law of nations imposed, and no such custom attached to non-European prisoners in other lands.[46] As the Enlightenment progressed, philosophers writing about natural rights became less comfortable with the traditional justifications for slavery. John Locke believed that man was naturally entitled to the fruits of his own labour, and though he accepted that slavery might be justifiable in a situation where a man might otherwise rightly be slain, he called it a 'vile and miserable' state of man.[47] Not much later, Jean-Jacques Rousseau asserted that slavery was entirely contrary to natural right. He argued that slavery could not arise from voluntary contract because '[t]o renounce one's liberty is to renounce one's humanity, the rights of humanity and even its duties'; nor could slavery justly arise from warfare, because there was no right to kill the vanquished and no right to enslave as a lesser measure.[48]

Perhaps equally important were religious arguments and changes in the ideology and institutional structure of Christianity. While Christianity had always had a strand of egalitarianism, religious beliefs had long been used to justify, rather than condemn, slavery. However, in younger Protestant sects there emerged new understandings of sin and bodily and spiritual liberty. Among the Quakers in particular, slave holding came to be seen as sinful.[49] A strain of philanthropic tradition also ran through British Protestantism, was linked to the emergence of capitalism, and was a response to problems created by economic change.[50] Surges in religious enthusiasm and participation fostered the spread of anti-slavery thought and an organizational infrastructure for antislavery work.

While slavery was a lynchpin of the economy in new world colonies at the periphery of empire, it was not a practice that was legally encouraged in the metropolitan centre, even for non-Europeans. While the occasional African slave might reach Western Europe in the company of a well-travelled master, chattel slavery was not part of daily life. William Blackstone's famous *Commentaries on the Laws of England* thus suggested in the 1765 edition that 'a slave or negro, the moment he lands in England, falls under the protection of the laws and with regard to all natural rights becomes *eo instanti*

[45] Davis, *The Problem of Slavery in Western Culture* (n 28) 83.

[46] See eg Hugo Grotius, *The Rights of War and Peace* (AC Campbell tr, M Walter Dunne 1901) 346–47.

[47] John Locke, *Two Treatises of Government: A Critical Edition with an Introduction and Apparatus Criticus* (2nd edn, CUP 1967) 159; Davis, *The Problem of Slavery in Western Culture* (n 28) 119–20.

[48] Alan Ritter and Julia Conaway Bondanella (eds), *Rousseau's Political Writings* (Julia Conaway Bondanella tr, WW Norton 1988) 88–91.

[49] Davis, *The Problem of Slavery in Western Culture* (n 28) 308–309.

[50] Davis, *The Problem of Slavery in Western Culture* (n 28) 334–36.

a freeman' (though, curiously, the 1769 edition retreated somewhat from this assertion).[51] The same was true, at least some of the time, in France.[52]

In 1772, the landmark British case of *Somerset v Stewart* made clear that slaves who set foot on British soil would, in fact, be free, on the grounds that slavery was contrary to natural law and was not legally authorized within the United Kingdom proper (as opposed to its colonial possessions).[53] James Somerset, a slave from Virginia, had arrived in England with his master, Charles Stewart; Stewart intended to continue to hold Somerset as a slave and eventually to return with him to America. Granville Sharp, a lawyer known to be opposed to slavery, and who had helped other Africans in London defend their freedom, became aware of Somerset's presence and helped him file a petition for habeas corpus seeking his release.[54] The lawyer argued that slavery was contrary to natural law and inalienable human rights, as well as to the customary liberties of English law. He suggested that slavery could not lawfully be based on a contract, for a man could not consent to 'dispose of all the rights vested by nature and society in him and his descendants' without 'ceasing to be a man; for these rights immediately flow from, and are essential to, his condition as such; they cannot be taken from him'.[55] Nor did capture in war justify slavery; the right to kill in battle did not translate into the right to enslave instead, he argued. On the other hand, Stewart's attorneys emphasized conventional conflict of laws doctrine and suggested that Somerset's legal status as a slave should follow him to England. These lawyers also argued that it would be impractically idealistic to find in Somerset's favour.

The court held that slavery was 'so odious' and contrary to natural law that it could only be justified by 'positive law'.[56] While slavery was recognized in other territories, the law of England itself did not allow or approve of it. Thus, despite the practical 'inconvenience' that might follow from the decision, the court ordered Somerset's release.[57]

Somerset was an important symbolic victory. However, it was a relatively isolated event. Granville Sharp was a lawyer who supported abolition, yet at the time there existed no NGOs that would allow for a more widespread movement against slavery to gain momentum. Such a civil society emerged only in the late eighteenth century, when religious organizations began translating their antislavery

[51] Davis, *The Problem of Slavery in the Age of Revolution* (n 28) 485 (quoting Blackstone).

[52] Sue Peabody, *'There are No Slaves in France': The Political Culture of Race and Slavery in the Ancien Régime* (OUP 1996) 23–40, 88–93.

[53] For a discussion of similar cases in French courts, see Peabody (n 52).

[54] Hochschild (n 33) 48–51 (describing the role of abolitionists in bringing Somerset's case).

[55] *Somerset v Stewart* 502.

[56] *Somerset* (n 55) 510. For a discussion of the natural law underpinnings of *Somerset* and other anti-slavery cases, see Robert M Cover, *Justice Accused: Antislavery and the Judicial Process* (Yale UP 1984) 8–30. Positive law generally refers to man-made laws promulgated by a particular sovereign or authority and specific to a certain time or place, rather than to inherent rights of natural law.

[57] *Somerset* (n 55) 509.

ideas into practical action and reform. Quakers were some of the first to organize against slavery. In 1787, a mixed group of Quakers and members of the Anglican Church and other denominations in Britain, came together to form a committee and launch a campaign that would, over the next two decades, change both mass and elite opinion concerning the slave trade. It was a novel undertaking. As one scholar has described, in Britain, NGOs of this sort 'were unknown in 1750, novel in 1780, commonplace in 1830'.[58]

It was not yet politically feasible to try to abolish slavery in British colonial possessions. Attacking the trade was more practical, although British merchants who participated in the trade, as well as those who owned slaves in the West Indies, resisted the effort. But it was easier to portray the slave trade as cruel and unjust than to attack the image of benign plantation masters. Newspapers and pamphlets carried stories by sailors and freed slaves of the horrors of the transiting the Atlantic in the hold of a slave ship, and slave ship crews were not made up of the best kinds of men, but instead of characters who were easy to demonize. Abolitionists also argued that plantation owners would treat their existing slaves better, and thus reduce horrific mortality rates on plantations, if there was not a plentiful supply of new captives from Africa.

Civil society actors used a number of different tactics to organize around anti-slavery. One of the key strategies for conveying popular sentiment in Britain was the petition to Parliament. At a time when voting rights were limited to a small segment of property-owning elites, the petition was a way in which ordinary people could express their political opinions. It was a mechanism for translating civil society's aspirations into political action. A mass petition drive concerning the slave trade in Britain in 1788 gathered 60–100,000 signatures, followed by 390,000 in 1792, and 750,000 in 1814.[59] The strategy was used again at various times. In 1833, some 1.3 million people in the UK signed a petition in support of immediate emancipation of slaves in British colonies.[60] Petitions were also used in other countries, including the US and France, though not on the same scale or with the same positive effects on legislative action.[61] Other modes of organizational action that were developed and perfected included public meetings and rallies, as well as placement of newspaper articles.[62]

[58] Charles Tilly, *Popular Contention in Great Britain: 1758–1834* (Harvard UP 1995) 142.

[59] Margaret E Keck and Kathryn Sikkink, *Activists Beyond Borders: Advocacy Networks in International Politics* (Cornell UP 1998) 44; Hochschild (n 33) 137, 230.

[60] Drescher, 'Women's Mobilization in the Era of Slave Emancipation' (n 35) 106.

[61] On petitions in the US, see S Higginson, 'A Short History of the Right to Petition Government for the Redress of Grievances' (1986) 96 *Yale LJ* 142, 158 (discussing 'crisis' over how Congress should respond to abolitionist petitions in the 1830s). On the much smaller scale of petitioning in France, see Drescher, 'Women's Mobilization in the Era of Slave Emancipation' (n 35) 106.

[62] Drescher, 'Women's Mobilization in the Era of Slave Emancipation' (n 35) 112.

As the early abolition movement sought to mobilize greater numbers of supporters, activists in some places eagerly sought out women's involvement.[63] As one scholar has noted, women 'were targeted as, and credited with, having an inherent sensitivity to the sufferings of slavery, especially its female victims'.[64] In 1791, British abolitionists launched a boycott of slave-grown sugar, introducing a new tool into the activists' toolbox (one particularly suited to a capitalist economy). This was a moment that would prove important, both in the history of anti-slavery activism and in the involvement of women in abolitionist causes.[65] The boycott began following the failure in Parliament of a measure that abolitionist leader William Wilberforce introduced to abolish the British slave trade. As scholars have described, '[i]t was an attempt to overcome a failure in politics by action in the spheres of civil society and the market', and '[t]he initiators of the movement believed that women were both susceptible to the message and essential to the campaign'.[66] An estimated 300,000 people participated in the boycott, and women were considered particularly important in its success, as they determined their families' purchasing and consumption decisions.[67]

Abolitionist organizations thus gained traction in British politics. With the leadership of William Wilberforce, the House of Commons passed anti-slave trade legislation in 1792, but conservative forces in the House of Lords blocked the measure.[68] The movement stalled, and other events overtook abolition in importance. Political agitation was viewed as dangerous and threatening in the wake of the bloody French Revolution, and the public meetings and petition campaigns that had galvanized Wilberforce's campaign could not continue.[69] Wilberforce dutifully introduced antislavery legislation each year, but the legislation was dead on arrival and received little attention.

In the spring of 1806, a change in strategy broke the log jam. The Foreign Slave Trade Act[70] prohibited British subjects from participating in the slave trade with the current or former colonies and possessions of France and its allies, with whom England was at war.[71] The act easily passed the House of Commons, framed as part of the war effort. Conservative forces finally noticed the measure and submitted a petition opposing the act to the House of Lords with more than 400 signatures from

[63] Clare Midgley, *Women Against Slavery: The British Campaigns: 1780–1870* (Routledge 1992); Clare Midgley 'Slave Sugar Boycotts, Female Activism and the Domestic Base of British Anti-Slavery Culture' (1996) 17 *Slavery and Abolition* 137.

[64] Drescher, 'Women's Mobilization in the Era of Slave Emancipation' (n 35) 101.

[65] Midgley, *Women Against Slavery* (n 63) 35–50; Midgley, 'Slave Sugar Boycotts, Female Activism and the Domestic Base of British Anti-Slavery Culture' (n 63).

[66] Drescher, 'Women's Mobilization in the Era of Slave Emancipation' (n 35) 99.

[67] Midgley, *Women Against Slavery* (n 63) 35–37.

[68] Hochschild (n 33) 233–34.

[69] Hochschild (n 33) 241–55.

[70] See Act to Prevent the Importation of Slaves 1806 (46 Geo 3 c 52).

[71] Drescher, 'Whose Abolition?' (n 33) 141, 142; Hochschild (n 33) 302–303.

the key trading centre of Manchester. The abolition forces proved their growing organizational sophistication and responded within hours with a counter-petition from Manchester bearing more than 2,300 signatures.[72] The act passed the House of Lords.[73] The slave trade proved an issue in key parliamentary elections in the fall of 1806.[74] In early 1807, both houses of Parliament finally passed the Act for the Abolition of the Slave Trade.[75] The law prohibited participation in the slave trade by British subjects and the importation of slaves to British possessions.

With strong enforcement by the Royal Navy, slave trading soon became an intolerably risky venture for British ships.[76] At the same time, it quickly became clear that the slave trade ban would have little constructive effect unless other countries followed. If Portugal, for example, did not prohibit the trade, Portuguese slave traders would simply pick up the slack created by the British exit from the market. In addition, Portuguese colonies would continue to import slaves, making their plantations more productive than those in British colonies. Accordingly, absent a repeal of the legislation (which seemed improbable), the best hope for British West Indian plantation owners was a re-levelling of the playing field through the abolition of the slave trade by other countries, as well. In other words, activism against the slave trade could not be solely confined within one nation, but would eventually have to address the transnational nature of the slave trade and the existence of slavery in many different nations. This would eventually take the forms of transnational civil society organizing for abolitionism, as well as the use of international law in the form of treaties to facilitate multi-country cooperation.

Across the Atlantic, legislation against the slave trade was also working its way through the American political system. Individual states took measures against the slave trade starting in the late eighteenth century. Between 1776 and 1787, ten of the thirteen states banned importation of slaves from abroad. Two others imposed high tariffs or had very low rates of import.[77] The Constitutional Convention in 1787 did not resolve the slave trade question; it deferred it, providing that the federal congress could not ban the importation of persons until 1808.[78] In the early 1790s, abolition societies began petitioning Congress for national anti-slave trade legislation. A statute passed in 1794 prohibited slave ships in American ports from being fitted out for slave trade abroad.[79] In 1800, Congress passed an act that outlawed US

72 Drescher, 'Whose Abolition?' (n 33) 142.

73 Drescher, 'Whose Abolition?' (n 33) 142–44.

74 Drescher, 'Whose Abolition?' (n 33) 145–48.

75 Act for the Abolition of the Slave Trade 1807 (47 Geo 3 c 36) (repealed 1824).

76 David Eltis, 'The Nineteenth-Century Transatlantic Slave Trade: An Annual Time Series of Imports into the Americas Broken down by Region' (1987) 67 *Hispanic American Historical Review* 109, 136 table V.

77 Keith L Doughtery and Jac C Heckelman, 'Voting on Slavery at the Constitutional Convention' (2008) 136 *Public Choice* 293, 294–95; Martinez (n 18) 40.

78 Martinez (n 18) 39.

79 Act of 22 March 1794, ch 11, 1 Stat 347, 349. See Martinez (n 18) 41.

citizen involvement on slave ships, and slavery-related trips, abroad.[80] These statutes allowed for a number of civil forfeitures and criminal prosecutions in federal court in the following years.[81] Congress then passed legislation fully prohibiting the slave trade on 2 March 1807, effective in January 1808.

The anti-slavery movement in the United States had begun to emerge in the aftermath of the American Revolution.[82] The Quakers played a central role in its emergence, speaking out against slavery starting in the latter half of the eighteenth century.[83] Early anti-slavery activism focused on attempts to gradually emancipate slaves, as well as suggestions of colonizing Liberia with free blacks, in order to end slavery in the south.[84] More radical efforts soon developed. By 1838, there were about 1,350 anti-slavery societies, which together had as many as 250,000 members, in the United States.[85] These associations were deeply rooted in American communities of Quakers, Methodists, Presbyterians, and Unitarians.[86]

2. International Action against the Slave Trade

2.1. Civil society networks

A rich transnational network flourished between abolitionist organizations in Britain and the United States. Activists in the two countries 'frequently exchanged letters, publications, and visits', drawing on 'a tradition of transatlantic networking and information exchange that had flourished among them during the last decades before American independence'.[87] These links were particularly rooted in the relationships that Quakers had built over the course of the eighteenth century.[88] Activists shared tactics, including petitioning, boycotting goods produced by slaves,

[80] Act of 10 May 1800, ch 51, 2 Stat 70, 70–71. See Martinez (n 18) 42.

[81] Martinez (n 18) 42.

[82] Clapp, 'Introduction' (n 36) 5.

[83] David Brion Davis, 'The Quaker Ethic and the Antislavery International' in Bender (n 29) 29; S Drescher, 'Women's Mobilization in the Era of Slave Emancipation' (n 35) 112; Sally G McMillen, *Seneca Falls and the Origins of the Women's Rights Movement* (OUP 2008) 56.

[84] Clapp, 'Introduction' (n 36) 6.

[85] Herbert Aptheker, *Abolitionism: A Revolutionary Movement* (Twayne Publishers 1989) 56 (cited in Keck and Sikkink, *Activists Beyond Borders* (n 59) 44).

[86] Keck and Sikkink, *Activists Beyond Borders* (n 59) 44.

[87] Keck and Sikkink, *Activists Beyond Borders* (n 59) 44 (citing Alison Gilbert Olson, *Making the Empire Work: London and American Interest Groups: 1690–1790* (Harvard UP 1992).

[88] Midgley, *Women Against Slavery* (n 63) 127.

and hiring abolitionist speakers, which were often transmitted from Britain to the United States.[89] Several key abolitionist figures were crucial to solidifying these links in the 1830s, including William Lloyd Garrison, Charles Stuart, and George Thompson.[90] Garrison, for example, started the American Anti-Slavery Society. He sought British assistance, which came in the form of the Universal Abolition Society defining one of its aims as 'aiding American abolitionists and campaigning against foreign involvement in the slave trade'.[91] Stuart and Thompson also prioritized establishing more links between the two countries. Upon his return from one tour in the United States, Thompson encouraged the creation of more universal abolition societies.[92]

The World Anti-Slavery Convention, held in 1840, was central to solidifying the ties between British and American abolitionist organizations.[93] As one scholar has noted, '[t]he 1840 conference was built on efforts of women and men working on both sides of the Atlantic, in Calcutta, Sierra Leone, and the Cape of Good Hope'.[94] The conference 'represented a joint English and American undertaking' that key antislavery leaders in both countries attended.[95]

2.2. State-to-state action: international treaties and courts

At the same time as civil society actors in various countries were working together to further the abolitionist agenda, developments were taking place on the state-to-state level. Influenced by domestic pressure groups, Britain in particular made suppressing the slave trade a pillar of its foreign policy. Over the course of the nineteenth century, a network of treaties against the slave trade were put in place and played a significant role in solidifying the international consensus against slavery. The international legal effort against the slave trade began with declarations that the slave trade was contrary to the interests of humanity, in instruments such as the Treaty of Ghent (between the US and Britain at the end of the War of 1812) and in a non-binding declaration by European powers at the Congress of Vienna.[96] These were followed by more binding forms of international law-making, including treaties against the slave trade and even provisions for international judicial enforcement of those treaties.

[89] Keck and Sikkink, *Activists Beyond Borders* (n 59) 45.

[90] Midgley, *Women Against Slavery* (n 63) 127.

[91] Midgley, *Women Against Slavery* (n 63) 126.

[92] Midgley, *Women Against Slavery* (n 63) 128.

[93] Keck and Sikkink, *Activists Beyond Borders* (n 59) 46.

[94] Resnik (n 14) 22.

[95] Douglas H Maynard, 'The World's Anti-Slavery Convention of 1840' (1960) 47 *Mississippi Valley Historical Review* 452.

[96] Vienna Congress Treaty, Act XV, Declaration Relative to the Universal Abolition of the Slave Trade.

The late eighteenth century had seen the emergence of arbitral commissions for settling disputes between countries, such as the 1794 Jay Treaty between Britain and the United States[97] to settle claims that arose from the American Revolutionary War, and the November 1815 peace treaty addressing claims from the Napoleonic Wars.[98] From such institutions emerged the idea of establishing courts to enforce the new treaties against the slave trade. By 1817, Britain had established bilateral treaties with the Netherlands, Portugal, and Spain that allowed for 'mutual rights of search and established mixed courts to try and condemn captured slave ships'. These treaties were formulated using language that clearly condemned slavery as an offence against humanity and can thus be understood as 'the world's first international courts directed at the protection of human rights'.[99]

These courts were set up in possessions of each of the four treaty member countries: Freetown, Sierra Leone; Havana, Cuba; Rio de Janeiro, Brazil; and Suriname.[100] Other countries, including Brazil, Chile, the Argentine Confederation, Uruguay, Bolivia, Ecuador, and the United States, eventually joined and established additional courts.[101] The courts initially struggled with uncertainties about procedural rules and substantive law, further complicated by the high absenteeism of European judges and arbitrators who would fall victim to tropical diseases.[102] But ultimately, the international courts condemned more than 600 illegal ships, and freed more than 80,000 slaves.[103] In addition, national courts operating under national laws and sometimes theories of universal jurisdiction also took action at various times to enforce the international slave trade ban.[104]

While the international treaties and the international court system did not alone end the slave trade, they played an important role in solidifying the consensus against the slave trade and provided a mechanism for cooperation between nations.[105] While abolitionist organizations were not predominantly focused on the international legal regime, they did recognize it was a tool that could aid in their fight. The delegates at the 1840 World Anti-Slavery Convention, for example, voted in favour of a proposal for dramatically expanding the jurisdiction of the mixed courts, and the British government in turn drafted a treaty that would have done just that, although that particular draft was never adopted.[106] Ultimately, however, the campaign for abolition of the slave trade stands as a milestone in the history of international human rights law, both conceptually, as the first time international treaties were seen as a proper mechanism for countries to address the violation of the rights of persons who were not their citizens, as well as practically, as in the first instance in which international treaties were successfully used to change global practices in relation to a human rights issue.

[97] Treaty of Amity Commerce and Navigation, between His Britannic Majesty; and The United States of America.

[98] Treaty of Paris.

[99] Martinez (n 18) 35–36.

[100] Martinez (n 18) 69.

[101] Martinez (n 18) 78–79.

[102] Martinez (n 18) 68–69.

[103] Martinez (n 18) 79.

[104] Martinez (n 18) 114–39.

[105] Martinez (n 18) 144–47.

[106] Martinez (n 18) 101.

2.3. Women and abolition

Historians have recognized that women were centrally involved in anti-slavery movements on both sides of the Atlantic, and there were strong connections between women's anti-slavery work and their eventual organizing in support of women's rights and other issues.[107] As one scholar noted:

> Some associations, women's antislavery organizations foremost among them, offered women opportunities to create institutions, to master the arts of debating, to formulate resolutions, to hold office, to negotiate with other branches, and to form contacts and alliances at the local, national, and international level. In short, they were a major pathway in the formation of what might be called feminine social capital, the art of building effective networks, coalitions, and leaders.[108]

Women could not vote at this point, and it was through non-governmental organizing in the context of civil society that they not only made their voices heard on the issue of slavery, but eventually organized themselves to demand greater political and civil rights. As previously noted, anti-slavery campaigns were closely entwined with religious activity, with Quakers and other Protestant denominations involved to varying degrees. Different religious sects, not surprisingly, had differing views on the role of women. Baptists, Congregationalists, and Methodists, for example, 'continued to emphasize women's role as godly wives and mothers, and their dependence on men'.[109] Other denominations, such as Unitarians, did not feel that women's role in the home was limited to 'maternal or domestic duties'.[110]

Women played an important part in abolitionist movements in many countries, 'especially in Great Britain and the United States, where the state did not regulate civil society or women's activism as much as it did in Germany or France', though some women were active in smaller anti-slavery movements at various moments in those countries, as well.[111] Historians have argued that abolition was a critical point for women's entry into the public space. The extent to which various abolitionists thought women should be involved varied. A striking example of this surrounded the controversy of American women and the 1840 London Conference, discussed in great detail below, where female delegates were not allowed to take a seat at the conference. Yet some abolitionists invited and rationalized women's involvement in the movement, as aspects of slavery were thought to be of particular concern to women, such as the ways in which slavery destroyed family structures (a traditional sphere of women) and the plight of women slaves.[112] While some have suggested that this reinforced the ideology of 'separate spheres' and distracted from more fundamental

[107] Clapp, 'Introduction' (n 36) 2–3.

[108] Drescher, 'Women's Mobilization in the Era of Slave Emancipation' (n 35) 113–14.

[109] Clapp, 'Introduction' (n 36) 15.

[110] Clapp, 'Introduction' (n 36) 15.

[111] Sklar and Stewart, 'Introduction' (n 37) xii.

[112] Drescher, 'Women's Mobilization in the Era of Slave Emancipation' (n 35) 110.

challenges to gender and class hierarchies,[113] it is not clear that women's voices could have entered the public sphere in a more radical way, at that moment in time, and met with any sort of success.

One of the factors that facilitated the entry of women into civil society, and eventually political activism, in both the US and Britain was the centrality of religion to abolitionist organizing. As one scholar has noted, churches—particularly those of newer, dissenting Protestant denominations—offered a structure for women to gather and interact, and 'women took strength from their church networks to become involved in collective activism for causes which, in the case of anti-slavery, took them into the political arena.'[114] Particularly in the US, 'religion, no longer supported by the state, became a competitive form of voluntarism that encouraged women's collective activism.'[115] Religious ideas and values heavily influenced abolitionist women, and the framework in which many of them experienced religion—that of evangelical conversion and dissent—created space for their work in challenging authority and existing social norms, whether related to gender norms or other issues, such as slavery.[116]

As historians have recounted: 'For over six decades, from the 1790s to the 1850s, religious women connected anti-slavery movements across the Atlantic, forging bonds of friendship, sharing strategies and resources, nurturing commitments, and constructing an international movement.'[117] But there were differences in the social and political contexts on opposite sides of the Atlantic. British women abolitionists emphasized 'political economy' and 'profitability' to a greater extent than Americans, who 'embraced a strategy whereby they sought to influence "public opinion" while avoiding any claim to "political" standing as such.'[118] In contrast to the British:

> American women did not, on the whole, take up an analysis of the economics of slavery or its abolition; instead they abstained from slave goods so that their behaviour (and their persons) reflected their souls…They paid homage to their British predecessors for formulating a basis for women's engagement in anti-slavery work, but, moved in part by the powerful evangelical currents that gave their abolitionism a wider audience, they embellished the emotionalism of their appeal.[119]

[113] Drescher, 'Women's Mobilization in the Era of Slave Emancipation' (n 35) 110.

[114] Clapp, 'Introduction' (n 36) 17.

[115] Sklar and Stewart, 'Introduction' (n 37) xii; K Offen, 'Feminist Campaign in "Public Space": Civil Society, Gender Justice, and the History of European Feminisms' in Gunilla Budde, Karen Hagemann, and Sonya Michel (eds), *Civil Society, Public Space, and Gender Justice* (Berghahn 2008).

[116] Sklar and Stewart, 'Introduction' (n 37) xii; Alison Twells, '"We Ought to Obey God Rather than Man": Women, Anti-Slavery, and Nonconformist Religious Cultures' in Clapp and Jeffrey (n 26) 67–68; Judie Newman, 'Writing Against Slavery: Harriet Beecher Stowe' in Clapp and Jeffrey (n 26) 176.

[117] Carol Lasser, 'Immediatism, Dissent, and Gender: Women and the Sentimentalization of Transatlantic Anti-Slavery Appeals' in Clapp and Jeffrey (n 26) 111.

[118] Lasser (n 117) 111, 113, 117, 130.

[119] Lasser (n 117) 130–31.

'Hundreds of female anti-slavery societies emerged in the 1830s' in the United States, mostly linked in some way to churches and emphasizing religious arguments, though in many instances 'women chose to join a female anti-slavery society despite the opposition of their church'.[120]

Mass national petitioning was key to women's anti-slavery activism. While petitioning was originally a male-driven form of activism, by 1830 British women were crucial to its success and essentially took it over.[121] Baptist and Methodist organizations asked for their involvement, and by 1838 more than two-thirds of signatures were from women.[122] Women also played a crucial role in American anti-slavery petition efforts. As one scholar notes, '[f]rom 1831 to 1863 women publicly expressed their opinion about slavery by affixing approximately 3 million signatures to petitions aimed at Congress'.[123]

It was also the case that women were 'responsible for the most massive antislavery action in Britain during the 1850s', when in 1852, in response to Harriet Beecher Stowe's visit to Britain, they authored two addresses to 'Their Sisters, the Women of the United States of America', for which more than 750,000 women's signatures were gathered.[124]

There were particularly strong ties between North American and British abolitionists, including between women abolitionists, and indeed some scholars have argued that the transatlantic networks that flourished, particularly from the 1830s to the 1850s, constituted 'the first international women's movement'.[125]

Many women involved in abolition campaigns became involved in other issues as well. Most notably, particularly in the United States, campaigners for abolition were transformed into campaigners for women's rights. As one abolitionist wrote, 'in striving to strike [the slaves'] irons off, we found most surely that we were manacled *ourselves*'.[126] At the time, 'married women could not own property, make contracts, bring suits, or sit on juries. They could be legally beaten by their husbands and were required at any moment to submit to their husbands' sexual demands'.[127] As early as the seventeenth century in France, the comparison between marriage and slavery was made by supporters of greater rights for women in novels and other literary

[120] Stacey Robertson, '"On the Side of Righteousness": Women, The Church, and Abolition' in Clapp and Jeffrey (n 26) 158, 165.

[121] Drescher, 'Women's Mobilization in the Era of Slave Emancipation' (n 35) 105.

[122] Drescher, 'Women's Mobilization in the Era of Slave Emancipation' (n 35) 106.

[123] Susan Zaeske, *Signatures of Citizenship: Petitioning, Antislavery, and Women's Political Identity* (University of North Carolina Press 2003) 2.

[124] Drescher, 'Women's Mobilization in the Era of Slave Emancipation' (n 35) 109–10.

[125] Bonnie S Anderson, *Joyous Greetings: The First International Women's Movement: 1830–1860* (OUP 2000). See also Margaret H McFadden, *Golden Cables of Sympathy: The Transatlantic Sources of Nineteenth-Century Feminism* (UP of Kentucky 1999).

[126] David Brion Davis, 'Declaring Equality: Sisterhood and Slavery' in Sklar and Stewart, *Women's Rights and Transatlantic Antislavery* (n 14) 11 (citing Anderson, *Joyous Greetings* (n 125) 122).

[127] Davis, 'Declaring Equality' (n 126) 11.

works, and eventually was invoked in countries including Germany, Britain, and the United States.[128] As one scholar has explained:

> [t]The power of the slavery analogy, for feminists, was its insistence that women, and particularly women who married, were individuals in their own right, that they possessed 'human rights' and free will and could not legally be disposed of like chattel or forced, even for family reasons, to do things against their will.[129]

More concretely, women delegates from the United States were denied official seats at the 1840 World Anti-Slavery Convention in London, an issue referred to as 'the woman question'.[130] This rejection highlighted an important difference in anti-slavery activism in Britain and the United States. While '[m]ost local anti-slavery societies in the United States before 1840 included both men and women', in Britain 'all anti-slavery societies were sex-segregated'.[131] This difference became salient when eight women presented themselves as delegates to the London Convention, invited as representatives of the American Anti-Slavery Society. The committee refused them, claiming that 'their presence constituted "an innovation on [British] customs and usages" that would subject the convention to ridicule'.[132] Debate on the issue dominated much of the first day of the conference.[133] In a vote at the end of the day, 90 per cent of male delegates voted against seating the women. Instead, the women observed the conference in a curtained-off area off of the main hall.[134]

The London Conference played a central role in the development of the women's movement.[135] Elizabeth Cady Stanton asserted that it was the experience of that convention that gave 'rise to the movement for women's political equality both in England and the United States'.[136] She claimed that their exclusion led her and Lucretia Mott to 'hold a convention as soon as we returned home, and form a society to advocate the rights of women'.[137] Eight years later, the Seneca Falls conference launched the American women's rights movement.[138] The issues discussed at Seneca Falls included women's suffrage, property rights for married women, equal wages,

[128] Karen Offen, 'How (and Why) the Analogy of Marriage with Slavery Provided the Springboard for Women's Rights Demands in France, 1640–1848' in Sklar and Stewart, *Women's Rights and Transatlantic Antislavery* (n 14) 59; Bonnie S Anderson, '*Frauenemancipation* and Beyond: The Use of the Concept of Emancipation by Early European Feminists' in Sklar and Stewart, *Women's Rights and Transatlantic Antislavery* (n 14) 82.

[129] Offen, 'How (and Why) the Analogy of Marriage with Slavery' (n 128) 72–73.

[130] McMillen (n 83) 72.

[131] Kathryn Kish Sklar, '"Women Who Speak for an Entire Nation": American and British Women Compared at the World Anti-Slavery Convention, London, 1840' (1990) 59 *Pacific Historical Review* 453, 464.

[132] Sklar, 'Women Who Speak for an Entire Nation' (n 131) 462.

[133] McMillen (n 83) 72.

[134] McMillen (n 83) 75.

[135] McMillen (n 83) 76.

[136] Midgley, *Women Against Slavery* (n 63) 160 (quoting Elizabeth Cady Stanton, *Eighty Years and More: Reminiscences 1815–1897* (T Fisher Unwim 1898) 82).

[137] Sklar, 'Women Who Speak for an Entire Nation' (n 131) 455 (quoting Stanton).

[138] Sklar, 'Women Who Speak for an Entire Nation' (n 131) 455.

education, and divorce.[139] The key actors involved in Seneca Falls and its aftermath came to the issue of women's rights through their abolitionist activities. They relied on their experiences in public speaking and organizing around anti-slavery in their involvement in the women's movement.[140]

In the immediate aftermath of the London Convention, American women turned their attention to women's rights, in order to create 'a new place within a civil and political society of equal citizens'.[141] In contrast, until the early 1850s, their British anti-slavery sisters 'were less inclined to form more radical feminist associations'.[142] Instead, they chose to focus their attention on 'the ever-broadening range of social problems being addressed by voluntary associations'.[143] Some scholars have noted that in the United States, race and gender 'were the two key determinants of full citizenship' that led to an intuitive linking of the issues;[144] women and blacks both did not have full enjoyment of the rights that the US Constitution granted to persons, leading to a natural analogy between their situations. In Britain, the picture was more complicated, because 'class was effectively the determinant of enfranchisement', with property ownership being the requisite for voting, and because slavery was an institution that existed at the periphery, not in the imperial centre of Britain proper, thus rendering less salient the equation between women and blacks as disenfranchised groups.[145] In addition, British women's activism occurred in the context of empire, as women activists linked their concern for women in the reaches of the British empire (framed in the troublesome context of imperial ideologies of superiority and obligation) to their domestic feminism and their supposed privileges as women. This included not only antislavery efforts, but also campaigns related to women in India and against the practice of *sati*.[146]

Women were also influential in various ways in the abolition movement in Brazil.[147] In early-nineteenth-century France, by contrast, there was no large-scale

[139] Keck and Sikkink, *Activists Beyond Borders* (n 59) 52; McMillen (n 83) 71.

[140] Kathryn Kish Sklar, '"The Throne of My Heart": Religion, Oratory, and Transatlantic Community in Angelina Grimke's Launching of Women's Rights, 1828–1838' in Sklar and Stewart, *Women's Rights and Transatlantic Antislavery* (n 14).

[141] Drescher, 'Women's Mobilization in the Era of Slave Emancipation' (n 35) 110.

[142] Drescher, 'Women's Mobilization in the Era of Slave Emancipation' (n 35) 114.

[143] Drescher, 'Women's Mobilization in the Era of Slave Emancipation' (n 35) 114.

[144] Clare Midgley, 'British Abolition and Feminism in Transatlantic Perspective' in Sklar and Stewart, *Women's Rights and Transatlantic Antislavery* (n 14) 125.

[145] Midgley, 'British Abolition and Feminism in Transatlantic Perspective' (n 144) 125.

[146] Antoinette Burton, *Burdens of History: British Feminists, Indian Women, and Imperial Culture, 1865–1915* (University of North Carolina Press 1994); Midgley, 'British Abolition and Feminism in Transatlantic Perspective' (n 144) 128. *Sati* is the practice of a widow self-immolating on her husband's funeral pyre.

[147] June E Hahner, 'Feminism, Women's Rights and the Suffrage Movement in Brazil, 1850–1932' (1980) 15 *Lat Am Res Rev* 65; Roger A Kittleson, '"Campaign All of Peace and Charity": Gender and the Politics of Abolitionism in Porto Alegre, Brazil, 1879–88' (2001) 22 *Slavery and Abolition* 83; Drescher, 'Women's Mobilization in the Era of Slave Emancipation' (n 35) 119 fn 48.

'organized mass movement either for the abolition of slavery or for the emancipation of women', though there was discussion and writing on both topics.[148] Women had participated actively in the French Revolution and had made demands for the franchise and other rights, but after the Revolution, the gains women made were quickly rescinded.[149] Even when abolitionists in France gathered 21,000 signatures in 1844 and 1847, they fell orders of magnitude short of the millions of signatures gathered in Britain at various times.[150] There were not distinct women's abolitionist societies in France, and women were not central to the small, male-dominated organizations.[151] In the late 1840s, the English Quaker and abolitionist Anne Knight 'participated in the efforts of the *Voix des Femmes* team to formulate their protests',[152] but overall there were not strong ties, in this time period, between French abolitionists and French women's groups campaigning for suffrage or other women's rights.[153] There was some participation by women in abolitionist organizations in Spain, and the 'Spanish Abolition Society published a series of letters in 1865 from British women's antislavery societies to the "Ladies of Madrid"', but again it was not as significant as in the Anglo-American countries.[154] In Spain, the trafficking of white women for the global sex trade was linked in public argument to the African slave trade. The same person (a man) who founded the *Sociedad Abolicionista* (Abolitionist Society) in 1865 (concerned with black slavery in the Antilles) later founded the *Sociedad para la Abolición de la Prostitución Legal o Tolerada* (Society for the Abolition of Legal or Tolerated Prostitution) in 1883 (concerned with prostitution, which was asserted to be a form of slavery).[155]

In the later part of the nineteenth and the early twentieth century, as the movement for women's rights advanced, some of the ties that had been forged between British and American abolitionist women were extended. These ties developed mainly around the issue of women's suffrage. A number of different tactics were shared transatlantically. For example, the British Women's Social and Political Union influenced more militant suffragettes in the United States.[156]

The international suffrage campaign was launched in 1904, with the founding of the International Woman Suffrage Association.[157] Eleven countries attended its

[148] Offen, 'How (and Why) the Analogy of Marriage with Slavery' (n 128) 70. See also Drescher, 'Women's Mobilization in the Era of Slave Emancipation' (n 35) 102.

[149] Offen, 'How (and Why) the Analogy of Marriage with Slavery' (n 128) 69; Drescher, 'Women's Mobilization in the Era of Slave Emancipation' (n 35) 104.

[150] Drescher, 'Women's Mobilization in the Era of Slave Emancipation' (n 35) 106.

[151] Drescher, 'Women's Mobilization in the Era of Slave Emancipation' (n 35).

[152] Offen, 'How (and Why) the Analogy of Marriage with Slavery' (n 128) 70–71.

[153] Drescher, 'Women's Mobilization in the Era of Slave Emancipation' (n 35) 108.

[154] Drescher, 'Women's Mobilization in the Era of Slave Emancipation' (n 35) 113.

[155] Pura Fernández, *Mujer Pública y Vida Privada: Del Arte Eunuco y la Novela Lupanaria* (Tamesis Books 2008) 233.

[156] Keck and Sikkink, *Activists Beyond Borders* (n 59) 55.

[157] Keck and Sikkink, *Activists Beyond Borders* (n 59) 53.

founding conference, a number that almost quadrupled by the time of the 1926 conference.[158] Shared tactics resembled those of the earlier abolitionists; '[a]s with the anti-slavery movement, these ideas spread through travel of key activists, family connections, and exchanges of letters, pamphlets, and newspapers'.[159] American suffrage activists played a particularly important role in shaping the demands of their British counterparts. Married women could not own property in Britain, and voting was tied to property ownership.[160] Americans such as Stanton pushed them to demand voting rights for married and single women. While only a minority of British activists originally held this position, it eventually became the dominant one in the country.[161]

Speaking tours played a central role in developing ties between women's organizations internationally, beyond Britain and the United States. During and in the immediate aftermath of the First World War, the United States, Canada, and many European countries granted women the right to vote. Shortly thereafter, these rights were extended throughout most countries in Latin America, Asia, and the Middle East.

2.4. Development of civil society and emergence of other transnational non-governmental organizations

Many of the organizations that flourished in the new space of civil society were geographically confined, either locally or within the context of the national state. However, as the abolition and women's suffrage movements demonstrate, there were some very significant ones with transnational reach. Churches and religious organizations, of course, had long had transnational reach. But although many of the new groups had some ties to religious organizations, their missions were in some ways broader than those of churches. For example, some point to the World Alliance of YMCAs, which was founded in 1855 with affiliated associations in eight countries, as another early example of an international non-governmental organization.[162] The YMCA was created in London to provide young migrant men refuge from the dangers of the city.[163] It gradually expanded to fulfilling its mission 'to

[158] Keck and Sikkink, *Activists Beyond Borders* (n 59) 56.
[159] Keck and Sikkink, *Activists Beyond Borders* (n 59) 56.
[160] Keck and Sikkink, *Activists Beyond Borders* (n 59) 57.
[161] Keck and Sikkink, *Activists Beyond Borders* (n 59) 57.
[162] Seary (n 22) 15.
[163] YMCA, 'The Story of Our Founding' <http://www.ymca.net/history/founding.html> accessed 27 August 2012.

bring social justice and peace to young people and their communities, regardless of religious, race, gender, or culture', in 125 countries, with over 45 million members.[164]

Transnational NGOs were also involved in the development of the international law of war. Henry Dunant founded the organization that became the International Committee of the Red Cross after he witnessed the suffering of the wounded at the Battle of Solferino in 1859. Dunant was born in Geneva, Switzerland, in 1828, the son of a well-to-do businessman.[165] Motivated in part by religious belief, he was involved in local charitable work from an early age, as were his parents.[166] Prior to founding the Red Cross, he participated in the founding of the Geneva chapter of the YMCA in 1852 and in the conference creating the international association of YMCAs in 1855. Relatedly, other NGOs in the early nineteenth century emerged and organized around the pursuit of peace, with over 425 peace societies active by 1900. These societies had important transnational reach. In 1840, the President of the American Peace Society, William Ladd, proposed a plan that would eventually become the Permanent Court of Arbitration (PCA).[167] Today, the PCA is 'a modern, multi-faceted arbitral institution that is now perfectly situated at the juncture between public and private international law to meet the rapidly evolving dispute resolution needs of the international community'.[168]

NGOs also expanded their transnational reach in other areas. These include worker solidarity, where '[t]ransnational worker activity increased in the 1870s'.[169] Groups focused on international labour issues and founded in the late nineteenth and early twentieth centuries the International Federation of Tobacco Workers, the International Federation for the Observation of Sunday, the Permanent International Committee on Social Insurance, the International Federation of Trade Unions, and the International Congress on Occupational Diseases.[170] Other organizations that emerged throughout the nineteenth century focused on issues of free trade, including the International Association for Customs Reform, founded in 1856.[171]

164 YMCA, 'Who We Are' <http://www.ymca.int/who-we-are> accessed 27 August 2012.

165 Pierre Boissier, *History of the International Committee of the Red Cross: from Solferino to Tsushima* (Henry Dunant Institute 1978) 9.

166 Boissier (n 166) 11.

167 Steve Charnovitz, 'Two Centuries of Participation: NGOs and International Governance' (1997) 18 *Mich J Int'l L* 183, 193.

168 Permanent Court of Arbitration, 'About Us' <http://www.pca-cpa.org/showpage.asp?pag_id=1027> accessed 27 August 2012.

169 Charnovitz (n 168) 193.

170 Charnovitz (n 168) 193–94.

171 Charnovitz (n 168) 194.

2.5. Connections between early NGOs and those active today

Not only did a number of the early NGOs develop organizing tactics and strategies still used by transnational NGOs today, some of these organizations have had a more or less continuous organizational life, even as their agendas have developed and changed with the times. A number of major human rights organizations, active in the post-Second World War period, can trace their genealogy to the nineteenth-century abolition campaigns and women's movement. For example, the organization currently called Anti-Slavery International has been called 'the world's oldest and most enduring nongovernmental organization monitoring human rights'.[172] The current entity is the organizational successor of early organizations that grew out of the British and Foreign Anti-Slavery Society that was formed in 1839 by British abolitionist Thomas Clarkson and others, and had ties to the 1823 Anti-Slavery Society. Its members played a crucial role in the 1840 London conference and the subsequent sugar boycott. It was also involved in the 1890 Brussels Act, an early anti-slavery treaty. In the early twentieth century, it campaigned against King Leopold's slavery practices in the Congo, and participated in the movement against indentured labour in British colonies. Since the end of the twentieth century, it has worked on anti-trafficking and slavery activities throughout the world, including Western Europe, Nepal, Niger, Brazil, and the Gulf States.[173]

Some of the founding members of the National Association for the Advancement of Colored People (NAACP) in 1909, such as Mary White Ovington and Oswald Garrison Villard, were descendants of individuals actively involved in the anti-slavery and women's movements.[174] In addition, WEB DuBois wrote his doctoral dissertation on the suppression of the slave trade,[175] and through his attendance at several Pan-African Congresses in the early decades of the twentieth century, he coupled his work on behalf of African Americans with broader international efforts to promote human rights. DuBois attended the founding convention of the United Nations as a representative of the NAACP.[176]

Other prominent twenty-first century organizations also had links to the nineteenth-century abolition and women's movements. Carrie Chapman Catt, who

[172] Drescher, 'Women's Mobilization in the Era of Slave Emancipation' (n 35) 105.

[173] Anti-Slavery International, 'History of Anti-Slavery International' <http://www.antislavery.org/english/what_we_do/our_history.aspx> accessed 27 August 2012.

[174] NAACP, 'NAACP: 100 Years of History' <http://www.naacp.org/pages/naacp-history> accessed 27 August 2012.

[175] DuBois (n 28).

[176] C Anderson, *Eyes Off the Prize: The United Nations and the African American Struggle for Human Rights, 1944–1955* (CUP 2003) 38–43.

founded the League of Women Voters in 1920, was a key player in the American suffrage movement. She had previously been head of the National American Woman Suffrage Organization, which was in turn a product of the merger of earlier women's suffrage organizations that had close ties to abolitionist organizations.[177] Crystal Eastman, who with Roger Baldwin founded the organization that would eventually become the American Civil Liberties Union (ACLU), came from a family actively involved in abolition and women's rights movements.[178] Interestingly, the history of the ACLU shows how even an institution that is today largely viewed as a domestic civil rights organization had important transnational ties. As one scholar has noted, the domestic American civil liberties movement, including the ACLU, 'arose out of a pre-World War I transatlantic internationalism that transcended the national boundaries of the United States'.[179]

This chapter underscores how the contemporary dialogue around international human rights law has roots in nineteenth-century activism that emerged first around the issues of the slave trade and slavery, and shortly after around the women's rights movement. As demonstrated here, one key similarity between these historical antecedents and modern human rights activism is the importance of transnational ties to successful mobilization. In addition, there also exist concrete links between contemporary human rights organizations and the abolitionist and women's rights organizations of the nineteenth century. In underscoring these shared tactics and ties, this chapter shows the benefits of considering specific issue areas across history in order to make convincing claims about the emergence of today's human rights movement. Such a case study approach to the question of when international human rights law emerged makes it difficult to deny the deep historical roots of contemporary law and practice.

Further Reading

Charnovitz S, 'Two Centuries of Participation: NGOs and International Governance' (1997) 18 *Mich J Int'l L* 183

Clapp EJ and Jeffrey JR (eds), *Women, Dissent and Anti-Slavery in Britain and America, 1790–1865* (OUP 2011)

Davis DB, *The Problem of Slavery in Western Culture* (OUP 1966)

[177] Resnik (n 14) 19–22; The National League of Women Voters was the offspring of the National American Woman Suffrage Organization. See League of Women Voters, 'About Us: Our History' <http://www.lwv.org/AM/Template.cfm?Section=Our_History&Template=/TaggedPage/TaggedPageDisplay.cfm&TPLID=36&ContentID=1501> accessed February 28, 2011.

[178] John Fabian Witt, 'Crystal Eastman and the Internationalist Beginnings of American Civil Liberties' (2004) 54 *Duke LJ* 705, 709, 712.

[179] Witt (n 179) 709.

Hochschild A, *Bury the Chains: Prophets and Rebels in the Fight to Free an Empire's Slaves* (Mariner Books 2005)
Keck ME and Sikkink K, *Activists Beyond Borders: Advocacy Networks in International Politics* (Cornell UP 1998)
Martinez JS, *The Slave Trade and the Origins of International Human Rights Law* (OUP 2012)
Midgley C, *Women Against Slavery: The British Campaigns: 1780–1870* (Routledge 1992)
Sklar KK and Stewart JB (eds), *Women's Rights and Transatlantic Antislavery in the Era of Emancipation* (Yale UP 2007)
Zaeske S, *Signatures of Citizenship: Petitioning, Antislavery, and Women's Political Identity* (University of North Carolina Press 2003)

CHAPTER 10

DIPLOMATIC PROTECTION AS A SOURCE OF HUMAN RIGHTS LAW

ANNEMARIEKE VERMEER-KÜNZLI

1. Introduction

Diplomatic protection, or the protection of nationals abroad, has been a traditional feature of international law. It has influenced many other areas of international law, such as the law of state responsibility, investment law, and human rights law. This chapter explores the extent to which the law of diplomatic protection and its development have influenced the formation of human rights law. After a general introduction, the discussion examines the legal rules concerning diplomatic protection, which are designed to respect the sovereignty of the receiving state—that is, the state where the (alleged) injury to an alien occurred. Although modern human rights law has not adopted the rule on nationality of claims, the requirement of exhausting local remedies is part of human rights law, based on similar underlying considerations. The third part will consider the international minimum standard and its relevance for the formation of modern human rights law.

In the eighteenth century, the Swiss scholar Emmerich de Vattel wrote:

Quiconque maltraite un Citoyen offense indirectement l'Etat, qui doit protéger ce Citoyen. Le Souverain de celui-ci doit venger son injure, obliger, s'il le peut, l'aggresseur à une entière réparation, ou le punir; puisqu'autrement le Citoyen n'obtiendroit point la grande fin de l'association Civile, que est la sûreté.[1]

Although this certainly is not the first reference to the rights of individuals or human rights, it is commonly considered the first doctrinal source on what became 'diplomatic protection'. Other important early sources include a wealth of case law that the various mixed claims commissions of the nineteenth and early twentieth centuries produced, as well as the works of scholars such as Borchard, Dunn, and Freeman, and the case law of the Permanent Court of International Justice (PCIJ) and its successor, the International Court of Justice (ICJ). Today's approach to diplomatic protection, as can be found in the Draft Articles on Diplomatic Protection adopted by the UN International Law Commission (ILC) in 2006,[2] largely reflects the notion as Vattel expressed it. Diplomatic protection still allows an injured individual's state of nationality to present a claim against the state responsible, based on indirect injury, with a view to obtain reparation—in the words of the ILC, the 'implementation of such responsibility'.[3] This is not to say that no important developments have taken place in the law of diplomatic protection, quite to the contrary, but these changes affect the conditions for the exercise of diplomatic protection and the allocation of the rights protected, not the notion that a state may protect its injured nationals as such.[4] In addition, they primarily occurred after the emergence of human rights law and thus have limited relevance for the present study.

Prior to the emergence of specific human rights instruments in international law, and institutions such as the European and Inter-American Courts on Human Rights and the UN treaty monitoring bodies, diplomatic protection was the most important or even the only means by which claims could be made and reparation could be

[1] Translation: 'Whoever mistreats a citizen, indirectly offends the state, which is bound to protect the citizen; and the sovereign of the latter should avenge his injury, if possible, obliging the aggressor to make full reparation; since otherwise the citizen would not obtain the great end of the civil society, which is, security.' (Trans by ed.) Emer de Vattel, *Le Droit des Gens ou Principes de la Loi Naturelle Appliqués à la Conduite et aux Affaires des Nations et des Souverains*, vol I (A Leide 1758) para 71 published in English as: Emer de Vattel, *The Law of Nations* (first published 1758, J Chitty (tr), 6th edn, T & JW Johnson 1844) para 71.

[2] ILC, 'Text of the Draft Articles on Diplomatic Protection and Commentaries Thereto' in ILC, 'Report of the International Law Commission' (8 August 2006) UN Doc A/61/10.

[3] ILC, 'Draft Articles' (n 2) Art 1.

[4] Developments in the law on diplomatic protection, as the ILC Draft Articles on Diplomatic Protection reflect, include the acknowledgment that states protect the rights of individuals, not primarily their own rights; the abandonment of the requirement of genuine nationality and the adoption of continuous nationality; the protection of refugees, stateless persons, and ships' crews; certain exceptions to the local remedies rule; and recommendations regarding the decision whether and by what means to resort to diplomatic protection. See ILC, 'Draft Articles' (n 2) Arts 1, 3, 5, 8, 10, 15, 18, and 19, respectively.

sought for injuries to individuals. Diplomatic protection was used to address claims arising from individual injury, resulting both from situations of revolution, war, and armed conflict, for which specific claims tribunals were often created, and for injuries arising in peacetime, which diplomatic negotiation or arbitration dealt with.[5] In this sense, diplomatic protection was an instrument for the protection of human rights *avant la lettre*, because the rights that diplomatic protection protected were not always classified as *human* rights, and because individuals were not considered holders of rights. Nevertheless, diplomatic protection proved an effective means to protect individuals against abuses at the hands of states. While this chapter will discuss the influence of diplomatic protection on human rights law, the opposite has also occurred. The ILC Draft Articles on Diplomatic Protection stress, for example, that the acquisition of nationality may not be contrary to international law, with reference to the Convention on the Elimination of All Forms of Discrimination against Women's prohibition of the automatic change of nationality upon marriage.[6] In addition, the explanatory commentary on the exceptions to the local remedies rule frequently refers to decisions of human rights courts to support the (customary) status of the exceptions.[7] The jurisprudence and case law of the various human rights bodies has undoubtedly greatly influenced the form of these exceptions and their customary status.

The influence of diplomatic protection on human rights law will be analysed from two perspectives: a formal one and a material one. This chapter first examines how the territorial and nationality-related rules on diplomatic protection have contributed to the development of human rights law. Second, it demonstrates how the basis for diplomatic protection claims *ratione materiae* has long been the 'international minimum standard', which in turn has informed many civil and political rights. The formal perspective may appear to have been less important in the development of human rights law than the material one, but the analysis will show two influences; on the one hand, the requirement to exhaust local remedies, a means to preserve the sovereignty of states, has been included in those human rights instruments which provide for individual claims. On the other hand, restricting diplomatic protection to nationals of the claimant state has successfully been eliminated in modern

[5] Examples of claims commissions instituted in response to armed hostilities are the France-Venezuela Mixed Claims Commission of 1902 and the US-Germany Mixed Claims Commission of 1933. Somewhere in between are claims commissions established in response to *internal* disturbances affecting foreign nationals, such as the US-Mexico General Claims Commission of 1926–27. However, during the negotiations on the British-Mexican Claims Commission it was initially proposed to limit the jurisdiction of the Commission to claims related to the revolution in Mexico and to create a second, and separate, claims commission for claims not related to the revolution, if such claims could not be settled diplomatically. This suggested that situations unrelated to armed conflict were also subject to international settlement. See *British-Mexican Claims Commission* (1930) V RIAA 3. Numerous other arbitral awards have been reported in the Reports of International Arbitral Awards (RIAA) for claims based on individual injury.

[6] ILC, 'Draft Articles' (n 2) 33–34.

[7] ILC, 'Draft Articles' (n 2) 72, 78–86.

human rights law. These two issues may be qualified as a positive and a negative influence, respectively.

2. The Territorial and Nationality Dimension of Diplomatic Protection

In 1919, Edwin Borchard, wrote:

> [W]hatever rights the individual has in a state not his own are derived from international law, and are due him by virtue of his nationality. As a matter of fact, the alien derives most of his rights—fundamental or human rights and others—by grant from the territorial legislature, international law fixing a minimum which cannot be overstepped and authorizing certain agencies, usually the national state, to remedy and punish a breach.[8]

The starting point for the enjoyment of rights is thus nationality, but the relevant territorial sovereign determines the contents of these rights, while being enjoined to respect the international minimum standard. These three elements—nationality, locus, and the international minimum standard—largely determined whether a claim based on diplomatic protection was admissible and, if so, the scope of the claim on the merits. Reference to the state of nationality of the individual concerned, of course, primarily settles the issue of nationality, since that state determines who its nationals are.[9] Borchard suggested that, to the contrary, the receiving state, taking the international minimum standard into account, primarily determines the rights an individual may claim (the merits).

To some extent, the construct presented is no longer the case, because the international minimum standard is no longer the only source for international human rights. Yet even today, the application of rules still depends on consent, or in Borchard's words, the 'grant from the territorial legislature'.[10] The limitations thus created considerably influenced the scope of diplomatic protection, and by extension, the protection of individual rights in general. Before the rise of universal human rights, this meant that states' application of the international minimum standard was limited to foreigners within their territory or jurisdiction. In addition, as will

[8] Edwin M Borchard, *Diplomatic Protection of Citizens Abroad or the Law of International Claims* (Banks Law Publishing Co 1915) 13.

[9] Provided, of course, that its granting of nationality is not contrary to international law. The discussion on the validity under international law of nationality is beyond the scope of the present chapter. For some general rules, see ILC, 'Draft Articles' (n 2) 31–35 (Art 4 and accompanying text).

[10] Borchard, *Diplomatic Protection* (n 8) 13.

be discussed in Section 3, the rights that could be claimed also largely depended on the regime applicable in the receiving state, the minimum standard being somewhat of a residual standard. The ILC Draft Articles on Diplomatic Protection also reflect the limitation *ratione personae*, both with respect to the protected individual and with respect to the state against which the claim is presented, even if the rights that can be claimed are no longer limited to the international minimum standard. As is stipulated in Article 1, states may present an international claim based on injury inflicted on their nationals against another state (allegedly) responsible for this injury.[11] The link between nationality and rights has long been a defining feature of diplomatic protection and stands in stark contrast to the modern approach to human rights. The law on diplomatic protection had (and still has) very little to say about the treatment of nationals in their state of nationality or about general situations of abuse that do not involve nationals of a potential claimant state.[12] The relevance of nationality will be discussed first, followed by a brief section on territory and rights in the context of diplomatic protection.

2.1 The bond of nationality

In the exercise of diplomatic protection, states are allowed to protect their nationals only.[13] This is the nationality of claims rule, which is derived from the bond of nationality. This bond, or link, between an individual and his or her state of nationality, is the basis for protection by the latter in favour of the former. In the *Panevezys-Saldutiskis Railway* case, the PCIJ expressed this principle as follows:

> it is as a part of the function of diplomatic protection that the right to take up a claim and to ensure respect for the rules of international law must be envisaged. Where the injury was done to the national of some other State, no claim to which such injury may give rise falls

[11] Article 1 reads: 'For the purpose of the present draft articles, diplomatic protection consists of the invocation by a State, through diplomatic action or other means of peaceful settlement, of the responsibility of another State for an injury caused by an internationally wrongful act of that State to a natural or legal person that is a national of the former State with a view to the implementation of such responsibility.'

[12] The still-not-very-successful international law response to the latter situation is an invocation of responsibility *erga omnes*, as stipulated in Art 48 of the Articles on State Responsibility. ILC, 'The Implementation of the International Responsibility of a State' [2001] UNYBILC 116, 126–28.

[13] There are some exceptions, which the ILC Draft Articles have included by way of progressive development; under Art 8, states are allowed to protect refugees and stateless persons under certain circumstances. While a human rights approach clearly inspired this provision, it is considered *de lege ferenda* and therefore outside the development of human rights law and diplomatic protection. See *R (Al Rawi) v Foreign Secretary* [2006] EWHC 972 (Admin), para 63, where the Court held that Art 8 was *de lege ferenda* 'not yet part of international law'. If anything, it is the influence of human rights law on diplomatic protection that explains this provision.

within the scope of the diplomatic protection which a State is entitled to afford nor can it give rise to a claim which that State is entitled to espouse.[14]

The nationality of claims rule constitutes an important limit to the range of situations susceptible to diplomatic protection, because the bond of nationality is a *conditio sine qua non* for the exercise of diplomatic protection. First and foremost, this is a procedural requirement; the nationality of the injured individual must be of the protecting state. However, the *Panevezys-Saldutiskis* judgment quoted above reveals a more fundamental point: no claim can exist when the nationality of claims rule is not satisfied. This suggests that the foreign nationality of an individual is a requirement of substance in relation to the alleged breach; it is not just that the claim is not admissible, but no international responsibility will exist without satisfaction of the nationality of claims rule. The international minimum standard only applies to foreign nationals and gives rise to international state responsibility when breached. In this sense, nationality is more than a formal requirement unconnected to the substance of the claim. It reflects the rule (pre-existing human rights law) that states are not internationally responsible for the treatment of their own nationals. This rule, while now largely abandoned, was more widely supported in the past.[15] As Borchard also stated, the enjoyment of rights was dependent on nationality, and the distinction between foreigners and nationals in this respect had serious consequences for the legal regimes applicable to individuals.[16] Provided their state of nationality was willing to resort to diplomatic protection, foreign nationals could enjoy a more advanced set of individual human rights. As was made clear in the *Roberts* claim,[17] foreigners enjoyed the rights under the international minimum standard, even if local nationals were not treated in accordance with this standard.[18] Although states may have been presumed to apply this standard to their own nationals, and the likes of Borchard strongly believed in the civilizing mission of the international minimum standard,[19] no other state had standing to hold a state responsible for violations of the rights of its own nationals.

[14] *Panevezys-Saldutiskis Railway Case (Estonia v Lithuania)*, para 68.

[15] Borchard, *Diplomatic Protection* (n 8) 588. A formal source of this rule is the Convention on Certain Questions relating to the Conflict of Nationality Laws. It is interesting to note that this provision apparently reflects a compromise and that, at the time, various delegations preferred alternatives allowing the protection of dual nationals. See RW Flournoy, 'Nationality Convention, Protocols and Recommendation Adopted by the First Conference on the Codification of International Law' (1930) 24 *AJIL* 467, 471. See also the ICJ Advisory Opinion, *Reparation for Injuries Suffered in the Service of the United Nations* 186.

[16] See n 8 and accompanying text.

[17] *Roberts v United Mexican States.*

[18] This case will be discussed more extensively below, see n 103 and accompanying text.

[19] See Borchard, *Diplomatic Protection* (n 8) 14, in which he explains that only states that respect the rights of humanity will be called civilized states and can be members of the international community, and that even if a state disrespects such rights 'habitually', 'one or more states may intervene in the name of the society of nations' with a view to enforcing respect for 'human rights'. See also Edwin Borchard, 'The "Minimum Standard" of the Treatment of Aliens' (1939) 33 *ASIL Proc* 51, 56.

Nationality, therefore, was essential to ensure the enjoyment of human rights, because the minimum standard only applied to foreign nationals. The invocation of responsibility was a privilege granted to states on behalf of their nationals, for the protection of their rights, providing both the standard and the standing. This notion often led to the preferential treatment of foreigners and ensuing resentment against intervening foreign states. The broad means allowed for intervention, which could and sometimes did include the use of force,[20] aggravated such resentment, resulting in 'gunboat diplomacy'.[21] States receiving claims of diplomatic protection often considered the actions by states on behalf of their nationals as intrusive incursions into their domestic affairs. Responses emerged in the form of the Drago Doctrine, the Calvo clause, and the principle of national treatment, discussed in further detail below.[22] It is important to note, however, that states have attempted to limit the enhanced status of foreign nationals, by providing for treatment equal to that of their own nationals, and to force foreign nationals to renounce the possibility of invoking protection by their state of nationality. Such attempts have not been successful,[23] even if understandable in light of the sometimes-abusive nature of diplomatic protection and tension between the realm of domestic affairs and the rules that international law imposes (and enforces). Although the enjoyment of rights today is no longer dependent on nationality—indeed, human rights instruments largely prohibit differentiation on the basis of nationality[24]—the next section will demonstrate that traces of a desire to preserve sovereignty in this realm remain.

The unequal treatment between nationals and foreigners in the law of diplomatic protection, with foreigners sometimes enjoying a higher standard of protection, has provided a source of inspiration for the abandonment of nationality as a basis for the enjoyment of rights in human rights law. Garcia Amador, the first ILC Special Rapporteur on State Responsibility, opined that fundamental rights should be vested in the individual as such and not be derived from the state of nationality.[25] Higgins similarly

[20] As Borchard stated, 'the army or navy has frequently been used for the protection of citizens or their property in foreign countries'. Borchard, *Diplomatic Protection* (n 8) 448.

[21] On the use of force and diplomatic protection, see UNGA, 'First Report on Diplomatic Protection by John M R Dugard, Special Rappoteur' (7 March 2000) UN Doc A/CN.4/506, paras 47–60; Borchard, *Diplomatic Protection* (n 8) 448. However, see also Richard B Lillich, 'The Current Status of the Law of State Responsibility for Injuries to Aliens' in Richard B Lillich (ed), *International Law of State Responsibility for Injuries to Aliens* (UP of Virginia 1983), who argued that diplomatic protection was not as abusive as is often contended. See also Frederick Sherwood Dunn, *The Protection of Nationals: A Study in the Application of International Law* (Johns Hopkins Press 1932) 19, asserting that 'the normal case of protection seldom gets beyond the stage of diplomatic negotiation'.

[22] See generally Donald R Shea, *The Calvo Clause: A Problem of Inter-American and International Law and Diplomacy* (U Minnesota Press 1955).

[23] *North American Dredging Company of Texas v United Mexican States.*

[24] It should be noted that discrimination between nationals or citizens, and non-nationals or non-citizens, is allowed. The right to vote, for instance, or entitlement to education and social security may be, and often is, limited to nationals or citizens. However, the discrimination that is allowed in such instances is only between citizens or nationals and 'others', not between the various 'others'.

[25] FV García Amador, 'International Responsibility' [1956] *UNYBILC* 173, 194.

wrote that 'the individual has in fact been badly served by the nationality-of-claims rule', but suggested that states would not act on behalf of the interest of the individual.[26] Others have suggested that the international imposition of the minimum standard was no luxury, since foreign individuals usually were treated significantly less favourably than nationals, and that 'national treatment' would lead to discrimination, rather than to equal treatment.[27] Clearly all would benefit from a system in which rights were owed to individuals, not to the state of nationality of foreign nationals.

A further observation must be made in the light of the bond of nationality and the source of rights. The traditional law of diplomatic protection, though not the final approach in the ILC Draft Articles on Diplomatic Protection, often assumed that the protecting state was claiming its *own* rights. The *locus classicus* for this doctrine is the *Mavrommatis Palestine Concessions* case, in which the court states that the state is 'in reality asserting its own rights—its right to ensure, in the person of its subjects, respect for the rules of international law'.[28] Modern human rights law rejected the notion that individuals had no rights of their own, another 'negative' influence of the law of diplomatic protection on human rights law. A clear example is the American Declaration on the Rights and Duties of Man, which states in its preamble that: 'The American States have on repeated occasions recognized that the essential rights of man are not derived from the fact that he is a national of a certain state, but are based upon attributes of his human personality.'[29] In the light of the foregoing, it should be noted that the early scholars writing about diplomatic protection demonstrated some recognition of 'universal' rights, or the rights attached to human beings qua human beings rather than foreign nationals. Borchard stated that 'the individual, as a human being, is accorded certain fundamental rights by all states professing membership in the international community'.[30] Yet, these rights were meaningless unless the state of nationality of the individual protected them. In his more detailed discussion of the relevant rights, Borchard assessed them only from the perspective of the foreign national, not the human being as such. As he continued:

Whatever the origin, therefore, of the rights of the individual, it seems assured that these essential rights rest upon the ultimate sanction of international law, and will be protected,

[26] Rosalyn Higgins, *Problems and Process: International Law and How We Use It* (OUP 1994) 52.

[27] MS McDougal, HD Lasswell, and Lung-Chu Chen, 'The Protection of Aliens from Discrimination and World Public Order: Responsibility of States Conjoined with Human Rights' (1976) 70 *AJIL* 432. The right to vote may seem to be not particularly relevant for the daily enjoyment of human rights. However, when they are not allowed to vote, foreigners cannot meaningfully participate in or influence the government of the host state. More importantly, the host state's politicians do not need to seek the support of these individuals in elections. The possibility of support from their state of nationality should compensate for this. See also Erik JS Castrén, 'Some Considerations upon the Conception, Development, and Importance of Diplomatic Protection' (1962) 11 *GYIL* 37, 41.

[28] *Mavrommatis Palestine Concessions Case (Greece v Britain)* 12.

[29] American Declaration of the Rights and Duties of Man, preamble. The American Convention on Human Rights included the same consideration in its preamble.

[30] Borchard, *Diplomatic Protection* (n 8) 12.

in last resort, by the most appropriate organ of the international community—the national state of the individual or those states whose interests are most directly affected.[31]

We find here the beginnings of a legal order that is not purely bilateral, in the sense that the state was considered an organ (perhaps a subsidiary) of the international community empowered to look after the community's (and not only its own) interests. Yet, clearly no claim could exist without satisfying the nationality of claims rule; so even if there existed a notion that human beings enjoyed rights qua human beings, it did not lead to a lessening of the importance of nationality for the effectuation of those rights. In addition, in the exercise of the only available mechanism for protecting of these rights, the individual had no role. As Borchard explained, [the claimant] state, in demanding redress, does not represent the individual who has sustained the injury, and does not give effect to his right, but to its own right, the right, namely, that its citizen may be treated by other states in the manner prescribed by international law'.[32] Therefore, while individuals might have had international rights independent of their nationality, the claiming of such rights was reserved to the state of nationality. It was only in 1970, in its famous *Barcelona Traction* case, that the ICJ recognized standing for individual injury beyond diplomatic protection, even if it still remains to be applied in practice.[33]

2.2 The sovereignty of the territorial state

Under general international law, individual (or indirect) claims will only be admissible to international settlement once local remedies have been exhausted.[34] The law on diplomatic protection forms no exception and similarly requires the exhaustion of local remedies for the admissibility of claims, as is reflected in Articles 14 and 15 of the ILC Draft Articles on Diplomatic Protection. A thorough discussion of the local remedies rule is beyond the scope of this chapter, but the chapter will discuss briefly the role of the rule in preserving sovereignty and its presence in most human rights instruments today.[35] In the law of diplomatic protection, the rule has always been firmly established. Borchard recognized it, as did the PCIJ.[36] Many cases involved arguments on the admissibility of the claim based on alleged

[31] Borchard, *Diplomatic Protection* (n 8) 14.

[32] Borchard, *Diplomatic Protection* (n 8) 18.

[33] *Barcelona Traction, Light and Power Company Ltd* (*Belgium v Spain*) paras 33–34. See ILC, 'Articles on State Responsibility' (n 12) Art 48.

[34] See ILC, 'Articles on State Responsibility' (n 12) Art 44(b).

[35] On the local remedies rule in general, see Chittharanjan Felix Amerasinghe, *Local Remedies in International Law* (2nd edn, CUP 2004).

[36] Borchard, *Diplomatic Protection* (n 8) 332.

non-exhaustion of local remedies.[37] Indeed, the rule was well established to such an extent that the ICJ in the *Interhandel* case did not feel required to substantiate its affirmation of the rule's existence.[38]

The primary purpose of the rule is to preserve the sovereignty of the respondent state by allowing it to discharge in its own way its responsibility to do justice, to investigate and adjudicate in its own tribunals the questions of law and fact which the claim involves and then, on the basis of this adjudication, to fulfil its international responsibility in meeting or rejecting the claim accordingly.[39]

A state can thus delay, or deny, the transformation of an individual claim on the domestic level to an international dispute. It can delay or avoid a pronouncement of an international dispute settlement body on the legality of its conduct within its own territory. Apart from reasons of efficiency—relevant evidence is often more easily available in the local judicial system, and international procedures can be more costly—the local remedies rule thus serves to give a state the chance to address the claim internally, without outside interference.[40] Borchard listed the preservation of sovereignty and the opportunity of 'doing justice to the injured party in its own regular way' as primary rationales for the rule.[41] As the ICJ stated in the *Interhandel* case, 'the State where the violation occurred should have an opportunity to redress it by its own means, within the framework of its own domestic legal system'.[42]

The nature of indirect claims, which may be invoked by means of diplomatic protection, justifies the application of the local remedies rule in another way, too. An indirect claim primarily concerns a domestic dispute, except for the fact that the injured party happens to have a foreign nationality and that the breach complained of is based on a rule of international law. The rule breached, however, finds application in the domestic legal order, and the foreign national is present in the relevant state. The situation giving rise to an indirect claim is thus strongly linked to the territorial state, which is the respondent to the claim. International law, then, grants that state the right to settle the matter domestically before having to answer on an international level.

When the relation between the foreign national and the respondent state is tenuous, or even absent (as in cases of transboundary harms), the primarily domestic nature of the dispute is somewhat weakened. One could even argue that when the injured individual has no relevant connection to the territorial state responsible for the injury, the respondent state loses its right to claim domestic settlement first,

[37] See eg the *Panevezys-Saldutiskis Railway* Case (n 14); *Mavrommatis Palestine Concessions* Case (n 28); *Chorzow Factory* Case (*Germany v Poland*).

[38] *Interhandel* Case 6, 27.

[39] *Claim of Finnish Shipowners against Great Britain in Respect of the Use of certain Finnish Vessels during the War* (*Finland v Great Britain*) 1501.

[40] See also Amerasinghe (n 35) 56–61.

[41] Borchard, *Diplomatic Protection* (n 8) 817.

[42] *Interhandel* Case (n 38) 27.

since the absence of a connection between the injured individual and the respondent state diminishes the domestic nature of the dispute. The ILC considered that this should then also affect the application of the local remedies rule. Article 15(c), by way of progressive development, provides that individuals with 'no relevant connection' to the respondent state will not be required to exhaust local remedies.[43] The example given was related to nuclear fallout; after the Chernobyl accident, Scottish farmers sustained injury, because their crops had been contaminated. Assuming for the sake of argument that the Chernobyl accident constituted an internationally wrongful act, which could be attributed to the then Soviet Union, it would be unreasonable to require that these farmers apply to the Soviet judicial authorities before the United Kingdom could espouse their claim.[44] It is important to note the rationale the ILC presented for this exception. It focuses entirely on the situation of the injured individual and the particular hardship or unreasonableness that may ensue due to a requirement to exhaust local remedies. This, in turn, is inspired by modern developments. In fact, the commentary contrasted its approach by reference to the 'old' approach to the rule and stated that:

> the early history of diplomatic protection was characterized by situations in which a foreign national resident and doing business in a foreign State was injured by the action of that State and could therefore be expected to exhaust local remedies in accordance with the philosophy that the national going abroad should normally be obliged to accept the local law as he finds it, including the means afforded for the redress of wrong.[45]

This is somewhat of an overstatement. Even in Borchard's day, the rule was not absolute and allowed for exceptions in case of denial of justice or when, as he stated, 'no hope may be entertained of obtaining justice from them [ie the judicial remedies]'.[46] In addition, the local law was not the only law applicable to a foreign national, who also enjoyed the international minimum standard. To the extent that this standard prescribed standards of justice, to be discussed below, a foreigner could challenge the requirement to exhaust local remedies.

The local remedies rule is also applicable to human rights regimes. The Inter-American system,[47] the UN monitoring bodies and their complaints procedures,[48] the European Court of Human Rights,[49] and the African Commission on Human and Peoples' Rights,[50] all require the exhaustion of local remedies prior to the admissibility of an individual complaint. The relevant provisions of these

[43] ILC, 'Draft Articles' (n 2) Art 15(c).
[44] ILC, 'Draft Articles' (n 2) commentary to Art 15, paras 7 and 8.
[45] ILC, 'Draft Articles' (n 2) commentary to Art 15, para 8.
[46] Borchard, *Diplomatic Protection* (n 8) 822.
[47] American Convention on Human Rights, Art 46(1)(a).
[48] Eg First Optional Protocol to the International Covenant on Civil and Political Rights, Art 5(1)(b).
[49] See eg ECHR, Art 35(1).
[50] African Charter on Human and Peoples' Rights, Art 56(5).

conventions often stipulate that local remedies must be exhausted 'according to the generally recognised rules of international law'.[51] This is a direct *renvoi* to the rule applied to diplomatic protection, since it is in this area of international law that the rule has developed. In fact, the Inter-American Commission on Human Rights, in its first inter-state complaint, declared the case inadmissible, because it found that Nicaragua was presenting an indirect claim to which the local remedies rule applied and not, as it had tried to argue, a direct claim based on systematic violations of the Inter-American Convention.[52] The Commission held that:

> Having been unable to corroborate *prima facie* the existence of a generalized practice of discrimination against the Nicaraguan migrant population in Costa Rica, it would be inappropriate for the Commission to assume that no suitable and effective remedies exist to repair the violations alleged in this interstate communication. Accordingly, the exception to the rule set forth in Article 46 of the Convention [which contains the obligation to exhaust local remedies] does not apply.[53]

While this decision clearly demonstrates that the local remedies rule will apply to all cases brought on the basis of indirect injury (in other words diplomatic protection), many of the human rights treaties also contain specific exceptions to the requirement of exhausting local remedies, giving more precision to the rule. In addition, the human rights courts and bodies have now developed their own approach to the local remedies rule, and this has in turn influenced its application in the field of diplomatic protection. Without entering into too much detail, one could expect issues related to the exhaustion of local remedies presented in new diplomatic protection claims to rely on the case law of the various human rights procedures, especially when the merits of the claim concern human rights violations. Although the ICJ did not refer to human rights law when discussing the local remedies rule in the *Diallo* case,[54] the ILC referred to case law and jurisprudence of the European Court of Human Rights, the Inter-American Court, and the Human Rights Committee to explain and support the rule and its exceptions in its commentary to Articles 14 and 15.[55]

[51] ECHR, Art 35(1). See eg ACHR, Art 46(a)(a).

[52] *Nicaragua v Costa Rica.*

[53] *Nicaragua* (n 52) para 306.

[54] *Ahmadou Sadio Diallo (Republic of Guinea v Democratic Republic of the Congo)* (Preliminary Objections). Due to the parties' arguments and the lack thereof, the Court only applied the rule applicable to the claim based on the allegedly illegal expulsion of Mr Diallo from the Democratic Republic of the Congo (DRC). The Court considered that based on estoppel, the DRC was prevented from relabelling the 'refusal of entry' as 'expulsion' and that a 'refusal of entry' was not 'appealable under Congolese law'. The only 'remedy' left to Mr Diallo was applying for grace, but this did not constitute a legal remedy that must be exhausted for the claim to be admissible. It then rejected the DRC's objection based on non-exhaustion of local remedies, paras 46–48.

[55] ILC, 'Draft Articles' (n 2) 71–86, on Arts 14 and 15, with commentaries.

3. The International Minimum Standard

The law and practice of diplomatic protection has arguably been most significant for the development of human rights law with respect to the content of the rules. The international minimum standard applicable to aliens, laying down the rules binding upon states with regard to the treatment of foreign nationals on their territory, has informed human rights law in many ways. Most obvious is perhaps the prohibition of a denial of justice, which has been translated into rules on fair trials, such as Article 6 of the European Convention of Human Rights and Fundamental Freedoms (ECHR), Article 14 of the International Covenant on Civil and Political Rights, and Article 8 of the American Convention on Human Rights. Other elements of the international minimum standard have led to rights such as the prohibition on arbitrary detention; the prohibition on torture, inhuman, cruel, and degrading treatment and punishment; the right to property; and the right to life. In the following section, the content of the international minimum standard will be presented first, followed by a discussion of its function.

3.1 The 'international standards that every reasonable and impartial man would readily recognize'[56]

There can be no doubt that the introduction of the international minimum standard in international law fundamentally changed the perception of individual rights, which together with other movements such as the protection of minorities, inspired modern human rights systems. The international minimum standard was the first step in a process leading to international law, and not municipal law, as the source of individual rights. This process, however, did not achieve its end overnight. In the early years of the twentieth century, Borchard could still write with authority that:

> [I]t may be agreed that the so-called Rights of Man are not a product of international law and that the primary source of the alien's rights is municipal law. But the argument overlooks the fact that treaty and custom have in the course of the 18th and 19th centuries placed limitations on the arbitrary power of a state to deprive aliens of elementary rights, and that international tribunals enforce these claims... [T]he body of international law developed by diplomatic practice and arbitral decision, vague and indefinite as it may be, represents the minimum which each state must accord the alien whom it admits. Whether called the fundamental, natural, or

[56] *LFH Neer and Pauline Neer (USA) v United Mexican States* 62.

inherent rights of humanity or of man or of the alien, this minimum has acquired a permanent place in the protective ambit of international forums.[57]

The title of this section is taken from the *Neer* case[58] that the Mixed Claims Commission, which settled claims between (nationals of) the United States and Mexico, decided in 1926. The case law of this Claims Commission is famous for its express adoption of the international minimum standard, not only in the *Neer* case, but also in the *Roberts* and *Chattin* cases.[59] The claims commission saw no apparent difficulty in applying the standard to the facts presented before it, and it would sometimes admit, sometimes dismiss, a claim based on conduct (allegedly) contrary to the international minimum standard. Nonetheless, as Dunn wrote in 1932:

> One finds, however, that the efforts of the authorities to give specific content to this 'very simple, very fundamental' standard have resulted in the utmost confusion and vagueness. One finds in fact a wide divergence among the members of the family of nations in systems of protection and methods of administering justice, as well as in ideas of human values and social ends.[60]

According to him, states had two obligations towards aliens: due diligence and not to deny them justice. States must observe due diligence in their treatment of aliens and must prevent injury where possible. The conduct of official organs towards aliens must further be in accordance with standards of due process and not lead to denial of justice.[61] In this way, his approach is somewhat different from Borchard. Borchard considered that the minimum standard had a prohibition on discrimination at its core, which could be made more specific.[62] While he also acknowledged that the standard was far from clear (describing it as 'mild, flexible and variable'),[63] he did engage in a discussion of substantive rights, rather than describing the authorities' general approach. As he phrased it: 'International law is concerned not with the specific provisions of the municipal legislation of states in the matter of aliens, but with the establishment of a *somewhat indefinite* standard of treatment which the state cannot violate without incurring international responsibility.'[64] This is an understatement. Borchard went on at some length to spell out the rights aliens enjoyed, but in doing so he merely reported the opinions of various writers, without firmly establishing that they were correct or that case law supported their views. The following citation, which is worth giving in full, demonstrates his writing's lack

[57] Borchard, 'The "Minimum Standard"' (n 19) 53 (footnotes omitted).

[58] *LFH Neer* (n 56).

[59] *LFH Neer* (n 56); *Roberts* (n 17); *BE Chattin (USA) v United Mexican States*. For further detail, see Section 3.2 of this chapter.

[60] Dunn (n 21) 141.

[61] Dunn (n 21) 143–56. Eagleton also supported this view. See Clyde Eagleton, 'Denial of Justice in International Law' (1928) 22 *AJIL* 538.

[62] Borchard, 'The "Minimum Standard"' (n 19) 62.

[63] Borchard, 'The "Minimum Standard"' (n 19) 61.

[64] Borchard, *Diplomatic Protection* (n 8) 39 (emphasis added).

of clarity surrounding individual rights prior to the emergence of a human rights movement proper:

'Civil rights' being a term of uncertain definition, numerous publicists have adopted a category of rights, which they call public rights, the enjoyment of which must be granted to every alien. A list of these rights is difficult to draw. They include personal and religious liberty and inviolability of domicil [sic], liberty of the press, and other rights. In particular, the alien has the right to equal protection of the laws, which involves access to the courts and the use of the executive arm of the government in the enforcement of the rights granted.[65]

Borchard, then, considered that human beings had fundamental rights, which all states must uphold.[66] He suggested that the minimum standard includes 'the right to personal security, to personal liberty and to private property'.[67] Later on, he referred to Fiore and Martens, who had also included the 'right to exercise civil rights in conformity with the public law of the state[,]... the right to religious worship',[68] and the 'right to live and procure the means to live[,] the right to develop intellectual faculties[,] the freedom of emigration and intercourse[,] and the right to be respected in person, life, honor, health and property'.[69] In a similar vein, Friedmann considered that the international minimum standard included the right to life, the right to liberty of the person, and the right to protection of private property.[70] Sadly, Friedmann noted in 1938 that those rights no longer enjoyed the international support they used to enjoy, due to the changed political climate in Europe, and he despaired of 'the disintegration and destruction of those standards of Christian morality which, even ten years ago, no nation would have contested in principle'.[71] This confirms the position that some agreement existed on a core list of rights applicable to aliens, but also that the international minimum standard's foundations were not unshakable and that they clearly suffered in the political turmoil leading up to the Second World War.

The hesitations and lack of clarity concerning material rules as part of the international minimum standard applied less to the procedural dimension. Borchard felt more secure in this respect. According to him, the international minimum standard clearly prescribed fair administration of justice and due process.[72] Eagleton also seemed to support a more formal content of the standard. He wrote that:

There is, and must be, an international standard for the administration of local justice for aliens, demanding the promulgation of laws, and their proper enforcement, and the creation

[65] Borchard, *Diplomatic Protection* (n 8) 42–43.

[66] Borchard, *Diplomatic Protection* (n 8) 13–15.

[67] Borchard, *Diplomatic Protection* (n 8) 12.

[68] Borchard, *Diplomatic Protection* (n 8) 15.

[69] Borchard, *Diplomatic Protection* (n 8) 15.

[70] W Friedmann, 'The Disintegration of European Civilisation and the Future of International Law: Some Observations on the Social Foundations of Law' (1938) 2 *MLR* 194, 201–208.

[71] Friedmann (n 70) 202.

[72] Borchard, 'The "Minimum Standard"' (n 19) 63.

of machinery, and its efficient operation, for the protection of aliens…This international standard is, in effect, a sort of international due process of law.[73]

Many other scholars writing on diplomatic protection in the first half of the twentieth century focused on the denial of justice as the basis for international claims, resulting in a vivid debate on the scope of the term—whether it should include all acts of government or only those of the judiciary, and how badly the judiciary must behave to give rise to a denial of justice—but producing the first steps in the direction of the right to a fair trial.[74] It was, then, perhaps easier to decide that a wrongful conviction was the result of an unfair trial and thus contrary to the prohibition on denial of justice, than to determine at what moment treatment of a prisoner became inhuman.[75]

These writings might have led to the start of an international bill of rights, at first enforceable in the case of injuries to aliens only, but with the potential of applying to humankind in general. After all, if only international law could induce those 'backward' countries to adopt the Western style, soon their populations would enjoy the same level of civilization, complete with the civil and political rights that are part of liberal democracies.[76] While many scholars and states professed clear views on the level of civilization of other states,[77] analysis of the case law of the claims commissions of the early years of the twentieth century does not demonstrate a clear concept of rights. As the next section will show, the international minimum standard

[73] Eagleton (n 61) 557.

[74] Eg Dunn (n 21); Eagleton (n 61); JW Garner, 'International Responsibility of States for Judgments of Courts and Verdicts of Juries Amounting to Denial of Justice' (1929) 10 *Brit Ybk Int'l L* 181; GG Fitzmaurice, 'The Meaning of the Term "Denial of Justice"' (1932) 13 *British Ybk Int'l L* 93; Oliver J Lissitzyn, 'The Meaning of the Term Denial of Justice in International Law' (1936) 30 *AJIL* 632; Alwyn V Freeman, *The International Responsibility of States for Denial of Justice* (Longmans, Green & Co 1938).

[75] In this respect, the rules of one of the very first international courts, the Central American Court of Justice, are interesting. Article II of the Convention for the Establishment of a Central American Court of Justice provides that: 'This Court shall also take cognizance of the questions which individuals of one Central American country may raise against any of the other contracting Governments, because of the violation of Treaties or Conventions, and other cases of an international character; no matter whether their own Government supports said claim or not; and provided that the remedies which the laws of the respective country provide against such violation shall have been exhausted *or that denial of justice shall have been shown*' (emphasis added). This demonstrates two things: first, a denial of justice already constituted an exception to the requirement to exhaust local remedies in the first decade of the Twentieth Century; and second, claims based on a denial of justice were directly admissible without further attempts to exhaust local remedies for the denial of justice.

[76] See Martti Koskenniemi, *The Gentle Civilizer of Nations, the Rise and Fall of International Law 1870–1960* (CUP 2001) generally and 54–76 in particular. Although beyond the scope of the present chapter, there is no doubt that even modern human rights law presupposes some measure of liberal democracy for its implementation.

[77] Eg Borchard (n 8) 25–26, distinguishing between the Orient and semi-civilized states, and the highest type of civilized government. See more generally, Koskenniemi (n 76); Antony Anghie, *Imperialism, Sovereignty and the Making of International Law* (CUP 2004) 84–96.

was a *standard* indeed: a yardstick used to measure conduct without imposing a regime in full.

The law on diplomatic protection did thus not move beyond the international minimum standard for the treatment of aliens, resulting in the continued application of the nationality of claims rule and a not very articulate list of rights. With the arrival of the human rights movement, a paradox emerged between the 'old' and the 'new': the former state-centred order in which only the state of nationality of a foreign national was entitled to enforce a minimum standard without judgment on the treatment of the rest of the population in the respondent state, and the dawn of 'human rights' irrespective of nationality and existing above national systems. This clearly troubled the first ILC Special Rapporteur on State Responsibility, Francisco Garcia Amador. As he stated: 'The traditional view [ie that rights were only held by states, not individuals] is *a fortiori* incompatible with the present international recognition of the fundamental human rights and freedoms.'[78] To him, the discriminatory nature of diplomatic protection constituted an insurmountable problem if diplomatic protection were to continue the way it had in the past.[79] He therefore suggested a synthesis of the two regimes (human rights and diplomatic protection), which should eventually lead to the demise of diplomatic protection. By suggesting a *synthesis* of the two regimes, the presumption must have been that there were indeed two separate regimes that could be merged: human rights, which were universally applicable to all human beings and which comprised more rules *ratione materiae*, and diplomatic protection, which would implement the international minimum standard, but was only applicable to foreign nationals, and which was limited *ratione materiae* to what he called 'essential or fundamental' rights.[80] This, in turn, presumes that their development was separate, too.

To some extent, it is undeniable that the concept of the rights of man differs from the protection of nationals. Even so, the list that García Amador presented as the fundamental rights includes the right to life, liberty, and security of person; to the inviolability of privacy, the home, and correspondence; to freedom of thought, conscience, and religion; to own property; to recognition everywhere as a person before the law; and to access to the court, a fair trial, and the presumption of innocence.[81] As this chapter presents above, many of these rights are already featured in the lists that earlier scholars writing on diplomatic protection presented, but they are also the core civil and political rights found in universal and regional human rights treaties. This continuity *ratione materiae* cannot be a coincidence. Indeed, as García Amador stated, the international minimum standard 'has also been pleaded

[78] García Amador, 'First Report' (n 25) 194.

[79] García Amador, 'First Report' (n 25) 199–203; FV Garcia-Amador, 'Second Report on International Responsibility' [1957] UNYBILC 104.

[80] García Amador, 'Second Report' (n 79) 115.

[81] García Amador, 'Second Report' (n 79) 113. In light of modern fundamental rights statements, it is interesting to note that this list does not include freedom of expression, or an express prohibition on torture or inhuman and degrading treatment and punishment, but does include the right to property.

and applied precisely in order to show that an alien has certain fundamental rights which the State wherein he resides cannot violate without incurring international responsibility'.[82] What had changed was not so much the content of the rights, but the fact that they were no longer dependent on nationality: 'Aliens (and even stateless persons) are on a par with nationals in that all enjoy these rights not by virtue of their particular status but purely and simply as human beings. In the recent international recognition of the right of the individual, nationality does not enter into consideration.'[83] Thus the relevance of diplomatic protection for human rights law is undeniable, even if human rights law has now successfully eliminated the nationality of claims rule as a bar on the enjoyment of rights.

3.2 The international minimum standard as a safety net

The indeterminacy of the content of the international minimum standard and the focus on states and their sovereignty, inherent in the law of diplomatic protection of the first half of the twentieth century, limited the scope of the protection afforded to individuals. An analysis of the methodology of the various authorities of this era, confronted with claims based on injury to individuals, demonstrates the immaturity of the system with regard to the protection of individuals. International law was still in the process of finding a balance between the sovereignty of states in their internal organization and the imposition of rules in the international community. The arbitrators vacillated between the two sources of law. In the context of diplomatic protection, this issue was particularly relevant, because the protection was not against an injury that the state of nationality caused but against that caused by another state, to which the foreigner had travelled or emigrated voluntarily. The extent to which international law could determine how this foreign national was to be treated was a constant issue of debate, even if this debate was not yet very articulate.

Borchard made clear that aliens must abide by the local rules and customs and may be subjected to treatment different from that to which they are accustomed. In the context of a denial of justice, he concluded that protection is not allowed just because the treatment is different (or harsher) than in the state of nationality, but only 'if the laws themselves, the methods provided for administering them, and the penalties prescribed are in derogation of the principles of civilized justice as universally recognised or if, in a specific case, they have been wrongfully subverted by the courts so as to discriminate against him as an alien'.[84] What this reveals is the paradox that was part of the international minimum standard and the thinking of diplomatic protection. State sovereignty prescribed that states were free to

[82] García Amador, 'First Report' (n 25) 194.
[83] Garcia Amador, 'First Report' (n 25) 194.
[84] Borchard, *Diplomatic Protection* (n 8) 334.

determine their own internal affairs. Migrants were supposed to take for granted the risks involved in travelling and in being subjected to a foreign administration. Yet, states were simultaneously supposed to treat foreign nationals in accordance with the international minimum standard, even when this standard required better treatment than the one usually bestowed upon nationals. This standard of 'civilised justice', as Borchard phrased it in the citation just above, was 'universally recognised'.[85] This 'universe', however, consisted of the international community of civilized states, to the exclusion of non-civilized states (ie colonial entities and other non-Western states).[86]

Without wishing to enter into the debate on colonialism, civilizing missions, and cultural relativism, it is worth noting that the issue of who determines the standard was just as controversial then as now. Whereas states can decide today not to ratify human rights treaties or enter reservations to avoid unwelcome provisions, during Borchard's time it was more difficult to avoid the application of the (Western-style) international minimum standard. International legal scholarship, and some states, responded to this problem by rejecting the existence of a minimum standard. The writings of Carlos Calvo, the doctrine of national treatment, and the insertion of Calvo clauses in contracts with foreigners, were largely unsuccessful efforts to counter the majority position, even if these attempts received sympathy.[87] Case law from the Mexico-United States Mixed Claims Commission provides examples in this regard. The international minimum standard was thus upheld. Yet, due to its indeterminacy, it served not an absolute source of rights, but as a safety net to hold a state responsible in case of egregious behaviour, in an attempt to balance national sovereignty and international expectations. A discussion of three leading cases, the *Chattin*, *Neer*, and *Robert* cases, in this regard, will demonstrate the complexities.

The *Chattin*[88] case is sometimes presented as the leading case on the international minimum standard and the inception of international human rights law. For instance, Steiner, Alston, and Goodman cite this case as an example of the roots of human rights law.[89] Yet, a close reading of the decision reveals that the Commission was not very clear on the origin of the norms it applied and that it sometimes relied on domestic (Mexican) law and sometimes on an international standard, without, however, always being explicit in this regard. The fact that of the three commissioners, one attached a separate opinion and another a dissenting opinion to the decision and that these opinions primarily concerned the applicable law, only supports the position that the issue was far from clear. Mr Chattin, a US national, was accused of embezzlement. More specifically, he was accused of producing and selling false

[85] Borchard, *Diplomatic Protection* (n 8) 334. [86] See Koskenniemi (n 76) 176–78.

[87] See Garcia-Amador, 'First Report' (n 25) 201–202. [88] *Chattin* (n 59).

[89] Henry J Steiner, Philip Alston, and Ryan Goodman, *International Human Rights in Context: Law, Politics, Morals* (3rd edn, OUP 2008) 85–93.

railway tickets and pocketing the revenues. He was on trial together with other individuals of US or Mexican nationality. He complained of wrongful arrest, unduly long procedures, an unfair trial due to the impossibility of reviewing evidence and questioning witnesses, and a wrongful conviction based on this untested evidence. Some claims were dismissed on the facts. Most interesting is the manner in which the Commission relied on domestic and international law to consider the claims. First, the commission considered that the arrest, and in particular the basis for it, were compatible with domestic requirements. Interestingly, the Commission added weight to this finding by stating that the Mexican law was similar to laws of 'many other countries'.[90] The claim was dismissed. The issue of the denial of justice was more complicated. The Commission not only considered it necessary to (re)define 'denial of justice' and to explain that the present case concerned the malfunctioning of the judiciary (as opposed to malfunctioning of other government agencies), but also to explain that such conduct must be measured against the international standard:

It is true that *both* categories of government responsibility—the direct one and the so-called indirect one—should be brought to the test of international standards in order to determine whether an international wrong exists... It is moreover true that, as far as acts of the *judiciary* are involved, the view applies to *both* categories that 'it is a matter of the greatest political and international delicacy for one country to disacknowledge the judicial decision of a court of another country'... and to *both* categories the rule applies that state responsibility is limited to judicial acts showing outrage, bad faith, wilful [sic] neglect of duty, or manifestly insufficient governmental action.[91]

Yet, for the ultimate analysis, this distinction was largely irrelevant.[92] What mattered was whether the conduct attributable to Mexico (directly or indirectly) was in breach of its own rules or the international minimum standard. In applying the international minimum standard, however, the Commission revealed an aspect of it that is not common in modern human rights law. In the final part of the decision, the Commission stated that:

[T]he Commission would render a bad service to the Government of Mexico if it failed to place the stamp of its disapproval and even indignation on a criminal procedure so far below international standards of civilization as the present one. If the wholesome rule of international law as to respect for the judiciary of another country... shall stand, it would seem of the utmost necessity that appellate tribunals when, in exceptional cases, discovering proceedings of this type should take against them the strongest measures possible under constitution and laws, in order to safeguard their country's reputation.[93]

This refers to the relative nature of the international minimum standard; it is not a standard with absolute obligations, but one that will be applied when the injury

[90] *Chattin* (n 59) 285. [91] *Chattin* (n 59) 288 (emphasis in original).

[92] A fact that Commissioner MacGregor acknowledged in his dissenting opinion in *Chattin*. *Chattin* (n 59) 309–10.

[93] *Chattin* (n 59) 292–93.

reaches a certain level of seriousness.[94] Both the separate and dissenting opinions clarify this further; Nielsen stated that: 'Positive conclusions as to the existence of some irregularities in a trial of a case obviously do not necessarily justify a pronouncement of a denial of justice.'[95] McGregor considered that: '[T]o delay the proceedings somewhat, to lay aside some evidence, there existing other clear proofs, to fail to comply with the adjective law in its secondary provisions and other deficiencies of this kind, do not cause damage nor violate international law.'[96]

Importantly, even though human rights are not always absolute, a different analytical structure is used to determine whether a violation has occurred. Most non-absolute rights, such as the freedom of expression, are not necessarily breached simply based upon *interference* with the government's exercise of the right, but the fact of the interference brings the government's act within the scope of the relevant international rule and requires that it be further examined. When a state imposes a ban on publications by a journalist, for example, this will constitute interference in the right to freedom of expression, regardless of the motivation or severity of the ban. Whether the ban constitutes a violation of the right will depend on further considerations, including whether the ban was prescribed by law, intended to protect a legitimate purpose, or necessary and proportionate in a democratic society. If the ban can be thus justified, there will be no breach of the right to freedom of expression, despite the interference, and the matter will still fall within the scope of the right to freedom of expression.

The *Chattin* claim demonstrated that certain conduct, even when in breach of the domestic standard, will not reach the international level, unless it can be qualified as 'outrageous', 'in bad faith, in wilful neglect of their duties, or in a pronounced degree of improper action', as the Commission in the *Neer* case, discussed hereafter, found.[97] Short of excess, the situation will thus not fall within the scope of the international minimum standard. This is a different approach; it is not a justified interference, but no interference at all. The characterization of the international minimum standard as one of degree was important; only then could the balance be struck between the (strong) emphasis on sovereignty and non-interference in

[94] A similar analysis has been applied to the denial of justice itself. Fitzmaurice has argued that: 'Without attempting any enumeration of the acts or omissions which are intended to be covered by this interpretation of the term denial of justice, it may be said that they include not only a failure to hear a case, but all other palpable irregularities on the part of a court, e.g. a flagrant abuse by the court of its own rules of procedure, the extraction or procuring by the court of evidence by forcible or fraudulent means, or by threats or bribes, &c., and finally the delivering of a judgment which no honest and competent court could have given (though not a mere erroneous judgment if given in good faith' Fitzmaurice (n 74) 103.

[95] *Chattin* (n 59) 301 (concurring opinion of Commissioner Nielsen).

[96] *Chattin* (n 59) 312 (dissenting opinion of Commissioner MacGregor).

[97] *LFH Neer* (n 56) 62.

domestic affairs, and the first steps of an international movement of human rights. In fact, Commissioner MacGregor provides a clear example of this ambivalence. He disagreed with the majority, because he considered that 'the judicial decision of a sovereign cannot be attacked by another state before an arbitral tribunal'[98] and that the way trials are conducted 'are matters of internal regulation and belong to the sovereignty of States'.[99]

In the *Neer* case, individuals in Mexico killed Mr Paul Neer, an American national, while he was out riding with his wife. Mrs Neer and her daughter subsequently claimed indemnities, since Mexico had allegedly failed to investigate the murder properly. While the Claims Commission eventually dismissed the claim, because it found that the Mexican authorities had not acted contrary to their obligations, it did discuss the standard applicable to the situation at hand. It stated that:

> [T]he propriety of governmental acts should be put to the test of international standards, and (second) that the treatment of an alien, in order to constitute an international delinquency, should amount to an outrage, to bad faith, to wilful neglect of duty, or to an insufficiency of governmental action so far short of international standards that every reasonable and impartial man would readily recognize its insufficiency.[100]

The Commission would not consider whether alternative approaches to the investigation into the murder of Mr Neer would have been more effective, but only whether the actual approach was just. In the words of the Commission:

> It is not for an international tribunal such as this Commission to decide, whether another course of procedure taken by the local authorities at Guanaceví might have been more effective. On the contrary, the grounds of liability limit its inquiry to whether there is convincing evidence either (1) that the authorities administering the Mexican law acted in an outrageous way, in bad faith, in wilful neglect of their duties, or in a pronounced degree of improper action, or (2) that Mexican law rendered it impossible for them properly to fulfil their task.[101]

Although this case is much more explicit on the source of the obligation and the fact that domestic laws and practices cannot be brought forward in defence of certain behaviour that is contrary to international standards, a similar logic is applied here: conduct will only violate the international minimum standard when of a certain degree. International law, in other words, was not concerned with 'minor' offences against individuals. Those offences should be dealt with under national law. This approach also inspired the so-called 'Fourth Instance Rule', as human rights tribunals apply it and which prescribes, in the words of the Human Rights Committee, that the particular international tribunal 'is not a "fourth instance" competent to re-evaluate findings of fact or to review the application of domestic legislation', but

[98] *Chattin* (n 59) 304. [99] *Chattin* (n 59) 307. [100] *LFH Neer* (n 56) 61–62.
[101] *LFH Neer* (n 56) 62.

rather an instance under which to consider whether a violation of international law has occurred.[102]

The *Roberts* claim applied the standard on the merits, imposing a level of protection not provided by domestic law. In addition to an excessive period of detention without charge, Mr Roberts, an American national, was detained in a very small cell with many other prisoners, poor sanitary conditions, and virtually no chance to exercise and to clean.[103] Mexico explicitly argued that the prison conditions under which Mr Roberts was detained were no different from the conditions generally applicable to detainees in Mexico and that therefore the claim should fail on the merits. In addition, even though Mexican law stipulated that charges must be brought within six months of arrest, longer periods of detention without charge were no exception. Mexico saw no reason to treat Mr Roberts differently from its own nationals. The Claims Commission found that foreigners 'are obliged to submit to proceedings properly instituted against them in conformity with local laws'.[104] International law did not (yet) impose an absolute limit on pre-trial detention, and it was thus up to Mexico to determine the term. It did impose a prohibition on the denial of justice, including treatment unreasonably contrary to local law.[105]

Up to this point in the case, the Claims Commission used international law only to find responsibility for the violation of local laws, not to impose an external standard against which to test the local law. This changed when the Commission turned to the claim on inhuman treatment. Instead of taking the local customs as the standard and using the international minimum standard as a means to check whether the foreign national received fair treatment, the Claims Commission used the standard as an absolute measure and found that the treatment Mr Roberts suffered failed to meet the requirements. As the Claims Commission stated:

> Facts with respect to equality of treatment of aliens and nationals may be important in determining the merits of a complaint of mistreatment of an alien. But such equality is not the ultimate test of the propriety of the acts of authorities in the light of international law. That test is, broadly speaking, whether aliens are treated in accordance with ordinary standards of civilization.[106]

The Commission did not explain exactly what this standard prescribed or how it related to national rules and regulations. Without much hesitation, the Claims

[102] *Van Meurs v Netherlands*, para 7.1. The HRC and other international human rights bodies have widely applied this rule. To give two further examples, see *Wright v Jamaica*, para 5; *García Ruiz v Spain*, para 28.

[103] *Roberts* (n 17) 80. [104] *Roberts* (n 17) 79. [105] *Roberts* (n 17) 80.

[106] *Roberts* (n 17) 80.

Commission concluded its consideration that 'the treatment of Roberts was such as to warrant an indemnity on the ground of cruel and inhumane imprisonment'.[107]

4. Conclusion

As a precursor to human rights law, the law on diplomatic protection has played an important role in setting some benchmarks for the protection of individuals. The most important element has not only been the international minimum standard itself, but also the acceptance, already in place by the mid-1920s, that this standard prevailed over national law. No longer could states claim that 'equal treatment' meant that everyone received inhuman treatment for which no international responsibility ensued. The international minimum standard suffered, however, from indeterminacy and weakness. Not only was there no internationally agreed list of rights and obligations, but international responsibility only arose in cases of blatantly abusive behaviour. The standard was, thus, more of a safety net than an absolute source of rights. This was due to the immaturity of the system and an inability—or unwillingness—to move away from national sovereignty and non-intervention in domestic affairs towards international human rights. Nevertheless, the first steps were taken, and the 'fundamental' rights of the human person were recognized.

The law on diplomatic protection influenced human rights law in other ways, too. First, the growing unease with its discriminatory nature—foreign nationals were sometimes receiving better treatment than locals—resulted in a clear move away from the attribution of rights by virtue of nationality in human rights law. What remained was the local remedies rule, which most systems for the protection of human rights have accepted.

The arrival of human rights law and the accompanying instruments for its enforcement have greatly benefitted individuals in their capacity to claim their rights. The influence of diplomatic protection on this system in its early days was important. Today, the two systems are increasingly intertwined. States support the claims of their nationals against other states before human rights courts,[108] and they claim the rights of their nationals under international human rights conventions by

[107] *Roberts* (n 17) 80.

[108] Eg *Selmouni* v *France*, in which the Netherlands supported its national against France; *Soering v United Kingdom*, in which Germany (the applicant's state of nationality) supported the applicant.

exercising diplomatic protection.[109] This simultaneous existence and development is to be supported, as long as human rights protection is not effective throughout the world.

Further Reading

Borchard EM, *Diplomatic Protection of Citizens Abroad* (Banks Law Publishing Co 1915)
UNGA, 'First Report on Diplomatic Protection by John Dugard, Special Rappoteur' (7 March 2000) UN Doc A/CN.4/506
Freeman AV, *The International Responsibility of States for Denial of Justice* (Longmans, Green & Co 1938)

[109] Eg *Case Concerning Ahmadou Sadio Diallo (Republic of Guinea v Democratic Republic of the Congo)* (Judgment), in which Guinea claimed violations of the International Covenant on Civil and Political Rights and the African Charter on behalf of its national, Mr Diallo.

CHAPTER 11

HUMANITARIAN LAW AS A SOURCE OF HUMAN RIGHTS LAW

GERD OBERLEITNER

1. Humanity in War: Ancient Roots and the European Middle Ages

Centuries before the creation of the modern international human rights regime, international humanitarian law (or the law of war, as it was then known) had postulated that individual human beings deserve protection from cruelty and abuse in time of war. With its roots in antiquity and its long history of codification, humanitarian law seems a natural foundation of and precursor to human rights. But despite their common aim of preserving human dignity, the interplay of humanitarian law and human rights has been more complex historically, as well as from a contemporary perspective. The view that the two legal regimes have evolved 'along entirely different and totally separate lines'[1] seems untenable in light of their continuous interaction over time, in particular the interaction of the ideas, customs, and rules

[1] Dietrich Schindler, 'International Committee of the Red Cross and Human Rights' (1979) 19(208) *International Review of the Red Cross* 3, 5. This separatist view was still held in the 1995 edition of the *Encyclopaedia of International Law*. See Karl Josef Partsch, 'Human Rights and Humanitarian Law' in Rudolf Bernhardt (ed), *Encyclopedia of Public International Law* vol II (Elsevier 1995) 911.

that formed their respective bases. On the other hand, although many features of humanitarian law have made this legal regime a 'trailblazer'[2] for human rights, international humanitarian law is not simply an early version of human rights. The two fields have mutually influenced each other and continue to interact with each other, but there is no linear development from humanitarian law to human rights: throughout history, the humanitarian strand of the law of war has helped to inspire the idea of human rights, but the emerging concept of individual human rights has also affected the law of war.

Rules on how to behave in war are perhaps as old as mankind. Prescriptions on how warriors ought to act can be found in the earliest philosophical and religious texts of African, Asian, and European origin. The rules on warfare in ancient India, eg in the *Mahabharata*, one of the two major Sanskrit texts written in the fourth century BCE, pre-date their counterparts in Western and Mediterranean cultures.[3] Specific rules supplemented the general demands to exercise compassion in warfare. The Hindu *Code of Manu* (500–100 BCE), for example, outlawed using barbed or poisoned weapons and striking a sleeping or naked enemy or one who carries no arms.[4] In a similar spirit, King Cyrus of Persia, when taking Babylon in 538 BCE, ordered his soldiers to respect the sanctity of holy shrines. Elaborate rules on warfare can be found in early and classic Greek history, including in Homer's writings.[5] Roman law developed differentiated rules for different types of warfare, too, and pre-colonial Africa and Latin America knew detailed humanitarian regulations. Sacred texts of religions, including the Old Testament, the Qur'an, and Deuteronomy (the fifth book of the Torah), also deal with questions of warfare,[6] and Buddhist humanitarian principles had decisive influence on accentuating the humanitarian duties in warfare in ancient times in South Asia.[7]

Humanitarian law of today is, however, largely a product of the European Middle Ages. Between the beginning of the second millennium CE and the mid-fifteenth century, Christian faith and the medieval ideal of chivalry became the major sources of the emerging law of war. The religiously inspired idea of mercy and the

[2] Walter Kälin and Jörg Künzli, *The Law of International Human Rights Protection* (OUP 2009) 10.

[3] See BC Nirmal, 'International Humanitarian Law in Ancient India' in VS Mani (ed), *Handbook of International Humanitarian Law in South Asia* (OUP 2007) 37–38.

[4] See Manoj Kumar Sinha, 'Hinduism and International Humanitarian Law' (2005) 87 *International Review of the Red Cross* 285, 291.

[5] See Josiah Ober, 'Classical Greek Times' in Michael Howard, George J Andreopoulos, and Mark R Shulman (eds), *The Laws of War: Constraints on Warfare in the Western World* (Yale UP 1994).

[6] See Zidane Meriboute, 'Humanitarian Rules and Sanctions in the Major Philosophical and Religious Traditions' in Liesbeth Lijnzaad, Johanna van Sambeek, and Bahia Tahzib-Lie (eds), *Making the Voice of Humanity Heard: Essays on Humanitarian Assistance and International Humanitarian Law in Honour of HRH Princess Margriet of the Netherlands* (Martinus Nijhoff 2004) 374–79; Leslie C Green, 'Human Rights in Peace and War: An Historical Overview' in Horst Fischer and others (eds), *Crisis Management and Humanitarian Protection: Festschrift für Dieter Fleck* (Berliner Wissenschafts-Verlag 2004) 178.

[7] See CG Weeramantry, 'Buddhism and Humanitarian Law' in Mani (n 3) 12–13.

status-based code of honour, together with the reciprocal self-interest of the emerging class of *chevaliers*, led to ever more elaborate rules on warfare. Decrees, bilateral pacts, and agreements between warring parties later expressed and formalized what started as customary rules. The Council of Narbonne in 1045 is often cited as one of the earliest attempts to declare unlawful certain acts of war, such as attacks on clerics, monks, and nuns; women and pilgrims; merchants and peasants; and churches, cemeteries, cloisters, and the land of the clergy, as well as agricultural goods.[8] Faith dictated that bloodshed should not stain certain holy days, and faith was a measuring tool for restraint in warfare: those who would convert to one's belief could be spared but not necessarily others.

The emergence of a noble class of warriors in possession of horses and weapons also necessitated rules to guarantee that hostilities were carried out honourably, because only such behaviour could guarantee the continued social status of knights. The rules applicable to such gentlemen (and to them only) thus became a secular concern. Although chivalry was seen as expressing God's will, the church gradually lost its say in matters of warfare. Key concepts, such as justice, loyalty, courage, honour, and mercy, could now be derived from social status rather than faith.[9] Those rules were first and foremost intended to authorize a privileged aristocratic class to fight wars and benefit from them; the protection of the population was a beneficial side effect. The codes of chivalry were subsequently written down, with texts such as Richard II of England's *Articles of War*, promulgated in 1385, among the earliest examples.[10] Such professional ethos was self-sufficient and not necessarily concerned with the idea of a broadly shared humanitarianism. Humanitarian ideals were promulgated, but in the end it was the threat of shame and dishonour that ensured some restraint on the battlefield.[11] More pragmatic considerations of reciprocity, military advantage, and the food security in agricultural societies at all times accompanied the high-minded ideals of mercy, compassion, and honour, by leading to special protective regimes for mills, bakeries, barns, agricultural equipment, farms, fields, and gardens.[12]

Concerns for universal human dignity informed neither humanitarian ideals nor pragmatism as sources of the rules, even though mercy could, exceptionally, be extended beyond one's own belief.[13] 'Humanness' at this time was grounded in religion, class, or ethnicity and was not universally shared. European medieval 'humanity' was thus exclusionist: 'Had medieval Europeans given any serious thought to

[8] See Green, 'Human Rights in Peace and War' (n 6) 179.

[9] See Theodor Meron, *Bloody Constraint: War and Chivalry in Shakespeare* (OUP 1998) 4–5.

[10] See Green, 'Human Rights in Peace and War' (n 6) 180.

[11] See Theodor Meron, 'Shakespeare's Henry V and the Law of War' in Theodor Meron (ed), *War Crimes Law Comes of Age: Essays* (Clarendon Press 1998).

[12] See Leslie C Green, 'The Contemporary Law of Armed Conflict and the Protection of Human Rights' in Gerald L Gall (ed), *Civil Liberties in Canada: Entering the 1980s* (Butterworths 1982) 167–68.

[13] See Meron, 'Shakespeare's Henry V and the Law of War' (n 11) 65.

the idea of equal legal and political rights for all human beings, they would have seen them as a moral abomination, a horrid transgression against divinely ordained order.'[14] Justice, however, was an important concern, and wars were seen as either just or unjust. While the just war theory was mainly concerned with identifying the just cause for war and less with its specific conduct, it had two important repercussions for the laws of war: first, war was not a contest between equals in which both sides could benefit from the same protection; and second, war was not a separate condition clearly set apart from peace, but rather a specific means to guarantee or restore that very peace. In such a view, there was little room for elaborate rules on warfare. The unjust party had little to expect in terms of protection while the killing of a just warrior was a crime. The overriding principle of warfare was that of necessity: whatever force was necessary to bring the injustice to an end was justified, but not more. Nonetheless, theorists of natural law, such as Thomas Aquinas (1225–74), emphasized the importance of the right intention in warfare, irrespective of the enemy's behaviour. For such scholars, affording protection to those that war affected should not depend on adherence to a specific culture or class, but was based in, and represented, universal humanness.[15] While this was not the dominant view, it allowed for additional rules to develop in the Middle Ages, such as those for the protection of cultural objects, as a matter of common interest.[16]

The reality of warfare and the ever more sophisticated intellectual framework of the just war theory, and the demands of natural law, generated new practical rules for the many types of wars known in the Middle Ages. Different codes began to emerge in the late fourteenth century in Italy, France, and England. They resulted in comprehensive regulations, such as the *Laws and Ordinances of Warre* of 1639.[17] They were well received by the *chevaliers*, while 'free-lancing' knights (in the literal sense of the word) felt no inclination to exercise restraint in using armed force against civilians. Furthermore, because gentlemen soldiers had to supply their own equipment and servants, they consequently depended on the profits of pillage to cover their expenses, including ransom in cases of capture. Warfare between noblemen was a profoundly personal matter, and prior legal arrangements between them were seen as more useful to ensure physical safety than appeals to humanity. Even captivity could be a negotiated arrangement governing suitable conditions of detention, the prohibition of the death penalty, and protection from ill-treatment. It thereby became obvious that the rules on warfare were not necessarily dependent

[14] Jack Donnelly, *International Human Rights: Dilemmas in World Politics* (3rd edn, Westview Press 2006) 42.

[15] See Bertrand G Ramcharan, *Contemporary Human Rights Ideas* (Routledge 2008) 21–25.

[16] See Howard M Hensel, 'Theocentric Natural Law and Just War Doctrine' in Howard M Hensel (ed), *The Legitimate Use of Military Force: The Just War Tradition and the Customary Law of Armed Conflict* (Ashgate 2008) 16.

[17] See Leslie C Green, *The Contemporary Law of Armed Conflict* (3rd edn, Manchester UP 2008) 32.

on shared faith or nobility but could become a matter of law; war could be a contractual arrangement.

2. National Wars and Individual Rights

The medieval law of war thus emerged from and developed as a combination of ecclesiastical teaching, military practice and custom, natural and divine law, and aristocratic self-interest. This changed in the wake of the Thirty Years War of 1618 to 1648, when the Westphalian system of statehood allowed the law of nations to emerge. Religion and knightly honour could no longer provide sufficient guidance on what was right and wrong in wars which now became contentions between sovereign nation-states. Intellectually, the seventeenth century witnessed a struggle over the meaning of (just) war and peace and their associated legal frameworks. It was Hugo Grotius (1583–1646) who finally rearranged the rules on warfare in his *De Jure Belli ac Pacis Libri Tres*,[18] published in 1625. Under the emerging international law, those rules expressed the mutual consent of the nation-states, and wars between such states were no longer penal acts against wrongdoers who had disturbed an eternal peace, but rather a legal state and condition clearly set apart from peace. Grotius remained, however, ambiguous on the rationale for exercising restraint in warfare. While the framework he had helped to create allowed the law of war to become a special legal regime that states made, he still rested his arguments for restraint in warfare on the Christian virtue of charity, while at the same time holding forth on the natural law and allowing for 'a certain element of human rights ideology' to protect civilians and prisoners of war.[19]

By the eighteenth century war had become a 'public activity'[20] fought by professional and well-supplied armies in need of discipline. The continued rise of the nation-state, the onset of industrialization, and the emergence of a middle class in Europe, meant that war was no longer an aristocratic pastime. Advances in weapons technology and ever more complex, and costly military operations confirmed the usefulness of rules to avoid collapsing into total wars which even the strongest

[18] Hugo Grotius, *De Jure Belli Ac Pacis Libri Tres* (first published 1625, Clarendon Press 1925).

[19] Ove Bring, 'Hugo Grotius and the Roots of Human Rights Law' in Jonas Grimheden and Rolf Ring (eds), *Human Rights Law: From Dissemination to Application: Essays in Honour of Göran Melander* (Martinus Nijhoff 2006) 131.

[20] Green, *The Contemporary Law of Armed Conflict* (n 17) 30.

nations would not survive. On European soil, wars were fought in a way that provoked contemporary observers to suggest that 'war is made with little animosity, and battles are fought without any personal exasperation of those who are engaged; so that parties are, almost in the very heat of a contest, ready to listen to the dictates of humanity or reason'.[21] The age-old idea of fairness as the hallmark of the professional soldier was held in high esteem, but the virtues of humanity, reason, and fairness did not necessarily extend to warfare beyond Europe or against rebels challenging a monarch's authority. Cool military professionalism was not reflective of a more humane society, either,[22] but the rationality upon which the laws of war were now founded fit comfortably into the Age of Enlightenment throughout the eighteenth century and up to the Napoleonic Wars (1803–15). Although this was not a pacific age, professional discipline and restraint in warfare were notable.[23] In addition, warring forces concluded bilateral treaties on the mutual respect for hospitals and the treatment of wounded on both sides, without consideration of their nationality, with some frequency.

At this time, human rights began emerging as part of the intellectual and political struggle against absolute rulers. The movement was, however, primarily concerned with assigning the individual a new place in society and not so much with matters of warfare.[24] In his 1762 book on the Social Contract (*Du Contrat Social ou Principes du Droit Politique)*, Jean-Jacques Rosseau (1712–78), for example, referred to the laws of war only in passing, under the rubric of slavery, where he pleaded for rationality as the ultimate source of restraint in warfare.[25] He also argued for the individual rights of those that war affected: 'Even in the midst of war, a just prince, seizing what he can of public property in the enemy's territory, nevertheless respects the persons and possessions of private individuals: he respects the principles on which his own rights are based.'[26] In general, then, the proponents of human rights paid little attention to humanizing warfare and to the military codes and humanitarian agreements of the time, grounded in professional ethos and Christian compassion, as they were. The latter seem to have had little, if any, influence on the rising concept of inalienable human rights.

[21] The eighteenth century Scottish philosopher and historian Adam Ferguson, quoted from Stephen C Neff, *War and the Law of Nations: A General History* (CUP 2005) 90.

[22] See Geoffrey Parker, 'Early Modern Europe' in Howard, Andreopoulos, and Shulman (n 5) 40.

[23] See AJP Taylor, 'War and Peace' (1980) 19(2) *London Review of Books* 3. During this period, some sixteen wars were waged between European nations, in addition to religious and ethnic wars in Eastern and South-Eastern Europe and colonial wars and revolts outside the continent. See Gunther Rothenberg, 'The Age of Napoleon' in Howard, Andreopoulos, and Shulman (n 5) 86; Neff (n 21) 83–93.

[24] See Roger Normand and Sarah Zaidi, *Human Rights at the UN: The Political History of Universal Justice* (Indiana UP 2008) 11.

[25] Jean-Jacques Rousseau, *The Social Contract* (first published 1762, Maurice Cranston (tr), Penguin 1968) book 4, ch I.

[26] Rousseau (n 25) 57.

When the French Revolution descended into the Revolutionary Wars from 1792 to 1802, followed by the Napoleonic Wars from 1803 to 1815, war became an all-consuming enterprise. In these wars, people were at the service of the state again, rather than asserting rights against it. The conscript armies of Europe's great nations could project armed force across time and space with devastating effects on the civilian population and the fight over colonies led to genocidal violence against their native inhabitants.[27] Attempts to moderate warfare in such circumstances were largely an academic exercise, with limited influence on the battlefield; there was little incentive to grant mercy to the enemy or the civilian population.[28] Finally, the conservative and nationalist approach to war in the counter-Enlightenment of the late eighteenth century ended any considerations of humanizing warfare through ideas of individual entitlements to human dignity. Carl von Clausewitz (1780–1831) was perhaps the most influential in rejecting any cosmopolitan ethos and instead emphasized the role of war as a means to further the interest and policies of the nation-state. War was simply an act of unlimited force to compel the enemy. Humanitarian considerations, let alone natural rights, were of no concern.[29] To him, even the existing laws of war merely meant 'certain self-imposed, imperceptible limitations hardly worth mentioning, known as international law and custom'.[30]

3. The Science of Warfare and the Progress of Civilization

In the late nineteenth century, the law of war revived. From a European perspective, this century was an era of belief in human evolution and technical advances. Scientific progress was omnipresent, and warfare itself became a science. Legal positivism allowed consolidating the rules on warfare (hitherto scattered among customary principles, military codes, and legal treatises) into public international law, which was largely preoccupied with questions of war anyway.[31] The laws and customs of war turned into highly technical norms, created by nation-states at the

[27] See Normand and Zaidi (n 24) 348. [28] See Rothenberg (n 23) 87.

[29] See Howard Hensel, 'The Rejection of Natural Law and Its Implications for International Relations and Armed Conflict' in Hensel, *The Legitimate Use of Military Force* (n 16) 76.

[30] Carl von Clausewitz, *On War* (first published 1832, Michael Eliot Howard and Peter Paret (eds), Princeton UP 1976) 75.

[31] See Adam Roberts, 'Land Warfare: From Hague to Nuremberg' in Howard, Andreopoulos, and Shulman (n 5) 119.

prime of their sovereignty. War was seen as the normal state of affairs in a competitive world, needing practical and technical rules based on state consent and utilitarian considerations. More liberal and cosmopolitan views, which preserved the legacy of the Enlightenment, believed in individual rights, and expressed empathy for non-European peoples, only intermittently challenged this prevailing approach.[32]

In 1868, nineteen European states adopted the Declaration of St Petersburg, one of the first legal texts to be drafted in this scientific spirit, combining the skills of professional warriors and positivist lawyers. The purpose of the Declaration was to have 'by common agreement fixed the technical limits at which the necessities of war ought to yield to the requirements of humanity'.[33] The document was also meant to 'alleviat[e] as much as possible the calamities of war',[34] thus balancing humanitarian motives with the freedom of states to go to war. In this scientific age of mathematical calculation, military necessity became the key concept for this balancing act. It was hoped that unlike ill-defined ideas of 'humanity', military necessity could be described with a degree of precision, as the full title of the Declaration of St Petersburg: 'Declaration Renouncing the Use, in Time of War, of Explosive Projectiles under 400 Grammes Weight' demonstrated.[35] This duality of military necessity and humanity—that for humanitarian reasons, wars have limits which need to be defined in a dispassionate calculation of military gain against human lives, rather than by reference to justice or human dignity—stands at the beginning of the codification of the laws of war in the 1860s.

The Lieber Code, which Francis Lieber (1789–1872), the German-born professor of history and political science, prepared in 1863, became the blueprint for the codification of the law of war. United States President Abraham Lincoln asked Lieber to compile a set of instructions to provide guidance in the American Civil War, then in its second year. The President signed the resulting text on 24 April 1863.[36] The motivation for drafting the text was more utilitarian than humanitarian; the confrontation between American soldiers was seen in need of rules which

[32] See Matti Koskenniemi, 'The Legacy of the Nineteenth Century' in David Armstrong (ed), *Routledge Handbook of International Law* (Routledge 2009) 143.

[33] Declaration Renouncing the Use, in Time of War, of Explosive Projectiles Under 400 Grammes Weight, preamble (St Petersburg Declaration).

[34] St Petersburg Declaration (n 33), preamble.

[35] The document was a response to the emergence of a new type of weapon; small explosive rifle projectiles had proven their worth against enemy material. However, when used against enemy soldiers, they were no more useful in disabling them than any other type of bullet, but they caused particularly heavy injuries. The drafters of the Declaration argued that the use of such projectiles would exceed the legitimate aim of weakening enemy armed forces and inflict unnecessary and superfluous injuries, and that they should be banned from the battlefield. The dividing line between lawful and unlawful explosive ammunition was set at 400 grams. See Frits Kalshoven and Liesbeth Zegveld, *Constraints on the Waging of War: An Introduction to International Humanitarian Law* (4th edn, CUP 2011) 9–10.

[36] US Adjutant-General's Office, 'General Order No 100: Instructions for the Government of Armies of the United States in the Field' (24 April 1863) (Lieber Code).

made civilized fighting possible, in contrast to the violent encounters with Native Americans, where humanitarian rules were seen as dispensable. It was thought that atrocities ought to be avoided in the Civil War, with a view towards some form of peaceful coexistence of the two sides after hostilities.

The Code contained provisions on the behaviour of armed forces, care for wounded and captured soldiers, and on the protection of civilians and civilian property. Lieber was, however, not completely the pragmatist. He invoked ideas of justice, honour, and humanity; the emancipatory spirit of the fight against slavery and the slave trade also influenced him, and he added provisions on non-discrimination in the Code.[37] Nonetheless, he was still a child of his age when he argued that '[t]he more vigorously wars are pursued, the better it is for humanity'.[38] The Code was influential beyond the American Civil War, just as Lieber had intended.[39] It inspired the Brussels Project of an International Declaration concerning the Laws and Customs of War of 1874[40] and the Oxford Manual on the Laws of War on Land (which the Institute of International Law in 1880 drafted),[41] which eventually led to the adoption of the Hague Conventions and Regulations of 1899, the first comprehensive internationally binding set of rules for warfare.[42] They were followed and revised by the Hague Conventions and Regulations of 1907,[43] which contained rules on prisoners of war, the acceptable means and methods of warfare, protection of the wounded and sick, and territory under occupation.

The law of war, which began to emerge at the turn of the nineteenth to the twentieth century, was also on a *mission civilisatrice* (civilisatory mission). Restraint in warfare was no longer God's will or a chivalric attitude, nor was it only a rational calculation, but it demonstrated Europe's desire to advance civilization. Many of the texts adopted since the Declaration of St. Petersburg of 1868 explicitly refer to the civilizing force of law, including the Declaration itself.[44] The Hague Conventions of 1899 and 1907 echoed this language when they presented themselves as 'animated

[37] In Art 57, for example, the Lieber Code stipulates that belligerents must not be treated as a public enemy based on class, colour, or condition, when properly organized as soldiers. Lieber Code (n 36).

[38] Lieber Code (n 36) Art 29.

[39] Indeed, only nine out of 157 Articles dealt with insurrection, civil war, and rebellion, and even those Lieber had added reluctantly.

[40] Final Protocol and Project of an International Declaration Concerning the Laws and Customs of War.

[41] Gustave Moynier, *Oxford Manual of the Laws of War on Land* (Institute of International Law 1880).

[42] Convention (II) with Respect to the Laws and Customs of War on Land and its Annex: Regulations Concerning the Laws and Customs of War on Land; Convention (III) for the Adaptation to Maritime Warfare of the Principles of the Geneva Convention of 22 August 1864; Declaration to Prohibit, for the Term of Five Years, the Launching of Projectiles and Explosives from Balloons, and Other Methods of Similar Nature; Declaration Concerning Asphyxiating Gases; Declaration Concerning Expanding Bullets.

[43] The most important being Convention (IV) Respecting the Laws and Customs of War on Land and its Annex: Regulations Concerning the Laws and Customs of War on Land.

[44] The preamble of the St Petersburg Declaration declares that, 'the progress of civilization should have the effect of alleviating as much as possible the calamities of war'.

by the desire to serve ... the interests of humanity and the ever increasing requirements of civilization'.[45] While such language was meant to push back the dominant requirement of military necessity, it did not necessarily reflect a commitment to universal human dignity. Civilization was seen as the hallmark of industrialized Europe, with its professional armies, and thus, like medieval references to humanity, exclusive and open to abuse; any religiously or ideologically inspired racist and intolerant worldview could dehumanize its opponents as being outside 'civilization' and unworthy of protection by the law.[46] Acting civilized in war was also useful from the military point of view, as it allowed the conduction of war in an environment that the peace movement of the nineteenth century increasingly influenced. Nations at war wanted to know how to carry out military campaigns so as to avoid critique, as the Oxford Manual of 1880 made clear:

> so long as the demands of opinion remain indeterminate, belligerents are exposed to painful uncertainty and to endless accusations. A positive set of rules, on the contrary, if they are judicious, serves the interests of belligerents and is far from hindering them.[47]

In this blend of legal positivism, civilizing spirit, military requirements, and charitable impetus, the law of war was codified. The tension between the military and humanitarian perspective remained, with proponents of the latter seeking to protect war victims, push back extensive invocations of military necessity, and introduce the humanitarian imperative in all texts. They were partly successful, and their work is often seen as expressing an emerging tradition of human rights advocacy.[48] Elements of the human rights language began to appear in the respective texts, such as in Article 46 of the Hague Regulations of 1907.[49] But the absence of a wider range of protective norms for civilians, together with ambiguous references to 'rights and honours' (as in the provision just quoted), reflect uncertainty over whether or not the individual's entitlement to human dignity or the *chevaliers'* obligation to act honourably should form the basis for protecting war victims.[50] The Hague Conventions of 1899 and 1907 were no human rights documents, unequivocally defending inalienable rights, but rather sought to balance military needs and humanitarian demands. At the most, one can argue that the birth of human rights in these documents was 'premature but not stillborn'.[51] The texts foreshadowed the

[45] Convention (II) with Respect to the Laws and Customs of War on Land and Its Annex, preamble; Convention (IV) Respecting the Laws and Customs of War on Land, 1907, preamble.

[46] See Hensel, 'The Rejection of Natural Law' (n 29) 85–88.

[47] Moynier (n 41) preface.

[48] See Dietrich Schindler, 'International Humanitarian Law: Its Remarkable Development and Its Persistent Violation' (2003) 5 *Journal of the History of International Law* 165; Normand and Zaidi (n 24) 35.

[49] Hague Regulations, Art 46: 'Family honour and rights, the lives of persons, and private property, as well as religious convictions and practice, must be respected.'

[50] See George H Aldrich, 'The Laws of War on Land' (2000) 94 *AJIL* 42, 50; Christian Tomuschat, *Human Rights: Between Idealism and Realism* (2nd edn, OUP 2008) 16.

[51] Normand and Zaidi (n 24) 42.

possibility of directly protecting individuals through international treaty law and cut back on states' absolute sovereign prerogative under international law.

Another element in the Hague Conventions, however, speaks more audibly of a human rights perspective on the laws of war. In the 1899 Hague Peace Conference, Fedor Fedorovich (Frédéric) Martens (1845–1909), a German-speaking Estonian employed to represent Russia, drafted an ambiguous clause that was later named after him. It was adopted by unanimous vote as part of the 1899 Hague Convention and repeated in the 1907 Hague Convention, where it reads:

> Until a more complete code of the laws of war has been issued, the High Contracting Parties deem it expedient to declare that, in cases not included in the Regulations adopted by them, the inhabitants and the belligerents remain under the protection and the rule of the principles of the law of nations, as they result from the usages established among civilized peoples, from the laws of humanity, and the dictates of the public conscience.[52]

The clause has since become 'one of the legal myths of the international community'[53] and lends itself to different interpretations.[54] The more extensive of them see the clause as 'an origin of international human rights law in the positivistic sense',[55] while more sceptical commentators consider it as 'not much more than a swallow announcing a summer still some way off'.[56] Martens surely had no intention to resort to human rights when suggesting his compromise formula. Yet, the clause does open up the law of armed conflict to considerations beyond the axiomatic and schematic balance of military necessity and humanitarian concerns as introduced in the late nineteenth century, by giving more weight to humanitarian considerations.[57] By invoking natural law, it responds to and corrects the technocratic and positivist approach. It suggests that the law of armed conflict is not solely the prerogative of states, but reflects community interests and values beyond positive law

[52] Hague Convention (IV) Respecting the Laws and Customs of War on Land, preamble. The clause was a compromise formula to overcome a deadlock in the negotiations on the status of civilians who had taken up arms against an occupying force. Some delegations wanted them to be shot as *francs-tireurs*, while others saw their behaviour as lawful. Martens suggested that, as a minimum, they should be entitled to basic protection and proposed a text vague enough to allow delegates to accept it. See Kalshoven and Zegveld (n 35) 11.

[53] Antonio Cassese, 'The Martens Clause: Half a Loaf or Simply Pie in the Sky?' (2000) 11 *EJIL* 187, 188.

[54] For an account of the various positions, see Cassese (n 53) 189–92; Rupert Ticehurst, 'The Martens Clause and the Laws of Armed Conflict' in Naorem Sanajaoba (ed), *A Manual of International Humanitarian Laws* (Regency 2004) 312–13.

[55] Jeremy Sarkin, 'The Historical Origins, Convergence and Interrelationship of International Human Rights Law, International Humanitarian Law, International Criminal Law and Public International Law and Their Application since the Nineteenth Century' (2007) 1 *Human Rights and International Legal Discourse* 125, 128.

[56] Geoffrey Best, *War & Law since 1945* (OUP 1997) 250.

[57] See Ticehurst (n 54) 319, who argues that in light of the clause, the law of armed conflict is not just a positive legal but also a moral code.

and even irrespective of the will of states.[58] It has convincingly been argued that in a modern interpretation, the 'usages established among civilized peoples, from the laws of humanity, and the dictates of the public conscience'[59] can and need to be derived from international human rights law.[60]

4. *Inter Arma Caritas*: Henri Dunant and the Red Cross

It was not the governmental delegates in the Hague conferences but practical humanitarians, who advocated effectively for humanity on the battlefield: the Swiss businessman and 'idea entrepreneur'[61] Henri Dunant (1818–1910) represents this humanitarian strand of the law of war like no other. Dunant's motivation to assist war victims was both deeply humanitarian and practical at the same time. Appalled by the wounded and dying soldiers left unattended on the battlefield of Solferino in 1859, he rallied support for setting up a private agency to care for wounded and sick soldiers. He succeeded, and in 1863 the International Committee of the Red Cross (ICRC) was established. A year later, the first Geneva Convention was adopted, obliging states to offer basic protection to the wounded and sick.[62] The text was revised in 1906 and 1929.[63] From now on, the 'Hague Law' (named after the outcome of Hague Peace Conferences) was accompanied by the 'Geneva law', with its emphasis on humanity. Christian humanism and a practical sense for social change sufficed to create this strand of law and its practical arrangements,[64] bringing the fate of individuals into treaty law. The Geneva Convention of 1864 was indeed the first instance that international law protected 'human values as such'.[65]

[58] See Ticehurst (n 54) 319; Mika Nishimura Hayashi, 'The Martens Clause and Military Necessity' in Hensel, *The Legitimate Use of Military Force* (n 16) 151.

[59] Hague Convention (IV), preamble.

[60] See eg Hans-Joachim Heintze, 'On the Relationship between Human Rights Law Protection and International Humanitarian Law' (2004) 86 *International Review of the Red Cross* 789, 797–98.

[61] David P Forsythe, *The Humanitarians: The International Committee of the Red Cross* (CUP 2005) 15.

[62] Convention for the Amelioration of the Condition of the Wounded in Armies in the Field (1864).

[63] Convention for the Amelioration of the Condition of the Wounded and Sick in Armies in the Field (6 July 1906); Convention for the Amelioration of the Condition of the Wounded and Sick in Armies in the Field (27 July 1929); Convention Relative to the Treatment of Prisoners of War (1929).

[64] See Jean Guillermand, 'The Historical Foundations of Humanitarian Action' in Sanajaoba (n 54) 4, 15–16. On Dunant's humanitarian perspective, see also 75–79.

[65] Daniel Thürer, *International Humanitarian Law: Theory, Practice, Context* (Martinus Nijhoff 2011) 197–98.

It seems nevertheless important to recall that, at this period, 'humanity' was a grace and not a right. Despite their humanitarian ethos, charity, and not individual human rights, informed the Geneva Conventions of 1864, 1906, and 1929. *Inter arma caritas* ('in war, charity') was thus chosen as (and remains) the motto of the ICRC.[66] The organization's original aim was to remedy the recklessness of states, which would provide more veterinarians for horses used in warfare than doctors to care for wounded soldiers. At the same time, the ICRC was diffident towards the idea of individual human rights as they were discussed in the 1860s (in matters such as the fight against slavery and slave trade). As a private charity organization and as guardian of humanitarian law, the ICRC considered itself as a neutral, confidential, and impartial relief organization, broker, and mediator—'more the expert drafting secretariat than the vociferous advocate prepared to duel publicly with states'.[67] On the other hand, it found itself soon tasked with safeguarding the dignity and welfare of individuals during conflicts. This tension may explain the ICRC's cautious and lasting approach to human rights; it shares the liberal and moral impetus of human rights without participating in or, perhaps, even approving of its radical egalitarian spirit and partisan approach.

5. The United Nations, Human Rights, and Humanitarian Law

'The 19th century formulated the laws of war; the 20th century was expected to apply them'[68]—this anticipation was shattered in the First (1914–18) and Second (1939–45) World Wars. They were traumatic experiences not only for all concerned, but also for the law of war; its technocratic rules could either be easily circumvented[69] or used to justify morally abhorrent episodes, such as the mass slaughter at the Western Front and elsewhere, carried out strictly in accordance with the law.[70] The ideas firmly held in the nineteenth century—that civilized nations fight

[66] Statutes of the International Red Cross and Red Crescent Movement (adopted 1986, as amended) preamble.

[67] Forsythe (n 61) 261.

[68] Taylor (n 23) 5.

[69] The German armed forces' first use of poison gas in 1915, for example, was seen as compatible with the 1899 Declaration on Asphyxiating Gases, as the gas was released from thousands of cylinders along 6 kilometres of frontline, rather than diffused by projectiles, which the Convention would prohibit. See Roberts (n 31) 123.

[70] See Roberts (n 31) 125.

civilized wars and that wars could be regulated so as to constitute an acceptable element of politics—were shattered. With its fifty million victims, the Second World War shifted the perception of war (and the laws governing it) 'away from a focus on fairness and mutuality as between the warring states, to a primary concern with relieving the suffering of victims of war'.[71] The inadequacy of humanitarian rules had clearly been demonstrated; in the First World War, five per cent of all victims had been civilians, while in the Second World War, the number rose to fifty per cent; at the same time, the casualties among soldiers were lower in the Second than in the First World War.[72] As a consequence, the perspective on war was now that of the victims and no longer that of the military.

The prohibition of war in the UN Charter reflected this new era,[73] leaving the question of where to put the law of war now that war was illegal. The UN turned its back on the law of war, and the International Law Commission (the UN's codification unit) struck the laws of war from its programme of work, because its members thought that any further codification in this area would show 'lack of confidence in the efficiency of the means at the disposal of the United Nations for maintaining peace'.[74] When the UN General Assembly invoked international humanitarian law in the Korean War (1950–53), however, its continued importance was confirmed.[75] In the same resolution, the Assembly also said that such incidents are not only a matter of international humanitarian law, but are also 'affronting human rights and the dignity and worth of the human person'.[76] This argument rested on the other important response to the atrocities of the preceding years: the creation of the international human rights regime.

Like the Hague and Geneva Conventions, the 1948 Universal Declaration of Human Rights was a response to a previous war, but it was not limited in its sources. Inspired by the peace movement of the late nineteenth and early twentieth centuries and informed by the idea of universally shared inalienable rights, rather than being motivated by charitable impulses, the Declaration renounced war and postulated human rights as a means to secure peace. The drafters of the Universal Declaration largely ignored the established law of war when creating this altogether new field of international law, but many of the same states adopted the four Geneva Conventions

[71] Neff (n 21) 315.

[72] See Schindler, 'International Humanitarian Law' (n 48) 170; Roberts (n 31) 128–31.

[73] UN Charter, Art 2(4): 'All Members shall refrain in their international relations from the threat or use of force against the territorial integrity or political independence of any state, or in any other manner inconsistent with the Purposes of the United Nations.'

[74] International Law Commission, 'Report of the International Law Commission to the General Assembly on the Work of the First Session' (12 April–9 June 1949) UN Doc A/CN.4/SER.A/1949, 281.

[75] See UNGA, 'Question of Atrocities Committed by the North Korean and Chinese Communist Forces against United Nations Prisoners of War in Korea' (3 December 1953) UN Doc A/Res/804, preamble, para 2.

[76] UNGA, 'Question of Atrocities' (n 75) para 2.

of 1949 less than a year after the Declaration.[77] Modestly presented as a revision of the law of war, they effectively confirmed the idea that the whole of the law of war is humanitarian by nature, leading to a renaming of this branch of law as 'international humanitarian law'.[78] Now two fields of international law expressed a similar goal—protecting individual human dignity, life, and livelihood. Seemingly, the tacit consensus was that one was meant for times of peace and the other for times of war, with both operating independently. They would have to coexist; human rights law was not a rebranded humanitarian code, and international humanitarian law was not absorbed in human rights.

The role of human rights during the writing of the Geneva Conventions was more ambiguous than such a separatist view would assert. Although there was only occasional reference to human rights in the drafting process,[79] human rights found their way into the texts.[80] Their impact is most visible in three areas in which the Conventions broke new ground: first, the minimum rules of Article 3 common to all four Conventions on armed conflicts, which offers protection in all circumstances.[81] To most observers, this article is a human rights provision which grants minimum humanitarian guarantees to everyone at all times.[82] Second, the fourth Geneva Convention on the protection of civilians extends guarantees to everyone in the hands of the enemy and has been hailed as a 'manifesto of human rights

[77] Convention for the Amelioration of the Condition of the Wounded and Sick in Armed Forces in the Field; Convention for the Amelioration of the Condition of the Wounded, Sick and Shipwrecked Members of the Armed Forces at Sea; Convention Relative to the Treatment of Prisoners of War; Convention Relative to the Protection of Civilian Persons in Time of War.

[78] The origins of the term 'humanitarian law' remain shrouded in mystery. It had not been widely used before 1949, and Jean Pictet, who had been so influential in drafting the Geneva Conventions, is usually credited with its invention. See Schindler, 'International Humanitarian Law' (n 48) 171.

[79] See Robert Kolb, 'The Relationship Between International Humanitarian Law and Human Rights Law: A Brief History of the 1948 Universal Declaration of Human Rights and the 1949 Geneva Conventions' (1998) 38 *International Review of the Red Cross* 409.

[80] See Best (n 56) 144–45; Sergey Sayapin, 'The International Committee of the Red Cross and International Human Rights Law' (2009) 9 *HRL Rev* 95, 97.

[81] Article 3 common to the Geneva Conventions: 'In the case of armed conflict not of an international character occurring in the territory of one of the High Contracting Parties, each Party to the conflict shall be bound to apply, as a minimum, the following provisions: (1) Persons taking no active part in the hostilities, including members of armed forces who have laid down their arms and those placed 'hors de combat' by sickness, wounds, detention, or any other cause, shall in all circumstances be treated humanely, without any adverse distinction founded on race, colour, religion or faith, sex, birth or wealth, or any other similar criteria. To this end, the following acts are and shall remain prohibited at any time and in any place whatsoever with respect to the above-mentioned persons: (a) violence to life and person, in particular murder of all kinds, mutilation, cruel treatment and torture; (b) taking of hostages; (c) outrages upon personal dignity, in particular humiliating and degrading treatment; (d) the passing of sentences and the carrying out of executions without previous judgment pronounced by a regularly constituted court, affording all the judicial guarantees which are recognized as indispensable by civilized peoples. (2) The wounded and sick shall be collected and cared for…'

[82] See eg Cordula Droege, 'Elective Affinities? Human Rights and Humanitarian Law' (2008) 90 *International Review of the Red Cross* 501, 504.

for civilians during armed conflict'.[83] And finally, the provisions on grave breaches of the Conventions are, in essence, a list of individual human rights, as contained in the Universal Declaration of Human Rights.[84] Contrary to the separatist view (under which human rights apply only in peacetime, and humanitarian law is the sole framework for armed conflicts), human rights informed international humanitarian law from 1948 onwards. With this, the idea of humanity in warfare underwent yet another transformation, from being a grace extended by noble *chevaliers*, pious officers, and kind-hearted businessmen, to a set of individual entitlements laid down in the growing international human rights law.

6. Human Rights in Armed Conflict

For decades, this view was one to which few subscribed. From 1949 to 1968, international humanitarian law and human rights law, and with them their epistemic communities, including the ICRC and the UN, went strictly separate ways.[85] The World Conference on Human Rights in Tehran in 1968 ended this separatist approach when it adopted a resolution entitled 'Human Rights in Armed Conflict'.[86] While ambiguously worded and not overly ambitious in its content (the resolution only asked the UN Secretary General to study steps for enhancing international humanitarian law, including the drafting of new conventions), it brought the UN back onto the playing field of the law of armed conflict and suggested a role for human rights in regulating warfare. Not everyone was convinced this was a good idea, but the debate on the role of human rights in armed conflict had been triggered and continues to date.[87]

The experiences of the wars of the 1950s and 1960s, first and foremost the Vietnam War, and the ICRC's pressure to reaffirm and develop international humanitarian law, led to the adoption of the two Additional Protocols of 1977 to the Geneva

[83] Green, 'The Contemporary Law of Armed Conflict' (n 12) 179. Disagreement over other issues only hindered direct reference to human rights in a planned, but not realized, preamble to the Convention. See Best (n 56) 72.

[84] See Leslie C Green, 'Human Rights and the Law of Armed Conflict' (1980) 10 *Isr YB Hum Rts* 9.

[85] See Charles Garraway, 'Occupation Responsibilities and Constraints' in Hensel, *The Legitimate Use of Military Force* (n 16) 268.

[86] International Conference on Human Rights, 'Res XXIII: Human Rights in Armed Conflict' (Tehran 12 May 1968).

[87] For a critical view on the outcome of the Tehran conference, see eg Keith D Suter, 'An Enquiry into the Meaning of the Phrase "Human Rights in Armed Conflict"' (1976) 15 *Revue de Droit Pénal Militaire et de Droit de la Guerre* 393, 400.

Conventions on international and non-international armed conflicts.[88] They were drafted in a different spirit than any previous humanitarian law document; the UN was involved, the newly independent UN member states had their own views of the rules of warfare, political and ideological divisions ran deep, and the idea and law of human rights had greater impact than before.[89] Many provisions of Additional Protocol I on international armed conflicts drew heavily on human rights law.[90] The fundamental guarantees of Article 75 (on non-discrimination, the right to life and physical integrity, prohibition of torture and inhuman and degrading treatment, fair trial, and detention conditions), for example, were carried over from the International Covenant on Civil and Political Rights; reprisals were perceived as incompatible with a human rights-oriented view of civilian protection; and some derogable human rights, such as medical care and prisoners' rights, were made non-derogable in the Protocol.[91] In Additional Protocol II on non-international armed conflicts, Articles 4 to 6 on humane treatment also reproduced provisions from the International Covenant on Civil and Political Rights.[92]

The prevailing view at present sees human rights and humanitarian law not as mutually exclusive, but as applying complementarily in times of armed conflict (except where human rights treaties allow for derogations from certain provision in situations of emergency), with international humanitarian law as the *lex specialis* in relation to human rights law.[93] The International Court of Justice has summed up this position by stating that:

> [S]ome rights may be exclusively matters of international humanitarian law; others may be exclusively matters of human rights law; yet others may be matters of both these branches of international law. In order to answer the question put to it, the Court will have to take into

[88] Protocol Additional to the Geneva Conventions of 12 August 1949 and Relating to the Protection of Victims of International Armed Conflicts; Protocol Additional to the Geneva Conventions of 12 August 1949 and Relating to the Protection of Victims of Non-International Armed Conflicts.

[89] See Forsythe (n 61) 261.

[90] See Louise Doswald-Beck and Sylvain Vité, 'International Humanitarian Law and Human Rights Law' (1993) 33 *International Review of the Red Cross* 94, 113.

[91] See Schindler, 'International Humanitarian Law' (n 48) 173, 183; Cordula Droege, 'The Interplay between International Humanitarian Law and International Human Rights Law in Situations of Armed Conflict' (2007) 40 *Is LR* 310, 316.

[92] See René Kosirnik, 'The 1977 Protocols: A Landmark in the Development of International Humanitarian Law' in Sanajaoba (n 54) 74.

[93] See eg Noelle Quénivet, 'Introduction: The History of the Relationship between International Humanitarian Law and Human Rights Law' in Roberta Arnold and Noelle Quénivet (eds), *International Humanitarian Law and Human Rights Law: Towards a New Merger in International Law* (Martinus Nijhoff 2008); Christian Tomuschat, 'Human Rights and International Humanitarian Law' (2010) 21 *EJIL* 15; Orna Ben-Naftali, 'Introduction: International Humanitarian and International Human Rights Law—Pas De Deux' in Orna Ben-Naftali (ed), *International Humanitarian and International Human Rights Law* (OUP 2011).

consideration both these branches of international law, namely human rights law and, as *lex specialis*, international humanitarian law.[94]

While the precise relationship between the two legal regimes remains to be settled,[95] the jurisprudence of the European and Inter-American Courts of Human Rights and UN treaty bodies support this principled position—which the United States and Israel protest.[96] The UN Security Council also regularly resorts to international humanitarian law and human rights law in parallel,[97] and the ICRC, while emphasizing the differences between international humanitarian law and international human rights law, invokes human rights in its seminal study on customary international law.[98]

7. Conclusion

For centuries, international humanitarian law (in its early form as the law of war) was the only international legal framework which accommodated the fate of individuals, at least to some extent. Its legal force and practical impact, albeit only in situations of war, was way ahead of the lofty ideas and academic debates on human rights, before they became a legal reality in 1945. In this sense, humanitarian law was a predecessor of and model for human rights. Humanitarian law has foreshadowed parts of the human rights discourse, eg on the place of individuals in international law; their natural right to security, dignity, and well-being; the respect which

[94] *Legal Consequences of the Construction of a Wall in the Occupied Palestinian Territory*, para 106. The Court had considered the matter also in *Legality of the Threat or Use of Nuclear Weapons* and in *Armed Activities on the Territory of the Congo*. Reference to the *lex specialis* principle is seen, however, increasingly sceptically. Eg Nancie Prud'homme, '*Lex Specialis*: Oversimplyfing a More Complex and Multifaceted Relationship?' (2007) 40 *Is LR* 355, 378.

[95] See eg Alexander Orakhelashvili, 'The Interaction between Human Rights and Humanitarian Law: Fragmentation, Conflict, Parallelism, or Convergence?' (2008) 19 *EJIL* 161.

[96] See eg Hans-Joachim Heintze, 'The European Court of Human Rights and the Implementation of Human Rights Standards During Armed Conflicts' (2002) 45 *Germ Yrbk Intl L* 6; David Weissbrodt, 'The Role of the Human Rights Committee in Interpreting and Developing Humanitarian Law' (2010) 31 *U Pa J Int'l L* 1185; Christina M Cerna, 'The History of the Inter-American System's Jurisprudence as Regards Situations of Armed Conflict' (2011) 2 *Journal of International Humanitarian Legal Studies* 3.

[97] See eg Robert Cryer, 'The Security Council and International Humanitarian Law' in Susan C Breau and Agnieszka Jachec-Neale (eds), *Testing the Boundaries of International Humanitarian Law* (British Institute of International and Comparative Law 2006).

[98] Chapter 32 of the Study, entitled 'Fundamental Guarantees', identifies nineteen rules which combine humanitarian law and human rights law. See Jean-Marie Henckaerts and Louise Doswald-Beck, *Customary International Humanitarian Law: Volume I: Rules* (CUP 2005) 299–383.

the sovereign nation-state owes to those under its jurisdiction; and the protective obligations states owe towards individuals in distress. But the law's nexus with war meant that it could not simply serve as a blueprint for human rights as the emerging regulatory framework for societies in peace. There is thus no direct lineage; instead, the ideas and concepts out of which humanitarian law and human rights would later arise, communicated with each other, audibly at times and inaudibly at others.

Humanitarian law allowed the forerunners of the human rights movement to put individual needs and rights on the international agenda and to formulate them as part of international law. But the aim of humanitarian law has always been to mitigate the consequences of war by balancing military requirements and humanitarian concerns. The law's rationale and the perception of humanity changed over time, comprising religious belief and compassion, honour and professional fairness, self-interest and civilizing ethos, practical humanitarianism, and charitable impulses. When humanitarian law was codified, humane treatment in war was the grace of God or gentlemen, or compassionate fellow humans. Such humanity did not necessarily reflect the idea of universal and inalienable human rights. In this sense, humanitarian law was less a source from which human rights could draw than an essential stage and platform for developing, challenging, and refining the concept of human dignity in an international legal framework.

And human rights influenced and shaped humanitarian law, too. To claim that 'the idea of human rights, though perhaps not under that name, lies at the root of all the conscious attempts at codifying the law of war, undertaken since the Conference of Brussels of 1874',[99] may perhaps be too benevolent, as the motivations to create humanitarian norms were manifold. But an undercurrent of human rights ideas was certainly able to challenge the military tradition and perception of the law of war on many occasions throughout history, swirling the waters of the legal mainstream without always changing its course.

Now that human rights have become the 'hegemonic moral discourse'[100] in international affairs, the situation has changed. Human rights have secured a place for themselves in armed conflicts, supporting the mission of humanitarian law to humanize warfare, but also challenging some foundational conceptions of humanitarian law. Since 1945, humanity in warfare can no longer be seen as a grace, but is an entitlement, a fact which the prevailing nineteenth-century deep structure of humanitarian law fails to fully accommodate. In light of the history of humanitarian law and human rights, their current convergence should not come as a surprise, nor is it an aberration, but reflects the much-quoted 'humanization of international law'.[101] While the precise contours and the legal, political, and operational

[99] Frits Kalshoven, 'Human Rights, the Law of Armed Conflicts, and Reprisals' (1971) 11 *International Review of the Red Cross* 183, 183.

[100] See Normand and Zaidi (n 24) 8.

[101] Theodor Meron, *The Humanization of International Law* (Martinus Nijhoff 2006).

consequences of a human rights-based law of armed conflict are yet to be discerned, the contours of humanity in warfare are being redrawn once again.

Further Reading

Bederman DJ, 'International Law in the Ancient World' in Armstrong D (ed), *Routledge Handbook of International Law* (Routledge 2009) 115–25

Green LC, 'Human Rights in Peace and War: An Historical Overview' in Fischer H and others (eds), *Crisis Management and Humanitarian Protection: Festschrift für Dieter Fleck* (Berliner Wissenschafts-Verlag 2004) 159–94

—— *The Contemporary Law of Armed Conflict* (3rd edn, Manchester UP 2008)

Henckaerts JM, 'The Development of International Humanitarian Law and the Continued Relevance of Custom' in Hensel HM (ed), *The Legitimate Use of Military Force: The Just War Tradition and the Customary Law of Armed Conflict* (Ashgate 2008) 117–20

Jocknick C and Normand R, 'The Legitimation of Violence: A Critical History of the Laws of War' (1994) 35 *Harv Int'l LJ* 49

Mani VS (ed), *Handbook of International Humanitarian Law in South Asia* (OUP 2007)

Meriboute Z, 'Humanitarian Rules and Sanctions in the Major Philosophical and Religious Traditions' in Lijnzaad L, van Sambeek J, and Tahzib-Lie B (eds), *Making the Voice of Humanity Heard: Essays on Humanitarian Assistance and International Humanitarian Law in Honour of HRH Princess Margriet of the Netherlands* (Martinus Nijhoff 2004) 366–68

Meron T, 'Francis Lieber's Code and Principles of Humanity' in Charney JI, Anton DK, and O'Connell ME (eds), *Politics, Values and Functions: International Law in the 21st Century: Essays in Honour of Professor Louis Henkin* (Martinus Nijhoff 1997) 249–60

Neff SC, *War and the Law of Nations: A General History* (CUP 2005)

Ramcharan BG, *Contemporary Human Rights Ideas* (Routledge 2008)

Schmitt MN and Green LC (eds), *The Law of Armed Conflict: Into the Next Millennium* (Naval War College 1998).

Sigg A, *International Human Rights Law, International Humanitarian Law, Refugee Law: Geneva from Early Origins to the 21st Century* (Swiss Federal Department of Foreign Affairs 2003)

Stacey RC, 'The Age of Chivalry' in Howard M, Andreopoulos GJ, and Shulman MR (eds), *The Laws of War: Constraints on Warfare in the Western World* (Yale UP 1994) 27–39

Veuthey M, 'Public Conscience in International Humanitarian Law Today' in Fischer H and others (eds), *Crisis Management and Humanitarian Protection: Festschrift für Dieter Fleck* (Berliner Wissenschafts-Verlag 2004) 613–14

CHAPTER 12

SOCIAL JUSTICE, RIGHTS, AND LABOUR

JANELLE M DILLER[1]

1. Introduction

The rise of the international labour movement at a time of growing economic globalization and cooperation tells the story of how a permanent international organization emerged to defend workers in a world dominated by sovereign states. Wartime collaboration among national labour movements in the early twentieth century spurred the idea of international cooperation for the public rather than sovereign interest, which evolved in the form of a growing body of international labour law. States' mutual recognition of their obligations to ensure work-related rights and entitlements through international labour standards influenced the development of international human rights law thirty years later.

The international labour movement emerged in the nineteenth century, as labour unions struggled against capital's increasingly cross-border influence. The use of regulatory and policy methods to achieve social goals first gained ground

[1] Deputy Legal Adviser, International Labour Office, Geneva. The views expressed here are those of the author and should not necessarily be attributed to the International Labour Office.

at the national level, based on natural law principles. As international trade increased, international social legislation did as well, with early efforts resulting in two international labour conventions in 1906. During the First World War, public appreciation for the working classes' war efforts grew, as did concerns over the specter of revolution arising from labour unrest. The importance of labour issues, and the apex of influence that labour unions enjoyed, led labour and capital to have a direct role in working with governments to draft the post-war Peace Treaty[2] that declared a Labour Charter and set up the International Labour Organization (ILO).

The structural machinery and guiding principles of the ILO, which resulted from the labour movement's early international efforts, have served for nearly a century as the global reference point for setting and supervising standards on workers' rights, freedoms, and entitlements. In the mid-twentieth century, as changing economic and social realities challenged the ILO's ability to achieve its goals, the organization expanded its constitutional mandate to include policy and programmatic areas. Further ILO innovations in response to modern-day forms of economic globalization led to authoritative International Labour Conference Declarations in 1998 and 2008, ultimately espousing an umbrella concept of 'decent work'. Decent work is to be achieved by promoting fundamental principles and rights at work, as well as employment, social protection, and social dialogue—all guided by international labour standards.

The ILO experience serves as a historical and legal precedent for human rights law, although international labour standards are based on distinctive legal theories and methods of action. While workers' rights and international human rights share certain normative content, mutual deference is required to ensure that no harm is done to either system. In situations where labour issues overlap with more general application of international human rights law, special care should be given to recognize the meaning that ILO bodies have given to international labour standards. Better coordination between the ILO and United Nations (UN) systems, together with an appreciation of the similarities and differences between the two systems, are required for states to give effect to obligations on the same subject matter in both spheres, without prejudice to the more favourable standard that may apply in a particular situation.

[2] Treaty of Peace between the Allied Powers and Germany (Treaty of Versailles).

2. The Emergence of International Labour Law

2.1 Development of an international labour movement

Unions developed during the nineteenth century in countries affected by industrialization's sweeping impact on the national economic and social fabric. By 1830, humanitarian and religious ideals motivated social groups to form associations for international cooperation in political, economic, and cultural matters. In the same period, the democratic ideals of the French and American Revolutions, and the early doctrines of socialism that enlightened business interests, inspired a set of common values on the rights and guarantees necessary to economic and social progress. As industry expanded and international trade grew, workers on strike faced the importation of foreign workers as strikebreakers, which stimulated international labour contacts to counteract the threat. In 1847, Karl Marx and Friedrich Engels declared that the struggle of workers, though national in form, was international in essence, and that the combined action of workers across countries was needed to establish a new society, in which the means of production would be owned in common and used to foster greater economic and social equality and democracy.[3]

The international solidarity of organized labour grew as workers recognized the similar interests of working classes of people worldwide.[4] Common aims created strong international links among the national unions. Together, they called for peace, prosperity, better working conditions, an eight-hour day, higher wages, protection for working women, and freedom from child labour. The early international labour movement agreed that workers could not entrust the solution of international problems to other social groups or to official diplomacy; they had

[3] Marx based his claim, 'from each according to his ability, to each according to his needs', on John Locke's argument that capitalists' payment did not adequately reflect the value of workers' labour. The association of the labour theory of value with Marxism may have diminished the respect given to economic claims of workers in contemporary human rights discourse. Tonia Novitz and Colin Fenwick, 'The Adoption of Human Rights Discourse to Labour Relations: Translation of Theory into Practice' in Colin Fenwick and Tonia Novitz (eds), *Human Rights at Work: Perspectives on Law and Regulation* (Hart 2010) 1, 10.

[4] The 1836 People's Charter of the London Working Men's Association, which William Lovett led, exemplified the trend toward class-consciousness across borders. It called for universal suffrage and other democratic measures, reflecting an assumption that political reform and organization were necessary for workers to obtain economic and social progress. In 1843, the French unionist, Flora Tristan, presented a concrete plan for an international association of workers united to obtain political and economic power in *L'Union Ouvrière*. Lewis L Lorwin, *The International Labor Movement: History, Policies, Outlook* (Harper 1953) 3, 5.

to build their own international organizations to act as an independent force. The national unions differed, however, on whether the working classes should rely only on their own influence or combine with political and socialist parties. These differences led to the formation of various international associations and persistent frictions within the international labour movement.[5]

2.2 Sources and the theory of social legislation

The labour unions' claims to improve working conditions gathered influence as the expansion of political participation became possible through universal compulsory education and the extension of the right to vote. The confluence of these social factors led to political action in the form of social legislation for better working conditions and a higher standard of living. Motivating these trends was the central idea that workers were entitled to rights and freedoms as human beings, an idea grounded in the intellectual tradition of the Enlightenment and its philosophical roots of natural law.[6] The view of workers' rights as natural rights belonging to all people, equal and independent in the original state of nature, is attributed to John Locke, while the further appeals of Thomas Paine and John Thelwall stressed natural rights as the basis for the entitlements of working people.[7] Catholic social teachings of the time stressed the human dignity of the worker,[8] a concept rooted in the writings of St Augustine and St Thomas Aquinas affirming workers' claims to a living wage within the limits that social responsibility set.

The theoretical foundation of social legislation also drew upon the natural law principles of equality, mutuality, and justice.[9] Aristotle posited horizontal and vertical dimensions of these principles: commutative justice, which operates within the sphere of relations between private individuals or groups involving individual

[5] Before the First World War, the labour movements in Great Britain and the United States (US) took a pragmatic and functional approach to international problems, focusing on issues like migration and mutual aid in strikes. Social reformist trade unions in many Western European countries espoused immediate improvements in labour conditions and faith in socialism. The French and various minorities of other national labour movements advocated radical methods of class struggle to abolish capitalism but, with the advent of the First World War and the Bolshevik Revolution in Russia, the French labour movement shifted toward the social reformist views. Lorwin (n 4) xii.

[6] See the other chapters in Part II of this *Handbook*.

[7] Paine argued for governmentally enforceable rights to justice and Thelwall for 'equal participation of all the necessaries of life, which are the product of their labour' resulting from an original social contract that entitled labour to a proportionate share in the profits of capital as a 'partner'. Fenwick and Novitz, 'The Adoption of Human Rights Discourse' (n 3) 7–9.

[8] *Rerum Novarum*, Encyclical of Pope Leo XIII on the Condition of the Working Classes (15 May 1891) para 19.

[9] On solidarity and equality, see Chapters 17 and 18 of this *Handbook*. See also Janelle M Diller, *Securing Dignity and Freedom through Human Rights: Article 22 of the Universal Declaration of Human Rights* (Martinus Nijhoff 2011) 100–106, 112–16, 121–25.

well-being in community; and distributive justice, which regulates the actions between the social whole and the citizens and groups which are its parts. The concept of distributive justice spawned further theories for distributing resources, opportunities, profits and advantages, responsibilities, taxes, and burdens. Those theories supported the evolution of the term 'social justice', which came into use in the mid-nineteenth century, particularly in Catholic thought.[10]

The assumption that, without compulsion, humanitarian principles would not be able to prevail over pecuniary interests, practically motivated the adoption of social legislation, beyond its philosophical roots. Labour laws represented 'a strengthening of the public conscience' by imposing regulation on the private interests of manufacturers for reasons of the life, health, safety, morals, and liberty of the workers. Originally rooted in private economic law, national legislation in employment and labour law grew in scope and took on public law characteristics.

2.3 The idea of transnational labour law

At the turn of the twentieth century, as labour questions occupied an increasingly prominent place in national policies and programs, legislation extended to factories, mines, and other industries. Initially, lawmakers focused on the national interest in the health and morals of workers and their family life and did not take into account the charge on industry and increased costs of production. However, as international trade increased, foreign competition between manufacturers in different countries generated concerns about production costs. Soon, the idea of some limitation on freedom of competition emerged, based on the precedence of humanitarian ideals over considerations of economic profit. A Swiss manufacturer in France, Daniel Legrand, advocated that governments consider 'an international law to protect the working-classes against premature and excessive labour, which is the prime and principal cause of their physical deterioration, their moral degradation and their being deprived of the blessings of family life'.[11] Thereafter, social reformers and philanthropists, as well as international congresses, called for international labour legislation.

The Swiss Government was the first to take official action toward international labour law, in a series of initiatives lasting from 1876 to 1891. In 1889, the Swiss invited European governments to a preparatory conference on international cooperation in regard to labour questions; the motive was to help neutralize the influence

[10] The term 'social justice' reportedly first appeared in Luigi Taparelli d'Azeglio, *Saggio Teoretico di Diritto Naturale Apogiatto Sul Fatto* (Palermo, 1845) 347–56, cited in Leo W Shields, 'The History and Meaning of the Term Social Justice' (PhD Dissertation, University of Notre Dame 1941).

[11] Ernest Mahaim, 'The Historical and Social Importance of International Labor Legislation' in James T Shotwell (ed), *The Origins of the International Labour Organization*, vol I (Columbia UP 1934) 3 (from memorandum of Legrand, 1847).

and possible revolutionary agitation expected of a subversive pan-European workers' movement. Although the outcome of the initiative was hortatory, due primarily to German resistance, the Swiss proposal to develop international obligations for labour law, and a centralized organ to prepare conferences and disseminate information, foreshadowed a new era and a new attitude that placed labour questions in the field of diplomacy.

With the failure of official means, French and German intellectuals held an international congress on labour legislation that established the International Association for Labour Legislation in 1897. Operating in Basel from 1901, an International Labour Office (different from the present day ILO), comprised of former high government officials led the Association which convened a committee of governments. Following much the same approach that the ILO uses today, the Office identified possible subjects for international law-making through careful study, based on information and consultations with associated national sections, and reported the information to a general assembly. In 1901, the first assembly selected two subjects for discussion and possible adoption of labour legislation: the prohibition of women performing night work and of the use of white phosphorus in the manufacture of matches. Following a technical conference for a first discussion of the subjects at Berne in 1905, a diplomatic conference held at the invitation of the Swiss Government reviewed the drafts of conventions that ultimately gained acceptance.[12] This work broke ground on a number of legal issues relevant to international labour standard-setting today.[13]

Although the Association identified more topics for discussion after the Berne conventions of 1906, its efforts failed to achieve consensus before it dissolved in the First World War. As an organ on industrial questions, its unofficial composition prevented its access to official sources beyond official publications. This fundamental weakness left unresolved the question of a method for supervising and controlling the realization of conventions. Nonetheless, the Association gave birth to three leading elements which shaped the design of the ILO after the war: (1) the holding of periodic conferences; (2) the creation of a central organ; and (3) the supervision and enforcement of states' observance of conventions.

[12] The double discussion method for standard-setting is still the approach International Labour Conference uses most frequently, as it permits preparation with careful study of the diversity of law and practice across member countries. See ILO, Standing Orders of the International Labor Conference, art 39, reprinted in ILO, *Constitution of the International Labour Organisation and Selected Texts* (ILO 2011).

[13] The discussion included such issues as exemption of small establishments; demarcation between industry, agriculture, and commerce; and derogations and exceptions in case of accidents, seasonable pressure, and other exceptional circumstances.

2.4 Preparing the way: workers' rights in the interest of humanity

The First World War I elevated the position of labour in society and drew workers' and employers' associations into closer relations with governments, as the organization of industry and the maintenance of essential community services required tripartite consultation, cooperation, and agreement. Under strong pressure to produce military and civilian necessities, the working classes' sacrifices intensified public appreciation of their claims to a higher standard of living, and labour gained a new position of political and social prominence. Despite their national loyalties, organized labour movements did not forget their pre-war cross-border relationships. Indeed, the need for international labour legislation as an essential method of organizing peace became evident. Before the war few workers' organizations had supported the Association's efforts to secure international labour legislation. Now, the growing cooperation with governments, and concern over the Bolshevik revolution in Russia and its influence on the working classes in other countries, motivated a number of labour organizations to seek a solution to industrial problems at the coming Peace Conference—through evolution, not revolution.

A remarkable war-time collaboration of international conferences among various leading national unions and international union federations directly contributed to the design of the labour programme in the Peace Treaties and the creation of the ILO. From 1914 to 1919, the various labour movement conferences agreed on the need for international relations to ensure not only the interest of wage earners, but also the rights of humanity.[14] However, the labour leaders differed on whether to achieve this by direct workers' participation in the Conference or by outside advocacy. They also differed on whether the treaties should directly establish minimum guarantees for workers' rights, or whether they should create international machinery to fix international labour legislation and oversee its compliance. In the end, the British trade unions played a powerful role in shaping the design that the Peace Treaty ultimately adopted, which included international machinery and rights. In addition, the American Federation of Labor (AFL) advocated a Magna Carta of principles for organized labour to establish social justice and assist 'in laying the foundation for a more lasting peace'.[15] The Labor Commission of the Preliminaries of the Peace Conference, over which the AFL leader Gompers presided as a US delegate, later debated many of the principles.

[14] During WWI, various labour congresses passed influential resolutions, including those at Philadelphia (American Federation of Labor), Leeds (British, French, Belgian, and Italian representatives), Berne (parallel international conferences of socialist and International Federation of Trade Unions), and London (Inter-Allied Labour and Socialist unions). For the original texts, see James T Shotwell (ed), *The Origins of the International Labor Organization*, vol II (Columbia UP 1934) doc nos 1, 2, 4, 7, 8, 9.

[15] See Mahaim (n 11) 17; Shotwell, *Origins* II (n 14) doc no 1, at 3.

Above all, broad human rights considerations guided the labour leaders in the warring countries. Rather than demand recognition for itself as a class, labour was aware that it 'spoke not merely for itself but for humanity at large... It is to the lasting credit of the labor leaders that during the War labor was not so narrowly preoccupied'[16] with the protection of its own interests. Labour's programmes dealt with social justice the world over, rather than with the narrow issues of domestic economic welfare. In advocating action, British unionist William Appleton stated: 'The time has arrived for... the consideration of the common rather than the particular interest [in peace treaties]; *for the wide conception of human rights rather than the narrow one*'.[17] Similarly, AFL leader Samuel Gompers argued that:

> There is so much inherent dignity and sacredness about the demands that the organized labor movement makes in the name of humanity that they preclude ridicule or rejection by those with understanding of human purpose and the forces that have directed the wider ideals of all nations.[18]

Like the unionists, the governments preparing the Preliminaries of the Peace Conference recognized that the Peace Treaties presented an opportunity to resolve labour unrest. In elevating labour issues to the international plane, governments accepted a new era of international cooperation and more limited sovereignty over issues that domestic interests had previously driven. The specter of revolution motivated governments to accept the treaty-based labour concessions, a fact reflected in the compelling defence of the Labor Commission's proposals in the plenary of the Preliminaries of the Peace Conference by the Belgian delegate M Vandervelde:

> [T]he work of the Labor Commission has been one of fairness and moderation, one of give and take, and, if I may say so, one of transition between the absolutism of the employers, which was the rule of yesterday, and the sovereignty of labor, which, I am ardently convinced, will be the rule of tomorrow. For passing from the one to the other there are many roads: some are beset with violence and insurrection; others, on the contrary, give just as quick a journey, but without clashes and shocks.... [T]here are two methods of making the revolution which we feel is happening throughout the world, the Russian [violent revolution] and the British method [drafters of labour chapter in the Peace Treaty]. It is the British method which has triumphed in the labor Commission; it is the one which I greatly prefer.[19]

2.5 Principles and machinery for lasting peace

The organization created at the end of the First World War to support international cooperation on labour issues bore a 'significance which reaches far outside

[16] Carol Riegelman, 'War-Time Trade-Union and Socialist Proposals' in Shotwell, *Origins* I (n 14) 56.

[17] Riegelman (n 16) 65, fn 17 (emphasis added).

[18] Riegelman (n 16) 62.

[19] Edward J Phelan, 'The Commission on International Labour Legislation' in Shotwell, *Origins* I (n 11) 208–209 (quoting Mr Vandervelde, Belgian Minister of Justice).

the particular field of labor'.[20] Intended for 'conference and study in the largest and most contentious field of economic relations', the creation of the ILO was even considered as:

much more important than the tracing of frontiers as part of the drama of war and peace... the problem of the day's work is the one outstanding problem in all lands... the alignments of the future both between nations and within them are conditioned by economics. The deepest and truest note in the whole peace settlement was that which introduces the labor section of each of the Peace Treaties: that universal peace can be established only if it is based on social justice.[21]

In this light, the title of the Organization was overly narrow in referring only to 'labour'. In reality, labour had declared its readiness to cooperate with capital in a new global enterprise, in a way which promised advantages to capital, as well as the elimination of unfair competition. The ILO was truly an international economic organization that dealt with labour problems.

The new vision of international cooperation that the ILO pioneered was intended not to intrude on the government of sovereign states, but to 'coordinate the public opinion of the world in matters of common concern and frame... a program of reform that would ensure higher standards of social justice throughout the world'.[22] The Peace Treaty reflected a compromise between having no specialized organization, but only direct obligations under the League machinery, and having only specialized machinery for later incorporation of direct obligations. The treaty provided for a dedicated, specialized organization to secure labour reforms and an international Labor Charter of rights and reforms to guide the Organization and its members. Workers' proposals were at the root of the Labour Charter.[23] Although the legal effect of the Charter principles in the Peace Treaty was never completely clear, its principles have shaped the work of the ILO since its first International Labour Conference in 1919.

Work began on the Labour Section of the Peace Treaty soon after the Peace Conference opened in Paris.[24] On 25 January 1919, the Conference appointed a Commission for International Labour Legislation:

to inquire into the conditions of employment from an international aspect, and to consider the international means necessary to secure common action on matters affecting

[20] John T Shotwell, 'Introduction' in Shotwell, *Origins* I (n 11) xxii.

[21] Shotwell, 'Introduction' (n 20) xxii.

[22] Shotwell, 'Introduction' (n 20) xx.

[23] The AFL had prepared a Magna Carta for organized labour that it believed would establish social justice in the world. The US, Belgian, and Italian Delegations also submitted drafts. The French Delegation communicated a manifesto of the International Trade Union Confederation, developed at the Berne international labor conference in 1919, suggesting insertion of an international Labor Charter into the Treaty of Peace. See Phelan (n 19) 185–86.

[24] David Fromkin, 'A Peace to End All Peace' in Michael S Neiberg (ed), *The World War I Reader: Primary and Secondary Sources* (New York UP 2007) 340. The Treaty of Versailles contained the Labour Section and the Labour Charter. Covenant of the League of Nations, Pt XIII and Art 427, respectively.

conditions of employment, and to recommend the form of a permanent agency to continue such inquiry and consideration in cooperation with and under the direction of the League of Nations.[25]

The Commission's composition was comprised of two representatives from each of the five Great Powers[26] and five other representatives, which the Powers with special interests appointed.[27] In a surprise move that greatly influenced the outcome, the United States appointed two non-governmental representatives—one from labour and the other from industry—foreshadowing the tripartite character of the ILO today.

The draft convention that the United Kingdom presented to the Commission envisaged the world's first permanent organization to legislate and oversee international treaties to regulate labour conditions. Its major elements still comprise the ILO's unique structure today. The proposals included: a permanent bureau; a tripartite Governing Council; an annual Conference with delegations of governments; employers' and workers' representatives, each with the right to a separate vote;[28] a procedure for selecting issues for conference discussion based on government vetting and careful preparatory studies; and a procedure for special investigations that the Conference would order. The draft was based on a memorandum that addressed the structural and guiding principles still foundational to the ILO and to international organizations.

2.5.1 *Structural principles of the organization*

The ILO's creation forged unprecedented limits to state sovereignty that paved the way for the now-established principles common to the structure of international organizations today. Those principles included international cooperation and accountability among states. Another principle, subsidiarity,[29] ordered the relationship between international and domestic levels of action and ensured deference to each state's competence to add value to the international norm in its own way. The further principle of democratic participation, which at the time was increasing at

[25] Commission on International Labour Legislation, 'Report of the Commission on International Labor Legislation of the Peace Conference' (24 March 1919). The Commission held eighteen meetings from 1 to 28 February 1919 and seventeen more meetings from 11 to 24 March 1919.

[26] France, Italy, Japan, the United Kingdom, and the United States of America.

[27] Charles Picquenard, 'The Preliminaries of the Peace Conference: French Preparations' in Shotwell, *Origins* I (n 11) 92. The smaller Powers decided that Belgium should send two representatives, and Cuba, Czechoslovakia, and Poland one representative each.

[28] The right to a separate vote was agreed so that 'the decision of the Conference should have the greatest possible authority... [and to avoid] that the labor delegates might leave the Conference'. Phelan (n 19) 133–40. The power of the General Conference of the ILO—convening states together for discussion and action—remains central to the Organization's structure and functioning.

[29] For subsidiarity in human rights law, see Chapter 15 of this *Handbook*. See also Paolo G Carozza, 'Subsidiarity as a Structural Principle of International Human Rights Law' (2003) 97 *AJIL* 38.

the national level through the extension of the franchise, was applied in the new context of an international organization. For the ILO, democratic participation took the form of tripartism.

International cooperation and accountability. The true test of the will of the nations in setting terms of peace proved to be the self-denying measures that the victorious countries accepted for themselves. The recognition that matters of domestic concern justified international action provoked a substantial debate in the Labour Commission on two questions of ILO structure: (1) whether the instruments to be adopted would be advisory or mandatory, and (2) whether only governments or also non-state actors would bring complaints against states for non-compliance. On the first question, US opposition to the proposal for adoption only of treaties resulted in a compromise by which the Conference could adopt both binding Conventions and also guiding (non-binding) Recommendations. Ratification of adopted Conventions was made subject to the consent of the competent national authorities.[30] On the second question, some objected to allowing any delegate of the International Labour Conference to initiate complaints against states for non-compliance with ratified Conventions, on the ground that states might refuse to ratify conventions if unions could accuse their own governments. Others argued that it would be in the states' interests to be aware of any non-observance of ratified provisions, which allowing any delegate to accuse a government would aid. In the end, a robust system of complaints that any delegate of the Conference could bring survived and remains a potent reminder of the power of labour and capital in the international economic relations between states.[31]

Subsidiarity. In a particular expression relevant to subsidiarity, the final result at the Peace Conference explicitly provided that no Recommendation or Convention could diminish protection that existing national legislation afforded. The Labour Charter of the Treaty of Versailles also reflects the ILO's attentive balance of

[30] From the start, the adoption of conventions by two-thirds of the Conference was proposed, with an obligation on all states to communicate ratification within one year, unless the national legislature opposed. The US preferred to have only Recommendations, with the same obligation to submit them to competent authorities, but with each state able to give effect to them in their own way and to report that effect to the organization. The referral to the competent national authorities accommodated federal states with limited power to enter into Conventions on labour matters. Phelan (n 19) 145–63. The compromise is reflected in the ILO Constitution, Art 19(7)(b)(iv).

[31] The ILO's constitutionally based system of representations and complaints differs from UN human rights mechanisms in the breadth of persons with standing to bring such actions, the lack of a specific requirement for exhaustion of domestic remedies, and the well-operating follow-up through the ILO supervisory system or appointment of Commissions of Inquiry. Compare Section 3 with Chapters 26 and 27 of this *Handbook*. In case of a failure to comply with the recommendations of a Commission of Inquiry after its review, the sanctions originally adopted by the Peace Conference as 'measures against the commerce of a defaulting State' were amended thirty years later to 'measures of an economic character', upon establishment of the United Nations and its Security Council. Compare Treaty of Versailles, pt XIII, Art 418, with ILO Constitution, Art 33 in ILO, *Selected Texts* (n 12).

particularity and universality; the opening text recognizes that 'differences of climate, habits and customs, of economic opportunity and industrial tradition, make strict uniformity in the conditions of labour difficult of immediate attainment'.[32] At the same time, the Labour Charter enumerates methods and principles to regulate labour conditions of 'special and urgent importance', which all industrial communities should apply 'so far as their special circumstances will permit'.[33] A constitutional requirement still applies to ILO's standard-setting, by which

> the Conference shall have due regard to those countries in which climatic conditions, the imperfect development of industrial organization, or other special circumstances make the industrial conditions substantially different and shall suggest the modifications, if any, which it considers may be required to meet the case of such countries.[34]

Democratic participation by tripartism. Unparalleled in composition, the ILO pioneered the principle of democratic governance through the equal participation of member states, in tripartite representation, in its governing organs and in its machinery for review of states' implementation of international labour standards. The choice of tripartite representation at the Conference assures the balanced participation of public and private interests in producing acts of the International Labour Conference that serve as both diplomatic decisions and popular resolutions. To ensure tripartism, members are constitutionally required to nominate and pay the expenses of Conference delegates representing the government and the employers and workers of their countries.[35] The Governing Body of the International Labour Office also has a tripartite structure, with a fixed number of seats reserved for members of 'chief industrial importance' and other government members that government delegates elect at the Conference.[36]

Democratic participation presumes equality of voting power, and the method of exercising this voting power proved to be a controversial issue at the Peace Conference. A government proposal for government and non-government delegates to share decision-making power on a 50/50 basis prevailed over a worker-supported proposal for equal weight to be given each of the three partners' votes. In the debate over voting power, different views were heard on whether only governments, or also

[32] Article 427.

[33] 'Final Texts of the Labor Section', art 427, in Shotwell, *Origins* I (n 11) 448–50, App B.

[34] ILO Constitution, Art 19(3). This type of flexibility, directly embodied in Conventions, has supported the practice of the Organization to prohibit reservations in the ratification of international labor Conventions. See eg Guido Raimondi, 'Réserves et Conventions du Travail' in G Politakis (ed), *Les Normes Internationales du Travail: Un Patrimoine pour l'Avenir* (ILO 2004) 527.

[35] ILO Constitution, Arts 3, 7.

[36] The Governing Body now determines the method for determining Members of chief industrial importance, a task originally granted to the Executive Council of the League of Nations, as Art 7 of the ILO Constitution lays out. Reforming the Governing Body's composition is the subject of a Constitutional amendment adopted in 1986 that has not entered into force. ILO, 72nd Session, Prov Rec No 36, 39/21 (vote) (1986).

workers and employers, represented the interests of society as a whole. Although workers' organizations subsequently protested the plenary voting outcome, the 2:1:1 system remains the defining structure of the final votes of the Conference. Nonetheless, a voting system with 1:1:1 equality, like the one the workers in Versailles demanded, is embedded in the operation of the Conference committees that elaborate proposals to submit for Conference decision, including for texts of international labour standards.[37] The same power-sharing ratios apply in the Governing Body plenary and committees, respectively.[38] The question of who best represents the public interest continues to challenge the ILO as it seeks to fulfil its mandate in a globalized world in which an increasing multiplicity of social and economic actors have expanded in form and influence relative to those of labour unions.

2.5.2 *Guiding principles of the organization*

Along with structural principles, the treaty establishing the ILO contained a number of fundamental principles to guide the work of the Organization, including social justice, equality, freedom, and dignity. Various forms of these guiding principles motivate international human rights law, as well.

Social justice. A reference to the ILO's now-famous guiding principle of social justice was missing from the Peace Treaty's original text,[39] but the Labour Commission amended the original draft wording from 'such peace [the League of Nations' object] can be established only if it is based upon *the prosperity and contentment of all classes in all nations*' to 'such peace can be established only if it is based upon *social justice*'.[40] Although the record contains no reason for the amendment, the preambular provisions that follow give further meaning to the term 'social justice' *in pari materia*, by invoking the need to improve labour conditions and avoid unrest due to deprivation, improving specific terms and conditions of work, preventing unemployment, and providing for social protection and the recognition of freedom of association.[41] As part of the Peace Treaty framework informing the term 'social justice', the

[37] Phelan (n 19) 139. The Standing Orders of the International Labour Conference set out the 1:1:1 voting power in Conference committees. Article 65.

[38] In a move by governments for more influence, the Governing Body recently eliminated most committee structures in favour of plenary work. See ILO Governing Body, 'Amendments to the Compendium of Rules Applicable to the Governing Body and to Decisions Attributing Function to Committee Structure or Officers' (June 2011) ILO Doc GB.311/7/1, para 9. Notably, the principal remaining committee is the powerful standing Committee on Freedom of Association, created to review cases alleging violations of the constitutional principle of freedom of association.

[39] Shotwell, *Origins* I (n 11) 424–25, preamble to the Labour Section. After the demise of the League of Nations, the text was amended to read in its current form: 'Whereas universal and lasting peace can be established only if it is based upon social justice.' ILO Constitution, preamble, para 1.

[40] Shotwell, *Origins* II (n 14) 216–17, doc no 34 (emphasis added).

[41] Shotwell, *Origins* II (n 14) 424–25, preamble to the Labour Section, para 2.

Labour Charter opened by invoking the 'supreme international importance [of] the well-being, physical, moral, and intellectual, of industrial wage-earners'.[42]

Equality. The fundamental principle of equality is at the origin of ILO's structure and aims. The Labour Commission was of the view that women should be appointed to Conference delegations on an equal footing with men. The Constitution itself provides affirmatively for the participation of women in Conference delegations and among the Office staff.[43] The Labour Charter similarly recognized the equality of every human being, both in general and in relation to gender. The Charter's first principle famously recognized that 'labour should not be regarded merely as an article of commerce',[44] a formulation later enhanced in the Declaration of Philadelphia by less qualified words: 'labour is not a commodity'.[45] Similarly, equitable treatment regardless of nationality motivated the eighth general principle that national labour laws 'should have due regard to the equitable economic treatment of all workers lawfully resident therein'.[46] As to gender equality, the seventh principle affirmed 'that men and women should receive equal remuneration for work of equal value', and the ninth principle provided that 'women should take part' in governmental systems of labour inspection.[47] Since then, in a number of resolutions, the International Labour Conference has reaffirmed the principle of gender equality, including in the use of language for ILO official texts and instruments.[48]

Freedom. Together with equality, human freedom constituted a foundational principle of the ILO, essential to fulfilling its mandate. The preamble of the constitutional section referred to 'recognition of the principle of freedom of association' as a way to improve labour conditions. Likewise, the Labour Charter's second principle affirmed the 'right of association for all lawful purposes by the employed as well as by the employers'.[49] The freedom of children to pursue educational and physical

[42] At the demise of the League of Nations, the Labour Charter was not directly incorporated into the ILO Constitution, which took up the articles providing for the structure and functioning of the Organization.

[43] Article 3, para 2 of the ILO Constitution requires that women be included as advisers on Conference 'questions specially affecting women'—a phrase now deemed to include all questions, in light of the increased participation of women in the work force. ILO, 'Resolution Concerning the Participation of Women in ILO Meetings' (11 June 1981) reprinted in ILO, *Women and Work: Selected ILO Documents* (ILO 1994). Article 9, para. 3 of the ILO Constitution provides that a 'certain number of [the staff of the International Labour Office] shall be women'.

[44] Article 427.

[45] See ILO, Declaration of Philadelphia, pt I(a) (1944), annex to ILO Constitution.

[46] Labour Charter (n 24) Art 427.

[47] Labour Charter (n 24) Art 427.

[48] ILO, 'Resolution Concerning Gender Equality and the Use of Language in Legal Texts of the ILO' (11 June 2011), reprinted in ILO, 'Resolutions Adopted by the International Labour Conference at Its 100th Session' (June 2011) <http://www.ilo.org/wcmsp5/groups/public/---ed_norm/---relconf/documents/meetingdocument/wcms_162049.pdf> accessed 26 May 2012.

[49] Labour Charter (n 24) Art 427.

development justified the 'abolition of child labour' and other limitations declared in the Charter's sixth principle.

Dignity in life and work. The principle of human dignity took specific form in the Peace Treaty's validation of the dignity of workers through just terms and conditions of work, which reflected the demands of the international labour movement. In the Labour Section's preamble, the ILO's mandate included the regulation of hours of work, the provision of an 'adequate living wage' and protection in matters of occupational safety and health, as well as insecurity due to old age or injury.[50] The principles adopted in the Labor Charter to guide the Organization's work offered specific inspiration, including the 'payment of a wage adequate to maintain a reasonable standard of life', the 'adoption of an eight-hours day or a forty-eight-hours week' and of 'a weekly rest of at least twenty-four hours'.[51] ILO Conventions and Recommendations regulating hours of work and rest, including for specific sectors of industry, express those principles.

3. ILO Action and Innovation

The structural machinery and guiding principles adopted nearly a century ago have continued to serve as the foundation of ILO action. Since its creation, the ILO has developed and applied a 'corpus juris of social justice',[52] which now includes nearly two hundred international labour Conventions and more than two hundred Recommendations. After a number of efforts by the Office and the Governing Body to classify ILO instruments,[53] the Conference definitively adopted an overarching organization in 2008, which resulted in the establishment of four principal categories of instruments.[54] As discussed below, the four categories provide for action to promote fundamental rights at work, employment creation, social protection, and

[50] Covenant of the League of Nations, pt XIII, preamble, para 2. See also ILO Constitution, preamble, para 2.

[51] Covenant of the League of Nations, pt XIII, paras 'Third', 'Fourth', and 'Fifth'. The words 'as this is understood in their time and country' builds flexibility to national circumstances into the term 'reasonable standard of life'.

[52] C Wilfred Jenks, *A New World of Law? A Study of the Creative Imagination in International Law* (Longmans 1969) 53, citing C Wilfred Jenks, *Law, Freedom and Welfare* (Stevens & Sons 1963) 101–36.

[53] See ILO, 'Subjects Covered by International Labor Standards' <http://www.ilo.org/global/standards/subjects-covered-by-international-labour-standards/lang--en/index.htm> accessed 29 June 2012.

[54] ILO, 'Declaration on Social Justice for a Fair Globalization' (10 June 2008) <http://www.ilo.org/global/meetings-and-events/campaigns/voices-on-social-justice/WCMS_099766/lang--en/index.htm> accessed 26 May 2013.

social dialogue—which comprise four constitutionally based 'strategic objectives' that together achieve 'decent work'. The ILO has used standard-setting and supervision, advisory services, technical cooperation, research, and other means to act in innovative ways to develop the Organization's mandate to keep pace with changes and challenges in the world of work.

3.1 ILO in operation: international labour standards and the oversight machinery

Across the decades, as changes in international economic patterns affected the world of work, the ILO adopted and supervised an extensive body of international labour standards to address a broad range of challenges facing its Members. The breadth of subjects treated in the 'International Labour Code' required arrangement by subject matter, which in turn determined the classification of the instruments for institutional purposes, such as frequency of reporting. The instruments now known as 'fundamental conventions' address obligations to respect, promote, and realize basic human rights and freedoms, in such areas as freedom of association and collective bargaining, and elimination of forced and child labour and employment discrimination.[55] Another set of conventions, now identified as 'priority' or 'governance conventions', guide the establishment of systems to ensure states' compliance with the ILO's objectives in areas covering employment policy and promotion, labour administration and inspection, and tripartite consultation.[56] Many other Conventions and Recommendations cover obligations concerning human rights in specific fields of work or for certain groups of workers.[57] These instruments fix either specific international standards or principles and goals at the international level, upon which governments are to decide the national standard in or after consultation with representative organizations of employers and workers at the national level.

[55] Eight main Conventions address the fundamental principles and rights that the International Labour Conference identified formally in its 1998 Declaration on Fundamental Principles and Rights at Work. ILO Declaration on Fundamental Principles and Rights at Work (18 June 1998, annex revised 15 June 2010), para 2 <http://www.ilo.org/declaration/thedeclaration/textdeclaration/lang--en/index.htm> accessed 18 February 2013. See ILO, 'List of Instrument by Subject and Status', ss 1–4 <http://www.ilo.org/dyn/normlex/en/f?p=1000:12030:1777344826332100::NO:::> accessed 27 May 2012.

[56] Along with the fundamental Conventions, the ILO, 'Declaration on Social Justice' (n 54), stressed the key role of governance instruments, identifying those then in existence: Convention Nos 81, 122, 129, and the Tripartite Consultation (International Labour Standards) Convention (No 144).

[57] Obligations concerning human rights are found in instruments on social security, the right to work and adequate terms and conditions of work, occupational safety and health, and maternity protection. Specific categories of workers include migrant or domestic workers, seafarers, fishers, dockworkers, and indigenous and tribal peoples. See ILO, 'List of Instruments' (n 55) ss 8–15 (fields), 16–22 (workers).

The emphasis on national-level consultation and decision-making builds flexibility into ILO standards, in line with the ILO Constitution.[58] Rather than aiming for uniformity of legislation across countries, the goal of ILO Conventions is equivalence, based on minimum guarantees that 'mark the progress of a uniform movement for social reform throughout the world'.[59] The 'cumulative effect is to ensure that the network of treaty obligations embodying international labour standards... cannot reasonably be regarded as jeopardizing either national or individual freedom'.[60] So-called 'flexibility measures' in ILO Conventions provide specific possibilities for Members to adjust the scope of application of an instrument when necessary; this practice has justified the ILO's insistence in practice that Members ratify Conventions without reservations. Similarly, ILO Conventions contain no standard limitation or derogation clauses, unlike certain provisions in human rights treaties. In addition, obligations arising under ILO Conventions are considered non-derogable, even in public emergency and except as the Convention concerned may expressly provide, though a plea of impossibility to perform such as force majeure may arise in emergency or war which, if independently verified, may justify non-compliance limited in extent and time to what is immediately necessary.[61]

Closely connecting international- and national-level action promotes the effective implementation of international labour standards through a wide range of ILO procedures. Members adopt, not sign, Conventions, which are subject to immediate submission for ratification as foreseen in the Peace Treaty compromise.[62] Members have constitutional obligations to submit reports on the effect given to the Conventions they have ratified,[63] as well as to ILO Recommendations[64] and even to provisions of Conventions they have not ratified.[65] A Committee of Experts examines their reports and prepares an annual report for the Governing Body on the application of ILO standards.[66] The International Labour Conference then submits this report through a tripartite standing Committee. The Conference Committee notes situations of special concern and makes other recommendations to the

[58] ILO Constitution, Art 19(3) (due regard for modifications required by special local conditions in standards of general application). See also C Wilfred Jenks, *Human Rights and International Labour Standards* (Stevens & Sons 1960) 130–31.

[59] Shotwell, 'Introduction' (n 20) xix (uniform movement part).

[60] Phelan (n 19) 131.

[61] See eg International Labour Code 1951, Vol I, Explanatory Note, XCVI–XCVII.

[62] ILO Constitution, Art 19.

[63] ILO Constitution, Art 22.

[64] ILO Constitution, Arts 19(6)(d), 19(7)(b)(b). ILO Recommendations contain guidance for all ILO members.

[65] ILO Constitution, Arts 19(5)(e), 19(7)(b)(iv). The purpose is to show the extent to which effect has been given and to state the difficulties which prevent ratification.

[66] At the request of the Conference in 1926, the Governing Body established a Committee of Experts on the Application of Conventions and Recommendations to operate in an independent technical expert capacity. The Committee of Experts now has twenty members that the Governing Body appoints from different regions and legal systems. ILO, *ILC Proceedings* (ILO 1926) 243–44 (Appendix VII).

Conference.[67] The intended result is a 'highly effective form of mutual supervision of the application of obligations'[68] undertaken by the Members. Along with the examination of states' reports, the special procedures set up at the Peace Conference still allow governments, and employers' and workers' representatives to allege a state's failure to apply ratified conventions by lodging representations[69] and complaints.[70] In contrast to the rarity of interstate complaints in human rights law, the willingness of the ILO Governing Body, as well as employers' and workers' representatives, to use the ILO procedures[71] may be due to the distinctive tripartite working relationship and to the economic effects in one country of non-compliance with ILO standards by another country.[72]

Across the years, the ILO has supplemented its constitutional arrangements with ad hoc and standing procedures focused on human rights-related international labour standards and constitutional obligations. Notably, in 1951, the Governing Body established a standing Committee on Freedom of Association to review allegations of violations of freedom of association against any ILO member; its broad

[67] See ILO, *The Committee on the Application of Standards of the International Labour Conference: A Dynamic and Impact Built on Decades of Dialogue and Persuasion* (ILO 2011) <http://www.ilo.org/wcmsp5/groups/public/---ed_norm/---normes/documents/publication/wcms_154192.pdf> accessed 26 May 2011.

[68] Jenks, *Human Rights* (n 58) 21. Members' compliance with their reporting obligations is notably higher than in the UN human rights treaty system; in 2011, nearly seventy per cent of Members delivered their reports on ratified Conventions on time. ILO, '2011 Report of the Committee of Experts on the Application of Conventions and Recommendations' (2011) ILC.100/III/1A, 12 (2,084 reports received of 3,013 requested).

[69] ILO Constitution, Art 24.

[70] ILO Constitution, Art 26.

[71] Under the Constitution, the right to file representations belongs to industrial associations of employers and workers, and the right to file complaints belongs to any Member, any delegate of the Conference, or the Governing Body on its own motion. The Governing Body takes direct action on representations; with complaints, it may appoint a Commission of Inquiry to report on the matter prior to taking action. ILO Constitution, Arts 24, 25 (representation procedure); 26–34 (complaints procedure). Since 1924, more than 140 representations have been filed under Art 24 of the ILO Constitution, and since 1934, more than twenty-five complaints under Art 26 of the ILO Constitution, some of which Governments brought in the ILO's first fifty years. See 'Representations' and 'Commissions of Inquiry' in ILO, *Rules of the Game: A Brief Introduction to International Labour Standards* (ILO 2009) 84–87.

[72] Despite the volume of Art 26 complaints, constitutionally-based sanctions have been used only once—in the case of Myanmar's non-compliance with the recommendations of a Commission of Inquiry on forced labour, in violation of the country's obligations under the ILO Convention on Forced Labour (No 29). See Janelle Diller, 'UN Sanctions—The ILO Experience' in Vera Gowlland-Debbas (ed), *United Nations Sanctions and International Law* (Kluwer Law 2001). After the Conference imposed sanctions on Myanmar in 2000, the Government agreed to an ILO in-country presence, which received complaints of forced labour and liaised with authorities for appropriate action. In 2012, the Conference lifted a number of the sanctions and provided for further review of the situation. ILO, 'Resolution Concerning the Measures Recommended by the Governing Body under Article 33 of the ILO Constitution on the Subject of Myanmar' (2000), reprinted in ILO, 'Provisional Record' (2012) appendix III <http://www.ilo.org/wcmsp5/groups/public/---ed_norm/---relconf/documents/meetingdocument/wcms_181314.pdf> accessed 18 February 2013.

mandate reflects the principle that all members hold obligations respecting freedom of association directly under the Constitution, as well as under any ratified Conventions on the subject.[73] In addition, the Conference has long-established legal procedures to examine the representative character of delegates that the governments have nominated to the International Labour Conference. Under the Conference's Standing Orders, a tripartite Credentials Committee considers and decides on objections, as well as other forms of allegations, affecting the tripartite nature of delegations.

3.2 Changing economic and social realities: ILO constitutional innovation

In its early decades, the ILO pursued an ambitious standard-setting agenda which the international labour movement promoted actively, but ratifications were slow and labour's disillusionment grew. The turbulence of the Great Depression and two World Wars made clear that the regulation of workplace conditions and relations could not alone achieve social justice. As a result, the ILO formally expanded its constitutional objectives and means of action to cover social and economic policies and programmes, including the promotion of full employment and higher standards of living at both national and international levels. This innovation was achieved largely by the Conference adopting the Declaration of Philadelphia in 1944 and later annexing it to the ILO Constitution.

The Declaration of Philadelphia identified the ILO's 'fundamental objective' as the right of all human beings to material well-being and spiritual development,[74] thus launching a 'rights-based approach' to social and economic development decades before that term was actually coined. Under the Declaration, the ILO resolved that all national and international policies and measures should be accepted only insofar as they promoted and did not hinder the achievement of that fundamental rights-based objective. The ILO also assumed ambitious programmatic commitments to assist Members in achieving employment promotion, skills training, wages and other terms and conditions of work, effective recognition of the right to collective bargaining, social security, and equality of educational and vocational opportunity. These priorities led to the adoption of standards guiding states to develop and implement policy-making mechanisms, and offering ILO assistance through country-based activities.[75] Overall,

[73] Prior to creation of the Committee on Freedom of Association in 1951, the tripartite Officers of the Governing Body—a chair and two vice-chairs—exercised authority to examine allegations concerning infringements of trade union rights. ILO (1951) 34 Official Bulletin 208, 208–209.

[74] ILO, Declaration of Philadelphia (n 45), pt II(a).

[75] After the 1964 adoption of the Employment Policy Convention (No 122), corollary field-based work, through the World Employment Programme, started in 1969 and spawned a research arm in 1976. Other policy-oriented standards encourage occupational safety and health policies and programmes, and fixing minimum wages. See eg ILO, 'Convention Concerning Minimum Wage Fixing (No 131)'

from the 1950s to the 1980s, the ILO's emphasis on direct and facilitative action, including advisory services and technical cooperation, shifted the 'balance between making rules and making things happen through direct interventions or facilitations'.[76]

Even as the ILO expanded its mandate, the changing economic and social realities after the Second World War continued to underscore the limitations of labour law's private law roots. Free market theory argued that legislation designed to protect the collective action and interests of workers distorted economic markets and infringed on individual freedom. Times of economic and financial crisis brought support for deregulation, management choice, and improved productivity for competitiveness. This tendency provoked questions about the effectiveness of international labour standards as 'an orderly framework for economic life, a mutually accepted discipline within which freedom can flourish without leaving the weak at the mercy of the strong'.[77] The ascendancy of the human rights movement in the second half of the twentieth century reflected 'to a very large extent... the failure of the promise of democracy, and of the capture of the democratic process by economic power'.[78]

The approach to rights and social justice, including through international labour standards, significantly shifted as theories of social rights expanded beyond the conventional understanding of claims to resources in the form of income, services, or employment. In the 1990s, the economist Amartya Sen and others developed the idea that capabilities, freedoms, and opportunities, as well as material resources such as access to health, wealth, information, and education, determine the economic functioning of individuals.[79] In such theories, opportunities for capabilities take the form of social rights that do not operate simply as claims to public resources; they also serve as ways to grow free markets through productive employment and to individual wealth. The question remains whether such an approach can extend to support collective capabilities, such as those necessary to trade union action. In practice, however, the idea that sustainable growth in the international economic order relies on economic and social rights, and in particular on labour rights, spawned increasingly practical forms of ILO innovation.

(1970) <http://www.ilo.org/dyn/normlex/en/f?p=NORMLEXPUB:12100:0::NO:12100:P12100_ILO_CODE:C131> accessed 18 February 2013; ILO, 'Promotional Framework for Occupational Safety and Health Convention (No 187)' (2006) <http://www.ilo.org/public/english/region/eurpro/moscow/areas/safety/docs/rep_iv1.pdf> accessed 18 February 2013.

[76] Jill Murray, 'The ILO and the Core Rights Discourse' in Fenwick and Novitz, *Human Rights at Work* (n 3) 359–60.

[77] Jenks, *Human Rights* (n 58) 131.

[78] KD Ewing, 'Foreword' in Fenwick and Novitz, *Human Rights at Work* (n 3) x.

[79] See eg Amartya Sen, *Inequality Reexamined* (Harvard UP 1992); Amartya Sen, *Development as Freedom* (OUP 1999); Amartya Sen, 'Work and Rights' (2000) 139 *Int'l Labour Rev* 119; Amartya Sen, *The Idea of Justice* (Harvard UP 2009).

In the face of challenges to the role of international labour standards from economic globalization and international trade,[80] the ILO developed a global minimum set of 'core' labour standards the 1998 ILO Declaration on Fundamental Principles and Rights at Work formally recognized. In principle, core labour standards served as enabling prerequisites for the realization of other international labour standards. The UN World Conference on Social Development and the World Trade Organization's Ministerial Singapore Declaration recognized the concept of core labour standards.[81] The minimalist approach to ILO standards that the 1998 ILO Declaration crafted tackled a market hungry for reductions in regulatory action. Consequently, a number of multilateral development bank policies and regional and bilateral trade and aid agreements incorporated the ILO fundamental principles and rights at work as minimum requirements for rights at work.[82] Nonetheless, the 1998 Declaration received criticism for setting unequal priorities among labour rights.[83]

Ten years after the 1998 Declaration, the ILO reaffirmed the full breadth of international labour standards, while still reducing their complexity. In the Social Justice Declaration, adopted in 2008, the Conference recognized the promotion of fundamental principles and rights at work as one of four 'interrelated, interdependent and mutually supportive' strategic objectives.[84] The four objectives converged to create the 'Decent Work Agenda', launched in 2000 as a policy and programmatic orientation of the Organization. The concept 'decent work' required the promotion of full employment, social protection, and social dialogue, along with fundamental principles and rights at work which were considered 'both rights and enabling conditions' necessary to realize the other strategic objectives. As a soft law instrument,

[80] The relationship of trade and labour standards was not addressed directly when the World Trade Organization was established in 1992. Marrakesh Agreement Establishing the World Trade Organization. The ILO has not concluded any standing relationship agreements with the World Trade Organization, nor with the World Bank or the International Monetary Fund, although ad hoc cooperation occurs. See Janelle Diller, 'Taking Account of Human Values in the International Economic Legal Order: Law and the Legal Counsel in the International Labour Organization' in Asif H Qureshi and Xuan Gao (eds), *International Economic Organizations and Law: The Perspective and Role of Legal Counsel* (Kluwer Law 2012) 82–84.

[81] Eg 'Copenhagen Declaration on Social Development', introduction para 5, in World Summit for Social Development, 'Report of the World Summit for Social Development' (19 April 1995) UN Doc A/Conf.166/9; World Trade Organization, 'Singapore Ministerial Declaration' (13 December 996) WT/MIN(96)DEC, para 4.

[82] Eg 'The OECD Guidelines for Multinational Enterprises' in Organization for Economic Co-operation and Development (OECD), *The OECD Declaration and Decisions on International Investment and Multinational Enterprises: Basic Texts* (8 November 2000) DAFFE/IME(2000)20; International Financial Corporation, 'Performance Standards on Environmental and Social Sustainability' (2012) 10 <http://www1.ifc.org/wps/wcm/connect/c8f524004a73daeca09afdf998895a12/IFC_Performance_Standards.pdf?MOD=AJPERES> accessed 18 February 2013.

[83] Eg Philip Alston, '"Core Labour Standards" and the Transformation of the International Labour Rights Regime' (2004) 15 *EJIL* 457.

[84] ILO, 'Declaration on Social Justice' (n 54) pt I(A), I(B).

the Social Justice Declaration relied on the constitutional grounding of each of the four objectives to declare that all Members are to achieve the objectives with 'due regard...to the...principles and provisions of [all] international labour standards'.[85] The evolving 'decent work' approach of the ILO seeks to affirm the relevance of the wide scope of ILO human rights standards beyond core labour standards, including those that contain positive or aspirational obligations. At the same time, an annual review focuses on the diverse realities and needs of the ILO Members in seeking to achieve the objectives, including through the use of information from state reports under ILO instruments. In its review, the Conference aims to better calibrate ILO's standards, policies, and programmes, to enhance the achievement of 'decent work' in countries around the world.

3.3 ILO standards, international human rights law, and the so-called 'generations'

The fact that international labour standards provided early inspiration for the development of international human rights law refutes the idea that economic and social rights emerged after civil and political rights as a later 'generation' of international human rights. The ILO's integrated emphasis on international- and national-level action to address economic and social as well as civil and political rights and freedoms is reflected in the human rights clauses of the United Nations Charter that link international cooperation with the efforts of each Member to solve economic and social problems and respect human rights and freedoms. The basic aims of the ILO's mandate—established in 1919 and expanded in 1944—are also restated in the Universal Declaration of Human Rights (UDHR). Its preamble, for example, asserts that 'recognition of [human] dignity and...equal...rights of all...is the foundation of freedom, justice and peace in the world'. The UDHR's introduction of economic, social, and cultural (ESC) rights in its article 22 further echoes the Declaration of Philadelphia's fundamental objective that 'all human beings...pursue both their material well-being and their spiritual development in conditions of freedom and dignity, and of economic security and equal opportunity'.[86] As an umbrella for the ESC rights in articles 23 to 27, article 22 recognizes that everyone, as a member of society, has the right to social—not technical, but social—security and 'is entitled to realization, through national effort and international co-operation...of the economic, social and cultural rights indispensable for...dignity and the free development of [the] personality'. Other fundamental principles underlying international labour standards also appear in the UDHR, including universality, non-discrimination and equality, participation, and solidarity.

[85] ILO, 'Declaration on Social Justice' (n 54) pt I(C)(iii).

[86] ILO, Declaration of Philadelphia (n 45) pt II(a).

The ILO itself recognized that 'certain important fundamental principles laid down in the [UDHR] have largely been inspired by and are closely interrelated with those contained in the [ILO] Constitution...and in the Declaration of Philadelphia',[87] and the protection of human rights and fundamental freedoms was 'of fundamental importance for the fulfillment of the objectives of the International Labour Organisation'.[88]

The popular misconception that economic, social, and cultural rights came after civil and political rights confuses the different sequences that occurred at national and international levels. In national constitutions and laws, civil liberties have had a longer legal history than economic and social rights. By the eighteenth century, legal protection was accorded to civil liberties—particularly as a heritage of the English, American, and French revolutions—while political participation rights appeared in the nineteenth century and social rights in the twentieth century, particularly as a result of the Mexican, Russian, and German revolutions. In contrast to national legal developments, the legal recognition of social and workers' rights at the international level, and international cooperation for social justice, was given effect through the ILO Constitution and machinery some thirty years before the Universal Declaration of Human Rights, as set out above. The UDHR's integrated set of civil, political, economic, social, and cultural rights—adopting this same approach—also appeared in a draft Covenant and in a set of implementation proposals that were proposed to the UN General Assembly along with the UDHR. After adopting the UDHR in 1948, the General Assembly sent the other proposals back to the Economic and Social Council for further examination. For nearly two decades, the UDHR remained the only authoritative articulation of the human rights clauses of the UN Charter.

In the UN effort to finalize a legally binding treaty based on the UDHR, Cold War political alignments supported the idea of bifurcating the integrated 1948 draft Covenant into two separate Covenants: the International Covenant on Civil and Political Rights (ICCPR), and the International Covenant on Economic, Social and Cultural Rights (ICESCR). The Soviet-style social welfare system of the time gave priority to economic and social rights, to the detriment of civil and political freedoms, and the West emphasized civil and political rights. Decades later, despite the fall of Soviet-style communism and authoritative international statements about the indivisible nature of all human rights,[89] the politically motivated idea of the

[87] ILO, 'Resolution Concerning Action by the International Labour Organisation in the Field of Human Rights and in Particular with Respect to Freedom of Association' (24 June 1968) preamble, reprinted in ILO, *Resolutions Adopted by the International Labour Organization in Its 52nd Session* (ILO 1968).

[88] ILO, 'Resolution Concerning Human Rights' (20 June 1958) International Labour Conference 42nd Session, preamble II.

[89] Eg 'Economic Development and Human Rights' (12 May 1968) preamble, in International Conference on Human Rights, 'Final Act of the International Conference on Human Rights' (1968) UN Doc A/CONF.32/41; Vienna Declaration and Programme of Action, para I.5. International labour

primordial nature of civil and political rights persists (particularly in the United States), as does its corollary: the 'generations' of human rights. In turn, tensions between individual and collective or group rights remain, as exemplified by human rights law decisions restricting the exercise of freedom of association for trade unions and their members because the right is viewed as limiting the right of other workers not to associate.[90]

3.4 ILO and UN human rights: distinctive approaches to common aims

A dichotomy has long been evident in relation to UN human rights instruments and international labour standards; although common normative principles and rights underlie their general object and purpose, the distinctive contexts and traditions of their elaboration and implementation import differences in their content, enforcement, and remedies.[91] At the time the Covenants were adopted, the ILO noted with concern that 'the Covenants and the international labour Conventions differ in their scope and in the nature and extent of the protection they provide'.[92] Presaging the risk of divergence, the ILO called for 'a common understanding of human rights [as being] of the greatest importance for the full realisation of the pledge embodied in the [UDHR]'. It recognized that 'ILO human right standards' include not only those Conventions concerning discrimination, forced labour, and freedom of association, but also 'standards concerning other basic human rights, including income maintenance and security, the protection of ageing workers and equality of treatment for migrant workers'.[93] In a study comparing the Covenant provisions to ILO standards, the ILO noted the contribution that ILO instruments could make 'to defining more clearly the nature and level of protection required for the enjoyment of the rights recognized in the Covenants'.[94]

standards, in turn, rely on a combination of civil liberties and freedoms, on the one hand, and the protection of the state and society, on the other hand, to guarantee adequate standards of living and social rights that permit individual well-being and development.

[90] For the impact of human rights law decisions on labour standards, one author concludes that 'particular forms of human rights protections are no guarantee of respect for labour standards'. Ewing (n 78) x.

[91] See Opinion of the Legal Adviser, 'Fundamental Principles and Rights at Work: From Commitment to Action' (2012) ILC.101/VI, paras 199–204. See also Colin Fenwick and Tonia Novitz, 'Regulating to Protect Workers' Human Rights' in Fenwick and Novitz, *Human Rights at Work* (n 3) 590, 594.

[92] ILO, 'Resolution Concerning the International Covenants on Human Rights and the Measures Which the International Labor Organization Should Adopt in Regard Thereto' (1967) 50 Official Bulletin 40, 49–50.

[93] ILO, 'Resolution Concerning the International Covenants' (n 92) para 4(d).

[94] ILO, 'Comparative Analysis of the International Covenants on Human Rights and International Labour Conventions and Recommendations' (1969) 52 Official Bulletin 181, paras 155–56.

A brief review of linkages between the two regimes illustrates how international labour conventions 'provide, in a more specific and detailed manner, for the practical implementation, at the national level, of the series of principles embodied in more general terms in the [ESC] Covenant',[95] as well as the UDHR and even the ICCPR. Fundamental principles and rights at work deal with specific threats to personal freedoms or upon an individual's actions or opportunities; these core labour standards contribute to respect for the more general human rights to life, liberty, and security of person, and to freedom of association; and, in turn, the ILO has stressed the importance of civil liberties to the exercise of freedom of association. Similarly, ILO standards on discrimination in employment and equal remuneration give specific expression to the human rights recognized in UN and regional instruments to freedom from discrimination and to equality, as well as the rights to work, to free choice of employment, and to equal pay for equal work. In addition to negative freedoms and rights, international labour law also addresses positive entitlements to freedom from want that are generally associated with international economic and social rights. For example, the right to social security recognized in international human rights law is expressed in international labour standards as both a complex of rights governing the operation of a social security scheme and, more recently, as a right to a nationally defined set of social security guarantees, including at a minimum, access to essential healthcare and basic income security.[96] In like concrete manner, ILO occupational safety and health standards provide for workplace arrangements that contribute to achieve the right to the highest attainable standard of health, including measures to improve industrial hygiene and combat occupational diseases, which provide means for promoting health at work.[97]

Distinctively, international labour standards address states' obligations to take steps to remove social and economic barriers, as well as legal measures to achieve the agreed aims.[98] For example, governments are to develop a policy to promote equality and nondiscrimination in society, rather than merely prohibiting discrimination by law, and are to ensure application of the principle of equal remuneration by appropriate

[95] Nicholas Valticos, 'International Labor Standards and Human Rights: Approaching the Year 2000' (1998) 37 *Int'l Lab Rev* 140.

[96] See ILO, 'Recommendation Concerning National Floors of Social Protection' (2012) No 14A. The Recommendation's insistence on the universality of basic social protection rebuts concerns that the ILO approach on social security had potential for social exclusion, by providing that only certain branches or workers be covered. See eg Lucie Lamarche, 'The Right to Social Security in the International Covenant on Economic, Social and cultural Rights' in Audrey Chapman and Sage Russell (eds), *Core Obligations: Building a Framework for Economic, Social and Cultural Rights* (Intersentia 2002) 87.

[97] Compare Convention concerning Occupational Safety and Health Convention and the Working Environment, with ICESCR, Art 12.

[98] Although the UN's 'respect, protect, fulfill' approach used for states' obligations to ensure economic, social, and cultural rights similarly aims for states to address societal conduct, the scope and methods of implementation differ from the ILO approach.

means.[99] Similarly, practical means are recommended to stimulate national social security policy and programmes to overcome particular problems, as well as achieve equality of treatment between nationals and aliens.[100] International labour standards also approach the right to work as a challenge that requires adequate national machinery for economic policy, as well as effective employment services and educational and vocational training.[101]

3.5 ILO and UN human rights cooperation

At the time of the Covenants' adoption, it was noted that 'the specialized agencies and in particular the ILO, by reason of the number and importance of the economic and social rights falling within its field, are the *executing agencies of the [ESC] Covenant* with a major share of the responsibility for its effective implementation' and the 'bridge from principle to practice'.[102] The task involved 'a wholly new series of arrangements for cooperation between the United Nations and the specialized agencies in the implementation of the Covenant's provisions', which could determine 'the extent to which the law of nations as a whole, as distinguished from the *corpus juris* administered by the ILO, reflects the contemporary insistence on social justice'.[103]

The ILO's direct role as an executing agency for the relevant provisions of the Covenant has not been realized, although an early Charter-based review system relied on reports, not only from states, but also from the ILO and other specialized agencies on the effect given to their relevant provisions in the UDHR.[104] At that time, agencies across the UN System were seen to engage in human rights

[99] Discrimination (Employment and Occupation) Convention (No 111). Specific steps include seeking the cooperation of employers and workers, enacting legislation and educational programmes designed to secure policy acceptance, and repealing laws and regulations inconsistent with the policy. See also Equal Remuneration Convention (No 100).

[100] Eg Social Security (Minimum Standards) Convention (No 102); Equality of Treatment (Social Security) Convention (No 118); Maintenance of Social Security Rights Convention (No 157). For further social security instruments, see ILO, 'Social Security' <http://www.ilo.org/global/standards/subjects-covered-by-international-labour-standards/social-security/lang--en/index.htm> accessed 27 May 2012.

[101] Compare eg Employment Policy Convention (No 122) and Human Resources Development Convention (No 142), with UDHR, Arts 23 (work), 26 (education) and ICESCR, Arts 6, 7 (work), 13 (education).

[102] Wilfred Jenks, *Social Justice in the Law of Nations: The ILO Impact after Fifty Years* (OUP 1970) 79, citing Wilfred Jenks, 'Human Rights, Social Justice and Peace' in August Schoon and Asbjörn Eide (eds), *Nobel Symposium VII: International Protection of Human Rights: Proceedings of the Seventh Nobel Symposium* (Almqvist & Wiksell 1967) (emphasis added).

[103] Jenks, *Social Justice in the Law of Nations* (n 102) 79.

[104] The periodic reporting system was founded in 1954, on the basis of Art 64 of the UN Charter, and later adapted to Art 56 of the UN Charter, until its discontinuance in 1973. See Diller, *Securing Dignity* (n 9) fns 445, 503, 517, 696, and accompanying text.

implementation to the extent that their mandates concerned the rights the UDHR recognizes. After adoption of the Covenants, the integrated system was replaced with reporting, through human rights treaty bodies and other UN Charter-based procedures. In principle, article 18 of the ESC Covenant provides for arrangements with the specialized agencies to report on 'observance of the provisions of the Covenant falling within the scope of their activities', and the Migrant Workers' Convention notably provides that state reports be transmitted to the ILO in order that the ILO may provide expertise regarding matters dealt with by the Convention 'that fall within the sphere of competence' of the ILO.[105]

In practice, the ILO participates in some UN Charter and treaty body activities by providing information on ILO standards and activities, in particular to ensure consistency with ILO standards in draft UN instruments. It also informs treaty body conclusions or observations relevant to the ILO's mandate.[106] Joint UN–ILO technical assistance has focused primarily on economic and social development, without specific reference to human rights standards, except for initiatives to which the ILO and the Office of the UN High Commissioner for Human Rights directly agreed.[107]

4. *Quo Vadis*: International Human Rights and International Labour Standards

In today's increasingly complex globalized economy, union power has declined from its apex a century ago, and the increasing attempts to prioritize workers' claims by reference to human rights reflect this trend. Human rights are based on principles of public law that have the potential to expand the application of labour law beyond its traditional private law roots. However, the degree of success or risk for

[105] International Convention on the Protection of the Rights of All Migrant Workers and Members of their Families, GA Res 45/158 of 18 December 1990, Art 74(2) and (5).

[106] Eg the ILO has reported mixed results of its inter-institutional dialogue with UN human rights bodies, which it attributed, among other factors, to a lack of knowledge about the ILO's work in human rights. Eg ILO, 'Cooperation with the United Nations in the Field of Human Rights' (1994) GB.261/LILS/8/6, paras 15, 19–21.

[107] The lack of integration of human rights and labour interventions at the country level reflects a general shortcoming in mainstream UN technical cooperation efforts. See eg Philip Alston, 'Ships Passing in the Night: The Current State of the Human Rights and Development Debate Seen Through the Lens of the Millennium Development Goals' (2005) 27 *Hum Rts Q* 755.

workers' claims in such innovation depends on how the two distinctive sets of rules are coordinated. Coordination should ensure that no harm is done to the specific obligations of member states under either set of rules. This goal requires reforms in ILO and UN approaches to account for the mandates, regulatory mechanisms, and actors involved.

The ILO is in a 'regulatory conversation'[108] with tripartite representatives of states that is influenced by many actors and processes at the local and transnational levels. With its activities affecting labour, employment, trade, development, and human rights, the ILO also engages with private and public interest groups; groups of states, like the G-20; business actors influencing governments; and other international organizations. These new actors do not share decision-making power in the tripartite structure yet their influence may create momentum toward new standards or toward reforms for methods of work.[109] To be achieved, the Social Justice Declaration's goal of 'decent work' requires innovative responses to significant changes in the world of work and, by its own terms, the Declaration calls on the ILO to inform and mobilize these new actors 'in consultation with' ILO constituents and to encourage other international organizations to contribute to the goal of decent work when their mandates affect labour. The ILO should use states' reports under articles 19 and 22 to help target national-level needs for assistance to achieve decent work, and should convert regulatory standards into operational guidance for business to apply.

In contrast to the ILO's tripartite dialogue with its members, the UN has expanded its own 'conversation' with states into areas central to the ILO's mandate and business actors in recent years. The UN Global Compact and the Guiding Principles on Human Rights and Business, which the UN Human Rights Council adopted,[110] incorporate fundamental principles and rights at work and other ILO human rights standards, but they do so without the ILO's tripartite mechanisms for interpretation and application. The follow-up systems to build state and corporate accountability under these soft-law mechanisms, to the extent they exist, are not tripartite in nature. Nor do they recognize the primacy of ILO machinery in interpreting and applying their provisions involving labour rights.

The mixed results to date from general ILO–UN human rights cooperation give cause for concern. In pursuing its business-related initiatives, the UN will be faced with situations that require the application of ILO standards or the exercise of the tripartite regulatory conversation. This dilemma will arise on issues involving labour standards in the informal economy, in employment relationships across supply chains, and other significant changes in the world of work. The UN efforts,

[108] Murray (n 76) 378, fn 67 (crediting Julia Black, Australian Society of Legal Philosophy Conference, 2003).

[109] For example, non-governmental organizations which were outside the ILO's system of representation wielded influence in the development of the Worst Forms of Child Labour Convention (No 182).

[110] UN Human Rights Council, Res 17/4 (16 June 2011).

if not adequately coordinated with the ILO, risk doing harm to existing ILO standards and encroaching on areas rightly within the ILO's standard-setting expertise, and possibly weakening the UN's own human rights foundation. Indeed, the implementation of the Guiding Principles risks a selective approach urging companies to exercise 'due diligence' to satisfy their human rights responsibilities and to focus on the 'most severe... human rights impacts'.[111] As such, the soft 'alternatives' may even dilute the indivisibility of international human rights and the corresponding duties of non-state actors that the UDHR recognizes.

Better coordination of UN and ILO action on human rights lies in recognition of common interests and in respect for differences in the content, scope, machinery, and actors engaged in each system. The UN should defer to the ILO's primary mandate for human rights in the world of work when selecting or developing new subjects for UN human rights standard-setting, whether in treaties or through soft-law means like the Guiding Principles on Human Rights and Business. In the past, coordination between UN and ILO instruments has been exemplary in such areas as the rights of indigenous peoples, the right to social security, and the rights of migrant workers. Similarly, when reviewing states' reports or individual complaints involving ILO issues, or developing interpretative comments, UN treaty bodies and Charter mechanisms should give due effect to ILO standards, using the meaning that the ILO supervisory machinery has given them. This would be the case, for example, where international labour standards apply to the situation in question, and human rights law does not articulate specific provisions in relation to the world of work. Where human rights law permits limitations that international labour standards for the right concerned do not recognize, the application of *lex specialis* should guide the action of states parties to the relevant ILO Conventions, to avoid prejudice to the greater rights granted under ILO law. Such coordination requires knowledge and understanding of the scope and aims of ILO's action in the field of human rights, including through ILO engagement in UN human rights bodies at a consistent and high level. The ultimate aim is for the many states that have ratified both ILO Conventions and human rights treaties to give full effect to their obligations under both systems in order to respect human rights at work.

Further Reading

Cooney S, 'Testing Times for the ILO: Institutional Reform for the New International Political Economy' (1998) 20 *Comparative Labor Law and Policy Journal* 365

[111] Office of the High Commissioner for Human Rights, *Guiding Principles on Business and Human Rights: Implementing the United Nations 'Protect, Respect and Remedy' Framework* (UN 2011) Principles 15 and 24 (in pertinent part) <http://www.ohchr.org/Documents/Publications/GuidingPrinciplesBusinessHR_EN.pdf> accessed 18 February 2013.

Diller J, 'Taking Account of Human Values in the International Economic Legal Order: Law and the Legal Counsel in the International Labour Organization' in Asif H Qureshi and Xuan Gao (eds), *International Economic Organizations and Law* (Kluwer Law 2012) 77–104
Fenwick C and Novitz T (eds), *Human Rights at Work: Perspectives on Law and Regulation* (Hart 2010)
Fudge J, 'The New Discourse of Labour Rights: From Social to Fundamental Rights?' (2007) 29 *Comparative Labor Law and Policy Journal* 29
Alston P (ed), *Labour Rights as Human Rights* (OUP 2005)
Lee E, 'The Declaration of Philadelphia: Retrospect and Prospect' (1994) 133 *Int'l Lab Rev* 467
Lorwin L, *The International Labor Movement: History, Policies, Outlook* (Harper 1953)
Shotwell JT (ed), *The Origins of the International Labour Organization*, 2 vols (Columbia UP 1934)
Webb S and Webb B, *History of Trade Unionism* (first published 1894, AMS Press 1976)

CHAPTER 13

THE PROTECTION OF MINORITIES UNDER THE AUSPICES OF THE LEAGUE OF NATIONS

PÉTER KOVÁCS

THE League of Nations Woodrow Wilson[1] envisaged was not intended to be a specialized (or a priori mandated) institution for considering the grievances of national, linguistic, or religious minorities. It only gained entitlement to examine these problems as a consequence of the Versailles Peace Conference (1919–20).

The principle of self-determination shaped the outcome of the conference. Although the drafters formulated the principle rather vaguely[2] in the Fourteen Points, it became a powerful weapon in media and war propaganda and was soon invoked as a *right* to self-determination or even a right to secede, thus contributing to the dismemberment of the double monarchy of Austria–Hungary. Even some of

[1] Note the last of Wilson's Fourteen Points: 'XIV. A general association of nations must be formed under specific covenants for the purpose of affording mutual guarantees of political independence and territorial integrity to great and small states alike.'

[2] The original texts contained a phrase guaranteeing only the 'opportunity to autonomous development' in reference to the peoples of Austria–Hungary and the Turkish Empire. 'President Woodrow Wilson's Fourteen Points' (*The Avalon Project*, 2008) <http://avalon.law.yale.edu/20th_century/wilson14.asp> accessed 7 October 2012.

Wilson's closest collaborators[3] advocated new borders and state-based assertions of such rights. The President himself tried to convince the other leaders of this need at the Peace Conference,[4] but ultimately the outcome of the deliberations on territorial claims generally confirmed the existing military occupation of the areas in question.

The drafters drew the borders of the newly created[5] or territorially enlarged[6] countries much more in accordance with historical memories and military status quo than existing ethnographical realities. According to Henry Kissinger, the outcome was that:

> At the end of this process, which was conducted in the name of self-determination, nearly as many people lived under foreign rule as during the days of the Austro-Hungarian Empire, except that now they were distributed across many more, much weaker, nation-states which, to undermine stability even further, were in conflict with each other.[7]

Moreover, these states generally adopted the nation-state philosophy and very often tried to take vengeance for prior history or putative historical injustices.

1. The Birth of the Mechanism in the Settlement of Peace after the First World War

In order to promote ratification of the peace treaties in the states emerging from the defeated Central Powers and to prevent these countries and their co-nationals, which now suddenly found themselves on the other side of a new boundary, from

[3] See the commentary of presidential advisor Colonel House. His remarks on the phrase 'opportunity to autonomous development' began: 'This proposition no longer holds. Instead we have [today] the following elements' to which he appended a list of minorities found within the various states, 'for whom... provision must be made' by adjusting boundaries on the basis of ethnicity. Colonel House, 'Interpretation of President Wilson's Fourteen Points' <http://www.mtholyoke.edu/acad/intrel/doc31.htm> accessed 7 October 2012 (text, numbering, and orthography, as in the above document).

[4] Even in 1919, Wilson imagined 'an equitable distribution of territories according to the race, the ethnographic character of the people inhabiting those territories'. Woodrow Wilson, 'Speech at the Plenary Session, 31 May 1919' in HW Temperly (ed), *History of the Peace Conference of Paris* (vol 5, Frowde & Hodder & Stoughton 1921) 130, cited by Thomas Smejkal, 'Protection in Practice: The Minorities Section of the League of Nations Secretariat, 1919–1934' (Senior Thesis, Columbia University 2010) 11.

[5] Poland (reborn after her partition in the eighteenth century among Prussia, Austria, and Russia) or Estonia, Latvia, and Lithuania.

[6] Eg Romania or the SHS-Kingdom (after 1929: Yugoslavia).

[7] Henry Kissinger, *Diplomacy* (Simon & Schuster 1994) 241.

basing their future only on the establishment and promotion of expansive territorial claims and thus threatening peace, some American[8] and European diplomats and politicians launched a campaign to grant the League of Nations competence over minority issues. It was a 'fragile compromise between American utopianism and European paranoia', as Kissinger puts it.[9]

This endeavour resulted in the creation of a complex mechanism which concerned neither Europe in its totality, nor the world as a whole; indeed, obligations whose observance the League monitored linked mostly Central European and Balkan countries. From the beginning, states—especially the newly created or territorially enlarged ones subject to such duties—sharply criticized this differential treatment. Reluctant to accept international control, they tried to avoid it inter alia by complaining about discrimination in favour of the Great Powers.

The French Prime Minister, George Clémenceau, had the task of convincing the reluctant countries that this differential approach was the price of their independence or territorial gain. In a famous letter that he sent to the Polish Prime Minister Paderewski, Clémenceau explained the legal reasoning with an explicit reference to well-established practice.

> In the first place, I would point out that this Treaty does not constitute any fresh departure. It has for long been the established procedure of the public law of Europe that when a state is created, or even when large accessions of territory are made to an established state, the joint and formal recognition by the Great Powers should be accompanied by the requirement that such state should, in the form of a binding international convention, undertake to comply with certain principles of government... The Principal Allied and Associated Powers are of the opinion that they would be false to the responsibility which rests upon them if on this occasion they departed from what has become an established tradition... There rests, therefore, upon these Powers an obligation, which they cannot evade, to secure in the most permanent and solemn form guarantees for certain essential rights which will afford to the inhabitants the necessary protection whatever changes may take place in the internal constitution.[10]

2. The Main Principles and Structures of the League of Nations Mechanism

Legal scholars of the period divided the relevant law of the League of Nations into material minority law, on the one hand, and formal minority law, on the other hand.

[8] For an expression of the importance of minority protection, see the paper of Colonel House (n 3).

[9] Kissinger (n 7) 240.

[10] (1919) 13 *AJIL Suppl* 416, 417–18.

The system's legal sources and, in particular, the relevant treaty law, comprised *material minority law*. These treaties were: (i) peace treaties with defeated countries (Hungary, Austria, Bulgaria, and Turkey);[11] (ii) treaties contracted by the Principal Allied and Associated Powers with enlarged or newly created countries (Poland, Czechoslovakia, Romania, Yugoslavia, and Lithuania);[12] and (iii) a few bilateral treaties (contracted, eg by Germany with Poland, Free City of Danzig with Poland, Austria with Czechoslovakia, and Sweden with Finland). Parties voluntarily placed the monitoring of some of the commitments[13] under the League of Nations, while other agreements,[14] although similar in content, were left in the context of improving neighbourly relations.

Some states proclaimed very similar obligations in the form of unilateral declarations or binding promises (Estonia, Latvia, Lithuania, Albania, and Iraq).[15] They generally made these promises because the parties considered them to be a precondition to admission into the League of Nations. The treaty contracted between Poland and the Allied and Associated Powers, in some cases modified with special clauses and generally linked to issues of autonomy, influenced or sometimes provided the basis for the commitments made.

The general commitments concerned mainly: (i) the right to citizenship and the right to opt in favor of the maintenance of the previous citizenship;[16] (ii) the prohibition of discrimination; (iii) freedom of religion and belief; and (iv). the right to,

[11] Signed with Austria in Saint Germain en Laye (10 September 1919), with Bulgaria in Neuilly (27 November 1919), with Hungary in Trianon (4 June 1920), and with Turkey first in Sèvres (20 August 1920, but not ratified) and finally in Lausanne (24 July 1923).

[12] Poland (28 June 1919), Czechoslovakia (10 September 1919), Romania (9 December 1919), Yugoslavia (10 September 1919), and Lithuania about the Memel-region (8 May 1924) signed the treaties. The Turkish peace treaties of Sèvres and Lausanne also imposed some obligations on Greece vis-à-vis her Muslim minority.

[13] Treaty between Sweden and Finland (27 June 1921); Treaty between Germany and Poland concerning Upper Silesia (15 May 1922).

[14] Treaty between Austria and Czechoslovakia (7 June 1920), amended later with an additional protocol (23 August 1920); Treaty between Free City of Danzig and Poland (9 November 1920); Treaty between Bulgaria and Greece (27 November 1919) and its protocol (29 September 1924); Treaty between Czechoslovakia and Poland (25 April 1925); Treaty between Romania and Yugoslavia (10 March 1933).

[15] Declaration by the government of Albania (2 October 1921); Declaration by the government of Lithuania (12 May 1922); Declaration by the government of Latvia (19 July 1923); Declaration by the government of Estonia (27 September 1923); Declaration by the government of Bulgaria (29 September 1924); Declaration by the government of Greece (29 September 1924); Declaration by the government of Iraq (30 May 1932).

[16] The philosophy underlying these rules was that persons living in the newly acquired territories should get *ipso facto* citizenship irrespective of their ethnic or religious identity. The rule was extremely important first and foremost in Orthodox countries where former citizenship was recognized only for Orthodox believers. If a person wished to maintain his previous citizenship, he had the right to express his will within two years (this was the right to opt in favour of the maintenance of previous citizenship which extended to the wife and minor children). The 'optant' could thus maintain his previous citizenship. He could then be obliged to leave the country of residence, but he could maintain his immobile property. In the 1920s several interstate disputes emerged from the fact that the agrarian reforms in these countries affected the real property of the 'optants', often formerly well-off aristocrats.

or in some cases the 'facilities' related to, the use of minority languages in school, in judicial or administrative proceedings, and also in daily communication. The special clauses concerned either various situations of territorial autonomy[17] or personal autonomy.[18]

The expression *formal minority law* covered the League of Nations' procedural rules for monitoring the implementation of commitments states made in favor of minorities. The minority treaties or declarations contained a rather general reference in their final articles to oversight by the Council of the League of Nations. Article 12 of the Polish treaty, for example, provided as follows:

> Poland agrees that the stipulations in the foregoing articles, so far as they affect persons belonging to racial, religious or linguistic minorities, constitute obligations of international concern and shall be placed under the guarantee of the League of Nations. They shall not be modified without the assent of a majority of the Council of the League of Nations. The United States, the British Empire, France, Italy and Japan hereby agree not to withold their assent from any modification in these Articles which is in due form assented to by a majority of the Council of the League of Nations.
>
> Poland agrees that any member of the Council of the League of Nations, shall have the right to bring to the attention of the Council any infraction, or danger of infraction, of any of these obligations, and that the Council may thereupon take such action and give such direction as it may deem proper and effective in the circumstances.

The above-mentioned commitments were fundamental law,[19] ie superior to simple legal acts parliaments adopted. Moreover, the commitments could not change without the approval of the Council, and they did not constitute internal affairs that fell under the exclusive domestic jurisdiction of the countries concerned. As the system evolved, the Council adopted several resolutions based upon detailed reports some of its members submitted,[20] and the General Assembly also contributed to the development of the infrastructure and functional complex.[21]

[17] The autonomy provided for in the Swedish-speaking Aland islands, and the Ruthenians in Czechoslovakia (never realized) included a regional parliament and a regional government according to the competences attributed to these territories. In contrast, the local judiciary and administration remained competences of the state.

[18] See eg the freedom of Jews to hold their religious holidays (in the Polish treaty), the religious and cultural autonomy of the kutzo-valach (Aromanian) community, the special status of the monks of the monastery at Mount Athos (Greece), or the religious and schooling autonomy of Saxon and Szekler public bodies in Romania (between the eleventh and nineteenth centuries, the Hungarian speaking Szeklers had enjoyed a special status of collective nobility in Transylvania, when it belonged to Hungary).

[19] Today, they would be called dispositions of constitutional value.

[20] See eg Resolution of 22 October 1920 of the Council, based on the so-called Tittoni report. See also the Resolution of 25 October 1920; the Resolution of 27 June 1921; the Resolution of 5 September 1923; or the Resolution of 10 June 1925, based on the Mello-Franco report.

[21] See eg the five resolutions adopted on 21 September 1922, on the basis of the Murray Report, as well as the Resolution of 26 September 1923.

The top political organ of the League of Nations (ie the Council) was primarily empowered to undertake the monitoring of state commitments, but the Permanent Court of International Justice (PCIJ), which—in contrast to today's UN institutional framework—was a special institution acting in cooperation with the League of Nations, rather than one of its permanent organs, could also contribute to the monitoring activity. First, it could deliver advisory opinions at the request of the Council, if the issues examined were interrelated with basic questions of international law.[22] Second, disputes over the implementation of the above-mentioned bilateral treaties could often be referred to the PCIJ, because many states accepted its jurisdictional competence over interstate disputes.[23] Generally, the minority treaties contained an explicit provision concerning the settlement of disputes arising out of the implementation of commitments. Third, after 1930, the Paris Agreement of Hungary, Romania, Yugoslavia, and Czechoslovakia, further empowered the PCIJ to act as an appellate body over the individual decisions of the Mixed Arbitral Tribunals that peace treaties established with the aim of verifying their implementation.[24]

2.1 The complaints procedure

A state or a person alleging a violation of his protected rights could file a complaint with the League of Nations. Before the Council decided to place the complaint on its agenda (and only members of the Council could add an item to the agenda), it

[22] The following advisory opinions concerned minority problems:
a. *Settlers of German Origin in Poland*;
b. *Acquisition of Polish Nationality*;
c. *Exchange of Greek and Turkish Populations*;
d. *Interpretation of the Greco-Turkish Agreement of 1 December 1926*;
e. *Greco-Bulgarian Communities*;
f. *Access to German Minority Schools in Upper Silesia*;
g. *Treatment of Polish Nationals and Other Persons of Polish Origin or Speech in the Danzig Territory*;
h. *Interpretation of the Greco-Bulgarian Agreement of 9 December 1927*;
i. *Minority Schools in Albania*;
j. *Consistency of Certain Danzig Legislative Decrees with the Constitution of the Free City*.

[23] The PCIJ gave the following judgments linked directly or indirectly to minority issues:
a. *Certain German Interests in Polish Upper Silesia* (*Germany v Poland*);
b. *Factory at Chorzów*;
c. *Rights of Minorities in Upper Silesia (Minority Schools)* (*Germany v Poland*);
d. *Interpretation of the Statute of the Memel Treaty* (*UK v Lithuania*);
e. *Administration of Prince von Pless* (*Germany v Poland*);
f. *Polish Agrarian Reform and German Minority* (*Germany v Poland*).

[24] The PCIJ gave the following judgment as an appellate body over the Mixed Arbitral Commission in agrarian/optant issue: *Pajzs, Czáky, and Esterházy Case (Hung v Yugo)*.

followed a special filtering procedure. Resolutions of the Council and also of the General Assembly set forth the criteria for filtering complaints.

An individual 'communication' had to exactly fulfil important formal requirements of admissibility, namely:

(i) the communication had to be linked to an international legal commitment of the state;[25]
(ii) the communication could not be anonymous;
(iii) the communication had to concern a precise legal or administrative problem and not be politically motivated or contain propagandistic language;
(iv) the communication had to deal with a matter that the Council had not decided on yet.

Surprisingly, the process did not make the prior exhaustion of local remedies a legal precondition, unlike the standard practice of human rights bodies today. Nevertheless, in practice, petitioners usually submitted complaints concerning issues which had not been resolved domestically.[26]

In order to avoid overburdening the Council, the League established the so-called 'committees of three' to filter complaints. The acting chairman of the Council presided, while the other two members of the committee were chosen from the members of the Council. The members could not come from a neighbouring country, the country against which the complaint was directed, or a country speaking the same language as the petitioner (referred to as a kin-state).

Experts of the Secretariat checked each communication for prima facie satisfaction of the criteria. For those that were satisfactory, the Council communicated with the government of the relevant state and asked it to reply within two months. If the government recognized its fault and provided an adequate remedy, the Council could adopt a decision ending the procedure.

If the respondent government did not agree with the factual or legal considerations in the petition, it presented its own arguments. The Council would then assign a committee of three to examine the respective documents, prepare a report, and

[25] As we have presented above, the minority instruments of the League of Nations were similar but not totally identical, especially concerning the eventual territorial or personal autonomies. On the one hand, the geographical scope of application could be different; most of the Central European and Balkan states were under obligation concerning the totality of their territory, but some states were only under partial obligation. For example, Germany was only under obligation vis-à-vis that part of the divided Upper Silesian territory which belonged to her as a result of the Versailles Treaty. On the other hand, even in Poland, the details of the commitments for the German speaking population of Upper Silesia and other minorities living elsewhere were not totally identical, and, as we have presented above, even the legal sources were not the same in this case.

[26] See in this sense the recapitulation of the history of the petitions of the Hungarian minority in Attila Varga, 'A jövő idejű múlt [Past in the Future]', in Balogh Artúr, *A kisebbségek nemzetközi védelme a kisebbségi szerződések és a békeszerződések alapján című kötethez [The international legal protection of minorities according to the minority and peace treaties]* (Kájoni Press 1997) 20.

send it to the government for observation. In the meantime, the petition and the government's reply were communicated *ex officio* to all the members of the Council; in addition, any member of the General Assembly could receive the materials upon request.

During the examination of the complaint, Eric Colban and Pablo de Azcarate, chief administrators of the Minorities Section of the Secretariat of the League of Nations, followed a practice of avoiding open and bitter discussions. Instead they held discreet talks with the aim of settling the issues with an equitable result—what today's international human rights mechanisms refer to as a friendly settlement or *règlement à l'amiable*.[27]

If the government accepted the draft report of the Council, usually because the Council adopted the government's position, the case ended. If the government proposed changes in the draft, the procedure continued. No time limits governed the procedure, nor were there limits on the number of drafts and responses. Governments could also request postponements. Thus, very often only ongoing monitoring emerged from the process, without the Council reaching a final decision on the merits of the case.

If the Council concluded that an important question of international law required interpretation before it could decide a case, the Council was entitled to submit the question to the PCIJ for a consultative opinion, after which the Council could continue its analysis of the matter. Generally, a consultative opinion accelerated and influenced the outcome of the procedure *de facto*, if not *de jure*.

3. The Perception of Minority Protection by States and Minorities: Dissatisfaction Followed by Paralysis

The subject matter of individual and state grievances in minority issues that the Council and the PCIJ examined mainly concerned: (i) land confiscation or restrictions on use, generally linked to agrarian reform policies whose execution was often perceived as manifestly discriminatory; (ii) harassment of parents who sought to have their children schooled in minority languages; (iii) problems of curriculum and textbooks; (iv) religious freedom, either in the context of the nationalization

[27] Smejkal (n 5) 28.

of the agricultural property of churches or respecting schools; (v) obstacles to the use of minority language in daily activities (commerce, advertisement, etc); and (vi) intervention in the functioning of autonomous administrations.[28] With respect to the last-mentioned concern, states often claimed that they acted for the preservation of public order against the abuse of minority rights.

While gaining political sympathy among the political and scientific elite of the period, the minority protection system of the League of Nations became the subject of increasing criticism. Minorities, their representatives, and individual petitioners first mainly complained about the length of the procedure. Second, they objected to the fact that their governments were in a much better position procedurally, because the petitioner did not enjoy a clear legal status as a subject of international law; consequently, the petitioner was not granted standing in the procedure and could be notified only informally about the status of the complaint. However, members of the Council, their collaborators, and eventually the staff of the Secretariat of the League of Nations, could inform the petitioner about the usefulness of sending additional memoranda in order to contest a given element of the government's position paper. A third criticism was that persons and countries having little knowledge of the Central European reality were involved in the procedure—even though this was the consequence of the desire for impartiality in the committees of three. Finally, critics also complained that only a small percentage of the submitted petitions ended in satisfaction and/or a final settlement.[29]

The governments of countries having lost territories (the 'kin-states') were even less satisfied; they often complained in favour of their 'optants' and against the agrarian reforms and undue interventions of the new governments in the personal choice of the individuals who sought recognition as members of the minority group. Both aspects were especially important in minority schooling; first, the agrarian reforms limited the economic capacity of minority elites to subsidize minority schools. States distributed nationalized parcels of land not only among local peasants but also among new settlers, which resulted in a change in the ethnic composition of the given territories. Second, government analysis of the etymological origin of names and forenames could shift into a source of pressure on individuals, to convince them that in fact they were the descendants of a 'germanized' Pole or of a 'magyarized' Slovak or Romanian. Once this succeeded, the state rewrote the names according to the spelling rules of the official language, and by this means could

[28] The German-speaking Memel Territory (today: Klaipeda) of Lithuania was often the source of complaints of such a nature.

[29] According to Varga, between 1925 and 1937, twenty-nine petitions concerned grievances of the Hungarian minority in Romania, twelve emanating from individuals, two from Hungarian churches, and fifteen from the Party of Hungarians of Romania. Of the twenty-nine, only three were settled at the end of the procedure, while three others were put on the agenda of the Council but did not reach a settlement. At the same time, fifty-three complaints were directed against Yugoslavia and 155 against Poland. Varga (n 26) 20.

reduce the number of children eligible for minority schooling to below the necessary threshold for continuing teaching in minority languages in schools.

The governments of the kin-states also discovered the persistent problem of the length of the procedure and the inherent handicap that only members of the Council could submit a proposal to include an item on the Council's agenda. If the respondent state was a member of the Council, its position became even more favourable compared to the 'kin-state,' and it could seek to make political alliances with other members afraid of the so-called hidden—but often only alleged—revanchism behind the petitions.

The governments whose minority policies were challenged before the Council were, of course, even less satisfied. They complained about the relativism of the system (ie that the Council of the League of Nations only continuously examined a dozen Central European and Balkan states). The allegations of discrimination were not heard or accepted during the first decade of the League of Nations, and this contributed to the paralysis of the system in the mid-1930s. It must be underlined, however, that the League of Nations did pay attention to the minority policy of the defeated states of the First World War. Hungary, for example, had to answer complaints about its policy towards its Jewish minority,[30] and in 1926 it ultimately found that it was better to promise the repeal of a criticized piece of legislation.

The Council also paid attention to Germany. Weimar-Germany cooperated rather loyally with the mechanism and cannot be blamed for the abuse of the right of petition for revanchist purposes. The situation changed dramatically with Hitler's arrival to power in 1933. After the promulgation of the racial laws of Nuremberg, the Council had to consider Franz Bernheim's petition. The new German policies directly affected him as a member of the Jewish community in German Upper Silesia. The Council expressed surprise when, in May 1933, the German delegation qualified the injuries Bernheim suffered, including a restriction on the exercise of some fields of the legal profession, and *numerus clausus* in high schools, as a local misinterpretation of the law or as an administrative error. In the autumn of 1933, the Council was ready to deal with German anti-Semitism. The Reich first declared this an intervention into domestic affairs and, some days later, decided to leave the League of Nations. Hitler also worked at and succeeded in radicalizing the German minority living abroad, instilling the Nazi ideology through the Volksbund movement his regime manipulated from Berlin.

In 1934, Poland decided that under the new circumstances, the state would no longer reply to petitions submitted about its minority policy, petitions which nearly always concerned the German-speaking minority of Silesia. Romania soon

[30] This was linked to the so-called *numerus clausus* law, an act the parliament adopted in 1920 that aimed to alter the composition of the intelligentsia by restricting the number of enrolled students to the percentage of their religious community in the national census. The evident and quasi-officially proclaimed aim was to diminish the number of Jews among students.

followed the Polish example (in 1935), and subsequently the minority protection system of the League of Nations became de facto dead, years before the paralysis of the organization itself.

4. The Funeral: The Memorandum of the Secretary General of the United Nations

During the talks of the 'Big Three' allied leaders in the Second World War, Franklin Roosevelt, Winston Churchill, and Josef Stalin made clear that they were thinking of creating a new world organization instead of revitalizing the League of Nations. The new organization could have taken over the League of Nations' minority protection system, but the leaders made a political decision not to place this in the hands of the United Nations. The publicly expressed reasons were somewhat contradictory. On the one hand, they claimed it to be useless, while on the other hand, they asserted that a special minority regime would be dangerous. They viewed such a mechanism as unnecessary because the new prohibition of genocide and racial discrimination, together with the protection of human rights, would suffice.[31] A minority regime by itself could be 'dangerous' because it might destabilize states, lead to intervention in domestic affairs, and hide territorial revanchism.[32]

It became clear surprisingly soon that the United Nations had nonetheless become a successor to the League in many more ways than originally thought, particularly with

[31] Eleanor Roosevelt, the first US ambassador to the UN and promoter of the Universal Declaration of Human Rights, and the French Nobel Peace Prize winner, René Cassin, were the prominent representants of this approach.

[32] (i) Manifestly, on the one hand. French and British politicians who wanted to make people forget their capitulation in Münich (1938) by the artificial assimilation of the policy of Weimar Germany in the League of Nations with Hitler's revanchism. France and the United Kingdom were also afraid that a comprehensive international minority protection system could hamper them in the stabilization of their power over colonies in Africa or Southeast Asia.

(ii) For special reasons, the territorially re-established Czechoslovakia, Yugoslavia, and Romania backed the French and British approach while in 1945/1946, they retaliated by attempts at ethnic cleansing, to the detriment of German and Hungarian minorities.

(iii) The Soviet Union tried to strengthen her position in the strategic game; while she took a stand for the inclusion of a minority clause in the Universal Declaration of Human Rights, she was against any form of strong international monitoring mechanism, and in this respect she evoked the legal doctrine of absolute sovereignty. She also opposed any special dispositions protecting minorities in the peace treaties.

respect to the system of mandates. When Italy and Austria reached an agreement[33] about the territorial autonomy of the German speaking inhabitants of South Tyrol and a quasi-protecting power status for Austria, the Economic and Social Council of the United Nations asked the Secretary General to prepare a comprehensive report about the status of the minority instruments of the League of Nations.

Trygve Lie's report[34] was negative; with the exception of the Swedish–Finnish treaty on Aaland autonomy, the report concluded that the minority agreements had ceased to exist, basically because of the fundamental changes in circumstances[35] and the terminating effect of war on bilateral treaties between belligerents.[36] Even if its legal reasoning is in part rather superficial,[37] states did not contest this memorandum. This acquiescence did not change even later when, eg Austria announced that because of a confirmation in the constitution of 1955, the Saint Germain Treaty vis-à-vis the Croatian and Slovenian minorities still bound the state.[38]

5. Our Common Heritage: Historical and Practical Lessons

The minority protection efforts of the League of Nations with their semi-successes and inherent problems are appreciated much more today than they were in the

[33] Gruber–De Gasperi Agreement (Paris Agreement) of 5 Sept 1946.

[34] Memorandum of the Secretary General, 'Study of the Legal Validity of Undertakings Concerning Minorities' (1951) UN Doc E/CN.4/367.

[35] The Secretary General referred eg to the changes in the ethnic configuration of territories, changes in borders, differences between the structure and the competences of the League of Nations and the United Nations, as well as the above-metioned legal approach of the UN, emphasizing human rights, interdiction and punishment of genocide, and racial discrimination.

[36] As long as Sweden could preserve her neutrality, WWII could not induce the termination of the Swedish–Finnish treaty.

[37] Eg contrary to the assumptions of the Memorandum (n 34), a considerable part of the German-speaking minority did stay in Poland, where they were legally recognized in the 1990s. As long as Turkey was also neutral in WWII, the effect of war vis-à-vis Greece was not so simple. In the 1970s and 1980s, sometimes Turkey and sometimes Greece referred to the continuity of these commitments. Before the International Court of Justice, Bosnia-Herzegovina also made reference to the validity of the minority commitments of the SHS Kingdom and Yugoslavia. *Application of the Convention on the Prevention and Punishment of the Crime of Genocide (Bosnia and Herzegovina v Yugoslavia)* 619–20.

[38] See Austria Constitution, chapter VIII, Art 149, [Old Laws] connected to that choice of minorities according to the minority and peace treaties: '(1) In addition to the present law, the following laws, with the modifications necessitated by this law, shall, within the meaning of Article 44 (1), be regarded as constitutional law: ... Section V of Part III of the Treaty of Saint-Germain of 10 Sep 1919'.

1930s, 1940s, or the 1950s. The contributions of the system became clearer when problems of the coexistence of different linguistic, ethnic, or religious communities repeatedly emerged in the latter part of the twentieth century. In a tragic way, when former African or Asian colonies became free and formed independent states, genocide and ethnic hatred, inspired by the desire to build up nation-states modelled after those from which they had seceded, often overshadowed the first decades of their existence.

In Europe, the progressive economic and political integration first in its Western half and then in its Central and Balkan parts, slowly brought about the critical reappraisal of the model of the nation-state. After the 1990s these countries became more open to renouncing the principle of national and linguistic uniformity or predominance, progressively permitting the establishment in Europe of something similar to the League of Nations.

Under the auspices of the Council of Europe, an instrumental complex founded on three pillars was built up for minorities: the European Convention on Human Rights, the European Charter for Regional or Minority Languages, and the Framework Convention for the Protection of National Minorities.[39] This complex embraces nearly the whole continent. In the United Nations, as well, important steps were taken with the General Assembly's adoption of two important resolutions, namely its Declaration on the Rights of Persons Belonging to National or Ethnic, Religious and Linguistic Minorities[40] and Declaration on the Rights of Indigenous Peoples.[41]

In substantive law, by the 1920s and 1930s, the PCIJ had already formulated the doctrine of freedom of choice of identity and the notion of affirmative action, ie that the adoption of special measures in favour of genuine social equality is compatible with the prohibition of discrimination. On identity, taking into account double identity and lacunas in the knowledge of literary languages, the PCIJ emphasized:

> If the authorities wish to verify or dispute the substance of a declaration by a person, it is very unlikely that in such cases they would be able to reach a result more nearly corresponding to the actual state of fact. Such a proceeding on the part of the authorities would, moreover, very easily assume in public opinion the aspect of a vexatious measure which would inflame political passions and would counteract the aims of pacification which are also at the basis of the stipulations concerning the protection of minorities.[42]

[39] See Péter Kovács: *International Law and Minority Protection: Rights of Minorities or Law of Minorities?* (Akadémiai 2000).

[40] UNGA, 'Declaration on the Rights of Persons Belonging to National or Ethnic, Religious and Linguistic Minorities' (18 December 1992) UN Doc A/Res/47/135.

[41] UNGA, 'Declaration on the Rights of Indigenous Peoples' (13 September 2007) UN Doc A/Res/61/295.

[42] *Rights of Minorities in Upper Silesia* (n 23) 34.

As the PCIJ rightly stated about the requirement of genuine equality:

There must be equality in fact as well as ostensible legal equality in the sense of the absence of discrimination in the words of the law.[43]

The idea underlying the treaties for the protection of minorities is to secure for certain elements incorporated in a State, the population of which differs from them in race, language or religion, the possibility of living peaceably alongside that population and cooperating amicably with it, while at the same time preserving the characteristics which distinguish them from the majority, and satisfying the ensuing special needs. In order to attain this object, two things were regarded as particularly necessary, and have formed the subject of provisions in these treaties. The first is to ensure that nationals belonging to racial, religious or linguistic minorities shall be placed in every respect on a footing of perfect equality with the other nationals of the State. The second is to ensure for the minority elements suitable means for the preservation of their peculiarities, their traditions and their national characteristics.[44]

The same logic can be found when examining the interpretive activity of the monitoring organs established by the United Nations, beginning with the Committee for the Elimination of all Forms of Racial Discrimination[45] and the International Committee on Civil and Political Rights.[46] The two UN resolutions[47] referred to above, and the Council of Europe's Charter[48] and Framework Convention[49] have also incorporated the affirmative action, or positive discrimination, principle. These legal instruments all emphasize that self-identification by the individual is the basis for deciding on minority membership, and the individual should be protected

[43] *German Settlers in Poland* (n 22) 24. [44] *Minority Schools in Albania* (n 22) 17.

[45] This monitoring Committee, the CERD, formulated in this sense its 'General Recommendation No 32: The Meaning and Scope of Special Measures in the International Convention on the Elimination of All Forms of Racial Discrimination' (24 September 2009) UN Doc CERD/C/GC/32.

[46] The Human Rights Committee (HRC) formulated its interpretation of the non-discrimination principle in HRC, 'General Comment No 18: Non-Discrimination' (10 November 1989) para 10 <http://www.unhcr.org/refworld/type,GENERAL,,,453883fa8,0.html> accessed 7 October 2012; HRC, 'General Comment No 23: The Rights of Minorities' (8 April 1994) UN Doc CCPR/C/21/Rev.1/Add.5, para 6.2.

[47] See in particular Art 8(3) of the Declaration on the Rights of Persons Belonging to National or Ethnic, Religious and Linguistic Minorities: 'Measures taken by States to ensure the effective enjoyment of the rights set forth in the present Declaration shall not *prima facie* be considered contrary to the principle of equality contained in the Universal Declaration of Human Rights.'

See also Art 21 of the Declaration on the Rights of Indigenous Peoples:

1. Indigenous peoples have the right, without discrimination, to the improvement of their economic and social conditions, including, *inter alia*, in the areas of education, employment, vocational training and retraining, housing, sanitation, health and social security.

2. States shall take effective measures and, where appropriate, special measures to ensure continuing improvement of their economic and social conditions....

[48] Article 7(2) of the European Charter for Regional or Minority Languages.

[49] Article 4(2)–(3) of the Framework Convention for the Protection of National Minorities.

against forced assimilation, as well as against discriminatory treatment, as a result of the personal choice.[50]

While these specific measures are significant in their own right, the most important contribution of the League of Nations' system may be as a precursor and critical contributor to the general evolution of international human rights mechanisms; one can easily see the logic and the main elements of the former filtration system in the procedures of treaty bodies like the Committee established under the International Covenant of Civil and Political Rights of the United Nations (1966), as well as those of the regional conventions on human rights.

A number of lessons drawn from the experience of the League of Nations, both its successes and failures, have helped shape modern human rights law. First, the facts that the norms related to minorities were nearly the same in all respective cases (with the exception of the local 'extras' described above) and that organs of an international organization undertook the monitoring, represented a radically different approach from the pre-League practice of drafting special rules attributing compliance monitoring to a single protector country or to a great power. The experience of the League of Nations helped states realize that sovereignty can coexist with the acceptance of common rules promoting and protecting the individual's position vis-à-vis state authority.

Another legacy of the League of Nations minority system arose in response to the many criticisms it faced because of the unclear position of the individual. The limited procedural status that was afforded individuals is not surprising, given that contemporary scholars did not recognize individuals as a subject of public international law, and states were even less ready to share their privileged status with any other actor. The experience of the League of Nations contributed to the metamorphosis of international law with respect to the legal status of individuals.

Although even after the Second World War, the necessity of recognizing the individual as a special subject of international law still divided UN member states, governments opposing the concept had to give way during the progressive establishment of a complex mechanism for the protection of human rights. The new treaties adopted for the protection of human rights contained well-detailed rules concerning the individual's procedural capacity, even if the regimes (at least at the UN) were generally of an optional nature. It became clear for scholars, and probably for politicians as well, that the recognition of a certain international legal capacity

[50] See Art 3(2) of the Declaration on the Rights of Persons Belonging to National or Ethnic, Religious and Linguistic Minorities (n 45): 'No disadvantage shall result for any person belonging to a minority as the consequence of the exercise or non-exercise of the rights set forth in the present Declaration.' See also Art 3(1) of the Framework Convention for the Protection of National Minorities (n 47): 'Every person belonging to a national minority shall have the right freely to choose to be treated or not to be treated as such and no disadvantage shall result from this choice or from the exercise of the rights which are connected to that choice.'

for individuals is not only compatible with the need for preserving integrity, stability, and order at home, but it can also contribute to better or more far-reaching interstate cooperation. In this way—but also due to the bitter experiences of totalitarianism—the present-day international monitoring system can be considered part of the legacy of the League of Nations.

The one-sided approach of the League of Nations was also transformed. While it may appear at first glance that double standards entirely disappeared, close examination reveals that underlying divisions can still be discovered in the United Nations' human rights mechanisms, albeit in a more elegant and more sophisticated manner. The UN Charter proclaimed a general rule requiring observance of human rights for all member states, but governments have retained discretion in choosing among human rights treaties and deciding on the degree of scrutiny they will accept, from agreeing to rather weak monitoring (typically through filing periodic reports) to accepting stronger mechanisms (interstate or, most effectively, individual complaints). Many of the great powers who objected to or failed to accept obligations towards minorities in the League of Nations system have also abstained from ratifying or acceding to strong human rights treaties and their protocols. Universality of equal obligations is far from accomplished.

The current human rights regimes have largely rectified another perceived failure of the League of Nations system. At the League, the involvement of the top political organ (the Council) purportedly politicized the monitoring itself. Governments of permanent or elected members of these organs generally based their voting and decisions on political considerations and opportunism—at least equally important in their way of thinking as purely legal assessments. In contrast, the United Nations and regional human rights bodies base their decisions mostly on reports of either civil society or independent experts. An organization's primary 'executive' organ (the Security Council or its regional equivalent) typically takes action only after having seen a persistent failure to correct the discovered faults, or in cases of extreme urgency.

In retrospect, the foremost consequence of the League of Nations minority protection system in the international legal order is most certainly the changed perception of what issues belong 'solely within the domestic jurisdiction' of a state. The fact that not all of the League of Nations member countries were under minority commitments did not undermine the legal perception that minority issues in those states that *had* made commitments belonged to the realm of common concern, where standard-setting and monitoring were to be exercised. Subsequently, even though the minority issue was to some extent a taboo topic in the early years of the United Nations, the fact that the UN Charter contains human rights commitments for all member states means that human rights matters do not fall within the UN Charter provision barring intervention in 'matters which are essentially within the domestic jurisdiction of any state'. Thus, emerging from the League of Nations precedents, human rights generally has become a matter of legitimate international concern, with the result that the international community can monitor how a state behaves towards those within its jurisdiction.

To sum up, the protection of national minorities under the auspices of the League of Nations undoubtedly contributed to the evolution of international human rights law. It is an early example of how a multilateral framework could institutionalize this issue. Even if it left behind bitter remembrances, partly due to wilful misinterpretations as an element of post-War policies of the former Allies who sought to have their policy of appeasement in 1938/1939 forgotten, it should be considered with all its advantages and disadvantages, strengths and weaknesses. Today, universal and regional approaches are trying to benefit from these experiences in order to contribute to the standardization of a law-based protection system where different linguistic communities can live together while each preserves its own identity.

Further Reading

de Azcarate P, *League of Nations and National Minorities: An Experiment* (Eileen E Brook (tr), Carnegie Endowment for International Peace 1945)

Fink C, 'The League of Nations and the Minorities Question' (1995) 157(4) *Wld Aff* 197

Kovács P, *International Law and Minority Protection: Rights of Minorities or Law of Minorities?* (Akadémiai 2000)

Lauren PG, *The Evolution of International Human Rights: Visions Seen* (U Pennsylvania Press 1998) 82–138

Mazower M, 'Minorities and the League of Nations in Interwar Europe' (1997) 126 *Daedalus* 47

Smejkal T, 'Protection in Practice: The Minorities Section of the League of Nations Secretariat, 1919–1934' (Senior Thesis, Columbia University 2010)

Szalay-Sándor E, 'The Role of the League of Nations and the UN in the Protection of Minorities under International Law' (1999) *Minorities Research* 1, 108–22 <http://www.hhrf.org/kisebbsegkutatas/mr_01/cikk.php?id=1180> accessed 7 October 2012

PART III

STRUCTURAL PRINCIPLES

CHAPTER 14

HUMAN DIGNITY

PAOLO G CAROZZA

HUMAN dignity is one of the most pervasive and fundamental ideas in the entire corpus of international human rights law. From 1948 to the present, the formal instruments of international human rights make consistent reference to dignity. Interpretive and adjudicative bodies employ the concept regularly. Doctrinal commentary and scholarly literature invoke and advance its use. For these reasons, one cannot deny that human dignity is properly regarded as a basic principle of international human rights law. At the same time, the meaning and use of human dignity in contemporary international human rights law is a subject of much debate and is open to considerable controversy, primarily because of the multiplicity of different possible understandings of dignity that diverge from and sometimes contradict one another. As a consequence, the practical usefulness of the principle of human dignity in international human rights law is contested.

While many scholars applaud human rights law's reliance on the idea of human dignity[1] and urge even greater development of its role, especially in judicial

[1] Eg Jeremy Waldron, 'Dignity, Rank, and Rights: The 2009 Tanner Lectures at UC Berkeley' (2009) NYU School of Law, Public Law & Legal Theory Research Paper Series Working Paper No 09-50 <http://ssrn.com/abstract=1461220> accessed 3 February 2013; Jeremy Waldron, 'Dignity, Rights, and Responsibilities' (2010) Public Law & Legal Theory Research Paper Series Working Paper No 10-83 <http://ssrn.com/abstract=1710759> accessed 3 February 2013.

interpretation,[2] other commentators are less enthusiastic. Critics see it as a vacuous term that has no stable meaning and which can be given any content.[3] The alleged absence of meaning in turn raises concerns about the degree of discretion that an invocation of human dignity provides to judges and about the degree of ideological manipulation to which the concept can be subject.[4] Some judges of the European Court of Human Rights have even suggested that human dignity is therefore a 'dangerous' concept.[5] However, relatively little of the enormous and rapidly expanding philosophical literature on human dignity has dealt directly with the meaning and use of the principle in international human rights law—a paradox, given the foundational and structural place that the recognition of human dignity has in the canon of human rights treaties and other instruments.

Part of the difficulty of delineating, and reaching greater consensus on, the meaning and implications of human dignity in international human rights law is that the idea refers to both a foundational premise of human rights and also to a principle having an impact on the way that specific human rights are interpreted and applied. Human dignity, as it is used in international human rights law, is, in the first instance, an ontological claim about the *status* of human persons: an affirmation that every human being has an equal and inherent moral value or worth. Interrelated with this status claim is the idea of human dignity in international human rights law, as a normative and meta-legal *principle* affirming that all human beings are entitled to have others respect this status of equal worth (including, in particular, the state in its law and policy). As an affirmation of the equal moral value of all human beings, the idea of human dignity has emerged as the single most widely recognized and frequently invoked basis for grounding the idea of human rights generally, since the mid-twentieth century. As a principle to be employed in the interpretation and application of specific rights, human dignity also occupies a commonly accepted central place, although it can provoke greater disagreement—especially in its more extensive use in areas beyond a small core of specific rights relating to physical integrity.

[2] Eg Christopher A Bracey, 'Dignity in Race Jurisprudence' (2005) 7 *U Pa J Const L* 669, 719; Gay Moon, 'From Equal Treatment to Appropriate Treatment: What Lessons from Canadian Equality Law on Dignity and on Reasonable Accommodation teach the United Kingdom?' (2006) 6 *EHRLR* 695.

[3] Justin Bates, 'Human Dignity—An Empty Phrase in Search of Meaning?' (2005) 10 *JR* 165; Mirko Bagaric and James Allen, 'The Vacuous Concept of Dignity' (2006) 5 *JHR* 257; Neomi Rao, 'On the Use and Abuse of Dignity in Constitutional Law' (2008) 14 *Colum J Eur L* 201.

[4] Bates (n 3) 165; John Harris, *Clones, Genes, and Immortality: Ethics and the Genetic Revolution* (OUP 1998) 31; Paolo G Carozza, 'Il Traffico dei Diritti Umani nell'Età Post-Moderna' ('Trafficking in Human Rights in the Post-Modern Age') in Luca Antonini (ed), *Il Traffico Dei Diritti Insaziabili* (*Trafficking in Insatiable Rights*) (Rubbettino 2007); Christopher McCrudden, 'Human Dignity and Judicial Interpretation of Human Rights' (2008) 19 *EJIL* 655.

[5] *Vereinigung Bildender Künstler v Austria*, Spielman and Jebens dissent, para 9.

1. The Function of Human Dignity in the Universal Declaration of Human Rights

The central importance of the status and principle of human dignity in international human rights law has been evident, at least since the drafting and adoption of the Universal Declaration of Human Rights (UDHR). The five references to human dignity the short text of the Declaration contains provide a unifying key to that document's vision of human rights. The preamble affirms that 'recognition of the inherent dignity and of the equal and inalienable rights of all members of the human family is the foundation of freedom, justice and peace in the world', and also (echoing the Charter of the United Nations) 'reaffirm[s]...faith in fundamental human rights, in the dignity and worth of the human person and in the equal rights of men and women'. Article 1, an introduction to the subsequent specification of rights in the first part of the document, states that 'All human beings are born free and equal in dignity and rights'. Similarly, Article 22, the *chapeau* to the second section of specified rights, provides that 'Everyone...is entitled to realization...of the economic, social and cultural rights indispensable for his dignity'.[6] Finally, in connection with the right to work in Article 23(3), the Declaration claims that 'Everyone who works has the right to just and favourable remuneration ensuring for himself and his family an existence worthy of human dignity'. In sum, dignity serves both to indicate the foundation of rights in the Universal Declaration (the status of equal and inherent human worth) and also to highlight some of the normative implications of that status (eg the equal rights of men and women; the realization of certain social and material needs; the right to work and to be paid adequately to support a family). This deliberate construction of the Declaration around the status and principle of human dignity clearly situates the document in the 'large family of dignity-based rights instruments that were adopted after the Second World War'.[7]

[6] See generally Janelle M Diller, *Securing Dignity and Freedom through Human Rights: Article 22 of the Universal Declaration of Human Rights* (Martinus Nijhoff 2012).

[7] Mary Ann Glendon, *A World Made New: Eleanor Roosevelt and the Universal Declaration of Human Rights* (Random House 2002) 175. As Glendon goes on to explain, 'most of the constitutions and treaties of the latter half of the twentieth century belong to the dignitarian family', citing in particular the highly influential German Basic Law of 1949 (at 263). In fact, much of the development of the idea of human dignity in international human rights law is attributable to its widespread and more thickly developed status as a constitutional principle in a wide variety of legal systems, starting with the Irish Constitution of 1937. Samuel Moyn, 'The Secret History of Constitutional Dignity' (2012) Paper <https://papers.ssrn.com/sol3/papers.cfm?abstract_id=2159248> accessed 3 February 2013. Although the present chapter will focus on the place of human dignity specifically in international human rights law, rather than on its role in constitutional law, the analytical separation of the two dimensions is admittedly somewhat artificial, as they inevitably interrelate and influence one another. See eg Paolo

Before tracing the further development of the status and principle of human dignity in subsequent human rights instruments, it is helpful to pause and ask *why* dignity played such a vital role in the framing of the Universal Declaration. Part of the answer undoubtedly lies in dignity's capacity to evoke an ideal that could have broad and enduring application and appeal, and which so clearly rejects the mid-twentieth century totalitarian ideologies that in both theory and practice massively denied the equal moral worth of all human beings. Another significant part of the explanation, however, lies in human dignity's capacity to signify a shared foundational commitment that peoples belonging to a wide range of different cultural, ethical, religious, and political traditions could accept.

As has been well documented, the framers and first proponents of the Universal Declaration were acutely conscious of the difficulty of articulating a list of rights capable of securing universal acceptance in a pluralistic world. The generation of jurists, scholars, and politicians who drew up and secured approval for the Universal Declaration of Human Rights all came to the discussion with profoundly different first principles concerning the nature and destiny of the human person, the authority of the state, the meaning of justice, and the role of law. Around the table, there were secular Western liberals and committed communists, Islamic scholars and Catholic intellectuals, and Jewish lawyers and democratic socialist diplomats. Their consensus on a declaration of basic human rights was not based on substantive agreement about foundations, nor on the discovery and acceptance of a transcendent global ethic that unified them. Rather, it was based on a more modest and limited aim: to reach a practical agreement on the articulation of specific human rights, while setting aside the goal of attaining any thicker consensus about the origins of those rights and why we should regard them as pertaining to human persons.[8] Whenever he was asked how it was possible that adherents of such radically opposed philosophies could reach agreement on a declaration of fundamental rights, Jacques Maritain—a Thomist philosopher and French diplomat who was heavily involved in the adoption of the Universal Declaration of Human Rights—liked to say, 'Yes, we agree about the rights, but on condition that no one asks us why. It is with the "why" that all the disagreements begin'.[9]

This context provides an important insight into the structural function that dignity plays in the Universal Declaration and, subsequently, in international human

G Carozza, '"My Friend Is a Stranger": The Death Penalty and the Global Ius Commune of Human Rights' (2003) 81 *Tex L Rev* 1031, 1069. For an overview of the status and principle of human dignity within comparative constitutional law, see Paolo G Carozza, 'Human Dignity in Constitutional Adjudication' in Tom Ginsburg and Rosalind Dixon (eds), *Comparative Constitutional Law* (Edward Elgar 2011).

[8] Glendon (n 7) 175; Johannes Morsink, *The Universal Declaration of Human Rights: Origins, Drafting, and Intent* (U Pennsylvania Press 1999).

[9] Jacques Maritain, 'Introduction' in United Nations Educational, Scientific and Cultural Organization, *Human Rights: Comments and Interpretations* (Greenwood Press 1949) 9.

rights law more generally; it represents the intersection of a variety of different ethical traditions, each of which provides a distinct grounding for the human rights listed in the document, but all of which can converge on a limited and general affirmation of the equal moral worth of all human persons. It therefore serves as the indicator of the minimal degree of overlapping consensus regarding the foundations of human rights that is necessary for the project of a universal declaration and international law to proceed. The capaciousness of the word 'dignity' allows it to represent an affirmation belonging to a wide array of different traditions, while the generality of the term, standing alone without further elaboration, does not decisively signify any one of those traditions.

Seen from a slightly different angle, this also means that 'human dignity' within the Universal Declaration does not by itself have a clear, univocal meaning, but is subject to a multiplicity of different (and to some extent even mutually contradictory) understandings with varied historical roots. The word's origin is Latin, but ancient Romans primarily used it in a context that referred to the respect due to those who were in an elevated social status—for example, senators had *dignitas*, but women, slaves, and common men did not. It was a term that drew status distinctions between people, rather than suggesting universal moral equality. In contrast, the Judeo-Christian notion of human dignity, deriving from the traditional belief that man is made in the image of God, identifies an inherent worth in every individual. Kantian philosophy is often closely associated with discussions of human dignity, particularly those contemporary understandings of dignity that place a heavy emphasis on individual autonomy and on not treating a person merely as a means to other ends. Other Enlightenment philosophers, such as Rousseau, have bequeathed a slightly different emphasis to the idea of dignity, associating it with more communitarian and republican ideals. Outside of European and Mediterranean traditions, human dignity has been linked to other concepts, like *ubuntu* or *dharma*, which belong to distinctive philosophical, religious, and cultural traditions; they may arguably serve in their particular contexts as functional analogues to the idea of human dignity, or as alternative ways of giving content and meaning to human dignity.[10] The point is not to catalogue all possible sources of the idea of dignity, and even less to enter into their details or merits, but simply to highlight both that dignity's roots are highly diverse and emerge from traditions that represent deeply divergent ideas about *why* human persons have an inherent value that demands the respect of others (the status of dignity), and what respecting the moral worth of another entails (the principle of dignity).

[10] See eg Thaddeus Metz, 'Human Dignity, Capital Punishment, and an African Moral Theory: Toward a New Philosophy of Human Rights' (2010) 9 *JHR* 81. See also the Indian Supreme Court's very interesting discussion of India in *M Nagraj v Union of India*, philosophizing at length about the relationship between Indian conceptions of human dignity and the German understanding of dignity, and the extent to which German ideals thus inform their decision.

The narrative of human dignity in international human rights law, from the Universal Declaration onwards, can be understood to be an ongoing story about this dual character of the idea. On the one hand, it signifies a wide consensus about the status of human dignity as the generic foundation of human rights across the pluralistic landscape of the human family. On the other hand, almost paradoxically it contains within itself the very diversity of understandings it seeks to overcome or set aside. That internal, structural, and to some extent even deliberate, indeterminacy of the source and implications of human dignity becomes more apparent the more one seeks to develop and expand upon the requirements of human dignity as a normative principle.

2. Dignity and Human Rights in Other International Instruments

Subsequent international treaties and declarations on human rights have consistently followed the Universal Declaration's dignitarian framework for human rights. A few examples suffice to illustrate what is a nearly exceptionless canonical inclusion of references to dignity. Among the core universal human rights treaties, the two International Covenants[11] both recognize that 'these rights derive from the inherent dignity of the human person', and each refers to dignity in relationship to certain specific rights thereafter.[12] The 1965 Convention on the Elimination of all Forms of Racial Discrimination invokes dignity (in connection with equality, in particular) three times in its preamble, as does the 1979 Convention on the Elimination of All Forms of Discrimination against Women. The 1984 Convention Against Torture affirms that 'the equal and inalienable rights of all members of the human family... derive from the inherent dignity of the human person',[13] while the 1989 Convention on the Rights of the Child has no fewer than eight separate references to human dignity.[14] Even more recently, the 2006 Convention on the Rights of Persons with Disabilities uses human dignity nine times in its preamble and substantive articles.[15]

[11] International Covenant on Civil and Political Rights (ICCPR), International Covenant on Economic, Social and Cultural Rights (ICESCR).

[12] See eg ICCPR, Art 10; ICESCR, Art 13.

[13] Convention against Torture and Other Cruel, Inhuman or Degrading Treatment or Punishment, preamble.

[14] Preamble and Arts 23, 28, 37, 39, 40.

[15] Preamble and Arts 1, 3(a), 8(1)(a), 16(4), 24(1)(a), 25(d). Tellingly, the original working title of this treaty was the International Convention on the Protection and Promotion of the Rights and Dignity of Persons with Disabilities.

The regional human rights treaties follow a similar pattern. Both the Inter-American instruments and the African ones make repeated use of the idea of dignity throughout their texts. The European Convention on Human Rights is the only major treaty, and one of the very few international human rights instruments of any kind, to make no mention of dignity. The European Convention is, however, expressly founded on the Universal Declaration of Human Rights, which the preamble invokes repeatedly as the source of the rights that the Convention includes. Other human rights instruments that the Council of Europe has adopted make ample use of human dignity, including, most notably, the Convention on Human Rights and Biomedicine.[16] Moreover, as will be seen below, the idea of dignity has become a significant part of European human rights case law, notwithstanding its absence from the text of the treaty; the European Court has gone so far as to declare that 'the very essence of the Convention is respect for human dignity'.[17]

Consistent with the text of the Universal Declaration of Human Rights, the most common use of the idea of human dignity in other human rights instruments is as a generic reference to the foundation and source for the human rights that are thereafter more explicitly articulated. This is true through different time periods, across various subject areas, and spanning all parts of the world.

The Convention on the Rights of Persons with Disabilities, however, seems to mark a certain shift in this respect. Although saturated with references to dignity, it conspicuously does not repeat the standard phrase that rights are 'derived from' the inherent dignity of the human person. Instead, it consistently refers to respect for the 'rights and dignity' of persons with disabilities, suggesting implicitly that they are separate matters, instead of human dignity being a way of grounding human rights as a whole. One also finds that Article 3 lists respect for dignity among the general principles of that, alongside individual autonomy and independence, participation in society, respect for difference, equality, accessibility, and evolving capacities; that is, dignity is presented as one among a list of basic animating principles of the treaty, rather than the main overarching and integrating principle of the whole. In a certain sense, then, that treaty uses dignity more frequently, but less comprehensively, than is seen in previous treaties. It is too early to tell whether the approach of the Convention on the Rights of Persons with Disabilities will, in retrospect, be a watershed in the invocation of dignity in future human rights treaties.

For the present, almost all of the major human rights treaties go beyond recognizing the foundational role of the status of human dignity, to link the principle of human dignity to other principles or to specific rights. One use of dignity in this way is in its relationship to physical and personal integrity, particularly in situations

[16] Full title: Convention for the Protection of Human Rights and Dignity of the Human Being with regard to the Application of Biology and Medicine.

[17] *Goodwin v United Kingdom*, para 90; *Pretty v United Kingdom*, para 65; *VC v Slovakia*, para 105. See also *SW v United Kingdom*; *CR v United Kingdom*, para 44.

where persons are deprived of liberty. Article 10(1) of the ICCPR requires that all persons deprived of liberty 'be treated with... respect for the inherent dignity of the human person'. The American Convention on Human Rights uses virtually identical language, while Article 5 of the African Charter of Human and Peoples' Rights ties a general reference to 'the dignity inherent in a human being' to the prohibition of 'slavery, slave trade, torture, cruel, inhuman or degrading punishment and treatment'. Other treaties, including the Convention on the Rights of the Child[18] and the International Convention on the Protection of the Rights of All Migrant Workers and Members of Their Families,[19] similarly call for respecting dignity in contexts where persons are deprived of their liberty or subjected to punishment of any sort.

Another connection often found in the human rights treaties is between dignity and equality. This is, in part, merely an expression of the implicit content of the ontological claim about the status of human persons (that they have *equal* moral worth), and in part results from the very prosaic fact that many of the human treaties cite the Charter of the United Nations in their preambles. In its own preamble, the Charter refers to 'faith in fundamental human rights, in the dignity and worth of the human person, [and] in the equal rights of men and women'. The Universal Declaration's reference to all human beings being 'born... equal in dignity and rights'[20] also receives frequent mention in subsequent instruments' preambles. Other indications of the close connection between human dignity and equality go beyond mere repetition of the Charter and UDHR. For instance, the Convention on the Elimination of All Forms of Discrimination against Women recalls that 'discrimination against women violates the principles of equality of rights and respect for human dignity'.[21] The Convention on the Rights of Persons with Disabilities states even more forcefully and clearly that, 'discrimination against any person on the basis of disability is a violation of the inherent dignity and worth of the human person'.[22]

While equality and physical integrity are the rights that the major international human rights instruments most commonly link in an explicit way to the principle of human dignity, a range of other rights can also be found to be tied overtly to dignity, in one treaty or another. The American Convention on Human Rights provides that 'Everyone has the right to have his honor respected and his dignity recognized'.[23] More than one treaty specifies that fulfillment of the right to education requires particular respect for human dignity.[24] The Convention on the Rights of the Child codifies the need to ensure that criminal processes respect the human dignity of children,[25] and the same treaty mandates particular respect for the dignity of disabled children.[26] The Convention on Migrant Workers and their Families

[18] Articles 28, 37. [19] Article 17. [20] Article 1.
[21] Preamble. [22] Preamble. [23] Article 11(1).
[24] ICESCR, Art 13; Convention on the Rights of Persons with Disabilities, Art 24.
[25] Article 40. [26] Article 23.

(fittingly, in light of the basic purposes of the treaty) links dignity to work conditions,[27] while the Convention on the Rights of Persons with Disabilities (also reflecting one of the core concerns of that treaty) ties the quality of healthcare for persons with disabilities explicitly to the recognition of their dignity.[28] The African Charter, interestingly and uniquely, links dignity to certain collective rights and interests, in addition to individual ones, by referring in its preamble to the goal of 'the total liberation of Africa, the peoples of which are still struggling for their dignity and genuine independence'.

One notable absence in all of the major international human rights treaties is any 'right to dignity' in and of itself. Because several constitutional systems do recognize a right to dignity as such (most prominently Germany and Israel),[29] considerable jurisprudence and scholarly discussion has addressed the meaning, scope, and limits of such a right in constitutional contexts.[30] However, that discussion has not yet entered directly into international human rights discourse in any substantial way.

3. The Further Specification of the Principle of Human Dignity

Beyond its general invocation as the foundation for claims of human rights generically, the principle of human dignity (ie the requirement, including in law and policy, that human beings always be treated with respect for their equal and inherent moral value) has a bearing on the interpretation and application of specific rights, as evidenced in the decisions and judgments of a variety of international human rights bodies.[31]

The most consistent and widespread invocation of human dignity by international tribunals (and other organs with interpretive roles in international human rights law) arises in connection with the prohibition on cruel, inhuman, and degrading treatment. In fact, the European Court of Human Rights, notwithstanding the absence of any reference to human dignity in the European Convention, first introduced the principle into its jurisprudence in a 1978 decision that found the corporal

[27] Article 70. [28] Article 25.

[29] Article 1 GG; Israel Ministry of Foreign Affairs, Basic Law: Human Dignity and Liberty (17 March 1992) <http://www.mfa.gov.il/MFA/MFAArchive/1990_1999/1992/3/Basic%20Law-%20Human%20 Dignity%20and%20Liberty-> accessed 4 February 2013.

[30] See eg Otto Lagodny, 'Human Dignity and Its Impact on German Substantive Criminal Law and Criminal Procedure' (1999) 33 *Is LR* 575.

[31] The examples that follow are meant to be illustrative rather than exhaustive of the loose and broad categories of cases referring to dignity.

punishment of a child in school to be a violation of Article 3. The Strasbourg Court observed that:

> [A]lthough the applicant did not suffer any severe or long-lasting physical effects, his punishment—whereby he was treated as an object in the power of the authorities—constituted an assault on precisely that which it is one of the main purposes of Article 3 (art. 3) to protect, namely a person's dignity and physical integrity.[32]

Since then, the European Court has emphasized that treatment or punishment is 'considered to be "degrading" when it humiliates or debases an individual, showing a lack of respect for, or diminishing, his or her human dignity'.[33] The Inter-American Court of Human Rights makes similarly sweeping assertions that cruel, inhuman, and degrading treatment violates persons' human dignity.[34]

Specifying in more detail the generic connection between the principle of human dignity and the prohibition on cruel, inhuman, and (especially) degrading treatment, various human rights bodies have used human dignity to help explain or justify why some particular forms of punishment or conditions of detention must be prohibited. The Inter-American Court, going beyond the bare affirmation that 'persons detained have the right to live in prison conditions that are in keeping with their dignity as human beings',[35] has held that prolonged isolation and deprivation of communication violate a detainee's 'inherent dignity as a human being',[36] while excessive force in controlling inmate behaviour 'constitutes an assault on the dignity of the person'.[37] Dignity is compromised also by prohibiting persons in detention from using their native language[38] and by forcing prison inmates to be naked for extended periods.[39] The case law of the European Court of Human Rights regards both the use of excessive force against detainees and nakedness as a form of humiliation that violates human dignity.[40]

In human rights jurisprudence, as in the treaty texts, equality and non-discrimination constitute a second significant area in which the link between the principle of human dignity and rights has received more explicit attention and development. Again, this is particularly clear in the case law of the European and Inter-American courts. In *Cyprus v Turkey*, for example, the Strasbourg Court emphasized not only that, in general, 'a special importance should be attached to

[32] *Tyrer v United Kingdom*, para 33.

[33] *MSS v Belgium and Greece*, para 220. See also *Peers v Greece*, para 75; *Kuznetsov v Ukraine*, para 126 ('the conditions of detention, which the applicant had to endure in particular until May 1998, must have caused him considerable mental suffering, diminishing his human dignity'); *Ramirez Sanchez v France*, para 119 ('Article 3 requires the State to ensure that prisoners are detained in conditions that are compatible with respect for their human dignity').

[34] See eg *Cabrera García and Montiel Flores v Mexico*, para 199. See also *Maritza Urrutia v Guatemala*, para 87.

[35] *'Juvenile Reeducation Institute' v Paraguay*, para 151.

[36] *Velásquez-Rodríguez v Honduras*, para 156. See also *El Salvador*, a 1994 case of the Inter-American Commission of Human Rights.

[37] *Loayza Tamayo v Peru*, para 57.

[38] *López-Álvarez v Honduras*, para 169.

[39] *Miguel Castro-Castro Prison v Peru*, paras 305, 306.

[40] *Ribitsch v Austria*, para 38; *Wiktorko v Poland*, para 54.

discrimination based on race and that publicly to single out a group of persons for differential treatment on the basis of race might, in certain circumstances, constitute a special affront to human dignity', but also that in the facts of the case, '[t]he conditions under which that population is condemned to live are debasing and violate the very notion of respect for the human dignity of its members'.[41] The European Court has made the same point with respect to racial violence and discrimination against sexual minorities.[42] The Inter-American Court has even more forcefully affirmed the connection between equality and dignity in its case law. In an early Advisory Opinion, the Court declared that 'the notion of equality springs directly from the oneness of the human family and is linked to the essential dignity of the individual'.[43] A later Advisory Opinion on migrant workers went so far as to describe the equal protection of the law as a peremptory norm of international law 'linked to the essential dignity of the individual'.[44]

Already in the Universal Declaration of Human Rights, one of the principal references to human dignity was in the *chapeau* to the UDHR's articles on economic, social, and cultural rights; and the General Comments of the Committee on Economic, Social and Cultural Rights (CESCR) has further developed this theme considerably. The CESCR has, in general, argued that the principle of human dignity requires an expansive interpretation of a whole range of Covenant rights. With respect to housing:

> '[T]he inherent dignity of the human person' from which the rights in the Covenant are said to derive requires that the term 'housing' be interpreted so as to take account of a variety of other considerations, most importantly that the right to housing should be ensured to all persons irrespective of income or access to economic resources.[45]

The right to adequate food, according to the Committee, 'is indivisibly linked to the inherent dignity of the human person and is indispensable for the fulfillment of other human rights enshrined in the International Bill of Human Rights',[46] as is the right to the highest attainable standard of health.[47] The Committee describes

[41] *Cyprus v Turkey*, paras 306, 309.

[42] *Goodwin* (n 17) paras 90, 91 ('society may reasonably be expected to tolerate a certain inconvenience to enable individuals to live in dignity and worth in accordance with the sexual identity chosen by them at great personal cost'); *Nachova and Others v Bulgaria*, para 145 ('Racial violence is a particular affront to human dignity').

[43] See also *Atala Riffo and Daughters v Chile*, para 79 (a case involving discrimination on the basis of sexual orientation).

[44] *Juridical Condition and Rights of the Undocumented Migrants*, para 100.

[45] UN Committee on Economic, Social and Cultural Rights (CESCR), 'General Comment No 4: The Right to Adequate Housing (Art 11(1) of the Covenant)' (13 December 1991) UN Doc E/1992/23, para 7.

[46] CESCR, 'General Comment No 12: The Right to Adequate Food (Art 11)' (12 May 1999) UN Doc E/C.12/1999/5, para 4.

[47] CESCR, 'General Comment No 14: The Right to the Highest Attainable Standard of Health (Art 12)' (11 August 2000) UN Doc E/C.12/2000/4.

the right to work as 'an inseparable and inherent part of human dignity',[48] and the right to social security as being 'of central importance in guaranteeing human dignity for all persons when they are faced with circumstances that deprive them of their capacity to fully realize their Covenant rights'.[49] Somewhat different from all the examples above, the CESCR has also made an explicit link between dignity of individuals and the (collective) right to culture:

> The full promotion of and respect for cultural rights is essential for the maintenance of human dignity and positive social interaction between individuals and communities in a diverse and multicultural world...The protection of cultural diversity is an ethical imperative, inseparable from respect for human dignity. It implies a commitment to human rights and fundamental freedoms, and requires the full implementation of cultural rights, including the right to take part in cultural life.[50]

Interestingly, although the American Convention on Human Rights only protects economic and social rights very weakly,[51] the Inter-American Court has attached a robust notion of dignity to its interpretation and application of the right to life that allows that right to include a guarantee of the minimal socio-economic conditions for a life lived with dignity.[52]

Beyond physical integrity, equality, and basic material needs, the principle of dignity clearly touches also on notions of human freedom generally. Here, however, unlike in the previous areas, there is considerably less consistency or consensus on what rights dignity requires, protects, and justifies, especially insofar as freedom is understood to mean the protection of individual autonomy. The European Court explicitly rejected a claim that respect for human dignity can support the proposition that Article 2 of the European Convention on Human Rights implies a right to choose the time and manner of one's death, even while acknowledging the centrality of dignity to the meaning and content of the Convention as a whole.[53] On the other hand, the same court strongly affirmed that post-operative transsexuals have a right 'to live in dignity and worth in accordance with the sexual identity chosen by them at great personal cost'.[54] Similarly, a patient's autonomy to make his own medical decisions, according to the Court, flows from a respect for human dignity.[55] The Committee on the Elimination of All Forms of Discrimination against Women has recognized, in a comparable way, the basis of the right to choose a

[48] CESCR, 'General Comment No 18: The Right to Work' (6 February 2006) UN Doc E/C.12/GC/18, para 1.

[49] CESCR, 'General Comment No 19: The Right to Social Security (Art 9)' (4 February 2008) UN Doc E/C.12/GC/19, para 1.

[50] CESCR, 'General Comment No 21: Right of Everyone to Take Part in Cultural Life (Art 15, Para 1a of the Covenant on Economic, Social and Cultural Rights)' (21 December 2009) UN Doc E/C.12/GC/21 [1], para 40.

[51] Article 26.

[52] *Case of the Yakye Axa Indigenous Community v Paraguay* (Indigenous peoples deprived of adequate food, water, and healthcare, suffered violation of right to life).

[53] *Pretty* (n 17) para 65.

[54] *Goodwin* (n 17) para 91 (emphasis added).

[55] *VC v Slovakia* (n 17) para 105.

spouse and enter freely into marriage in human dignity.[56] Yet, the Human Rights Committee, in deciding one of the most famous controversies regarding the use of human dignity in constitutional adjudication, concluded that a French judicial judgment forbidding dwarf-throwing as a violation of the human dignity of the participants notwithstanding their free consent, did not violate the ICCPR's guarantees of liberty.[57]

Finally, in addition to the themes described above, in which human dignity plays a relatively recurrent or even persistent role, there is a miscellaneous collection of issues and cases in which one international organ or another has made some ad hoc link to human dignity. These include, among others:

- freedom of expression;[58]
- the rights of the child generally and especially with regard to the principle of the best interests of the child;[59]
- the obligation to recognize juridical personality;[60] and
- democratic rule of law.[61]

Overall, despite the range of these uses of dignity, when seen from the perspective of the use of human dignity in various constitutional jurisdictions around the world, the jurisprudence of dignity in international human rights law appears decidedly thinner and less developed in its substantive content.[62]

4. The Functions of Human Dignity

Another way of considering the overall body of jurisprudence on the principle of human dignity in international human rights law is to take what may be considered a functional approach; in addition to looking at the meaning given to the notion of dignity, look at how the bodies invoking the principle use it. What purpose does it serve in reasoning about international human rights norms? Again, one finds a narrower set of those uses, and a decidedly less overt reflection on those functions,

[56] UN Committee on the Elimination of Discrimination against Women, 'CEDAW General Recommendation No 21: Equality in Marriage and Family Relations' (1994) UN Doc A/49/38, para 16.

[57] *Wackenheim v France.* [58] *Juan José López (Argentina)*, para 43.

[59] *Gómez-Paquiyauri Brothers v Peru*, para 163; *Leydi Dayán Sánchez (Colombia)*, para 49.

[60] *Case of the Yean and Bosico Children v Dominican Republic.*

[61] *Rodolfo Robles Espinoza and Sons (Peru)*, para 103.

[62] Compare the comparative constitutional case law described and analysed in Carozza, 'Human Dignity in Constitutional Adjudication' (n 7).

in international human rights decisions than in many of the constitutional jurisdictions employing the principle.[63] In the great majority of cases, dignity appears to make a merely rhetorical appearance, without actually doing any work in the process of reaching or justifying the decision of the interpreting body in question.

In at least three ways, however, the principle of human dignity can be seen to contribute to the arguments. First, the principle of dignity seems to help justify expansive interpretations of human rights. This is most evident in the general comments of the Committee on Economic, Social and Cultural Rights cited earlier. In those examples, the implied value of linking the rights in question to the broader idea of human dignity is that the latter's breadth and comprehensiveness opens up the narrow right, connects it to a unifying and universalizing ideal, and thus offers a counterweight to any more restrictive or cramped understanding of the right under discussion. The second function is similar: strengthening the centrality and importance of the right in question and limiting possible exceptions or limitations to that right. Here, one of the clearest examples appears in the Inter-American Court's advisory opinion on migrant workers, described above.[64] Although rights to non-discrimination and equal treatment are undoubtedly at the heart of the idea of human rights, they are not usually regarded as exceptionless *jus cogens* norms (at least in the absence of systematic and *de jure* form of discrimination, like apartheid). The Court's insistence on the intimate connection between human dignity, as the unifying and universally grounding ideal of human rights as a whole, and equality, arguably helps to justify the elevation of the equal treatment for migrants to a higher plane than most other human rights norms. Taking both of those functions together reveals a third possible use of the principle of human dignity; it serves generally as a normative reference point textually within the treaties, and yet it points beyond them to some supra-positive value and therefore can be a way of bringing new content to the treaty norms through interpretation.

Still, there are few examples in international human rights decisions where any of these functions is clearly evident. It is possible that the limited set of examples stems from the fact that all three of the identified functions presume that there is enough of a stable, consensual, and determinable meaning to human dignity, beyond any specific right or treaty provision. In view of the overall survey of the meanings of dignity—even across constitutional jurisdictions, let alone in international human rights bodies—the validity of this premise can reasonably be questioned, at least insofar as dignity is used beyond the narrow area of rights pertaining to personal integrity, such as the prohibitions on degrading treatment or slavery.

63 Carozza, 'Human Dignity in Constitutional Adjudication' (n 7).

64 *Rights of the Undocumented Migrants* (n 44).

5. Conclusion

The difficulty in identifying any clear role for the use of human dignity in relationship to specific human rights does not deny the importance and centrality of the principle more generally. Rather, it points back to the broad, structural place of human dignity at the core of the human rights enterprise, with which this discussion began. Agreement surrounding the generic recognition of the inherent and equal value of all human persons, and the affirmation that certain practical implications should flow from that status, has allowed the task of proposing and developing universal human rights norms to proceed, even in the face of deeply rooted differences in the philosophical origins of that belief. Dignity's role as a mediating concept among varied traditions places it at the starting point of the international human rights enterprise. That same susceptibility that dignity has to a multiplicity of foundations and meanings, however, also makes it vulnerable to great ambiguity and thus less clearly useful in the detailed application of international human rights norms.

Further Reading

Carozza PG, 'Human Dignity and Judicial Interpretation of Human Rights: A Reply' (2008) 19 *EJIL* 931

Kretzmer D and Klein E (eds), *The Concept of Human Dignity in Human Rights Discourse* (Kluwer Law International 2002)

McCrudden C, 'Human Dignity and Judicial Interpretation of Human Rights' (2008) 19 *EJIL* 655

McCrudden C (ed), *Understanding Human Dignity* (British Academy 2013)

CHAPTER 15

SUBSIDIARITY

GERALD L NEUMAN[1]

SUBSIDIARITY both is, and is not, a principle of international human rights law. Subsidiarity manifests itself in various forms in structural, substantive, and procedural aspects of the human rights system. The observation that international protection of human rights is subsidiary to national protection asserts a fundamental fact about the system's architecture. Certain human rights can also be interpreted as illustrations of a broader, substantive 'social subsidiarity' principle, although the corpus of human rights law does not include this more general principle. Specific international mechanisms for the protection or promotion of human rights apply procedural rules that reflect their subsidiary character. Whether all these phenomena should be grouped under a single term, and whether they all result from an underlying principle, is subject to debate.

1. What is Subsidiarity?

According to the Oxford English Dictionary, the neologism 'subsidiarity' entered the English language in the 1930s, as the analogue of an older German word (*Subsidiarität*) that was used in the translation of a Latin phrase in the papal

[1] The author is writing in his personal capacity.

encyclical *Quadragesimo anno*.[2] The English noun has acquired wider currency only in recent decades. The older adjective 'subsidiary' has a range of meanings, including 'serv[ing] to help, assist, or supplement'.[3] In general terms, 'subsidiarity' describes a relationship between two institutions or norms, by which one supplements the other in appropriate circumstances. That loose formulation covers a broad range of conceivable principles, positive or negative, weak or strong, substantive or procedural, relating pairs of proposed actions.

The most prominent legal example is the EU principle of subsidiarity, introduced in 1993 by the Maastricht Treaty on European Union—a strong, negative substantive principle under which the Union may employ certain of its powers only when action by the member states would be insufficient to achieve the purpose. As reformulated by the Lisbon Treaty, Article 5(3) of the Treaty on European Union provides:

> Under the principle of subsidiarity, in areas which do not fall within its exclusive competence, the Union shall act only if and in so far as the objectives of the proposed action cannot be sufficiently achieved by the Member States, either at central level or at regional and local level, but can rather, by reason of the scale or effects of the proposed action, be better achieved at Union level.

The EU version of subsidiarity treats action at a hierarchically higher level (the Union) as subsidiary to action at a hierarchically lower level (the member states), in order to place the making of decisions closer to the individual. It shares this feature with two of its intellectual ancestors: the subsidiarity principle of Catholic social doctrine, whose roots can be traced back to Aristotle,[4] and a territorial version of subsidiarity that certain forms of federalism apply. Catholic social doctrine calls for protection of the autonomy of smaller associations, including the family, from unnecessary intervention by larger associations, including the state. The encyclical *Rerum novarum*[5] asserted this doctrine in 1891, with special emphasis on associations formed for the protection of the interests of workers, as a Christian alternative to laissez-faire liberalism and socialism. The encyclical *Quadragesimo anno* of 1931 restated the doctrine against the historical background of Fascism and Communism, and included the following influential passage:

> The supreme authority of the State ought, therefore, to let subordinate groups handle matters and concerns of lesser importance, which would otherwise dissipate its efforts greatly. Thereby the State will more freely, powerfully, and effectively do all those things that belong to it alone because it alone can do them: directing, watching, urging, restraining, as occasion

[2] The Latin phrase in the Encyclical, more literally 'the principle of subsidiary function' in English, is '"*subsidiarii*" *officii principio*'.

[3] 'Subsidiary' in *Oxford English Dictionary* (3rd edn, OUP 2012).

[4] Ken Endo, 'The Principle of Subsidiarity: From Johannes Althusius to Jacques Delors' (1994) 44 *Hokkaido LJ* 553, 646; John Finnis, *Natural Law and Natural Rights* (OUP 1980) 144–47.

[5] *Rerum novarum*, Encyclical of Pope Leo XIII on Capital and Labor (15 May 1891).

requires and necessity demands. Therefore, those in power should be sure that the more perfectly a graduated order is kept among the various associations, in observance of the principle of 'subsidiary function', the stronger social authority and effectiveness will be [and] the happier and more prosperous the condition of the State.[6]

To describe its purpose in religiously neutral terms, this doctrine of subsidiarity (herein referred to as 'social subsidiarity') serves human dignity by enabling individuals to gain fulfilment through social interaction within a hierarchy of freely chosen associations, each performing its proper tasks, and with the larger associations aiding but not superseding the smaller ones.[7]

Some federal systems pursue a vision of territorial subsidiarity that restricts the national government's exercises of power to situations in which the action of the political subunits (regions, provinces, or states) would not be sufficient. Drafters of a constitution can implement this strategy *ex ante*, by allocating powers to the central and local levels with this criterion in mind, or *ex post*, by making satisfaction of the criterion an express condition for the national government's exercise of certain powers. The United States illustrates the *ex ante* version,[8] whereas Germany illustrates both the *ex ante* and *ex post* versions.[9] In contrast to social subsidiarity, which restrains government action in order to protect private associations, federalism establishes a priority between two governmental units.[10] Territorial subsidiarity can be applied more deeply, setting relative priorities among a long chain of nested governmental units, or it can stop at the first two levels.

Additionally, the notion of 'subsidiarity' may be applied in other contexts, where closeness to the individual is not the issue. German constitutional law, for example, also uses the term to describe aspects of the relationship between the constitutional court and the ordinary courts, and the displacement of a more general right by a more specific right.[11] Italian constitutional law uses it to describe the limitation of the criminal sanction to being employed only as a last resort when other sanctions fail.[12]

[6] *Quadragesimo Anno*, Encyclical of Pope Pius XI on Reconstruction of the Social Order (15 May 1931) para 80, quoted in Paolo G Carozza, 'Subsidiarity as a Structural Principle of International Human Rights Law' (2003) 97 *AJIL* 38, 42. [7] Carozza (n 6) 42–44.

[8] Jack N Rakove, *Original Meanings: Politics and Ideas in the Making of the Constitution* (Vintage Books 1997) 177–80.

[9] Greg Taylor, 'Germany: The Subsidiarity Principle' (2006) 4 *ICON* 115; cf Greg Taylor, 'Germany: A Slow Death for Subsidiarity?' (2009) 7 *ICON* 139 (discussing later amendment narrowing the scope of *ex post* subsidiarity).

[10] NW Barber, 'The Limited Modesty of Subsidiarity' (2005) 11 *OJLS* 308, 309–10.

[11] Hans D Jarass and Bodo Pieroth, *Grundgesetz für die Bundesrepublik Deutschland: Kommentar* (8th edn, Verlag CH Beck 2006) 55, 890.

[12] Augusto Barbera, Francesco Cocozza, and Guido Corso, 'Le situazioni soggettive. Le libertà dei singoli e delle formazioni sociali. Il principio di eguaglianza' in Guiliano Amato and Augusto Barbera (eds), *Manuale di diritto pubblico* (5th edn, Mulino 1997) vol 1, 249; cf Nils Jareborg, 'Criminalization as Last Resort (*Ultima Ratio*)' (2004) 2 *Ohio St J Crim L* 521.

The EU principle of subsidiarity illustrates the subspecies of 'negative subsidiarity' by *prohibiting* action at a higher level when action at the lower level would be sufficient; this may be contrasted with 'positive subsidiarity,' which affirmatively calls for action at the higher level when action at the lower level would *not* be sufficient.[13] Some conceptions of subsidiarity, including Catholic social doctrine, combine both the positive and negative aspects.

The EU principle, being a legal criterion for action, can be described as a 'strong' subsidiarity principle, when viewed on a spectrum that extends to weaker subsidiarity principles that treat subsidiarity as merely one relevant consideration among many. Subsidiarity principles may also differ in the metrics they use to evaluate the justification for action at a higher level.[14] Sufficiency may be evaluated in terms of its efficacy in attaining the objective, in terms of economic efficiency, or in terms of a balance between the objective and other values, such as autonomy.

Making subsidiarity operational may also require the specification of a decision maker, or a more complex mechanism, that determines whether the criteria for negative or positive subsidiarity have been met.[15] The determination can be made *ex ante*, as in the drafting of a treaty, or *ex post*, as in the application of a treaty. The power to determine may be placed at the higher level, or the lower level, or shared.

Against this taxonomic background, one may ask which forms of subsidiarity are operative in international human rights law. Some authors see social subsidiarity as the underlying principle that unites seemingly disparate examples of subsidiarity.[16] Other authors doubt that the meaning and rationale of these different examples are the same.[17]

2. Subsidiarity of International Institutions as a Structural Fact

Since its creation in the 1940s, the international human rights system has placed primary reliance on states to ensure the protection of human rights. International institutions facilitate that protection in a variety of ways—by providing guidance,

[13] Endo (n 4) 641–42. [14] Endo (n 4) 637.

[15] George A Bermann, 'Taking Subsidiarity Seriously: Federalism in the European Community and the United States' (1994) 94 *Columbia L Rev* 331, 366–67.

[16] Carozza (n 6); Dinah Shelton, 'Subsidiarity, Democracy and Human Rights' in Donna Gomien (ed), *Broadening the Frontiers of Human Rights: Essays in Honour of Asbjørn Eide* (Scandinavian UP 1993) 43.

[17] Barber (n 10) 309; Jonas Christoffersen, *Fair Balance: Proportionality, Subsidiarity and Primarity in the European Convention on Human Rights* (Martinus Nijhoff 2009) 241.

assistance, monitoring, and back-up—but without replacing states as the primary guarantors. Positive subsidiarity motivates the existence of these institutions, although they clearly lack the resources to assist wherever assistance is needed.

Human rights treaties impose obligations directly on states, including obligations to protect individuals against certain harms that other individuals and groups inflict. Reporting procedures under the principal global human rights treaties require states to account for their performance of these obligations through dialogue with international treaty bodies. Communications procedures enable individuals (or other states) to bring complaints against states that have failed to fulfil their obligations in concrete instances. Regional human rights treaties in Africa, the Americas, and Europe similarly oblige states and create petition mechanisms before commissions and courts in which states figure as respondents.

States implement their human rights obligations through their constitutions, criminal laws, civil codes, courts, administrative agencies, and public services. Some human rights obligations are defined specifically in relation to state-based institutions, such as political elections, criminal justice systems, and nationality laws. Others expressly require states to provide legal protection against acts such as discrimination, attacks on reputation, or exploitation of children.

In consequence, states have the obligation and the opportunity to adopt legislation and other measures for the implementation of human rights within their territory (and sometimes elsewhere), and states have administrative, judicial, and law enforcement personnel in place to carry out those measures. These personnel may not be designated as human rights officers, and some of them may even be unaware that their duties correspond to the implementation of international obligations. Nonetheless, from the human rights perspective, they form part of a vast corps of national officials constrained by and contributing to the realization of the human rights of their populations. The principal function of the far smaller number of personnel at the international level is to assist the national officials in performing those responsibilities. That assistance includes the articulation of standards, provision of training and funding, monitoring of performance, and sometimes the adoption of stronger incentives. The goal of these activities, directly or indirectly, is the implementation of human rights at the national level. In short, international action for human rights is normally subsidiary to national action.

The observation that international human rights law operates on and through states does not assert a logical necessity or a rule without exceptions. Some treaties define certain human rights violations as international criminal offences that apply directly to individuals. Some human rights instruments include chapters that define the duties of individuals in addition to their rights. Sometimes international organizations provide human rights assistance directly to individuals, either with the permission of states or in the temporary absence of state authority. In a variation from the usual practice of treaty bodies, the United Nations Interim Administration

Mission in Kosovo engaged in state reporting to the Human Rights Committee in 2006.[18]

The pattern of subsidiarity results in part from the fact that many activities for the protection of human rights require presence on state territory, which implicates the territorial sovereignty of states. Human rights treaties do not generally grant international officials unlimited access to the territory of states parties in order to investigate, enforce, or implement human rights. On the other hand, some activities for the promotion of human rights in a state do not require access to state territory, and it is not clear that any implicit negative principle of subsidiarity restricts the authority of international institutions to perform such actions. To take a minor example, the Office of the High Commissioner for Human Rights maintains translations of the Universal Declaration of Human Rights into more than three hundred languages on its website; this activity probably does not need to be justified in response to a hypothetical objection that states have a prior claim to educate their own populations about human rights.

3. Substantive Subsidiarity within the State

Some leading experts have considered the principle of social subsidiarity fundamental to human rights law. For example, Professor Shelton has described subsidiarity as a 'necessary component of democratic rule and human rights law', defining it as follows:

> Broadly conceived, subsidiarity divides decision-making in society, considering values of efficiency, liberty, and justice. It thus calls for non-interference with the activities of individuals or smaller groups when these are capable of the tasks appropriate to them, and assistance to individuals and lesser societies when these are not able to perform appropriate or necessary tasks.[19]

Another future President of the Inter-American Commission on Human Rights, Professor Carozza, has argued for subsidiarity as a 'structural principle of international human rights law', offering as a simplified summary the principle 'that each social and political group should help smaller or more local ones accomplish their respective ends without, however, arrogating those tasks to itself'.[20]

[18] Yogesh Tyagi, *The UN Human Rights Committee: Practice and Procedure* (CUP 2011) 182.

[19] Dinah Shelton, 'Subsidiarity and Human Rights Law' (2006) 27 *HRLJ* 4, 5.

[20] Carozza (n 6) 38, fn 1 (I quote these simplified definitions merely as confirmation that the principle both these authors champion is a version of 'social subsidiarity').

The substance of international human rights law does include several elements that correlate with mandates that a principle of social subsidiarity would place upon the state. Freedom of association and rights of the family resonate with aspects of negative subsidiarity; numerous positive state duties embody notions of positive subsidiarity. Whether these correlations support a broader identification of human rights law with social subsidiarity at the present time, however, may be questioned.

The configuration of family rights in human rights treaties clearly evokes a programme of both negative and positive subsidiarity. Article 23(1) of the International Covenant on Civil and Political Rights (ICCPR) echoes the Universal Declaration of Human Rights in affirming that: 'The family is the natural and fundamental group unit of society and is entitled to protection by society and the State.' Article 10(1) of the International Covenant on Economic, Social and Cultural Rights (ICESCR) further specifies that: 'The widest possible protection and assistance should be accorded to the family, which is the natural and fundamental group unit of society, particularly for its establishment and while it is responsible for the care and education of dependent children.' Article 13(3) of the ICESCR expands on the liberty of parents to choose private schools for their children and to 'ensure the religious and moral education of their children in conformity with their own convictions'. These guarantees do not wholly preclude state intervention in family matters; the ICCPR also addresses the equality of spouses in marriage and at its dissolution,[21] and a child's right to protection[22] entails a right to protection against his or her parents when necessary. These limits on the autonomy of the family received further development in the Convention on the Elimination of All Forms of Discrimination Against Women[23] and the Convention on the Rights of the Child.[24] Whether or not the resulting allocation of rights and responsibilities accords with the particular conclusions of various proponents of social subsidiarity, the design clearly expresses the negative subsidiarity approach of family autonomy subject to necessary intervention, and the positive subsidiarity approach of state support for families when needed.[25]

Guarantees of freedom of association in both Covenants also express important themes of social subsidiarity. The ICESCR specifically addresses the freedom of trade unions,[26] while the ICCPR mentions trade unions as an example of a much broader right to freedom of association.[27] Both Covenants explicitly prohibit unnecessary state interference with freedom of association. But the Covenants do not protect associations from competition by the state in carrying out their chosen goals; the negative subsidiarity norm that the state should not perform tasks that private

[21] Article 23(4). [22] Article 24(1). [23] Eg Art 16. [24] Eg Arts 3, 5.

[25] It is more difficult to categorize the subsidiarity principle of Art 21(b) of the Convention of the Rights of the Child, which subordinates inter-country adoption to suitable placement in the child's country of origin, as an issue of social subsidiarity, territorial subsidiarity, or something else.

[26] Article 8. [27] Article 22.

associations could adequately perform does not currently appear to operate in human rights law, either weakly or strongly. Furthermore, the state's positive duties toward associations appear to be far more limited than the state's positive duties toward families. The state may be obliged to protect private associations against private violence, but it is not generally obliged, or even encouraged, to fund them. Thus, the human rights approach to associations may correspond only partially to the negative and positive dictates of social subsidiarity.

As these examples illustrate, international human rights law—at both the global and the regional levels—imposes many positive duties on the state. Negatively expressed duties, such as certain civil and political rights, often spawn positive duties of prevention and remedy. Some civil and political rights directly express positive duties, such as a criminal defendant's right to 'the free assistance of an interpreter'.[28] Economic and social rights impose positive duties on the state to foster the provision of goods and services to individuals. A common typology of such duties distinguishes between the state's obligation to respect and protect individuals' access to existing goods or services and the state's obligation to fulfil the right by facilitating access and by providing the good or service directly. Interpretations that apply the obligation to provide directly 'whenever an individual or group is unable, for reasons beyond their control, to enjoy the right',[29] convey the message of positive subsidiarity.

The ICESCR also evokes the concept of positive subsidiarity on the international plane, in several references to international cooperation and assistance. Perhaps the clearest example occurs in Article 11(2), in which states parties agree to

> take, individually and through international co-operation, the measures...which are needed...(a) [t]o improve methods of production, conservation and distribution of food...[and] (b) [t]aking into account the problems of both food-importing and food-exporting countries, to ensure an equitable distribution of world food supplies in relation to need.

The positive duties in human rights law, however, are rarely limited by negative subsidiarity. Human rights law does not discourage states from giving individuals assistance that private associations could have provided, in order to reserve space for private charity. Nor does it clearly discourage states from giving individuals more assistance than they need, in order to foster self-reliance. Inefficient or wasteful government programmes may be subject to criticism on human rights grounds, to the extent that they undermine the ability of the state to meet the full range of its rights obligations to the maximum of its available resources. But criticism based on

[28] ICCPR, Art 14(3)(f).

[29] UN Committee on Economic, Social and Cultural Rights (UNCESCR), 'General Comment No 12: The Right to Adequate Food (Art 11)', in 'Compilation of General Comments and General Recommendations Adopted by Human Rights Treaty Bodies' (27 May 2008) UN Doc HRI/GEN/1/Rev.9, 58.

such empirical evidence of unfulfilled rights would differ from criticism based on a commitment in principle that the state should aid its citizens only as a last resort.

The example of education may reinforce this observation. The ICESCR does recognize the liberty to establish private schools, subject to appropriate regulation, and the liberty of parents to choose private education for their children.[30] The state cannot enforce a legal monopoly on education, but the state's right to offer education does not depend on the absence of religious, commercial, or charitable alternatives. The treaty does not disparage public education, and the Committee on Economic, Social and Cultural Rights interprets Article 13 as giving the state 'principal responsibility for the direct provision of education in most circumstances'.[31]

More generally, international human rights law does not mandate privatization of government services or enterprises, on the theory that it has intrinsic value. Privatization may achieve aggregate efficiencies in the delivery of services and thereby contribute to the realization of economic and social rights, but markets often deny vulnerable populations access to services, creating a need for state vigilance to regulate and supplement private distribution.[32] Treaty bodies have more often cautioned states to study the effects of privatization carefully and to ensure that they do not achieve the savings by decreasing the rights of the beneficiaries.[33] Where state or private agencies could provide a service equally well, the state is not obliged to leave the field to private initiative.

Similarly, international human rights law does not currently provide strong support for a requirement of *territorial* subsidiarity *within* the state, as a claim for federalism or local government. Human rights law ordinarily takes the political subunits of the state, and the allocation of powers among them, as a given. Local government may be desirable as an opportunity for citizens to exercise the right to political participation, but there are many ways to structure political participation. The principal human rights treaties do not give local governments autonomy rights against regions or states, or require that the larger units refrain from regulating matters that the local governments could address. Special issues involving the right to self-determination of peoples or the rights of indigenous peoples do arise, but these are not instances of a general right to territorial subsidiarity. The distance between territorial subsidiarity and human rights is particularly clear in Europe,

[30] Article 13(3), 13(4).

[31] UNCESCR, 'General Comment No 13: The Right to Education (Art 13)', in 'Compilation of General Comments and General Recommendations Adopted by Human Rights Treaty Bodies' (27 May 2008) UN Doc HRI/GEN/1/Rev.9, 72.

[32] UNCESCR, 'General Comment No 14: The Right to the Highest Attainable Standard of Health (Art 12)', in 'Compilation of General Comments and General Recommendations Adopted by Human Rights Treaty Bodies' (27 May 2008) UN Doc HRI/GEN/1/Rev.9, 86–87.

[33] Eg UN Committee on the Rights of the Child, 'General Comment No 5: General Measures of Implementation of the Convention on the Rights of the Child (Arts 4, 42 and 44, para 6)', in 'Compilation of General Comments and General Recommendations Adopted by Human Rights Treaty Bodies' (27 May 2008) UN Doc HRI/GEN/1/Rev.9, 431.

where the right to political participation under the regional human rights convention applies only to elections for 'the legislature', which is understood as excluding municipal elections.[34] Meanwhile, the Council of Europe has a separate Charter of Local Self-Government that is not integrated into its human rights system, but that does assert a version of subsidiarity on behalf of the local authorities.[35] In other regions, and at the global level, the rights to political participation in human rights treaties are defined more abstractly and could someday be construed as implying a human right to local government. For the present, however, the subsidiarity of the international regime to the prerogatives of states in structuring their political systems appears to inhibit a mandate for deep territorial subsidiarity.

4. Procedural Doctrines of Subsidiarity

Mechanisms for the international protection of human rights at the global or regional level often employ procedural doctrines that have been described in terms of subsidiarity. Among those doctrines are: the requirement of the exhaustion of domestic remedies, the 'fourth instance' formula, the notion of remedial subsidiarity, and the margin of appreciation doctrine. Some notes of caution, however, may be justified. First, some of these doctrines may not be applied by all international law mechanisms, and some of these doctrines may relate especially to international adjudicatory mechanisms; one such doctrine is associated specifically with the European regional system. Second, the relevant notion of subsidiarity may vary from doctrine to doctrine. Third, the highly contested doctrine of the margin of appreciation may incorporate multiple strands, either procedural or substantive.

4.1 Exhaustion of domestic remedies

A typical procedural expression of subsidiarity is the doctrine of exhaustion of domestic remedies. Where it applies, the requirement of exhaustion ensures that a petitioner will not resort to an international court, commission, or body until the petitioner has given the authorities of the respondent state the opportunity to provide a remedy for the wrong done. The exhaustion requirement implements

[34] Protocol to the Convention for the Protection of Human Rights and Fundamental Freedoms, Art 3.

[35] European Charter of Local Self-Government, Art 4(3) ('Public responsibilities shall be exercised, in preference, by those authorities which are closest to the citizen. Allocation of responsibility to another authority should weigh up the extent and nature of the task and requirements of efficiency and economy').

the subsidiary character of international protection as supplementing the primary responsibility of states to implement human rights. It is often expressly included in human rights treaties by the drafters, and thus imposed by the 'lower' level. Taken together with such exceptions as ineffectiveness and excessive delay, the exhaustion doctrine embodies a strong negative subsidiarity principle that the international tribunal should not intervene when the state's own remedies are sufficient to address the violation. The principle is limited in its stringency, however, to the extent that it merely postpones international adjudication; the existence of an adequate procedural mechanism in the state does not shield the state from further adjudication of the cases in which the domestic mechanism has denied relief.

The exhaustion requirement could be viewed as an illustration of territorial subsidiarity, limiting action by institutions of the larger territorial unit out of deference to the smaller territorial unit. It is worth observing, however, that the exhaustion requirement also resembles the common doctrine of the subsidiarity of the individual complaint procedures of national constitutional courts, which makes prior resort to the ordinary courts a prerequisite for invoking the special constitutional jurisdiction, for functional rather than territorial reasons.

Moreover, it should be recalled that the exhaustion doctrine applies primarily in international adjudication, either between states or in proceedings individuals bring against a state. Other less judicialized mechanisms for the protection of human rights, such as Special Rapporteurs on thematic mandates appointed by the Human Rights Council, are not subject to the exhaustion doctrine.[36] Neither are the inquiry procedures of several treaty bodies, or the preventive visiting system of the Optional Protocol to the Convention Against Torture. When treaty bodies monitor compliance with human rights obligations through the state reporting process, they also issue concluding observations on matters of concern, irrespective of any prior submission of those matters to domestic remedies. Thus, the doctrine of exhaustion, though widespread in courts and similar procedures, does not amount to a pervasive subsidiarity norm for international protection.

4.2 The 'fourth instance' doctrine

Another adjudicatory doctrine that has been described in terms of subsidiarity is the 'fourth instance' rule, which addresses the allocation of responsibility between international and national tribunals for resolving issues of fact and issues of domestic law.[37] The maxim states that an international court does not sit as a fourth

[36] Sir Nigel Rodley, 'The United Nations Human Rights Council, Its Special Procedures, and Its Relationship with the Treaty Bodies: Complementarity or Competition?' in Kevin Boyle (ed), *New Institutions for Human Rights Protection* (OUP 2009) 65.

[37] Jo M Pasqualucci, *The Practice and Procedure of the Inter-American Court of Human Rights* (CUP 2003) 92–95; Herbert Petzold, 'The Convention and the Principle of Subsidiarity' in Ronald St J

instance of the national legal system to correct mere errors in the finding of fact or the interpretation or application of national law. Rather, the international court sits for the specific purpose of resolving the human rights claim and re-examines issues of fact or national law only to the extent it considers necessary in order to ensure respect for the human rights norm.

Like the exhaustion doctrine, the 'fourth instance' rule can be viewed as embodying a negative territorial subsidiarity principle, expressing the international court's respect for the authority of the state's own courts in construing the state's own laws. And similarly, it is worth observing that the 'fourth instance' rule also resembles a norm that some national systems use to allocate responsibility between specialized constitutional courts and the ordinary courts (in the case of Germany, the *Fachgerichte*), for functional rather than territorial reasons.[38] The US Supreme Court pursues a similar practice with regard to interpretation of state law in constitutional cases, reflecting both functional and federalism considerations (and hence territorial subsidiarity).[39]

4.3 Remedial subsidiarity

When an international tribunal finds that a state has violated a human rights obligation, the duty to implement a remedy falls on the state, and the state may enjoy a substantial degree of discretion in how it fulfils that duty. The European Court of Human Rights (ECtHR) has had occasion—particularly in its early years—to refer to remedial measures as a subject of subsidiarity.[40] Nonetheless, the practice of the ECtHR is not uniform and has been evolving, and the approaches of other tribunals vary considerably.

The European Convention expressly confers authority on the ECtHR to award 'just satisfaction'.[41] Initially, the ECtHR described its findings of violation as a form of declaratory remedy and ordered financial redress as compensation for pecuniary and non-pecuniary injury and costs of litigation. Rather than remitting prevailing applicants to the domestic legal system for a calculation of their damages, the ECtHR held hearings of its own and conducted its own evaluation, under its own autonomous standards, of the monetary amount to be awarded. At the same time, the ECtHR denied its authority to award the applicant in-kind relief, such as release

Macdonald, F Matscher, and H Petzold (eds), *The European System for the Protection of Human Rights* (Martinus Nijhoff 1993) 50.

[38] Ernst Benda and Eckart Klein, *Lehrbuch des Verfassungsprozeßrechts* (CF Müller 1991) 249–51.

[39] Henry Paul Monaghan, 'Supreme Court Review of State-Court Determinations of State Law in Constitutional Cases' (2003) 103 *Columbia L Rev* 1919.

[40] Dinah Shelton, *Remedies in International Human Rights Law* (2nd edn, OUP 2005) 194–200; Petzold (n 37) 48.

[41] Convention for the Protection of Human Rights and Fundamental Freedoms, Art 41.

from custody or reversal of a judgment.[42] The ECtHR also declined to strike down statutes, or order their repeal, or to order other steps to be taken for the benefit of unrelated third parties as a result of the finding of the violation. These specific and general forms of reparation were left to the discretion of the respondent state, acting under the supervision of the Council of Ministers, a political body of the Council of Europe.[43]

As the ECtHR became more established, and states grew more accustomed to its condemnations of their practices and legislation, the ECtHR asserted more expansive interpretations of its remedial powers. With the encouragement of the Council of Europe, the ECtHR began to order specific non-monetary remedies on behalf of some applicants.[44] Next, the ECtHR adopted innovative methods for dealing with large classes of similar cases resulting from a common structural defect in a respondent state and overcame its prior reluctance to order systemic reforms in the operative part of its judgment.[45] The outcome of all these developments has been a narrower conception of the remedial discretion of the respondent state and an enlarged sense of the remedial discretion of the ECtHR itself.

The remedial role of the ECtHR can still be described as subsidiary, but the criteria for evaluating its subsidiarity have clearly evolved. The ECtHR addresses both the substantive reforms that would prevent similar violations from occurring later and the procedural reforms at the national level that would ensure that domestic courts provide any needed remedies for violations that do occur. The ECtHR exercises a greater degree of authority in the present, in the hope of playing a more subsidiary role in the future. Trade-offs of this kind illustrate the complexity of drawing conclusions from a general principle of subsidiarity in human rights law.

In the regional human rights system for the Americas, the conception of the remedial power of the Inter-American Court of Human Rights (IACtHR) evolved more rapidly. From the outset, the IACtHR has exercised the authority to award compensation for material and moral damages, based on its own understanding of international standards.[46] Article 63 of the American Convention on Human Rights makes clear that the remedial authority of the IACtHR extends beyond ordering compensation, and the IACtHR has made expansive use of this authorization. In one of its earliest decisions on reparations, it ordered the establishment of a foundation to administer a trust on behalf of murdered victims' families and the reopening

[42] Georg Ress, 'The Effects of Judgments and Decisions in Domestic Law' in Ronald St J Macdonald, F Matscher, and H Petzold (eds), *The European System for the Protection of Human Rights* (Martinus Nijhoff 1993) 802.

[43] The Council of Europe is the regional organization under whose auspices the ECtHR operates.

[44] Shelton, *Remedies* (n 40) 198–99; Luzius Wildhaber, 'The Execution of Judgments of the European Court of Human Rights: Recent Developments' in Pierre-Marie Dupuy and others (eds), *Völkerrecht als Wertordnung: Festschrift für Christian Tomuschat* (Engel 2006) 674–76.

[45] Lech Garlicki, 'Broniowski and After: On the Dual Nature of "Pilot Judgments"' in Lucius Caflisch (ed), *Liber Amicorum Luzius Wildhaber: Human Rights: Strasbourg Views* (Engel 2006).

[46] Pasqualucci (n 37) 254–72.

of a school and a medical dispensary in their village.[47] Since then, the IACtHR has ordered a wide range of detailed remedies, specifically on behalf of victims and their families, or generally for the benefit of persons similarly situated, including retrial, release, commutation of sentences, restoration to office, public apologies, commemoration of victims by naming a street or a school or by erecting a monument, prosecution of perpetrators, nullification of amnesties, establishment of development projects for villages where massacres occurred, restoration of control over indigenous lands, improvements in prison conditions, creation of websites and genetic databases to facilitate identification of disappeared children, provision of human rights training to officials and judges, and reform of legislation that caused the violation.[48]

It appears that considerations of subsidiarity play a fairly small role in the IACtHR's remedial practice. The IACtHR feels free to select remedies over the objection of the respondent state, without demonstrating that they are the only method, or even the best method, for making restitution to the victims and preventing future violations. Some advocates would like to see the IACtHR go further in specifying the details of its remedies, because imprecision fosters secondary disputes that delay compliance, but the IACtHR may already be operating at the limits of its knowledge of local conditions in some cases.[49] The imprecision that remains could be considered a consequence of subsidiarity.

The remedial practice of the regional human rights courts may be juxtaposed with the practice of international treaty bodies. The Human Rights Committee (HRC) has the most voluminous body of decisions (known as 'views') on individual communications under the Optional Protocol to the ICCPR. Article 2(3) of the ICCPR requires states parties to provide an effective remedy for violations of the enumerated rights, and the HRC has usually referred to this obligation in the remedial paragraph of its views.[50] On some occasions, after finding a violation, the HRC has merely stated in general terms that the state is obliged to provide an effective remedy for the victim and to take steps to ensure that similar violations do not occur in the future.[51] From its earliest years, however, there have been decisions

[47] *Aloeboetoe et al v Suriname (Reparations).*

[48] Thomas M Antkowiak, 'An Emerging Mandate for International Courts: Victim-Centered Remedies and Restorative Justice' (2011) 47 *Stan J Int'l L* 279, 292–304; Gerald L Neuman, 'Import, Export, and Regional Consent in the Inter-American Court of Human Rights' (2008) 19 *EJIL* 101, 104.

[49] Antkowiak (n 48) 312–14.

[50] UN Human Rights Committee, 'General Comment No 33: The Obligations of States Parties under the Optional Protocol to the International Covenant on Civil and Political Rights' (5 November 2008) UN Doc CCPR/C/GC/33 para 14; Martin Scheinin, 'The Human Rights Committee's Pronouncements on the Right to an Effective Remedy—An Illustration of the Legal Nature of the Committee's Work under the Optional Protocol' in Nisuke Ando (ed), *Towards Implementing Universal Human Rights: Festschrift for the Twenty-Fifth Anniversary of the Human Rights Committee* (Martinus Nijhoff 2004) 102.

[51] Jakob Th Möller and Alfred de Zayas, *United Nations Human Rights Committee Case Law 1977–2008: A Handbook* (Engel 2009) 499–500.

in which the HRC identified specific remedies that the state should afford to the victim, such as compensation, release, retrial, medical care, permission to leave the country, and bringing to justice those responsible for a disappearance.[52] The less frequent practice of calling explicitly for changes to the state's legislation, either for the benefit of the particular victim or to avoid similar violations in the future, also dates to these early years.[53] With regard to compensation, in contrast to the regional courts, the HRC does not attempt to calculate the amount of compensation to be paid, although it sometimes specifies particular elements that should be involved in the calculation.[54] Moreover, the HRC's standard phrasing in terms of an obligation to provide an effective remedy 'including' compensation or other elements suggests that the HRC leaves the task of identifying any additional measures that might be required to the state.[55]

Thus the remedial practice of the HRC in its views leaves greater discretion to states for implementation than the practice of the IACtHR, and on the issue of compensation it leaves greater discretion to states than the ECtHR. Given the general absence of explicit reasons accounting for the HRC's selection of remedies, the contribution of a principle of subsidiarity to producing this pattern of outcomes is uncertain.

The practice of the HRC may be contrasted with the practice of another treaty body, the Committee on the Elimination of Discrimination Against Women (CEDAW). The recently adopted Optional Protocol that created an individual communication procedure for CEDAW expressly authorizes that body to transmit 'its views on the communication, together with its recommendations, if any, to the parties concerned'.[56] CEDAW's recommendations of remedies have been 'more detailed than those of other human rights treaty bodies', especially with regard to broader legal and administrative reforms for the prevention of future violations.[57] As of January 2012, however, CEDAW had not taken on the task of calculating the compensation owed to victims.

Thus the subsidiarity of international remedies for human rights violations, in regional courts and treaty bodies, takes a wide variety of forms. None of these tribunals execute their own orders; all rely on national implementation. Some remedies are fully specified and need only be enforced, while others leave significant room for adaptation or judgment, and some are quite open-ended. The precision provided for a particular kind of remedy can vary from system to system.

52 Möller and de Zayas (n 51) 457–62.

53 Möller and de Zayas (n 51) 460.

54 Möller and de Zayas (n 51) 481–82; Tyagi (n 18) 556.

55 Möller and de Zayas (n 51) 457.

56 Optional Protocol to the Convention on the Elimination of All Forms of Discrimination Against Women, Art 7(3).

57 Jane Connors, 'Optional Protocol' in Marsha Freeman, Christine Chinkin, and Beate Rudolf (eds), *The UN Convention on the Elimination of All Forms of Discrimination Against Women: A Commentary* (OUP 2012) 656.

4.4 The margin of appreciation

The European doctrine of the margin of appreciation entails deference by the ECtHR to determinations by national authorities regarding the compatibility of national measures with internationally protected rights. Both the meaning and the justifiability of this doctrine are highly contested. Arguably the label 'margin of appreciation' covers different practices that serve different functions, thereby further complicating its relationship with the notion of subsidiarity.

The ECtHR delivered a foundational judgment on the doctrine in *Handyside v United Kingdom*. The compatibility of a conviction for publishing a book that advised schoolchildren on sexual matters with freedom of expression turned on whether the restriction was necessary in a democratic society for the protection of morals. The ECtHR observed that national authorities were in a better position than international judges to decide on both the question of necessity and the exact content of the requirements of morals, given that there was no uniform European conception of morals. The ECtHR accorded the legislature and the national judges a margin of appreciation in assessing these issues, subject to a European supervision.

The ECtHR has since extended a broader or narrower margin of appreciation (implying greater or lesser deference, respectively) in evaluating various claims of violation, invoking a number of factors, such as the nature or importance of the right implicated, the nature of the interest proffered to justify the restriction, the technicality of the subject matter, the degree of consensus existing in national policies on the subject, and the state's need for urgent action.[58] Sometimes the phrase is used, perhaps mistakenly, when the ECtHR independently agrees that the state's chosen action was justified, and hence permissible.[59] Sometimes the phrase expresses the deference of the ECtHR, as a distant judicial body, to the superior empirical understanding of the national authorities regarding local conditions relevant to the proportionality of a restriction.[60] At other times, it suggests the deference of the ECtHR to the superior ability of the national authorities to strike a culturally and/or democratically legitimate balance between conflicting claims of rights, or claims of a right and other interests.[61] Commentators have also expressed concern that the

[58] Paul Mahoney, 'Marvellous Richness of Diversity or Invidious Cultural Relativism?' (1998) 19 *HRLJ* 1; Jeroen Schokkenbroek, 'The Basis, Nature and Application of the Margin-of-Appreciation Doctrine in the Case-Law of the European Court of Human Rights' (1998) 19 *HRLJ* 30.

[59] Ronald St J Macdonald, 'The Margin of Appreciation' in Ronald St J Macdonald, F Matscher, and H Petzold (eds), *The European System for the Protection of Human Rights* (Martinus Nijhoff 1993) 84–85; George Letsas, 'Two Concepts of the Margin of Appreciation' (2006) 26 *OJLS* 705, 706.

[60] MacDonald (n 59) 94, 102–103, 122; Luzius Wildhaber, 'A Constitutional Future for the European Court of Human Rights?' (2002) 23 *HRLJ* 161, 162.

[61] MacDonald, (n 59) 122–23; Wildhaber (n 60) 162; Letsas (n 59) 722–23; cf Robert Alexy, *A Theory of Constitutional Rights* (Julian Rivers (tr), OUP 2002) 420–22 (discussing normative epistemic discretion in balancing).

ECtHR affords national authorities leeway in varying the definition of a protected right.[62]

The practice of extending a margin of appreciation is explicitly linked to the subsidiary character of the ECtHR's review. The empirical version of the margin of appreciation could be understood as a consequence of the limited capacity of international litigation procedures to ensure accurate finding of the facts relevant to policy judgments; to this extent the doctrine bears some analogy to the fourth instance rule.[63] The more challenging questions concern the elements of cultural relativism and majoritarian control involved in other versions of the doctrine, and how they are compatible with the purposes of a human rights court.

Some aspects of the doctrine are defended as pragmatic.[64] The regional court, dependent on the cooperation of the states parties, can avoid confrontation over certain particularly sensitive issues. Furthermore, given the ECtHR's practice of an evolutive interpretation of human rights, a wide margin of appreciation for issues on which states are highly divergent allows the court to postpone a definitive response, and then to adopt a more progressive interpretation after substantial convergence has occurred.

Variable margins of appreciation enable the ECtHR to defer action with regard to some rights while maintaining strict standards for others. The latter includes certain non-derogable rights, such as the right to life and the right not to be tortured, as well as rights of democratic participation that supply some of the legitimacy of the judgments to which the regional court defers.[65]

Another partial justification rests on the incompleteness of balancing as a methodology for resolving conflicts among rights and interests. When proportionality analysis does not unambiguously point to the correct solution, the international court owes respect to the outcome of a properly structured democratic deliberative process. President Luzius Wildhaber has observed that in such cases, an 'area of discretion is a necessary element inherent in the nature of international jurisdiction when applied to democratic States that respect the rule of law'.[66] Arguably, however, this explanation justifies a conclusion of non-violation rather than an occasion for mere deference.[67]

Emphasizing the democratic presuppositions of the margin of appreciation provides one clue as to why the doctrine remains anchored in Europe. Jurists in other regions may not have similar confidence in the democratic credentials of national laws and the progressive character of local legislative consensus.

[62] Janneke Gerards and Hanneke Senden, 'The Structure of Fundamental Rights and the European Court of Human Rights' (2009) 7 *ICON* 619; cf Schokkenbroek (n 58) 36 (insisting that 'the margin has no normative content relating to the interpretation of the provisions of the Convention').

[63] Letsas (n 59) 723; Wildhaber (n 60) 162.

[64] MacDonald (n 59) 123.

[65] Mahoney (n 58) 4–5; Wildhaber (n 60) 162.

[66] Wildhaber (n 60) 162.

[67] Letsas (n 59) 714–15.

A different defence of the margin of appreciation, not limited to situations of balancing, embeds the concept in a fuller theory of social subsidiarity.[68] On this account, the international human rights regime should be subsidiary to the plurality of human communities and therefore should respect the diverse interpretations of human rights treaty norms that these communities generate. International institutions should temper abstract universalism with concrete pluralism, deferring to national interpretations that instantiate the broadly worded norms. This account not only defends the European margin of appreciation, but favors its application globally.[69]

A few reasons for hesitation might be noted concerning this broader defence. First, its persuasiveness may be greatest to those who believe that social subsidiarity does pervade international human rights law. Second, one might question to what extent social subsidiarity would justify deference to national interpretations of human rights norms rather than to the rights claims of members of substate communities.[70] Third, just as one may ask how the democratic justification of the margin of appreciation applies to non-democratic states, one might ask how the social subsidiarity justification applies in a world where many states do not respect the principle of social subsidiarity.

5. Conclusion

Subsidiarity plays important roles in international human rights law, and the use of the concept is likely to expand and evolve in the future. Unquestionably, the international protection of human rights is subsidiary to national protection, serving to help, assist, and supplement it. Working out the consequences of this subsidiarity takes us into more contested terrain. Some authors have argued that one underlying principle unites the different forms of subsidiarity in human rights law, while others have denied it. Still other authors, and some judges, may have taken the single term unreflectively as denoting a single concept. Even if different applications of the term are being mistakenly conflated, that may only increase its power.

[68] Carozza (n 6) 68–73. [69] Carozza (n 6) 75.

[70] cf Eyal Benvenisti, 'Margin of Appreciation, Consensus, and Universal Standards' (1999) 31 *NYU J Int'l L & Pol* 843.

Further Reading

Barber NW, 'The Limited Modesty of Subsidiarity' (2005) 11 *OJLS* 308
Benvenisti E, 'Margin of Appreciation, Consensus, and Universal Standards' (1999) 31 *NYU J Int'l L & Pol* 843
Bermann GA, 'Taking Subsidiarity Seriously: Federalism in the European Community and the United States' (1994) 94 *Columbia L Rev* 331
Carozza PG, 'Subsidiarity as a Structural Principle of International Human Rights Law' (2003) 97 *AJIL* 38
Christoffersen J, *Fair Balance: Proportionality, Subsidiarity and Primarity in the European Convention on Human Rights* (Martinus Nijhoff 2009)
Endo K, 'The Principle of Subsidiarity: From Johannes Althusius to Jacques Delors' (1994) 44 *Hokkaido LJ* 553
Gerards J and Senden H, 'The Structure of Fundamental Rights and the European Court of Human Rights' (2009) 7 *ICON* 619
Letsas G, 'Two Concepts of the Margin of Appreciation' (2006) 26 *OJLS* 705, 706.
Macdonald R St J, 'The Margin of Appreciation' in Ronald St J Macdonald, F Matscher, and H Petzold (eds), *The European System for the Protection of Human Rights* (Martinus Nijhoff 1993) 84
Neuman GL, 'Import, Export, and Regional Consent in the Inter-American Court of Human Rights' (2008) 19 *EJIL* 101
Petzold H, 'The Convention and the Principle of Subsidiarity' in Ronald St J Macdonald, F Matscher, and H Petzold (eds), *The European System for the Protection of Human Rights* (Martinus Nijhoff 1993) 50
Schokkenbroek J, 'The Basis, Nature and Application of the Margin-of-Appreciation Doctrine in the Case-Law of the European Court of Human Rights' (1998) 19 *HRLJ* 30
Shelton D, 'Subsidiarity, Democracy and Human Rights' in Donna Gomien (ed), *Broadening the Frontiers of Human Rights: Essays in Honour of Asbjørn Eide* (Scandinavian UP 1993) 43
Shelton D, 'Subsidiarity and Human Rights Law' (2006) 27 *HRLJ* 4

CHAPTER 16

SOVEREIGNTY

JOHAN D VAN DER VYVER

In 1933, when the League of Nations questioned the treatment of Jews in Germany, Joseph Goebbels, who was to become the *Reich* Minister of Propaganda, responded: 'A man is master in his own home.'[1] By 1949, the world appeared transformed, as the International Law Commission (ILC) proclaimed in its Draft Declaration on Rights and Duties of States that: 'Every State has the duty to conduct its relations with other States in accordance with international law and with the principle that the sovereignty of each State is subject to the supremacy of international law.'[2]

Today, the contents of that supreme body of international law undoubtedly include respect for human rights. Recently, Lord Millet succinctly affirmed this in the British House of Lords, with reference to atrocities that Chile's President Pinochet committed toward the end of the twentieth century: '[T]he way in which a state treat[s] its own citizens within its own borders ha[s] become a matter of legitimate concern to the entire international community.'[3] The Appeals Chamber of the International Criminal Tribunal for the Former Yugoslavia (ICTY) similarly and passionately avowed that: 'It would be a travesty of law and a betrayal of the universal need for justice, should the concept of State sovereignty be allowed to be raised successfully against human rights.'[4]

[1] See Robert Badinter, 'International Criminal Justice: From Darkness to Light' in Antonio Cassese, Paola Gaeta, and John RWD Jones (eds), *The Rome Statute of the International Criminal Court: A Commentary* (OUP 2002).

[2] Draft Declaration on Rights and Duties of States, art 14 (1949), reprinted in United Nations, *The Work of the International Law Commission*, 165–67 (5th edn, United Nations 1996).

[3] *R v Bow Street Metropolitan Stipendiary Magistrate & Others* 177.

[4] *Prosecutor v Duško Tadić*, para 58.

Goebbels's firm assertion of state sovereignty still echoes today, however; some political leaders express it, and the constitutional systems of many countries affirm it. Zimbabwe, for example, adopted a constitutional amendment in 2005, authorizing the compulsory acquisition by the government of farms owned by white farmers only, without compensation, and without granting the farmers access to the courts of law to contest the taking of their property.[5] The Southern African Development Community (SADC) Tribunal condemned the government for (a) depriving the farmers of their property without compensation, (b) taking these lands in a racially discriminatory manner, and (c) denying the landowners access to a court of law to contest the expropriation, in each instance in violation of the Treaty of the Southern African Development Community, to which Zimbabwe is a party.[6] The High Court of Zimbabwe declined to enforce the judgment of the SADC Tribunal, because in Zimbabwe, the Constitution is the supreme law of the land,[7] the Supreme Court of Zimbabwe had upheld the constitutionality of the 'land reform program' at issue,[8] and 'notwithstanding the international obligations of the Government,... registration and consequent enforcement of that judgment would be fundamentally contrary to the public policy of this country'.[9]

The 'international obligations of the Government', given second place in this judgment, are proclaimed as superior in Article 27 of the Vienna Convention on the Law of Treaties, which provides that a party to a treaty 'may not invoke provisions of its own internal law as justification for failure to carry out an international agreement'. In turn, the agreement in question, the Protocol to the Treaty of the Southern African Development Community, through which the SADC Tribunal was established, is explicit in Article 32 that: 'Decisions of the Tribunal shall be binding upon the parties to the dispute... and enforceable within the territories of the States concerned.'[10] It imposes on member states the obligation to 'take forthwith all measures necessary to ensure execution of the decisions of the Tribunal'.[11]

The United States, too, has subordinated its international legal obligations to domestic law, as evidenced by the judgment of the Supreme Court of the United States (SCOTUS) in the case of *Medellín v Texas*.[12] The International Court of Justice (ICJ)[13] and the Inter-American Commission on Human Rights

[5] Constitution of the Republic of Zimbabwe (2005).

[6] *Campbell (Pvt) Ltd and Others v The Republic of Zimbabwe*.

[7] Constitution of the Republic of Zimbabwe (1980) art 3.

[8] *Campbell (Pvt) Ltd and Another v Minister of National Security Responsible for Land, Land Reform and Resettlement*.

[9] *Gramara (Pvt) Ltd and Another v Government of the Republic of Zimbabwe and Others* 16.

[10] SADC 'Protocol on Tribunal and Rules of Procedure Thereof' (2000) art 32(3).

[11] SADC 'Protocol on Tribunal' (n 10) art 32(2).

[12] *Medellín v Texas*. See also Johan D van der Vyver, *Implementation of International Law in the United States* (Peter Lang GmbH 2010) 129–58.

[13] *Case Concerning the Vienna Convention on Consular Relations (Paraguay v United States)*; *LaGrand Case (Germany v US)*; *Avena and Other Mexican Nationals (Mexico v United States)*.

(IACHR)[14] have held against the United States several times for its failure to comply with the commitments contained in Article 36 of the Vienna Convention on Consular Relations to inform foreigners that it arrested or detained, in prison or in custody in the United States, of their right to consular assistance.[15] In *Medellín*, SCOTUS declined to use judicial action to implement an ICJ instruction that the United States remedy, 'by means of its own choosing', the consequences of non-compliance with Article 36. SCOTUS also held that President George W Bush acted unconstitutionally when he instructed state Attorneys General to give effect to the ICJ judgment in the case of *Mexico v The United States of America*.[16] This occurred despite the President's duty under Article II, Section 3 of the Constitution to 'take Care that the Laws be faithfully executed',[17] where 'laws' include the treaties that the United States enters into, as they are designated as part of the supreme law of the land.[18] The result left the US in violation, at least temporarily,[19] of Article 94(1) of the Charter of the United Nations, pursuant

[14] *Case of Ramón Martinez Villareal*. See also *Case of Cesar Fierro*, noting that executing the convicted individual would constitute an arbitrary deprivation of his right to life.

[15] Vienna Convention on Consular Relations, Art 36 (placing an obligation on the state concerned: (a) upon the request of the detainee, to inform the consular post of the state of nationality of the person arrested, in prison, custody, or detention, without delay, of the arrest or detention of that person; (b) to forward, without delay, any correspondence addressed by the person arrested, in prison, custody, or detention, to the consular post of his or her national state; and most importantly, (c) to inform the person arrested, in prison, custody or detention, without delay, of his or her rights under this provision).

[16] Memorandum for the Attorney General (28 February 2005) 44 ILM 964, with reference to *Avena* (n 13). An undertaking of the United States in an earlier case to, in the future, comply with Art 36 of the Vienna Convention on Consular Relations clearly prompted the President's instruction. See *LaGrand Case* (n 13) para 124.

[17] US Constitution, art II, s 3. See also Joshua J Newcomer, 'Messing with Texas? Why President Bush's Memorandum Order Trumps State Criminal Procedure' (2006) 79 *Temple L Rev* 1029, 1044.

[18] Louis Henkin, 'International Law as Law in the United States' (1984) 82 *Mich L Rev* 1555, 1567 ('There can be little doubt that the President has the duty, as well as the authority, to take care that international law, as part of the law of the United States, is faithfully executed'); Jules Lobel, 'The Limits of Constitutional Power: Conflicts Between Foreign Policy and International Law' (1985) 71 *Va L Rev* 1071, 1119 ('The President has a constitutional obligation to execute international law because it is the law of the land'); Arthur S Miller, 'The President and Faithful Execution of the Laws' (1987) 40 *Vand L Rev* 389, 405 (referring to the President's duty 'to faithfully execute the laws—in this instance, international law'); Newcomer (n 17) 1045 (noting that the 'faith execution' Clause empowered the President to enforce the treaty); Jordan J Paust, '*Medellin, Avena*, the Supremacy of Treaties and Relevant Executive Authority' (2008) 31 *Suffolk Transnat'l L Rev* 301, 311 (referring to the constitutionally-based mandate under which 'the President must faithfully execute... treaties of the United States').

[19] On 7 March 2005, the United States withdrew from the Protocol to the Vienna Convention on Consular Relations, under which disputes emanating from the Convention must be submitted to the ICJ. A bill '[t]o facilitate compliance with Article 36 of the Vienna Convention on Consular Relations' is currently pending before Congress and will, if enacted, afford to federal courts 'jurisdiction to review the merits of a petition claiming a violation of Article 36(1)(b) or (c) of the Vienna Convention on Consular relations... or a comparable provision of a bilateral international agreement addressing consular notification and access'. Consular Notification Compliance Act of 2011, s 1194, 112th Cong (2011) s 4(a)(1).

to which every member state 'undertakes to comply with the decision of the International Court of Justice in any case to which it is a party'.[20]

The reasoning of the US Supreme Court has relevance to the discussion of sovereignty because of its references to Article 94(2) of the UN Charter. That article addresses the possible consequences should a party to a case before the ICJ fail to comply with the Court's judgment. It affords to the Security Council the power to 'make recommendations or decide upon measures to be taken to give effect to the judgment'.[21] The plurality observed that the President and the Senate 'were undoubtedly aware' of this 'diplomatic—that is, nonjudicial—remedy' when they ratified the Optional Protocol to the Vienna Convention on Consular Relations.[22] The so-called 'diplomatic remedy' affords to the United States 'the unqualified right to exercise its veto of any Security Council resolution'.[23] SCOTUS appears to be saying that the United States, through actions of the President and the Senate, submitted to the compulsory *ipso jure* jurisdiction of the ICJ, with the knowledge and upon the deliberate understanding that the United States—and presumably other permanent members of the Security Council who hold a veto—can disregard judgments of the Court at will and without adverse consequences. If true, this elevates considerations of sovereignty to a level of profound cynicism.

1. The Concept of Sovereignty

Jean Bodin (1530–95) is commonly regarded as 'the founder of the modern doctrine of sovereignty'.[24] Attempts to create a unitary national state in France following the Hundred Years War (1350–1450), triggered the first theoretical exposition of the concept of sovereignty in Bodin's *Six Livres de la République*.[25] The gist of Bodin's concept of sovereignty is reflected in the adage: *Summa in cives ac subditos legibusque solute potest* ('[sovereignty is] the supreme power over citizens and subordinates, which [supreme power] is not subject to the law'). Wolfgang Friedmann tells us that Bodin's theory 'was mainly concerned with securing and consolidating the legislative power of the monarch in France against the rival claims of estates,

[20] Charter of the United Nations, Art 94 (UN Charter). [21] UN Charter, Art 94(2).

[22] *Medellín* (n 12) 509.

[23] *Medellín* (n 12) 510. See also David J Bederman, 'Medellin's New Paradigm for Treaty Interpretation' (2008) 102 *AJIL* 529, 534 (noting that applying 'the probative impact of Senate ratification debates and understandings in creating a "legislative history" for international agreements' was unprecedented and in itself 'the most astonishing interpretative move in Medellin').

[24] Wolfgang Friedmann, *Legal Theory* (5th edn, Columbia UP 1967) 573.

[25] See HJ van Eikema Hommes, *Hoofdlijnen van de Geschiedenis der Rechtsfilosofie* (2nd edn, Kluwer 1981) 63.

corporations, and the Church'.[26] The contemporary meaning and significance of sovereignty goes well beyond this, of course.

Sovereignty operates in at least three quite distinct venues in human society. In international law, it primarily denotes 'the international independence of a state, combined with the right and power of regulating its internal affairs without foreign dictation',[27] or 'the right of a state to pursue whatever policies it wishes within its own borders'.[28] In constitutional law, sovereignty denotes the 'supreme political authority' within the body politic, or '[t]he supreme, absolute, and uncontrollable power by which any independent state is governed', [29] or 'the power and authority of the State over all persons, things, and territory within its reach',[30] and which includes 'powers of the...government in respect of foreign or external affairs and those in respect of domestic or internal affairs'.[31] Social entities other than the state (for example, church institutions) can also lay claim to sovereign powers to regulate their internal affairs, without interference by the power base of other social institutions that are of a different kind (for example, the state).[32] Here, we are primarily concerned with the sovereignty of states as governed by international law.

The sovereignty of states has several dimensions, including (a) political independence; (b) exclusive control of the sovereign state over the persons and objects within its territory and under its control; (c) territorial integrity, or the inviolability of national borders; and (d) immunity of the sovereign state and certain high-ranking state officials from the exercise of jurisdiction by the courts of other states or international tribunals.

1.1 Political independence

Sovereignty in the international context means, in part, 'an autonomous state in no way subordinate to any other country'.[33] An influential line of thought, reflected in a statement by Judge Huber in the *Island of Palmas Case* of 1928, [34] and the separate

[26] Friedmann (n 24) 573–74.

[27] See Henry Campbell Black, *Black's Law Dictionary* (6th edn, West 1990).

[28] See Johan D van der Vyver, 'Sovereignty and Human Rights in Constitutional and International Law' (1991) 5 *Emory Int'l L Rev* 321, 392 (citing Richard Lillich).

[29] Black (n 27). As to political sovereignty in the constitutional context, see Van der Vyver, 'Sovereignty and Human Rights' (n 28) 355–92.

[30] JES Fawcett, *The Law of Nations* (Basic Books 1968) 39.

[31] *United States v Curtiss-Wright Export Corp* 315 (Sutherland, J, delivering the opinion of the Court).

[32] See Van der Vyver, 'Sovereignty and Human Rights' (n 28) 342–55; Johan D van der Vyver, *Leuven Lectures on Religious Institutions, Religious Communities and Rights* (Peeters 2004) 35–66; Johan D van der Vyver, 'Sphere Sovereignty of Religious Institutions: A Contemporary Calvinistic Theory of Church-State Relations' in Gerhard Robbers (ed), *Church Autonomy* (Peter Lang 2001) 645.

[33] *Harris v Minister of the Interior* (Centlivres, CJ, delivering the judgment of the Court).

[34] *Island of Palmas Case (United States v The Netherlands)*.

opinion of Judge Anzilotti in the *Austro-German Customs Case* of 1931,[35] identified 'sovereignty' with the 'internal and domestic power' of the state and defined sovereignty in the international context as 'independence'. Judge Huber explained that '[s]overeignty in the relations between States signifies independence. Independence in regard to a portion of the globe is the right to exercise therein, to the exclusion of any other State, the functions of a State'.[36] Judge Anzilotti, in a statement described by James Crawford as the *locus classicus* on the subject,[37] proclaimed that: 'Independence... may also be described as sovereignty (*suprema potestas*), or external sovereignty, by which is meant that the State has over it no other authority than that of international law.'[38]

James Fawcett likewise identified sovereignty in the external and international context as 'independence',[39] defining an independent state as 'a community of people, living together in a defined territory under an organized government not subordinate to any other government'.[40] Clive Parry argued that sovereignty in international law 'no longer conveys the idea of supremacy but rather that of independence' and that in a secondary sense, sovereignty denotes 'the authority of the state over its territory or its citizens'.[41]

A trend emerged in international law in the twentieth century to promote the national independence of subordinated entities by creating new states. This first became evident at the peace negotiations following the First World War (1914–18). In his Fourteen Points Address of 8 January 1918, President Woodrow Wilson contemplated:

> [a] free, open-minded, and absolutely impartial adjustment of all colonial claims, based upon a strict observance of the principle that in determining all such questions of sovereignty the interests of the population concerned must have equal weight with the equitable claims of government whose title is to be determined.[42]

Wilson's statement has come to be regarded as the basis of the mandate system under which the League of Nations regulated the future political

[35] *Customs Régime between Germany and Austria.*

[36] *Island of Palmas Case* (n 34) 838. See also p 839 ('[t]erritorial sovereignty... involves the exclusive right to display the activities of a State').

[37] James Crawford, 'The Criteria of Statehood in International Law' (1976–77) 48 *British YB Int'l L* 93, 122.

[38] *Customs Régime between Germany and Austria* (n 35) 57 (individual opinion by Anzilotti, J).

[39] Fawcett, *Law of Nations* (n 30) 41.

[40] Fawcett, *Law of Nations* (n 30) 46. See also JES Fawcett, 'General Course on Public International Law' (1971) 132 *RCADI* 363, 381 (maintaining that '[i]ndependence and sovereignty can be seen as the *external and internal aspects* of the State').

[41] Clive Parry, 'The Function of Law in the International Community' in Max Sørensen (ed), *Manual of Public International Law* (St Martin's Press 1968) 13.

[42] President Wilson, 'Fourteen Points' (Address to Congress, Washington DC, 8 January 1918) point 5. See Ray Stannard Baker and William E Dodd (eds), *Public Papers of Woodrow Wilson: War and Peace* (Harper 1927) 155–59.

dispensation of nation-states that had been part of the Ottoman, German, Russian, and Austro-Hungarian empires,[43] eventually 'transforming self-determination into a universal right'.[44] Following the Second World War (1935–45), the aim of the international community with respect to self-determination expanded to include 'bringing all colonial situations to a speedy end'.[45] Colonized peoples thus acquired the right to self-determination, substantively denoting political independence.[46] The United Nations Millennium Declaration reaffirmed the principle of decolonization as 'the right to self-determination of peoples which remain under... foreign occupation'.[47]

It should be emphasized at the outset that the concept of 'self-determination' is not confined to communities subject to colonial rule or foreign occupation, but is also attributed to ethnic, religious, and linguistic minorities within the body politic. Here, the substance of the right is not a matter of political independence, but is confined to the entitlement of an ethnic community to promote its culture, of a religious community to practice its religion, and of a linguistic community to speak its language, without undue state interference or legal restrictions. The International Covenant on Civil and Political Rights (ICCPR) thus provides: 'In those States in which ethnic, religious or linguistic minorities exist, persons belonging to such minorities shall not be denied the right, in community with the other members of their group, to enjoy their own culture, to profess and practise their own religion, or to use their own language.'[48]

1.2 Exclusive control within national borders

The 1970 United Nations Declaration on Principles of International Law concerning Friendly Relations and Cooperation among States in Accordance with the Charter of the United Nations ('the 1970 Declaration') contains an impressive exposition of '[t]he principle concerning the duty not to intervene in matters within the domestic

[43] Vernon van Dyke, *Human Rights, the United States,and World Community* (OUP 1970) 86.

[44] Robert A Friedlander, 'Self-Determination: A Legal-Political Inquiry' (1975) 1 *Det CL Rev* 71, 73.

[45] *Western Sahara*, para 55. See also *Legal Consequences for States of the Continued Presence of South Africa in Namibia (South West Africa) Notwithstanding Security Council Resolution 276 (1970)*, para 52 (in which the Court holds that the right to self-determination was applicable to 'territories under colonial rule' and that it 'embraces all peoples and territories which "have not yet attained independence"').

[46] Nathaniel Berman, 'Sovereignty in Abeyance: Self-Determination and International Law' (1988) 7 *Wis Int'l LJ* 51, 54. See also van Dyke (n 43) 87; Rupert Emerson, 'Self-Determination' (1971) 65 *AJIL* 459, 463; Oscar Schachter, 'The United Nations and Internal Conflict' in John Norton Moore (ed), *Law and Civil War in the Modern World* (Johns Hopkins UP 1974) 406–407; Gebre Hiwet Tesfagiorgis, 'Self-Determination: Its Evolution and Practice by the United Nations and its Application to the Case of Eritrea' (1987) 6 *Wis Int'l LJ* 75, 78–80; Antonio Cassese, *Self-Determination of Peoples: A Legal Reappraisal* (Grotius 1995) para 43.

[47] United Nations Millennium Declaration, para 4.

[48] ICCPR, Art 27.

jurisdiction of any State, in accordance with the Charter'. The principle includes the following directives:

No State or group of States has the right to intervene, directly or indirectly, for any reason whatever, in the internal or external affairs of any other state....

No State may use or encourage the use of economic, political or any other type of measures to coerce another State in order to obtain from it the subordination of the exercise of its sovereign rights and to secure from it advantages of any kind.

...

Every State has an inalienable right to choose its political, economic, social and cultural systems, without interference in any form by another State.[49]

The Declaration also included under the '[p]rinciple of sovereign equality of States', the right of each state 'freely to choose and develop its political, social, economic and cultural systems'.[50]

Although the Declaration makes no attempt—nor does any other international instrument—to define what constitutes the internal affairs of a state, one aspect of internal sovereignty has received explicit recognition: exclusive control of the state over its natural wealth and resources. The United Nations has repeatedly proclaimed the 'inalienable right of all states freely to dispose of their natural wealth and resources in accordance with their national interests',[51] with occasional reminders that developing countries are in need of encouragement 'in the proper use and exploitation of their natural wealth and resources'.[52] Article 1(2) common to the human rights covenants of 1966 goes further, by adding that the right has to be exercised 'without prejudice to any obligations arising out of international economic co-operation, based upon the principle of mutual benefit, and internationals law'.[53]

The inclusion of this principle in the Covenants could be seen as limited to the colonial context or as a grant of the right to peoples (indigenous and tribal) existing within a state. In either case, it marks a shift away from designating the right over natural resources as an integral part of state sovereignty, and toward proclaiming it more specifically as a component of the human right of peoples to

[49] The 1970 Declaration. [50] The 1970 Declaration.

[51] See eg UNGA Res 626 (21 December 1952) UN Doc A/2361; UNGA Res 1515 (15 December 1960) UN Doc A/4648; UNGA Res 1803 (14 December 1962) UN Doc A/5217; UNGA Res 2158 (25 November 1966) UN Doc A/6316; UNGA Res 3016 (18 December 1972) UN Doc A/8730; UNGA Res 3171 (17 December 1973) UN Doc A/9030. See also Trade and Development Board, Res 88 on Permanent Sovereignty over Natural Resources (19 October 1972) UN Doc A/8715?/Rev.1, endorsed by the General Assembly in UNGA Res 3041 (19 December 1972) UN Doc A/8730, para 16. There was up to date reaffirmation in the 1992 Convention on Biological Diversity, at least insofar as biological resources are concerned.

[52] UNGA Res 626 (21 December 1952) UN Doc A/2361. See eg ESC Res 1737 (1973) UN ESCOR Supp 54; UNGA Res 1803 (14 December 1962) UN Doc A/5217, para 6; UNGA Res 2158 (28 November 1966) UN Doc A/6316, para 3.

[53] ICCPR, Art 1(2); International Covenant on Economic, Social and Cultural Rights, Art 1(2).

self-determination. As early as 1958, the General Assembly, in the Resolution establishing the Commission on Permanent Sovereignty over Natural Resources,[54] stated that the 'permanent sovereignty over natural wealth and resources' of states is 'a basic constituent of the right to self-determination'.[55] In the colonial context, the General Assembly decided in 1967 that the 'inalienable right' to natural resources, and the right to dispose of those resources in territories subject to colonial rule, belonged to the peoples of the colonized territories,[56] adding:

> [T]he colonial Powers which deprive the colonial peoples of the exercise and the full enjoyment of those rights, or which subordinate them to the economic or financial interests of their own nationals or of nationals of other countries, are violating the obligations they have assumed under... the Charter of the United Nations.[57]

At the regional level, Article 21(1) of the African Charter on Human and Peoples' Rights provides: 'All peoples shall freely dispose of their wealth and natural resources. This right shall be exercised in the exclusive interest of the people. In no case shall a people be deprived of it.'[58] In the 2001 *Ogoni decision*, the African Commission on Human and Peoples' Rights (ACHPR) traced the historical basis of this provision to colonialism, 'during which the human and material resources of Africa were largely exploited for the benefit of outside powers'.[59] The decision made clear, however, that the peoples' rights in the African Charter are no longer coextensive with the state or limited to the colonial context, but extend to all 'peoples' within the states of Africa. In a recent path-breaking decision, the ACHPR decided that an indigenous community that had been displaced from their ancestral land in Kenya almost half a century ago (the *Endorois*), still constitute a distinct people within the meaning of Article 21(1) and that their right to 'freely dispose of their wealth and natural resources' has been violated.[60] The Inter-American system has similar jurisprudence with respect to the rights of indigenous and tribal peoples over their ancestral lands and natural resources.[61]

The right of indigenous peoples to their ancestral lands or territories, and in particular in connection with the development of mineral, water, or other resources, have been afforded prominence in the United Nations Declaration on the Rights of

[54] UNGA Res 1314 (12 December 1958) UN Doc A/4090.

[55] See also United Nations Declaration on the Granting of Independence to Colonial Countries and Peoples, para 2; United Nations Declaration on the Right to Development, para 1.2. See also UNGA Res 2288 (7 December 1967) UN Doc A/6716.

[56] UNGA Res 2288 (n 55) para 2.

[57] UNGA Res 2288 (n 55) para 3.

[58] The African Charter on Human and Peoples' Rights, Art 21(1).

[59] *Social and Economic Rights Action Center (SERAC) v Nigeria*, para 58.

[60] *Centre for Minority Rights Development (Kenya) and Minority Rights Group International v Kenya*. See also Margaret Beukes, 'The Recognition of "Indigenous Peoples" and Their Rights as "a People": An African First' (2010) 35 *South Afr YB Int'l L* 216.

[61] See eg *Case of the Indigenous Community Yakye Axa v Paraguay*, para 137; *Case of the Indigenous Community Sawhoyamaxa v Paraguay*, para 118; *Case of the Saramaka People v Suriname*, para 121.

Indigenous Peoples,[62] and in several other human rights instruments.[63] These rights evidently place a damper on state sovereignty over such territories and resources, based on human rights concerns.

1.3 Territorial integrity

International law has been adamant in proclaiming the sanctity of post-Second World War national borders. The Organization of African Unity (now the African Union), sensitive to the chaotic situation that might emerge with any effort to redraw the (quite irrational) national borders that colonial powers established in Africa, played a leading role in emphasizing the salience of the existing frontiers. Its Charter of 1963 prompted member states to 'solemnly affirm and declare' their 'respect for the sovereignty and territorial integrity of each State and for its inalienable right to independent existence'.[64] A Resolution of the Assembly of Heads of State and Government adopted at its first ordinary session, held in Cairo in 1964, called on all member states 'to respect the borders existing on their achievement of national independence'.[65]

The principle of upholding the territorial integrity of states has been emphatically endorsed in other international instruments, including the 1970 Declaration, which proclaimed that, 'any attempt aimed at the partial or total disruption of the national unity and territorial integrity of a State or country or at its political independence is incompatible with the purposes and principles of the Charter [of the United Nations]', without exception.[66] The Helsinki Final Act[67] likewise endorsed the principle of 'respect for the sovereignty and territorial integrity of each State and for its inalienable right to independent existence'.[68] It has now come to be accepted that 'the principle of territorial integrity is an important part of the international legal order and is enshrined in the Charter of the United Nations'.[69] The principle of territorial integrity of states has two elements, one strictly prohibiting the acquisition of territory by force, and the second generally denouncing secession from the territory of an existing state.

[62] UN Declaration on the Rights of Indigenous Peoples, Art 32.

[63] See eg the Indigenous and Tribal Peoples Convention of the International Labour Organization, Convention No 169, Art 15(2); Office of the High Commissioner for Human Rights (OHCHR), 'General Comment 23: The Rights of Minorities' (1994) CCPR/C/21/Rev.1/Add.5, para 7; OHCHR 'General Recommendation XXIII: Indigenous Peoples' (1997) UN Doc A/52/18 Annex V, para 5.

[64] Charter of the Organization of African Unity, Art III(3).

[65] Organization of African Unity (1964) AHG/Res. 16(I), para 2.

[66] The 1970 Declaration, preamble.

[67] Final Act of the Conference on Security and Co-operation in Europe, Art III.

[68] UN Charter, Art III(3).

[69] *Accordance with International Law of the Unilateral Declaration of Independence in respect of Kosovo*, para 80 (*Kosovo Case*).

1.3.1 *The forceful acquisition of a territory*

During much of history, military invasions, conquest, annexation, and occupation established and modified national borders, almost at random. Today, the acquisition of a territory by force is inadmissible in international law and its inadmissibility is often asserted to be a *jus cogens* norm.[70] The UN Charter places predominant emphasis on the maintenance of international peace and security,[71] through the peaceful settlement of disputes[72] and the obligation of member states to refrain from the threat or use of force.[73] The 1970 Declaration endorsed and further specified this central theme of international relations and coexistence.

The General Assembly confirmed the unconditional proscription on the acquisition of territory by force in its definition of aggression.[74] Aggression includes '[t]he invasion or attack by the armed forces of a State of the territory of another State, or any military occupation, however temporary, resulting from such invasion or attack, or any annexation by the use of force of the territory of another State or part thereof'.[75] The Resolution further provides: 'No consideration of whatever nature, whether political, economic, military or otherwise, may serve as a justification for aggression';[76] and, '[n]o territorial acquisition or special advantage resulting from aggression is or shall be recognized as lawful'.[77] General agreement during the 2010 Review Conference of the International Criminal Court (ICC), held in Kampala, Uganda, endorsed this definition of aggression.[78]

States responsible for the invasion of any other state are liable for human rights violations committed in the occupied territory. Following the invasion of Northern Cyprus by Turkey, the European Court of Human Rights decided that Turkey's responsibility for human rights violations in Cyprus derived from its effective control of the occupied territory and was not dependent on the legality or illegality of such control.[79] Following the attempted annexation of Kuwait by Iraq on 2 August 1990, the Security Council likewise demanded that Iraq accept 'in principle its liability under international law for any loss, damage or injury arising in regard to

[70] See eg James Fawcett, *Law and Power in International Relations* (Faber and Faber 1982) 91; Ian Sinclair, *The Vienna Convention on the Law of Treaties* (Manchester UP 1984) 222; Eduardo Jiménez de Aréchaga, General Course in Public International Law (1978) 159 *RCADI* 1, 64; Jochen Frowein, 'Jus Cogens' (1984) 7 *Encyclopedia of International Law* 327, 329; Giorgio Gaja, 'Ius Cogens Beyond the Vienna Convention' (1981) 172 *RCADI* 271, 287–88. See also Erika de Wet's chapter in this *Handbook*.

[71] UN Charter, Art 1(1). [72] UN Charter, Art 2(3). [73] UN Charter, Art 4.

[74] UNGA Res 3314 (14 December 1974) UN Doc A/9631. [75] UNGA Res 3314 (n 81) Art 3(a).

[76] UNGA Res 3314 (n 81) Art 5(1).

[77] UNGA Res 3314 (n 81) Art 5(3). See also the UNGA 'Declaration on the Inadmissibility of Intervention in the Domestic Affairs of States and The Protection of Their Independence and Sovereignty' (21 December 1965) UN Doc A/Res/20/2131, para 3.

[78] ICC 'Resolution on the Crime of Aggression' (11 June 2010) ICC-ASP/RC/Res.6, Annex 1, para 2.

[79] *Loizidou v Turkey*, paras 54–57.

Kuwait and third States and their nationals and corporations, as a result of the invasion and illegal occupation of Kuwait by Iraq'.[80]

1.3.2 *Secession*

International law is also, in principle, not favourably disposed toward the dismemberment of existing states, particularly if the purpose of the separation is to establish homogenous ethnic, religious, or linguistic communities. The international community of states has thus censured attempts at secession by Katanga, Biafara, and the Turkish Republic of Northern Cyprus.[81] As explained by Vernon van Dyke, 'the United Nations would be in an extremely difficult position if it were to interpret the right to self-determination in such a way as to invite or justify attacks on the territorial integrity of its own members'.[82]

It must be emphasized that the right to self-determination of ethnic, religious, and linguistic communities is confined to the right of such communities to promote and protect their culture, to practise their religion, and to speak their language, without undue state restrictions. It does not include a right to secession. The 1992 Declaration expressly states that its provisions must not be taken to contradict the principles of the United Nations pertaining to, inter alia, 'sovereign equality, territorial integrity and political independence of States'.[83] The 2007 United Nations Declaration on the Rights of Indigenous Peoples reiterated that, by virtue of their right to self-determination, indigenous peoples are entitled to 'freely determine their political status and freely pursue their economic, social and cultural development'.[84] Lest this provision be interpreted to denote political independence, the Declaration stipulates that '[n]othing in this Declaration may be... construed as authorizing or encouraging any action which would dismember or impair, totally or in part, the territorial integrity or political unity of sovereign and independent States'.[85] The 1995 Framework Convention for the Protection of National Minorities of the Council of Europe fixes the same outer limit:

> Nothing in the present framework Convention shall be interpreted as implying any right to engage in any activity or perform any act contrary to the fundamental principles of international law and in particular of the sovereign equality, territorial integrity and political independence of States.[86]

[80] UNSC Res 686 (2 March 1991) UN Doc S/Res/686, Art 2(b).

[81] See Van der Vyver, 'Sovereignty and Human Rights' (n 28) 403–407. For greater detail, see James Crawford, *The Creation of States in International Law* (Clarendon Press 1979) 235–36 (Katanga), 265 (Biafara); John Dugard, *Recognition and the United Nations* (Grotius 1987) 86–90 (Katanga), 84–85 (Biafara), 108–111 (Turkish Republic of Northern Cyprus); Johan D van der Vyver, 'Statehood in International Law' (1991) 5 *Emory Int'l L Rev* 9, 35–37 (Katanga), 42–44 (Turkish Republic of Northern Cyprus).

[82] Van Dyke (n 43) 102.

[83] Declaration on the Rights of Persons Belonging to National or Ethnic, Religious and Linguistic Minorities, Art 8(4).

[84] Declaration on the Rights of Indigenous Peoples, Art 3.

[85] Declaration on the Rights of Indigenous Peoples, Art 46(1).

[86] European Framework Convention for the Protection of National Minorities, Art 21.

Secession is sanctioned by international law in two instances only: (i) if a decision to secede is 'freely determined by a people'[87]—that is, it is submitted, a cross section of the entire population of the state to be divided, and not only to the inhabitants of the region wishing to secede;[88] and (ii) if, following an armed conflict, national boundaries are redrawn as part of a peace settlement.[89] The reunification of Germany, the break-up of the Soviet Union, the parting of constitutional ways of the Czech Republic and Slovakia, and the recent secession of Southern Sudan,[90] exemplify the first of these two principles, while the secession of Eritrea from Ethiopia exemplifies the second. The disintegration of the former Yugoslavia represents a complicated conglomeration of both principles.

On 17 February 2008, a substantial majority of the Assembly of Kosovo adopted a unilateral declaration of independence from Serbia. The General Assembly followed this act by requesting an advisory opinion from the ICJ—a request, which the court noted did not call upon it 'to take a position on whether international law conferred a positive entitlement on Kosovo unilaterally to declare its independence or, a fortiori, on whether international law generally confers an entitlement on entities situated within a State unilaterally to break away from it'.[91] Instead, the ICJ concluded that the Security Council Resolution which authorized the Secretary General to establish an interim administration for Kosovo with a view, inter alia, to oversee 'the development of provisional democratic self-governing institutions'[92] did not preclude this declaration of independence,[93] and somewhat obscurely, that the declaration of independence did not violate general international law.[94]

The United Nations' 1993 World Conference on Human Rights, in its declaration on self-determination, reiterated that this right 'shall not be construed as authorizing or encouraging any action which would dismember or impair, totally or in part, the territorial integrity or political unity of sovereign and independent States', but seemingly only made this assertion applicable to states 'conducting themselves in compliance with the principle of equal rights and self-determination of peoples and thus possessed of a Government representing the whole people belonging to

[87] The 1970 Declaration, proclaiming under the heading 'The Principle of Equal Rights and Self-Determination of Peoples' that: 'The establishment of a sovereign and independent State, the free association or integration with an independent State or the emergence into any other political status freely determined by a people constitute modes of implementing the right of self-determination by that people.'

[88] See the Canadian case, *Reference re: Secession of Quebec*, para 93 (deciding that secession of Quebec from Canada will require 'clear' majorities on two fronts: the population of the province of Quebec and the population of Canada as a whole). See also the 1970 Declaration, para 152.

[89] Cassese, *Self-Determination of Peoples* (n 46) 359–63.

[90] The referendum that sanctioned the secession of Southern Sudan was confined to residents of that region, but the legislation of Sudan that authorized the referendum sanctioned it.

[91] *Kosovo Case* (n 69) para 56.

[92] UNSC Res 1244 (10 June 1999) UN Doc S/Res/1244, Art 10.

[93] *Kosovo Case* (n 69) paras 114, 119.

[94] *Kosovo Case* (n 69) para 122.

the territory without distinction of any kind'.[95] Does this mean that secession would also be legitimate as a remedial right, founded on violations of the right of indigenous peoples to self-determination? Some years ago, the African Commission on Human and Peoples' Rights suggested by way of obiter dictum that Katanga would have been entitled to secede from Zaire if 'concrete evidence [existed] of violations of human rights to the point that the territorial integrity of Zaire should be called to question and ... that the people of Katanga are denied the right to participate in government as guaranteed by article 13(1) of the African Charter'.[96] The fallacy of this reasoning is that the right to self-determination belongs to a people while it is a territory that secedes. In the final analysis, a general agreement or a peace treaty must sanction secession. It is, of course, quite possible that gross human rights violations could culminate in a referendum or an armed conflict that would eventually constitute the basis of secession; however, the legality of secession will depend on the referendum or peace treaty, and not on the human rights violations per se—at least not within the current confines of international law and state sovereignty.

There are indeed compelling reasons to avoid the disjunction of territorial frontiers. First, a multiplicity of economically non-viable states will further contribute to a decline in the living standards in the world community. Second, the belief that people sharing a common language, culture, or religion are inherently politically compatible is clearly a myth, and disillusionment after the event might provoke profound resentment and further conflict. A third reason lies in the fact that the migration of people across territorial divides has largely dismantled any previously existing homogeneity in the population of all regions, rendering impossible any demarcation of borders based on specific demography. Fourth, affording such political relevance to ethnic, cultural, or religious affiliations carries with it the potential for the repression of minority groups within the nation, and excludes political standing for persons who, on account of mixed parentage or marriage, do not and cannot be identified with any particular faction of the group-conscious community, as well as those who, for whatever reason, do not wish to be identified under any particular ethnic, religious, or cultural label. In consequence of the above, an ethnically, culturally, or religiously defined state would, more often than not, create its own 'minorities problem', and secession based on ethnicity, culture, or religion, would almost invariably result in profound discrimination against those who do not belong, or worse still, in a strategy of ethnic cleansing.

[95] Vienna Declaration and Programme of Action, Art I(2).

[96] *Katangese People's Congress v Zaire*, para 6. See in general, Ernest Duga Titanji, 'The Right of Indigenous Peoples to Self-Determination Versus Secession: One Coin, Two Faces?' (2009) 9 *Afr Hum Rts LJ* 52, 68–72, 73–74.

1.4 Sovereign immunity

Foreign sovereign immunity, derived from the norm of sovereign equality, has several dimensions. First, under the act of state doctrine, the courts of one country will not inquire into the validity of public acts of another recognized, foreign sovereign, when committed within that first sovereign's territory.[97] The act of state doctrine is a principle of international comity, based on respect for the sovereignty of foreign nations on their own territory and a desire to avoid embarrassing the executive branch of government in its conduct of foreign relations.[98] It has been held in the United States that the act of state doctrine is confined to declaring invalid the official acts of the foreign sovereign power within its own territory and will not preclude the exercise of jurisdiction to pronounce upon certain unlawful transactions, such as receiving bribes in the performance of an official act—at least when Congress directs the Courts to decide.[99]

State immunity, which legislation regulates in many states,[100] applies to preclude the exercise of jurisdiction by national courts over foreign states. As discussed in the chapter on immunities, such laws often contain a 'commercial activities exception', which provides no jurisdictional immunity to a foreign state in respect of a commercial activity the foreign state carries out while acting as would a private actor.[101] Most states now accept that sovereign immunity is limited in this respect. Other exceptions are more controversial, including the 'territorial tort exception', which excludes the jurisdictional immunity of a foreign state in instances of tortious conduct, attributable to the state, being committed in the state exercising jurisdiction.[102]

In the case of *Germany v Italy: Greece Intervening*, the ICJ considered the existence and scope of a 'territorial tort exception' under the rules of customary international law applicable to state immunity. The ICJ affirmed that state immunity 'derives from the principle of sovereign equality of States' and 'occupies an important place in international law and international relations'.[103] As have many national courts, the ICJ determined that the immunity is 'essentially procedural in nature'[104] and that it applies only to *acta jure imperii* (the exercise of sovereign powers) of a state.[105]

[97] *Underhill v Hernandez* 252; *Banco Nacional de Cuba v Sabbatino* 416–39.

[98] *Kirkpatrick Co v Environmental Tectonics Corp International* 408.

[99] *Kirkpatrick* (n 98) 409–10.

[100] See *Jurisdictional Immunities of the State* (*Germany v Italy*), para 70 (referring to legislation of nine states that includes a 'tort exception' in legislation regulating the act of state doctrine).

[101] 28 USC § 1605(a)(2) (2006).

[102] 28 USC § 1605(a)(5) (2006). As to exceptions to jurisdictional immunities of states and their property, see also United Nations Convention on Jurisdictional Immunities of States and Their Property, Arts 10–17.

[103] *Jurisdictional Immunities of the State* (n 100) para 57.

[104] *Jurisdictional Immunities of the State* (n 100) para 58.

[105] *Jurisdictional Immunities of the State* (n 100) para 59.

Under the rules of customary international law, *acta jure imperii* includes acts of a state's armed forces,[106] and the law thus entitles the state to immunity despite claims of a territorial tort exception.[107] Moreover, since the immunity is procedural in nature, the gravity of the offence is irrelevant.[108]

As to state officials, the immunity from foreign jurisdiction is an inherent part of state sovereignty and, accordingly, vests in the state and not in a state official. It can therefore be waived by the state, in which event the state official concerned can be sued or brought to trial in the courts of a foreign state.[109]

2. Sovereignty and Human Rights

In *Prosecutor v Tadić*, the ICTY pointed to a development in international law whereby '[a] State-sovereignty-oriented approach has been gradually supplanted by a human-being-oriented approach'.[110] Bruce Broomhall has highlighted a certain tension in contemporary international law between the Nuremberg legacy, with its 'sovereignty-limiting rationale' (rule of law), and the Westphalian tradition, with its emphasis on 'the sovereignty-based control [of national states] over enforcement'.[111] It was accordingly decided in the Lotus Case that state jurisdiction to prosecute a crime is to be presumed, and the other state, claiming that a rule of customary international law restricts the prosecuting state's competence to do so, bears the burden of proof to establish such a rule.[112]

[106] *Jurisdictional Immunities of the State* (n 100) para 72.

[107] *Jurisdictional Immunities of the* State (n 100) para 75.

[108] *Jurisdictional Immunities of the State* (n 100) para 84. In the European Court of Human Rights, *Al-Adsani v United Kingdom*, para 61 (upholding the immunity from civil suit in the courts of another state where acts of torture are alleged); *Kalogeropoulou and Others v Greece and Germany* 417 (upholding the immunity from civil suit in the courts of another state, where crimes against humanity are alleged). See also, Erika de Wet's chapter on *jus cogens* in this *Handbook*.

[109] *Arrest Warrant of 11 April 2000 (Democratic Republic of the Congo v Belgium)*, para 61.

[110] *Prosecutor v Tadić*, para 97. See Kai Ambos, 'Völkerrechtliche Bestrafungspflichten bei schweren Menschenrechtsverletzungen' (1999) 37 *Archiv des Völkerrechts* 318, 355; Hans-Peter Kaul and Claus Kreß, 'Jurisdiction and Cooperation in the Statute of the International Criminal Court: Principles and Cooperation' (1999) 2 *YIHL* 143, 171; Kai Ambos, 'Zur Bestrafung von Verbrechen im internationalen und Internen Konflikt' in Jana Hasse, Erwin Müller, and Patricia Schneider (eds), *Humanitäres Völkerrecht: Politische, Rechtliche und Strafgerichtliche Dimensionen* (Nomos 2001) 325, 327; Theodor Meron, 'How Do Human Rights Humanize the Law of War?' in Morten Bergsmo and Asbjørn Eide (eds), *Human Rights and Criminal Justice for the Downtrodden: Essays in Honour of Asbjørn Eide* (Brill 2003) 163.

[111] Bruce Broomhall, *International Justice and the International Criminal Court: Between Sovereignty and the Rule of Law* (OUP 2004) 2.

[112] *The Lotus Case (France v Turkey)*.

The United Nations, established in 1945 on the basis of 'faith in fundamental human rights',[113] committed itself to promoting '*universal* respect for, and observance of, human rights and fundamental freedoms for all without distinction as to race, sex, language, or religion'.[114] Member states solemnly pledged themselves to take joint and separate action in cooperation with the Organization for the achievement of that commitment.[115] The Universal Declaration of Human Rights afforded substance to the concept of human rights and fundamental freedoms, and served as the basis for defining the exact meaning of those concepts. In retrospect, it is fair to conclude that, in those formative years, the Organization succeeded in mustering universal support for the affirmation of faith in human rights.

Louis Henkin correctly affirmed that, '[t]he idea of human rights is accepted in principle by all governments regardless of other ideology, regardless of political, economic, or social condition'.[116] The fact is, though, that state sovereignty has remained the basic norm of international law and international relations. The UN Charter prohibits the United Nations from 'interven[ing] in matters which are essentially within the domestic jurisdiction of any state'.[117] Thus, while through its creation, the UN embarked on a programme of standard-setting for the protection of human rights, states remained free to accept or refrain from contracting binding obligations through voluntary ratification of the conventions and covenants that the United Nations sponsored. The Vienna Convention on the Law of Treaties provides further scope for state discretion; in the exercise of their sovereignty, states have the right to add reservations, understandings, and declarations (RUDs) to their instruments of ratification to exclude the binding effect of certain provisions, or to attach to provisions a special meaning, according to their own subjective interests. The freedom to make reservations is subject only to any restrictions the states themselves write into the specific treaty or to a general test that precludes reservations contrary to the object and purpose of an agreement.[118] States can also avoid the binding force of human rights norms that have matured into rules of customary international law (short of *jus cogens*), by entering into a treaty with another state or states that deviate from the customary law provision. Their agreement will prevail *inter se*, although it cannot affect the rights and duties vis-à-vis third party states. Customary international law itself, being based on the conduct and will of a cross section of the international community of states, is therefore not at odds with the notion of state sovereignty.

Like the issue of ratifying or acceding to human rights treaties, the issue of incorporating international human rights norms into the municipal law of a state is, to

[113] UN Charter, preamble.

[114] UN Charter, Art 55(c) (emphasis added).

[115] UN Charter, Art 56.

[116] Louis Henkin, *The Rights Of Man Today* (Westview Press 1978) 28.

[117] UN Charter, Art 2(7).

[118] Article 19(c) of the Vienna Convention on the Law of Treaties prohibits reservations that are 'incompatible with the object and purpose of the treaty'.

a large extent, conditional upon historical, cultural, and religious specificity. The South African Constitution of 1996 affords protection to almost the entire range of internationally proclaimed human rights and fundamental freedoms. The United States is often commended for being the primary entrepreneur as far as the constitutional protection of human rights is concerned, but its Federal Bill of Rights affords protection to civil and political rights only, to the exclusion of the most fundamental natural rights of the individual, of economic and social rights, and of solidarity rights.[119] Social and economic rights are included in the 1937 Constitutions of the Republic of Ireland and the 1949 Constitution of India as (unenforceable) Directive Principles of Social Policy (Ireland) or Directive Principles of State Policy (India). In general, how a state chooses to implement its human rights obligations is a matter of its own choice.

State consent—a vital component of sovereignty—remains the most fundamental condition for subjecting a state to internationally proclaimed human rights and fundamental freedoms. State consent is also required for the exercise of jurisdiction in interstate disputes by the ICJ and other (regional) international tribunals and arbitration bodies.[120] With the establishment of the UN, however, the requirement of state consent as a precondition for imposing binding obligations on states has changed quite radically. The UN Charter subjects the principle of sovereign equality of all member states[121] to several mandatory rules, which the overall purpose of the United Nations of maintaining international peace and security, dictates. Member states must 'settle their international disputes by peaceful means'[122] and must 'refrain in their international relations from the threat or use of force against the territorial integrity or political independence of any state'.[123] Member states agree 'to accept and carry out the decisions of the Security Council'.[124]

In executing its 'primary responsibility for the maintenance of international peace and security',[125] the Security Council has been entrusted with wide powers under Chapter VII of the UN Charter to determine that a situation in any part of the world constitutes a threat to the peace, a breach of the peace, or an act of aggression.[126] It can then impose punitive measures against the culprit state, in order to bring an end to the threat or breach of the peace or the act of aggression, including sanctions of various kinds[127] and, in extreme cases, even armed intervention.[128] In the 'Uniting for Peace Resolution' of 1950, the General Assembly took upon itself the power to take action in cases where a situation constitutes a breach of the peace or an act of aggression.[129] UN bodies, mostly the Security Council, have thus far

119 As to these different categories of human rights, see van der Vyver, *Leuven Lectures* (n 32) 91–99.

120 See eg Statute of the International Court of Justice, Art 36.

121 See UN Charter, Art 2(1).

122 See UN Charter, Art 2(3).

123 See UN Charter, Art 2(4).

124 See UN Charter, Art 25.

125 See UN Charter, Art 24(1).

126 See UN Charter, Art 39.

127 See UN Charter, Art 41.

128 See UN Charter, Art 42.

129 UNGA 'Uniting for Peace Resolution' (3 November 1950) UN Doc A/Res/377.

invoked the Resolution on ten occasions, to authorize 'Emergency Special Sessions' of the General Assembly to deal with a variety of crisis situations involving human rights violations.[130]

What might seem to be the most radical intervention in state sovereignty for the protection of human rights is the power vested in the ICC to prosecute 'the most serious crimes of concern to the international community as a whole'.[131] The power of the ICC to prosecute sitting heads of state or government, and other state officials who might be entitled to immunity against prosecution under the rules of national or international law, implicates state sovereignty. In the *Arrest Warrant Case*, the ICJ stated that state officials with sovereign immunity may be subject to criminal prosecution in certain international criminal courts, such as the ICC.[132] The Appeals Chamber of the Special Court for Sierra Leone (SCSL) gave this cautious assessment definitive substance in the case against Charles Taylor.[133] Taylor, a former President of neighbouring Liberia, claimed sovereign immunity. The SCSL noted that the *Arrest Warrant Case*, affording immunity to the minister of foreign affairs of the Democratic Republic of the Congo, applied to prosecutions of an official of state A in state B; that the SCSL is not a national court of Sierra Leone but an international criminal court;[134] and that the principle of sovereign immunity 'derives from the equality of sovereign states and therefore has no relevance to international criminal tribunals which are

[130] The first Emergency Special Session of the General Session was convened at the request of the Security Council on 1–10 November 1956, to deal with a crisis in the Middle East following Egypt's annexation of the Suez Canal; the second Emergency Special Session of the General Session was convened at the request of the Security Council on 4–10 November 1956, to deal with a crisis in Hungary following the Soviet Union's invasion; the third Emergency Special Session of the General Session was convened at the request of the Security Council on 8–21 August 1958, to deal with a crisis in the Middle East in consequence of the deployment of foreign troops in Lebanon and Jordan; the fourth Emergency Special Session of the General Session was convened at the request of the Security Council on 17–19 September 1960, to deal with the situation in the Democratic Republic of the Congo; the fifth Emergency Special Session of the General Session was convened at the request of the Security Council on 17–18 June 1967, to deal with measures taken by Israel to change the status of east Jerusalem; the sixth Emergency Special Session of the General Session was convened at the request of the Security Council on 10–14 January 1980, to deal with a crisis in Afghanistan; the seventh Emergency Special Session of the General Session was convened at the request of Senegal on 22–29 July 1980, 20–28 April 1982, 25–26 June 1982, 16–19 August 1982, and 24 September 1982, to deal with the situation in Palestine; the eighth Emergency Special Session of the General Session was convened at the request of Zimbabwe on 13–14 September 1981, to deal with the situation in Namibia; the ninth Emergency Special Session of the General Session was convened at the request of the Security Council on 29 January–5 February 1982, to deal with the situation in occupied Arab territories; and the tenth Emergency Special Session of the General Session was convened at the request of Qatar for its first session in April 1997, to deal with illegal Israeli action in occupied East Jerusalem and the rest of the occupied territories.

[131] See Rome Statute of the International Criminal Court, preamble (Rome Statute).

[132] *Arrest Warrant Case* (n 109) para 61. Also see para 36 (Van den Wyngaert, J, dissenting, holding that '[i]mmunity should never apply to crimes under international law, neither before international courts nor national courts'). See also John Dugard and Garth Abraham, 'Public International Law' (2002) *ASSL* 140, 165–66.

[133] *Prosecutor v Taylor.*

[134] *Taylor* (n 133) para 42.

not organs of a state but derive their mandate from the international community'.[135] The Rome Statute of the ICC expressly provides that the normal immunities attaching to the official capacity of sitting heads of state and other government officials do not bar the ICC from exercising jurisdiction over such persons.[136]

In the final analysis, drafters of the ICC Statute were fully sensitive to the principle of state sovereignty. Cooperation of states with the ICC in bringing perpetrators of crimes within the jurisdiction of the Court to justice is, as a matter of principle, based on state consent.[137] Except in cases deriving from a Security Council referral, the ICC's exercise of jurisdiction is conditional upon the consent of the national state of the suspect or of the state where the crime was allegedly committed.[138] In all cases, the exercise of jurisdiction by the ICC is complementary to investigations and prosecutions in a nation-state with a special interest in the matter.[139] The ICC will only exercise jurisdiction if the nation-state fails to take action,[140] or if it did, the ICC will only investigate or prosecute if the investigation or prosecution of the nation-state turned out to be a sham.[141]

The ICC has gone beyond the above deference to state sovereignty by endorsing a strategy of 'positive complementarity',[142] defined by the Assembly of States Parties as:

> all activities/actions whereby national jurisdictions are strengthened and enabled to conduct genuine national investigations and trials of crimes included in the Rome Statute, without involving the Court in capacity building, financial support and technical assistance, but instead leaving these actions and activities for States, to assist each other on a voluntary basis.[143]

[135] *Taylor* (n 133) para 51.

[136] Rome Statute, Art 27(2). As to the current dispute between the ICC and the African Union relating to the sovereign immunity of a sitting head of state, see Johan D van der Vyver, 'Prosecuting the President of Sudan: A Dispute between the African Union and the International Criminal Court' (2011) 11 *Afr Hum Rts LJ* 683–98.

[137] Rome Statute, pt IX. See also Rome Statute, Art 12(3) (making provision for non-party states to agree to cooperate with the Court on an ad hoc basis).

[138] Rome Statute, Art 12.

[139] Rome Statute, Art 1.

[140] ICC Office of the Prosecutor, 'Paper on Some Policy Issues before the Office of the Prosecutor' (September 2003) 4; ICC Office of the Prosecutor, 'Informal Expert Paper: The Principle of Complementarity in Practice' (2003) paras 17–18; *Prosecutor v Katanga and Chui*, paras 2, 74–79, 80.

[141] Rome Statute, Art 17; Darryl Robinson, 'The Mysterious Mysteriousness on Complementarity' (2010) 21 *Crim LF* 67. See also Sarah MH Nouwen, 'Fine-Tuning Complementarity' in Bartram S Brown (ed), *Research Handbook on International Criminal Law* (Edward Elgar 2011) 209.

[142] ICC Res RC/Res.1 (8 June 2010) reprinted in ICC, *Review Conference of the Rome Statute of the International Criminal Court* (ICC 2010) RC/9/11, adopted by the Review Conference of the ICC held in Kampala, Uganda on May 31 through 11 June 2010. See also Office of the Prosecutor, 'Prosecutorial Strategy: 2009–2012' (1 February 2010) paras 16, 17.

[143] ICC 'Report of the Bureau on Stocktaking: Complementarity' (18 March 2010) ICC-ASP/8/51, para 16. See also William W Burke-White, 'Proactive Complementarity: The International Criminal Court and National Courts in the Rome System of International Justice' (2008), 49 *Harv Int'l LJ* 53, 54 (appealing to the ICC to 'participate more directly in efforts to encourage national governments to prosecute international crimes themselves').

Positive complementarity promotes, through capacity building, a national infrastructure that empowers nation-states, and not the ICC, to bring perpetrators of crimes within the subject-matter jurisdiction of the ICC, to justice. As ICC Prosecutor Luis Moreno-Ocampo stated, the success of the ICC is not dependent on the number of cases that reach the Court: 'On the contrary, the absence of trials before this Court, as a consequence of the regular functioning of national institutions, would be a major success.'[144]

3. Conclusion

In our day and age, human rights have come to be accepted worldwide as a basic norm of commendable state–subject relations; and although state sovereignty may still be an obstacle to the implementation of human rights and fundamental freedoms within many municipal legal systems, governments engaging in serious violations of the internationally accepted human rights norms will inevitably bear the brunt of their unbecoming laws and practices. Leaving aside the instances of human rights violations that might provoke Security Council interventions, individual complaints under international human rights instruments and in regional institutions for the promotion of human rights, or criminal prosecutions of perpetrators of gross violations of human rights, the major deterrent remains decisive condemnation by (a) institutions established for the promotion or protection of human rights, and (b) the international community of states. Reprobation might seem quite ineffective in bringing about change in the short term, but persistent condemnation will bear fruit in the long run; no state likes to be seen as a perpetrator of institutionalized practices that are at odds with international perceptions of good governance.

Apartheid South Africa is a case in point. The South African racial policies had been on the agenda of the General Assembly since its first session in 1946; initial support for the South African defences, based on state sovereignty as guaranteed under Article 2(7) of the UN Charter, declined over time; international condemnation

[144] Luis Moreno-Ocampo, 'Statement' (Ceremony for the Solemn Undertaking of the Chief Prosecutor of the International Criminal Court, The Hague, 16 June 2003) <http://www.iccnow.org/documents/MorenoOcampo16June03.pdf> accessed 25 November 2012. See also ICC, 'Statement of the Prosecutor Luis Moreno Ocampo to the Diplomatic Corps' (The Hague, 12 February 2004) <http://www.iccnow.org/documents/OTPStatementDiploBriefing12Feb04.pdf> accessed 25 November 2012 (including 'a positive approach to complementarity' in key strategic decisions taken and defining that approach as encouraging 'national proceedings wherever possible' in preference to 'competing with national systems for jurisdictions').

persisted and escalated; and in the end, South Africa capitulated—albeit almost half a century later—and through peaceful means transformed itself into 'an open and democratic society based on human dignity, equality and freedom'.[145]

State sovereignty is thus no longer an absolute right. Even insofar as it remains a prominent principle in international relations, its implementation has, at least de facto if not *de jure*, become subordinate to the values embedded in the human rights doctrine.

Further Reading

Cassese A, *Self-Determination of Peoples: A Legal Reappraisal* (Grotius 1995)
Fawcett JES, *The Law of Nations* (Basic Books 1968)
Friedmann W, *Legal Theory* (5th edn, Columbia UP 1967)
Van der Vyver JD, 'Sovereignty and Human Rights in Constitutional and International Law' (1991) 5 *Emory Int'l L Rev* 321
—— 'Statehood in International Law' (1991) 5 *Emory Int'l L Rev* 9
—— 'Sphere Sovereignty of Religious Institutions: A Contemporary Calvinistic Theory of Church-State Relations' in Gerhard Robbers (ed), *Church Autonomy* (Peter Lang 2001)
Van Dyke V, *Human Rights, the United States, and World Community* (OUP 1970)

[145] Constitution of the Republic of South Africa (1996), s 36(1). See also s 7(1).

CHAPTER 17

SOLIDARITY

RÜDIGER WOLFRUM*

1. Introduction

An acknowledgement that the principle of solidarity exists in international law and is having an impact on the structure of the law reflects the transformation of the international system from a network of bilateral commitments into a value-based global legal order. This development stands in stark contrast to the traditional view of public international law of the nineteenth and early twentieth centuries.[1]

Traditionally, public international law developed to define areas of jurisdiction for states in respect of others and to coordinate state activities, when such

* This chapter expands upon the author's previous work 'Solidarity amongst States: An Emerging Structural Principle of International Law' in Pierre-Marie Dupuy and others (eds), *Common Values in International Law: Essays in Honour of Christian Tomuschat* (Engel 2006). I am very grateful to Katja Göcke, Senior Research Fellow at the Max Planck Institute for Comparative Public Law and International Law, who has very creatively contributed to this chapter.

[1] Rüdiger Wolfrum, 'Solidarity amongst States: An Emerging Structural Principle of International Law' in Pierre-Marie Dupuy and others (eds), *Common Values in International Law: Essays in Honour of Christian Tomuschat* (Engel 2006). There is a growing literature on the principle of solidarity. See in particular Ronald St J Macdonald, 'Solidarity in the Practice and Discourse of Public International Law' (1996) 8 *Pace Int'l L Rev* 259; Karel Wellens, 'Solidarity as a Constitutional Principle: Its Expanding Role and Inherent Limitations' in Ronald St J Macdonald and Douglas M Johnston (eds), *Towards World Constitutionalism: Issues in the Legal Ordering of the World Community* (Brill 2005); Peter Hilpold, 'Solidarität als Rechtsprinzip: Völkerrechtliche, Europarechtliche und Staatsrechtliche Betrachtungen' (2007) 55 *JoR* 195; Karel Wellens, 'Revisiting Solidarity as a (Re-)Emerging Constitutional Principle: Some Further Reflections' in Rüdiger Wolfrum and Chie Kojima (eds), *Solidarity: A Structural Principle of International Law* (Springer 2010).

activities might interfere with the interests of other states. Positing the existence of a structural principle of solidarity among states seems totally alien to a legal system devoted merely to the coordination of independent state activities. The introduction of the principle of solidarity as a structural principle of international law reorients international law from a set of rules for preserving the present state of existing international relations, into a regime for fulfilling a certain mission, namely the promotion of international social justice among states. This is because, at its heart, solidarity strives for the amelioration, or at least the acknowledgement, of inequalities among states.

The reference to the principle of solidarity as a structural principle is actually not a new one. As Ulrich Scheuner has pointed out in his contribution to the *Festschrift for Eberhard Menzel*,[2] the idea that the principle of solidarity should guide states in their relations was discussed between the sixteenth and nineteenth centuries. The perception of a *universitas christiana* based upon common Christian values significantly influenced the early development of international law.[3] After the severance of international law's connection with its religious roots, attempts were made in the eighteenth century to construe a state community on the basis of a common perception of the human being. For example, Samuel von Pufendorf (1632–94) refers to the obligations each individual has towards all other human beings in his book, *De Officio Hominis et Civis (On The Duty of Man and Citizen According to the Natural Law)*.[4] From there, he deduces obligations among states. Christian Wolff (1679–1754) further elaborated upon this concept in his book, *Ius Gentium Methodo Scientifica Pertractatum (The Law of Nations Treated According to Scientific Method)*.[5] He argued that each individual had obligations with respect to him or herself and to others, and that obligations among states developed from there. This obligation existed in particular as between *gentes doctae et cultae* and *gentes barbarae et incultae*.[6] Finally, Emer de Vattel (1714–67) advocated the same ideas.[7] While referring to

[2] Ulrich Scheuner, 'Solidarität unter den Nationen als Grundsatz in der Gegenwärtigen Internationalen Gemeinschaft' in Jost Delbrück (ed), *Recht im Dienst des Friedens: Festschrift für Eberhard Menzel* (Duncker & Humblot 1975) 251, 265 *et seq*. See also VM Rangel, 'The Solidarity Principle, Francisco de Vitoria and the Protection of Indigenous Peoples' in Holger P Hestermeyer and others (eds), *Coexistence, Cooperation and Solidarity: Liber Amicorum Rüdiger Wolfrum* (Martinus Nijhoff 2012).

[3] cf, although with objections, Wilhelm Grewe, *Epochen der Völkerrechtsgeschichte* (Nomos Verlagsgesellschaft 1984) 30 *et seq*. However, concurring, Scheuner (n 2) 256 *et seq*.

[4] Samuel von Pufendorf, *De Officio Hominis et Civis Juxta Legem Naturalem* (first published 1673, OUP 1927) book I, chs 5–6. For further details see Scheuner (n 2) 266.

[5] Christian Wolff, *Ius Gentium Methodo Scientifica Pertractatum* (first published 1749, Clarendon Press 1934) s 162. 'Genti unicuique constans et perpetua esse debet voluntas felicitatem aliarum Gentium promovendi' ('Each nation should be a constant and perpetual will to promote the happiness of other nations').

[6] Wolff (n 5) ss 167–68.

[7] Emer de Vattel, *Le Droit des Gens, ou Principes de la Loi Naturelle* (Paris 1758) book II, ch 1, ss 2–3.

a *société civile* (civil society), he formulates that: 'Un Etat doit à tout autre Etat, ce qu'il se doit à soi-même, autant que cet autre a un véritable besoin de son secours, et qu'il peut le lui accorder sans négliger ses devoirs envers soi-même.'[8] As an example, Emer de Vattel referred to assistance in the case of aggression or famine.

It is evident that international law has not reached this stage of development. However, the principle of solidarity in fact governs certain areas of international law. Looking at them from this point of view may open new ways to interpret the respective legal regimes. Furthermore, it is worth considering whether the principle of solidarity may also be used for other international legal regimes.

The principle of solidarity may serve different objectives. It is particularly relevant in regulating concerns common to the international community. Such matters include, for example, commons areas (the high seas, outer space); the environment (the atmosphere, the availability of safe drinking water); the protection and implementation of internationally agreed upon human rights standards; economic development; social justice; and the preservation of international peace and security.[9] All such concerns can only be successfully managed by the common action of all members of the international community—which means, by their cooperative efforts—and not by the individual actions of one or more states. Hence, one can say that solidarity operates to achieve common objectives through common action.

The changes international law is undergoing, or has undergone in recent years, are due to the transformation of international relations from a system governed by the coexistence of states[10] and in which the acceptance that all forms of government are considered equal, into a system following the law of cooperation,[11] and then, in a third stage, into a legal system based upon common values. The latter development has transformed the society of states (*Staatengesellschaft*) into a community of states (*Staatengemeinschaft*).[12] This is why the principle of solidarity has emerged (or rather re-emerged) and is gaining relevance.

Solidarity may mean that a state has to sacrifice, or at least limit, its individual interests, in favour of the overarching interest of the international community; however, because every member of the international community, including the self-sacrificing ones, accrues the benefits of such cooperation, the term self-centred

[8] de Vattel (n 7) book II, ch 1, s 3. ('A state owes to each other State that which it owes to itself, to the extent that the other states has a real need of its help and that it can help the other state without neglecting its duties to itself ').

[9] Andreas L Paulus, *Die Internationale Gemeinschaft im Völkerrecht: Eine Untersuchung zur Entwicklung des Völkerrechts im Zeitalter der Globalisierung* (CH Beck 2001) 250 *et seq*.

[10] Wolfgang Friedmann, *The Changing Structure of International Law* (Stevens & Sons 1964) 15 *et seq*, 60 *et seq*.

[11] Rüdiger Wolfrum, 'International Law of Cooperation' in Rudolf Bernhardt (ed), *Encyclopedia of Public International Law* (Elsevier 1995) vol II, 1242–47; Georges Abi-Saab, 'Whither the International Community?' (1998) 9 *EJIL* 248.

[12] Hermann Mosler, 'The International Society as a Legal Community' (1974) 140 *RdC* 1, 17 *et seq*.

solidarity has been coined.[13] Sacrificing individual interests does not necessarily mean, however, that the contributions of all states are bound to be equal. The relative capacities of the individual states may be of relevance when trying to achieve a common goal. This means that, the contributions of some states may exceed the contributions of others.

In certain cases, solidarity-based actions may be designed to benefit some states or particular groups of states, or even a single state. This type of solidarity may be described as altruistic, although the realization of the benefit is also, in the long term, in the interest of the international community.[14] Such balancing seems to be contrary to the traditional understanding of the general matrix of international law but, as will be shown, it has become reality in a few international legal regimes. However, for these regimes, the principle of solidarity is quite determinative.

On the basis of the foregoing, one may distinguish three different aspects to solidarity: the achievement of common objectives, the achievement of common objectives through differentiated obligations, and the adoption of actions to benefit particular states or groups thereof.

Accepting the existence of the principle of solidarity in the matrix of international relations means that, generally speaking, states should consider not only their own individual interests, but also the interests of other states, the community of states as a whole, or both, when shaping their positions. This is true for both types of solidarity.

Some international treaties contain legal norms, which explicitly refer to the principle of solidarity. One example may suffice as an introduction. Article 3 of the UN Convention to Combat Desertification states:

> In order to achieve the objective of this Convention and to implement its provisions, the Parties shall be guided, *inter alia*, by the following: ... (b) the Parties should, in a spirit of international solidarity and partnership, improve cooperation and coordination at subregional, regional and international levels, and better focus financial, human, organizational and technical resources where they are needed....[15]

This chapter examines United Nations pronouncements on solidarity and the impact that solidarity has had on the specific international legal regimes concerned with peace, environmental law, and trade law, before turning to its role in relation to human rights law, where it not only provides a theoretical underpinning for the very internationalization of concern for human rights, but also has shaped modern doctrines of humanitarian assistance, the responsibility to protect, and reparations for human rights violations.

[13] Holger P Hestermeyer, 'Reality or Aspiration?: Solidarity in International Environmental and World Trade Law' in Holger P Hestermeyer and others (eds), *Coexistence, Cooperation and Solidarity: Liber Amicorum Rüdiger Wolfrum* (vol I, Martinus Nijhoff 2012) 45, 50 *et seq*.

[14] Hestermeyer, 'Reality or Aspiration?' (n 13) 45, 50 *et seq*.

[15] Article 3.

2. United Nations Pronouncements on Solidarity

The UN Millennium Declaration refers to solidarity as a fundamental value, stating:

> Global challenges must be managed in a way that distributes the costs and burdens fairly in accordance with basic principles of equity and social justice. Those who suffer or who benefit least deserve help from those who benefit most.[16]

Several resolutions of the UN General Assembly reaffirmed the principle of solidarity. Resolution 64/157 of 18 December 2009 on the 'Promotion of a Democratic and Equitable Democratic Order' is of particular relevance.[17] It mentions the principle of solidarity twice, namely solidarity among states[18] and solidarity as a right of peoples and individuals.[19] The context in which it refers to the principle of solidarity is remarkable, namely the protection of human rights; the preservation of peace, social, and economic development; and the protection of the environment.[20] The forerunner to this resolution was the 2006 UN General Assembly Resolution on the 'Promotion of a Democratic and Equitable International Order'.[21] Its emphasis was different, because it did not mention the right of peoples and individuals to solidarity, but rather reiterated the Millennium Declaration.[22]

3. Solidarity in the International System

3.1 The protection of peace

The most significant change to international law was the prohibition of resorting to armed force in the Kellogg–Briand Pact of 27 August 1928, which entered into force on 25 July 1929,[23] and whose prohibition Article 2(4) of UN Charter has expanded.

[16] United Nations Millennium Declaration, para 6.

[17] UNGA Res 64/157 (18 December 2009) UN Doc A/Res/64/157.

[18] UNGA Res 64/157 (n 17) para 4(e). 'The right to an international economic order based on equal participation in the decision-making process, interdependence, mutual interest, solidarity and cooperation among all States.'

[19] UNGA Res 64/157 (n 17) para 4(g).

[20] The discussion surrounding this resolution has been controversial; it received 127 votes in its favour, but all industrialized States voted against it.

[21] UNGA Res 61/160 (19 December 2006) UN Doc A/Res/61/160.

[22] This resolution, too, was controversial, and it was adopted against the vote of industrialized States.

[23] General Treaty for Renunciation of War as an Instrument of National Policy.

The principle of non-use of force in international relations is also rooted in customary international law.[24] There are two exceptions to this prohibition which are of relevance to the issue of this contribution, namely the right to self-defence and the right to military actions that the UN Security Council undertakes or mandates under the system of collective security. Article 51 of the UN Charter recognizes that every state has the inherent right to individual or collective self-defence. This is not the place to delve into the intricacies of the scope of the right to self-defence;[25] it is sufficient to state that the right to self-defence reflects the inherent right of each state to preserve its existence and its position as a sovereign and equal member in the community of states.

It is important to examine, however, the underlying rationale of Article 51 of the UN Charter when it refers to an 'inherent right of... collective self-defence'. Historically, the roots of this provision lay in the desire to protect regional pacts of mutual assistance in cases of armed attack. According to Stephen C Schlesinger (1942–),[26] the first version of this provision, which Latin American states endorsed, tried to immunize the Chapultepec Pact and the Monroe Doctrine from veto in the Security Council. On the insistence of the US delegation in particular, at the Conference of San Francisco, the direct reference to regional pacts was dropped, and the more neutral terminology was introduced. The accomplishment inherent to Article 51 of the UN Charter, in retrospect, was providing the legal framework for the establishment of a series of security pacts around the world, such as the North Atlantic Treaty Organization or the South East Asia Treaty Organization.

Article 51 of the UN Charter goes beyond preserving the rights of such security pacts, however. Apart from being a mechanism to preserve the existence of a particular state, self-defence is a mechanism for countering armed attacks in general. Since the state that is lending support to another state that has been the victim of an armed attack, does not have to pursue an interest of its own, it performs an act of solidarity by making the second state's case its own, when it intervenes for the second state's protection. That such intervention may qualify as an act of solidarity is well expressed in Article 5 of the North Atlantic Treaty,[27] as well as in

[24] For more on the scope of this prohibition, see Christian Tomuschat, 'International Law: Ensuring the Survival of Mankind on the Eve of a New Century: General Course on Public International Law' (1999) 281 *RdC* 13, 203 *et seq*, with further references. It is acknowledged that the prohibition on resorting to armed force is one of the central values of the community of States. The Atlantic Charter, as well as the Declaration of Four Nations on General Security of 30 October 1943, clearly emphasized that the preservation of peace was not only an end in itself, but was meant to safeguard human rights and justice, as well as life, liberty, independence, and religious freedom in general.

[25] See Albrecht Randelzhofer, 'Article 51' in Bruno Simma (ed), *The Charter of the United Nations* (vol I, 2nd edn, OUP 2002).

[26] Stephen C Schlesinger, *Act of Creation: The Founding of the United Nations* (Westview Press 2003) 182–83.

[27] Article 5 reads: 'The Parties agree that an armed attack against one or more of them in Europe or North America shall be considered an attack against them all and consequently they agree that, if such

other safety pacts. Technically speaking, the provision creates the legal fiction that an attack launched against one of the parties is an attack against all of them. The rationale for this construction of the notion of collective self-defence is, first and foremost, the promotion of a common value, namely the prohibition of armed force in international relations. The altruistic aspect of solidarity is also relevant, though, because security pacts, in particular, may shield states that are less powerful militarily against military action from more powerful neighbours.

The system of collective security also includes elements of solidarity. The basic idea underlying the concept of collective security is the replacement of individual states' recourse to self-help with a collective response system. The distinguishing lines between systems of collective self-defence and collective security have blurred. More generally, the regime of collective security also invokes the principle of solidarity, as it obliges states to act in the interest and defence of a common value—namely the preservation of peace. However, in this case, the principle of solidarity is of a self-centred nature only.

3.2 International environmental law

The preamble to the Rio Declaration of 1992[28] emphasizes the integral and interdependent nature of the Earth, and on this basis, calls upon states to establish a new and equitable partnership. This Declaration, which summarizes the objectives meant to guide and pre-structure the progressive development of international environmental law, clearly indicates the need for states to cooperate in order to meet common objectives. International environmental law covers various issues, such as transboundary pollution; the protection of wildlife; the use and protection of areas beyond national jurisdiction, such as the high seas or Antarctica; and the management of environmental problems of global relevance. The latter category embraces measures against climate change and for the protection of the ozone layer and biological diversity. International environmental law (treaty law, as well as customary law) has developed on the basis of several principles, two of which have a bearing on the role of solidarity in international law—namely, the principles of sustainable development and common but differentiated responsibility.

an armed attack occurs, each of them, in exercise of the right of individual or collective self-defence recognised by Article 51 of the Charter of the United Nations, will assist the Party or Parties so attacked by taking forthwith, individually and in concert with the other Parties, such action as it deems necessary, including the use of armed force, to restore and maintain the security of the North Atlantic area.'

[28] Rio Declaration on Environment and Development.

The principle of the sustainable development of natural resources is generally considered to be comprised of four elements or needs:[29] to preserve natural resources for the benefit of future generations;[30] to exploit natural resources in a rational manner; to use natural resources equitably, which means taking into consideration the needs of other states; and to ensure that environmental considerations are integrated into development plans or policies.

In spite of the controversy over the exact meaning of the scope[31] and implications of sustainable development, it is evident that the principle embraces an element of solidarity, because intergenerational equity requests that the present generation limit its use of natural resources so as to leave future generations with equal living conditions. It goes without saying that its other aspects also imply a principle of solidarity among states, most notably the obligation to use natural resources in a way that also takes into account the needs of other states.

Similarly, the principle of common but differentiated responsibility, pervasive in climate change law and negotiations, reflects a principle built upon the principle of interstate solidarity. The first of several clearly distinguishable elements[32] is that of common responsibility for the world's climate, which means that all states have an obligation to cooperate for the preservation of the climate. A further aspect of the principle of common but differentiated responsibility is that the preservation of the world's climate is not only for the present benefit, but also for the benefit of future generations, bringing in a certain element of intergenerational equity. Moreover, the state obligations may differ[33] and entail, as some legal regimes provide, that one group of states may have to provide financial transfers to another.[34]

To summarize, it should be noted that international environmental law is based upon the structural principle of solidarity. This legal regime, in particular, combined the two aspects of this principle: the achievement of a common objective and the amelioration of the deficits of certain states.

[29] Rüdiger Wolfrum, 'International Environmental Law: Purposes, Principles and Means of Ensuring Compliance' in Fred L Morrison and Rüdiger Wolfrum (eds), *International, Regional and National Environmental Law* (Kluwer 2000) 3, 20 *et seq*; Philippe Sands, *Principles of International Environmental Law* (2nd edn, CUP 2003) 252 *et seq*.

[30] See, in particular, Edith Brown Weiss, *In Fairness to Future Generations: International Law, Common Patrimony and Intergenerational Equity* (Transnational Publishers 1989) 17 *et seq*.

[31] Edith Brown Weiss, 'Environmentally Sustainable Competitiveness: A Comment' (1993) 102 *Yale LJ* 2123; U Beyerlin, 'Rio-Konferenz 1992: Beginn einer Neuen Globalen Umweltrechtsordnung?' (1994) 54 *ZaöRV* 124.

[32] See, in detail, Bettina Kellersmann, *Die Gemeinsame, Aber Differenzierte Verantwortlichkeit von Industriestaaten und Entwicklungsländern für den Schutz der Globalen Umwelt* (Springer 2000) 35 *et seq*.

[33] The Framework Convention on Climate Change refers, among other things, to the capacity of industrialized States to justify their heightened obligation to contribute to combating climate change. Article 3(1).

[34] See eg Convention on Biological Diversity.

3.3 World trade law

In its first consideration, the preamble of the World Trade Organization Agreement[35] lists several overall and paramount objectives, namely raising standards of living, ensuring full employment, ensuring a large and steadily growing volume of real income and effective demand, and expanding the production of goods and services. The objectives contained in the World Trade Organization (WTO) preamble define a common value, namely the enhancement of economic development. Combined therewith is the second aspect of the principle of solidarity, namely the amelioration of existing deficiencies through the promotion of economic development in developing countries.

It is occasionally overlooked that the principle of solidarity has helped structure the world trade order. Although its objective, the liberalization of world trade, is pursued through individually negotiated steps on the basis of reciprocity, there are several exceptions to the concept of reciprocity. First and foremost, it must be emphasized that the WTO subjects its reciprocally negotiated concessions to most-favoured nation treatment for a multitude of reasons.[36] The most-favoured nation principle leads to a multiplication of liberalization efforts, which, as soon one state concedes them, benefit all other states.[37]

In particular circumstances, the WTO legal system provides for exceptions to the principle of most-favoured nation treatment. Particularly relevant in this respect is the preferential treatment accorded to developing countries, which the so-called Enabling Clause justifies.[38] Besides the Enabling Clause, special arrangements in favour of developing countries can also be secured by means of exceptional authorizations—the so-called waivers.[39] The preference system of the European Union vis-à-vis the ACP countries (African, Caribbean, and Pacific Group of States), as established under the Cotonou Agreement,[40] provides an example of such a waiver.[41]

It is evident that the structural principle of solidarity can be identified in the WTO legal regime. Altruistic solidarity is, however, dominant only insofar as developing countries are concerned. In this context, it even provides for a deviation from one structural mechanism of that regime—namely reciprocity.

[35] Marrakesh Agreement Establishing the World Trade Organization.

[36] The General Agreement on Tariffs and Trade, Art I(1).

[37] For details, see Peter Tobias Stoll and Frank Schorkopf, *WTO-Welthandelsordnung und Welthandelsrecht* (Heymann 2002) 46 *et seq*.

[38] See Abdulqawi A Yusuf, '"Differential and More Favourable Treatment": The GATT Enabling Clause' (1980) 14 *JWTL* 488; John H Jackson, *The World Trading System* (2nd edn, MIT Press 1997) 164.

[39] Isabel Feichtner, 'Waiver', *The Max Planck Encyclopedia of Public International Law* (2012) vol X, 747–54.

[40] Partnership Agreement between the Members of the African, Caribbean and Pacific Group of States of the one Part, and the European Community and its Member States of the other Part (Cotonou Agreement).

[41] Stoll and Schorkopf (n 37) 58 *et seq*.

4. Solidarity as a Basis for the Protection of Human Rights

Since the beginning of the human rights movement, it has been recognized that the effective realization of individual rights constitutes a community interest[42] requiring international solidarity.[43] Article 1 of the *Institut de Droit International*'s (International Law Institute's) 1989 resolution on the 'Protection of Human Rights and the Principle of Non-Intervention in Internal Affairs of States' states that the states' obligation to protect human rights 'implies a duty of solidarity among all States to ensure as rapidly as possible the effective protection of human rights throughout the world'.[44] Referring to the distinction which has been made between self-centred solidarity and altruistic solidarity, it should be emphasized that in the context of human rights, all attempts to safeguard and promote human rights in other countries reflect altruistic solidarity. The driving motif does not predominantly rest on the national interests of the intervening state (although occasionally the interest to avoid a flow of refugees may exist), but on the desire to uphold and consolidate a high human rights standard. This can be clearly established from the fact that states with a satisfactory human rights record are particularly interested in bringing up the standard in other states.

Karel Vasak developed the concept of solidarity rights comprising inter alia the right to development, the right to a healthy environment, and the right to peace, in his inaugural lecture at the International Human Rights Institute in Strasbourg in 1979. The particularity of such rights is that they impose on states joint obligations that are structurally different—as they require positive action—from the obligations the International Covenant on Civil and Political Rights contains, which, to a large extent, are in principle obligations of abstention. Solidarity rights also recognize, as an important element, an individual obligation to contribute to the realization of such rights. While other human rights impose obligations primarily on states, solidarity rights cannot be realized 'without the concerted efforts of all the actors on the social scene', including the individual.[45]

For the protection of human rights, the concept of solidarity is particularly relevant in two areas; one is humanitarian assistance, and the other one is the responsibility to protect. A third area, which has recently developed, is reparations for

[42] This is particularly evident for the movement on the suppression of slaves and the slave trade.

[43] Abdul G Koroma, 'Solidarity: Evidence of an Emerging International Legal Principle' in Holger P Hestermeyer and others (eds), *Coexistence, Cooperation and Solidarity: Liber Amicorum Rüdiger Wolfrum* (Martinus Nijhoff 2012) 108.

[44] Institut de Droit International, 'The Protection of Human Rights and the Principle of Non-Intervention in Internal Affairs of States' (1989) 63 *Annuaire* 338, art 1.

[45] Carl Wellmann, 'Solidarity, the Individual, and Human Rights' (2000) 22 *Hum Rts Q* 639, 642–43.

victims of gross and systematic violations of human rights, as referred to in the 'UN Basic Principles and Guidelines on the Right to a Remedy and Reparations for Victims of Gross Violations of International Human Rights Law and Serious Violations of International Humanitarian Law' of 16 December 2005.[46]

4.1 Humanitarian assistance

As indicated above, the early writings dealing with the principle of solidarity referred to assistance in cases of natural disasters. This issue has been discussed in the United Nations. For example, on 8 December 1988, the General Assembly adopted the 'Resolution on Humanitarian Assistance to Victims of Natural Disasters and Similar Emergency Situations'.[47] While reaffirming the sovereignty of states and their primary role in the initiation, organization, coordination, and implementation of humanitarian assistance within their respective territories, the General Assembly:

> [u]rges States in proximity to areas of natural disasters and similar emergency situations, particularly in the case of regions that are difficult to reach, to participate closely with the affected countries in international efforts with a view to facilitating, to the extent possible, the transit of humanitarian assistance.[48]

This does not give states the right to intervene, but it indicates at least a moral obligation to render assistance if the affected state so requests. General Assembly Resolution 45/100 of 14 December 1990 reaffirmed this appeal and additionally called upon the state having suffered the natural disaster to facilitate the work of states and non-governmental organizations by providing access possibilities (relief corridors) to the population in need of assistance.[49]

Beyond the context of natural disasters, the Security Council has implemented this approach in armed conflicts involving Sudan and Croatia, and involving the protection of the Kurds in Iraq.[50] There is, however, a significant difference between the resolutions of the Security Council and those of the General Assembly.[51] Whereas the General Assembly invokes, although not explicitly, the principle of

[46] UNGA Res 60/147 (21 March 2006) UN Doc A/Res/60/147. See Theo van Boven, 'The United Nations Basic Principles and Guidelines on the Right to a Remedy and Reparation for Victims of Gross Violations of International Human Rights Law and Serious Violations of Inernational Humanitarian Law' (United Nations 2010).

[47] UNGA Res 43/131 (8 December 1988) UN Doc A/Res/43/131.

[48] UNGA Res 43/131 (n 47) para 7.

[49] UNGA Res 45/100 (14 December 1990) UN Doc A/Res/45/100, paras 4, 8.

[50] UN Security Council (UNSC), Res 688 (5 April 1991) UN Doc S/Res/688. See also UNSC Res 733 (23 January 1992) UN Doc S/Res/733; UNSC Res 770 (13 August 1992) UN Doc S/Res/770; UNSC Res 1590 (24 March 2005) UN Doc S/Res/1590.

[51] See also Pierre-Marie Dupuy, *Droit International Public* (10th edn, Dalloz 2010) 135.

solidarity as the basis for its call for assistance, including the call to accept assistance, the Security Council acts on the basis of its powers under Chapter VII of the UN Charter. Therefore, one may argue that one may refer only to the resolutions of the General Assembly as an indication that the structural principle of solidarity is evolving. This, however, does not sufficiently take into account that the powers of the Security Council under Chapter VII of the UN Charter are based upon the structural principle of solidarity. Therefore, it is quite pertinent to compare the actions of the General Assembly, which has to invoke solidarity as a basis of legitimacy, with the actions of the Security Council, which may act on the basis of its institutional powers.

There is, furthermore, a second lesson to learn from the General Assembly's resolutions. The principle of solidarity is embedded in international law. It cannot be used as a means to enforce an action against a state, unless, as provided under Chapter VII of the UN Charter, public international law explicitly provides for such an enforcement measure.

4.2 Responsibility to protect

Perhaps the most controversial manifestation of the notion of solidarity in the context of human rights is the emerging concept of the responsibility to protect.[52] The International Commission on Intervention and State Sovereignty developed the concept in September 2001.[53] Concerns raised by UN Secretary General Kofi Annan and debates in the General Assembly triggered the report. Secretary General Kofi Annan had referred to the great failure of the international community to handle gross and systematic violations of human rights, such as those perpetrated in Rwanda and Srebrenica, and emphasized that the international community could not stand idle while such incidents occurred.[54] The concept of the responsibility to protect has its roots in the concept of a *droit d'ingérence* (right to intervene)

[52] As to the development of this concept and its potential consequences for the Security Council, see Ramesh Thakur, *The United Nations, Peace and Security: From Collective Security to the Responsibility to Protect* (CUP 2006); Gareth Evans, 'From Humanitarian Intervention to the Responsibility to Protect' (2006) 24 *Wis Int'l LJ* 703; Gareth Evans, *The Responsibility to Protect: Ending Mass Atrocity Crimes Once and For All* (Brookings Institution Press 2008); Alex J Bellamy, *The Responsibility to Protect: The Global Effort to End Mass Atrocities* (Polity Press 2009); Anne Peters, 'The Responsibility to Protect: Spelling Out the Hard Legal Consequences for the UN Security Council and Its Members' in Ulrich Fastenrath and others (eds), *From Bilateralism to Community Interest: Essays in Honour of Judge Bruno Simma* (OUP 2011); Ramesh Thakur, *The Responsibility to Protect: Norms, Laws, and the Use of Force in International Politics* (Routledge 2011). See also Thakur, Chapter 32 in this *Handbook*.

[53] International Commission on Intervention and State Sovereignty, 'The Responsibility to Protect' in UNGA 'Letter Dated 26 July 2002 from the Permanent Representative of Canada to the United Nations Addressed to the Secretary-General' (14 August 2002) UN Doc A/57/303 Annex (2002).

[54] UNGA 'Report of the Secretary-General on the Work of the Organization' (2007) UN Doc A/62/1, 48. See also UNGA 'Report of the Secretary-General Pursuant to General Assembly Resolution A53/35' (15 November 1999) UN Doc A/54/549, para 501.

that developed in French academic literature in the 1990s.[55] The dogmatic basis of the concept of the responsibility to protect rests on states' responsibility for the well-being of their inhabitants.

According to the Commission on Intervention and State Sovereignty, the concept of the responsibility to protect embraces three different elements: the responsibility to prevent, the responsibility to respond, and the responsibility to rebuild, with prevention being considered the single most important dimension of the responsibility to protect. As far as military intervention—the most controversial aspect of the concept—is concerned, the Commission identified various thresholds, namely that the intervention must react to serious and irreparable harm that is currently happening to human beings or that is imminently likely to happen. It mentioned large-scale loss of life and large-scale 'ethnic cleansing' as examples.[56] The intention of the intervention must be to avert human suffering; it must be a means of last resort, and it must be conducted in a proper way, with a reasonable chance of achieving the desired result.[57] Although not ruling out military action by individual states, the Commission clearly advocated that actions be undertaken by the Security Council or under its authority.[58]

The concept of the responsibility to protect has subsequently been adopted or referred to in multiple contexts, such as the Security Council debate concerning Resolution 1556 on Darfur.[59] The representative of the Philippines made a direct reference to the concept of the responsibility to protect when he stated that sovereignty also entailed a state's responsibility to protect its people. If the state was unable or unwilling to live up to this obligation, the international community had the responsibility to assist an unable state to gain the needed capacity or to induce an unwilling state to assume its responsibility. If that proved fruitless, the international community, in extreme situations, had the responsibility to intervene.[60] The United Kingdom similarly referred to the 'most basic of a government''s [sic] obligations to its own people: the obligation to protect them—something that the Government of Sudan has so far failed to do.'[61]

Furthermore, the Report of the High-Level Panel on Threats, Challenges and Change referred to an emerging norm of collective international responsibility to protect, stating:

> [T]here is a growing acceptance that while sovereign Governments have the primary responsibility to protect their own citizens from such catastrophes, when they are unable

[55] See eg Mario Bettati and Bernard Kouchner (eds), *Le Devoir d'Ingérence: Peut-on Les Laisser Mourir?* (Denoël 1987).

[56] International Commission on Intervention and State Sovereignty (n 53) 31–32.

[57] International Commission on Intervention and State Sovereignty (n 53) 37.

[58] International Commission on Intervention and State Sovereignty (n 53) 47–55.

[59] UNSC 'Report of the Secretary-General on the Sudan' (30 July 2004) UN Doc S/2004/453.

[60] UNSC 'Verbatim Record of the 5015th Meeting' (30 July 2004) UN Doc S/PV 5015, 10–11.

[61] UNSC 'Verbatim Record' (n 60) 5.

or unwilling to do so that responsibility should be taken up by the wider international community....[62]

The Secretary General also referred to this concept in a statement to the High-Level Panel in March 2005, qualifying the concept as an emerging norm of international law.[63]

In September 2005, the World Summit Outcome Document endorsed the concept, stating:

Each individual State has the responsibility to protect its populations from genocide, war crimes, ethnic cleansing and crimes against humanity. This responsibility entails the prevention of such crimes, including their incitement, through appropriate and necessary means. We accept this responsibility and will act in accordance with it...

The international community, through the United Nations, also has the responsibility to use appropriate diplomatic, humanitarian and other peaceful means, in accordance with Chapters VI and VIII of the Charter, to help protect populations from genocide, war crimes, ethnic cleansing and crimes against humanity. In this context, we are prepared to take collective action, in a timely and decisive manner, through the Security Council, in accordance with the Charter, including Chapter VII, on a case-by-case basis and in cooperation with relevant regional organizations as appropriate, should peaceful means be inadequate and national authorities are manifestly failing to protect their populations from genocide, war crimes, ethnic cleansing and crimes against humanity.[64]

In addition, UN Secretary General Ban Ki-moon issued three special reports on the responsibility to protect, further developing and refining the concept.[65]

4.2.1 *Security Council action with respect to the responsibility to protect?*

In its operative part, Security Council Resolution 1674 of 28 April 2006 on the Protection of Civilians in Armed Conflict referred to paragraphs 138 and 139 of the World Summit Outcome Document, which contain the concept of a responsibility to protect,[66] but did not instrumentalize the concept later. In its Resolution 1769 of 31 July 2007 on the situation in Darfur,[67] the Security Council referred to Security

[62] UN High-Level Panel on Threats, Challenges and Change (ed), *A More Secure World: Our Shared Responsibility* (2 December 2004) UN Doc A/59/565, para 201.

[63] UNGA 'In Larger Freedom: Towards Development, Security and Human Rights for All' (21 March 2005) UN Doc A/59/2005, para 135.

[64] UNGA Res 60/1 (16 September 2005) UN Doc A/Res/60/1, paras 138–39.

[65] UNGA 'Report of the Secretary-General: Implementing the Responsibility to Protect' (12 January 2009) UN Doc A/63/677; UNGA 'Report of the Secretary-General: Early Warning, Assessment and the Responsibility to Protect' (14 July 2010) UN Doc A/64/864; UNGA/UNSC 'Report of the Secretary-General: The Role of Regional and Sub-Regional Arrangements in Implementing the Responsibility to Protect' (27 June 2011) UN Doc A/65/877–S/2011/393.

[66] UNSC Res 1674 (28 April 2006) UN Doc S/Res/1674, para 4.

[67] UNSC Res 1769 (31 July 2007) UN Doc S/Res/1769.

Council Resolution 1674 without mentioning the concept of a responsibility to protect. The concept was used, at least in part, though, in the resolutions concerning Libya. In its Resolution 1970 of 26 February 2011,[68] the Security Council emphasized the Libyan authorities' responsibilities for protecting its population in its preambular paragraphs. The Security Council reiterated this statement in Resolution 1973 of 17 March 2011.[69] In a further preambular paragraph of Resolution 1973, the Security Council stated: 'Expressing its determination to ensure the protection of civilians and civilian populated areas and the rapid and unimpeded passage of humanitarian assistance and the safety of humanitarian personnel.' There is no explicit link to the concept of a responsibility to protect. But this paragraph fits into the concept, since the Security Council indicates that it will intervene if the government of Libya does not live up to its responsibility. In fact, the Security Council takes such action by authorizing 'Member States that have notified the Secretary-General, acting nationally or through regional organizations or arrangements,... to take all necessary measures... to protect civilians and civilian populated areas under threat of attack....'[70]

However, these few references in Security Council Resolutions are not yet conclusive evidence that the concept of a responsibility to protect has already been accepted in all its facets. It is more than doubtful whether the military intervention in Libya has—seen in the long term—fostered the acceptability of the concept of the responsibility to protect, as far as it concerns military intervention based on Chapter VII of the UN Charter. It is a matter of discussion whether the military intervention was proportional and whether the intervention has led to a better environment for the protection of international human rights standards.

4.2.2 *New developments*

As indicated above, a third area is developing—namely the responsibility for the treatment of victims of gross and systematic violations of human rights according to the UN Basic Principles and the Guidelines on the Right to a Remedy and Reparations.[71] These instruments provide that states should modify or amend their national law so as to ensure that victims of gross violations of human rights are treated with dignity and get the assistance they need.

[68] UNSC Res 1970 (26 February 2011) UN Doc S/Res/1970.

[69] UNSC Res 1973 (17 March 2011) UN Doc S/Res/1973.

[70] UNSC Res 1973 (n 69) para 4. In this context, it should be noted that UN Secretary General Ban Ki-moon called on Libya to respect the concept of a responsibility to protect human rights, and the obligations under international humanitarian law. UNSC 'Press Statement on Lybia' (22 February 2011) UN Doc SC/10180, AFR/2120 <http://www.un.org/News/Press/docs/2011/sc10180.doc.htm> accessed 15 April 2012.

[71] See UNGA Res 60/147 (n 46).

4.2.3 *Assessment*

It is evident that the concept of a responsibility to protect has undergone a decisive change since its original development. It has been limited in several respects. It now relates only to the most serious crimes, such as genocide, war crimes, crimes against humanity, and ethnic cleansing. Furthermore, the possible reactions are limited to a responsibility for the concerned state, international assistance and capacity-building to enable the state concerned to live up to its protection responsibilities, and a timely and decisive response by the international community.

It is not the objective of this contribution to discuss whether the responsibility to protect has already developed into positive international law.[72] The question of interest here is whether the responsibility to protect is based on the principle of solidarity.

According to Judge Abdul G Koroma, the concept of a responsibility to protect is legally distinguishable from humanitarian intervention.[73] For him, the basis for international community intervention in favour of a suffering or suppressed population lies in the international community's solidarity with that population. In contrast thereto, humanitarian intervention derives from one state's claim of superiority over another.

In the context dealt with here, this means a significant shift in the matrix of solidarity as briefly outlined before. So far, the principle of solidarity has been accepted in the form of solidarity among states, whereas the responsibility to protect would mean the international community's solidarity with the population of a particular state. Is this change of addressee acceptable? The answer to this question should be sought in the concept of the principle of solidarity, as well as in the relevance of the protection of human rights in the matrix of international law.

As has been pointed out, the structural principle of solidarity was distilled from several legal regimes that enshrined, or even explicitly referred to, it. It means, generally speaking, that states have to take into account community interests when shaping their national policies. The reference to community interests embraces interests whose realization would benefit the whole international community or a particular state or group of states, in case the international community has accepted these interests as its own. The fact is that, seen from this perspective, solidarity does not result in an infringement of the sovereignty of those states that benefit from a solidarity action. Considering solidarity as a basis for a responsibility to protect would change that situation, since any action in favour of a population bypassing, or even forcing the state concerned, definitely means an infringement on the sovereignty of the latter.

However, it has been established by now, and does not have to be argued in depth again, that the recognition of human rights and their protection has become one of

[72] On this see Peters (n 52) 300 *et seq*, who answers this question in a differentiated manner, but as for the responsibility of the state in question, affirmatively. [73] Koroma (n 43) 122–23.

the core elements of the present international legal order, and states can no longer claim that the treatment of their populations is an internal affair immune from international interference.[74]

5. Concluding Remarks

The legal regimes briefly analysed in this contribution are based on, or reflect, the structural principle of solidarity. This shows that international law certainly has moved away from a legal regime dedicated to merely coordinating the activities of states. The acknowledgement of this principle, and its introduction into several legal regimes dealing with different aspects of international relations, clearly show that in formulating their decisions in the respective areas, states must take into consideration that the respective legal regime aims at the protection or management of common goods. However, an assessment of modern international agreements shows that they are based upon a structural principle of solidarity that displays a further aspect, namely the amelioration of deficits, which certain states or a particular state also pursue as an objective in the interest of the community of states.

The fact that some international legal regimes are based upon the structural principle of solidarity induces the question whether different rules concerning adherence or termination may be warranted for such regimes. The respective international agreements do not point in this direction, although this would be a matter of consequence.

One may question whether a state may refrain from adhering to a treaty regime whose objective and purpose is to pursue the interests of the world community. If one were to argue that the adherence to such a regime is obligatory, one would, in fact, vest the respective State Conference with legislative power. International law has not yet developed into such a direction, making it difficult to adequately describe the international community's formulation of values or interests, although such formulation is a fact.[75] However, it is possible to argue that states that refrain from acceding to regimes which are meant to protect the interests of the international community, are under an obligation not to undermine such efforts.

Applying the principle of solidarity to human rights means another step forward in the evolution of this principle, since it means broadening the scope of potential addressees. As far as human rights are concerned, the addressee of any

[74] Tomuschat (n 24) 220 *et seq*.

[75] See Paulus (n 9) 254 *et seq*, who proceeds on the basis that such common values are based upon consent.

solidarity-based action would be the population, rather than a given state. But such development is in line with the relevance of international human rights standards in public international law and with a more modern view of the meaning of statehood. States are not a means of themselves, but instead are a means of serving the well-being of their populations. This is exactly what the first pillar of the concept of the responsibility to protect emphasizes. Therefore, this concept correctly incorporates the principle of solidarity into the international human rights regime, while also adding to its means of implementation.

Further Reading

Abi-Saab G, 'Whither the International Community?' (1998) 9 *EJIL* 248

Bellamy AJ, *Responsibility to Protect: The Global Effort to End Mass Atrocities* (Polity 2009)

Bettati M and Kouchner B (eds), *Le Devoir d'Ingérence: Peut-on les Laisser Mourir?* (Denoël 1987)

Beyerlin U, 'Rio-Konferenz 1992: Beginn Einer Neuen Globalen Umweltrechtsordnung?' (1994) 54 *ZaöRV* 124

Brown Weiss E, *In Fairness to Future Generations: International Law, Common Patrimony and Intergenerational Equity* (Transnational Publishers 1989)

—— 'Environmentally Sustainable Competitiveness: A Comment' (1993) 102 *Yale LJ* 2123

Dupuy PM, *Droit International Public* (10th edn, Dalloz 2010)

Evans G, 'From Humanitarian Intervention to the Responsibility to Protect' (2006) 24 *Wis Int'l LJ* 703

—— *The Responsibility to Protect: Ending Mass Atrocity Crimes Once and For All* (Brookings Institution Press 2008)

Feichtner I, 'Waiver', *The Max Planck Encyclopedia of Public International Law* (2012) vol X

Friedmann W, *The Changing Structure of International Law* (Stevens & Sons 1964)

Grewe W, *Epochen der Völkerrechtsgeschichte* (Nomos Verlagsgesellschaft 1984)

Hestermeyer HP, 'Reality or Aspiration?: Solidarity in International Environmental and World Trade Law' in Hestermeyer HP and others (eds), *Coexistence, Cooperation and Solidarity: Liber Amicorum Rüdiger Wolfrum* (vol I, Martinus Nijhoff 2012)

Hilpold P, 'Solidarität als Rechtsprinzip: Völkerrechtliche, Europarechtliche und Staatsrechtliche Betrachtungen' (2007) 55 *JoR* 195

Jackson JH, *The World Trading System* (2nd edn, MIT Press 1997)

Kellersmann B, *Die Gemeinsame, Aber Differenzierte Verantwortlichkeit von Industriestaaten und Entwicklungsländern für den Schutz der Globalen Umwelt* (Springer 2000)

Koroma AG, 'Solidarity: Evidence of an Emerging International Legal Principle' in Hestermeyer HP and others (eds), *Coexistence, Cooperation and Solidarity: Liber Amicorum Rüdiger Wolfrum* (Martinus Nijhoff 2012)

Macdonald RSJ, 'Solidarity in the Practice and Discourse of Public International Law' (1996) 8 *Pace Int'l L Rev* 259

Mosler H, 'The International Society as a Legal Community' (1974) 140 *RdC* 1

Paulus AL, *Die internationale Gemeinschaft im Völkerrecht: Eine Untersuchung zur Entwicklung des Völkerrechts im Zeitalter der Globalisierung* (CH Beck 2001)

Peters A, 'The Responsibility to Protect: Spelling Out the Hard Legal Consequences for the UN Security Council and Its Members' in Fastenrath U and others (eds), *From Bilateralism to Community Interest: Essays in Honour of Judge Bruno Simma* (OUP 2011)

von Pufendorf S, *De Officio Hominis et Civis Juxta Legem Naturalem* (first published 1673, OUP 1927)

Randelzhofer A, 'Article 51' in Simma B (ed), *The Charter of the United Nations* (vol I, 2nd edn, OUP 2002)

Rangel VM, 'The Solidarity Principle, Francisco de Vitoria and the Protection of Indigenous Peoples' in Hestermeyer HP and others (eds), *Coexistence, Cooperation and Solidarity: Liber Amicorum Rüdiger Wolfrum* (Martins Nijhoff 2012)

Sands P, *Principles of International Environmental Law* (2nd edn, CUP 2003)

Scheuner U, 'Solidarität unter den Nationen als Grundsatz in der Gegenwärtigen Internationalen Gemeinschaft' in Delbrück J (ed), *Recht im Dienst des Friedens: Festschrift für Eberhard Menzel* (Duncker & Humblot 1975)

Schlesinger SC, *Act of Creation: The Founding of the United Nations* (Westview Press 2003)

Steiner HJ and Alston P, *International Human Rights in Context: Law, Politics, Morals* (2nd edn, OUP 2000)

Stoll PT and Schorkopf F, *WTO-Welthandelsordnung und Welthandelsrecht* (Heymann 2002)

Thakur R, *The United Nations, Peace and Security: From Collective Security to the Responsibility to Protect* (CUP 2006)

—— *The Responsibility to Protect: Norms, Laws, and the Use of Force in International Politics* (Routledge 2011)

Tomuschat C, 'International Law: Ensuring the Survival of Mankind on the Eve of a New Century: General Course on Public International Law' (1999) 281 *RdC* 13

de Vattel E, *Le Droit des Gens, ou Principes de la Loi Naturelle* (Paris 1758)

Wellens K, 'Revisiting Solidarity as a (Re-)Emerging Constitutional Principle: Some Further Reflections' in Wolfrum R and Kojima C (eds), *Solidarity: A Structural Principle of International Law* (Springer 2010)

—— 'Solidarity as a Constitutional Principle: Its Expanding Role and Inherent Limitations' in Macdonald RSJ and Johnston DM (eds), *Towards World Constitutionalism: Issues in the Legal Ordering of the World Community* (Brill 2005)

Wellmann C, 'Solidarity, the Individual, and Human Rights' (2000) 22 *Hum Rts Q* 639

Wolff C, *Ius Gentium Methodo Scientifica Pertractatum* (first published 1749, Clarendon Press 1934)

Wolfrum R, 'International Law of Cooperation' in Bernhardt R (ed), *Encyclopedia of Public International Law* (Elsevier 1995) vol II

—— 'International Environmental Law: Purposes, Principles and Means of Ensuring Compliance' in Morrison FL and Wolfrum R (eds), *International, Regional and National Environmental Law* (Kluwer 2000)

—— 'Solidarity amongst States: An Emerging Structural Principle of International Law' in Dupuy PM and others (eds) *Common Values in International Law: Essays in Honour of Christian Tomuschat* (Engel 2006)

Yusuf AA, '"Differential and More Favourable Treatment": The GATT Enabling Clause' (1980) 14 *JWTL* 488

CHAPTER 18

EQUALITY

JARLATH CLIFFORD

EQUALITY is an immensely challenging, complex, and dynamic concept. Although most persons have an intuitive understanding of equality,[1] their diverse characteristics and range of experiences mean that they are likely to reach very different conclusions when asked to explain equality. In other words, equality means many things to many people. These various perspectives are made manifest both positively and negatively in society. Often, the human diversity that should be promoted, embraced, and cherished, instead triggers prejudice, discrimination, and oppression. Laws and policies may draw conscious and unconscious distinctions that discriminate against particular groups or individuals.[2] The net effect of *de facto* and *de jure* discrimination is that those perceived as different are unable to enjoy fundamental human rights on an equal basis with others, and they continue to be abused and denied basic social goods, benefits, and public safeguards.

Against this backdrop, international human rights law has developed a multi-dimensional relationship with the principle of equality. As a structural principle, equality provides a conceptual framework through which to understand and analyse human rights issues—and through which to justify human rights decisions. It provides a spotlight for identifying key issues in complex cases and acts as a moral lever for explaining human rights protections.[3] Thus, equality (together with the related

[1] Sandra Fredman, *Discrimination Law* (1st edn, OUP 2002) 1.

[2] Dinah Shelton, 'Prohibited Discrimination in International Human Rights Law' in Aristotle Constantinides and Nikos Zaikos (eds), *The Diversity of International Law: Essays in Honour of Professor Kalliopi K. Koufa* (Martinus Nijhoff Publishers 2009).

[3] See eg the United Kingdom case of *A and others v Secretary of State for the Home Department* (Belmarsh case).

principle of non-discrimination) provides a moral and analytical mechanism for ensuring that all people effectively enjoy human rights guarantees. The principle of equality also binds human rights norms and embellishes them with both a procedural and substantive content. Taking stock of these dimensions, this chapter will examine the normative and philosophical bases of the principle of equality. Second, it explores and maps out how contemporary international human rights law transposes and applies the principle, especially as it relates to the prohibition of discrimination. Finally, the chapter will explore the claim that a right to equality exists in international law and will attempt to identify some of the benefits of this right.

The principle of equality in international human rights law is multifaceted. At the theoretical level, when scholars talk of equality, they often talk about different concepts which, while rooted in the same overarching framework, frequently can have very different implications for human rights. These discussions broadly encompass the concepts of formal and substantive equality. Formal equality refers to the idea that things that are the same or similar should be treated in the same or similar ways. As Section 2 will discuss, this concept is linked to the notion that equality requires consistent treatment of all. On the other hand, substantive equality refers to the idea that equality provisions should be sensitive to the informal arrangements and barriers that cause inequality for some, and account for them by requiring different treatment for persons who are disadvantaged in society. Section 2 of this chapter sets out that one or more conceptions of equality based on these two concepts, such as equality of opportunity, equality of outcomes, or transformative equality, are generally adopted when formulating equality law and policy. Alongside this theoretical discourse, international human rights law transposes these concepts within the principle of equality primarily through the dynamic of equality and non-discrimination. Thus, in practice the prohibition of discrimination, defined in Article 1(1) of the 1965 International Convention on the Elimination of All Forms of Racial Discrimination (CERD), the requirement to take some form of positive or special measures found in Article 1(4) of CERD, and so forth, represent the key articulations of the principle of equality in international human rights law. Sections 3 and 4 discuss in greater detail how these two strands of the principle of equality have been transposed in international human rights instruments and interpreted within its jurisprudence.

1. The Philosophical Foundations of Equality

Equality is a common cornerstone of many contemporary democracies. To appreciate why it occupies a cherished position in contemporary legal orders, it is necessary to examine how the understanding of equality has evolved over time.[4] The United Nations Educational, Scientific, and Cultural Organization's (UNESCO) *Birthright of Man* illustrates that the idea of equality has preoccupied social thinkers and philosophers from all civilizations throughout history.[5] Some scholars contend that even social philosophies such as Confucianism, which they traditionally perceived as promoting societal difference and inequality, have made important contributions to our current understanding of the idea of equality.[6]

An understanding of why contemporary rights-based democracies have appropriated equality as a constitutional norm begins with classical Greece.[7] Thucydides proposed that equality prescriptively indicates how law ought to operate in a democracy.[8] In particular, he suggested that procedural equality is instrumental for social justice—a key component of the democratic order. Plato, on the other hand, argued that the key differences which existed between individuals, for example, on the basis of sex, should be accounted for in exigent times.[9] Greek philosophy's most significant contribution to the notion of equality is provided by Aristotle's maxim that 'things that are alike should be treated alike',[10] with an implicit corollary that the unlike should be treated according to the relevant differences.

Aristotle's maxim directly underpins the formal ideas of equality that are important for addressing specific human rights concerns, for instance, how the legal system should react when laws on their face treat some people unfavourably because of a shared characteristic. Yet, classical Greek notions have leaned towards procedural forms of equality and lack many characteristics that are integral to modern human rights norms. One such characteristic is universality. This basic human rights principle is absent from Greek thinking, which envisaged equality between citizens of the state, but not between citizens and non-citizens. Indeed, the idea of equality was applied differently to different people, depending on their political status. The idea of universal citizenship, a concept with which international human rights law and contemporary constitutions struggle today, was absent from classical Greek philosophy.[11]

Universalism was critical to Christian thinking on equality. St Thomas Aquinas emphasized an approach to equality that united everyone under God's direction in

[4] Jarlath Clifford, 'Locating Equality: from Historical Philosophical Thought to Modern Legal Norms' (2008) 1 *The Equal Rights Rev* 11.

[5] Jeanne Hersch (ed), *Birthright of Man* (UNESCO 1969). The collection shows that social, political, and philosophical thinkers from Africa, Asia, the Middle East, and Europe have considered equality to be a fundamental component of a society.

[6] See AT Nuyen, 'Confucianism and the Idea of Equality' (2001) 11 *Asian Philosophy* 61. See also Clifford (n 4) 12.

[7] George L Abernethy, *Introduction to the Idea of Equality: An Anthology* (John Knox Press 1959) 15–24. [8] Abernethy (n 7) 38.

[9] Abernethy (n 7) 41.

[10] Aristotle, *Ethica Nicomachea* (JL Ackrill and JO Urmson (eds), W Ross (tr), OUP 1980) 112–17, 1131a–31b. [11] Abernethy (n 7) 18.

a common bond of happiness. Aquinas' concept of divine law commanded that all unite in mutual love of God.[12] Thus, in contrast to Greek philosophers who limited the application of the principle of equality to members of set democratic orders, Aquinas presupposed that by divine design and law the principle of equality applied to everyone.

Natural law theorists added to the body of knowledge which has shaped modern understanding of the principle of equality. In *Leviathan*, for instance, Hobbes set out his vision of equality within natural law:

> Nature hath made men so equal in the faculties of body and mind as that, though there be found one man sometimes manifestly stronger in body or of quicker mind than another, yet when all is reckoned together the difference between man and man is not so considerable as that one man can thereupon claim to himself any benefit to which another may not pretend, as well as he.[13]

Hobbes thus suggested that despite the inevitability of individual differences with respect to physical and mental talents, such differences should not by themselves imbue benefits. Conor Gearty has argued that Hobbes's basic premise with respect to equality is that if everybody is equal in terms of natural rights, they must be able to use their equal natural rights to make choices regarding their participation in society. Furthermore, he argues that the natural law discourse of Hobbes's time created a progressive vision of equality that provides direction for modern law-making in facilitating 'real' equality.[14] As with other natural law thinkers, Hobbes believed that equality imparted natural rights on the basis of an individual's humanity. John Locke asserted that, under natural law, all men were equal in the sense that every man had an equal right to his natural freedom without being subjected to the will or authority of any other man. Yet, he did not suggest that all men were equal in everything: 'I cannot be supposed to understand all sorts of equality: age or virtue may give men a just precedency: excellency of parts and merit may place others above the common level.'[15] Likewise, Thomas Paine declared that through the will of God all men are born equal with equal natural right, and the only basis of distinction is that between the sexes.[16] By applying this position, natural law theorists were situating the discourse of equality within rights-based language, thereby enabling individuals to assert the principle of equality for political and legal ends.

[12] Abernethy (n 7) 73.

[13] Thomas Hobbes, *Leviathan*, (first published 1651, Forgotten Books 2008) 84.

[14] Conor Gearty, 'Can Human Rights Deliver Real Equality?' (5th Annual LAG Lecture, London, 19 November 2007) <http://www.conorgearty.co.uk/pdfs/Legal_Action_group_GEARTY2007.pdf> accessed 13 February 2012.

[15] John Locke, *Second Treatise of Government* (C B Macpherson (ed), first published 1689, Hackett Publishing 1980) 31.

[16] Thomas Paine, *The Rights of Man* (eBooks@Adelaide 2009) <http://ebooks.adelaide.edu.au/p/paine/thomas/p147r/index.html> accessed 10 March 2012.

Many contemporary political and legal philosophers have contested the normative relevance of equality for underpinning modern legal norms. Some scholars, such as Nozick, suggest that equality is normatively defunct and cannot be used to underwrite governmental interference in the distribution of resources.[17] Others recognize that different notions exist when people talk of equality. Berlin, for example, analyses two of these notions: (i) equality as rules and (ii) equality proper.[18] After balancing the two against each other, Berlin concludes that equality as rules is a more convincing notion of equality, because even in conditions where a moderate form of equality proper is permitted to flourish:

> the criterion of equality has plainly been influenced by something other than the mere desire for equality as such, namely, desire for liberty or the full development of human resources, or the belief that men deserve to be as rich or as powerful or as famous as they can make themselves—beliefs which are not connected with the desire for equality at all.[19]

Other scholars, such as Peter Westen[20]—and later Christopher Peters[21]—argue that equality is merely a tautology, entirely 'circular', because it tells us to treat like people alike, but it is completely silent about what is meant by 'like people'. As with Berlin's observation about equality proper, they assert that equality without further moral guidance says nothing about how we should act and is anterior to and dependent upon rights to give it form and function.[22]

The contributions of John Rawls, Amartya Sen, and Ronald Dworkin perhaps have been the most significant to the contemporary understandings of equality's normative importance in the democratic order. All three agree on equality's normative worth but approach it in different ways. John Rawls, for instance, sets out that a sound model of justice requires adherence to two overarching principles:

1. Equality in terms of basic rights and liberties; and
2. Equality in respect to primary social goods.[23]

Equality is thus a necessary and common component of Rawls's justice equation. Amartya Sen's seminal work contends that focusing on the equalization of social goods is not the correct approach. Instead, Sen suggests that we should attempt to equalize individual capabilities because 'there is evidence that the conversion of goods to capabilities varies from person to person substantially, and the equality of the former may still be far from the equality of the latter'.[24]

[17] Robert Nozick, *Anarchy, State, and Utopia* (Basic Books 1974) ch 8.

[18] Richard Wollheim and Isaiah Berlin, 'Equality' (1956) 56 *Proceedings of the Aristotelian Society* 281.

[19] Wollheim and Berlin (n 18) 317.

[20] Peter Westen, 'The Empty Idea of Equality' (1982) 95 *HLR* 537.

[21] Christopher J Peters 'Equality Revisited' (1997) 110 *HLR* 1211.

[22] Westen (n 20) 547.

[23] John Rawls, *A Theory of Justice* (Harvard UP 1971) 60.

[24] Amartya Sen, 'Equality of What' (The Tanner Lecture on Human Values, Stanford University, 22 May 1979) 219 <http://www.uv.es/~mperezs/intpoleco/Lecturcomp/Distribucion%20Crecimiento/Sen%20Equaliy%20of%20what.pdf> accessed 13 February 2012.

Dworkin's work also has been hugely influential to understanding the intrinsic worth of the principle of equality in law and policy. He argues that equality is not anterior to rights or liberties at all, but that:

[L]iberties must be recognized only when the fundamental right to treatment as an equal can be shown to require these rights. If this is correct then the right to distinct liberties does not conflict with any supposed competing right to equality, but on the contrary follows from a conception of equality conceded to be more fundamental.[25]

Dworkin asserts that it is a primary obligation of government not only to treat people with concern and respect, but to treat them with *equal* concern and respect.[26] He proceeds, in later work, to advocate for what he terms 'equality of resources'.[27] Under his construct of equality of resources:

[W]e must, on pain of violating equality, allow the distribution of resources at any particular moment to be (as we might say) ambition-sensitive... But on the other hand, we must not allow the distribution of resources at any moment to be endowment-sensitive, that is, to be affected by differences in ability of the sort that produce income differences in a laissez-faire economy among people with the same ambitions.[28]

In other words, a choice/endowment distinction is integral to Dworkin's model of equality, in which distinctions or inequalities that the errant choices of an individual cause are morally acceptable, but those which are the result of a specific endowment of an individual are not. Part of the attraction of Dworkin's model of equality is its simplicity. Everyone has an intuitive understanding of what it means to be concerned for, or to respect, others. Consequently, the principle of equality in this sense underscores that human rights are based on basic and common human values which everyone understands, shares, and approves.

Jack Donnelly has applied Dworkin's model of equality within international human rights law and has argued that 'the Universal Declaration [of Human Rights] model is rooted in an attractive moral vision of human beings as equal and autonomous agents living in states that treat each citizen with equal concern and respect'.[29] Moreover, he asserts that the basic moral equality of all human beings, together with the counterparts of equal respect and equal concern, has provided the foundation for a convergence on the rights of the Universal Declaration of Human Rights,[30] a basis to understand the right to personal liberty,[31] and a justification for requiring states to implement social and economic rights.[32]

25 Ronald Dworkin, *Taking Rights Seriously* (Harvard UP 1977) 274.
26 Dworkin, *Taking Rights Seriously* (n 25) 272–73.
27 Ronald Dworkin, 'What is Equality? Part 2: Equality of Resources' (1981) 10 *Phil & Pub Aff* 283.
28 Dworkin, 'What is Equality?' (n 27) 311.
29 Jack Donnelly, *Universal Human Rights in Theory and Practice* (2nd edn, Cornell UP 2003) 38.
30 Donnelly (n 29) 41. 31 Donnelly (n 29) 44. 32 Donnelly (n 29) 46.

Equality is integral to our moral, philosophical, and political understanding of the idea of democracy. Our common awareness regarding the need for equality (of some form) may be one reason why equality is so often the backbone of contemporary justice systems. Classical Greek philosophy believed that some formal notion of equality was fundamental to the successful operation of the democratic order. While this notion of equality has clearly advanced over time, the transition to realizing an egalitarian purpose for equality has been slow. Nevertheless, over time political and legal philosophers have incrementally recognized equality's potential to combat disadvantage and enable everyone to share in the benefits of democratic membership. Contemporary human rights law's reliance on the principle of equality is evident.

2. Equality and Non-Discrimination Concepts in Human Rights Law

Although, linguistically, the opposite of equality is inequality, in legal terms non-discrimination or anti-discrimination are often preferred to frame the legal or policy action used to achieve equality. Ellis, writing about this legal corollary, states that 'the non-discrimination principle is essentially the non-dynamic part of the equality package; it works only in conjunction with dynamic measures of social reorganization'.[33] The Inter-American Court of Human Rights has also referred to this special relationship stating:

> The element of equality is difficult to separate from non-discrimination. Indeed, when referring to equality before the law . . . this principle must be guaranteed with no discrimination.[34]

For such reasons, equality as non-discrimination is often promoted as a principle dynamic of international human rights law. In practice, while there is an underlying the concept of equality, there are several different conceptions of equality that apply in different contexts.[35] Claiming a violation of the right to non-discrimination or equality before the law thus often triggers an evaluation of one or more conceptions of equality. Indeed, in some cases it is not possible to fit the inequality or discrimination the victim experiences neatly into a distinct classification, and it is necessary

[33] Evelyn Ellis, 'The Principle of Equality of Opportunity Irrespective of Sex: Some Reflections on the Present State of European Community Law and Its Future Development' in Alan Dashwood and Siofra O'Leary (eds), *The Principle of Equal Treatment in EC Law* (Sweet & Maxwell 1997) 180.

[34] *Juridical Condition and Rights of the Undocumented Migrants*, para 83.

[35] Colm O'Cinneide, 'Fumbling Towards Coherence: The Slow Evolution of Equality and Anti-Discrimination Law in Britain' [2006] *NILQ* 57.

to analyse the particulars of a case through a number of sometimes-overlapping conceptions of equality.

This variety illustrates how problematic it is to apply the concepts of equality and discrimination in human rights discourse. Much academic literature has attempted to pinpoint the theoretical justifications for equality and non-discrimination provisions. Some works have sought to understand the justification of equality protections in national contexts. For example, Gardner has argued that anti-discrimination laws operating in national contexts promote individual autonomy.[36] Other research has attempted to understand how the concepts of equality and discrimination are operating within human rights contexts. For example, McCrudden and Kountouros identify four broad and porous approaches to equality and non-discrimination: (i) equality as 'rationality'; (ii) equality as protective of 'prized public goods'; (iii) equality as preventing 'status-harms' arising from discrimination on particular grounds; and (iv) equality as proactive promotion of equality of opportunity between particular groups.[37]

In the main, equality and non-discrimination provisions generally tend to adopt one or more of the following approaches: (i) equality as consistent treatment; (ii) equality of opportunity; (iii) equality of outcomes; or (iv) transformative equality. Some of these approaches are fluid and, in some cases, adopt characteristics of both formal and substantive equality. Consequently, rather than being distinct or isolated classifications, they are ranges in a spectrum which often blend into one another.

2.1 Equality as consistent treatment

This approach is closely associated with Aristotle's formal equality maxim that 'things that are alike should be treated alike'.[38] It represents the simplest understanding of equality today. Based on individual justice, its central ethical claim is that each individual is equal under laws that should apply to everyone equally. Hence, treating people unequally or inconsistently is unfair,[39] because a person's individual physical or personal characteristics (or status) should be irrelevant in determining whether he or she has a right to some benefit or gain. The prohibition against direct discrimination that is present in many legal systems, and can be defined as treating one person less favourably than another is, has been, or would be treated in a comparable situation on specific grounds, applies this approach in practice.

36 John Gardner, 'Liberals and Unlawful Discrimination' (1989) 9 *OJLS* 1.

37 Christopher McCrudden and Haris Kountouros, 'Human Rights and European Equality Law' in Helen Meenan (eds), *Equality Law in an Enlarged European Union: Understanding the Article 13 Directives* (CUP 2007).

38 Aristotle (n 10) 112–17, 1131a–31b.

39 Murray Wesson, 'Equality and Social Rights: An Exploration in Light of the South African Constitution' [2007] *PL* 748, 751.

Liberals defend this approach on the basis that it challenges arbitrary and irrational decision-making, for example, when policies or people selectively disadvantage others due to an irrelevant characteristic.[40] Thus, a key benefit is its ability to protect against arbitrary treatment that arises from irrational prejudice. But, on its own, requiring consistent treatment insufficiently addresses the disadvantage and inequality some individuals and groups experience. Suppose, for example, that a state passed a law which said that all brown-haired people—irrespective of any other criteria—are forbidden to attend university. Equality as consistent treatment tells us only to apply this law equally and says nothing about the inherent unfairness and arbitrariness of such a law. Consequently, without further substantive guidance, laws that are prima facie morally wrong could be applied equally, with the likely result that they would deepen inequality.

2.2 Equality of opportunity

Some have sought to solve some of the problems with the consistent treatment approach by equalizing the starting points for individuals from disadvantaged groups, so they can compete for social, economic, political, or other goods alongside other individuals. The equality of opportunity approach aims to strike an appropriate balance between formal and substantive notions of equality. To achieve this balance and equalize starting points, equality of opportunity approaches borrow some elements of the redistributive theory of justice, but do not cross over into pure utilitarian approaches.[41] Essentially these approaches aim to cultivate conditions which enable individuals to start at the same competitive position, regardless of their characteristics, background, or status. In this way, they account for the limited potential of formal equality to achieve full and effective equality for some groups. Injecting substantive equality-based mechanisms into the formal model addresses these limitations. In doing so, it permits certain forms of action in order to improve the lot of individuals or groups that are experiencing inequality. For example, it may allow individuals from traditionally disadvantaged groups to receive specialized education or training, or encourage them to apply for jobs in sectors or industries where the group is underrepresented.[42] Returning to the example of brown-haired people noted above, the equality of opportunity approach would require universities to encourage applications from brown-haired people in order to increase access among this group and redress formal or social exclusions that have previously existed.

[40] Paul Brest, 'In Defense of the Antidiscrimination Principle' (1976) 90 *HLR* 1.

[41] See for example, Fredman (n 1).

[42] Christopher McCrudden, 'The New Concept of Equality' (2003) 4 *ERA Forum* 9.

2.3 Equality of outcomes

An alternative substantive model of equality goes beyond equal access to opportunities and instead aims at a fair distribution of goods and benefits, in order to improve the lot of those who have been historically disadvantaged in society. Specific measures are adopted for them,[43] based on a belief that, due to historic disadvantages, individuals from some groups continue to suffer discrimination and marginalization and will be unable to overcome their situation unless mechanisms are put in place to equalize outcomes. In the case of the admission of brown-haired people to university, the equality of outcomes model would go further than the equality of opportunity approach by not just requiring the encouragement of applications, but by assuring that places are reserved for brown-haired people at university.

Some scholars and policy-makers reject equality of outcome policies, contending that they demand too many state resources (including state regulation) and impose too high a price on individual autonomy. Additionally, some scholars claim that the mechanisms equality of outcomes policies adopt, for instance quotas, overshadow the need for social change by adapting or reorganizing existing institutions and structures.[44] Another charge laid against this approach is that it tends to be under-inclusive, only improving the position of those who are best placed to take advantage of these polices within the broader disadvantaged group. Finally, some members of disfavoured groups oppose the idea of substantive redistribution because, in their view, it reinforces their status as 'victims' and thus perpetuates stereotypes that lead to discrimination.[45] Unsurprisingly, therefore, attempts to adopt and implement laws or policies based on this approach to equality are politically contentious, and opposition to such measures often ranges from those who abhor such action politically to those who charge that such policies will not sufficiently address the root causes of structural inequality.

2.4 Transformative equality

Legal systems such as those of the European Union (EU) and the United Kingdom have recently adopted mechanisms aimed at achieving what is referred to as transformative equality. Like equality of outcomes, transformative equality seeks to accelerate equality for disadvantaged groups. Unlike equality of outcomes, however, which prescribes outcomes to be achieved through providing benefits for

[43] Different terms, such as positive action, affirmative action, or special measures, are sometimes used to describe these measures. This chapter will use the term positive action.

[44] See eg Bhikhu Parekh, 'A Case for Positive Discrimination' in Bob Hepple and Erika M Szyszczak (eds), *Discrimination: The Limits of the Law* (Mansell Publishing Ltd 1992).

[45] See eg Mark A Drumbl and John DR Craig, 'Affirmative Action in Question: A Coherent Theory for Section 15(2)' (1997) 4 *Rev Const Stud* 80.

individuals, transformative equality aims to advance the position of disadvantaged groups through changing existing social structures and the way organizations and institutions function. Thus, transformative equality requires adaptive changes in the practices and structures of organizations and institutions, pursuant to an assessment of how they fail disadvantaged groups. The intent is to make organizations and institutions more inclusive, more representative, and more accessible to disadvantaged groups. This approach has been employed primarily when the strong equality guarantees already present in some legal systems have failed to create the necessary change. The EU's gender mainstreaming agenda and the imposition of public sector equality duties in the cases of Britain and Northern Ireland[46] are examples of transformative equality approaches in their infancy.

Locating the theoretical foundations upon which the principle of equality is implemented is a difficult task. Different conceptions of equality underscore different human rights protections, and often different forms of equality need to be applied to different contexts. To a large extent, each of these approaches reflects the different ways in which equality acts as a structural principle within human rights law. As will be set out below, the principle of equality manifests itself at many levels in international human rights law, and it is neither linear nor static; instead, it is a dynamic concept which is constituted within human rights architecture to reflect the complexity and diversity of humanity and to address the many ways inequality and discrimination are rooted in society.

3. Equality as a Structural Principle of International Human Rights Law

Well before the adoption of modern human rights instruments, equality was an important component of the international rule of law. In 1926, the Permanent Court of International Justice stated that the Treaty of Versailles required 'equality in fact as well as ostensible legal equality in the sense of the absence of discrimination in the words of the law'.[47] Further, in the *Minority Schools in Albania* case, it asserted that to ensure the equal footing of nationals belonging to racial, religious, or linguistic minorities with other nationals, and to maintain national minorities' particularities, traditions, and characteristics, true equality between a majority and a minority required the preservation of the minority's own institutions and the very

[46] See Bob Hepple, 'The New Single Equality Act in Britain' (2010) 5 *The Equal Rights Rev* 11; see also O'Cinneide (n 35).

[47] *Settlers of German Origin in Poland.*

essence of that which qualifies them as a minority.[48] These pre-United Nations (UN) commitments to the principle of equality were transposed into the UN Charter ('the Charter'). The Charter places the principle of equality front and centre as guiding principle for the UN's purpose and mandate. Article 1(2) of the Charter states that the purpose of the UN is to develop friendly relations among nations based on respect for the principle of equal rights and self-determination of peoples, and Article 1(3) sets out that the UN must promote and encourage 'respect for human rights and for fundamental freedoms for all without distinction as to race, sex, language, or religion'. It is the only right that the Charter specifically mentions, and indeed, the Charter makes the principle of equality an original structural foundation upon which to guarantee, secure, and develop human rights. One may plausibly contend that the principle of equality is so wedded to the Charter and the Universal Declaration of Human Rights (UDHR) that its absence would make the landscape of human rights look fundamentally different.

Most of the major human rights instruments explicitly express a commitment to equality as a justification for the adoption of international standards and many extralegal human rights initiatives, such as the 1993 Vienna Declaration on Human Rights, have ensured that equality and non-discrimination are at the heart of developments in human rights policy. But what makes the principle of equality a 'structural' one in international human rights law? The first step in answering this question is to examine how the principle of equality has been transposed into the architecture of international human rights law. The second step is to appreciate how the principle of equality has been interpreted and applied.

Turning to the first step, it seems the transposition process has taken shape in three distinct ways, namely: (i) equality as a preambular objective of international human rights treaties; (ii) equality's implicit descriptive function in the normative understanding of the scope and application of human rights; and (iii) equality's codification in the substantive articles of human rights treaties.

3.1 Equality as a preambular objective

A preamble in international treaty law is used to 'establish the general "philosophy" of the text as well as to set its general purpose'.[49] In other words, it introduces the spirit and the general objectives that the treaty aims to achieve. Equality is a defining feature of all international human rights preambles. The international order continually returns to the need to achieve equality as a justification for introducing human

48 *Minority Schools in Albania*, paras 48–52.

49 Audrey Guichon, 'Some Arguments on the Universality of Human Rights in Islam' in Javaid Rehman and Susan Breau (eds), *Relgion, Human Rights and International Law: A Critical Examination of Islamic State Practices* (Martinus Nijhoff 2007) 186.

rights standards. The preamble to the UDHR, for example, refers to the 'equal and inalienable rights of all members of the human family' and the 'equal rights of men and women'. Likewise, the 'the equal and inalienable rights of all members of the human family' is mentioned in the preambles to the International Covenant on Civil and Political Rights (ICCPR) and the International Covenant on Economic, Social and Cultural Rights (ICESCR). The Convention on the Elimination of All Forms of Racial Discrimination (CERD), the Convention on the Elimination of All Forms of Discrimination against Women (CEDAW), the Convention on the Rights of the Child and most recently the Convention on the Rights of Persons with Disabilities (CRPD) go further by expressing a broader range of ways that equality underscores the text of the respective treaties. For example, CERD's preamble states that all human beings are equal before the law and are entitled to equal protection of the law and CEDAW's preamble speaks to promoting women's equality with men in all fields. The CRPD's preamble refers to the barriers persons with disabilities face in their participation as equal members of society and the need for persons with disabilities to have equal enjoyment of rights and equal opportunities.

The overarching preambular commitment to equality suggests that alongside other principles, such as dignity, achieving greater equality is a principal purpose that the international order aims to achieve through the international human rights movement. Indeed, realizing the equal rights of all people is one of the few common declarations made throughout international human rights law. Thus, by being a core reason for adopting international human rights standards, equality acts as a cohesive instrument which enables states and individuals to take stock of the conceptual origins of these human rights standards and realize why they are necessary.

3.2 Equality serving an implicit descriptive function

At a secondary level, equality serves an implicit descriptive function with respect to the nature and scope of human rights obligations. Commonly, the language of human rights states that they must be enjoyed by all human beings. Treaties continually use phrases such as 'everyone', 'all', or 'nobody' to frame the scope and contours of human rights. Describing human rights in this way ensures that the principle of equality is interwoven into the human rights fabric. Without this simple yet extremely important direction, the human rights landscape would be a much more contested domain. It appears that the drafters of human rights instruments have taken cognizance of the need to guarantee human rights through an equality paradigm. It is thus unsurprising that Articles 1 and 2 of the UDHR stress unequivocally that '[a]ll human beings are born free and equal in dignity and rights' and that the rights within the UDHR are an entitlement of everyone without 'distinction of any kind, such as race, colour, sex, language, religion, political or other opinion, national or social origin, property, birth or other status', respectively. It is clear from more recent human rights instruments that equality continues to drive how human rights guarantees are framed. Thus, the Charter of Fundamental Rights of the European Union guarantees that '[e]veryone has the right to respect for his or her physical and mental integrity';[50] '[e]veryone has the right to respect for his or her private and family life, home and communications';[51] and '[e]veryone is equal before the law'.[52] Noting the prevalence of the principle of equality in framing human rights norms, Shelton has written:

> Equality and non-discrimination are implied in the fact that human rights instruments guarantee rights to 'all persons', 'everyone', or 'every human being'. In fact, the right to be free from discrimination has been called 'the most fundamental of the rights of man…the starting point of all other liberties'.[53]

Consequently, the right to life;[54] freedom from torture, cruel, inhuman or degrading treatment or punishment;[55] and many more basic human rights, must be enjoyed by 'everyone'. The importance of this instructive aspect of human rights law should not be underestimated. As noted above, without this instructive function, human rights would be a far more contested domain, and the principle of universality would have a less solid foundation. It must be accepted that although some rights, such as marriage or voting rights, have limits imposed upon them, their application is still subject to the principle of equality. In such cases, the need to apply different conceptions of equality in different contexts becomes clear. For example, substantive conceptions of equality recognize the need to treat people that are in different situations differently. This mirrors social norms in many countries which proscribe people from voting or marrying until the have the capacity to make fully informed decisions and understand the consequences of these decisions. When individuals attain this capacity to enjoy such rights they benefit from the formal concept of equality that ensures that no one is arbitrarily denied access to these rights. Thus, human rights law recognizes the necessity of making relevant distinctions and allows people to be treated differently when compelling reasons justify this.

3.3 Equality codification in the substantive articles of human rights treaties

Equality also serves an extremely important instructive function through its codification in the substantive articles of human rights treaties. First amongst these substantive articles is Article 7 of the UDHR, which states that '[a]ll are equal before

[50] EU Charter Fundamental Rights, Art 3(1).
[51] EU Charter Fundamental Rights, Art 7.
[52] EU Charter Fundamental Rights, Art 20.
[53] Shelton (n 2) 1. Furthermore, Singh considers that the most important word in the UDHR is 'everyone'. See, Rabindher Singh, 'Equality: The Neglected Virtue' (2004) 2 *EHRLR* 141.
[54] ICCPR, Art 6(1).
[55] ICCPR, Art 7.

the law and are entitled without any discrimination to equal protection of the law'. Analysing the UDHR from an equality perspective reveals the many ways equality is necessary to protect, promote, and fulfil human rights adherence.[56]

Stating clearly at the earliest opportunity that human rights have to be applied equally to the entire human family and that they are an entitlement of everyone, the UDHR sets an equality agenda which has been transposed throughout international human rights law. Article 26 of the ICCPR reasserts Article 7 of the UDHR, stating that everyone is entitled to 'equality before the law and without any discrimination to equal protection of the law'. Article 2(1) guarantees the enjoyment of rights without distinction of any kind. In fact, the UN Human Rights Committee has added that unlike Article 2(1), which confines the principle of non-discrimination to the application of the rights in the ICCPR, 'article 26 ... provides in itself an autonomous right. It prohibits discrimination in law or in fact in any field regulated and protected by public authorities'.[57] Equality's influence in the ICCPR is also apparent in Article 3, requiring equal treatment of men and women in the enjoyment of the ICCPR's rights; Article 14(1), providing that all people shall be equal before courts and tribunals; and Article 23(4), requiring that states must take 'appropriate steps to ensure equality of rights and responsibilities of spouses as to marriage, during marriage and at its dissolution'.

The ICESCR is also imbued with commitments to the principle of equality. Article 2(2) proclaims that the rights in the ICESCR will be guaranteed without discrimination of any kind. Article 3 requires states to ensure that men and women will enjoy the economic, social, and cultural rights equally. Article 7 introduces equality in the workplace, including equal pay for equal work and equal opportunity for everyone to be promoted. Similarly, the ICESCR requires equality of rights in respect to education[58] and health.[59] General Comment No 20 to the ICESCR recognizes that non-discrimination is an immediate and cross-cutting obligation in the Covenant.[60] Non-discrimination and equality are the fundamental components of international human rights law, essential to the enjoyment of economic, social, and cultural rights.[61] General Comment No 20 stresses that in order to fulfil the rights the ICESCR guarantees, it is not enough to end formal, or *de jure*, discrimination; positive action is also necessary. Therefore, states must 'adopt the necessary

[56] For example, Arts 10, 16, 21(2), 21(3), 23(2), and 26(1) require equal treatment in the application of the rights to a fair and public hearing, marriage, access to public service, universal suffrage, pay for equal work and access to education respectively.

[57] United Nations Commission on Human Rights (UNCHR), 'General Comment No 18: Nondiscrimination' in 'Compilation of General Comments and General Recommendations Adopted by Human Rights Treaty Bodies' (29 July 1994) UN Doc HRI/GEN/1/Rev.1), para 12.

[58] ICESCR, Art 13(c). [59] ICESCR, Art 12(1).

[60] UN Committee on Economic, Social and Cultural Rights (UNCESCR), 'General Comment No 20: Nondiscrimination in economic, social and cultural rights' (ICESCR, Art 2, para 2), 2 July 2009, E/C.12/GC/20.

[61] UNCESCR (n 60) para 2.

measures to prevent, diminish and eliminate the conditions and attitudes which cause or perpetuate substantive or *de facto* discrimination'.[62]

Of course, CERD and CEDAW deal exclusively and respectively with eliminating racial discrimination and discrimination against women. The two conventions have common standards to accelerate equality for those protected and to safeguard against discrimination in particular fields, for example, with respect to civil, political, economic, and social rights.[63] In addition, both conventions require states parties to take positive steps in order to reduce the inequality.[64] Hence, while many of the equality and non-discrimination guarantees contained in the UDHR are translated directly into the provisions of the ICCPR, the international legal order has recognized the context-dependent nature of providing equality to specific groups that are vulnerable to inequality and discrimination.

More recently, the CRPD has relied upon equality as an underlying principle.[65] Article 1 states that the purpose of the CRPD is 'to promote, protect and ensure the full and equal enjoyment of all human rights and fundamental freedoms by all persons with disability'. Equality is deeply rooted within the general principles of the convention, under Article 3 in particular with relation to: non-discrimination, full and effective participation and inclusion in society, respect for difference and acceptance of persons with disabilities as part of human diversity and humanity, equality of opportunity, and equality between men and women. These principles are further reflected in substantive provisions of the CRPD. For instance, Article 5 provides for equality before and under the law, equal protection and benefit of the law, as well as non-discrimination, reasonable accommodation, and specific means to accelerate or achieve *de facto* equality. Article 12(2), which states 'that persons with disabilities enjoy legal capacity on an equal basis with others in all aspects of life', is critically important for addressing long term structural inequalities that have denied basic legal rights to persons with disabilities. The CRPD also provides for equality in rights for persons with disabilities in a range of other ways, including access to justice,[66] liberty of the person,[67] and right to respect for their physical and mental integrity.[68]

The 1989 ILO Convention 169 Concerning Indigenous and Tribal Peoples in Independent Countries also contains a number of provisions which codify the principle of equality and emphasize equality based on respecting differences. Article 2(1) sets out that governments have the responsibility to develop coordinated and

[62] UNCESCR (n 60) para 8. [63] See CERD, Art 5; CEDAW, Art 4.

[64] CERD, Art 2(2); CEDAW, Art 4.

[65] Council of Europe Commissioner for Human Rights, *Who Gets to Decide? Right to Legal Capacity for Persons with Intellectual and Psychosocial Disabilities* (Issue Paper, CommDH/IssuePaper (2012) 2). See also Jarlath Clifford, 'The UN Disability Convention and its impact on European Equality Law' (2011) 6 *The Equal Rights Rev* 11.

[66] Convention on the Rights of Persons with Disabilities, Art 13(1) (CRPD).

[67] CRPD (n 66), Art 14. [68] CRPD (n 66), Art 17.

systematic action to respect indigenous and tribal peoples' integrity. Article 2(2)(a) explains that such action includes ensuring that members of these peoples benefit from the rights and opportunities which national laws and regulations grant to other members of the population on an equal footing. Article 3(1) states that '[i]ndigenous and tribal peoples shall enjoy the full measure of human rights and fundamental freedoms without hindrance or discrimination'. Furthermore, Article 4(1) requires the adoption of special measures for safeguarding the persons, institutions, property, labour, cultures, and environment of indigenous and tribal peoples.

In Europe equality has been codified in Article 14 of the European Convention on Human Rights (ECHR), which protects against discrimination in the enjoyment of convention rights. A similar clause is contained in Article E of the Revised European Social Charter. It is noteworthy that these provisions only operate in conjunction with other treaty rights and do not stand alone. The later Protocol 12 to the ECHR added a broader right to non-discrimination applicable to any right set forth by law. Thus, as in the case of Article 26 of the ICCPR, Protocol 12 does not require the engagement of other convention rights.

Alongside these mechanisms the EU has the power to address discrimination[69] in certain fields through Article 19 (and Article 157) of the Treaty on the Functioning of the European Union. The EU has administered these powers through the adoption of equality directives including Council Directive 2000/78/EC,[70] Council Directive 2000/43/EC,[71] and Council Directive 2006/54/EC.[72] Some scholars have suggested that the use of different directives to address different forms of discrimination has fragmented EU law and made it inconsistent and hierarchical.[73] The grounds of race and gender have broader legal protection from discrimination than the grounds of disability, age, sexual orientation, or religion and belief. As a result, civil society and equality experts have consistently urged the EU to adopt a new equality directive that would harmonize EU anti-discrimination law.

Other regional human rights treaties also have codified equality in their guarantees. Article 1(1) of the American Convention on Human Rights contains a general non-discrimination provision. In addition, Article 24 (like Article 7 of the UDHR) states that '[a]ll persons are equal before the law. Consequently, they are entitled,

69 On grounds of race, sex, disability, sexual orientation, age, and religion or belief.

70 Council Directive 2000/78/EC of 27 November 2000 establishing a general framework for equal treatment in employment and occupation [2000] OJ L303/16.

71 Council Directive 2000/43/EC of 29 June 2000 implementing the principle of equal treatment between persons irrespective of racial or ethnic origin [2000] OJ L180/22.

72 Council Directive 2006/54/EC of 5 July 2006 on the implementation of the principle of equal opportunities and equal treatment of men and women in matters of employment and occupation (recast) [2006] OJ L 204/23.

73 Mark Bell, 'A Patchwork of Protection: The New Anti-discrimination Law Framework' (2004) 67 *MLR* 465.

without discrimination, to equal protection of the law'. The African Charter of Human and Peoples' Rights contains further strong guarantees to equality and non-discrimination. Important amongst these are Article 3, which stipulates that '[e]very individual shall be equal before the law... Every individual shall be entitled to equal protection of the law', and Article 2, which guarantees the Charter rights without distinction of any kind.

The structural importance of the principle of equality is visible if one unravels the various interwoven strands of the human rights fabric to see how equality is employed to frame and substantiate human rights standards. As is clear from the human rights treaty preambles equality is a core reason why human rights standards exist. Furthermore, it serves both a procedural function, by prescribing how human rights must be applied, and a substantive function, by setting out the scope and nature of human rights obligations. Reflecting on its multidimensional role, the Inter-American Court of Human Rights has placed the principle within the highest order of human rights guarantees, stating:

> the principle of equality before the law, equal protection before the law and non-discrimination belongs to *jus cogens*, because the whole legal structure of national and international public order rests on it and it is a fundamental principle that permeates all laws.[74]

4. The Scope and Interpretation of the Principle of Equality in Contemporary International Human Rights Law

Having examined equality in human rights law architecture, the next step is to consider how it is interpreted and applied by international human rights bodies. At this point it is worth noting that international law has rarely defined or interpreted a right to equality *per se*. More frequently, the interpretation pertaining to the principle of equality has focused on the right to non-discrimination or equal treatment and the core components of: (i) the definition and scope of discrimination and equal treatment and (ii) the scope of permissible measures to accelerate *de facto* equality

[74] *Juridical Condition and Rights of the Undocumented Migrants* (n 34) para 101.

4.1 The definition and scope of discrimination and equal treatment

Among the core international human rights treaties, only CERD, CEDAW, and CRPD define discrimination.[75] Within these definitions there is a common reference to 'purpose or effect' which implies that the definition includes indirect as well as direct forms of discrimination.[76] The reference to 'effect' also suggests that discrimination need not be intentional. Harassment and instruction to discriminate are also forms of prohibited discrimination under international and regional human rights law.

Although other international and regional human rights instruments have not defined discrimination, treaty bodies' decisions and comments have defined prohibited discrimination. In General Comment No 18, the UN Human Rights Committee (UNHRC) set out a definition which largely mirrors the definition contained in CERD, CEDAW, and CRPD.[77] It has also set out that under Article 26, '[a] differentiation which is compatible with the provisions of the Covenant and is based on objective and reasonable grounds does not amount to prohibited discrimination'.[78] This definition accords with the Article 14 jurisprudence of the ECHR, wherein discrimination 'means treating differently, without an objective and reasonable justification, persons in relevantly similar situations'.[79] Some key questions for establishing discrimination, therefore, appear to be: (i) has there been a difference in treatment, (ii) is the difference in treatment objectively and reasonably justifiable, and (iii) are persons in comparable situations? In practice, a factual approach is often taken to determine what constitutes both difference in treatment and an objective and reasonable justification.[80] It is also worth noting that a difference in treatment on grounds such as race, sex, disability, and nationality, is typically subject to strict scrutiny and requires 'very weighty reasons' to comply with the objective and reasonable justification component of the test for discrimination.[81]

As practices of discrimination evolve, legal action has shed light on the complex ways inequality and discrimination appear in society. In the EU case of *Coleman v Attridge Law*, for example, the Court of Justice of the European Union held that

[75] CERD, Art 1(1); CEDAW, Art 1; CRPD, Art 2.

[76] UNCESCR (n 60) para 10 affirms that indirect forms of differential treatment can amount to discrimination. Regionally, indirect discrimination is prohibited under the ECHR, see *DH and Others v Czech Republic* para 184.

[77] UNCHR 'General Comment No 18' (n 57) para 7.

[78] See *Zwaan-de Vries v Netherlands*, para 13.

[79] See *Willis v UK*, para 48.

[80] In *Broeks v Netherlands*, *Zwaan-de Vries* (n 78), *Pauger v Austria*, and *Vos v Netherlands*, it was held that distinctions on the grounds of sex in social security laws had no reasonable or objective aims and thus violated Article 26 of the ICCPR. In *Young v Australia*, the UNHRC held that the state had failed to show how the denial of benefits to same-sex partners, while granting the same benefits to unmarried heterosexual partners, was based on 'reasonable and objective' criteria.

[81] For a good overview of the strict scrutiny principle, see Dagmar Schiek, Lisa Waddington, and Mark Bell (eds) *Cases, Materials and Text on National, Supranational and International Non-Discrimination Law* (Hart 2007).

the scope of direct discrimination within Council Directive 2000/78/EC prohibited discrimination by association. To address discrimination as a human rights issue understanding the implications of such forms of discrimination is extremely important. People responsible for caring, for example, for elderly, disabled, or ill relatives or friends, often experience a special vulnerability that results in a cycle of discrimination and inequality. Research has shown that this vulnerability and subsequent inequality and discrimination are acutely felt in developing countries.[82]

The concept of multiple discrimination, that is, discrimination based on more than one of a person's characteristics,[83] has also been subject to much international scrutiny. The Durban Declaration and Plan of Action, as well as special procedures of the Human Rights Council, have called on states to combat multiple discrimination.[84] In *Teixeira v Brazil*, it was recently held that a failure to provide necessary and emergency care to the applicant constituted discrimination on the multiple grounds of her sex, her status as a woman of African descent, and her socio-economic background, which ran contrary to Brazil's obligations under CEDAW.

Human rights bodies thus are increasingly taking an expansive approach to the definition of discrimination. Some treaty bodies seem prepared to match the emergence of new forms of discrimination with strong legal safeguards. In this process, the principle of equality is a key, as it enables bodies to assess the human rights issues through an equality paradigm and thus cut straight to the core of the concern. At the same time, it provides bodies with practical justification for declaring that these emerging forms of discrimination contravene basic human rights.

4.2 Permitted measures to accelerate and achieve *de facto* equality

In most human rights systems, not all differential treatment will amount to discrimination. Instead, they accept that measures may be necessary to achieve full and effective equality. For instance, under the ECHR '[t]he right not to be discriminated against in the enjoyment of the rights guaranteed under the Convention is also violated when States without an objective and reasonable justification fail to

[82] Ann Elwan, 'Poverty and Disability: A Survey of the Literature' (18 December 1999) WDR Background Paper 2000/2001 <http://siteresources.worldbank.org/INTPOVERTY/Resources/WDR/Background/elwan.pdf> accessed 10 March 2012.

[83] For an analysis of this phenomenon, see Sarah Hannett, 'Equality at the Intersections: The Legislative and Judicial Failure to Tackle Multiple Discrimination' (2003) 23 *OJLS* 65.

[84] See Durban Declaration and Programme of Action, paras 2 or 69; UNHRC 'Promotion and Protection of all Human Rights, Civil, Political, Economic, Social and Cultural Rights, Including the Right to Development—Report of the Independent Expert on Minority Issues, Gay McDougall' (27 February 2009) UN Doc A/HRC/10/11/Add.2.

treat differently persons whose situations are significantly different'.[85] 'Reasonable accommodation', the denial of which CRPD, Article 2 defines as discrimination, is another example of permitted positive action measures. Within international and regional human rights systems, a growing consensus is developing that legislative and policy measures are sometimes necessary to accelerate progress towards equality for certain groups. Positive action measures are usually presented as social and economic rights mechanisms that aim to redistribute resources or wealth, but viewing positive action solely in these terms dampens its potential to redress structural inequalities that arise from the denial of civil and political opportunities. Hence, political shortlists for women and minority groups are sometimes proposed to increase their political representation and their status within politics.[86] The former UN Sub-Commission on the Promotion and Protection of Human Rights explained that justifications for positive action are not limited to economic redistribution and include remedying historical injustices, remedying social discrimination, creating diversity or proportional group representation, pre-empting social unrest, and implementing means for nation building.[87]

Human rights bodies have called for measures to address cases where systemic disadvantage has affected particular groups. The UN Human Rights Committee, for example, has called for the adoption of positive action measures, such as quotas, to improve the situation of particularly disadvantaged groups.[88] Similarly, the ICESCR Committee has stated that '[s]tates parties may be, and in some cases are, under an obligation to adopt special measures to attenuate or suppress conditions that perpetuate discrimination'.[89] The Committee clarified that these measures are legitimate as long as they represent a reasonable, objective, and proportionate means of redressing *de facto* discrimination. Such measures will ordinarily be temporary, but they can be permanent in exceptional cases, such as in making reasonable accommodations for people with sensory impairments.[90] Likewise, CERD may require positive action measures be taken. In General Recommendation No 32, the CERD Committee set out that the concept of special measures is based on the principle that the Convention requires states, when circumstances warrant, to adopt temporary special measures designed to secure to disadvantaged groups the full and equal

85 *Thlimmenos v Greece*, para 44.

86 Commission 'Report on Positive Action Measures' (Directorate-General for Employment and Social Affairs 2005) <http://ec.europa.eu/justice/gender-equality/files/report_on_positive_action_final_en.pdf> accessed 14 February 2012.

87 UNCHR, 'Prevention of Discrimination and Protection of Indigenous Peoples and Minorities: The Concept and Practice of Affirmative Action' (26 June 2001) UN Doc E/CN.4/Sub.2/2001/15.

88 See eg UNHRC, 'Consideration of Reports Submitted by States Parties under Article 40 of the Covenant: International Covenant on Civil and Political Rights: Concluding Observations of the Human Rights Committee: Japan' (18 December 2008) UN Doc CCPR/C/JPN/CO/5, para 12.

89 UNCESCR (n 60) para 9.

90 UNCESCR (n 60) para 9.

enjoyment of human rights and fundamental freedoms.[91] Furthermore, the General Recommendation makes it plain that special measures are not an 'exception to the principle of non-discrimination but are integral to its meaning and essential to the Convention project of... advancing... effective equality'.[92] In sum, reasonable, objective and proportionate positive or special measures are an integral part of the principle of equality and must be applied temporarily or (exceptionally) permanently, when it is necessary to achieve equality.

Regionally, the Inter-American Court, the European Court of Human Rights, and the European Committee on Social Rights have all confirmed that a state's failure to implement positive action measures can contravene their equality and non-discrimination obligations.[93] In spite of their legitimacy in international human rights law, positive action measures remain contentious in many national systems. This is partly due to the idea that they are an affront to individual autonomy and partly because adopting such policies can reduce the advantages that those in the dominant group enjoy. In light of the tension behind such measures, it is perhaps unsurprising that EU anti-discrimination law adopts a more cautious approach. Under EU law, in cases where there is a need for a tiebreaker, an employer can favour employing a woman over a man if there is no reason which would favour the man's appointment,[94] but an employer cannot automatically and unconditionally favour the employment of a woman in the recruitment process.[95] Research indicates that in some legal systems such positive action measures have been successfully implemented, without resorting to contentious measures such as quotas, through agreements between state regulators and private enterprises. The agreements outline procedural and substantive requirements that a private enterprise must meet to accelerate the position of disadvantaged groups.[96] Thus it seems human rights law and policy has begun to approach such political contexts with more nuanced solutions in order to achieve effective results.

Equality also has a pivotal role in the practical application of human rights. It has consistently underscored justifications for the decisions of human rights bodies, the defence of human rights victims, and the basis for holding states to account for human rights violations. Equality's dual functions as a foundation for human rights

[91] CERD 'General Recommendation No 32, The Meaning and Scope of Special Measures in the International Convention on the Elimination of All Forms Racial Discrimination' (24 September 2009) UN Doc CERD/C/GC/32, para 11.

[92] CERD, General Recommendation No 32 (n 91) para 20.

[93] See *Juridical Condition and Rights of the Undocumented Migrants* (n 34) in respect of the Inter-American system; *Glor v Switzerland* in respect to the ECHR; and Collective Complaint no. 51/2008 *European Roma Rights Centre (ERRC) v France* (2009) with respect to the European Committee on Social Rights.

[94] *Badeck and others.*

[95] *Kalanke v Freie Hansestadt Bremen* and *Marschall v Land Nordrhein Westfalen.*

[96] Christopher McCrudden and others, 'Affirmative Action without Quotas in Northern Ireland' (2010) 4 *The Equal Rights Rev* 7.

norms and a guide for their implementation and application continue to be at the core of contemporary human rights law.

5. A Right to Equality in International Human Rights Law?

The steady development of the principle of equality and its influence on international and regional human rights law have led some to suggest that an independent right to equality exists in international human rights law.[97] As noted above, international human rights treaties do not provide for a right to equality *per se*, but examining the interpretation of human rights norms indicates that such a right is alive when human rights bodies discuss non-discrimination or equality before the law. Has international human rights jurisprudence thus fashioned a substantive right to equality in all but name? Answering this question first demands consideration of what is meant by a substantive right to equality. Perhaps the closest approximation of an agreed definition of a right to equality is contained in the Declaration of Principles on Equality. Principle 1 states:

> The right to equality is the right of all human beings to be equal in dignity, to be treated with respect and consideration and to participate on an equal basis with others in any area of economic, social, political, cultural or civil life. All human beings are equal before the law and have the right to equal protection and benefit of the law.[98]

Holistic consideration of international human rights jurisprudence leads to a strong presumption that a right to equality exists. Many of the characteristics that would be associated with this right, such as promoting equal respect and giving it autonomous and universal application, have previously been read into key elements of international human rights law. As noted in Section 4 above, human rights treaty bodies, courts, and more recently treaties, have adopted an expansive definition of discrimination which includes, for example, a failure to take positive action measures and (under the CRPD) the denial of reasonable accommodation for persons with disabilities.[99] These examples demonstrate a shift from the formal conceptions of equality towards the substantive conception of equality. The obligation to take positive action measures indicates that a principal aim of international human rights law is rooted in substantive equality. Therefore, while human rights treaty law does not provide for a right to equality per se, in practice the human

[97] See The Equal Rights Trust, *Declaration of Principles on Equality* (London 2008).
[98] The Equal Rights Trust (n 97) Principle 1.
[99] CRPD (n 66), Art 2.

rights bodies' interpretations of these norms suggest that the right has developed organically.

Several benefits may result from accepting the existence of a right to equality. First, such recognition reinforces the existing jurisprudence of many international human rights bodies that a significant purpose of human rights is to help those who are most vulnerable and disadvantaged. Inequality is often the seed of long term, systematic human rights violations. Social, economic, and political inequality is a feeding ground for mistrust, anger, hatred, exclusion, and violence that cultivates prejudice, separation, and stigma among close communities and individuals, as occurred for example, in Sri Lanka, Northern Ireland, and the former Yugoslavia. A right to equality aimed at addressing the position of the vulnerable and the disadvantaged benefits not only the individual as a right holder, but also broader society, by nurturing social harmony through seeking improvements in democratic institutions.

Second, equality as a substantive right fits more logically with the development of current jurisprudence. It enables human rights practitioners to move away from viewing equality and non-discrimination provisions as largely last resort procedural provisions. Instead, the provisions indicate something greater about the purpose and function of human rights law, setting out how a state must substantively treat everyone who is subject to its jurisdiction.

Third, the substantive model of equality provides a sophisticated mechanism to analyse potential human rights violations and to evaluate the justifications offered for differential treatment and status. A right to equality based on equal respect or consideration for the individual will be more representative for those who have experienced inequality or discrimination than formal notions of equality that are largely based on a comparative rationalist approach. In some cases, the latter approach can disadvantage the victim by requiring them to explain how their treatment has been more adverse than another person's treatment because of a characteristic that the other does not have. Basing the analysis on equal respect, or consideration, allows the justice system to assess whether adverse treatment because of a characteristic is inherently wrong, irrespective of how another person is treated.

An added benefit is that substantive equality may transcend the historical polemics that exist between civil, political, economic, and social rights, promoting the interconnectedness and universality of all human rights. Emerging from the jurisprudence are techniques and concepts that provide important bridges between traditional classifications of rights. Political distinctions within human rights often collapse when considered through the lens of equality. Finally, in complex cases of national importance, equality arguments often bring added, even decisive, weight to the legal debate. For example, it has been central to ending the criminalization of same sex relationships in countries such as India;[100] in other jurisdictions, such as

[100] *Naz Foundation v Government of NCT of Delhi.*

the United Kingdom, it has been crucial for defending the right to liberty.[101] In this way, equality arguments may help to depoliticize issues, or at least to make them more politically digestible. In contentious cases, the principle of equality is there to remind courts that at the heart of the case is a victim wishing to live an ordinary life with the equal concern and consideration that is afforded to others.

6. Concluding Remarks

This chapter has addressed the manner in which equality operates as a structural principle in contemporary human rights law. As a basic principle of democracy, equality dates back at least to classical Greece. Today, equality still infuses modern ideas about democracy, the rule of law, and the role of individuals in society. While notions of equality sometimes differ due to political disagreement about which conception of equality to apply to a particular situation, most contemporary constitutions agree that a right to equality is a necessary ingredient for democracy.

This chapter has also shown that the principle of equality has two main structural functions. First, it is a foundation upon which the architecture of human rights has been designed. The principle of equality provides justification for the adoption of human rights standards, gives instruction about how human rights norms must be applied, and is applied directly through its transposition into substantive rights, such as non-discrimination and equality before the law. Viewing the impact of the principle of equality from this perspective demonstrates how it is instrumental in reinforcing other fundamental human rights principles, such as universality. Second, in addition to this, equality serves an immensely important interpretative and guidance function for policy-makers, courts, and human rights bodies charged with applying and developing human rights standards. Recent human rights developments, in particular the adoption of the CRPD, demonstrate that equality continues to underpin the way forward for guaranteeing and protecting human rights. It is not merely as a procedural mechanism that equality performs this task, but more significantly as a genuine normative instrument that illustrates why human rights standards are necessary and how they ought to be interpreted. Without the principle of equality's guiding hand, the landscape of human rights would look fundamentally different, and it is likely that human rights standards would be poorer in both content and form.

[101] Belmarsh case (n 3).

Further Reading

Abernethy GL, *Introduction to the Idea of Equality: An Anthology* (John Knox Press 1959)
Clifford J, 'Locating Equality: from Historical Philosophical Thought to Modern Legal Norms' (2008) 1 *The Equal Rights Rev* 11
Dashwood A and O'Leary S (eds), *The Principle of Equal Treatment in EC Law* (Sweet & Maxwell 1997)
McCrudden C, 'The New Concept of Equality' (2003) 4 *ERA Forum* 9
Shelton D, 'Prohibited Discrimination in International Human Rights Law' in Aristotle Constantinides and Nikos Zaikos (eds), *The Diversity of International Law: Essays in Honour of Professor Kalliopi K Koufa* (Martinus Nijhoff 2009)

CHAPTER 19

PROPORTIONALITY

YUTAKA ARAI-TAKAHASHI

1. Introduction

The following analytical account of the principle of proportionality in the context of international human rights law (IHRL) begins by briefly tracing its historical origins and development in German public laws and its subsequent 'transplantation' into European Union (EU) law[1] and human rights adjudication. Second, it examines the intrinsic nature and underlying rationales for applying the principle of proportionality. Third, the chapter distinguishes the different proportionality analyses undertaken by regional human rights bodies and the UN Human Rights Committee (HRC). Finally, it engages in a theoretical exploration of the critiques of proportionality in human rights adjudication. The aim is to help construct a coherent explanatory framework for the principle of proportionality as a shared analytical tool designed to enhance the effective protection of human rights. In doing so, the analysis draws on the theories on proportionality that constitutional

[1] For analysis of the principle of proportionality in European Union law, see: Gráinne de Búrca, 'The Principle of Proportionality and its Application in EC Law' (1993) 13 *YEL* 105; Nicholas Emiliou, *The Principle of Proportionality in European Law: A Comparative Study* (Kluwer 1996); George Gerapetritis, *Proportionality in Administrative Law: Judicial Review in France, Greece, England and in the European Community* (Sakkoulas 1997); Evelyn Ellis (ed), *The Principle of Proportionality in the Laws of Europe* (Hart 1999); Yutaka Arai-Takahashi, '"Scrupulous but Dynamic": The Freedom of Expression and the Principle of Proportionality under European Community Law' (2005) 24 *YEL* 27; Tor-Inge Harbo, 'The Function of the Proportionality Principle in EU Law' (2010) 16 *ELJ* 158.

lawyers expound,[2] while taking into account the structural differences between the roles and remits of international and national judges. It also reflects on the affinities between proportionality analysis and the application of variable standards of review, such as a margin of appreciation and judicial deference to executive and legislative discretion.[3]

2. Genesis and Development

The principle of proportionality traces its origin to Prussian poilce law at the end of the eighteenth century, from which the principle then developed as a rudimentary facet of the *Rechtsstaat* principle in the late nineteenth century, but without a precise formula or test for its application.[4] After the traumas of the Holocaust and the Second World War, the German polity emerged with a special constitutional consciousness that recognized the elevated value of human dignity. This drastic transformation of underlying values came with a flourishing of proportionality analysis as a 'constitutional' vehicle for ensuring enhanced effectiveness in safeguarding individual rights.[5] Indeed, the German Federal Constitutional Court has recognized that 'the principle of proportionality possesses constitutional status'.[6]

The extensive German experience in applying the principle of proportionality has influenced the jurisprudence of the European Court of Justice (ECJ), the European Court of Human Rights (ECtHR),[7] and other human rights tribunals.

[2] See inter alia Julian Rivers, 'Proportionality and Variable Intensity of Review' (2006) 65 *CLJ* 174; Dieter Grimm, 'Proportionality in Canadian and German Constitutional Jurisprudence' (2007) 57 *UTLJ* 383; Alec Stone Sweet and Jud Mathews, 'Proportionality Balancing and Global Constitutionalism' (2008) 47 *Colum J Transnat'l L* 72; Moshe Cohen-Eliya and Iddo Porat, 'American Balancing and German Proportionality: The Historical Origins' (2010) 8 *ICON* 263; Charles-Maxime Panaccio, 'In Defence of Two-Step Balancing and Proportionality in Rights Adjudication' (2011) 24 *CJLJ* 109.

[3] Rivers argues that '[d]iscretion is hidden in complex ways in the interstices of the law', adding that '[i]n the context of proportionality, the language of discretion and judicial deference is often used interchangeably'. Rivers (n 2) 191.

[4] Cohen-Eliya and Porat, 'American Balancing' (n 2) 271–75, discussing in detail the historical roots and evolution of proportionality in Prussian administrative law.

[5] Donald P Kommers, 'German Constitutionalism: A Prolegemenon' (1991) 40 *Emory LJ* 837, 852–53, 861; Moshe Cohen-Eliya and Iddo Porat, 'The Hidden Foreign Law Debate in Heller: The Proportionality Approach in American Constitutional Law' (2009) 46 *San Diego L Rev* 367, 387–90.

[6] *Wencker*, Constitutional Court, 19 BVerfG 342, 348–49, 15 December 1965.

[7] See inter alia Marc-André Eissen, 'The Principle of Proportionality in the Case-Law of the European Court of Human Rights' in Ronald St J Macdonald, Franz Matscher, and Herbert Petzold (eds), *The European System for the Protection of Human Rights* (Martinus Nijhoff 1993) ch 7; Jeremy McBride, 'Proportionality and the European Convention on Human Rights' in Evelyn Ellis (ed), *The Principle of Proportionality in the Laws of Europe* (Hart 1999) 23; Yutaka Arai-Takahashi, *The*

The ECJ has recognized proportionality as one of the 'general principles of law deriving from the rule of law'.[8] Since the entry into force of the Maastricht Treaty,[9] Article 5 of the Treaty Establishing the European Economic Community (Treaty of Rome) embodies the principle of proportionality, providing that '[a]ny action by the Community shall not go beyond what is necessary to achieve the objectives of this Treaty'. Article 3(b)(1) of the Treaty of Lisbon, amending the Treaty on EU and the EC Treaty, has now reinforced this. The Inter-American Court of Human Rights (IACtHR) and the Inter-American Commission of Human Rights (IACHR) have also solidified proportionality analysis into their methodology. Even the HRC, long reluctant to incorporate methodologies developed by a regional tribunal, is showing a readiness to integrate proportionality analysis.

3. The Principle of Proportionality as a General Principle of IHRL

3.1 Overview

The first question to be examined is whether proportionality can be described as a general *principle* governing the entire corpus of IHRL. To answer this query, it is necessary to undertake a brief inquiry into what features characterize *principles* in the normative order, built on the presupposition that it is possible to classify or differentiate various types of norms.[10] In this regard, Dworkin stresses that many standards other than 'rules' are operative within the legal order. Principles or polices are not part of the law but are treated as 'extra-legal standards'.[11] Dworkin describes a principle as 'a standard that is to be observed, not because it will advance or secure an economic, political, or social situation deemed desirable, but because it is a requirement of justice or fairness or some other dimension of morality'.[12]

The foremost special trait of a principle is the malleable nature of its normative force. Robert Alexy's idea of principles as 'optimization requirements' that 'can be

Margin of Appreciation Doctrine and the Principle of Proportionality in the Jurisprudence of the ECHR (Intersentia 2002).

[8] See eg *Fédération Charbonnière de Belgique v High Authority of the European Coal and Steel Community* 298; *Nold v Commission of the European Communities* 512–13.

[9] Treaty on European Union.

[10] For sceptics to the existence of legal principles as such, and concerning their distinction from norms, see Robert Alexy, 'The Construction of Constitutional Rights' (2010) 4 *Law & Ethics of Human Rights* 20, 24–26.

[11] Ronald Dworkin, *Taking Rights Seriously* (Duckworth 1977) 35.

[12] Dworkin, *Taking Rights Seriously* (n 11) 22.

satisfied to varying degrees' can illustrate this.[13] According to Alexy, if a principle clashes with other principles, they ought to be subjected to balancing.[14] The amenable nature of a principle suggests its capacity for greater resilience. It can survive intact, even in circumstances where it cannot provide a basis for a precise normative outcome.[15] A diachronic implication of this feature is that a principle is capable of metamorphosing according to vicissitudes of social forces. In other words, principles embody the essential dimension of law as 'a living social construct'[16] that can change over time to accommodate different social values. This may partly account for the development of evolutive interpretation as a method for reinforcing a robust form of proportionality appraisal in respect to the limitation clauses of the European Convention on Human Rights (ECHR).

The term 'general principles of international law' ought to be distinguished from general principles derived from municipal law. The former are 'sweeping and loose standards of conduct' that can be deduced from customary and treaty rules by way of extraction, distillation, and generalization of some of their most significant common denominators.[17] In the EU legal order, one can understand 'general principles' as 'fundamental unwritten principles of law which underlie the Community law edifice'.[18] Such general principles are derived from the rule of law and equipped with (quasi-)constitutional functions.[19] The similar line of arguments can be adduced to justify the recognition of 'general principles' in the context of the ECHR. The word 'general' also indicates the potential for universal applicability.[20]

3.2 The principle of proportionality as a general principle of IHRL

The role of proportionality in guiding judicial reasoning can foster legal predictability, certainty, and coherence, all these being intrinsic properties of the substantiated understanding of the rule of law.[21] Moreover, proportionality can serve as an analytical vehicle for assessing how national authorities have employed their margin of

[13] Alexy, 'The Construction of Constitutional Rights' (n 10) 21.

[14] Kai Möller, 'Balancing and the Structure of Constitutional Rights' (2007) 5 *ICON* 453, 463. Alexy seems to find a logical or necessary connection between principles, balancing, and proportionality: 'The Construction of Constitutional Rights' (n 10) 459, 461.

[15] This can be contrasted with rules, which may be changed or fall into desuetude when drastically failing to dictate normative direction and outcome, such as in the case in which a contrary result continues. Dworkin, *Taking Rights Seriously* (n 11) 35–36.

[16] Margit Cohn, 'Legal Transplant Chronicles: The Evolution of Unreasonableness and Proportionality Review of the Administration in the United Kingdom' (2010) 58 *AJIL* 583, 587.

[17] Antonio Cassese, *International Law* (2nd edn, OUP 2005) 186.

[18] Takis Tridimas, *The General Principles of EC Law* (OUP 1999) 3–4.

[19] Tridimas (n 18) 2. [20] Harbo (n 1) 159. [21] Harbo (n 1) 162–63.

appreciation to delineate rights in practice.[22] In other words, it can be deployed as a yardstick for appraising whether or not the state has overstepped the bounds of its discretion. As such, the notion of proportionality can be conceived as a 'general principle' that has emerged in IHRL.

The principle of proportionality is fully embedded in the normative bedrock of the two parallel European legal systems (EU law and the ECHR) and the American Convention on Human Rights (ACHR). It is now making a progressive inroad into the case law of the HRC. The African Commission on Human and Peoples' Rights (AfCHPR) has also integrated proportionality as an analytical vehicle for assessing encroachments on human rights. After first testing whether a limitation constitutes a law of general application, the AfCHPR will weigh the impact, nature, and extent of the limitation against the legitimate state interest, to determine whether the limitations are 'strictly proportionate with and absolutely necessary for the advantages which are to be obtained'.[23] The AfCHPR also demands that states adopt the less restrictive means of achieving an objective when there is more than one available alternative.[24]

Despite the growing and potential role of proportionality in creating a shared language within the standard-based structure of IHRL,[25] its operational modality varies in the case law of the international monitoring bodies, as will be discussed below.

4. Three Tests of Proportionality

4.1 Overview

Human rights tribunals tend to follow a two-tier structure of analysis in respect to alleged human rights violations. Their examination focuses firstly on whether there exists an interference (infringement) with a specific human right as claimed by an applicant. Once such interference is identified, the analysis then turns to the question of whether such interference can be justified in the light of specific criteria of assessment. At this second stage, the onus of proof shifts to the respondent government to adduce grounds to justify such interference. The proportionality

[22] Stone Sweet and Mathews (n 2) 151.

[23] *Media Rights Agenda and others v Nigeria*, para 69 (right to receive information and free expression). See also *Law Office of Ghazi Suleiman v Sudan*, paras 62–63, 65; *Prince v South Africa* (right to freedom of religion); Frans Viljoen, *International Human Rights Law in Africa* (2nd edn, OUP 2012) 331.

[24] *Interights and others v Mauritania*, para 82; *Media Rights* (n 23) para 75.

[25] See Michel Rosenfeld, 'Rethinking Constitutional Ordering in an Era of Legal and Ideological Pluralism' (2008) 6 *ICON* 415.

analysis that the ECtHR, the Organization of American States (OAS) organs, and the AfCHPR conduct is usually preceded by two preliminary inquiries: (i) whether the interference has a basis in national law (the legality test); and (ii) whether the impugned measure is pursuant to, or consonant with, a particular legitimate aim/purpose (legitimate aim test). The limitation clauses in the International Covenant on Civil and Political Rights (ICCPR), ECHR, ACHR, and AfCHPR list acceptable public interest grounds, such as the protection of public health, public order, national security, and the rights of others, or the prevention of disorder or crime.[26]

In their case law, once the two preliminary questions are answered, the regional tribunals apply the principle of proportionality using a three-part test: (i) the test for suitability, or rationality, which examines whether a disputed measure that interferes with an individual's right is suitable for achieving the legitimate aim; (ii) the test of necessity or less restrictive alternative (LRA), or 'minimal impairment', which obliges the state to choose the measure that is least restrictive of the person's right; and (iii) the test for proportionality in the strict sense, which requires that any detriment to the person not be excessive as compared with the benefits to be obtained (no disproportionate burden). Notably, the first two tests deal with efficiency, while the third makes an empirical evaluation of the relative weights and trade-offs of the competing values.[27] If the impugned measure does not satisfy the first or second test, then examination of the third part is generally unnecessary, although OAS organs sometimes use the third test to corroborate their findings with respect to the first two parts.

4.2 Suitability (rational connection)

Panaccio describes two variations of this inquiry, summarized here.[28] In its less taxing form, the proponent must demonstrate that the measure in question can be considered 'causally able' to achieve the stated aim/objective. It is unlikely that a state authority's measure would fail to meet this standard, because it only prohibits 'absurdly irrational' laws or measures. In its more demanding form, a determination of 'suitability' requires more extensive reasoning or 'moral balancing' that examines whether a contested measure or law can be considered irrational or unreasonable because it generates a disproportionate degree of deleterious effects.

[26] In the case of anti-discrimination clauses, the legitimate aim test that Art 14 ECHR develops is not based on such express listing; this may be considered inherent in testing, whether or not a distinction the contested national measure or law makes is arbitrary.

[27] Moshe Cohen-Eliya and Iddo Porat, 'Proportionality and the Culture of Justification' (2011) 59 *Am J Comp L* 463, 469–70.

[28] Panaccio (n 2) 112.

4.3 Necessity (less restrictive alternative or least restrictive means)

The test of necessity asks if the measure deployed by the government encroaches on rights more than necessary to achieve the legitimate aim or policy goal sought. Put differently, an international tribunal must investigate if there is any other alternative that is less restrictive of rights while being equally effective in attaining the stated policy objective.[29] As will be analysed below, the OAS organs have applied the subtest of necessity in a robust manner in their detailed assessment of impugned national measures.

4.4 Proportionality in the strict sense

Proportionality *stricto sensu* requires 'measuring the relative intensity of the interference with the importance of the aim sought'.[30] Analytically, the process by which this occurs consists of assessing the means to achieve desired social ends in a particular factual setting.[31] According to Robert Alexy, this analysis embodies 'the Law of Balancing', by which he means that '[t]he greater the degree of non-satisfaction of, or detriment to, one principle, the greater must be the importance of satisfying the other'.[32] Aharon Barak similarly argues that this test 'examines the proper ratio between the benefit stemming from attainment of the object and the deleterious effect upon the human right'.[33]

Even the least injurious solution suitable to attain an envisaged objective may be deemed to entail an excessive detrimental impact on a person's rights, when compared to the beneficial outcomes of the measure. Rupprecht von Krauss, in his 1953 dissertation, argued that 'if the measure [of legality] is only necessity, then a quite negligible public interest could lead to a severe right infringement, without being unlawful'.[34] Many commentators thus suggest that the essence of proportionality analysis lies in this third prong.[35]

[29] Stone Sweet and Mathews (n 2) 75.

[30] Stavros Tsakyrakis, 'Proportionality: An Assault on Human Rights?' (2009) 7 *ICON* 468, 474.

[31] Yuval Shany, 'Toward a General Margin of Appreciation Doctrine in International Law?' (2005) 16 *EJIL* 907, 917, 935.

[32] Robert Alexy, *A Theory of Constitutional Rights* (OUP 2002) 102. See also Alexy, 'The Construction of Constitutional Rights' (n 10) 28.

[33] Aharon Barak, 'Proportional Effect: The Israeli Experience' (2007) 57 *UTLJ* 369, 374. Barak adds that: 'Whereas the rational connection test and the least harmful measure test are essentially determined against the background of the proper objective, and are derived from the need to realize it, the test of proportionality (*stricto sensu*) examines whether the realization of this proper objective is commensurate with the deleterious effect upon the human right': 374.

[34] Rupprecht von Krauss, *Der Grundsatz der Verhältnismäßigkeit im seiner Bedeutung für die Notwendigkeit des Mittels im Verwaltungsrecht* (Appel 1955) 15, as cited in Stone Sweet and Mathews (n 2) 105.

[35] Tsakyrakis (n 30) 474.

5. Proportionality Analysis by the European Court of Human Rights

5.1 Overview

It can be observed that the proportionality analysis that the ECtHR conducts in most cases does not strictly follow the three-pronged test observed in the case law of the ECJ and the two OAS organs, although the ECtHR has repeatedly held that the notion of balancing, in a general sense, is inherent in the normative edifice of the ECHR. The former president of the ECtHR, Roly Ryssdal, noted that '[t]he theme that runs through the Convention and its case law is the need to strike a balance between the general interest of the community and the protection of the individual's fundamental rights....'[36] Indeed, Rivers argues that: 'In practice, the European Court [of Human Rights] engages in balancing in the context of almost every Convention right.'[37] Other authors willingly recognize that the balancing approach, as an intrinsic feature of the principle of proportionality, 'has acquired the status of general principle in the Convention system.'[38]

Apart from balancing, however, the principle of proportionality in the ECHR context remains unsystematically applied,[39] as compared to the refined structure of proportionality appraisal the ECJ devised.[40]

The ECtHR has relied on the test of proportionality in the narrow sense in assessing limitations on rights in diverse areas: limitation clauses, derogation clauses, non-discrimination, and restrictions on due process guarantees. Brief inquiries will be made into each of them.

5.2 Limitation clauses and proportionality analysis under the ECHR

The principle of proportionality comes into play most significantly in respect to the limitation clauses attached to several specific rights: the right to private and family life,[41] freedom of religion,[42] freedom of expression,[43] freedom of assembly

[36] Tsakyrakis (n 30) 475, referring to Rolv Ryssdal, 'Opinion: The Coming Age of the European Convention on Human Rights' (1996) 1 *EHRLR* 18, 26.

[37] Rivers (n 2) 182.

[38] Tsakyrakis (n 30) 475, citing Pieter van Dijk and others (eds), *Theory and Practice of the European Convention on Human Rights* (3rd edn, Martinus Nijhoff 1998) 81.

[39] See eg Arai-Takahashi, *The Margin of Appreciation Doctrine* (n 7) 193–205; Eissen (n 7) 125.

[40] See eg de Búrca (n 1); Emiliou (n 1); Tridimas (n 18) 89–162.

[41] ECHR, Art 8.

[42] ECHR, Art 9.

[43] ECHR, Art 10.

and association,[44] the right to property,[45] freedom of movement,[46] and the procedural rights concerning expulsion of aliens.[47] These limitations clauses have provided the ECtHR with experimental grounds for judicial reasoning. In this context, the Court's preliminary inquiries into legality and legitimate aim(s) precede the proportionality appraisal. As regards legality, case law has well established that the domestic measure in question must be adequately accessible and foreseeable—that is, formulated with sufficient precision to allow any individual person to foresee the consequences of his or her conduct.[48]

With regard to the limitation clauses, several 'derivative' principles, or subtests, associated with proportionality have emerged, taking several patterns. Still, it is proportionality in a narrow sense, namely balancing between a means chosen and a legitimate aim pursued, that has played a decisive role in constraining the discretion that national authorities exercise. In this context, as noted above, the Court has had recourse (albeit unsystematically) to the doctrine of less restrictive alternatives (necessity).

The Court has interpreted the phrase 'necessary in a democratic society' in the limitation clauses as suggesting the existence of a 'pressing social need'. According to the case law, the term 'pressing social need' requires a reasonable or proportionate balance between the interfering measure and the legitimate aim(s).[49] However, in its early and seminal decision in the *Handyside* case,[50] the Court blunted the edge of this proportionality analysis by introducing the doctrine of a margin of appreciation. This deferential rhetoric becomes incorporated as part of the formula for assessing the phrase 'necessary in a democratic society'.[51] Worth noting is the variability of the margin of appreciation doctrine, which can range from very narrow to exceedingly wide.

Two accessory subtests have emerged. First, the respondent state bears the onus of proving both the relevance and sufficiency of the reasons justifying the interfering

[44] ECHR, Art 11.

[45] Protocol No 1 to the Convention for the Protection of Human Rights and Fundamental Freedoms, Art 1.

[46] Protocol No 4 to the Convention for the Protection of Human Rights and Fundamental Freedoms, Securing Certain Rights and Freedoms Other than Those Already Included in the Convention and the First Protocol Thereto, Art 2.

[47] Protocol No 7 to the Convention for the Protection of Human Rights and Fundamental Freedoms, Art 1.

[48] See inter alia *Sunday Times v UK (No 1)*, paras 47–49 (Art 10); *Malone v UK*, paras 66–68 (Art 8); *Lithgow and Others v UK*, para 110 (Art 1, Protocol 1).

[49] See inter alia *Handyside v UK*, paras 48–49 (Art 10); *Silver and Others v UK*, para 97 (Art 8); *The Socialist Party and Others v Turkey*, para 49 (Art 11); *Serif v Greece*, paras 49, 54 (Art 9); *Baumann v France*, para 67 (Art 2, Protocol 4).

[50] The Court recognized that the national authorities were accorded a margin of appreciation that was 'certain but not unlimited' in ascertaining such 'pressing social need'. *Handyside* (n 49) paras 48–49.

[51] See eg *Gorzelik and Others v Poland*, para 96 (Art 11).

measure.[52] The demand for a 'relevant reason' bears close affinity to the test of suitability, the first limb of proportionality analysis under EU law and the ACHR. Still, in the ECHR context, the preliminary inquiry into the legitimate purpose of an impugned measure (legitimate aim), where it has played hardly any meaningful role, may subsume the 'relevant reason' test. The Court's preference is to engage in closer scrutiny of the 'sufficient reason', which relates to the onus and standard of proof in the Court's appraisal of the third test. The Court has shown a proclivity to demand that the government adduce weighty rationales for the contested measure.[53] Second, the assessment of 'pressing social need' (proportionality in a narrow sense) is *contextual*, in harmony with evolution of social forces and public opinions. This leaves room for a teleological interpretive method, such as evolutive interpretation and an autonomous 'European consensus' approach.[54]

5.3 Necessity and proportionality *stricto sensu* under the limitation clauses

Necessity (or the doctrine of less restrictive alternatives) has yet to mature under the ECtHR into a standardized device for constraining the national government's discretion. Even so, one can discern a gradual move towards integrating this test into the analytical framework pertinent to the limitation clauses. In the *Otto-Preminger-Institut* case,[55] a minority of three of the nine ECtHR judges on the case held that the seizure and confiscation of the film *Das Liebeskonzil* (*Council in Heaven*) was tantamount to a complete prevention of freedom of expression. In their view, such a far-reaching restriction could be justified only where the impugned speech was so abusive as to stultify the right of others to freedom of religion. They considered that the seizure was all the more disproportionate because there was no likelihood of adult viewers confronting the objectionable scenes unwillingly, due to the age restriction, admission fees, and public warning given in advance of the film's showing.[56] The view of the minority is in striking contrast to the majority's lax review based on a broad margin of appreciation.

[52] See inter alia *Handyside* (n 49) para 50; *Sunday Times (No 1)* (n 48) para 62; *Dudgeon v United Kingdom*, para 54; *Lingens v Austria*, para 40 (Art 10); *Olsson v Sweden (No 1)*, para 68; *Olsson v Sweden (No 2)*, para 87 (Art 8); *United Communist Party of Turkey and Others v Turkey*, paras 46–47 (Art 11).

[53] See eg *Incal v Turkey*.

[54] This means that when assessing the legality of a contested measure in one of the member states, the Court has not relied on the practice of the empirical majority of the member states. The Court reserves to itself the right to set forth its own objective and autonomous standards, independent of the meanings national jurisdictions give to particular legal terms.

[55] *Otto-Preminger-Institut v Austria*.

[56] *Otto-Preminger-Institut* (n 55) paras 9–11 (Joint Dissenting Opinion of Judges Palm, Pekkanen, and Makarzczyk).

In more recent cases involving freedom of expression, the Court has exhibited a greater willingness to engage in critical proportionality analysis, by combining the two subtests of necessity and proportionality in a narrow sense. One hallmark of the robust methodology is the application of a 'chilling effect' doctrine,[57] emerging in cases relating to political expression, applied in tandem with the doctrine of a less restrictive alternative. In *Ahmet Sadik v Greece*,[58] a Greek parliamentarian was convicted of the criminal offence of deceiving electors, after circulating communiqués referring to Muslim minorities in Western Thrace as 'Turkish'. The former European Commission of Human Rights considered such a measure to be clearly excessive, because there was no indication of incitement to violence, and the penalty, though low, was deemed sufficient to deter the councillor's political expression.[59] The Commission placed the onus on the government to prove the overriding weight of countervailing social ends. Analyses of other recent cases demonstrate the Court's close scrutiny of restrictions on speech,[60] even with respect to statements that may be interpreted as a threat to national security and public order, or to the territorial integrity of member states. Even in such cases, the ECtHR has examined whether the contested measure is the least injurious.[61]

5.4 Derogations (Article 15) and proportionality in a narrow sense

Proportionality *stricto sensu* is ingrained in the text of the derogation clause, under Article 15(1) ECHR, which provides that: 'any High Contracting Party may take measures derogating from its obligations under this Convention to the extent strictly required by the exigencies of the situation'. In fact, it was in the context of derogation and national emergencies that the ECtHR set in motion the tandem doctrines of the margin of appreciation and proportionality. The ECtHR not only recognizes a wide margin of appreciation for the national authorities to assess the existence of a national emergency, but also grants a margin in respect of the 'scope of derogations' suspending rights. This suggests that national authorities themselves assess the proportionality of responses to the exigency.[62] This is a methodological

[57] See eg *Castells v Spain*, para 46; *Ceylan v Turkey*, para 34; *Erdoğdu and İnce v Turkey*, para 50; *Sürek and Özdemir v Turkey*, para 60; *Dammann v Switzerland*, para 57.

[58] On the non-exhaustion of the domestic remedies before the Court.

[59] *Lombardo and Others v Malta*, para 61.

[60] See eg *Piermont v France*.

[61] *Incal* (n 53).

[62] For instance, in the case of *Ireland v UK*, the Court held that:

> It falls in the first place to each contracting state, with its responsibility for 'the life of [its] nation', to determine whether that life is threatened by a 'public emergency' and, if so, how far it is necessary to go in attempting to overcome the emergency. By reason of their direct and continuous contact with the pressing needs of the moment, the national authorities are

dislocation. The better approach would be for the ECtHR to deploy the principle of proportionality as a yardstick for assessing whether a specific measure that the national government takes remains within the appropriate (narrow or wide) margin of appreciation.[63]

5.5 Non-discrimination (Article 14) and proportionality *stricto sensu*

Proportionality in the narrow sense serves as a crucial device for ascertaining if difference in treatment amounts to discrimination under Article 14 of the ECHR. Since its early decision in the *Belgian Linguistic* case,[64] the Court has engaged in rigorous scrutiny based on the third limb of proportionality, infusing it into a structured form of assessment of all discrimination issues. Along the sliding scale of the standard of review, difference in treatment relating to birth,[65] race (ethnicity),[66] sex,[67] sexual orientation,[68] and religion[69] are among the so-called 'suspect categories' that invite the most intense form of proportionality scrutiny.[70] According to the Court, the existence of 'an objective, reasonable justification' must corroborate differential treatment on any of these grounds and requires twofold analysis. First, as in the case of analyses under the limitation clauses, the Court conducts a preliminary inquiry into whether the differential treatment pursues a legitimate aim. Second, if this question is answered in the affirmative, the Court ascertains if there is reasonable proportionality between the means chosen (the contested measure) and the legitimate end to be realized.[71] When 'suspect categories' are involved, the Court requires the respondent government to adduce robust justifications for the impugned difference. Similar proportionality-bound reasoning appears in the case law concerning non-discrimination in the field of economic, social, and cultural rights under Article E of the 1996 revised European Social Charter.[72]

> in principle in a better position than the international judge to decide both on the presence of such an emergency and on the nature and scope of derogations necessary to avert it. In this matter [Art 15(1)] leaves the authorities a wide margin of appreciation. [para 207.]

[63] Arai-Takahashi, 'Scrupulous but Dynamic' (n 1).

[64] *Belgian Linguistic Case*, para 10.

[65] *Marckx v Belgium*; *Inze v Austria*; *Mazurek v France*; *Camp and Bourimi v Netherlands*; *Merger and Cros v France*. See also *Pla and Puncernau v Andorra*.

[66] See eg *Timishev v Russia*, para 58; and *DH and Others v Czech Republic*, para 176.

[67] See eg *Abdulaziz, Cabales, and Balkandali v United Kingdom*, para 78. Contrast with *Spöttl v Austria* (European Commission of Human Rights); *Petrovic v Austria*.

[68] *Salgueiro da Silva Mouta v Portugal*; *L and V v Austria*; *Karner v Austria*; *EB v France*.

[69] *Hoffman v Austria*.

[70] See David J Harris and others (eds), *Law of the European Convention on Human Rights* (2nd edn, OUP 2009) 590–600.

[71] Harris and others (n 70).

[72] See eg *Syndicat National des Professions du Tourisme v France* (difference in treatment between the approved lecturer guides on one hand, and interpreter guides and national lecturers with a state

5.6 Due process guarantees and proportionality in a narrow sense

Judicial reliance on the test of proportionality in the strict sense is visible when examining the case law on 'due process guarantees', namely, the rights of liberty and security under Article 5, and the right to a fair trial, including the right of access to courts, under Article 6. The application of this test appears most frequently in relation to the implied right of access to court, and elsewhere it remains sporadic. Two patterns are evident in the judgments. First, the Court uses the principle of proportionality as a synonym for the general notion of balancing. Second, it has adopted the concept of minimum core rights, referring to the 'very essence' of a right that can never be abridged.[73] The Court's reasoning has yet to clarify the meaning and ramifications of this approach, but thus far the case law suggests that the impairment of such 'very essence' is no more than a reiteration of the fact that an impugned measure is disproportionate to the legitimate end.[74]

5.7 Evaluation of the ECtHR's proportionality analysis

Overall, the tripartite form of proportionality analysis prevalent in the EU law is missing from the case law of the ECtHR. The insufficient development of the second limb of proportionality, the necessity test, compounds this. Nevertheless, the case law dealing with the limitation clauses discloses an elaborate and systemic analytical framework that draws on a third subtest of proportionality. This framework can help embolden the assertive judicial policy in furtherance of European standards of human rights. Such a dynamic judicial strategy is set against the deferential pull of the variable margin of appreciation doctrine, which respondent states may plead in light of their national interests[75] or distinct historical experience.[76]

diploma on the other, in relation to the right to work (Art 1) and the right to vocational training (Art 10)). In that case, assessment of the difference in treatment hinged on: (i) whether the two categories were in comparable situations; and (ii) whether there was reasonable and objective justification for distinction.

[73] This notion seems to originate from the notion of *Wesensgehalt* in the German constitutional theory. It has been frequently relied upon in the context of Arts, 6, 11, and 12. See Arai-Takahashi, *The Margin of Appreciation Doctrine* (n 7) 36–37. See *Winterwerp v Netherlands*, para 60 (Art 5(4)); *Young, James and Webster v UK*, paras 52, 56–57; *Rees v UK*, paras 49–50; *Sibson v UK*, para 29 (Art 11); *Levage Prestations Services v France*, paras 42–43 (Art 6(1)); *Sheffield and Horsham v UK*, para 66 (Art 12).

[74] Rivers (n 2) 184–85.

[75] See eg *The Sunday Times v UK (No 2)*, paras 52–56.

[76] In this case, see, for instance, *Lehideux and Isorni v France*, Dissenting Opinion of Judges Foighel, Loizou, and Sir John Freeland.

6. Proportionality as Applied by the UN Human Rights Committee

6.1 Overview

Overall, the tripartite and structured form of proportionality has yet to come into play in the case law of the HRC. At times, the HRC identifies the violation of a right without invoking the language of proportionality.[77] This does not mean that the HRC decisions are lacking in elaborate reasoning. On the contrary, the HRC, like the AfCHPR,[78] has, expressly or implicitly, recognized specific doctrines, including the 'chilling effect' doctrine related to freedom of expression,[79] which serve to scrutinize carefully government actions. Moreover, the principle of proportionality is fully ingrained in the textual structure of some salient provisions of the ICCPR, including the limitations clauses[80] and the derogation clause.[81] In its 'General Comment No 29', the HRC observed that 'the obligation to limit any derogations to those strictly required by the exigencies of the situation reflects the principle of proportionality which is common to derogation and limitation powers'.[82] In other General Comments the HRC explicitly endorses disaggregated elements of proportionality, including the less restrictive alternative doctrine.

With respect to the derogation clause, in its 'General Comment No 29', the HRC articulates a balancing test, utilizing proportionality in a narrow sense, as an important vehicle for constraining the national authorities' discretion.[83] Such a duty to undertake proportionality assessments must focus on 'the duration, geographical coverage and material scope' of derogating measures.[84] The HRC criticizes states' periodic reports for lacking such detailed proportionality analysis.[85]

[77] *Aduayom et al v Togo*, para 7.4.

[78] See eg *Media Rights* (n 23).

[79] *Aduayom* (n 77).

[80] See eg Arts 12(3) (freedom of movement); 19(3) (freedom of expression); 21 (freedom of peaceful assembly); 22(2) (freedom of association).

[81] ICCPR, Art 4. When critically examining issues of indefinite detention, Alfred de Zayas argues that:

> Temporary derogation from some provisions of the applicable legal regimes is possible, but subject to specified conditions, notably the criterion of 'public emergency threatening the life of the nation', and the principle of proportionality, which limits such derogation 'to the extent strictly required by the exigencies of the situation'. Derogations cannot be open-ended, but must be limited in scope and duration. Legal analysis of the justification proffered by States for the limitations of rights frequently reveals that such derogations are not valid under either municipal or international law.

Alfred de Zayas, 'Human Rights and Indefinite Detention' (2005) 87(857) *IRRC* 15, 16.

[82] HRC, 'General Comment No 29: States of Emergency (Art 4)' (31 August 2001) UN Doc CCPR/C/21/Rev.1/Add.11, para 4.

[83] HRC, 'General Comment No 29' (n 82) para 4.

[84] HRC, 'General Comment No 29' (n 82) para 4.

[85] HRC, 'General Comment No 29' (n 82).

6.2 Necessity as developed by the HRC

The HRC has gradually come to confirm the essence of the necessity test. In *Faurrisson v France*, the individual opinions of the members of the HRC expressly constructed their reasoning with references to necessity.[86] In that case, a French academic was penalized on the basis of a French law (the Gayssot Act) for his anti-Semitic comments, including his claim that the gas chambers were fictions the Jewish people concocted. The individual opinions of Evatt and Kretzmer, in which Klein joined, criticized the sweeping nature of the impugned law by reference to necessity and proportionality in a narrow sense. They stated that even if the Gayssot Act was apposite to the legitimate end of preventing incitement to anti-Semitism, it was couched in such broad terms as to prevent even bona fide Holocaust research. They added that:

> [T]he legitimate object of the law could certainly have been achieved by *a less drastic provision* that would not imply that the State party had attempted to turn historical truths and experiences into legislative dogma that may not be challenged, no matter what the object behind that challenge, nor its likely consequences.[87]

However, the case did not concern the Gayssot Act in the abstract, but the *specific* encroachment on the petitioner's freedom of expression. On this matter, the three Committee members agreed with the other members of the HRC, who found that the restriction did not hamper the core of Faurisson's free speech rights. In their view, the necessity test was satisfied for the purpose of safeguarding an equally important countervailing interest:

> The restrictions placed on the author did not curb the core of his right to freedom of expression, nor did they in any way affect his freedom of research; they were intimately linked to the value they were meant to protect—the right to be free from incitement to racism or anti-semitism; *protecting that value could not have been achieved in the circumstances by less drastic means.*[88]

The endeavour by individual members of the HRC to inject proportionality reasoning into the structure of analyses has gradually borne fruit. In relation to the limitation clause on freedom of movement,[89] the HRC, in its 'General Comment No 27', expressly endorsed the necessity test as part of proportionality analysis:

> Article 12, paragraph 3, clearly indicates that it is not sufficient that the restrictions serve the permissible purposes; they must also be necessary to protect them. Restrictive measures must conform to the principle of proportionality; *they must be appropriate to achieve their*

[86] *Faurisson v France*, paras 9.5–9.6.

[87] *Faurisson* (n 86) para 9, individual opinion by Elizabeth Evatt and David Kretzmer, co-signed by Eckart Klein (concurring). Emphasis added.

[88] *Faurisson* (n 86) para 10. Emphasis added.

[89] Article 12(3).

protective function; they must be the least intrusive instrument amongst those which might achieve the desired result; and *they must be proportionate to the interest to be protected.*[90]

As shown by the last sentence of this paragraph, the HRC expressly recognizes the threefold components of proportionality: 'appropriateness'; less restrictive alternatives; and proportionality *stricto sensu*. In *Bakhtiyari v Australia*, the HRC interweaves the two subtests of necessity and proportionality *stricto sensu*:

[T]he State Party has not, in the Committee's view, demonstrated that their [the applicant family's] detention was justified for such an extended period. Taking into account in particular the composition of the Bakhtiyari family, *the State Party has not demonstrated that other, less intrusive, measures could not have achieved the same end of compliance with the State Party's immigration policies by, for example, imposition of reporting obligations, sureties or other conditions which would take into account the family's particular circumstances*. As a result, the continuation of immigration detention for Mrs Bakhtiyari and her children for the length of time described above, without appropriate justification, was arbitrary and contrary to Article 9, paragraph 1, of the Covenant.[91]

So far, the HRC has rarely referred to the case law of regional tribunals. Still, it is safe to surmise that the HRC's incremental recognition of the triple analytical structure of proportionality reflects the growing influence of the case law of the regional human rights organs. This can be described as an upward, vertical transplantation of proportionality, as opposed to a horizontal transplantation of proportionality as has initiated the process of 'normative cross-fertilization' between the European and OAS systems.

7. Proportionality Analysis in the Inter-American System

7.1 Overview

The Inter-American Commission on Human Rights (IACHR) and the Inter-American Court of Human Rights (IACtHR), two bodies set up under the auspices of the Organization of American States (OAS), have come to stress the importance of the principle of proportionality.[92] The case law of the OAS organs

[90] HRC, 'General Comment No 27: Freedom of Movement (Art 12)' (2 November 1999) UN Doc CCPR/C/21/Rev.1/Add.9, para 14. Emphasis added.

[91] *Mr Ali Aqsar Bakhtiyari and Mrs Roqaiha Bakhtiyari v Australia*, para 9.3. Emphasis added.

[92] See eg Paolo G Carozza, 'Human Dignity and Judicial Interpretation of Human Rights: A Reply to Christopher McCrudden' (2008) 19 *EJIL* 931, 931.

reveals a refined analysis and elaborate reasoning, peppered with the component elements of the threefold proportionality test.[93] Article 29 of the ACHR[94] in fact incorporates the principle of proportionality as part of the *general* clause that governs the entire corpus of the ACHR. According to IACHR, this provision denotes 'the notion of proportionality in a broad sense as a synonym for the non-arbitrariness of the State's intervention and its compatibility with the American Convention'.[95] The application of proportionality in this provision is envisaged in a horizontal manner (*Drittwirkung*), as well. The IACHR has expressly invoked it to deduce the general principle of proportionality within the normative framework of the ACHR. Furthermore, the OAS organs have displayed greater readiness to rely on a 'comparative method' than their European counterparts. They have adverted to the interpretive methods and principles crafted by the UN treaty-based bodies, the ECtHR, and the AfCHPR.[96]

7.2 The Structure of Proportionality Analysis under the ACHR

The IACHR and the IACtHR have suggested that their structure of analysing human rights infringements is fivefold, including: legality, legitimate aim, suitability, necessity, and proportionality in a narrow sense.[97] The first two tests, legality and legitimate aims, correspond to the modality of analysis the ECtHR follows.[98] The latter three tests dovetail with the tripartite form of proportionality devised in the realms of EU law. Consistent with the earlier discussion, the first two tests can be considered precursory questions. With respect to the other three tests, analysis will focus on the second and third; as in the case of ECJ's decisions, the first test of suitability has hardly featured as a stringent criterion.

7.3 Necessity

In the Advisory Opinion on *Juridical Condition and Rights of Undocumented Migrants*, the IACtHR examined restrictions on the rights of undocumented migrant

[93] *Newspaper 'La Nación' v Costa Rica*. See also *Dudley Stokes v Jamaica*.

[94] This provision reads: 'No provision of this Convention shall be interpreted as: (a) permitting any State Party, group, or person to suppress the enjoyment to exercise of the rights and freedoms recognized in this Convention or to restrict them to a greater extent than is provided for herein.'

[95] *Murillo et al v Costa Rica (In Vitro Fertilization)*, para 86.

[96] See eg *Case of Herrera-Olloa v Costa Rica*, paras 113–114.

[97] *Case of Escher et al v Brazil*, para 129 (interception of telephone conversations); *Case of Tristán-Donoso v Panama*, para 76. See also *Murillo* (n 95) para 89.

[98] Indeed, these two tests are expressly embodied in the limitations clauses of the ICCPR, as well as the ECHR and ACHR.

workers, in particular, their right to remuneration. In doing so, the Court employed the second limb of proportionality (necessity or less restrictive alternatives):

Human rights, such as the right to equality or the right to remuneration may be restricted, but limitations must respond to criteria of necessity and proportionality in order to attain a legitimate objective. Implementing measures to control irregular immigration into a State's territory is a legitimate objective. However, if such measures are intended to strip irregular migrant workers of the right to receive remuneration for work performed, it is urgent to examine the proportionality and the need and, to do this, we must consider whether there are other measures that are less restrictive of the said right.[99]

In the *Costa Rican in Vitro Fertilization* case, which concerned a complete ban on the assisted reproductive technique of *in vitro* fertilization, the Commission engaged in an in-depth proportionality analysis. It duly evaluated whether less restrictive alternatives to the outright ban on *in vitro* fertilization existed. After surveying the practice of many states in Europe and the Americas, the Commission found that the state should favour 'some other form of regulation that could produce results that more closely resemble the natural process of conception, such as a regulation that diminishes the number of fertilized ovules' over the comprehensive prohibition.[100] Once it found that the state had not carried out a quest to discover a less drastic means, it held that the impugned measure was excessive.[101]

7.4 Proportionality in a narrow sense

In the aforementioned *Costa Rican In Vitro Fertilization* case, the Commission went on to undertake an elaborate analysis of proportionality in a narrow sense, even though it had found that the state in question had not fulfilled the necessity requirement. Generally, the failure to meet the second limb of the proportionality test eliminates the need for further inquiries. In that sense, the Commission's examination of the third prong was redundant; however, it was instrumental in highlighting the aggravated nature of the impugned measure. The Commission emphasized the onerous standard of proof imposed on the respondent government, which was bound to adduce 'particularly compelling' reasons and 'strict criteria' to justify the contested ban.[102] The rationale for requiring such bold proportionality analysis was that the ban affected one of the most intimate aspects of private and family life.[103] The Commission gave due weight to how the interdiction had produced concrete and personal effects on the alleged victims.[104]

[99] *Juridical Condition and Rights of the Undocumented Migrants* 57.
[100] *Murillo* (n 95) para 110. [101] *Murillo* (n 95) paras 110–111.
[102] *Murillo* (n 95) para 90. [103] *Murillo* (n 95) para 90.
[104] The Commission stated that: 'For the victims who suffer from infertility conditions that make any other assisted reproductive technique unviable, the ban on *in vitro* fertilization represented a

Proportionality in the narrow sense has been rigorously scrutinized in cases involving the general non-discrimination clause embodied in Article 1 of the ACHR. As is true of the structured analysis developed by the ECtHR, under ECHR Article 14, the reasoning process is two-tiered, including the onus to show (1) a legitimate objective and (2) 'a reasonable relationship of proportionality' between the impugned means (the difference in treatment at issue) and the aim to be realized.[105] Still, the IACtHR's methodology can be considered more elaborate than its European counterpart. Its elaborations of the legitimate aim test provide evidence of this feature. The pursued objectives demonstrated by the respondent state 'may not be unjust or unreasonable, that is,...not be arbitrary, capricious, despotic or in conflict with the essential oneness and dignity of humankind'.[106] The exacting scrutiny imposed on the national government, both in respect of the legitimate aim test and the test of proportionality in a narrow sense, is stated in terms reminiscent of natural law; such a difference in treatment must 'not lead to situations which are contrary to justice, to reason or to the nature of things'.[107]

8. Critiques of Proportionality Analysis

Several strands of criticisms reviewed herein have been levelled at utilizing the principle of proportionality to assess limitations on human rights. The bulk of the criticism relates to how a proportionality appraisal *stricto sensu* may undermine the fundamental idea of human rights.

Some critics claim that use of the principle of proportionality transposes human rights discourse into a rather simplistic process of cost-benefit analysis. This critique presupposes that conflicts of diverse values operative in human rights discourse are reduced to balancing them, based on a 'a common metric' that compares

complete suppression of their personal identity and individual free will to decide to have biological children and control their own reproductive capacity.' *Murillo* (n 95) para 113.

[105] In its Advisory Opinion on *Juridical Condition and Rights of Undocumented Migrants*, several interveners in their submissions expressly relied on the case law of the ECtHR and stressed 'a reasonable relationship of proportionality' between the impugned means (the difference in treatment at issue) and the aim to be realized: *Juridical Condition and Rights of Undocumented Migrants* 38, 59, 62. See also Opinions of Judge AA Cançado Trindade, para 60 and Judge Hernán Salgado Pesantes, paras 6, 8, 9.

[106] *Juridical Status and Human Rights of the Child*, para 47; *Proposed Amendments to the Naturalization Provisions of the Constitution of Costa Rica*, para 57; *Juridical Condition and Rights of Undocumented Migrants* (n 105) para 91.

[107] *Juridical Status and Human Rights of the Child* (n 106) para 47; *Proposed Amendments to the Naturalization Provisions of the Constitution of Costa Rica* (n 106) para 57; *Juridical Condition and Rights of Undocumented Migrants*, para 91.

the intensity of interference to the benefit of public interests accruing from a contested measure. As such, the structure of proportionality analysis (and balancing) focuses on 'the *technical* weight, cost, or benefit of competing interests', to the exclusion of more substantive arguments relating to 'the *moral* correctness, goodness, or rightness of a claim'.[108] Such a balancing exercise *is assumed* to be 'objective, neutral, and totally extraneous to any moral reasoning',[109] although in a critic's mind, assessing the relative merits of interest, cost, and weight, cannot be reduced to a technical question free of substantive moral judgments.[110] Such analysis shows the 'substantive emptiness' and 'manipulability' of the notion of proportionality,[111] one of which gives a false impression of 'accuracy' while 'camouflaging' the actual process of rights reasoning.[112] Such an implication risks sacrificing profound discussions on the scope of the rights protection,[113] as next discussed.

The most robust criticism levelled at a proportionality analysis relates to the 'depoliticization and de-moralization' of the 'rights discourse'.[114] Such a method of analysis is said to risk side-stepping the need for substantive rationalization based on political morality, or worse even, devaluing the importance of it.[115] The balancing mechanism the third proportionality prongs requires is censured for downplaying the complexity of the moral discourses on human rights.[116] Proportionality is rebuked for de-politicizing rights claims and transforming moral and political discourses into technicalities of weight and balance.[117] The gist of this line of criticism turns on the perceived impossibility of undertaking a proportionality appraisal apolitically and amorally.[118] Further, proportionality in a narrow sense (or balancing) might be criticized for bypassing a fundamental epistemic problem: the inability to quantify diverse values in a complex 'moral universe'.[119] Its tendency to assume the comparisons of only two clashing interests overlooks the generally polycentric nature of rights claims in the social reality,[120] undermining any alternative modes of reasoning that can better integrate a moral understanding of rights.[121]

Finally, Tsakyrakis argues that the fundamental problem of the balancing approach proportionality considerations require is that, by reducing conflicts between allegedly competing rights or conflicts between a right and a social end to evaluations of relative weights, one undermines the 'justification-blocking function' of human

[108] Grégoire Webber, 'Proportionality, Balancing, and the Cult of Constitutional Rights Scholarship' (2010) 23 *CJLJ* 179, 180. Emphasis in original.

[109] Tsakyrakis (n 30) 474. See also the criticism raised by Jürgen Habermas, *Between Facts and Norms* (MIT Press 1998) 259.

[110] Webber (n 108) 194.

[111] *Panaccio* (n 2) 114.

[112] *Panaccio* (n 2) 114.

[113] *Panaccio* (n 2) 114–15.

[114] Webber (n 108) 179, 191; Panaccio (n 2) 114–115. See also Pamela A Chapman, 'The Politics of Judging: Section 1 of the Charter of Rights and Freedoms' (1986) 24 *Osgoode Hall LJ* 867; Norman Siebrasse, 'The *Oakes* Test: An Old Ghost Impeding Bold New Initiatives' (1991) 23 *Ottawa L Rev* 99.

[115] See eg Tsakyrakis (n 30) 191.

[116] Tsakyrakis (n 30) 475, 493.

[117] Webber (n 108) 191.

[118] Webber (n 108).

[119] Tsakyrakis (n 30) 475.

[120] Webber (n 108) 192.

[121] Webber (n 108) 191, 193.

rights.[122] The idea of 'justification-blocking function' of human rights is akin to Dworkin's view of human rights as 'trumps' possible of being deployed against policy arguments in legal discourse.[123] It is also similar to Thomas Nagel's idea of human rights as having a 'special type of inviolability' because of their 'nonderivative and fundamental' natures.[124] Such anti-balancing theoretical stock can be found in the work of an array of different theorists.[125] Rawls argues that: 'Each person possesses an inviolability founded on justice that even the welfare of society as a whole cannot override.'[126] Habermas cautions against reducing the idea of human rights to policy arguments, observing that: '[I]f in cases of collision *all* reasons can assume the character of policy arguments, then the fire wall erected in legal discourse by a deontological understanding of legal norms and principles collapses.'[127] Underpinning the anti-utilitarian justification for human rights is the idea that human rights are not to be surrendered for efficiency or 'for any aggregate of lesser interests under the heading of the public good'.[128] In essence, the proportionality *stricto sensu* (balancing appraisal) is criticized for trivializing the distinctly morality-laden nature of human rights claims that are predicated on the status of individuals as moral agents.[129]

9. Conclusion

Proportionality as a form of balancing reflects 'a manifestation of the perennial quest to invest adjudication with precision and objectivity'.[130] The principle of

[122] Tsakyrakis (n 30) 489. For instance, in his view, when confronted with a case like the ECtHR's *Otto-Preminger-Institut* case (n 55), religious feelings and the right to freedom of expression should never be put on any scale: 489.

[123] Ronald Dworkin, 'Rights as Trumps' in Jeremy Waldron (ed), *Theories of Rights* (OUP 1984) 153. See also Habermas (n 109) 259.

[124] Thomas Nagel, 'Personal Rights and Public Space' (1995) 24 *Phil & Pub Aff* 83, 86–87.

[125] Webber (n 108) 201.

[126] John Rawls, *A Theory of Justice* (Harvard UP 1971) 3. He adds that: 'For this reason justice denies that the loss of freedom for some is made right by a greater good shared by others... the rights secured by justice are not subject to political bargaining or to the calculus of social interests... Being first virtues of human activities, truth and justice are uncompromising' 3–4.

[127] Habermas (n 109) 258–59. Emphasis in original.

[128] Jeremy Waldron, 'A Right-Based Critique of Constitutional Rights' (1993) 13 *OJLS* 18, 30.

[129] Tsakyrakis (n 30) 390. See also Webber, who within the context of a discussion of national constitutional law, observes that: 'Constitutional rights scholarship should seek to cleanse itself of the yoke of the contemporary cult of rights reasoning and aspire to struggle more explicitly with the moral and political reasoning inherent to all rights. The danger of neglecting to redirect efforts in this way is nothing short of the loss of the vocabulary of rights.' Webber (n 108) 201.

[130] Tsakyrakis (n 30) 469. According to him, as such, proportionality is vulnerable to criticisms raised in the American debate on balancing.

proportionality is an analytical and structural method for assessing national decisions and is instrumental in enhancing certainty, coherence, transparency, and legitimate expectations—all essential ingredients for the rule of law.[131] Some authors argue that by securing a measure of non-arbitrariness and 'relative objectivity' in the monitoring bodies' reasoning in a transparent manner, the principle of proportionality fosters trust in the international judicial and quasi-judicial bodies' supervisory roles.[132] Furthermore, from a practical point of view, proportionality has a special advantage because it provides 'a simple, structured, and manageable method to adjudicate human rights issues that does not embroil judges in deep moral questions with all their complexity and contestability'.[133] In other words, the principle of proportionality serves as an expediently un-taxing device that exonerates the supervisory organs of IHRL treaties from engaging in intricate moral discourses. It might be argued that precisely because of the need to mask the discomfort inherent to confrontation with both substantive moral reasoning and the intractable question of moral disagreements, the language of proportionality/balancing is pervasively deployed in our discourses on human rights.[134]

With respect to the robust criticism based on the 'morality-bypassing' role of balancing (or proportionality in a narrow sense), one can counter that it plays much more than a rhetorical role insofar as it requires the judiciary to engage in substantive moral evaluations.[135] Indeed, proportionality analysis is never value-neutral. Political and moral questions are inherent in rights reasoning. What may appear a mechanical process of judicial reasoning that proportionality has propelled is ineluctably value-laden. There is always at least a relative assessment of conflicting (but commensurable) interests and rights 'in a crude manner'. Because of its sliding scale of intensity, proportionality can serve as a vehicle for securing dynamic and diverse human rights claims, reflecting evolving social forces in different context.

Many IHRL treaties are equipped with catalogues of non-derogable rights that cannot be abridged under any circumstance. Further, even when applying the 'state-limiting conception of proportionality', the monitoring bodies prefer to leave space for moral arguments by recognizing the notion of 'an absolute minimum' of the derogable rights (or the 'very essence' of the rights, in the language of the ECtHR),[136] which must never admit of any scope of relativization or balancing.[137] In other words, those rights designated as 'absolute' are immune from balancing exercises (proportionality in a narrow sense). Any debates over such notions of 'absolute rights' or minimum intransgressible cores require us to examine how to identify

[131] *Harbo* (n 1) 162–63. [132] *Harbo* (n 1) 164. [133] Tsakyrakis (n 30) 490.

[134] Tsakyrakis (n 30) 493.

[135] Rivers (n 2) 177–82. He contends that 'all the court does is maintain an efficiency-based oversight to ensure that there are no unnecessary costs to rights, that sledgehammers are not used to crack nuts, or rather, that sledge-hammers are only used when nutcrackers prove impotent', 180.

[136] This notion has been frequently relied upon in the context of Arts 6, 11, and 12. See Arai-Takahashi, 'Scrupulous but Dynamic' (n 1) 36–37. [137] Rivers (n 2) 180.

them and to what extent evolutive interpretation in the furtherance of individual persons' rights can expand their scope. Such a task presupposes that the monitoring bodies are always poised to engage, even inadvertently, in reasoning processes imbued with substantive moral and political discourses.[138]

Further Reading

Arai-Takahashi Y, *The Margin of Appreciation Doctrine and the Principle of Proportionality in the Jurisprudence of the ECHR* (Intersentia 2002)

de Búrca G, 'Principle of Proportionality and its Application in EC Law' (1993) 13 *YEL* 105

Carozza PG, 'Subsidiarity as a Structural Principle of International Human Rights Law' (2003) 97 *AJIL* 38

Cohen-Eliya M and Porat I, 'Proportionality and the Culture of Justification' (2011) 59 *Am J Comp L* 463

Stone Sweet A and Mathews J, 'Proportionality Balancing and Global Constitutionalism' (2008) 47 *Colum J Transnat'l Law* 72.

Van Drooghenbroeck S, *La Proportionnalité dans le Droit de la Convention Européenne des Droits de l'Homme: Prendre l'Idée Simple au Sérieux* (Publications Fac Saint-Louis 2001)

[138] Tsakyrakis (n 30) 492.

CHAPTER 20

DEMOCRACY AND THE RULE OF LAW

CHRISTIAN TOMUSCHAT

1. Introduction

Human rights are not abstract legal concepts that flourish easily in any environment. In order to flourish, they need an appropriate climate fostering their operation. More often than not, state acceptance of an international instrument for the protection of human rights, by itself, brings few significant changes in actual governmental practices vis-à-vis persons in the state. The drafters of the UN Charter recognized this in particular. They were well aware of the necessity of promoting the objective of international peace as the foundation of all human rights that the Charter solemnly proclaimed by creating favourable conditions in the lives of ordinary people, in particular through 'social progress and better standards of life in larger freedom'.[1] Human rights, once introduced, however, can exert a considerable impact on the condition of a society. To the extent that human rights are realized for every human being without any discrimination, they produce salutary effects for society as a whole. Thus, slowly, law and fact influence one another until reaching a symbiosis—which, understandably, will never be fully perfect.

Human rights are a living force that imposes demands not only on government agents, but also on private individuals. When violence and crime anchored

[1] Charter of the United Nations, preamble.

in conscious and unconscious traditions plague society, human rights have great difficulty producing responsible governments free from such deep-seated ills. Accordingly, human rights must be conceived of as a permanent challenge whose desired outcome depends on the endeavours of the relevant human community in its entirety. One can neither 'import' nor 'export' human rights; in essence and in the long run, societies themselves must determine the fate of human rights within their own historical and political framework.

2. Formal Recognition of the Rule of Law and Democracy

The preambles of many of the relevant international instruments state in unequivocal terms an awareness of this social complexity. They mention three pillars time and again, namely human rights, the rule of law, and democracy. First, the preamble to the Universal Declaration of Human Rights (UDHR) proclaims in its third recital: 'Whereas it is essential, if man is not to be compelled to have recourse, as a last resort, to rebellion against tyranny and oppression, that human rights should be protected by the rule of law.'[2] Along similar lines, the second recital of the preamble to the Statute of the Council of Europe outlines the intentions of the free nations of Western Europe following their liberation from dictatorship and the infernal atrocities of the Second World War: 'Reaffirming their devotion to the spiritual and moral values which are the common heritage of their peoples and the true source of individual freedom, political liberty and the rule of law, principles which form the basis of all genuine democracy.'

Article 3, which establishes the criteria for membership in the Organization, reinforces this general statement of principle:

> Every member of the Council of Europe must accept the principles of the rule of law and of the enjoyment by all persons within its jurisdiction of human rights and fundamental freedoms, and collaborate sincerely and effectively in the realisation of the aim of the Council as specified in Chapter I.[3]

The Council applies the Article in practice. For more than a decade, it has found that Belarus does not fulfil the membership criteria and has refused to accept the country's application for membership. Earlier, after the 1967 putsch of the military junta in Greece, the Council of Europe seriously considered terminating Greek membership

[2] UDHR, preamble. [3] Statute of the Council of Europe, Art 3.

in accordance with Article 8 of the Statute. In order to pre-empt this severe sanction, Greece declared its withdrawal from the Council on 12 December 1969. It rejoined the Council after the restoration of democracy in 1974.[4] The Parliamentary Assembly similarly debated the exclusion of Turkey after the military coup in 1980, but did not take the step because a majority felt that it would be easier to exert a positive influence on political developments while Turkey retained its membership. Nonetheless, during the three years of the military dictatorship, the Council's Parliamentary Assembly did not seat the Turkish members of the Assembly.

The criteria that the Statute of the Council of Europe sets forth were also chosen to reflect the spirit prevailing when the European Convention on Human Rights (ECHR) was launched in 1950. In paragraphs 4 and 5 of the preamble, one finds a 'declaration of faith' that has withstood the conflicts of the twentieth century and become a leitmotif for the nations of central and eastern Europe as they joined the common European endeavour after the demise of their communist governments:

> Reaffirming their profound belief in those fundamental freedoms which are the foundation of justice and peace in the world and are best maintained on the one hand by an effective political democracy and on the other by a common understanding and observance of the human rights upon which they depend;
>
> Being resolved, as the governments of European countries which are like-minded and have a common heritage of political traditions, ideals, freedom and the rule of law, to take the first steps for the collective enforcement of certain of the rights stated in the Universal Declaration.[5]

For decades, officials of the socialist systems sought to denigrate the ECHR as a purely 'Western European' undertaking. After the fall of the Berlin wall, the easy and even enthusiastic welcoming of the ECHR made it obvious that the premises of the ECHR reflected the common understanding of most peoples and also most governments in Europe.

In 1990, in order to give greater emphasis to its guiding principles of democracy, human rights, and the rule of law, the Council of Europe created the European Commission for Democracy through Law (Venice Commission), an advisory body of individual experts that acts as an independent legal think-tank.[6] Its first task was to provide constitutional assistance to the former members of the socialist bloc after they embraced pluralist democracy. The Venice Commission is also open to non-European states, and as of 2012 it has fifty-nine full members.[7] Through its studies and opinions,

[4] Council of Europe (Committee of Ministers) 'Invitation to Greece to Rejoin the Council of Europe' (28 November 1974) Res (74)34.

[5] Convention for the Protection of Human Rights and Fundamental Freedoms (ECHR), preamble.

[6] For an overview, see <http://www.venice.coe.int/WebForms/pages/?p=01_Presentation> accessed 31 May 2013.

[7] In addition to the forty-seven members of the Council of Europe, Kyrgyzstan joined in 2004, Chile in 2005, the Republic of Korea in 2006, Morocco and Algeria in 2007, Israel in 2008, Peru and Brazil in 2009, Tunisia and Mexico in 2010, Kazakhstan in November 2011, and the United States in early 2013. The Council has accepted Belarus as an associate member, while Argentina, Canada, the Holy See,

the Commission has been able to pinpoint major shortcomings in the constitutional structure in a number of individual countries.

Elsewhere on the regional level, the American Convention on Human Rights (ACHR) and the African Charter on Human and Peoples' Rights (AfChHPR) do not include the term 'rule of law', though both instruments refer to democracy as the framework within which a people can best enjoy human rights. Thus, the ACHR states in its preamble the intention of the state parties to consolidate, 'within the framework of democratic institutions, a system of personal liberty and social justice based on respect for the essential rights of man'. The Charter provides that one of the essential purposes of the Organization of American States (OAS) is to 'promote and consolidate representative democracy',[8] a proposition reconfirmed as one of the basic 'Principles': 'The solidarity of the American States and the high aims which are sought through it require the political organization of those States on the basis of the effective exercise of representative democracy.'[9] In September 2001, the legal architecture was completed when the OAS adopted the Inter-American Democratic Charter, which specifies in elaborate detail the requirements of a democratic system of government.

The AfChHPR places its emphasis on self-determination and the fight against remnants of colonialism on African soil. It makes no mention in general terms of internal democracy as a condition for the enjoyment of human rights, but Article 13 takes up the main elements by stating that '[e]very citizen shall have the right to participate freely in the government of his country, either directly or through freely chosen representatives…'.

Reconfirming and strengthening this principle, the 2007 Charter on Democracy, Elections and Governance[10] provides in simple and straightforward language: 'State Parties shall commit themselves to promote democracy, the principle of the rule of law and human rights.'[11]

Both the OAS and the African Union provide for suspending the participation of any government that comes to power through undemocratic means, and each organization has voted to do so.[12]

The European integration process merits additional attention, having created entities with a current status not far removed from statehood. The member states originally saw no need to articulate an obligation for the organs of this process

Japan, and Uruguay are observers. For a complete list, see 'Documents by Opinion and Study' (*Venice Commission*) <http://www.venice.coe.int/WebForms/members/countries.aspx> accessed 31 May 2013.

[8] Charter of the Organization of American States (OAS Charter), Art 2(b).

[9] OAS Charter, Art 3(d).

[10] African Charter on Democracy, Elections and Governance (African Charter on Democracy). The Charter entered into force on 15 February 2012, after having attained the minimum threshold of fifteen ratifications.

[11] African Charter on Democracy, Art 4.

[12] The OAS suspended Honduras following a *coup d'état* in 2009, readmitting the government in 2011. The African Union similarly suspended Mauritania in 2005 and 2009.

to respect human rights and the rule of law. Neither the Treaty Establishing the European Coal and Steel Community,[13] nor the subsequent Treaties of Rome,[14] contained any specific reference to human rights as a yardstick for Community action. The legal position changed with the Treaty of Maastricht,[15] which transformed the substance of the Community from a marketplace to a political body that recognized the nationals of the member states as 'Citizens of the Union' holding rights corresponding to their status.[16] Accordingly, the new Treaty on European Union (TEU) placed the Union under the aegis of democratic principles and instructed it to respect fundamental rights as guaranteed by the ECHR and as they result from the common constitutional tradition of all member states.[17]

Upon the Maastricht Treaty's entry into force in 1993, European leaders realized the necessity of further consolidating and strengthening the institutional structure. After a series of attempts, the Treaty of Lisbon, encompassing the Treaty on European Union (TEU) and the Treaty on the Functioning of the European Union (TFEU), received approval in 2009.[18] Article 2 TEU contains a comprehensive formula that enunciates the core principles and values of the European Union under its new constitutional arrangement:

> The Union is founded on the values of respect for human dignity, freedom, democracy, equality, the rule of law and respect for human rights, including the rights of persons belonging to minorities. These values are common to the Member States in a society in which pluralism, non-discrimination, tolerance, justice, solidarity and equality between women and men prevail.[19]

The inclusion once again of democracy, the rule of law, and human rights manifests the drafters' conviction that those concepts count among the core principles of the European integration process. The European Union finished adjusting its institutional structure to match the requirements of a political entity with extensive powers by the adoption of the Charter of Fundamental Rights of the European Union. The Charter's preamble states in straightforward language that the Union 'is based on the principles of democracy and the rule of law', once more affirming the close alliance of the principles.[20]

At the global level, the UN's two International Covenants of 1966[21] do not explicitly refer to the rule of law, but their substance can be seen to reflect the principle. Article 25 of the International Covenant on Civil and Political Rights (ICCPR)

[13] Treaty Establishing the European Coal and Steel Community (Treaty of Paris).

[14] Treaty Establishing the European Economic Community (Treaty of Rome).

[15] Treaty of Maastricht on European Union (TEU).

[16] TEU, Art 8(2).

[17] TEU, Art 6(2).

[18] Consolidated versions of the Treaty on European Union and the Treaty on the Functioning of the European Union.

[19] TEU, Art 2.

[20] For a comprehensive study, see Laurent Pech, '"A Union Founded on the Rule of Law": Meaning and Reality of the Rule of Law as a Constitutional Principle of EU Law' (2010) 6 *EU Const* 359, 367.

[21] International Covenant on Civil and Political Rights (ICCPR); International Covenant on Economic, Social and Cultural Rights (ICESCR).

contains guarantees of political rights essential to democratic pluralism. More generally, the organization has long expressed concern with the rule of law and with democracy, in particular their actual implementation. Since at least 1988, the UN has had on its agenda assisting the building of democratic institutions in sovereign states.[22] By 1992, a famous and influential article by Thomas Franck[23] could assert that democracy had become a binding precept, indeed a right, under international law.

The World Conference on Human Rights, held in Vienna in June 1993, emphasized, albeit in a somewhat disorganized fashion,[24] the importance of the rule of law and democracy, together with an extensive bundle of other principles and objectives, in the preamble to its Declaration and Programme of Action.[25] Paragraph 8 of the Declaration contains a more elaborate reference to democracy as a factor promoting and sustaining human rights. Thereafter, the General Assembly's Millennium Declaration in 2000 devoted a large section of part V to 'Human rights, democracy and good governance'.[26] In a resolute fashion, it proclaimed the member states' intention to 'spare no effort to promote democracy and strengthen the rule of law, as well as respect for all internationally recognized human rights and fundamental freedoms, including the right to development'.[27]

Significantly, the Assembly placed this proposition at the top of the section, which underlines the intimate relationship between the three elements.

The chain of UN instruments focusing on these principles reached its highpoint with the World Summit Outcome of 2005, where paragraph 134 extensively examines the scope and meaning of the rule of law and the consequences to be drawn therefrom, with a view to operative action. The two subsequent paragraphs endorse democracy as a model for all countries, with the proviso, however, that 'there is no single model of democracy',[28] a formula leaving wide room for diverse forms of government. This proviso is complemented by the further exhortation that it is necessary to respect 'sovereignty and the right of self-determination',[29] a phrase that while essentially correct, is nonetheless couched deliberately in ambiguous terms.

Based on the instructions of the Summit Outcome paragraph 134(e),[30] the Secretary General produced a report on the prospect of a 'rule of law assistance unit within the Secretariat'[31] in 2007, followed by subsequent annual reports. The

22 UNGA Res 43/157 (8 December 1988).

23 Thomas Franck, 'The Emerging Right to Democratic Governance' (1992) 86 *AJIL* 46.

24 '[P]eace, democracy, justice, equality, rule of law, pluralism, development, better standards of living and solidarity.'

25 Vienna Declaration and Programme of Action.

26 Millennium Declaration, UNGA Res 55/2 (8 September 2000).

27 Millennium Declaration, Art 24.

28 UNGA Res 60/1 (24 October 2005), Art 135 (World Summit Outcome).

29 World Summit Outcome (n 28) Art 135.

30 UNGA Res 61/39 (4 December 2006) and UNGA Res 62/70 (6 December 2007) reiterated the request for action.

31 Report of the Secretary-General, 'The Rule of Law at the National and International Levels' (2007) UN Doc A/62/261.

General Assembly reviews the activities undertaken under those auspices each year.[32] Moreover, the General Assembly decided to hold a high-level event on the rule of law at the beginning of the 67th session in 2012.[33] The conclusion is thus warranted that the rule of law has taken centre stage in international discourse on the legal elements of a satisfactory international order.

3. A Closer Look at the Rule of Law and Democracy in Relation to Human Rights

3.1 The rule of law

To date, no official definition of the 'rule of law' has emerged, although 'law' is generally understood as the embodiment of justice and fairness, and governance by precepts that are intended to serve the public good on the basis of a fair balancing of the interests at stake. History reveals many expressions of the desire to see such a system of government, acting on the basis of norms applicable to everyone, replace despotic arbitrariness. It is a perennial theme of constitutional philosophy.[34] In 1780, when he drafted the Constitution of Massachusetts, John Adams, later the second President of the United States, famously uttered that there should be 'government of laws and not of men'.[35] This simple formula raises legitimate questions, however, about what law is. Is it a parliamentary statute, a regulation that the executive branch of government enacts, or simply an instruction that a superior authority imparts to an inferior one? Does a law need any substantive qualities, such as compliance with requirements of justice and equity, or is it sufficient that a competent rule-setting authority passes it?

Without a definition or binding normative precepts on the rule of law, debate has inevitably arisen in the field of jurisprudence, where different conceptions rival each other for paramountcy. An initial query is whether the rule of law is a concept that derives exclusively from Anglo-American legal tradition or whether it is

[32] Latest Resolution: UNGA Res 67/97 (14 December 2012).

[33] Report of the Secretary-General, 'Strengthening and Coordinating United Nations Rule of Law Activities' (2011) UN Doc A/66/133, para 77.

[34] The generality of law was the key element in Immanuel Kant's philosophical doctrine, cf Immanuel Kant, 'Methodenlehre der reinen praktischen Vernunft' in W Weischedel (ed), *Werke in sechs Bänden*, vol IV (Wissenschaftliche Buchgesellschaft 1956) 337. On the history of the rule of law cf Simon Chesterman, 'An International Rule of Law' (2008) 56 *Am J Comp L* 333.

[35] Const Massachusetts, Pt 1, Art XXX.

a general principle spanning various legal cultures. In the German legal tradition the concept of *Rechtsstaat* and *Rechtstaatlichkeit* emerged during the late eighteenth and early nineteenth centuries,[36] and today it constitutes the core element of the constitutional system, after the abominable crimes committed during the Nazi period.[37] The Basic Law of 1949 establishes that 'the legislature shall be bound by the constitutional order, the executive and the judiciary by law and justice' ('*Gesetz und Recht*'),[38] a proposition that encapsulates the essence of the rule of law. It is significant that the text does not confine itself to manifesting confidence in the law (*Gesetz* as statutory law), but specifies that 'justice' ('*Recht*') as a concept including both customary law and elements of legitimacy, that may, if need be, correct undue rigors of the law (in the Anglo-American system, the principles of equity serve a similar function), binds government institutions. In France, the concept of '*état de droit*', originally derived from the German '*Rechtsstaat*', has also taken its place in the legal literature.[39] Despite learned examinations of the different virtues, shortcomings, overlappings, incongruences, and minor inconsistencies of the various terms mentioned, it appears that they have a largely identical content.[40]

The main ongoing debate about rule of law is between advocates of a 'lean', 'minimalist', or formal concept, on the one hand, and a 'thick' or substantive concept, on the other hand. Scholars have observed that HLA Hart has generally avoided speaking of the rule of law in his writings, in particular in his seminal work *The Concept of Law*.[41] Hart's analytic aim easily explains this omission. He has focused on law as an instrument actually used in society, which can be seen as a fact of life, both empirically and conceptually. He has not examined the law as a technique and strategy of good governance. In contrast, the term 'rule of law' is the centrepiece of a constitutional theory that seeks to build a legal framework for a community of human beings in search of freedom from arbitrariness. This connotation is totally lacking in Hart's analytical thinking. He deliberately confines himself to analysing the law's characteristic features, not unlike Hans Kelsen in his 'Pure Theory of the Law'.[42]

[36] cf Eberhard Schmidt-Assmann, 'Der Rechtsstaat' in Josef Isensee and Paul Kirchhof (eds), *Handbuch des Staatsrechts*, vol II (3rd edn, CF Müller 2004) 540, s 26; Karl-Peter Sommermann, 'Commentary on Article 20(3) of the Basic Law' in von Mangoldt and others (eds), *GG Kommentar zum Grundgesetz*, vol II (5th edn, Franz Vahlen 2005) 95–96.

[37] On the attempts to pervert the notion of the '*Rechtsstaat*' during that time cf Walter Pauly, 'Grundrechtstheorien in der Zeit des Nationalsozialismus und Faschismus' in Detlef Merten and Hans-Jürgen Papier (eds), *Handbuch der Grundrechte in Deutschland und Europa*, vol I (CF Müller 2004) 575 fn 16.

[38] Article 20(3) GG.

[39] cf Dominique Colas, *L'Etat de Droit* (Presses Universitaires de France 1987).

[40] cf, for instance, Luc Heuschling, *Etat de Droit = Rechtsstaat = Rule of Law* (Dalloz 2002); Gianluigi Palombella, 'The Rule of Law as an Institutional Ideal' in Leonardo Morlino and Gianluigi Palombella (eds), *Rule of Law and Democracy. Inquiries into Internal and External Issues* (Brill 2010) 11–13.

[41] HLA Hart, *The Concept of Law* (2nd edn, Clarendon Press 1994).

[42] Hans Kelsen, *Reine Rechtslehre* (2nd edn, Franz Deuticke 1960).

For Hart, the central distinction is between law and morality, the law as it is and the law as it ought to be.[43] Classic philosophical categories appear to govern Hart's writings, without taking cognizance of (or simply ignoring?) the dramatic changes in the legal universe that the UN Charter and the holdings of the International Military Tribunal at Nuremberg initiated. The latter had dismissed all legislative acts of Nazi Germany as irrelevant, instead prosecuting the defendants directly on the basis of rules of international law that moral concepts, later codified in Article 7(2) ECHR[44] and Article 15(2) ICCPR,[45] starkly impacted. Although one of Hart's leading articles discussed the responses of the judiciary of the new democratic Germany to accusations of crimes arising from acts that had been lawful under Nazi legislation,[46] he did not seem to realize that it was possible to refer to the higher authority of international law, ie to a source within the proper realm of law, and that it was not necessary to rely on morality.

In deliberate opposition to Hart's approach, Lon L Fuller's monograph *The Morality of Law*[47] considers the concept of law as more than a technical device. Convinced that the strict separation of law and morality that Hart advocated constituted a fatal error, and being fully aware of the crucial relevance of law within society, Fuller pleads for a broader concept of the rule of law. In a carefully defined catalogue he presents eight points aimed at the elimination of governmental arbitrariness. He begins by asserting that there must first be laws ensuring equality among citizens. The subsequent seven demands are: the promulgation of laws, lack of retroactive effect, clarity, elimination of contradiction, laws that do not require the impossible (*impossibilium nulla obligatio*), constancy of the law throughout time, and, as the crowning element, congruence between official action and declared rules. This catalogue refrains from explicitly requiring laws to correspond to specific substantive values. It displays an inventory of all devices available *in abstracto* to prevent recourse to the law as an instrument for capricious abuse by governmental powers. Fuller also holds that a system of governance can become so barbarous and shameful, lacking any ambition to orient itself towards the common good, that it should be denied characterization as a legal system.[48]

John Rawls follows Fuller's ideas on many points, but he explicitly emphasizes, as an element of the rule of law, the regular and fair administration of the law in

[43] HLA Hart, 'Positivism and the Separation of Law and Morals' (1958) 71 *Harv L Rev* 593 *et seq*.

[44] 'This article shall not prejudice the trial and punishment of any person for any act or omission which, at the time when it was committed, was criminal according to the general principles of law recognised by civilised nations.'

[45] 'Nothing in this article shall prejudice the trial and punishment of any person for any act or omission which, at the time when it was committed, was criminal according to the general principles of law recognized by the community of nations.'

[46] Hart, 'Positivism' (n 43) 613–21.

[47] Lon L Fuller, *The Morality of Law* (rev edn, Yale UP 1969).

[48] Lon L Fuller, 'Positivism and Fidelity to Law—A Reply to Professor Hart' (1958) 71 *Harv L Rev* 630, 660.

accordance with the principle of legality, which to Fuller seems self-evident.[49] It is undeniable that by heeding the standards that Fuller identifies to define the rule of law, many abuses can be forestalled. Nonetheless, the total perversion of a bureaucratic system that utilizes the law as an instrument of repression must be combatted by other means.[50]

When the Secretary General of the United Nations presented his first report on the rule of law,[51] he provided a definition that did not depart greatly from the position that Fuller and Rawls espoused, although he took an important step further, positing the need for adherence to international human rights standards, including a few elements of democratic governance:

> The rule of law is a concept at the very heart of the Organization's mission. It refers to a principle of governance in which all persons, institutions and entities, public and private, including the State itself, are accountable to laws that are publicly promulgated, equally enforced and independently adjudicated, and which are consistent with international human rights norms and standards. It requires, as well, measures to ensure adherence to the principles of supremacy of law, equality before the law, accountability to the law, fairness in the application of the law, separation of powers, participation in decision-making, legal certainty, avoidance of arbitrariness and procedural and legal transparency.[52]

None of the main political organs of the United Nations has ever adopted this definition. Moreover, a later report of the Secretary General[53] far exceeds the limits the above quotation suggesting and including almost anything that might contribute to the well-being of a nation, such as issues of disarmament and non-proliferation.[54] This expansion is due, in part, to its adopting a comprehensive understanding of the rule of law as a legal precept to govern not only relations between each state and its citizens, but also the relations between states themselves. The following discussion suggests that a narrower approach to interrelating the rule of law and human rights promises to yield better, more fruitful results.[55]

At the outset, it is perhaps obvious, but nonetheless true, that the recognition and legal consolidation of human rights is the first and perhaps most important step in

[49] John Rawls, *A Theory of Justice* (Harvard UP 1971) 235–43.

[50] Thus, Joseph Raz takes the view that the rule of law can be 'consistent with gross violations of law'. 'The Rule of Law and its Virtue' in Joseph Raz, *The Authority of Law: Essays on Law and Morality* (OUP 1979) 211, 224.

[51] Report of the Secretary-General, 'The Rule of Law and Transitional Justice in Conflict and Post-Conflict Societies' (2004) UN Doc S/2004/616.

[52] Report of the Secretary-General, 'The Rule of Law' (n 51) para 6.

[53] Report of the Secretary-General, 'Strengthening and Coordinating United Nations Rule of Law Activities' (2011) UN Doc A/66/133.

[54] Report of the Secretary-General on Strengthening (n 53) para 9.

[55] Rightly, Raz (n 50) 211 observes that '[i]f the rule of law is the rule of good law then to explain its nature is to propound a complete social philosophy. But if so the term lacks any useful function'. For a 'formal' core definition, see also Chesterman (n 34) 342. On the other hand, M Cherif Bassiouni advocates the inclusion of substantive values in the rule of law concept. 'Challenges Facing a Rule-of-Law-Oriented World Order' (2010) 8 *Santa Clara J Intl L* 1, 9.

establishing the rule of law. Civil and political rights generally have a simple structure; they set limits to governmental action by requiring the state and its organs to respect the freedom of the individual. Large zones of societal life are consequently withdrawn from governmental interference; civil rights and freedoms erect walls that must not be breached. Such rights in law determine the legitimate space within which governmental power may operate.

Since the origin of the constitutional movement in the Western world at the end of the eighteenth century, the idea of the constitution has been inextricably bound up with the guarantee of human rights. Protecting the individual by limiting the government by way of constitutionally guaranteed human rights (or fundamental rights) is all the more effective as a strategy since most states enshrine rights in constitutional instruments that they endow with superior rank. The constitutions take primacy and therefore trump ordinary legislative rule-making or regulation. Even democratically legitimated parliamentary bodies are prevented from overriding such rights by vote and a stroke of the pen. In this regard, no distinction between human rights and the rule of law are perceivable; human rights are a (or the) core element of the rule of law.

Of course, human rights are rarely sacrosanct, establishing rigid and intransgressible prohibitions. Only a few rights, like the right not to be tortured, are absolute and permit of no derogation. A limitations (or claw-back) clause that permits interference for purposes of the public weal, complements most human rights, but only under the rule of law. Under the ICCPR, the ECHR, and the ACHR, such interferences generally presuppose authorization by law. The text of the AfChHPR does not reveal such a consistent pattern of a requirement of legality. A careful reading of the Charter makes clear, however, that authorization by law is upheld as a minimum condition in all instances where a right is subject to express limitations, including Article 6, which governs the right to liberty and to the security of person. Here it explicitly stipulates: 'No one may be deprived of his freedom except for reasons and conditions previously laid down by law.'[56] Other provisions simply state that certain rights may be exercised only 'subject to law and order', 'within the law', or if the person concerned 'abides by the law'.[57] In the jurisprudence of the African Commission on Human and Peoples' Rights (AfCHPR), it is clear that governmental interference with protected rights requires a valid legal foundation that must be in conformity with the international obligations of the country concerned.[58] In sum, one may conclude that confidence is placed in the law by entrusting it with the function of guardian of the citizens' rights and freedoms, requiring it to balance, in each and every instance, the interest of the individual in exercising his rights fully with society's interest in ensuring achievement of certain paramount public interests.

[56] AfChHPR, Art 6. [57] AfChHPR, Arts 8, 9, 10, 12.

[58] See *Constitutional Rights Project et al v Nigeria*, para 40; *Jawara v The Gambia*, para 59; *Article 19 v Eritrea*, para 92; *Scanlen and Holderness v Zimbabwe*, paras 115–116.

Nowhere does state power exclusively threaten individuals. Indeed, the most plausible explanation for the existence of the state is the need of everyone to be protected from criminality or abuse by other members of society. Without appropriate safeguard mechanisms, human beings cannot live a life free from fear. From this perspective, all international human rights bodies called upon to adjudicate cases have evolved a doctrine of 'positive' state duties, ie a duty of the state to take measures with a view to shielding core rights from attack by any private actor.[59] For that purpose, standard measures are required. Every entity desirous of recognition as a truly functioning state must, at a minimum, enact criminal laws, set up judicial mechanisms, and ensure effective execution of the judgments its courts render. This whole complex of enforcement and implementation also pertains to the rule of law. Indeed, for many authors, effective remedies make up the core substance of the rule of law.[60]

In the Western hemisphere, the term 'citizen security' has been coined to refer to the duty of protection incumbent upon state authorities. In a report from 31 December 2009,[61] the Inter-American Commission on Human Rights derives a corresponding right to be secure from crime or violence from the obligation of the state to guarantee the security of the individual. It considers that 'a normative core demanding the protection of rights particularly vulnerable to criminal or violent acts', in particular 'the right to life, the right to physical integrity, the right to freedom, the right to due process and the right to the use and enjoyment of one's property' binds states.[62] With regard to these rights, the elementary function of the state as a survival group must come into operation, and it is not only justified, but imperative that the concept of the rule of law include such core elements of the governmental purpose.[63]

Civil and political rights, on the one hand, and economic, social, and cultural rights, on the other, have many features in common,[64] but they also differ in many important respects. It is undeniable that the right to work, the right to social security, and the right to education, to name but a few, are essential foundations for a life of dignity. Joblessness, or a lack of assistance after a loss of income, may reduce an individual to a life of misery and may even threaten death by starvation or exposure

[59] *Marckx v Belgium*, para 31; *Young, James and Webster v UK*, paras 48, 49; *Velásquez Rodríguez v Honduras*, para 166; AfCHPR, *Commission Nationale des droits de l'homme et des libertés v Chad* (1995) Communication No 74/92, para 22; HRC, 'General Comment No 31: Nature of the General Legal Obligation on States Parties to the Covenant' (29 March 2004) UN Doc CCPR/C/21/Rev.1/Add.13, para 8. See also Frans Viljoen, *International Human Rights Law in Africa* (OUP 2007) 239.

[60] See, for instance, Jeremy Waldron, 'The Concept and the Rule of Law' (2008) 43 *Ga L Rev* 1, 20.

[61] IACHR, 'Report on Citizen Security and Human Rights' (31 December 2009) OEA/Ser.L/V/II Doc 57.

[62] IACHR, 'Report on Citizen Security' (n 61) paras 5, 18.

[63] Rightly, protection against disappearance has found increased protection through international agreements both at the regional and the universal level in that forced disappearances encroach upon the right to freedom and the right to life at the same time. International Convention for the Protection of All Persons from Enforced Disappearance; Inter-American Convention on the Forced Disappearance of Persons.

[64] cf eg Christian Tomuschat, 'Civil and Political Rights—Economic, Social and Cultural Rights. Complementarity and Opposition' in *Thesaurus Acroasium* XXXV (2007) 3–48.

to the elements. The modern welfare state has assumed the burden of assisting every member of society when such existential need arises. National budgets in developed nations provide public allowances to everyone in order to avert the worst consequences threatening human existence. In less developed states, the capacities of the governmental machinery are frequently unable to provide the necessary assistance for survival. Obviously, issues of life and death belong to the most crucial ones societies must address. The question is, however, whether it may appear useful to include this field of activity under the heading of the rule of law. To many, serious doubts emerge in this regard.

In the first place, it is obvious that the law plays only a secondary role in providing public services to citizens. Under the International Covenant on Economic, Social and Cultural Rights (ICESCR), states must establish comprehensive mechanisms for the furtherance of the objectives set forth in its provisions. Thus, Article 6(2) ICESCR, which details the measures a government must take for the implementation of the right to work, provides:

> The steps to be taken by a State Party to the present Covenant to achieve the full realization of this right shall include technical and vocational guidance and training programmes, policies and techniques to achieve steady economic, social and cultural development and full and productive employment under conditions safeguarding fundamental political and economic freedoms to the individual.[65]

This call for action is the common thread which runs generally through the rights the ICESCR proclaims. Public authorities are enjoined to take a specific sector of societal life under their authority in order to provide services of a substantive character in accordance with the general performance level of the national economy. In most developed nations today, however, controversies about the size and volume of public services have become the central theme of political debate, in particular during electoral campaigns. Thus, there is manifestly no lack of importance, but the programmes devised for the attainment of such purposes do not relate to their legal format. They can be decided and implemented in the most diverse forms, and national methods differ widely. Only highly developed legal systems require legal regulation of the provision of crucial public goods and services. Scholars like Hilary Charlesworth[66] insist that the concept of the rule of law should include the instruments of such public welfare services, but one may counter that such extension requires abandoning the transnational connotation of the rule of law as a concept applicable on the global scale. Therefore, it appears preferable to confine the scope of the rule of law to configurations where, indeed, the law maintains a central position.

[65] cf also 'General Comment No 18: The Right to Work (art 6)' in 'Human Rights Instruments' (27 May 2008) UN Doc HRI/GEN/1/Rev.9 (Vol I), 139.

[66] Hilary Charlesworth, 'Human Rights and the Rule of Law after Conflict' in Peter Cane (ed), *The Hart-Fuller Debate in the Twenty-First Century* (Hart 2010) 46.

In sum, two criteria seem determinative: the rule of law obliges the state to regulate its action by law, and the law must be founded on the principles of equality and non-discrimination. The rule of law does not allow for exceptionalism.[67] A state embracing the rule of law must react to any challenges, including threats of terrorism, in a thoughtful and measured way and not itself resort to terrorist methods.[68]

It seems clear that research on the rule of law should not remain fixed on the normative level where the law operates to command, because laws are not ends in themselves. As already pointed out, the rule of law serves the specific purpose of protecting persons against any form of abuse or arbitrariness. In other words, legal rules, in particular human rights, must deploy their effects in practice by shaping relationships in societal life in accordance with their aim. It is a standing dictum of the European Court of Human Rights, shared by all similar bodies, that the provisions of international human rights instruments are designed to be effective forces in society and should not remain theoretical or illusory.[69] Accordingly, those instruments do not confine themselves to proclaiming human rights; they also regularly create mechanisms suited to vindicate the rights concerned. The extent to which these lofty proclamations gain real substance in the daily lives of citizens provides a benchmark to measure the real enjoyment of human rights and, accordingly, the true meaning of the rule of law.[70] Accordingly, effective remedies must be available—a demand which has found its reflection in all international treaties for the protection of human rights.[71] This again presupposes guarantees of the independence and impartiality of judges; normative proclamations that lack fulfilment in the daily fight for law and justice would create no more than a hollow façade.

3.2 Democracy

The concept of democracy also lacks an official definition. Like the rule of law, it is a concept in constant motion. Despite the indeterminacy of many of its component elements, however, very few words are necessary to circumscribe its essence. Government is a human creation, and the recognition that human beings are equals removes any justification for granting a privileged position to a limited group to rule or as rulers. Everyone should be able to contribute to framing the political

[67] cf *Article 19* (n 58) paras 99, 102.

[68] The General Assembly has firmly called upon states to heed the rule of law while countering terrorism. Protection of Human Rights and Fundamental Freedoms while Countering Terrorism, UNGA Res 65/221 (21 December 2010), paras 10, 13, 14, 18.

[69] *Stafford v UK*, para 68; *Goodwin v UK*, para 74; *Sabeh El Leil v France*, paras 46, 50; *Palomo Sánchez et al v Spain*, paras 56, 59; *Al-Khawaja and Tahery v UK*, para 127.

[70] This procedural aspect of the rule of law is underlined by most authors dealing with the concept, see Rawls (n 49) 239–41; Waldron (n 60) 5, 7.

[71] See UDHR, Art 8; ECHR, Arts 6(1), 13; ICCPR, Arts 2(3), 14(1); ACHR, Art 25; AfChHPR, Art 26.

order under which the polity lives. Where true democratic participation is ensured, one may normally assume that the acts of government reflect the needs and aspirations of the people as a whole. Majoritarian rule is no panacea, however. History has taught the bitter lesson that majorities are often tempted to discriminate massively against minorities. In this regard, the interaction between human rights and democracy operates as a check to prevent majoritarian as well as dictatorial abuses.

When the UN Charter was adopted in 1945, one could hardly claim democracy as the only legitimate form of government. Two of the founding nations, France and the United Kingdom, permanent members of the Security Council, held large colonial empires that the metropolitan power centres dominated. Many countries lived under dictatorial regimes, and the establishment of the apartheid regime in South Africa openly defied democratic ideals. Although the Charter mentions self-determination among the purposes and principles of the Organization, this was only a half-hearted acknowledgement; Chapter XI, regarding non-self-governing territories, did not open the path to true self-determination of colonized peoples, but limited itself to stating the objective of self-government—without fixing any deadline for its attainment. The doctrine of exclusive domestic jurisdiction set forth in Article 2(7) deemed that, for most observers and governments, the way in which peoples organized themselves under their national constitutions lay outside any international interference. Moreover, the pretensions of the United Nations to be an organization of universality meant that it was considered unacceptable to exclude nations from membership, whatever their form of government.

The adoption of the UDHR in 1948 marked a breakthrough, as it refers to a democratic society in two places implicitly or explicitly. Article 21 confers on everyone rights of political participation, and its third paragraph states explicitly that '[t]he will of the people shall be the basis of the authority of government'.[72] Article 29, the general limitations clause, further specifies that any limitations must be consonant with the requirements of 'a democratic society'.[73] The process embarked upon was by no means a self-fulfilling one. In 1960, after the admission of many former colonial nations to the UN, the General Assembly adopted Resolution 1514 (XV), the Declaration on the Granting of Independence to Colonial Countries and Peoples, which states that '[a]ll peoples have the right to self-determination' by virtue of which they 'freely determine their political status'.[74]

[72] UDHR, Art 21(3). [73] UDHR, Art 29(2).

[74] Declaration on the Granting of Independence to Colonial Countries and Peoples, UNGA Res 1514 (XV) (14 Dec 1960) (adopted by 89 votes to none; 9 abstentions), para 2. No State voted against the Resolution, but nine States (Australia, Belgium, the Dominican Republic, France, Portugal, Spain, South Africa, the United Kingdom, and the United States) abstained. UNGA 'Declaration on Granting Independence to Colonial Countries and Peoples' [1960] UNYB 49. Portugal entered a reservation in its explanation after the vote on A/PV.947 referring to its earlier declaration in A/PC.934, also reprinted by James Summers, *Peoples and International Law: How Nationalism and Self-Determination Shape a Contemporary Law of Nations* (Martinus Nijhoff 2007) 198, fn 286.

The intimate connection between democracy and self-determination should have made it possible, in the subsequent years, to refer to the requirements of a democratic society in an open way. Indeed, the two International Covenants of 1966 open with guarantees of self-determination in Article 1, a welcome consolidation of what, in 1945 and 1960, had essentially remained no more than a political goal. At the same time, the right to political participation, which the UDHR characterized as a 'common standard of achievement',[75] obtained the full binding force of a conventional commitment in ICCPR Article 25. Still, some of the limitations clauses refrain from inserting the requirement of a 'democratic society' as a condition for the admissibility of restrictive measures, in a clear departure from the rule established under Article 29 UDHR. The drafting history indicates that there was a clear reluctance during the negotiations to accept that condition. Only in a few provisions do the words 'in a democratic society' appear.[76] Article 19, freedom of expression, fails to include the phrase, despite its obvious necessity.[77] Notably, the Human Rights Committee has embraced an understanding of freedom of expression that does not differ from the views held within the framework of the ECHR,[78] where the words do appear.

In the ECHR, the criterion of a democratic society pervades the entire text. The preamble affirms that human rights and fundamental freedoms are 'best maintained' by an 'effective political democracy' and by a 'common understanding and observance of the human rights upon which they depend'.[79] Throughout, limitations clauses contain references to a democratic society.[80] Oddly, however, the original ECHR did not include a right of political participation; it came in two years later, when Protocol No 1 introduced the right of free elections, a right narrower in scope than the corresponding right that Article 21 UDHR enshrined.

The ACHR is somewhat more cautious in appealing to democratic principles. Its preamble affirms the intention to consolidate, 'within the framework of democratic institutions', a system of personal liberty and social justice.[81] However, the limitation clauses do not generally make the exigencies of a democratic society the yardstick for permissible restrictive measures.[82] The jurisprudence of the Inter-American Court of Human Rights has made clear, however, that the principle of democracy

[75] UDHR, preamble. [76] ICCPR, Arts 14(1), 21, 22.

[77] In 1950 and 1952, the Commission on Human Rights rejected France's motions to include the phrase 'in a democratic society' in Art 19, by votes of 8:5 and 8:8. cf Manfred Nowak, *UN Covenant on Civil and Political Rights: CCPR Commentary* (2nd edn, Engel 2005) 460.

[78] cf HRC, 'Article 19: Freedoms of Opinion and Expression' (2011) UN Doc CCPR/C/GC/34, paras 20, 23. [79] ECHR, preamble.

[80] ECHR, Arts 6(1), 8(2), 10(2), 11(2), 2(3); Protocol No 4 to the ECHR.

[81] ACHR, preamble.

[82] In ACHR Arts 15 (right of assembly), 16 (freedom of association), and 22 (freedom of movement and residence), such references are present, but the guarantee of freedom of expression, following the model of the ICCPR, abstains from referring to the requirements of a democratic society.

pervades the ACHR in its entirety.[83] Indeed, the Convention expressly provides a rule of interpretation that prohibits any provision in the text from being interpreted so as to 'preclud[e] other rights or guarantees that are inherent in the human personality or derived from representative democracy as a form of government'.[84]

The 1981 AfChHPR makes no mention of democratic principles as hurdles to governmental interference with human rights. The lacuna has been filled, however, by subsequent instruments which unequivocally embrace democracy as the only legitimate system of government in Africa, in particular the 2000 Constitutive Act of the African Union[85] and the 2007 Charter on Democracy, Elections and Good Governance. The African Commission on Human Rights has also contributed to effectuating democratic principles.[86] One of the Commission's relevant decisions addressed the King of Swaziland's assumption of all governmental powers and his ban on the formation of political parties. The Commission characterized the measures as unequivocally infringing on the right of every citizen, guaranteed in Article 13 AfChHPR, to participate freely in the government of the country.[87] In a consistent fashion, the regional organizations in Africa condemn military coups, denying such de facto governments international recognition. Thus, in March 2012, both the African Union (AU)[88] and the Economic Community of Western African States (which imposed severe economic and financial sanctions on the military regime)[89] unanimously criticized the overthrow of the civilian Government in Mali.

Three prominent global instruments capable of shedding light on the mutual relationship between human rights and democracy have been mentioned above: the Vienna Declaration and Programme of Action of the 1993 World Conference on Human Rights, the Millennium Declaration of 8 September 2000, and the World Summit Outcome of 16 September 2005. Another text dealing exclusively with the democratic system, General Assembly Resolution 55/96 of 4 December 2000, comprehensively particularizes the inferences which may be drawn from the concept of democracy.[90] It praises the virtues of liberal democracy through a partisan pamphlet, and its adoption encountered some resistance within the General Assembly. While no states voted against the resolution, sixteen developing states, largely in the Asian region, abstained[91] and deprived the resolution of an international consensus.

[83] *The Word 'Laws' in Article 30 of the American Convention on Human Rights*, para 34; *Yatama v Nicaragua*, para 192; *Claude-Reyes et al v Chile*, para 84; *Kimel v Argentina*, para 87.

[84] ACHR, Art 29(c).

[85] Constitutive Act of the African Union, Arts 3(g), 4(m).

[86] *Interights et al v Islamic Republic of Mauritania*, para 80; *Article 19* (n 58) para 106; *Zimbabwe Lawyers for Human Rights v Zimbabwe*, paras 92, 95.

[87] *Lawyers for Human Rights v Swaziland.*

[88] Mali's membership was immediately suspended.

[89] Economic Community of West African States (ECOWAS), 'ECOWAS Joint Chiefs of Defence Staff Hold Emergency Meeting on Mali Crisis' (5 April 2012) Press Release No 098/2012 <http://news.ecowas.int/presseshow.php?nb=098&lang=en&annee=2012> accessed 15 July 2012.

[90] UNGA, 'Promoting and Consolidating Democracy' (4 December 2000) UN Doc A/Res/55/96.

[91] cf UNGA, 'Reports of the Third Committee' (2000) UN Doc A/55/PV.81, para 16: Bahrain, Bhutan, Brunei Darussalam, China, Cuba, Democratic Republic of the Congo, Honduras, Lao People's

It is significant, in this regard, that the subsequent World Summit Outcome characterizes democracy as a 'value' only, not as a legal norm.[92]

In reference to the recent democratic uprisings in the Arab world ('Arabellion'), the Security Council has clearly favoured endeavours aimed at democratic reform. Although it seems not to consider democracy a legally binding precept in the same manner as some of the regional organizations, it does not hesitate to support democratic aspirations if the population concerned has manifested its desire to change the governing regime. This leaves the democratic principle in a somewhat hybrid twilight situation. Although not constituting a legal requirement, it has become a legitimate guideline for international community action in reshaping the domestic legal order of a country in danger of anarchy.

The Security Council also views the establishment of democratic institutions as a strategy to discharge its mandate of securing international peace and security, as seen in regard to Haiti[93] and Côte d'Ivoire.[94] With regard to Libya after the fall of the dictatorship, the Security Council expressed its support for the 'Libyan-led transition and rebuilding process aimed at establishing a democratic, independent and united Libya'.[95] For Syria, as well, agreement was reached on a Presidential Statement which identifies the introduction of democratic institutions as one of the key aims of international action.[96]

The democratization of the international order has become a controversial counterweight to the demands for democracy in domestic settings. Under that heading, the developing countries have sought a greater say in the regulation of international matters. On 19 December 2011, the General Assembly approved a Resolution on 'Promotion of a democratic and equitable international order'[97] by a vote of 130 in favour to fifty-four against, with six abstentions. Western states cast all the opposing votes.[98] In turn, the Human Rights Council has appointed an independent expert

Democratic Republic, Libyan Arab Jamahiriya, Maldives, Myanmar, Oman, Qatar, Saudi Arabia, Swaziland, and Viet Nam.

92 UNGA, '2005 World Summit Outcome' (16 September 2005) UN Doc A/Res/60/1, para 135.

93 UNSC Res 2012 (14 October 2011) UN Doc S/Res/2012, para 6.

94 UNSC Res 2000 (27 July 2011) UN Doc S/Res/2000, preamble, para 11.

95 UNSC Res 2040 (12 March 2012) UN Doc S/Res/2040, para 12.

96 UNSC Presidential Statement 6 (2012) UN Doc S/PRST/2012/6: 'The Security Council expresses its full support for the efforts of the Envoy to bring an immediate end to all violence and human rights violations, secure humanitarian access, and facilitate a Syrian-led political transition to a democratic, plural political system, in which citizens are equal regardless of their affiliations or ethnicities or beliefs, including through commencing a comprehensive political dialogue between the Syrian government and the whole spectrum of the Syrian opposition.'

97 UNGA Res 66/159 (19 December 2011) UN Doc A/Res/66/159. A long list of similar resolutions in earlier years, starting with UNGA Res 55/107 (4 December 2000) UN Doc A/Res/55/107, preceded it.

98 See UNGA 'General Assembly Adopts More than 60 Resolutions Recommended by Third Committee, Including Text Condemning Grave, Systematic Human Rights Violations in Syria' (19 December 2011) Press Release GA/11198, Annex X. The six abstentions came from Argentina, Armenia, Chile, Costa Rica, Mexico, and Peru.

to explore that problematique.[99] The new mechanism may not yield any concrete results, given the measure of disunity the voting pattern has shown, which reflects more on a conflict about leadership at the world level and less on any disagreement over the democratic principle.

4. The Legal Nature of the Rule of Law and Democracy

Ultimately, the question is whether the rule of law and democracy exert any positive impact on the realization of human rights. While this may be the most useful test in examining their interrelationships, it is necessary to examine the general connotation of the two concepts before undertaking such an assessment.

4.1 The rule of law

Regarding the rule of law, a clear alternative exists. On the one hand, one may view the rule of law as a principle that has autonomous content as a binding legal rule. Thus, it might be possible to examine a specific set of facts with the rule of law as a yardstick, concluding eventually that a given action was lawful or unlawful. Since no international instrument enshrines the rule of law as an independent proposition, one would have to look for its legal foundation in the general principles of international law, as mentioned in Article 38 of the Statute of the International Court of Justice.[100] One may question, however, whether that specific class of rules really covers the concept. The legal precepts the concept of the rule of law encompasses do indeed contain rules of conduct, but it is not the concept in and of itself which imparts orders on how to behave correctly.

Everything militates for conceiving the rule of law as a common denominator which has an exclusively descriptive value. It embodies a call for action as a matter of legal policy. As soon as such a demand has been satisfied, it takes on its own identity. It may still reflect the rule of law, but the rule of law then essentially appears as the philosophical background of the new rule. Essentially, the rule of law is the synthesis of all the more detailed rules, regulations, and mechanisms which, derived from the key idea of protecting the individual through the instrument of law, seek to establish an environment where he or she can live without fear. It is significant,

[99] At its 19th session on 23 March 2012, the Human Rights Council appointed Mr Alfred de Zayas as Special Rapporteur. [100] UN Charter, annex.

in this regard, that the scholarly articles concerning the rule of law provide long lists of legislative acts and judicial decisions which may be assembled under the all-encompassing roof of the rule of law.

From a general perspective, one may view the combination of the rule of law and democracy as a structural device designed to ensure the rationality of the law. Law should be the outcome of a well-pondered process involving the population in its entirety. Statutes that parliamentary assemblies adopt have necessarily gone through a process of public scrutiny where the pros and cons of the planned regulation have been scrutinized. The parliamentary process permits of no concealment. Thus, the combination of the rule of law and democracy is not only directed against secret law-making, but also against traditional rules that have never been put to the test of rational reflection, deriving their authority from their traditional and historical roots.

For many Western states, where the process of government modernization started in the eighteenth century, this does not amount to a challenge to their identity. For some developing nations, however, that still found their internal stability, to a great extent, on ancestral patterns of life, the requirements that the rule of law and democracy establish can lead to a clash of values which it may be hard to overcome. One should not abdicate in front of claims that the modernity of the rule of law destroys good order and national stability. More often than not, such complaints mask the arbitrariness of a dictatorial regime that does not wish to have any rational rule bind it, invoking instead ossified patterns of predominance of one group over the others which society should have reviewed or abandoned long since. Not all traditions are good per se. Those that conflict with human dignity and grossly discriminate against a specific group of the population do not merit being maintained in a world where human dignity and equality have become the leading parameters for societal development.

4.2 Democracy

Democracy has a different nature. Democracy is a mechanism for the generation of legitimate governments able to make claims for general obedience. In the Europe that has united under the auspices of the Council of Europe and the European Union, democracy is a legally binding standard. Article 7 TEU provides for a special procedure under which states that grossly infringe the common values of the EU, among them the principle of democracy, may be investigated. As a sanction, specific rights of the State concerned may be suspended, including voting rights in the Council. Thus, effective mechanisms are available to ensure that democracy remains a living reality in all member States. It stands to reason that legislation enacted by bodies that do not fulfil the requirements of democratic legitimacy is structurally subject to suspicion. In particular, under such circumstances, the assumption that fundamental human rights are no longer well safe-guarded is inescapable.

Some have pointed out that democracy does not have the same quality as a binding legal principle at the universal level. The fact that some of the limitation clauses of the ICCPR refer to the standard of a democratic society cannot be taken to mean that any non-democratic regime is automatically contrary to international law. As long as the UN is open to all states, one may not draw any such inference. On the other hand, one may safely take the view that democracy today is considered the only truly legitimate form of government.

5. Taking Stock

This last section is devoted to ascertaining what the rule of law and the democratic principle may mean for the status of human rights in practice.

5.1 The rule of law

Many times throughout history, societies have lost their internal cohesiveness and developed into dictatorships that maintain their power by adopting laws or issuing decrees suppressing all political opposition, including through extensive use of the death penalty. In Nazi Germany, the government could sanction any criticism of the government by death, on the basis of officially promulgated legal enactments. The regime openly threatened its own people with deprivation of liberty and with capital punishment. On the other hand, the Nazi leadership did not publicly announce its intention to exterminate the Jewish people, and the instructions directing the security forces to kill the Jewish population in the occupied territories never received the formal hallmark of a legal statute. Hitler's Order No 1 of 11 January 1940 declared the extermination strategy top secret.[101]

The law as an instrument of oppression constitutes a fundamental challenge to the rule of law. In such instances, the law, losing its dignity, degenerates into a tool that power wielders handle exclusively for their own interests and, possibly in their eyes, for the interest of the nation as they interpret it. Calling such enactments 'laws' is justified only in an empirical, sociological sense as long as it can be observed that an obedient judiciary applies them. Lawyers may shy away from lending the label of law to commands that are devoid of any trace of goodness. In any event, the management of public affairs in a given country can be so far away from justice

[101] See Alfred de Zayas, *Völkermord als Staatsgeheimnis* (Olzog 2011) 47. On Hitler's camouflage strategy in general, see Sarah Gordon, *Hitler, Germans, and the 'Jewish Question'* (Princeton UP 1984) 142.

and equity that the concept of the rule of law may become a mockery. Whoever has endured injustice by law for decades, and perhaps even centuries, will not easily praise the rule of law.

Seen from the viewpoint of international human rights, the rule of law requires that the domestic legal orders of the contracting states effectively implement the international guarantees. The old doctrine still prevails, however, that except for specific stipulations ordering otherwise, states are free to execute their international commitments as they see fit. They are not obligated to transpose the international texts *tels quels* into their domestic legal orders.[102] The United States refrained from making the ICCPR part of its domestic law. In a 'Declaration' appended to its instrument of ratification it specified 'that the provisions of Articles 1 through 27 of the Covenant are not self-executing'.[103] At the same time, it declined to ratify the Optional Protocol providing for individual communications to be submitted to the Human Rights Committee. While the US Declaration is lawful,[104] its consequences have proved fatal to efforts to enforce the ICCPR.[105]

International supervisory bodies have decided hundreds of cases, finding that a national statute infringed one or another of the guarantees in the relevant international instrument. The essential demand in such cases is that the domestic instrument be corrected and brought into line with the international commitment. One may glean the richest yield, measured in practical terms, from the jurisprudence of the ECtHR regarding the requirements that must be met to lawfully enforce a legal rule meant to restrict a human right or fundamental freedom.[106] As already pointed out, the ECtHR is particularly demanding with respect to the justification of such restrictive measures. In all of the provisions which permit interference, a law that satisfies the criteria of a 'democratic society' is necessary for that purpose. In one

[102] *James et al v UK*, para 84; *Observer and Guardian v UK*, para 76. The United Kingdom insisted on that position when the ECHR was adopted, and only after many years did the British Parliament integrate the ECHR into the internal legal order of the United Kingdom through the Human Rights Act 1998.

[103] Reprinted in Hurst Hannum and Dana Fischer (eds), *US Ratification of the International Covenants on Human Rights* (Transnational Publishers 1993) 329.

[104] The Human Rights Committee implicitly acknowledged this when examining the first US Report. 'Report of the Human Rights Committee, Vol I' (1996) UN Doc A/50/40, para 279.

[105] In the proceedings that were conducted with respect to the inmates of the military detention centre established in Guantánamo (Cuba), the ICCPR could not play a significant role. It appears that it was never mentioned in any of the relevant judgments. Apart from the exclusion of the self-executing character of the instrument, the US government has made an argument that the ICCPR does not apply extra-territorially. UNHRC, 'Consideration of Reports Submitted by States Parties under Article 40 of the Covenant: United States of America' (28 November 2005) UN Doc CCPR/C/USA/3, para 109. The Human Rights Committee has convincingly refuted this contention. HRC, 'General Comment No 31: Nature of the General Legal Obligation on States Parties to the Covenant' (29 March 2004) UN Doc CCPR/C/21/Rev.1/Add.13, para 10.

[106] For a comprehensive overview, see Jens Meyer-Ladewig, 'The Rule of Law in the Case Law of the Strasbourg Court' in Hermann-Josef Blanke and Stelio Mangiameli (eds), *The European Union after Lisbon: Constitutional Basis, Economic Order and External Action* (Springer 2012) 233–49.

of its earlier decisions, the ECtHR specified that laws restricting a guaranteed right must serve a 'pressing social need', thereby initiating a consistent jurisprudence.[107] With respect to freedom of expression, this formula has been translated as requiring pluralism, tolerance, and broadmindedness.[108] Thus all laws restricting a guaranteed right must be the outcome of a careful balancing process, weighing the public interest at issue, relevant on account of the claw-back clause concerned, against the private interest that guarantee protects.

The ECtHR does not accept national doctrines according to which the executive branch may do anything that is not specifically forbidden. A prominent early case (*Malone*) concerned telephone wiretapping in the United Kingdom, where it was clear that the authorities had no legislative mandate for their actions.[109] The judges in the United Kingdom were fully aware of the violation of the ECHR, but they could not issue a judgment on that ground, because the ECHR was not part of domestic law at that time. Later cases reiterated the proposition *Malone* set forth,[110] which now stands very firm: any interference with one of the rights and freedoms under the ECHR requires a legal basis. The Inter-American Court of Human Rights has based its jurisprudence on the same premise.[111] It emphasizes legality as one of the pillars of the system for the protection of human rights.[112] The African Commission on Human Rights has also adopted this method.[113]

This principle of legality requires determining whether a formal act of the legislature is required or whether other forms of legal regulation are sufficient to limit the exercise of a human right or freedom. In general, only legal rules that a democratic parliamentary body has enacted have gone through a process of public scrutiny providing opportunities to detect any possible shortcomings with the proposed legal norm. In the jurisprudence of the ECtHR, the *Sunday Times* case[114] required a determination as to whether British common law, ie rules having developed as a result of judicial practice, provided a suitable legal foundation for imposing fines. The *Sunday Times* newspaper had been fined for reporting, in the public interest, on a case still pending before the British courts. The government justified the fines as sanctions deriving from contempt of court, for which no statutory regulation existed. The ECtHR, faced with having to interpret the concept of law, stated in a straightforward manner that the word covered not only statutory but also unwritten law.[115] Later, the Court explained in its judgment in *Kruslin* that had it declared

[107] *Handyside v UK*, para 48. The IACtHR has also adopted the phrase. See *Fontevecchia and D'Amico v Argentina*, para 54.

[108] See eg from the recent jurisprudence *Palomo Sánchez* (n 69) para 53.

[109] *Malone v UK*, para 67. [110] *Khan v UK*, paras 27, 28; *Copland v UK*, paras 47, 48.

[111] *The Word 'Laws' in Article 30* (n 83) paras 21, 22, 24.

[112] See, from the most recent jurisprudence, *Fontevecchia* (n 107) para 52.

[113] See Viljoen (n 59) 348–53. [114] *Sunday Times v UK*.

[115] *Sunday Times* (n 114) para 49. See also *Casado Coca v Spain*, para 43. The HRC shares this view: HRC 'Dissanayake v Sri Lanka: Views' (22 July 2008) UN Doc CCPR/C/93/D/1373/2005, para 8.2.

common law as not fulfilling the requirement of 'law', it would have 'struck at the very roots' of the UK's legal system.[116]

In contrast, the Inter-American Court of Human Rights (IACtHR) has held that the word 'laws' in Article 30 ACHR 'can have no other meaning than that of formal law, that is, a legal norm passed by the legislature and promulgated by the Executive Branch, pursuant to the procedure set out in the domestic law of each State'.[117] The IACtHR also admits restrictions enacted on the basis of valid delegations of law-making authority,[118] but, despite the fact that it mentions the *Sunday Times*, seems to have rejected customary law in the form of common law as capable of authorizing restrictive measures.

The ECtHR continues to manifest a high degree of liberalism—or carelessness—in accepting any form of legal rule. Thus, in *Sanome Uitgevers v Netherlands*,[119] it held that the term 'law' is to be understood in its substantive sense, including written law, ie parliamentary acts, enactments of lower-ranking statutes, and regulatory measures that professional regulatory bodies take under independent rule-making powers that parliament delegates to them, and unwritten law.[120] Additionally, the ECtHR counts as law any judge-made rules. 'In sum, the "law" is the provision in force as the competent courts have interpreted it.'[121] This proposition may well be acceptable with regard to ordinary cases lacking any particular gravity. However, the ECtHR has also embraced the same doctrine with regard to instances of criminal offences, considering also that with regard to the establishment of such offences, all legal norms are of the same value, none of them having to be excluded.[122] As a matter of principle, however, one should not accept that criminal offences may be established in any manner whatsoever. In this field, in particular, democratic legitimacy is an indispensable requirement. As already pointed out, the IACtHR has shown a more acute awareness of this aspect.[123] In those cases which have come before it, the AfCHPR has also insisted that only laws which are compatible with the obligations that the AfChHPR enshrines may restrict those rights that that instrument guarantees.[124]

The Human Rights Committee (HRC) under the ICCPR shares the view of the ECtHR that laws do not have to be of parliamentary origin. It explicitly acknowledges rules of common law, such as those providing penalties for contempt of court,

[116] *Kruslin v France*, para 29. For the most recent reflection of the case law, see *Huhtamäki v Finland*, paras 43–44. [117] *The Word 'Laws' in Article 30* (n 83) para 27.

[118] *The Word 'Laws' in Article 30* (n 83) para 36. [119] Paragraph 83.

[120] See also *Şahin v Turkey*, para 88; *Kononov v Latvia*, para 185; *Huhtamäki* (n 116) paras 43–44.

[121] *Şahin* (n 120) para 88. [122] *Kafkaris v Cyprus*, para 139.

[123] See, in particular, *Fontevecchia* (n 107) para 86, where the Court emphasizes that restrictions on freedom of expression based on criminal law 'must be formulated previously, in an express, accurate, and restrictive manner'.

[124] See *Jawara* (n 58) paras 58–68; *Ouko v Kenya*; *The Law Office of Ghazi Suleiman v Sudan*; *Zegveld and Ephrem v Eritrea*, para 62.

as capable of limiting freedom of expression.[125] On the other hand, the HRC has explicitly stated that it is not compatible with the ICCPR to impose restrictions enshrined in 'traditional, religious or other such customary law'.[126]

Since its beginnings, the ECtHR has insisted on the requisite inherent qualities of a law. Whatever its origin, a legal rule purporting to interfere with a human right or fundamental freedom must be accessible to the public, and second, the rule must be formulated with the requisite degree of precision.[127] For the citizen, what is demanded must be foreseeable so that the person can behave accordingly. The IACtHR has also embraced this line of reasoning.[128]

The ECtHR has acknowledged from early on that an emphasis on precision and predictability may lead to excessive rigour which is then likely to considerably impede the application of the law in practice. There must be some margin of interpretation. The law must keep pace with developments, and an abstract legal text can never meet all the characteristics of a case that is located in a borderline area.[129] In principle, this acceptance of some cautious degree of flexibility is warranted, although it involves obvious dangers if the judicial function is entrusted to judges not truly independent or committed to the common weal.

The ECtHR has found in some cases that a specific regulation did not reach the required degree of precision—most often, curiously enough, in matters relating to wiretapping. In *Kruslin*, the Court found that the applicable French regime was exceedingly complex, did not provide sufficient legal certainty, and lacked adequate safeguards against various possible abuses.[130] In a case brought against Switzerland, the Court similarly held that the rules to which public authorities had resorted were not sufficiently clear and detailed to afford appropriate protection against interference with the applicant's right to respect for private life and correspondence.[131]

Attention must be drawn, finally, to a judgment on issues of principle with regard to laws enacted under a dictatorial regime. In *Streletz, Kessler, and Krenz*,[132] the ECtHR had to delve into the past. Former state agents of the German Democratic Republic (GDR) applied against their convictions for involvement in killing persons trying to flee the country by climbing over the wall of separation. One of the main defence arguments was that all the individuals involved had acted in accordance with the legislation in force. In the first place, the Court dismissed the contention

[125] HRC, 'Dissanayake' (n 115) para 8.2. [126] *Article 19* (n 78) para 24.

[127] *Sunday Times* (n 114) para 49; *Silver et al v UK*, paras 87–88; *Malone* (n 109) para 70; *Kruslin* (n 116) para 30; *De Geouffre de la Pradelle v France*, paras 33–35. From the most recent jurisprudence, see *Atanasovski v Former Yugoslav Republic of Macedonia*, para 38 (but no right to the maintenance of an established jurisprudence); *Dadouch v Malta*, para 52; *A et al v Ireland*, para 220; *Huhtamäki* (n 116) para 43.

[128] *López Mendoza v Venezuela*, paras 199–202; *Barrios Family v Venezuela*, para 49.

[129] See *Silver* (n 127) para 88; *Hasan and Chaush v Bulgaria*, para 84; *Şahin* (n 120) para 91; *Kafkaris* (n 122) para 141; *Scoppola v Italy*, para 100; *Kononov* (n 120) para 185.

[130] *Kruslin* (n 116) paras 34, 35. See also *Fontevecchia* (n 107) paras 89–90.

[131] *Amann v Switzerland*, paras 55–62 [132] *Streletz et al v Germany*.

that the applicable legal GDR statutes enjoined shooting fleeing persons to death. Secondly, however, the Court introduced a principled argument: even if the legislation had contained such a command, it would have been devoid of any legal force:

> The Court considers that a State practice such as the GDR's border-policing policy, which flagrantly infringes human rights and above all the right to life, the supreme value in the international hierarchy of human rights, cannot be covered by the protection of Article 7 § 1 of the Convention. That practice, which emptied of its substance the legislation on which it was supposed to be based, and which was imposed on all organs of the GDR, including its judicial bodies, cannot be described as 'law' within the meaning of Article 7 of the Convention.[133]

This statement is also in full accordance with paragraph 2 of the same provision, which provides that the ban on retroactivity does not apply to offences which are criminal 'according to the general principles of law recognised by civilised nations'.[134] On similar grounds, in *Kononov v Latvia* the ECtHR came to the conclusion that the respondent had not acted unlawfully by convicting Kononov of committing a war crime, since the acts underlying the conviction had constituted a gross infringement of international humanitarian law. The ECtHR has made clear that a dictatorship cannot prevent criminal prosecution of its members by clothing its misdeeds with the formal coat of a 'law' before surrendering to democratic forces.

In sum, the rule of law, as embodied in the ECHR, contains elements which contribute considerably to strengthening the protection of the individual. However, as a judicial body, the ECtHR cannot introduce sweeping reforms since it is bound to adjudicate the requests submitted to it.[135] Decisions of the politically responsible authorities will remain necessary to bring about system change—getting rid of habits that give political considerations precedence over legal rules.

5.2 Democracy

The requirements connected with a 'democratic society' have also played an important role in the case law of the ECtHR. The Court coined the felicitous formula that a democratic society distinguishes itself by three criteria: pluralism, tolerance, and broadmindedness. Accordingly it held that, in particular, freedom of expression covers not only ideas 'that are favourably received or regarded as inoffensive or as a matter of indifference, but also . . . those that offend, shock or disturb the State or any sector of the

[133] *Streletz* (n 132) para 87. [134] ECHR, Art 7(2).

[135] To some extent, the ECtHR has gone beyond individual decision-making through the use of pilot judgments, where governments are enjoined to deal in the same manner with specific factual patterns bearing identical features, even with regard to cases which were not yet pending. *Broniowski v Poland*; *Hutten-Czapska v Poland*, paras 231–39.

population'.[136] For the Court, extreme vigilance is called for where the genuineness of the political process is at stake. Any ban on political parties must therefore be submitted to strict scrutiny. This firm position has led the Court into an acrimonious confrontation with Turkey on some occasions. It declared many such bans incompatible with the obligations under the ECHR.[137] The African Commission on Human Rights also pronounced a verdict on the dissolution of a political party in Mauritania, holding it to be contrary to freedom of association under Article 10 AfChHPR.[138] As noted above, it made the same assessment with regard to a general ban on political parties issued by the King of Swaziland.[139]

Generally, the ECtHR acknowledges that the states parties to the ECHR enjoy a certain margin of appreciation when assessing whether a restrictive measure is necessary according to the relevant limitations clause.[140] The Court has relied mainly on two arguments to justify limiting its review of such measures. On the one hand, it has observed that national authorities are in more direct and continuous contact with the vital forces of the country concerned, so they can better assess the local needs and conditions.[141] On the other hand, the ECtHR has also stressed its subsidiary role, derived from the direct democratic legitimation of the national authorities.[142] Accordingly, the ECtHR does not rigorously or strictly scrutinize the balancing of the interests involved. The Court has applied the doctrine of the margin of appreciation essentially to societal phenomena with typically national features, in particular with respect to sensitive issues of ethics and morals, primarily sexual morals.[143] By contrast, whenever issues relating directly to the democratic process in a society are concerned, the Court has unwaveringly upheld a common standard, not permitting any deviations. It has explicitly stated that there is little scope under Article 10(2) for restrictions on political speech or on the debate of questions of public interest.[144] Thus, it has become one of the staunchest supporters of democratic institutions in Europe.

Like the ECtHR, the IACtHR has, from its inception, emphasized the crucial importance of freedom of expression in a democratic society. From this perspective, it has always held that persons in public life cannot claim the same level of

[136] *Handyside* (n 107) para 49. This line of reasoning has been consistently maintained, see ultimately *Bayatyan v Armenia*, para 126; *Palomo Sánchez* (n 69) para 53.

[137] *United Communist Party of Turkey et al v Turkey*; *Socialist Party v Turkey*; *Freedom and Democratic Party v Turkey*. Only in one case was the dissolution of a political party considered justifiable under the ECHR: *Refah Partisi (the Welfare Party) v Turkey*. A similar verdict was rendered against Russia on account of the dissolution of the Republican Party of Russia. *Republican Party of Russia v Russia*.

[138] *Interights* (n 87) para 80.

[139] *Lawyers for Human Rights v Swaziland* (n 88) para 53.

[140] The point of departure was the judgment in *Handyside* (n 107) para 48.

[141] *Handyside* (n 107) para 48. From the more recent jurisprudence, see *A et al* (n 127) para 232; *Van der Heijden v Netherlands*, para 55.

[142] *Hatton v UK*, para 97; *Van der Heijden* (n 141) para 55.

[143] *Handyside* (n 107) para 48; *Müller et al v Switzerland*, para 36; *A et al* (n 127) para 232; *Van der Heijden* (n 141) para 60. A stricter control yardstick was applied in *Vereinigung Bildender Künstler v Austria*.

[144] *Sürek v Turkey (No 1)*, para 61; *Feldek v Slovakia*, para 74; *Fratanoló v Hungary*, para 24.

protection of honour and reputation as ordinary citizens. In an open democracy, judicial injunctions must not stifle criticism on matters of public interest.[145] The AfCHPR has followed this line without reservations.[146] One may conclude that the jurisprudence of the ECtHR has set the tone that is now generally accepted. Democratic governance requires public accountability, for which freedom of speech, in particular freedom of the press, is the primary instrument.

6. Conclusion

The rule of law and democracy are elements that constitute essential pillars promoting real enjoyment of human rights. However, on their part, too, they are dependent on the general conditions prevailing within society. Supervision by international bodies has emerged as one of the primary forces able to ensure the effectiveness of the guarantees set forth in today's international instruments for the protection of human rights.

Further Reading

Chesterman S, 'Rule of Law' in *The Max Planck Encyclopedia of Public International Law*, Vol VIII (Rüdiger Wolfrum (ed), OUP 2012) 1014–22
Fitschen T, 'Inventing the Rule of Law for the United Nations' in *Max Planck Yearbook of United Nations Law* 12 (2008) 347–80
Fuller LL, *The Morality of Law* (revised edn, Yale UP 1969)
Peerenboom RP, 'Varieties of Rule of Law: An Introduction and Provisional Conclusion' in Peerenboom RP (ed), *Asian Discourses of Rule of Law* (RoutledgeCurzon 2004) 113–45
Rawls J, 'The Rule of Law' in *A Theory of Justice* (Harvard UP 1971) 235–43
Raz J, 'The Rule of Law and its Virtue' in *The Authority of Law. Essays on Law and Morality* (OUP 1979) 210–29
Sen A, 'Human Rights and Global Imperatives' in *The Idea of Justice* (Allen Lane 2009) 355–87

[145] *Compulsory Membership in an Association Prescribed by Law for the Practice of Journalism*, paras 42, 44; *'The Last Temptation of Christ' (Olmedo Bustos et al) v Chile*, paras 68–69; *Ivcher-Bronstein v Peru*, paras 149–155; *Ricardo Canese v Paraguay*, para 82; *Palamara-Iribarne v Chile*, paras 79–88; *Claude-Reyes* (n 93) para 85; *Ríos et al v Venezuela*, para 105; *Perozo et al v Venezuela*, para 116; *Usón Ramírez v Venezuela*, para 47; *Fontevecchia* (n 107) paras 44–45.

[146] See above decisions to which n 123 refers.

PART IV

NORMATIVE EVOLUTION

CHAPTER 21

THE LAW-MAKING PROCESS: FROM DECLARATION TO TREATY TO CUSTOM TO PREVENTION

BERTRAND G RAMCHARAN

1. Introduction

The law-making process in the area of the international law of human rights has special characteristics that set it apart from most other areas of international law. It shares with international law in general the idea of the international rule of law and a quest for justice for humanity, but its focus is on individuals, on groups, and on people. This people-based, missionary character of the international law of human rights has influenced the law-making processes; an idea originates within the human rights movement, it is formulated as a possible draft declaration or convention, a draft is floated, and there is lobbying for the relevant United Nations (UN) body to take up the proposal. After all of this occurs, there are different contributors to the drafting process: individuals, experts, organizations, governmental experts or representatives, members of the UN Secretariat, and the deliberative bodies of the UN. The contributions culminate in the UN General Assembly, where governments are in charge, but where the lobbying of human rights actors is influential.[1] Unlike in the case of the International Law Commission, for example, for the most part there is no mid- or long-term plan of action for law-making and no conscious process of drafting in an expert body prior to the government level taking up the draft. The former Sub-Commission of the then Commission on Human Rights did do some expert studies and recommend drafts to the Commission; and if the current Human Rights Council so chooses, its Advisory Committee may prepare a draft, as it did recently with a draft declaration on human rights education.[2] At the outset in 1947, the former Commission on Human Rights adopted a plan for an International Bill of Human Rights[3] and subsequently produced drafts of the Universal Declaration of Human Rights (UDHR) and of the two Covenants.[4] The UN Secretariat contributed to this process, as did member states and civil society organizations. However, unlike in the example of the UN Commission on International Trade Law, the adoption of legal instruments is largely a process of innovation and improvisation, bearing the imprints of the members of the international human rights movement.[5]

Solid examples of initiatives within the human rights movement are the Declaration[6] and then the Convention against Torture (CAT). Amnesty International judged that anti-torture efforts would be helped if there were a UN Declaration against Torture. It lobbied for the UN Committee on Crime Prevention and Control to undertake work on this proposal and provided drafting suggestions. Based on the work within this Committee, the quinquennial UN Crime Congress adopted the Declaration against Torture. Amnesty International followed up by lobbying for a Convention against Torture. Another forum, the then Commission on Human Rights, took up this work. After negotiations within the Commission—with drafting inputs from Amnesty International—the General Assembly adopted the Convention against Torture and opened it for signature and ratification, or accession. This pattern has

[1] International relations specialists have described this process as a 'constructivist' approach to norm formation in the international community. See Thomas Risse, Stephen C Ropp, and Kathryn Sikkink (eds), *The Power of Human Rights: International Norms and Domestic Change* (CUP 1999).

[2] Based on the work of the Advisory Committee and the Human Rights Council, the General Assembly subsequently adopted a Declaration on Human Rights Education and Training. UNGA Res 66/137 (16 February 2012) UN Doc A/Res/66/137.

[3] See the Report of the Commission on its First Session in 1947. UN Economic and Social Council, 'Report of the Commission on Human Rights' (1947) UN Doc E/259.

[4] The International Covenant on Civil and Political Rights; the International Covenant on Economic, Social and Cultural Rights.

[5] For a discussion of the multilateral treaty-making process in the field of human rights, see Vera Gowlland-Debbas (ed), *Multi-lateral Treaty-making* (Martinus Nijhoff 2000).

[6] Declaration on the Protection of All Persons from Being Subjected to Torture and Other Cruel, Inhuman or Degrading Treatment or Punishment.

been repeated on numerous occasions, including, more recently, the drafting and passage of the Convention against Enforced and Involuntary Disappearances.

Based on the foundations of the present international human rights normative order, it might be appropriate for the UN Human Rights Council to consider the creation of periodic work plans for new standard-setting backed by expert studies, before it decides to commence a drafting exercise.[7] Considerations of planning and orderliness could support such an approach. However, nothing should be done to diminish a special and invaluable feature of the law-making process—namely, that when the human rights movement determines that there is a problem and that drafting standards could help deal with the problem, it may mount an initiative to draft such standards. The law-making process is, and should remain, in the hands of members of the human rights movement.

With the foregoing observations in mind, this chapter proposes to proceed along the following course: first, to give a conspectus of the drafting process, in relation to both declarations and conventions; second, to consider the contributions of declarations and conventions to the codification and progressive development of international law; third, to consider the transformation of declaration provisions into international customary law; fourth, to perform the same analysis in respect of convention provisions; and fifth, to offer some general reflections on the human rights law-making process.

2. The Drafting Process for Declarations and Conventions

From the outset, the UN has followed flexible approaches with regard to drafting declarations and conventions. The former Commission on Human Rights, its former Sub-Commission (upon request), the Committee on Crime Prevention and Control, the quinquennial Congresses on Crime Prevention and Control, the Commission on the Status of Women, and the Third (Social and Humanitarian) and Sixth (Legal) Committees of the UN General Assembly have prepared drafts of declarations and treaties. In most instances, the General Assembly has been the final adopting body, but sometimes other arenas have taken this role, as in the case of the UN Crime Congress and the Declaration against Torture. There have been few if any instances of drafting conferences, such as the UN conferences on the law of treaties, diplomatic relations, or the law of the sea. At one stage, the Office of the

[7] See Bertrand G Ramcharan, *The UN Human Rights Council* (Routledge 2011).

High Commissioner for Refugees convened a worldwide conference on the issue of the definition of asylum, but the conference did not reach any agreement.

Some years ago, the UN disseminated a publication on the multilateral treaty-making process, with an extensive chapter that this author wrote on the multilateral treaty-making process in the field of human rights.[8] That chapter examined the drafting process of human rights-related treaties, from the time of the League of Nations until the mid-1980s, and found great diversity in the approaches and processes followed. The same findings would, in all probability, hold true today (some twenty-five years later). One can therefore note the principle of flexibility in the drafting of both declarations and conventions. Going beyond this insight, it is helpful to touch on some thematic issues related to the drafting process.

2.1 Plans of action for drafting new norms

When the United Nations International Law Commission began its work shortly after the establishment of the UN, the UN Secretariat commissioned Professor Sir Hersch Lauterpacht to prepare an expert survey of international law which extensively reviewed topics that the Commission could possibly consider for inclusion in its work programme.[9] The Commission eventually adopted a long-range work plan to which it more or less adhered. There has been at least one other expert Secretariat survey thereafter, as well as periodic updates of the Commission's work-plans.

The human rights field has not followed this approach. The then Commission on Human Rights began its work with a mandate to prepare an International Bill of Human Rights that would eventually contain the Universal Declaration of Human Rights, the two Covenants, and some measures for implementation. This vision guided the Commission in its first decade. While working on the International Bill, however, the Commission did prepare other normative drafts, and the process of drafting of declarations and conventions continues today.

A certain measure of planning could be detected in the former Sub-Commission of the Commission. Massive human rights problems plagued the early days of the UN. The Sub-Commission, at the request of the Commission, conducted a series of studies on the rights of minorities and indigenous populations—including on issues of equality. The Commission guided the work-plan of the Sub-Commission, inasmuch as it was the Commission which decided for the most part whether

[8] See the UN Legislative Series: International Law Commission, 'Review of the Multilateral Treaty-Making Process' (23 July 1979) UN Doc A/CN.4/325.

[9] UN General Assembly, 'Survey of International Law in Relation to the Work of Codification of the International Law Commission' (1949) UN Doc A/CN.4/1/Rev.1.

the Sub-Commission should work on a topic. The Commission, from time to time, requested that the Sub-Commission update it on the status of its work and, in particular, on studies under consideration. This was more a form of rationalization, but there were some shades of planning in it. The Sub-Commission's successor, the Advisory Committee of the Human Rights Council, may take up topics only at the request of the Council. As far as the normative drafting process is concerned, there has not, so far, been an Advisory Committee work plan for the drafting of new norms.

Similarly, other human rights bodies have not followed a practice of drafting normative work plans. Nor, unlike in the International Labour Organization (ILO), have there been instances of expert reports from the United Nations Secretariat reviewing or discussing the normative drafting processes. Keeping in mind the flexibility that has so far characterized the drafting process, a case could be made for periodic UN Secretariat studies or Expert Surveys that might influence bodies like the Human Rights Council in their choice of topics to work on in the future. There has been no such study to date.

A particular recurring issue concerns proposals for protocols or supplementary treaties to existing treaties. When the initiative for the drafting of what is now the Convention against Torture arose, the Government of Sweden proposed that the initiative could be a supplement to the International Covenant on Civil and Political Rights and that the Human Rights Committee could supervise it. The Centre for Human Rights studied this issue, in particular the question of whether a new treaty could add monitoring responsibilities to an existing treaty organ. Eventually, the sponsors opted to draft a separate treaty with its own monitoring body: today's Committee against Torture. More recently, the UN has adopted quite a few additional protocols to existing treaties, such as the Convention on the Rights of the Child and the International Covenant on Economic, Social and Cultural Rights. The initiatives for such protocols have come from within the human rights movement, and the drafting processes have followed those for human rights instruments generally. It might be useful, when an optional protocol or supplementary convention is proposed, for the UN Secretariat to prepare an expert study, so that the drafters can take issues of compatibility into account.

The views of existing treaty bodies are also relevant. While they usually find a way of making any views they have on the proposed protocols or supplementary instruments known, a case could be made for the formalizing of this process, with a view to assuring the integrity and coordination of related instruments. In a recent instance, the drafting of supplementary standards to the International Convention on the Elimination of All Forms of Racial Discrimination has been the subject of different views. Some governments and the monitoring body favour preparing supplementary standards, while other governments disagree. A Human Rights Council working group was considering the issue at the end of 2012.

2.2 Expert studies

Some expert studies were done prior to the initiation of a drafting process in the Sub-Commission of the former Commission on Human Rights,[10] in the former Commission itself,[11] and in the Committee on Crime Prevention and Control; however, for a great number of treaties, no such expert studies were realized prior to the commencement of the drafting process. Human rights non-governmental organizations (NGOs) that initiate many drafting exercises often base them on expert reports that they have drawn up, including in the case of what eventually became the International Convention for the Protection of All Persons from Enforced Disappearance. Human Rights NGOs called for such an instrument for years and did a number of reports on the concept and the need for standards. Keeping in mind the principle of flexibility, as well as the possible contributions of expert studies to the drafting process, on the one hand, and, on the other hand, the relationship between protection strategies and drafting processes, one should avoid generalizing on the need for expert studies before commencing a normative drafting process.

2.3 The collection of relevant materials

In drafting global instruments, it is important to keep in mind the circumstances and experiences of countries and societies all over the world. When the UN Secretariat commenced its work on the Universal Declaration of Human Rights, it collected materials and provisions from the constitutions and laws of some fifty countries, nearly all of the independent states of the time. This helped the Secretariat to prepare its first draft of the Declaration. The former Sub-Commission's global studies on topics such as the rights of minorities and the rights of indigenous populations were based on monographs about numerous countries. More recent practice varies, and sometimes relevant materials or insights are injected into the discussions of a body like the Human Rights Council after a draft is put forward.

At some stage during the drafting process it is appropriate to ask whether enough attention has been paid to drawing on experiences and insights from around the world, even though the relevance of the materials from different countries might vary from topic to topic. One might expect that during the discussion of drafts in different governmental bodies, especially the UN General Assembly, insights from countries the world over are brought to bear on the drafts under consideration. Of course, when one is seeking to raise the level of protection against torture, for

[10] See United Nations, 'United Nations Action in the Field of Human Rights' (1994) UN Doc ST/HR/2/Rev.4.

[11] For an example on the right to development, see a prior study by the UN Secretariat: UN Economic and Social Council, 'Report of the Secretary-General' (2 January 1979) UN Doc E/CN.4/1334.

example, the insights and experiences of numerous countries might be negative. In any event, it is also important to retain the flexibility that members of the human rights movement have to propose the drafting of new instruments.

2.4 The role of the Secretariat and Office of Legal Affairs

The role of the Secretariat is invariably a supportive one both substantively and in the provision of services. The Secretariat is a partner for consultations and for expert opinions. At times, the role of the Secretariat might be mainly one of providing services, as when a Working Group of the Third Committee of the General Assembly drafted what became the International Convention on the Protection of the Rights of All Migrant Workers and Members of Their Families. In this instance, the Mexican delegation suggested the initiative, chaired a working group of the General Assembly on the topic, provided a draft convention, and pressed for its adoption—in many instances over the objections of some other delegations. Notably, the Convention has not been widely ratified to date.

For the future, should the international community perceive a need to systematize the extensive International Code of Human Rights, consisting of declarations, bodies of principle, treaties, and other instruments, it would be natural to expect the UN Secretariat to contribute in this respect. Moreover, ideally, there should be an entity watching over the integrity and coordination of the diverse instruments that have been adopted, and as well as those that will be proposed in the future. In the future, this proposition should be kept in mind.

Another UN contributor to the drafting process is the United Nations Office of Legal Affairs (OLA). The Office has consistently provided, upon request, legal opinions on issues arising during the drafting of human rights instruments. In practice, there has been a distinction between the substantive human rights department and the OLA, with the substantive department playing a broader role. The role of OLA is to provide independent and unbiased legal opinions on issues with regard to considerations of existing international law.

2.5 Stages in the deliberations process

Governments are involved almost throughout the drafting process. These governments, as well as international organizations and NGOs, have many opportunities to comment on drafts during the various stages of the drafting process. In some instances, they may make such comments in writing on a case-by-case basis, and their views are circulated formally. Even when topics are being discussed in expert bodies like the Advisory Committee of the Human Rights Council, governments have opportunities or avenues for making their views known. They control the deliberations in the Human Rights Council; however, because the Council's membership is much smaller than that of the UN General Assembly, when a Council draft reaches the Assembly, the passage is not always smooth. Membership in the General Assembly is four times that of the Council, and drafts have to attract the agreement of the wider membership. When the UN Declaration on Religious Freedom[12] was being discussed, a draft reached the General Assembly after working its way through the then Sub-Commission and the then Commission, but its passage through the General Assembly came about only after protracted discussions and the good offices of the Chairperson of the Third Committee.

2.6 Final adoption

In the UN General Assembly, the Third (Social and Humanitarian) Committee usually scrutinizes drafts before they reach the Plenary. In most instances, issues are worked out before they reach the Plenary, where they are formally adopted and, in the instances of treaties, opened for signature and ratification or accession, depending on the provision of the particular treaty in question. Sometimes there is fanfare at the time when an instrument is adopted, as happened with the Universal Declaration and the Covenants. At other times, the general public largely does not notice the event.

3. The International Law of Human Rights

Human rights instruments, declarations, bodies of principle, and conventions represent a major chapter of international law, as is evident from a glance at the UN's *Human Rights: A Compilation of International Instruments.*[13] Human rights instruments elaborated and adopted within the UN system, as well as in regional organizations, cover practically every aspect of the relationship between the individual and the state, and the process of discussing and elaborating new normative instruments continues.

[12] Declaration on the Elimination of All Forms of Intolerance and of Discrimination Based on Religion or Belief.

[13] Office of the High Commissioner for Human Rights (OHCHR), *Human Rights: A Compilation of International Instruments* (UN 2002).

Many of these instruments probably represent the progressive development of the international law of human rights. As discussed herein, only selected parts of these instruments have attained the status of customary international law. There has not been much codification of the international law of human rights as such, unless one considers the various treaties to be codifications of the law. The numerous instruments cover different issues, and to date there has been little effort at systematization or comprehensive codification. With regard to political complexities, it may not be wise to attempt any comprehensive codification of the international law of human rights, because some parties may be tempted to try to renegotiate salient provisions of instruments such as the Universal Declaration. There would, however, be a strong case for an academic systematization or Restatement of the International Law of Human Rights.

Human rights norms, like other norms of international law, have their origins in customary international law, human rights treaties, and principles of law which the world's main legal systems share. As a general matter, the 1993 Vienna World Conference on Human Rights reaffirmed the solemn commitment of all states to fulfil their obligations to promote universal respect for, and observance and protection of, all human rights and fundamental freedoms, in accordance with the Charter of the United Nations, other instruments relating to human rights, and international law.

The Restatement (Third) of the Foreign Relations Law of the United States is considered a highly authoritative summary of the current state of international law. A group of American international and international human rights lawyers of great renown produced it.[14] It describes the obligation of states to respect human rights as follows:

> A state is obliged to respect the human rights of persons subject to its jurisdiction (a) that it has undertaken to respect by international agreements; (b) that states generally are bound to respect as a matter of customary international law (§ 702); and (c) that it is required to respect under general principles of law common to the major legal systems of the world.[15]

The International Court of Justice (ICJ) has recognized the existence of peremptory norms of international law, or norms of international public policy, which take precedence over all other norms of international law.[16] In other words, these peremptory norms are binding on all states, regardless of their internal structure

[14] The late Professor Louis Henkin of the Columbia Law School, author of several leading books on international human rights, was the Editor.

[15] American Law Institute, 'Restatement (Third) of the Foreign Relations Law of the United States' (1986) s 701.

[16] See Erika de Wet, Chapter 23 in this *Handbook*.

or other commitments. The ICJ has recognized the prohibition of genocide as an example of such a peremptory norm of international law.[17]

There are those who argue that the UN Charter represents international constitutional law, thereby according it special status in international law.[18] This argument has particular relevance when it comes to assessing member states' obligations to respect, protect, and ensure human rights under the Charter and the UDHR. It is thus helpful to review the human rights provisions of the UN Charter.

3.1 The United Nations Charter

The preamble to the UN Charter expressed the determination of the peoples of the UN to reaffirm their faith in fundamental human rights, the dignity and worth of the human person, and the equal rights of men and women and of nations large and small. The purposes of the UN include the achievement of international cooperation in solving international economic, social, cultural, or humanitarian problems and in promoting and encouraging respect for human rights and for fundamental freedoms for all, without distinction as to race, sex, language, or religion. The UN was created as a centre for harmonizing the actions of nations towards attaining these ends.[19]

All members of the UN pledge to fulfil in good faith the obligations they undertook in accordance with the Charter.[20] Articles 55 and 56 of the Charter elaborate on this duty. Article 55 charges the UN with promoting 'universal respect for, and observance of, human rights and fundamental freedoms for all without distinction as to race, sex, language, or religion'.[21] Article 56 adds that all members pledge 'to take joint and separate action in cooperation with the Organization for the achievement of the purposes set forth in Article 55'. For the present, it suffices to indicate that Article 56, when combined with Article 55, presents binding legal obligations on member states, the content of which the provisions of the UDHR spell out in more detail.

A state's international obligation to uphold human rights thus begins with the UN Charter, with the UDHR constituting an elaboration of the Charter's human rights provisions. The second port of call is customary international law.

[17] See eg *Application of the Convention on the Prevention and Punishment of the Crime of Genocide (Bosnia and Herzegovina v Yugoslavia)*.

[18] See generally Ronald St John Macdonald and Douglas M Johnston, *Towards World Constitutionalism: Issues in the Legal Ordering of the World Community* (Martinus Nijhoff 2005).

[19] UN Charter, Art 1. [20] UN Charter, Art 2. [21] UN Charter, Art 55(c).

3.2 Customary international law

The Restatement (Third) of the Foreign Relations Law of the United States contains a succinct statement of states' human rights obligations under customary international law:

> A state violates international customary law if, as a matter of state policy, it practices, encourages, or condones (a) genocide; (b) slavery or slave trade; (c) the murder or causing the disappearance of individuals; (d) torture or other cruel, inhuman, or degrading treatment or punishment; (e) prolonged arbitrary detention; (f) systematic racial discrimination; or (g) a consistent pattern of gross violations of internationally recognized human rights.[22]

This list was drawn up some two decades ago. In light of subsequent experiences and legal developments, one could probably add forced disappearances, systematic gender discrimination, and ethnic cleansing to the list of acts prohibited under customary international law.

3.3 Human rights treaties

The League of Nations began the practice of concluding treaties to protect people from slavery and slavery-like practices and to protect minorities. The UN has continued the practice of making treaties to protect individuals and groups from abuse, to the point that there are now dozens of international treaties that states have duly accepted and by which they have become bound. The most widely accepted treaty is the Convention on the Rights of the Child, which (as of the writing of this chapter) is binding on 189 states Parties. Other major treaties, which the UN refers to as 'core' instruments, are the International Convention on the Elimination of All Forms of Racial Discrimination; the International Convention on the Elimination of All Forms of Discrimination against Women; the International Covenant on Civil and Political Rights (ICCPR); the International Covenant on Economic, Social and Cultural Rights; the Convention against Torture; and the International Convention on the Protection of the Rights of All Migrant Workers and Members of Their Families.[23] The UN's *Compilation of International Instruments*[24] lists ninety-four such global instruments. Since the issuance of the publication, the UN has adopted further instruments, including the Convention for the Protection of All Persons from Enforced Disappearance.

[22] American Law Institute, 'Restatement' (n 15) s 702.

[23] For the latest state of ratifications see the OHCHR website. OHCHR, 'Monitoring the Core International Human Rights Treaties' <http://www.ohchr.org/EN/HRBodies/Pages/TreatyBodies.aspx> accessed 12 February 2013.

[24] OHCHR, *Human Rights: A Compilation of International Instruments* (n 13).

Stated summarily, the international treaties contain norms to which the states parties have consented to be bound. Depending on the treaty, the states have also agreed to submit reports periodically, to engage in dialogue with the treaty body that each treaty has established, to consider the advice and recommendations of the treaty body, and to generally make the treaty provisions part of their national orders in law and in practice. Some states have also agreed to be bound by petitions procedures or state-to-state complaints procedures.

The adhering or ratifying governments have thus freely accepted human rights treaties. They are therefore the most solid consensual bases on which to build national, regional, and international human rights work in the twenty-first century. Debates are ongoing as to whether to consolidate the treaties or combine the different human rights treaty bodies, but it bears repeating that the human rights treaties and the body of jurisprudence arising from their treaty bodies represent the broadest consensual ground on which to build future human rights work.

The practical inference to be drawn from this conclusion is that the bulk of the resources of the UN and of regional organizations should be deployed in support of the implementation of human rights treaties. The ultimate rationale for the human rights treaty regime is to provide the basis for building effective national protection systems. The human rights treaty regime often provides a solid basis for dealing with new problems or threats, such as global terrorism, even if supplements may be necessary to deal with new issues. In General Comment No 31,[25] the Human Rights Committee of the International Covenant on Civil and Political Rights spelled out the obligations of states parties to the Covenant. Although based on the provisions of the Covenant, the principles contained therein are reflective of the general obligations of a state party to a human rights treaty.

As set forth in Article 2 of the Covenant, each state party undertakes to respect and ensure the rights recognized in the Covenant to all individuals within its territory and subject to its jurisdiction, without distinction of any kind, including distinction based on 'race, colour, sex, language, religion, political or other opinion, national or social origin, property, birth or other status'. Similar language appears at the beginning of most human rights treaties. The Human Rights Committee observed that every state party has a legal interest in every other state party's performance of its obligations. This follows from the fact that the 'rules concerning the basic rights of the human person are *erga omnes* obligations' and that there is a UN Charter obligation to promote universal respect for and observance of human rights and fundamental freedoms.[26]

[25] Human Rights Committee (HRC), 'General Comment No 31: Nature of the General Legal Obligation Imposed on State Parties to the Covenant' (26 May 2004) UN Doc CCPR/C/21/Rev.1/Add.13.

[26] HRC, 'General Comment No 31' (n 25) para 2 (internal quotations omitted).

States' obligations to respect the guaranteed rights and to ensure them to all individuals in their territory and subject to their jurisdiction, as well as to give effect to the rights and obligations in good faith, are binding on every state party. All branches of government (executive, legislative, and judicial) and all other public or governmental authorities at whatever level—national, regional, or local—are in a position to engage the responsibility of the state party. This understanding flows directly from the principle contained in Article 27 of the Vienna Convention on the Law of Treaties according to which a state party may not invoke the provisions of its internal law as justification for its failure to fulfil a treaty obligation.

The legal obligation is both negative and positive in nature. States parties must refrain from violating the recognized rights, and any restrictions on any of these rights must be permissible under the relevant treaty provisions. When they restrict these rights in some fashion, states must demonstrate the necessity of the restrictions and must only take such measures as are proportionate to the pursuance of legitimate aims to ensure continuous and effective protection of rights. In no case may the restrictions be applied or invoked in a manner that would impair the essence of a right.

States parties are required to respect and ensure the Covenant rights to all persons—that is, anyone within the power or effective control of that state party, even if not situated within the state's territory. The enjoyment of human rights is not limited to citizens of states parties, but must also be available to all individuals, such as asylum seekers, refugees, migrant workers, and other persons who may find themselves in the territory or subject to the jurisdiction of the state party, regardless of nationality or statelessness. This principle also applies to those within the power or effective control of the forces of a state party acting outside its territory, including forces constituting a national contingent of a state party assigned to an international peace-keeping or peace-enforcement operation, regardless of the circumstances through which the State obtained such power or effective control.

Human rights treaties also apply in situations of armed conflict to which the rules of international humanitarian law are applicable. While, in respect of certain rights, more specific rules of international humanitarian law may be especially relevant for interpreting human rights, both spheres of law are complementary and not mutually exclusive.

The states parties' obligation to respect and ensure the Covenant rights for all persons in their territory and all persons under their control, entails an obligation not to extradite, deport, expel, or otherwise remove a person from their territory where there are substantial grounds for believing that there is a real risk of irreparable harm, either in the country to which removal is to be effected or in any country to which the person may subsequently be removed.

States parties must take the necessary steps to give effect to the Covenant rights in their domestic order. It follows that, unless their domestic law or practices already protect the guaranteed rights, upon ratification states parties are required to make such changes to their domestic laws and practices as are necessary to ensure conformity with the treaty. Where there are inconsistencies between domestic law and international obligations, the state must change the domestic law or practice to meet the standards the treaty requires.

In addition to ensuring effective protection of rights, states parties must ensure that individuals also have accessible and effective remedies to vindicate those rights. Such remedies should be appropriately adapted so as to take account of the special vulnerability of certain categories of person—children, in particular. States parties should establish appropriate judicial and administrative mechanisms for addressing claims of rights violations under domestic law.

Also reflecting the provisions of other human rights agreements, Article 2, paragraph 3 of the ICCPR requires states parties to make reparations to individuals whose Covenant rights have been violated. Reparation can involve restitution, rehabilitation, and measures of satisfaction (such as public apologies, public memorials, guarantees of non-repetition, and changes in the relevant laws and practices), as well as bringing the perpetrators of the human rights violation(s) to justice.[27]

There is widespread concern about impunity and an emphasis on a state's obligation to take measures to prevent the recurrence of violations, an obligation that is integral to ICCPR Article 2. Accordingly, when considering individual petitions, the Committee has frequently included in its Views the need for the state to adopt measures beyond a victim-specific remedy, in order to avoid the recurrence of the type of violation in question. Such measures may require that states parties change their laws or practices.

When investigations reveal certain rights violations, states parties must ensure that those responsible are brought to justice. As with a failure to investigate, a failure to bring the perpetrators of such violations to justice could, in and of itself, give rise to a breach of the treaty. These obligations notably arise in respect of those violations that either domestic or international law recognize as criminal, such as torture and similar cruel, inhuman, and degrading treatment;[28] summary and arbitrary killing;[29] and enforced disappearance.[30] Indeed, the problem of impunity for these violations may well be an important contributing element in the recurrence of the violations. When committed as part of a widespread or systematic attack on a civilian population, these violations are crimes against humanity.[31]

Accordingly, where public officials or state agents have committed violations of the rights to which this author just referred, the states parties concerned may not relieve perpetrators from personal responsibility. Furthermore, no official status justifies

[27] See Fiona McKay, Chapter 38 in this *Handbook*.

[28] ICCPR, Art 7.

[29] ICCPR, Art 6.

[30] ICCPR, Arts 7, 9, and frequently 6.

[31] Rome Statute of the International Criminal Court, Art 7.

the persons accused of such violations being held immune from legal responsibility. Other impediments to the establishment of legal responsibility should also be removed, such as the defence of obedience demonstrated to the orders of superiors or unreasonably short statutory limitation periods in cases where such limitations are applicable. States parties should also assist each other in bringing to justice individuals suspected of the commission of these acts punishable under domestic or international law.

The Committee further took the view that the right to an effective remedy may, in certain circumstances, require states parties to provide for and implement provisional or interim measures, in order to avoid continuing violations, and to endeavour to repair at the earliest possible opportunity any harm that such violations may have caused. General Comment No 31 is a magisterial summary of the idea of international obligations under international human rights treaties. It represents, in many respects, the heart of international human rights law. As summarized above, its principles are applicable, subject to textual variations, to human rights treaties in general.[32]

3.4 General principles of law and international declarations or guidelines

In instances in which an international decision-making body is called upon to decide a human rights case or in which no clear norm is identifiable under customary international law or a human rights treaty, recourse may be had to general principles of law common to the principal legal systems.

In the *Chorzow Factory Case*, the World Court remarked 'that it is a principle of international law, and even a general conception of law, that any breach of an engagement involves an obligation to make reparation'.[33] Brownlie discusses considerations of humanity[34] as part of the general principles of law and notes that the provisions of the UN Charter that concern the protection of human rights and fundamental freedoms, as well as references to the 'principles' of the Charter, have been used as a more concrete basis for considerations of humanity in recent years—'for example in matters of racial discrimination and self-determination'.[35]

[32] See Section 3.3 in this chapter.

[33] *Chorzow Factory Case (Germany v Poland)* 29. See generally Ian Brownlie, *Principles of Public International Law* (6th edn, OUP 2003) 15–18.

[34] In the *Corfu Channel Case (UK v Albania)* 22, the World Court invoked 'elementary considerations of humanity, even more exacting in peace than in war'. See also *Military and Paramilitary Activities in and against Nicaragua (Nicaragua v United States)* 112–14.

[35] Brownlie (n 33) 27.

General principles of law may be deduced from national law and jurisprudence, as well as from the numerous declarations, bodies of principles, and guidelines that the UN adopts.[36] In theory, a declaration, body of principle, or guideline is not a legally binding instrument at the time of its adoption, but a particular provision could evolve into a rule of customary international law. It would be perfectly normal to look at the provisions of such instruments when seeking to identify a general principle of law. The declarations, bodies of principle, and guidelines are usually adopted by consensus and therefore reflect a good synthesis of the thinking of the collective governments and civil society on a particular issue.

4. The Passage of Declaration and Convention Provisions into Customary International Law

The emergence of customary international law through international law-making processes has been the subject of long-standing jurisprudence of the International Court of Justice, notably the *North Sea Continental Shelf Cases* of 1969. The principles the Court enunciated could also govern the passage of provisions of declarations and conventions to customary international law.

In the *North Sea Continental Shelf Cases*, the International Court of Justice concluded that the 1958 Geneva Convention on the Continental Shelf did not embody or crystallize any pre-existing or emergent rule of customary law according to which the delimitation of continental shelf areas between adjacent states must, unless the parties otherwise agreed, be carried out on an equidistance-special circumstances basis. While Article 6 of the Convention contained a rule, it was as a purely conventional rule. The Court then proceeded to consider whether it had since acquired a broader basis.

Denmark and the Netherlands argued that even if at the date of the Geneva Convention there was no rule of customary international law in favour of the equidistance principle, and even if Article 6 of the Convention did not crystallize any such rule, nevertheless such a rule had come into being since the drafting of the Convention, partly because of the Convention's impact and partly because of subsequent state practice. They further argued that this rule, being a rule of customary international law binding on all states, should be declared applicable to the

[36] OHCHR, *Human Rights: A Compilation of International Instruments* (n 13) contains several such instruments.

delimitation of the boundaries between the parties' respective continental shelf areas in the North Sea.

The Court commented that insofar as the Danish and Dutch based their contention on the view that Article 6 of the Convention had had the influence and had produced the effect described, it clearly involved treating that Article as a norm-creating provision. Such a provision, it commented, would constitute the foundation of or generate a rule which, while only conventional or contractual in its origin, would pass into the general corpus of international law and be accepted as *opinio juris*, so as to become binding even for countries, such as Germany, that had never become parties to the Convention. The Court declared:

There is no doubt that this process is a perfectly possible one and does from time to time occur: it constitutes indeed one of the recognized methods by which new rules of customary international law may be formed. At the same time this result is not lightly to be regarded as having been attained.[37]

This reasoning would undoubtedly be equally applicable in the area of international human rights law. The further reasoning of the ICJ therefore holds particular significance to this subject matter.

The Court eventually found that the Convention's equidistance rule had not passed into international customary law. Its reasoning provides guidance on the possible process of the passage of a treaty rule into customary international law. In the first place, in order to prove the passage of a normative provision (whether a treaty or a declaratory provision) into the corpus of customary international law, it would be necessary for the provision concerned to be of a fundamentally norm-creating character in potentially all events, such as could be regarded as forming the basis of a general rule of law. Second, even without the passage of any considerable period of time, very widespread and representative participation in the convention might of itself suffice, provided it included the participation of those states whose interests it especially affected.

The Court further clarified:

As regards the time element, the Court notes that it is over ten years since the Convention was signed, but that it is even now less than five since it came into force in June 1964, and that when the present proceedings were brought it was less than three years, while less than one had elapsed at the time when the respective negotiations between the Federal Republic and the other two Parties for a complete delimitation broke down on the question of the application of the equidistance principle. Although the passage of only a short period of time is not necessarily, or of itself, a bar to the formation of a new rule of customary international law on the basis of what was originally a purely conventional rule, an indispensable requirement would be that within the period in question, short though it might be, State practice, including that of States whose interests are specially affected, should have been both extensive and virtually uniform in the sense of the provision invoked;—and should

[37] *North Sea Continental Shelf Cases*, para 71.

moreover have occurred in such a way as to show a general recognition that a rule of law or legal obligation is involved.[38]

The Court examined the particular facts of the case and found that these tests had not been met.

In the case of *Nicaragua v United States (Military and Paramilitary Activities in and Against Nicaragua)*, the Court considered the Nicaraguan submission that, leaving aside the United Nations Charter in the particular circumstances of the case, the non-use of force was a principle of customary law similar in content to the law of the UN Charter.[39] The Court held as follows:

It is not to be expected that in the practice of States the application of the rules in question should have been perfect, in the sense that States should have refrained, with complete consistency, from the use of force or from intervention in each other's internal affairs. The Court does not consider that, for a rule to be established as customary, the corresponding practice must be in absolutely rigorous conformity with the rule. In order to deduce the existence of customary rules, the Court deems it sufficient that the conduct of States should, in general, be consistent with such rules, and that instances of State conduct inconsistent with a given rule should generally have been treated as breaches of that rule, not as indications of the recognition of a new rule. If a State acts in a way prima facie incompatible with a recognized rule, but defends its conduct by appealing to exceptions or justifications contained within the rule itself, then whether or not the State's conduct is in fact justifiable on that basis, the significance of that attitude is to confirm rather than to weaken the rule.[40]

There has been lively discussion in the literature about the process of passage of provisions of human rights declarations or conventions into customary law.[41] Three observations may be offered in this regard. In the first place, the International Court of Justice is the most authoritative body from which to take guidance. As seen in the two cases discussed above, the Court has affirmed that the passage from declarations or conventions to customary law is possible and that it is a matter to be determined on a case-by-case basis.

In the second place, the Court has on occasion expressly held that a norm, eg a norm in the Universal Declaration of Human Rights, has become a norm of customary law. In the case of *United States Diplomatic and Consular Staff in Tehran*, the Court stated the following:

Wrongfully to deprive human beings of their freedom and to subject them to physical constraint in conditions of hardship is in itself manifestly incompatible with the principles of the Charter of the United Nations, as well as with the fundamental principles enunciated in the Universal Declaration of Human Rights.[42]

38 *Continental Shelf Cases* (n 37) para 74.

39 *Nicaragua v United States* (n 34).

40 *Nicaragua v United States* (n 34) para 186.

41 See generally, eg (1996) 25 *Ga J Int'l & Comp L*. The introductory article by the late Professor Richard Lillich is particularly illuminating. Richard B Lillich, 'The Growing Importance of Customary International Human Rights Law' (1996) 25 *Ga J Int'l & Comp L* 1.

42 *United States Diplomatic and Consular Staff in Tehran*, para 91.

In the third place, if authoritative organs, such as human rights treaty bodies, express a view on the customary law status of a particular norm or set of norms, and if the international community widely acquiesces to this assertion, it would provide fairly convincing evidence of the customary nature of the rule or rules in question. Further, even if one or a few states indicate a contrary understanding, the presumption should still stand in favour of the interpretation of the authoritative human rights treaty organ. This is because the entire history of international human rights law since the establishment of the United Nations has been one of dynamic advances in the articulation of norms and in authoritative human rights treaty organs' confirmation of the binding status of a particular norm or norms. This is as it should be. Human rights norms are distilled from the experiences and views of states worldwide, and this distillation of norms must be supported and defended. Otherwise, what remains are the narrow-minded views of conservative or reactionary governments. To the contrary, clear evidence of the objection of a large enough group of states will generally obviate the conclusion that a customary law norm exists. Nonetheless, if there is widespread acquiescence in understanding the law as an authoritative human rights treaty body states it, then the dissent of one or of a few states should not stand in the way of the concretization of a customary norm representing the higher view of the international community as a whole.

As an example, the UN Human Rights Committee, in its General Comment No 24 on reservations to the ICCPR, affirmed that states parties to the Covenant could not make reservations to provisions that represented customary international law:

> [A] State may not reserve the right to engage in slavery, to torture, to subject persons to cruel, inhuman or degrading treatment or punishment, to arbitrarily deprive persons of their lives, to arbitrarily arrest and detain persons, to deny freedom of thought, conscience or religion, to presume a person guilty unless he proves his innocence, to execute pregnant women or children, to permit the advocacy of national, racial or religious hatred, to deny to persons of marriageable age the right to marry, or to deny to minorities the right to enjoy their own culture, profess their own religion, or use their own language.[43]

On 28 March 1995, the Legal Adviser of the US Department of State wrote to the Chairman of the Human Rights Committee, stating that the Committee had asserted in a conclusive fashion that a number of propositions were customary international law which, 'to speak plainly, [were] not'.[44] He thought that such 'a cavalier approach to international law [raised] serious concerns about the methodology of the Committee as well as its authority'.[45]

[43] HRC, 'General Comment No 24: Issues Relating to Reservations Made upon Ratification or Accession to the Covenant or the Political Protocols Thereto, or in Relation to Declarations under Article 41 of the Covenant' (4 November 1994) UN Doc CCPR/C/21/Rev.1/Add.6, para 8.

[44] HRC, 'General Comments—Government Responses: Observations on General Comment No 24' (3 October 1995) UN Doc A/50/40, vol 1, annex VI(a)(3).

[45] HRC, 'Government Responses' (n 44) annex VI(a)(3).

In instances such as this, one should accord persuasive value to the views of the Human Rights Committee, and there should be a rebuttable presumption of the customary nature of the norms in question—unless other states express similar opposition. If the issue were to arrive before the International Court of Justice, for example, any country could assert its dissent and attempt to convince the Court that norms of customary international law had not emerged. As the ICJ states in the *Nicaragua* case, the Court does not consider that, for a rule to be established as customary, the corresponding practice must be in absolutely rigorous conformity with the rule. In order to deduce the existence of customary rules, the Court deems it sufficient that the conduct of states should, in general, be consistent with such rules and that instances of state conduct inconsistent with a given rule should generally have been treated as breaches of that rule, not as indications of the recognition of a new rule. If a state acts in a way that is prima facie incompatible with a recognized rule, but defends its conduct by appealing to exceptions or justifications contained within the rule itself, then the attitude confirms rather than weakens the rule, regardless of whether the state's conduct is in fact justifiable on that basis.[46]

5. Reflections on Improving Human Rights Law-Making: Moving to Prevention

Keeping in mind the foregoing discussion, it is appropriate to reflect on whether the process has room for improvement. For a start, it is important to keep open and flexible the initiative to propose new standards, because one of the key ways in which the international human rights movement can respond to emerging human rights problems is by examining the adequacy of standards and proposing new standards.

In the second place, it might be useful to have a systematic, thematic compilation of the existing standards. The academic and research community should perform the task to begin. A good example is the Restatement (Third) of the Foreign Relations Law of the United States, which is in need of updating and a more universal approach. An objective research institute could do this, with input from human rights law scholars of many nationalities. Third, it could be useful to have an academic compilation of core norms of customary international law, both containing pre-existing customary international law and identifying norms that might have passed from declarations or treaties to customary international law. Fourth, by the

[46] *Nicaragua v United States* (n 34) para 186.

same token, an academic compilation of general principles of international human rights law would be helpful. Fifth, a periodic survey of international human rights law, similar to the periodic surveys done for the International Law Commission, could be useful to governmental bodies such as the Human Rights Council. Sixth, it would be beneficial for the UN Secretariat to publish digests, similar to the ILO's Digest of Decisions on Freedom of Association, of the jurisprudence of UN human rights bodies.[47] Seventh, the UN Secretariat could also initiate a Repertory of the Practice of the Human Rights Council so as to facilitate the identification of the emergence of norms of customary international law, if any, in the practice of that body. Eighth, the human rights treaty bodies functioning under the principal human rights treaties could be encouraged to comment on the passage of provisions of their treaties into customary international law.

The foregoing reflections may apply to the law-making process seen in classical perspectives. However, at the advent of the twenty-first century, one cannot leave the matter there; international lawyers in general, and human rights lawyers in particular, must add a new category when discussing the law-making process: prevention. In a generic sense, it could be argued that the whole of international law already has a preventive rationale. By inviting governments to respect the rule of law, international law seeks to head off conflicts and problems in the relations among states. The international law of human rights has a similar rationale when it comes to preventing human rights violations, and some treaties, such as the Convention against Torture and the Optional Protocol to the Convention, seek to prevent the commission of this international crime—but this will not suffice in the future.

In a chapter in *The Oxford History of the Twentieth Century*, Professor Ralph Dahrendorf offers three moral principles for the twenty-first century.[48] First, only open societies can be good societies. Second, acknowledgment of a duty to future generations and of the necessity of the 'responsibility principle' in the 'risk society' of the present is required. Third, humans may be living in an uncertain environment and may not know for sure what is right, good, and just, but they must try to find out and must never give up trying to enhance the quality of life.[49]

Former UN High Commissioner for Human Rights, Mary Robinson, devoted her 2000 annual report[50] to the then Commission on Human Rights to a discussion of preventive human rights strategies. The report, which specialists in Office of the High Commissioner for Human Rights (OHCHR) drafted and which this author

[47] See ILO, *Freedom of Association: Digest of Decisions and Principles of the Freedom of Association Committee of the Governing Body of the ILO* (5th rev edn, ILO 2006).

[48] Ralf Dahrendorf, 'Towards the Twenty-First Century' in Michael Howard and Wm Roger Louis (eds), *The Oxford History of the Twentieth Century* (OUP 2006).

[49] Dahrendorf (n 48) 342–43.

[50] Economic and Social Council, 'Report of the United Nations High Commissioner for Human Rights and Follow-Up to the World Conference on Human Rights' (28 December 1999) UN Doc E/CN.4/2000/12.

coordinated as the then Deputy High Commissioner, contained chapters offering strategies for the prevention of the crime of genocide, the prevention of racism and racial discrimination, the right to development, the prevention of human rights violations, the prevention of gross violations of civil and political rights, the fundamental standards of humanity, the prevention of slavery, the prevention of trafficking in women and children, the prevention of violations through human rights education, and the combating of impunity as a preventive approach. The report concluded:

> [T]he prevention of gross violations of human rights and of conflicts is a defining issue of our time. As we begin the new millennium, it must be a matter of the utmost priority that we seek, at the national, regional and international levels, to develop societies fashioned in the image of the international norms on human rights.[51]

The law-making process of the future endeavours to deal with the grievous threats facing humanity.

5.1 Threats to humanity that call for the articulation of their human rights dimensions

Global threats, such as climate change, natural disasters, and global competition for depleting resources, make it imperative to address and articulate their human rights dimensions and the need for responses that are anchored in respect for human rights and fundamental freedoms. Depending on the degree of global warming, up to 300 million people could be forced to seek refuge on safer ground. Responses to natural disasters, such as Hurricanes Katrina and Sandy in the USA, demand thoughtful and equitable policies, in which the human rights dimension is at the forefront. Following the devastation that Hurricane Sandy caused in November 2012, the policy community in the USA began to sound the call for more prevention, preparedness, and planning.

The UN Human Rights Council has taken some incipient steps towards the discussion of future preventive human rights strategies, but this has yet to develop much traction. The work on preventive human rights strategies included discussion of a dozen threats to humankind that would warrant consideration of their human rights dimensions beforehand.[52]

[51] Economic and Social Council, 'Report of the United Nations High Commissioner' (n 50) para 92. The report is reproduced in Bertrand Ramcharan, *A UN High Commissioner in Defence of Human Rights* (Martinus Nijhoff 2004) appendix III.

[52] Bertrand G Ramcharan, *Preventive Human Rights Strategies* (Routledge 2011). See also Bertrand G Ramcharan, *Preventive Diplomacy at the UN* (Indiana UP 2008). The Human Rights Council has, since its establishment, adopted two general resolutions on prevention and a few other resolutions dealing with, eg the prevention of maternal mortality. The Council has not yet worked out a clear-cut policy on preventive human rights strategies. See generally Ramcharan, *The UN Human Rights Council* (n 7).

5.2 The protection of vulnerable groups

In the contemporary world, minorities, indigenous populations, and migrants have numerous vulnerabilities. There are normative instruments and UN bodies devoted to promoting and protecting their human rights. The UN High Commissioner's role is to spearhead and crystallize. At any one time, the world should be put on notice through alert statements and studies from OHCHR that draw attention to the dangers particular communities face. Such alerts can be brought to the attention of the General Assembly, the Security Council, and the Human Rights Council, as well as to the attention of the regional bodies. The aim should be to head off and prevent human rights violations. Vulnerable groups facing imminent problems should be able to address the High Commissioner and to seek the articulation of their concerns. This would be prevention in action.

5.3 The preventive dimensions of the responsibility to protect

The high-level group of experts that first advocated the doctrine of the responsibility to protect saw it as having three core components: the responsibility to prevent, the responsibility to react, and the responsibility to rebuild.[53] The UN Secretary-General has established the positions of the Special Adviser on the Responsibility to Protect and the Special Adviser on the Prevention of Genocide. They have both made useful contributions.

The concept of the responsibility to protect, as approved by the UN General Assembly in 2000, covered genocide, ethnic cleansing, crimes against humanity, and war crimes. As a political choice, this was understandable in the circumstances. But the responsibility to prevent, generically, must reach far beyond these four offences and to the entire gamut of threats to human rights. The UN High Commissioner for Human Rights must surely shoulder the responsibility for the responsibility to prevent worldwide, drawing upon the complementary efforts of the Secretary-General's Special Advisers and of regional officials such as the Organization for Security and Co-operation in Europe (OSCE) High Commissioner on National Minorities.

5.4 The preventive roles of national protection systems

A national human rights system should consist of constitutional, legislative, judicial, educational, institutional, and preventive pillars. The OHCHR has a good

[53] See Rudiger Wolfrum, Chapter 17 and Ramesh Thakur, Chapter 32 in this *Handbook*.

programme of cooperation with national human rights institutions, both regionally and internationally. But the cooperation has been generic up to this point. There has, to date, been little or no highlighting of the preventive pillar of national protection systems.

This is the key to the future protection of human rights worldwide. Competent national human rights institutions should be expected to take the lead in heading off and preventing gross human rights violations. As soon as possible, the OHCHR needs to commission a study of the preventive pillar of national human rights systems and to place this issue in the spotlight. The High Commissioner should take personal charge of efforts to highlight the importance of the preventive dimension of national protection systems and to foster their development in every country of the world.

5.5 Using the Universal Periodic Review process to advance prevention

Universal Periodic Review (UPR) has valuable features, inasmuch as, once every four-and-a-half years, every member state of the UN prepares a report, which two reports from the OHCHR supplement, on its efforts to advance human rights domestically and on the problems it is encountering in the process. The Human Rights Council reviews the report with the participation of the country concerned and, at the plenary stage, with the participation of NGOs. The system is now only in its second cycle, and one must withhold judgment on its eventual efficacy. There are strong political currents that make this more of a diplomatic than a legal process, in comparison to the consideration of reports by human rights treaty bodies.

The OHCHR is still in the process of developing a policy of building on the UPR. So far, its efforts have veered in the direction of capacity-building within countries (which is understandable), but the OHCHR can make a decisive difference by focusing on strengthening national protection systems and on national efforts to prevent gross violations of human rights. The OHCHR could, for example, commission a global study on national policies, strategies, and institutions for the prevention of human rights violations. The study could be cast in terms of sharing experiences among countries and identifying good practices.

At the end of the day, however, the aim should be to assist each country to define and operate a policy of prevention. That would be genuine human rights protection at work. Capacity building sounds good and can be useful. However, it can also be vague and ephemeral. Prevention is concrete and will make a real effect on human rights protection.

5.6 Injecting human rights dimensions into regional preventive regimes

Regional mechanisms for the prevention of conflict and violence exist today in the Association of South-East Asian Nations (ASEAN), the African Union (AU), the Economic Community of West African States, the Southern African Development Community, the Organization of American States (OAS), OSCE, and other regional and sub-regional organizations.[54] The AU Charter specifically supports AU action in the event of gross violations of human rights. In addition to these conflict and violence-prevention mechanisms, regional institutions for the promotion and protection of human rights exist in ASEAN, AU, the Council of Europe, OAS, and OSCE.

The OHCHR and the High Commissioner have spasmodic cooperation with some of these bodies, but there is no evidence that the High Commissioner has provided spearheading and leadership. For this to happen, there must be policy choices. General cooperation can degenerate into courtesies. We suggest that the policy choice should be for prevention. The High Commissioner should periodically visit each of the regional preventive mechanisms and address them with human rights insights and recommendations. The High Commissioner should also periodically visit regional and sub-regional human rights institutions and encourage them toward stronger preventive efforts. The thrust of prevention would define the relationship and help give sharper definition to the OHCHR in the process.

[54] See generally BG Ramcharan (ed), *Conflict Prevention in Practice: Essays in Honour of Jim Sutterlin* (Martinus Nijhoff 2005). See also International Peace Institute, *Preventive Diplomacy: Regions in Focus* (International Peace Institute 2011). See further UN Security Council, 'Preventive Diplomacy: Delivering Results' (26 August 2011) UN Doc S/2011/552, para 52:

> In the past five years, we have deepened existing or established new conflict prevention and mediation partnerships with the African Union, the European Union, OSCE, OAS, the Caribbean Community (CARICOM), ECOWAS, SADC, ASEAN, OIC and others. Partly through the use of extra budgetary resources, we have been able to undertake initiatives to help build regional capacities and learn from regional experiences. Joint training programmes on a broad range of peace and security issues are now available. Still, synergies take time and hard work to attain and are not rendered easier by the fact that, with very few exceptions, the United Nations, regional organizations and other actors have no shared mechanism or procedure to decide, in real time, who should do what in a given case. As we work to improve our formal institutional channels and protocols in that regard, we are also investing in key personal relationships with regional partners, which form the bedrock of closer cooperation. [Citations omitted.]

The question that deserves to be posed is: Where does the OHCHR fit into all of this? So far, the answer would be in very few places. This should change in the future. The OHCHR should be a key player in all of these processes.

5.7 Leadership on preventive treaties such as the Optional Protocol to CAT

Historically, the relationship between the High Commissioner and the human rights treaty bodies has been an ambiguous one. This chapter does not address this broader relationship. Rather, it makes the case that High Commissioners should take a special interest in (and place their shoulders to the wheel when it comes to) treaties with pronounced preventive thrusts. The Optional Protocol to CAT (OPCAT), for example, provides for states parties to establish national preventive mechanisms, regular visits by national bodies, and regular visits by the OPCAT sub-committee. In their contacts with national authorities, High Commissioners should highlight the importance of the OPCAT arrangements and seek to use their influence to strengthen these arrangements. There can be no more important human rights work than preventing torture, and High Commissioners should be identified with this. This would, again, help sharpen the definition of the OHCHR.

5.8 Cooperating with partners to advance prevention

This chapter has already argued for stronger emphasis on preventive strategies by the OHCHR and by High Commissioners, and it has already made the point that High Commissioners should develop cooperative relationships with regional preventive and human rights mechanisms, in order to help prevent gross violations of human rights worldwide. There are other actors active in the field of prevention, with whom the OHCHR and High Commissioners should also have more pronounced cooperation. These include the major human rights NGOs and organizations with a pronounced preventive focus. The OHCHR could invite these organizations to periodic meetings on cooperation for prevention, with a view to drawing insights and suggestions from them and to building up a culture of cooperation for the prevention of human rights violations.

With a view to demonstrating that there is fertile ground for the OHCHR to work with these partners on future preventive strategies, this chapter sets out below the preventive focus of a number of them—it being understood that there are other organizations that also support preventive human rights work.

5.9 Using the voice of the UN High Commissioner

Finally, whenever the UN High Commissioner for Human Rights considers that a group or people are in particular danger, she or he should be ready to utilize the power of the voice of the High Commissioner by issuing public statements, calling for the attention of the Human Rights Council, the Security Council, the Secretary-General, or of the leadership of regional or sub-regional organizations, with a view to heading off the danger of gross violations. As a result of such a practice, over time the High Commissioner and the OHCHR would become more sharply defined as a preventive organization.

5.10 Making prevention the decisive rationale of a human rights grand strategy

Human rights work has an inherent preventive rationale. Human rights work can be grouped under categories such as seed-planting, fire-brigade, or preventive. The various High Commissioners and the OHCHR have done much in the areas of seed-planting and fire-brigade reactions. However, so far few efforts address prevention, which should become a defining priority of the OHCHR and High Commissioners. Global threats to humanity make this imperative, and there are other areas where there is room for the development of preventive policies and strategies.

Secretary-General Ban Ki-moon made a strong case for more prevention in his 2011 report on preventive strategies:

> We should build on the improvements that have been made in the United Nations and in various regional and subregional organizations in developing early warning mechanisms. The establishment of regular and informal early warning dialogues between the United Nations and regional and other partners would allow us to pool information and help us to anticipate 'threshold moments' when key actors might decide to use violence. However, early warning is useful only if it leads to early action, and we need to consider a broader range of options for addressing an emerging threat, including seemingly small steps, such as multi-actor statements of concern or fact-finding missions, which can affect the calculations of parties on the ground early on.[55]

6. Conclusion

This chapter has taken a thematic approach to discussing the international human rights law-making process—focusing on sources and methods for the creation of norms and the transition from declarations and treaties to customary international

[55] UN Security Council, 'Preventive Diplomacy' (n 54) 18.

law. More general discussions of the actual norms drafted exist in the literature.[56] Textbooks on international human rights law also cover the ground amply.

As stated earlier, it could be useful to have an academic compilation of core norms of customary international law in the field of human rights, as well as an academic compilation of general principles of international human rights law.

Finally, the chapter makes a strong appeal for the law-making process to embrace a greater preventive role in the future. The challenges facing humankind demand this step. The international law of the future, including international human rights law, must rise to the challenges of the times.

Further Reading

Lillich RB, 'The Growing Importance of Customary International Human Rights Law' (1996) 25 *Ga J Int'l & Comp L* 1

Ramcharan BG, *Preventive Human Rights Strategies* (Routledge 2011)

—— *The UN Human Rights Council* (Routledge 2011)

Risse T, Ropp SC, and Sikkink K (eds), *The Power of Human Rights: International Norms and Domestic Change* (CUP 1999)

Macdonald RSJ and Johnston DM, *Towards World Constitutionalism: Issues in the Legal Ordering of the World Community* (Martinus Nijhoff 2005)

[56] See eg Dinah Shelton, *Commitment and Compliance: The Role of Non-Binding Norms in the International Legal System* (OUP 2003).

CHAPTER 22

CORE RIGHTS AND OBLIGATIONS

MARTIN SCHEININ

THIS chapter presents and discusses three different approaches to identifying a core within the normative framework of human rights law. First, the chapter discusses efforts to define *some* human rights as superior or more fundamental than other human rights, hence forming a category of 'core rights' as compared to 'plain human rights'. Second, it presents a theory of *each* human right encompassing an essential core that is not subject to permissible limitations. Third, the discussion turns to efforts to define the core *obligations* of the state in relation to the enjoyment of human rights. The chapter compares the relative merits of the three approaches and makes an effort to reconcile them.

1. Some Human Rights as Core Rights

The idea of some human rights being more fundamental, or even sacred, compared to other human rights is intuitively both appealing and problematic. A human rights expert, or any member of the public, feels tempted to classify some human rights violations as 'grave' or 'gross', because they are manifestly in breach of a shared universal understanding about the essence of human rights. The right to life and the prohibition against torture, and violations of human dignity reminiscent of Nazi practices are strong candidates for such special status.

At the same time, a human rights expert, and probably also a lay person, would identify a problem in that all human rights are supposed to be universal and fundamental, and therefore the elevation of some human rights to a special status would pose a risk to the normative force of a broader catalogue of human rights. While it is fully defendable to be restrictive with regard to the emergence of 'new' human rights, even a fairly traditional catalogue of human rights, such as that contained in the 1948 Universal Declaration of Human Rights (UDHR), would include a broader set of rights than would a 'core rights' approach.

As to the moral foundation of (legally binding) human rights, efforts have been made to derive all human rights from one, or just a small number of, moral values. For instance Henry Shue identified a limited set of 'basic rights' that must be firmly established as a precondition for other rights and therefore require primacy in relation to 'non-basic rights'.[1] For Shue, the basic rights are the right to physical security, the right to subsistence, and the right to liberty.[2] Interestingly, Shue's category of basic rights has a close connection with economic and social rights, in contrast to the long line of followers of John Locke, who afford special status to civil rights such as liberty and property.[3] These and many other theories may result in the identification of a limited number of human rights as core rights or in a distinction between the two categories of derivative and non-derivative human rights. While non-derivative human rights protect the core moral values behind human rights thinking, other (derivative) human rights serve the function of protecting the non-derivative rights. A possible outcome of these approaches may also be the creation of a priority order of moral values underlying human rights, resulting in a hierarchy, or at least relative priority order, between human rights. Such hierarchies could then be relied upon, for instance, in resolving conflicts between human rights, by giving primacy to the hierarchically superior right.

The codification of human rights, from the UDHR to the current network of universal, regional, and specialized human rights treaties, does not give much support to the existence of a defined category of core rights or of an established hierarchical order between human rights. Positive human rights law more highly favours the universality, indivisibility, and equal value of all human rights.[4] However, there

[1] Henry Shue, *Basic Rights: Subsistence, Affluence, and US Foreign Policy* (Princeton UP 1980) 18.

[2] Shue (n 1) 18–20.

[3] 'Man being born, as has been proved, with a Title to perfect Freedom, and an uncontrolled Enjoyment of all the Rights and Privileges of the Law of Nature, equally with any other Man…hath by Nature a Power…to preserve his Property, that is, his Life, Liberty and Estate.' John Locke, *Two Treatises of Government* (first published 1689, CUP 1965) 366–67, discussing the Second Treatise s 87.

[4] This position was formulated in the Vienna Declaration and Programme of Action, which the 1993 World Conference on Human Rights adopted as follows: 'All human rights are universal, indivisible and interdependent and interrelated', para I.5.

are multiple ways in which the philosophical thinking behind those constructions reflects the text of human rights treaties. Although three different variations of the theme can be identified, the overall conclusion to be drawn is that positive human rights law does not support the existence of a defined category of core rights that would include some, but not all, human rights. The three variations are as follows:

(i) Instead of proclaiming human dignity as a distinct human right, many human rights treaties refer to it in their preamble, thereby elevating human dignity to the status of a background value common to all human rights—perhaps even a function they are supposed to serve. For instance, the preambles to the 1966 Covenants[5] proclaim that the respective rights under the two Covenants 'derive from the inherent dignity of the human person'. The idea of some or even all specific human rights being derivative in relation to a common background value suggests that human dignity can be used as an overarching interpretive principle that will help to resolve possible tensions or collisions between human rights. This solution turns to the substantive interpretation of the content of each human right, instead of their subordination to a hierarchically higher right.

(ii) Some human rights documents, notably the International Covenant on Civil and Political Rights (ICCPR), proclaim a limited set of the protected rights as non-derogable, ie as rights from which no exception is allowed, even during a state of emergency.[6] There are both common elements and variations in the list of non-derogable human rights under different treaties,[7] as well as many human rights treaties that do not provide such a category.[8] One of the main reasons why certain rights are regarded as non-derogable is their background as *jus cogens* norms in customary international law.[9] In General Comment No 29, the Human Rights Committee (HRC) carefully analysed the relationship between peremptory norms and non-derogable rights. It started by stating

[5] International Covenant on Civil and Political Rights (ICCPR); International Covenant on Economic, Social and Cultural Rights (ICESCR).

[6] The Human Rights Committee (HRC) has paraphrased the ICCPR Art 4(2) list of non-derogable rights as follows: 'article 6 (right to life), article 7 (prohibition of torture or cruel, inhuman or degrading punishment, or of medical or scientific experimentation without consent), article 8, paragraphs 1 and 2 (prohibition of slavery, slave-trade and servitude), article 11 (prohibition of imprisonment because of inability to fulfil a contractual obligation), article 15 (the principle of legality in the field of criminal law, ie the requirement of both criminal liability and punishment being limited to clear and precise provisions in the law that was in place and applicable at the time the act or omission took place, except in cases where a later law imposes a lighter penalty), article 16 (the recognition of everyone as a person before the law), and article 18 (freedom of thought, conscience and religion).' HRC, 'General Comment No 29: States of Emergency (Art 4)' (31 August 2001) UN Doc CCPR/C/21/Rev.1/Add.11, para 7.

[7] Compare the ICCPR list, which the preceding footnote provides, with Art 15 of the European Convention on Human Rights and Art 27 of the American Convention of Human Rights.

[8] See, notably, the African Charter of Human and Peoples' Rights; ICESCR.

[9] On human rights norms of *jus cogens* nature, see Erika de Wet, Chapter 23 in this *Handbook*.

that the enumeration of non-derogable provisions in ICCPR Article 4 is 'related to, but not identical with', the question of whether certain human rights obligations bear the same nature as peremptory norms of international law.[10] In some cases, the proclamation of certain provisions of the Covenant as non-derogable was to be seen as recognition of the peremptory nature of those rights; here, the Committee mentioned as examples the right to life (Article 6) and the prohibition against torture or other inhuman treatment (Article 7).[11] However, the Committee clearly states that the two categories are not identical. First, 'it is apparent' that some other provisions of the Covenant were included in the list of non-derogable provisions simply because a state of emergency can never necessitate derogation from these rights (eg Articles 11 and 18).[12] Second, the Committee also emphasizes that the category of peremptory norms extends beyond the list of non-derogable provisions.[13]

The Human Rights Committee had already earlier taken the view that the proclamation of some rights as non-derogable during a state of emergency does not entail a 'hierarchy of importance of rights under the Covenant'.[14] In its General Comment No 29, the Committee elaborated an approach of treating derogations from human rights during a genuine state of emergency merely as a specific form of permissible restrictions to some human rights, rather than as a regime for their suspension.[15] The Committee discussed and emphasized the category of non-derogable rights,[16] but also clearly demonstrated that other rights, those that are subject to permissible derogations, nevertheless contain aspects that are not subject to lawful derogation. The Committee made clear and concretized that position through a non-exhaustive list of examples, with multiple references to provisions of the ICCPR that are not non-derogable under Article 4(2), as such, but which nevertheless contain 'elements that in the Committee's opinion cannot be made subject to lawful derogation'.[17]

[10] HRC, 'General Comment No 29' (n 6) para 11.

[11] HRC, 'General Comment No 29' (n 6) para 11.

[12] HRC, 'General Comment No 29' (n 6) para 11.

[13] HRC, 'General Comment No 29' (n 6) para 11. As to the latter point, the Committee gives four examples of prohibited conduct that would not relate to any of the non-derogable provisions of the ICCPR, but which nevertheless would violate either peremptory norms or international humanitarian law: hostage-taking, collective punishment, arbitrary deprivation of liberty, and deviation from fundamental principles of a fair trial, including the presumption of innocence. It is to be noted that the Committee does not specify which, if any, of these prohibitions represent peremptory norms.

[14] HRC, 'General Comment No 24: Issues Relating to Reservations Made upon Ratification or Accession to the Covenant or the Optional Protocols Thereto, or in Relation to Declarations under Article 41 of the Covenant' (4 November 1994) UN Doc CCPR/C/21/Rev.1/Add.6, para 10.

[15] See, above all, HRC, 'General Comment No 29' (n 6) para 4.

[16] HRC, 'General Comment No 29' (n 6) para 7.

[17] See HRC, 'General Comment No 29' (n 6) para 13, wherein the examples given relate to non-derogable elements of, inter alia, Arts 9, 12, and 27 of the ICCPR. See also HRC, 'General Comment

The Committee also emphasized that there are elements or dimensions of the right to non-discrimination that do not permit derogation in any circumstance.[18]

All in all, the position of the Human Rights Committee supports the conclusion that the non-derogability of a limited set of human rights does not create a hierarchical relationship between these and other rights. There are good grounds otherwise to maintain a cautious and critical approach to proposals for creating a hierarchical order between different human rights.[19]

(iii) A third possible basis for declaring some human rights as core rights, as compared to other human rights, is the category of so-called absolute rights, ie rights that do not allow for any limitation. This distinction is separate from the question of non-derogability, as some absolute rights have not been proclaimed non-derogable and, conversely, some non-derogable rights may permit limitations during normal times but not allow for an additional layer of exceptions through the introduction of derogations during a state of emergency.[20]

In the ICCPR, only some of the provisions contain a separate clause on permissible limitations. Those are Articles 12 (freedom of movement), 18 (freedom of thought, conscience, and religion), 19 (freedom of expression), 21 (freedom of assembly), and 22 (freedom of association).

This does not mean that all other provisions would represent absolute rights, ie exclude all restrictions or limitations. For example, although Article 26 prohibits in categorical terms all discrimination, the fact that reasonable and objective differentiations do not amount to discrimination forms a part of the established interpretation of that provision.[21] Similarly, Article 27's prohibition of 'denying' members of minority groups the right to use their language, practise their religion, or enjoy their culture, is understood as permitting interferences that remain below the threshold of denial. Instead of a full-fledged permissible limitations clause, Article 17 on privacy, family life, and correspondence prohibits unlawful or arbitrary attacks, implicitly allowing for non-arbitrary limitations that have a proper legal basis. The prohibition against arbitrary deprivation of liberty or life appears also, respectively, in Articles 9 and 6. Its inclusion in the non-derogable right to life provision of Article 6, together with the multiple restrictions (but not total prohibition)

No 29' (n 6) paras 14–16, relating to the non-derogability of procedural protections for non-derogable rights, an interpretive position analogous to the explicit wording of Art 27 of the American Convention on Human Rights.

[18] HRC, 'General Comment No 29' (n 6) para 8.

[19] See eg Theodor Meron, 'On a Hierarchy of International Human Rights' (1986) 80 *AJIL* 1.

[20] HRC, 'General Comment No 29' (n 6) para 7, mentioning the obvious case of ICCPR Art 18 (freedom of religion, thought, and conscience) as a provision that includes a permissible limitations clause, but which is nevertheless non-derogable.

[21] See HRC, 'General Comment No 18: Non-Discrimination' (adopted 10 November 1989) reprinted in 'Compilation of General Comments and General Recommendations Adopted by Human Rights Treaty Bodies' (1994) UN Doc HRI/GEN/1/Rev.1, para 13.

on the use of capital punishment, demonstrate that even non-derogable rights may be subject to some restrictions and are not absolute in that sense.

The clearest example of a human right that is absolute in not allowing for any restrictions is the ICCPR's Article 7 prohibition against torture and any form of inhuman treatment. While the provision is, of course, subject to interpretation, such interpretation only relates to the question of whether certain treatment of a person amounts to torture or to cruel, inhuman, or degrading treatment, without leaving any room to accept such treatment. The same can be said about the prohibitions against slavery and servitude in Article 8 of the ICCPR, but not of the prohibition against forced labour in the same provision; unlike slavery, the prohibition against forced labour is subject to qualifications in paragraph 3, which leave room for permissible forms of compulsory work.

The International Covenant on Economic, Social and Cultural Rights (ICESCR) does not include a derogations clause and hence no list of non-derogable rights, either. Nor do there appear to be any absolute rights in the ICESCR, meaning rights that do not allow for restrictions, as the Covenant includes a general clause about limitations.[22] The provision acknowledges that states may subject (all) ICESCR rights to limitations, provided that such limitations are determined by law, compatible with the nature of these rights, and introduced solely for the purpose of promoting the general welfare in a democratic society.

None of the three sub-approaches for the special higher status of some rights presented above (namely their relation to underlying fundamental moral values, their status as non-derogable rights with or without *jus cogens* character, or their quality as absolute rights), supports a hierarchical relationship between these and other human rights. In short, there are various reasons for the special characteristics of one or the other human right, but they do not justify any order of superiority or primacy between human rights.

2. Each Human Right Contains an Essential Core

We are now turning to a totally different perspective: identifying a core in human rights protections. Instead of searching for *core rights*, we are now looking for the *core of a right*, asking whether all or many human rights contain an inviolable core, ie one or more essential elements that are not subject to limitations or exceptions.

[22] ICESCR, Art 4.

Although this chapter will still present a third approach—that of focusing on *core obligations* of the state—below, the reader is already herein informed that this second approach of viewing each human right as containing an essential core is the one the current author favours.

Some of the General Comments by the Human Rights Committee, acting under the ICCPR, support the position that all or many human rights contain an essential, inviolable core. In its 1999 'General Comment No 27: Freedom of Movement (Art 12)', the Committee for the first time explained its approach to permissible limitations to a human right that provides for a proper limitations clause in its ICCPR formulation.[23] As a part of its elaboration of an analytical, step-by-step test for the permissibility of restrictions, the Committee used the notion of 'the essence' of a human right and emphasized that restrictions must never impair that essence.[24] The same position was repeated in relation to all of the ICCPR rights in a subsequent 'General Comment No 31: The Nature of the General Legal Obligation Imposed on States Parties to the Covenant': 'In no case may the restrictions be applied or invoked in a manner that would impair the essence of a Covenant right.'[25] And in 'General Comment No 32: Right to Equality before Courts and Tribunals and to a Fair Trial (Art 14)', the Committee also identified an essential core in ICCPR Article 14 by outlawing such restrictions to the right to access to court that would 'undermine the very essence of the right'.[26] Finally, in its 'General Comment No 34: Freedoms of Opinion and Expression (Art 19)', the most recent General Comment available as of the time of the finalization of this chapter, the Committee identified freedom of opinion as the essential core of ICCPR Article 19:

> although freedom of opinion is not listed among those rights that may not be derogated from pursuant to the provisions of article 4 of the Covenant, it is recalled that, 'in those provisions of the Covenant that are not listed in article 4, paragraph 2, there are elements that in the Committee's opinion cannot be made subject to lawful derogation under article 4'. Freedom of opinion is one such element, since it can never become necessary to derogate from it during a state of emergency. [27]

and, 'Paragraph 1 of article 19 requires protection of the right to hold opinions without interference. This is a right to which the Covenant permits no exception or restriction.'[28]

Building upon the practice of the Human Rights Committee, and in particular its General Comment No 27, in his capacity as United Nations Special Rapporteur,

[23] HRC, 'General Comment No 27: Freedom of Movement (Art 12)' (2 November 1999) UN Doc CCPR/C/21/Rev.1/Add.9.

[24] HRC, 'General Comment No 27' (n 23) para 13.

[25] HRC, 'General Comment No 31: The Nature of the General Legal Obligation Imposed on States Parties to the Covenant' (26 May 2004) UN Doc CCPR/C/21/Rev.1/Add.13, para 6.

[26] HRC, 'General Comment No 32: Right to Equality before Courts and Tribunals and to a Fair Trial (Art 14)' (23 August 2007) UN Doc CCPR/C/GC/32, para 18.

[27] HRC, 'General Comment No 34: Freedoms of Opinion and Expression (Art 19)' (12 September 2011) UN Doc CCPR/C/GC/34, para 5.

[28] HRC 'General Comment No 34' (n 27) para 9.

the current author has proposed that the inviolability of the essential core of any human right—in that case the right to privacy—is one of the steps in an analytically rigorous test of the permissibility of restrictions. In that context, the elements of a permissible limitations test were condensed as follows:

(a) Any restrictions must be provided by the law...;
(b) The essence of a human right is not subject to restrictions...;
(c) Restrictions must be necessary in a democratic society...;
(d) Any discretion exercised when implementing the restrictions must not be unfettered...;
(e) For a restriction to be permissible, it is not enough that it serves one of the enumerated legitimate aims; it must be necessary for reaching the legitimate aim...;
(f) Restrictive measures must conform to the principle of proportionality; they must be appropriate to achieve their protective function; they must be the least intrusive instrument amongst those which might achieve the desired result; and they must be proportionate to the interest to be protected...;
(g) Any restrictions must be consistent with the other rights guaranteed in the Covenant...[29]

Many national constitutions include positive law formulations of all or many fundamental rights containing an essential or inviolable core.[30] Moreover, the Charter of Fundamental Rights of the European Union, which the Treaty of Lisbon elevated to the status of part of the constituting treaties of the European Union, corresponds to that approach by proclaiming as follows:

Any limitation on the exercise of the rights and freedoms recognised by this Charter must be provided for by law and respect the essence of those rights and freedoms. Subject to the principle of proportionality, limitations may be made only if they are necessary and genuinely meet objectives of general interest recognised by the Union or the need to protect the rights and freedoms of others.[31]

One way to relate the idea that each human right contains an inviolable core to rights theories is to explain that a human right, formulated in broad and morality-based terms, would constitute a principle in the meaning of Robert Alexy's theory of rights[32] when positivized in law, but would at the same time carry a more narrow rule as its essential and inviolable core. While principles allow for optimization

[29] UNGA, 'Report of the Special Rapporteur on the Promotion and Protection of Human Rights and Fundamental Freedoms while Countering Terrorism, Martin Scheinin' (28 December 2009) UN Doc A/HRC/13/37, para 17 (footnotes omitted, emphasis added). The pin-pointed characteristics reference HRC, 'General Comment No 27' (n 23) paras 11–12, 13, 14–15, and 18, respectively.

[30] The best known example is Art 19(2) of the German Basic Law of 1949, addressing restrictions to fundamental rights: 'In no case may the essence of a basic right be affected', Art 19(2) GG.

[31] OJ [2007] C303/1, Art 52(1) (emphasis added).

[32] Robert Alexy, *Theorie der Grundrechte* (Suhrkamp 1994). See also the postscript in Robert Alexy, *A Theory of Fundamental Rights* (OUP 2002) (English edition of *Theorie der Grundrechte*); Robert

through a process of weighing and balancing against competing principles, a rule either determines the outcome of a case, or it does not apply at all. The interpretation of legal norms with the character of a principle is primarily a matter of assessing its weight in relation to other, competing principles. In contrast, as rules are applied in an all-or-nothing fashion, defining their scope of application is the most important question in their interpretation. If a rule applies, it also determines the outcome of a case. As the validity of principles pertains to the legal order as a whole, they will always apply; however, their concrete effect in a case depends on a process of optimization in relation to all other factors, including possibly competing principles. As a rule determines the outcome of a case within its own scope of application, there can never be genuine conflict between rules. Rather, rules are applied to determine the proper scope of application of each other, such as in the case of a main rule and an exception.[33]

In short, every human right contains a core with the quality of a rule. When a case falls within the properly defined scope of application of that rule, the rule determines the outcome without any further operation of balancing. Hence, the inviolability of the essential core of any human right is an important step in the assessment of permissible limitations to the broader human right surrounding that core.

As a final word concerning the approach of each human right containing an essential or inviolable core, it needs to be emphasized that the notion of a core is, of course, just a metaphor. Some human rights are complex umbrella concepts that host a number of quite different substantive elements, or attributes.[34] For instance ICCPR Article 17's provision on the right to privacy lists family, home, correspondence, honour, and reputation, in addition to privacy itself, as spheres protected as human rights. It is quite understandable that all or several of such interconnected, but nevertheless separately identifiable, attributes of a complex human right may contain their own core areas and therefore a single human rights treaty provision multiple 'cores'.

Alexy, 'Constitutional Rights and Legal Systems' in Joakim Nergelius (ed), *Constitutionalism: New Challenges: European Law from a Nordic Perspective* (Martinus Nijhoff 2008).

[33] For the author's elaboration and application of Robert Alexy's theory on rules and principles, see Martin Scheinin and others, 'Law and Security—Facing the Dilemmas' (2009) *EUI Working Papers Law* 2009/11 <http://cadmus.eui.eu/bitstream/handle/1814/12233/LAW_2009_11.pdf?sequence=3> accessed 1 February 2013.

[34] The notion of 'attributes' was chosen to refer to the main substantive dimensions of a human rights provision in a project with the UN Office of the High Commissioner for Human Rights, to identify indicators for the assessment of compliance with human rights treaties. The methodology for defining the attributes representing each human right was based, inter alia, on the General Comments of the respective treaty body and on an effort to find attributes that, as far as possible, are at the same time mutually exclusive and, when taken together, comprehensive in relation to the substantive scope of the treaty provision. See, in particular, UN Office of the High Commissioner, Human Rights Indicators: A Guide to Measurement and Implementation (2012) UN Doc HR/PUB/12/5, 31 <http://www.ohchr.org/Documents/Publications/Human_rights_indicators_en.pdf> accessed 2 February 2013.

3. Core Obligations

There is one more general approach through which the issue of a core is addressed in human rights law: it focuses on the state as the duty-bearer in relation to the human rights of its population (or any other individuals with human rights entitlements vis-à-vis that state) and tries to identify whether some of the state's human rights obligations are more burning, more immediate, or more compelling than some others. Hence, the question is whether core obligations, or minimum core obligations, can be identified.

The commonly used typologies of state obligations under human rights law are well known, most often combining the dichotomy of positive and negative obligations with the tripartite typology to respect, to protect, and to fulfil. There may be differences of emphasis (but not of category) between civil and political rights, on the one hand, and economic, social, and cultural rights, on the other—such that the negative obligation not to violate a human right, which is closely associated with the duty to respect it, resides predominantly under civil and political rights, while positive obligations pertaining to the duty to fulfil are primarily in focus when dealing with economic, social, and cultural rights. Another point of discussion relates to the drafting of the 1966 Covenants, in that the one on civil and political rights calls for immediate and full compliance upon entry into force through a state's voluntary ratification,[35] while the sister Covenant on economic, social, and cultural rights allows for progressive realization to the maximum of available resources,[36] even if, as a matter of law, its entry into force as a legally binding treaty is as clear-cut as the case of the ICCPR.

Originally, a political body, the Economic and Social Council (ECOSOC), was to monitor the ICESCR.[37] In 1985, ECOSOC decided to establish an eighteen-member expert committee to monitor the ICESCR, including through the consideration of periodic state reports.[38] Quite soon that expert committee, following the example of the Human Rights Committee, started to issue General Comments on provisions of, or issues arising under, the ICESCR. Since its General Comment No 3, the Committee on Economic, Social and Cultural Rights has adopted an approach under which it tries to define minimum core obligations under the ICESCR. This approach can be seen as an effort to respond to the challenge the Article 2

[35] ICCPR, Art 2(1) on general state obligations is based on the idea of immediate compliance, as a State Party 'undertakes to respect and to ensure... the rights recognized in the present Covenant'.

[36] ICESCR, Art 2(1) contains the progressive realization clause according to which a State Party 'undertakes to take steps... to the maximum of its available resources, with a view to achieving progressively the full realization of the rights recognized in the present Covenant'.

[37] See, ICESCR, Arts 16(2), 21.

[38] Economic and Social Council, Res 1985/17 (28 May 1985) UN Doc E/Res/1985/17.

progressive realization clause and its reference to 'available resources' have posed. When identifying something as a minimum core obligation, the Committee appears to assert that those dimensions of ICESCR rights are immediate, not conditioned by the possible lack of resources, and even directly applicable (justiciable). A consequence of the immediate nature of the core obligations is that retrogressive measures within their scope will entail a violation of the ICESCR. These features of the Committee's understanding of the notion of core obligations can be illustrated by reference to some of its General Comments.[39]

In 1990, the Committee adopted its General Comment No 3.[40] This General Comment refers to the minimum core obligation 'to ensure the satisfaction of, at the very least, minimum essential levels of each of the rights' and then gives examples related to specific ICESCR rights—listing here essential foodstuffs, essential primary healthcare, basic shelter and housing, or the most basic forms of education.[41] In relation to the reference in Article 2(1) to available resources, the Committee imposes upon states the heavy burden of justifying any failure to meet their core obligations:

> In order for a State party to be able to attribute its failure to meet at least its minimum core obligations to a lack of available resources it must demonstrate that every effort has been made to use all resources that are at its disposition in an effort to satisfy, as a matter of priority, those minimum obligations.[42]

Several of the General Comments related to specific ICESCR rights have followed this approach to minimum core obligations. For instance, in 'General Comment No 12: The Right to Adequate Food (Art 11)', the Committee first conceded that the right to food is subject to the progressive realization clause also, but then used the core obligations approach to define the mitigation or alleviation of hunger as a core obligation that must be met irrespective of the level of resources and made justiciable through courts.[43]

> The right to adequate food will have to be realized progressively. However, States have a core obligation to take the necessary action to mitigate and alleviate hunger as provided for in

[39] For a thorough analysis of the notion of core obligations under the ICESCR, see Katharine G Young, 'The Minimum Core of Economic and Social Rights: A Concept in Search of Content' (2008) 33 *Yale J Int'l L* 113. Similarly to the current chapter, she structures her analysis around a typology of three different approaches to a 'core' of human rights. While Young's analysis contains elements that also appear in the current discussion, they are presented in the context of an assessment of the way the Committee on Economic, Social and Cultural Rights (CESCR) addresses the minimum core obligations of the state. That said, Young also discusses what she calls the 'Essence Approach', which is related to the position the current author prefers.

[40] CESCR, 'General Comment No 3: The Nature of States Parties' Obligations (Art 2, para 1)' (14 December 1990) UN Doc E/1991/23, annex III.

[41] CESCR, 'General Comment No 3' (n 40) para 10.

[42] CESCR, 'General Comment No 3' (n 40) para 10.

[43] CESCR, 'General Comment No 12: The Right to Adequate Food (Art 11)' (12 May 1999) UN Doc E/C.12/1999/5.

paragraph 2 of article 11, even in times of natural or other disasters... Courts would then be empowered to adjudicate violations of the core content of the right to food by direct reference to obligations under the Covenant.[44]

'General Comment No 14: The Right to the Highest Attainable Standard of Health (Art 12)' draws the conclusion that retrogressive measures constitute a violation of the ICESCR in relation to core obligations.[45] 'The adoption of any retrogressive measures incompatible with the core obligations under the right to health, outlined in paragraph 43 above, constitutes a violation of the right to health.'[46]

The minimum core obligations approach developed under the ICESCR combines the consequences of immediate effect, immunity from the excuse of insufficient resources, non-retrogression, and direct applicability. The ICESCR contains no underlying 'deep theory' or positive law basis for the approach. Even if this approach has been here presented as a separate and third one, due to its focus on state obligations rather than individual entitlements, the core obligations approach is actually highly compatible with the second approach—the idea of each human right containing essential core content that is not subject to exceptions or limitations. The examples and arguments the ICESCR Committee uses are very much in line with efforts to locate such an essential core within the broader scope of treaty provisions on economic, social, and cultural rights. Hence, the third approach can be seen as a methodology for how to operationalize the second approach in relation to the states parties of the ICESCR.

4. Discussion

Each of the three approaches presented above appears to possess some merit in furthering a thorough understanding of the normative quality and content of human rights as legal rights. That said, it is proposed herein that the best way to reach such an understanding is to reconcile and merge the three approaches. The second and third approach, relating respectively to each human right having an essential core and to a focus on core obligations of the state, enable a comprehensive and holistic view on human rights. And as just explained, the third approach can be understood as a methodology for operationalizing the second approach in relation to state obligations.

[44] CESCR, 'General Comment No 12' (n 43) paras 6, 33.

[45] CESCR, 'General Comment No 14: The Right to the Highest Attainable Standard of Health (Art 12)' (11 August 2000) UN Doc E/C.12/2000/4, para 48.

[46] CESCR, 'General Comment No 14' (n 45) para 48.

All human rights are fundamental and therefore result in inviolable entitlements of the human person and inescapable state obligations. These considerations lead us to dismiss as an unnecessary and unfounded extrapolation of the first approach (related to a distinct category of core rights), that there would be a fixed hierarchy among human rights. If each human right includes an essential and inviolable core, then there is no abstract order of primacy between human rights. Rather, potential tensions and even conflicts between human rights must be addressed by granting each human right primacy within the defined scope of its essential core, the non-core dimensions of other human rights having therefore to yield in those situations. Using once again the language of rules and principles, it is possible to utilize weighing and balancing to resolve tensions or collisions between human rights where the two (or more) rights operate as principles, ie the case or issue does not fall within the scope of the essential core of any of them. But when a situation does fall within the essential core of a human right, applicable as a rule, then that right determines the outcome, without any further recourse to balancing against other human rights or against any other considerations, including national security. Certainly, this kind of a categorical approach advocates caution in determining the scope of the essential core of any human right, so that its integrity will be worthy of full respect even in difficult circumstances. One consideration in defining the respective cores of various human rights is that these cores must never end up in a conflict with each other. If a seeming (prima facie) conflict arises between two rules, it must be resolved through redefining each rule's proper scope of application, so that an all-things-considered conflict is avoided.

The obvious merit of the first approach, even if dismissed as such here, rests in its reliance upon notions of non-derogable rights and *jus cogens* norms, and hence its appeal to the moral values behind positive law human rights provisions. That said, there is also a way to reconcile the first approach with the idea that every human right contains an inviolable essential core. What is typical for human rights falling in the two overlapping categories of non-derogable rights and *jus cogens* norms is that they can often be formulated in the form of a prohibition. This suggests that the particular human right at issue may contain a core that is proportionally wider than an average situation under any human right. While a right subject to permissible derogation and permissible limitations may be described as a broad principle with a narrow inviolable core, rights that are of an absolute, non-derogable, or *jus cogens* nature tend to include a core that is, comparatively speaking, wide in scope. And even if the core obligations of the state, which the third approach covers, cannot be reduced to the negative obligation not to violate a human right (the duty to respect), that dimension of a negative right still will be more prominent in the case of absolute, non-derogable, or *jus cogens* rights.

What results from the above discussion is a model based on the second approach, but informed by the first and the third. Perhaps the most important conclusion to be drawn from this reconciliation is the importance of interpretation for the proper understanding and application of human rights. The application of concepts, such as rules, principles, attributes, scope, and weight, will not be self-evident on the basis of the mere wording of a human rights treaty provision. Rather, they are methodological tools for making sense of the substantive content—rights and obligations—flowing from complex formulations of human rights treaty provisions, often relying in their wording upon direct references to moral values. In accordance with the established rules concerning treaty interpretation, reflected in Articles 31 and 32 of the Vienna Convention on the Law of Treaties, and with due regard to the special characteristics of human rights treaties,[47] the identification of the essential core content of various human rights will be a matter for the institutionalized practices of interpretation existing under the human rights treaties in question to affirm.

Further Reading

Alexy R, *A Theory of Fundamental Rights* (OUP 2002)

Meron T, 'On a Hierarchy of International Human Rights' (1986) 80 *AJIL* 1

Scheinin M and others, 'Law and Security—Facing the Dilemmas' (2009) *EUI Working Papers Law* 2009/11

Shue H, *Basic Rights: Subsistence, Affluence, and US Foreign Policy* (Princeton UP 1980)

Young KG, 'The Minimum Core of Economic and Social Rights: A Concept in Search of Content' (2008) 33 *Yale J Int'l L* 113

[47] See, Martin Scheinin, 'Impact on the Law of Treaties' in Menno T Kamminga and Martin Scheinin (eds), *The Impact of Human Rights Law on General International Law* (OUP 2009). See, also, the chapters by Jonas Christoffersen (on treaty interpretation) and Ineke Boerefijn (on reservations) in the same volume.

CHAPTER 23

JUS COGENS AND OBLIGATIONS *ERGA OMNES*

ERIKA DE WET

1. The Concept of *Jus Cogens*

The notion of peremptory norms in international law is reminiscent of the distinction in Roman law between *jus strictum* (strict law) and *jus dispositivum* (voluntary law), as well as the natural law thinking of the seventeenth and eighteenth centuries, according to which certain rules existed independent of the will of states and law-makers.[1] It found its way into positive international law through Article 53 of the Vienna Convention on the Law of Treaties of 1969 (VCLT).[2] As is well known, this article determines that:

> [a] treaty is void if, at the time of its conclusion, it conflicts with a peremptory norm of general international law. For the purposes of the present Convention, a peremptory norm of general international law is a norm accepted and recognized by the international community of States as a whole as a norm from which no derogation is permitted and which can be modified only by a subsequent norm of general international law having the same character.

[1] ILC, Report of the Study Group on Fragmentation of International Law: Difficulties arising from the Diversification and Expansion of International Law (13 April 2006) UN Doc A/CN.4/L.682, para 361 (Fragmentation Report).

[2] Reprinted in (1969) 8 *Intl L Materials* 679.

In addition, Article 64 of the VCLT declares that '[if] a new peremptory norm of general international law emerges, any existing treaty which is in conflict with that norm becomes void and terminates'.

The work of Albert Verdross, who himself was strongly influenced by natural law, particularly influenced the definition in the VCLT. In accordance with Verdross's line of reasoning, general principles of morality or public policy common to the legal orders of civilized states would constitute a limitation on contradicting treaty obligations.[3] In his view, immoral treaties would include those preventing the maintenance of law and order within a state, defence against external attack, care for the bodily and spiritual welfare of citizens, as well as the protection of foreigners abroad.[4]

The definition in Article 53 VCLT does not identify any norms having peremptory status. This relates to the fact that at the time of its adoption the concept was regarded with suspicion by some Western countries (notably France[5]), while it enjoyed more support amongst the (then) socialist and newly independent states.[6] Article 53 VCLT was thus negotiated so as to leave it to the 'international community as a whole' to identify those international law norms belonging to the category of *jus cogens*. In essence, this implies that a particular norm is first recognized as customary international law, whereafter the international community of states as a whole further agrees that it is a norm from which no derogation is permitted.[7] The international community of states as a whole would therefore subject a peremptory norm to 'double acceptance'.[8]

[3] Alfred Verdross, 'Forbidden Treaties in International Law' (1937) 31 *AJIL* 571, 572. See also Alfred Verdross, 'Jus Dispositivum and Jus Cogens in International Law' (1966) 60 *AJIL* 55, 56. He further suggested that customary rules of international law, such as freedom of the high seas, would invalidate treaties in which two or more states excluded other states from the use of the high seas. But see Dinah Shelton, 'Normative Hierarchy in International Law'(2006) 100 *AJIL* 291, 298. She accurately points out that that it is unclear why one would need the notion of peremptory norms under these circumstances. Customary international law has long recognized the *pacta tertiis* rule, according to which states cannot limit the rights of third states without their consent. Articles 34 and 35 VCLT also codify it.

[4] Verdross 'Forbidden Treaties' (n 3) 574; Shelton (n 3) 299.

[5] France has still not ratified the VCLT in large part due to opposition to *jus cogens*.

[6] Eric Suy, 'Article 53 Treaties conflicting with a peremptory norm of general international law ("jus cogens")' in Olivier Corten and Pierre Klein (eds), *The Vienna Convention on the Law of Treaties: A Commentary Volume II* (OUP 2011) 1225. The Soviet international law doctrine regarded the principles of peaceful coexistence, which also found their way into the Declaration on Principles of International Law concerning Friendly Relations and Co-operation among States in accordance with the Charter of the United Nations, UNGA Res 2625 (XXV) (24 October 1970), as peremptory in nature. See also Jure Vidmar, 'Norm Conflicts and Hierarchy in International Law: Towards a Vertical International System?' in Erika de Wet and Jure Vidmar (eds), *Hierarchy in International Law: The Place of Human Rights* (OUP 2012) 26; Christine Chinkin, 'Jus Cogens, Article 103 of the UN Charter and Other Hierarchical Techniques of Conflict Solution' (2006) XVII *FYBIL* 63, 68.

[7] Shelton (n 3) 300. It is of course possible that a norm of *jus cogens* finds its way into a treaty, as is the case with most of the obligations on the ILC's list referred to in (the text leading up to) n 13.

[8] Vidmar (n 6) 25.

This threshold for gaining peremptory status is high, for although it does not require a consensus among all states (and a single state would not be able to block the recognition of a peremptory norm), it does require the acceptance of a large majority of states.[9] The fact that complete consensus amongst states is not a requirement for the emergence of a peremptory norm further implies that the peremptory obligation can nonetheless bind the (very small number of) states not in agreement against their will.[10] For example, the claim of South Africa's government that it was a persistent objector to the prohibition of racial discrimination and apartheid was universally rejected with the argument that peremptory law does not exempt persistent objectors.[11] In the case of a peremptory norm, the collective will, underpinned by shared values of the international community of states, can overrule the will of an individual state.[12]

2. The Content of *Jus Cogens*

Since the late 1990s, increased acceptance of the concept of *jus cogens* can be observed in doctrine, the case law of international courts and tribunals and the work of the United Nations International Law Commission (ILC). According to the ILC, the most frequently cited candidates for *jus cogens* status include: (a) the prohibition of aggressive use of force; (b) the right to self-defence; (c) the prohibition of genocide; (d) the prohibition of torture; (e) crimes against humanity; (f) the prohibition of slavery and slave trade; (g) the prohibition of piracy; (h) the prohibition of racial discrimination and *apartheid*, and (i) the prohibition of hostilities directed at a civilian population ('basic rules of international humanitarian law').[13]

[9] Elsewhere this author has argued that *jus cogens* norms would be obligations *erga omnes*, ie would affect the international community as a whole (to be understood as states and other subjects of international law). See Erika de Wet, 'The International Constitutional Order' (2006) 55 *ICLQ* 51, 61. Support for this position can be found in *Barcelona Traction, Light and Power Company Ltd* 32. Although the ICJ did not expressly refer to *jus cogens*, it implied as much by the types of norms it mentioned as examples of *erga omnes* norms (ie prohibition of unilateral use of force, genocide, and the prohibition of slavery and racial discrimination). For an analysis of the relationship between *jus cogens* and *erga omnes* obligations, see the contribution of Olivier de Schutter in this Handbook.

[10] Vidmar (n 6) 26. [11] Vidmar (n 6) 26.

[12] See Shelton (n 3) 299, who also notes that the notion of *jus cogens* deviates from the notion of a strictly voluntarist view of international law.

[13] Fragmentation Report (n 1) para 374. See also ILC, Official Records of the General Assembly, Fifth-sixth Session (5 May–6 June and 7 July–8 August 2003) UN Doc A/56/10, 283–84; 'Commentary to Article 26' in 'Draft articles on the Responsibility of International Organizations with Commentaries' (2011) 2 *YB of Intl L Com.*

This list features predominantly human rights obligations and, as will be discussed below, in particular the prohibition of genocide and the prohibition of torture. Judicial bodies have widely recognized these prohibitions as constituting *jus cogens*. Some decisions and judgments have also extended the list of human rights that have acquired peremptory status beyond what is included in the ILC's list. A common feature of most of these decisions is the absence of any systematic reference to state practice and/or *opinio juris* to buttress the conclusion that the norm(s) in question are *jus cogens*.

This lack of supporting evidence was apparent, for example, when then International Court of Justice (ICJ) for the first time explicitly referred to *jus cogens* in a majority opinion.[14] In the 2006 decision *Democratic Republic of Congo v Rwanda*, pertaining to armed activities in the territory of the Congo,[15] the ICJ described genocide as 'assuredly' being a peremptory norm of general international law, without engaging in any analysis of state practice.[16] The same lack of systematic analysis can be witnessed in the *Furundzija*[17] and *Al Adsani*[18] decisions of, respectively, the International Criminal Tribunal for the Former Yugoslavia (ICTY) and the European Court of Human Rights (ECtHR), when concluding that the prohibition of torture constitutes a *jus cogens* norm.

The 2003 advisory opinion of the Inter-American Court of Human Rights (IACtHR) on undocumented migrants[19] cited nineteen treaties and fourteen soft law instruments in an attempt to illustrate the 'universal acceptance' of the obligation of non-discrimination.[20] However, in support of its conclusion that the obligation also enjoyed peremptory status, the IACtHR seems to have relied on natural law. It linked equality before the law to the dignity of the individual, claiming that all persons have attributes inherent to their human dignity that those in power may not disregard.[21]

The Inter-American Commission on Human Rights has also relied on natural law in motivating its position that the right to life has *jus cogens* status. It stated that *jus cogens* derives from a higher order of norms established in ancient times and which

[14] In *Military and Paramilitary Activities in and against Nicaragua*, para 190 the court did not explicitly refer to *jus cogens* norms, even though this is often claimed. Instead the ICJ referred to some rules of international humanitarian law as 'intransgressible' principles of customary international law. Shelton (n 3) 305.

[15] *Armed Activities on the Territory of the Congo* 32.

[16] Shelton (n 3) 306.

[17] *Prosecutor v Anto Furundzija*, para 153.

[18] *Al-Adsani v UK*, para 55.

[19] *Juridical Condition and Rights of the Undocumented Migrants*.

[20] *Undocumented Migrants* (n 19) para 99; Shelton (n 3) 310.

[21] *Undocumented Migrants* (n 19) paras 45, 73, 99. See also the position of the Inter-American Commission of Human Rights, which intervened in the case. It submitted that the principle of non-discrimination constitutes *jus cogens*, given its 'fundamental importance' in all international laws, despite admitting that the international community has not yet reached consensus on prohibiting discrimination based on motives other than racial discrimination. *Undocumented Migrants* (n 19) para 47. See also Shelton (n 3) 310.

the laws of man or nations cannot contravene.[22] The Inter-American Commission on Human Rights further suggested, without additional analysis, that non-derogable treaty rights constitute an important starting point for identifying *jus cogens* norms.[23] On the one hand, the quality of non-derogability does suggest that the right in question has special significance.[24] For example, the prohibition of slavery and torture, which are generally regarded as peremptory norms, are also recognized as non-derogable in the International Covenant on Civil and Political Rights of 1966 (ICCPR), the European Convention of Human Rights and Fundamental Freedoms of 1950 (ECHR) and the Inter-American Convention on Human Rights (ACHR). On the other hand, the lists of non-derogable rights in the three conventions are not identical, with the ACHR in particular containing a very extensive list.[25]

Overlap exists only in relation to the right to life (prohibition of the arbitrary deprivation of life); the prohibition of torture, inhuman and degrading punishment; the prohibition of slavery; and the prohibition of retroactive application of criminal offences. While a case can be made that (most of) these rights have acquired peremptory status, it is doubtful whether one could say this of the other rights listed as non-derogable in one or more of these instruments, such as the prohibition against imprisonment for breach of a contractual obligation (non-derogable according to ICCPR), or the right to a name or the right to a nationality (non-derogable according to the ACHR). In essence, therefore, the depiction of a right as non-derogable in an international human rights instrument would be a factor to be taken into account when determining whether the right has acquired *jus cogens*, but is not in itself decisive.[26]

[22] *Victims of the Tugboat '13 de Marzo' v Cuba*, para 79.

[23] See *Dominques v United States*, para 49; Shelton (n 3) 314.

[24] The Human Rights Committee, 'General Comment No. 29: States of Emergency (article 4)' (31 August 2001), UN Doc No CCPR/C/21/Rev.1/Add.11 described the proclamation of certain rights as being of a non-derogable nature as partial recognition of their peremptory character. But see Harmen van der Wilt, 'On the Hierarchy between Extradition and Human Rights' in De Wet and Vidmar (n 6) at 154. He suggests that the non-derogable (absolute) quality of a norm such as the prohibition of torture gives it a special quality, as a result of which the (additional) qualification of *jus cogens* would have little added value.

[25] Article 4(2) ICCPR recognizes as non-derogable: Art 6 (the right to life); Art 7 (prohibition of torture, inhuman or degrading treatment); Art 8(1) and (2) (prohibition of slavery); Art 11 (prohibition of imprisonment for contractual obligations); Art 15 (prevention of retroactive application of criminal offences); Art 16 (the right to recognition as a person before the law); and Art 18 (freedom of thought, conscience and religion). Art 15 ECHR recognizes as non-derogable: Art 2 (right to life); Art 3 (prohibition of torture, inhuman or degrading treatment); Art 4(1) (prohibition of slavery); and Art 7 (prevention of retroactive application of criminal offences). Art 27(2) ACHR recognizes as non-derogable: Art 3 (right to recognition before the law), Art 4 (right to life), Art 5 (prevention of torture, inhumane or degrading treatment), Art 6 (prohibition of slavery), Art 9 (prevention of retroactive application of criminal offences); Art 12 (freedom of conscience and religion); Art 17 (rights of the family); Art 18 (right to a name); Art 19 (rights of the child); Art 20 (right to nationality); and Art 23 (right to participate in government); or the judicial guarantees essential for the protection of such rights.

[26] The Human Rights Committee has similarly assessed the quality of non-derogable rights in its 'General Comment No 24: Issues relating to reservations made upon ratification or accession

The same natural law approach present in the above decisions underpinned the sweeping approach of the (then still) Court of First Instance (CFI) of the European Union in the first *Kadi* decision.[27] The case concerned the targeted sanctioning of individuals the United Nations Security Council suspected of involvement with Al Qaeda, in accordance with Security Council Resolution 1267 of 15 October (1999) and subsequent resolutions, without the possibility of a fair trial.[28] According to the CFI, it followed from Articles 25 and 103 of the Charter that United Nations Security Council obligations prevailed over any other conflicting obligation of international treaty law. In addition, the CFI did not have the right in cases appropriately before it to examine (incidentally) the legality of Security Council resolutions.[29] At the same time, the CFI claimed that an exception existed to these principles with respect to *jus cogens* obligations. It would have the right to review (incidentally) the legality of Security Council Resolutions which conflicted with *jus cogens* obligations, as these obligations were binding on all subjects of international law, including the organs of the United Nations.[30]

In determining which norms constitute *jus cogens*, the CFI seems to have relied on a natural law argument, according to which the United Nations Charter itself presupposed the existence of mandatory principles of international law, in particular the protection of the fundamental rights of the human person. By following this line of argument, the CFI elevated the entire body of human rights law to the peremptory level from which neither states nor the organs of the United Nations may derogate.[31] However, the fact that the CFI also seems to have elevated the limitations attached to the rights in question to the peremptory level immediately quashed any expectation that this sweeping approach would result in effective judicial and other human

to the Covenant or the Optional Protocols thereto, or in relation to declarations under article 41 of the Covenant' (4 November 1994) UN Doc CCPR/C/21/Rev.1/Add.6. In para 10 it noted that the non-derogable character of a right does not necessarily mean that it is absolute and exempt from reservations.

[27] *Kadi v Council and Commission.*

[28] See Erika de Wet, 'Human Rights Considerations and the Enforcement of Targeted Sanctions in Europe: The Emergence of Core Standards of Judicial Protection for overview and analysis of literature' in Bardo Fassbender (ed), *Securing Human Rights? Achievements and Challenges of the UN Security Council* (OUP 2011), 141 *et seq.*

[29] *Kadi* (n 27) paras 181–183 and paras 224–225; see also Shelton (n 3) 311.

[30] *Kadi* (n 27) para 226. It is now accepted in doctrine and practice that *jus cogens* binds the United Nations Security Council. However, the challenge remains to determine which norms would constitute *jus cogens* and therefore bind the Council. See extensively Antonios Tzanakopoulus, 'Collective Security and Human Rights' in Erika de Wet and Jure Vidmar (n 6) 49 *et seq.*

[31] *Kadi* (n 27) para 231; Shelton (n 3) 312. Compare also *Youssef Nada v State Secretariat for Economic Affairs and Federal Department of Economic Affairs* para 7.3. In this instance, the court followed the reasoning of the *Kadi* decision, but limited the range of peremptory norms—without any explanation—to the right to life, the protection from torture and humiliating treatment, the freedom from slavery and human trafficking, the prohibition on collective punishment, the principle of personal responsibility in criminal prosecution, and the principle of non-refoulement. It did not include in its list the right to a fair trial.

rights protection for the targeted individuals.[32] As a result, the CFI granted the Security Council extensive discretion in limiting (inter alia) the rights to a fair trial and the right to property, and concluded that no violation of any *jus cogens* obligation occurred through the UN's listing procedure.[33] Although the European Court of Justice (ECJ) overturned the CFI's decision on appeal, the ECJ did not engage with or explicitly overturn the CFI's *jus cogens* reasoning. Instead, the ECJ followed a dualist approach in the sense that it granted judicial protection exclusively on the basis of European Union law, which it treated as a domestic (in the sense of autonomous) legal system.[34] As the *jus cogens* reasoning of the CFI remains untouched, its ghost may continue to haunt debate over the content of *jus cogens*.

The vague natural law arguments of the courts above, combined with their scant reliance on state practice, arguably pose some of the biggest threats to the credibility of peremptory norms as representing the core values of the international community as a whole.[35] The decisions open the door for the inclusion of a wide variety of arbitrarily selected norms on the *jus cogens* list and for potential abuse by courts, states, and other actors claiming to serve the interests of the international community.[36]

3. The Practical Impact of *Jus Cogens*

An overview of case law, some of which is cited below,[37] reveals that despite the categorical fashion in which some judicial bodies acknowledge the peremptory status of certain norms, very few judgments have thus far given extensive effect to the normative ambition of *jus cogens*.[38] This reluctance is evidenced by the limited role that peremptory norms play in the resolution of norm conflicts before international and domestic judicial bodies. This applies to norm conflicts between treaty obligations,

[32] See also Carlo Focarelli, 'Promotional Jus Cogens: A Critical Appraisal of Jus Cogens' Legal Effects' (2008) 77 *Nord J Intl L* 429, 436.

[33] *Kadi* (n 27) paras 286, 288; Shelton (n 3) 312.

[34] See *Kadi and Al Barakaat International Foundation v Council and Commission*.

[35] Shelton (n 3) 313; Andrea Bianchi, 'Human Rights and the Magic of Jus Cogens' (2008) 19(3) *EJIL* 491, 506.

[36] Focarelli (n 32) 440; Chinkin (n 6) 68. For a critique of the notion of universal values, see also Martti Koskenniemi, 'International Law in Europe: between Tradition and Renewal' (2005) 16 *EJIL* 113, 113 *et seq*.

[37] For an extensive overview, see de Wet and Vidmar (n 6).

[38] Jutta Brunnée, 'The Prohibition on Torture: Driving Jus Cogens Home?' (2010) 104 *Proceedings of the Annual Meeting of the American Society of International Law* 454.

which constitute the original context in which Article 53 VCLT developed,[39] as well as norm conflicts between treaty and customary obligations.

In general, judges do not seem to be convinced that peremptory norms would have the legal effects that the various protagonists of the cause would attribute to them.[40] This follows inter alia from the narrow scope of most peremptory obligations, as well as the fact that courts rely on conflict avoidance techniques that obscure the relevance or added value of the peremptory status of (one of) the norms in question. The question also arises of why one would need to rely on the 'special' character of *jus cogens*, when one could achieve a similar result by relying on 'ordinary' customary international law.

3.1 Limiting the scope of *jus cogens* norms

In accordance with Article 53 VCLT, a treaty is null and void if it is concluded to be in conflict with a peremptory norm of general international law (ie *jus cogens*). To give a concrete example, a treaty between two countries aimed at committing genocide against a particular ethnic group on one or both of their territories would be null and void. The state parties would also have to eliminate as far as possible the consequences of acts performed in reliance on provisions in conflict with the peremptory norm, and should bring their mutual relations in conformity with the peremptory norm.[41] Where a treaty itself does not violate a *jus cogens* norm, but the execution of certain obligations under the treaty would have such effect, the state is relieved from the need to give effect to the obligation in question. The treaty itself would, however, not be null and void. For example, the obligations existing under an extradition treaty would fall away if they resulted in the extradition of a person to a country where he or she faced torture. [42] The treaty itself would nonetheless remain intact.[43]

In practice, however, the main threat to *jus cogens* norms does not result from (particular obligations within) bilateral or multilateral treaties, but from acts of

[39] Some authors regard the application of *jus cogens* outside of the treaty context as an over-extension of its original role. Andreas Zimmermann, 'Sovereign Immunity and Violations of International *Jus Cogens*—Some Critical Remarks' (1995) 16 *Michigan J Intl L* 433, 438; Wladyslav Czaplinski, 'Concepts of *Jus Cogens* and Obligations *Erga Omnes* in International Law in the Light of Recent Developments' (1999) 23 *Polish YB Intl L* 87, 88.

[40] Brunnée (n 38) 455.

[41] VCLT (n 2) Art 71; see also AJJ de Hoogh, 'The Relationship between *Jus Cogens*, Obligations *Erga Omnes* and International Crimes: Peremptory Norms in Perspective' (1991) 42(2) *Österreichische Zeitschrift für öffentliches Recht und Völkerrecht* 183, 190.

[42] After 9 September 2011, there have been allegations of agreements between the USA and Egypt facilitating the transport of detainees from the USA to Egypt, where they were subjected to torture during interrogation. See Erika de Wet, 'The prohibition of torture as an international norm of jus cogens and its implications for national and customary law' (2004) 15(1) *EJIL* 97, 99.

[43] De Wet (n 42) 99–100. The Swiss Federal Supreme Court has asserted that non-refoulement in itself constitutes *jus cogens*, The Canadian, Kenyan, and New Zealand courts for their part have been less inclined to adopt this view. See *Spring v Switzerland*; *Ktaer Abbas Habib Al Qutaifi and Another v Union of India and Others*, para 18; *Suresh v The Minister of Citizenship and Immigration and the*

state organs or officials towards individuals or groups on their territory.[44] In these circumstances, norm conflicts can arise which are sometimes perceived as existing between a peremptory norm and a norm under customary international law. A pertinent example concerns the violation of the prohibition of torture, which can result in proceedings in foreign courts against the state in which the torture took place, or against (a) state official(s) involved in its commission. The court would then need to confront the norm conflict between the torture victim's right to a trial (eg under Article 6(1) of the European Convention of Human Rights and Fundamental Freedoms of 1950) and the obligation under customary international law to provide immunity to foreign states and their officials. Closer scrutiny reveals that there is no direct conflict between the law of immunity and *jus cogens*, as the normative scope of the peremptory obligation only encompasses the prohibition of torture as such (a negative obligation not to engage in torture).[45] It does not yet encompass an ancillary obligation to deny immunity.[46] Put another way, access to a court is not seen as a peremptory norm.

In recent Italian decisions pertaining to immunities, notably *Ferrini* and *Lozano*, the courts gave significant weight to the values underpinning *jus cogens* obligations and the need for effective enforcement of these obligations and the values that they represent.[47] This *effet utile* argument, which then results in the lifting of immunity and potential widening of the scope of the peremptory norm, was also inherent in the minority decision in the *Al Adsani* case of the ECtHR.[48] However, these cases remain exceptions to the rule and are not yet representative of the case law of international or domestic jurisdictions. In fact, when the *Ferrini* case subsequently culminated in proceedings between Germany and Italy before the ICJ in 2012, the ICJ explicitly rejected the *effet utile* line of argument. The ICJ saw no basis for the proposition that a rule lacking the status of *jus cogens* may not be applied, even if that would hinder the enforcement of a *jus cogens* norm.[49]

In this context, one may also recall the reluctance of the ICJ to accept the *effet utile* argument in relation to its own jurisdiction in the *Congo v Rwanda* decision. The ICJ

Attorney General of Canada; *Abdulkadir Al-dahas v Commissioner of Police et al*; *Attorney-General v Zaoui et al*, para 51; Van der Wilt (n 24) 154.

[44] Theodor Meron, 'On a Hierarchy of International Human Rights' (1986) 80 *AJIL* 1, 14.

[45] Vidmar (n 6) 36.

[46] *Jones v Ministry of the Interior of the Kingdom of Saudi Arabia*, paras 44–45; *Al-Adsani* (n 18) para 61; *Bouzari v Islamic Republic of Iran*, para 90; *Schreiber v Germany and Canada*.

[47] *Ferrini v Republica Federale di Germania*; *Criminal Proceedings against Milde*; *Lozano v Italy*. See also *Lord Millet in R v Bow Street Metropolitan Stipendiary Magistrate ex parte Pinochet Ugarte* 177; Riccardo Pavoni, 'Human Rights and the Immunities of Foreign States and International Organizations' in De Wet and Vidmar (n 6) 86–87.

[48] *Al-Adsani*, Joint Dissenting Opinion of Judges Rozakis and Caflisch, Joined by Judges Wildhaber, Costa, Cabral Barreto, and Vajic (n 18) para 3. The obiter dictum statement of the ICTY in *Furundzija* supported a similar approach. Paragraphs 155–157.

[49] *Jurisdictional Immunities of the State*, para 95. See also Philippa Webb, 'Human Rights and the Immunities of State Officials' in De Wet and Vidmar (n 6) 122–23.

was not prepared to accept that the *jus cogens* characterization of the prohibition of genocide could in itself provide a basis for jurisdiction. It concluded that a reservation to its jurisdiction is not invalid on the ground that it withholds jurisdiction over *jus cogens* violations. Rwanda's exclusion of the ICJ's jurisdiction through a reservation to Article IX of the Convention on the Prevention and Punishment of the Crime of Genocide of 1948 only excluded a particular method of dispute settlement and had no bearing on that country's substantive obligations concerning the prohibition of genocide. The prohibition of genocide is a matter distinct from jurisdiction over disputes pertaining to genocide, and there is no peremptory norm in international law that would oblige a state to accept the ICJ's jurisdiction in a case involving genocide.[50]

The above-mentioned examples pertaining to the perceived conflict between immunities and the prohibition of torture expose what is arguably one of the most important reasons for the limited impact of peremptory norms in all types of norm conflicts, namely the narrow scope that judicial bodies tend to attribute to them. Most judicial bodies, whether international or domestic, have the inclination to avoid or reduce norm conflict through interpretation. By limiting the scope of a *jus cogens* obligation, the judicial body in question reduces the possibility of a norm conflict arising between a peremptory obligation and any other obligation. This also necessarily reduces the impact of peremptory norms on norm conflict resolution and their ability to provide effective protection for the values which they represent.

Another illuminating example in this context concerns diplomatic assurances in extradition law.[51] Courts have allowed extradition to countries known for engaging in torture practices in instances where the receiving country has given an assurance that this would not occur in the case of the specific extraditee.[52] The courts have thereby prevented the conflict between the obligation to extradite and the rule prohibiting refoulement by narrowing the scope (including the absolute character) of the prohibition. Circumstances only trigger the latter if the extraditing state agrees to send a person to a requesting state notorious for torture practices *without* having received assurances that said state will not subject the extraditee to torture. The prohibition therefore does not apply broadly in the sense that it always prohibits extradition to such a state. In the process, the absolute character of the prohibition of torture itself may also be undermined, as the extraditee might still be tortured, if the diplomatic assurances are not honoured subsequent to the extradition.[53] Similarly, when faced with extradition or deportation requests, courts tend to apply a high threshold when determining

[50] *Armed Activities on the Territory of the Congo* (n 15) paras 67, 69; Shelton (n 3) 307.

[51] Van der Wilt (n 24) 164 *et seq*.

[52] *Al Moayed v Germany*, para 67 *et seq*; *Judge v Canada*, para 10.9; *United States v Burns*, [2001]; *Mohamed and another v President of the Republic of South Africa and others*, para 3.1.1; *Short v Netherlands*.

[53] Similarly, in the area of refugee law, states have defined refugee status in a very narrow manner. As a result, the duty not to refoule under the 1951 Refugee Convention rarely arises. See Geoff Gilbert, 'Human Rights, Refugees and Other Displaced Persons in International Law' in De Wet and Vidmar (n 6) 190.

what constitutes torture, or inhuman or degrading treatment,[54] as well as requiring evidentiary proof that the risk to the individual is specific and personal.[55] These requirements can result in further narrowing the scope of the peremptory prohibition.

3.2 Other techniques for avoiding *jus cogens*

In addition to techniques of interpretation that affect the substance (scope) of conflicting rights and obligations, courts also engage in formalistic techniques of conflict avoidance that by implication avoid the need to give full effect to the applicable peremptory norm. One such technique consists of distinguishing substantive and procedural law, in particular as applied in relation to the law of immunities.[56] In making and applying this distinction, obligations pertaining to immunities cannot conflict with the *jus cogens* norm encompassed in the prohibition of torture, as the former is a matter of procedural law while the latter constitutes substantive law.[57] By insisting that no conflict can exist between procedural and substantive norms, the court avoids the need to deal openly with the issue of norm conflicts and, by extension, the relevance of the higher status of peremptory norms in resolving the conflict.

Another formalistic conflict avoidance mechanism applied in relation to the law of immunities concerns the distinction between private and official acts, when the immunity *ratione materiae* of a state official is in question. By arguing that crimes under international law (such as the prohibition of torture) cannot constitute 'official' acts, but instead qualify as 'private acts' of the individual, one excludes the act in question from the scope of the *immunity ratione*. As a result, a norm conflict

[54] For example, in *R (on the application of Bary) v Secretary of State for the Home Department*, the House of Lords did not, under the circumstances, accept harsh prison conditions combined with the possibility of life without parole in a Florida prison as a bar to extradition.

[55] See eg *Chipana v Venezuela*, para 3; *Maksudov, Rakhimov, Tashbaev and Pirmatov v Kyrgystan*, para 12.4; *Saadi v Italy*, paras 138, 139.

[56] Domestic cases that upheld immunity *ratione personae* of state officials and (implicitly) supported the procedural-substantive distinction include inter alia *Affaire Kadhafi*, *L'Association Fédération Nationale des victimes d'accidents collectifs 'Fenvac sos catastrophe' et L'association des familles des victimes du 'Joala'*; *The Hague City Party and Others v Netherlands and Others*; *Re Mofaz*; *Re Mugabe*; *Re Sharon* and *Yaron*.

[57] See generally Webb (n 49) 118; Pavoni (n 47) 74. The ICJ also followed this line of argument in the *Jurisdictional Immunities* case (n 49) para 93: 'Assuming for this purpose that the rules of the law of armed conflict which prohibit the murder of civilians in occupied territory, the deportation of civilian inhabitants to slave labour and the deportation of prisoners of war to slave labour are rules of *jus cogens*, there is no conflict between those rules and the rules on State immunity. The two sets of rules address different matters. The rules of State immunity are procedural in character and are confined to determining whether or not the courts of one State may exercise jurisdiction in respect of another State. They do not bear upon the question whether or not the conduct in respect of which the proceedings are brought was lawful or unlawful.'

with the right to access to court or the right to a remedy will not arise.[58] However, it is doubtful whether the labelling of torture as a private act is convincing, since the treaty definition of torture is limited to acts of state officials,[59] and such acts almost invariably involve the support of the state apparatus which should also incur state responsibility.[60] Of particular importance for the current analysis is the fact that the *jus cogens* status of the prohibition of torture does not provide the basis for excluding *immunity ratione*, as any norm conflict involving a peremptory norm lacks acknowledgment.

3.3 Resorting to 'ordinary' custom instead of *jus cogens*

A further factor that may account for the limited impact of peremptory norms in judicial practice would be the fact that the 'ordinary' customary status of a (human rights) norm can usually suffice in protecting the human rights interests at stake. For example, one could argue that in relation to the prohibition of torture an exception has developed under customary international law, in accordance with which state immunity does not apply before foreign courts.[61] If one accepts that such a customary exception is recognized, the exception would bind states—unless they were persistent objectors at the time the customary exception developed—regardless of whether the exception has also acquired *jus cogens* status.[62]

One can find support for this line of reasoning in the *Distomo* decision of the Greek Supreme Court (*Areios Pagos*), which concerned a compensation claim against members of the SS for the massacre of 218 civilians and the destruction of Greek property in June 1944.[63] The Supreme Court claimed the existence of a new rule of customary international law, in accordance with which states could not rely on sovereign immunity for those violations of international law which its organs committed while present in the territory of the forum state. The Court thus seemed to rely on the existence of a *customary international* exception to sovereign immunity in instances where the forum state coincided with the state on whose territory the illegal behaviour occurred, rather than on the hierarchical nature and scope of the prohibition against torture.[64]

[58] See inter alia Lord Hutton in *Pinochet (No 3)* (n 47); *Bouterse*, para 4.2.; *Arrest Warrant of 11 April 2000 (Democratic Republic of the Congo v Belgium)*, Joint Separate Opinion of Judges Higgins, Kooijmans and Buergenthal, para 85.

[59] Article 1 of the United Nations Convention against Torture defines torture as prohibited acts 'inflicted by or at the instigation of or with the consent or acquiescence of a public official or other person acting in an official capacity'.

[60] Webb (n 49) 119–20.

[61] De Wet (n 42) 108.

[62] See Gilbert (n 53) 88.

[63] *Germany v Prefecture of Voiotia*, representing 118 persons from Distomo village.

[64] But see *Germany v Margellos*, Petition for cassation, Special Supreme Court (Anotato Eidiko Dikastirio) Case no 6/2002, 17 September 2002; ILDC 87 (GR 2002). In this decision the Supreme

In addition, the threshold for recognizing a right or obligation as constituting customary law is lower than that of *jus cogens*. Focusing on the customary nature of the rights and obligations in question rather than their *jus cogens* character could therefore be equally if not more effective. Moreover, as this author has argued elsewhere, by bypassing ordinary customary law in favour of arguing for *jus cogens*, litigants and scholars give the impression that customary law has no value in itself. This could severely undermine the binding force of international law in general. This criticism touches on one of the major controversies relating to the recognition of a hierarchy of norms in international law, namely the fear that the recognition of superior norms will engender back-sliding on commitments already assumed and a devaluation of norms that fail to achieve the elevated ranking.[65] On the other hand, it might be overly pessimistic to assume that such an undesirable outcome would necessarily follow from the recognition of a hierarchy of norms in international law. To the extent that the full realization of peremptory norms would also depend on the realization of non-peremptory norms of international law, the recognition of a hierarchy of norms could actually serve as a catalyst for a better realization of international law in general.[66]

4. The Relationship Between *Jus Cogens* and *Erga Omnes* Obligations

4.1 Identifying *erga omnes* norms

The ICJ introduced the concept of *erga omnes* into positive law in the *Barcelona Traction* case of 1970, determining that *erga omnes* obligations are the concern of all states because of the importance of the obligations involved, which means all states

Special Court determined widespread and consistent state practice did not support such an exception, regardless of whether the acts constituted a violation of *jus cogens* norms or not. The ICJ took a similar position in the *Jurisdictional Immunities* case (n 49) para 78, at least in relation to acts that the armed forces of a foreign state committed on the territory of the forum state. It concluded that customary international law continued to require that a state be accorded immunity in proceedings for torts its armed forces and other organs of State allegedly committed on the territory of another state in the course of conducting an armed conflict.

[65] De Wet (n 42) 118–19. See generally for a critique of hierarchy in international law, Prosper Weil, 'Towards Relative Normativity in International Law' (1983) 77 *AJIL* 413, 413 ff.

[66] The *jus cogens* dimension of a particular norm could, through its moral appeal, accelerate the development of the state practice and *opinio juris* required for the emergence of a new customary international obligation. See Focarelli (n 32) 449, 457.

can be held to have a legal interest in their protection.[67] This concept of obligations that are directed towards the international community as a whole further finds recognition in the law of state responsibility. The 2001 Articles on State Responsibility draw a distinction between breaches of bilateral obligations and obligations of a collective nature, which include obligations towards the international community as a whole.[68] Breaches of a bilateral nature may arise where the performance of an obligation involves two states, even though the treaty framework or customary rule in question imposes obligations on all states (parties).[69] In such an instance the nature of the obligations stemming from the multilateral treaty or customary rule can be described as 'bundles of bilateral obligations'.[70] An example in point would be Article 22 of the Vienna Convention on Diplomatic Relations of 1961, where the obligation to protect the premises of a diplomatic mission is owed by the individual receiving state to the individual sending state.[71]

Breaches deemed to be of a collective nature are those that concern obligations established for the protection of the collective interest of a group of states (*erga omnes partes*) or indeed of the international community as a whole (*erga omnes*).[72] Concrete examples of *erga omnes partes* obligations can be found in particular in human rights treaties. Obligations stemming from regional or universal human rights treaties would have *erga omnes partes* effect towards other states parties, as well as *erga omnes* effect to the extent that they have been recognized as customary international law.[73] The same would apply to the obligations articulated in the Statute of the International Criminal Court (ICC) that grant the ICC jurisdiction over the most serious crimes of concern to the 'international community as a whole', namely genocide, crimes against humanity, and war crimes.

Particularly relevant for this chapter is the question if and to what extent *jus cogens* and *erga omnes* obligations overlap. The *Barcelona Traction* decision of the ICJ provides authority for the conclusion that *jus cogens* obligations would have *erga omnes* effect.[74] Without expressly referring to *jus cogens* the ICJ implied as much

[67] *Barcelona Traction, Light and Power Company Ltd* (Second Phase) 3, 32; See also *Case Concerning East Timor (Portugal v Australia)* 90, 102; *Legal Consequences of the Construction of a Wall in the Occupied Palestinian Territory* 136, 199.

[68] See Arts 42 and 48 of the Articles on State Responsibility available in James Crawford *The International Law Commission's Articles on State Responsibility* (CUP 2002) 257.

[69] Crawford (n 68) 257.

[70] Crawford (n 68) 258.

[71] See *United States Diplomatic and Consular Staff in Tehran* 3 *et seq*; see also Crawford (n 68) 257–58.

[72] Crawford (n 68) 277.

[73] Pierre-Marie Dupuy 'L'unité de l'ordre juridique international' (2002) 297 *Recueil des Cours de l'académie de droit international* 382, 384; Crawford (n 68) 277–78; International Law Institute, *The Protection of Human Rights and the Principle of Non-intervention in Internal Affairs of States*, Resolution adopted during the Session of Santiago de Compostela 1989 Art 1 available at <http://www.idi-iil.org>. See Human Rights Committee General Comment No 31 [80] *Nature of the General Legal Obligation Imposed on States Parties to the Covenant* CCPR/C/21/Rev.1/Add.13 of 26 May 2004, para 2.

[74] *Barcelona Traction* decision (n 67) 32.

by the types of obligations it mentioned as examples of *erga omnes* norms. These included the outlawing of the unilateral use of force, genocide, and the prohibition of slavery and racial discrimination. Given the fact that these same prohibitions are widely regarded as being of a peremptory nature, it follows that when an obligation is recognized as one from which no derogation is permitted due to its fundamental nature, all states (and other subjects of international law) have a legal interest in its protection.[75]

One should be careful however, not to assume that the opposite also applies, namely, that all *erga omnes* obligations necessarily also have *jus cogens* status.[76] For example, the human rights obligations contained in the ICCPR and ICESCR would arguably all have *erga omnes* effect to the extent that they have acquired customary international law status.[77] Their collective interest nature gives the international community as a whole an interest in their performance and reflects that they amount to more than mere 'bundles of bilateral obligations'. At the same time, this fact does not in and of itself elevate all *erga omnes* human rights obligations to peremptory norms. The peremptory character of the prohibition of genocide and torture, for example, resulted from their specific recognition as such by a large majority of states.

4.2 The implications of *erga omnes* status for the enforcement of *jus cogens* obligations

The conclusion that *jus cogens* obligations possess *erga omnes* status raises the question whether the legal interest that all states have in compliance with *jus cogens* obligations could contribute to their more effective enforcement. The first avenue through which *erga omnes* status can impact the enforcement of peremptory norms concerns Article 48 of the Articles on State Responsibility, which has created a system of responsibility for serious violations of international obligations towards the international community as a whole (*erga omnes*). In accordance with Article 48, states other than injured states are entitled to invoke responsibility

[75] Barcelona Traction decision (n 67) 32; Jochen A. Frowein 'Collective Enforcement of International Obligations' (1987) 47 *Zeitschrift für Ausländisches Öffentliches Recht und Völkerrecht* 71; Karl Zemanek, 'New Trends in the Enforcement of *erga omnes* Obligations' (2000) 4 *Max Planck Yearbook of United Nations Law* 6–7. See generally on the relationship between *jus cogens* and *erga omnes* obligations Cherif Bassiouni, 'International Crimes: Jus Cogens and Obligations Erga Omnes' (1996) 59 *Law and Contemporary Problems* 63 *et seq*; André De Hoogh 'The Relationship between Jus Cogens, Obligations Erga Omnes and International Crimes: Peremptory Norms in Perspective' (1991) 42 *Österreichische Zeitschrift für öffentliches und Völkerrecht* 183 *et seq*; Claudia Annacker 'The Legal Regime of Erga Omnes Obligations in International Law' (1994) 46 *Austrian Journal of Public International Law* 131 *et seq*.

[76] Dupuy (n 73) 385.

[77] Those rights in the ICCPR and ICESCR which have not yet acquired customary status would nonetheless have *erga omnes partes* effect towards other states parties.

where the obligation breached is owed to the international community as a whole. When invoking responsibility in this fashion, the invoking state may claim from the responsible state cessation of the internationally wrongful act, as well as performance of the obligation or reparation in the interest of the beneficiaries.

Second, there are indications that the ICJ may increasingly be confronted with contentious proceedings concerning the protection of peremptory norms, due to the evolving impact of the concept of *erga omnes* on the nature of the 'legal interest' that states need to show for purposes of standing before the ICJ. The ICJ gave a very restricted interpretation of 'legal interest' in the *South West Africa* decision of 1966. It was unwilling to assume that a state may have a legal interest in vindicating a principle of international law where it has not suffered harm—unless this was explicitly provided for in an international text or instrument.[78]

The ICJ gave some indications in the 1995 *Case Concerning East Timor (Portugal v Australia)* that it may have broadened its understanding of 'legal interest', despite the fact that it declined to rule on whether Australia had behaved unlawfully in concluding a treaty with Indonesia pertaining to the East Timorese continental shelf while East Timor was de facto administered by Indonesia. Although Portugal and Australia had accepted the ICJ's compulsory jurisdiction in accordance with Article 36(2) of the ICJ Statute, Indonesia had not done so. According to the ICJ, a ruling in this case would inevitably result in a ruling on the lawfulness of Indonesia's behaviour, in violation of the ICJ Statute which only foresees jurisdiction in instances where states have consented to it.[79]

In reaching its conclusion the ICJ acknowledged the *erga omnes* status of the right to self-determination and in particular the right of self-determination of the East-Timorese people.[80] The ICJ nonetheless underscored that regardless of the nature of the obligations invoked, it could only rule on the lawfulness of the conduct of a state which had consented to its jurisdiction.[81] The ICJ thus made clear that the *erga omnes* status of a right did not in and of itself oblige states to accept its jurisdiction. However, implicit in the ICJ's argument was the assumption that had Indonesia accepted the ICJ's jurisdiction, Portugal would have been able to invoke the right of self-determination of the East Timorese people against Indonesia before the ICJ. Portugal would have had a legal interest in the protection of the right of self-determination of the East-Timorese people on the basis of the *erga omnes* character of this right.

An expanded notion of 'legal interest' has since been endorsed explicitly in the decision on *Questions relating to the Obligation to Prosecute or Extradite (Belgium v*

[78] *South West Africa* Second Phase (Judgment) ICJ Rep 1966, para 44. At para 88 the ICJ further underscored that its Statute did not provide for an *actio popularis* that would allow any members of the international community to initiate proceedings in vindicating the violation of community interests.

[79] *East Timor* decision (n 67) 102.

[80] *East Timor* decision (n 67) 102–103.

[81] *East Timor* case (n 67) 102.

Senegal), also known as the *Habré* case.[82] In deciding whether Senegal has breached its obligations under the United Nations Convention against Torture and Other Cruel, Inhuman or Degrading Treatment or Punishment of 10 December 1984 (the Convention against Torture), in accordance with which it either had to prosecute former Chadian President Hissène Habré without delay or extradite him, the issue of Belgium's standing before the ICJ arose. Belgium relied both on the compromissary clause in Article 30(1) of the Convention against Torture and on the declarations made by both parties under Article 36(2) of the ICJ Statute.[83]

In confirming Belgium's standing, the ICJ determined that all state parties to the Convention against Torture have a common interest in compliance with the obligation to initiate prosecution by the state on whose territory an alleged offender is present. That common interest implies that the obligations in question are owed by any state party to all the other states parties to the Convention. All the states parties have a 'legal interest' in the protection of these 'obligations *erga omnes partes*'.[84] Therefore, each state party to the Convention can make a claim concerning the cessation of an alleged breach by another state party, without proving any special interest.[85]

It is noteworthy that this broadened notion of 'legal interest' for the purposes of standing arose in a case concerning states parties to the Convention against Torture. The ICJ tailored its decisions towards the common interest of the parties to the Convention and explicitly referred to *erga omnes partes* obligations. It remains to be seen whether the ICJ would also allow standing in situations where states base their claims exclusively on the fact that torture is forbidden and criminalized under customary international law, as a result of which all states would have a legal interest in its cessation and prosecution. Such a claim would then be based on the *erga omnes* character of the prohibition of torture. A claim of this nature would only succeed, however, between states which have both accepted the compulsory jurisdiction of the ICJ according to Article 36(2) of the ICJ Statute.[86] In the *Habré* decision the court refrained from addressing this issue and focused instead on the fact that both Senegal and Belgium are parties to the Convention against Torture.

It is also unclear whether the *jus cogens* status of the prohibition of torture had a decisive impact on the ICJ's decision. Although it referred in passing to the

[82] *Questions relating to the Obligation to Prosecute or Extradite (Belgium v Senegal)*, IJC 20 July 2012, available at <http://www.icj-cij.org>. See also *Armed Activities on the Territory of the Congo* (n 15), separate opinion of Judge Simma, para 38 *et seq*. See also Alain Pellet 'The Draft Articles of the International Law Commission on the Responsibility of States for Internationally Wrongful Acts: A Requiem for States' Crime?' (2001) 32 *Netherlands Yearbook of International Law* 77.

[83] *Habré* decision (n 82) para 42.

[84] *Habré* decision (n 82) para 68.

[85] *Habré* decision (n 82) para 69.

[86] The ICJ can only exercise jurisdiction over disputes if and to the extent that states have accepted its jurisdiction in accordance with Art 36(1) or 36(2) of the ICJ Statute. This condition is not affected by the broadening of the notion of 'legal interest'.

peremptory nature of the prohibition of torture,[87] this did not feature in relation to its reasoning pertaining to the *erga omnes partes* nature of the obligations in the Convention against Torture. Instead, the ICJ found the common legal interest of countries in prosecuting torture on the shared values embodied in the Convention.[88] One can therefore argue that since all human rights treaty obligations constitute obligations *erga omnes partes*,[89] this expanded notion of 'legal interest' could facilitate standing before the ICJ in relating to disputes between states that that are based on a human rights treaty containing a promissory clause regarding the ICJ's jurisdiction.

In essence therefore it seems that the ICJ has accepted that the common interest ('community oriented character') underpinning peremptory human rights obligations—and perhaps also other human rights obligations which have not yet acquired peremptory status—constitutes a sufficient 'legal interest' for the purpose of standing before the ICJ. However, this standing would only come into play once it is clear that the states in question have also consented to the ICJ's jurisdiction. This would notably be the case where the peremptory or other human rights obligations form the object of a treaty ratified by all parties to the dispute and which provides for the jurisdiction of the ICJ in relation to disputes concerning the treaty's interpretation or application.

Where no such treaty is in place between states parties, but they have nonetheless accepted the compulsory jurisdiction of the ICJ in terms of Article 36(2) of the ICJ Statute, another avenue for standing may exist. This would be where the claim between these parties is based on the customary nature of a particular human rights obligation, ie the *erga omnes* proper character of the particular human rights norm.

5. The Relevance of *Jus Cogens* Within The Domestic Legal Order

From the perspective of domestic law, reliance on peremptory norms may serve as a means to try to ensure that domestic law does not set aside international law. In many common law countries, incorporated treaties and customary international law have a status equivalent to that of ordinary national legislation.[90] The legislature can therefore set aside international law by enacting inconsistent domestic legislation, though the state remains responsible on the international level in accordance with the principles

[87] *Habré* decision (n 82) para 99.
[88] *Habré* decision (n 82) para 68.
[89] See text leading up to n 73.
[90] Shelton (n 3) 315.

of state responsibility. By emphasizing the peremptory nature of a norm, litigators (in particular in the United States) have attempted to avoid these constitutional ramifications, thus far without success.[91]

A more reliable way of protecting *jus cogens* norms of international law within the domestic legal order would be to provide constitutional recognition of them. This was done in Switzerland in the revised Swiss Federal Constitution of 1999.[92] A new provision explicitly states that no People's Initiative (referendum) aimed at achieving a constitutional amendment may be in conflict with the norms of *jus cogens*.[93] Swiss authorities must invalidate any initiative that violates *jus cogens*.[94] Such explicit recognition can serve as an 'emergency break' aimed at securing respect for core international obligations at all times.

The Swiss Federal Supreme Court has taken the position that in the case of conflicting obligations arising from national and international law respectively, the latter enjoys precedence unless the national legislature explicitly intended to adopt

[91] Shelton (n 3) 315.

[92] For a discussion, see Daniel Thürer, 'Verfassungsrecht und Völkerrecht' in Daniel Thürer et al (eds), *Verfassungsrecht der Schweiz* (Schulthess 2001), 179–205 and sources quoted therein.

[93] The text of the Swiss Federal Constitution is available at <http://www.admin.ch/ch/d/sr/101/index.html> accessed 23 March 2012. The English translation is available at <http://www.admin.ch/ch/e/rs/1/101.en.pdf>. The relevant clauses read as follows:

Artikel 139 Volksinitiative auf Teilrevision der Bundesverfassung

3. Verletzt die Initiative die Einheit der Form, die Einheit der Materie oder zwingendes Völkerrecht, so erklärt die Bundesverfassung sie für ganz oder teilweise ungültig

[*Article 139—Popular initiative requesting a partial revision of the Federal Constitution in specific terms*

3. If the initiative fails to comply with the requirements of consistency of form, and of subject matter, or if it infringes mandatory provisions of international law, the Federal Assembly shall declare it to be invalid in whole or in part.]

Artikel 193 Totalrevision

4. Die zwingenden Bestimmungen des Völkerrechts dürfen nicht verletzt werden.

[*Article 193—Total Revision*

4. The mandatory provisions of international law must not be violated.]

Artikel 194 Teilrevision

2. Die Teilrevision muss die Einheit der Materie wahren und darf die zwingenden Bestimmungen des Völkerrechts nicht verletzen.

[*Article 194—Partial Revision*

2. The partial revision must respect the principle of cohesion of subject matter and must not violate mandatory provisions of international law.]

[94] In fact, by 1996, three years before the formal anchoring of *jus cogens* in the Swiss Federal Constitution, both chambers of the Swiss Federal Parliament invalidated a People's Initiative (*Volksinitiative*) that proposed a constitutional amendment that violated the prohibition of refoulement, which Switzerland acknowledges as a peremptory norm. See (n 43). See also *Bundesbeschluss über die Volksinitiative 'für eine vernünftige Asylpolitik'*, 14 March 1996, BBl 1996 I 1355. The People's Initiative, which was submitted to the federal authorities in July 1992, inter alia proposed a constitutional clause determining that asylum seekers who entered the country illegally would be deported summarily and without the possibility of appeal. See discussion in de Wet (n 42) 101–102.

contradicting legislation.[95] This approach is therefore similar to the one followed in many common law countries in the sense that, within the domestic legal order, the democratic will of the people supersedes international law. However, through the explicit constitutional protection of *jus cogens*, the core values of the international community remain beyond the reach of the will of the people (unless the constitution itself is amended to reverse this position).[96]

6. Concluding Remarks

The above analysis illustrates that there is increasing formal recognition in state practice and doctrine of a hierarchy of norms in international law in the form of *jus cogens*. This, in turn, implies increased recognition of core values, especially of fundamental human rights, throughout the international community of states. At the same time, the international consensus regarding the number of *jus cogens* norms, their scope and their utility as a mechanism for norm conflict resolution, remain disputed. Practice has illustrated that the recognition of the peremptory status of a particular norm is no guarantee of effective enforcement of the norm and the values it represents. It also remains unclear if and to what extent peremptory norms can provide protection beyond what is also guaranteed by ordinary customary and/or treaty law. It is therefore fair to conclude that the jury is still out on whether increased recognition of human rights norms as peremptory norms in international law will enhance their effective enforcement internationally and domestically. Although one can no longer say that *jus cogens* is '[the] vehicle that hardly ever leaves the garage' (as it is increasingly invoked in international and domestic litigation),[97] its excursions into the open have not yet resulted in a change of the rules of the road.

[95] The so called '*Schubert-Praxis*' was introduced in BGE 99 1b 39 and affirmed in BGE 111 V 201; BGE 112 II 13; BGE 116 IV 269; BGE 117 IV 128. The *Schubert* case concerned the potential conflict of legislation regulating the acquiring of property in Switzerland by persons abroad with a Swiss-Austrian bilateral agreement. See also Thürer (n 69) at 189–90; Thomas Cottier and Maya Hertig, 'Das Völkerrecht in der neuen Bundesverfassung: Stellung und Auswirkung' in Ulirch Zimmerli (ed), *Die neue Bundesverfassung. Konsequenzen für Praxis und Wissenschaft* (Stämpfli Verlag 2000) 13 *et seq.*

[96] Although some Swiss authors suggest that the notion of peremptory norms should be interpreted broadly on the national level, the Swiss federal Supreme Court has not yet followed this approach. Instead, it limits the range of peremptory norms to those most frequently cited in international law. See *Nada* (n 31); *A v Federal Department of Economic Affairs*, para 8.2.

[97] Ian Brownlie, 'Comment' in Antonio Cassese and JHH Weiler (eds), *Change and Stability in International Law-Making* (de Gruyter 1988) 110. See also Alain Pellet, 'Comments in Response to Christine Chinkin and in Defense of Jus Cogens as the Best Bastion against the Excesses of Fragmentation' (2006) 17 *FYBIL* 83, 85.

Further Reading

Bianchi A, 'Human Rights and the Magic of Jus Cogens' (2008) 19(3) *EJIL* 491

Byers M, 'Conceptualising the relationship between Jus Cogens and Erga Omnes Rules' (1997) 66 *Nord J Intl L* 211

Chinkin C, 'Jus Cogens, Article 103 of the UN Charter and Other Hierarchical Techniques of Conflict Solution' (2006) XVII *FYBIL* 63

Czaplinski W, 'Concepts of *jus cogens* and Obligations *erga omnes* in International Law in the Light of Recent Developments' (1999) 23 *Polish YB Intl L* 87

De Wet E, 'The prohibition of torture as an international norm of jus cogens and its implications for national and customary law' (2004) 15(1) *EJIL* 97

De Wet E and Vidmar J (eds), *Hierarchy in International Law: The Place of Human Rights* (OUP 2012)

Dupuy P, 'Some Reflections on Contemporary International Law and the Appeal to Universal Values: a Response to Martti Koskenniemi' (2005) 16(1) *EJIL* 131

Focarelli C, 'Promotional Jus Cogens: A Critical Appraisal of Jus Cogens' Legal Effects' (2008) 77 *Nord J Intl L* 429

Hannikainen L, *Peremptory Norms (Jus Cogens) in International Law: Historical Development, Criteria, Present Status* (Finnish Lawyers' Publishing Company 1988)

Kadelbach S, *Zwingendes Völkerrecht* (Dunker & Humblot 1992)

Kolb R, 'Théorie du ius cogens international' (2003) 36(3) *RBDI* 5

Koskenniemi M, 'International Law in Europe: between Tradition and Renewal' (2005) 16(1) *EJIL* 112

Meron T, 'On a Hierarchy of International Human Rights' (1986) 80 *AJIL* 1

Oeter S, 'Ius cogens und der Schutz der Menschenrechte' in Breitenmoser Stephan et al (eds), *Human rights, democracy and the rule of law: liber amicorum Luzius Wildhaber* (Nomos 2007) 499

Shelton D, 'Normative Hierarchy in International Law'(2006) 100 *AJIL* 291

Seiderman I, *Hierarchy in International Law: The Human Rights Dimension* (Intersentia 2001)

Tams C, 'Schwierigkeiten mit dem Ius Cogens' (2002) 40 *Arch Völkerrechts* 331

Verdross A, 'Forbidden Treaties in International Law' (1937) 31 *AJIL* 571

—— 'Jus Dispositivum and Jus Cogens in International Law' (1966) 60 *AJIL* 55

Weil P, 'Towards Relative Normativity in International Law' (1983) 77 *AJIL* 413

CHAPTER 24

POSITIVE AND NEGATIVE OBLIGATIONS

DINAH SHELTON

ARIEL GOULD

1. Introduction

Human rights law has a dual nature, because it is not sufficient simply to proclaim rights; it is also necessary to identify duty-holders and their obligations. In international human rights instruments, this means specifying the obligations of the states parties.[1] The right to freedom of expression, for example, has its counterpart in the state obligation to respect the right and ensure that that individual is in some way able to exercise the guarantees it proclaims. This formulation suggests that the scope of state obligations is both negative and positive in nature, imposing not only a state duty to abstain from interfering with the exercise of the right, but also to protect the right from infringement by third parties. *Positive* obligations are therefore generally considered to be obligations 'requiring member states to ... take action',[2]

[1] Jean-François Akandji-Kombe, 'Positive Obligations under the European Convention on Human Rights: A Guide to the Implementation of the European Convention on Human Rights' (2007) *Human Rights Handbook* No 7, at 5 <http://echr.coe.int/NR/rdonlyres/1B521F61-A636-43F5-AD56-5F26D46A4F55/0/DG2ENHRHAND072007.pdf> accessed 23 February 2013.

[2] Judge Martens in *Gul v Switzerland* 165, as quoted in Alastair Mowbray, *Human Rights Law in Perspective: The Development of Positive Obligations under the European Convention on Human Rights by the European Court of Human Rights* (Hart 2004) 2.

imposing a duty upon states to take affirmative steps to ensure rights protections.[3] Negative obligations, on the other hand, 'essentially require states not to interfere in the exercise of rights'.[4]

This chapter assesses the development of positive and negative obligations in human rights law. In so doing, the chapter examines the textual bases and jurisprudence regarding these obligations in the universal and regional systems. It devotes particular attention to the issue of the due diligence standard of care in the field of international human rights law.

The concept of responsibility as encompassing both positive and negative obligations largely originated in the law of diplomatic protection prior to the development of human rights law.[5] More generally, the law of state responsibility has long required a state to cease the breach and make reparations when it fails to comply, through an act or omission attributable to it, with an obligation under international law.[6] The breach may come from the injurious actions of state officials directly or from the failure of the state to perform its international duty to take all reasonable and adequate measures to prevent private wrongs, including the duty to arrest and bring an offender to justice. The state is not held directly and primarily responsible for the private wrongs, because such an approach would have the effect of making the state an insurer of the safety and well-being of aliens. Lack of due diligence of state organs nevertheless renders the state responsible for private wrongs, that is, when the state 'has failed to take such measures as in the circumstances should normally have been taken to prevent, redress or inflict punishment for the acts causing the damage'.[7]

The Permanent Court of Arbitration referenced unlawful acts and omissions in a 1912 decision,[8] and in 1949, the International Court of Justice held Albania responsible for violations of international law due to a failure to act when it knew (or should have known) that a violation had occurred or was about to occur.[9] Global and regional human rights bodies have since then adopted the duality of positive and negative duties in judging a state's compliance with its human rights obligations. The chapter concludes that positive obligations have become increasingly important in international human rights law.

[3] See eg *Kemaloğlu v Turkey.* [4] Akandji-Kombe (n 1) 5.

[5] See Vermeer, Chapter 10 in this *Handbook*. See also Edwin M Borchard, *The Diplomatic Protection of Citizens Abroad or the Law of International Claims* (Banks Law Publishing Co 1915); Richard B Lillich (ed), *International Law of State Responsibility for Injuries to Aliens* (UP of Virginia 1983).

[6] UNGA, 'Responsibility of States for Internationally Wrongful Acts' (12 December 2001) UN Doc A/RES/56/83.

[7] Text approved at the 1930 Hague Conference, 560. Quoted in Shabtai Rosen (ed), *The International Law Commission's Draft Articles on State Responsibility: Part 1, Articles 1–35* (Martinus Nijhoff 1991) 15.

[8] *Russian Indemnity Case (Russia v Turkey)* 543.

[9] *Corfu Channel Case (United Kingdom v Albania)* 23.

2. The Textual Statements of Obligation

Although the 1948 universal and inter-American declarations of human rights set forth comprehensive catalogues of civil, political, economic, social, and cultural rights, without specifying the nature of the corresponding state obligations, the global and regional treaties subsequently drafted were divided into two categories, on the mistaken belief that civil and political rights, on the one hand, and economic, social, and cultural rights on the other hand, were inherently different and imposed quite dissimilar state obligations. Civil and political rights were perceived to be freedoms that could be enjoyed so long as the state did not interfere with their exercise. States therefore could comply with the right to freedom from torture, for example, by abstaining from acts of torture. In contrast, economic rights, such as the right to education, were deemed to demand state action and resources to create a system of schools to ensure the enjoyment of the right. The debate over this distinction was a primary consideration in dividing the rights in the Universal Declaration of Human Rights into two treaties: the International Covenant on Economic, Social and Cultural Rights (ICESCR) and the International Covenant on Civil and Political Rights (ICCPR).[10]

Despite the adoption of separate Covenants, the language of obligations in both treaties suggests a rapprochement, as both instruments impose positive and negative obligations. The ICCPR requires states parties not only to 'respect', but also to 'ensure', the rights contained therein[11] and to adopt such laws or other measures as may be necessary to give effect to the rights recognized in the Covenant.[12] Article 2(3) requires each state party to provide and enforce remedies for human rights violations, including developing the possibilities of judicial remedy. Several substantive rights in the ICCPR also require states to act. Article 6, for example, requires states to protect 'by law' the right to life; Article 17 does the same with respect to the right to privacy, while Article 26 requires the state by law to prohibit discrimination. Articles 9 and 14 provide guarantees against arbitrary arrest and for due process, include establishing and maintaining an independent judiciary, providing access to justice, and ensuring the right to legal assistance. Conditions

[10] Silvia Borelli, 'Positive Obligations of States and the Protection of Human Rights' (2006) 15 *Interights Bulletin* 1, 1. '[I]t has been asserted that the obligations under the International Covenant on Economic, Social and Cultural Rights (ICESCR) are 'positive' obligations in that on their face they require states to take action, in contradistinction to the obligations arising under the International Covenant on Civil and Political Rights (ICCPR), which are said to contain essentially 'negative' obligations, or duties of abstention.'

[11] Article 2(1). [12] Article 2(2).

of detention are regulated in Article 10 and impose positive obligations on states regarding the prison system. Article 25 obliges the state to organize genuine periodic elections by secret ballots. In sum, a state cannot comply with the ICCPR simply by abstaining from action. As the UN Human Rights Committee has concluded, the ICCPR contains states' obligations that are 'both negative and positive in nature'[13] and states may be responsible for failure to ensure rights against infringement by private actors.[14]

The ICESCR has a more lengthy and programmatic set of obligations to 'achiev[e] progressively' the full realization of the rights in that treaty.[15] At the same time, there are provisions set forth in terms of immediate obligation and state abstention. These include the duty of non-discrimination in respect to the rights guaranteed, equal rights of men and women, and various trade union freedoms.[16] With the passage of time, it has increasingly been recognized that the supposedly clear-cut distinctions between 'positive' and 'negative' obligations do not exist.[17]

2.1 Positive and negative obligations in the universal system

Human rights bodies have long deemed both acts and omissions to be sources of state liability for breach of human rights obligations.[18] By 1970, one United Nations (UN) report concluded that the number of cases against states based on omissions far outweighed those based on acts.[19] Two decades later, the Human Rights Committee commented that a state can only effectively guarantee ICCPR rights 'by a combination of negative and positive State obligations',[20] a claim which the Committee on Economic, Social, and Cultural Rights (CESCR) has mirrored with respect to the ICESCR.[21]

[13] Human Rights Committee, 'General Comment No 31: The Nature of the General Legal Obligation Imposed on States Parties to the Covenant' (26 May 2004) UN Doc CCPR/C/21/Rev.1/Add.13.

[14] Viviana Waisman, 'Human Trafficking: State Obligations to Protect Victims' Rights, the Current Framework and a New Due Diligence Standard' (2010) 33 *Hastings Int'l and Comp L Rev* 385, 407.

[15] ICESCR, Art 2(1) provides: 'Each State Party to the present Covenant undertakes to take steps, individually and through international assistance and cooperation, especially economic and technical, to the maximum of its available resources, with a view to achieving progressively the full realization of the rights recognized in the present Covenant by all appropriate means, including particularly the adoption of legislative measures.'

[16] See ICESCR, Arts 2(2), 3, 8.

[17] Borelli (n 10) 1.

[18] Dinah Shelton, 'Private Violence, Public Wrongs, and the Responsibility of States' (1989) 13 *Fordham Int'l LJ* 1, 17.

[19] Shelton, 'Private Violence' (n 18) 17.

[20] Manfred Nowak, *UN Covenant on Civil and Political Rights: CCPR Commentary* (2nd edn, Engel 2005) xxi.

[21] See eg CESCR, 'General Comment No 3: The Nature of States Parties Obligations' (14 December 1990) UN Doc E/1991/23. Note that in this General Comment, rather than using the terms

The Human Rights Committee's General Comment No 31, adopted in 2004, updates and details the Committee's views on the legal obligations of states parties to the ICCPR. The negative obligation requires such states to refrain from violating the rights recognized by the Covenant, and to restrict such rights only as permitted by relevant provisions of the treaty. This means states must demonstrate the necessity of any restriction and only take such measures as are proportionate to the pursuit of legitimate aims. As to ensuring the recognized rights, the Committee notes that obligations do not, as such, have direct horizontal effect as a matter of international law and are therefore not a substitute for domestic criminal or civil law.

> [T]he positive obligations on States Parties to ensure Covenant rights will only be fully discharged if individuals are protected by the State, not just against violations of Covenant rights by its agents, but also against acts committed by private persons or entities that would impair the enjoyment of Covenant rights in so far as they are amenable to application between private persons or entities.[22]

States may be held responsible if they permit or fail to take appropriate measures or to exercise due diligence to prevent, punish, investigate, or redress harm caused by acts by private persons or entities.[23] Even freedom from torture requires implicitly that the state take positive measures to ensure that persons or entities do not inflict torture or cruel, inhuman, or degrading treatment, or punishment on others within their power.

In a more nuanced conceptualization of negative and positive obligations, the universal system of human rights developed the triad of obligations to respect, protect, and fulfil,[24] to which others sometimes add 'promote' as a fourth obligation.[25] The obligation to respect is a negative obligation, requiring states to refrain from interfering with or curtailing the enjoyment of human rights.[26] The obligation to protect is a positive obligation, requiring states to protect individuals and groups against human rights abuses by others.[27] The obligation to fulfil is also a positive obligation, requiring states to take positive action to facilitate the enjoyment of human rights.[28]

'positive' and 'negative' obligations, the CESCR used the terms 'obligations of conduct' and 'obligations of result'.

22 Human Rights Committee, 'General Comment No 31' (n 13) para 9.

23 Human Rights Committee, 'General Comment No 31' (n 13) para 9.

24 Nowak (n 20) xxi.

25 See *Social and Economic Rights Action Center (SERAC) v Nigeria*, para 44 (*Ogoniland* Case).

26 Nowak (n 20) xxi. See also UN Office of the High Commissioner for Human Rights, 'International Human Rights Law' <http://www.ohchr.org/en/professionalinterest/Pages/InternationalLaw.aspx> accessed 1 March 2013. 'The obligation to respect means that States must refrain from interfering with or curtailing the enjoyment of human rights.'

27 Waisman (n 14) 406. See also UN Office of the High Commissioner for Human Rights, 'International Human Rights Law' (n 26). 'The obligation to protect requires States to protect individuals and groups against human rights abuses.'

28 Nowak (n 20) xxi. See also UN Office of the High Commissioner for Human Rights, 'International Human Rights Law' (n 26). 'The obligation to fulfil means that States must take positive action to facilitate the enjoyment of basic human rights.'

These three type of obligations play out in different ways in the universal system. The so-called 'triad of State obligations'[29] is relevant with respect to several rights. Both Article 20 (the prohibition of war propaganda and advocacy of national, racial, or religious hatred) and Article 8 (the prohibition of slavery and servitude) are largely 'horizontal' in nature and require extensive state efforts to protect the right from violations by private individuals.[30] Other rights require significant institutional protection by way of specific procedural guarantees.[31] With regard to elections, mentioned above:

> Citizens have not only the right but also the 'opportunity'... to take part in the conduct of public affairs. This sets up a duty on States Parties to guarantee with *positive measures* that all formally eligible persons have the *actual opportunity to exercise their political rights.* For instance, it is not enough to extend formal voting eligibility to all citizens...when it is no simultaneously ensured that these citizens are truly able to make use of their right to vote.[32]

The case law and commentary surrounding Articles 6(1) and 25[33] of the ICCPR provide examples of the assessment of positive and negative obligations in the universal human rights system. The Committee has expanded its consideration of Article 6(1) beyond traditional conceptions of the right to life as merely the 'right to protection against arbitrary killing', to 'include other threats to human life, such as malnutrition, life-threatening illness, nuclear energy or armed conflict'.[34] In doing so, the Human Rights Committee has focused on the state's duty, imposed by the ICCPR, to both 'ensure' and 'protect'. The state's duty to ensure, it has stated, is 'relative', meaning that 'the national legislature has broad discretion in fulfilling its duty'.[35] The duty to protect corresponds to the passage of sufficient legislation 'as measured against the actual threat'.[36] When read in conjunction with Article 2, this positive obligation under Article 6(1) extends beyond criminal sanctions and to judicial, administrative, or other measures that may be necessary to deter violations and provide redress to victims.[37]

[29] Nowak (n 20) xxi.

[30] Nowak (n 20) xxi.

[31] Eg Art 14 (right to a fair trial), Art 16 (recognition of legal personality), Art 23 (protection of marriage, and the family), and Art 25 (guarantee of political rights). See eg Nowak (n 20) xxi; Mowbray (n 2) 1.

[32] Nowak (n 20) 569. See also Art 6 (the right to life) and Art 8 (the prohibition of slavery and servitude).

[33] Article 25: 'Every citizen shall have the right and the opportunity, without any of the distinctions mentioned in article 2 and without any unreasonable restrictions: (a) To take part in the conduct of public affairs, directly or through freely chosen representatives; (b) To vote and to be elected at genuine periodic elections which shall be by universal and equal suffrage and shall be held by secret ballot, guaranteeing the free expression of the will of the electors; (c) To have access, on general terms of equality, to public service in his country.'

[34] Nowak (n 20) 123.

[35] Nowak (n 20) 123. For a discussion of the relative nature of a right with regard to voting rights, see also Nowak (n 20) 569.

[36] Nowak (n 20) 123.

[37] Nowak (n 20) 124.

Article 25 of the ICCPR relates to the opportunity to exercise political rights.

> States must take effective measures to ensure that all persons entitled to vote are able to exercise that right... Positive measures should be taken to overcome specific difficulties, such as illiteracy, language barriers, poverty, or impediment to freedom of movement which prevent persons entitled to vote from exercising their rights effectively.[38]

In the *Mauritian Women* case, the Committee noted that legal provisions may inappropriately limit an individual's ability to exercise these rights 'in practice'.[39] This implies that a *de jure* right to exercise political rights is not sufficient; a *de facto* right must exist, as well.[40]

An important positive obligation developed in the jurisprudence is that of investigating and sanctioning violations of human rights, a requirement articulated not only in global bodies and instruments, but also in regional human rights systems. In General Comment No 31, the Human Rights Committee refers to the general obligation to investigate allegations of violations promptly, thoroughly, and effectively through independent and impartial bodies. Failure to do so can give rise to a separate breach of the Covenant. Where the investigations reveal violations of certain Covenant rights, states parties must ensure that those responsible are brought to justice; the obligation pertains most notably in respect of those violations recognized as criminal under either domestic or international law.[41] The Committee's statement of obligation in this respect has been reinforced by the UN's adoption of the 'Basic Principles and Guidelines on the Right to a Remedy and Reparation for Victims of Gross Violations of International Human Rights Law and Serious Violations of International Humanitarian Law'.[42]

The Committee on Economic, Social and Cultural Rights also issued a General Comment No 3 on the nature of states parties' obligations,[43] in which it notes the significant similarities in the obligations contained in the two Covenants. In particular, there are obligations of immediate effect, largely of a positive nature. There is also the negative obligation to avoid any deliberately retrogressive measures in the area of economic, social, and cultural rights.

[38] Human Rights Committee, 'General Comment No 25: The Right to Participate in Public Affairs, Voting Rights and the Right of Equal Access to Public Service' (27 August 1996) UN Doc CCPR/C/21/Rev.1/Add.7, paras 11, 12.

[39] *Mauritian Women v Mauritius*, para 9.2(c)(2).

[40] Nowak (n 20) 569.

[41] Human Rights Committee, 'General Comment No 31' (n 13). Such violations would include torture (Art 7), summary and arbitrary killing (Art 6), and enforced disappearance (Arts 6, 7, 9).

[42] UNGA, 'Basic Principles and Guidelines on the Right to a Remedy and to Reparation for Victims of Gross Violations of International Human Rights Law and Serious Violations of International Humanitarian Law' (21 March 2006) UN Doc A/RES/60/147. See also Commission on Human Rights, 'Report of the Independent Expert to Update the Set of Principles to Combat Impunity, Diane Orentlicher' (8 February 2005) UN Doc E/CN.4/2005/102/Add.1.

[43] CESCR, 'General Comment No 3' (n 21).

2.2 Positive and negative obligations in the European system

The European Convention on Human Rights (ECHR) requires its contracting parties to 'secure' to everyone the rights and freedoms defined in the Convention,[44] a verb that encompasses negative and positive duties. In the case law of the European Court of Human Rights, state authorities have been deemed obliged to adopt some measure that safeguards a right, or to implement 'reasonable and suitable'[45] measures to protect the right in question.[46] The European system has always generally assumed that negative obligations are inherent in the Convention, which is limited almost entirely to guarantees of civil and political rights.[47] The Court began attributing positive obligations to states through judgments issued starting in the 1960s.[48] It has developed this jurisprudence largely through applying the principle of 'effectiveness' as a standard for treaty interpretation.[49]

Interpreting the obligation in Article 1 of the ECHR to secure rights, together with the guaranteed rights contained in subsequent provisions, the Court has over time implied and imposed a detailed set of positive, as well as negative, obligations on contracting parties.[50] The Court originally referenced positive obligations in the *Belgian Linguistics Case*,[51] but cemented the idea of such obligations in respect to the right to private life (Article 8) in the *Marckx* case.[52]

[44] Convention for the Protection of Human Rights and Fundamental Freedoms.

[45] Akandji-Kombe (n 1) 7.

[46] See eg *Vgt Verein Gegen Tierfabriken v Switzerland.*

[47] Economic, social and cultural rights are contained in the European Social Charter of 18 October 1961.

[48] Akandji-Kombe (n 1) 5.

[49] *Öneryildiz v Turkey*, para 69. '[T]he Court reiterates, firstly, that its approach to the interpretation of Art 2 is guided by the idea that the object and purpose of the Convention as an instrument for the protection of individual human beings requires its provisions to be interpreted and applied in such a way as to make its safeguards practical and effective.'

[50] *Gegen Tierfabriken* (n 46) para 45. '[I]n addition to the primarily negative undertaking of a State to abstain from interference in Convention guarantees, "there may be positive obligations inherent" in such guarantees. The responsibility of a State may then be engaged as a result of not observing its obligation to enact domestic legislation.'

[51] Case 'Relating to Certain Aspects of the Laws on the Use of Languages in Education in *Belgium*' *v Belgium* 28. '[I]t cannot be concluded from this that the State has no positive obligation to ensure respect for such a right as is protected by Article 2 of the Protocol (P1-2). As a "right" does exist, it is secured, by virtue of Article 1 (art. 1) of the Convention, to everyone within the jurisdiction of a Contracting State.'

[52] *Marckx v Belgium*, para 31. 'By proclaiming in paragraph 1 the right to respect for family life, Article 8 (art. 8-1) signifies firstly that the State cannot interfere with the exercise of that right otherwise than in accordance with the strict conditions set out in paragraph 2 (art. 8-2). As the Court stated in the Belgian Linguistic case, the object of the Article is "essentially" that of protecting the individual against arbitrary interference by the public authorities. *Nevertheless it does not merely compel the State to abstain from such interference: in addition to this primarily negative undertaking, there may be positive*

Following these precedents, the Court has repeatedly interpreted Article 8 to include positive obligations.[53] Article 8 states that:

1. Everyone has the right to respect for his private and family life, his home and his correspondence.
2. There shall be no interference by a public authority with the exercise of this right except such as is in accordance with the law and is necessary in a democratic society in the interests of national security, public safety or the economic well-being of the country, for the prevention of disorder or crime, for the protection of health or morals, or for the protection of the rights and freedoms of others.[54]

With regard to this provision, the Court has argued that the duty to 'respect'[55] implies a positive obligation on the part of the state.[56] These obligations are not to be analysed in a vacuum,[57] because the guarantees of the Convention, including Article 8, develop within the confines of that which is necessary according to the reigning ideas of 'contemporary European societies'.[58]

Under the doctrine of 'implied positive obligations' that *Marckx* and the *Belgian Linguistics Case* initiated,[59] other Convention guarantees have been interpreted to impose some form of positive, as well as negative, obligation upon states,[60] especially Articles 2,[61] 3,[62] and 11.[63] As one commentator has noted:

> resorting to the concept of positive obligation has enabled the Court to strengthen, and sometimes extend, the substantive requirements of the European text and to link them to procedural obligations which are independent of Articles 6 and 13 and additional to those covered by those articles.[64]

In certain instances, the text of a provision itself provides a basis for imposing positive obligations. An example of such an article is Article 2 of the ECHR: 'Everyone's right to life shall be protected by law. No one shall be deprived of his life intentionally save in the execution of a sentence of a court following his conviction of a crime for which this penalty is provided by law.'[65] The article itself directly outlines the role

obligations inherent in an effective "respect" for family life.' (emphasis added; internal citations omitted). See also *Gaskin v United Kingdom*.

[53] See eg *Savda v Turkey*; *Chapman v United Kingdom*. [54] Article 8. [55] Article 8(2).

[56] Akandji-Kombe (n 1) 8. [57] See eg *Marckx* (n 52) 53 [58] *Marckx* (n 52) 53.

[59] Hugh Tomlinson and Matrix Chambers, 'Positive Obligations under the European Convention on Human Rights' (2012) <https://www.google.com/url?sa=t&rct=j&q=&esrc=s&source=web&cd=1&ved=0CDUQFjAA&url=http%3A%2F%2Fwww.adminlaw.org.uk%2Fdocs%2FSC%25202012%2520by%2520Tomlinson%2520QC.docx&ei=KisxUZjJCYfV0gGB8IH4Bg&usg=AFQjCNGIfphLexyU_SefygKtUvUMLff_-g&sig2=Rs3gZk2h9Sqm1VMfwF5Maw&bvm=bv.43148975,d.dmQ> accessed 1 March 2013.

[60] Akandji-Kombe (n 1) 6. [61] See eg *McCann and Others v United Kingdom*.

[62] See eg *Assenov and Others v Bulgaria*. [63] See eg *Plattform 'Ärzte für das Leben' v Austria*.

[64] Akandji-Kombe (n 1) 6. [65] Article 2(1).

that the government shall play in proactively protecting the right in question. Article 6 similarly contains explicit 'substantive' positive obligations.[66]

Positive obligations of a so-called procedural nature have proven particularly important in European jurisprudence especially in respect to the right to life[67] and the prohibitions on ill-treatment[68] and slavery.[69] Case law has established that when these articles are interpreted in conjunction with Article 1,[70] there is not only a substantive dimension, but also a positive procedural obligation to investigate any alleged violation that occurs and sanction those responsible, as appropriate.[71] The substantive dimension of the right to life, for example, requires the state to take all appropriate steps to safeguard life; this entails a primary duty on the state to put in place a legislative and administrative framework designed to provide effective deterrence against threats to the right to life.[72] The procedural dimension entails that where lives have been lost in circumstances potentially engaging the responsibility of the state, the state has a duty to ensure, by all means at its disposal, an adequate response, judicial or otherwise, so that the legislative and administrative framework set up to protect the right to life is properly implemented and any breaches of that right are repressed and punished.[73]

More generally ECHR Article 1 provides the basis for imposing positive obligations.[74] The Court's judgments in *Assanidze v Georgia* and *Ilaşcu and Others v Moldova and Russia* exemplifies the Court's interpretation of Article 1 as containing independent general (and positive) obligations.[75]

These general obligations may be described as quasi-autonomous. They are autonomous in so far as they arise solely by virtue of Article 1 of the Convention. But they are not wholly so, because their observance can be tested only on the occasion of an application alleging violation of one of the substantive rights secured by the European Convention.[76]

[66] See eg ECHR, Art 6(3): Everyone charged with a criminal offence has the following minimum rights:

(a) to be informed promptly, in a language which he understands and in detail, of the nature and cause of the accusation against him;
(b) to have adequate time and facilities for the preparation of his defence;
(c) to defend himself in person or through legal assistance of his own choosing or, if he has not sufficient means to pay for legal assistance, to be given it free when the interests of justice so require;
(d) to examine or have examined witnesses against him and to obtain the attendance and examination of witnesses on his behalf under the same conditions as witnesses against him;
(e) to have the free assistance of an interpreter if he cannot understand or speak the language used in court.

[67] Article 2. See eg McCann (n 61). [68] Article 3. [69] Article 4.

[70] Article 1 states: 'Every natural or legal person is entitled to the peaceful enjoyment of his possessions. No one shall be deprived of his possessions except in the public interest and subject to the conditions provided for by law and by the general principles of international law. The preceding provisions shall not, however, in any way impair the right of a State to enforce such laws as it deems necessary to control the use of property in accordance with the general interest or to secure the payment of taxes or other contributions or penalties.'

[71] See eg *Assenov* (n 62). [72] *Öneryildiz* (n 49) para 89. [73] *Öneryildiz* (n 49) para 91.

[74] See eg *Gegen Tierfabriken* (n 46); *Broniowski v Poland*. [75] Akandji-Kombe (n 1) 9.

[76] Akandji-Kombe (n 1) 9.

The Court in *Ilaşcu* provided guidance for determining the scope of positive obligations, indicating that the Court or state must consider what would constitute a 'fair balance ... between the general interest and the interests of the individual, the diversity of situations ... in Contracting States and the choices which must be made in terms of priorities and resources'.[77] Obligations should not impose an 'impossible or disproportionate burden' on states.[78] Though the Court will not outline the specific measures to be taken in any given case, it will evaluate whether the measures adopted were 'appropriate and sufficient'.[79]

The Court's development of procedural obligations has led to a significant expansion of the public's right to information. The Court's jurisprudence has consistently held that ECHR Article 10 guarantees only the negative 'freedom to receive information'. In the case of *Leander v Sweden*, the Court unanimously stated:

> [T]he right to receive information basically prohibits a Government from restricting a person from receiving information that others wish or may be willing to impart to him. Article 10 ... does not, in circumstances such as those of the present case, confer on the individual a right of access to a register containing information on his personal position, nor does it embody an obligation on the Government to impart such information to the individual.[80]

In *Anna Maria Guerra and 39 others against Italy*,[81] the Court maintained this interpretation in a case alleging the government's failure to inform the public of the risks and the measures to be taken in case of a major industrial accident at a hazardous chemical plant. A Grand Chamber of the European Court of Human Rights affirmed that Article 10 generally only prohibits a government from interfering with a person's freedom to receive information that others are willing to impart. However, the Court recharacterized the claim and unanimously found a violation of an affirmative procedural obligation deemed implicit in Article 8, the right to family, home, and private life. Its judgment observed that the individuals waited throughout the operation of fertilizer production at the company for essential information 'that would have enabled them to assess risks they and their families might run if they continued to live at Manfredonia, a town particularly exposed to danger in the event of an accident at [the] factory'.[82] In *Öneryildiz v Turkey*, the Court similarly found implicit in the right to life an obligation on government authorities to provide information about hazardous activities.[83] Thus, through articulating positive procedural obligations, the Court has effectively expanded the right to information beyond its limited formulation in ECHR Article 10.

[77] *Ilaşcu and others v Moldova and Russia*, para 332. [78] *Ilaşcu* (n 77) para 332.
[79] *Ilaşcu* (n 77) para 334. [80] *Leander v Sweden*, para 74. [81] *Guerra and Others v Italy*.
[82] *Guerra* (n 81) iii.
[83] 'Where such dangerous activities are concerned, public access to clear and full information is viewed as a basic human right.' *Öneryildiz* (n 49) para 62.

2.3 Positive and negative obligations in the Inter-American system

American Convention on Human Rights (ACHR) Article 1(1) lays out the main basis for establishing many of the positive state obligations to protect and ensure human rights in the Inter-American system.[84] Under this article:

> [t]he States Parties to this Convention undertake to respect the rights and freedoms recognized herein and to ensure to all persons subject to their jurisdiction the free and full exercise of those rights and freedoms, without any discrimination for reasons of race, color, sex, language, religion, political or other opinion, national or social origin, economic status, birth, or any other social condition.[85]

The article imposes on states parties the 'fundamental duty' of respecting and protecting all of the rights that the Convention recognizes.[86]

The obligations to 'respect' and to 'ensure' vary in nature and scope. The principle of respecting human rights involves restrictions on state actions, as no state actor can act in such a manner as to violate a Convention right.[87] The obligation to ensure 'implies the duty of States Parties to organize the governmental apparatus and, in general, all the structures through which public power is exercised, so that they are capable of juridically ensuring the free and full enjoyment of human rights'.[88] This implies duties both of prevention and investigation.[89] The duty to prevent includes 'all those means of a legal, political, administrative and cultural nature that promote the protection of human rights and ensure that any violations are considered and treated as illegal acts'.[90] In *Velásquez Rodríguez*, the first contentious matter decided by the Court, the tribunal detailed three distinct sets of obligations binding the states by virtue of Article 1's requirement to 'respect' and 'ensure': '(1) abstention from violating guaranteed human rights; (2) prevention of violations by state and non-state actors; and (3) investigation and punishment of both state and private human rights infringements.'[91] In cases like *Velásquez Rodríguez*, the state has been held responsible for actions carried out by non-state actors where the state did not exercise due diligence to prevent or punish the violations;[92] the due diligence standard is discussed below.[93]

In the text of ACHR Article 2, the states undertake proactively to 'adopt such legislative or other measures as may be necessary' to give full respect to recognized

[84] See *Velásquez Rodríguez* (n 95) para 164.
[85] Article 1(1).
[86] *Velásquez Rodríguez* (n 95) para 164.
[87] *Velásquez Rodríguez* (n 95) para 165.
[88] *Velásquez Rodríguez* (n 95) para 166.
[89] *Velásquez Rodríguez* (n 95) para 166. See also Shelton, 'Private Violence' (n 18) 13.
[90] *Velásquez Rodríguez* (n 95) para 175.
[91] Shelton, 'Private Violence' (n 18) 2, referencing *Velásquez Rodríguez* (n 95) paras 164, 174–77.
[92] Shelton, 'Private Violence' (n 18) 16.
[93] See also *Godínez Cruz* (n 100) para 182. 'An illegal act which violates human rights and which is initially not directly imputable to a State (for example, because it is the act of a private person or

rights, by guaranteeing them '*de facto* and *de jure*... within [a State's] jurisdiction'.[94] The requirement extends beyond mere *de jure* guarantees, however, because the simple fact that a state has designed its legal system in such a manner as to provide for the exercise of rights does not guarantee their free exercise; the existence of legal provisions does not guarantee that states parties and their citizens will not violate human rights.[95]

The Inter-American Court has consistently held that the Convention imposes upon states the duty to respect, protect, ensure, and promote the rights contained therein.[96] With regard to the obligation to respect rights, neither a state nor a state actor can act in such a manner as to violate a Convention right, regardless of any intent to violate said right.[97] The obligation to protect 'is the duty to prevent third parties from interfering with, hindering or barring access to the resources that are the object of that right'.[98] The obligation to 'ensure' a right requires a state to 'organize the governmental apparatus and, in general, all the structures through which public power is exercised, so that they are capable of juridically ensuring the free and full enjoyment of human rights'.[99] Incorporated within this obligation are state duties to prevent rights violations and, when unable to prevent them, to investigate, punish the perpetrators, and provide the appropriate compensation to victims.[100] Under this system:

> The State has a legal duty to take reasonable steps to prevent human rights violations... This duty to prevent includes all those means of a legal, political, administrative and cultural nature that promote the protection of human rights and ensure that any violations are considered and treated as illegal acts, which as such, may lead to the punishment of those responsible and the obligation to indemnify the victims for damages.[101]

because the person responsible has not been identified) can lead to international responsibility of the State, not because of the act itself, but because of the lack of due diligence to prevent the violation or to respond to it as required by the Convention.' Shelton, 'Private Violence' (n 18) 16.

94 IACHR, 'Access to Justice for Women Victims of Violence in the Americas' (20 January 2007) OEA/Ser.L/V/II, para 26.

95 Shelton, 'Private Violence' (n 18) 12. See *Velásquez Rodriguez v Honduras*, para 167 ('The obligation to ensure the free and full exercise of human rights is not fulfilled by the existence of a legal system designed to make it possible to comply with this obligation—it also requires the government to conduct itself so as to effectively ensure the free and full exercise of human rights').

96 *Velásquez Rodríguez.* See also Inter-American Commission on Human Rights (IACHR), 'Report on Citizen Security and Human Rights' (31 December 2009) OEA/Ser.L/V/II, para 35.

97 *Velásquez Rodríguez* (n 95) paras 165, 169–70. See also Shelton, 'Private Violence' (n 18) 12–13; IACHR, 'Report on Citizen Security' (n 96) para 35.

98 IACHR, 'Report on Citizen Security' (n 96) para 35.

99 *Velásquez Rodríguez* (n 95) para 166. See also Shelton, 'Private Violence' (n 18) 13.

100 *Velásquez Rodriguez* (n 95) para 166; *Godínez Cruz v Honduras*, para 175. See also Shelton, 'Private Violence' (n 18) 13.

101 *Velásquez Rodriguez* (n 95) paras 174–75. See also Andrew Clapham and Mariano Garcia Rubio, 'The Obligations of States with Regard to Non-State Actor in the Context of the Right to Health' (2002) Health and Human Rights Working Paper Series No 3, at 8 <http://www.who.int/hhr/Series_3%20 Non-State_Actors_Clapham_Rubio.pdf> accessed 25 February 2013.

Meanwhile, the obligation to 'promote' connotes a duty to foster conditions such that the individual may access and benefit from the right.[102]

The negative obligation to protect, once a violation occurs, is largely centred around 'access to adequate and effective judicial remedies... [as] the first line of defense to protect basic rights',[103] which are largely housed in Article 18 of the American Declaration and Articles 8 and 25 of the ACHR. Together, they guarantee that 'every person has the right to resort to a court and the right to a hearing, with due guarantees and within a reasonable time, by a competent, independent and impartial tribunal when that person believes his or her rights have been violated'.[104] The duty to investigate and to prevent individuals from controverting the human rights of others with impunity, which also fall under this obligations prong, are not absolute.[105] 'Nevertheless, [the investigation] must be undertaken in a serious manner and not as a mere formality preordained to be ineffective.'[106]

The positive obligations imposed on a state are not limited to those referenced in the seminal *Velásquez Rodríguez* decision, but can also extend to other provisions of the ACHR. A recent trend in the Inter-American system jurisprudence has been to 'infer positive obligations from a combination of standard-setting provisions and the general principle of the "rule of law" or "state governed by the rule of law"'.[107] The Court regards the rule of law as a fundamental principle of any democratic society and a characteristic 'inherent in all the articles of the Convention'.[108] Utilizing this approach, the Inter-American Commission has recognized a positive state obligation under Article 13(1) (freedom of thought and expression),[109] where it concerns victims of human rights violations.[110] '[T]he State has the positive obligation to guarantee essential information to preserve the rights of the victims, to ensure transparency in public administration and the protection of human rights.'[111] It is also relevant with regard to Article 13(3),[112] under which a state has an obligation not only to refrain from instituting policies that would violate the right, but also to 'ensure that the violation does not result from the "private controls"' to which the article refers.[113]

[102] IACHR, 'Report on Citizen Security' (n 96) para 35.

[103] IACHR, 'Access to Justice for Women' (n 94) para 23.

[104] IACHR, 'Access to Justice for Women' (n 94) para 24.

[105] *Velásquez Rodríguez* (n 95) paras 176–77.

[106] *Velásquez Rodríguez* (n 95) para 177.

[107] Akandji-Kombe (n 1) 9

[108] *Matheus v France*, para 70.

[109] Everyone has the right to freedom of thought and expression. This right includes freedom to seek, receive, and impart information and ideas of all kinds, regardless of frontiers, either orally, in writing, in print, in the form of art, or through any other medium of one's choice.

[110] *Barrios Altos v Peru.*

[111] *Barrios Altos* (n 110) para 45.

[112] The right of expression may not be restricted by indirect methods or means, such as the abuse of government or private controls over newsprint, radio broadcasting frequencies, or equipment used in the dissemination of information, or by any other means tending to impede the communication and circulation of ideas and opinions.

[113] *Compulsory Membership in an Association Prescribed by Law for the Practice of Journalism*, para 48.

2.4 Positive and negative obligations in the African system

The African Commission on Human and Peoples' Rights has similarly developed the concept of positive and negative obligations as applicable to state action and the protection of human rights. In so doing, it has referenced the jurisprudence of other regional as well as global human rights institutions and articulated four categories of obligations, in particular citing to the ICESCR: to 'promote', to 'protect', to 'respect', and to 'fulfil'.[114] In its leading case on this topic, the African Commission outlined government responsibility to 'respect' the Charter's enumerated rights (life, dignity, health, and property) and implied rights (shelter and food). The Commission commented that 'there is no right in the African Charter that cannot be made effective'.[115] The requirements to 'protect' and 'fulfil' connote positive obligations on the part of the state.[116] These include a duty to investigate and punish, even where the rights violations in question were not performed by state actors.[117] As to the duty to 'fulfil', the *Ogoniland* case and the case of the *Free Legal Assistance Group and Others v Zaire* outline the standard to be applied, in particular respecting individuals to whom the state owes a special duty of care. The Charter contains no provision that would measure compliance with the duty according to the availability of resources, in contrast to the ICESCR.[118] However, cognizant of the 'problem of poverty', the Commission has read such a qualification into the right to health,[119] while still demanding that the state adopt some concrete steps toward the fulfilment of the right.[120]

To give an example of the scope of positive obligations in respect to two rights, Article 16 (physical and mental health) and 24 (satisfactory environment) of the African Charter, the Commission determined that:

> The right to a general satisfactory environment, as guaranteed under Article 24 of the African Charter... imposes clear obligations upon a government. It requires the State to take reasonable and other measures to prevent pollution and ecological degradation, to promote conservation, and to secure an ecologically sustainable development and use of natural resources... The State is under an obligation to respect the just noted rights and this entails largely non-interventionist conduct from the State for example, not from carrying out, sponsoring or tolerating any practice, policy or legal measures violating the integrity of the individual. Government compliance with the spirit of Articles 16 and 24 of the African

[114] *Ogoniland Case* (n 25). See also Frans Viljoen, *International Human Rights Law in Africa* (2nd edn, OUP 2012).

[115] *Ogoniland Case* (n 25) para 68.

[116] Viljoen (n 114) 216. See also *Commission Nationale des Droits de l'Homme et des Libertés v Chad*, para 22.

[117] Viljoen (n 114) 216–17.

[118] Viljoen (n 114) 217.

[119] *Purohit and another v the Gambia*, para 84.

[120] Viljoen (n 114) 217. See also CESCR, 'General Comment No 3' (n 21).

Charter *must also include ordering or at least permitting independent scientific monitoring of threatened environments, requiring and publicising environmental and social impact studies prior to any major industrial development, undertaking appropriate monitoring and providing information to those communities exposed to hazardous materials and activities and providing meaningful opportunities for individuals to be heard and to participate* in the development decisions affecting their communities.[121]

Such a ruling was developed, even though Article 24 (unlike Article 16) does not directly charge the governments with any positive or affirmative duties.[122]

3. The Due Diligence Standard

States are responsible for ensuring that neither government officials nor anyone acting as an agent of the state, within the scope of duty, act in such a way as to violate an individual's human rights.[123] This duty of respect (abstention) imposes a strict standard of liability, requiring that the state redress any such violation attributable to it without regard to the intent or motive of the actor. Such a standard is not appropriate to positive obligations, which requires the state to take affirmative measures to protect individuals from the actions of others not acting in an official capacity. The state cannot ensure that no homicides or assaults will occur, or that other violations of guaranteed rights will always be prevented. Yet, at the other extreme, the state cannot stand by idly while death squads roam the country, killing with impunity. Somewhere between these extremes lies the standard for judging whether a state has fulfilled its affirmative obligations to 'ensure' or 'secure' rights. Most commonly, international tribunals refer to due diligence as the appropriate standard.[124] Without necessarily having a single, concrete definition of this term, it is generally held to mean: 'the reasonable measures of prevention that a well-administered government could be expected to exercise under similar circumstances.'[125]

[121] *Ogoniland Case* (n 25) paras 52–53, as cited in Clapham and Rubio (n 101) 10 (internal citations omitted, emphasis added).

[122] Compare Art 16:

> 1. Every individual shall have the right to enjoy the best attainable state of physical and mental health. 2. States Parties to the present Charter shall take the necessary measures to protect the health of their people and to ensure that they receive medical attention when they are sick.

With Art 24:

All peoples shall have the right to a general satisfactory environment favorable to their development.

[123] Waisman (n 14) 406.

[124] See eg *Velásquez Rodríguez* (n 95).

[125] Shelton, 'Private Violence' (n 18) 23.

3.1 Development of the due diligence standard

In one form or another, not always related directly to human rights, due diligence has been a long-standing concept in international law. As early as the late sixteenth century, Gentili wrote that a state could be held responsible for private actions violating rights, where 'the state, which knows because it has been warned, and which ought to prevent the misdeeds of its citizens, and through its jurisdiction can prevent them, will be at fault and guilty of a crime if it does not do so'.[126] International tribunals were analysing cases against a due diligence standard at least as early as 1872.[127] More recently, the International Court of Justice applied the standard in the *Iranian Hostage Case*.[128]

This standard was applied most frequently in diplomatic protection cases involving injury to aliens.[129] In these instances, the government at fault was deemed liable either for actively violating an applicable norm benefiting the alien or for failing to fulfil some duty or obligation. As pointed out in the *Noyes* case:

> [t]he mere fact that an alien has suffered at the hands of private persons an aggression, which could have been averted by the presence of a sufficient police force on the spot, does not make a government liable for damages under international law. There must be shown special circumstances from which the responsibility of the authorities arises: either their behavior in connection with the particular occurrence, or a general failure to comply with their duty to maintain order, to prevent crimes or to ... punish criminals.[130]

Thus, a state's diligence is not legally deficient because of the act that causes the injury, but rather because of what was lacking in the authorities' prevention of or response to said act.[131] As stated in the Harvard Draft on State Responsibility:

> Failure to exercise due diligence to apprehend, or to hold after apprehension as required by the laws of the State, a person who has committed against an alien any act referred to in paragraph 1 of this Article is wrongful, to the extent that such conduct deprives that alien or any other alien of the opportunity to recover damages from the person who has committed the act.[132]

126 Shelton, 'Private Violence' (n 18) 21, citing Gentili, *De Jure Belli Libri Tres* (John Rolfe (tr), OUP 1933) 100.

127 See eg *Alabama Claims (United States v Great Britain)*.

128 *United States Diplomatic and Consular Staff in Tehran*.

129 See eg Shelton, 'Private Violence' (n 18).

130 *Noyes (United States) v Panama* 311.

131 See Shelton, 'Private Violence' (n 18) 23; FV García-Amador, Louis Bruno Sohn, and Richard Reeve Baxter, *Recent Codification of the Law of State Responsibility for Injury to Aliens* (Brill 1974) 27. 'In other words, a State is not responsible unless it is displayed, in the conduct of its organs or officials, patent or manifest negligence in taking the measures which are normally taken in the particular circumstances to prevent or punish the injurious acts.'

132 Harvard Law School, 'Draft Convention on the International Responsibility of States for Injuries to Aliens', Art 13(2), reprinted in García Amador, Sohn, and Baxter (n 131).

This is not the same as saying the state is complicit in the wrongful act;[133] it is the state's own behaviour that is judged wrongful.

Since the founding of modern human rights law, the Inter-American Commission and Court have been called upon more than other human rights body to apply the due diligence standard to judge whether a state has lived up to its positive obligations in human rights cases. This is largely a consequence of the nature of the cases that have been presented, cases that have concerned disappearances, extrajudicial killings, forced displacements, and other violations for which the state has denied all responsibility. Serious factual questions have arisen about attribution, but it has also been necessary to develop the law to determine the scope of state responsibility in such cases.

3.2 Developing and applying the due diligence standard

Associated with the duty to 'ensure' rights, as set forth in ACHR Article 1, the case law of the Inter-American system[134] has applied the standard of due diligence to hold that '[i]n order for the state to be liable... there must be a harmful act committed by an individual or group. In addition, it must also be possible to attribute to the state some conduct with respect to the act that implies the non-performance of an international duty'.[135] The case of *Velásquez Rodríguez v Honduras* largely propelled the discussion and set forth the framework. In general, this standard requires a state to take 'reasonable steps' necessary to prevent or address potential rights violations.[136]

In this first contentious case, the Court held that:

An illegal act which violates human rights and which is initially not directly imputable to a State (for example, because it is the act of a private person or because the person responsible

[133] See eg *James et al (United States) v Mexico* paras 19–20. 'At times international awards have held that, if a State shows serious lack of diligence in apprehending and/or punishing culprits, its liability is a derivative liability, assuming the character of some kind of complicity with the perpetrator himself and rending the State responsible for the very consequences of the individual's misdemeanor... The reasons upon which such a finding of complicity is usually based in cases in which a Government could not possibly have prevented the crime, is that the nonpunishment must be deemed to disclose some kind of approval of what has occurred, especially so if the Government has permitted the guilty parties to escape or has remitted the punishment by granting either pardon or amnesty. A reasoning based on presumed complicity may have some foundation in cases of nonprevention where a Government knows of an *intended* injurious crime, might have averted it, but for some reason constituting its liability did not do so. The present case is different; it is one of nonrepression... [T]he Government is liable for not having measured up to its duty of diligently prosecuting and properly punishing the offender... Even if the nonpunishment were conceived as some kind of approval—which in the Commission's view is doubtful—still approving of a crime has never been deemed identical with being an accomplice to that crime; and even if non-punishment of a murderer really amounted to complicity in the murder, still it is not permissible to treat this derivative and remote liability not as an attenuate form of responsibility, but as just as serious as if the Government had perpetrated the killing with its own hands.'

[134] See Section 1.3 in this chapter.

[135] Shelton, 'Private Violence' (n 18) 21.

[136] See *Velásquez Rodríguez* (n 95) para 174.

has not been identified) can lead to international responsibility of the State, not because of the act itself, but because of the lack of *due diligence* to prevent the violation or to respond to it as required by the Convention.[137]

As a baseline:

> [T]he State has a legal duty to take reasonable steps to prevent human rights violations and to use the means at its disposal to carry out a serious investigation of violations committed within its jurisdiction, to identify those responsible, to impose the appropriate punishment and to ensure the victim adequate compensation.[138]

The Court's role, with respect to this standard, is to establish whether or not the rights violation that occurred at the hands of the private actors is the result of a state's failure to comply with its Article 1(1) obligations to 'respect' and 'guarantee' the right in question.[139] In examining whether or not the state has acted with due diligence, the state's actions should not be examined in a vacuum or outside of the context of a given situation or series of events. In *Maria da Penha Maia Fernandes v Brasil*, the Court examined not only the situation of the violence in question, but also the general state of affairs at the time, in finding that the asserted violence was 'part of a general pattern of negligence and lack of effective action by the State in prosecuting and convicting aggressors'.[140] Similarly, in the case of *González ('Cotton Field') et al v Mexico*, which concerned state responsibility for the unsolved deaths of many women in Mexico, the Court identified specific steps that should be taken to combat such violence and that would comply with the due diligence standard.[141]

> States should adopt comprehensive measures to comply with due diligence in cases of violence against women. In particular, they should have an appropriate legal framework for protection that is enforced effectively, and prevention policies and practices that allow effective measures to be taken in response to the respective complaints. The prevention strategy should also be comprehensive; in other words, it should prevent the risk factors and, at the same time, strengthen the institutions that can provide an effective response in cases of violence against women. Furthermore, the State should adopt preventive measures in specific cases in which it is evident that certain women and girls may be victims of violence.[142]

In so doing, the system has provided guidance (though neither exhaustive nor exclusive) to states on how to meet their affirmative obligations under the due diligence standard.

The European Court of Human Rights has also adopted the due diligence standard, although it was late in naming it as such.[143] Nonetheless, the European Court

[137] *Velásquez Rodríguez* (n 95) para 172 (emphasis added).

[138] *Velásquez Rodríguez* (n 95) para 174.

[139] *Velásquez Rodríguez* (n 95) para 173.

[140] *Maria da Penha Maia Fernandes v Brasil*, para 56.

[141] *González ('Cotton Field') et al v Mexico*, para 258.

[142] *'Cotton Field' Case* (n 141) para 258.

[143] Commission on Human Rights, 'Report of the Special Rapporteur on Violence Against Women, Its Causes and Consequences, Yakin Ertürk' (20 January 2006) UN Doc E/CN.4/2006/61, para 22; Waisman (n 14) 415.

often takes as a starting point the elements as outlined in *Velásquez Rodríguez*.[144] In *Osman v United Kingdom*, although the Court did not use the term 'due diligence', it required the state to '[comply with] Article 1 of the Convention and the obligations of Contracting States under that Article to secure the practical and effective protection of the rights and freedoms laid down therein, including Article 2'.[145] The Court has also suggested that a higher standard of diligence is required on the part of the state when serious human rights violation have occurred, without explaining or defining what are 'serious' violations.[146]

Over time, standards have developed for determining whether or not a state has complied with the due diligence requirement. '[D]ecisive is whether a violation of the rights recognized... has occurred with the support or the acquiescence of the government, or whether the State has allowed the act to take place without taking measures to prevent it or to punish those responsible.'[147] 'Liability may also result from "complicity" [that is] demonstrated by establishing that the State condones a pattern of abuse through pervasive non-action.'[148]

The due diligence standard has been important in recent years in respect of gender-based violence. Significantly, the Convention regulating violence against women in the Inter-American system[149] expressly includes the due diligence standard in its Article 7:

> The States Parties condemn all forms of violence against women and agree to pursue, by all appropriate means and without delay, policies to prevent, punish and eradicate such violence and undertake to... (b) apply due diligence to prevent, investigate and impose penalties for violence against women.

Applying this standard in the *'Cotton Field'* case, the Commission stated directly that:

> States should adopt comprehensive measures to comply with due diligence in cases of violence against women. In particular, they should have an appropriate legal framework for protection that is enforced effectively, and prevention policies and practices that allow effective measures to be taken in response to the respective complaints.[150]

[144] See eg *Bevacqua and S v Bulgaria* (citing *Velásquez Rodriguez* (n 95)); *Opuz v Turkey* (citing *Velásquez Rodriguez* (n 95)). For a further discussion of the use of Inter-American system case law in the case law of the European system, see Council of Europe, 'References to the Inter-American Court of Human Rights in the Case-Law of the European Court of Human Rights' (2012) Research Report <http://www.echr.coe.int/NR/rdonlyres/7EB3DE1F-C43E-4230-980D-63F127E6A7D9/0/RAPPORT_RECHERCHE_InterAmerican_Court_and_the_Court_caselaw.pdf> accessed 1 March 2013.

[145] *Osman v United Kingdom* 33. See also *Opuz* (n 144); *Z and Others v United Kingdom*.

[146] See *Isayeva and Others v Russia*, paras 208–13

[147] *Velásquez Rodríguez* (n 95) para 173.

[148] Commission on Human Rights, 'Report of the Special Rapporteur on Violence against Women, Its Causes and Consequences, Ms Radhika Coomaraswamy, Submitted in Accordance with Commission on Human Rights Resolution 1995/85' (6 February 1996) UN Doc E/CN.4/1996/53, para 33.

[149] Convention on the Prevention, Punishment and Eradication of Violence against Women (Convention of Belém do Pará).

[150] *'Cotton Field' Case* (n 141) para 258.

The Convention on the Elimination of All Forms of Discrimination against Women (CEDAW) Commission adopted this requirement in relation to gender-motivated violence earlier, when it expressed the opinion that states could be responsible when violations occurred at the hands of private actors with said states did not exercise due diligence to prevent or investigate the violations.[151] The UN Rapporteur has outlined a similar standard, declaring that a state is obligated under a due diligence standard with regard to acts of violence against women performed by private actors.[152]

> States whose Governments leave private violations of human rights unaddressed breach their duty under international law to protect human rights. States must also facilitate realization of these rights by employing governmental means to afford individuals the full benefit of human rights, including taking appropriate legislative, administrative, judicial, budgetary, economic and other measures to achieve women's full realization of their human rights.[153]

In this way, the due diligence standard emerging from the general law of state responsibility and the case law of the Inter-American system has come to play a large role in protecting human rights regionally and globally.

4. Conclusion

Over the past several decades, the ideas of positive and negative obligations in the universal and regional systems have become a major part of human rights law, in some instances extending both rights and obligations beyond the strict textual confines of international instruments. As litigation and investigations have transformed human rights courts, commissions, and other monitoring bodies, due diligence has emerged as the prevalent standard to measure positive obligations. Adopted from the law of state responsibility for injury to aliens, it has emerged as a prevalent standard in regional and universal systems, and has become particularly wide-spread in efforts to protect women against gender-motivated violence. Positive obligations, negative obligations, and due diligence are largely concepts developed in jurisprudence and they may further develop into effective and detailed legal standards that

[151] CEDAW Committee, 'General Recommendation No 19: Violence Against Women' (1992) UN Doc HRI/GEN/1/Rev.1, para 9. 'Under general international law and specific human rights covenants, States may also be responsible for private acts if they fail to act with due diligence to prevent violations of rights or to investigate and punish acts of violence, and for providing compensation.'

[152] Commission on Human Rights, 'Report of the Special Rapporteur on Violence Against Women, Its Causes and Consequences, Ms Radhika Coomaraswamy, in Accordance with Commission on Human Right Resolution 1997/44' (21 January 1999) UN Doc E/CN.4/1999/68/Add.4.

[153] Commission on Human Rights, 'Report of the Special Rapporteur' (n 152) para 47.

protect individuals from human rights violations, whether committed by state or non-state actors.

Further Reading

Borelli S, 'Positive Obligations of States and the Protection of Human Rights' (2006) 15 *Interights Bulletin* 1, 1

Mowbray A, *Human Rights Law in Perspective: The Development of Positive Obligations under the European Convention on Human Rights by the European Court of Human Rights* (Hart 2004)

Shelton D, 'Private Violence, Public Wrongs, and the Responsibility of States' (1989) 13 *Fordham International Law Journal* 1

PART V

INSTITUTIONS AND ACTORS

CHAPTER 25

FROM COMMISSION TO THE COUNCIL: EVOLUTION OF UN CHARTER BODIES

MILOON KOTHARI

1. Introduction

WHILE all United Nations principal organs address human rights issues within their respective spheres of action, the General Assembly created the United Nations Human Rights Council ('Council') on 15 March 2006, to be the world's premier human rights body.[1] The formative resolution called on the Council to promote universal respect and protection of all human rights and fundamental freedoms.[2] This was not, however, the first attempt by the UN to establish a mechanism to strengthen and promote human rights globally; in fact, the Council replaced the Commission on Human Rights ('Commission') that had been created for this purpose in 1946, but had come under increasing criticism that politicization of its work had compromised its effectiveness.

As discussed in this chapter, the Council acts as a political forum to discuss, address, decide, make recommendations, and report on all thematic human rights issues and situations throughout the world.[3] It is additionally tasked with

[1] UN GA Res 60/251 of 15 March 2006. [2] Res 60/251 (n 1) para 2.
[3] Res 60/251 (n 1) para 5.

mainstreaming human rights within the United Nations system and promoting coordination amongst United Nations entities when tackling human rights issues.[4] The Council is required to fulfil this mandate while being guided by the principles of universality, impartiality, objectivity, non-selectiveness, and cooperation.[5] The Council's Institution Building Package of 2007 further elaborated these principles, enshrining the concepts of predictability, flexibility, transparency, accountability, balance, inclusion, comprehension, and a gender perspective.[6]

In order to achieve its mandate the Council has a range of procedures, mechanisms and structures at its disposal, listed here and discussed in more detail below. These various elements include a system of 'Special Procedures',[7] Universal Periodic Review (UPR),[8] complaints procedure,[9] an Advisory Committee,[10] an expert mechanism on the Rights of Indigenous Peoples, and three Forums: on Minority Issues, Business and Human Rights, and Social Issues. Section 2 of this Chapter explores the creation and work of the Council. Section 3 examines the Council's procedure of universal periodic review in order to provide a practical critique on the effectiveness and development of this unique human rights mechanism. Section 4 reviews the work of the Council's Special Procedures and their critical role in upholding, through normative and practical work, the high standards set by international human rights instruments. The remaining section before the conclusion addresses some of the proposals for reform of the Council and how it might be improved in the future.

[4] Res 60/251 (n 1) para 3.

[5] Res 60/251 (n 1) para 4.

[6] Human Rights Council Res 5/1: Institution-Building of the United Nations Human Rights Council.

[7] Special Procedures are individual experts or groups of experts whose mandates are to examine a specific global human rights issue or a particular country that is of concern to the international community. Following examination of the relevant issues, each Special Procedure mandate holder reports to the Council in order to enable the latter to make informed decisions on how to proceed. See Section 4 of this chapter.

[8] UPR is a peer-review system whereby the international community, represented by the members of the Council, regularly assesses the human rights record of all United Nations member states. The state under review is required to report to the Council on the human rights situation in the country and the actions taken to improve the situation. Civil society organisations, national human rights institutions and other human rights bodies are given an opportunity to contribute to this process by providing observations on the State under review. The Council then publicly reports on the state and makes recommendations for improving its human rights record. See Section 3 of this Chapter.

[9] The Council's complaint procedure allows victims, and people or organizations with direct knowledge of victims, to bring situations of human rights violations to the Council's attention.

[10] The Advisory Committee operates as the Council's think tank. It consists of a group of human rights experts whose role is to provide expert advice to the Council on human rights issues when requested to do so.

2. The Demise of the Commission and Creation of the Council

The Commission, precursor to the Council, was established in 1946 by the Economic and Social Council (ECOSOC).[11] The Commission was a means by which ECOSOC could discharge its Charter mandate to promote universal respect for, and observance of, human rights and fundamental freedoms.[12] The initial tasks of the Commission focused on preparing and submitting to ECOSOC studies, information, proposals, recommendations, reports, and drafts on the proposed international bill of rights and on international declarations or conventions on civil liberties, the status of women, freedom of information, the protection of minorities, and the prevention of discrimination.[13] This mandate was extended four months later to include a reference to 'any other matter concerning human rights'.[14]

The Commission operated for sixty years, and undoubtedly contributed to international human rights protection by, for example, providing an international framework for protection of human rights.[15] Its latter years were marred, however, by criticisms and loss of credibility due to actions by member states that had politicized and paralysed some of its work, preventing the Commission from being able to perform its most pressing function: responding to mass human rights violations. When atrocities came to the attention of the Commission, the voting patterns of member states, particularly the practice of block voting, prevented the Commission from taking action. The lack of response by the Commission to the genocide in Rwanda provides a prominent illustration. In 1994, before the killings began, one of the Commission's Special Procedures had alerted the Council to the potential for development of a situation of mass atrocities stemming from rising ethnic tensions and violence within the country[16]. The Council took no action after receiving this report and subsequently approximately

[11] Economic and Social Council res 5 (I) of 16 February 1946. Article 68 of the UN Charter provided the mandate for ECOSOC to create a commission for the promotion of human rights.

[12] See UN Charter Art 62(2) ("The Economic and Social Council... may make recommendations for the purpose of promoting respect for, and observance of, human rights and fundamental freedoms for all').

[13] Economic and Social Council res 5 (I) of 16 February 1946.

[14] Economic and Social Council res 9 (II) of 21 June 1946.

[15] The framework consists of the Universal Declaration on Human Rights, the International Covenant on Civil and Political Rights, the International Covenant on Economic, Social and Cultural Rights (together known as the International Bill of Rights) and other core human rights treaties.

[16] Report by Mr. BW Ndiaye. Special Rapporteur, on his mission to Rwanda from 8 to 17 April 1993, UN Doc E/CN.4/1994/7/Add.1 (11 August 1993).

800,000 people were massacred and many inhabitants were subjected to other gross human rights violations.[17]

In addition to the standard political considerations of national interests that constrain the actions of all United Nations bodies composed of state representatives, the Commission was further reliant on the consent of particular human rights violators before it could respond to human rights abuses. Election of a country to serve on the Commission did not require a reasonable human rights record as a pre-requisite. As such, some states with a questionable commitment to human rights, even for their own citizens,[18] controlled the action of the international community when responding to the human rights violations of other states. In addition to making action less likely, such membership also raised questions of credibility and legitimacy in terms of the Commission's recommendations, statements, and standard setting. A major review of the United Nations by a high level panel noted that 'standard-setting to reinforce human rights cannot be performed by States that lack a determined commitment to their promotion and protection'.[19] The fact that Sudan was elected to the Commission during the government's campaign of violence in Darfur created the troubling situation that Sudan thus obtained voting privileges and influence over decisions concerning this matter. Such examples led some commentators and states to claim that membership on the Commission had ceased to be a demonstration of commitment to human rights but merely served as a shield for human rights violators. In effect, through membership on the Commission, states could perpetrate human rights violations against their own citizens with impunity.[20]

Critics further claimed that the voting pattern of the Commission reflected a North-South divide. Some states argued that the balance of power in the Commission meant that more powerful developed nations were able to condemn the weaker developing nations without the possibility of reciprocity.[21] A uniting factor in all the criticisms, pointed out by the High Level Panel in their 2004 report,[22] was the member state involvement. The flaws of the Commission resulted from

[17] Report of the Independent Inquiry into United Nations actions during the 1994 Rwanda genocide, p 1 presented 15 December 1999 by Ingvar Carlsson former Swedish Prime Minister, Han Sung-Joo, former South Korea Foreign Minister (1993-94) and M Kupolati, retired Nigerians lieutenant general. Available at <http://daccess-dds-ny.un.org/doc/UNDOC/GEN/N99/395/47/IMG/N9939547.pdf?OpenElement>. See also OHCHR, 'Human Rights Experts Have a Key Role in Early Warning,' available at <http://www.ohchr.org/EN/NewsEvents/Pages/KeyRoleEarlyWarning.aspx>.

[18] Prominent examples given by commentators are Libya under Khaddafi and Uganda during the regime of Idi Amin.

[19] Report of the High-level Panel on Threats, Challenges and Change, *A More Secure World: Our Shared Responsibility* (United Nations 2004) para 283 ('A More Secure World').

[20] See eg the Statement by the USA official at the 16th General Assembly Plenary 72nd Meeting held on 15 March 2006 on the creation of the Council available at GA/10449.

[21] See eg the Statement by the Cuban official at the General Assembly meeting on the creation of the Council.

[22] A More Secure World (n 19) para 283.

these states failing to respect their commitments, respond to warnings or use their power in a balanced manner.

The intent in creating the Council was to correct these flaws. Following a growing crescendo of criticisms, the first notable move towards reform came in 2004 with the proposals of the High Level Panel on Threats, Challenges and Change, in their report *A More Secure World: Our Shared Responsibility*.[23] The High Level Panel asserted that the Commission had lost its credibility and required reform. Noting that the majority of the difficulties faced by the Commission derived from its membership, the report recommended that the Commission should instead be opened up to universal membership of all United Nations member states. Another important recommendation called for ensuring greater interaction between the Commission, the Security Council and the Peace-building Commission, through regular briefings. The General Assembly did not accept these recommendations from the report of the High Level Panel when it adopted the resolution leading to the formation of the Council. Other recommendations came to fruition, however, including upgrading the status of the new body to a council so that it would became a Charter body, and establishing an advisory council.[24]

The UN Secretary General at the time, Kofi Annan, followed the 2004 report in 2005 with his own report, entitled 'In Larger Freedom'. This report coined the term 'credibility deficit' to describe the Commission's declining credibility and professionalism and the resulting impact upon the Commission's work and the reputation of the United Nations.[25] The solution the Secretary General proposed was to replace the Commission with a smaller standing Council.[26] An Addendum to the Report noted that the establishment of a Council would increase the prominence given to human rights within the UN system, bringing human rights into line with security and development matters. It further noted that major benefit would be derived from a change of status from a Commission to a Council, because a Council would be a standing body. It would thus be able to meet at any time, allowing it to respond quickly to emerging situations and providing it time to look into matters in more depth, as well as allowing increased time for follow-up. A reform of the election process to require a two-thirds majority of the General Assembly would also increase the accountability and authority of the body. Contrary to the 2004 High Level Panel report, the 2005 report recommended that membership be reduced, the motivation being to allow for more focused discussion.[27] The Secretary General's proposals were further elaborated in his Statement to the Commission on 7 April 2005 where he proposed a system of peer review within the framework of

[23] A More Secure World (n 19) para 283.

[24] A More Secure World (n 19) para 291.

[25] 'In Larger Freedom: Towards Development, Security and Human Rights for All,' UN Doc. A/59/2005) para 182

[26] 'In Larger Freedom' (n 25) para 183.

[27] 'In Larger Freedom' (n 25) para 183.

his proposed Council. This proposal provided the foundation for the establishment of the system of Universal Periodic Review (UPR).

The UN's World Summit in 2005 agreed to establish the Council and articulated the purpose for the new body, which would be 'to promote universal respect for the protection of all human rights and fundamental freedoms for all, without distinction of any kind in a fair and equal manner'.[28] Member states of the General Assembly then held some thirty rounds of negotiations over a five-month period in order to facilitate the drafting of resolution 60/251, whose adoption formally established the Council and its framework for operation.[29]

Despite the near unanimity of states voting in favour of the resolution, the text was not without its critics. The predominant criticism related to the process of gaining Council membership. Most of the objections concerned the imposition of a criterion that required states who wished to stand for election to have a good human rights record. For some observers, this criterion did not go far enough to exclude the worst violators from membership,[30] while others felt that the definition was too vague,[31] or held the view that to impose a membership criterion of any description went against the universal right of United Nations member states to stand for election to any UN body.[32] Others objected that the size of the proposed Council was too small for adequate participation.[33] In relation to the membership vote, some states favoured a two-thirds majority for election instead of a simple majority.[34] Similarly concern was expressed regarding the vote to expel a state from the Council (exclusion procedure) on the grounds of its human rights record. Critics noted that although the resolution specified that a two-thirds majority was required for expulsion, it failed to specify a minimum number of votes to be cast.[35]

A more general criticism of the resolution contended that it failed to achieve its objective, which was to replace a hampered politicized body with one secure from the threat of politicization. Some states expressed concern about the lack of safeguards aimed at addressing the causes of politicization,[36] the potential for politicization of the exclusion procedure,[37] and the potential that political considerations would govern the adoption of country specific resolutions.[38]

[28] World Summit Outcome. General Assembly resolution 60/1 of the 16 September 2005, para 158.

[29] GA Resolution 60.125 adopted by a vote of 170 in favour to 4 against (Israel, Marshall Islands, Palau, and USA voting against).

[30] The USA, Chile, New Zealand, Canada, and Australia comments in the press Statement on draft resolution 60/251.

[31] Israel and Iran press Statement on draft resolution 60/251.

[32] Comments by Russia, Iran, and Cuba in the press Statement on draft resolution 60/251.

[33] African group press Statement on draft resolution 60/251.

[34] USA, EU, Argentina, Japan press Statement on draft resolution 60/251.

[35] Cuba press Statement on draft resolution 60/251.

[36] African group, Sudan, Pakistan, and Cuba press Statement on draft resolution 60/251.

[37] Iran press Statement on draft resolution 60/251.

[38] China press Statement on draft resolution 60/251.

Finally, another major criticism of the resolution related to the proposed geographical distribution of member states. Criticism on this ground came solely from the Latin America and Caribbean countries, who as a group, were due to lose 27 per cent of their seats as a result of the change to the geographical distribution of membership.[39]

2.1 Structure and functioning of the Council

The Council debated and decided on its internal workings through preparing the Institutional Building Package of 2007 and the Rules of Procedures drafted and adopted during this process.[40] These Rules of Procedure and the Rules applicable to the main committees of the General Assembly are the main normative sources that govern the Council.

The Council consists of forty-seven member states who are elected for three-year terms by secret ballot.[41] In order to be eligible for election, the state is required to have a good human rights record and make appropriate commitments for the further promotion and protection of human rights in their country. Eligible states are elected also with respect to the geographical balance. The Council must comprise thirteen members from Africa, thirteen members from Asia, six members from Eastern Europe, eight from Latin American and the Caribbean, and seven from the Western European and other states.[42] States elected to the Council may serve for a maximum of two terms before stepping down for a minimum of one year. As noted above, a state may be expelled by a two-thirds majority if it fails to maintain a good domestic human rights record or if it fails to cooperate with the

[39] Press Statement on draft resolution 60/251. Other criticisms of the resolution included lack of emphasis on the need for cooperation and dialogue when dealing with non-compliant States; lack of a strong development commitment; the potential overlap between the UPR, Special Procedures and Treaty bodies, the burden of which may most keenly impact upon developing nations; the Council not being given Principal organ status; lack of flexibility in convening mechanisms to enable a faster response to changing global circumstances; lack of specification of the duration and frequency of Council meetings; insufficient focus on all forms of intolerance and incitement to religious hatred; lack of reference to the right of self-determination for people living under colonial rule; insufficiently robust reference to the role of civil society; lack of a global annual reporting; and the reference to humanitarian action caused concern in relation to potential infringement of State Sovereignty on the grounds of humanitarian intervention. See the explanations during the General Assembly debate and press statements following the vote on the resolution.

[40] Human Rights Council Resolution 5/1 of 18 June 2007. [41] Resolution 60/251, para 7.

[42] The President of the Council is also elected on the basis of rotation among the geographical group and the vice presidents are drawn from the remaining geographical groups. The President of the Council and the four Vice Presidents together form the Council's Bureau, which is responsible for organisational and procedural matters. The President and Vice Presidents are elected at the Council's first meeting of the year, by the Member States who are present, for a one year period and are not eligible for immediate re-election. See Rules of Procedure, Rule 14.

UPR process.[43] The Office of the United Nations High Commissioner for Human Rights (OHCHR) acts as the Council's secretariat and provides all support functions including translations, printing, storage, and circulation of materials.[44]

The Council can convene three types of meetings: organizational meetings, working sessions and special sessions. Organizational sessions take place prior to working sessions, sometimes referred to as regular sessions, where the majority of Council business is undertaken. The Council sets its agenda and priorities at its first meeting of the year.[45] In addition to regular sessions, the Council can convene, at the request of one-third of its members, special sessions to address and respond to human rights violations and emergency situations.[46] Numerous Special Sessions of the Council have been held to address specific country situations as well as thematic issues that have assumed global crisis proportions.[47] As a general rule meetings are held in public unless the Council decides that exceptional circumstances require a closed meeting.[48] The General Assembly directed that the Council's operations should be transparent, impartial, equitable, fair, and pragmatic; and lead to clarity, predictability, and inclusiveness.[49] The Council may adopt resolutions, decisions, recommendations, conclusions, summaries of discussions, Presidential Statements, and its annual report to the General Assembly, prepared by the Secretariat. The Council's process of decision-making requires a quorum of one-third of states and is based on a majority of states that are present and voting.

In order to fulfil its mandate the Council may draw upon its mechanisms of special procedures, UPR and complaints and may seek advice from its advisory committee or committees of inquiry established to investigate emerging situations. Each Council mechanism is introduced below, but only a brief overview is provided of the UPR, because it is addressed in detail below.

Special procedures are mechanisms inherited from the Commission and used by the Council to investigate and address either the human rights situation in a particular country (country situation) or a particular global human rights problem (thematic concern). When the Council identifies the existence of such a country or a theme it is entitled to establish a Special Procedure mandate by way of a resolution. As of April 2013, there were thirty-six thematic[50] and thirteen country

[43] Resolution 60/251 para 9. [44] Rules of Procedure Rule 14.

[45] The Council holds no fewer than three regular sessions per year comprising of a minimum of ten weeks.

[46] <http://www.ohchr.org/EN/HRBodies/HRC/Pages/Sessions.aspx>.

[47] Special Sessions have been held on Syria in 2011–12, Libya in 2011, the Côte d'Ivoire following the elections in 2010, Haiti following the Earthquake in 2010, the Occupied Palestinian territory in 2006, 2008 and 2009, Sri Lanka in 2009, on the global financial crisis in 2009, the Democratic Republic of the Congo in 2008, the negative impact of worsening world food crisis in 2008, Myanmar in 2007, Darfur in 2006, and Lebanon in 2006. For details see: <http://www.ohchr.org/EN/HRBodies/HRC/Pages/Sessions.aspx>.

[48] Rules of Procedure Rule 16. [49] General Assembly resolution 60/251.

[50] <http://www.ohchr.org/EN/HRBodies/SP/Pages/Themes.aspx> accessed on 10 June 2013.

mandates[51] approved and functioning. Following creation of a mandate, the Council appoints an expert or a working group (usually consisting of five experts) to investigate, examine, monitor, advise, publicly report, and make recommendations to the Council on the subject of their mandate.

The peer review process of UPR envisages assessment every four-and-a-half years of the human rights situation in, and record of, every member state of the United Nations. The review aims to analyse the country according to the norms contained in the United Nations Charter, Universal Declaration of Human Rights, human rights instruments to which the state is a party, voluntary state commitments, and international humanitarian law. Through this assessment process that applies equally to all states, regardless of their willingness to adopt human rights commitments, it is expected that the Council will have the ability to promote the universality, interdependence, indivisibility, and interrelatedness of all human rights, increase international compliance with human rights obligations, accurately assess the challenges being faced by states in relation to human rights, and to assist states with capacity building through the provision of technical assistance and sharing of best practice to support the state in implementing the outcome of the review.

The Advisory Committee of the Council replaced the former Sub-Commission on the Promotion and Protection of Human Rights, an independent expert body that engaged in studies, recommendations, and standard-setting. The new Advisory Committee is the think tank of the Council, serving as its research body, providing expertise when required and asked by the Council. The Advisory Committee comprises eighteen experts who serve on the Advisory Committee in their personal capacity. These experts are appointed following an election. All United Nations member states are eligible to nominate a candidate from their own region to serve on the Advisory Committee. Following the nomination process the Council will elect candidates through a secret ballot considering gender balance, geographical and legal system representation, competence, moral standing, impartiality, and independence. The term of appointment for experts is three years with a maximum of two consecutive terms permitted. The Advisory Committee sits for two sessions per year totalling a maximum of ten days.

The Council's complaints procedure is based on the previous procedure of the Commission, established in 1970 by ECOSOC resolution 1503;[52] however the Council's Complaint Procedure is more victim-oriented in response to criticisms of the former process. The procedure is designed to be more transparent and efficient, with the Council required to keep complainants informed of the progress of their complaint and to address complaints in a timely manner.[53] In addition to a focus

[51] <http://www.ohchr.org/EN/HRBodies/SP/Pages/Countries.aspx> accessed on 10 June 2013.

[52] Economic and Social Council res. 1503 (XLVIII), 27 May 1970.

[53] Following transmission of a complaint to the State concerned the matter must come before the Council within twenty-four months; the 1503 procedure had no requirements or guidelines on the time for consideration of a complaint.

on the victim, the principles of the new complaints procedure include confidentiality, impartiality, objectivity, and efficiency. The procedure allows victims, or those aware of the existence of victims, to draw human rights violations to the attention of the Council by sending a communication detailing their complaint. Two working groups of five persons deal with such complaints: the Working Group on Communications and the Working Group on Situations. They meet for a minimum of two sessions per year consisting of five working days in total. The Working Group on Communications screens out inadmissible complaints and passes admissible ones to the state concerned for comment. A complaint is inadmissible if it is manifestly politically motivated; the object of the complaint is not consistent with the applicable human rights law; the complaint does not contain a factual description of the alleged violation and the rights that were violated; the complaint contains abusive language; the complaint was not submitted by an identified individual or group that asserts direct and reliable knowledge of the violation; the complaint is already being dealt with by a Special Procedure, a treaty body or regional human rights complaint mechanism; or domestic remedies have not been exhausted (provided effective remedies exist and are not unreasonable prolonged).

After receiving a response from the state—or not receiving a response as the case may be—the Working Group assesses the merits of the complaint in order for appropriate cases to be forwarded to the Working Group on Situations. The Working Group on Situations, in private session, meets with the Council in order to present the latter with a report on consistent patterns of gross and reliably attested violations of human rights and fundamental freedoms, discuss the contents of the report and make recommendations to the Council on the course of action it should take in response to the allegations—normally in the form of a draft resolution or decision. The Council may then decide to dismiss the complaint, keep the situation under review, appoint an expert to investigate and report back to the Council, discontinue private consideration to take up public consideration (if the state is not cooperating with the Council), or recommend that the OHCHR provide technical cooperation, capacity building assistance, or advisory services to the state concerned.

In practice, it is clear that the Council does not favour establishing country rapporteurs or investigations. Yet, the Council has publicly debated and adopted country-specific resolutions as a response to grave human rights crises, for example, regarding Libya, Belarus, and Syria. The country resolutions have at times led to the formation of Inquiry Commissions and fact-finding missions, for example regarding Libya, Ivory Coast and Syria, Israel in relation to Gaza, and the independent international fact-finding mission to investigate the implications of the Israeli settlements.[54]

[54] For a full listing of Commissions of Inquiry and fact-finding missions of the Council see: <http://www.geneva-academy.ch/docs/news/HR-council-inquiry-conference-brief.pdf>.

The Council has, however, also failed to respond to grave human rights situations in other countries, such as Bahrain and Afghanistan.

The Council has established standing bodies on a range of thematic issues. The Social Forum engages in dialogue across sectors on different themes every year;[55] the Minority Forum seeks to identify initiatives for the further implementation of the Declaration on the Rights of Persons belonging to National or Ethnic, Religious and Linguistic Minorities;[56] the Forum on Business and Human Rights has been tasked with discussing trends and challenges in the implementation of the Guiding Principles on Business and Human Rights;[57] the Expert Mechanism on the Rights of Indigenous Peoples conducts work on issues relating to indigenous peoples throughout the world.[58]

Significant thematic resolutions adopted by the Council have focused on the prevention of maternal mortality from a human rights perspective and a landmark resolution on sexual orientation and gender equality. Controversial resolutions, however, that contradict basic human rights principles continue to be adopted, such as the resolution on traditional values of humankind.[59]

2.2 Five year review of the Council

Resolution 60/251 made provision for the Council to be reviewed after five years in order to reflect on the strengths and weaknesses of the system and to make appropriate amendments. An open-ended inter-governmental working group began this review in 2011, completing it in one year, after which the General Assembly voted to maintain the Council.[60] The process generated much debate about possible significant changes to the Council, but in the end there were no major alterations. Instead, the General Assembly voted by an overwhelming majority to maintain the Council's status as a subsidiary organ of the General Assembly, making only minor

[55] Themes taken up by the Social Forum in recent years include: Negative impacts of economic and financial crises on efforts to combat poverty (2009); climate change and human rights (2010) and the effective realisation of the right to development (2011). For more details see <http://www.ohchr.org/EN/Issues/Poverty/SForum/Pages/SForumIndex.aspx>.

[56] For more information and a compilation of recommendations from the first four sessions of the Forum (2008–11) see <http://www.ohchr.org/EN/HRBodies/HRC/Minority/Pages/ForumIndex.aspx>.

[57] See <http://www.ohchr.org/EN/Issues/Business/Pages/ForumonBusinessandHR2012.aspx>.

[58] See <http://www.ohchr.org/EN/Issues/IPeoples/EMRIP/Pages/EMRIPIndex.aspx>.

[59] For a full listing of resolutions adopted by the Council see <http://www.ohchr.org/EN/HRBodies/HRC/Pages/Documents.aspx>.

[60] General Assembly Resolution 5.2 of 23 March 2011 154 States voted for this resolution and four voted against (Canada, USA, Israel, and Palau voting against).

procedural changes to its functioning. During discussions after the vote it appeared that states, despite voicing opinions on how to reform the Council, feared losing the Council altogether and preferred an imperfect system to no system at all.[61] The General Assembly did somewhat strengthen the role of the Advisory Committee, in deciding that there should be an increased engagement between the Council and Committee through seminars, panels, working groups and feedback sessions, and the Council was urged to provide more guidance regarding the work priorities of the Committee.[62]

2.3 Comparing the Council and the Commission

As has been previously discussed, the Council was created to replace what was viewed by many as a dysfunctional Commission. It is worth asking, then, whether the changes that were enacted have been sufficient to protect the Council from the political manipulations that doomed the Commission.

First, the Council has been given membership criteria that had no equivalent for members of the Commission and, indeed, the Commission was heavily criticized because a number of its states had particularly poor human rights records. The current criteria require states to uphold the highest standards in the protection and promotion of human rights, to make appropriate voluntary human rights commitments and to fully cooperate with the council and the UPR system. These criteria are expected to guide the General Assembly when electing members to the Council and the Council's members themselves throughout their term in office; failing to comply with these criteria could in theory lead to a vote of expulsion. These measures obviously were intended to prevent such a situation from occurring on the Council, although it is far from clear that the reform has been entirely successful in this respect.[63]

Limitation as to the length of time a state can be a member also distinguishes the Council from the Commission. The two-term limit (six years) is meant to avoid a criticism that other United Nations bodies face: that particular states maintain a quasi-permanent seat on them. Now, 'for the first time in the history of the

[61] Report of the open-ended intergovernmental working group on the review of the work and functioning of the Human Rights Council 11–17.

[62] Other reform proposals that were adopted included the creation of a half-day yearly panel discussion with other United Nations agencies and funds in order to fulfil the Council's mandatory commitment to mainstream human rights; the creation of the Office of the President to support the president and enhance efficiency; enhancement of disabled access to the Council and its resources; and to make the Council more accessible through increased use of information technology.

[63] As with the Commission, Council membership continues to include countries whose human rights record is subject to considerable criticism. A list of the member states can be found at <http://www.un.org/en/rights>.

Organization, the Assembly had decided that no state could have a de facto permanent membership in the new Council. That set a very important precedent for the future'.[64]

The final significant change, requiring equitable geographical representation amongst member states, was aimed at redressing a perceived imbalance between developed and developing nations, particularly by increasing the representation of Asian and developing countries. The effect of this change, it could be argued, is a reduction in initiatives, particularly controversial initiatives, by Western states. While this is certainly a trend, as noted by some commentators,[65] it could be argued that this was a trend even prior to the establishment of the Council.[66]

Advocates have perceived the elevation of the Council to a subsidiary body of the General Assembly as an important change that could impact positively on the Council's functioning and credibility and demonstrate the United Nations' commitment to mainstreaming human rights. While it is true that the institutional status of the Council is higher than what the Commission held, the Commission in fact had a very high status and considerable autonomy. The change may in fact reduce the authority and autonomy of the Council due to the change in oversight from ECOSOC to the General Assembly, because the General Assembly appears to be taking a more active role in assessing the work of the Council than ECOSOC did with the Commission. This is illustrated by the General Assembly's treatment of the Council's Declaration on the Rights of Indigenous People,[67] which encountered delays and amendments prior to its ultimate adoption.[68] ECOSOC, in contrast, rarely involved itself in Commission business. The result of this change ultimately could be either positive or negative. On the one hand, monitoring of decisions has an important role to play when a relatively small body is taking action that may have an impact on the global community as a whole. An increased role for the General Assembly in this regard may improve the Council's status, moral authority, and moral legitimacy. On the other hand, such involvement could cripple the ability of the Council to respond to situations in a timely manner and increase the political nature of the Council's actions. Analysts have correctly pointed out that the

[64] Comment by the Lichtenstein delegation at the vote on Resolution 60/251 reported in the press Statement.

[65] See eg the comments made by Dr Lempinen and Prof Scheinin, 'The New Human Rights Council: The First Two Years (2007) p.4, available at <http://www.eui.eu/Documents/DepartmentsCentres/AcademyofEuropeanLaw/Projects/HRCReport.pdf>.

[66] Dr Lempinen and Prof Scheinin (n 65).

[67] United Nations Declaration on the Rights of Indigenous Peoples, GA Res 61/295, Annex, UN Doc A/RES/61/295 (13 September 2007).

[68] For the history and application of the Declaration, see James Anaya, 'The Right of Indigenous Peoples to Self-Determination in the Post-Declaration Era,' in Claire Chartres and Rodolfo Stavenhagen (eds), *EDS., Making the Declaration Work: The United Nations Declaration on the Rights of Indigenous Peoples* 184 (IWGIA 2009).

Council, as the United Nations main human rights body, should be free to operate within the confines of its mandate and rules without interference from other United Nations bodies.[69]

In terms of working arrangements the Council meets more frequently than the Commission did and has the ability to call special sessions, making it easier to act speedily in response to global emergencies or emerging situations. The Commission was permitted special sessions only under exceptional circumstances with the agreement of a majority of Commission states. In contrast, the Council permits special sessions to be called at the request of one-third of member states whenever they are required.

A further change in practice relates to the Council's treatment of economic, social, and cultural rights (ESCR). The Council has given more prominence to these rights, as can be seen in the continued support given to the ESCR mandates inherited from the Commission, as well as in the development of new thematic mandates related to these human rights. The Council has expressly recognized the right to development and has increased its focus on cultural rights through the establishment of the forum for minorities, declaration on the rights of indigenous people, multiple declarations on religious tolerance, resolution on globalization and its resolutions on cultural diversity, protection of culture during armed conflict, and protection of cultural heritage.

The most significant change from the Commission to the Council was undoubtedly the establishment of the UPR system. As a universal peer review system it directly responds to one of the major criticisms of the Commission: that membership on the Commission could act to shield a state from scrutiny in respect to its human rights record. While the UPR system certainly has potential to bring needed change to the system by allowing consistent and uniform treatment, it requires the cooperation of states to succeed. The example in January 2013 of Israel, the first state to refuse to cooperate with the UPR, is therefore a troubling event that could jeopardize the system should it be taken as an acceptable precedent.

In relation to the special procedures, the Council has improved the system for the appointment of mandate holders, which was largely a closed political process under the Commission. The process has become more open and transparent and there has been a strengthening of the selection criteria.

Despite the changes, the purpose of the Council remains the same as that of the Commission: to serve as a forum for political discussion, placing human rights on the agenda of states. Furthermore most of the tools available to the Council are those previously utilized by the Commission; no radically different or additional power has been added, such as providing the Council with a quasi-judicial status. It is therefore the responsibility of the Council member states to use the existing tools

[69] See eg 'In Larger Freedom (n 25) Addendum 1, para 1.

to fulfil the mandate of the Council, while steering away from actions that could give rise to renewed criticisms.

3. The Universal Periodic Review (UPR)

The establishment in 2008 of the peer-review mechanism known as UPR is potentially one of the most significant changes occurring in the move from the Commission to the Council.[70] Under this process all UN member states face a review of their human rights record.[71] This section will outline the guidelines for conducting the UPR, based on the Council's Rules of Procedure.[72]

During the UPR, the Council conducts the human rights assessment based on the legal norms contained in the UN Charter, Universal Declaration of Human Rights, human rights instruments to which the state is a party, voluntary state commitments, and international humanitarian law. This approach, a unique feature of the UPR, allows a much wider canvas of review by going well beyond examining state responsibility as limited to treaties ratified by the respective state.

UPR is based on the principles of promotion of the universality, interdependence, indivisibility, and interrelatedness of all human rights, cooperation, use of objective and reliable information, and equal treatment of states. It is intended to be member driven, action-oriented, and fully involve the country under review. It should

[70] UN General Assembly resolution 60/251 mandated UPR when it created the Council. The UPR, while path-breaking and unique, is not an entirely new procedure. Between 1956 and 1981, the Commission requested states to submit periodic reports on measures they had taken to implement human rights, focusing on positive developments within states. The system was a failure, however, as governments paid it little attention.

[71] By May 2012 all 192 member states completed the UPR. At the time of writing the second cycle of the UPR is well under way. Information on the UPR process and reports of all member states and other actors are available at: <http://www.ohchr.org/EN/HRBodies/UPR/Pages/UPRMain.aspx>. Another very useful website for documents and analysis of the UPR is <http://www.uprinfo.com>.

[72] See in particular Resolution adopted by the General Assembly: 6/251, Human Rights Council, Sixtieth session, Agenda items 46 and 120, 3 April 2006, A/RES/60/251; Resolution adopted by the Human Rights Council: 16/21, Human Rights Council, Sixteenth session, Agenda item 1, 12 April 2011, A/HRC/RES/16/21; Decision adopted by the Human Rights Council: 17/119—Follow-up to the Human Rights Council resolution 16/21 with regard to the universal periodic review, Seventeenth session, Agenda item 1, 19 July 2011, A/HRC/DEC/17/119; Decision adopted by the Human Rights Council: 6/102—Follow-up to Human Rights Council resolution 5/1, 20th meeting, 27 September 2007 and Human Rights Council, Modalities and practices for the universal periodic review process, President of the Council Statement 8/PRST/1, 9 April 2008. All documents available at: <http://www.ohchr.org/EN/HRBodies/UPR/Pages/BackgroundDocuments.aspx>.

complement and not duplicate other human rights mechanisms, be objective, transparent, and constructive. There are negative requirements as well: it should not be selective, confrontational or politicized; not overly burdensome or time consuming; and must not diminish the Council's capacity to respond to urgent human rights situations. Finally, it must fully integrate a gender perspective, take into account the stage of development of the concerned country, and take into account the views of all relevant stakeholders.

The objectives of the UPR are to increase compliance with human rights obligations, assess the challenges faced by states, provide capacity building through technical assistance and sharing of best practices, support cooperation as a tool to protect and promote human rights, encourage full support for the Council and other human rights bodies, provide an opportunity for states to declare what actions they have taken in respect of human rights in their country, and remind states about their obligations.

UPR occurs over a four-and-a-half year cycle following a schedule that is drafted in accordance with the principle of equal treatment and geographical representation. States are considered in alphabetical order from the different geographical groups.

The documentation for the UPR consists of three key reports: (i) a national report of up to twenty pages prepared by the state containing relevant information as outlined and encouraged by guidelines from the Council;[73] (ii) a ten-page report by the OHCHR compiling all relevant information from treaty bodies, special procedures and other UN documents; and (iii) an OHCHR summary of information received from stakeholders, also not to exceed ten pages. These documents are reviewed by a working group comprised of all members except the country being reviewed, chaired by the President of the Council. Other relevant stakeholders may attend. A troika of three rapporteurs (appointed based on geographical representation and drawing of lots) facilitate the process and prepare the review. They present a report for adoption by the working group. All of the review takes place in a time period of three hours per country within the working group and another hour for consideration of the outcome by the Council.[74]

The outcome report summarizes the assessment of country situation, including positive developments and challenges, provides conclusions and/or recommendations and the voluntary commitments of the state concerned. The state is given the opportunity to reply before the working group adopts of the outcome report. Both the state and stakeholders may express their views prior to the plenary Council adopting the report and taking action.

[73] See n 72. Council Resolution A/HRC/RES/16/21. This resolution also encourages states to prepare the national report in broad consultations with all stakeholders (para 15 (1)). The state report and other documents have to be submitted six weeks prior to the review.

[74] Following the five-year review this time period for the working group was extended to three-and-a-half hours.

The Council decides if and when any particular follow up is required. The individual state is responsible for implementing the outcome of the review, but if it so requests the international community will provide technical assistance and capacity building to aid implementation. Subsequent cycles of the UPR will provide an opportunity for review, but there is also a system of voluntary mid-term progress updates. In addition, the Council may address consistent non-compliance with the review process.

The Council adopted a number of amendments to the UPR at its session in 2011, following the five-year review.[75] These are summarized below. While the changes dictated by the resolution are not as transformative as civil society activists and independent human rights experts hoped, they provide some pointers to a potentially path-breaking evolution.

3.1 Five-year review of the Council: enhancing participation

Among the significant amendments adopted during the review process, the General Assembly decided to focus the second UPR cycle on evaluating the implementation of recommendations arising from the initial cycle. In this vein it was decided to encourage states as a matter of policy to conduct extensive consultations with stakeholders on the outcome of their UPR and to cooperate with the voluntary mid-term follow-up process. The General Assembly further decided that comments from the national human rights institutions (NHRI) submitted as part of UPR should be included in a separate section of the stakeholder summary of information and that the NHRIs should be entitled to intervene immediately after the state during the adoption of the outcome of the UPR and Special Procedure Report. It was decided that the recommendations adopted in the outcome of a UPR would henceforth be clustered thematically for ease of use. In terms of the amount of time devoted to the UPR process it was decided that the sessions of the working group would be extended by thirty minutes each, taking them to three-and-a-half hours. Furthermore it was agreed that the UPR voluntary Trust Fund and the fund for financial and technical assistance should be strengthened to facilitate the participation of developing countries and islands in the UPR process. The linkage of the UPR system with other United Nations entities was strengthened by the decision to allow states to request assistance from their United Nations country representative in implementing the UPR outcome.

[75] See Council decision A/HRC/DEC/17/119 adopted on 17 June 2011. This resolution was a follow-up to the Council Resolution A/HRC/RES/16/21HRC. See n 72.

The UPR process is essentially driven and led by states, but in the actual review of the report and during the follow-up a number of other actors play a significant role.

First, national civil society groups have an important role in the UPR process by contributing content to the country report if there are national consultations held by the state. They may also submit information to the OHCHR for inclusion in the stakeholders report. They may hold their own national and regional consultations to gather information and case studies for the stakeholders report.[76] Information from the stakeholders report and other information transmitted to states may be used to formulate questions and recommendations during the review. Then, once the recommendations are made, civil society can monitor their implementation and can develop tools for doing so. International NGOs also contribute to the UPR process by providing information on states and by providing training to national NGOs and by sharing tools and strategies developed by national and international NGOs.[77]

Obstacles remain for active and influential involvement of NGOs in the UPR process. UPR sessions are spread out over the year and it is often difficult for NGOs to travel to Geneva for the review. The fact that each country's review is a two-stage process separated by several months also makes it difficult to attend all sessions. Notably, among the suggestions for reform it has been proposed to have one annual session focused only on UPR, rather than continue the current practice of undertaking UPR review during several Council sessions throughout the year. In relation to participation, NGOs presently have no active role in the initial review and are only allowed to formally intervene with an oral statement in the closing stages of the UPR. Despite these obstacles, the UPR process gives credibility and a formal standing to the work of NGOs by including their information and analysis of a national human rights situation in the stakeholders report. The recommendation of the Council to states to involve NGOs in the preparation of reports and in the implementation of UPR recommendations also provides an important avenue for NGOs to influence the UPR process, including the content of the recommendations.

Second, NHRCs have a similar opportunity to contribute to the stakeholders report. Moreover, unlike NGOs, they may deliver an oral statement directly after the presentation of the country report. The UPR report can be used by NHRCs to demonstrate their independent nature by not following the positions taken by

[76] See eg the work of the Working Group on Human Rights in India and the UN (WGHR) at <http://www.wghr.org>.

[77] See Working Group on Human Rights in India and the UN (n 76), such as the development of a monitoring tool for UPR recommendations. See also A Guide to the Universal Periodic Review Process for NGOs and NHRIs, International Women's Rights Action Watch Asia Pacific (IWRAW Asia Pacific) at http://www.iwrawap.org/aboutus/documents/factsheetupr.pdf. For more examples see <http://www.upr-info.org>.

their respective states.[78] In the follow-up period NHRCs can assist in monitoring the UPR recommendations and in mobilizing civil society and other independent institutions to institute a collective process of monitoring.[79]

Third, UN agencies operating at the national level can submit information for the OHCHR compilation of information from UN sources. Agencies can submit information individually or in a consolidated UN country team report. As with NHRCs and NGOs, UN agencies can also monitor implementation of UPR recommendations. The opportunity to contribute their information and analysis to the UPR process allows UN agencies to further the unfinished task of 'mainstreaming' human rights into their work.

3.2 Proposals for reform of the UPR process

States, civil society, and independent sources continue to develop proposals for a more effective UPR. First, in the preparation of state reports, it is very important that states provide details on the implementation of UPR recommendations in their subsequent reports. During preparation of a state's UPR report, a number of suggestions have emphasized the importance of holding national consultations in a timely manner with various actors, but in particular with NHRIs, parliamentarians, and civil society groups. It would be helpful for the Council to adopt mandatory guidelines for the national consultations. Many observers have indicated a need to increase the time allocated by the working group session for the UPR reviews, including increasing the time available for questions from states. Any such expansion of time should include reconsideration of limited time allocated to NHRIs and NGOs. Currently, NGOs can only make a short statement at the end of the review process in the second UPR session.

Other suggestions point to the need to draw on the expertise of the mandate-holders of relevant Special Procedures during UPR reviews and to refer systematically to recommendations from Special Procedures and treaty bodies in the questions raised during the review. Currently this is ad hoc and depends on the willingness and knowledge of the states posing the questions and making recommendations.

A critical component of the UPR process is the outcome, the recommendations made to the state at the end of the process. Some states have suggested reducing the number of recommendations and clustering them thematically. Another proposal

[78] See eg the reports of the NHRC's of India and Bangladesh. India NHRC report: <http://nhrc.nic.in/disparchive.asp?fno=2523>; Bangladesh NHRC report: <http://www.nhrc.org.bd/PDF/Stakeholder%20Report%20Universal%20Periodic%20Review.pdf>.

[79] See, in this context, the ongoing work of the Indian NHRC in collaboration with other Indian National Commissions and WGHR and other civil society organisations.

is for the OHCHR to undertake an independent review of the findings of the working group, to check that the recommendations comply with international human rights law. Finally, states now commonly express consent or dissent to the recommendations between the two UPR sessions. A useful suggestion in this regard has been to make it mandatory for states to consult NHRIs and civil society groups in this intermission period.

Various proposals have been put forward to create financial and technical support for states to implement the UPR recommendations. The role of the OHCHR may also be strengthened in identifying areas of international cooperation stemming from the UPR recommendations. Other proposals suggest instituting a mandatory mid-term report on implementation of UPR recommendations two years after the review and requiring states to develop a national action plan for the implementation of UPR recommendations, including through a process of national consultation.

In addition to the above outlined suggestions for reform of the UPR process, a number of general recommendations have also been made, including extending the UPR review cycle to five years, maintaining the four-year cycle and having a gap year after the four-year cycle ends. To make the UPR process truly representative particular attention should be given to the least developed and landlocked states and small developing islands that face particular challenges, including the need to strengthen the UPR voluntary trust fund.

Assessment of the effectiveness of the UPR in creating positive change on the ground is at a nascent stage. Several important reports,[80] however, give insights into the impact of the UPR process at the end of the first cycle, including the implementation records of states and an overall evaluation of state performance in the first cycle, including nature of human rights issues covered.[81] If such studies already demonstrate the effectiveness of the UPR, it is likely that adoption of reform measures outlined above can lead to the UPR becoming a key factor in the evolution of UN Charter bodies towards a robust system of monitoring states' human rights records. Such an evolution can also open a critical pathway, through the implementation of UPR recommendations, to the internationalization of action to meet the challenge of realizing the human rights for the world's most vulnerable populations, beyond national borders.

[80] See *On the road to implementation*, UPR-INFO at <http://www.upr-info.org>. This publication reviews the implementation records of 66 countries and concludes that 40 percent of the recommendations have been implemented. For an up-to-date listing of publications on the UPR see <http://www.upr-info.org/-Library-.html>.

[81] See Edward R McMahon, *The Universal Periodic Review: A Work in Progress*, Friedrich Ebert Stiftung at <http://www.fes-globalization.org/geneve>.

4. The Council's Special Procedures

'Special procedures' (SPs) refer to the mechanisms the Council established to address specific country situations or pervasive human rights issues or themes. The Council derives this authority from the UN's mandate to promote the observance of human rights and fundamental freedoms, indicated throughout the UN Charter. The Council thus willingly assumed the former Commission's SP system and has appointed individuals or groups to investigate human rights issues or countries. This section will focus on the varied dimensions of the system, explain the unique nature of SPs within the UN system, and briefly discuss the potential contributions to human rights that remain to be developed in the work of the SPs.

The Council creates the mandates and appoints an expert or a working group of five experts, who are given the title of Special Rapporteur or independent expert. The experts investigate, examine, monitor, advise, and publicly report and make recommendations to the Council on the subject of the mandate. The Council may welcome or take note of SPs work in resolutions that inform the activities of the mandate holder. The indispensability of the SPs to the UN human rights programme is reflected in descriptions such as 'crown jewel of the system'[82] or 'the pillars of the UN's human rights system'.

In 1967 the Commission established the first ad hoc working group to assess the country situation in South Africa,[83] part of a growing and ultimately successful global effort to end apartheid. In 1975 the Commission established an ad hoc working group for Chile,[84] replaced in 1979 by a Special Rapporteur and two experts to study the fate of that country's disappeared persons. In 1980, the Commission decided to appoint a working group to investigate the phenomenon of forced disappearances generally.[85] Since these early ad hoc efforts, the idea of using such procedures to address specific situations has become the norm. From 1980 until 1995, the Commission created most thematic mandates on topics concerning civil and political rights, but after the Vienna World Conference on Human Rights the majority of new thematic mandates focused on economic, social, and cultural rights.[86]

[82] 'The Special Procedures are the crown jewel of the system. They, together with the High Commissioner and her staff, provide the independent expertise and judgment which is essential to effective human rights protection. They must not be politicized, or subjected to governmental control.' UN Secretary General Kofi Annan, speech at the Time Warner Center, New York, December 2006.

[83] Resolution 2 (XXIII), document E/259, 1947, para 22.

[84] See 'Special Procedures Fact Sheet', OHCHR at: <http://www.ohchr.org/Documents/Publications/FactSheet27en.pdf>.

[85] 'Special Procedures Fact Sheet' (n 84).

[86] 'Special Procedures Fact Sheet' (n 84). Since 2006, new thematic mandates have been created on the following issues: Special Rapporteurs in the field of cultural rights; on the rights to freedom of peaceful assembly and of association; on the promotion of truth, justice, reparation, and guarantees of non-recurrence; on contemporary forms of slavery, including its causes and its consequences; on

In creating the Council in 2007, the General Assembly called upon it to assume, review and where necessary improve and rationalize all of the Commission's mandates, mechanisms, functions, and responsibilities in order to maintain the system of special procedures. The review was guided by the same principles of universality and impartiality that govern all the Council's functions, intended to ensure equal attention to all human rights, avoid duplication of work, and determine the most effective means of increasing human rights protection.[87] After the review, the Council adopted resolution 5/1 concerning the selection of mandate holders and the rationalization and improvement of all special procedure mandates.[88] The resolution did not fundamentally modify the system, being mostly concerned with the quality of mandate holders (selection criteria) and not the mandates themselves. In fact, there was almost no change to the list of thematic and country mandates inherited from the Commission. Later, during the five-year review of the Council, some states previously criticized by SPs attempted to rein in the mandate holders by introducing new means of oversight and scrutiny. The effort was defeated due to vigorous opposition from other Council members, the coordination committee of the SP mandate holders, and civil society. All were concerned about limiting the independence and function of the mandate holders through excessive procedural requirements and scrutiny.

The only major change that occurred during the review carried out on the role of SPs in 2007 was the creation of a code of conduct for SPs.[89] While no other major changes emerged either in 2007 or in 2011, a number of important proposals were adopted that parallel those applicable to UPR.[90] First, the Council has given increased importance to the role of national human rights institutions in addressing the Council during sessions where SP reports are discussed. Secondly, the appointment procedure for the SPs has been made more transparent and space opened up for increased contribution of a range of actors in the process of appointing SPs, including through nominating individuals for any of the mandates.[91]

the human right to safe drinking water and sanitation and independent experts on the promotion of a democratic and equitable international order and on the issue of human rights obligations relating to the enjoyment of a safe, clean, healthy, and sustainable environment. The Council has also appointed country mandates on: the situation of human rights in Belarus; Côte d'Ivoire; Eriteria; Islamic Republic of Iran; Sudan; and the Syrian Arab Republic. The Council also appointed new Working Groups on the issue of human rights and transnational corporations and other business enterprises and on the issue of discrimination against women in law and in practice.

87 See GA res A/RES/60/251, 15 March 2005.

88 UN Human Rights Council, 'Institution-Building of the United Nations Human Rights Council' A/HRC/RES/5/1, 18 June 2007.

89 UN Human Rights Council, 'Code of Conduct for Special Procedures Mandate-Holders of the Human Rights Council' A/HRC/RES/5/2, 18 June 2007. See discussion, on the impact of the code of conduct, below.

90 In addition to the governments, a number of actors also contributed actively to this discussion. Special note needs to be made of the Coordinating Committee of SPs. See <http://www2.ohchr.org/english/bodies/chr/special/docs/cclettertechnical.pdf>.

91 The range of the entities who can nominate a candidate are diverse: Governments; Regional Groups operating within the United Nations human rights system; international organizations or

4.1 Functions of the mandate holders

The SPs are appointed for a maximum of two terms of three years each. During their mandates, the SPs are required to submit to the Council annual reports reporting violations but also addressing thematic issues of global importance.[92] They also: conduct country missions,[93] initiate or respond to communications,[94] contribute to the further development of international law through the formulation of principles and guidelines, develop collaborative initiatives, and carry out research.

SPs utilize country visits to meet with national and local authorities, non-governmental organizations, civil society organizations, the UN and other inter-governmental agencies, and the media. SPs will usually hold meetings with

their offices; non-governmental organizations; other human rights bodies; individual nominations; and national human rights institutions in compliance with the Paris Principles. Certain criteria are set for nomination, selection, and appointment of mandate holders, such as, expertise; experience in the field of the mandate; independence; impartiality; personal integrity; and objectivity. While compiling the public list of nominees, due consideration is given to gender balance and equitable geographic representation, as well as to an appropriate representation of different legal systems. A Consultative Group prepares shortlists and interviews the nominees for each mandate. On the basis of the recommendations made by the Consultative Group and in particular through the regional coordinators, the President of the Council, after the broad consolations, appoints each of the upcoming mandates.

92 The annual thematic reports discuss general issues concerning: working methods, theoretical analysis, general trends and developments, facts and violations, positive developments with regard to their respective mandates, and may contain general recommendations. Numerous SPs attempt to highlight one theme each year that may be an obstacle to the realization of the human right within their mandate. The first SP on Adequate Housing, for example, prepared annual reports on the following themes: discrimination and the impact of globalization; homelessness; forced evictions; emerging issues including water and sanitation. See: <http://www.ohchr.org/EN/Issues/Housing/Pages/AnnualReports.aspx>. The second SP on Violence against Women, for example, covered issues such as: standards of due diligence; indicators on violence against women and state response; intersection between culture and violence against women. See: <http://www.ohchr.org/EN/Issues/Women/SRWomen/Pages/AnnualReports.aspx>. Some SPs are requested to present an interim report annually to the UN General Assembly. Country mandate holders report annually to the Council, usually based on visits to the country, except for those rapporteurs who are not allowed to enter the country (eg North Korea and Iran). These SPs rely on information from UN sources, neighbouring country governments, and interviews with refugees in the neighbouring countries or anywhere in the world.

93 One to two week missions to countries form a critical part of the work of SPs. The visits are based on requests from SPs which then may or may not result in invitations by countries to carry out the mission. A significant number of states (92) have issued standing invitations to SPs. For the full list see <http://www.ohchr.org/EN/HRBodies/SP/Pages/Invitations.aspx>. Reports on country visits made by the thematic SPs are usually presented as addenda to the annual reports. SPs have their own criteria for selecting which countries to visit. Factors influencing decisions to make field visits – national developments, availability of reliable information, geographical balance, expected impact of the visit, willingness of national actors to cooperate, likelihood of follow-up on the recommendations, upcoming examinations by treaty bodies, visits by other mandate holders and date of the country's UPR. Country visits are also an opportunity to follow-up on the status of treaty body and UPR recommendations related to the theme being examined by the respective SP.

94 Most SPs are able to receive information on human rights violations and other situations of human rights from a range of sources. Based on these communications the SPs can, in turn, send letters to governments requesting information on particular cases of human rights.

government authorities in charge of the visit at the beginning, to brief the government representatives on the most significant issues to be addressed during the visit, and prior to departure, to share the SP's preliminary findings and recommendations. A critical dimension of SP country visits is the interaction with victims in the field. This can take the form of hearing testimonies at regional consultations and/or directly seeking evidence on the ground while witnessing the adverse conditions faced by victims.

During the visits, the host countries are expected to guarantee the freedom of movement of the mandate holder and team; freedom of inquiry through access to all prisons, detention centres and places of interrogation; and freedom to contact central and local authorities of all branches of government and others. The government must also assure confidential and unsupervised contact with witnesses and other private persons, including persons deprived of their liberty, and full access to all documentary material relevant to the mandate and the safety of all who talk with the SR, the security and safety of the SR and all staff assisting the SR during the visit. A mission report must be submitted to the Council subsequent to each visit, including findings and recommendations. The SP presents the country report at a session of the Council during the debate on the mandate and takes part in an interactive dialogue with governments, UN agencies, and civil society. There are also a number of examples of joint missions amongst SPs either on their own initiative[95] or at the request of the Council.[96] It is expected that joint missions will become more commonplace as the collaborative work of SPs grows.

SPs engage in standard-setting for the further development of human rights law. Several noteworthy examples include the Guiding Principles of Internal Displacement[97] and the Basic Principles and Guidelines on the Right to a Remedy and Reparation for Victims of Violations of International Human Rights and Humanitarian Law.[98] Under the Council, two types of standards have developed. First, standards have been developed as a result of requests from the Council, such

[95] Joint report of the independent expert on the question of human rights and extreme poverty, Magdalena Sepúlveda Cardona, and the independent expert on the issue of human rights obligations related to access to safe drinking water and sanitation, Catarina de Albuquerque. Mission to Bangladesh (3–10 December 2009) at: <http://daccess-dds-ny.un.org/doc/UNDOC/GEN/G10/154/51/PDF/G1015451.pdf?OpenElement>.

[96] Report of the Special Rapporteur on extrajudicial, summary or arbitrary executions, Philip Alston; the Special Rapporteur on the right of everyone to the enjoyment of the highest attainable standard of physical and mental health, Paul Hunt; the Representative of the Secretary-General on human rights of internally displaced persons, Walter Kälin; and the Special Rapporteur on adequate housing as a component of the right to an adequate standard of living, Miloon Kothari. Mission to Lebanon and Israel (September 2006). A/HRC/2/7 at: <http://daccess-dds-ny.un.org/doc/UNDOC/GEN/G06/141/95/PDF/G0614195.pdf?OpenElement>.

[97] Guiding Principles on Internal Displacement (E/CN.4/1998/53/Add.2).

[98] Basic Principles and Guidelines on the Right to a Remedy and Reparation for Victims of Gross Violations of International Human Rights Law and Serious Violations of International Human Rights Law, GA Res 60/147, at 1, UN Doc A/RES/60/147 (21 March 2006).

as the Guiding Principles on Foreign Debt and Human Rights coordinated by the Independent Expert[99] and the Guiding Principles on Extreme Poverty and Human Rights.[100] Secondly, some SPs have developed standards on their own initiative, such as the Basic Principles and Guidelines on Development-based Evictions and Displacement[101] and the Guiding Principles on Human Rights Impact Assessments of Trade and Investment Agreements.[102] Some of these standards, over time, have become influential in the development of policies and laws at national and regional levels, are routinely used as a basis for court judgments across the world, and have been translated into dozens of languages. Examples of such influential non-binding instruments are the IDP Guidelines[103] and the guidelines on development-based displacement.[104] The SPs also contribute to the formulation of standards developed by other human rights bodies, such as general comments and general recommendations, and assist the efforts of UN agencies,[105] independent expert groups,[106] and civil society initiatives.[107]

SPs can communicate directly with states apart from the country visits. Urgent appeals are used to communicate information about a violation that is imminent or already underway, in order to prompt action by states to halt or prevent the violation. Letters of allegation are sent to states based on information received by the SP

[99] For the text of these guidelines coordinated by the Independent Expert on the effects of foreign debt and other related international financial obligations of states on the full enjoyment of all human rights and endorsed by the Council in June 2012 see: <http://www.ohchr.org/EN/Issues/Development/IEDebt/Pages/GuidingPrinciples.aspx>.

[100] For a text of these guidelines coordinated by the Special Rapporteur on Extreme Poverty and Human Rights. Adopted by the Council on 27 September 2012 see: <http://www.ohchr.org/EN/Issues/Poverty/Pages/DGPIntroduction.aspx>.

[101] For a text of these principles and guidelines developed by the Special Rapporteur on Adequate Housing and acknowledged by the Council in 2007 see: <http://www.ohchr.org/Documents/Issues/Housing/Guidelines_en.pdf>.

[102] For the text of these Guiding Principles developed by the UN Special Rapporteur on the Right to Food and presented to the Council in 2011 see: <http://www.ohchr.org/Documents/HRBodies/HRCouncil/RegularSession/Session19/A-HRC-19-59-Add5_en.pdf>.

[103] For an overview of the impact of the IDP Guidelines see Allehone Mulugeta Abebe 'Special rapporteurs as law makers: the developments and evolution of the normative framework for protecting and assisting internally displaced persons' (2011) 15:2 *The International Journal of Human Rights* 286–298.

[104] For an overview of the impact of the Guidelines on Development-based Evictions see: Handbook on the Guidelines at: <http://hic-sarp.org/documents/Handbook%20on%20UN%20Guidelines_2011.pdf>.

[105] Eg The Voluntary Guidelines on the Responsible Governance of Tenure of Land, Fisheries and Forests in the Context of National Food Security at: <http://www.fao.org/nr/tenure/voluntary-guidelines/en>.

[106] Eg Maastricht Principles on Extraterritorial Obligations of States in the area of Economic, Social and Cultural Rights at: <http://www2.lse.ac.uk/humanRights/articlesAndTranscripts/2011/MaastrichtEcoSoc.pdf>.

[107] Such as Yogyakarta Principles—Principles on the application of international human rights law in relation to sexual orientation and gender identity, at: <http://www.unhcr.org/refworld/category,REFERENCE,ICJRISTS,,,48244e602,0.html>.

after the human rights violations have already occurred. Both these forms of communications are confidential and a reply from the authorities is expected.[108] The vast majority of communications are responses to violations, impending or having already occurred. There are examples, however, where SPs have issued communications that raise concerns about laws and policies in the state of formulation at the national level or on national policy matters.[109] The SPs, either singly or jointly, occasionally issue public statements in the form of press releases. These public statements often play a critical role in highlighting attention to egregious human rights violations or critical ongoing debates on policy matters.[110]

Unlike the complaint mechanisms of treaty bodies or the Council's 1503 procedure, SPs can receive information from sources that have not exhausted domestic remedies, making them a powerful avenue for victims, or their defenders, to reach an international mechanism and contribute to pressure being placed on governments to halt violations and to overhaul weak and cumbersome national mechanisms for access to justice. These modes of information taken together with the increasing role being played by the Council's Inquiry Commissions and the increasing credibility that pronouncements of the Inquiry Commissions and SPs receive globally, arguably means that adjudication and a quasi-judicial function for SPs is becoming accepted standard practice at the Council.[111]

In 2005, a meeting of mandate holders resulted in the creation of a Coordination Committee. The Coordination Committee played an active role during the review of mandates conducted in 2007 by the Human Rights Council Working Group on the issue of improving and rationalizing all mandates, mechanisms, functions, and responsibilities in order to maintain the system of special procedures. The Coordination Committee also contributed to the subsequent process of the review, rationalization, and improvement of mandates undertaken by the Council in 2008.

[108] Until 2011, these communications were summarized in an addendum to the SP's annual reports. Since September 2011, however, SPs have been submitting a joint report on their communications to each regular session of the Human Rights Council. These periodical reports include short summaries of allegations communicated to the respective state or other entity. The intention of a joint report was also to prevent inconsistencies among mandate holders reporting on the same communications to the Council; avoid duplication, rationalize documentation and to ensure that the content of communications and any follow-up would feed into the universal periodic review process more effectively.This decision was taken at the fifth annual meeting of the SPs in 2008 but not put into practice until 2011. See see A/HRC/10/24, para 34–35.

[109] See communication to Mexico by the SP on Adequate Housing and Indigenous Peoples at: Reflexiones sobre algunas implicaciones en material de derechos humanos del Proyecto Hidroeléctrico de La Parota, Estado de Guerrero, México, Informe del Relator Especial para el Derecho a una Vivienda Adecuada Señor Miloon Kothari, 4 de marzo de 2008, A/HRC/7/16/Add.1, párrafo 82.

[110] See examples on the 'Human Rights in the News' section of the OHCHR home page: <http://www.ohchr.org/EN/Pages/WelcomePage.aspx>.

[111] See for example: Dapo Akande and Hannah Tonkin: 'International Commissions of Inquiry: A New Form of Adjudication?' in the blog of the European Journal of International Law at: <http://www.ejiltalk.org/international-commissions-of-inquiry-a-new-form-of-adjudication>.

The aim was to ensure that the process of review of mandates would result in a more effective and strengthened system of special procedures. At the second and fourth session of the Human Rights Council, the Coordination Committee held meetings with the President of the Human Rights Council, the facilitators of the institution-building working groups of the Council, and the coordinators of regional groups to discuss issues concerning the review of mandates. The Chair of the Coordination Committee also participated in the meetings of the Council Working Group on the review of mandates. The Coordination Committee also played a proactive and defining role in ensuring that the code of conduct that emerged from the Council, discussed below, would not be intrusive of the independence the SPs enjoyed and would be based on collaborative thinking with the SPs.[112]

The SPs also work with other bodies. Among the UN human rights system, this includes treaty bodies (standard setting and follow-up work on country missions, dialogues on thematic issues, annual meetings with treaty body chairpersons, and development of indicators), UN country teams (including OHCHR field offices), and UN agencies such as WHO, FAO, and UN Habitat).[113] The role of NGOs is crucial for the success of the many dimensions of the SP's work and collaboration with them can take place during country visits, in Council meetings, and during the development of standards and follow-up work after SP country visits.[114]

The Council adopted a code of conduct for mandate holders during its 2007 review, claiming its aim was to 'enhance effectiveness by defining the standards of ethical behavior and personal conduct'.[115] The code of conduct outlines the key

[112] See: <http://www2.ohchr.org/english/bodies/chr/special/docs/note_code_of_conduct.pdf>.

[113] For numerous examples of such collaborations see: Ted Piccone, *Catalysts for Change: How the UN Independent Experts Promote Human Rights* (Brookings Institution Press, Washington DC 2012).

[114] Piccone (n 113).

[115] These include: **principles of conduct**: independence; furthering Council mandate (universal human rights); compliance with mandate (not exceeding), regulations and code of conduct; integrity; efficiency; competence; impartiality; equity; and good faith; **status**: personal capacity, entitled to privileges and immunities (but must comply with country laws); **perogatives**: facts must be established on an objective basis with cross-checking to ensure reliability and credibility of sources. The principles that should be considered in relation to the use of sources are transparency, even handedness, impartiality, and discretion. Furthermore confidential sources must be protected. Information provided by the state must be considered in a timely manner. The mandate holder must provide states with the opportunity to pass comments on their findings; **letters of allegation**: must not be manifestly ill-founded or politically motivated. Must contain factual description, language should not be abusive, based on report by victim or third party in good faith (not extensively based on media reports); **urgent appeals**: should only be used if the matter is time sensitive eg loss of life, grave damage to victims that cannot be addressed by letters of allegation; **field visits**: ensure consent of state is received. Mission should be prepared in close collaboration with the state delegation, share programme with host state, and seek to establish dialogue with government departments; **private matters and the public nature of the mandate**: mandate holders must: maintain constraint, discretion and moderation throughout appointment; ensure all public statements reflect government responses; ensure when reporting they are encouraging constructive dialogue; ensure states are the first to receive reports and given adequate time to respond; communications with governments should be through diplomatic channels unless

standards according to which SPs should conduct their many activities. The code has not caused a perceptible change in the manner in which SPs carry out their activities. Nonetheless, the code of conduct is seen by some as a negative development in terms of the independence and effective functioning of the SPs. In contrast, other analysts believe that the code has strengthened the legal basis for SP operations by introducing 'criteria of admissibility' for SPs when dealing with allegations, including a 'standing' requirement that complaints can be considered only when they're submitted by victims, or persons or groups claiming to have direct knowledge of these violations.[116] Such a view is consistent with the point previously made that aspects of the work of SPs can qualify as being of a quasi-judicial nature.

4.2 Reform of the Special Procedures

The system of SPs as it has evolved and strengthened during the course of the Council has proven to be extremely valuable to the UN human rights system and, more importantly, to the victims of human rights abuse across the world. The SPs therefore need to be strengthened and protected. To achieve this aim a number of areas need urgent improvement if the SPs are expected to continue to contribute to the enjoyment of human rights in an effective manner. The following proposals for reform of the SP system have been collated from discussions that emerged during the Council's five-year review and subsequent research work done by a number of analysts.

The concern so evident at the Commission that there was a politicization of the appointment process of SPs has considerably subsided with the more transparent process in evidence now at the Council. There are, however, examples of the consultative committee's preferred list of candidates being overruled by the President of the Council without adequate explanation, as required by the new appointment procedure of the Council. There is a need, therefore, for increased protection of mandate holders from political interference at all stages, including appointment.

Interaction of the SPs with the Council is limited and there is a need to increase the time given for such interaction. In the same spirit, the Council needs to provide greater support to SPs in adopting their recommendations. The Council and OHCHR also need to institutionalize a mechanism to follow-up the recommendations made

otherwise agreed; mandate holders are accountable to the Council. For the full text see: Resolution 5/2 'Code of Conduct for Special Procedures Mandate-holders of the Human Rights Council'. Adopted without a vote on 18 June 2007.

[116] See Elvira Dominguez Redondo, 'Rethinking the legal foundations of control in international human rights law—the case of the Special Procedures' (2011) 29:3 *Netherlands Quarterly of Human Rights* 261–88.

in the SPs' thematic and country reports. Follow-up to the work of the SPs, as well as that of treaty bodies and the UPR recommendations, remains a major weakness of the UN human rights system. OHCHR needs to devote more resources to this important task and to encourage UN offices at the national level to take more seriously the task of following up on SP recommendations.

Communications form an important part of the work of SPs although the response from states to urgent appeals and allegation letters remains weak and inconsistent.[117] There is a need, therefore, for the Council to ensure that the communication of SPs through diplomatic channels does not create delays when responding to urgent situations.

The rise in the number of states offering open invitations to SPs to visit their countries on official mission, as noted earlier in this chapter, is a welcome development. There are, however, numerous cases where states, both those that have offered open invitations and those that have not, fail to respond to requests for visits or inordinately delay such visits, through repeated postponements.

There are a number of other areas where reform is necessary including tackling the perennial question of insufficient and uneven staff support for SPs at OHCHR and the perennial unresolved question of whether the SPs should be remunerated for the time spent on their mandates.

4.3 Impact of the work of SPs

A copius amount of anecdotal evidence is available on the positive impact that SPs have made to the realization of human rights across the world. In addition, the Brookings Institute undertook the first major attempt at understanding the impact of the work of SP.[118] A number of analysts have also carried out research on the impact of the work of certain groups of SPs[119] and a major international Conference to assess the impact of the work of SPs, particularly to standard setting, resulted in an important compilation of articles dealing with different themes and mandates.[120]

The studies referred to and thousands of victims and defenders of human rights across the world agree that the international community has created in the SPs a mechanism that is unique and increasingly indispensable as the world faces

[117] See *Catalysts for Change* (n 113). [118] See *Catalysts for Change* (n 113).

[119] See, Christophe Golay, Claire Mahon and Ioana Cismas 'The impact of the UN special procedures on the development and implementation of economic, social and cultural rights' (2011) 15:2 *The International Journal of Human Rights* 299–318.

[120] 'The Role of the Special Rapporteurs of the United Nations Human Rights Council in the Development and Promotion of International Human Rights Norms' (2011) 15:2 *The International Journal of Human Rights* 155–61 (Special Issue).

increasing numbers of challenges to the realization of human rights. SPs play a unique role and carry an enormous responsibility in mediating between victims and the Human Rights Council—and indeed the world. SPs place the protection of those in need high among priorities and pursue a victim-oriented perspective. They have the enormous task of analysing human rights situations, making relevant recommendations, and striving for justice for the victims, actual and threatened. They represent the UN yet are independent; they can officially visit countries, conduct on-site investigations of their choice and take direct testimony from victims on the ground; they are able to publicly denounce human rights violations across the world and even criticize, if warranted, UN actors, in a manner no UN employee can. Over the course of the forty year history of the SPs they have become the voice of objectivity in a deeply politicized UN inter-governmental system and a deeply politicized world order. In this context, the SPs provide, with their objectivity and commitment, clarity of purpose otherwise hard to find in the international human rights system.

5. Reform of the Council

During the review of the Council after its first five years, persistent criticisms emerged in the discussions of different stakeholders.[121] They resulted in suggestions that may stimulate further appropriate changes in the Council and its work:

(1) Size and distribution of membership. Some observers suggest that that the current membership of forty-seven countries makes the operation of the Council 'unwieldy.' In contrast, others have called for universal membership in order to underline the fact that the protection of human rights is the responsibility of all states, but also to focus debate on the substantive issues and away from who is voting on them and to remove the politicization of membership.[122] A cross-country group at the Council has further asserted that the regional distribution of Council membership results in under representation of small and developing countries Council.

(2) Membership criteria. The system of voluntary pledges and review of individual state human rights records has reduced the possibility of 'serial violators'

[121] In addition to the documents from the UN cited above see, for example, the joint *NGO Proposal on the Structure for the 2011 Review of the Human Rights Council's work and Functioning*, Appendix 1 in: Human Rights Watch, Curing the Selectivity Syndrome.

[122] A More Secure World (n 19) para 285.

of human rights gaining membership of the Council. Nevertheless, there remains deficiency in the application of rigorous membership criteria, with the result that numerous states become and remain Council members even though they fail to maintain the 'highest standards of human rights' during membership.

(3) Voting patterns. The Council continues to engage in block voting, one of the main factors leading to the 'politicization' of human rights issues in the Council, just as it did during the life of the Commission.

(4) Status of the Council. As a subsidiary body of the UN General Assembly there is every possibility that the Council's actions can be overruled. Many have argued that if human rights are central to the message of the UN, then the Council should stand independent of any oversight body, similar to the Security Council or a specialized agency. One consequence of dependency on the General Assembly is that the Council lacks a structure for interaction with other UN bodies.

(5) Participation of non-state actors. Numerous states and civil society organizations see a need to increase the participation of non-governmental organizations and national human rights institutions in the work of the Council.

(6) Role of the Advisory Committee. The roster of experts on the Advisory Committee could be replaced with experts commissioned for specific research projects. If the Advisory Committee remains in its current configuration, some states argue that it should be able to take independent initiatives regarding areas of research; others continue to insist that the Committee should only undertake work under the express direction of the Council.

(7) Complaint procedure. Suggestions on the complaints procedure have ranged from eliminating it entirely, from those who claim it lacks transparency, impartiality, and efficiency, to merging the two working groups, to the possibility of abolishing the working group on situations, and to separating the working group on communications from the Advisory Committee.

Many of these proposals appeared in the 2004 high-level panel report and the five-year Council review mandated and undertaken by the GA. The 2004 report included other wide-ranging proposals that are important to consider, such as the recommendation that the Council conduct a mandatory periodic briefing of the Security Council and the peacebuilding commission to enable focused intervention and monitoring. Presently, the Security Council may call on the Council or mandate holders to brief it.[123] Another useful proposal in the 2004 report was the need for a global annual human rights report that would assist focused debates at the Council.

[123] Rule 39 of Rules of Procedure.

6. Conclusion

The UPR, which the Council initiated in 2007, is likely to be institutionalized as a permanent human rights mechanism of the United Nations. This means that it is now possible, for the first time at the international level, to contemplate a *triangulation* of reporting, recommendations, and implementation of the human rights obligations and accountability of the vast majority of UN member states (see Figure 1).

The universal nature of the UPR, covering all 193 UN member states, the fact that all member states have ratified one or more UN human rights treaties and that 93 member states have issued standing invitations[124] to UN Special Procedures (indicating at least two country visits a year), means it has become possible to ensure continuous monitoring at the international level of the human rights obligations of states. If, as recommended in the Council's five-year review, states can be convinced to submit mid-term reviews[125] of their implementation of UPR recommendations every two years, then consistent international human rights monitoring comes close to reality.

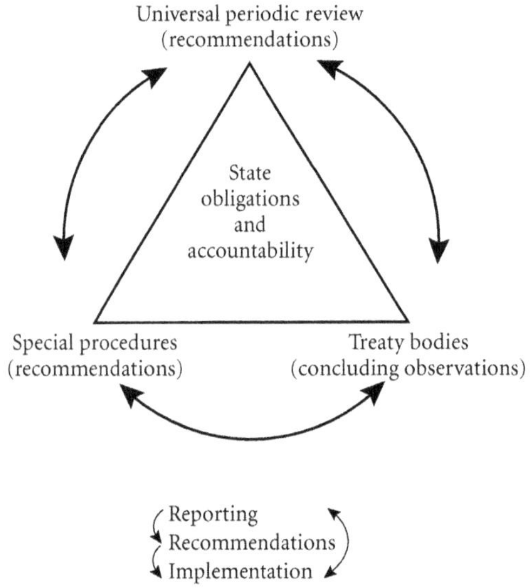

FIGURE 1 Universal Periodic Review

[124] As of 15 April 2013. It is important to note here that the number of countries that have issued standing invitations to SPs has increased at a faster rate since the onset of the UPR as states want to demonstrate results to their peers when they come up for the UPR.

[125] Thirty states from across the world have voluntarily submitted implementation reports to the Council. See <http://www.ohchr.org/EN/HRBodies/UPR/Pages/UPRImplementation.aspx> accessed 10 June 2013.

Such a triangulation should aim to ensure that states are not able to halt the continuous process of implementation of international human rights commitments. Such triangulation should thus seek to break the habit, sometimes chronic, of some states taking little action on the ground during the gap period (four to four-and-a-half years) between reports to the treaty bodies.

The UN human rights system ensures the active, and legitimate, role of non-state actors, particularly civil society and national human rights commissions, in the process of monitoring recommendations emanating from the three nodal points of the UN human rights system. This suggests a range of dynamic opportunities for national level action on human rights. Such action can take the form of human rights trainings across sectors, human rights education at all levels of society and government including within ministries charged with human rights mandates (most of which, prior to UPR, have been only marginally involved in the reporting process), and local and national level mechanisms for monitoring the states human rights commitments. If this process of active national level participation to ensure state compliance, guided by the triangulation, can involve national parliaments and political and non-political formations, then state accountability can perhaps be ensured at the national level where it matters the most. This in turn can lead to the strengthening and institutionalization of implementation mechanisms informed by the domestication of international human rights commitments.

The UN as a whole, but particularly the human rights system, has a critical role to play in ensuring the establishment and the success of this triangulation dynamic. OHCHR has an especially key leadership role to play in this process in deciding, and acting upon, its position as a driving force to ensure triangulation. The dynamic, now increasingly operational, provides a remarkable opportunity for OHCHR to institutionalize follow-up procedures for energetic and systematic tracking of treaty body concluding observations, UPR recommendations, and the recommendations contained in the reports of SPs. OHCHR has to take on the mantle of providing leadership directly and play a catalytic role where necessary to ensure that the entire UN system, including UN agencies[126] operating at the national level, participates actively in this triangulation process.

It is now possible to put into practice the triangulation dynamic proposed above, precisely because of the evolution of the UN human rights bodies, including the treaty bodies and the maturing of the Council, the UN's premier inter-governmental human rights body, Council through the operations of the UPR and the SPs. The institutionalization of the triangulation dynamic would then be the best outcome of the evolution of the UN human rights system.

Given these embryonic developments towards the 'universalization of the applicability of international human rights instruments', it is possible to contemplate a

[126] Amongst the UN agencies UNDP, given its coordinating role for UN teams at country levels including the preparation of country reports for the UPR, has a particularly important role to play.

new world for the global human rights system. This is the evolution of UN Charter bodies which the world's disadvantaged urgently require and which their dignity and their struggles demand.

Further Reading

A More Secure World: Our Shared Responsibility, Report of the High Level Panel on Threats, Challenges and Change (United Nations 2004)

Golay C, Mahon C, and Cismas I, 'The Impact of the UN Special Procedures on the Development and Implementation of Economic, Social and Cultural Rights' (2011) 15:2 *The International Journal of Human Rights* 299–318

In Larger Freedom: Towards Security, Development and Human Rights For All, Report of the UN Secretary General of the United Nations, UN Doc A/59/2005

McMohan ER, *The Universal Periodic Review: A Work in Progress* (Friedrich Ebert Stiftung 2012)

Piccone T, *Catalysts for Change: How the UN's Independent Experts Promote Human Rights* (Brookings Institution Press 2012)

Ramacharan BG, *The Protection Role of UN Human Rights Special Procedures* (Martinus Nijhoff 2008)

'The Role of the Special Rapporteurs of the United Nations Human Rights Council in the Development and Promotion of International Human Rights Norms' (2011) 15:2 *The International Journal of Human Rights* Special Issue

The Universal Periodic Review: On the Road to Implementation (UPR-INFO 2012) <http://www.upr-info.org 2012>

Tracking Implementation: A Monitoring Tool for Recommendations from the Universal Periodic Review (Working Group on Human Rights in India and the UN (WGHR) 2013) <http://www.wghr.org>

CHAPTER 26

THE ROLE AND IMPACT OF TREATY BODIES

NIGEL S RODLEY

1. Introduction

At the founding of the United Nations (UN), it was generally understood that the UN could not monitor states' compliance with human rights. The dominant approach was that the Charter of the United Nations (UN Charter) Article 2(7), prohibiting intervention in matters falling 'essentially within the domestic jurisdiction' of states, protected states from human rights scrutiny. This relied on the theory that human rights were, indeed, a matter of domestic jurisdiction and that even discussing critically states' human rights performance was impermissible intervention.

Accordingly, it was believed that states could only be held to any form of account for their human rights behaviour by voluntarily accepting international supervision.[1] It followed that this could only be achieved by virtue of a treaty obligation that each state freely assumed upon becoming a party to a treaty providing for some sort of supervision.

It was thus that the International Bill of Human Rights was conceived. The Bill would consist first of the Universal Declaration of Human Rights (UDHR),

[1] See eg Vratislav Pechota, 'The Development of the Covenant on Civil and Political Rights' in Louis Henkin (ed), *The International Bill of Rights: The Covenant on Civil and Political Rights* (Columbia UP 1981) 35.

followed by treaty-based obligations. The UDHR, as a resolution of the General Assembly, could only have the formal status of a recommendation and so would not be binding per se.[2] Meanwhile, the emergent, legally binding treaties, namely, the International Covenant on Economic, Social and Cultural Rights (ICESCR) and International Covenant on Civil and Political Rights (ICCPR), would give further specificity to (most of) the rights in the UDHR and have supervisory machinery. The ICCPR provided for the establishment of the Human Rights Committee, which was expected to become the first human rights treaty body.

There are now nine core human rights treaties. It is usual to speak of the United Nations 'treaty body system' when referring to the committees that have been empowered to monitor states parties' compliance with their obligations under these treaties. In fact, there was no consciousness that any such system was being created when the first two such committees were being contemplated. The first to come into existence was the Committee on the Elimination of Racial Discrimination (CERD Committee) after the adoption in 1965 of the International Convention on the Elimination of All Forms of Discrimination (CERD).[3] The drafting of the CERD was initiated within the context of the seemingly endless process of drafting the two covenants. In fact, it was modelled on the draft of what a year later would become the ICCPR. It is often forgotten that not even the International Covenant on Economic, Social and Cultural Rights (ICESCR), adopted contemporaneously with the ICCPR, provided for such a committee. Rather, the function was assigned to the intergovernmental 'principal organ' of the UN, the Economic and Social Council (ECOSOC).

As is often the case, an instance becomes a precedent.[4] So, in 1979, the Convention on the Elimination of Discrimination against Women (CEDAW) was adopted,[5] followed by the Convention against Torture and Other Cruel, Inhuman or Degrading

[2] Under UN Charter Art 10, the General Assembly only has the power to make recommendations to member states. However, from the time of the UDHR's adoption, there were those who argued that its provisions articulated the human rights and fundamental freedoms to which the UN Charter referred, especially Art 1 (purposes) and Arts 55 and 56, which were said to contain (and have since become accepted as containing) an obligation to comply with human rights. Eg Hersch Lauterpacht, *International Law and Human Rights* (Stevens & Sons 1950) 145–54 (arguing for the binding force of the Charter provisions), 408–17 (disagreeing with the 'indirect' legal authority thesis at that time). cf Nigel S Rodley, 'Human Rights and Humanitarian Intervention: The Case Law of the World Court' (1989) 38 *ICLQ* 321, 324–27 (some forty years after the adoption of the UDHR, suggesting that the UDHR had been found to have legal authority). See also Olivier de Schutter, 'The Status of Human Rights in International Law' in Catarina Krause and Martin Scheinin (eds), *International Protection of Human Rights: A Textbook* (Åbo Akademi University Institute for Human Rights 2009) 39–41.

[3] See generally Natan Lerner, *The UN Convention on the Elimination of All Forms of Racial Discrimination: A Commentary* (2nd edn, Sijthoff & Noordhoff 1980).

[4] Another example of this in the UN context was the creation in 1980 of the Working Group on Enforced or Involuntary Disappearances, the first thematic mechanism of the UN Commission on Human Rights. It became, without any prior design, the precedent for a network of thirty-five 'thematic special procedures' (see previous chapter in this *Handbook*).

[5] See generally Lars Adam Rehof, *Guide to the Travaux Préparatoires of the United Nations Convention on the Elimination of All Forms of Discrimination against Women* (Martinus Nijhoff 1993);

Treatment or Punishment (CAT) in 1984.[6] The UN Convention on the Rights of the Child (CRC) in 1989[7] and the International Convention on the Protection of the Rights of All Migrant Workers and Members of Their Families (ICRMW) in 1990 followed this.[8] In 2006, two more treaties were added: the Convention on the Rights of Persons with Disabilities (CRPD)[9] and the International Convention for the Protection of All Persons from Enforced Disappearances (CPED).[10]

Each of these conventions provided for the establishment of its own monitoring committee, which will be referred to here, in order of treaty adoption, as the CEDAW Committee, the Committee against Torture (or CAT), the CRC Committee, the CMW Committee (CMW), the CRPD Committee and the Committee on Enforced Disappearances (CED). Meanwhile, ECOSOC, an intergovernmental body, found that it was not able to engage in effective monitoring of the ICESCR, and in 1985 created its own Committee on Economic, Social and Cultural Rights (CESCR), composed of individuals, based on the model of the other committees.[11] Each of the nine so-called 'core' human rights treaties thus has its own treaty body. This chapter touches on some of the reasons for this in Section 7, below.

At this point it should be noted that there is a tenth treaty body, in the form of a Sub-Committee for the Prevention of Torture (SPT), established under a 2002 Optional Protocol to UNCAT (OPCAT).[12] It is a *sui generis* body, whose functions are wholly unlike those of the other treaty bodies and so cannot be considered as a normal part of the 'system'. For the sake of completeness, these functions will be briefly described below, but the SPT will not be the subject of further comment.

Marsha A Freeman, Christine Chinkin, and Beate Rudolf (eds), *The UN Convention on the Elimination of All Forms of Discrimination against Women: A Commentary* (OUP 2012).

[6] See generally J Herman Burgers and Hans Danelius, *The United Nations Convention against Torture: A Handbook on the Convention against Torture and Other Cruel, Inhuman or Degrading Treatment or Punishment* (Martinus Nijhoff 1988); Ahcene Boulesbaa, *The UN Convention on Torture and the Prospects for Enforcement* (Martinus Nijhoff 1999); Manfred Nowak and Elizabeth McArthur, *The United Nations Convention against Torture: A Commentary* (OUP 2008); Nigel S Rodley and Matt Pollard, *The Treatment of Prisoners under International Law* (3rd edn, OUP 2009).

[7] See generally Alfred Glenn Mower Jr, *The Convention on the Rights of the Child: International Law Support for Children* (Greenwood Press 1997); Sharon Detrick, *A Commentary on the United Nations Convention on the Rights of the Child* (Martinus Nijhoff Publishers 1999).

[8] Paul de Guchteneire, Antoine Pécoud, and Ryszard Cholewinski (eds), *Migration and Human Rights: The United Nations Convention on Migrant Workers' Rights* (CUP 2009).

[9] Oddný Mjöll Arnardóttir and Gerard Quinn (eds), *The UN Convention on the Rights of Persons with Disabilities: European and Scandinavian Perspectives* (Martinus Nijhoff 2009).

[10] Tullio Scovazzi and Gabriella Citroni, *The Struggle against Enforced Disappearance and the 2007 UN Convention* (Martinus Nijhoff 2007).

[11] ECOSOC Res 1985/17 (28 May 1985) UN Doc E/Res/1985/17. Meanwhile, the Optional Protocol to the ICESCR provides for a range of functions for the Committee, thus indirectly endowing it with treaty-based status.

[12] Optional Protocol to the Convention against Torture and Other Cruel, Inhuman or Degrading Treatment or Punishment. See generally Nowak and McArthur (n 6) 879–1192; Rachel Murray and others, *The Optional Protocol to the UN Convention against Torture* (OUP 2011).

2. Composition

The salient point about the composition of the treaty bodies, as evidenced by the action of ECOSOC in creating the CESCR, is that individual experts are more apt than government representatives to be able to bring independent judgement to bear on the neuralgic issue of states' respect (or otherwise) for their human rights obligations. Of course, interstate practices are such that the notion of the independent expert, which treaties do not define, may not always be evident in the candidates (which states parties nominate) or the members (which the same states parties elect). While the overwhelming membership of the Human Rights Committee over the years has been of individuals who have no formal connection with the governments that have nominated them, the membership of some committees has had a significant component of officials of their countries' executives, typically in the Foreign Service.

To minimize bias or the perception of it, treaty bodies will generally adopt rules of procedure that prevent members from participating in discussions of, or decision-making on, their own states' behaviour, or will at least limit such involvement.[13] Of course, these states have friends and allies, as well as adversaries, which might mean theoretically that a member holding a national public official function could find it difficult to treat such countries with the same impartiality as he or she would treat other states. That said, it is this author's experience that some holders of national office have been able to evince more evident and rigorous independence, not to mention genuine expertise, than some of those not formally holding any such office. It nevertheless remains desirable that states avoid presenting as candidates persons holding public office in the executive branch of government.[14]

The expertise sought tends to consist of 'high moral standing' and 'recognized competence' in the field covered by the treaty, but typically does not demand specifically legal training, albeit some treaties call for 'consideration being given to the usefulness of the participation of some persons having legal experience'.[15] Given that it falls to the treaty bodies to interpret their respective conventions, that is, solemn legal instruments, and apply them to sometimes complex factual situations, it appears incongruous that more weight is not given to the value of people trained in

[13] UNGA 'Implementation of Human Rights Instruments' (July 2012) UN doc A/67/28442, para 36, Annex 1 (Addis Ababa Guidelines).

[14] As the Human Rights Committee (HRC) pointed out, 'All branches of government (executive, legislative and judicial)...are in a position to engage the responsibility of the State Party'. UNHRC 'General Comment No 31: The Nature of the General Legal Obligation Imposed on States Parties to the Covenant' (29 March 2004) UN Doc CCPR/C/21/Rev.1/Add.13, para 4. Indeed, the courts have been found to have been responsible for ICCPR violations. See Nigel S Rodley, 'The *Singarasa* Case: *Quis Custodiet*...? A Test for the Bangalore Principles of Judicial Conduct' (2008) 41 *Is LR* 500. But it is the executive branch that is most apt to violate human rights.

[15] Eg ICCPR, Art 28(2). See also UNCAT, Art 17(1).

the discipline that lays down the canons of interpretation of international treaties.[16] In practice, certainly in the case of the Human Rights Committee, there may well be a predominance of members who are trained in or are otherwise familiar with legal work.

The variation in the numerical composition of the committees is incomprehensible. Membership ranges from ten to twenty-three, with the mean being eighteen. Some treaties provide for a base number when the treaty first enters into force and then for expansion after a given number of further ratifications. There can be no inherent reason why the CAT and CRC Committees have ten members each, while the CMW had an initial membership of ten, rising to fourteen, and the CEDAW Committee started with eighteen and expanded to twenty-three. The only explanation is that each decision reflected a tension between states' desire to keep costs down and the strength of their commitment to the subject matter of the convention. The influence of various civil society constituencies for a particular category of victim could also be relevant.

3. Decision-Making

The committees aspire to consensus in their decision-making. This started with the Rules of Procedure of the Human Rights Committee. Despite the fact that Article 39(2)(b) of the ICCPR envisages a majority voting for taking decisions, the Committee's Rules of Procedure specifically exhort the Committee to seek to operate by consensus where possible.[17] In practice, this has always been interpreted as requiring consensus decision-making on all substantive outputs except the adoption of 'views' on individual complaints, for which separate or dissenting opinions are common. Whether other treaties provide for majority voting (eg UNCAT Article 18 (2)(b)) or more typically leave the issue to the rules of procedure, the practice tends to follow that of the Human Rights Committee.

The original impulse towards consensus no doubt responded to the demands of Cold War realities. This could be frustrating for human rights advocates, who

[16] Mainly to be found in the 1969 Vienna Convention on the Law of Treaties, Arts 31, 32.

[17] UNHRC, 'Rules of Procedure of the Human Rights Committee' (11 January 2012) UN Doc CCPR/C/3/Rev.10, rule 51 fn. It should be noted that all the treaties provide for the treaty bodies to adopt rules of procedure that will spell out the modes of their operation—issues not usually extensively dealt with in the body of the treaty. Here, the bodies will often introduce methods of operation that the treaty does not foresee, but which are perceived as pertaining to necessarily implied powers of the body. Examples include the issuance of interim measures in respect of individual complaints and follow-up procedures, as discussed below.

chafed, for example, under the committees' inability to agree on country-specific evaluations. With the end of the Cold War, the practice changed.[18] Hindsight demonstrates that the consensus approach may have been beneficial. Constant voting on all aspects of the work could have been, and could still be, dysfunctional. More importantly, it invested the product of the committee with the authority that accompanies the corporate expression of a membership reflecting the broad cultural and political geography of the world. On balance, that product more resembles the highest common factor, rather than the lowest common denominator. This is no mean consideration in a world where East-West confrontation has transformed into one of North-South tension.

The periodicity and duration of meetings of treaty bodies vary from treaty to treaty or may be left to the determination of the specific treaty body in its rules of procedure. CERD addresses neither frequency nor duration. In practice, three of the committees meet three times a year for three-week sessions. All the others meet twice a year for sessions of one to four weeks.

4. Functions

There are five typical functions that the treaties may contemplate for the committees: first, review of reports that states undertake to submit after becoming party to the treaty; second, at least implicitly, general comments on the nature and scope of the treaties' provisions; third, interstate complaints; fourth, individual complaints; and fifth, inquiries into general practices that violate the respective treaty. Each will be considered separately, as will a small number of atypical functions found in two treaties.

4.1 Review of state reports

Reviewing state reports is generally understood as the core function of each treaty and the 'system' as a whole.[19] This is because it is the one monitoring element that is obligatory under each treaty. Each state party is obliged to submit a report to the

[18] See Section 4.1 in this chapter.

[19] See generally Michael O'Flaherty, 'The Concluding Observations of United Nations Human Rights Treaty Bodies' (2006) 6 *Human Rights LR* 27; Walter Kälin, 'Examination of State Reports' in Helen Keller and Geir Ulfstein (eds), *UN Human Rights Treaty Bodies: Law and Legitimacy: Studies on Human Rights Conventions* (CUP 2012).

particular committee on its compliance with the treaty's provisions; the committee then reviews it. It is customary to refer to this as review of periodic reports, because each treaty provides that, after the submission of an initial report, generally within one or two years of the state's ratification or accession to the treaty, states should submit future reports at intervals either laid down by the treaty or determined by the treaty body. Anomalously, the most recent treaty, the CPED, only contemplates the submission of an initial report, after which the CED has discretion as to whether it will require subsequent reports. No doubt this reflects the expectation that most states parties will not engage in the appalling practice of 'disappearing' people, and it would be vain and wasteful to require them to assume the burden of superfluous reporting and for the CED to engage in superfluous reviews.

There is no uniformity across the treaties and practice as regards the periodicity for submission of reports. It ranges from two to five years. There is no apparent reason for the inconsistency, nor is there any evident explanation as to why the periodicity is laid down in some treaties and, as in the case of the ICCPR, left to the treaty body in others. The Human Rights Committee (HRC) first established a standard period of four years in its Rules of Procedure. It later moved to a flexible one of (in practice) three to five years, and later three to six years, depending on the gravity and extent of its continuing concerns about each state party. The longer the period, the less pressing will be the Committee's concerns and vice versa.

The reporting system typically begins with the submission of the state report, which is sent for translation into the UN's five working languages (English, French, Spanish, Arabic, and Russian). Following a practice that the Human Rights Committee started, an increasing number of treaty bodies then review the report by utilizing a special rapporteur and/or a task force of a few members[20] to prepare an agreed 'list of issues' (LOI) to submit to the state party to alert it to the matters the Committee will wish to pursue as a priority. Indeed, to maximize the use of time during the actual review, the state party will be encouraged to respond to the LOI in writing. This is intended to permit the committee to move straight to an oral 'constructive dialogue', by way of follow-up to the replies to the LOI.

The dialogue usually takes place over a period of two to three half-day public meetings with a delegation sent by the state party. The state delegation will generally consist of officials from the operative ministries of the country, as well as members of the permanent mission in Geneva or New York, wherever the meeting is held. Predictably, delegations vary in size and expertise.

Although states are encouraged to share the difficulties they face in implementing their obligations with the committees,[21] in practice most reports tend to be self-congratulatory, focusing on the provisions of their constitutions and laws that

[20] The Human Rights Committee is the only one that keeps confidential the identities of its country rapporteurs or, as the case may be, its task force members.

[21] Eg ICCPR, Art 40(2); ICESCR, Art 17(2); CEDAW, Art 18(2).

are, in their view, consistent with those obligations. Reports tend to provide little information on how the rights are enjoyed in practice. It follows that committee members are in need of other sources of information to be able to evaluate the reality behind the report. Yet, except for two committees,[22] the (older) conventions failed to mention or grant authority to their committees to access other information. This was no accidental omission, but was part of the design of a procedure undoubtedly chosen as the least intrusive means available that could be considered consistent with any international monitoring. From the beginning, however, non-governmental organizations (NGOs) took the initiative of providing those members willing to receive it[23] with information on their concerns. This permitted those members to ask questions that tested the picture the official report presented. NGOs were also invited to meet informally with committee members.

As the procedures and committees have evolved, especially after the end of the Cold War and the abandonment of the earlier Soviet-camp allergy to unofficial (critical) information, recourse to information other than that contained in state reports has expanded. At present, the Secretariat makes available to all members information that NGOs specifically submit on the reports, as well as other relevant information, notably that from within the UN system itself, such as the reports of the UN Human Rights Council's special procedures and its Universal Periodic Review.[24] The availability of such independent information permits committee members to ask questions that will penetrate the facade that some states party present.

After the conclusion of the oral dialogue, the country rapporteur provisionally approves a draft report, which a confidential meeting of the plenary committee finalizes. The draft text contains what are generally called 'concluding observations', again following the practice of the Human Rights Committee. The power the ICCPR vests in the Committee to adopt 'general comments'[25] was interpreted for the first fifteen years as precluding the making of country-specific evaluations and only permitting comments on states' obligations in general (see below). Once the political will emerged to make such evaluations, the term 'concluding observations' was coined to describe them, so as to distinguish them from what had come to be understood as general comments. The concluding observations typically start with recognition of positive elements or advances since the prior report. The core of their content consists of an expression of 'concern' about certain issues, as well as

[22] The CESCR (as a sub-body of the ECOSOC, NGOs in consultative status have certain rights of written and oral intervention) and the CRC Committee (includes NGOs in the notion of 'other competent bodies' which it may consult under CRC Art 45(a)).

[23] Some were not and took the view that the Secretariat was not even permitted to distribute information that had no formal status under the Covenant.

[24] See the previous chapter in this *Handbook*; Nigel S Rodley, 'UN Treaty Bodies and the Human Rights Council' in Keller and Ulfstein (n 20).

[25] Article 40(4).

recommendations to address the concerns. The concluding observations are made public towards the end of the session.

Within the reporting system, some committees have introduced the practice of asking for special reports from states. This is essentially an emergency procedure, invoked when the above-mentioned independent sources make information available that suggests that a state is experiencing serious problems in complying with its treaty obligations. While it requested such special reports of some notorious regimes in the 1980s,[26] the Human Rights Committee has rarely followed the practice in recent times, because of the difficulty in agreeing from which states to request submissions. It is an area where members' backgrounds may play a role in their choices or their reaction to their colleagues' choices. It will be easier to agree on the usual pariahs than on other candidates. So, after seeking special reports from Israel and Yugoslavia (before it became ex-Yugoslavia) in the 1990s, the Human Rights Committee has not expressly availed itself of this option.[27]

There are two major temporal problems that treaty bodies can face. On the one hand, some states fail to submit their initial and/or subsequent reports on time—sometimes for up to two decades. On the other hand, contradictorily, committees themselves often develop a backlog when considering submitted reports. This leads to the anomaly that the more punctual states are in submitting their reports, the longer the backlog will become. As will be seen later, systemic proposals have been made to address this problem, but none has so far borne fruit.

Meanwhile, the committees themselves have taken measures to attenuate both sides of the problem. In 2001, the Human Rights Committee adopted a rule of procedure that allows it to review a country situation even in the absence of a report,[28] a rule adopted with the aim of inciting the state party to submit a report, or at least send a delegation to begin the dialogue (which would take place in closed session). Such a dialogue could be all the more productive after the LOI technique was available to frame a possible dialogue.[29] The aim was realized more frequently than not, because only a few states party failed to report, send a delegation for the hearing,

[26] Eg Iran and El Salvador: see Manfred Nowak, *UN Covenant on Civil and Political Rights: CCPR Commentary* (2nd edn, Engel 2005) 716.

[27] On 28 July 2005, after twelve months of correspondence relating to the (by now) seven-year overdue report of the United States of America, the Committee informed this State Party that unless the Committee received the report by 17 October 2005, the Committee would proceed to adopt an LOI regarding the human rights issues, domestic and extra-territorial, that arose out of its post-11 September 2001 anti-terrorist measures. (It was submitted on 21 October 2005.) While the Committee refrained from invoking specific rules of procedure, it may be inferred that (1) in the absence of a periodic report, it was seeking a special report; and (2) it was at the point of initiating a country situation review in the absence of a report pursuant to Rule 70 of the Rules of Procedure (n 17) below and text. UNHRC, 'Report of the Human Rights Committee: Vol I' (2005) UN Doc A/60/40, para 75.

[28] UNHRC, 'Rules of Procedure' (n 17) rule 70.

[29] Of course, where there is a hearing in the absence of a report, the LOI has to be compiled on the basis of other sources of information.

or respond to the LOI.[30] After the hearing, provisional concluding observations are sent to the state party concerned, with a view to making them public after a period of reflection, should the state party not undertake to present its overdue report. Since 2012, the whole exercise has taken place in public.

States parties to several human rights treaties often attribute the delays in submitting their reports to what they call the 'reporting burden', despite the fact that it is a burden they have voluntarily assumed, first, by drafting all the treaties to require reports and, second, by ratifying or acceding to them. Treating the concern seriously, two committees adopted a rule that would permit states, after review of their initial report, to dispense with further preparation of a global report[31] and instead to present a response to the LOI. Of course, the LOI itself could no longer be based on the state's report. Rather, the List of Issues prior to Reporting (LOIPR), as it is known, would be drafted on the basis of the concerns that the concluding observations in the previous report expressed, supplemented by more up-to-date information from the independent sources described earlier, as well as from the follow-up procedures (see below). It is too soon to assess how much this focused reporting procedure will lead to a reduction in the number of overdue reports or even to the amount of time they are overdue.

Measures aimed at reducing the backlog are hard won. The original purpose of adopting the LOIs was, it will be recalled, to streamline the reporting process, and perhaps this could have freed some meeting time for considering more reports. It may well be, however, that it merely permitted the use of the same amount of time for more effective consideration and analysis of each report. Another measure the Human Rights Committee tried was reinforcing the country rapporteur by establishing task forces of four or five members to agree on the LOI, with each of the members having primary responsibility for pursuing particular issues from the LOI. This could then relieve all the other Committee members of the sense of responsibility of being fully engaged in various aspects of each dialogue. While this may have achieved some success, it has not made a substantial dent in the backlog.

Another option is for committees to seek extra meeting time on an ad hoc basis, but in times of budgetary constraint (the rule rather than the exception), the General Assembly's Fifth Committee (on finance and budgetary matters) is reluctant to authorize the necessary funds. Even if it were to make the funds available, it is not easy for the committee members who receive no emoluments[32] to take the

[30] Gambia and Equatorial Guinea, each of which was eventually declared 'in non-compliance with its obligations under article 40 of the Covenant', as well as Seychelles, which did then submit comments on the provisional concluding observations (see immediately below) and promised a report. UNHRC, 'Report of the Human Rights Committee: Vol I' (2011) UN Doc A/66/40, paras 69 (Gambia), 71 (Equatorial Guinea), 78 (Seychelles). The most recent was Belize: UN Doc CCPR/C/BLZ/CO/1 (2013).

[31] The Human Rights Committee and CAT.

[32] Under ICCPR, Art 35; CEDAW, Art 17(8); and CRC, Art 43(12), the respective treaty bodies are supposed to receive 'emoluments'; calling them 'honoraria', the General Assembly decided to reduce these to USD 1.00. UNGA Res 56/272 (23 April 2002) UN Doc A/Res/56/272.

extra time from their ordinary working lives to donate to performing additional work for their committees.

4.2 General comments

ICCPR Article 40(4) authorizes the Human Rights Committee 'study the reports submitted by states parties' and then transmit its own reports 'and such general comments as it may consider appropriate' to the states parties.[33] As already mentioned, there was no agreement during the first decade and a half of the Committee's existence to make country-specific general comments, but the Committee did take seriously the challenge of making comments of a general nature. It saw the power to make general comments as an opportunity to give guidance to states parties on the content of their obligations under the Covenant, and thus as a means of assisting them in preparing their reports by alerting them to the Committee's expectations concerning the behaviour the provisions of the Covenant required.

Although some other treaties do not specifically authorize their committees to make general comments, or they make clear that the comments are meant to be country-specific, it is now the general practice of the treaty bodies to issue comments of a general nature because of their proven utility in clarifying expectations of what the conventions demand of states parties. The practice of CAT vividly illustrates the point. Article 19(3) of UNCAT was drafted in light of the Human Rights Committee's experience and empowered UNCAT to make 'general comments on the report'; the use of the singular ('report', not 'reports') was precisely aimed at encouraging the CAT to make comments on each state party's report. Nevertheless, the Committee did not in fact begin to adopt country-specific evaluations until the Human Rights Committee took that step with its first concluding observations, calling them 'conclusions and recommendations', while reserving the term 'general comment' for the same type of document as the same Committee produced.

The contents of the general comments may concern procedural[34] or substantive matters and, in either case, may indicate the sort of information being sought from states' reports, and/or they may simply describe the committees' interpretations of the law. The latter form is the predominant one. It tends to reflect each committee's accrued experience, both from its reviews of states' periodic reports and the 'views' it has issued on its examination of individual complaints. It will effectively amount to something close to a codification of evolving practice.

[33] See generally Helen Keller and Leena Grover, 'General Comments of the Human Rights Committee and Their Legitimacy' in Keller and Ulfstein (n 19).

[34] Eg UNHRC, 'General Comment No 33: The Obligations of States Parties under the Optional Protocol to the International Covenant on Civil and Political Rights' (5 November 2008) UN Doc CCPR/C/GC/33. See below.

The drafting process in the Human Rights Committee, which is similar to that in other treaty bodies, involves first deciding what issue or provision seems in most need of elucidation. The choice will not necessarily involve a new topic. It increasingly happens that the lapse of time and evolution of practice since the adoption of an earlier general comment makes it appropriate to revisit the topic. In this respect, at its March 2012 session, the Committee considered factors such as the Committee's frequency in applying a provision in its concluding observations and views on individual cases under the Optional Protocol, as well as the amount of time since the adoption of any previous general comment. Taking these factors into account, the Committee decided to prepare a new general comment on Article 9 (arbitrary arrest and detention) which had been the subject of a general comment in the 1980s.

After choosing the topic, the Committee appoints one of its members as rapporteur to present a draft to the whole committee which posts the draft text on its website, making it available to stakeholders, such as states parties and interested NGOs. A meeting may be held for the Committee to hear the views of such stakeholders. A 'first reading' text is eventually adopted, with stakeholders again being invited to comment. The Committee, taking account of suggestions that have been made, proceeds to a second (final) reading that can involve amendments and additions to, as well as deletions from, the first reading text. Apart from the intrinsic desirability of making the drafting process more transparent and better informed, the invitation to make suggestions at this key stage of the drafting process makes it possible to address and defuse potential problems. It is instructive to compare the negative reactions of three states to aspects of Human Rights Committee General Comment No 24 (on reservations to the ICCPR), adopted without outside consultation, to the absence of such reactions once General Comment No 33 (on states' obligations under the Optional Protocol) was adopted.[35] In the latter case, several states expressed concerns about language in the first reading text. The Committee was then able to take account of these at second reading, thereby avoiding what would certainly have been a similar reaction on adoption of the final text.

Once adopted, a general comment becomes a basic point of reference for the Committee. Like any codification, the Committee will invoke it as authority in its 'constructive dialogue' with states when considering their reports, in its concluding observations emerging from the dialogue, and in its subsequent views in individual complaints.

[35] See, on the reactions of France, the United Kingdom, and the United States of America to General Comment No 24, JP Gardner and Christine Chinkin (eds), *Human Rights as General Norms and a State's Right to Opt Out: Reservations and Objections to Human Rights Conventions* (British Institute of International and Comparative Law 1997).

4.3 Interstate complaints

Either the main treaty or an optional protocol related to all but one of the treaty bodies (the CEDAW Committee) provides the possibility of one state party making a complaint against another one. Uniquely, this function appears as an integral part of the CERD.[36] All the others establish it as an optional extra, either by virtue of depositing a declaration with the UN Secretary-General (as depository of the treaty itself) or by means of ratifying or acceding to the relevant protocol. The undertaking is reciprocal, meaning that only a state party that has accepted the jurisdiction of the treaty body with respect to itself can bring a claim against another such state.

No such complaint has been lodged with a treaty body since the inception of the system. One may only speculate on why this is so. It is a commonplace that states do not easily bring international claims against each other before international adjudicatory or quasi-judicial bodies. Their foreign ministries do not have standing institutions and resources for such ad hoc activities. Particularly in the field of human rights, the impugned state is likely to think of the initiation of the activity as unfriendly and thus disruptive of mutual relations. It also may be that a potential initiating state may fear a counter-claim in respect of its own behaviour.

Yet such claims have occasionally been brought before human rights instances outside the UN system, notably before regional mechanisms. This may well be because states feel more comfortable in such contexts of shared history and culture, *en famille* as it were. Even here they are infrequent. As far as the European Convention of Human Rights system is concerned, most interstate cases have involved issues that have already been bilateral irritants, for instance, in *Ireland v United Kingdom*, in respect of the 'troubles' in Northern Ireland, or *Cyprus v Turkey*, in respect of the northern Cyprus occupation. Cases that states with no direct interest in the impugned state bring, are the rarest of the rare.[37] In both cases mentioned, the situations were serious enough that their persistence represented a potentially existential challenge to the central ethos of the parent organization, the Council of Europe.

There is evidently room for research on the politics of bringing or, in the case of the UN human rights treaty bodies, failing to bring interstate complaints.[38]

[36] Article 12.

[37] The *Greek Case*, which Denmark, Norway, Sweden, and The Netherlands brought against the Greece of the post-1967 military junta, took place before the former European Commission of Human Rights. It could not reach the Court, as Greece had not accepted the (then optional) compulsory jurisdiction of the Court. The same applied to the case brought by Denmark, France, Norway, Sweden and The Netherlands against Turkey.

[38] cf the contrary practice the International Labour Organization, with its unique tripartite structure, in Janelle Diller's chapter in this *Handbook*.

4.4 Individual complaints

All nine core treaties and their protocols now provide for the possibility that their committees receive complaints of human rights violations submitted by or on behalf of individuals whose rights are claimed to have been violated. For most of the life of the system, that was the exception rather than the rule.

Dealing with individual complaints is the most court-like function of the treaty bodies, because it leads to a specific decision about claimed violations and can result in indications of appropriate redress. It is probably for that very reason that states have not easily accepted the idea of the individual complaint jurisdiction. They appear to be more comfortable with the state reports system, precisely because it is a mode of reviewing compliance with the treaties' obligations in a minimally intrusive manner. In any event, none of the treaties automatically provides for the treaty bodies to receive individual complaints. It is always a procedure into which states have to opt, either by becoming party to a protocol or by making a declaration with the UN Secretary-General pursuant to a provision of the treaty.

The Human Rights Committee was the first to begin dealing with individual complaints under the (First) Optional Protocol to the ICCPR, both instruments having entered into force at the same time. Although adopted nearly twenty years apart, the CERD (1965) and UNCAT (1984) were the next to acquire the necessary number of declarations of acceptance for their treaty bodies' jurisdiction over individual complaints in 1982 and 1987 respectively. It was not until the 2000s that individual treaties or protocols to other treaties brought the present across-the-board jurisdiction.[39]

The Human Rights Committee's accrued experience remains the most numerous and developed. That of the CERD Committee, under CERD Article 14, is more limited, followed by that of the CAT, under UNCAT Article 22. The much more recent experience of the CEDAW Committee under its 1999 Optional Protocol is also well under way. In general, the treaty provisions and treaty bodies have tended to be modelled on the ICCPR Optional Protocol and to follow the practice of the Human Rights Committee, so what follows is mainly based on that practice.

The proceedings are confidential, in the sense that all the Committee's deliberations under the Protocol take place in closed session. It is a written procedure. Authors of the communications (as the complaints are called) or the alleged victims, acting without representation, send the communication to the UN Secretariat (the Office of the High Commissioner for Human Rights). On receipt of a summary from the Secretariat, the Committee's Special Rapporteur for New Communications and Interim Measures decides whether or not there is the appearance of an arguable violation of the Covenant. If so, he or she will decide that the case should be registered.

[39] PR Ghandhi, *The Human Rights Committee and the Right of Individual Communication: Law and Practice* (Ashgate 1998); Geir Ulfstein, 'Individual Complaints' in Keller and Ulfstein (n 19) 73 and generally.

The Committee's Rules of Procedure allow it to grant interim measures of protection if there is a danger of irreparable harm to the alleged victim. Usually, such harm will entail the real risk of loss of life, as in the carrying out of a death sentence, or of other grave harm to the person, such as being sent to a country where there is a real risk of treatment in violation of the Article 7 prohibition of torture or cruel, inhuman, or degrading treatment or punishment. Other interim measures have responded to fears that the author or authors of the communications (other than the alleged victim) are at risk of serious harm to themselves. The same Special Rapporteur, acting on behalf of the Committee, makes the decision on interim measures. This is mainly because the urgency of the problem does not permit deferral of action to actual sessions of the Committee. If a state party fails to respect the requested measures, the Committee will consider that to be a grave violation, not of the Covenant itself, but of the Optional Protocol.[40] It considers such action to be incompatible with good faith compliance with the Optional Protocol process. It is the only example of the Committee's considering non-compliance with its decisions as being *ipso jure* a violation of a binding obligation. Interestingly, its practice here foreshadowed similar decisions by the International Court of Justice and the European Court of Human Rights. They, too, decided that, contrary to earlier doubts, their indications of provisional measures were binding.[41] The CAT followed suit in 2005.[42]

Theoretically, as is customary in international judicial or arbitral proceedings, there are two main phases in the Committee's handling of a case: admissibility and merits. The first deals with essentially procedural matters, such as whether domestic remedies have been exhausted; the second concerns the substance of the complained-of violation. To save the time of the Committee, the states parties, and the complainants, the two phases are usually telescoped into one. However, if the Special Rapporteur decides that there are serious admissibility questions to answer, he or she will split the phases, requesting the state party in question to respond first to those questions. Even where the initial decision is to stick with the usual practice of requesting observations on admissibility and merits together, states may request such a split. In that case, it falls to the Special Rapporteur to make the decision on behalf of the Committee.

Sometimes, it appears to the Special Rapporteur that, while there are sufficient grounds to register a case, there are such doubts as to its real admissibility that he or she will decide to prepare a draft inadmissibility decision without even referring the complaint to the state party for its comments. It will be up to the Committee to make the eventual decision.

[40] *Piandiong et al v Philippines*, para 5.2.

[41] *LaGrand Case (Germany v United States of America)*; *Mamatkulov and Askarov v Turkey*, para 129 (having cited *Piangdiong* (para 114) and *LaGrand* (para 117)).

[42] In respect of Art 22 (the complaints procedure): *Mafhoud Brada v France*.

Except for the latter kind of case, the next stage begins with a case rapporteur being charged with overseeing the treatment of the case. This rapporteur will receive a draft decision from the Secretariat. The rapporteur will then decide whether to follow the line the draft suggests or to request a different approach. He or she then submits a text to a Committee Working Group on Communications, generally consisting of eight to ten of the Committee's eighteen members, which meets in the week preceding each session. This is intended to, and probably does, permit a range of members to examine the issues at stake and reduce the amount of plenary time that has to be devoted to considering individual cases. However, there is no guarantee that other members of the Committee will not wish to discuss any particular case when it arrives at the plenary. The Working Group may deem that the solutions to some cases (or aspects of the cases) are so uncertain that alternative options are put to the plenary. The plenary will then make a decision, and, while consensus will be sought, it is not uncommon for a vote or at least a straw vote to be taken to settle the matter. In such cases, individual members will be free to express separate or, if necessary, dissenting opinions.

4.5 Inquiries

The adoption of UNCAT in 1984 brought with it a technique similar to that the inter-American system uses. Article 20 gave the CAT the power, of its own volition, to initiate an inquiry into an apparent systematic practice of torture. It was not, as such, a complaint-based procedure. There were no restrictions on the sources of information. There was only the objective requirement that the information be 'reliable' and the subjective one that the information 'contain well-founded indications' of the practice. This innovation was controversial from the beginning, and no agreement could be reached on it within the UN Commission on Human Rights, which oversaw the drafting process. It was only when the General Assembly was on the verge of adopting the draft instrument that a consensus was found that retained the provision but allowed states parties to make a reservation by which they could opt out of the procedure.[43] This was an improvement on the opt-in processes applicable to individual and most inter-state complaints procedures, as it placed the onus on the state to act if it wished to avoid being subject to the procedure.

Subsequent human rights treaties and optional protocols to earlier treaties also later adopted the power. So far, the only practice available is that of CAT and the CEDAW Committee, with CAT having had a substantial head start.

In fact, the UNCAT procedure has been relatively little used. In over a quarter of a century, the CAT has initiated only seven inquiries—or less than one every three

[43] Article 28.

years—that have reached the point of completion and thus publication.[44] This may in some measure be attributable to the original rule of procedure adopted to give effect to UNCAT Article 20. It is couched in terms that seem to require the submission of a complaint alleging the apparent systematic practice, rather than leaving it to the Committee to rely on other sources,[45] as originally contemplated. Other possible reasons, not excluding the quality of some CAT reports under Article 20, may explain the under-utilization of the procedure.[46]

4.6 Other functions

4.6.1 *Committee on Enforced Disappearances*

The CED is broadly modelled on the other treaty bodies, albeit—as noted—there is no automatic reporting requirement beyond that of submitting an initial report. It does, however, have two functions that are novel. The first is the power to refer a serious situation directly to the attention of the General Assembly. This is a reflection of the gravity with which the international community rightly regards the appalling phenomenon.

The second is the power to take an urgent action by intervening with a state party with a view to preventing any enforced disappearance or avoiding its prolongation. The intervention may also include a recommendation for the taking of interim measures.[47] This function is different from the interim measures that other Committees may indicate. The latter are merely designed to preserve the integrity of the individual complaints procedure. Indeed, the CED's urgent action procedure is independent of its power to deal with individual complaints which, as with other treaty bodies, is optional for the state in question.[48] It is also anomalous in another sense. The making of urgent appeals has long been a core function of the thematic 'special procedures' of the Human Rights Council. Indeed, the first special procedure, the Working Group on Enforced or Involuntary Disappearances created in 1980, developed the urgent appeal techniques. It is not clear whether the CED's urgent appeal procedure is meant to act alongside the Working Group's urgent action procedure or will be an alternative to it.[49]

[44] Turkey (1994), Egypt (1996), Peru (2001), Sri Lanka (2002), Mexico (2003), Serbia and Montenegro (2004), and Brazil (2008).

[45] Rule 75(1). Nowak quotes an interview with the Secretariat, according to which the Committee has begun to be more proactive and initiate inquiries without relying on a specially submitted request. Nowak and McArthur (n 6) 675; text accompanying (n 63).

[46] See Rodley and Pollard (n 6) 219. There is clearly room for much more detailed research and analysis into such use as has been made of the procedure and reasons why its use has been so limited.

[47] Article 30. [48] Article 31.

[49] Article 31(2)(c). See Nigel S Rodley, 'UN Treaty Bodies and the Human Rights Council' in Keller and Ulfstein (n 19) 343.

4.6.2 *Sub-Committee on the Prevention of Torture*

As earlier heralded, the Sub-Committee that OPCAT created has functions that are fundamentally different, both in nature and purpose, from those of the other treaty bodies. Intended to be preventive rather than reactive,[50] it is in fact aimed at engaging in and promoting a true monitoring function. Broadly patterned on the work of the Committee for the Prevention of Torture under the European Convention for the Prevention of Torture and Inhuman or Degrading Treatment or Punishment, it has the dual task of both visiting places of detention in states parties and cooperating with national preventive mechanisms that the parties are required to establish to engage in such visits at the domestic level. The reports of its visits are, in principle, confidential. The SPT is expected to make regular visits to states without the need for prior authorization. This distinguishes it from the inquiry procedure of several treaty bodies that begin with UNCAT Article 20. The only real element that the SPT has in common with the other treaty bodies is the very limited resources available for it to discharge its worldwide mandate.

5. Follow-Up Procedures

A number of treaty bodies have adopted follow-up procedures to encourage compliance with recommendations in their concluding observations on periodic reports and views on individual cases. As far as action on concluding observations is concerned, the stimulus is to avoid there being a vacuum between one set of concluding observations and the next report. As regards views, it is to encourage serious consideration of them, rather than letting them be forgotten.

There is nothing in the treaties contemplating follow-up activities, and their initiation would have to be seen as another deployment of what the committees consider their implied powers. States parties do not seem to have made any significant challenge to their implementation. On the contrary, most states seem willing to engage in the dialogue that the procedures entail.

Again drawing on the practice of the Human Rights Committee, the follow-up procedures work as follows. In the case of concluding observations, the observations themselves single out a small number of recommendations (usually three or four) that the Committee requests that the state party implement or begin to

[50] On the elusive meaning of prevention, see Nigel S Rodley, 'Reflections on Working for the Prevention of Torture' (2009) 6 *Essex Human Rights Review* 21, 26–29.

implement within a year. These are usually the recommendations arising out of the most serious concerns and which may have some prospect of being addressed (if not resolved) with reasonable rapidity. In the case of views on individual cases, states are given six months to respond on the effect they have given to the measures required to redress the violation.

The Committee appoints two Special Rapporteurs, one on concluding observations and one on views. If the state party has not already provided a response to the issues raised, the rapporteurs will contact them—in writing or, as necessary, in a direct meeting—with a view to eliciting a response or discussing the content of any response. The overall response obtained will then be evaluated on a scale ranging from satisfactory/partly satisfactory to unsatisfactory. At each Committee session, the Rapporteur gives an updated report, and the Committee then decides what further action to take. The process on Concluding Observations ceases once the next report is due, since the latter should be the repository of all information relevant to the state's compliance with its treaty obligations.

6. The Legal Nature and Effect of the Committees' Output

The outcomes of the committees' procedures (concluding observations, general comments, and jurisprudence) are not per se legally binding, but they have real legal significance. It should first be pointed out that in certain procedural matters, their decisions are binding. For example, where the treaty obliges a state party to provide a report at a time the Committee will determine, the Committee's decision of the time will *ipso jure* be binding on the state in question. It has already been seen that the Human Rights Committee and CAT consider their interim measures to be obligatory, if only to protect the integrity of the complaint process.

As regards the substantive outcomes, the legal impact must perforce be less direct. While their formal status is that of recommendations, that does not dispose of the matter. Resolutions of the UN General Assembly also only have the formal status of recommendations, yet their ability to affect the content of the law is substantial. Assembly resolutions, of course, can evince state practice. While that is not the case for treaty body determinations, they may contribute to community expectations of appropriate state behaviour under human rights treaty obligations.

This can be especially evident in actual judicial practice. The International Court of Justice (ICJ) has more than once illustrated the point. Famously, in the *Wall* case, it invoked the practice of the Human Rights Committee that considered the jurisdictional reach of Covenant obligations to extend beyond a state party's frontiers.[51] Both Israel, whose acts were at issue in the case, and the United States challenged this interpretation. The Court cited the Committee's 'constant practice', both in earlier Optional Protocol cases and its concluding observations on Israel, to support its own interpretation of the extra-territorial applicability of the Covenant.[52] It also invoked the Committee's General Comment No 27[53] in support of its interpretation of Article 12(3).[54]

In the subsequent *Diallo* case,[55] the Court elaborated on its view of the significance of the Committee's jurisprudence. Interpreting ICCPR Articles 13 and 12(4) (on freedom of movement) the Court invoked both an Optional Protocol case[56] and General Comment No 15.[57] Later in the same decision, the Court addressed issues under ICCPR Article 9 (liberty and security of person/arbitrary arrest and detention). Referring to their scope ('any form of arrest or detention decided upon and carried out by a public authority'), it invoked General Comment No 8.[58]

The Court explained its understanding of the significance of the Committee's work as follows:

Since it was created, the Human Rights Committee has built up a considerable body of interpretative case law, in particular through its findings in response to the individual communications which may be submitted to it in respect of States parties to the first Optional Protocol, and in the form of its 'General Comments'.

Although the Court is in no way obliged, in the exercise of its judicial functions, to model its own interpretation of the Covenant on that of the Committee, it believes that it should ascribe great weight to the interpretation adopted by this independent body that was established specifically to supervise the application of that treaty. The point here is to achieve the necessary clarity and the essential consistency of international law, as well as legal security, to which both the individuals with guaranteed rights and the States obliged to comply with treaty obligations are entitled.[59]

[51] *Legal Consequences of the Construction of a Wall in the Occupied Palestinian Territory* (*Wall* Case).

[52] *Wall* Case (n 51) paras 109–111.

[53] UNHRC, 'General Comment No 27: Freedom of Movement (Art 12)' (2 November 1999) UN Doc CCPR/C/21/Rev.1/Add.9.

[54] *Wall* Case (n 51) para 136.

[55] *Case Concerning Ahmadou Sadio Diallo (Republic of Guinea v Democratic Republic of the Congo)*; see Sandy Ghandhi, 'Human Rights and the International Court of Justice in the *Ahmadou Sadio Diallo Case* (2011) 11 Human Rights Law Review 536.

[56] *Diallo* (n 55) para 66, referring to *Maroufidou v Sweden*.

[57] *Diallo* (n 55) para 66, citing UNHRC, 'General Comment No 15: The Position of Aliens under the Covenant' (11 April 1986) reprinted in UNHRC, 'Compilation of General Comments and General Recommendations Adopted by Human Rights Treaty Bodies' (12 May 2004) UN Doc HRI/Gen.1/Rev.7.

[58] *Diallo* (n 55) para 77, citing UNHRC, 'General Comment No 8: Right to Liberty and Security of Persons (Art 9)' (30 June 1982) reprinted in UNHRC, 'Compilation of General Comments and General Recommendations Adopted by Human Rights Treaty Bodies' (12 May 2003) UN Doc HRI/GEN/1/Rev.6.

[59] *Diallo* (n 55) para 66.

This respectful understanding of the authority of the Committee's jurisprudence may owe something to the Committee's own approach to its activities under the Optional Protocol. In its General Comment No 33, the Committee explained that its views 'are arrived at in a judicial spirit, including the impartiality and independence of Committee members, the considered interpretation of the language of the Covenant, and the determinative character of the decisions'.[60] For the Committee, these were 'important characteristics of a judicial decision', albeit the Committee was 'not, as such... a judicial body'.[61] The Committee exercised its function of adopting its views in the belief that they represent an authoritative determination by the organ established under the Covenant itself charged with the interpretation of that instrument. These views derive their character, and the importance which attaches to them, from the integral role of the Committee under both the Covenant and the Optional Protocol.[62]

The substantial body of Human Rights Committee jurisprudence, accrued over some three decades, is also relevant to the authority with which the ICJ and, for that matter, the European and Inter-American Courts of Human Rights, which will frequently invoke Committee practice with approval, view it.[63] The more limited practices of the CERD Committee, CEDAW Committee, and CAT make it harder to conclude unambiguously that their case law would enjoy similar authority to that of the Human Rights Committee. There is nothing in principle to suggest that it should be treated any differently.[64] However, the output has not been such as to elicit the extent of authoritative judicial approval that that of the Human Rights Committee has acquired.

Meanwhile, the very important role of national courts must be stressed. Occasionally, a state party will even make a Committee decision directly enforceable in its courts or will permit the reopening of cases which have already concluded.[65] Many states' constitutions give various levels of authority to international treaties generally, or human rights treaties in particular. This leads to some invocation of Committee case law, as increasingly noted in comparative law scholarship.[66]

[60] UNHRC, 'General Comment No 33' (n 34) para 11.

[61] UNHRC, 'General Comment No 33' (n 34) para 11.

[62] UNHRC, 'General Comment No 33' (n 34) para 13.

[63] Eg *Mamatkulov* (n 41) para 114; *Case of Caesar v Trinidad and Tobago*, para 63 (corporal punishment).

[64] For instance, in *Questions Relating to the Obligation to Prosecute or Extradite (Belgium v Senegal)*, the Court had to choose between seemingly contradictory views of the CAT in respect of *ratione temporis* matters in UNCAT; it preferred the approach in which the Committee addressed the matter directly, even though it was an earlier case—indeed the first individual case the Committee decided. *Belgium v Senegal*, paras 100–102.

[65] Eg Colombia (enforceable) and Norway (re-openable). Rosanne Van Alebeek and André Nollkaemper, 'The Legal Status of Decisions by Human Rights Treaty Bodies in National Law' in Keller and Ulfstein (n 19) 363–67.

[66] See generally, the up-to-date article by Van Alebeek and Nollkaemper (n 65); Christof Heyns and Frans Viljoen *The Impact of the United Nations Human Rights Treaties on the Domestic Level* (Kluwer Law International 2002).

7. Problems the Treaty Body System Faces

The long-standing and intensifying central challenge confronting the system is that there is too much work to be done, in too short a time, with inadequate resources. It is not a new problem. On the contrary, the system has undergone three major reviews in as many decades.

As regards the reporting system, the most salient manifestations of the problem are that there are substantial delays in states submitting their reports; there are significant backlogs in the treaty bodies' examining the reports; the more the former problem is eased, the more serious the latter one will become; and, as regards the individual complaints system (for the three committees mainly engaged in this activity at present), there is a rough similarity. There is a significant backlog of cases waiting to be dealt with, despite the fact that the potential number of cases that could be brought before the bodies if the procedures were better known could overwhelm the whole system.[67] Meanwhile, there are many criticisms that the quality of the output needs improvement, such as more specific recommendation to government in concluding observations on their reports and better reasoned justifications of the views in individual cases.[68]

Different problems may result from different causes. For example, many states attribute the delays in their submission of reports to the 'reporting burden' (having to report regularly to eight treaty bodies),[69] even though it is a self-inflicted burden. Reasons for the backlog in processing reports may vary from Committee to Committee; some have more states parties than others (and so more reports); some have more meeting time than others (three, six, or nine weeks of plenary meetings annually); or the Secretariat does not have the resources to translate the reports promptly, or to translate at all states' written responses to the list of issues. Many of the issues the Committees deal with are duplicative, if only because much of the subject matter they deal with is relevant to more than one treaty. After all, there is no basic issue of concern to the specific subject or victim-group treaties that is not also of concern to the general treaties: the ICCPR and the ICESCR.[70]

[67] cf European Court of Human Rights, which, as of 30 June 2012, had 144,150 pending cases. Council of Europe, 'Pending Applications Allocated to a Judicial Formation' (31 October 2012) <http://www.echr.coe.int/NR/rdonlyres/D552E6AD-4FCF-4A77-BB70-CBA53567AD16/0/CHART_30062012.pdf> accessed 1 September 2012.

[68] See Henry J Steiner, 'Individual Claims in a World of Massive Violations: What Role for the Human Rights Committee?' in Philip Alston and James Crawford (eds), *The Future of UN Human Rights Treaty Monitoring* (CUP 2000) 38–45.

[69] It will be recalled that CED does not require regular reporting after the initial report.

[70] While duplicative activities may well be seriously burdensome for governments, from a human rights perspective, in which moral suasion is the only tool available, duplication may mean reinforced activity.

As regards individual complaints, some of the same reasons may apply. It is clear that in the last two or three years, the Secretariat has not been able to process the complaints to the point of being able to present as many draft outcomes as the HRC would have been able to deal with in the amount of time it typically allocates to this aspect of its functions. For a number of years there was a particularly large backlog of, and thus long delays in dealing with, cases from Russian-speaking countries, chiefly because the Secretariat lacked enough Russian-speaking human rights staff. The reasons for the Secretariat's problems are various, and space does not allow inquiry into them. One obvious one, however, is the expansion of the number of bodies dealing with individual cases and the number of cases being submitted to them, without commensurate new resources being put in place to process them.

Before considering the various proposals to resolve the problem(s), it is worth recalling that at the heart of it all is the multiplication of treaty bodies. Without that, there would not have had to be multiple reports, nor extensive duplication of concern. It may be speculated that the problem could have been avoided if the Covenants had taken less time to draft (which led to the adoption of CERD and its own treaty body), or if they had taken less time to enter into force—nearly a decade after their adoption (by which time the drafting of CEDAW had started).[71] An attempt was made to stop proliferation at the time of drafting the UNCAT, the original Swedish draft of which envisaged that the treaty body should be the Human Rights Committee. This attempt at rationality (and, it must be said, at saving money) stopped in its tracks when the UN Legal Counsel of the time advised the UN Commission on Human Rights working group responsible for drafting the Convention that, to give that Committee such functions would require an amendment to the Covenant.[72] Whether or not he was right with respect to the law,[73] the working group had no real choice but to make provision for a further treaty body. The last attempt to come to grips with the problem was during the drafting of the CPED. The Commission on Human Rights considered various options, including

[71] Note that CEDAW was drafted outside the human rights bodies. The Commission on the Status of Women (CSW) drafted it, whereas the (ex-) Commission on Human Rights drafted most of the other human rights treaties. Both of these bodies would then forward the texts, through ECOSOC, for adoption by the General Assembly (Third Committee). In any event, it would have been unlikely that a body (CSW), established because the Commission on Human Rights was not trusted to take proper account of gender issues, would have been willing to trust the generalist ICCPR treaty body to be appropriate for monitoring CEDAW.

[72] See Burgers and Danelius (n 6) 76.

[73] The basic argument of the Legal Counsel was that the functions of the Committee were limited to those for which the ICCPR provided. It may be noted that the same argument, if applied to the President of the International Court of Justice, would prevent that august officeholder, under the Court's Statute, from exercising such traditional functions as appointing arbitrators under international arbitral agreements.

making the Human Rights Committee or the CAT the treaty body, as well as a separate one.[74] In the end, pressure from constituencies that focused primarily on the issue persuaded the drafters that this most terrible phenomenon should have its own treaty body. Nevertheless, Article 27 of the CPED envisages the calling of a conference of states parties within between four and six years of the treaty's entry into force, to consider transferring the CED's powers to another body. This was agreed, in the context of the proposal being discussed at the time, to replace the existing panoply of committees with just one unified standing committee (see below). The failure of that proposal may be taken as ensuring that the CED will retain its separate existence.

8. Reviews and Proposals

In the 1990s, at the request of the General Assembly, then-CESCR member Philip Alston produced a series of reports.[75] In his 2002 report on strengthening the United Nations, after reviewing the whole UN system, the Secretary-General made suggestions in respect of the treaty bodies. In 2006, the High Commissioner for Human Rights, Louise Arbour, undertook a review of the treaty body system and presented a proposal that her 2005 Plan of Action had heralded. At the time of writing, a dual process is under way. The current High Commissioner, Navanethem Pillay, initiated and collaborated with a wide-ranging series of consultations with various 'stakeholders'—states, treaty body members, national human rights institutions, and civil society/NGOs—with a view to strengthening the system. The collaborative element has been the 'Dublin Process'. This consists of a series of meetings beginning and ending in the Irish capital, supported by the Irish government, at the initiative of the University of Nottingham's Human Rights Law Centre, led by its co-Director and HRC member Professor Michael O'Flaherty. Between the Dublin meetings, consisting predominantly of treaty body members, there were other meetings, including

[74] See the report that Mr Manfred Nowak, an independent expert charged with the examination of the existing international criminal and human rights framework for the protection of persons from enforced or involuntary disappearances. Report of Mr Manfred Nowak, 'Civil and Political Rights, Including Questions of: Disappearances and Summary Executions' (8 January 2002) UN Doc E/CN.4/2002/71.

[75] See Final report of the independent expert, Mr Philip Alston, on enhancing the long-term effectiveness of the United Nations human rights treaty system. Report of Philip Alston, 'Effective Functioning of Bodies Established Pursuant to United Nations Human Rights Instruments: Final Report on Enhancing the Long-Term Effectiveness of the United Nations Human Rights Treaty System' (27 March 1997) UN Doc E/CN.4/1997/74.

the Marrakesh, Poznan, Seoul, and Pretoria meetings. The product of the Dublin Process is the Dublin Outcome Document on the Strengthening of the United Nations Human Rights Treaty Body System,[76] which has 126 recommendations and which the chairs of all the treaty bodies have signed. The High Commissioner's own report was published in June 2012 offering twenty-three proposals.[77] Meanwhile, parallel to this process, the UN General Assembly initiated its own review.[78] As of the time of writing no substantive proposal had emerged, nor was it expected to until at least late-2013.

The best-known proposal for addressing a number of the problems postulated earlier is the idea of replacing the existing eight part-time treaty bodies (with unpaid members) with one unified, full-time professional treaty body. Alston cautiously mooted it, and then Louise Arbour championed it.[79] The advantages are evident. States would only have to report to one body (probably with one report), thus radically reducing the 'reporting burden', and the body would avoid unnecessary duplication. Given that currently treaty bodies together meet in plenary session for fifty-three weeks per year, involving members travelling to and from the meetings multiple times, it could well be that the proposal would not have major financial implications.

However, High Commissioner Arbour's proposal did not prosper. It is only possible to speculate as to the reasons why. The general perception was that the 'options paper' that contained the proposal only provided one option and in that sense was mis-labelled. Several of the treaty bodies and the constituencies supporting them, especially those whose treaties were victim-specific (racial group (CERD) gender (CEDAW), age (CRC)), also expressed clear opposition. There was a perceptible concern that their specificities would be submerged or at least lose prominence if left in the hands of what would perforce be a generalist body like the Human Rights Committee.

Another reason sometimes mooted was that some states feared that a unified body might become a precursor for a world human rights court. Certainly, this was a project that Manfred Nowak and Martin Scheinin (the latter then a Human Rights Committee member) had for some time been advocating. Indeed, the present

[76] UN High Commissioner for Human Rights, 'Outcome Document: Strengthening the United Nations Human Rights Treaty Body System' (11 November 2011) <http://www2.ohchr.org/english/bodies/HRTD/docs/DublinII_Outcome_Document.pdf> accessed 31 December 2012.

[77] UNGA, 'Report of the United Nations High Commissioner for Human Rights on the Strengthening of the Human Rights Treaty Bodies Pursuant to Assembly Resolution 66/254' (26 June 2012) UN Doc A/66/860.

[78] UNGA, 'Res 66/254: Intergovernmental Process of the General Assembly on Strengthening and Enhancing the Effective Functioning of the Human Rights Treaty Body System' (15 May 2012) UN Doc A/Res/66/254.

[79] Report by the Secretariat, 'Concept Paper on the High Commissioner's Proposal for a Unified Standing Treaty Body' (22 March 2006) UN Doc HRI/MC/2006/2.

writer also suggested that the High Commissioner might herself espouse it.[80] That, however, had to be seen as a separate idea. It would have been totally unrealistic to envisage that one treaty body performing all the functions of existing treaty bodies could easily evolve into a judicial body.

The CERD Committee made one original proposal during the Arbour-initiated review that would have hived off the function of adjudicating individual complaints to a single body.[81] Such a body could certainly have been a perceived as a potential stalking-horse for a world human rights court. No one took up that proposal, either.

Meanwhile, consultations were proceeding on the idea of a single consolidated report that would serve as the report on each treaty to each Committee. The Secretary-General in his 2002 report *Agenda for Further Change* had advised this.[82] After protracted consultations, the only notable outcome was an expanded 'common core document'.[83] Perhaps it is inevitable that, as long as there is one treaty body per treaty, each will feel more comfortable with a form and style of reporting reflecting the substantive specificities of each treaty and the accumulated experience of each body.

One ambitious proposal to emerge from the current review is that of a comprehensive reporting calendar. This would have each state expected to submit, say, two reports annually to each of the treaty bodies, which would then schedule and examine the reports according to a fixed timetable. The report would consist of responses to the LOIPR. Absent such responses, and therefore the report, the consideration of the country situation would proceed anyway. The proposal ignores the legal problem of the different periodicities for which the different treaties provide. Perhaps more challenging would be the states' willingness to accept such a strait-jacket in practice. At the last consultation of states that the High Commissioner convened

[80] Recollection of the present writer, during the 4th Inter-Committee Meeting discussion, at which Mme Arbour first broached the unified standing treaty body idea. See UNGA, 'Effective Implementation of International Instruments on Human Rights, Including Reporting Obligations under International Instruments on Human Rights' (19 August 2005) UN Doc A/60/278, Annex, para 34. See Julia Kozma, Manfred Nowak and Martin Scheinin, *A World Court of Human Rights: Consolidated Statute and Commentary* (Neue Wissenschaftlicher Verlag 2010).

[81] UN International Human Rights Instruments, 'Report of the Working Group on the Harmonization of Working Methods of Treaty Bodies' (9 January 2007) UN Doc HRI/MC/2007/2, para 5.

[82] UNGA, 'Report of the Secretary-General: Strengthening the United Nations: An Agenda for Further Change' (9 September 2002) UN Doc A/57/387, para 54.

[83] The common core document is one containing the basic backgrounds and institutional make-ups of states, which has information likely to be of concern to all the treaty bodies and in respect of which changes are unlikely to be frequent. The only substantive element is in relation to the principle of non-discrimination, itself a genuinely common concern of the treaty bodies. Report of the Secretary-General, 'Compilation of Guidelines on the Form and Content of Reports to Be Submitted by States Parties to the International Human Rights Treaties' (3 June 2009) UN Doc HRI/GEN/2/Rev.6, paras 31–59. The Committee unceremoniously dismissed a valiant effort by Australia in its fifth periodic report to the Human Rights Committee to pilot a consolidated report for failure to provide 'sufficient and adequate information'. UNHRC, 'Consideration of Reports Submitted by States Parties under Article 40 of the Covenant' (7 May 2009) UN Doc CCPR/C/AUS/CO/5, para 2.

before finalizing her report, which occurred in New York between 2 and 3 April 2012, however, a substantial number of states expressed interest in the idea.[84]

In reality, most of the changes in treaty body practice have come from the treaty bodies themselves seeking to be more effective, more efficient, and more productive, even with the ever inadequate resources available to them either directly or from the Secretariat. Salient examples in the reporting process include the original development of the list of issues drawn up after the submission of reports, the LOIPR system, and the country situation hearings in the absence of a report. Indeed, ingeniously, the comprehensive reporting calendar idea is predicated on the existence of these.

A constant goal of the treaty bodies in improving their effectiveness has been to seek a certain harmonization of work. This makes the Secretariat's task much easier, as well as making more predictable the experience of state officials who have to prepare and then defend their states' reports. It also permits, through the annual meetings of Committee chairpersons, a certain cross-fertilization and dissemination of new ideas and practices. There have been attempts to give the chairpersons' meeting decision-making power, and these need to be treated with caution. Apart from legal and even political obstacles, rigid harmonization could entail the sort of sclerosis that would prevent the kind of experimentation that has led to improving methodology.

It has been seen that no 'silver bullet' has so far commended itself to what many, especially the governments that created it, consider a dysfunctional system. That may not always be the case. Occasionally, a catalytic event or chain of events occurs that makes radical institutional change, considered unrealistic yesterday, become tomorrow's necessity. The experience in the 1990s that brought us the International Criminal Court, only a decade earlier the hobby-horse of a few visionaries, should remind us that something similar could happen with the world human rights court idea. If that were to materialize, it would probably lead to a root and branch re-appraisal of the current treaty body system.

Further Reading

Alston P and Crawford J (eds), *The Future of UN Human Rights Treaty Monitoring* (CUP 2000)

Bayefsky AF (ed), *The UN Human Rights Treaty System in the 21st Century* (Kluwer Law International 2000)

[84] Office of the High Commissioner for Human Rights, 'Consultation for States on Treaty Body Strengthening' (2–3 April 2012) para 17 <http://www2.ohchr.org/english/bodies/HRTD/docs/ReportConsultation2_3April2012.pdf> accessed 2 September 2012 (consulted 2 September 2012). The author served as a 'resource person' from the treaty bodies at this consultation.

—— *The UN Human Rights Treaty System: Universality at the Crossroads* (Kluwer Law International 2001)

Conte A and Burchill R, *Defining Civil and Political Rights: The Jurisprudence of the United Nations Human Rights Committee* (2nd edn, Ashgate 2009)

Craven M, *The International Covenant on Economic, Social and Cultural Rights: A Perspective on Its Development* (OUP 1995)

Ghandhi PR, *The Human Rights Committee and the Right of Individual Communication: Law and Practice* (Ashgate 1998)

Hanski R and Scheinin M, *Leading Cases of the Human Rights Committee* (2nd rev edn, Åbo Akademi University 2007)

Ingelse C, *The UN Committee against Torture: An Assessment* (Martinus Nijhoff 2001)

Joseph S, Schultz J, and Castan M, *The International Covenant on Civil and Political Rights: Cases, Materials, and Commentary* (2nd edn, OUP 2004)

Keller H and Ulfstein G (eds), *UN Human Rights Treaty Bodies: Law and Legitimacy: Studies on Human Rights Conventions* (CUP 2012)

McGoldrick D, *The Human Rights Committee: Its Role in the Development of the International Covenant on Civil and Political Rights* (OUP 1994)

Möller JT and de Zayas A, *The United Nations Human Rights Committee Case Law 1977-2008: A Handbook* (Engel 2009)

Nowak M, *UN Covenant on Civil and Political Rights: CCPR Commentary* (2nd edn, Engel 2005)

Odello M and Seatzu F, *The UN Committee on Economic, Social and Cultural Rights: The Law, Process and Practice* (Routledge 2012)

Yogesh Tyagi, *The UN Human Rights Committee: Practice and Procedure* (CUP 2011)

CHAPTER 27

THE ROLE OF INTERNATIONAL TRIBUNALS: LAW-MAKING OR CREATIVE INTERPRETATION?

CECILIA MEDINA[1]

1. Introduction

An assessment of the role of the international decision-maker serving on a human rights body raises the particular question of whether such an individual interprets the applicable treaty, or whether he goes beyond interpretation and application to create new rights and obligations the drafters did not foresee. Legal literature has debated the general matter of judicial law-making, in contrast to law interpretation

[1] This chapter is based on the author's experience in international tribunals. She served as a member of the Human Rights Committee, an organ that the International Covenant on Civil and Political Rights (ICCPR) established. The author was also a judge on the Inter-American Court of Human Rights. The Inter-American Court had its first meeting in 1979, after the American Convention on Human Rights (ACHR) established it. The author wishes to thank Daniela Ortega for her research and comments.

and application, extensively and at length. It will be discussed herein in reference to the theory and practice of human rights law. The following examination of the matter begins from a theoretical point of view and then evaluates the relevant practice.[2] It may be noted at the outset that the norms themselves might suggest an invitation to monitoring bodies to 'make' law when they apply the treaties.

2. Law-Making or Interpretation?

From the point of view and experience of a former international decision-maker, having observed numerous colleagues in different international bodies, it appears that the interpretation of any rule involves an act of 'creative interpretation'.[3] Some rules require a significant amount of construction for their interpretation and application, and others demand very little in this respect. Differences of opinion arise between the members of a collective decision-making organ, but it seems clear that none of the individuals seeks to overturn the law in order to invade the functions of another organ or to be unfaithful to the mandate and powers conferred on the decision-makers. Each position taken with regard to a norm is based on an understanding of the 'right way' to read it. The difficulty arises regarding the permissible scope of 'creativity' in interpreting the rights the treaty guarantees. The resolution depends on a number of factors examined below.

There are certain limits on judges and members of treaty bodies in interpreting 'creatively'. In international human rights law, the treaty-drafters set forth the rights that states are bound to respect and ensure; it would not be possible for a decision-maker to create new rights; neither would such a person be allowed to create new state obligations. The interpretation has to fit legally within the sphere of the rights in the treaty and the sphere of the obligations of states. The point—and problem—is to decide which interpretation fits and which does not; of course, disagreements may arise in tracing the dividing line between law-making and interpretation, but that is a problem that cannot be decided in the abstract. Only a careful

[2] I have had to apply and to interpret international human rights law in two different bodies, first as a member of a global supervisory organ and subsequently a regional one. The first gave me a wide range of thought and vision, being as I served with seventeen colleagues from various continents. The second post placed me in the more limited region of Latin America, where I could deepen my knowledge of the continent to which I belong and whose characteristics I share, or at least understand. The privilege of having seen other mores allowed me to take what I thought was valuable for my task and to have a sharper eye to assess critically my own continental culture and traditions.

[3] HLA Hart, *The Concept of Law* (2nd edn, Clarendon Press 1994) 126–28.

examination of the facts of each case and an equally careful application of the rules of interpretation will allow a conclusion to be reached.

In general, it may be that any conclusion about whether a decision is law-making or interpretive will rest in the eyes of the beholder. Judges and members of treaty bodies tend to be inconsistent in terms of their restraint or expansiveness in undertaking interpretation; they may approach certain issues conservatively in certain cases and behave progressively in others, according to different factors and circumstances. Yet categorization is important, because to call a decision 'law-making' is meant to and serves to reject the decision's legality as falling outside the scope of the decision-maker's functions. It can also affect the legitimacy of the organ. However, as shown below, if the focus of the analysis is put on whether or not the decision exceeds the boundaries of the powers of the organ, there is arguably very little that human rights decision-makers cannot do in the matter of creative interpretation, short of establishing new rights or obligations completely unrelated to the text of the treaty.

In the field of international human rights law, there are strong reasons to support the idea that considerable latitude is given to international decision-makers to exercise their functions creatively. There is not only ample opportunity, but also a duty, for such decision-makers to ensure that the content of a human right remains up to date and to apply it to situations that those who drafted the treaty did not specifically envision. The rules of treaty interpretation, applied to human rights law, make it intrinsically part of the judicial mandate to do this.[4]

Starting from the premise that the applicable treaty text establishes the legal framework constraining a decision-maker, interpretation begins by examining the wording of the norm, as the rules for interpretation of treaties in the Vienna Convention on the Law of Treaties (VCLT) require. Significantly, however, international human rights law is formulated invariably as principles and general norms, which necessarily require further development when applying them to specific circumstances. Thus, it is inherent in the interpreter's task to elaborate, detail, and develop the norm, and such action does not exceed the judicial function or the powers of the organ.

Consideration of the object and purpose of the treaty is a fundamental rule of interpretation that governs how the decision-maker takes what is needed from the text, to apply the norm to a specific situation. The rule implies, first, that Committee members and judges must keep in mind that the norms and principles they are applying have been adopted in order to protect the human rights of human beings; interpretation should thus be *pro persona*. From the point of view of potential victims, this approach gives interpreters a clear interpretive mandate, with considerable

[4] The term 'judicial' herein refers not only to judges serving on courts, but also to the members of treaty bodies who decide cases and exercise interpretive functions akin to judicial officers. See the chapter by Fitzmaurice in this *Handbook*.

latitude to develop the norm in favour of the alleged victim, which of course does not mean doing it without sufficient legal grounds.

Such interpretations will change over time; the way to protect a person today may be, and frequently is, different from what was required in the past; the perception of what is impermissible for states to do and permissible in a person's conduct similarly varies with the passing of time. This requires that interpretations be dynamic. Human rights decisions are supposed to protect a person from actions that violate human rights in the present;[5] threats to human rights fluctuate, as human inventiveness is fertile not only with respect to improving life but also in harming or destroying it. It is telling in this regard that the *travaux préparatoires* are clearly only a supplementary means to determine the meaning of a norm.[6]

Another relevant consideration is the fact that human rights law forms an integral, universal system, allowing and encouraging interpreters to reach into the melting pot where national and international legal orders and jurisprudence mix and enrich human rights, with the purpose of improving the consistency and reach of the norms they have to apply. Finally, international human rights systems are new in historical terms, so almost each case sets a precedent. There are few established ways to apply norms, and often there is no trodden path. It is necessary to develop the law, and international human rights decision-makers must be creative by the very essence of their function and the powers they exercise.

Nevertheless, there remain limits on elaborating a human rights provision. These limits mark the difference between norm interpretation and norm creation. Treaty drafters in international human rights law set forth the rights that states are bound to respect and ensure; it is not the function of an interpreter to do so. In perceiving the limits of creative interpretation, several factors will play a part. First, those decision-makers who exercise restraint in interpretation do so with the conviction that going further would take them beyond their powers. Second, they may also think that, in respect to certain issues, it is advisable to let society change at its own pace; therefore, although there might be room for interpreting a legal provision creatively, they will tend to follow and not precede the attitudes of the culture with which they identify. In contrast, others believe that it is in their power, and it is their duty, to read the law with less consideration to its origins and to the usual way in which it has been applied. In order to fulfil the purpose of the law to protect each person's human rights, protection must at times challenge the predominant culture in the state concerned.

In sum, whether decision-makers are restrictive or creative is not a legal, but a political, decision in the widest sense. In principle, then, it is possible to dismiss the categorization of a judicial or quasi-judicial decision in the field of human rights as

[5] See *Interpretation of the American Declaration of the Rights and Duties of Man within the Framework of the Article 64 of the American Convention on Human Rights*, para 37.

[6] VCLT, Arts 31.1, 32.

law-making; instead, usually the content of a right necessarily evolves as new possibilities of its application are unveiled.

3. Factors Potentially Influencing the Interpretation of Human Rights Norms

Those deciding human rights cases and those litigating before human rights tribunals should know the factors that may influence the exercise of the decision-making function; such awareness can help maintain judicial impartiality and confidence in the process, whether the approach to any specific question of interpretation is creative or restrained. Certain factors are intrinsic, stemming from the personal traits of those who decide, and some are extraneous to them.

The personal attributes and backgrounds of judges and committee members are important. International norms have to be applied irrespective of the legal order of each state, and a decision-maker must therefore transcend the familiar domestic system to arrive at an international standard. The personal makeup of each person determines whether this will be achieved easily or with more difficulty. It is probable that the characteristics of the state of origin are relevant, whether it is a 'first world country' or a 'third world country'; one found in the East, West, South, or North; or whether the country is highly religious, whatever the religion may be. State reports coming from a decider's own region, or from states sharing a religious affinity, may produce empathy in the member and result in a tendency not to notice possible incompatibilities with the norms, which are evident to others. Decision-makers coming from the academic world may approach issues very differently from those who served in the national judiciary or diplomatic corps. The first are likely to have more difficulty in yielding to a certain interpretation, advanced because of its political or social consequences. Instead, they will try to insist on international legal arguments. Former officials will have difficulty transcending their national legal systems and methodological approaches to reach a result different from their own laws, while diplomats will tend to look at the large picture and evaluate how a particular interpretation might correspond to the international political stage and interfere as little as possible with state parties. Gender also matters, as does personal contact with human rights violations, especially if the decider, a family member, or a friend, was a victim of a violation. Finally, the personality of the individual also figures in—whether the person is cautious, daring, willing to override tradition and the majority, or mistrustful of authority and power.

Among the extraneous factors relevant to interpretation, is the economic, social, political, and ideological context in which a treaty is drafted. This factor significantly influences the road that supervisory organs will follow when applying the treaty to specific situations, one example being the issue of democracy and human rights. Both the Human Rights Committee (HRC) and the Inter-American Court (IACtHR) base their work on the understanding that human rights operate in and for democratic states, and the standards they develop are based on what human rights in a democracy need. Yet, textual and contextual elements shape their different approaches to the issue.

In the case of the Court, consideration of democracy is supported by the preamble of the American Convention on Human Rights (ACHR), which begins by reaffirming that the states of the Organization of American States have the 'intention to consolidate in this hemisphere, *within the framework of democratic institutions*, a system of personal liberty and social justice based on respect for the essential rights of man'.[7] Members of the IACtHR and the Inter-American Commission (IACHR) thus have a robust mandate to develop human rights, with a focus on building democracy, and are encouraged to construe human rights to maximize individuals' enjoyment of them, on the basis of the existence of a democratic legal order. The International Covenant on Civil and Political Rights (ICCPR), to the contrary, does not refer to democracy in its preamble, although it asserts that human rights are the foundation of freedom, justice, and peace in the world. The concept of democracy is mentioned only in relation to freedom of the press,[8] freedom of assembly,[9] and freedom of association[10]—freedoms generally linked with the possibility of free and informed elections, a typical feature of participatory democracy.

Notably, the ICCPR came to life during the Cold War, among states with highly different cultures and perceptions of democracy, and when there were profound divisions between East and West. The text needed twenty years to be concluded and adopted, and ten additional years to enter into force. Moreover, it has never been possible to establish a human rights court to deal with violations of the diverse human rights treaties in force within the framework of the universal system. So, despite the efforts of the Committee, democracy is not always at the forefront of some aspects of the Committee's work. The ACHR, in contrast, came to life as a strong response against dictatorships and the appalling situation of human rights in many of the OAS member states, and was adopted by states with mostly similar legal systems and a similar understanding of what 'liberal' democracy meant, even if it does not always show in the practice of all the member states. The emphasis on democracy in the interpretation of human rights is clear in the jurisprudence, and

[7] ACHR, preamble (emphasis added). [8] Article 14. [9] Article 21.
[10] Article 22.

judges have taken care to consider each right in its relationship with the democratic process.[11] Broad contextual factors, then, are important to consider when examining the interpretation and application of a treaty.

Another factor that influences the outcome of a decision is the collective nature of the deciding organ. A collective organ arrives at solutions with the input of each member of the organ, producing some form of agreement—at least a majority agreement, if not one of consensus or unanimity—as to the decision or an opinion. The homogeneity or heterogeneity of the composition of the body is significant; it is not the same to debate and agree among colleagues who are all lawyers as it is among those coming from various disciplines. It is different, as well, to debate and agree among peers who have relatively similar cultures, languages, and legal systems, compared to debating and reaching agreement among people who are diverse in all these aspects.

Most of these external factors contribute to forming the culture of the organ; the 'personal' factors make up the culture of the member. Together, they interweave to produce an amalgam, whose different elements usually cannot be distinguished and measured. No specific instances can be cited wherein it is possible to identify the various factors operating distinctly in the exercise of the Committee's function, but it may be possible to perceive differences in the individual opinions regarding individual complaints, both in the Committee and the Court.

Two remaining factors are powerful enough to have a considerable bearing on the limits of the organs' creative interpretation of a human rights treaty, particularly in regard to certain human rights. One is the cultural changes in the world resulting from the actions and reactions of those on whose behalf human rights were established. The cultural changes resulting from the struggle of human beings to enjoy human rights without discrimination almost invariably have had a bearing on the interpretation of rights and obligations emerging from the ICCPR and the ACHR, widening the vision of universality, even of those whose personal culture would make their approach more restrictive. The other factor is the new threats that ideological, economic, and political world events pose. These two factors will often greatly influence the perception of decision-makers. On the one hand, the reaction of the international community to the narrowness of some interpretation is bound to have an effect on judges and will perhaps lead them to feel the need to review their former stand. On the other hand, new, clear, potential, or actual threats that the changes occurring in the world pose, necessitate a response, if the object and purpose of human rights law is not to be undermined.

[11] The ACHR is the only human rights treaty that includes as non-derogable those state obligations emerging from Art 23 (Right to Participate in Government).

4. The Practice of the Human Rights Committee

The Committee, composed of eighteen members coming from Africa, Asia, Europe, the Middle East, Australia, and the Americas, purports to represent different forms of civilization and of the world's principal legal systems.[12] The members thus emerge from an enormous variety of languages, legal orders, cultures, ideologies, and religions. Members do not necessarily have to have legal experience.[13] The Committee has two main functions: examining state reports and handling individual communications. From the first function has derived—using a creative interpretation—the drafting of General Comments, where the Committee gives instructions to the States on how to report. General Comments have developed into a powerful source of jurisprudence as they are based on what the Committee has said in Concluding Observations at the end to the examination of reports and its Views on individual petitions.

Article 40 of the ICCPR sets forth an undertaking by state parties to submit reports to the Committee 'on the measures they have adopted which give effect to the rights recognized herein and on the progress made in the enjoyment of those rights',[14] providing also information on 'the factors and difficulties, if any, affecting the implementation'[15] of the ICCPR. The Committee is directed to study the reports and 'transmit its [own] reports, and such general comments as it may consider appropriate, to the States Parties'.[16] The Committee receives reporting states in a public hearing, during which members may submit oral questions to the delegation that they request the latter to answer. To develop questions, Committee members depend on information the state's report contains and on what they know in their expert capacity about the situation in a country. They also rely on information that non-governmental organizations produce in written form, a feature that the cryptic Article 40 does not mention, but which has developed in practice. Non-governmental organizations and individuals do not have a right to oral participation in the hearing. The issues the Committee members ultimately examine are thus not necessarily the most important ones for a specific state, and the amount of available information varies with consequences on the concerns expressed and mode of expression.

In examining a state report, the Committee automatically weighs the entire human rights situation in the country and the level of the state's compliance with

[12] ICCPR, Art 31(2).

[13] ICCPR, Art 40; *Optional Protocol to the International Covenant on Civil and Political Rights*, Art 9.

[14] ICCPR, Art 40(1). [15] ICCPR, Art 40(2). [16] ICCPR, Art 40(4).

the ICCPR. Consideration is also given to the impact that it would have on that state or others, were the Committee to express its concern over a particular issue. All this sets a particular tone to the exercise, which has become known as a 'constructive dialogue'. The Committee voices both its praises and its worries or concerns with regard to the state of affairs in the country. What is said and what is omitted during the process is determined as the result of a thoughtful process, in pursuit of the best way to convey a message that could be of influence in the future conduct of the state, due either to its own initiative or the demands of civil society armed with the legitimacy that pronouncements of the Committee confer. Since this exercise is a 'friendly' affair, the position of the Committee member is softer than when dealing only with written, often succinct information, to produce views on an individual case. This does not mean that the function is not ultimately one of interpreting the law and applying it; it only means that the approach is different and less adversarial.

It is clear that in the examination of state reports, legal and non-legal considerations play a part. The factors mentioned above play a role, each one to a different degree. Since deliberations are confidential, it is not possible to show their influence in achieving one or another result, but they can be identified in reading the minutes of the hearings and observing which member asked what questions to the delegation. Leaving aside the personal traits, it can be perceived that changes due to creative interpretation are very linked to certain human rights that are particularly susceptible to fluctuations in the world situation and to the evolution of the culture of the international community.

In its second function, the Committee acts as a quasi-judicial body, interpreting and applying the ICCPR to individual cases. A dispute is submitted, and the Committee member has to give views on the matter. The (First) Protocol to the Convention regulates the procedure, and it is conducted under the framework of legal principles and norms. The procedure is written; the alleged victim and the state are never seen or heard in person. In this function, the member of the Committee has a role similar to that of a judge. The petition contains facts and arguments, which the Committee must consider in order to apply the ICCPR to the specific case. Each Committee member has considerable freedom to assert his or her position with regard to the way to apply the ICCPR to the case, because individual dissenting or concurring opinions are permitted. The sex, religion, legal system, ideology, or other characteristics of the member play an important role, and it may be hard to transcend these individual features to reach an agreement that could be called universal. Personal traits and political views, in a wide sense, sometimes can be detected in the views of the Committee on an individual case, either in the result or in the considerations set forth to interpret the scope and content of a human right.

A good illustration of the prior points, among many possible examples, is how the Committee has dealt with the matter of women in relation to the right to life[17] and

[17] Article 6.

the right not to be tortured or to suffer cruel, inhuman, or degrading treatment or punishment.[18] A review of the Committee's decisions reveals a significant expansion of interpretation in the jurisprudence. The Committee has not been shy, in general, in interpreting creatively the right to life. Already in 1982, General Comment No 6 criticized states for providing the Committee with limited information concerning this provision, 'to only one or other aspect of this right'.[19] The Committee stressed that this is a right 'which should not be interpreted narrowly' and proceeded to inform states that it 'considers that it would be desirable for States parties to take all possible measures to reduce infant mortality and to increase life expectancy, especially in adopting measures to eliminate malnutrition and epidemics'.[20] Neither has there been a lack of enthusiasm in the Committee, or within the UN as a whole, to protect persons from the prohibition in Article 7 of the ICCPR.[21]

Women, however, struggled for a long time to receive their place within the shelter of the ICCPR. Interpretations of the meaning of 'everyone' and 'no one' as the holder of rights has varied throughout time, eventually leading to a progressive inclusion of women and others in a situation of vulnerability and discrimination, as potential victims of human rights violations; only cultural changes can be posited as the basis of this new reading of the ICCPR rights. In turn, women have instigated the changes in culture, taking an 'up in arms' attitude to defend their understanding of the extent and scope of their rights and of state obligations.[22] For a long time previously, women's human rights violations were invisible, sometimes even not intentionally, due to the blind failure to recognize certain state conduct or omissions as potential violations of human rights when the alleged victims were women, because of the manner in which the content and extent of rights were construed or read.

[18] Article 7.

[19] UNHRC, 'CCPR General Comment No 6: The Right to Life (Art 6)' (30 April 1982), para 1, reprinted in 'Note by the Secretariat: Compilation of General Comments and General Recommendations Adopted by Human Rights Treaty Bodies' (2003) UN Doc HRI/GEN/1/Rev.7, 128.

[20] HRC, 'General Comment No 6' (n 19) paras 1, 5.

[21] The Committee has issued two General Comments on Art 7: HRC, 'CCPR General Comment No 20: Article 7 (Prohibition of Torture, or Other Cruel, Inhuman or Degrading Treatment or Punishment' (10 March 1992), replacing HRC, 'CCPR General Comment No 7: Article 7 (Prohibition of Torture or Cruel, Inhuman or Degrading Treatment of Punishment' (30 May 1982) reprinted in 'Note by the Secretariat: Compilation of General Comments and General Recommendations Adopted by Human Rights Treaty Bodies' (27 May 2008) UN Doc HRI/GEN/1/Rev.9. There is also a Convention against Torture and Other Cruel, Inhuman or Degrading Treatment or Punishment, with its own Committee, and an Optional Protocol to the Convention, with a significant emphasis on prevention.

[22] Since the Vienna Conference of 1993 and the 1995 Beijing Conference, the vertiginous change is noticeable. See R Christopher Preston and Ronald Z Ahrens, 'United Nations Convention Documents in Light of Feminist Theory' (2001) 8 *Mich J Gender & L* 1; Stephanie Farrior, 'Human Rights Advocacy on Gender Issues: Challenges and Opportunities' (2009) 1 *JHRP* 83; Dianne Otto, 'Women's Rights' in Daniel Moeckli, Sangeeta Shah, and Sandesh Sivakumaran (eds), *International Human Rights Law* (OUP 2010).

The Committee now views female genital mutilation as a violation of the right of all human beings not to be 'subjected to torture or to cruel, inhuman or degrading treatment or punishment'[23] and of the right of children to request measures of protection from the state.[24] Linking this practice with Article 7 appears to have been done only in the concluding observations made to Sudan in 1997.[25] General Comment No 28 of 2000 then commanded the attention of states in which this egregious violation was occurring, asking them to provide the Committee with information on its extent and on measures to eliminate it, as well as the measures of protection 'for women whose rights under Article 7 have been violated'.[26] In further action, the Committee made an important decision against Canada involving creative interpretation of Article 7. The case concerned a young girl and the risk of female genital mutilation should she be removed from Canada to Guinea.[27] The Committee stated that 'there is no question that subjecting a woman to genital mutilation amounts to treatment prohibited under article 7 of the Covenant', and it recalled that states parties are under an obligation not to extradite, expel, or refouler, individuals who as a consequence would be exposed to a real risk of being killed or being subjected to torture or cruel, inhuman or degrading treatment or punishment.[28] It thus found a violation by Canada.

The same evolution can be seen with regard to the law on the total or partial criminalization of abortion. The Committee did not mention the problem of criminalized abortion until 1996, apparently on the legal basis that the ICCPR does not include a right to have an abortion. This justification started to disappear in 1996.[29] From that year on, the issue of abortion started to be mentioned, for example in the concluding observations to the Reports of Peru, Ecuador, Chile, Costa Rica, Lesotho, and Tanzania.[30] Now, according to General Comment No 28, it is the Committee's view that criminalization of abortion may violate the right to life of Article 6 and/or the right to personal integrity of Article 7.[31] Making abortion a

[23] Article 7. [24] Article 24.

[25] HRC, 'Concluding Observations: Sudan' (19 November 1997) UN Doc CCPR/C/79/Add. 85, para 10.

[26] HRC, 'General Comment No 28: Equality of Rights between Men and Women (art 3)' (29 March 2000) UN Doc CCPR/C/21/Rev.1/Add/10, para 11.

[27] *Kaba v Canada.* [28] *Kaba* (n 27) para 10.1.

[29] Again, the momentum acquired by the women's movement after Vienna (1993) and Beijing (1995) must be mentioned.

[30] HRC, 'Concluding Observations: Peru' (18 November 1996) UN Doc CCPR/C/79/Add.72, paras 15, 22; HRC, 'Concluding Observations: Ecuador' (18 August 1998) UN Doc CCPR/C/79/Add.92, para 11; HRC, 'Concluding Observations: United Republic of Tanzania' (18 August 1998) UN Doc CCPR/C/79/Add.97, para 15; HRC 'Report to the General Assembly' (1999) UN Doc A/54/40 Vol I, para 211 (Chile), para 254 (Lesotho), para 254 (Costa Rica).

[31] HRC, 'General Comment No 28' (n 26) paras 10, 11.

criminal offence has serious consequences on these two rights, particularly for poor women, something that has been well known for quite some time.[32]

This new interpretation has remained constant and particularly associated with the threat that criminalization of abortion poses for women's right to life.[33] General Comment No 28 was a welcome signal for women affected by state actions in the area of their sexual and reproductive lives. In 2002, the first case on denial of abortion was presented to the Committee against Peru. An under-aged girl, whom a public hospital had denied her legal right to terminate the pregnancy of an anencephalic foetus due to the risk for life of the mother, brought the case.[34] The girl gave birth to an anencephalic daughter who was (forcibly) breast-fed by the mother until the baby died, four days later, leading to the mother's deep depression. She claimed the violation of Articles 6, 7, 17, and 24 of the ICCPR, among other rights.[35] The Committee, invoking General Comment No 20 on the fact that Article 7 also relates to mental suffering, found a violation of this right and did not consider it necessary to make a finding on Article 6.[36] The Committee also found violations of Article 17, on privacy, and Article 24, on the rights of the child.[37]

A second case, against Argentina,[38] dealt with a rape and the subsequent pregnancy of a permanently impaired young woman. A public hospital refused to terminate the pregnancy, although Article 86, paragraph 2 of the Criminal Code described the situation at hand as one allowing a non-punishable abortion. The mother of the victim had to appeal to the Supreme Court to obtain an affirmative answer to her petition, after which the hospital denied her the abortion, because the pregnancy was too advanced. The family managed to arrange a clandestine abortion. The facts of the case showed the extreme lengths to which Argentinean society and public officers went to deny this young woman her legal right, starting with an injunction to prevent a procedure that was about to be performed. The Rector of the Catholic University and the spokesperson of the Corporation of Catholic Lawyers exerted strong pressure on the situation; religion undoubtedly exercised enormous influence on doctors from public hospitals and member of the judiciary.[39] In spite

[32] In 1967, the World Health Assembly (WHA) already acknowledged abortion as a serious health problem. WHA Res 20.41 (25 May 1967), quoted in World Health Organization (WHO), 'Safe Motherhood: Studying Unsafe Abortion: A Practical Guide' (1996) WHO/RHT/MSM/96.25.

[33] HRC, 'Concluding Observations: Argentina' (31 March 2010) UN Doc CCPR/C/ARG/CO/4, para 13; HRC, 'Concluding Observations: Mexico' (17 May 2010) CCPR/C/MEX/CO/5, para 10; HRC, 'Concluding Observations: Colombia' (4 August 2010) UN Doc CCPR/C/COL/CO/6, para 19; HRC, 'Concluding Observations: Poland' (15 November 2010) UN Doc CCPR/C/POL/CO/6, para 12; HRC, 'Concluding Observations: El Salvador' (18 November 2010) UN Doc CCPR/C/SLV/CO/6, paras 9, 10.

[34] *Llantoy Huamán v Peru.*

[35] *Llantoy Huamán* (n 34) para 6.3.

[36] There was a dissenting opinion in that regard from one member of the Committee, Hipolito Solari Irigoyen.

[37] *Llantoy Huamán* (n 34) paras 6.4, 6.5.

[38] *LMR v Argentina.*

[39] *LMR* (n 38) paras 2.4, 2.7–2.9.

of this and the arguments of the state, the Committee found violations of Articles 7, 17, and 2.3, in relation to Articles 3, 7, and 17 of the ICCPR.[40]

An under-aged, indigenous victim, complaining of rape and the unacceptable treatment she had received at the hands of the state's agents, also initiated the case *LNP v Argentina*. The Committee found an additional violation of Article 26, due to 'discrimination based on the author's gender and ethnicity', because she was subjected to tests to determine whether or not she was a virgin and was investigated to see if she was a prostitute, to conclude that she had not demonstrated lack of consent to the sexual act.[41] Violations of Articles 7, 14, 17, and 24 were also found.[42]

To sum up, concluding observations at the end of the examination of state reports and general comments—developed on the basis of these observations and the Committee's views in individual communications—are instruments that develop creatively the understanding of the rights in the ICCPR. Since the examination of reports ends with a unanimous conclusion, personal factors play a minor role. Committee members have to be open to the points of view of others and clear in insisting on what they consider important. The Committee has apparently deemed it more important to find a proper manner to carry out its function in a way that will produce more effective results in promoting and defending human rights, than to risk the criticism that it is exceeding the boundaries of its powers, providing that there is clear support for its position in the international community and a significant number of states. The Committee's views on individual petitions generally have been subsequent to the creative interpretations that concluding observations and General Comments have elaborated and developed. In the exercise of all of its functions, the Committee has been creative almost always when the existing international circumstances support the new interpretation. None of the examples reveals that the Committee has exceeded its powers, but have rather revealed the contrary.

5. The Practice of the Inter-American Court

The Court is composed of judges, and therefore its essence, like any other judicial body, is to interpret and apply the law in individual cases. As stated in Article 63 of the ACHR, the Court is directed to decide if there has been a violation of a right or freedom that the ACHR protects. Its function, thus, is to interpret and apply the

40 *LMR* (n 38) para 10.

41 *LMR* (n 38) para 13.3.

42 *LNP v Argentina*, paras 13.3–13.8.

ACHR to the set of circumstances that forms a case. The composition of the Court is more homogeneous than that of the Committee. Judges must all be lawyers, and of the seven judges, six have always come from the Latin American region, with comparable legal systems and almost all Spanish-speaking;[43] the seventh judge has been elected from the English-speaking Caribbean islands.

The Court has a strong sense of unity, and its jurisprudence has a clear Latin American accent. Many of the judges have a past linked to the defence of human rights. The record of the Court as a whole, and of certain judges in particular, demonstrates that they have consistently felt the need to apply the ACHR as creatively as possible to counter the authoritarian tendencies of those who have ruled the continent and the tendency of society to maintain privileges that lead to discrimination. The Court's approach has been to interpret its powers, and the human rights set forth in the ACHR, understanding that its judicial mandate is to flesh out the provisions of the ACHR for the true enjoyment of human rights by the people in the continent. This has been neither unwise, nor has it exceeded the Court's powers. Aside from the fact that its functions required this approach, if the Court was to be effective as a human rights organ, the text of the ACHR points in that direction through the ample formulation of Article 29.[44]

The Court reads and applies the ACHR based on a set of premises, all coming from accepted rules of interpretation. First, it views the ACHR as a living instrument. The Court has used this term many times, explaining that an evolutionary interpretation of international instruments of protection is consistent with the general rules of treaty interpretation in the 1969 VCLT. This means that the interpretation of human right treaties 'must consider the changes over time and present-day conditions'.[45] Second, the Court operates to apply the *corpus juris* of international human rights law, comprising a set of international instruments of varied content and juridical effect (treaties, conventions, resolutions, and declarations), which leads the Court to interpret the ACHR 'in the context of the evolution of the fundamental rights of the human person in contemporary international law'.[46] This premise has allowed the Court to enrich its interpretation of human rights and the ACHR's obligations for states by incorporating advancements made in other treaties relevant to the subject matter. Article 29 of the ACHR has aided it in this.

[43] It is possible for one of these judges to be a Portuguese speaker from Brazil. Brazil shares most of the characteristics of Spanish-speaking Latinos, except for the language. Usually, Brazilians can understand and speak Spanish.

[44] See ICCPR, Art 29(b), (c).

[45] See eg *The Right to Information on Consular Assistance in the Framework of the Guarantees of the Due Process of Law*, paras 112–114, where it quotes, inter alia, the advisory opinion *On the Legal Consequences for States of the Continued Presence of South Africa in Namibia* of the International Court of Justice and judgments of the European Court of Human Rights.

[46] *The Right to Information on Consular Assistance* (n 45) para 115.

Third, the use of the concept *effet utile* to find the correct interpretation has played a significant part in the evolution of norms. The understanding is that the Court should not interpret a treaty in a way that renders the provision totally or partially ineffective. In contrast to the Committee's jurisprudence in cases and in concluding observations on reports, the Court has not advanced much in developing this continent's 'values',[47] but has instead focused more on what is needed to strengthen democracy, with a strong emphasis on the improvement of courts and due process, as well as on ensuring full rights to significant groups of people left out by discriminatory practices and a limited conception of the scope and content of rights. In this practice, the history of Latin America and sometimes powerful global and regional social movements, have strongly influenced the Court.

A few examples will show how much the Court has developed the inter-American human rights system. The first is the judgment in the *Velásquez* case,[48] which had to address a major problem regarding the attribution of responsibility to the state of Honduras for human rights violations perpetrated with the utmost care not to leave any trace behind that might implicate the state. If states must ensure the free and full 'exercise' of rights,[49] it seems obvious that they will have to intervene not only through the enactment of laws, but also through changing administrative practices, adjusting judicial decisions to make them compatible with the ACHR, and even seeing to it that society changes its discriminatory practices.[50] These ideas are behind paragraphs 166 and 167 of the *Velásquez* judgment, on the obligations of states to respect and to ensure human rights. Here, the Court used its powers to interpret the ACHR to give it an *effet utile*.[51] *Velásquez*'s interpretation of Article 1 has developed greatly in different contexts and has had a pivotal role in the development of all ACHR rights, particularly in the area of reparations.

In the same spirit, the Court decided several cases alleging violations of the rights of indigenous peoples. A major aspect of these cases related to the interpretation of Article 21 on the right to property. The facts revealed the serious straits of

[47] Values here refer to terms of the sexual conduct of individuals, from women's new roles to abortion, sexual orientation biases, and the like, which evidently are not considerations that a modern, integrated society might wish to entertain.

[48] *Velásquez-Rodríguez v Honduras.*

[49] See ACHR, Art 1: 'The States Parties to this Convention undertake to respect the rights and freedoms recognized herein and to ensure to all persons subject to their jurisdiction the free and full exercise of those rights and freedoms, without any discrimination for reasons of race, color, sex, language, religion, political or other opinion, national or social origin, economic status, birth, or any other social condition.'

[50] See Cecilia Medina Quiroga, *La Convención Americana: Teoría y Jurisprudencia: Vida, Integridad Personal, Libertad Personal, Debido Proceso y Recurso Judicial* (Universidad de Chile, Centro de Derechos Humanos 2005) 16–21.

[51] A form of interpretation of treaties and other instruments, derived from French administrative law which looks to the object and purpose of a treaty, as well as the context, to make the treaty more effective. John P Grant and J Craig Baker (eds), *Encyclopaedic Dictionary of International Law* (3rd edn, OUP 2009).

indigenous people in several countries of the continent: problems of malnutrition, lack of medical care and food, and discriminatory treatment. At the core of the problem was the lack of land, denying them the ability to acquire their food and carry out the community life that was the basis of their cultural and spiritual world, and of their economic subsistence. Several other human rights were implicated as well as the right to property. Indigenous peoples gathered[52] and began to reclaim their human rights, developing and invoking, among other instruments, ILO Convention No 169 and the UN Declaration on the Rights of Indigenous Peoples. This changed the legal and political context in which the struggle of indigenous peoples—who are not mentioned as such in the regional instruments—was being carried out until the cases reached the Court.

The judgments illustrate the importance of transcending national legal orders and the set conceptions that derive from the types of societies in which such orders were established. The concept of property common in the Civil Codes of the American continent is that of private individual property; that could have been mechanically applied as such to Article 21. It was clear, however, that there were significant human settlements or communities in that continent composed of people who had a different concept, particularly over the relationship of individuals with land, which played an essential role in their spiritual and social life.

Article 21 was first interpreted in the case of the *Mayagna Community (SUMO) Awas Tingni v Nicaragua*. Nicaragua, which recognized communal property and indigenous peoples,[53] had failed to regulate the procedure to realize this right. This situation additionally was causing the Community a significant vulnerability regarding access to food, medical attention, and sanitary services, all of which constituted a continuous threat to their survival and integrity.[54] The Court resorted for guidance to the *travaux préparatoires* of the ACHR and observed that the concept of the right 'to the use and enjoyment of his property' had replaced the right to 'private property' in the draft.[55] It also explained that the terms of an international human rights treaty are autonomous, a reasonable assumption since the standards the regional organ is to develop must transcend national laws.[56] The Court reasoned that the ACHR is a living instrument, and the Court could not ignore the reality to which it had to apply the treaty norms. It examined the indigenous conception of property as communal in nature and the tight bond of the Community with their ancestral lands, this being the fundamental basis of their culture, spiritual life, integrity, and economic survival. Basing itself also on national law, the Court stated that '[a]s a result of customary practices, possession of the land should suffice for

[52] The first Conference on Aboriginal peoples, which the United Nations organized, took place in 1977.

[53] *Mayagna Community (SUMO) Awas Tingni v Nicaragua*, para 150.

[54] *Mayagna Community* (n 53) para 83 (expert opinion of Rodolfo Stavenhagen Gruenbaum).

[55] *Mayagna Community* (n 53) para 145.

[56] *Mayagna Community* (n 53) para 146.

indigenous communities lacking real title to property of the land to obtain official recognition of that property, and for consequent registration'.[57]

The Court was thus faced with one interpretation of a human right as traditionally understood, but which left aside the protection of many people. It therefore decided to apply carefully all of the possibilities offered by the rules of interpretation, among others that of *effet utile*, to try to find out or uncover the true meaning of a right to which 'everyone' was entitled, so that in fact everybody would be able to enjoy the right. As a conclusion, the Court stated that:

> [I]t is the opinion of this Court that article 21 of the Convention protects the right to property in a sense which includes, among others, the rights of members of the indigenous communities within the framework of communal property, which is also recognized by the Constitution of Nicaragua.[58]

Consequent to this definition, the Court ordered Nicaragua, inter alia, to delimit, demarcate, and title the Mayagna territory, and in the meantime to abstain from actions that might lead state agents to affect or to acquiesce to third parties affecting the territory in any way.[59]

In the *Yakye Axa* case,[60] a similar situation occurred,[61] so the conclusion was bound to be the same.[62] The Court expanded its examination, however, by making use of ILO Convention No 169[63] as it dealt with a different aspect of the state's obligations with regard to land. It had to do so, because there were conflicting claims by other private owners in the territory.[64] It also decided that it was necessary to recognize a legal status for the indigenous community in Paraguay, in order for them to enjoy their land. The Court included this finding under the state's obligations with regard to Article 21.[65]

In the two cases examined above, the Court applied not only the ACHR, but also the national legal order of the state concerned; in one it also applied ILO Convention 169. In two cases involving Suriname, however, neither the national legal order nor the ILO Convention No 169 helped in the analysis.[66] In Suriname, land not belonging to registered individuals belongs to the state by default.[67] In the case of *Moiwana*, the N'djuka clans living in Moiwana Village fled following a military attack and were internally displaced or living as refugees in French Guiana. As the state did not

57 *Mayagna Community* (n 53) para 151.

58 *Mayagna Community* (n 53) para 148.

59 *Mayagna Community* (n 53) para 153.

60 *Case of the Yakye Axa Indigenous Community v Paraguay.*

61 *Yakye Axa* (n 60) paras 140, 141.

62 For similar cases, see *Case of the Sawhoyamaxa Indigenous Community v Paraguay*; *Case of the Xákmok Kásek Indigenous Community v Paraguay.*

63 See *Yakye Axa* (n 60) paras 126, 127, 130.

64 *Yakye Axa* (n 60) paras 143–148.

65 *Yakye Axa* (n 60) paras 81–86.

66 *Case of the Moiwana Community v Suriname*; *Case of the Saramaka People v Suriname.*

67 *Moiwana Community* (n 66) paras 129–130.

present arguments regarding Article 21,[68] the Court used documentary and expert evidence to prove the attachment of the N'djuka clans to Moiwana Village and the unique and enduring ties that bound the community to the territory. It concluded that it considered the Moiwana Community 'the legitimate owners of their traditional lands', having therefore 'the right to the use and enjoyment of that territory'.[69] In order that the Moiwana Community could enjoy their land, the Court ordered Suriname to adopt all necessary measures to ensure the property rights of the community's members, including inter alia a mechanism for the delimitation, demarcation, and titling of the territories, and to ensure the safety of the community when returning to the land.[70]

In the case of *the Saramaka People v Suriname*, the legal situation in the country was similar to that of the Moiwana case. The Court used Article 29 of the ACHR and examined the two International Covenants to which Suriname was a party,[71] the ICCPR and the International Covenant on Economic, Social and Cultural Rights. The Court read Article 21 in terms of Article 1 of the latter, on the right to self-determination, and in terms of Article 27 of the former, on the rights of members of minorities,[72] to come to the conclusion that Article 21 imposes a duty on states to adopt all measures 'to recognize, respect, protect and guarantee the communal property right of the members of the Saramaka community' to the land which they had traditionally occupied.[73]

Another remarkable example of creative interpretation is what the Court has done in the area of reparations; the possible clash between the Court and the state does not happen only in regard to the legislative powers, but also in relation to the domestic executive branch and judiciary. It is not a matter of allegedly establishing new rights; it is the logical consequences the Court extracts from the obligations of states, particularly the obligation to ensure the effective enjoyment of guaranteed rights.

In the development of reparations law, the Committee has been less creative than the Court. However, the wording of Article 63 of the ACHR facilitates the task of the Court and has no equivalent in the ICCPR. Instead of stating, as the Optional Protocol to the ICCPR does, that '[t]he Committee shall forward its views to the State Party concerned and to the individual',[74] Article 63(1) of the ACHR directs the Court to order 'that the consequences of the measure or situation that constituted the breach of such right or freedom be remedied and that fair compensation be paid to the injured party'.[75] On this ground, the Court has made the ACHR effective

[68] *Moiwana Community* (n 66) para 124. [69] *Moiwana Community* (n 66) paras 132–134.

[70] *Moiwana Community* (n 66) paras 209, 212.

[71] *Saramaku People* (n 66) para 93. [72] *Saramaka People* (n 66) para 95.

[73] *Saramaka People* (n 66) paras 95–96. [74] ICCPR Optional Protocol, Art 5(4).

[75] Full text: 'If the Court finds that there has been a violation of a right or freedom protected by this Convention, the Court shall rule that the injured party be ensured the enjoyment of his right or freedom that was violated. It shall also rule, if appropriate, that the consequences of the measure or

in terms of the lives of the victims and the incorporation of international human rights standards in the domestic legal order and practice of states. This has taken place in a continent where, aside from its history of *caudillismo* and dictatorship, extreme inequalities prevail, particularly on grounds of poverty, ethnicity, sex, and sexual orientation. The Court's conception of reparations is well explained in the *Sawhoyamaxa* case.[76] It is clear that the Court conceives of reparations as a way to make states comply with the obligation the ACHR imposes to ensure rights in each specific case. It touches aspects such as needed cultural changes[77] and the creation of state organs[78] that are necessary to comply with health objectives (because of the threat to the right to life) or with educational ones (to combat discrimination).

With regard to the judiciary, the development of the 'right to the truth', subsumed by the Court under Articles 8 and 25, has permitted family members of the disappeared, for example, to instigate criminal investigations.[79] It has given guidelines to the national courts to include the gender perspective in criminal trials for disappearances, ill-treatment, and deprivation of life that occurred in a context of mass violations of the rights of young, poor, and vulnerable women.[80] It has ordered training for judges and other judiciary bodies.[81] As to the impact on governments, the Court has ordered measures, such as providing indigenous communities with water, medical assistance, food, and financial and human resources for schools, among others.[82] Guarantees of non-repetition also form part of the reparations the Court requires, and much has been done in that regard.[83]

Examples of this type of decision abound. Has the Court exceeded its powers? It has not, given that the whole point of international human rights law is to ensure the enjoyment of rights in the domestic legal order and practice every day and in every moment. It is clear that states in Latin America are slowly complying with

situation that constituted the breach of such right or freedom be remedied and that fair compensation be paid to the injured party.'

[76] *Sawhoyamaxa Indigenous Community* (n 62) paras 195–198.

[77] *Case of González et al ('Cotton Field') v Mexico*, paras 541, 602.23.

[78] *Case of Aloeboetoe et al v Suriname*, para 96; *Case of Vélez Loor v Panama*, para 272.

[79] See eg I/A Court HR, *Case of Durand and Ugarte v Peru*, para 130; *Case of Bámaca-Velásquez v Guatemala*, para 201; Case of Barrios Altos *v Peru*, para 48; *Case of Humberto Sánchez v Honduras*, para 136; *Velásquez-Rodríguez* (n 48) paras 181, 188; *Case of Blake v Guatemala*, para 97; *Case of the Serrano-Cruz Sisters v El Salvador*, paras 64, 65; *Case of Gomes Lund et al v Brazil*, para 180.

[80] *'Cotton Field'* (n 77) para 455. See also *Case of Fernández Ortega et al v Mexico*.

[81] *Case of the* Caracazo *v Venezuela*, para 143.4.a; *Case of Myrna Mack Chang v Guatemala*, para 282; *Case of Gelman v Uruguay*, paras 276–278; *Vélez Loor* (n 78) para 272; *Gomes Lund* (n 79) para 283; *Case of Ibsen-Cárdenas and Ibsen-Peña v Bolivia*, para 258.

[82] *Sawhoyamaxa Indigenous Community* (n 62) paras 230–233; *Xákmok Kásek Indigenous Community* (n 62) paras 300–309.

[83] See eg *Case of 'The Last Temptation of Christ' (Olmedo-Bustos et al) v Chile*; Case *of Trujillo-Oroza v Bolivia*, paras 94–97; *Case of Palamara-Iribarne v Chile*, paras 269.14, 269.15; Fernández Ortega (n 80) para 271; *Case of Usón Ramírez v Venezuela*, paras 199.7–199.9; *Case of Dacosta-Cadogan v Barbados*, para 128.9; *Case of Rosendo-Cantú et al v Mexico*, para 295.16.

this obligation enunciated by the Court and, what is more important, recognizing the authority of the Court to do what it is doing, even as they do not as yet fully observe many judgments. States, through the treaty, gave the Court its powers; if a significant majority agrees to the manner in which the Court exercises these powers, there is no reason to wonder if this is law-making or policy-making. Were the states' acceptance to dwindle, the situation would have to be reviewed.

6. Conclusions

The function of judicial or quasi-judicial bodies is to interpret and to apply the law to a set of factual circumstances that constitute the situation or case under examination. This task is, therefore, different in essence from that of creating a norm when interpreting it. If the body concerned exceeds the boundaries surrounding the provision it is supposed to apply (*ratione materiae*), we can properly speak of a deviation of its powers. However, within the boundaries set by the legal provisions, judicial or quasi-judicial bodies have variable latitude (and obligations) to interpret the norm in a creative way. The nature of the legal corpus to be applied and the regulations given to the body by its statute of creation, determine this latitude.

International human rights treaty bodies have not, in general, exceeded their powers, because international law gives them the directive to determine the most suitable interpretation to guarantee the rights of individuals and, at the same time, the capacity and the rules to interpret law creatively. States parties have the obligation not only to respect the rights the treaties recognize, but also to ensure and give them effect (as set forth in Article 2 of the ICCPR), or to give them effect while respecting and ensuring their free and full exercise (according to Articles 1 and 2 of the ACHR). The Inter-American Court, more than the Committee, has made use of these powers to improve rights and make stricter obligations, with the aim of allowing human beings the full enjoyment of their rights. The examples given here have also shown that the development of creative interpretation is usually dependent on the cultural changes of the international community.

The above assessment is not a detailed study of what the Committee and the Court have done from the perspective of this analysis, but nonetheless it is possible to conclude that it would be difficult to find judicial or quasi-judicial decisions of these organs that go beyond the confines of creative interpretation to engage in law-making. In the field of international human rights law, there would be little point in establishing committees, commissions, and courts that did not have the power to develop and flesh out principles and general norms, because it is this capacity that helps influence states to comply with their international human rights obligations.

Further Reading

Boschiero N (ed), *International Courts and the Development of International Law* (TMC Asser Press 2013)

Grant JP and Baker JC (eds), *Encyclopaedic Dictionary of International Law* (3rd edn, OUP 2009)

Hart HLA, *The Concept of Law* (2nd edn, Clarendon Press 1994)

Medina Quiroga C, *La Convención Americana: Teoría y Jurisprudencia: Vida, Integridad Personal, Libertad Personal, Debido Proceso y Recurso Judicial* (Universidad de Chile, Centro de Derechos Humanos 2005)

Shelton D, 'Form, Function and the Powers of International Courts' (2009) 9 *Chi J Int'l L* 537

CHAPTER 28

UNIVERSALITY AND THE GROWTH OF REGIONAL SYSTEMS

CHRISTOF HEYNS
MAGNUS KILLANDER[1]

1. Introduction

INTERNATIONAL human rights law has, in the course of the last sixty years, grown into the closest approximation the world has to a globally accepted and enforced code of ethics. Violations clearly continue to occur, but those who depart from human rights standards in exercising power must increasingly justify themselves and come under pressure to change their behaviour to conform to the adopted norms. Human rights could perhaps be seen, then, as a universal language on the acceptable use of power. Whether this metaphor is accurate or not (some comments thereon will be made in the course of this contribution), it is clear that human rights has become a central organizing principle of the modern era.

The main argument for the legitimacy of human rights lies in its universality, reflected, for example, in the name of the Universal Declaration of Human Rights. The appeal of human rights is widely understood to derive from the universality

[1] We thank Frans Viljoen and Dinah Shelton for their comments on an earlier draft.

of norms that it posits—broadly speaking, it sets the same standards for everyone. This uniform application, however, is qualified by the fact that human rights law sets only minimum standards in respect of a number of core interests; it does not present a comprehensive normative system. In fact, one of the reasons for its wide acceptance is that, unlike eg religion, it claims space for people to pursue freely their own conceptions of what constitutes a good life.[2] Human rights also holds out the promise of norm enforcement, in the sense that 'something will be done' to protect the values that it recognizes, in the form of legal remedies or other forms of pressure and accountability. Such an idea will have an obvious appeal to people from all backgrounds, who are looking for common ground while retaining their own identities.

By promising to treat everyone alike, human rights is an idea that is highly 'communicable'—it is imminently suitable to spread through communication and persuasion. In a world largely constituted by the easy flow of communication across the globe, it is understandable that the concept of human rights gained rapid acceptance. Universality of norms, however, has its limitations.[3] The mere fact that the same norms are formally applicable to everyone does not necessarily imply that they resonate with the values of the people to whom they apply. While some of the core interests that human rights protect clearly enjoy protection in terms of the higher values of the main normative systems of the world (such as the right to life and the dignity of all people), other values (for example, freedom of expression or non-discrimination on the basis of gender or sexual orientation) may lack the same support at present. Moreover, consensus does not necessarily exist on how to interpret these values in practice, how and why to limit the exercise of rights, or on their relative importance when they come into conflict. Disagreement also attends the issue of norm enforcement: on how to apply them in particular cases. Perceived 'external' ideas may offend local custom.

Legitimacy requires foundations. Where consensus is not possible, meaningful participation by all parties in the process to determine the standards, institutions, and procedures adopted provides at least a starting point—not a panacea, but probably the strongest point of departure—for a sense of ownership of and commitment to human rights. Thus, for human rights to make a credible claim to legitimacy in the world community, universality of participation is required, in respect of both norm recognition and norm enforcement. Participation will remain a central challenge—and credential—for human rights in the future, if it is to retain its relevance.

A scan of the human right environment today shows that human rights is driven by formal or legal, as well as informal or extra-legal, actions alike. A multiplicity of

[2] See eg Amartya Sen, *Development as Freedom* (OUP 1999).

[3] For a discussion of various critiques of human rights, see eg David Kennedy, *The Dark Sides of Virtue: Reassessing International Humanitarianism* (Princeton UP 2005).

state and non-state actors engage in and contribute to the setting and enforcement of authoritative standards in the field of human rights.[4]

On the global level, the United Nations (UN) largely drives the human rights law system, supplemented by international humanitarian law and international criminal law. The United Nations has seen a significant expansion in the number of its active participants since it foundations were laid at the end of the Second World War. This has included a considerable expansion in the number and geographical representation of the UN member states, as a result of the independence of former colonies. These newly formed states in many respects changed the balance of power in the UN's human rights work, or at least have the potential to do so.[5] Active participation by non-state actors, such as non-governmental organizations (NGOs), in the work of the UN and beyond, is also a central feature of the global human rights project. It has been argued that the system as it exists today only emerged during the 1970s, due to the formation of the leading human rights NGOs.[6]

Parallel to the global human rights structures, regional initiatives form part of the international human rights system. In fact, even before the main components of the United Nations human rights machinery were set up, the Council of Europe and the Organization of American States established regional systems. In the 1980s, a system for Africa was established by the then Organization of African Unity. These three systems add an important feature to international human rights law that the global or universal system—the United Nations—does not provide: they give individuals access to international courts that make legally binding decisions in respect of human rights.

Other regional (including sub-regional) inter-governmental organizations around the world have also started incorporating human rights into their objectives in recent years. Some have created human rights initiatives, if not fully equipped human rights systems. These include initiatives in Asia and the Arab-speaking world, as well as sub-regional bodies in Europe, the Americas, and Africa that have also taken human rights on board.

The emergence of regional systems and initiatives constitutes an important dimension of broader participation in the international human rights project. These systems provide platforms to states and civil society, where people from all parts of the world can potentially make their voices heard in the global human rights discourse, often with greater likelihood of success than if they were to compete among themselves and with others in the conference rooms of the UN. Regional systems are in a position to play an important role in ensuring that the international human

[4] See in this regard, Janet Levit, 'Bottom-Up International Lawmaking: Reflections on the New Haven School of International Law' (2007) 32 *Yale J Int'l L* 393.

[5] See further Lynn Hunt, *Inventing Human Rights: A History* (Norton 2007); Mark Mazower, *No Enchanted Palace: The End of Empire and the Ideological Origins of the United Nations* (Princeton UP 2009).

[6] See Samuel Moyn, *The Last Utopia: Human Rights in History* (Harvard UP 2010).

rights project is more responsive to local needs and concerns, and as such they can add to the legitimacy of international human rights. This potential has only been realized to a limited extent.

A common lament about the UN human rights system is that 'Geneva is very far away'. Regional systems help to cross this distance and benefit from their position closer to the ground. This proximity accounts in large part for the feasibility of establishing supervisory mechanisms that take legally binding decisions; there are regional human rights courts, but not a world human rights court. Regional mechanisms are generally closer to the people they serve—the governments involved, the complainants, those who act on their behalf, and the sources of information. It is, in many cases, easier to gain a working consensus about the specific norms to protect and how to interpret them in a particular region than on the global level. The same applies to ensuring compliance with the decisions of such courts through the ties between these societies. It has also been noted that in some cases, repressive regimes are more willing to accept regional than global human rights supervision.[7]

As a result, regional human rights mechanisms can serve to make the international human rights project as a whole more responsive and more democratic. The opportunities for participation that the regional systems offer can help bridge the gap between the universality of human rights norms, on the one hand, and the cultural-rootedness of norms, on the other. Human rights develop as a response to specific historical circumstances and should be understood primarily not as the pursuit of abstract notions of justice, but rather as a reaction to concrete experiences of injustice.[8] The inclusion of regional human rights systems in the broader body of international human rights law can therefore serve to ensure that the global system more closely reflects the historical, and often localized, concrete experiences of humanity as a whole.[9] This is not to prioritize the regional over the global, but rather to say that both play important roles.

There are also limits to regional initiatives, necessary in order not to undermine the global human rights project. The UN began to support the formation of regional systems only after the Covenants were in place in the 1970s; it previously viewed them as 'breakaway movements' that could weaken the claim of universality.[10] Even

[7] See eg in respect of the willingness of the Pinochet government in Chile to accept an Organization of America States (OAS), but not a UN, fact-finding mission, Thomas Buergenthal 'International and Regional Human Rights Law and Institutions: Some Examples of Their Interaction' (1977) 12 *Tex Int'l LJ* 321, 326.

[8] Christof Heyns, 'A "Struggle Approach" to Human Rights' in Christof Heyns and Karen Stefiszyn (eds), *Human Rights, Peace and Justice in Africa: A Reader* (Pretoria University Law Press 2006).

[9] According to Helen Stacy, 'regions are also communities of memory'. Helen Stacy, *Human Rights for the 21st Century: Sovereignty, Civil Society, Culture* (Stanford UP 2009) 146.

[10] UNGA 'Regional Arrangements for the Promotion and Protection of Human Rights' (20 March 2009) UN Doc A/Res/63/170. See Karel Vasak and Philip Alston (eds), *The International Dimension of Human Rights* (Greenwood Press 1982) 451.

now, there is a danger that the emergence of regional systems and initiatives might undermine the standards set at the global level. Precisely because human rights language is so dominant, states may pay lip service to it in regional systems, while undercutting the system from the inside. Such regional initiatives, taken under the banner of human rights, and established institutions may in fact be so-called 'pretenders', rather than 'protectors' of human rights that aim to shield states from global supervision.[11]

The first Arab Charter on Human Rights of 1994, for example, was widely considered to represent a retreat from global norms, and as a result it did not gain international traction. The Arab League later requested some Arab members of UN treaty bodies to prepare a new draft of the Charter, more in line with international standards. Adopted in 2004, even the new Charter has been criticized for not being fully in line with international human rights law.[12] In another example, in late 2012 the African Union has been pursuing the establishment of a regional criminal court that could potentially undermine the global system of personal accountability for some of the most egregious crimes and violations of human rights.[13] It is noticeable that the draft protocol does not refer to the International Criminal Court and does not present its role as complementary to the global institution.

Initiatives in Asia are also being monitored. The Association of South-East Asian Nations (ASEAN) established an Intergovernmental Commission on Human Rights that drafted a Declaration on Human Rights adopted by the ASEAN Summit in November 2012.[14] The UN High Commissioner, in commenting on this development, has noted that regional instruments 'should complement and reinforce international human rights standards'.[15] She further stated that '[t]he process through which this crucial Declaration is adopted is almost as important as the content of the Declaration itself', and called for extensive civil society engagement before adoption of the Declaration.[16]

[11] See Human Rights Watch, *Protectors or Pretenders? Government Human Rights Commissions in Africa* (Human Rights Watch 2001).

[12] Louise Arbor, 'Statement by the UN High Commissioner for Human Rights on the Entry into Force of the Arab Charter on Human Rights' (Geneva, 30 January 2008) <http://www.unhchr.ch/huricane/huricane.nsf/view01/6C211162E43235FAC12573E00056E19D?opendocument> accessed 5 January 2013.

[13] The Draft Protocol extending criminal jurisdiction to the African Court was deferred at the AU Summit in July 2012. The Draft Protocol is further discussed below.

[14] <http://aichr.org/documents/> accessed 24 May 2013. See also I Gede Ngurah Swajaya, 'ASEAN Declaration Should Be "Equally Powerful" to UN's' *The Jakarta Post* (28 June 2012) <http://www.thejakartapost.com/news/2012/06/28/asean-declaration-should-be-equally-powerful-un-s.html> accessed 5 January 2013.

[15] 'Pillay Urges ASEAN to Set the Bar High with Its Regional Human Rights Declaration' *United Nations Human Rights News* (Geneva, 11 May 2012) <http://www.ohchr.org/en/NewsEvents/Pages/DisplayNews.aspx?NewsID=12142&LangID=E> accessed 5 January 2013.

[16] 'Pillay Urges ASEAN to Set the Bar High' (n 15).

The challenge lies in expanding the reach of international human rights, while avoiding devolution of the concept to the point that it becomes everything to everyone and therefore ceases to set substantive standards, or that regions create human rights mechanisms that pose lower standards than those the UN sets, in order to protect themselves from global scrutiny. Standards can be adopted and used to evaluate the extent to which emerging regional systems contribute to or undermine the global system. While there are challenges, regional systems are important access points for participation in the global human rights project. A brief overview of the current status of regional protection provides a basis for assessing its role in the human rights project as a whole.

2. The Three Established Regional Systems

The regional human rights systems of Europe, the Americas, and Africa were each developed as part of the activities of regional intergovernmental organizations (IGOs): respectively, the Council of Europe, the Organization of American States, and the Organization of African Unity/African Union. Each system developed in response to its own unique set of circumstances.

2.1 Europe

After the Second World War, the focus in Western Europe was to prevent further conflict on the continent, to avoid a recurrence of dictatorships, and to provide an ideological alternative to communism, based on individual freedoms. The Council of Europe was established in 1949 to pursue these aims, chief among which was the pursuit of human rights. In 1950, ten 'like-minded' governments adopted the European Convention for the Protection of Human Rights and Fundamental Freedoms (European Convention on Human Rights) in Rome, taking 'the first steps for the collective enforcement of certain of the rights stated in the Universal Declaration'.[17] The European initiative can be seen as a response to the lack of agreement on an implementation framework for the Universal Declaration within the United Nations, inter alia, because of the paralyzing effect of the Cold War. This

[17] Convention for the Protection of Human Rights and Fundamental Freedoms, preamble (European Convention on Human Rights).

is an example of the benefit of diversity in the system—where when the one level (here, the global) falters, the other (the regional) can take over.

The European Convention on Human Rights established two supervisory institutions to ensure enforcement of the rights: a European Commission on Human Rights and a European Court of Human Rights. Initially, these institutions had limited jurisdiction, with both the right of individual petition and the jurisdiction of the Court made optional for states parties. Nonetheless, they were the first international bodies to provide remedies to persons whose rights, recognized under the Convention, a state party had violated. These remedial powers, which would also become the hallmarks of the enforcement mechanisms of the two regional systems in the Americas and Africa, had significant implications for traditional international law. The individual would become a subject of international law, capable of lodging complaints and holding states accountable, through the binding decisions of an international court, in respect of what would earlier have been seen as a domestic matter. Space was opening up for much broader participation in shaping the human rights project, which would also find resonance in the other regional and UN mechanisms.

The European system evolved by gradually strengthening its institutions and procedures. Initially, the European Commission was very cautious and placed emphasis on friendly settlement,[18] but it developed its complaints procedure over the years. In 1998, Protocol 11 to the European Human Rights Convention[19] entered into force; it reformed the system by abolishing the European Commission and providing for a full time Court. The new Court was given compulsory jurisdiction over all state parties to the European Convention, and individual victims were given direct access to the Court. The system thus was initially, and remains largely, litigation-orientated, as the central role of the European Court of Human Rights and the fact that the Commission did not have a general promotional mandate comparable to that of its counterparts in the other regions, exemplify.

The European Committee on Social Rights, established under the European Social Charter, adopted in 1961 and revised in 1991, provides for a state reporting system similar to that adopted under the UN human rights treaties. A committee to monitor conditions in places of detention was established through the European Convention for the Prevention of Torture and Inhuman or Degrading Treatment or Punishment, which was adopted in 1987 and entered into force in 1989. In 1999, the Council of Europe created the post of Commissioner for Human Rights, with a promotional and monitoring mandate.

[18] Ed Bates, *The Evolution of the European Convention on Human Rights: From Its Inception to the Creation of a Permanent Court of Human Rights* (OUP 2010) 260.

[19] Protocol No 11 to the Convention for the Protection of Human Rights and Fundamental Freedoms, Restructuring the Control Machinery Established Thereby.

The European system traditionally covered a relatively homogenous group of countries and did not generally deal with large-scale human rights violations. A few cases dealing with massive violations in Greece, Turkey, and Cyprus were exceptions, confirming the general rule. This changed in the early 1990s, when Russia and other countries from Eastern Europe joined the system, bringing challenges that were more reminiscent of those faced in the other regional systems. In addition, and tied to the problem of widespread violations, a major challenge to the European Court is keeping up with the ever-increasing number of individual complaints submitted to the Court. Many of these cases deal with systemic violations, such as excessive delays in judicial proceedings.[20]

2.2 The Americas

The Organization of American States (OAS) pursues a wide range of objectives in the Americas, which includes human rights. From its establishment in the late 1800s, the Pan-American Union, the predecessor to the OAS, took a number of initiatives with regard to the rights of members of various groups, for example women and children.[21] The American Declaration of the Rights and Duties of Man was adopted on 2 May 1948, simultaneously with the Charter of the OAS. The Declaration was one of the documents that the drafters of the Universal Declaration of Human Rights, adopted a few months later, considered. It should also be noted that Latin American states had been instrumental in promoting the inclusion of references to human rights in the UN Charter, which had been adopted three years earlier.[22]

The OAS did not immediately put in place an implementation framework for the American Declaration. However, in 1959 the OAS General Assembly created the Inter-American Commission on Human Rights (IACHR) as an autonomous body. The IACHR became a Charter body when the Protocol of Buenos Aires, which amended the OAS Charter, entered into force in 1970.

In 1969, the American Convention on Human Rights (ACHR) was adopted in San José, Costa Rica. Before it was adopted, the Inter-American Commission and OAS member states scrutinized the Convention to ensure that it was compatible

[20] See European Court of Human Rights, 'Violation by Article and by State 1959–2011' (31 December 2011) <http://www.echr.coe.int/NR/rdonlyres/2B783BFF-39C9-455C-B7C7-F821056BF32A/0/TABLEAU_VIOLATIONS_EN_2011.pdf> accessed 5 January 2013; European Court of Human Rights, 'Statistics on Judgments by State: Statistics 1959–2010' (September 2011) <http://www.echr.coe.int/NR/rdonlyres/E6B7605E-6D3C-4E85-A84D-6DD59C69F212/0/Graphique_violation_en.pdf> accessed 5 January 2013 (showing that article 6 violations constitute the largest category of subject matter judgments).

[21] On the early history of the Inter-American system, see Anna P Schreiber, *The Inter-American Commission on Human Rights* (Sijthoff 1970).

[22] Mary Ann Glendon, 'The Forgotten Crucible: The Latin American Influence on the Universal Human Rights Idea' (2003) 16 *Harv Hum Rts J* 27.

with the two UN Covenants. The IACHR noted that the ACHR 'could coincide in certain respects with the United Nations Covenants... with such additions as are necessary and it could, in addition, include other rights... the international protection of which is demanded because of conditions peculiar to the Americas'.[23]

On the advice of the IACHR,[24] socio-economic rights were only included with reference to the progressive realization of the 'basic goals' set out in the OAS Charter.[25] The ACHR was thus left essentially devoted to the protection of civil and political rights. More detailed protection of socio-economic rights came in 1988, with the adoption of the Protocol to the American Convention on Human Rights in the Area of Economic, Social and Cultural Rights (Protocol of San Salvador). This Protocol adds trade union rights and the right to education to the individual petition system,[26] but both the IACHR and the Inter-American Court of Human Rights have dealt with socio-economic rights more broadly.[27] While the American Declaration on the Rights and Duties of Man recognized duties, the ACHR did not repeat this.

Other human rights treaties that the OAS has adopted deal with torture,[28] the death penalty,[29] forced disappearance,[30] violence against women[31] and disabilities.[32] The conventions concerning forced disappearances and violence against women were the first in the world on these topics and led the UN and other regions to adopt similar instruments. The OAS has also adopted important political declarations, for example the Inter-American Democratic Charter of 2001.

When it entered into force in 1978, the ACHR made the IACHR its treaty-based mechanism (it also continues to function as an OAS Charter body) and created an Inter-American Court of Human Rights. The time when the Convention entered into force, however, coincided with the heyday of gross human rights violations in large parts of Latin America. The regional human rights system had to combat a

[23] IACHR, 'Comparative Study of the United Nations Covenants on Civil and Political Rights and on Economic, Social, and Cultural Rights and the Draft Inter-American Convention on Human Rights' (1968) OEA/Ser.L/V/II.9, para v, reprinted in IACHR, 'Report on the Work Accomplished during Its Eighteenth Session, 1–17 April 1968' (12 September 1968) OEA/Ser.L/V/II.19, Docs 30, 31.

[24] IACHR, 'Comparative Study' (n 23) para vi.

[25] American Convention on Human Rights, Art 26. See also Charter of the Organization of American States, Arts 34, 45.

[26] Additional Protocol to the American Convention on Human Rights in the Area of Economic, Social and Cultural Rights, Art 19(5).

[27] Tara J Melish, 'The Inter-American Court of Human Rights: Beyond Progressivity' in Malcolm Langford (ed), *Social Rights Jurisprudence: Emerging Trends in International and Comparative Law* (CUP 2008).

[28] Inter-American Convention to Prevent and Punish Torture.

[29] Protocol to the American Convention on Human Rights to Abolish the Death Penalty.

[30] Inter-American Convention on Forced Disappearance of Persons.

[31] Inter-American Convention on the Prevention, Punishment and Eradication of Violence against Women.

[32] Inter-American Convention on the Elimination of All Forms of Discrimination against Persons with Disabilities.

'regional network of repression' epitomized by Operation Condor, through which the leaders of countries in the Southern Cone helped each other to eliminate opponents.[33] The IACHR played a leading role in exposing the atrocities that the juntas of the Western hemisphere committed.[34]

Challenges to the Inter-American system include a lack of political will from OAS member states, both with regard to funding the system and to putting pressure on states to comply with the findings of the Commission and the Court. The system has also been under pressure because of the unwillingness of some states to accept precautionary measures[35] and of others to acknowledge the findings that they have engaged in systematic human rights violations. A number of states have threatened to renounce the system (and in the past some have attempted to do so).[36] Another concern is the fact that the Inter-American Court effectively functions as a Latin American human rights court, as very few of the Anglophone states of the hemisphere have accepted its jurisdiction.

2.3 Africa

When the Charter of the Organization of African Unity (OAU) was adopted in 1963, it did not explicitly recognize the pursuit of human rights as one of its objectives. However, in 1981 the member states adopted the African Charter on Human and Peoples' Rights (AfCHPR).

Despite being the first of the regional instruments adopted with the active encouragement of the UN, the text of the Charter differs more from the Universal Declaration and the Covenants than is the case with the earlier established systems. In addressing the drafters of the Charter, President Senghor of Senegal implored them to:

> [N]either copy, nor strive for originality, for the sake of originality. We must show imagination and effectiveness. We could get inspirations from our beautiful and positive traditions.

[33] Sonia Cardenas, *Human Rights in Latin America: A Politics of Terror and Hope* (University of Pennsylvania Press 2010) 67.

[34] Tom J Farer, 'The Rise of the Inter-American Human Rights Regime: No Longer a Unicorn, Not Yet an Ox' (1997) 19 *Hum Rts Q* 510.

[35] See eg Conectas, 'Condemnation of the Government's Response to the Precautionary Measures Issued by the IACHR in the Belo Monte Case' (Public Statement, São Paulo, 15 April 2011) Public Statement 1/2011 <http://www.conectas.org/en/institutional/condemnation-of-the-government undefineds-response-to-the-precautionary-measures-issued-by-the-iachr-in-the-belo-monte-case?tipo=AUDIO> accessed 5 January 2013.

[36] Trinidad and Tobago denounced the American Convention on Human Rights in 1998, but it remains subject to the IACHR as a Charter-based organ. See Natasha Parassram Concepcion, 'The Legal Implications of Trinidad & Tobago's Withdrawal from the American Convention on Human Rights' (2001) 16 *Am U Int'l L Rev* 847. Alberto Fujimori purported to withdraw Peru from the jurisdiction of the Court without denouncing the Convention; the Court rebuffed this effort. Venezuela denounced the ACHR in September 2012, effective one year later.

Therefore, you must keep constantly in mind our values of civilization and the real needs of Africa.[37]

Recognizing that the Charter was not intended to limit the rights set out in the UN human rights instruments, in the preamble to the Charter, the member states of the OAU reaffirmed their commitment to the human rights instruments of the United Nations. The Charter explicitly tasks the expert body established to monitor compliance with the Charter to 'draw inspiration from international law on human and peoples' rights', including instruments that the UN adopts.[38]

The fact that Africa established a regional system when it did may be attributed in part to the desire of the recently independent former colonies to establish themselves as part of the world community. Moreover, the OAU Charter included the 'eradicat[ion of] all forms of colonialism from the continent' as one of the organization's objectives.[39] In the pursuit of this objective in international fora and due to the opposition to apartheid in Southern Africa, the use of human rights language was inevitable. It was also the time when a central tenet of US President Jimmy Carter's foreign policy was human rights. Closer to home, and perhaps more directly linked, was the fact that the process to draft the African Charter was initiated against the background of the fall of some particularly murderous regimes on the continent, including that of Idi Amin in Uganda.[40] An invasion of troops from neighbouring Tanzania brought about the downfall of the latter.[41]

Against the backdrop of the Ugandan experience, it is perhaps not surprising that the Charter largely focused on the possibility of interstate communications regarding human rights violations, a mechanism which could (at least in aspiration) serve to prevent or diffuse interstate conflict. However, in practice the individual complaints system has played a much more important role, with only one interstate communication submitted and decided by the African Commission.[42] A protocol on the rights of women supplemented the Charter in 2003.[43] The 1990 African Charter on the Rights and Welfare of the Child entered into force in 1999,

[37] Leopold Senghor, President of the Republic of Senegal, 'Address' (Meeting of African Experts preparing the draft African Charter, Dakar, Senegal, 28 November–8 December 1979), reprinted in Christof Heyns (ed), *Human Rights Law in Africa 1999* (Kluwer Law International 2002) 79.

[38] African Charter on Human and Peoples' Rights, Art 60.

[39] Article 2(d).

[40] Amin was elected Chairman of the OAU at the height of his murderous regime in 1975, a post which he held for a year, in line with OAU practice.

[41] For the history of the adoption of the African Charter, see Olusola Ojo and Amadu Sesay, 'The OAU and Human Rights: Prospects for the 1980s and Beyond' (1986) 8 *Hum Rts Q* 89, 89–95; Frans Viljoen 'The African Charter on Human and Peoples' Rights: The *Travaux Préparatoires* in the Light of Subsequent Practice' (2004) 25 *HRLJ* 313.

[42] *Democratic Republic of the Congo v Burundi, Rwanda and Uganda.*

[43] Protocol to the African Charter on Human and Peoples' Rights on the Rights of Women in Africa.

following which the Committee of Experts on the Rights and Welfare of the Child was established in 2001.[44]

The African Charter recognizes a wide range of norms additional to those that other regional systems recognize; it upholds not only individual rights, but also peoples' rights; not only rights, but also duties; and not only civil and political rights, but also socio-economic rights and so-called solidarity rights (such as a right to development,[45] peace,[46] and a satisfactory environment[47]). The sole supervisory body that the African Charter foresaw was the African Commission of Human and Peoples' Rights, which held its first session in 1987.

In 2002 the African Union (AU), which recognizes human rights as one of its objectives, replaced the OAU.[48] In 2004, a protocol establishing the African Court on Human and Peoples' Rights, designed to 'supplement' the work of the Commission, entered into force; its first judges were elected in 2006.[49] The Court is scheduled to merge with the African Court of Justice when a new protocol enters into force.[50] After the merger, the Court would have two sections: one to deal with general affairs and one with human rights.

The AU has launched a subsequent initiative to add individual and corporate criminal jurisdiction to the jurisdiction of the merged court, against the background of the disquiet of many African leaders about the focus of the International Criminal Court (ICC) on Africa. None of the other regional courts have such jurisdiction, and it is doubtful whether the Court is well placed to deal with this expansion of its role.[51] The question may also be asked whether such an initiative will not undermine the role of the global ICC.

One of the flagship projects of the AU has been the establishment of the African Peer Review Mechanism (APRM), a voluntary process that involves African heads of state in mutual scrutiny of the human rights records of and other governance issues in the thirty African states that have signed up for the process.[52]

[44] On the Children's Charter and the work of the Committee, see eg Frans Viljoen, *International Human Rights Law in Africa* (2nd edn, OUP 2012) 391–409.

[45] AfCHPR, Art 22. [46] AfCHPR, Art 23. [47] AfCHPR, Art 24.

[48] Constitutive Act of the African Union, Art 3(h).

[49] Protocol to the African Charter on Human and Peoples' Rights on the Establishment of an African Court on Human and Peoples' Rights.

[50] Protocol on the Statute of the African Court of Justice and Human Rights. The African Court of Justice was provided for in a protocol adopted in 2003 but has not been established.

[51] See eg Chacha Bhoke Murungu 'Towards a Criminal Chamber in the African Court of Justice and Human Rights' (2011) 9 *JICJ* 1067; Frans Viljoen, 'AU Assembly Should Consider Human Rights Implications before Adopting the Amending Merged African Court Protocol' (*AfricLaw*, 23 May 2012) <http://africlaw.com/2012/05/23/au-assembly-should-consider-human-rights-implications-before-adopting-the-amending-merged-african-court-protocol> accessed 5 January 2013.

[52] See Magnus Killander, 'The African Peer Review Mechanism and Human Rights: The First Reviews and the Way Forward' (2008) 30 *Hum Rts Q* 41.

The main challenges that the African system faces include the deep levels of poverty on the continent, the weakness of many of its states, little domestic commitment to the rule of law and human rights in the region, lack of a proper administrative system for either the Commission or the Court, constant changes to the composition and jurisdiction of the Court, and inadequacies in the Charter itself.[53] Some of those who work inside the system also sketch a gloomy picture about competition between the Commission and the Court (something also perceived in the Inter-American system).

3. Thematic Comparison

A number of the features of the systems dealt with above are best understood by thematically comparing the position of the three regions.[54]

3.1 Institutional functioning

In all three cases, there is a wide level of participation among states that are members of the parent IGOs in the regional human rights systems, at least on a formal level. All forty-seven members of the Council of Europe are state parties to the European Convention and thus are subject to the jurisdiction of the Court; indeed, this is de facto required of all members. In the Americas, twenty-five of thirty-five member states of the OAS have ratified the American Convention. However, Trinidad and Tobago and Venezuela have denounced the Convention. All member states of the OAS are subject to supervision by the IACHR in terms of the American Declaration of the Rights and Duties of Man. Twenty-one states have accepted the jurisdiction of the Inter-American Court of Human Rights.[55] In Africa, fifty-three of fifty-four AU member states have ratified the African Charter and as such are subject to supervision by the African Commission.[56] A total of twenty-six African states have accepted the jurisdiction of the African Court of Human and Peoples' Rights.

[53] Such as Art 59, which requires the Assembly's authorization to publish certain Commission reports and makes the complaints procedure confidential. See Magnus Killander 'Confidentiality Versus Publicity: Interpreting Article 59 of the African Charter on Human and Peoples' Rights' (2006) 6 *AHRLJ* 572.

[54] See also Dinah Shelton 'The Promise of Regional Human Rights Systems' in Burns H Weston and Stephen Marks (eds), *The Future of International Human Rights* (Transnational Publishers 1999).

[55] 'Multilateral Treaties—American Convention on Human Rights' <http://www.oas.org/dil/treaties_B-32_American_Convention_on_Human_Rights_sign.htm> accessed 24 May 2013.

[56] The exception is South Sudan, which seceded from the Sudan in July 2011 and by July 2012 had not yet ratified the Charter. Arguably, the Charter applies to South Sudan even absent ratification.

The European system, as it is today, contains the fewest obstacles for individuals to access the Court; anyone claiming to be a victim of a violation may approach the Court directly, provided the admissibility criteria (which are to a large measure the same for all three systems) are met. In the Americas, the way to the Court is through the Commission. Although the Commission used to submit few cases to the Court, since 2001 there has been a general rule of referral.[57] Moreover, the Court has amended its rules to provide separate representation for victims and their representatives during its proceedings. In Africa, as a general rule, the Commission or states have the power to refer cases to the Court. States have to make a special declaration to allow individuals to take their cases directly to the Court, thereby bypassing the Commission.[58] Only a small number of states have done so.[59]

In Europe, only the victim of an alleged violation (including legal persons) has standing to bring a case to the Court.[60] The African and American systems recognize *actio polularis*, and anyone may bring a case to the Commission in the Americas or Court in Africa (against the states which have made the declaration).[61] However, in the Americas a victim or victims must be named.

A difference between the European system, on the one hand, and the Inter-American and African systems, on the other, is that a judge from the state under scrutiny will always be on the bench of the European Court,[62] while commissioners and judges in the two other systems must recuse themselves when a case is against a state of which they are a national.[63]

All three systems provide for advisory jurisdiction by their courts. While the Inter-American Court has delivered more than twenty advisory opinions on a variety of topics,[64] the European Court has only delivered two advisory opinions, both

[57] IACHR, 'Rules of Procedure of the Inter-American Commission on Human Rights' (adopted 13 November 2009, modified 2 September 2011) Art 45 (IACHR Rules of Procedure) <http://www.oas.org/en/iachr/mandate/Basics/rulesiachr.asp> accessed 8 January 2013.

[58] Protocol to the African Charter on Human and Peoples' Rights on the Establishment of an African Court on Human and Peoples' Rights, Art 34(6).

[59] As of May 2013, six of the twenty-six states that had ratified the Protocol establishing the Court, had made the required declaration in terms of Art 34(6).

[60] European Convention on Human Rights, Art 34.

[61] AfCHPR, Art 55. See also *Social and Economic Rights Action Centre (SERAC) v Nigeria*, para 49; IACHR Rules of Procedure (n 57) Art 23; Laurence Burgorgue-Larsen and Amaya Úbeda de Torres, *The Inter-American Court of Human Rights: Case Law and Commentary* (OUP 2011) 47.

[62] European Convention on Human Rights, Art 43.

[63] IACHR Rules of Procedure (n 57) Art 17(2)(a); IACHR, 'Rules of Procedure of the Inter-American Court of Human Rights' (adopted 31 January 2009) Art 19 (national judges may participate, or an *ad hoc* judge may be appointed in interstate complaints) (IACtHR Rules of Procedure); African Commission on Human and Peoples' Rights, 'Rules of Procedure of the African Commission on Human and Peoples' Rights' (entered into force 18 August 2010) rule 101 (AfCHPR Rules of Procedure); Protocol to the African Charter on Human and Peoples' Rights on the Establishment of an African Court on Human and Peoples' Rights, Art 22.

[64] Inter-American Court of Human Rights, 'Opiniones Consultivas' ('Advisory Opinions') <http://www.corteidh.or.cr/index.php/16-juris/22-casos-contenciosos> accessed 24 May 2013.

dealing with lists of candidates for election to the Court. Only the Committee of Ministers may bring requests to the European Court for advisory opinions.[65] The African Court has wide advisory jurisdiction, but as of May 2013 it had not delivered any advisory opinion.

The role the commissions play in the various systems can be described as follows. In all three cases, the Commissions have (or in the case of Europe, had) a quasi-judicial function in respect of individual and interstate complaints. While the African Commission is unique in also requiring the states to submit regular reports, a substantial part of the work of the Inter-American Commission consists of considering the country and thematic reports that it prepares at its own initiative. Both systems also have rapporteurs, and the African system has working groups. The European Court of Human Rights obviously does not fulfil such functions. However, the European Commissioner for Human Rights does have a promotional function.

The remedies the three systems provide in respect of individual complaints differ. In Europe, the focus has traditionally been on judgments that declare whether a violation has occurred in the particular case and, if so, compensatory damages. In the Americas, the power of the human rights court is much wider, and states may be ordered to take specific remedial steps, such as changing the law or engaging in symbolic actions such as apologies. The African Court is also granted wide powers in this regard. The Inter-American and African Commissions similarly indicate a wide variety of remedies.

The use of provisional measures, also known as interim or precautionary measures, to prevent irreparable harm varies among the systems. The European Court has a dedicated fax line to quickly respond to requests for interim measures. However, the Court is restrictive in granting such measures and in 2011 only granted 342 out of 2,778 requests for interim measures it received.[66] The Inter-American Commission issues about one in seven requests for precautionary measures. In addition, the American Convention allows the IACHR to request provisional measures from the Inter-American Court; in practice, it generally does so only after the state has failed to implement recommended precautionary measures. The African Commission has given itself the power in its Rules of Procedure to issue interim relief and has done so in several cases.[67] The African Court issued its first order for provisional measures in 2011.[68] In the European and African systems, a request for provisional

[65] Protocol No 2 to the Convention for the Protection of Human Rights and Fundamental Freedoms, Conferring upon the European Court of Human Rights Competence to Give Advisory Opinions.

[66] European Court of Human Rights, 'Interim Measures—Practical Information' <http://www.echr.coe.int/ECHR/EN/Header/Applicants/Interim+measures/Practical+information/> accessed 7 January 2013.

[67] See rule 98.

[68] In terms of the Court Protocol Art 27(2). See Judy Oder, 'The African Court on Human and Peoples' Rights' Order in Respect of the Situation in Libya: A Watershed in the Regional Protection of Human Rights?' (2011) 11 *AHRLJ* 495.

measures must be linked to a petition, which the Inter-American system does not require because of its more pro-active stance in regard to preventing violations.

The European system is generally recognized as having the highest level of compliance with decisions on individual complaints, in particular with regard to monetary compensation. For general measures, in particular in the context of massive or systemic violations, compliance has been harder to achieve.[69] Of course, it is much harder to comply with and to evaluate compliance with the mandated implementation of these measures, which usually require legal and other reforms, than other forms of implementation.[70]

Compliance with the orders of the Inter-American Commission and Court has been rather mediocre, though this fact should not detract from the influence of the Court's jurisprudence in the development and application of international human rights law.[71] By May 2013, the African Court had not handed down any substantive judgment. A study of compliance with the recommendations of the African Commission indicates that full compliance is rare.[72] Compliance with the African Court's judgments may in theory be higher, as the Protocol establishing the Court foresees a system where the political bodies of the AU play a major role in ensuring compliance, but the recent experience with the South African Development Community (SADC) Tribunal discussed below suggests that some caution may be warranted.

The systems vary greatly in terms of the scale of their operations and their capacity. This is evident from the case loads. The European Court hands down more than 1,500 judgments each year,[73] while the Inter-American Court delivered thirteen judgments on the merits in 2011,[74] although it should be noted that the number of victims in each case before the Inter-American Court can reach into the hundreds, something not seen in the European Court. The African Commission only decided one case on the merits in 2010 and one in 2011. The African Human Rights Court has delivered only a few judgments, all dealing with the same procedural issue, namely submission of a case against a state or international organization not party to the Protocol that established the Court. There do not seem to be many cases heading to the Court at the moment.

[69] See Gisella Gori, Chapter 37, in this *Handbook*.

[70] David C Baluarte and Christian M De Vos, *From Judgment to Justice: Implementing International and Regional Human Rights Decisions* (Open Society Foundations 2010) 21.

[71] Fernando Basch and others, 'The Effectiveness of the Inter-American System of Human Rights Protection: A Quantitative Approach to Its Functioning and Compliance with Its Decisions' (2010) 7(12) *SUR Int'l J Hum Rts* 9.

[72] Frans Viljoen and Lirette Louw 'State Compliance with the Recommendations of the African Commission on Human and Peoples' Rights, 1993–2004' (2007) 101 *AJIL* 1.

[73] Council of Europe, *The European Court of Human Rights in Facts and Figures 2011* (Council of Europe 2012).

[74] Inter-American Court of Human Rights, 'Casos Contenciosos' ('Contentious Cases') <http://www.corteidh.or.cr/index.php/16-juris/22-casos-contenciosos> accessed 27 May 2013.

The comparative budgets are as follows. The European Court's budget for 2011 was almost 59 million euros (USD 74 million), more than a quarter of the total Council of Europe budget.[75] The financial resources provided to the two Inter-American human rights bodies are clearly inadequate in relation to their workload, in particular the processing of an ever-increasing number of individual complaints. In 2011, the Inter-American Commission received USD 4.3 million from the OAS (5 per cent of the OAS budget) and USD 5.1 million from other donors.[76] The Inter-American Court received USD 2 million from the OAS. This can be compared to the African Commission, which received USD 3 million from the AU (less than 3 per cent of the AU budget) and USD 2 million from donors in 2010, while the African Court received more than USD 6 million from the AU budget and USD 1.7 million from donors in 2010.[77] When the budgets of the Inter-American and African systems are compared, a huge discrepancy seems to appear between their outputs. In particular, the allocation to the African Court is inexplicably high considering the small number of cases before the Court even six years after it started functioning. Judged on a cost per case basis, it must be one of the most expensive courts in the world.

The point was made earlier that proximity can play a role in allowing international human rights mechanisms, and in particular regional systems, to be more interactive with the affected population, for example through the participation in its activities by local NGOs and lawyers, news coverage, etc. The European Court is based in Strasbourg and does not convene in other parts of Europe. The Inter-American Commission is based in Washington, DC, but occasionally meets elsewhere, and individual members of the Commission travel frequently to make on-site visits to member states. The Inter-American Court has its seat in San José, Costa Rica, but has also held sessions elsewhere. The African Commission has been the most mobile and regularly has meetings in capitals other than Banjul, The Gambia, where its headquarters are located, though in recent years it has held most sessions in (the rather inaccessible) Banjul. The African Court, based in Arusha, Tanzania, and the African Children's Committee, based in Addis Ababa, had held one session each outside of their headquarters by May 2012.[78]

In addition to location, time in session is also an indicator of opportunities for interaction and participation. The European Court is a permanent body; the Inter-American Commission sits around six to seven weeks, in three regular sessions per year,[79] and the Inter-American Court is in session around seven weeks

[75] The budget for the Council of Europe as a whole was 217 million euros for 2011.

[76] OAS, 'Financial Resources' (2011) <http://www.cidh.oas.org/recursos.eng.htm> accessed 8 January 2013.

[77] African Union Executive Council, 'Decision on the Budget of the African Union for the 2010 Financial Year' (1 February 2010) EX.CL/Dec.524 (XVI).

[78] In 2011, the Committee held a session in Algiers, Algeria, and in 2012, the Court held a session in Accra, Ghana.

[79] OAS, 'IACHR Session' <http://www.oas.org/en/iachr/activities/sessions.asp> accessed 8 January 2013.

per annum.[80] The African Commission convenes for four weeks of regular sessions per year. The Rules of the African Court provides that it should hold four ordinary fifteen-day sessions per year,[81] an excessive amount considering the Court's current caseload.[82] The Rules should rather provide that the Court will decide at each session when, and for how long, it should next meet, as the rules of the Inter-American Court provide.[83]

Participation in the proceedings of the respective systems takes different forms. The European Court decides cases on the basis of written submissions, though it does hold hearings in exceptional cases. The Inter-American Commission holds one-hour hearings in some, but not all, cases. The African Commission can hold hearings in private session at the request of one of the parties or at the initiative of the Commission.[84] The Inter-American and African Courts hold public hearings.

Diversity in the ranks of decision-makers could serve to facilitate participation, even if the various 'constituencies' do so indirectly. As of May 2013, a majority of the members of the African Commission and Inter-American Commission were women, and there was racial diversity, as well. However, at the judicial level, the situation is different. Only two of eleven judges on the African Court are women, in 2013 none of the seven judges on the Inter-American Court were women, and in 2012 only eleven of the more than forty-five judges on the European Court were women. The European Court has a member from each state party, while the political organs that elect the members of the Inter-American and African bodies are supposed to ensure geographical diversity in the membership (though some sub-regions, such as Arabic- or Portuguese-speaking Africa, have lacked representation).

NGO participation in the three systems also differs. NGOs are involved in a much smaller percentage of cases before the European Court than before the Inter-American and African Commissions.[85] This is linked to the possibility of *actio popularis* in the latter systems. The African Commission arguably provides for the greatest level of engagement of the system with civil society.[86] A clear difference is

[80] Inter-American Court of Human Rights, 'Comunicados de Prensa' <http://www.corteidh.or.cr/index.php/comunicados> accessed 29 May 2013.

[81] African Union, 'African Court on Human and Peoples' Rights: Rules of Court' (adopted 2 June 2010) r 14.

[82] The Court has just a handful of cases on the docket, see African Court on Human and Peoples' Rights, 'Pending Cases' <http://www.african-court.org/en/index.php/2012-03-04-06-06-00/pending-cases> accessed 15 January 2013.

[83] IACtHR Rules of Procedure (n 63) Art 11.

[84] African Union, 'Rules of Court' (n 81) r 99.

[85] Lloyd Hitoshi Mayer, 'NGO Standing and Influence in Regional Human Rights Courts and Commissions' (2011) 36 *Brook J Int'l L* 911, 913.

[86] Nobuntu Mbelle, 'The Role of Non-Governmental Organisations and National Human Rights Institutions at the African Commission' in Malcolm Evans and Rachel Murray (eds), *The African Charter on Human and Peoples' Rights: The System in Practice: 1986–2006* (CUP 2008) 289.

the NGO accreditation system at the African Commission, which has no parallel in the other institutions.

Considering the importance of the role of public awareness as a precondition for participation, it is instructive to look at the websites of the different systems. The website of the Council of Europe is highly organized and accessible.[87] New websites of the Inter-American Commission[88] and African Commission[89] were launched in early 2012 and Inter-American Court in 2013. These are generally great improvements, when compared with the past, and make information about the work of these commissions available to a wider audience.

In the larger perspective, the three systems are similar in that they are all part of the inter-governmental bodies of the particular region, aimed at regional integration in one form or another. Member states have the option—and in practice are expected—to become state parties to the central human rights treaties that the IGOs accepted. The success of the human rights mechanisms seems to be closely tied to the overall level of integration in the region concerned.

Standing in the IGO, and the benefits that this entails, is one of the main motivations for states to comply with the human rights standards set within the system. Membership in the parent IGO may be tied to human rights in two ways. In the first place, states could be expected to reach a certain level of human rights compliance before they are allowed to join the IGO.[90] Secondly, states that are members of the IGO may be expelled, or find themselves subject to other sanctions, based on a poor human rights record.[91]

3.2 Jurisprudence

The jurisprudence of the European and, to some extent, the Inter-American system has become part and parcel of international human rights jurisprudence.

There has been a remarkable convergence in the jurisprudence of the three systems, despite some differences in the texts of the treaties. They have all endorsed the

[87] Council of Europe, 'Home Page COE' (2012) <http://www.coe.int> accessed 8 January 2013.

[88] OAS, 'Inter-American Commission on Human Rights' <http://www.oas.org/en/iachr> accessed 8 January 2013.

[89] AfCHPR, 'Home' (2013) <http://www.achpr.org> accessed 8 January 2013.

[90] The Council of Europe required far-reaching legal reform, also in the area of human rights, and ratification of the European Convention of Human Rights, before allowing former communist countries to join the Council.

[91] The Council of Europe has never used suspension, though its Parliamentary Assembly has suspended Greece (1967–74), Turkey (1980–84), and Russia (2000–01). Suspension for an unconstitutional change of government has occurred in both the OAS and AU. Syria was suspended from the Arab League in November 2011. See David Batty and Jack Shenker, 'Syria Suspended from Arab League' *The Guardian* (12 November 2011) <http://www.guardian.co.uk/world/2011/nov/12/syria-suspended-arab-league> accessed 8 January 2013.

idea that politicians are less protected against robust free speech than other members of the public, that military courts should not try civilians, that corporal punishment is inhuman, and that the rights the treaties enshrine not only require states to abstain from violating them, but also obligate states to take certain positive measures to ensure their realization.[92] The rules on and exceptions to the exhaustion of local remedies pre-condition to filing a complaint have also converged. Differences remain, however, in the recognition and scope of certain rights. For example, while the European jurisprudence focuses largely on civil and political rights, the African system and the Inter-American system give recognition to other rights, as well. Sexual orientation and gender identity remain contested issues in the work of the African system, while the regional systems of Europe and the Americas have made substantial progress towards ending discrimination on this ground.[93]

Sometimes a change in approach spreads from one system to the other, both vertically (from the global to the regional) and horizontally (between the regional systems). The UN Human Rights Committee and European Court initially did not recognize conscientious objection to military service as protected under the right to freedom of conscience. The Human Rights Committee changed its stance on this issue in 1993,[94] and the Grand Chamber of the European Court followed suit in 2011.[95] The case law of the Inter-American Commission still reflects the old position.[96] It remains to be seen whether the Commission will change its position should a case of conscientious objection again come before it.

The African system's ground-breaking inclusion of, and jurisprudence on, environmental rights has been echoed increasingly in the case law of the other systems, while in turn the Inter-American jurisprudence on indigenous peoples has marked the development of human rights law in the African system.

The European system has gone further towards the abolition of the death penalty than the global system or the other regional systems.[97] Moreover, the European Court of Human Rights has held that the death row phenomenon can constitute inhuman treatment,[98] while the UN Human Rights Committee has held that the

[92] See Magnus Killander, 'Interpreting Regional Human Rights Treaties' (2010) 7(13) *SUR Int'l J Hum Rts* 145.

[93] The European Court of Human Rights has adopted numerous judgments dealing with discrimination based on sexual orientation, starting with *Dudgeon v United Kingdom*, which prohibited the criminalization of homosexual acts between consenting adults. The Inter-American Commission recently handed down its first decision dealing with sexual orientation and child custody in *Atala and Daughters v Chile*.

[94] Human Rights Committee, 'General Comment No 22: The Right to Freedom of Thought, Conscience, and Religion (Art 18)' (30 July 1993) UN Doc CCPR/C/21/Rev.1/Add.4, para 11.

[95] *Bayatyan v Armenia*.

[96] *Sahli Vera et al v Chile*, para 100.

[97] Article 6(2) of the ICCPR provides that states may retain the death penalty under certain closely defined circumstances. In the European system, Protocol 13 (ratified by all but five states, of which three have signed it) provides for the complete abolition of the death penalty.

[98] *Soering v United Kingdom*, para 111.

death row phenomenon in itself does not constitute a violation of the International Covenant on Civil and Political Rights (ICCPR).[99]

This also raises the question of the formal relationship between the regional systems and the UN. The first and obvious point is that they are not part of the same hierarchical structure. As a general rule, once regional courts have adjudicated a case, the complainants may still approach UN treaty bodies, but complaints that are pending before the UN system may not be brought to the regional level.[100] At the request of the Council of Europe, however, many European countries have entered reservations to the ICCPR, under the terms of which they will not allow cases to go to the Human Rights Committee after the European Court of Human Rights has given a judgment.

There is considerable collaboration and cross-referencing between the different levels. In light of the persistence of torture, ill-treatment, and inadequate conditions of detention, the Inter-American Commission and relevant UN bodies, such as the Special Rapporteur on Torture, the Committee against Torture, and the Office of the High Commissioner for Human Rights (OHCHR) have joined forces to promote a more effective implementation of recommendations.[101] Such collaboration is particularly important in light of the OHCHR's field presence in many countries. The Office of the High Commissioner for Human Rights is currently actively involved in engagement with the regional systems.[102]

In general, it would be fair to say that the global system has led the way in terms of norm recognition, but there are exceptions where the regional bodies have innovated in ways that the global institutions later followed. Regional systems are well placed to put specific human rights concerns from their part of the world on the international agenda. An example in this regard would be the issue of disappearances, which rose from being a matter of specific concern in Latin America, reflected in the 1994 Inter-American Convention on Forced Disappearance of Persons, to being taken up by the UN, where it is now reflected in the 2006 International Convention for the Protection of All Persons from Enforced Disappearance.

The African Charter is the only treaty to include such peoples' rights as the right to a safe and healthy environment and the right to development. The Arab Charter is the only international legal instrument to explicitly discuss rights of the elderly.[103] In light of the absence of explicit provisions on violence against women,

[99] *Johnson v Jamaica*, para 8.1.

[100] AfCHPR, Art 56(7); European Convention on Human Rights, Art 35(2)(b).

[101] IACHR, 'International Mechanisms against Torture Agree to Elaborate Joint Report in Light of High Level of Non-Compliance with Their Recommendations' (30 November 2011) Press Release 124/11 <http://www.cidh.oas.org/Comunicados/English/2011/124-11eng.htm> accessed 8 January 2013.

[102] UN Human Rights Council, 'Report of the Office of the United Nations High Commissioner for Human Rights on the International Workshop on Enhancing Cooperation between International and Regional Mechanisms for the Promotion and Protection of Human Rights' (9 August 2010) UN Doc A/HRC/15/5.

[103] Article 38. See also Paul De Hert and Eugenio Mantovani, 'Specific Human Rights for Older Persons? The Inevitable Colouring of Human Rights Law' (2011) 4 *EHRLR* 398.

the OAS adopted the Inter-American Convention on the Prevention, Punishment and Eradication of Violence against Women in 1994. The Protocol to the African Charter on the Rights of Women in Africa also included provisions on violence against women.

Progress is, however, sometimes quicker at the global level than the regional level. For example, the OAS has been negotiating an American Declaration on the Rights of Indigenous Peoples for many years now, while the UN General Assembly adopted the Declaration on the Rights of Indigenous Peoples in 2007, albeit after two decades of negotiations.

4. Other Regional Human Rights Initiatives

Put together, the three established regional systems provide more than a billion people with the possibility of individual recourse to regional courts, and hundreds of millions more are given the protection of a commission or other mechanism.[104] This still leaves around 5 billion people, mainly in Asia, without such a layer of international protection. In many states that fall outside the areas that the systems discussed above cover, some regional and sub-regional intergovernmental organizations are including human rights in their lists of aims and objectives. The UN General Assembly and the Human Rights Council now regularly welcomes new regional initiatives.

4.1 Asia and the Pacific

During the period leading up to the 1993 World Conference on Human Rights, the notion of a so-called 'Asian exception' to human rights gained prominence.[105] However, recent years have seen the emergence of regional human rights initiatives in this region, and less emphasis will presumably be placed on this variety of

[104] As noted below, individuals in many African states have access to sub-regional courts with a human rights mandate, while they lack access to the African Court.

[105] UNGA, 'Final Declaration of the Regional Meeting for Asia of the World Conference on Human Rights' (7 April 1993) UN Doc A/CONF.157/ASRM/8A/CONF.157/PC/59 (Bangkok Declaration). See also Amartya Sen, 'Human Rights and Asian Values' *The New Republic* (14 July 1997) 33–40; Vitit Muntarbhorn, 'Human Rights Monitoring in the Asia-Pacific Region' in Gudmundur Alfredsson and others (eds), *International Human Rights Monitoring Mechanisms: Essays in Honour of Jakob Th Möller* (2nd edn, Brill 2009) 641–48.

exceptionalism in future. The UN has been active in helping to establish regional human rights mechanisms in Asia. The most progress has been achieved in South East Asia, where ASEAN has adopted a number of human rights instruments.[106]

In 2007, the ASEAN Charter was adopted. Its article 14 calls for the establishment of an ASEAN human rights body for the 'promotion and protection of human rights and fundamental freedoms of peoples in ASEAN'.[107] The Terms of Reference of the ASEAN Intergovernmental Commission on Human Rights (AICHR) were adopted in 2009. As the name indicates, AICHR is an inter-governmental body that is fundamentally different than that of the three established systems. AICHR is made up of representatives of ASEAN member states who are not independent experts as in the case of the other regional systems. It is largely a promotional body and has a mandate which includes 'promot[ing] the full implementation of ASEAN instruments related to human rights'.[108] The Terms of Reference does not provide AICHR explicitly with the power to consider individual communications.

The first Commissioners were appointed in 2009. They then embarked on drafting an ASEAN Human Rights Declaration which was finally adopted by ASEAN in November 2012. The Terms of Reference for the Drafting Group on the ASEAN Human Rights Declaration noted that the Declaration should 'reflect ASEAN peculiarities and specificities and accommodate different political, religious, historical and cultural backgrounds from ASEAN Member States', but at the same time 'not be less or go lower than international human rights standards, including the Universal Declaration of Human Rights'.[109] The process of drafting the Declaration has been criticized for a lack of transparency.

In 2004, the South Asian Association for Regional Cooperation (SAARC) adopted a Social Charter[110] with commitments to eradicate poverty; improve health services; foster educational access; and promote the status of women and children, population stabilization, and drug addiction rehabilitation. However, the institutional framework for implementation is limited to the participating national coordination committees.

The Pacific Islands Forum has taken steps to establish a regional human rights mechanism for the Pacific island states.[111]

[106] Eg ASEAN Declaration against Trafficking in Persons Particularly Women and Children; The Declaration on the Elimination of Violence against Women in the ASEAN Region; The Declaration on the Protection and Promotion of the Rights of Migrant Workers.

[107] See Yung-Ming Yen, 'The Formation of the ASEAN Intergovernmental Commission on Human Rights: A Protracted Journey' (2011) 10 *Journal of Human Rights* 393.

[108] ASEAN, 'Terms of Reference of ASEAN Intergovernmental Commission on Human Rights' (20 July 2009) art 4.6.

[109] ASEAN, 'Terms of Reference (TOR) AICHR's Regional Seminar on the ASEAN Human Rights Declaration' (December 2011) (on file with authors).

[110] SAARC Social Charter. For the full text of the Charter, see: SAARC, 'SAARC Charter' <http://www.saarc-sec.org/SAARC-Charter/5> accessed 8 January 2013.

[111] Asia Pacific Forum, 'Pacific Islands Forum Secretariat' <http://www.asiapacificforum.net/working-with-others/project-partners/pacific-islands-forum-secretariat> accessed 8 January 2013;

4.2 The Arab League and the Organization of Islamic Cooperation

In the Arab world, the revised Arab Charter on Human Rights of 2004 entered into force in 2008.[112] The Charter elaborates a catalogue of rights and makes provision for the appointment of an expert Committee. The first members were appointed in March 2009. States are required to submit reports to the Committee, but there is no complaints mechanism. It remains to be seen whether the Arab Spring will invigorate the Arab human rights system.

Despite some defects, the Arab League system probably bears more promise than the initiatives of the broader-based Organization of Islamic Cooperation (previously known as the Organization of the Islamic Conference), which has adopted instruments that restrict universally agreed upon norms.[113] The Organization of Islamic Cooperation (OIC) Independent Permanent Commission on Human Rights held its first session in Jakarta, Indonesia, in February 2012.[114] The Commission is virtually powerless and seems to have been established to defend a particular view of human rights. This is illustrated by the fact that one of the objectives of the Commission is to 'support the OIC's position on human rights at the international level'.[115] Saudi Arabia, Iran, and Indonesia are competing to host the Commission.[116]

4.3 Other regional and sub-regional bodies

Within Europe, the Council of Europe institutions are joined in taking up human rights issues by the Organization for Security and Cooperation in Europe and the European Union (EU), which in some respects overlap with the work of the European Court of Human Rights. The EU has adopted the Charter of Fundamental Rights of the European Union, which includes civil, political, economic, social, and

Asia Pacific Forum, 'Concept Note: Regional Consultation on Advancing a Pacific Regional Human Rights Mechanism' (21–24 November 2011) (on file with authors).

112 See Mervat Rishmawi, 'The Arab Charter on Human Rights and the League of Arab States: An Update' (2010) 10 *HRL Rev* 169.

113 See Kamran Hashemi, 'Muslim States, Regional Human Rights Systems and the Organization of the Islamic Conference' (2009) 52 *Germ Yrbk Intl L* 75.

114 The Statute of the OIC Independent Permanent Commission on Human Rights is available at: OIC, 'Statute of the OIC Independent Permanent Commission on Human Rights' (7 June 2012) <http://www.oicun.org/75/20120607051141117.html> accessed 8 January 2013.

115 Statute of the OIC Independent Permanent Commission on Human Rights (n 114) Art 13.

116 Human Rights in Islamic Countries, 'Indonesia Wants to Be Host of OIC Human Rights Commission' *Tempo Interactive* (Jakarta, 23 February 2012) <http://oichumanrights.wordpress.com/2012/03/15/indonesia-wants-to-be-host-of-oic-human-rights-commission> accessed 8 January 2013.

cultural rights. The Charter is binding on member states and EU institutions, and national courts, as well as the European Court of Justice, can enforce it.[117]

In the Americas, sub-regional organizations have in general deferred to the work of the regional human rights bodies. The most active sub-regional human rights body is the Human Rights Public Policy Institute of the Mercado Común del Sur (MERCOSUR).[118] In addition, there is the Caribbean Court of Justice, established in 2006 to replace the Judicial Committee of the Privy Council as the final court of appeal for the independent countries of the Commonwealth of the Caribbean. So far, its jurisprudence has served to amend, but not to upset in any dramatic way, that of the Privy Council.[119]

At the sub-regional level in Africa, the Economic Community of West African States (ECOWAS), the East African Community, and the SADC have all been involved in the human rights standard-setting and enforcement of sub-regional courts, although with regard to the latter, only the ECOWAS Community Court of Justice has an explicit human rights mandate.[120] The ECOWAS Court is unique among human rights tribunals in that it does not require the exhaustion of local remedies. The SADC Tribunal's judgments on human rights cases against Zimbabwe eventually led to the tribunal's suspension by SADC,[121] setting a worrying precedent for the continental African Court of Human Rights.

5. Conclusion

The preceding overview demonstrates the depth and the breadth of the work of the regional dispensations, as well as their important role in ensuring wider participation in the human rights project and in making human rights more responsive and effective. There can be little doubt that the regional human rights systems now are an integral part of the global human rights system and an avenue for the effective participation of millions of people.

117 For a further analysis, see Wolfgang Weiß, 'Human Rights in the EU: Rethinking the Role of the European Convention on Human Rights after Lisbon' (2011) 7 *EU Const* 64.

118 OAS, 'IACHR and MERCOSUR Coordinate Joint Efforts' (21 October 2011) Press Release 109/11 <http://www.cidh.oas.org/Comunicados/English/2011/109-11eng.htm> accessed 8 January 2013.

119 See Derek O'Brien, 'The Caribbean Court of Justice and Its Appellate Jurisdiction: A Difficult Birth' [2006] *Public Law* 344; Derek O'Brien, 'Attorney General of Barbados v Joseph and Boyce: The Caribbean Court of Justice Answers Its Critics?' [2007] *Public Law* 189.

120 See Solomon Ebobrah, 'Litigating Human Rights before Sub-Regional Courts in Africa: Prospects and Challenges' (2009) 17 *AJICL* 79.

121 Human Rights Watch, 'SADC: Q&A on the Tribunal' (11 August 2011) <http://www.hrw.org/news/2011/08/11/sadc-qa-tribunal> accessed 8 January 2013.

It seems that the dangers of the fragmentation of international human rights law by breakaway movements have not come to pass. On the contrary, there has been a considerable amount of convergence in the approaches the different regional systems have followed and between them and the United Nations. The threat regional systems pose to the coherence of human rights may thus be more feared than real.[122] Nevertheless, the overview above suggests that this convergence has been achieved not by coincidence, but rather through constant vigilance. The coherence may also provide support for the contention that human rights are universal.

Given the convergence in terms of norms, it is clear that an important aspect of the work of regional systems lies in norm enforcement. It is a feature of the modern human rights approach across these systems that remedies, in one form or another, are tied to rights, either through judicial proceedings or through other forms of pressure. In this context, regional systems are playing an important role in advancing a world-wide conception of human rights wherein respecting human rights norms is expected, and people have a right to human rights enforcement.

The active human rights systems and initiatives described above are all located within IGOs as part of a wider integrative project within the region concerned. This serves as an indicator against the attempts to establish regional human rights initiatives in areas where such IGOs do not exist—for example, in Asia as a whole.

In the same way that the norms the different regions recognize reflect regional particularities, the mechanisms for norm enforcement are also regionally specific. Calls have been made for the abolition of the Commissions in the Americas and in Africa and the retention merely of a Court, as is the case in Europe. Such an approach appears to ignore the fact that commissions are often the best way of dealing with gross and systematic violations of human rights, as the Inter-American system has so vividly illustrated. Likewise, the African Court of Human and Peoples' Rights still needs to show a practical impact on the continent.

Courts and commissions, and those who shape them, need to be attuned to the environment in which they operate. Within the context of the Inter-American system, it has been remarked that decision-makers, and even judges, need to take cognizance of the environment in which they function on a continuous basis, in order to ensure the maximum impact of their decisions, inter alia, through the opportunities that they create for further engagement by other actors, especially on the domestic level.[123]

Promoting engagement by all role players in human rights initiatives appears to be particularly important where legitimacy is in question. In the African context,

[122] For a discussion of the dynamics that lead members of IGOs to converge their interests and approaches, see David H Bearce and Stacy Bondanella, 'Intergovernmental Organizations, Socialization, and Member-State Interest Convergence' (2007) 61 *International Organization* 703.

[123] See James L Cavallaro and Stephanie Erin Brewer, 'Reevaluating Regional Human Rights Litigation in the Twenty-First Century: The Case of the Inter-American Court' (2008) 102 *AJIL* 768.

the low level of domestic enforcement of human rights norms likely suggests that the legitimacy of the African human rights system may be under pressure. On a number of fronts, there is evidence of an awareness of the need to ensure greater participation in the system, to enhance the system's legitimacy. Great care is taken, for example, to achieve gender diversity in the composition of the Commission. The central role of NGOs in the same system is another example, as is the Commission's tradition of holding its sessions in different parts of the continent. On the other hand, the cases that the African Court has heard so far have not captured the imagination about the future of the Court, compared, for example, to the lasting impact of the cases of *Velásquez-Rodríguez v Honduras* or *Lawless v Ireland* in the other regional systems. It must, however, be noted that it took the Inter-American and European Courts some years before they started to hand down such seminal judgments.

The strength of the regional contribution to international human rights jurisprudence is evident from the number of individuals who seek its protection, the NGOs who focus their attention on these institutions, and—to a varying degree—the collaboration of states. But perhaps the best illustration of their vibrancy was alluded to earlier: the fact that each of the three regional systems has a court that makes legally binding decisions, at its apex. The idea that the UN treaty bodies would make legally binding decisions similar to those of a court—or that the UN would create a world court of human rights—has so far failed to gain wide support and is not about to be implemented.[124]

The proximity that regional human rights systems have to the people they serve while still forming part of international law, places them in a uniquely strong position to promote and protect universal human rights, understood here to entail a universality of norms, as well as a universality of participation.

The shortcomings of some of the emerging systems and initiatives cannot be denied. However, they provide potentially valuable entry points in the quest to make the human rights project more responsive. The ASEAN and Arab League initiatives may currently be limited and limiting in their focus, but it is clear that this was the case, for example, with the European and Inter-American systems in their early years, as well. The history of human rights has incorporated the stories of people from all walks of life—members of civil society, in some cases officials and judges—who have engaged with the opportunities that such entry points offer, however limited, and who have enabled the systems to live up to their promise.

[124] On the global level, the International Court of Justice deals with human rights issues only in a peripheral way. The work of the International Criminal Court, for its part, does have concrete implications for some rights, such as the right to life, but its jurisdiction is confined to individual criminal responsibility in respect of those rights. On the idea of a world human rights court, see Manfred Nowak, 'The Need for a World Court of Human Rights' (2007) 7 *HRL Rev* 251.

For human rights to be successful as a universal project, it has to be rooted in the daily lives of people—universality has to be participatory; it has to grab people's imagination and therefore their actions and commitment. Geneva, for all its importance, is indeed very far from where most people live. Human rights may truthfully be seen as an international language for the use of power, which finds expression and is claimed in many tongues. It is a language that is all the more compelling and vibrant because of its regional dialects.

Further Reading

Bates E, *The Evolution of the European Convention on Human Rights* (OUP 2010)

Burgorgue-Larsen L and Úbeda de Torres A, *The Inter-American Court of Human Rights: Case Law and Commentary* (OUP 2011)

Faúndez Ledesma H, *The Inter-American System for the Protection of Human Rights: Institutional and Procedural Aspects* (Inter-American Institute of Human Rights 2008)

Harris D and others, *Law of the European Convention on Human Rights* (2nd edn, OUP 2009)

Heyns C, Padilla D, and Zwaak L, 'A Schematic Comparison of Regional Human Rights Systems' in Gómez Isa F and de Feyter K (eds), *International Human rights Law in a Global Context* (Deusto UP 2009) 927–39

Heyns C and Killander M, 'Towards Minimum Standards for Regional Human Rights Systems' in Arsanjani MH and others (eds), *Looking to the Future: Essays on International Law in Honor of W Michael Reisman* (Martinus Nijhoff 2011) 527–58

Pasqualucci J, 'The Americas' in Moeckli D, Shah S, and Sivakumaran S (eds), *International Human Rights Law* (OUP 2010) 433–53

Shelton D and Carozza P, *Regional Protection of Human Rights* (2nd edn, OUP 2013)

van Dijk P and others (eds), *Theory and Practice of the European Convention on Human Rights* (4th edn, Intersentia 2006)

Viljoen F, *International Human Rights Law in Africa* (2nd edn, OUP 2012)

CHAPTER 29

NATIONAL IMPLEMENTATION AND INTERPRETATION

NISUKE ANDO

1. Introduction

The implementation of international human rights law is realized through the domestic legal systems of states. It is important, therefore, to clarify how treaty and (the relatively few) customary rules and principles of human rights law are brought into national or domestic legal systems of states, by what mechanisms the rules and principles are implemented within the national or domestic legal systems and, in those processes, what specific problems arise. International human rights standards, both customary law and treaty norms, may be implemented or interpreted by state organs in all branches of government (legislative, executive, judicial) and at any level of governance. The term 'implemented' usually indicates acts of legislative or executive organs, while the term 'interpreted' indicates acts of judicial organs. The distinction is not always maintained, however, because legislative and executive organs also interpret rules and principles of international human rights law and interpretation by judicial organs may be based on incorporating acts of legislative or executive organs. Consequently, the term 'implementation' may embrace 'interpretation' as well.

Large numbers of multilateral treaties concern human rights. Some of them set forth a comprehensive catalogue of human rights, others contain more limited guarantees, and still others concern only a specific human right, such as freedom from torture. Some treaties are aimed at global acceptance, while the scope of others is regional or sub-regional. The following discussion uses the examples of the global International Covenant on Civil and Political Rights (ICCPR) and the European Convention for the Protection of Human Rights and Fundamental Freedoms (ECHR) to examine issues of national implementation and interpretation. One big difference between the two is that the ECHR is equipped with a judicial body that may render a decision binding on states parties, although how that decision is carried out is left to the domestic authorities. In contrast, ICCPR monitoring results in non-binding decisions called 'views' or 'concluding observations' whose implementation is left to the discretion of states parties.

2. Reception of International Human Rights Law in National Legal Systems

2.1 Ratification, accession, and succession

The initial phase of reception of an international human rights treaty in national legal systems ordinarily takes the form of ratification, accession,[1] or succession.[2]

Ratification is usually preceded by signature of the treaty by a state's representative, followed by a procedure to endorse its content in accordance with domestic constitutional requirements. In the case of the United States, for example, the federal Constitution establishes a requirement that a treaty receive the approval of the

[1] The term 'accession' means that a state is expressing its consent to be bound by a multilateral treaty after the treaty itself has entered into force. For example, the International Covenant on Civil and Political Rights (ICCPR) came into force in 1976, when the thirty-fifth instrument of ratification was deposited with the Secretary General; states have adhered to the Covenant since that point.

[2] With the demise of the Soviet Union, Russia succeeded to the ICCPR, thereby becoming a party. In contrast, the three Baltic states, Belarus, and the Ukraine joined the same treaty by accession for the purpose of emphasizing their own identity separate from that of the Soviet Union. The ten Commonwealth of the Independent States (CIS) states followed suit. Another unique problem of state succession arose with the transfer of Hong Kong from the United Kingdom to China. The agreement of transfer required China to continue applying the ICCPR to Hong Kong, although China itself is not a party to the treaty. The succession of Macao to the ICCPR followed the same pattern on the basis of agreement between Portugal and China.

Senate by a two-thirds majority before the President ratifies the agreement. After the approval of the treaty through the relevant procedure, the government submits an instrument of ratification, which confirms the final consent of the state. Multilateral human rights treaties adopted by the United Nations usually provide for the instrument of ratification to be submitted to the United Nations Secretary-General.

2.2 Reservation, derogation, and denunciation

When ratifying or acceding to a treaty, a state may formulate one or more 'reservations' that purports to exclude or modify the legal effect of a provision of the treaty. The United States, for example, ratified the ICCPR with a reservation to exclude the application of Article 6(5), which prohibits the imposition of the death penalty on persons who committed their crimes before they were eighteen years old. At the time, the criminal law of some states within the United States retained the death penalty for persons above sixteen years of age (that practice no longer exists).[3] France formulated a reservation to prevent ICCPR Articles 9 and 14, which provide for the security of persons and the details of criminal procedure, from applying to military disciplinary measures. Germany also entered a reservation to Article 14, paragraph 5, to exclude higher courts' appellate review for 'every' criminal offence of minor gravity. In another example, the United Kingdom formulated a reservation to Article 10, paragraph 2(a) and paragraph 3, in order to modify mandatory separation of adult from juvenile detainees in prisons.

The domestic scope of application of international human rights standards is thus narrowed, to the extent of the reservations, but not every reservation is permissible under international law. The VCLT Article 19 prohibits reservations inconsistent with the text of a treaty and prohibits those inconsistent with the agreement's object and purpose, in the event the treaty text does not regulate the scope of permissible reservations,. In fact, the above-mentioned US reservation met with objections from many European states parties to the ICCPR that the reservation was incompatible with the object and purpose of the treaty.

The VCLT defines a reservation as any unilateral statement that changes a legal right or obligation contained in a treaty, whatever the name the state attaches to its document. Egypt made the following 'declaration' when it ratified the ICCPR: 'Taking into consideration the provisions of the Islamic Shariah and the fact that they do not conflict with [the Covenant], we accept, support and ratify it.' Whether this amounts to a reservation or remains a mere interpretative declaration cannot be determined by the text alone. Many members of the Human Rights Committee that

[3] The United States Supreme Court subsequently held that application of the death penalty to juvenile offenders was unconstitutional, citing in part international consensus on the topic. *Roper v Simmons.*

monitors implementation of the ICCPR, pointed out to the Egyptian delegation discrepancies between provisions of the Covenant and Egyptian laws and customs, recommending either clarification of the declaration or its withdrawal altogether.

Treaty articles foreseeing 'derogations' also may allow a state party to a human rights treaty to limit temporarily the internal application of some of its provisions. According to ICCPR Article 4, a state party may take measures to derogate from certain guaranteed rights in time of public emergency threatening the life of the nation.

However, the party should limit such measures to those strictly required by the exigencies of the situation, and the actions taken may not be discriminatory or inconsistent with the state's other obligations under international law, and should be immediately notified to the other states parties to the Covenant through the UN Secretary-General. The ECHR Article 15 contains a similar permission for temporary suspension of some rights during an emergency and a requirement for a state party to inform fully the Secretary-General of the Council of Europe of the derogation measures taken. Both the ICCPR and the ECHR (as well as the American Convention on Human Rights) prohibit any derogation with respect to certain basic rights such as freedom from arbitrary deprivation of life, torture or slavery and retroactive application of criminal law.

Derogation concerns a temporary suspension of human rights guarantees contained in a treaty, whereas 'denunciation' means permanent withdrawal from the entire agreement. Whether human rights treaties allow denunciation in the absence of a provision permitting it has been discussed in the context of the ICCPR. The treaty contains no provision concerning denunciation, although the ICCPR's First Optional Protocol, Article 12, paragraph 1, explicitly provides for the right of any state party to denounce it. Invoking this provision, Jamaica in 1997 and Trinidad and Tobago in 1998 and 2000 denounced the Optional Protocol, without raising any issue of the legality of their action under international law. The permissibility of denouncing the ICCPR itself arose in April 1997, when the Democratic People's Republic of Korea (North Korea) sent a note to the Human Rights Committee purporting to denounce the Covenant. In reply to the note, the Committee issued a General Comment on the matter,[4] in which it noted that the ICCPR and the Optional Protocol were adopted by the UN General Assembly at the same time in 1966, with the latter instrument providing for the right to denounce but not the former. According to the Human Rights Committee (HRC), this evidenced the drafters' deliberate intention to exclude the possibility of denunciation of the ICCPR. Moreover, the HRC deemed the ICCPR by nature not to be the type of treaty for which it is possible to imply a right of denunciation,[5] because once people are

[4] UN Human Rights Committee, 'General Comment No 26: Continuity of Obligations (8 December 1997) UN Doc CCPR/C/21/Rev.l/App.B/Rev.l

[5] In the absence of a specific provision in a treaty providing for denunciation, the VCLT Article 56 provides that it is prohibited, unless it is established that the parties intended, to admit the possibility or the right of denunciation 'may be implied by the nature of the treaty'.

accorded the protection of human rights under the Covenant such protection continues despite change in government of the state concerned as an objective legal regime. Thus, international law does not permit a state which has ratified or acceded or succeeded to the Covenant to denounce it or withdraw from it. The General Comment made clear that North Korea's purported denunciation had no effect on its obligations under the Covenant. North Korea apparently acquiesced to this treaty interpretation, because it submitted its second periodic report in December 1999.

3. Incorporation

3.1 Modalities of incorporation

Treaty provisions, including those of a human rights treaty, need to be incorporated into the national or domestic legal system of a state before a litigating party may invoke those provisions in the state's courts, because such courts, as creations of the domestic legal order, can apply only that law that is part of the same legal order. International law leaves it to the domestic legal system of each state to determine the method of incorporating treaty provisions and customary international law. Roughly speaking, there are two modalities of such incorporation: an 'automatic' or 'general acceptance' of treaty provisions and a 'specific or individual acceptance' of the same.

Automatic or general acceptance, sometimes called the French formula, allows treaty provisions to be invoked before national courts once the final consent of the state to be bound by the treaty is granted either by ratification, accession or succession and the treaty provisions are published in the official journal of the state. The United States,[6] Japan, and many other states adhere to this formula. The British and many former British colonies, in contrast, require enactment of a specific national or domestic law in addition to and after granting final consent of the state to be bound by a treaty. Many Scandinavian and some European states have a similar constitutional framework.

In the area of human rights, the United Kingdom adopted a Human Rights Act in 2000, allowing litigants to plead ECHR treaty rights against any public authority; courts have jurisdiction to enforce all the Convention rights except when they

[6] Article VI of the US Constitution provides that treaties made under the authority of the United States are the supreme law of the land. See *Ware v Hylton*.

conflict with Parliamentary statutes, although appellate court judges are authorized to declare such statutes as incompatible with the Convention. Similarly, in 2003, Ireland incorporated the European Convention to supplement its own detailed domestic Charter of Rights. In 1994, Sweden adopted a proposal for Parliament to incorporate the European Convention, although parties had invoked and Swedish courts had adjudicated ECHR rights rather than its own Bill of Rights during the previous two decades, seemingly making incorporation unnecessary.

In fact, European states parties to the ECHR have incorporated the treaty in their domestic legal systems in one way or another; this practice is not as widespread with the International Covenant on Civil and Political Rights. When these states appear before the HRC to review the conformity of their domestic laws and practices with the Covenant, they defend their non-incorporation on the basis that they do not consider such action necessary because their existing domestic laws (and the ECHR) have provisions equivalent to those of the Covenant. Nonetheless, it often turns out that it is indeed necessary for them to amend some existing law or enact a new one.

3.2 Rank of the treaty in national or domestic legal systems

When a state incorporates a human rights treaty in its national or domestic legal system, the question arises as to the hierarchy of the treaty in the system, particularly in relation to constitution and national laws. International law also leaves this matter to each state to determine. Roughly speaking, there are three different variations in constitutional provisions.

The Netherlands Constitution provides an example of the highest ranking. According to the Constitution of the Netherlands, a treaty which may contravene a Constitutional provision is valid if it is concluded with the consent of a two-thirds majority of the both Houses of Parliament.[7] However, since the Constitution itself may be amended with the same majority, it can be regarded that the Constitutional provision at issue has been amended in line with the treaty. The constitutions of some African states incorporate the Universal Declaration of Human Rights and the International Covenant on Civil and Political Rights, while some Latin American constitutions give constitutional rank to some or all human rights treaties, but not treaties regulating other topics.[8] There appears to be a trend to give human rights treaties preferential treatment in domestic

[7] Article 91(3).

[8] In 2011, for example, Mexico adopted an amendment to Article I of its constitution to give constitutional standing to international human rights treaties.

constitutions.[9] Those countries that have experienced dictatorships or foreign occupation generally reveal greater receptivity to international law, often incorporating or referring to specific international texts in their post-repression constitutions. The failures of the domestic legal order appear to have inspired these countries to turn towards an international 'safety net'. This is evident not only in the new constitutions of Central and Eastern Europe, but also in those of Argentina, South Africa, and, from an earlier period, Spain and Portugal. In any event, in these systems, provisions of a human rights treaty has a constitutional rank.

In many states including France and Japan, a treaty is subordinate to the Constitution, but superior to legislation.[10] In such systems, a treaty in contravention of a Constitutional provision may not be concluded without Constitutional amendment. At the same time, an international treaty or agreement duly ratified or recognized has superiority over an ordinary law. Consequently, provisions of a human rights treaty in contravention of the Constitution may not be enforceable, although they may be enforced against a conflicting prior or subsequently-enacted law.

In a third model, represented by the United States, a treaty may not contravene the Federal Constitution and is ranked at the same level as a Federal law. Therefore, when a treaty is concluded that contravenes an existing Federal law, the later in time treaty prevails; the reverse is also true, in that a later statute can override an earlier treaty. Here, the principle *lex posterior derogate priori* holds, although it is substantially mitigated by the rule that whenever possible the treaty and legislation should be read so that the domestic law complies with US treaty obligations.[11]

A few constitutions appear to leave the issue of hierarchy between treaties and domestic law unresolved,[12] either failing to mention the topic or doing so in terms that are ambiguous about the place of international law in the domestic legal system.

[9] In Argentina, Slovakia, and Venezuela, special status is given to human rights treaties. The Argentine Constitution mentions a number of human rights treaties, giving them constitutional status; they cannot be repealed by the legislature. Similarly, Art 23 of the 1999 Venezuelan Constitution grants human right treaties a high level in the constitutional hierarchy, to the extent that those treaties contain provisions more favorable than domestic legislation. Austria and Italy require a parliamentary supermajority to give treaties the same status as constitutional provisions. Article 154(c) of Slovakia's Constitution provides that human rights treaties adopted prior to I July 2001 have this status only if the rights are of greater scope than those provided in the constitution. For further examples, see Thomas Buergenthal, 'Modem Constitutions and Human Rights Treaties' (1997) 36 *Colum J Transnat'l L* 211. See the reports contained in Dinah Shelton (ed), *International Law in Domestic Legal Systems* (OUP 2011).

[10] Other states in this category include Bulgaria, France, Germany, Greece, Portugal, and Russia.

[11] *The Charming Betsy* case.

[12] Article 98 of the Japanese Constitution provides, without further elaboration in the text, that the Constitution is the supreme law of the land and that 'The treaties concluded by Japan... shall be faithfully observed'.

Some constitutions simply make reference to the principles and norms of international law or to international obligations.[13]

As for customary law, many countries lack a clear rule on the place of custom in the domestic legal order.[14] For example, whether or not customary international law overrides common law precedent in Canada is unclear, but it does yield to clearly inconsistent statutory language. To avoid conflict, courts in Canada as well as some other common law countries, have developed and entrenched an interpretive doctrine that presumes legislative intent to conform domestic law to international customary as well as treaty law. As a consequence, courts must interpret domestic law in conformity with international legal obligations where possible. Domestic legislation continues to prevail, however, when it cannot be reconciled with international law. Indeed most systems, whether common law or civil law in origin, privilege written law over unwritten custom.

In contrast, customary international law has the force of constitutional law in some countries. In Italy, for example, any domestic law in conflict with custom is held to violate indirectly the Italian Constitution and can be repealed by the Constitutional Court; however, the Constitution and basic human rights guarantees prevail over the observance of international customary law in case of conflict. In Greece as well, the generally recognized rules of international law are stated in the Constitution to be an integral part of domestic Greek law and to prevail over any contrary provision of the law.

3.3 Self-executing character of a treaty provision

The term 'self-executing' ordinarily means that a treaty provision is capable of immediate judicial enforcement. In contrast, rights or obligations of a general or ambiguous content need legislative enactment of specific or clear content before a court will be able to apply them. The doctrine of self-executing treaties developed as judicial doctrine, rooted in notions of separation of powers; Constitutions rarely speak to this issue. Most courts look for (1) expressions of the intent of the parties, (2) whether or not the agreement creates specific rights in private parties, and (3) whether the provisions of the treaty are capable of being applied directly.

In the states that follow an automatic incorporation model, the ICCPR provisions are, in principle, applicable without specific national legislation. However, Article 23, Paragraph 2, of the Covenant stipulates 'The right of men and women

[13] Examples include the constitutions of the Czech Republic, the Republic of Hungary, Portugal, and Slovakia.

[14] Like that of many other constitutions, the Netherlands' Constitution is silent on customary international law. The Portuguese Constitution also does not clearly indicate hierarchy. Authors almost unanimously ascribe a superior value to general international law, but opinions are divided as to its hierarchical position in relation to the constitution.

of marriageable age to marry and found a family shall be recognized'; national legislation is required to clarify what 'marriageable age' is. Except for instances like this, the ICCPR presents numerous rights capable of immediate judicial application. Perhaps in order to avoid this result, the US Senate appended a declaration to its approval of the ICCPR to assert that the Covenant provisions of Articles 1 through 27 require specific national or domestic legislation in order to grant 'rights and obligations' to individuals. Considerable debate revolves around the question of whether or not this declaration is in fact a reservation to the Covenant.

In any event, the self-executing character of a human rights treaty provision needs to be examined with respect to any state party having this doctrine, in order to determine whether a specific national law will be required for the domestic implementation of that provision. In this connection, it is interesting to note that the Constitution of the Republic of South Africa[15] has a stipulation to the effect that, while an international agreement needs to be incorporated by legislation to constitute part of the law of the Republic, no such incorporation is necessary regarding an international agreement of self-executing character which has been recognized by the Parliament and does not contravene domestic law of the Republic.

European courts tend to discuss 'direct applicability' or 'direct effect' rather than self-execution, but the courts behave similarly in examining the question of whether the treaty provision in question is capable of judicial enforcement or whether an intervening legislative or executive act is required.[16] The factors utilized by national courts in deciding on the direct application of a treaty provision are strikingly similar,[17] relying on the language of the treaty and an assessment of whether or not the provision can be applied directly consistent with the appropriate functions of the judiciary. While courts often refer to the intent of the parties, the decisive criterion most commonly

[15] Section 231(4).

[16] Even those countries where treaties must be incorporated into domestic law face this issue. The exception seems to be Israel, where it has been accepted that treaties are not automatically accepted into domestic law, but instead need to be implemented by primary legislation, or even by secondary legislation—provided such implementation was previously authorized in principle by primary legislation. Non-implemented treaties are not devoid of any legal effect, though, since the courts have adopted a rule of interpretation and a rule of presumption which ensure, to the extent possible, the compatibility of Israeli domestic law with Israel's international commitments. The incorporation doctrine and practice means there is very limited scope for the notion of self-executing treaties in Israel.

[17] In the Czech Republic, as in most other states, a ratified treaty is regarded as self-executing if the rights and obligations stipulated therein are sufficiently specific that such a treaty can be applied in the legal order without any further legislative specification in a separate act. In Greece, similarly, international agreements have a 'self-executing' character if their provisions have achieved a letter of sufficiency and fullness, recognize the rights of private persons capable of supporting legal actions before tribunals, or prescribing the obligations of the executive branch, which private persons can invoke before tribunals. 'Non-self-executing' treaties are those international conventions which do not produce direct legal effects in the internal legal order, either because their application requires the promulgation of supplementary measures in the internal field, or because their purpose is not the recognition or the attribution of rights capable of being pursued by judicial procedures.

cited is whether or not the provision is sufficiently precise to be capable of judicial enforcement.[18] Some courts have referred to this test as one of the 'self-sufficiency' of the provision.[19]

Judges from British Commonwealth and other common law countries participating in a series of colloquia on the relationship between international and domestic law adopted a statement in 1998 that 'the universality of human rights derives from the moral principle of each individual's personal and equal autonomy and human dignity. That principle transcends national political systems and is in the keeping of the judiciary'.[20]

It is striking that such a statement issued from judges whose legal systems are traditionally dualist. Melissa Waters correctly reads this declaration to imply that the international law of human rights is the 'primary, authoritative source for human rights norms: Domestic legal sources are merely derivative of international human rights law'.[21] Under this approach, the role of judges is to harmonize domestic law with the superior law in an integrated legal order, a role that recent case law indicates some judges are fulfilling by implying rights, presuming that statutes are intended to conform to international norms (even those not in force for the state), and developing the normative content of the common law.[22]

4. Mechanism of Implementation and Interpretation

4.1 Basic commitments

The VCLT incorporates the fundamental principle of treaty law: *pacta sunt servanda*. The specific obligations of states parties are spelled out in the global and regional human rights treaties. ICCPR Article 2(1), for example, requires each state party 'to respect and to ensure all individuals within its territory and subject to

[18] cf Administrative Court, Collection No 5819 F, 21 October 1983; Supreme Court, Decision No 70bl/86, 20 February 1986.

[19] (1995) 5 Ann dr lux 307.

[20] 'The Challenge of Bangalore: Making Human Rights a Practical Reality' in Commonwealth Secretariat, *Developing Human Rights Jurisprudence, Volume 8: Eighth Judicial Colloquium on the Domestic Application of International Human Rights Norms* (Commonwealth Secretariat 2002) 268.

[21] Melissa A Waters, 'Creeping Monism: The Judicial Trend Toward Interpretive Incorporation of Human Rights Treaties' (2007) 107 *Colum L Rev* 628, 648.

[22] See Waters (n 21); Vicki Jackson, 'Constitutional Comparisons: Convergence, Resistance, Engagement' (2005) 119 *Harv L Rev* 109; Francis G Jacobs and Shelley Roberts (eds), *The Effect of Treaties in Domestic Law* (Sweet & Maxwell 1987).

its jurisdiction the rights enshrined in the present Covenant'. Paragraph 2 adds that where the rights are not already provided for by existing legislative or other measures, each state party 'undertakes to take the necessary steps... to adopt such legislative or other measures as may be necessary to give effect to the rights'. A further obligation, set forth in paragraph 3, demands that each state party 'ensure any person whose rights or freedoms as herein recognized are violated shall have an effective remedy' and that those remedies will be determined by competent judicial, administrative or legislative authorities. Article 1(1) of the American Convention on Human Rights is similar.[23] The ECHR stipulates, in Article 1, that 'The High Contracting Parties shall secure to everyone within their jurisdiction the rights and freedoms' defined in the Convention. The Convention has no provision equivalent to the ICCPR and ACHR requirement of legislative incorporation.

All of the treaties mentioned have monitoring bodies to oversee compliance by states parties with the obligations assumed. The European Convention and the American Convention each created a regional court that may give a binding decision in a case presented to it,[24] in contrast to the ICCPR, which has no such system. Instead, Article 1 of the ICCPR's first Optional Protocol provides for a system of communications from individuals who claim to be victims of a violation by that state party of any of the rights set forth in the Covenant. Once the Committee's views are expressed on a case against a state party, it is up to that state party if and how the state party will respond to the Committee's decision.

The findings of the HRC can nonetheless have impact. The Republic of Korea's National Security Law, enacted after the Korean War to guard against communist or socialist concept or influence, was criticized by the HRC after Korea became a state party to the ICCPR and its Optional Protocol. The Human Rights Committee adopted views which found a violation of the right to freedom of expression enshrined in the Covenant, after which both the Korean Government and the judiciary started moving towards an interpretation of the law more in conformity with the ICCPR. At the same time, a big question for Korea was the principle of *res judicata* in its domestic legal system. Because of this principle, once the Supreme Court of Korea handed down a judgment, it is legally impossible to implement the Human Rights Committee's decision even if the Committee finds a violation of the Covenant provision. The only way out is for the Korean legislature to adopt a new law enabling the implementation of the Committee decision.

[23] 'The States Parties to this Convention undertake to respect the rights and freedoms recognized herein and to ensure to all persons subject to their jurisdiction the free and full exercise of those rights and freedom' and in Art 2: 'Where the exercise of the rights or freedoms... is not already ensured by legislative or other provisions, the States Parties undertake to adopt... such legislative or other measures as may be necessary to give effect to those rights and freedoms.'

[24] Jurisdiction of the European Court is automatic with respect to all states parties to the ECHR, whereas states parties to the American Convention must file a separate declaration accepting the contentious jurisdiction of the Court. All but three states parties have done so.

4.2 Choice of means of implementation

A state party to a human rights treaty is generally free to choose from among various domestic organs and operations in implementing its treaty obligations. States often create an independent organ such as an Ombudsman to monitor their actions, in particular the actions of police agents, so that they comply with international human rights standards. An Ombudsman may be entitled to receive complaints from citizens and report to another state agent or to bring an action on behalf of the complainants. Alternatively, in accordance with the so-called Paris Principles[25] adopted by the UN General Assembly in 1993, a state may establish a National Human Right Commission with the power to advise the Government, Parliament or any other competent state agency on matters concerning the promotion and protection of human rights. In fact, many states have instituted an Ombudsman office or National Human Rights Commission or both. Other existing administrative and judicial organs of a state may perform to give effect to international human rights standards in the performance of their functions.

The Korean case above suggests that state legislatures often play a decisive role in implementing international human rights standards, important in any democratic system. For example, when in 1981 the Japanese initial report was considered by the ICCPR's Human Rights Committee, some of its members found a discrepancy between the Japanese Nationality Law and the principle of sexual equality enshrined in the Covenant, because the law stipulated that a child could inherit Japanese nationality from the father, whereas the mother's Japanese nationality could be inherited only when the father's nationality law would make the child stateless. Following the dialogue that took place between the state and the HRC, the Japanese government consulted a board of legal experts. Upon Japan's ratification of the Convention on the Elimination of All Forms of Discrimination against Women in 1985, the Nationality Law was amended to enable a child to inherit mother's nationality on the same footing as that of the father's.

A change in national legal norms to conform to international human rights standards often involves more than a single state organ. The case of Dutch Unemployment Benefit Law presents a good example. The law used to require that, in order to receive the unemployment benefit, a married woman must prove that she was the 'breadwinner of the family' whereas a married man or a single woman could receive the benefit without such proof. Two Dutch married women submitted a communication under the ICCPR's Optional Protocol, claiming that the law violated the principle of equality on the ground of sex as well as social status. The HRC decided in their favour, relying on Article 26 which provides for equality before the law and equal protection of the law. The Dutch government, while opposing the Committee's decision because the Committee dealt with the case of a 'social

[25] UNGA Res 48/134 (20 December 1993), UN Doc A/Res/48/134.

right' (unemployment benefit) in regards to a treaty that guaranteed civil and political rights, offered compensation not only to the two women, but to all others in the same position. It must not be overlooked that some Dutch lower courts had rendered judgments similar to that of the HRC and that the law was subsequently amended in line with the Committee decision. Here, it is obvious that the executive, the judiciary and the legislature were all involved in changing the legal norm.

4.3 Exhaustion of domestic remedies

The rule concerning the exhaustion of domestic or local remedies originally developed in the law of state responsibility where it barred a state from exercising the right of diplomatic protection of a citizen who had suffered injury attributable to a wrongful state act abroad, until the citizen had exhausted all remedies locally available in the country where the injury occurred. Its purpose was to allow the state committing the wrong to redress the injury before being brought to an international venue. The ECHR and all subsequent human rights treaties adopted this rule as one of the preconditions before victims can submit a claim to the relevant international organ for protection.

With respect to the requirement of exhaustion of domestic remedies, three issues need to be noted. The first is that the domestic remedies should not only be 'available' but also 'effective'. In many cases domestic remedies are available in form but not in substance. For example, if the higher court's precedent in respect to a similar claim has been firmly established against the claim, then it is not necessary for the claimant to appeal because the domestic remedies should be regarded as exhausted in substance. Also, if a higher court is entitled to look into issues of law only but not those of facts while the dispute at a lower court concerns facts, then the appeal may be available in form but not in substance. In such a situation, the remedies should be regarded as exhausted at the lower instance.

The second is the issue of the time limit for admissibility. ECHR Article 35, Paragraph I, stipulates 'The Court may only deal with the matter after all domestic remedies have been exhausted and within a period of six months from the date on which the final decision was taken'. In contrast, Article 5, Paragraph 2 (b), of the Optional Protocol attached to the Covenant on Civil and Political Rights stipulates 'The [Human Rights] Committee shall not consider any communication unless it has ascertained that: [t]he individual has exhausted all available domestic remedies. This shall not be the rule where the application of the remedies is unreasonably prolonged'. The question is what constitutes the time-limit for the HRC to admit a communication on the ground of 'unreasonably prolonged' remedies. Sometimes a communication comes from a prisoner who has been in death row for longer than ten years. The lengthy period results from the time necessary to deal with the prisoner's appeal, request for re-trial, or habeas corpus challenges to the constitutionality of the proceedings, all matters within the control of the prisoner. But because, unlike the ECHR, the Optional Protocol itself does not specify the time-limit for admissibility of the claim, it is difficult for the Human Rights Committee to determine how long the remedies may be delayed before constituting "unreasonably prolonged' ones.

The third is the issue of retrial or revision of a final domestic decision. As indicated by the above-mentioned Korean experience in respect to the Supreme Court's *res judicata* doctrine, an international legal decision in conflict with the final decision of a domestic court, in particular that of the highest judicial authority of a state, causes difficulty for implementation of the international decision. One way out is to treat the international decision as a new fact which requires retrial under the existing domestic legal system. The other is to amend an existing domestic law or to enact a new domestic law which enables the implementation of the international decision. In any event, a retrial may help to alleviate the tension between an original domestic final decision and the conflicting international decision.

In 1997 the European Court of Human Rights decided that the Dutch court had violated the ECHR because it convicted the applicant on the basis of statements by anonymous witnesses.[26] The case involved a particularly brutal armed robbery, but he was quickly released after the European Court's decision and received damages from the Dutch government, although he was unable to alter the criminal conviction and the Dutch society was dissatisfied with the release of the person because his innocence remained seriously in doubt. Later in 2002 the Dutch Code of Criminal Procedure came to recognize explicitly that the judgment of the European Court in favour of the person criminally convicted in the domestic proceedings should enable the reopening of the proceedings. If the *Mechelen* case had been put to retrial, it would have been less dissatisfactory to everyone involved.

5. National Implementation of Jurisprudence

The implementation of international human rights decisions or recommendations at the national or domestic level raises various problems. For the sake of convenience, this 'jurisprudence' will be examined in two separate categories: (1) treaty bodies that deliver non-binding decisions, and (2) judicial bodies that make binding decisions.

[26] *Van Mechelen et al v Netherlands.*

5.1 Under the international legal system with non-binding decisions

As noted above, a representative international treaty with a monitoring body that issues non-binding decisions is the International Covenant on Civil and Political Rights and the Optional Protocol attached to the Covenant. The Human Rights Committee, the monitoring body under the Covenant, examines the reports of each state party that present the state's domestic implementation of the Covenant provisions. Following study of the report and a hearing, the Committee adopts Concluding Observations, indicating where problems lie in the implementation and what should be done to overcome the problems. The Committee also examines individual complaints under the Optional Protocol and, when it finds a violation of a Covenant provision by the state party concerned, adopts final views on the merits and indicates the remedies the state party should afford the applicant. Neither the Concluding Observations nor the final views have binding legal force, although the role conferred on the HRC suggests that states parties should pay due regard in good faith to its authoritative views and observations. The state party nonetheless retains discretion to implement the Committee's decisions.

The international human rights law or standards indicated by the Committee are given consideration by the states party. It has been observed that the Japanese Nationality Law was amended following the indication of some Committee members. The Committee's views on the Dutch Unemployment Benefit Law were implemented by the Netherlands. Likewise, Finland consistently follows the Committee's Observations as well as its final views. Furthermore, several states of Latin America have enacted what they call 'Enabling Law' that obligates them to implement the Committee's views. At the same time, generally speaking, much remains to be done with respect to national or domestic implementation of the International Covenant on Civil and Political Rights and its attached Optional Protocol. The periodic state reports and 'shadow' reports of non-governmental organizations, as well as widespread media reports, attest to human rights concerns in every country that is a Party to the ICCPR.

5.2 Under the international legal system with binding decisions

The European Convention on Human Rights and Fundamental Freedoms, with its full time court issuing more than 1000 judgments a year, has certainly had considerable impact on the domestic implementation of international human rights law or standards in its states parties. The United Kingdom, France, and Germany provide examples of this impact.

- The United Kingdom

The United Kingdom was among the first states to ratify the European Convention in 1951 (two years before the Convention came into force in 1953) but it was only in 1966 that it accepted the then-optional right of individuals of international petition under the Convention. Two basic features characterize the British legal system: (1) Parliamentary supremacy and (2) no written Constitution with a Bill of Rights. Both of these two characteristics seem to have been affected by the interpretation and application of the European Convention.

British law courts initially were rather reluctant to refer to, interpret and apply provisions of the Convention, probably in consideration of Parliamentary supremacy. However, a succession of the European Court decisions holding that the United Kingdom had violated the ECHR, prompted more and more British judges to refer to the Convention and to Parliamentary action. In particular, the rejection in 1979 by the European Court[27] of the decision to punish the *Sunday Times* for reporting on thalidomide babies attracted high public attention because of its effort at censoring an issue of public interest. The judgment led Parliament to adopt the Contempt of Court Act in 1991[28] to clarify the components of this crime that had been left to the courts' discretion as a common law crime.

The Human Rights Act of 1998 does not entitle the law courts to nullify Parliamentary enactments but allows the courts to make 'declaration of incompatibility'.[29] The declaration is an invention which enables the courts to declare a Parliamentary legislation incompatible with the European Convention while retaining formal Parliamentary supremacy. Such a declaration was made in 2001 in respect of the indefinite detention of a foreign terrorist suspect before prosecution under Anti-terrorism Crime and Security Act, and Parliament proceeded to enact the Prevention of Terrorism Act in 2005.[30] The Human Rights Act thus authorizes the judiciary to prod the legislature to adopt a new law or amend an existing one, somewhat reducing Parliamentary Supremacy in practice.

The incorporation of the ECHR into the domestic law of the United Kingdom may foreshadow a further change in the British legal system. The Constitutional Reform Act of 2000 reviewed the total structure of the system, foreseeing the establishment of Supreme Court in 2009 which would take over the function of the Law Lords of the House of Lords. In addition, under Equality Act of 2006,[31] it is not improbable that a single Commission for Equality and Human Rights might be established which would integrate various existing organs dealing with issues of equality and discrimination. As a result, the European Convention on Human Rights and Fundamental Freedoms may work as a Bill of Rights for the United Kingdom, a step towards constitutionalizing the European Convention.

[27] *Sunday Times v UK.* [28] Contempt of Court Act 1981, ch 49 (UK).
[29] Article 4(2). [30] Prevention of Terrorism Act 2005, ch 2 (UK). [31] Article 1.

- France

France was heavily involved in drafting the European Convention on Human Rights and Fundamental Freedoms, but it did not ratify the agreement until 1974 and it took another seven years before France recognized individuals' right to petition under the Convention.

As in the case of the United Kingdom, the traditional approach of the French judiciary towards the European Convention was dominated by the concept of 'national sovereignty' which militates against 'supra-nationalism'. The courts tended to interpret obligations under the Convention restrictively and characterized them as subsidiary to the French legal system. Thus the courts allowed the payment of damages awarded by the European Court of Human Rights but considered that the implementation of the remaining parts of the judgment was left for other branches of government.

One characteristic of the French legal system is the triple structure of the highest courts: the Constitutional Council (*Conseil Constitutionelle*) deals with constitutional issues; the Supreme Court (*Cour de Cassation*) handles civil and criminal issues; and the State Council (*Conseil d'Etat*) adjudicates administrative matters. As noted above, France adopts a general or automatic incorporation of a treaty and ranks a treaty below the constitution but above ordinary legislation. In this connection, the Constitutional Council decided in 1975 to make the constitution the only criterion by which it would judge the constitutionality of legislation.[32] This means that Constitutional Council will not adjudicate the compatibility of legislation with the European Convention, leaving the determination of such compatibility to Supreme Court and State Council.

As the ECHR became more widely known, complaints against France greatly increased after France granted individuals' right of international petition under the European Convention in 1981, and particularly after its ratification of ECHR Protocol 11 in 1998. In turn, there resulted an increased number of judgments finding violations of the European Convention by France. This necessitated measures to avoid repetitious cases alleging similar violations on the part of the state. After the European Court held in 1990 that the French legislative provisions on phone-tapping were incompatible with the Convention,[33] a new law reformed the practice to conform to the decision within a year.[34] Also noticeable was the change of the role of the government commissioner (*Commissaire du gouvernement*) in administrative cases. A long established tradition of the State Council allowed such a commissioner to attend proceedings and participate in the deliberation of cases,

[32] *Administration des Douanes v Société 'Cafés Jacques Vabre'.*

[33] *Huvig v France.*

[34] Loi no 91-646 du 10 juillet 1991 relative au secret des correspondences émises par la voie des communications électroniques.

but after the European Court condemned the practice in a judgment of 2001[35] a decree of 2006[36] excluded the commissioner from deliberation.

Until rather recently French lawyers as well as magistrates were not well informed of the ECHR, but now many of them are aware of the Convention and its judicial system. They are also learning rapidly about the jurisprudence of the European Court of Human Rights. As of May 2007, it was reported that about half of the State Council decisions referred to the European Convention. The Supreme Court mentioned the Convention in less than five percent of its decisions, but sixty percent of those were adopted after 2000. Even at the Constitutional Council, there seems to be a move to reconsider the above-mentioned decision of 1975. In its decision of 22 January 1999 concerning the Statute of the International Criminal Court, the Constitutional Council indicated that the categorical refusal to review legislation for compatibility with a treaty, as it does with respect to the constitution, might not be applicable in case of a treaty of humanitarian character.[37] Considering the close relations between humanitarian law and human rights law, the decision may imply a possibility for the Constitutional Council to refer to the European Convention as well.

- Germany

Germany ratified the ECHR in 1951 and slightly before the ratification enacted a federal law incorporating the Convention in substance. In 1955, Germany recognized individuals' right to petition under the Convention. These moves reflect two things: first, the Basic Law (Grundgesetz) of the state, adopted in 1949, which provides extensive guarantees of fundamental rights as well as a detailed system for their protection; second, post-war Germany's strong political will to demonstrate to the international community its commitment to democratization and human rights protection. The German legal system guarantees individuals standing to submit constitutional complaints to the Federal Constitutional Court, the supreme judicial organ to judge on the constitutionality of legal acts, against infringement of their fundamental rights by any public authorities, including courts.

As to the ranking of a treaty in the German domestic legal system, a treaty occupies the same position as federal legislation, thus involving the principle *lex posterior derogate priori*. In a decision of 26 March 1987, however, reaffirmed by another decision in 2004, the Federal Constitutional Court stated that 'the text of the [European] Convention and the case-law of the European Court of Human Rights serve, on the level of constitutional law, as guides to interpretation in determining the content and scope of fundamental rights and constitutional principles of the Basic Law'.[38]

35 *Kress v France*. 36 Code of Admin Just, R 732-2.

37 Decision 98-4087 DC of 22 January 1999, Approval of the Treaty on the Statute of the International Criminal Court, para 12.

38 *Görgülü v Germany*.

Thus, German laws 'are to be interpreted and applied in harmony with [German] commitments under international law, even when such laws were enacted posterior to an applicable international treaty'.[39] The first decision concerned the principle of presumption of innocence and the Federal Constitutional Court explicitly referred to Article 6, paragraph 2, of the European Convention.

A question remains whether the above statement of the Constitutional Court covers all the rights and freedoms enshrined in the European Convention. With respect to the issue of retrial after the European Court has found that a proceeding failed to conform to ECHR standards, Germany amended its Code of Criminal Procedure in 1998, to allow a retrial of all domestic criminal proceedings which are found in violation of the ECHR. In civil and administrative proceedings, however, German laws have rejected the reopening or retrial of cases, mainly on the basis of legal stability, despite the advice of the Council of Ministers of the European Council and the report of the Parliamentary Assembly.

In Germany, the ECHR is considered as basically supplementary to the German domestic federal legal system for the protection of fundamental rights, but nonetheless, Germany ranks near the bottom among states as concerns the number of cases submitted to the European Court of Human Rights. The European Court issued its first judgment with respect to Germany in 1968.[40] Between then and 2010, the Court issued 234 judgments concerning Germany of which 66 per cent found a violation of the Convention; notably 99 per cent of all applications were declared inadmissible or struck out. Slightly more than half of the judgments finding a violation concerned the right to be tried within reasonable time (lengthy proceedings).[41] About 10 per cent of the cases concerned other issues of fair proceedings, such as the right for foreigners to have interpretation without charge.[42] Other judgments addressed the right to be released from detention within certain period (unlawful detention),[43] the right to respect private and family life,[44] prohibition of discrimination,[45] and freedom of expression.[46] Considering the comparatively small number of such cases, it appears that the international human rights standards set forth in the ECHR as interpreted by the European Court have had an impact on the domestic legal system of Germany and that, generally speaking, the state has implemented the standards to a large extent.

[39] BVerfGE 74, 358 (370).

[40] *Wemhoff v Germany.*

[41] See eg *Buchholz v Germany*; *Eckle v Germany.*

[42] Eg *Luedicke, Belkacem, and Koç v Germany.*

[43] Eg *Haidn v Germany.*

[44] Eg *Kutzner v Germany; von Hannover v Germany.*

[45] Eg *Brauer v Germany; Zaunegger v Germany.*

[46] Eg *Axel Springer AG v Germany.*

The review of the national implementation of European human rights standards in the United Kingdom, France, and Germany indicates that the ECHR and its Court have encouraged the three states parties to amend or revise their domestic legislation, where necessary, in line with the requirements of the Convention. The Convention system in which a Court issues binding decisions has prompted the states parties to avoid a repetition of violations. While there are numerous problems with newer states parties from Central and Eastern Europe, it nonetheless seems clear that compared to international human rights treaties that allow only non-binding decisions, fully judicialized systems are more effective in promoting national implementation of international human rights standards.

6. Concluding Remarks

Three concluding remarks are in order. First, the two human rights treaties analysed above guarantee civil and political rights, whose common characteristics in general are non-action by state authorities with respect to citizens' activities (freedom from intervention). In contrast, economic, social and cultural rights largely require action by state authorities with respect to private or non-state activities (necessity of state action to realize rights). Although this chapter has not addressed the second category of rights, much of the analysis is relevant to implementing these human rights as well.

The second remark is that a multilateral human rights treaty should not be the only forum to analyse the implementation of human rights by the national legal system of a state. Obligations arising under a general treaty such as the United Nations Charter may also have an impact. Universal Periodic Review (UPR) instituted by the Human Rights Council serves to review human rights situation of all the UN member states over a four-year period. UPR may provide a valid forum, though much needs to be done to ensure achievement of that purpose.

Third, national or domestic implementation of international human rights law or standards inevitably reflects the 'national legal culture' of each state with its own tradition, religion, society, and history, and this fact should be recognized for objective analysis of implementation. The national implementation of universal human rights law and standards requires practical balancing of reality with ideals, usually a difficult and time-consuming endeavour but an inescapable, necessary process to reach a meaningful outcome.

Further Reading

Burgorgue-Larsen L and Ubeda de Torres A, *The Inter-American Court of Human Rights: Case Law and Commentary* (OUP 2011)

Keller H and Stone-Sweet A (eds), *A Europe of Rights: The Impact of the ECHR on National Legal System* (OUP 2008)

Kyoto Human Rights Research Institute, 'Effectiveness of the Human Rights Committee's Follow-up Procedure' (Proceedings of the International Symposium, Kyoto, 31 January 2010)

Nowak M, *UN Covenant on Civil and Political Rights: CCPR Commentary* (2nd rev edn, Engel 2005)

Joseph S, Schultz J, and Castan M, *The International Covenant on Civil and Political Rights: Cases, Materials, and Commentary* (2nd edn, OUP 2004)

Sciotti-Lam C, *L'Applicabilité des Traités Internationaux Relatifs aux Droits de l'Homme en Droit Interne* (Bruylant 2004)

Shelton D, *Remedies in International Human Rights Law* (2nd edn, OUP 2005)

Viljoen F, *International Human Rights Law in Africa* (2nd edn, OUP 2012)

CHAPTER 30

ROLES AND RESPONSIBILITIES OF NON-STATE ACTORS

DAVID WEISSBRODT[1]

1. Introduction

International law and human rights law have principally focused on protecting individuals from abuse of power by governments. Human rights law's traditional focus on states as violators and individuals as victims insufficiently addressed the major impact that non-state actors have on the protection of human rights—both positively and negatively. Increasing attention is now being paid to individual responsibility for war crimes, genocide, and other crimes against humanity. Following the Nuremberg,[2] Tokyo,[3] and Control Council Law No 10[4] tribunals in the 1940s, the tribunals established in the 1990s for the former Yugoslavia[5] and Rwanda revived

[1] The author wishes to thank Joshua Wetzel of the University of Minnesota Law School Class of 2013 for his assistance in the preparation of this chapter.

[2] Agreement for the Prosecution and Punishment of the Major War Criminals of the European Axis.

[3] Charter of the International Military Tribunal for the Far East.

[4] Control Council, 'Law No 10: Punishment of Persons Guilty of War Crimes, Crimes against Peace and against Humanity' (1946) 3 *Official Gazette Control Council for Germany* 50.

[5] Statute of the International Criminal Tribunal for the Former Yugoslavia.

international criminal law;[6] the establishment of the International Criminal Court,[7] to which over one hundred twenty states are party, further developed it.

Private individuals are non-state actors, but so are such diverse entities as non-governmental or civil society organizations (NGOs), transnational corporations and other business entities, and armed opposition groups. NGOs may be formed to promote and protect human rights locally or around the world; transnational corporations and other commercial entities may violate or further human rights through their business practices; and armed opposition or terrorist groups may violate human rights and humanitarian law, particularly in situations of armed conflict.

States as the principal subjects of international law play a primary role in the formulation of international law and must obey the law they have created. Non-state actors are generally not the subjects of international law, but they can be the objects of it; even though they generally do not play a primary or direct role in formulating the law, they cannot argue that they lack recognition in international law. Similarly, individuals within a society do not necessarily endorse the law, but they must follow it.

Since the formation of the United Nations (UN), a growing body of law has emerged to regulate the roles and responsibilities of non-state actors in regards to human rights. The adoption of the Universal Declaration of Human Rights (UDHR), in 1948, recognized the relevance of human rights law to non-state actors. The UDHR calls itself:

> a common standard of achievement for all peoples and all nations, to the end that every individual and every organ of society, keeping this Declaration constantly in mind, shall strive by teaching and education to promote respect for these rights and freedoms and by progressive measures, national and international, to secure their universal and effective recognition and observance, both among the peoples of Member States themselves and among the peoples of territories under their jurisdiction.[8]

The phrase 'every organ of society' includes non-state actors within the UDHR's scope. Common Article 3 of the 1949 Geneva Conventions adds additional standards for non-state actors in the context of an armed conflict not of an international character.[9] The UN has also articulated roles and responsibilities of non-state actors in human rights treaty and non-treaty instruments.[10]

[6] Statute of the International Criminal Tribunal for Rwanda.

[7] Rome Statute of the International Criminal Court. As of 26 August 2012, 121 states have become parties to the Rome Statute

[8] UDHR, preamble.

[9] Common Article 3 of the Geneva Conventions of 12 August 1949: Geneva Convention for the Amelioration of the Condition of the Wounded and Sick in Armed Forces in the Field; Geneva Convention for the Amelioration of the Condition of Wounded, Sick and Shipwrecked Members of Armed Forces at Sea; Geneva Convention Relative to the Treatment of Prisoners of War; Geneva Convention relative to the Protection of Civilian Persons in Time of War.

[10] See eg International Covenant on Economic, Social and Cultural Rights (ICESCR); International Covenant on Civil and Political Rights (ICCPR); Convention on the Rights of the Child; Declaration on the Right and Responsibility of Individuals, Groups and Organs of Society to Promote and Protect Universally Recognized Human Rights and Fundamental Freedoms; International Convention on the Elimination of All Forms of Racial Discrimination.

Although NGOs, businesses, and armed opposition groups are all non-state actors, unique human rights obligations govern each type of non-state actor. The standards vary greatly in both the degree to which they have been elaborated and the success with which they have been implemented. The greater the power of non-state actors, the more necessary is the development of human rights law to govern them.

2. Non-Governmental or Civil Society Organizations

Human rights NGOs often register as non-profit organizations under the domestic laws of the state where they have their principal headquarters. Their members are individuals who work to promote human rights and prevent human rights abuses by governments, individuals, armed opposition groups, and others.[11] There are thousands of NGOs engaged in the promotion and protection of human rights at the international, regional, national, and local levels.[12] They engage in standards development, violations monitoring, advocacy, campaigns, education, conciliation, and assistance to victims.[13]

The contributions of NGOs to the development of human rights law are undeniable and indispensable. Non-governmental organizations are active in nearly every aspect of international human rights practice. They have advocated for and helped to draft international human rights standards in multilateral treaties and resolutions. They have assisted intergovernmental organizations and governments with the implementation of human rights norms. Non-governmental organizations have also engaged in various measures, which directly encourage improvements in human rights compliance.[14]

From the beginning of the United Nations, NGOs were active in lobbying for human rights standards. The drafters of the UN Charter benefitted from the lobbying of a dozen or more human rights organizations,[15] most of them based in the United States, and some of them officially part of the US delegation. They successfully

[11] Ann Marie Clark, 'Nongovernmental Organizations: Overview' in David P Forsythe (ed), *Encyclopedia of Human Rights* (OUP 2009).

[12] Clark (n 11). [13] Clark (n 11).

[14] Margret E Keck and Kathryn Sikkink, *Activists beyond Borders: Advocacy Networks in International Politics* (Cornell UP 1998).

[15] Theo van Boven, 'The Role of Non-Governmental Organizations in International Human Rights Standard-Setting: A Prerequisite of Democracy' (1990) 20 *Cal W Int'l LJ* 207, 210.

advocated for human rights provisions in Articles 1, 55, and 56 of the Charter.[16] NGOs also participated in the drafting of the UDHR,[17] the two human rights Covenants,[18] and subsequent human rights treaties and other instruments. Their expertise on particular subjects and their perseverance in the drafting process have made them very influential in preparing treaties, such as the Convention on the Rights of the Child, where they worked closely with the government taking the lead on this topic.

In order to be effective in advocating for human rights standards, NGOs must remain informed of human rights conditions and applicable legal principles. NGOs receive information from human rights victims, families, and friends; interview witnesses; visit places of detention, refugee camps, camps for internally displaced persons, hospitals, morgues, and psychiatric institutions; examine injuries and physical evidence; record incidents or distribute cameras to witnesses willing to record abuses; disinter and help perform autopsies on the bodies of persons who have been killed; observe events such as elections, trials, and demonstrations; perform tests as to housing or job discrimination; undertake meetings with government officials; monitor the conduct of corporations or other non-state actors; assess governmental budgets to determine how they will provide for children, women, or other human rights concerns; pursue legal research; and formulate recommendations for corrective action.[19]

Human rights NGOs may work toward the improvement of human rights situations in a number of ways. They meet with or lobby governments and international governmental organizations; testify in favour of legislation; issue media statements and reports; publish newsletters; post material on websites; prepare videotapes; initiate law suits; file amicus curiae and other briefs in court; promote international tribunals and truth commissions; petition or provide information to UN human rights bodies; and encourage investors, banks, universities, and city councils to avoid investing in companies that abuse human rights.

NGOs also mobilize their members and others to support and promote human rights campaigns. For example, NGOs organize individuals and groups to write letters, telegrams, faxes, emails, text messages, and blogs; get petitions signed and submitted; run listserves; post information on websites; hold meetings, teach-ins, seminars, and other discussions; distribute leaflets; put up posters; hold rallies and demonstrations; organize silent vigils, debates, and mock trials; run film screenings and theatre performances; erect museums; and engage in non-violent civil disobedience.[20] Some NGOs develop and distribute curricula and educational materials.

[16] Charter of the United Nations, Arts 1, 55, 56.

[17] Van Boven (n 15) 211.

[18] ICCPR; ICESCR.

[19] Specific examples of tactics used by NGOs and other human rights advocates available from 'Tactics' (*New Tactics in Human Rights*) <http://www.newtactics.org/en/tactics> accessed 20 December 2011.

[20] 'Tactics' (n 19).

They might even teach classes and seminars, as well as provide training for teachers, police, prison guards, military officers, and other government officials.

Those NGOs that are well known for their knowledge of human rights conditions and have a reputation for impartiality may become involved in reconciliation and mediation. They may help to resolve conflicts or other disputes, facilitate negotiations between ethnic communities, develop confidence-building measures, and encourage exchanges of prisoners in the context of armed conflict.[21]

NGOs can further assist human rights victims by responding to requests for emergency aid, food aid, food production techniques and tools, housing or emergency shelter, medicine, healthcare, water, sanitation, protection, and logistics. They may provide rehabilitation to torture victims and give psychological care to other survivors of human rights abuses. NGOs also help feed and house refugees and displaced persons, provide blankets and other necessities to prisoners, seek compensation for human rights victims, give legal advice and assistance, and accompany persons at risk in travelling to dangerous locations.[22]

There is a complex relationship between the work of local, national, and international NGOs. International NGOs—centred mainly in Geneva, London, New York, Paris, and Washington—often rely on information and inspiration from grassroots organizations that are aware of local conditions. At the same time, local and national organizations are often at greater risk of retaliatory action and rely for credibility on international organizations such as the United Nations.[23]

The United Nations Economic and Social Council (ECOSOC), the International Labour Organization,[24] United Nations Educational, Scientific and Cultural Organization (UNESCO),[25] and several regional organizations,[26] have developed official consultative arrangements with NGOs. Article 71 of the UN Charter authorizes ECOSOC to make 'suitable arrangements for consultation with non-governmental organizations'. In order to participate in the Human Rights Council, NGOs must seek consultative status through the ECOSOC Committee on NGOs, which is comprised of nineteen government representatives. Almost all the human rights procedures of the United Nations rely heavily, or even exclusively, upon information and arguments that NGOs supply.

[21] See Clark (n 11). [22] Clark (n 11).

[23] Michael H Posner and Candy Whittome, 'The Status of Human Rights NGOs' (1994) 25 *Colum Hum Rts L Rev* 269, 285.

[24] International Labour Organization (ILO), 'Partnerships and Development Departments: "Civil Society"' <http://www.ilo.org/public/english/bureau/pardev/civil/index.htm> accessed 20 December 2011, containing information on the ILO's relationships with NGOs and lists of NGOs with which the ILO maintains standing consultative agreements.

[25] UNESCO, 'Directives Concerning UNESCO's Relations with Non-Governmental Organizations' <http://erc.unesco.org/ong/en/Direct_ONG.htm> accessed 20 December 2011.

[26] Organization of American States (OAS), 'Manual for Civil Society Participation in OAS Activities' (OAS 2009) <http://www.oas.org/en/ser/dia/civil_society/docs/Civil_Society_Manual%28English%29.pdf> accessed 21 December 2011.

Over the last thirty years, there has been a tremendous increase in the number of NGOs that focus on human rights issues. One way of measuring the growth in the number of NGOs is to note that in 1974 there were about 600 international NGOs in consultative status with ECOSOC; by 2011, there were more than 3,000 international and national NGOs in consultative status.[27]

Some NGOs are very small—essentially just the lengthened shadow of one individual focusing on a single issue. Others have millions of members, in many countries, with democratic decision-making procedures, and many activities. There is tremendous diversity among human rights NGOs in their structures, activities, and supporters. Most NGOs, however, have a central office or secretariat. International NGOs usually have national sections, or chapters, in several countries. National NGOs may be located in the country's capital city or other large city. A Secretary-General, Executive Director, or other head officer, who directs the staff and is guided as to policy matters by a board, executive committee, or similar group, leads most NGOs. Many NGOs make use of volunteers.[28]

Anti-Slavery International is one of the oldest NGOs, formed in the United Kingdom in 1839.[29] The organization was originally founded as the Anti-Slavery Society, and was an abolitionist group, which continues to focus on the slave trade, human trafficking, and related issues today. Amnesty International, one of the most influential NGOs, was founded in London in 1961.[30] Amnesty International began as a group focusing on prisoners of conscience and has since expanded its operations into other areas of human rights. Human Rights Watch, originally Helsinki Watch, was founded in New York in 1978 to monitor the Soviet Union's human rights violations, but now works to prevent human rights violations around the world.[31]

The International Committee of the Red Cross (ICRC)[32] occupies a unique position in the international system. The ICRC, in addition to its other functions as an NGO, fulfills treaty obligations that include monitoring compliance with the four Geneva Conventions and two Additional Protocols. Its delegates visit places of detention, approach authorities, use its right of humanitarian initiative, and receive complaints about breaches of international humanitarian law. The ICRC visits prisoners of war and civilian internees; interviews them without witnesses, repeats such visits to ensure that the detainees are not killed or ill-treated, and supplies prisoners

[27] UN, 'Basic Facts about ECOSOC Status' <http://csonet.org/?menu=100> accessed 23 May 2013.

[28] Clark (n 11).

[29] Anti-Slavery International, 'History of Anti-Slavery International' <http://www.antislavery.org/english/what_we_do/our_history.aspx> accessed 21 December 2011. For further information on its work, see the chapter in this volume by Jenny Martinez.

[30] Amnesty International, 'History of Amnesty International' <http://www.amnesty.org/en/who-we-are/history> accessed 21 December 2011.

[31] Human Rights Watch, 'Our History' <http://www.hrw.org/en/node/75134> accessed 20 December 2011.

[32] David P Forsythe, *The Humanitarians: The International Committee of the Red Cross* (CUP 2005).

of war and political detainees with basic supplies of blankets, medicines, medical care, clothing, and food.

NGOs provide an invaluable service for the protection of human rights. By helping to formulate human rights standards and increasing awareness of abuses, NGOs pressure international bodies, as well as national governments, to address human rights issues. Because of the vital role NGOs play, it is important that they are protected from government repression that inhibits their worthwhile activities. The UN Declaration on Human Rights Defenders is an example of the standards needed to protect NGOs and to ensure the effectiveness of their human rights work.[33]

NGOs also must remain credible and legitimate in their work; unfortunately, not all are ethical or effective. As a consequence, in addition to standards protecting NGOs from interference by human rights abusers, there have also been some attempts at creating standards regulating NGOs' behaviour in monitoring human rights. Such standards aim to ensure that NGOs engaged in human rights work remain unbiased, independent, and legitimate. *The Code of Conduct for the International Red Cross and Red Crescent Movement and Non-Governmental Organisations (NGOs) in Disaster Relief*,[34] which the International Federation of Red Cross and Red Crescent Societies and the ICRC developed, is an example of a set of voluntary standards for NGO behaviour.[35] The Code of Conduct calls on NGOs, inter alia, to refrain from seeking to further a political or religious agenda through their work and to refrain from discrimination based on race or other factors in giving aid. Transparency is also cited increasingly as a goal for NGOs. The promulgation of such standards could potentially make NGOs' work more effective by ensuring ethical behaviour and fairness, thereby increasing their legitimacy, even at the cost of slowing down some of their operations.

3. Transnational Corporations and Other Business Entities

The relationship between business entities and human rights is a domain of increasing focus in intergovernmental organizations, NGOs, and states. The notion that

[33] Declaration on the Right and Responsibility of Individuals, Groups and Organs of Society to Promote and Protect Universally Recognized Human Rights and Fundamental Freedoms.

[34] The International Federation of Red Cross and Red Crescent Societies (IFRCRCS) and ICRC, *The Code of Conduct for the International Red Cross and Red Crescent Movement and Non-Governmental Organisations (NGOs) in Disaster Relief* (IFRCRCS 1994) <http://www.ifrc.org/Global/Publications/disasters/code-of-conduct/code-english.pdf> accessed 20 December 2011.

[35] The IFRCRCS lists 472 humanitarian organizations that have agreed to follow the code, as signatories to the Code of Conduct.

businesses should respect human rights and consider the social and environmental effects of their actions has gained acceptance. The largest Transnational Corporations (TNCs) are extremely powerful international actors. Generally, the term 'transnational corporation' refers to a corporation with affiliated business operations in more than one country. A more specific definition deems an enterprise a transnational corporation if 'it has a certain minimum size, if it owns or controls production or service plants outside its home state and if it incorporates these plants into a unified corporation strategy.'[36]

The need to address the human rights responsibilities of businesses arose from the growing power of corporations and their complicity in human rights abuses. As early as the Nuremberg Trials following World War II, German industrialist Alfried Krupp and nine other officials of the huge Krupp industrial firm were convicted of charges relating to, inter alia, the use of slave labour.[37] The Krupp firm was an inextricable part of the German policy for occupied countries such as France, Norway, and Poland. The Nuremburg Tribunal sentenced the Krupp corporate officers to terms of imprisonment, sentencing Krupp himself to twelve years imprisonment. In addition, all his properties—public and private—were forfeited. In a subsequent case, twenty-four directors and officers of the German conglomerate IG Farben Industry were convicted for using slave labour, for designing and producing poison gas used in the concentration camps of the Third Reich, and for other crimes.[38] The tribunal found thirteen IG Farben corporate defendants guilty and sentenced them to terms of imprisonment.

Companies may violate human rights not only in periods of armed conflict, but also by employing child labourers; discriminating against certain groups of employees (such as union members and women); attempting to repress independent trade unions and discouraging the right to bargain collectively; failing to provide safe and healthy working conditions; and limiting the broad dissemination of appropriate technology and intellectual property. Companies also dump toxic wastes, and their production processes may have consequences for the lives and livelihoods of those people

[36] Luzius Wildhaber, 'Some Aspects of the Transnational Corporation in International Law' (1980) 27 *Neth Int'l L Rev* 79, 80.

[37] *United States v Krupp*, as described by the trial court in *Doe v Unocal Corp*, 110 F Supp 2d 1294, 1310 (CD Cal 2000), *aff'd*, 395 F3d 932 (9th Cir 2002) (citations omitted): 'The Tribunal found the defendants guilty of employing slave labor because their will was not overpowered by the Third Reich "but instead coincide[d] with the will of those from whom the alleged compulsion emanate[d]." Moreover, the "Krupp firm had manifested not only its willingness but its ardent desire to employ forced labor."' (citations omitted) (citing *United States v Krupp* 1439–40).

[38] *United States v Krauch* 35: 'While the Farben organisation, as a corporation, is not charged under the indictment with committing a crime and is not the subject of prosecution in this case, it is the theory of the prosecution that the defendants individually and collectively used the Farben organisation as an instrument by and through which they committed the crime enumerated in the indictment. All of the members of the Vorstand or governing body of Farben who were such at the time of the collapse of Germany were indicted and brought to trial.'

in neighbouring communities. One of the most visible examples of a devastating corporate impact on human well-being occurred in Bhopal, India, in 1984, when a plant owned by Union Carbide Corporation released forty-one tons of methyl isocyanate.[39] The chemicals killed at least 15,000 people and left more than 120,000 people with severe health problems.[40] Local water and soil remain severely contaminated, and the local population continues to suffer birth defects as a result of the disaster. Five years after the disaster, the Indian Supreme court held Union Carbide legally accountable and ordered the company to pay civil claims of 470 million dollars.[41] More than twenty years after the disaster, however, many victims still have not received any compensation. Union Carbide has refused to release information about the chemicals that caused the harm, including the results of tests completed on the health effects of the spillage.[42] In 2001, Union Carbide became a subsidiary of the Dow Chemical Company, which claims that it has no responsibility for the prior actions of its new subsidiary.[43] In 2010, an Indian court sentenced seven former employees of Union Carbide to prison terms of two years and fines of two thousand dollars each after convicting them of causing death by negligence resulting from their involvement in the disaster.[44]

While corporations have the capacity to cause catastrophic damage, they also bring employment, capital, and technology capable of improving working conditions and raising local living conditions. For example, in 2010, Walmart stores reported sales of 405 billion dollars,[45] greater than the Gross Domestic Product (GDP) of 168 countries, including Denmark, Chile, and Thailand, in the same year.[46] They clearly have a great capacity to assert a positive influence in fostering development and achieving prosperity. The human rights objective becomes maximizing the good that companies do, while eliminating the abuses they commit.

Some human rights treaties and other law-making instruments may be interpreted to apply to non-state actors, including businesses (and NGOs). As noted above, the 1948 Universal Declaration of Human Rights first established an authoritative, worldwide definition of human rights. While the UDHR principally focuses

[39] Amnesty International, *India: Clouds of Injustice: Bhopal Disaster 20 Years On* (Amnesty International 2004) ASA 20/015/2004 <http://www.amnesty.org/en/library/info/ASA20/015/2004/en> accessed 21 December 2011.

[40] Amnesty International, *Clouds of Injustice* (n 39) 12.

[41] Amnesty International, *Clouds of Injustice* (n 39) 59.

[42] Amnesty International, *Clouds of Injustice* (n 39) 50.

[43] Amnesty International, *Clouds of Injustice* (n 39) 39.

[44] Amnesty International, 'First Convictions for 1984 Union Carbide Disaster Too Little, Too Late' (*Amnesty International News*, 7 June 2010) <http://www.amnesty.org/en/news-and-updates/first-convictions-1984-union-carbide-disaster-bhopal-too-little-too-late-2010-06-07> accessed 20 December 2011.

[45] Walmart, *2010 Annual Report* (Walmart Stores, Inc 2010) <http://cdn.walmartstores.com/sites/AnnualReport/2010/PDF/WMT_2010AR_FINAL.pdf > accessed 25 November 2012.

[46] International Monetary Fund, 'World Economic Outlook Database: April 2011: Nominal GDP List of Countries: Data for 2010' <http://www.imf.org/external/pubs/ft/weo/2011/01/weodata/index.aspx> accessed 20 December 2011.

on the obligations of states, the quoted paragraph from the preamble mentions the responsibilities of individuals and 'every organ of society',[47] which would include businesses.

Pursuant to the widely ratified International Covenant on Civil and Political Rights (ICCPR),[48] each state party 'undertakes to respect and to ensure to all individuals within its territory and subject to its jurisdiction the rights recognized in the present Covenant'.[49] Accordingly, if a corporation endangers the rights of an individual, the state has a duty to ensure respect for human rights and to take preventive action. In addition, the ICCPR indirectly covers the responsibilities of companies by declaring that '[n]othing in the present Covenant may be interpreted as implying for any State, group or person any right to engage in any activity or perform any act aimed at the destruction of any of the rights and freedoms recognized herein'.[50]

Other treaties express the idea that the state must ensure that non-state entities respect human rights. For example, Article 2(1)(d) of the International Convention on the Elimination of All Forms of Racial Discrimination (CERD) requires states to 'prohibit and bring to an end, by all appropriate means, including legislation . . . racial discrimination by any persons, group or organization'.[51] Hence, states have the indirect responsibility to prevent racial discrimination by corporations. Similarly, Article 2(e) of the Convention on the Elimination of All Forms of Discrimination against Women requires the 180 states parties to 'take all appropriate measures to eliminate discrimination against women by any person, organization or enterprise'. The Committee on the Elimination of Discrimination Against Women has interpreted that provision as including the states' responsibility 'for private acts if they fail to act with due diligence to prevent violations of rights or to investigate and punish acts of violence, and for providing compensation'.[52]

Accordingly, human rights treaties and the interpretive pronouncements of treaty bodies provide for businesses to have at least indirect human rights responsibilities.[53] The persistence with which businesses commit human rights abuses, however,

[47] UDHR, preamble.

[48] As of 26 August 2012, 167 states are party to the ICCPR.

[49] ICCPR, Art 2(1).

[50] ICCPR, Art 5(1). The same phrase also appears in Art 5 of the ICESCR.

[51] 170 states are party to CERD.

[52] UN Committee on the Elimination of all forms of Discrimination against Women, 'General Recommendation 19' reprinted in 'Note by the Secretariat: Compilation of General Comments and General Recommendations Adopted by Human Rights Treaty Bodies' (2003) UN Doc HRI/GEN/1/Rev.6, 243.

[53] For example, in interpreting the ICCPR, the Human Rights Committee observed that, 'Article 17 provides for the right of every person to be protected against arbitrary or unlawful interference with his privacy, family, home or correspondence as well as against unlawful attacks on his honour and reputation. In the view of the Committee this right is required to be guaranteed against all such interferences and attacks whether they emanate from State authorities or from natural or legal persons.' UNHCR 'General Comment No 16' reprinted in 'Compilation of General Comments and General Recommendations Adopted by Human Rights Treaty Bodies' (1994) UN Doc HRI/GEN/1/Rev.1, 21.

has prompted several international efforts to define the direct responsibilities of companies. For example, the UN Commission on Transnational Corporations unsuccessfully attempted to draft an international code of conduct for TNCs in the 1970s and 1980s.[54] The Organisation for Economic Cooperation and Development (OECD) undertook a similar effort in 1976 (updated in 2011), when it established its Guidelines for Multinational Enterprises to promote responsible business conduct consistent with applicable laws.[55] The original OECD Guidelines mentioned human rights only once in a single paragraph; however, the 2011 Guidelines revisions contain an expanded human rights section, which reflects the UN Human Rights Council's 'Protect, Respect, Remedy' Framework.[56] In 1977 (updated in 2000), the International Labour Organization (ILO) developed its Tripartite Declaration of Principles Concerning Multinational Enterprises, which calls upon businesses to follow the relevant labour conventions and recommendations.[57]

In January 1999, UN Secretary-General Kofi Annan proposed a 'Global Compact' of shared values and principles at the World Economic Forum in Davos, Switzerland.[58] The original Global Compact asked businesses to voluntarily support and adopt nine succinctly expressed core principles, which are divided into categories dealing with: general human rights obligations, standards of labour, and standards of environmental protection. In 2004 the Global Compact added a tenth core principle on corruption.[59] The ILO, OECD, and Global Compact initiatives all

[54] United Nations Draft International Code of Conduct on Transnational Corporations (1984) 23 ILM 626; 'Development and International Economic Cooperation: Transnational Corporations' (12 June 1990) UN Doc E/1990/94.

[55] Organisation for Economic Co-operation and Development (OECD), 'Guidelines for Multinational Enterprises' (1976) 15 ILM 967. The OECD updated these Guidelines in 2011. OECD, *OECD Guidelines for Multinational Enterprises: 2011 Edition* (OECD 2011) <http://www.oecd.org/daf/inv/mne/oecdguidelinesformultinationalenterprises.htm> accessed 11 July 2013.

[56] UN Commission on Human Rights (UNCHR) 'Protect, Respect and Remedy: A Framework for Business and Human Rights, Report of the Special Representative of the Secretary on issues of Human Rights, Transnational Corporations, and Other Business Enterprises' (7 April 2008) UN Doc A/HRC/8/5; see also UN Sub-Commission on the Promotion and Protection of Human Rights, 'Norms on the Responsibilities of Transnational Corporations and Other Business Enterprises with Regard to Human Rights' (2003) UN Doc E/CN.4/Sub.2/2003/12/Rev.2.

[57] ILO 'Tripartite Declaration of Principles Concerning Multinational Enterprises and Social Policy' (1978) 17 *ILM* 422, para 6.

[58] Secretary-General Kofi Annan, 'Markets for a Better World' (World Economic Forum, Davos, 31 January1999) UN Doc SG/SM/6448.

[59] The principles are that businesses should:

> [(1) S]upport and respect the protection of internationally proclaimed human rights [within their sphere of influence]; [(2)] make sure they are not complicit in human right abuses[;] ... [(3)] uphold the freedom of association and the effective recognition of the right to collective bargaining; ... [(4)] eliminat[e] all forms of forced and compulsory labour; ... [(5)] aboli[sh] child labour; ... [(6)] eliminat[e] discrimination in respect of employment and occupation[;] ... [(7)] support a precautionary approach to environmental challenges; ... [(8)] undertake initiatives to

indicate that they are voluntary, although they have established weak mechanisms for interpreting and encouraging compliance with their guidelines.[60]

The 1997 OECD Convention on Combating Bribery of Foreign Public Officials in International Business Transactions—commonly referred to as the OECD Anti-Bribery Convention—established more enforceable standards for business entities' interactions with foreign governments in order to fight corruption and create a level playing field for all businesses.[61] Corruption is increasingly part of the human rights agenda, as it affects, in particular, the enjoyment of economic, social, and cultural rights. Similarly, treaties establishing standards on the environmental impact of commercial activities may further the right to the highest attainable standard of health. One such agreement is the 1996 Protocol to the 1972 Convention on the Prevention of Marine Pollution by Dumping of Wastes and Other Matter,[62] in which the contracting parties agreed to attempt to end the dumping of industrial waste and other hazardous materials into the oceans.

In addition, civil society's scrutiny of the activities of global businesses and an emerging concern on the part of the companies, themselves, for social responsibility, have, since the 1980s, led hundreds of companies and several industry associations to adopt voluntary codes of conduct.[63] Some socially conscious businesspeople developed voluntary principles applicable to a broad range of companies. Although there is a very important educational value in company codes and other voluntary initiatives, they are often very vague in regard to human rights commitments and lack mechanisms for assuring continuity or implementation.

There may be business incentives for complying with voluntary human rights standards such as the Global Compact or company codes of conduct, as some investors now evaluate the social responsibility of the companies in which they invest. For example, in 2004 the Norwegian government began requiring the investments that the

> promote greater environmental responsibility;... [(9)] encourage the development and diffusion of environmentally friendly technologies[;]... [and (10)] work against all forms of corruption, including extortion and bribery.

UN Global Compact, 'The Global Compact's Ten Principles' <http://www.unglobalcompact.org/AboutTheGC/TheTenPrinciples/index.html> accessed 19 December 2011.

60 Andrew Clapham, *Human Rights Obligations of Non-State Actors* (OUP 2006) 207.

61 Convention on Combating Bribery of Foreign Public Officials in International Business Transactions. Thirty-eight countries are parties to the Convention, including the United States, which implemented the convention's principles through the International Anti-Bribery Act of 1998, amending the Foreign Corrupt Practices Act.

62 Protocol to the Convention on the Prevention of Marine Pollution by Dumping of Wastes and Other Matter, 1996.

63 Peter Frankental and Frances House, *Human Rights: Is It Any of Your Business?* (Amnesty International & The Prince of Wales Business Leaders Forum 2000) 23; University of Minnesota, Human Rights Corporate Codes of Conduct (*Human Rights Library*) <http://www1.umn.edu/humanrts/business/codes.html> accessed 29 December 2011.

Government Pension Fund,[64] the largest pension fund in Europe, made to meet certain ethical guidelines.[65] Since then, the Fund has declined to invest in companies, on ethical grounds, for reasons including human rights violations, environmental damage, arms production, and production of tobacco.[66]

In August 2003, the UN Sub-Commission on the Promotion and Protection of Human Rights unanimously approved the first attempt at creating a non-voluntary framework of human rights standards governing business entities, 'Norms on the Responsibilities of Transnational Corporations and Other Business Enterprises with Regard to Human Rights'.[67] The Norms represented a landmark step in holding businesses accountable for their human rights abuses and constituted a succinct, but comprehensive, restatement of the international legal principles applicable to businesses, with regard to human rights, humanitarian law, international labour law, environmental law, consumer law, anticorruption law, and so forth. The UN Commission on Human Rights responded to the Norms by appointing Professor John Ruggie as the Special Representative of the Secretary-General on Human Rights and Transnational Corporations and Other Business Enterprises.[68] In 2008, Professor Ruggie presented the UN Human Rights Council—the successor body to the UN Commission on Human Rights—with his report, detailing a three-part 'Protect, Respect, Remedy' framework.[69] Professor Ruggie's framework was based on three pillars—the duty of states to protect against human rights violations; the responsibility of businesses to respect and avoid violating human rights; and access to both judicial and non-judicial remedies for victims of human rights violations. The Human Rights Council responded to the framework by extending Professor Ruggie's mandate for an additional three years, under the title of the Secretary-General's Special Representative for Business and Human

[64] Norway's Government Pension Fund Global, formerly the Petroleum Fund of Norway, is a fund containing the proceeds from Norwegian oil production, which the Norwegian Ministry of Finance manages. See Norwegian Ministry of Finance, 'The Government Pension Fund' <http://www.regjeringen.no/en/dep/fin/Selected-topics/the-government-pension-fund.html?id=1441> accessed 29 December 2011.

[65] Norwegian Ministry of Finance, 'History' <http://www.regjeringen.no/en/dep/fin/Selected-topics/the-government-pension-fund/responsible-investments/History.html?id=434896> accessed 29 December 2011.

[66] Norwegian Ministry of Finance, 'Guidelines for Observation and Exclusion from the Government Pension Fund Global's Investment Universe' <http://www.regjeringen.no/en/dep/fin/Selected-topics/the-government-pension-fund/responsible-investments/guidelines-for-observation-and-exclusion.html?id=594254> accessed 29 December 2011.

[67] UN Sub-Commission on the Promotion and Protection of Human Rights, 'Norms on the Responsibilities of Transnational Corporations' (n 56).

[68] UN Press Release, 'Secretary-General Appoints John Ruggie of United States Special Representative on Issue of Human Rights, Transnational Corporations, Other Business Enterprises' (28 July 2005) UN Doc SG/A/934.

[69] UN Commission on Human Rights (UNCHR) 'Protect, Respect and Remedy: A Framework for Business and Human Rights, Report of the Special Representative of the Secretary on issues of Human Rights, Transnational Corporations, and Other Business Enterprises' (7 April 2008) UN Doc A/HRC/8/5.

Rights.[70] The product of this mandate was The Guiding Principles for Business and Human Rights,[71] which the UN Human Rights Council endorsed in June 2011.[72] The Human Rights Council also created a new working group to disseminate and promote implementation of the principles.[73]

The first section of the Guiding Principles deals with the duty of states to protect human rights and establishes the basic principle that states must protect against human rights abuses by third parties, such as businesses, within their jurisdiction. The second section of the Guiding Principles addresses the 'respect' portion of Professor Ruggie's framework, by encouraging business entities to adopt formal statements of their commitment to human rights and to actively examine the possible adverse impacts of their business activities on human rights. The final section of the Guiding Principles states that, as part of their human rights responsibilities, states must ensure that victims of human rights violations in their jurisdiction have access to effective judicial and non-judicial remedies.

The Guiding Principles provide a basic outline for human rights standards for states, intergovernmental organizations, and non-state actors. Some human rights organizations, however, believe that the UN Human Rights Council did not go far enough.[74] Furthermore, the Guiding Principles lack the thoroughness of the Sub-Commission Norm Relating to Human Rights, Humanitarian Law, International Labour Law, Environmental Law, and Anticorruption Law.

4. Armed Irregular Groups

A third major type of non-state actor in human rights law is non-state armed groups, including terrorists, insurgents in opposition to the government, and death squads, or militias, that support repressive regimes. In addition to state responsibility and individual criminal responsibility, international law has placed direct obligations on such

[70] UN Human Rights Council (UNHRC), Res 8/7 (18 June 2008) UN Doc A/HRC/RES/8/7.

[71] Report of the Special Representative of the Secretary-General on the Issue of Human Rights and Transnational Corporations and Other Business Enterprises, 'Guiding Principles on Business and Human Rights: Implementing the United Nations "Protect, Respect and Remedy" Framework' (21 March 2011) UN Doc A/HRC/17/31.

[72] UNHRC Res 17/4 (6 July 2011) UN Doc A/HRC/RES/17/4.

[73] UNHRC Res 17/4 (n 72) para 6.

[74] Representatives of Human Rights Watch denounced the Council's refusal to endorse binding standards by saying, 'In effect, the council endorsed the status quo: a world where companies are encouraged, but not obliged, to respect human rights.' Human Rights Watch, 'UN Human Rights Council: Weak Stance on Business Standards' <http://www.hrw.org/en/news/2011/06/16/un-human-rights-council-weak-stance-business-standards> accessed 22 December 2011.

armed groups—particularly in the context of non-international armed conflicts. Like NGOs and businesses, the category non-state 'armed group' includes a great variety of different entities. These groups can range from loosely organized terrorist organizations to revolutionary movements and groups seeking self-determination with well-defined leadership structures.[75]

Some armed groups impact the lives of individuals, as do states or businesses entities, exercising day-to-day control over populations or territories. They may even have limited administrative procedures, like states.[76] Because of the power such armed groups have over individuals, they can also be responsible for grave human rights abuses.[77] During conflicts, they may violate the human rights of the prisoners they capture; they can also violate the rights of civilian populations in a variety of ways, including using forced labour to support the armed opposition group's activities and engaging in kidnapping children to become child soldiers.[78] Some armed groups amount to organized criminal enterprises participating in drug and human trafficking, as well as other criminal activities, to finance their operations.[79]

In response to the human rights concerns that non-state armed groups raise, international human rights law and humanitarian law have been interpreted as setting standards for the conduct of organized armed groups. International humanitarian law often applies to their actions and has provided an additional legal foundation for accountability.[80] In some cases, international humanitarian law may even provide a stronger basis for response than the UDHR or the ICCPR. In cases of human rights violations committed by non-state armed groups during internal armed conflicts, application of both international humanitarian law and human rights law can help to combat gaps in protection that could arise from the application of either legal regime alone.[81] Common Article 3 of the Geneva Conventions states, 'In the case of armed conflict not of an international character occurring in the territory of one of the High Contracting Parties, each Party to the conflict shall be bound to apply, as a minimum, the following provisions',[82] which require armed groups—at a minimum—to treat '[p]ersons taking no active part in the hostilities'[83] humanely by abstaining from

75 Liesbeth Zegveld, *Accountability of Armed Opposition Groups in International Law* (CUP 2002) 1.

76 Zegveld (n 75) 1. See also Sandesh Sivakumaran, 'Courts of Armed Opposition Groups: Fair Trials or Summary Justice?' (2009) 7 *JICJ* 489.

77 Zegveld (n 75) 2.

78 Joseph N Madubuike-Ekwe, 'The International Legal Standards Adopted to Stop the Participation of Children in Armed Conflicts' (2005) 11 *Ann Surv Int'l & Comp L* 29, 33.

79 Ravi Nair, 'Confronting the Violence Committed by Armed Opposition Groups' (1998) 1 *Yale Hum Rts & Dev LJ* 1, 4, discussing the criminal activities of armed opposition groups in India.

80 Yoram Dinstein, 'Human Rights in Armed Conflict: International Humanitarian Law' in Theodor Meron (ed), *Human Rights in International Law: Legal and Policy Issues*, vol 2 (OUP 1984) 345.

81 Fionnuala Ni Aolain, 'Parallel Applicability of International Humanitarian Law and International Human Rights Law: The No-Gaps Approach to Parallel Application in the Context of the War on Terror' (2007) 40 *Is L Rev* 563.

82 Common Article 3 (n 9).

83 Common Article 3(1) (n 9).

murder, cruel treatment, torture, hostage-taking, degrading treatment, and carrying out sentences without the judgment of a regularly constituted court; and to collect and care for the sick and wounded. Common Article 3 has been interpreted to distinguish non-international armed conflicts from unorganized and short-lived insurrections, or mere acts of banditry. The authoritative ICRC commentary on Common Article 3, however, mentions a number of non-obligatory, but convenient, criteria for applying Common Article 3.[84] The commentary's list of criteria for the applicability of Common Article 3 to armed groups includes control of territory by the armed group; however, even if some of the criteria are not met, the ICRC believes that parties should apply Common Article 3 as widely as possible. The drafters intended that Common Article 3 would protect those basic and fundamental rights that deserve respect at all times. Accordingly, the standards articulated in Common Article 3 can bind armed groups, even when they do not meet all the criteria listed in the commentary.

Additional Protocol II to the Geneva Conventions adds more responsibilities on organized armed groups, beyond those limits Common Article 3 contains. However, Additional Protocol II is more limited in its scope of application than Common Article 3.[85] The standards in Additional Protocol II apply to states, as well as to 'armed groups which, under responsible command, exercise such control over a part of its territory as to enable them to carry out sustained and concerted military operations and to implement this Protocol'.[86] Since this language restricting Protocol II's scope to groups that control territory appears in the text of the treaty, rather than in the commentary like in Common Article 3, Protocol II's standards are limited to armed opposition groups exercising day-to-day control over territory. Additional Protocol II imposes many more detailed standards on armed groups than Common Article 3 in three areas: humane treatment, including treatment of persons not taking part in hostilities, children, and persons detained or imprisoned as part of the conflict; treatment of wounded, sick, and shipwrecked persons, or personnel involved in caring for such persons, such as medical personnel; and treatment of the civilian population, including protection from attacks targeting civilians. These standards reflect the greater burden which the international community places on groups seeking or exercising territorial control regarding human rights violations.

Additional Protocol I to the Geneva Conventions[87] also applies standards to some armed opposition groups, but only with regard to armed groups seeking self-determination. Additional Protocol I applies the full range of humanitarian law

[84] Jean Pictet (ed), *Commentary on the Geneva Conventions of 12 August 1949* (ICRC 1952) 49–50.

[85] Protocol Additional to the Geneva Conventions of 12 August 1949, and Relating to the Protection of Victims of Non-International Armed Conflicts (Protocol II).

[86] Protocol II, Art 1(1).

[87] Protocol Additional to the Geneva Conventions of 12 August 1949, and Relating to the Protection of Victims of International Armed Conflicts (Protocol I).

provisions in the four Geneva Conventions to armed opposition groups seeking statehood.

International criminal law also creates standards for the human rights responsibilities of organized armed groups. The Statute of the International Criminal Tribunal for the Former Yugoslavia, which created the tribunal to address crimes committed in the former Yugoslavia after 1991, states that, 'A person who planned, instigated, ordered, committed or otherwise aided and abetted in the planning, preparation or execution of a crime ... shall be individually responsible for the crime'.[88] The International Criminal Tribunal for Rwanda was created to prosecute crimes against humanity and other crimes committed in, and around, Rwanda in 1994, and has the authority to impose individual responsibility for crimes against humanity, as well as for violations of Common Article 3 and Additional Protocol II.[89] The International Criminal Court has jurisdiction to prosecute individuals for certain war crimes committed during 'conflicts not of an international character'.[90] These international bodies all allow for the prosecution of individual members and leaders of armed opposition groups for their role in human rights violations,[91] placing additional responsibilities and incentives on such groups to respect human rights.

5. Conclusion

NGOs, business entities, and armed non-state groups each play a role in the protection and violation of human rights. Each type of non-state actor has unique standards regarding human rights, governing its behaviour; however, there also remains work to be done with regard to each type of non-state actor. International bodies must continue working to identify and close gaps in the protection of human rights relating to non-state actors. Gaps still exist in both the protection of individuals from human rights abuses committed by non-state actors, as well as the protection of non-state actors from abuses committed against them. The development of new standards and expansion of existing standards to groups and individuals they do not currently cover can help to close these gaps and offer greater protection against human rights violations.[92] NGOs provide a valuable service in helping

[88] Statute of the International Criminal Tribunal for the Former Yugoslavia, Art 7(1).

[89] Statute of the International Criminal Tribunal for Rwanda, Art 4.

[90] Rome Statute, Art 8(2)(d). [91] Zegveld (n 75) 97.

[92] International Council on Human Rights Policy, *Human Rights Standards: Learning From Experience* (International Council on Human Rights Policy 2006) 7 <http://www.ichrp.org/files/reports/31/120b_report_en.pdf> accessed 22 December 2011.

intergovernmental bodies protect human rights; however, the international community must do more to protect NGOs, so they can continue to carry out their activities. Business entities have a great deal of economic power, which can be used either to abuse or protect human rights, and standards governing their behaviour are beginning to develop, but more detailed, binding standards, with adequate implementation mechanisms, are still needed. Well-established humanitarian and human rights standards govern armed opposition groups participating in armed conflicts. However, enforcement of those standards remains inadequate. There is a trend toward placing more responsibilities directly on non-state actors in international law, rather than relying on states to ensure non-state actors within their territory do not abuse human rights. Nonetheless, a need for the further development of standards and enforcement mechanisms relating to non-state actors remains.

Further Reading

Blitt RC, 'Who Will Watch the Watchdogs? Human Rights Nongovernmental Organizations and the Case for Regulation' (2004) 10 *Buff Hum Rts L Rev* 261.

Clapham A, *Human Rights Obligations of Non-State Actors* (OUP 2006)

Lyons GM and Mayall J (eds), *International Human Rights in the 21st Century: Protecting the Rights of Groups* (Rowman & Littlefield 2003)

McBeth A, 'Every Organ of Society: The Responsibility of Non-State Actors for the Realization of Human Rights' (2008) 30 *Hamline J Pub L & Pol'y* 33

Posner MH and Whittome C, 'The Status of Human Rights NGOs' (1994) 25 *Colum Hum Rts L Rev* 269

Sikkink K and Keck ME, *Activists beyond Borders: Advocacy Networks in International Politics* (Cornell UP 1998)

United Nations Office of the High Commissioner for Human Rights, *The Corporate Responsibility to Respect Human Rights: An Interpretive Guide* (United Nations 2012)

PART VI

HUMAN RIGHTS AND GENERAL INTERNATIONAL LAW

CHAPTER 31

INTERPRETATION OF HUMAN RIGHTS TREATIES

MALGOSIA FITZMAURICE

1. Introduction

The interpretation of human rights treaties is a matter both complex and, to a certain extent, obscure. It involves multiple issues, each of which poses difficult questions to which there are few clear answers. In turn, these separate issues interrelate in a multitude of ways that neither practice nor doctrine fully clarifies. The interpretive techniques applied to human rights treaties begin with the application of the provisions of the 1969 Vienna Convention on the Law of Treaties (VCLT), but also require consideration of the extent to which human rights courts and human rights treaty bodies have introduced new techniques of interpretation. In this context, the issue of whether human rights treaties constitute a special category of treaty, a form of *lex specialis*, has proven particularly divisive.

Human rights treaties undoubtedly fall within the definition of a treaty for the purposes of the VCLT. Although most of them were concluded before the entry into force of the non-retroactive VCLT, human rights fora have generally acknowledged the applicability of the VCLT rules of interpretation as customary international law. Indeed, human rights tribunals frequently assert that their interpretive methods are consistent with the relevant VCLT provisions. At the same time, these fora have adopted positions concerning interpretation that are hard to reconcile with the provisions. Such positions are generally viewed as at least expanding on traditional methods of interpretation, if not as introducing interpretive techniques outside the VCLT provisions. This critique is difficult to evaluate, in large part because the relevant provisions of the VCLT are themselves far from clear and are fluid in their relationship to each other. In addition, the concept of human rights and the treaty formulations of such rights are frequently general, vague, and subjective.

The next section discusses some approaches to the classification of human rights treaties, in particular noting those aspects that are important to questions of interpretation. Section 3 introduces briefly the provisions of the VCLT relating to interpretation, noting in particular the potential expansion of certain of these provisions in relation to the interpretation of human rights treaties. Section 4 provides a very brief introduction to the main human rights conventions this chapter will discuss. Section 5 introduces their provisions relating to interpretation. Section 6 reviews the jurisprudence of human rights tribunals on these issues.

2. Human Rights: A Self-Contained Regime?

A perception that human rights treaties may have a distinctive legal character has triggered interest their interpretation. This perception gives human rights law a special relevance in the current discourse on 'self-contained regimes' and the fragmentation of international law. The general topic of fragmentation has given rise to a vast body of literature,[1] from which the primary question for purposes of this chapter is whether or not human rights treaties comprise a separate category of treaty constituting a broad, 'self-contained' regime subject to a uniform '*lex specialis*'. If they do constitute such a regime, the analysis then becomes a matter of deciding, with respect to each specific treaty, whether or not the treaty belongs to this category. Should the decision on this issue be affirmative, certain specific rules of interpretation may apply as part of the *lex specialis* of the category.

There are great uncertainties, however, as to what constitutes a self-contained regime, and, indeed, as to whether such regimes exist at all. Assuming such regimes do exist, there are further uncertainties as to whether, compared to all other kinds of treaty, human rights treaties exhibit such distinctive characteristics that they amount to a self-contained regime. An International Law Commission (ILC) Study Group studied

[1] See eg Matthew Craven, 'Legal Differentiation and the Concept of the Human Rights Treaty in International Law' (2000) 11 *EJIL* 489.

the topic of self-contained regimes[2] and devoted some of its findings to the issue of human rights in this context. The Study Group identified a set of rules that it believed addressed particular problems differently from the way in which the application of the rules of general international law would address them. One example of this different approach was the methodology that the European Court of Human Rights (ECtHR) applied when interpreting the European Convention on Human Rights (ECHR), seeing that treaty as an instrument of *ordre publique* intended for the protection of human beings. This may indeed be the treaty's purpose, but attempts to classify international instruments according to the perceived fields they regulate may prove to be little more than a futile exercise.[3]

Yet, international legal fields, such as human rights law, World Trade Organisation law, European law, humanitarian law, and environmental law, are frequently identified as 'special' in the sense that they modify or exclude certain rules of general international law in their administration.[4] Less ambitiously, the label of 'self-contained regime' could simply involve providing interpretive guidance in some ways that depart from the interpretive principles of general international law. In either instance, such a notion of self-contained regimes may be seen as giving too much credence to the 'separateness' of a particular field of law, such as 'human rights law'.[5]

The relationship between any such regime and general international law—ie the degree to which it is self-contained—is predominately a matter of interpretation.[6] No such regime is ever completely separated from general law, as can be seen in the numerous examples of reliance on general international law by the ECtHR and the Inter-American Court, including references to general rules regarding treaty interpretation, statehood, and immunity.[7] The ECtHR has not assumed a priori that

[2] ILC, 'Report of the Study Group of the International Law Commission: Fragmentation of International Law: Difficulties Arising from Diversification and Expansion of International Law' (13 April 2006) UN Doc A/CN.4/L682, 65–101. See also Bruno Simma, 'Self-Contained Regimes' (1985) 16 *NYIL* 111; Erik Castrén, *Annual Report: 2007* (U Helsinki 2007). Note, too, that Art 55 of the 2001 Articles on State Responsibility recognizes the phenomenon of self-contained regimes.

[3] As Koskenniemi aptly noted, 'Terms such as "human rights law", "trade law" or "environmental law" and so on are arbitrary labels of forms of professional specialization. There are no rules on how to qualify particular treaty regimes and most regimes could be qualified from a number of such perspectives. Human rights treaties, for example, are often used to further environmental objectives and trade regimes presuppose and are built upon the protection of human rights (in particular the right to property)'. ILC, 'Fragmentation of International Law' (n 2) 129–30. 'The characterizations have less to do with the "nature" of the instrument that the interest from it which it is described' ((n 2) 17).

[4] ILC, 'Fragmentation of International Law' (n 2) 68.

[5] ILC, 'Fragmentation of International Law' (n 2) 70.

[6] ILC, 'Fragmentation of International Law' (n 2) 85.

[7] Eg *Velásquez Rodrígez v Honduras*, para 184. ILC, 'Fragmentation of International Law' (n 2) 86: '[t]he Convention cannot be interpreted...in a vacuum. The Court must be mindful of the Convention's special character as a human rights treaty, and it must take the relevant rules of international law into account. The Convention should so far as possible be interpreted in harmony with other rules of international law of which it forms a part, including those relating to the grant of State immunity' (citing *McElhinney v Ireland*, para 36).

the rules of the ECHR trump those of general international law; on the contrary, it has given effect, for example, to the law on sovereign immunity when the issue has come before it.[8] From existing practice, it is not possible to designate human rights treaties overall as a special category to which special rules, ipso facto, apply. In the end, to determine how particular treaties will be interpreted, it is necessary to examine the language of the specific instrument and the practices of particular forum in relation thereto.

In the absence of a clear theoretical basis to distinguish human rights treaties from the general body of treaties, the present chapter will examine specific regional and universal treaties, which their own terms call 'human rights' conventions. They share certain characteristics which, to some extent, distinguish them from the general body of treaties, and which may affect the manner in which these treaties may be interpreted.

The first shared characteristic of human rights treaties relates to their so-called 'constitutional' nature and in particular to the non-reciprocal nature of the rights and obligations set forth therein. Among other effects, this nature may lead to reductions in the importance of the actual text of the treaty in relation to other factors relevant to interpretation—in particular enhancing the importance of the object and purpose of the treaty.

The second shared characteristic is their subject matter. To an extent, the subject matter of all treaties has a bearing upon their interpretation, but aspects related to the nature of human rights seem to have had a fundamental impact well beyond that found in relation to most, if not all, other treaties. This nature gives rise to a particular approach in relation to interpretation, sometimes referred to as the '*pro homine*' approach. It also reinforces the so-called 'constitutional' or '*ordre publique*' nature of human rights treaties, arising from a concept that the parties to a human rights treaty do not create the rights that the treaties protect; rather, they recognize rights that arise from the very nature of man, quite independently of the will or volition of the parties.

The possibility that certain treaties or treaty provisions can have a special legal character is well established. In 1951, the International Court of Justice (ICJ) rendered its influential Advisory Opinion on *Reservations to the Genocide Convention*, in which it noted the non-reciprocal or 'unilateral' international humanitarian obligations included in this Convention[9]—in contrast to the previous classification based mainly on the distinction between bilateral and multilateral obligations.[10] Sir Gerald

[8] *McElhinney* (n 7) para 36; *Al-Adsani v United Kingdom*, para 55 (cited in ILC, 'Fragmentation of International Law' (n 2) 86, fn 215).

[9] '[I]n a convention of this type one cannot speak of individual advantages or disadvantages to States, or of the maintenance of a perfect contractual balance between rights and duties. The high ideals which inspired the Convention provide, by virtue of the common will of the parties, the foundation and measure of all its provisions.' *Reservations to the Convention on the Prevention and Punishment of the Crime of Genocide* 23.

[10] On the typology of international obligations, see: Joost Pauwelyn, *Conflict of Norms in Public International Law: How WTO Law Relates to Other Rules of International Law* (CUP 2003); Joost Pauwelyn, 'A Typology of Multilateral Treaty Obligations: Are WTO Obligations Bilateral or Collective

Fitzmaurice, as Special Rapporteur on the Law of Treaties, developed this idea during the process of codifying the law of treaties.[11] He noted that a certain kind of multilateral obligation was of a non-reciprocal nature, in the sense that the obligations of each party to a treaty were independent of other parties' performance of their obligations under the treaty, even in the event of one of those other parties' breach of its obligations. He termed such obligations 'absolute' or 'integral' obligations.[12] A related development, having potential importance in the field of human rights, has been the emergence of the concepts of obligations *erga omnes* and *jus cogens*.[13]

The concept of 'unilateral' obligations applies, however, to certain types of provision within a treaty, rather than to a class of treaties as a whole. Alain Pellet, during his work on the 'Guide to State Practice on Reservations to Treaties', rejected the claim of distinctiveness in relation to human rights treaties as a whole. He took the view that no treaty contains only provisions of a normative unilateral character; each also has provisions of a reciprocal, contractual nature.[14] Pellet, a staunch supporter of the view that international law constitutes a single overarching regime, described assertions of the need for a separate system in relation to reservations of human rights treaties as 'parochial'.[15] Human rights treaties clearly do contain traditional reciprocal obligations (such as dispute resolution provisions), and some agreements are based almost entirely on reciprocity, such as the 1949 Geneva Conventions and their Additional Protocols.

It remains the case that 'reciprocity will remain the principal leitmotiv, a constructive, mitigating and stabilizing force, the importance of which can hardly be overestimated'.[16] Thus, despite the views human rights bodies and tribunals have expressed on the need for different rules of interpretation for these treaties, scholars often reject such an approach in favour of a uniform system of interpretation, based on VCLT provisions concerning the interpretation of treaties.[17] Nevertheless, the

in Nature?' (2003) 14 *EJIL* 907; Dinah Shelton, 'Normative Hierarchy in International Law' (2006) 100 *AJIL* 291.

[11] ILC, 'Second Report on the Law of Treaties by Mr GG Fitzmaurice, Special Rapporteur' (15 March 1957) UN Doc A/CN.4/107, 30–31 (Arts 18 and 19). See also ILC, 'Third Report by GG Fitzmaurice' (18 March 1958) UN Doc A/CN.4/115, 27 (Art 18).

[12] Fitzmaurice formulated a set of principles of treaty interpretation, which he submitted had developed in customary international law and which the jurisprudence of the ICJ had largely endorsed. He identified the following principles of interpretation: I. Principle of actuality (or textuality); II. Principle of the natural and ordinary meaning; III. Principle of integration (which incorporates the principle that treaties should be interpreted in accordance with their object and purpose—the teleological principle); IV. Principle of effectiveness; V. Principle of subsequent practice; VI. Principle of contemporaneity. Sir Gerald Fitzmaurice, *The Law and Procedure of the International Court of Justice* (Grotius Publications 1986) 345–46.

[13] See Erika de Wet, Chapter 23 in this *Handbook*.

[14] Alain Pellet, Special Rapporteur 'Second Report on Reservations to Treaties' (13 June 1996) UN Doc A/CN.4/477/Add.1, para 85.

[15] Pellet (n 14).

[16] Bruno Simma, 'From Bilateralism to Community Interest' (1994) 250 *RCADI* 217, 400.

[17] Jonas Christoffersen, 'Impact on General Principles of Treaty Interpretation' in Menno T Kamminga and Martin Scheinin (eds), *The Impact of Human Rights Law on General International Law* (OUP 2009) 43, 50.

non-reciprocal character of human rights obligations has been identified as probably the most important feature for distinguishing them from other treaties, even in the views of authors who have a careful, if not sceptical, view of the claim that human rights treaties constitute a special category of treaty.[18]

Determining precisely the nature of the non-reciprocal character of human rights treaties remains an unresolved doctrinal problem concerning the relationship between human rights treaties and general international law. For some authors, differentiation between various types of reciprocity appears to be the answer. Legal reciprocity, ingrained in the VCLT, characterizes human rights treaties, even though they lack any well-defined material or sociological exchange, unlike eg commercial treaties.[19]

3. Canons of Interpretation and the VCLT

3.1 Interpretation of treaties prior to the VCLT

In order to understand the approach of the human rights fora to the relevant VCLT provisions, it is necessary to examine briefly the canons of interpretation as they existed before the conclusion of the VCLT, because the latter is regarded as a codifying treaty, largely embodying the pre-existing state of customary law.[20] Its provisions were adopted after a lengthy and frequently contentious discussion among scholars, and in many respects the main issues in this discussion remained unresolved. As a result, the articles of the VCLT concerning interpretation were ultimately drafted in a way which left them open to widely varying constructions, allowing human rights fora to continue the debate while their different contentions arguably remain within the boundaries of the VCLT.

Prior to the VCLT negotiations, an underlying controversy related to whether there should, in fact, be defined principles (or rules or canons) of interpretation at all. One view posited that 'in the last resort all interpretation must consist in the exercise of common sense by the judge, applied in good faith and with intelligence'.[21] Plainly,

[18] Mark Toufayan, 'Human Rights Treaty Interpretation: A Postmodern Account of its Claim to "Speciality"' (2005) NYU Center for Human Rights and Global Justice Working Paper No 2, 5–6.

[19] Simma, 'From Bilateralism' (n 16) 401.

[20] Some interpretive methods of customary international law, which the ICJ recognizes as such, survived independently of the codification that the VCLT undertook and re-emerged as important factors in the development of new techniques to interpret human rights treaties (eg the 'principle of effectiveness' discussed below).

[21] Sir G Fitzmaurice, 'The Law and Procedure of the International Court of Justice: Treaty Interpretation and Certain Other Treaty Points' (1951) 28 *BYBIL* 1, 3.

this view was not adopted, but shades of it do sometimes emerge in some of the more extreme approaches to the interpretation of human rights treaties. Other issues continued to be debated up to the conclusion of the VCLT. They concerned, first, what the rules of interpretation should be, and second, their inter-relationship—in particular whether there should be some form of hierarchy or order of precedence between them, and if so, what it should be.

Broadly, there were three schools of thought. According to the first of these, the objective of interpretation was to ascertain the intention of the parties, as a result of which this school laid great emphasis on the importance of the *travaux préparatoires*, to the extent of according them almost a priority over the actual text of the treaty. This theory of interpretation did not prevail during the course of further discussion, and the term 'intention of the parties' did not feature as a principle of interpretation in the VCLT or its earlier drafts. The concept of the intention of the parties, in a different and more objective sense, remains, however, a fundamental concept for illuminating the bounds of allowable interpretation within the terms of the VCLT. It has emerged as a live issue in relation to the interpretive methods of human rights fora, which critics claim sometimes ignore the original intention of the parties to human rights treaties, as discussed in Section 6, below.

The other two major approaches were 'textual' and 'teleological', the latter placing greatest emphasis on the 'object and purpose' of the treaty. These interpretive methods were generally accepted as valid and expressly incorporated into the provisions of the VCLT. The priority to be accorded to each of them remained an open issue. On the face of it, this issue appeared to have been fairly conclusively decided in favour of the text being the primary source of interpretation. The ILC Draft Articles that formed the basis of the final VCLT negotiations were quite clear as to the primacy of the text, a position that a number of ICJ judgments also endorsed. Arguably, Article 31(1) of the VCLT incorporates this primacy, but the wording is not categorical in this respect, and it has been frequently, even generally, interpreted as according equal weight to the two elements mentioned. This possible ambiguity in the provisions of the VCLT is the source of one of the major areas of distinctiveness in the interpretive methodology of human rights fora, as discussed in the following sections.

Two other aspects of treaty interpretation that prevailed prior to the VCLT are relevant to the subsequent development of the methodology, in relation to human rights treaties. In the first place, there was broad recognition of the particular importance of the teleological method of interpretation in relation to 'general multilateral conventions, particularly those of the social, humanitarian and law-making type'.[22] In the second place, the textual approach, as incorporated in the various formulations, was less rigid than is sometimes supposed, due to the principle of

[22] Maja Kirilova Eriksson, *Reproductive Freedom: In the Context of International Human Rights and Humanitarian Law* (Martinus Nijhoff 2000) 303.

integration.[23] The principle of integration is relevant to the provisions of the VCLT and important in the present context in relation to treaty interpretation by human rights fora. Special Rapporteur Sir Humphrey Waldock adopted the ICJ principles that Fitzmaurice synthesized, including integration, as the basis of his Draft Articles, which the ILC took up to form the origin of the VCLT provisions concerning interpretation. Waldock, while endorsing the basic concept of textual primacy[24] was open to the view that this approach did not exclude a 'discretionary element' of interpretation.[25] This view, as well as the requirements of relative brevity for a treaty text and the difficulty of obtaining state agreement on detailed rules, influenced the contents of the final VCLT provisions.

3.2 The articles of the VCLT

The general rule of interpretation is contained in Article 31(1), which begins as follows:

Article 31—General rule of interpretation

1. A treaty shall be interpreted in good faith in accordance with the ordinary meaning to be given to the terms of the treaty in their context and in the light of its object and purpose.

This provision[26] merges the principles of textuality, ordinary meaning, and integration, as well as the teleological principle of 'object and purpose' (which is itself generally regarded as incorporating the principle of 'effectiveness'), into a single rule. Even though they are presented in an order that may accord some primacy to the text, if only as a starting point, a hierarchy among the various components of the rule is far from categorically, or even clearly, expressed.

Two general points in the VCLT drafting have a bearing on the methodology of human rights tribunals:

(a) The International Law Commission approach has been referred to as the 'crucible approach', according to which the various interpretive elements of Articles 31 and 32 are thrown together in a 'single combined operation'.[27] It has been suggested, therefore, that the 1969 VCLT rules are not step-by step formulas for producing a conclusive interpretation in each and every case. The rules instead indicate factors or elements that one should take into consideration

[23] See Fitzmaurice, 'The Law and Procedure of the ICJ: Treaty Interpretation' (n 21).

[24] Sir Humphrey Waldock, Special Rapporteur, 'Third Report on the Law of Treaties' (1964) reprinted in [1964] UNYBILC 5.

[25] Waldock (n 24).

[26] It is pertinent to note that the title of the Article is 'General Rule' in the singular.

[27] Richard Gardiner, *Treaty Interpretation* (OUP 2008) 10.

(text, preamble, annexes, related agreements, *travaux préparatoires* etc). Although the rules contain a certain inherent logical sequence, they should not all necessarily be used in every case, nor should they always be sequentially applied.[28] The International Court of Justice,[29] other international courts and tribunals, and national courts have endorsed this provision on interpretation. Indeed, it has rightly been said that the ICJ's application of the Vienna rules is 'virtually axiomatic'.[30] It remains the case that the ICJ's starting point for interpreting a treaty is still the ordinary meaning, taking into account 'all the consequences which normally and reasonably flow from that text'.[31] The ordinary meaning is not an abstract notion, but instead must be interpreted in the light of 'the place which that phrase occupies in the text to be interpreted'.[32] 1969 VCLT Article 31(2) defines the context of a treaty.

(b) The formulations of principles, both before and during the course of the drafting of the VCLT, omitted any reference to the agreed-upon intention of the parties to the treaty, previously an absolutely fundamental element of treaty interpretation. In a world with nearly two hundred states drafting and adhering to treaties and given the growing importance of multilateral treaties, finding a common intention of the parties in any subjective sense has become increasingly difficult, if not impossible. Thus, 'a search for the common intentions of the parties can be likened to a search for the pot of gold at the end of a rainbow'.[33]

The shift from bilateral to multilateral treaties thus led to the formulation of an interpretive methodology concentrated on more objective and ascertainable principles. The intention of the parties remains a crucial factor in relation to interpretation, with a focus on the battle between the objective (textual) and the subjective (intent) schools.[34] Adhering to 'the intention of the parties' is still one of the final litmus tests of traditional interpretive techniques.

Article 31(1) widens the scope of 'ordinary meaning' by incorporating the principle of integration, of great importance in relation to human rights interpretation. Article 31(2) adds to this, defining the 'context' so that it extends beyond the text of the treaty (including its preamble and annexes) to include other related agreements. Article 31(3) opens the scope of interpretive methodology still further, by requiring that important additional matters be taken into account. Article 31(3) has played a critical role in the development of the so-called 'evolutive concepts'

[28] Gardiner (n 27) 9.

[29] See eg *Avena and Other Mexican Nationals (Mexico v United States)*, para 83.

[30] Gardiner (n 27) 15.

[31] Ian Sinclair, *The Vienna Convention on the Law of Treaties* (2nd edn, Manchester UP 1984) 121.

[32] Sinclair (n 31) 121.

[33] Sinclair (n 31) 130.

[34] Michael Waibel, 'Demystifying the Art of Interpretation' (2011) 22 *EJIL* 571, 572.

of treaty interpretation, which have become so important in relation to human rights. The article provides that:

3. There shall be taken into account, together with the context:

   ...

   (b) any subsequent practice in the application of the treaty which establishes the agreement of the parties regarding its interpretation;

   (c) any relevant rules of international law applicable in the relations between the parties.

Article 31(4) further provides that 'A special meaning shall be given to a term if it is established that the parties so intended'. Finally, mention must also be made of Article 32, which provides for '[s]upplementary means of interpretation'. The extent to which these interpretive tools may legitimately be used, in particular the *travaux préparatiores*, is also a divisive issue in the general law of treaties.[35]

In practice, in the field of human rights, it may prove particularly difficult to arrive at an acceptable 'ordinary meaning' of difficult abstract concepts or general terminology that may apply to many different situations or include many particular elements or principles. Another major problem relates to 'contemporaneity', as the ordinary meaning of a term develops with time through the subsequent practice of the parties. Similarly, establishing the 'object and purpose' of a treaty can be a daunting task, due to uncertainty surrounding the concept and the method of its determination.[36] Indeed, the Judgment of the International Court of Justice in the 1996 *Oil Platform* case[37] relied on the entire context of the interpreted instrument,[38] not just Article 1 of the Treaty, to ascertain its object and purpose.

[35] See *Marine Delimitation and Territorial Questions between Qatar and Bahrain (Qatar v Bahrain)* (1994); *Marine Delimitation and Territorial Questions between Qatar and Bahrain (Qatar v Bahrain) (Jurisdiction and Admissibility)* (1995). See also Judge Stephen's powerful dissenting opinion, *Marine Delimitation* (1995) 27; Stephen M Schwebel, 'May Preparatory Work be Used to Correct Rather than Confirm the "Clear" Meaning of a Treaty Provision?' in Jerzy Makarczyk (ed), *Theory of International Law at the Threshold of the 21st Century: Essays in Honour of Krysztof Skubiszewski* (Kluwer Law 1996); Panos Merkouris, '"Third Party" Considerations and "Corrective Interpretation" in the Interpretive Use of Travaux Préparatoires—Is it Fahrenheit 451 For Preparatory Work?' in Malgosia Fitzmaurice, Olufemi Elias, and Panos Merkouris (eds), *Treaty Interpretation and the Vienna Convention on the Law of Treaties: 30 Years On* (Brill 2010). Generally, on supplementary means of interpretation, see Gardiner (n 27) ch 8; Detlev F Vagts, 'Treaty Interpretation and the New American Ways of Law Reading' (1993) 4 *EJIL* 472, 486. Many commentators view the preparatory work as one of the main interpretive tools, reflecting the shared intentions of the parties. The ICJ, however, has always been adamant that the text of the treaty evidences the intentions of the parties, and the use of *travaux préparatiores* has to be approached with great caution.

[36] Isabelle Buffard and Karl Zemanek, 'The "Object and Purpose" of a Treaty: An Enigma?' (1998) 3 *ARIEL* 311.

[37] *Case Concerning Oil Platforms (Islamic Republic of Iran v United States)* (1996), para 31.

[38] The Court said: 'the Court considers that the objective of peace and friendship proclaimed in Article I of the Treaty of 1955 is such as to throw light on the interpretation of the other Treaty

It is far from clear what conclusions can be drawn from looking at the VCLT provisions as to their utility in relation to the interpretation of human rights treaties. It is generally accepted that human rights instruments require a more expansive attitude towards their interpretation than has been applied when interpreting other types of international law treaties, but views vary vastly as to the efficacy of the provisions of the VCLT in this respect. On the one hand, Article 31 has been termed a straightjacket of interpretation, representing an unreal regime of treaty interpretation in the contemporary world.[39] On the other hand, the VCLT is said to be so flexible that it is almost impossible to arrive at an 'illegal' interpretation when applying its provisions.[40] Views similarly diverge about the extent to which human rights fora apply the VCLT provisions.

VCLT Article 31(3)(c), which requires that treaties be interpreted while taking into account 'any relevant rules of international law applicable in the relations between the parties', has gained a renewed interest due to reliance on it by the ICJ[41] and the World Trade Organization (WTO).[42] In very broad terms, this provision is based on the premise that no treaty exists in a legal vacuum, but instead has to be interpreted within the wider background of international law. The reference to 'any relevant rules of international law' is understood broadly to encompass both applicable treaties and customary international law. Article 31(3)(c) can thus be said to refer to the principle of systematic integration, based on the premise that any relevant rule of international law must be taken into account in the interpretive process; the VCLT's definition of 'treaty' as an agreement governed by international law further supports this.[43]

The ILC decided to include the temporal element of treaty interpretation in Article 31(3)(c) as well, it 'being an element extrinsic both to the text and to the

provisions, and in particular of Articles IV and X. Article I is thus not without legal significance for such an interpretation, but cannot, taken in isolation, be a basis for the jurisdiction of the Court.' *Oil Platforms*—1996 (n 37) para 31.

[39] Joseph Weiler, 'Prolegomena in a Meso-theory of Treaty Interpretation at the Turn of the Century' (IILJ International Legal Theory Colloquium, New York, 14 February 2008) 5–6 <http://iilj.org/courses/documents/2008Colloquium.Session5.Weiler.pdf>.

[40] Birgit Schlütter, 'Aspects of Human Rights Interpretation by the UN Treaty Bodies' in Helen Keller and Geir Ulfstein (eds), *Human Rights Treaty Bodies: Law and Legitimacy* (CUP 2012) 317.

[41] *Case Concerning Oil Platforms (Iran v United States)* (2003), para 41; Campbell McLachlan, 'The Principle of Systemic Integration and Article 31(3)(c) of the Vienna Convention' (2005) 54 *ICLQ* 279; Duncan French, 'Treaty Interpretation and the Incorporation of Extraneous Legal Rules' (2006) 55 *ICLQ* 281. See Alexander Orakhelashvili, 'Restrictive Interpretation of Human Rights Treaties in the Recent Jurisprudence of the European Court of Human Rights' (2003) 14 *EJIL* 529, 537.

[42] WTO, 'European Communities—Measures Affecting the Approval and Marketing of Biotech Products: Reports of the Panel' (29 September 2006) WT/DS291/R, WT/DS292/R, WT/DS293/R; Benn McGrady, 'Fragmentation of International Law or "Systemic Integration" of Treaty Regimes: EC-Biotech Products and the Proper Interpretation of Article 31(3)(c) of the Vienna Convention on the law of Treaties' (2008) 42 *Journal of World Trade* 589. See also generally, Pauwelyn, *Conflict of Norms in Public International Law* (n 10).

[43] McLachlan (n 41) 289.

"context" as defined in [Article 31] paragraph 2'.[44] The ICJ addressed how the inevitable evolution of international law should affect the interpretation of a treaty, especially in cases where a considerable passage of time may occur between the conclusion of the treaty and its interpretation[45] in its 1971 Namibia advisory opinion:

> the Court must take into consideration the changes which have occurred in the supervening half-century, and its interpretation cannot remain unaffected by the subsequent development of law, through the Charter of the United Nations and by way of customary law. Moreover, an international instrument has to be interpreted and applied within the framework of the entire legal system prevailing at the time of the interpretation. In the domain to which the present proceedings relate, the last fifty years, as indicated above, have brought important developments.[46]

In several contentious cases, the ICJ similarly embraced the evolutive, temporal aspect of treaty interpretation.[47] Each new case brings elucidation and development to this doctrine. In the *Costa Rica v Nicaragua* case, the ICJ stated that evolutive obligations 'must be understood to have the meaning they bear on each occasion on which the Treaty is to be applied, and not necessarily their original meaning'.[48] While the ICJ has thus recognized evolutionary interpretation as part of general international law, the approach has mainly developed through the interpretation of human rights treaties. One leading scholar has objected that such interpretive methodology may only be adopted if the parties so intended and that such intention cannot be presumed; any contrary practice amounts to judicial legislation.[49] Arato

[44] Sinclair (n 30) 139. In the *Island of Palmas* arbitration, Judge Huber set forth the leading doctrine on intertemporality, formulating it as follows: 'A[a] juridical fact must be appreciated in the light of the law contemporary with it, and not of the law in force at the time when a dispute in regard to it arises or falls to be settled.' *Island of Palmas Case (United States v Netherlands)* 845. There is a vast literature on this subject: TO Elias, 'The Doctrine of Intertemporal Law' (1980) 74 *AJIL* 285; Hugh Thirlway, 'The Law and Procedure of the International Court of Justice: 1960–1989' (1980) 60 *BYBIL* 1; Rosalyn Higgins, 'Some Observations on the Inter-Temporal Rule in International Law' in Makarczyk (n 34); DW Greig, *Intertemporality and the Law of Treaties* (British Institute of International and Comparative Law 2003); Daniel-Erasmus Khan, 'Max Huber as Arbitrator: The Palmas (Miangas) Case and Other Arbitrations' (2007) 18 *EJIL* 145; Afshin Akhtarkhavari, 'The Passage of Time in International Environmental Disputes' (2003) 10 *Murdoch University Electronic Journal of Law*.

[45] See Pauwelyn, *Conflict of Norms in Public International Law* (n 10) 264–65.

[46] *Legal Consequences for States of the Continued Presence of South Africa in Namibia (South-West Africa) Notwithstanding Security Council Resolution 276*, para 53. The Court also adopted the evolutive approach to treaty interpretation in the *Dispute Regarding Navigational and Related Rights (Cost Rica v Nicaragua)*, especially para 63.

[47] See eg *Aegean Sea Continental Shelf Case (Greece v Turkey)*, para 77; *South Africa in Namibia* (n 46) para 53; *Case Concerning the Gabčíkovo-Nagymaros Project (Hungary/Slovakia)*, para 112; *Navigational and Related Rights* (n 46). See also *Iron Rhine Case (Belgium v Netherlands)* 37.

[48] *Navigational and Related Rights* (n 46) para 70.

[49] In case of a lack of evidence regarding the parties' intention to allow evolutive interpretation, the only acceptable interpretive practice regarding some terms of a treaty is recourse to the principle of 'contemporaneity'—ie giving each term its historical meaning, not a modern one. Gerald Fitzmaurice, 'The Law and Procedure of the International Court of Justice, 1951–54: Treaty Interpretation and Other Treaty Points' (1957) 33 *BYBIL* 203, 223.

questioned how such intent is to be determined, ie whether it must be explicit or, if not, what evidence might provide the basis for claiming the evolutive character of a treaty provision.[50] The terms of a treaty only rarely contain the intention of the parties on this point, so courts have had recourse to a legal construct of the 'imputability' or 'presumption' of the intent of the parties. Even with this presumption, there remain inherent difficulties with determining the category of terms which can be deemed 'evolutive'. According to the ILC Working Group on Fragmentation, the view that highly technical or very general terms can be interpreted in such a way can be contentious, as the parties to a treaty may interpret such terms very differently.[51]

The ILC Working Group on Fragmentation also addressed the question of what evidence can be used to establish the substance of the term's contemporary meaning, suggesting that one available legal tool is application of Article 31(3)(c) to determine the international law 'applicable in the relations between the parties'.[52] However, the judicial practice of international courts indicates that they frequently ignore the strict requirements of the article, citing to instruments that are not in force or ones that are non-binding. In the well-known 1979 *Marckx* case, for example, the ECtHR interpreted a term in the ECHR on the basis of two other treaties that the majority of the parties to the ECHR had not ratified, nonetheless calling these treaties a 'common ground in this area amongst modern societies'.[53]

Evolutive interpretation based on the notion of the 'object and purpose' of a treaty is an interpretive tool that links Article 31(3)(c) and Article 31(1). The relationship between evolutive interpretation and teleological interpretation, a technique which puts great emphasis on the object and purpose, is far from clear. In the view of many authors, interpretation based on the object and purpose of a treaty should be treated with caution, as in extreme cases it can lead to meanings that extend beyond the bounds of textual interpretation.[54] Other scholars and judges are of the view that reliance on the object and purpose of a treaty is not only in accordance with VCLT Article 31(1), but it is particularly appropriate in the context of human rights obligations.[55] The object and purpose test is also related to the doctrine of effectiveness, captured in the maxim *ur res magis valeat quam pereat*—ie treaties are presumed

[50] Julian Arato, 'Subsequent Practice and Evolutive Interpretation: Techniques of Treaty Interpretation over Time and Their Diverse Consequences' (2010) 9 *LPICT* 443, 466.

[51] ILC, 'Fragmentation of International Law' (n 2) para 23. The ILC Working Group considered the following terms susceptible to evolutive interpretation: '(a) the concept is one which implies taking into account subsequent technical, economic or legal developments; (b) the concept sets up an obligation for further progressive development for the parties; or (c) the concept has a very general nature or is expressed in such general terms that it must take into account changing circumstances.'

[52] ILC, 'Fragmentation of International Law' (n 2) paras 443, 479 *et seq*.

[53] *Marckx v Belgium*, para 41; Malgosia Fitzmaurice, 'Dynamic (Evolutive) Interpretation of Treaties, Part I' (2008) 21 *Hague YB Int'l L* 101, 152.

[54] See Sinclair (n 30) 33.

[55] Lucius Caflisch and Antonio A Cançado Trinidade, 'Les Conventions Américaine et Européenne des Droits de L'Homme et le Droit International Général' (2004) 108 *RGDIP* 5, 12.

to have a definite force and effect; a treaty therefore may be interpreted expansively in order to ensure that all of its provisions have an independent (non-superfluous) meaning (*effet utile*).[56] Human rights courts and tribunals use these doctrines, although several complex issues arise regarding evolutive interpretation in relation to the object and purpose of a treaty. First, a treaty may have not one, but several, objectives and purposes; second, an object and purpose may be a general one relating to the treaty as whole, or it may be that individual provisions have their own different objects and purposes.

In general, the various considerations above lead to the conclusion that evolutive interpretation of treaties is still developing, and the legal features of the approach are not yet fully defined. It is a multi-faceted legal construct upon which international courts and tribunals elaborate in somewhat piecemeal fashion. Its application and relationship with other principles of interpretation is also itself evolving.

4. Introduction to the Treaties and Supervisory Bodies

This section examines several human rights treaties that fall into two categories. The first category comprises three major regional human rights conventions, each of which came into being under the auspices of a regional organization and sets up a substantial regime for the protection of human rights within the territories of the states parties. Each of these Conventions, moreover, sets up judicial or quasi-judicial entities to monitor and adjudicate parties' compliance with the provisions of the respective Conventions.

These Conventions are, in chronological order:

- The 1950 ECHR (entry into force 1953), concluded under the auspices of the Council of Europe. 'To ensure the observance of the engagements undertaken by…' the parties to the ECHR established the European Court of Human Rights;[57]
- The 1969 American Convention on Human Rights (ACHR, entry into force 1978), concluded within the framework of the Organization of American States. The ACHR established the Inter-American Court of Human Rights (IACtHR) and expanded the jurisdiction of the Inter-American Commission on Human Rights (IACHR);
- The 1981 African Charter on Human and Peoples' Rights (African Charter, entry into force in 1986), concluded under the auspices of the Organisation of African

[56] Fitzmaurice, 'The Law and Procedure of the ICJ: 1951–54' (n 49) 211.

[57] ECHR, Art 19.

Unity (now African Union). It established the African Commission on Human and Peoples' Rights (African Commission) 'to promote human and peoples' rights and ensure their protection in Africa'.[58] Subsequently, a 1998 Protocol to the African Charter, entry into force in 2004, established an African Court on Human and Peoples' Rights (African Court) to 'complement the protective mandate of the African Commission on Human and Peoples' Rights'[59] within the African Union.

Various provisions of these Conventions relate to, or have influenced, the methods of interpretation of the supervisory bodies, but it may be noted here that the jurisdictions of both the IACtHR and the African Court extend beyond just the interpretation of the above-mentioned Conventions, to cover interpretation of 'other treaties concerning the protection of human rights in the American states';[60] and 'any other relevant human rights instrument ratified by the States concerned'.[61]

The second category consists of the core United Nations conventions relating to the promotion of human rights. Each convention establishes a treaty body (committee) that produces various forms of pronouncements relating to the interpretation of their related Conventions.[62]

5. Provisions of Human Rights Conventions Relating to Interpretation

The mandates of the human rights tribunals and bodies require them to interpret the particular conventions under which they were established. They all therefore act

[58] Article 30.

[59] Protocol to the African Charter on Human and Peoples' Rights on the Establishment of an African Court on Human and Peoples' Rights, Arts 1, 2.

[60] ACHR, Art 64(1).

[61] Protocol to the African Charter, Art 3(1).

[62] They are: the Committee on the Elimination of Racial Discrimination (CERD Committee) for the International Convention on the Elimination of Racial Discrimination; the Human Rights Committee for the International Covenant on Civil and Political Rights; the Committee on Economic, Social and Cultural Rights (CESCR) for the International Covenant on Economic, Social and Cultural Rights; the Committee Against Torture (CAT) for the Convention Against Torture; the Committee on Elimination of Discrimination Against Women (CEDAW Committee) for the Convention on the Discrimination of All Forms of Discrimination Against Women; the Committee on the Rights of the Child (CRC Committee) for the Convention on the Rights of the Child; the Committee on Migrant Workers (CMW) for the Convention on the Protection of the Rights of All Migrant Workers and Members of Their Families; the Committee on the Rights of Persons with Disabilities (CRPD Committee) for the Convention on the Rights of Persons with Disabilities; the Committee on Enforced Disappearance (CED) for the International Convention for the Protection of All Persons from Enforced Disappearance.

in a theoretically discrete environment, wherein each convention's own particular tribunal or treaty body interprets the relevant convention. Nevertheless, there is a good deal of common ground, although there are significant differences in the different tribunals' approaches to interpretation.[63] The common ground arises from a number of factors.

First, the human rights bodies all recognize that they relate to the same subject matter, despite the divergent views on human rights and the different 'context' of the areas the regional conventions cover. In addition, it is generally recognized that the nature of that subject matter imposes certain approaches to interpretation, in particular in the form of the so-called '*pro homine*' emphasis in relation to human rights.

Second, all of the conventions are recognized as being of a more or less normative or constitutional nature, in which the major rights and obligations of the parties are non-reciprocal, justifying a more teleological approach to their interpretation. Third, frequent and deliberate cross-fertilization arises from each tribunal's use as persuasive, non-binding authority of each other's cases, as well as from other common sources—in particular the Universal Declaration of Human Rights and the UN Charter.

The development of this common ground involves, among other things, adoption by treaty bodies of relatively similar approaches to the VCLT provisions relating to interpretation. As mentioned above, there is major tension in VCLT Article 31(1) between the so-called 'textual' approach and the teleological approach that relies on the 'object and purpose' of a treaty. In the second place, the VCLT contains relatively vague provisions related to events or developments subsequent to the conclusion of a treaty, in particular respecting the relevance of the subsequent practices of states party to the interpretation of a treaty, and the provisions of Article 31(3)(c) relating to the use of rules of international law applicable in the relations between the parties. The approach of the human rights tribunals to these two aspects of the interpretive regime of the VCLT may constitute the most important aspect of their common ground, in relation to interpretation, and may also constitute the areas in which that common approach is seen as being distinctive from the traditional approach to treaty interpretation.

Section 6 considers the jurisprudence that the tribunals have developed in relation to each of these approaches. However, it is useful to consider first the actual Conventions, which reveal substantial relevant common ground. These Conventions do not expressly direct the manner of interpretation for the tribunals

[63] See eg *Compulsory Membership in an Association Prescribed by Law for the Practice of Journalism*, paras 42–52 (adopting a broader interpretation of freedom of expression than that which the ECHR guarantees, after expressly comparing the respective provisions and jurisprudence). See Fionnuala Ni Aolain, 'The Emergence of Diversity: Differences in Human Rights Jurisprudence' (1995) 19 *Fordham Int'l LJ* 101.

concerned to adopt, but a number of provisions are highly influential in relation to certain aspects of interpretation. The tribunals have used them to underpin and justify their election of certain approaches to interpretation. In this respect, particular provisions lead to the adoption of a teleological approach to interpretation and also are used to define the 'object and purpose' of the conventions. Some provisions are used to justify an exceptionally wide interpretation of the concept of 'relevant rules of international law' and have influenced the adoption of the *pro homine* approach of the human rights tribunals.

All three regional human rights conventions express themselves, in their preambles, as being concluded within the context of the UN Charter and the Universal Declaration of Human Rights. The ACHR cites the Charter of the Organization of American States, the American Declaration of the Rights and Duties of Man, the Universal Declaration of Human Rights, and 'other international instruments, worldwide as well as regional in scope'.[64] The quoted language is significant in that it points to an even wider context within which the rights that it upholds should be placed. The African Charter preamble takes this broader context even further; it not only refers to the UN Charter and Universal Declaration, but also affirms the parties' adherence to 'the principle of human and peoples' rights and freedoms contained in the declarations, conventions and other instruments adopted by the Organization of African Unity, the Movement of Non-Aligned Countries and the United Nations'.

These provisions not only provide a uniform source from which their objectives are said to derive, but also suggest that their objective relates to the upholding of rights which derive not only from the conventions themselves, but also from a wider, and in a sense higher, spectrum of instruments and rules. This tendency is enhanced by other provisions in the conventions, referred to below.

All three preambles also place the adoption of the conventions and the establishment of their respective tribunals within the context of a wider political order for the relative regions. The preamble to the ECHR, for instance, observes that the governments' signatories thereto are members of the Council of Europe and adds 'that the aim of the Council of Europe is the achievement of greater unity between its members and that one of the methods by which that aim is to be pursued is the maintenance and further realization of human rights and fundamental freedoms'. Both the ACHR and African Charter contain similar references to their institutional position in the context of, respectively, the Organization of American States and the African Union, in their preambles. Such provisions have been referred to in support of the 'public order' approach to interpretation.[65]

Third, the preambles to the ACHR and the African Charter contain provisions which, especially in the case of the IACtHR, have influenced the development of a

[64] Preamble.

[65] See eg *Golder v United Kingdom*; *Loizidou v Turkey*.

'*pro homine*' approach to interpretation by emphasizing that the source of human rights is not merely the Conventions themselves, nor even the wider context of other conventions and declarations, but the very nature of man. Thus, the second paragraph of the ACHR, reads: '*Recognizing* that the essential rights of man are not derived from one's being a national of a certain state, but are based upon attributes of the human personality'; while the African Charter contains the following paragraph: '*Recognizing* on the one hand, that fundamental human rights stem from the attributes of human beings, which justifies their national and international protection and on the other hand that the reality and respect of peoples rights should necessarily guarantee human rights.'[66]

Regard also must be given to Articles 17 and 18 of the ECHR, Article 29 of the ACHR, and Articles 60 and 61 of the African Charter. All of these, by requiring that rights restrictions be interpreted narrowly against the state, provide a '*pro homine*' framework of interpretation. In addition to preserving rights that domestic laws or other treaties to which the state is a party recognize, ACHR Article 29 provides, inter alia, that:

> [N]o provision of this Convention shall be interpreted as:
>
> . . .
>
> (c) precluding other rights or guarantees that are inherent in the human personality or derived from representative democracy as a form of government; or
>
> (d) excluding or limiting the effect that the American Declaration of the Rights and Duties of Man and other international acts of the same nature may have.

Thus Article 29 explicitly allows the Commission and Court to recognize rights not written into the Convention, and it gives a treaty basis for applying other treaties, as well as the American Declaration, the Universal Declaration of Human Rights, and other non-binding texts. More generally, its thrust is to apply the rule most favourable to the individual—the basis of the *pro homine* rule that the Court/Commission apply.

Article 60 of the African Charter is similarly expansive, providing as follows:

> The Commission shall draw inspiration from international law on human and peoples' rights, particularly from the provisions of various African instruments on human and peoples' rights, the Charter of the United Nations, the Charter of the Organization of African Unity, the Universal Declaration of Human Rights, other instruments adopted by the United Nations and by African countries in the field of human and peoples' rights as well as from the provisions of various instruments adopted within the Specialized Agencies of the United Nations of which the parties to the present Charter are members.

Article 61 continues:

> The Commission shall also take into consideration, as subsidiary measures to determine the principles of law, other general or special international conventions, laying down rules expressly

[66] Preamble.

recognized by member states of the Organization of African Unity, African practices consistent with international norms on human and peoples' rights, customs generally accepted as law, general principles of law recognized by African states as well as legal precedents and doctrine.

It is apparent immediately that in these provisions, the drafting states have provided a potent basis for widening the ambit of interpretation.

The spectrum of external legal or quasi-legal sources to which the ECtHR may look in interpreting the European Convention is somewhat narrower than in the case of the ACHR and the African Charter.[67] In addition, the ACHR and the African Charter both make reference to social and economic rights, opening the door, as it were, to the merger of such rights with political and civil rights. These two elements have made it easier for the IACtHR and the African Commission to broaden the scope of the rights they protect and the area across which they may look for consensus.

6. Jurisprudence

6.1 Applicability of the VCLT

The starting point for study of the interpretive methodology that the human rights tribunals have adopted is their attitude towards the VCLT provisions relating to interpretation. In this respect, the pronouncements of the regional human rights tribunals are both clear and uniform; all assert the applicability of those provisions to human rights treaties. The ECtHR, in its relatively early judgment in the *Golder* case[68] (discussed further below), said:

The Court is prepared to consider, as do the Government and the Commission, that it should be guided by Articles 31 to 33 of the Vienna Convention of 23 May 1969 on the Law of Treaties. That Convention has not yet entered into force and it specifies, at Article 4, that it will not be retroactive, but its Articles 31 to 33 enunciate in essence generally accepted principles of international law to which the Court has already referred on occasion. In this

[67] ECHR, Art 53: 'Nothing in this Convention shall be construed as limiting or derogating from any of the human rights and fundamental freedoms which may be ensured under the laws of any High Contracting Party or under any other agreement to which it is a Party.'

[68] *Golder* (n 65). The Court said as follows: 'In the way in which it is presented in the "general rule" in Article 31 of the Vienna Convention, the process of interpretation of a treaty is a unity, a single combined operation; this rule, closely integrated, places on the same footing the various elements enumerated in the four paragraphs of the Article.' ibid para 30. Although 1969 VCLT was not in force in 1975, the ECtHR stated that it represented the general principles of international law, which had to be taken into account.

respect, for the interpretation of the European Convention account is to be taken of those Articles subject, where appropriate, to 'any relevant rules of the organization'.[69]

The Inter-American Commission, in *Cases Nos 9777 and 9718 (Argentina)* and in their 1987/8 Annual Report,[70] held that an argument that the Petitioner put forward in relation to the interpretation of the Statute of the Inter-American Commission on Human Rights was not acceptable; it was not 'in agreement with the rules on interpretation of treaties set out in Article 31.2 of the Vienna Convention on Treaty Law (1969)',[71] a position which the IACtHR had already adopted in its Second Advisory Opinion, in relation to the interpretation of Article 75 of the American Convention.[72] The IACtHR's acknowledgement of the applicability of the provisions of the VCLT has continued in more recent cases, even when that Court is considering more innovative methods of interpretation and asserting their compatibility with the provisions of the VCLT. Thus, in the *Mapiripán Massacre* case, the Court said:

This evolutive interpretation is consistent with the general rules of interpretation set forth in Article 29 of the American Convention, as well those set forth in the Vienna Convention on Treaty Law.[73]

However, although the general positions of the three regional tribunals are clear, they have provoked widely differing reactions among scholars. In reference to the ECtHR, some authors firmly assert that the ECtHR endorses the rules of the VCLT;[74] others disagree. Letsas, for instance, considers that it was fair to say that the VCLT has not played a very significant role in the interpretation of the ECHR.[75] Sinclair contends that in fact the ECtHR pays only lip service to the VCLT rule of contextual interpretation and that it is instead engaged 'in a process of reasoning which pays scant respect to the principle of the "ordinary meaning" of the terms "in their context" '.[76] Though controversy remains, more recent scholarship appears to be moving towards some consensus that, subject to important limited exceptions, the interpretive methods of the human rights tribunals are consistent with the provisions of the

[69] *Golder* (n 65) para 29.

[70] IACHR, 'Annual Report of the Inter-American Commission on Human Rights: 1987–1988' (16 September 1988) OEA/Ser.L/V/II.74.

[71] 'Argentina' in IACHR, 'Annual Report 1987–88' (n 70) para 6.

[72] *The Effect of Reservations on the Entry into Force of the American Convention (Arts 74 and 75)*, Advisory Opinion OC-2/82, Sept 24, 1982, 2 Inter-Am.Ct.H.R. (Ser.A)(1982).

[73] *Case of the 'Mapiripán Massacre' v Colombia*, para 106.

[74] Daniel Rietiker, 'The Principle of "Effectiveness" in the Recent Jurisprudence of the European Court of Human Rights: Its Different Dimensions and Its Consistency with Public International Law—No Need for the Concept of Treaty *Sui Generis*' (2010) 79 *Nord J Int'l L* 245, 248.

[75] George Letsas, 'Strasbourg's Interpretive Ethic: Lessons for the International Lawyer' (2010) 21 *EJIL* 509.

[76] Sinclair (n 31) 131–32.

VCLT, albeit with a relatively wide interpretation of those provisions.[77] In order to see how, and to what extent, this view is justified, the sections below discuss first the attitudes of the human rights tribunals to particular provisions of the VCLT, and second the attitudes that those tribunals have developed toward certain principles, which appear to some extent special, or especially important, to their interpretive methods.

6.2 Special characteristics of human rights treaties

The conclusion that human rights treaties do not in themselves constitute a special form of treaty with their own discrete rules does not mean that they do not share certain special characteristics that impact their proper interpretation. In particular, human rights tribunals have been consistent in asserting the 'constitutional' nature of human rights treaties and the non-reciprocal nature of the rights and obligations that arise under them. This issue arose initially in relation to the assertion that a separate regime of reservations applies to human rights treaties. Human rights tribunals, in particular the ECtHR and the Inter-American Court,[78] have developed a distinctive jurisprudence regarding reservations. The Inter-American Court of Human Rights explicitly found the relevant provisions of the VCLT to be inapplicable, a conclusion it derived from the notion of the non-reciprocity of human rights obligations.[79] The Court stated as follows:

> The Court must emphasize, however, that modern human rights treaties in general, and the American Convention in particular, are not multilateral treaties of the traditional type concluded to accomplish the reciprocal exchange of rights for the mutual benefit of the contracting States. Their object and purpose is the protection of the basic rights of individual human beings irrespective of their nationality, both against the State of their nationality and all other contracting States. In concluding these human rights treaties, the States can be deemed to submit themselves to a legal order within which they, for the common good, assume various obligations, not in relation to other States, but towards all individuals within their jurisdiction.[80]

[77] See generally: Magnus Killander, 'Interpreting Regional Human Rights Treaties' (2010) 7(13) *SUR Int'l JHR* 145; Frédéric Vanneste, *General International Law Before Human Rights Court* (Intersentia 2010) ch 4; Magdalena Forowicz, *The Reception of International Law in the European Court of Human Rights* (OUP 2010); Başak Çali, 'Specialized Rules of Treaty Interpretation: Human Rights' in Duncan B Hollis (ed), *The Oxford Guide to Treaties* (OUP 2012).

[78] Alain Pellet, Special Rapporteur on reservations to treaties, found the regime of the 1969 VCLT sufficiently flexible to be applied to human rights treaties. Pellet (n 14). See also Human Rights Committee, 'General Comment No 24: Issues Relating to Reservations Made upon Ratification or Accession to the Covenant or the Optional Protocols Thereto, or in Relation to Declarations under Article 41 of the Covenant' (4 November 1994) UN Doc CCPR/C/21/Rev.1/Add.6, para 17; *Armed Activities on the Territory of the Congo (Democratic Republic of the Congo v Rwanda)*, dissention opinion.

[79] *Reservations on the Entry into Force of the ACHR* (n 69) para 10.

[80] *Reservations on the Entry into Force of the ACHR* (n 72) para 29.

In support of its opinion, the IACtHR cited decisions of the European Commission on Human Rights, the International Court of Justice's Advisory Opinion on *Reservations to the Genocide Convention*, and the Vienna Convention, particularly Article 60(5).

The Inter-American Court made further statements about its interpretive techniques in its Advisory Opinion, *Interpretation of the American Declaration of the Rights and Duties of Man within the Framework of Article 64 of the American Convention on Human Rights*. It developed these views in the *Mapiripán Massacre* case[81] and the *Case of Salvador Chiriboga v Ecuador*.[82] In the first of these cases, the Court reaffirmed the principles it had set forth in its early Advisory Opinions, emphasizing the special character of human rights obligations, as a consequence of which these obligations are independent from general international law.

A number of scholars have noted this reliance on human rights treaties' quasi-constitutional or non-reciprocal nature. Craven finds that recognizing human rights as having a quasi-constitutional character[83] may lead to the modification of, if not the complete disregard for, certain principles of general international law.[84] Indeed, the possible distinctiveness of human rights as having a formal or structural aspect relating to non-reciprocity, has been one of the major factors leading to human rights tribunals' adoption of a strong teleological approach to interpretation.

The distinctiveness also has a substantive aspect, relating to the nature and purpose of the content of human rights treaties. This aspect has had a major influence on human rights tribunals' interpretive approach in their emphasis on the principle of 'effectiveness' and the development of a so-called '*pro homine*' or '*ad personam*' approach, discussed below.

6.3 Approaches of human rights tribunals to the VCLT

6.3.1 *Article 31(1)*

The present subsection first examines the approach of human rights tribunals to certain particular principles, which were either embodied expressly in the provisions of the VCLT or recognized as existing principles of interpretation before the conclusion of the VCLT. The following subsection considers the development by human rights tribunals of certain principles, which are not expressly incorporated in the VCLT and which were, if known at all, were scarcely recognized at that time as legitimate interpretive techniques. However, both human rights tribunals and scholars widely assert their conformity with the provisions of the VCLT—although this assertion is subject to a good deal of debate.

[81] *Mapiripán Massacre* (n 73) paras 104–108.
[82] *Case of Salvador Chiriboga v Ecuador*, para 131.
[83] Craven (n 1) 493. [84] Craven (n 1) 491.

The characteristic, and some would say expansive, approach of the ECtHR to the provisions of the VCLT first emerged in the *Golder* case, in which the Court reasoned that the object and purpose of the ECHR, in particular as manifested in its preamble, outweighed what could have been considered to be the clear meaning of the text. The judgment in *Golder* signals the ECtHR's approach:

In the way in which it is presented in the 'general rule' in Article 31 of the Vienna Convention, the process of interpretation of a treaty is a unity, a single combined operation; this rule, closely integrated, places on the same footing the various elements enumerated in the four paragraphs of the Article.[85]

This 'crucible approach to interpretation', as discussed in section 2 above, posits the absolute equality of the elements in these Articles of the VCLT. However, it is not universally accepted in relation to general international law; the ICJ, for example, generally has given distinct precedence to the ordinary meaning of the text of the treaty, at least as the proper starting point for its interpretation. The ECtHR's unequivocal endorsement of the equality of all the elements in *Golder* thus takes on particular significance. It is, in fact, a foundational element in relation to the special approach that human rights tribunals have taken to interpretation, allowing a particular emphasis on the object and purpose of human rights conventions.

Golder concerned the interpretation of Article 6 of the Convention (the right of fair trial). The Court read into the Convention the right of access to a court, a right not expressly granted therein (sometimes referred to as an 'un-enumerated right').[86] The United Kingdom's government argued against implying any right that the Convention did not explicitly include. Although the Court's reasoning seemed to rely on the VCLT rules of interpretation, it interpreted Article 6 of the ECHR in a novel manner, by determining that the right was 'inherent' to another right which was enumerated in the Convention. The ECtHR did so on the basis that such a determination was necessary to achieve the object and purpose of the Convention and to render the expressly-guaranteed right 'effective'. The Court relied in particular on references to the 'rule of law' in the preamble:

It may also be accepted, as the Government have submitted, that the Preamble does not include the rule of law in the object and purpose of the Convention, but points to it as being one of the features of the common spiritual heritage of the member States of the Council of Europe. The Court however considers, like the Commission, that it would be a mistake to see in this reference a merely 'more or less rhetorical reference', devoid of relevance for those interpreting the Convention. One reason why the signatory Governments decided to 'take the first steps for the collective enforcement of certain of the Rights stated in the Universal Declaration' was their profound belief in the rule of law. It seems both natural and in conformity with the principle of good faith (Article 31 para. 1 of the Vienna Convention) to bear in mind this widely proclaimed consideration when interpreting the terms of Article 6

[85] *Golder* (n 65) para 30.

[86] Letsas, 'Strasbourg's Interpretive Ethic' (n 75).

para. 1 (art. 6-1) according to their context and in the light of the object and purpose of the Convention.[87]

Thus, even though provision for the rule of law is not expressly made the (or even an) object or purpose of the Convention itself, the ECtHR found that the parties' statement of 'profound belief' in the rule of law is sufficient to make it such.

Letsas provides a useful summary of the Court's line of reasoning in the *Golder* case:

1. In interpretation, one should look to the object and purpose of the law.
2. The object and purpose of the ECHR is to promote the rule of law.
3. One can scarcely conceive of the rule of law in civil matters without right of access to court.
4. The right of access to court is inherent in the right to fair trial under Article 6 ECHR.
5. The ECHR protects the right of access to court.[88]

In the *Golder* case, although the ECtHR implied a right that the ECHR did not expressly guarantee, the Court did not say it was doing so. Instead, it called the right 'inherent' to a right that *was* in the Convention. The ECtHR has generally been quite reluctant to imply rights not expressly in the Convention, although on a number of occasions it has upheld asserted rights which, though not expressly provided for in the ECHR, it finds to be 'inherent' in, or necessary to, rights which are expressly included. The Court will not find inherent or implied rights which have no such connection to Convention rights.[89]

In *Johnston and Others v Ireland*, for example, the ECtHR refused to hold that the right to marry implied, or had inherent in it, a right to divorce, even though it was the absence of a right to divorce in Ireland that prevented the Applicant from marrying. On the other hand, the Court has given support for environmental entitlements as part of rights that the Convention expressly includes. The Court has been assiduous, however, in declining to establish any new right to a clean environment, which the member states have refused to include in the Convention. In many of its judgments on this issue, the Court has observed that a right to a clean environment does not exist under the Convention.[90] In sum, the environmental element must be strictly linked to the rights which are expressly protected.

[87] *Golder* (n 65) para 34.

[88] Letsas, 'Strasbourg's Interpretive Ethic' (n 75) 517. The majority judgment of the Court in this case was subject to the severe criticism of Sir Gerald Fitzmaurice, who strongly objected to reading rights into the Convention that, according to him, were not expressly included or even implied within it.

[89] *Pretty v United Kingdom*. See also *Johnston and Others v Ireland*.

[90] *Budayeva and Others v Russia*; *Fadeyeva v Russia*. In the *Fadeyeva* case, the Court reiterated that Art 8 is only a ground for lodging 'environmental' cases if pollution directly and seriously affects the individual's right to private and family life.

The African Commission has been more open to the implication of rights not explicitly provided in the African Charter. In *SERAC v Nigeria*,[91] the Commission stated that although the African Charter does not explicitly provide for the right to housing or shelter or the right to food, the combination of provisions protecting the right to enjoy the best attainable state of mental and physical health, the right to property, and the protection accorded to the family, forbids the wanton destruction of shelter or food supplies, because when these are destroyed, it adversely affects the rights to property, health, and family life. Thus, the combined effect of Articles 14, 16, and 18(1) reads into the Charter other rights, which the Nigerian government violated.[92]

UN human rights bodies have similarly emphasized the object and purpose of the treaties. Mechlem has analysed the general interpretive techniques of the CESCR,[93] including the CESCR's use of the object and purpose criterion to establish the notion of the treaty's 'core obligations'. According to this author, the concept of 'core obligations' could, in practice, mean that many poorer countries fail to comply with the provisions of the CESCR. This result would conflict with the object and purpose of the CESCR, which, she posits, is to provide a progressive framework for all states parties to realize economic, social, and cultural rights. The CESCR introduced the concept of 'core obligations' in General Comment No 3 on the Nature of States' Parties Obligations.[94] The core obligations of states were initially well defined and precise, and related to 'true essentials',[95] but later General Comments, such as No 15 on the Right to Water[96] and No 14 on the Right to Health,[97] expanded the concept and significantly raised the risk of non-compliance with the CESCR's minimum obligations.[98] Mechlem critiques the CESCR, as well, for the references in its General Comments to the role of international organizations, because a textual interpretation of the International Covenant on Economic, Social and Cultural Rights clearly indicates that it only refers to states.[99] The conclusion is that the Committee's approach exceeds its mandate[100] and does not, in practice, follow the VCLT canons of interpretation.

In the course of this expansive approach, the human rights fora have made substantial use of the concept of effectiveness in interpretation—now regarded as

[91] *Social and Economic Rights Action Centre (SERAC) v Nigeria.* [92] *SERAC* (n 91).

[93] Kerstin Mechlem, 'Treaty Bodies and the Interpretation of Human Rights' (2009) 42 *V and J Transnat'l L* 905.

[94] CESCR, 'General Comment No 3: The Nature of States Parties' Obligations (Art 2, Para 1, of the Covenant)' (14 December 1990) UN Doc E/1991/123, para 10.

[95] Mechlem (n 93) 941.

[96] CESCR, 'General Comment No 15: The Right to Water (Arts 11 and 12)' (20 January 2003) UN Doc E/C.12/2002/11, para 37.

[97] CESCR, 'General Comment No 14: The Right to the Highest Attainable Standard of Health' (Art 12)' (11 August 2000) UN Doc E/C.12/2000/4, para 25.

[98] CESCR, 'General Comment No 14' (n 97).

[99] Mechlem (n 93) 931–32 [100] Mechlem (n 93) 933.

inherent in the VCLT reference to the 'object and purpose' of treaties. In fact, the reliance on the 'object and purpose rule' to interpret human rights treaties can be viewed as having as its primary aim the effective application of such treaties (*effet utile*) of the instrument.[101]

6.3.2 *Article 31(3)(c) of the VCLT*

The second VCLT provision that has played an important role in the development of a distinctive human rights approach to interpretation is Article 31(3)(c). Given its reference to general international law, human rights tribunals have offered and used this provision as a bridge to a wider context for the interpretation of human rights than that which solely the provisions of a particular convention provide. The ECtHR has repeatedly stated that the ECHR is not to be interpreted 'in a vacuum' and has used Article 31(3)(c) to justify looking for interpretive guidance outside the provisions of the ECHR. The first case in which it did so was *Golder*, in which the Court said:

> Article 31 para. 3 (c) of the Vienna Convention indicates that account is to be taken, together with the context, of 'any relevant rules of international law applicable in the relations between the parties'. Among those rules are general principles of law and especially 'general principles of law recognized by civilized nations' (Article 38 para. 1 (c) of the Statute of the International Court of Justice). Incidentally, the Legal Committee of the Consultative Assembly of the Council of Europe foresaw in August 1950 that 'the Commission and the Court must necessarily apply such principles' in the execution of their duties and thus considered it to be 'unnecessary' to insert a specific clause to this effect in the Convention (Documents of the Consultative Assembly, working papers of the 1950 session, Vol. III, no. 93, p. 982, para. 5).[102]

Numerous subsequent cases apply this approach. The 2008 ECtHR Grand Chamber judgment in the *Demir and Baykara* case,[103] in which the Court reviewed in detail its methodology for the first time since the permanent Court was inaugurated in 1998, has recently followed this approach. In this case, the Court observed that '[it] has never considered the provisions of the Convention as the sole framework of reference for the interpretation of the rights and freedoms enshrined therein'.[104] The Court further observed that:

> [I]n defining the meaning of terms and notions in the text of the Convention, [the Court] can and must take into account elements of international law other than the Convention, the interpretation of such elements by competent organs, and the practice of European States reflecting their common values.[105]

[101] Augusto Antônio Cançado Trindade, 'International Law for Humankind: Towards a New Jus Gentium: General Course on Public International Law' (2005) 317 *RCADI* 9, 60.

[102] *Golder* (n 65) para 35.

[103] *Demir and Baykara v Turkey*, para 54.

[104] *Demir* (n 103) para 67.

[105] *Demir* (n 103) para 85.

The IACtHR and the African Commission have also looked to an external context in interpreting their respective Conventions, as a result of the wide spectrum of instruments and concepts to which their texts refer. Applied in conjunction with the object and purpose approach to interpretation, the precise limits of Article 31(3)(c) have become somewhat blurred. The better view among international lawyers is that Article 31(3)(c) allows reference only to provisions which are binding on the parties to a particular dispute, if not to all the parties to the Convention in question, in aid of interpretation. On this basis, reference to 'soft law' instruments, or to the provisions of treaties that are not yet in force, would be deemed to fall outside the provisions of Article 31(3)(c). In the case of the ACHR and the African Charter, however, such reference is nonetheless justified, because the provisions on interpretation in ACHR Article 29 and African Charter Articles 60 and 61 explicitly allow it.

6.4 Special human rights rules/principles

6.4.1 *The* 'pro homine' *approach*

So far, discussion of the claimed special nature of human rights obligations has focused on their formal legal nature (reciprocity of obligations). Of equal importance, however, seems to be their substantive nature, as the ICJ's opinion in the *Reservations to the Genocide Convention* case indicated, when it said:

> The Convention was manifestly adopted for a purely humanitarian and civilizing purpose. It is indeed difficult to imagine a convention that might have this dual character to a greater degree, since its object on the one hand is to safeguard the very existence of certain human groups and on the other to confirm and endorse the most elementary principles of morality.[106]

The substantive nature and the content of human rights and obligations have been used as bases to distinguish them from other forms of rights and obligations; used to justify (sometimes expressly, sometimes tacitly) the application of approaches that differ from those of traditional international law. They may even be seen to form the basis of what may be a special human rights interpretive methodology, although the methodology now may be influencing other areas of international law.[107]

One of the characteristics of human rights interpretation, in the Inter-American Court in particular, but also in other human rights fora, is the existence of what has been referred to as the 'bias' of the Inter-American Court[108] or what the Court calls its '*pro homine*' approach—ie the emphasis on the Court's role in protecting human

[106] *Reservations to the Genocide Convention* (n 9) 23.

[107] National and international tribunals are exhibiting a trend towards the adoption of the principle '*in dubio, pro natura*' for cases involving environmental protection.

[108] Lucas Lixinski, 'Treaty Interpretation by the Inter-American Court of Human Rights: Expansionism at the Service of the Unity of International Law' (2010) 21 *EJIL* 585.

rights, which Convention Article 33 expressly sets forth.[109] Other human rights fora also have adopted a strong teleological approach to interpretation, by giving much weight in this respect to the preambles of the conventions and even to extraneous documents, such as human rights declarations, to which the preambles generally refer. This approach derives less from non-reciprocity in the obligations of the parties than from a more-or-less philosophical or moral understanding of a perceived overriding imperative to protect human rights. In the case of the IACtHR, Article 29 of the ACHR may justify, indeed require, this *pro homine* approach.

The judicial practice of the ECtHR has involved the development of two other fundamental concepts: (1) the status as 'living instruments' of the human rights conventions generally, and the ECHR in particular; and (2) the principle of 'common values' or 'commonly accepted standards'. The first of these concepts, whether or not allied to any principle relating to the intention of the parties, has been fundamental to the development of the ECtHR's concept of evolutive interpretation. The Court commented on both principles in the early and oft-quoted *Tyrer* judgment as follows:

> The Court must also recall that the Convention is a living instrument which, as the Commission rightly stressed, must be interpreted in the light of present-day conditions. In the case now before it the Court cannot but be influenced by the developments and commonly accepted standards in the penal policy of the member States of the Council of Europe in this field.[110]

The concept of evolutive interpretation has also been espoused by the IACtHr in its advisory opinion, *Interpretation of the American Declaration of the Rights and Duties of Man within the Framework of Article 64 of the American Convention on Human Rights*. In this Opinion, the Court declared that human rights law has to be interpreted according to present-day standards, according to the principle that the 1971 ICJ Advisory Opinion on Namibia elaborated, and that human rights law can be differentiated from classical international law to a certain degree.[111] Thus, the Inter-American Court, like the ECtHR, rejected the 'originalist' and 'intentionalist' approaches and applied the technique of evolutive interpretation,[112] relying on the principles that ACHR Article 29 and the rules that the VCLT elaborate. In the *Mapiripán Massacre* Judgment, the Court said as follows:

> The Court has pointed out, as the European Court of Human Rights has too, that human rights treaties are live instruments, whose interpretation must go hand in hand with evolving times and current living conditions. This evolutive interpretation is consistent with the

[109] ACHR, Art 33 provides that the IACHR and the IACtHR 'shall have competence with respect to matters relating to the fulfillment of the commitments made by the States Parties' to the ACHR.

[110] *Tyrer v United Kingdom*, para 31.

[111] 'The evolution of the here relevant "inter-American law" mirrors on the regional level the developments in "contemporary international law" and especially in human rights law, which distinguished that law from classical international law to a significant extent'. *Interpretation of the American Declaration*, para 38.

[112] However, see Toufayan (n 18).

general rules of interpretation set forth in Article 29 of the American Convention, as well those set forth in the Vienna Convention on Treaty Law. In this regard, when interpreting the Convention it is always necessary to choose the alternative that is most favorable to protection of the rights enshrined in said treaty, based on the principle of the rule most favorable to the human being.[113]

Finally, it may be noted that UN human rights bodies have also relied on the concept of dynamic interpretation of treaties—ie the treaty as a 'living instrument' to be interpreted according to contemporary standards. The Human Rights Committee, for example, expressly stated that the International Covenant on Civil and Political Rights should be interpreted 'as a living instrument' and further that the rights protected under the Covenant 'should be applied in context and in the light of present-day conditions'.[114]

6.4.2 *Margin of appreciation doctrine*

The ECtHR interpretation of the ECHR involves a nexus of other doctrines, such as proportionality and the margin of appreciation.[115] The margin of appreciation doctrine, which the Court developed and which the text of the ECHR does not contain, was initially introduced in the Court's first judgment—the 1961 *Lawless v Ireland* case[116]—and was further developed in the 1976 *Handyside v United Kingdom* case.[117] McInerney describes the policy underlying the doctrine in the following manner:

One of the most complex features of international human rights law is the challenge of balancing of international human rights norms and the particularity of the contexts in which their application arises. Aligned to this is the delicate task of mediating the tension between effective international supervision and the upholding of established human rights norms on the one hand, and primary domestic responsibilities and socio-cultural choices and contexts on the other.... [T]he balancing needed in relation to all human rights would appear to be heightened in the context of international human rights supervision, even in a relatively cohesive system such as the European Convention on Human Rights. These competing considerations form

[113] *Mapiripán Massacre* (n 73) para 106 (footnotes omitted).

[114] *Judge v Canada*, para 10.3. The CERD Committee made similar statements (*Hagan v Australia*, para 7.3), as did the CAT Committees (*VXN and HN v Sweden*, para 7.3).

[115] There is a vast literature on this subject, such as Paul Mahoney, 'Judicial Activism and Judicial Self-Restraint in the European Court of Human Rights: Two Sides of the Same Coin' (1990) 11 *HRLJ* 57; Ronald St J Macdonald, 'The Margin of Appreciation' in Ronald St J Macdonald, Franz Matscher, and Herbert Petzold (eds), *The European System for the Protection of Human Rights* (Martinus Nijhoff 1993); Howard Charles Yourow, *The Margin of Appreciation Doctrine in the Dynamics of European Human Rights Jurisprudence* (Martinus Nijhoff 1996); Eyal Benevisti, 'Margin of Appreciation, Consensus, and Universal Standards' (1999) 31 *NYU Journal of International Law* 843; Paul Mahoney, 'Speculating on the Future of the Reformed European Court of Human Rights' (1999) 20 *HRLJ* 1; Dinah Shelton, 'The Boundaries of Human Rights Jurisdiction in Europe' (2003) 13 *Duke J Comp & Int'l L* 95; James A Sweeney, 'Margins of Appreciation: Cultural Relativity and the European Court of Human Rights in the Post-Cold War Era' (2005) 54 *ICLQ* 459; George Letsas, 'Two Concepts of the Margin of Appreciation' (2006) 26 *OJLS* 705; Christoffersen (n 17) 37–61 and in particular 52–60.

[116] *Lawless v Ireland (No 3)* 15.

[117] *Handyside v United Kingdom*.

a symbiosis which an international supervisory body such as the European Court of Human Rights must continually define in its interpretative and supervisory role.[118]

The ECtHR has referred to its role as subsidiary in safeguarding human rights and has always insisted that the first and foremost responsibility for safeguarding human rights rests with national authorities and courts. In this regard, national authorities are seen as better equipped to assess local conditions and give effect to 'pressing social need[s]'.[119] They are best qualified to assess the notion of the 'necessity' (within the context of social needs) of 'restrictions' and 'penalties', due to their deep knowledge of the conditions prevalent in their countries.[120] Hence, they have a margin of appreciation or degree of discretion in adopting national measures. On the other hand, the Court also made it quite clear that the state's margin of appreciation is never unlimited. The ECtHR exercises a supervisory function, which 'concerns both the aim of the measure challenged and its "necessity"' in this context.[121] In certain cases, therefore, the ECtHR does not afford the state the sought-after margin of appreciation; one criticism is that the Court sometimes gives little or no explanation for its decision, which causes uncertainty for the states parties.[122]

The Court's deferential attitude to states through the margin of appreciation doctrine has caused a long-lasting debate among practitioners and theorists. The main objection raised has been that the doctrine mocks and undermines universal human rights standards by encouraging states to depart from these standards and to rely on local traditions.[123] In response, some scholars assert that the criticism misunderstands the margin of appreciation doctrine, because the Court leaves to states parties a measure of 'implementation freedom, discretion, or margin of appreciation not as a consequence of the Court's subsidiary review, but in the *absence* of international standards'.[124] The application of this doctrine is also subject to certain doubts, in particular due to the inconsistency with which the Court decides to defer to domestic authorities. A lack of transparency and depth of any rigorous standard in relation to a comparative approach to this doctrine is said to characterize the Court's application of the margin of appreciation.[125]

[118] Siobhan McInerney, 'Yourow, Howard Charles. *The Margin of Appreciation Doctrine in the Dynamics of the European Court of Human Rights Jurisprudence*' (1998) 9 *EJIL* 777.

[119] Shelton, 'The Boundary of Human Rights Jurisdiction' (n 115) 130.

[120] *Handyside* (n 117) para 48.

[121] *Handyside* (n 117) para 49.

[122] *Dudgeon v United Kingdom*; *Norris v Ireland*.

[123] See eg Benevisti (n 115) 844. See also less critical views on the Court's practice in relation to the margin of appreciation: Michael Walzer, *Thick and Thin: Moral Argument at Home and Abroad* (U Notre Dame Press 1994).

[124] Christoffersen (n 17) 55 (emphasis added).

[125] See also Shelton, 'The Boundaries of Human Rights Jurisdiction' (n 115) 134.

6.4.3 *Autonomous interpretation*

The European Court (as well as the Inter-American Court) has also insisted that terms in the Convention have their own meaning, regardless of national legislation, applying the principle of autonomous interpretation.[126]

6.4.4 *Principle of consensus*

The reliance on 'commonly accepted standards' greatly extended the nature of the 'context' upon which the ECtHR could draw in interpreting the scope of the guaranteed rights at any given time. It is closely related to the ECtHR's application of VCLT Article 31(3)(c). This device allows the ECtHR to seek common European values in other instruments of international law, both binding and non-binding.[127] The 2008 *Demir and Baykara* case spelled out such an approach.[128]

7. Conclusions: Towards a Uniform Holistic Approach to Interpretation

This Chapter examined the systems of interpretation of several international human rights treaties by their respective human rights tribunals. Many scholars have asserted that human rights tribunals do not follow or comply with the interpretive rules of the VCLT. However, among international scholars, a consensus is now emerging that: first, human rights tribunals do in fact follow the VCLT's rules of interpretation, possibly in a rather expansive, but nevertheless legitimate, manner; and second, though there are differences of approach between various human rights tribunals, these tribunals are moving towards a broadly similar methodology in interpreting human rights treaties—in particular through their reliance on

[126] See eg *Engel and Others v Netherlands* and *Mayagna Community (SUMO) Awas Tingni v Nicaragua*.

[127] See in-depth on this subject: Vassilis P Tzevelekos, 'The Use of Article 31(3)(c) of the VCLT in the Case Law of the ECtHR: An Effective Anti-Fragmentation Tool or a Selective Loophole for the Reinforcement of Human Rights Teleology? Between Evolution and Systemic Integration' (2010) 31 *Mich J Int'l L* 621.

[128] In this case, the Court observed that it 'has never considered the provisions of the Convention as the sole framework of reference for the interpretation of the rights and freedoms enshrined therein' and that 'in defining the meaning of terms and notions in the text of the Convention, [it] can and must take into account elements of international law other than the Convention, the interpretation of such elements by competent organs, and the practice of European States reflecting their common values'. *Demir* (n 103) paras 68, 85.

various human rights instruments, such as the Universal Declaration of Human Rights and the United Nations Charter.

It is also generally recognized that the approach has a holistic character, which the ECtHR judgment in *Rantsev v Cyprus and Russia* best exemplifies.

> The Convention was inspired by the Universal Declaration of Human Rights, proclaimed by the General Assembly of the United Nations in 1948, which itself made no express mention of trafficking. In its Article 4, the Declaration prohibited 'slavery and the slave trade in all their forms'. However, in assessing the scope of Article 4 of the Convention, sight should not be lost of the Convention's special features or of the fact that it is a living instrument which must be interpreted in the light of present-day conditions. The increasingly high standards required in the area of the protection of human rights and fundamental liberties correspondingly and inevitably require greater firmness in assessing breaches of the fundamental values of democratic societies.[129]

Similarly, the range of source material applied can be observed in the IACtHR's judgment of in the *Mapiripán Massacre* case:

> The preamble of the American Convention explicitly refers to the principles asserted and developed in international instruments, 'worldwide as well as regional in scope' (para. 3) and Article 29 requires that it be interpreted in light of the American Declaration and other international acts of the same nature' [sic]. Other provisions refer to obligations imposed by international law regarding suspension of guarantees (Article 27), as well as the 'generally recognized principles of international law' when defining exhaustion of domestic remedies (Article 46(1)(a)).[130]

There remains a certain degree of controversy concerning the breadth of interpretive methods that, in the view of some scholars and even some ECtHR Judges, are in danger of over-stepping the proper limits to the judicial function. There is an inherent tension between on the one hand the primary function of human rights courts to protect the rights of an individual and to regulate the behaviour of states, and, on the other hand, respecting the consensual basis of international law and state sovereignty, as classically expressed in the *Lotus* case.[131] In the case of ECtHR, this problem has been recognized and alleviated, to a certain extent, through the development of the margin of appreciation rule.

Further Reading

Çali B, 'Specialized Rules of Treaty Interpretation: Human Rights' in Duncan B Hollis (ed), *The Oxford Guide to Treaties* (OUP 2012)

Forowicz M, *The Reception of International Law in the European Court of Human Rights* (OUP 2010)

[129] *Rantsev v Cyprus and Russia*, para 277.

[130] *Mapiripán Massacre* (n 73) para 107, fn 186.

[131] *The Lotus Case (France v Turkey)*.

Killander M, 'Interpreting Regional Human Rights Treaties' 2010 7(13) *SUR Int'l JHR* 145

Rietiker D, 'The Principle of "Effectiveness" in the Recent Jurisprudence of the European Court of Human Rights: Its Different Dimensions and Its Consistency with Public International Law—No Need for the Concept of Treaty *Sui Generis*' (2010) 79 *Nord J Int'l L* 245

Schlütter B, 'Aspects of Human Rights Interpretation by the UN Treaty Bodies' in Keller H and Ulfstein G (eds), *Human Rights Treaty Bodies: Law and Legitimacy* (CUP 2012) 261–320

Vanneste F, *General International Law before Human Rights Court* (Intersentia 2010) ch 4

CHAPTER 32

ENFORCING HUMAN RIGHTS THROUGH ECONOMIC SANCTIONS

GEORGE A LOPEZ*

1. Introduction

SINCE the end of the Cold War, economic sanctions and human rights have each undergone a distinct, but equally remarkable, evolution in their conceptualization, their use by nation-states, and their institutionalization in new global processes involving multilateral agencies. Traditionally, sanctions operated as nation against nation general trade embargoes, often imposed before or during military conflicts. By the end of the 1990s, however, sanctions had become a diverse set of specialized, targeted, coercive measures involving finances, travel, arms, and selective commodities, which multilateral organizations most often imposed to achieve a wide array of goals. In addition to sanctions to protect human rights, these goals included ending international and civil wars, protecting innocents caught in war, extraditing international fugitives, controlling the spread of international terrorism, deterring the proliferation of weapons of mass destruction, and restoring democratically elected governments. Indicative of the expanded resort to sanctions and their diverse aims,

* The author thanks Alexandra dos Reis for her research assistance with portions of this chapter.

some analysts labeled the 1990s as a 'sanctions decade', while others worried the trend had become a 'sanctions epidemic'.[1]

As this volume attests, human rights advocacy and advancement, which blossomed in the 1970s and well before sanctions, also became more globalized and a powerful force against repressive governments in the post-Cold War decade.[2] It especially became fully operationalized in the work of numerous non-governmental organizations (NGOs), in far-reaching policy principles derived from the expansion of international human rights law, and has ultimately been enforced in new courts engaged in prosecutions of individuals for mass atrocities and genocide. This latter trend has led one prominent scholar to label this evolution as 'the justice cascade'.[3]

With both human rights and sanctions in this state of dynamic change, it is unsurprising that employing the latter to improve the former has progressed significantly. Sanctions mechanisms have evolved from a single donor nation withdrawing economic aid and trade to protest human rights violations, to multilateral organizations imposing targeted sanctions against individuals and entities to punish or constrain their specific role in human rights abuses and political killings, then ultimately to leveraging these more precise sanctions measures to protect fragile rights during the first years of democratic governance in post-civil war nations. Transnational human rights NGOs have increasingly advocated this use of multilateral economic sanctions, and their imposition and enforcement has occupied an increasingly prominent place in the coercive tool kit of national policymakers.[4]

Their operational form has taken shape most pronouncedly in United Nations Security Council Resolutions and has been strengthened, if not also extended in scope and enforcement, by sanctions that the European Union, the British Commonwealth, and ad hoc coalitions of states have adopted. Nothing may underscore the convergence between sanctions and human rights more than their parallel movement to focus increasingly on individuals and entities, and less often governments and states, as the responsible parties to indict for rights violations and target with smart sanctions.

These intersecting developments have not been without controversy and, sometimes, outright contradiction. As revealed in the five decades of US unilateral sanctions on Cuba and various 1980s Soviet sanctions against its satellite states,

[1] Richard N Haass, 'Sanctioning Madness' (1997) 76(6) *Foreign Aff* 74; David Cortight and George A Lopez, *The Sanctions Decade: Assessing UN Security Council Sanctions in the 1990s* (Lynne Rienner 2000).

[2] Jackie Smith and Ron Pagnucco, 'Globalizing Human Rights: The Work of Transnational Human Rights NGOs in the 1990s' (1998) 20 *Hum Rts Q* 379; David P Forsythe (ed), *Encyclopedia of Human Rights* (OUP 2009).

[3] Kathryn Sikkink, *The Justice Cascade: How Human Rights Prosecutions Are Changing World Politic* (WW Norton 2011).

[4] George A Lopez, 'Matching Means with Intentions: Sanctions and Human Rights' in William F Schulz (ed), *The Future of Human Rights: US Policy for a New Era* (U Pennsylvania Press 2008).

some economic sanctions that claim to be enforcing human rights norms were actually designed as a means to punish directly ideological foes, with significant negative impact on rights and the quality of life of the general population.[5] These cases of big power economic coercion, combined with the negative humanitarian consequences of the earliest cases of UN sanctions in the 1990s—Iraq (devastating humanitarian impact), Haiti and the Former Republic of Yugoslavia (varied from serious to minimal humanitarian impact)—led various analysts to question whether sanctions can ever be an ethical tool, or other than harmful, to human rights.[6]

With these trends and concerns in mind, this chapter focuses first on the international community's improvements in sanctions' strategy and the creation of those discrete tools called targeted—or smart—sanctions. These were forged, in part, to make possible improved sanctions design, implementation, and enforcement against those engaged in human rights violations. The second section summarizes some of the cases where smart sanctions were applied, devoting particular attention to the most recent controversies about sanctions and rights in the principles of the 'protection of civilians' (PoC) and 'the responsibility to protect' (R2P), and to the resort to targeted sanctions for counter-terrorism purposes. Third, reflections on the cases lead to several policy guidelines for the use of sanctions to protect and enhance rights and to stifle rights violators.

2. Getting Smarter about Sanctions Tools

Driven by the outcry against sanctions-induced negative humanitarian impact in the early 1990s, the UN Security Council undertook a multi-year sanctions reform process that included a series of research studies, diplomatic seminars, expert processes and conferences, and some trial and error in designing new sanctions instruments, methods for their implementation, and means for systematic monitoring of sanctions impact. The resulting period of sanctions development saw a shift from the use of comprehensive and general trade sanctions toward more targeted and specialized economic instruments that significantly advanced the sophistication of global sanctions.[7]

[5] See especially Michael Krinsky and David Golove (eds), *United States Economic Measures Against Cuba: Proceedings in the United Nations and International Law Issues* (Aletheia Press 1993).

[6] George A Lopez and David Cortright, 'Economic Sanctions and Human Rights: Part of the Solution or Part of the Problem?' (1997) 1(2) *IJHR* 1; Joy Gordon, 'Smart Sanctions Revisited' (2011) 25 *Ethics & International Affairs* 315.

[7] For an extensive discussion of the studies and UN processes summarized here, see George A Lopez and David Cortright, 'Sanctions as Alternatives to War' in Christopher J Coyne and Rachel L Mathers (eds), *The Handbook on the Political Economy of War* (Edward Elgar 2011).

In 1995, the UN Department of Humanitarian Affairs commissioned a series of reports on the impact of sanctions on humanitarian assistance efforts. The reports developed a methodology and series of specific indicators for assessing humanitarian impacts. Many of the recommendations in these studies became the basis for an ongoing humanitarian assessment methodology, which the successor agency of the Department of Humanitarian Affairs, the UN Office for the Coordination of Humanitarian Affairs, developed. Efforts to assess the humanitarian impact of particular sanctions cases became a regular feature of UN sanctions policy. Assessment reports and missions that examined the impact of sanctions provided the Security Council with an opportunity to anticipate and prevent potential humanitarian problems and to respond to adverse sanctions impacts in a timely manner.[8]

Also in 1995, the Security Council, anxious to know which individuals and entities were violating the Council's arms embargo for Rwanda, created a team of independent specialists to investigate sanctions violators and to report how these sanctions violators could be stifled and the sanctions better enforced. Subsequently, every new Security Council resolution that imposed sanctions also created such a 'Panel of Experts' for sanctions monitoring. Especially in cases of ongoing internal violence, these Panels have been instrumental in identifying and recommending more refined targeting of perpetrators and in advising a new or extended embargo of particular commodities—like diamonds or timber—that produced large revenues for violent actors.[9]

In the late 1990s, Switzerland, Germany, and Sweden sponsored working group meetings and a series of research conferences, with the aim of increasing the effectiveness of Security Council sanctions, strengthening the prospects for member state implementation and target state compliance, and refining the emerging use of targeted sanctions. The first of these policy initiatives, the Swiss Interlaken Process (1998–99), refined and adapted the methods utilized in combating money laundering to the challenge of implementing targeted financial sanctions. In particular, the Interlaken Seminars examined the extent to which financial sanctions could achieve their goal of cutting off the financial support crucial to sustaining abusive regimes and the decision-making elites who control such regimes.[10]

[8] A full summary of these reports and application of the case methodologies appeared in Thomas G Weiss, Larry Minear, George A Lopez and David Cortright, eds, *Political Gain and Civilian Pain: Assessing the Humanitarian Impact of Economic Sanctions* (Rowman & Littlefield 1997).

[9] The definitive study of Panels of Experts is Alix J Boucher and Victoria K Holt, *Targeting Spoilers: The Role of United Nations Panels of Experts* (Stimson 2009).

[10] As a part of the Swiss initiative, the Watson Institute for International Studies at Brown University developed model legislation for governments to strengthen their capacity to implement targeted financial sanctions. The Watson Institute also produced a handbook on the implementation of targeted financial sanctions, which the UN Secretariat subsequently distributed to member states. See TJ Biersteker, E Eckert, P Romaniuk, A Halegua, and N Reid (eds), *Targeted Financial Sanctions: A Manual for Design and Implementation* (Watson Institute for International Studies 2001).

Building on the Interlaken Process, the German Ministry of Foreign Affairs initiated a parallel effort to refine the implementation of travel bans and arms embargoes. The Bonn International Center for Conversion managed the German initiative, which included meetings in Bonn in 1999 and Berlin in 2000. This Bonn-Berlin Process provided rich detail about travel and arms embargos, with the latter being especially significant to the protection of innocents and human rights.[11] In 2001, the government of Sweden launched a further initiative in a series of meetings in Uppsala and Stockholm to develop recommendations for strengthening the monitoring and enforcement of Security Council sanctions. Known as the Stockholm Process on the Implementation of Targeted Sanctions, the Swedish conferences and research added to the work that the Swiss and German governments had already achieved, and helped to advance international understanding of the requirements for effectively implementing targeted sanctions.[12]

The cumulative result of these processes, policy relevant research, and the workings of Panels of Experts was the development and institutionalization of 'smart sanctions'—that is, an array of economic and other coercive measures that are precisely targeted in two ways. First, they take aim at the specific sub-national and transnational actors (such as companies, asset holding entities, or individuals) that are deemed most responsible for the policies or actions the imposer considers illegal or abhorrent. Rather than punishing general society through trade sanctions or punishing the national government as a catch-all actor, smart sanctions aim to constrain identifiable, culpable perpetrators. Second, smart sanctions isolate the arena of economic coercion to a specific micro-level economic activity that can be identified as contributing to increased human rights violations or, for example, to the development of a nation's weapons program.[13]

The measures below comprise the sanctions most readily available to constrain or end large-scale rights abuses and killing. They include:

- freezing financial assets that (a) the national government, (b) regime members in their individual capacity, or (c) those persons designated as key supporters or enablers of the regime, hold outside the country;
- suspending the credits, aid, and loans available to the national government, its agencies, and those economic actors in the nation who deal with monies involving international financial institutions;

[11] Michael Brzoska (ed), *Design and Implementation of Arms Embargoes and Travel and Aviation Related Sanctions: Results of the 'Bonn-Berlin Process'* (Bonn International Center for Conversion 2001). Further results were presented in Michael Brzoska and George A Lopez (eds), *Putting Teeth in the Tiger: Improving the Effectiveness of Arms Embargoes* (Emerald Press 2009).

[12] Peter Wallensteen, Carina Staibano, and Mikael Eriksson (eds), *Making Targeted Sanctions Effective: Guidelines for the Implementation of UN Policy Options* (Uppsala 2003).

[13] See David Cortright and George A Lopez (eds), *Towards Smart Sanctions: Targeting Economic Statecraft* (Rowman & Littlefield 2002).

- denying access to overseas financial markets, often to the target government's National Bank and other governmental entities, as well as to designated private banks, investors, and individual designees;
- restricting the trade of specific goods and commodities that provide power resources and revenue to the norm violating actors, most especially highly-traded and income-producing mineral resources;
- banning aid and trade of weapons, munitions, military replacement parts, and dual-use goods of a military nature, including computers and related communications technologies;
- banning flight and travel of individuals and/or specific air and sea carriers;
- denial of visa, travel, and educational opportunities to those individuals on the designee list; and
- denying the importation of, or other access to, goods labeled as 'luxury items' for the entities and individuals on the designated list.

Clearly smart sanctions make the political action of abusing rights and engaging in atrocities rather personal. The overseas 'rainy-day' funds of dictators become inaccessible, and children of perpetrators lose travel visas and access to tuition monies to attend Western schools. When time is of the essence in responding to unfolding rights violations and mass atrocities, some targeted sanctions are likely to be more appealing and effective than others. Due to economic circumstances, some sanctions imposers are likely to be more versatile in targeting certain measures than others. But in all cases, as will be illustrated below, sanctions' effectiveness in stifling human rights abuses demand a convergence of factors, anchored in the willingness of imposers to comply with the sanctions and to adapt them to patterns of violation by the targets.

3. Cases Involving Sanctions and Human Rights

Prior to imposing sanctions on Iraq for its invasion of Kuwait in August 1990, the UN's Permanent Five powers and a sufficient number of rotating Security Council members had reached agreement on sanctions only twice in the UN's first forty-five-year history. Significantly, each time involved a racial human rights case: Southern Rhodesia (1966) and South Africa (1977). In the fifteen years following the initial Iraq resolution, the majority of UN sanctions cases—Yugoslavia, Haiti, Somalia, Libya, Ethiopia, and Eritrea (which involved primarily governments); and Liberia,

Angola, Rwanda, Sudan, Sierra Leone, Afghanistan, the Democratic Republic of the Congo, and Côte d'Ivoire (which involved non-state, and often multiple, violent actors)—had some dimensions of rights concerns reflected in the resolutions.[14]

At the same time, sanctions have been fraught with inconsistencies regarding their design and 'clout', thus limiting their human rights impact. Put in its best light, over time the international community, acting through the UN Security Council, has made progress in some specific rights protection cases and has formulated at least two ongoing guiding themes—some would call them 'global norms': the protection of innocent civilians in armed conflict and the responsibility to protect civilians faced with mass atrocities.

The cases of Liberia, Côte d'Ivoire, and Libya (examined below) serve as reasonably positive recent examples of sanctions enforcing and protecting human rights, but they stand in contrast to the more troubling realities and significant historical cases in which UN sanctions activities failed to halt human rights abuses when civilians were under greatest attack—during genocide and in protracted bloody atrocities. In at least four cases—Yugoslavia, Rwanda, Liberia (until 2001), and Sudan/Darfur—UN sanctions resulted in little or no reduction in the killing, because the Council acted late and then imposed a limited and weakly-enforced arms embargo that it did not integrate with other, more powerful financial or other sanctions.[15] Similarly, the limited measures imposed in Afghanistan prior to 2001 also had no discernible impact on the policies of the Taliban regime regarding the treatment of cultural artifacts or women's rights.

Despite pleas of 'never again', the failure of the international community to use sanctions or other means to prevent ethnic cleansing in Bosnia in 1992 or genocide in Rwanda in 1994, was repeated with regard to Darfur a decade later. Without question, the Darfur case serves as a glaring example of too few sanctions imposed too late and without the broad targeting of a substantial number of elites, as would have maximized their effectiveness. Despite near-global condemnation of the Sudanese regime for its and its agents actions against the citizens of the Darfur region from 2003 to 2008, a rather watered-down set of financial asset freezes and travel restrictions were imposed against a small number of Sudanese officials in a series of Security Council resolutions. Most, but not all, of this back-tracking was due to the unwillingness of the Chinese and Russian representatives to support extensive sanctions. A draft Security Council resolution targeting more than thirty individuals responsible for killings and other brutal actions in the region faced serious opposition. Ultimately, the final resolution that the Security Council adopted only

[14] Regarding the historic dimensions of human rights in UN sanctions resolutions, see Andrew Clapham, 'Sanctions and Economic, Social and Cultural Rights' in Vera Gowlland-Debbas (ed), *United Nations Sanctions and International Law* (Kluwer Law International 2001).

[15] Boucher and Holt (n 9).

designated four individuals. The UN debate over sanctions continued for so long prior to their adoption that whoever was to face financial penalties surely avoided them.[16]

More positively, with the passage of resolution 1265 in 1999,[17] the Security Council recognized that civilians comprise the vast majority of casualties in armed conflicts and must be protected. In the context of obligations of the UN and member states under international humanitarian law, the confirmation of norms on PoC sparked a move toward sanctions regimes aimed directly at shielding innocent populations from harm.[18] It also established a pattern of designating as targets of sanctions those militant non-state actors (both groups and their individual leaders), like irregular armed groups, death squads, or paramilitary forces, that preyed on the civilian population, as well as those who bankrolled them.[19]

Since the passage of UN Security Council (UNSC) resolution 1265, PoC has emerged as a core directive of all humanitarian and human rights efforts and has been embedded in a number of Security Council resolutions dealing with armed conflict.[20] Complementary issues were acknowledged in Council resolutions on women, peace, and security,[21] children,[22] protection of humanitarian workers,[23] conflict prevention,[24] and sexual exploitation.[25] A significant factor that gave these sanctions 'more teeth' than their predecessors was the priority given the PoC concept in the work of many UN missions, including operations in Afghanistan, the Central African Republic, Côte d'Ivoire, Darfur, the Democratic Republic of the Congo, Haiti, Liberia, and the Sudan.[26]

[16] For an analysis of such patterns of sanctions preparation, see Michael Brzoska and George A Lopez, 'Sanctions Design and Security Council Dynamics' in Thomas Biersteker and Sue Eckert (eds), *UN Targeted Sanctions as Instruments of Global Governance* (2013).

[17] UN Security Council (UNSC), Res 1265 (17 September 1999) UN Doc S/Res/1265.

[18] Alexandra dos Reis and George A Lopez, 'Sanctions and the Responsibility to Protect' in Monica Serrrano and Thomas G Weiss (eds), *The International Politics of Human Rights: Rallying to the R2P Cause?* (Routledge 2013).

[19] 'Cross-Cutting Report on Protection of Civilians in Armed Conflict No 2' (20 July 2011) Security Council Report <http://www.securitycouncilreport.org/atf/cf/%7B65BFCF9B-6D27-4E9C-8CD3-CF6E4FF96FF9%7D/XCutting%20POC%202011.pdf> accessed 16 February 2013.

[20] See eg UNSC Res 1296 (19 April 2000) UN Doc S/Res/1296; UNSC Res 1674 (28 April 2006) UN Doc S/Res/1674; UNSC Res 1738 (23 December 2006) UN Doc S/Res/1738; UNSC Res 1894 (11 November 2009) UN Doc S/Res/1894; dos Reis and Lopez (n 18).

[21] UNSC Res 1325 (31 October 2000) UN Doc S/Res/1325; UNSC Res 1960 (16 December 2010) UN Doc S/Res/960.

[22] UNSC Res 1612 (26 July 2005) UN Doc S/Res/1612.

[23] UNSC Res 1502 (26 August 2003) UN Doc S/Res/1502.

[24] UNSC Res 1625 (14 September 2005) UN Doc S/Res/1625.

[25] UNSC Res 1820 (19 June 2008) UN Doc S/Res/1820.

[26] On the importance of sanctions and other aspects of UN operations in conflict zones being 'in sync', see David Cortright, George A. Lopez, and Linda Gerber-Stellingwerf, with Eliot Fackler and Joshua Weaver, 'Integrating UN Sanctions for Peace and Security: A Report Prepared for the Canadian Office of Foreign Affairs' (October 2010) Sanctions and Security Research Program <http://www.sanctionsandsecurity.org/wp-content/uploads/Integrating-UN-Sanctions-for-Peace-and-Security.pdf> accessed 13 February 2013.

In 2006, the protection-of-civilians agenda advanced considerably at the UN, when the Security Council made its historic first reference to the newly-endorsed construct called Responsibility to Protect.[27] As with UNSC Resolution 1265, this resolution acknowledged that civilians make up the majority of casualties in violent conflicts, but highlighted that states have the primary responsibility to protect their people from all acts of violence. The resolutions specifically mention provisions of paragraphs 138 and 139 of the 2005 World Summit Outcome document on R2P, to underscore the responsibility of all states to protect populations from four heinous human rights violations: genocide, war crimes, ethnic cleansing, and crimes against humanity.[28]

The evolution of PoC to R2P as a guiding theme for Council action reflects both the drive for more sanctions precision and the expanded Council concerns with the abuse of civilians during war. In 2007, this also led to the creation of two new positions of Special Representatives of the Secretary-General, one for the prevention of genocide and one for R2P—offices that would play a significant role in future sanctions cases. It also led to the development of new techniques and rationales for sanctions regimes and of the manner in which their Panels of Experts supported them.[29]

3.1 Liberia

The sanctions regime imposed on Liberia exemplifies how the Council can move from an ineffective, stand-alone arms embargo, to employing a range of targeted sanctions instruments. More than a decade of diverse sanctions culminated in protective measures that targeted those actors who were responsible for attacking peacekeepers and humanitarian workers, those who were impeding the delivery of humanitarian aid during the war, and those who undermined the peace process and the emergence of democratic institutions as the war ended. Replacing weak, initial sanctions measures, the UN Security Council adopted Resolutions 1521[30] and 1532,[31] thereby establishing a more stringent arms embargo on the forces of former President Charles Taylor, as well as extended financial and travel restrictions on Taylor and those of his supporters that represented a threat to the peace process

[27] UNSC Res 1674 (n 20).

[28] The Global Centre for the Responsibility to Protect, 'The Relationship between the Responsibility to Protect and the Protection of Civilians in Armed Conflict' (January 2009) Policy Brief 2 <http://www.ciaonet.org/pbei/gcr2p/0020021/f_0020021_17009.pdf> accessed 16 February 2013.

[29] Mark Notaras and Vesselin Popovski, 'The Responsibility to Protect' (*UN University*, 4 May 2011) <http://unu.edu/publications/articles/responsibility-to-protect-and-the-protection-of-civilians.html> accessed 17 February 2013.

[30] UNSC Res 1521 (22 December 2003) UN Doc S/Res/1521.

[31] UNSC Res 1532 (12 March 2004) UN Doc S/Res/1532.

in Liberia. In addition, certain trade restrictions for timber and diamonds were levied.[32]

Based on findings of the Panel of Experts and the work of the UN Mission, some of the sanctions were lifted following the election of Ellen Johnson Sirleaf. Those targeting timber were removed in 2006,[33] followed by those related to diamonds in 2007[34]—after it was clear that the financial profits from these industries no longer flowed to conflict actors. The remaining sanctions were meant to target actors that might disrupt the democratic process in the country. Thus, the sanctions were increasingly pre-emptive, protecting the new government and Liberian people from potential violent spoilers, leading some to refer to these protective measures as 'Sanctions for Peace', a label which more recently was used to protect the national reconciliation process in Côte d'Ivoire. However, the formula and background to the label is clearly consistent with sanctions for rights protection and enhancement.[35]

3.2 Côte d'Ivoire

The Security Council's response to changes in the long-standing civil war in Côte d'Ivoire in 2011 provides an example of how the lessons learned from Liberia and other cases informed subsequent sanctions regimes. Moreover, with the Côte d'Ivoire's crisis and the UN's response during the same period as the Council's Libyan action, the Council's full application of R2P as a principle guiding sanctions is clear. UN sanctions in Côte d'Ivoire began in 2004 and coincided with the deployment of the United Nations Operation in Côte d'Ivoire (UNOCI). The UN had hoped initially to assist in the preparation of general elections to be held in 2005 and to have a positive impact on the efforts to stabilize the West African sub-region as a whole. However, the protection-of-civilians mandate was very difficult to implement, because the arms embargo was weakly enforced due to the low number of troops and the large geographic area that needed to be covered.[36]

The opportunity for an explicit application of R2P arose in the bloody aftermath of the 2011 elections dispute between President Alassane Ouattara and former President Laurent Gbagbo. In response to a spike in ethnically-charged hate speech and allegations that the armed forces and militia groups from both sides were arming ethnic groups, the UN Secretary-General's special advisers on the prevention of genocide (Francis Deng) and on R2P (Edward Luck) released a joint statement

[32] For a more complete analysis of these sanctions and cases see, dos Reis and Lopez (n 18).

[33] UNSC Res 1689 (20 June 2006) Un Doc S/Res/1689.

[34] UNSC Res 1753 (27 April 2007) UN Doc S/Res/1753.

[35] Boucher and Holt (n 9) 89–108.

[36] Colum Lynch, 'UN Security Council Votes to Add 2,000 Peacekeepers in Ivory Coast' *The Washington Post* (UN, 19 January 2011) <http://www.washingtonpost.com/wp-dyn/content/article/2011/01/19/AR2011011905482.html> accessed 17 February 2013.

to UN Missions expressing grave concern about 'the possibility of genocide, crimes against humanity, war crimes and ethnic cleansing', and recommending that the Security Council take 'urgent steps... in line with the "responsibility to protect"'.[37]

In response to these concerns, Gbagbo's continued refusal to step down and the obstruction of UNOCI's mandate by his supporters, the Council unanimously adopted resolution 1975 in March 2011, reaffirming 'the primary responsibility of each State to protect civilians'.[38] Notably, the resolution authorized UNOCI to 'use all necessary means to carry out its mandate to protect civilians under imminent threat of physical violence', including the use of force.[39] The Council also imposed targeted economic sanctions on Gbagbo and his inner circle, and, significantly, stated its intent to impose similar sanctions 'against the media actors who fan tensions and incite violence',[40] a noteworthy innovation that acknowledges their role in perpetuating hate and violence.

3.3 Libya

Security Council action that authorized multifaceted smart sanctions, as well as North Atlantic Treaty Organization (NATO) bombing to protect Libyan civilians whom their government was about to attack, provides the classic case of R2P. Resolution 1970[41] targeted the Gaddafi regime institutionally, as well as individuals designated for their role in the brutal repression of protestors, also with the aim of sending a message to Gaddafi that he should halt future government attacks. In addition to an arms embargo, Resolution 1970 imposed an extensive assets freeze, other financial restrictions, and a travel and aviation ban. The sanctions also encompassed cargo inspections anywhere in the world, if freight were suspected of being bound for Libya. Significant for human rights advancement, the resolution also called for the International Criminal Court to investigate potential government atrocities and to issue indictments where appropriate.

Despite reservations on the part of some Council members, Resolution 1970 passed with remarkable unanimity and speed. The timely adoption of the resolution came after the defection of Libyan UN ambassador Mohammed Shalgham,

[37] Office of the Special Adviser on the Prevention of Genocide, 'Statement Attributed to the UN Secretary-General's Special Advisers on the Prevention of Genocide and the Responsibility to Protect on the Situation in Côte d'Ivoire' (19 January 2011) <http://www.un.org/en/preventgenocide/adviser/videos/video_8.shtml> accessed 17 February 2013.

[38] UNSC Res 1975 (30 March 2011) UN Doc S/Res/1975, preamble.

[39] UNSC Res 1975 (n 38) para 6.

[40] UNSC, 'Security Council Renews Mandate of Côte d'Ivoire Mission until End of 2010, Aiming to Get Electoral Process on Track, Shore Up Implementation of Political Accord' (30 June 2010) UN Doc SC/9969.

[41] UNSC Res 1970 (26 February 2011) UN Doc S/Res/1970.

who urged Security Council members to impose sanctions in response to the atrocities Gaddafi had committed.[42] Also influencing Council thinking were two developments that provided the teeth of enforcement just days before the resolution actually passed. The first was the endorsement for sanctions of member states in the region, supported by regional actors like Council of the League of Arab States. The second was that the extensive reach of the national sanctions that the United States and the European Union had imposed had already locked down the bulk of the assets of the Gaddafi regime and family, setting the stage for Security Council action.

Despite the effectiveness of these strong measures, it soon became clear that more stringent actions were needed in order to protect the lives of Libyan civilians—specifically in Benghazi, which Gaddafi had vowed to raze. In March 2011, Resolution 1973 expanded existing sanctions and authorized a no-fly zone and a ban on all Libyan flights.[43] The resolution also established a Panel of Experts to evaluate the enforcement of these measures. Arab support, critical to obtaining US consent to a military intervention, was quickly provided, when the Council of the League of Arab States called for a no-fly zone and the League of Arab States, Qatar, and the United Arab Emirates pledged to contribute to the NATO and international efforts in Libya.[44] Thus, resolution 1973 made clear that 'all necessary measures' other than an occupying force could be used to protect civilians.[45]

NATO implementation of the 'necessary measures' led to a full-scale bombing campaign to destroy Gaddafi's air defense units and command facilities. The success of these strikes, and the resulting rebel military victories, prompted the Council to pass resolution 2009, which established a support mission—the United Nations Support Mission in Libya—in the country. In support of its mandate to assist national efforts to extend state authority, strengthen institutions, and protect human rights, among other objectives, the Council also partly lifted the arms embargo previously imposed. It further began the complicated process of ending the asset freeze targeting entities connected to the previous regime and making these assets available to the opposition for the benefit of the Libyan people. With the capture and death of Gaddafi in October 2011, Security Council Resolution 2016[46] set a termination date for the provisions of Resolution 1973, which had formed the legal basis for NATO's military intervention. As an ongoing commitment to R2P

[42] Natalia Dannenberg and David Levitz, 'UN Security Council Unanimously Passes Sanctions against Gadhafi' *Deutsche Welle* (26 February 2011) <http://www.dw.de/un-security-council-unanimously-passes-sanctions-against-gadhafi/a-14876262-1> accessed 17 February 2013.

[43] UNSC Res 1973 (17 March 2011) UN Doc S/Res/1973.

[44] Jill Dougherty, Saad Abedine, Andreena Narayan, Reza Sayah, Yousuf Basil, Ben Wedeman and Barbara Starr, 'Italy, France Sending Troops to Advise Libyan Rebels' *CNN News* (Tripoli, 20 April 2011) <http://www.cnn.com/2011/WORLD/africa/04/20/libya.war/index.html> accessed 17 February 2013.

[45] UNSC Res 1973 (n 43) paras 4, 8.

[46] UNSC Res 2016 (27 October 2011) UN Doc S/Res/2016.

principles, the Panel of Experts continued to monitor the original arms embargo, assets freezes, and travel bans. In their reports to the Sanctions Committee, the Panel provided recommendations for areas of major concern and called for greater cooperation in repatriating any proceeds that it found from embezzlement and corruption that Gaddafi, other Libyan politicians, and their families had transferred to personal accounts or companies out of the country.[47]

Certainly the fall of the Libyan regime would not have occurred without an armed rebellion and NATO's military support, but the combination of UN, European Union, and US targeted sanctions played a considerable role in degrading both the regime's firepower and its support among Libya's elites. By cutting off nearly half of Gaddafi's usable monies—some USD 36 billion in Libyan funds were locked down in the first week of sanctions—the international community immediately denied the dictator the funds to import heavy weapons, to hire foot soldier mercenaries, or to contract with elite commando units bent on doing the killing Gaddafi would order. Had these sanctions not been successfully imposed and enforced, it is reasonable to assert that the war in Libya would have been longer and considerably more deadly for Libyan citizens. Tripoli, for example, was not destroyed in an all-out battle like that which engulfed and leveled major Syrian cities in 2012–13.[48]

4. Counter-Terrorism Sanctions and Human Rights

Throughout the 1990s, the Security Council extended the application of targeted sanctions explicitly to terrorist groups and to the state actors and agencies that were identified as their surrogate supporters. In UNSC Resolution 748,[49] the Council condemned Libyan terrorist actions against airlines and isolated the Gaddafi regime with a series of sanctions measures. UNSC Resolution 1054[50] sanctioned the Sudan for harboring and providing assistance to terrorists, specifically Osama bin Laden, and others implicated in the attempted assassination of Egyptian President

[47] cf UNSC, 'Final Report of the Panel of Experts Established Pursuant to Security Council Resolution 1973 (2011) Concerning Libya' (20 March 2012) UN Doc S/2012/163.

[48] For a debate on the issues of NATO's intervention in Libya, see David Cortright (ed), 'Military Interventionism in Libya: A Pandora's Box of Questions' (*Peace Policy*) <http://kroc.nd.edu/news-events/peace-policy/military-interventionism-libya-pandora-s-box-questions-1261> accessed 17 February 2013.

[49] UNSC Res 748 (31 March 1992) UN Doc S/Res/748.

[50] UNSC Res 1054 (26 April 1996) UN Doc S/Res/1054.

Mubarak. In UNSC Resolution 1267,[51] the Council required all member states to freeze the assets of, prevent the entry into or transit through their territories by, and prevent the direct or indirect supply, sale, and transfer of arms and military equipment to, any individual or entity associated with al-Qaida, Osama bin Laden and/or the Taliban.[52]

Following the al-Qaida attacks on the United States on 11 September 2001, the Council passed the most far reaching resolution in its history: Resolution 1373.[53] It mandated that all 191 member states participate in a global campaign to deny assets, safe haven, travel, or any other form of support to al-Qaida and other terrorist organizations, in accordance with what the newly-created Counter-Terrorism Committee (CTC) specified. One of the central features of this new counter-terrorism regime was the development of a listing procedure to include the names of individuals and entities suspected of engaging in terrorism or associating with terrorists. Until late 2006, any decision concerning listing and de-listing was left solely to the discretion of the '1267 Committee' and required the consent of all Committee members. By the end of 2008, UN member states had placed nearly five hundred individuals and entities on the '1267 Committee' list. [54]

International human rights groups, as well as leading legal scholars and practitioners, criticized this listing—and lack of de-listing—procedure from its inception, calling it 'black-listing'. There was broad consensus that the listing and closed procedures of the '1267 Committee' violated a number of fundamental human rights that the core international and regional human rights instruments guaranteed. These were—rang the clamour—the very legal documents and rights that the UN was meant to defend via resort to sanctions and not to be trampled in the name of security against terrorism.[55]

In particular, rights advocates claimed that the listing/delisting mechanisms of the Committee and Security Council lacked transparency and failed any serious accountability test for the Security Council or member states who had submitted the names of entities or individuals to be listed. Consequently, the due process rights of a listed individual were non-existent. An individual was neither made fully aware of the specific evidence, charges, associations, and behaviours which led the person to be listed, nor informed of the agencies that had submitted such information to

[51] UNSC Res 1267 (15 October 1999) UN Doc S/Res/1267.

[52] See Cortright and Lopez, *The Sanctions Decade* (n 1) 121–25.

[53] UNSC Res 1373 (28 September 2001) UN Doc S/Res/1373.

[54] In 1994, CTC transferred names in the hundreds to its successor committee, the Counter-Terrorism Executive Directorate. For an analysis of the workings of these UN Committees see, David Cortright et al, 'An Action Agenda for Enhancing the United Nations Program on Counter-Terrorism' (April 2004) Counter-Terrorism Evaluation Project <http://www.sanctionsandsecurity.org/wp-content/uploads/action-agenda-UN-counterterrorism.pdf> accessed 17 February 2013.

[55] International Commission of Jurists, *Assessing Damage, Urging Action: Report of the Eminent Jurists Panel on Terrorism, Counter-terrorism and Human Rights* (International Commission of Jurists 2009).

the Committee. Those listed had no due process rights to appeal this listing to the Council and thus there was no judicial review of the measures taken against them.[56]

By 2004, the issues of sanction-related listing, de-listing, and due process had become the subject of intense and parallel debate in policy and legal venues. Policy and institutional reforms were pressed in the Security Council, while individuals sought legal redress via national and regional courts, essentially challenging the Security Council's authority. The actions of the Council to address challenges to the 1267 machinery often emerged following new requirements that courts had mandated (although nearly all of these were under appeal), or they were attempts to pre-empt potential negative judgments via limited reform. The following analysis highlights the most significant ongoing case and presents a summary of the institutional and policy changes that the Council, as the sanctioning agent, made within the UN system.[57]

The case of *Kadi and Al Barakaat International Foundation*[58] has dominated both the discussion of the rights violations by the '1267 Committee' and the litigation through various regional and national court systems throughout the 2000s. By 2008, The European Court of Justice issued a ground-breaking ruling in the *Kadi* case, that the UN Security Council's refusal to abide by certain rights and processes that the EU system of rights guaranteed voided the obligation of European states to implement Security Council targeted sanctions against this individual. Reacting as a political and security forum for the region, the European Union Council later issued a ruling reinstating the restrictive measures placed on Kadi as a preventive counter-terrorism action permitted under European law. This see-saw battle between rights and security in counter-terrorism listing continues through similar cases in the US, Canada, and Europe.[59]

Disturbed by the rights insensitivity of the Council from 2001 to 2005, and convinced that decisions within the European court system raised serious questions about the adequacy of Security Council counter-terrorism sanctions, a group of 'like-minded states' dominated by European and Scandinavian members began to discuss with the Permanent Five Security Council members new resolutions administratively to remedy court adjudications. As a result of these pressures, the

[56] See George A Lopez, David Cortright, Alistair Millar, and Linda Gerber-Stellingwerf, 'Overdue Process: Protecting Human Rights while Sanctioning Alleged Terrorists' (April 2009) Report from the Fourth Freedom Forum and Kroc Institute for International Peace Studies <http://www.sanctionsandsecurity.org/overdue-process-protecting-human-rights-while-sanctioning-alleged-terrorists> accessed 17 February 2013.

[57] A full analysis of this diplomatic-legal dance is beyond the scope of this chapter, as is an assessment of all the cases and legal issues that comprise decided law. For further information on the *Kadi* case, see Erika de Wet's chapter in this *Handbook*.

[58] *Kadi and Al Barakaat International Foundation v Council and Commission*.

[59] On this tension, see David Cortright and Erika de Wet, 'Human Rights Standards for Targeted Sanctions' (January 2010) Policy Brief SSRP 1001-01 <http://www.sanctionsandsecurity.org/wp-content/uploads/10_01_HR_STANDARDS_FINAL_WEB.pdf> accessed 17 February 2013.

Council adopted stronger review mechanisms and enhanced procedures to ensure that listed individuals and entities are notified of the action taken against them. It also mandated that persons listed receive statements and narrative summaries of reasons for their listing. With Resolution 1730,[60] the Council established an office, 'The Focal Point', staffed by a Secretariat professional designated to facilitate and process the submission of requests for delisting. In a far-reaching action, Resolution 1822[61] directed the 1267 Monitoring Team to undertake a comprehensive review of all listed names in order to produce a clean and current list and to review each entry every three years. Without question, the impending European Court of Justice *Kadi* decision prompted the Security Council to adopt 1822.[62]

When reviews reported that the Focal Point mechanism did not meet the due process standards that court decisions were affirming, especially in not having the authority to conduct an independent review of petitioners' responses to charges and evidence, reformers pushed for further changes of a quasi-legal sort. These, in part, were realized in Resolution 1904,[63] wherein the Council created an independent and impartial Ombudsperson to replace the Focal Point for 1267 listing appeals. The resolution's annexes provided a template for improving the gathering of relevant information pertaining to listings, expanding the flow of information between the sanctions committee and listed persons and entities, and ensuring that the '1267 Committee' more fully considers requests for delisting. Although not a perfect mechanism, both petitioners and member states have been sufficiently satisfied with the procedures and results of the Ombudsperson's decisions. Thus, the office has been reaffirmed via Resolution 1989,[64] and with Resolution 2083[65] the Council extended the Ombudsperson's mandate for thirty months.

It is to be assessed fully if, how, where, and why these new mechanisms have contributed to improving the human rights responsiveness of the 1267 listing mechanism. The continuation of litigation attests to ongoing rights dilemmas, as does the critique of Council listing power. A November 2012 report that the Watson Institute released indicates that the UN Security Council measures have resulted in some welcome and effective reform. The 1267 Monitoring Team completed its systematic reevaluation of those placed on the list, taking more than the specified two years to finish. In this first review, 488 designated individuals on the list were re-examined, with thirty-five names of individuals removed/delisted based on the criteria for inclusion, while twenty-six individuals and organizations that were either deceased or defunct were delisted. In addition, the review process led to member states

[60] UNSC Res 1730 (19 December 2006) UN Doc S/Res/1730.
[61] UNSC Res 1822 (30 June 2008) UN Doc S/Res/1822.
[62] See George A Lopez et al, 'Overdue Process' (n 56).
[63] UNSC Res 1904 (17 December 2009) UN Doc S/Res/1904.
[64] UNSC Res 1989 (17 June 2011) UN Doc S/Res/1989.
[65] UNSC Res 2083 (17 December 2012) UN Doc S/Res/2083.

presenting more evidentiary bases for those remaining on the list, including summary statements that are available on a publicly-accessible website.[66]

As a result of the division of the al-Qaida and Taliban sanctions lists and committees, as mandated in Council Resolution 1988,[67] and the continued diligence of the Monitoring Team, the completed second list review of November 2012 now includes 295 names of individuals and entities—a significant reduction from the last review. Since its creation, the Focal Point delisted thirty-one petitioners out of eighty-five that were submitted for review; while the more intricate Ombudsperson process examined twenty cases, deciding to delist nineteen individuals and twenty-four entities.[68]

5. Making Sanctions Work

As this chapter has demonstrated, the type of sanctions imposed on rights abusers and the effectiveness of sanctions have varied over time. UN sanctions—despite counter-terrorism listing controversies—have the great advantage of being a foundational source of international law and, as such, impose obligations on all member states to comply with such coercive action. In practice, when powerful member states like the US or regional organization like the EU reinforce Council sanctions with further measures of their own, chances of success often increase. At the same time, however, Council sanctions suffer from taking time to mobilize, legislate, and implement. Experience shows that the very rumor of UN action may spark potential targets to hide their assets and begin to falsify companies, passports, and bank records.

Although practitioners and politicians frequently resort to sanctions to punish wrong-doers, the assessment of sanctions by analysts continues to be quite mixed. Most observers caution that the limited sanctions success rate, which social science researchers assess at about thirty-three percent, make sanctions a poor bet. This debate about the sanctions' effectiveness for punishing rights violators, or enhancing human rights in fragile political environments, has always been intense and diverse in policy circles. At present, the historical evidence about targeted sanctions is cautious at best; neither unilateral sanctions nor multilateral sanctions have

[66] Sue Eckert and Thomas Biersteker, 'Due Process and Targeted Sanctions: An Update for the "Watson Report"' (6 December 2012) Draft Discussion Paper 36 <http://www.watsoninstitute.org/pub/Watson_Report_Update_12_12.pdf> accessed 17 February 2013.

[67] UNSC Res 1988 (17 June 2011) UN Doc S/Res/1988.

[68] Eckert and Biersteker, 'Due Process' (n 66) 36.

ever toppled a targeted, rights-violating government. Nor have they, by themselves, ever forced rights violators to desist in their actions. When dictators change their behaviour, sanctions may be part of the mix of a set of foreign policy measures and domestic pressures that lead to an improved human rights situation. However, sanctions have more dramatic success in safeguarding fragile democracies, which protect the rights—respecting political climate of former non-democratic states. Generally, the most significant factors associated with effectiveness are the severity of the threats to rights, the degree of cooperation among national imposers, domestic politics within imposer and target states, and the diversity of economic entanglements between imposing nations and the target state or entity.[69]

Sanctions policy analysts tend to argue that these poor results arise from half-hearted purpose, weak sanctions design, and/or implementation, especially by the Permanent Five members of the UN Security Council. They suggest that a close scrutiny of the Kosovo, Sudan/Darfur, Zimbabwe, and especially the Syrian case, reveals that the reluctance of powerful states to enforce a full slate of coercive measures sabotaged what otherwise might have been effective sanctions for improving human rights. Among quantitative international relations scholars, there is a fairly consistent set of findings that economic trade sanctions are more detrimental to human rights than partial and selective sanctions, and generally, these studies find that economic coercion fails to attain its policy goal, even when sanctions are specifically imposed with the goal of improving human rights. Finally—and oddly—multilateral sanctions have a greater overall negative impact on human rights than unilateral sanctions.[70]

Lessons from the past two decades of multilateral cases of primarily targeted sanctions policy and mechanisms can be summarized succinctly regarding how sanctions can prompt, persuade, or force human rights improvements.[71] First, sanctions succeed when decision makers remember that sanctions are only tools—and thus *only one* of the multiple important tools that should be serving a clearly-specified policy goal and broader policy interest. When sanctions become *the* policy, or are maintained for so long that they *de facto* become *the* policy, they are no longer effective. This was the trap into which the US and UN had fallen by the mid-1990s with the sanctions on Iraq and with which they may be flirting with regard to Iran. It has been the dilemma of the US experience with Cuban sanctions for half of a century.

[69] I make a more extensive argument with cases to support it in George A Lopez, 'In Defense of Smart Sanctions: A Response to Joy Gordon' (2012) 26 *Ethics & International Affairs* 135.

[70] An example of such empirical analysis is provided in Dursun Peksen, 'Better or Worse? The Effect of Economic Sanctions on Human Rights' (2009) 46 *J Peace Res* 59.

[71] Here, I am succinctly summarizing generalizations developed in George A Lopez, 'Effective Sanctions: Incentives and UN-US Dynamics' (2007) 29 *Harvard International Review* 50–55; George A Lopez, 'Matching Means with Intentions' (n 4); George A Lopez, 'In Defense of Smart Sanctions' (n 56).

Second, and flowing from the first reality, despite their precision, smart sanctions seldom produce immediate and full compliance from targets. Rather, in a number of cases, sanctions produce partial compliance and generate pressure on targets and imposers to engage in more direct bargaining to achieve the sanctions objectives. Thus, the economic squeeze felt by the target comprises only the first tier of smart sanctions success. The political success of getting the target to change its behaviour results less over time from the economic pain it experiences, but more so from gains to be made at the bargaining table which the sanctions have set for the contending parties. Thus, sanctions work when they not only enrage, but actually engage their targets. Sanctions must provide a framework for continued dialogue between target and imposers.

When Libya was sanctioned for terrorist activities and support, the sanctions' impacts were a central factor in the ongoing negotiations from the mid-1990s until, a decade later, the actions brought suspected terrorists to trial and convinced the regime to reduce its support of international terrorism. In Angola, sanctions were initially ineffective, but became stronger over the years and combined with military and diplomatic pressures to weaken the National Union for Total Independence of Angola (UNITA) rebel movement. In Liberia, sanctions were designed to deny resources to Taylor and his allies. Then, after increased engagement by the imposers with the fighting factions, the sanctions helped to deny legitimacy to the Charles Taylor regime itself.

Third, sanctions as a means of punishment and isolation rarely succeed. In fact, sanctions form only half of the mix of mechanisms needed to alter the behaviour of stubborn targets, such as regimes or non-state groups engaged in human rights violations. Positive inducements—the proverbial carrots of international economic and political relations—are a necessary complement to the sticks of a sanctions strategy. Within this mix, the structure and use of sanctions to achieve the end-game desired from the target must be clear. The more effective sanctions are ones which detail a very clear and limited number of demands, and which are clear and credible. Both imposer and target must be in full agreement about what constitutes compliance. Moreover, the target must be confident that if it changes its human rights behaviour in accord with actions specified in the sanctions, it will result in a timely lifting of the coercive pressure and the extension of the promised benefits. When imposers shift the goal-posts (as has often been done in counter-proliferation sanctions), target compliance fails.

Finally, there is the generalization that many analysts shun, because they consider sanctions most useful as effective alternatives to war, firmly grounded in international law. This maxim states that unless the target understands that without some change in their behaviour, a sequence of stronger enforcement measures will follow—including the use of force—then sanctions become a bet that a bluffing hand supports. Haiti stands out as the exemplar of this maxim. Having overthrown the democratically-elected government, a sanctioned General Cedras did not act on verbal agreements to leave power until he clearly understood that he would be removed by force. The use of R2P in Libya—despite its negative outcome for the prospect of Syrian sanctions—with resulting military action, saved lives.

Two new emerging trends, maximizing commodity sanctions and targeting enablers, may not yet fall into the realm of generalizations about sanctions improving rights, but they should be noted. First, commodity-specific sanctions have increased in frequency and impact in diverse sanctions cases. Highly to moderately successful oil embargoes were imposed as part of the sanctions against Yugoslavia, Haiti, UNITA, and the military junta in Sierra Leone. After aid agencies and human rights NGOs documented the role of diamond smuggling in financing the civil wars in Angola and Sierra Leone, and in the recruitment and retention of child soldiers in other conflicts, the Security Council pushed the US and European states to take action to interdict the trade in so-called 'blood diamonds'. Diamond embargoes were imposed against UNITA in 1998, against the Revolutionary United Front areas of Sierra Leone in 2000, and against Charles Taylor's Liberian government in 2001. A log-export ban also was imposed against the government of Liberia, for its support of the Revolutionary Unified Front. There is increasing evidence that these commodity embargoes stifle the work of the criminal organizations that are often responsible for the rights abuses and murder of civilians in war-torn areas.[72]

Building from the reality that mass atrocities are organized crimes, reducing to the lowest possible level the means to organize and sustain them—that is, money, communications networks, and other resources—can disrupt their execution. A key element of such crimes, particularly relevant to international responses, is the role of third-parties who carry out the execution or genocidal orders of leaders. While atrocities vary in cause and method, and perpetrators are generally both creative and resourceful, a core set of activities can be identified that clearly *enable* and sustain the violence. By developing approaches to target the third-parties engaged in those activities, it may be possible to decrease or interrupt the perpetrators' access to necessary means. This may, in turn, alter their calculations regarding the commitment of atrocities against civilians.[73]

Examples of enablers in regard to the situation in Darfur, Sudan, involve transfers of arms by China, Russia, Chad, and other governments or state-owned entities, to government and rebel forces; these transfers have helped sustain the violence against civilians for six years. In the case of commercial entities, the range of enabling activities is potentially very broad. In Nigeria, multinational oil companies have faced lawsuits after being accused of hiring abusive security forces in the Niger Delta. In Darfur, the supply of Toyota trucks to which rebel groups had access was essential to their capacity to commit widespread attacks on civilians. The UN Panel

[72] Discussion of these commodity embargos can be found in David Cortright and George A Lopez, *Sanctions and the Search for Security: Challenges to UN Action* (Lynne Rienner 2002).

[73] The arguments regarding enablers are more extensively discussed in George A Lopez, 'Dealing with "Enablers" in Mass Atrocities: A New Human Rights Concept Takes Shape' (*Carnegie Council*, 26 June 2012) <http://www.carnegiecouncil.org/publications/ethics_online/0070.html>.

of Experts on the Sudan reported that Al-Futtaim Motors Company, the official Toyota dealership in the United Arab Emirates, was, along with second-hand dealers in the same country, the source of 'by far the largest number of vehicles that were documented as part of arms embargo violations in Darfur...'.[74] That dealership 'declined or replied...in a perfunctory manner' to three Panel requests for information about the buyers of the trucks identified in Darfur.[75]

Countries and commercial actors also act as enablers when they are engaged in the exploitation of natural resources that generate revenues for the perpetrators, thereby sustaining their capacity to abuse civilian populations. Examples include eastern Congo, where windfalls from the illicit mineral trade fuel the rebels' pursuit of arms and thus contribute to atrocities against civilians. In Burma, before the recent reforms, the country's military rulers derived massive export earnings from their gem mines, which helped to finance their severe repression of that country's citizens.

Syria stands as a brutal and recent example in which the UN's failure to impose and enforce multilateral sanctions has meant an inability to undercut the steadfast enablers of Mr Assad who work from Iran and Russia and as non-state actors in the regime. The porous nature of the borders surrounding the country has meant that those sanctions that the US and European Union have imposed have failed to pressure sufficiently the targeted Assad regime. Unlike in Libya, the serious, coordinated sanctioning of enablers needed to deny Assad the means to kill his own citizens has not emerged.

6. Conclusions

Short of military force, economic sanctions are the only major tool available to national leaders and multilateral institutions that will produce results essential to ending harsh repression and human rights abuses. By blocking access to financial assets, sanctions—sometimes slowly, but always surely—erode the regime's ability to purchase arms and mercenaries from abroad. Sanctions constrain guarantees that dictators can make to supporters that their government will meet the payroll. Monetary and travel sanctions placed on a growing number of government and military officials run a strong probability of sparking defections among the ruling elite.

[74] UNSC, 'Report of the Panel of Experts Established Pursuant to Resolution 1591 (2005) Concerning the Sudan' (29 October 2009) UN Doc S/2009/562, para 158.

[75] UNSC, 'Report of the Panel of Experts Established Pursuant to Resolution 1591' (n 74) para 158.

The continued fragility of human rights in nations emerging from internal war or economic crisis combines with the horrific mass atrocities of recent decades, to increase the likelihood that national policy-makers will turn to sanctions continually as a tool for coercion and persuasion. The emergence of the principles of protecting civilians and the responsibility to protect bolsters this prospect. Yet, the track record of the UN and the international community in addressing atrocities—as in the different responses to Libya and Syria, which occurred just one year apart—makes clear the complexity related to the problems and the challenges of mounting a fully successful action. It is a bitter irony that the quick success of the combination of coercive measures to protect the lives and rights of Libyans, in which NATO may have overstepped its military mandate, has led to big power disagreements over the application of the same principle and tools in Syria.[76]

The recent successes of sanctions in Libya, Côte d'Ivoire, and Liberia can be extended to other areas, if analysts dig deeper into the workings of repression and discover the revenue that the commodities supporting mass violence and the myriad enablers to human rights violations and mass atrocities generate. Targeting the diversity of these non-state actors early in an internal war, or as early warning signs of atrocities emerge, can increase the effectiveness of sanctions as a tool for human rights protection.

Finally, in many respects, the positive results of imposing targeted sanctions as proactive for human rights are counterbalanced by the ongoing rights controversies with counter-terrorism listing in the 1267 regime. While the latter has made some progress, fundamental disagreements remain. The weight of this contradiction has the potential—with other factors, like the push back against sanctions and Security Council reluctance to pass them—to undermine R2P and sanctions at the same time. Thus, the future of the relationship between sanctions and human rights will remain in question for some time to come.

Further Reading

Charron A, *UN Sanctions and Conflict: Responding to Peace and Security Threats* (Routledge 2011)

Cortright D and Lopez GA, *Sanctions and the Search for Security: Challenges to UN Action* (Lynne Rienner 2002)

Drezner D, *The Sanctions Paradox: Economic Statecraft and International Relations* (CUP 1999)

Gowlland-Debbas V (ed), *United Nations Sanctions and International Law* (Kluwer Law International 2001)

[76] By the beginning of 2013, the UN had certified that millions of Syrians are internally displaced or cross-border refugees, and more than 60,000 (many of the them innocent civilians) have died.

CHAPTER 33

TRANSNATIONAL LITIGATION: JURISDICTION AND IMMUNITIES

CHIMÈNE I KEITNER

1. INTRODUCTION AND OVERVIEW

TRANSNATIONAL human rights litigation involves the horizontal enforcement of human rights norms by national courts, rather than the vertical enforcement of those norms by international bodies. In the typical scenario, courts in State A are asked to adjudicate the lawfulness of conduct performed by individuals acting on behalf of, or in association with, the government of State B.[1] Section 2 of this chapter explores the bases for asserting jurisdiction in human rights cases. Section 3 focuses on human rights claims against foreign states, and the restrictions on these claims imposed by the principle of state immunity. Section 4 looks at civil and criminal proceedings against foreign officials. It emphasizes the distinction

[1] For a discussion of cases involving claims against State A's own government for extraterritorial rights violations, see Chimène I Keitner, 'Rights Beyond Borders' (2011) 36 *Yale J Int'l L* 55, and sources cited therein.

between status-based immunity (*ratione personae*) and conduct-based immunity (*ratione materiae*) and canvasses ongoing debates about the scope of conduct-based immunity for foreign officials. Section 5 discusses claims against non-state actors including private corporations for committing or assisting human rights violations.

Domestic courts play an important role in articulating and enforcing international legal rules, in particular those 'rules binding individuals for the benefit of other individuals'.[2] In the absence of international tribunals with appropriate jurisdiction and remedial powers, domestic courts can provide monetary compensation and symbolic vindication to victims who have been injured by internationally unlawful conduct. They can also impose a degree of accountability on defendants who might otherwise escape legal consequences for their acts. That said, domestic courts do not have an unlimited ability to act as transnational law enforcers. Political and territorial borders continue to carry international legal significance. Conflicts arise between the principles of state sovereignty and non-interference, on the one hand, and the goals of promoting accountability and providing remedies for victims, on the other.

The creation of the International Criminal Court (ICC) has prompted states parties to enact implementing legislation that, by and large, denies immunity from domestic prosecution for the crimes currently within the ICC's jurisdiction: war crimes, genocide, and crimes against humanity. The ICC does not recognize defenses based on the official capacity in which the conduct was performed.[3] In addition, domestic courts have found that a treaty obligation to extradite or prosecute an offender requires the denial of immunity, as in the UK House of Lords' decision denying immunity from extradition to former Chilean President Augusto Pinochet for torture.[4]

There is currently no comprehensive treaty governing individual immunities from transnational legal proceedings. The 2004 United Nations Convention on Jurisdictional Immunities of States and Their Property defines the term 'state' to include 'representatives of the State acting in that capacity', but the treaty does not apply to criminal proceedings,[5] and it has not yet attracted a sufficient number of ratifications to enter into force. Other treaties, such as the Vienna Convention on Diplomatic Relations, govern certain aspects of immunity, but they do not resolve persistent debates about the susceptibility of other categories of current and former officials to legal proceedings in foreign courts. While the customary international law of foreign *state* immunity is fairly well settled, as described in Section 3 below, consensus about the rules governing foreign *official* immunity has remained relatively more elusive. This chapter provides an overview of this evolving area of law.

[2] *Sosa v Alvarez-Machain* 715.

[3] Rome Statute of the International Criminal Court, Art 27.

[4] *R v Bartle, ex p Pinochet.*

[5] See UNGA Res 59/38 (16 December 2004) UN Doc A/RES/59/38.

2. Bases for Asserting Jurisdiction

A claim of immunity represents a defense to jurisdiction. In practice and in doctrine, jurisdiction falls into three basic categories: prescriptive (the authority to enact legal rules); adjudicatory (the authority to decide disputes by interpreting and applying legal rules); and enforcement (the authority to exert control over persons and property to implement legal rules). There are six recognized bases for exercising prescriptive jurisdiction. These are:

(1) territory (the location of the conduct);
(2) nationality (the citizenship of the actor);
(3) objective territoriality/effects jurisdiction (the location of the effects of the conduct);
(4) the protective principle (protection of the state's vital interests);
(5) passive personality (the citizenship of the affected party); and
(6) universality (particularly egregious conduct subject to regulation by the international community as a whole).

States need not exercise the full extent of jurisdiction permitted under international law and, indeed, jurisdictional conflicts arise with some frequency. Generally speaking, exercises of prescriptive jurisdiction on the basis of territoriality and nationality are less likely to elicit protests from other states than exercises of jurisdiction on other bases. This is because state jurisdiction is primarily—although not exclusively—territorial.[6]

If a domestic court is asked to apply international law directly, then it is exercising adjudicatory jurisdiction only, because the substantive legal rule that is being applied to the defendant's conduct has been prescribed by the international community as a whole (if the rule comes from customary international law) or by the states parties to an applicable treaty. If a court is asked to apply some form of its own domestic law (international law as incorporated into domestic law, or domestic law as informed by international law), then the forum state is arguably exercising a degree of prescriptive jurisdiction in addition to adjudicatory jurisdiction. If a domestic court applies foreign law to a defendant's conduct, it is again exercising adjudicatory jurisdiction only, because the applicable legal rule has been prescribed by the foreign state.

The exercise of prescriptive jurisdiction over extraterritorial conduct may elicit stronger protests than the exercise of adjudicatory jurisdiction, because common

[6] The European Court of Human Rights, for example, has observed frequently that a state's jurisdictional competence is 'primarily territorial'. *Al-Skeini and Others v United Kingdom*, para 131; *Soering v United Kingdom*, para 86; *Banković v Belgium and Others*, paras 66, 67; *Ilaşcu and Others v Moldova and Russia*, para 312.

understandings of the legitimate exercise of prescriptive jurisdiction remain largely territorial, notwithstanding the proliferation of conduct-regulating rules with extraterritorial reach. A myriad doctrines have emerged to contain and manage jurisdictional conflicts, including the common law doctrine of *forum non conveniens* and the civil law doctrine of *lis pendens*, requirements to exhaust local remedies in certain types of cases, choice of law rules, and the principle of 'comity' or deference to courts with more substantial connections to a particular legal dispute.

Immunity doctrines also curb the exercise of jurisdiction by one state over conduct performed by another state or its agents. While different types of immunities have different rationales, all serve to limit the exercise of jurisdiction by State A over conduct performed by or attributable to State B. The successful pursuit of a human rights claim in the courts of State A therefore depends not only on the existence of subject-matter jurisdiction over the claim and personal jurisdiction over the defendant, but also on the absence of an applicable immunity.

3. Claims against Foreign States

States themselves may be the subject of legal proceedings in another country's courts. In such situations, foreign states may claim an entitlement to jurisdictional immunity. The question of foreign state immunity arose in the late eighteenth century in the context of *in rem* proceedings against foreign ships. In 1795, French Minister Pierre-Auguste Adet protested the attachment of a French ship by a US court pursuant to the filing of a civil admiralty claim. Adet insisted that '[t]he party complaining should lay their complaints before [the Government of France], either directly, or through the medium of its own Government. Were it otherwise, one Government would become amenable to another; which would reverse the first principles of the rights of nations'.[7] The idea that one government should not be 'amenable' to another, captured by the maxim *par in parem no habet imperium* (an equal has no power over an equal), reached its apogee in the nineteenth century. In his often-cited opinion in the 1812 case *Schooner Exchange v McFaddon*, US Chief Justice John Marshall reasoned:

> This perfect equality and absolute independence of sovereigns, and this common interest impelling them to mutual intercourse, and an interchange of good offices with each other,

[7] Letter from PA Adet, Minister Plenipotentiary of the French Republic, to Mr Randolph, Secretary of State of the US (9 August 1795) in Walter Lowrie and Matthew St Clair Clarke (eds), *American State Papers: Foreign Relations*, vol 1 (Gales and Seaton 1832) 629.

have given rise to a class of cases in which every sovereign is understood to wave the exercise of a part of that complete exclusive territorial jurisdiction, which has been stated to be the attribute of every nation.[8]

According to Chief Justice Marshall, this 'class of cases' included situations in which the territorial sovereign had expressly or by implication consented to the entry into its ports of a friendly public ship of war.[9] Consequently, the Supreme Court held that a lower court could not adjudicate John McFaddon and William Greetham's claim to be the rightful owners of a French public ship of war that had sought repairs in the port of Philadelphia.[10]

The idea of sovereign equality and dignity has been understood to entail the 'absolute' immunity of foreign states from domestic jurisdiction, although at least in the Western legal tradition the absolute nature of this immunity has been arguably more rhetorical than real.[11] Moreover, the 'absolute' theory of foreign state immunity has been tempered in many countries to allow judicial enforcement of rights and duties created by commercial transactions. Under this 'restrictive' approach, a foreign state does not benefit from immunity with respect to its private or commercial acts (acts *jure gestionis*), although it generally retains immunity with respect to its public acts (acts *jure imperii*).[12] The pivotal distinction between commercial and public acts for the purpose of state immunity is codified in domestic legislation such as the US Foreign Sovereign Immunities Act of 1976 (FSIA), the UK State Immunity Act of 1978, the Canadian State Immunity Act of 1982, the Australian Foreign States Immunities Act of 1985, and others. It is also reflected in the 2004 United Nations Convention on Jurisdictional Immunities of States and their Property, which will enter into force after it has been ratified by thirty states.[13]

Under the restrictive theory, characterizing a state's alleged acts as acts *jure gestionis* or *jure imperii* determines whether or not the state may claim immunity from suit. In general, human rights violations are deemed to fall within the latter category; for example, in *Saudi Arabia v Nelson*, the US Supreme Court held that Scott Nelson and his wife could not invoke the FSIA's commercial activity exception to secure jurisdiction over Saudi Arabia for torture Mr Nelson allegedly suffered at the hands of Saudi officials in Saudi Arabia. The Court found that Saudi Arabia retained

[8] *Schooner Exchange v M'Faddon* 137.

[9] See *Schooner Exchange* (n 8) 144.

[10] This ruling was congenial from the perspective of US diplomacy, since the United States could not afford to alienate France while fighting a war with Britain.

[11] For example, David Bederman has observed that 'the absolute foreign sovereign immunity that *The Schooner Exchange* has often been cited as supporting, may not have been so "absolute" after all'. David J Bederman, *International Law Frameworks* (3rd edn, Foundation Press 2010) 198.

[12] This is so, even though, as Sir Hersch Lauterpacht has observed, 'the state always acts as a public person. It cannot act otherwise. In a real sense all acts *jure gestionis* are acts *jure imperii*'. Hersch Lauterpacht, 'The Problem of Jurisdictional Immunities of Foreign States' (1951) 28 *Brit YB Int'l L* 220, 224.

[13] United Nations Convention on Jurisdictional Immunities of States and Their Property.

its immunity because torture was not a 'commercial activity' within the meaning of the FSIA, even though the maltreatment allegedly occurred as the result of an employment relationship formed in the United States.[14]

UK courts have reached similar results under the UK State Immunity Act (SIA). In *Al-Adsani v Government of Kuwait*, the English Court of Appeal held that Sulaiman Al-Adsani could not proceed with a claim against the Government of Kuwait for torture that allegedly occurred in Kuwait because the Sovereign Immunity Act (SIA) does not contain an enumerated exception to state immunity for acts of torture.[15] A Grand Chamber of the European Court of Human Rights (ECHR) subsequently declined to find (by a vote of nine to eight) that the application of state immunity in this context impermissibly violated Mr Al-Adsani's right of access to a court under Article 6 of the European Convention on Human Rights. In the ECHR majority's view, 'the grant of sovereign immunity to a State in civil proceedings pursues the legitimate aim of complying with international law to promote comity and good relations between States through the respect of another State's sovereignty'.[16] The procedural limitations imposed by the doctrine of state immunity are 'generally accepted by the community of nations', the majority held, and therefore these limitations 'cannot in principle be regarded as imposing a disproportionate restriction on the right of access to a court'.[17]

The joint dissenting opinion advanced the contrary view that 'the *jus cogens* nature of the prohibition of torture entails that a State allegedly violating it cannot invoke hierarchically lower rules (in this case, those on State immunity) to avoid the consequences of the illegality of its actions'.[18] This opinion found unpersuasive the majority's view that state immunity is a procedural bar not subject to override by a substantive *jus cogens* rule (that is, a peremptory norm of international law). It was also not persuaded by the majority's attempt to distinguish the non-operation of immunity as a bar to individual criminal liability for torture in UK courts, on the one hand, and the continued existence of state immunity as a bar to civil proceedings against Kuwait, on the other.[19]

A decisive majority of the International Court of Justice in 2012 declined, like the European Court, to find that the *jus cogens* status of an alleged violation vitiates claims to state immunity that would otherwise exist as a matter of customary international law.[20] The ICJ held in *Germany v Italy* that claims arising from the conduct of Germany's armed forces on Italian territory during the Second World

[14] *Saudi Arabia v Nelson*. The Ontario Court of Appeal reached a similar conclusion on the non-application of the commercial exception in the Canadian State Immunity Act to claims of torture. *Bouzari v Islamic Republic of Iran*.

[15] *Al-Adsani v Kuwait*.

[16] *Al-Adsani v United Kingdom*, para 54.

[17] *Al-Adsani v UK* (n 16) para 56.

[18] *Al-Adsani v UK* (n 16) para 3 (joint dissenting opinion).

[19] *Al-Adsani v UK* (n 16) para 4 (joint dissenting opinion).

[20] *Jurisdictional Immunities of the State (Germany v Italy)*, paras 92–97.

War, which Italian courts had allowed to proceed, are barred from adjudication in Italian courts absent Germany's consent to Italian jurisdiction. The holding in *Germany v Italy* was limited to the context of litigation arising from armed activities on the territory of the forum state, based on a concern about the finality of post-war reparations agreements and the disruptive potential of unlimited claims against belligerent states. However, defendant states claiming immunity in foreign courts will likely attempt to invoke aspects of the ICJ's reasoning to support the proposition that customary international law requires state immunity for all acts *jure imperii* absent a waiver of immunity by the defendant state.[21]

Germany and Italy disagreed about the scope of state immunity, but they agreed that customary international law governs the matter. By contrast, the United States has traditionally viewed state immunity as a matter of 'grace and comity',[22] and has permitted further restrictions on immunity to be imposed by legislation. In 1996, for example, an amendment to the FSIA added jurisdiction over designated state sponsors of terrorism for civil actions seeking money damages for 'personal injury or death that was caused by an act of torture, extrajudicial killing, aircraft sabotage, hostage taking, or the provision of material support or resources for such an act' by the foreign state, even though these acts would ordinarily qualify as acts *jure imperii*.[23] Significant money damages have been awarded under this provision, although many of the awards remain unenforced.[24]

The ICJ's reasoning in *Germany v Italy* will not affect the validity of the state sponsors of terrorism exception as a matter of US law, but it will likely impede enforcement abroad of US judgments rendered under this provision. The ICJ's decision also found that state immunity barred Italian courts from giving effect to a judgment against Germany obtained in Greece, and defendants will no doubt argue that customary international law prohibits applying the state sponsors of terrorism exception to acts *jure imperii*.

[21] In the United States, the argument that *jus cogens* violations amount to an implied waiver of immunity from the jurisdiction of US courts under the FSIA also has not prevailed, notwithstanding Judge Patricia Wald's energetic dissent in support of the implied waiver theory. *Princz v Germany* 1176. The argument that *jus cogens* violations cannot benefit from state immunity had some success in Greek and Italian courts prior to the ICJ's judgment in *Jurisdictional Immunities* (n 20). *Prefecture of Voiotia v Federal Republic of Germany*; *Ferrini v Republica Federale di Germania*.

[22] *Verlinden v Central Bank of Nigeria* 486.

[23] FSIA, 22 USC s 1605(a). Even if state immunity were not viewed as a matter of comity, this explicit statutory provision would be sufficient to override state immunity as a matter of US domestic law. In March 2012, Canada enacted a similar exception to its State Immunity Act. See An Act to Enact the Justice for Victims of Terrorism Act and to Amend the State Immunity Act (13 March 2012) <http://www.parl.gc.ca/HousePublications/Publication.aspx?Language=E&Mode=1&DocId=5465759&File=53#8> accessed 17 February 2013.

[24] Jennifer K Elsea, 'Suits Against Terrorist States by Victims of Terrorism' (1 May 2008) Congressional Research Service Reports for Congress, Order Code RL31258 <http://www.fas.org/sgp/crs/terror/RL31258.pdf> accessed 17 February 2013.

4. Claims Against Current or Former Foreign Officials

Individuals may bear personal responsibility for acts they perform on behalf of states or under color of state law. International criminal tribunals and some treaties reject immunity defenses based on the official nature of the defendant's conduct.[25] The question is whether the domestic courts of other states can adjudicate the existence of such responsibility and impose legal consequences for unlawful acts. According to some, individual officials enjoy at least as much immunity as the state itself would enjoy in the same circumstances. Others take the view that individual officials may enjoy more or less immunity than the state itself. State practice is also divided.

The potential immunity of individual officials falls into two distinct categories. Individuals who claim immunity from foreign legal processes by virtue of their current official positions are claiming status-based immunity, or immunity *ratione personae*. Those who claim immunity by virtue of the official nature of their challenged acts are claiming conduct-based immunity, or immunity *ratione materiae*. The rationale for status-based immunity is to allow official representatives of the state to conduct foreign relations abroad without fear of arrest or suit. The rationale for conduct-based immunity involves a combination of not deterring legitimate state acts, not allowing one state to adjudicate the lawfulness of another state's acts, and not unduly impeding the freedom of travel of former foreign officials.

It is generally accepted that official immunities, which may be waived by the state, are not granted for the benefit of the individual, but rather to enable states to conduct relations with each other. As the International Court of Justice indicated in its *Arrest Warrant* decision, which contains its most explicit pronouncements on individual immunities: 'In customary international law, the immunities accorded to Ministers for Foreign Affairs are not granted for their personal benefit, but to ensure the effective performance of their functions on behalf of their respective States.'[26] The issue in the *Arrest Warrant* case was whether *ratione personae* immunity—that is, immunity attached to an individual's current official position—protects a sitting foreign minister from legal proceedings in the domestic courts of another country. A Belgian statute in effect at the time empowered Belgian courts to prosecute individuals for serious violations of international humanitarian law. A Belgian investigating judge issued an international arrest warrant against the Congolese minister for foreign affairs for alleged crimes against humanity. The warrant sought the

[25] Rome Statute, Art 27; Statute of the International Criminal Tribunal for the Former Yugoslavia, Art 7(2); Statute of the International Criminal Tribunal for Rwanda, Art 6(2); Convention on the Prevention and Punishment of the Crime of Genocide, Art 4.

[26] *Arrest Warrant of 11 April 2000 (Democratic Republic of the Congo v Belgium)* 53.

minister's provisional arrest pending a request for extradition to Belgium to face trial for his alleged crimes. Because the foreign minister was not a diplomat, he could not claim diplomatic immunity under the Vienna Convention on Diplomatic Relations.[27] The ICJ determined that his position came within the ambit of the customary international law immunity accorded heads of state because (1) like a head of state, a foreign minister's status as a representative of the state is established under international law 'solely by virtue of his or her office'; and (2) because a foreign minister is charged with conducting relations with other states, one state cannot exercise its authority in a way that would hinder another state's foreign minister 'in the performance of his or her duties' while in office.[28] Although the ICJ's decision related to criminal proceedings, its rationale would also apply to civil proceedings and other measures of constraint.[29]

In its *Arrest Warrant* decision, the ICJ emphasized that immunity does not always represent a bar to criminal prosecution for serious violations of international humanitarian law:

> First, [incumbent foreign ministers] enjoy no criminal immunity under international law in their own countries, and may thus be tried by those countries' courts in accordance with the relevant rules of domestic law.
>
> Secondly, they will cease to enjoy immunity from foreign jurisdiction if the State which they represent or have represented decides to waive that immunity.
>
> Thirdly, after a person ceases to hold the office of Minister for Foreign Affairs, he or she will no longer enjoy all of the immunities accorded by international law in other States. Provided that it has jurisdiction under international law, a court of one State may try a former Minister for Foreign Affairs of another State in respect of acts committed prior or subsequent to his or her period of office, as well as in respect of acts committed during that period of office in a private capacity.
>
> Fourthly, an incumbent or former Minister for Foreign Affairs may be subject to criminal proceedings before certain international criminal courts, where they have jurisdiction.[30]

The DRC had gone even further in its submissions, indicating that it did not 'deny the existence of a principle of international criminal law, deriving from the decisions of the Nuremberg and Tokyo international military tribunals, that the accused's official capacity at the time of the acts cannot, *before any court, whether domestic or*

[27] The Vienna Convention on Diplomatic Relations. The Vienna Convention on Consular Relations provides current and former consular officials with immunity for acts performed in the exercise of their consular functions, but not with immunity *ratione personae*.

[28] *Arrest Warrant* (n 26) 53–54.

[29] In *Certain Criminal Proceedings in France (Republic of the Congo v France)*, the ICJ found that provisional measures were not warranted where French courts had yet to take any measures of constraint against Congolese officials and where there was no risk of 'irreparable prejudice' to the Congolese head of state or minister of the interior. In *Certain Questions of Mutual Assistance in Criminal Matters (Djibouti v France)*, the ICJ reiterated that diplomatic agents and heads of state are inviolable, but found that France had not breached this inviolability by 'inviting' a visiting head of state to give evidence in a criminal investigation (paras 171–174).

[30] *Arrest Warrant* (n 26) para 61.

international, constitute a "ground of exemption from his criminal responsibility or a ground for mitigation of sentence" '.[31] In other words, the DRC's objection to Belgium's issuance of the arrest warrant was based on the foreign minister's position at the time the warrant was issued, not the nature of the acts under investigation.[32]

The functional rationale for *ratione personae* immunity has led states to recognize temporary status-based immunity for members of special diplomatic missions, either under the Convention on Special Missions, or on an ad hoc basis.[33] In sum, current diplomatic officials, sitting heads of state (including foreign ministers), and certain members of special diplomatic missions enjoy immunity *ratione personae* and cannot be sued or prosecuted by foreign states absent a waiver by the state they represent.

Former officials, and incumbent officials whose positions do not carry *ratione personae* immunity, cannot claim immunity *ratione personae*. Instead, they may attempt to claim immunity from foreign legal processes based on the official nature of their challenged acts (immunity *ratione materiae*). The scope of *ratione materiae* immunity remains contested, particularly with respect to alleged human rights violations and international crimes. Several approaches have emerged to delineate the scope of *ratione materiae* immunity from criminal and civil proceedings in a foreign country's courts.

4.1 Immunity from criminal prosecution

National courts apply different rules for securing jurisdiction over individual defendants in criminal cases. While certain legal systems permit criminal trials *in absentia*, the question of *ratione materiae* immunity arises most urgently where a potential criminal defendant faces the possibility of being taken into custody by national authorities by virtue of his or her presence on the forum state's territory. In one example, retired Israeli Major General Doron Almog stayed aboard an El Al plane when it landed at Heathrow airport upon learning that Scotland Yard detectives were waiting to arrest him for alleged war crimes; Almog returned to Israel without disembarking.[34] Several years later, the UK Foreign Office issued a

31 *Arrest Warrant* (n 26) para 48 (emphasis added).

32 See also *SOS Attentats v Gaddafi*, para 509 (a 2001 case from France, holding that Libyan leader Colonel Gaddafi was entitled to head-of-state immunity from charges of complicity in the destruction of a French civil aircraft in 1989).

33 See eg 'Suggestion of Immunity and Statement of Interest of the United States' in *Li Weixum v Bo Xilai* 11, fn 9 (suggesting immunity from service of process for an invitee of the Executive Branch). A UK Magistrates Court found Mikhail Gorbachev immune from arrest as a member of a 'special mission' in March 2011. 'Former Dissident Seeks Gorbachev's Arrest over "Soviet-era crimes"' (*RT.com*, 31 March 2011) <http://rt.com/politics/bukovsky-gorbachev-london-lawsuit>.

34 Vikram Dodd and Conal Urquhart, 'Israeli Evades Arrest at Heathrow Over Army War Crime Allegations' *The Guardian* (Tel Aviv, 12 September 2005) <http://www.guardian.co.uk/uk/2005/sep/12/israelandthepalestinians.warcrimes> accessed 17 February 2013.

certificate granting Israeli opposition leader Tzipi Livni special mission immunity (*ratione personae*) during a visit to the United Kingdom to allay concerns about her possible arrest.[35]

In several noteworthy cases, national courts have denied conduct-based immunity from criminal prosecution to former foreign officials accused of international crimes. The UK House of Lords denied Senator Augusto Pinochet immunity from extradition to Spain under an international arrest warrant to face charges of torture committed in Chile while Pinochet was head of state and after the United Kingdom, Chile, and Spain had all ratified the Convention Against Torture. Lord Browne-Wilkinson reasoned:

> How can it be for international law purposes an official function to do something which international law itself prohibits and criminalises?... [A]n essential feature of the international crime of torture is that it must be committed 'by or with the acquiesence of a public official or other person acting in an official capacity'. As a result all defendants in torture cases will be state officials... [I]f the implementation of a torture regime is a public function giving rise to immunity ratione materiae, this produces bizarre results.... Under the Convention the international crime of torture can only be committed by an official or someone in an official capacity. They would all be entitled to immunity. It would follow that there can be no case outside Chile in which a successful prosecution for torture can be brought unless the State of Chile is prepared to waive its right to its officials immunity. Therefore the whole elaborate structure of universal jurisdiction over torture committed by officials is rendered abortive and one of the main objectives of the Torture Convention—to provide a system under which there is no safe haven for torturers—will have been frustrated. In my judgment all these factors together demonstrate that the notion of continued immunity for ex-heads of state is inconsistent with the provisions of the Torture Convention.[36]

This reasoning is consistent with the International Court of Justice's holding in *Belgium v Senegal* that states parties to the Convention Against Torture have an obligation to prosecute suspected torturers, including former foreign officials, or to extradite them to face trial, because the object and purpose of the Convention Against Torture is to 'to make more effective the struggle against torture by avoiding impunity for the perpetrators of such acts'.[37]

In countries where the political branches are charged with initiating criminal proceedings, foreign relations considerations may influence the decision whether or not to pursue charges against individuals who acted under color of foreign law. For

[35] Owen Bowcott, 'Tzipi Livni Spared War Crime Arrest Threat' *The Guardian* (6 October 2011) <http://www.guardian.co.uk/world/2011/oct/06/tzipi-livni-war-crime-arrest-threat> accessed 17 February 2013. The United Kingdom subsequently modified its procedures for issuing privately-sought arrest warrants for universal jurisdiction offences. See Police Reform and Social Responsibility Act 2011, c 13 s 153(1) ('Where a person who is not a public prosecutor lays an information before a justice of the peace in respect of an offence to which this subsection applies, no warrant shall be issued under this section without the consent of the Director of Public Prosecutions').

[36] *Ex p Pinochet* (n 4) (Lord Browne-Wilkinson).

[37] *Questions Relating to the Obligation to Prosecute or Extradite (Belgium v Senegal)* 120.

example, the Paris Prosecutor declined to initiate criminal proceedings for torture against former US Secretary of Defense Donald Rumsfeld when Rumsfeld visited France.[38] The prosecutor explained that the French Ministry of Foreign Affairs held the view that customary international law required giving Rumsfeld immunity for acts performed in the exercise of his functions as secretary of defence.[39] By contrast, in *United States v Belfast*, a US court of appeals found that Chuckie Taylor, who lived under various aliases, was not immune from prosecution for torture committed in Liberia while his father was President. More recently, the Swiss Federal Criminal Court declined to follow the advice of the Swiss Directorate of Public International Law in the Federal Department of Foreign Affairs and denied immunity *ratione materiae* to a former Algerian Minister of Defense for war crimes committed during the Algerian civil war in a criminal case initiated by a private party.[40]

Courts may emphasize the presence, or absence, of a link between the forum state and the alleged conduct in determining whether to exercise jurisdiction or to recognize an immunity defense. For example, a UK court denied immunity from extradition to Khurts Bat, the Head of the Executive Office of the National Security Council of Mongolia.[41] Khurts was wanted in Germany for allegedly abducting a Mongolian national in France and imprisoning and drugging him in a basement flat in Berlin before forcibly sending him to Mongolia. The European Arrest Warrant issued for Khurts indicated that the kidnapping operation was authorized by the Mongolian Security Agencies.[42] Khurts sought to claim *ratione personae* immunity from the United Kingdom's jurisdiction under customary international law, either as a member of a special mission or as a high-ranking civil servant.

The court found that Khurts was not entitled to special mission immunity because the Foreign and Commonwealth Office had not consented to his visit as a special mission.[43] The court also found that, based on his job description and authority, Khurts was not within the 'narrow circle' of officials such as heads of state who are automatically entitled to *ratione personae* immunity.[44] With respect to *ratione materiae* immunity, which Khurts raised as a defense at the eleventh hour, the court adopted the conclusion of British solicitor Elizabeth Franey that 'State officials do not have immunity *ratione materiae* for criminal charges in respect of

[38] Letter from Jean-Claude Marin to Maître Patrick Baudouin (16 November 2007) <http://www.fidh.org/IMG/pdf/reponseproc23nov07.pdf> accessed 17 February 2013.

[39] Letter from Jean-Claude Marin (n 38). German authorities declined to prosecute Rumsfeld for torture that occurred in the Abu Ghraib prison in Iraq, on the grounds that German law does not permit the exercise of criminal jurisdiction in the absence of a 'domestic linkage' to Germany. See Order of the Prosecutor General at the Federal Supreme Court re Criminal Complaint against Donald Rumsfeld et al (5 April 2007) 3 ARP 156/06-2, 8 <http://ccrjustice.org/files/ProsecutorsDecision.pdf> accessed 17 February 2013 (English translation).

[40] *A v Ministère Public de la Confédération*.

[41] *Bat v The Investigation Judge of the German Federal Court*.

[42] *Bat* (n 41) 3.

[43] *Bat* (n 41) 24.

[44] *Bat* (n 41) 61.

acts committed on the territory of the Forum State, or the territory of a third State'.[45] This view is consistent with the approach to *ratione materiae* taken by the criminal court in Milan that sentenced 23 US CIA agents for their role in the abduction and rendition from Italy to Egypt of the Muslim cleric Abu Omar.[46]

4.2 Immunity from civil proceedings

The 2004 United Nations Convention on Jurisdictional Immunities of States and Their Property, which is not yet in force, defines the term 'state' to include 'representatives of the State acting in that capacity'.[47] This definition reflects the reality that states can only act through individuals. Most agree that claimants should not be able to circumvent state immunity simply by naming an individual official as the defendant in a civil suit. (States themselves are not generally subject to criminal prosecution, and the UN Convention does not apply to criminal proceedings.[48]) Some take the position that, as a result, individuals must enjoy civil immunity in national courts for all acts they perform on behalf of foreign states. Others agree that if the claimant seeks to obtain a judgment from the state's assets, rather than the individual's assets, then the state should be treated as the 'real party in interest'. However, under this view, if only the individual's assets are sought, then conduct-based immunity will not necessarily bar civil suits against individual officials who bear personal responsibility for the claimant's injuries.

Many of the cases invoked as precedents to support a more expansive version of individual civil immunity involve situations in which the individual does not bear personal responsibility, such as for commercial transactions entered into on behalf of the state.[49] In an early case, French consul-general Joseph Létombe signed several bills of exchange on behalf of the French Republic to France's purchasing

[45] *Bat* (n 41) [91], quoting Elizabeth H Franey, *Immunity, Individuals, and International Law: Which Individuals Are Immune from the Jurisdiction of National Courts under International Law* (Academic Publishing 2011) 284. Khurts was extradited to Germany in August 2011, but he was released from German custody less than two months later, on the eve of an official visit by German Chancellor Angela Merkel to Mongolia. Georg Bönisch and Sven Röbel 'Mongolian Murder Mystery: Release of Alleged Spy Angers German Investigators' (*Spiegel Online*, 12 October 2011) <http://www.spiegel.de/international/world/mongolian-murder-mystery-release-of-alleged-spy-angers-german-investigators-a-791009.html> accessed 17 February 2013. For an empirical analysis of the role of politics in universal jurisdiction prosecutions, see Máximo Langer, 'The Diplomacy of Universal Jurisdiction: The Political Branches and the Transnational Prosecution of International Crimes' (2011) 105 *AJIL* 1.

[46] *Adler et al.* See Micaela Frulli, 'Some Reflections on the Functional Immunity of State Officials' (2010) 19 *Ital YB Int'l L* 91.

[47] Convention on Jurisdictional Immunities.

[48] See UNGA Res 59/38 (16 December 2004) UN Doc A/RES/59/38.

[49] See generally Chimène I Keitner, 'Annotated Brief of Professors of Public International Law and Comparative Law as Amici Curiae in Support of Respondents' (2011) 15 *Lewis & Clark L Rev* 609, 622–30.

agent in the United States. In 1797, when France failed to pay the bills, their holder sued Létombe for the money owed. The Supreme Court found that 'there was no cause of action' against Létombe because 'the contract was made on account of the [French] government'.[50] Lady Hazel Fox has observed that, in similar suits for commercial transactions, a court cannot exercise jurisdiction over a foreign official not because the official is immune—there being no applicable immunity for this type of transaction—but because the law attributes responsibility to the state and not to the official.[51] Despite this distinction between jurisdictional immunity and the absence of a cause of action, some have reasoned that the inability to pursue a claim against an individual official in the commercial context supports claims to conduct-based immunity for any act that is attributable to the state.

Using the criterion of attribution as a touchstone for conduct-based immunity leads to a broad view of immunity, because in most instances involving action by state officials—including ultra vires action—the state itself will bear responsibility as a matter of international law.[52] This does not mean that the individual cannot also bear personal responsibility as a matter of both national and international law.[53] Nevertheless, in some jurisdictions, the concern with 'impleading' the state has led to a more expansive view of civil immunity, even with regard to actions for which individuals would be denied immunity from foreign or international criminal prosecution.

The expansive view of civil immunity is exemplified by the UK House of Lords' reasoning in *Jones v Saudi Arabia*, which has been followed by courts in Canada, Australia, and New Zealand.[54] In that case, Ronald Jones sought leave from an English court to serve a Saudi official outside the United Kingdom in a suit for torture inflicted upon him in Saudi Arabia.[55] The House of Lords found that the official enjoyed immunity

[50] *Jones v Le Tombe* 385. Not all courts have followed this approach. For example, in *Saorstat and Continental Steamship Co v Rafael de las Morenas*, the Supreme Court of Ireland found that a colonel in the Spanish army who had contracted to carry horses from Dublin to Lisbon for use by the Spanish army was not entitled to immunity, because '[h]e is sued in his personal capacity and the judgment which has been, or any judgment which may hereafter be, obtained against him will bind merely the appellant personally, and any such judgment cannot be enforced against any property save that of the appellant' (98).

[51] Hazel Fox, 'Imputability and Immunity as Separate Concepts: The Removal of Immunity from Civil Proceedings Relating to the Commission of an International Crime' in Kaiyan Homi Kaikobad and Michael Bohlander (eds), *International Law and Power: Perspectives on Legal Order and Justice* (Brill 2009) 172–73.

[52] See Draft Articles on Responsibility of States for Internationally Wrongful Acts, with Commentaries, Art 7, reprinted in ILC, 'Report of the International Law Commission on the Work of Its 53d Session' (23 April–1 June and 2 July–10 August 2001) UN Doc A/56/10.

[53] The Draft Articles state explicitly that the attribution of an individual's actions to the state for the purposes of state responsibility is 'without prejudice to any question of the individual responsibility under international law of any person acting on behalf of a State'. Draft Articles on Responsibility of States (n 52) Art 58.

[54] *Kazemi v Islamic Republic of Iran*, s 138; *Zhang v Zemin*, s 68; *Fang v Jiang*.

[55] *Jones v Ministry of the Interior of the Kingdom of Saudi Arabia*, para 2 (appeal taken from England).

ratione materiae because any other approach would enable claimants to circumvent the state's immunity for its non-commercial acts. Lord Hoffman distinguished the reasoning in *Jones* from the reasoning in *Pinochet*:

> It would be strange to say...that the torture ordered by General Pinochet was attributable to him personally for the purposes of criminal liability but only to the state of Chile for the purposes of civil liability. It would be clearer to say that the Torture Convention withdrew the immunity against criminal prosecution but did not affect the immunity for civil liability.[56]

Lord Phillips, who had participated in the House of Lords' decision in *Pinochet*, disagreed, joining the Court of Appeal's holding in *Jones* that Colonel Abdul Aziz did not enjoy immunity for torture. In his view, 'Once the conclusion is reached that torture cannot be treated as the exercise of a state function so as to attract immunity ratione materiae in criminal proceedings against individuals, it seems to me that it cannot logically be so treated in civil proceedings against individuals'.[57] Notwithstanding this compelling argument, the majority of the House of Lords found that the UK State Immunity Act, which does not apply to criminal proceedings, bars civil proceedings against individual officials for official acts including torture.

Like the claimants in *Al-Adsani v Kuwait*, Ronald Jones argued that the application of the UK SIA to prevent a civil suit against Saudi Arabia and its officials for torture violated his right of access to a court under the European Convention on Human Rights. The House of Lords rejected this argument. In so doing, it embraced the argument that acts for which a state bears responsibility under international law are shielded by immunity *ratione materiae* from adjudication in foreign courts, even when the named defendant is an individual official.[58]

Reports prepared by Special Rapporteur Roman Kolodkin under the auspices of the International Law Commission reflect this expansive view, even with respect to immunity from criminal prosecution.[59] This approach has sparked significant debate.[60] A resolution of the *Institut de droit international*, espousing a narrower approach to immunity *ratione materiae*, recommends the denial of conduct-based immunity for international crimes for which there exists universal jurisdiction in

[56] *Jones v Ministry of the Interior* (n 55) para 68 (Lord Hoffman).

[57] *Jones v Ministry of the Interior of Saudi Arabia* (Court of Appeal), para 127 (Lord Phillips).

[58] An application to the European Court of Human Rights challenging this conclusion was pending at the time of writing.

[59] See eg ILC, 'Second Report on Immunity of State Officials from Foreign Criminal Jurisdiction' (10 June 2010) UN Doc A/CN.4/631, para 24 (by Roman Anatolevich Kolodkin, Special Rapporteur on the Immunity of State Officials from Foreign Criminal Jurisdiction) ('The Special Rapporteur considers it right to use the criterion of the attribution to the State of the conduct of an official in order to determine whether the official has immunity *ratione materiae* and the scope of such immunity').

[60] ILC, 'Report on the Work of Its Sixty-Third Session' (26 April–3 June and 4 July–12 August 2011) UN Doc A/66/10 and A/66/10/Add.1.

treaty and custom.[61] While the debate continues, it seems likely that the lack of agreement on absolute immunity has given some former officials pause in planning foreign travel.

The US FSIA, unlike the UK SIA, does not prevent civil suits from proceeding against individual officials for alleged human rights violations.[62] As a doctrinal matter, the Executive branch has consistently taken the position that individual immunities fall outside the scope of the FSIA. For example, in *Matar v Dichter*, plaintiffs filed a civil suit against the former Director of Israel's General Security Service for injuries caused by a military strike on an apartment building in Gaza that resulted in multiple civilian casualties. The Executive branch took the position that, although the FSIA did not apply, '[a]llowing foreign officials to be sued in US courts for their official conduct would depart from customary international law, aggravate our relations with the foreign states involved, and potentially expose our own officials to similar suits abroad'.[63] In *Yousuf v Samantar*, plaintiffs filed suit against the former Prime Minister of Somalia, who now resides in the United States, for torture and other human rights violations committed in Somalia while he was a high-ranking government official there. Samantar claimed immunity. The Executive branch ultimately took the position that Samantar was not entitled to immunity even though he committed the alleged wrongdoing in the exercise of his official authority, and the trial and appellate courts agreed.[64]

In the *Samantar* litigation, the Supreme Court held decisively that the individual immunities foreign officials may enjoy in US courts are governed by the common law, not the Foreign Sovereign Immunities Act.[65] The Executive branch currently claims the authority to determine on a case-by-case basis whether or not a particular current or former foreign official is immune from suit on either *ratione personae* or *ratione materiae* grounds, taking into account a variety of factors.[66] The case-by-case nature

[61] The Institute of International Law, 'Resolution on the Immunity from Jurisdiction of the State and of Persons Who Act on Behalf of the State in Case of International Crimes' (2009) <http://www.idi-iil.org/idiE/resolutionsE/2009_naples_01_en.pdf> accessed 17 February 2013.

[62] For example, in *In re Estate of Marcos Human Rights Litigation*, the court found that the defendant did not benefit from immunity under the FSIA, because she 'has admitted acting on her own authority, not on the authority of the Republic of the Philippines', and the acts complained of were not 'public acts of the sovereign' (498, fn 10).

[63] Brief for the United States of America as Amicus Curiae in Support of Affirmance, *Matar v Dichter*.

[64] See Brief of the United States as Amicus Curiae Supporting Appellees, *Yousuf v Samantar* (2011).

[65] *Samantar v Yousuf*.

[66] For example, in *Doe v Zedillo*, the Executive Branch suggested immunity for former Mexican President Ernesto Zedillo, who now lives in New Haven, Connecticut, for allegations relating to 'lower level officials' tortious conduct' in carrying out a 1997 massacre of civilians in Acetal, Mexico. Contributions to the debate about the immunity regime in US courts post-*Samantar* include: John B Bellinger III, 'The Dog that Caught the Car: Observations on the Past, Present, and Future Approaches of the Office of the Legal Adviser to Official Acts Immunities' (2011) 44 *Vand J Transnat'l L* 819; Chimène I Keitner, 'Foreign Official Immunity After *Samantar*' (2011) 44 *Vand J Transnat'l L* 843; Harold Hongju

of immunity determinations under the current US State Department regime raises the question of the relationship between such determinations and customary international law. The State Department has indicated that, in making individual immunity determinations, it will take into account relevant principles of customary international law.[67] That said, doubts have been raised about the value of US practice as also providing evidence of *opinio juris* absent clearer statements about the role of customary international law in immunity determinations by authoritative decision-makers, including the Executive branch and US courts.[68]

5. Claims against Non-State Actors

Claims for human rights violations have also been brought against non-state actors. The precedent for claims against private actors in US courts is *Kadic v Karadzic*, an opinion by the Second Circuit Court of Appeals. The appeals court found that certain international law violations do not require state action, and that the state action requirement for other violations was satisfied by the fact that Karadzic acted on behalf of the republic of Srpska.[69] Karadzic was not, however, entitled to status-based immunity, either as a head of state or as an 'invitee' of the United Nations. The court also opined that the act of state doctrine, which prevents a court from invalidating the official acts of a foreign government within its own territory, would not bar adjudication of plaintiffs' claims in a US court: 'we doubt that the acts of even a state official, taken in violation of a nation's fundamental law and wholly unratified by that nation's government, could properly be characterized as an act of state'.[70]

Private corporations have also faced claims in US courts for complicity in human rights violations.[71] In 2012, the US Supreme Court considered two challenges to

Koh, 'Foreign Official Immunity After *Samantar*: A United States Government Perspective' (2011) 44 *Vand J Transnat'l L* 1141; Beth Stephens, 'Abusing the Authority of the State: Denying Foreign Official Immunity for Egregious Human Rights Abuses' (2011) 44 *Vand J Transnat'l L* 1163; Ingrid Wuerth, 'Foreign Official Immunity Determinations in US Courts: The Case Against the State Department' (2011) 51 *Va J Int'l L* 915.

[67] Brief for the United States as Amicus Curiae Supporting Affirmance, *Yousuf v Samantar* (2010).

[68] See Lori Fisler Damrosch, 'Changing the International Law of Sovereign Immunity Through National Decisions' (2011) 44 *Vand J Transnat'l L* 1185, 1188. A trial court in Quebec declined to follow the approach in *Samantar* and held that the Canadian SIA, unlike the US FSIA, provides *ratione materiae* immunity for individual officials. *Kazemi v Republic of Iran*, paras 132–133.

[69] *Kadic v Karadzic* 237. [70] *Kadic* (n 69) 250.

[71] On civil claims for aiding and abetting international law violations, see Chimène I Keitner, 'Conceptualizing Complicity in Alien Tort Cases' (2008) 60 *Hastings LJ* 61, and sources cited therein.

cases against private corporations: first, the challenge that corporations are not subjects of international law and thus cannot be held liable for aiding and abetting international law violations; and second, that US courts lack subject-matter jurisdiction over human rights violations that occur in other countries, even if they possess personal jurisdiction over a particular defendant. The second objection is the most salient for this chapter.

In *Kiobel v Royal Dutch Petroleum*, plaintiffs alleged that the defendant, acting through a Nigerian subsidiary, aided and abetted the Nigerian government's violent suppression of protests against oil exploration and development activities, including the execution in 1995 of the 'Ogoni Nine'. During oral argument at the US Supreme Court, Justice Anthony Kennedy raised a concern about the legitimacy of exercising 'universal civil jurisdiction over alleged extraterritorial human rights abuses to which the [forum] nation has no connection'.[72] The Supreme Court was concerned enough about this issue to order briefing and argument on the specific question of '[w]hether and under what circumstances the Alien Tort Statute, 28 USC §1350, allows courts to recognize a cause of action for violations of the law of nations occurring within the territory of a sovereign other than the United States'.[73] Although the United States is not unique in providing a forum for adjudicating claims for international law violations arising outside the territory of the forum state, US practice in this area has certainly been more extensive to date than that of other countries.[74] Five justices voted in *Kiobel* to rein in this practice by requiring that, in order for claims arising in a foreign country to proceed under the Alien Tort Statute, such claims must 'touch and concern the territory of the United States... with sufficient force to displace the presumption against extraterritorial application' of US statutes.

The debate over the legitimacy of exercising jurisdiction over extraterritorial human rights violations turns in part on the question of whether national courts are exercising prescriptive jurisdiction (that is, prescribing rules of conduct to apply to non-citizens abroad), or adjudicatory jurisdiction, with the substantive rules provided by either international law (which applies everywhere) or the law of the

[72] Transcript of Oral Argument, *Kiobel v Royal Dutch Petroleum Co et al* <http://www.supremecourt.gov/oral_arguments/argument_transcripts/10-1491.pdf> accessed 17 February 2013.

[73] *Kiobel v Royal Dutch Petroleum Co et al*, Order for Reargument (5 March 2012), <http://www.supremecourt.gov/orders/courtorders/030512zr.pdf> accessed 17 February 2013.

[74] As US Supreme Court Justice Breyer noted in his concurrence in *Sosa v Alvarez-Machain*, 'the criminal courts of many nations combine civil and criminal proceedings, allowing those injured by criminal conduct to be represented, and to recover damages, in the criminal proceeding itself... Thus, universal criminal jurisdiction necessarily contemplates a significant degree of civil tort recovery as well'. *Sosa* (n 2) 762–63. Judges Higgins, Kooijmans, and Buergenthal noted in their joint separate opinion in the *Arrest Warrant* case that, as of 2002, the United States' exercise of extraterritorial jurisdiction under the Alien Tort Statute 'has not attracted the approbation of States generally', but they also noted that '[t]he movement is towards bases of jurisdiction other than territoriality'. *Arrest Warrant* (n 26) Joint Separate Opinion, paras 47–48.

country where the acts occurred. The application of foreign law is fairly uncontroversial. The application of international law generates concern to the extent that its content might be perceived as indeterminate; hence the jurisdictional requirement in the United States that rules of customary international law must be concrete, specific, and universal in order to provide a basis for federal court jurisdiction.[75] As a matter of domestic law generally, legislatures may enact statutes that apply extraterritorially, and do so in a variety of contexts.[76] Legal proceedings initiated pursuant to these statutes may, however, spark diplomatic protests. This is especially likely when legal proceedings challenge conduct that was performed under color of foreign law, or when they pose an indirect challenge to conduct by a foreign state, for example by alleging that a private defendant aided and abetted an unlawful state policy.

Courts may increasingly require a link between the litigation and the forum state in order to adjudicate claims on the merits, especially with respect to multinational defendants such as corporations. This would be consistent with the policies underlying doctrines such as *forum non conveniens* and the exhaustion of local remedies, where such remedies exist. For example, the Canadian Supreme Court recently declined to review a decision by the Quebec Court of Appeal denying jurisdiction over claims against Anvil Mining for aiding and abetting human rights violations by the Congolese army.[77] Future cases will determine whether arguments that a Canadian court constitutes a 'forum of necessity' provides a sufficient basis for exercising jurisdiction in the absence of a 'real and substantial' link between the forum and the dispute.

6. Conclusions

The horizontal enforcement of human rights norms by national courts carries the potential for both salutary and disruptive effects. On the salutary side, it can provide an avenue for victims of human rights abuses to obtain redress for their injuries; it

75 *Sosa* (n 2) 731–32.

76 US examples in the human rights context include: Torture Victim Protection Act, 28 USC § 135 (2006); Genocide Accountability Act, Pub L No 110-151, 121 Stat 1821 (current version at 18 USC § 1091(e) (Supp IV 2006)); Torture Convention Implementation Act, 18 USC §§ 2340–2340(B) (2006); War Crimes Act, 18 USC § 2441 (2006); Child Soldiers Accountability Act, 18 USC § 2442 (Supp III 2006).

77 'Congolese Victims Pursuit of Justice against Canadian Company Goes to Supreme Court' (*Canadian Centre for International Justice*, 26 March 2012) <http://www.ccij.ca/media/news-releases/2012/index.php?DOC_INST=3> accessed 17 February 2013.

can help deny safe haven to human rights abusers; it can contribute to the articulation and entrenchment of binding human rights norms designed to promote human dignity; and it can reach defendants who might otherwise escape consequences for their actions, thereby forcing them to internalize the costs of non-compliance. On the disruptive side, it can interfere with the conduct of foreign relations with states that do not recognize the validity of national proceedings; it can subject defendants to uncertainty in the face of divergent accountability regimes; and it can compete with governmental attempts to resolve claims arising from the same set of facts. The potential for interference with the conduct of foreign relations is the most troubling. State immunity for acts *jure imperii*, and *ratione personae* immunity for heads of state and diplomatic officials, go a long way towards preventing this result. A purely territorially-based jurisdictional regime, and an expansive approach to *ratione materiae* immunity, would further reduce the possibility of disruption—but at the cost of reducing or eliminating many potential benefits of transnational human rights litigation. Such litigation, within limits, can perform an important role in articulating, diffusing, and enforcing international human rights norms.

Further Reading

Akande D and Shah S, 'Immunities of State Officials, International Crimes, and Foreign Domestic Courts' (2010) 21 *EJIL* 815

van Alebeek R, *The Immunity of States and their Officials in International Criminal Law and International Human Rights Law* (OUP 2008)

Bradley CA and Helfer LR, 'International Law and the US Common Law of Foreign Official Immunity' [2010] *Sup Ct Rev* 213

Caplan LM, 'State Immunity, Human Rights, and *Jus Cogens*: A Critique of the Normative Hierarchy Theory' (2003) 97 *AJIL* 741

Fox H, *The Law of State Immunity* (2nd edn, OUP 2008)

—— 'Imputability and Immunity as Separate Concepts: The Removal of Immunity from Civil Proceedings Relating to the Commission of an International Crime' in Kaikobad KH and Bohlander M (eds), *International Law and Power: Perspectives on Legal Order and Justice* (2009) 163–82

Higgins R, 'Certain Unresolved Aspects of the Law of State Immunity' (1982) 29 *NILR* 265

Keitner CI, 'Foreign Official Immunity and the "Baseline" Problem' (2011) 80 *Fordham L Rev* 605

—— 'The Forgotten History of Foreign Official Immunity' (2012) 87 *NYU L Rev* 704

Lauterpacht H, 'The Problem of Jurisdictional Immunities of Foreign States' (1951) 28 *Brit YB Int'l L* 220

McGregor L, 'Torture and State Immunity: Deflecting Impunity, Distorting Sovereignty' (2007) 18 *EJIL* 903

Orakhelashvili A, 'State Immunity in National and International Law: Three Recent Decisions of the European Court of Human Rights' (2002) 15 *LJIL* 703

Stephens B, 'The Modern Common Law of Foreign Official Immunity' (2011) 79 *Fordham L Rev* 2669

—— and others, *International Human Rights Litigation in US Courts* (2nd edn, Brill 2008)

Stewart DP, 'The Immunity of State Officials under the UN Convention on Jurisdictional Immunities of States and Their Property' (2011) 44 *Vand J Transnat'l L* 1047

Watts A, 'The Legal Position in International Law of Heads of States, Head of Governments and Foreign Ministers' (1995) 247 *RCADI* 1

Wright J, 'Retribution But No Recompense: A Critique of the Torturer's Immunity from Civil Suit' (2010) 30 *OJLS* 143

CHAPTER 34

THE USE OF INTERNATIONAL FORCE TO PREVENT OR HALT ATROCITIES: FROM HUMANITARIAN INTERVENTION TO THE RESPONSIBILITY TO PROTECT

RAMESH THAKUR

1. Introduction

NORMS are generally accepted standards of appropriate conduct, deviations from which are enforced by such social mechanisms as peer pressure, shaming, and ostracism. Laws are rules of behaviour enacted through accepted legislative processes and, at the domestic level, which the police and judicial authorities of the state enforce. The emergence of the international human rights norm has contributed to changes in the nature of state sovereignty, but in many instances there remains a dramatic discrepancy between commitments on paper and actual improvements in human rights conditions, producing tension between personal rights and the workings of the interstate system. So, while the human rights norm, including international humanitarian law (IHL), is ever more firmly established in international law, actual protections come under continual stress in state practice.[1]

The debate over when and how force may be used, including in defence of human rights or to protect against humanitarian atrocities, lies at the intersection of law, politics, and norms. The use and non-use of force alike have empirical consequences, shape the struggle for power, and help to determine the outcome of political contests. Under what circumstances, if ever, is the use of force by outsiders, without the consent of host governments, both lawful and legitimate, in order to provide effective international humanitarian protection to populations at apprehended risk of or being killed en masse?

The forum of choice for debating and deciding on collective action requiring the use of military force across borders and inside sovereign jurisdictions, is the United Nations (UN). Without consensus and clarity on this, the UN's performance will be measured against contradictory standards, exposing it to charges of ineffectiveness from some and irrelevance from others, increasing the probability of unauthorized interventions, and further eroding the UN's primacy in peace and security. This was evident from the controversies swirling around the UN corridors during the genocide in Rwanda in 1994, despite the presence of a frustrated and impotent UN peacekeeping force; the massacre of Muslims by Serbs, sheltering under the protection of shamefully passive UN peacekeepers in Srebrenica in 1995; the unilateral use of force by the North Atlantic Treaty Organization (NATO) in Kosovo in 1999; and the rampage of Indonesia-backed militias in violent protest at the pro-independence results of a UN-supervised plebiscite in East Timor in 1999. The controversies revived with the UN Security Council (UNSC)-authorized use of force to protect civilians in Libya and Côte d'Ivoire in 2011, and with the Chinese-Russian vetoes of draft resolutions for protecting civilians in Syria.

Rwanda's three-month genocide in 1994 that killed 800,000 people was a failure of political will, not of military capacity. In Kosovo in 1999, NATO took forceful action in the name of humanitarian intervention, but without UN authorization. In the aftermath of these controversies, Secretary-General Kofi Annan pushed for a new doctrine for taking forceful action against humanitarian atrocities. In 2001, the Canadian-sponsored, but independent, International Commission on Intervention and State Sovereignty (ICISS) formulated the innovative principle of

[1] See David P Forsythe, *Human Rights in International Relations* (3rd edn, CUP 2012).

the responsibility to protect (R2P).[2] Building on its report, in 2005 world leaders agreed unanimously that all states had the responsibility to protect people living in their territorial jurisdictions and that, where governments were manifestly failing in their sovereign duty, the international community, acting through the UN, would take 'timely and decisive' collective action to honour the international responsibility to protect people from atrocities.[3]

Thus R2P is the normative instrument of choice to convert a shocked international conscience into effective collective action. It navigates the treacherous shoals between the Scylla of callous indifference to the plight of victims and the Charybdis of self-righteous interference in others' internal affairs. R2P can be discussed as an analytical concept and studied with respect to its philosophical antecedents, theoretical coherence, and tensions and inconsistencies. Or it can be evaluated as a normative project that seeks to codify and shape international precepts and world order in order to realize the core UN mandate of a safer life for all peoples. As a third option, government and civil society organization criticisms of R2P for being overly permissive or, at the opposite end, much too restrictive, seek to highlight R2P's shortcomings and inadequacies as a policy template for triggering timely and effective international protective action.

This chapter is divided into four parts. The first locates humanitarian intervention in the context of the historical origins of sovereignty. The second section explains the reasons for the change to the less divisive terminology of the responsibility to protect, while the third sketches the progress of R2P from unanimous endorsement in 2005 to implementation in Libya in 2011. The final section, before concluding thoughts, calls for a global dialogue on how best to implement R2P.

2. 'Humanitarian Intervention' in a World of Sovereign States

Since the Treaty of Westphalia (1648), sovereignty has been the foundational principle of a world order resting on a system of states, as expressed in Article 2(1) of the Charter of the United Nations (UN Charter). Externally, sovereignty means the legal identity of the state in international law, an equality of status with all other states, and the claim to be the sole official agent acting in international relations on behalf of a society. The principle of non-intervention is the most important

[2] International Commission on Intervention and State Sovereignty Report, *The Responsibility to Protect* (International Development Research Centre (IDRC) for ICISS 2001).

[3] UNGA '2005 World Summit Outcome' (24 October 2005) UN Doc A/RES/60/1, paras 138–40.

embodiment of the notion that states are autonomous entities, and its ancestry, too, traces to Westphalia.[4]

Historically, sovereignty originated in the European search for a secular basis of state authority in the sixteenth and seventeenth centuries, and it postulated the sovereign as being above the law. While national sovereignty locates the state as the ultimate seat of power and authority, unconstrained by internal or external checks, constitutional sovereignty holds that the power and authority of the state are not absolute, but contingent and constrained, including internationally by globally legitimated institutions and practices. UN membership has been the final seal of sovereign statehood for newly independent countries. Article 2(7) of the Charter prohibits the UN from intervening in 'matters which are essentially within the domestic jurisdiction' of any member state.

Yet by the very fact of signing the Charter, a country accepts collective obligations and international scrutiny. The restrictions of Article 2(7) can be set aside when the UNSC decides to act under chapter seven's collective enforcement provision to meet threats to, or breaches of, international peace and security. The scope of what constitute such threats and breaches has widened to include such matters as HIV/AIDS, terrorism, and atrocity crimes. In any case, Article 2(7) is about matters 'essentially' within domestic jurisdiction, implying that the issue is subject to judgment, which may differ from one competent authority to another and may change over time. Moreover, the collapse of state authority, as in Somalia in the 1990s, means that there is no functioning government to fulfil an essential condition of sovereignty, on the one hand; and the violence, instability, and disorder can spill over from that failed state to others, on the other. This is why the UNSC dealt with Somalia under the coercive clauses of chapter seven, rather than the consensual chapter six.

In recent times, sovereignty has been reconceived as being instrumental. Its validation rests not in a mystical reification of the state, but in its utility as a tool for the state serving the interests of the citizens. Internal forms and precepts of governance must conform to international norms and standards of state conduct. That is, sovereignty must be exercised with due responsibility.[5]

2.1 The practice and theory of 'humanitarian intervention' until the 1990s

Traditional warfare is the use of force by rival armies of enemy states: us against them. Collective security rests on the use of force by the international community

[4] See Samuel Pefendorf, *De Jure Naturae et Gentium, Libri Octo* (first published 1688, CH Oldfather and WA Oldfather (trs), Clarendon Press 1934); Emerich de Vattel, *The Law of Nations or the Principles of Natural Law* (first published 1758, Charles G Fenwick (tr), Carnegie Press 1916).

[5] See Francis M Deng and others, *Sovereignty as Responsibility: Conflict Management in Africa* (Brookings Institution 1996).

to defeat or punish an aggressor nation: all against one. Peacekeeping involves the insertion of neutral and lightly armed third party soldiers as a physical buffer between combatants who have agreed to a ceasefire: us between enemies.[6]

'Humanitarian intervention' refers to the use of military force by outsiders for the protection of victims of atrocities: us between perpetrators and victims. It has a long, if not entirely distinguished, lineage. England, France, and Russia intervened in Greece in 1827 to stop massacres by Turkey, and France intervened again in Syria in 1860, to stop the killings of Maronite Christians. Various European powers also intervened in defence of Christians in Crete (1866–68), the Balkans (1875–78), and Macedonia (1903–08). Doctrine followed practice, with one analyst justifying humanitarian intervention as the use of force to protect victims of 'arbitrary and persistently abusive' treatment by their own governments.[7]

But in the growing anticolonial narrative after 1945, 'humanitarian intervention' was progressively discredited. The theory and practice of military intervention was circumscribed, also, by the gathering effort to put increasingly strict limits on the right of states to wage war as unilateral policy. The fetters of the Covenant of the League of Nations were reinforced normatively by the Kellogg-Brian Pact (1928), outlawing war, and which was followed by the proscriptions in the UN Charter on the use of force except for cases of self-defence or when the UNSC authorizes it.

The arguments against intervention hold up less easily on principle, that it violates sovereignty, than on pragmatism, that it can internationalize a local, morally ambiguous conflict, worsen the humanitarian plight of civilians, and camouflage ulterior commercial or geopolitical motives. Yet a decision not to intervene can have grave consequences too. The norm of non-intervention in the internal affairs of sovereign states in effect becomes a tyrant's licence to kill with impunity.

The supposed illegality of humanitarian intervention was neither uncontested in academic discourse,[8] nor abandoned in state practice. India sent troops into Bangladesh in 1971 to protect Bengalis from the murderous rampage of a military dictatorship in West Pakistan. In 1979, Tanzania intervened to overthrow Idi Amin in Uganda, and Vietnam sent troops into Cambodia to get rid of Pol Pot. Today, all three would be considered iconic cases of humanitarian intervention. But because

[6] See Ramesh Thakur and Albrecht Schnabel (eds), *United Nations Peacekeeping Operations: Ad Hoc Missions, Permanent Engagement* (United Nations UP 2001).

[7] Thomas G Weiss and Don Hubert, *The Responsibility to Protect: Research, Bibliography, Background* (IDRC for ICISS 2001) 17, quoting Ellery Stowell.

[8] See RJ Vincent, *Nonintervention and International Order* (Princeton UP 1974); Hedley Bull (ed), *Intervention in World Politics* (Clarendon Press 1984); Gene M Lyons and Michael Mastanduno (eds), *Beyond Westphalia? State Sovereignty and International Intervention* (Johns Hopkins UP 1995); Oliver Ramsbotham and Tom Woodhouse, *Humanitarian Intervention in Contemporary Conflict: A Reconceptualization* (Polity 1996); Fernando R Tesón, *Humanitarian Intervention: An Inquiry into Law and Morality* (2nd edn, Transnational 1997).

this was not an accepted doctrine, the actual justifications tended to be couched in the language of self-defence (the threat from regional instability the civil war raging in East Pakistan was causing in 1971) or demographic aggression (ten million refugees streaming into India).

The US has a long history of intervening in Latin America, essentially as within its sphere of influence, and in the Middle East, to effect regime change (Iran 1953, Lebanon 1958, Iraq 2003). Concerned with justifying the moral legitimacy of US support for insurgencies under certain circumstances, the Reagan doctrine rejected 'the inviolability of sovereignty'.[9] Yet some of the iconic events in Latin America—Cuba in the 1960s, Chile in the 1970s, and Nicaragua and Panama in the 1980s—show how difficult it is to pinpoint precisely what constitutes military intervention, let alone 'humanitarian' intervention.

In practice, the legitimacy of intervention often turned on the answer to four questions: who was the intervening *agent;* what was the *form* of intervention; who and how (il)legitimate was the *object* of intervention; and what was the motive or *goal* of intervention? The most immediately acceptable justification for intervention is the collectivist principle: it is not *why* intervention was undertaken, but *who* took the decision to intervene. Since 1945, the most widely accepted legitimator of international action has been the United Nations. But regional organizations might also be acceptable as authorizing agents for action within their area of jurisdiction—although there is always the risk of legitimizing the imperialism of the dominant power, as in Hungary in 1956 and Czechoslovakia in 1968.

The many examples of intervention in state practice throughout the twentieth century did not lead to an abandonment of the norm of non-intervention. Often the breaches provoked such fierce controversy and provided such little lasting benefit that their net effect was to reinforce the norm, not negate it. States have generally followed a restrictive view of the UN Charter's law on the use of force, with virtually every use of force since the Second World War being condemned or arousing strong controversy. In ruling against the US in the *Nicaragua* case[10] (1986), the International Court of Justice interpreted Article 2(4) broadly, to impose strict limits on the use of force, and Article 51 narrowly, to limit the use of force against another state to self-defence against armed attack from that state.

[9] Jeane J Kirkpatrick and Allan Gerson, 'The Reagan Doctrine, Human Rights, and International Law' in Louis Henkin and others (eds), *Right v Might: International Law and the Use of Force* (Council on Foreign Relations 1989) 21.

[10] *Military and Paramilitary Activities in and against Nicaragua (Nicaragua v United States).*

2.2 Changing world context and the emergence of new challenges

Under the impact of globalization, the total range of cross-border flows and activities has increased, while the proportion subject to control and regulation by the government has diminished. In today's seamless world, political frontiers have become less salient both for international organizations, whose rights and duties can extend beyond borders, and for states, whose responsibilities within borders can be subject to international scrutiny. The combined effect of these cumulative changes is to pose significant conceptual and policy challenges to the notion of state sovereignty.

The UN Charter contains an inherent tension between the intervention-proscribing principle of state sovereignty and the intervention-prescribing principle of human rights. Individuals became subjects of international law as bearers of duties and holders of rights under a growing corpus of human rights and international humanitarian law (IHL) treaties and conventions: the UN Charter, Universal Declaration of Human Rights, two covenants,[11] four Geneva Conventions, plus the two prohibiting torture and genocide, etc. At the same time, the cluster of norms inhibiting and prohibiting humanitarian intervention includes, alongside the norm of non-intervention, state sovereignty, domestic jurisdiction, pacific settlement of disputes, non-use of force, and impartiality.

In the decades after 1945, the nature of armed conflict transformed. Interstate warfare between uniformed armies gave way to irregular conflict between rival armed groups.[12] The nature of the state also changed from its idealized European version. Many communist and some newly decolonized countries were internal security states whose regimes ruled through terror. Increasingly, the principal victims of both types of violence were civilians. Advances in telecommunications brought the full horror of their plight into the world's living rooms. In the meantime, the goals of promoting human rights and democratic governance, protecting civilian victims of humanitarian atrocities, and punishing governmental perpetrators of mass crimes, became more important. The norm of non-intervention softened as that of human rights hardened.

All this presented the UN with a major difficulty: how to reconcile its foundational principle of member states' sovereignty with the primary mandate to maintain international peace and security, and the equally compelling mission to promote the interests and welfare of 'We the peoples of the United Nations'.[13] Annan

[11] International Covenant on Civil and Political Rights; International Covenant on Economic, Social and Cultural Rights.

[12] See Andrew Mack and others, *Human Security Report 2005: War and Peace in the 21st Century* (OUP 2005).

[13] UN Charter, preamble.

discussed the dilemma in the conceptual language of two notions of sovereignty, the one vesting in the state, the second in the people.[14]

3. From 'Humanitarian Intervention' to 'The Responsibility to Protect'

Going to war was once an acknowledged attribute of state sovereignty, and war was an accepted institution of the sovereign state's system, with distinctive rules, etiquette, norms, and stable patterns of practices.[15] Now there are significant restrictions on the authority of states to use force either domestically or internationally. Sovereignty is not static but has evolved over the centuries, and the use of force has been a central component in the historical evolution of the theory and practice of sovereignty. The state claimed, and was granted monopoly on, the legitimate use of domestic and international violence, in order to limit the excess of violence that had characterized pre-Westphalia anarchy. At the height of the Westphalian system, states considered it to be within their sovereign power to wage war on one another to protect nationals, co-religionists, and commercial interests; and to acquire colonies. The right to go to war was progressively anathematized in the twentieth century. The impact of the Holocaust also progressively curtailed the right to use violence internally. The expansion of permissive norms for the international community to use force within sovereign jurisdictions paralleled the increasing fetters placed on the right of states to use force within and across borders. While developing countries were the principal beneficiaries of the softening of the norms of sovereignty with regard to forcible conquest and colonization, they have also been the principal, but not exclusive, targets of the more recent softening norms of sovereignty with regard to the international scrutiny of excessive domestic violence within states.

After the Cold War, the proliferation of complex humanitarian emergencies, and the inappropriateness of the classical tenets of UN peacekeeping for dealing with them, dramatized the uneven impact of the neutrality of traditional peacekeeping on perpetrators and victims. In highlighting this, the Brahimi Report, in retrospect, was an important milestone on the road from humanitarian intervention to R2P.[16]

[14] Kofi A Annan, 'Two Concepts of Sovereignty' *The Economist* (18 September 1999) 49–50.

[15] See Kalevi J Holsti, *The State, War, and the State of War* (CUP 1996).

[16] UNGA/UNSC, 'Report of the Panel on United Nations Peace Operations' (21 August 2000) UN Doc A/55/305-S/2000/809, para 50.

It is easy to forget that the UN was never meant to be a pacifist organization. Its origins lie in the anti-Nazi wartime military alliance among Britain, the United States, and the Soviet Union. Its primary purpose is the maintenance of international peace and security. The UNSC is the world's one duly sworn-in sheriff for enforcing international law and order. In a number of cases in the 1990s, the UNSC endorsed the use of force, with the primary goal of humanitarian protection and assistance: in the (ineffectual) proclamation of UN safe areas in Bosnia, the delivery of humanitarian relief in Somalia, the restoration of the democratically elected government of Haiti, and the deployment of the multinational Kosovo Force.[17]

After the end of the Cold War, the UNSC experienced a spurt of enforcement activity to provide international relief and assistance to victims of large-scale atrocities from perpetrator or failing states, within civil war contexts.[18] A more activist UNSC engaged in de facto intervention in Iraq to protect the Kurds from Saddam Hussein's defeated regime, and Britain and the United States enforced a no-fly zone to protect the Kurdish minority in Northern Iraq throughout the 1990s, albeit with a questionable legal basis for their actions.[19] The international community explicitly recognized the conscience-shocking humanitarian catastrophes, from Liberia and the Balkans to Somalia, Kosovo, and East Timor, as threats to international peace and security requiring and justifying a forcible response by the international community. When the UNSC was unable to act due to a lack of enforcement capacity, it subcontracted the military operation to UN-authorized coalitions. And if it proved unwilling to act, sometimes groups of countries forged 'coalitions of the willing' to act anyway, even without UN authorization. Humanitarian crises in Somalia, Rwanda, Srebrenica, Kosovo, and East Timor, which revealed a dangerous gap in civilian protection mandates and capacities, and a sharp polarization of international opinion, ignited the debate on intervention, in particular.

3.1 Kosovo 1999

The first sustained questioning of the non-intervention norm came with NATO intervention in Kosovo.[20] An independent international commission concluded

[17] See Brian D Lepard, *Rethinking Humanitarian Intervention: A Fresh Legal Approach Based on Fundamental Ethical Principles in International Law and World Religions* (Pennsylvania State UP 2002) 7–23.

[18] Weiss and Hubert (n 7) 79–126.

[19] Washington and London grounded their declaration and enforcement of the no-fly zone on UNSC Res 688 (5 April 1991) UN Doc S/Res/688. But the resolution contains no obvious basis for such a claim and no relevant UN authority ever accepted it.

[20] See Albrecht Schnabel and Ramesh Thakur (eds), *Kosovo and the Challenge of Humanitarian Intervention: Selective Indignation, Collective Action, and International Citizenship* (United Nations UP 2000).

that, although NATO intervention was illegal, it was legitimate.[21] The crisis highlighted the need, in a world in which non-intervention is in practice impossible, for guidelines for determining the nature and gravity of threats that would justify external military intervention. Annan urged member states to come up with a new consensus on the 'challenge of humanitarian intervention'.[22] States 'bent on criminal behaviour', he declared, should know that frontiers are not an 'absolute defence'.[23] The response from the developing countries was that sovereignty was their final defence against the rules of an unjust world.[24] The Non-Aligned Movement—with 113 members, the most representative group of countries outside the UN—thrice rejected 'the so-called "right of humanitarian intervention" '.[25] Even American 'sovereigntists' launched three lines of counter-attack: the emerging international legal order is vague and illegitimately intrusive on domestic affairs; the international lawmaking process is unaccountable and the resulting law unenforceable; and Washington can opt out of international regimes, including those governing the use of force, as a matter of power, legal right, and constitutional duty.[26]

3.2 The International Commission on Intervention and State Sovereignty (ICISS)

ICISS adapted Deng's argument of sovereignty as responsibility and replaced the simple and familiar phrase 'humanitarian intervention' with the responsibility to protect.[27] Both the intergovernmental and non-governmental humanitarian actors

[21] Independent International Commission on Kosovo, *Kosovo Report: Conflict, International Response, Lessons Learned* (OUP 2000). Other works that can be traced to the debate launched in the aftermath of the Kosovo crisis include: Kofi A Annan, *The Question of Intervention: Statements by the Secretary-General* (UN Department of Public Information 1999); Danish Institute of International Affairs, *Humanitarian Intervention: Legal and Political Aspects* (Danish Institute of International Affairs 1999); Alton Frye, *Humanitarian Intervention: Crafting a Workable Doctrine* (Council on Foreign Relations 2000); *Humanitarian Intervention* (Advisory Council on International Affairs 2000).

[22] Kofi A Annan, *Facing the Humanitarian Challenge: Towards a Culture of Prevention* (UN Department of Public Information 1999). See also Nicholas Wheeler, *Saving Strangers: Humanitarian Intervention in International Society* (OUP 2000); Simon Chesterman, *Just War or Just Peace? Humanitarian Intervention and International Law* (OUP 2001).

[23] Kofi Annan, 'Annual Report to General Assembly' reprinted in UNGA Press Release (20 September 1999) UN Doc GA/9596.

[24] Weiss and Hubert (n 7) 7.

[25] Weiss and Hubert (n 7) 162. See also Philip Nel, 'South Africa: The Demand for Legitimate Multilateralism' in Schnabel and Thakur, *Kosovo* (n 20) 245–59.

[26] Peter J Spiro, 'The New Sovereigntists: American Exceptionalism and Its False Prophets' (2000) 79 *Foreign Aff* 9.

[27] See; Ramesh Thakur, *The United Nations, Peace and Security: From Collective Security to the Responsibility to Protect* (CUP 2006); Thomas G Weiss, *Humanitarian Intervention: Ideas in Action* (Polity 2007); Gareth Evans, *The Responsibility to Protect: Ending Mass Atrocities Once and For All* (Brookings Institution 2008); Alex J Bellamy, *Responsibility to Protect* (Polity 2009).

had complained that 'humanitarian intervention' was as much of an oxymoron as 'humanitarian bombing' (which is, indeed, what the NATO intervention in Kosovo was). In many non-Western minds, it conjures up historical memories of the strong imposing their will on the weak in the name of the prevailing universal principles of the day, from the civilizing mission of spreading Christianity to the cultivation and promotion of human rights. It focuses attention on the claims, rights, and prerogatives of the states that would potentially intervene, much more so than on the urgent needs of the putative beneficiaries of the action. The phrase is used to trump sovereignty with intervention at the outset of the debate, by labelling and delegitimizing dissent as anti-humanitarian.

By contrast, the 'responsibility to protect' implies an evaluation of the issues from the point of view of those seeking or needing support and acknowledges that the primary responsibility to protect rests with the state concerned. Only if the state is unable or unwilling to fulfil this responsibility, or is itself the perpetrator, does it become the responsibility of others to act in its place. Thus, R2P is more of a linking concept that bridges the divide between intervention and sovereignty, whereas the language of the right or duty to intervene is inherently more confrontational. R2P also incorporates the 'responsibility to prevent', the 'responsibility to react', and the 'responsibility to follow up'. It provides conceptual, normative, and operational linkages between assistance, intervention, and reconstruction. Moreover, the goal of protective intervention is not to wage war on a state in order to destroy it and eliminate its statehood, but instead to always protect victims of atrocities inside the state, to embed the protection in reconstituted institutions after the intervention, and then to withdraw all foreign troops.

Based on state practice, UNSC precedent, established and emerging norms, and evolving customary international law, ICISS held that the proscription against intervention is not absolute. The foundations of the international responsibility to protect lay in obligations inherent in the concept of sovereignty; the responsibility of the Council, under Article 24 of the UN Charter, for the maintenance of international peace and security; specific legal obligations under human rights and human protection declarations, covenants, and treaties; IHL and national law; and the developing practice of states, regional organizations, and the Council itself. The UN Charter is itself an example of an international obligation that member states voluntarily accepted. In granting UN membership, the international community welcomes the signatory state as a responsible member of the community of nations. Equally, however, by signing the Charter, the state accepts the responsibilities of membership flowing from that signature.

Even when there is agreement that military intervention may sometimes be necessary and unavoidable to protect innocent people from life-threatening danger by interposing an outside force between actual and apprehended victims and perpetrators, key questions remain about agency, lawfulness, and legitimacy. ICISS argued that the UN is the principal institution for building, consolidating, and using the authority of the international community, and it is particularly important that every effort be made to encourage the Council to exercise—and not abdicate—its responsibilities.

Annan's High-Level Panel reaffirmed the importance of changing the discourse from the deeply divisive 'humanitarian intervention' to the more reassuring 'responsibility to protect'. It endorsed the ICISS argument that 'the issue is not the "right to intervene" of any State, but the "responsibility to protect" of *every* State'.[28] It proposed five criteria of legitimacy: seriousness of threat, proper purpose, last resort, proportional means, and balance of consequences. Annan urged the UNSC to adopt a resolution 'setting out these principles and expressing its intention to be guided by them' when authorizing the use of force.[29] This would 'add transparency to its deliberations and make its decisions more likely to be respected, by both Governments and world public opinion'.[30]

At the 2005 UN world summit in New York, the agreed Outcome Document contained all UN members' clear, unambiguous acceptance of individual state responsibility to protect populations. In addition, member states declared they

> are prepared to take collective action, in timely and decisive manner, through the Security Council…and in cooperation with relevant regional organizations as appropriate, should peaceful means be inadequate and national authorities are manifestly failing to protect their populations.[31]

But they dropped the legitimacy criteria—which would simultaneously have made the UNSC more responsive to outbreaks of humanitarian atrocities and have made it more difficult for individual states and 'coalitions of the willing' to appropriate the language of humanitarianism for unilateral interventions.

3.3 From principle in 2005 to actionable norm in 2011

Thus R2P speaks eloquently to the need to change the UN's normative framework in line with the changed reality of threats and victims.[32] It attempts to strike a balance between unilateral interference, rooted in the arrogance of power, and institutionalized indifference, which dislocates the 'Other' from the 'Self'. It does not address the distribution of jurisdiction and authority among states, but between states and international actors. While it preserves to states the responsibility to protect their own populations, it strengthens the UN's responsibility for the international community as a whole, and in doing so 'represents one of the most significant

[28] UNGA 'Report of the High-Level Panel on Threats, Challenges and Change' (2 December 2004) UN Doc A/59/565, para 201, emphasis in original.

[29] UNGA 'In Larger Freedom: Towards Development, Security and Human Rights for All: Report of the Secretary-General' (21 March 2005) UN Doc A/59/2005, para 126.

[30] UNGA 'In Larger Freedom' (n 29) para 126.

[31] UNGA 'World Summit Outcome' (n 3) para 139.

[32] See Thakur, *The United Nations, Peace and Security* (n 27).

normative shifts in international relations since the creation of the UN in 1945'.[33] R2P was designed to help better prepare the world—normatively, organizationally and operationally—to meet the recurrent challenge of external military intervention wherever and whenever it arose again. To interveners, R2P offers the prospect of international legitimacy, reduced compliance and transaction costs, and more effective results. To potential targets of intervention, R2P offers the reassurance of a rules-based system, absent which there will be nothing to stop the powerful from intervening anywhere and everywhere.

R2P is narrow—it applies only to the four specified atrocity crimes—but deep; there exist no limits to what can be done when responding to these atrocity crimes. Far from hollowing out R2P as outlined by ICISS, the tweaking in 2005 added clarity, rigor, and specificity, limiting the triggering events to war crimes, genocide, ethnic cleansing, and crimes against humanity. Norms frame identities, interpretations, and behaviour. By realigning the emerging global norm of protection to existing international law on atrocity crimes, the 2005 formulation enhanced the prospect of the R2P principle becoming a norm robust enough to shape international behaviour.

There have been fairly tangible conceptual and political advances in R2P from 2001 to 2005 and again in 2011. Ban Ki-moon, Annan's successor as UN chief, identified himself closely with R2P, appointed a special adviser to develop and refine the principle, and articulated an agenda to convert R2P from promise to practice, from words to deeds. Ban's three special reports on R2P since 2009 have sustained and consolidated a new international consensus on the inherently controversial and contentious subject.[34] The world's comfort level is greater with action under Pillar One (building state capacity) and Pillar Two (international assistance to build state capacity) than Pillar Three (coercive international action, with the final option being military intervention).

Civil society organizations have promoted a vigorous process of R2P norm socialization and crystallization. The UN General Assembly's annual debates in 2009 to 2011 on Ban's three reports helped to forge a shared understanding of R2P, to distinguish it from humanitarian intervention and align it with building capacity to help states exercise their sovereignty more effectively. The debates showed the consensus that R2P is broadening, its legitimacy is strengthening, and most states more concerned with moving on to questions of implementation:[35] not if, but how. Although

[33] Anne Orford, *International Authority and the Responsibility to Protect* (CUP 2011) 41.

[34] UNGA 'Implementing the Responsibility to Protect: Report of the Secretary-General' (12 January 2009) UN Doc A/63/677; UNGA 'Early Warning, Assessment, and the Responsibility to Protect: Report of the Secretary-General' (14 July 2010) UN Doc A/64/864; UNGA/UNSC 'The Role of Regional and Sub-Regional Arrangements in Implementing the Responsibility to Protect: Report of the Secretary-General' (18 June 2011) UN Doc A/65/877-S/2011/393.

[35] Mónica Serrano, 'The Responsibility to Protect and Its Critics: Explaining the Consensus' (2011) 3 *Global Responsibility to Protect* 425.

R2P has not as yet been integrated and mainstreamed into a broader UN system, the widespread initial institutional resistance to it has abated and 'been replaced by a general willingness to explore how an atrocity-prevention perspective could help inform a wide range of UN operational activities'.[36]

Both the strengths and limitations of R2P as a politically powerful, but not legally robust, norm that circumscribes the internal use of force by states against people and permits but does not obligate the international use of force under UN-authorization against states ignoring the prohibition on internal atrocities, can be seen in the handling of the Darfur crisis.[37] On the one hand, R2P was an influential mobilizing pull on the world's conscience, which triggered UN activism when addressing the plight of the affected populations and alleviating their humanitarian suffering, and which led to the deployment of peacekeepers with more robust civilian protection mandates, the imposition of economic sanctions, and international criminal justice prosecution. On the other hand, it did not save strangers in peril. Given the logistical and other practical difficulties in using force against the Sudanese government, and the likely damaging consequences for humanitarian relief operations and the fragile peace process, Gareth Evans argues that, 'the failure has been in the application of other measures, not the non-application of coercive force'.[38]

3.4 International interventions and UN executive authority

Because R2P authorizes but does not mandate particular types of executive action, legal scholars believe that R2P imposes no new obligations on states or international organizations; 'it has no normative effect' and 'introduces no conceptual innovation'.[39] Anne Orford disagrees. Most political scientists are likely to share her judgment that R2P is a permissive and enabling, but not an obligating, new norm that confers authority, without imposing binding new duties.

Orford turns Ban's understanding on its head, arguing that R2P processed UN post-1945 deeds into words. In the period of decolonization after the Second World War, as European empires crumbled and retreated, the UN steadily expanded the range of executive actions it undertook, to fill actual or anticipated power vacuums in many newly-independent countries. Clearly articulated forms or bases of authority did not always accompany these 'practices of governing'. Instead, it fell to

[36] Edward C Luck, 'The Responsibility to Protect: The First Decade' (2011) 3 *Global Responsibility to Protect* 387, 391.

[37] See Nicholas J Wheeler, 'A Victory for Common Humanity? The Responsibility to Protect After the 2005 World Summit' (2005) 2 *JILIR* 95; Roberto Belloni, 'The Tragedy in Darfur and the Limits of the "Responsibility to Protect"' (2006) 5 *Ethnopolitics* 327; Alex de Waal, 'Darfur and the Failure of the Responsibility to Protect' (2007) 83 *Int'l Aff* 1039.

[38] Evans (n 27) 61. [39] Orford (n 33) 25.

ICISS to provide 'a detailed normative articulation' of the 'international authority to undertake executive action for protective ends'.[40] R2P is an effort to integrate existing and evolving, but dispersed, practices of protection, into a conceptually coherent account of international authority.

Secretary-General Dag Hammarskjöld justified a special and rapidly growing role for the UN based on its neutrality, impartiality, and technical competence. The UN's expansive responses to the more complex humanitarian emergencies after the Cold War could no longer contain the tensions inherent in his broadening conception and practice of UN executive action, kept dormant by the genius of his personality and diplomatic skills. The public setbacks and flaws of UN actions in Somalia, Rwanda, the Balkans, and East Timor raised questions about the organization's authority, credibility, and legitimacy with pressing urgency. According to Orford, ICISS stepped into the normative breach to provide the theoretical justification for the accumulated body of practices that Hammarskjöld bequeathed.

Just as Hammarskjöld's notions of preventive diplomacy and peacekeeping were meant to avert great power intervention by inserting the UN as a neutral presence, so R2P came about in opposition to efforts to justify interventions by non-UN coalitions of the willing, led by powerful states. It is a deliberate substitute for imperial visions and governance practices. Hammarskjöld's refusal to confront the reality of the collapse of state authority in Congo meant that he stubbornly resisted answering a fundamental question. If the UN was intervening with force, whose law and whose authority would it be upholding, if not its own? The logic of Hammarskjöld's conception and legacy of practices with respect to UN executive action culminated at the turn of the twentieth century in international administrations in the Balkans and East Timor.

As David Kennedy argues, 'The effort to intervene... without affecting the background distribution of power and wealth betrays this bizarre belief in the possibility of an international governance which does not govern'.[41] Orford makes the same argument, that international interventions, far from being above worldly interests and ideologies, can determine the winner among the rival claimants to authority.[42] Informed by a new global managerialism, international authority reaches deep into domestic jurisdictions to rearrange relations between the state, rulers, and people, with reference to external normative benchmarks.

The third component of the ICISS version of R2P, the responsibility to rebuild, at last tries to come to grips with this question. Hammarskjöld had preferred to operate with 'a very broad mandate... guided by a minimalist set of principles'.[43] He

[40] Orford (n 33) 1.

[41] David Kennedy, *The Dark Sides of Virtue: Reassessing International Humanitarianism* (Princeton UP 2004) 130.

[42] Orford (n 33) 195.

[43] Orford (n 33) 87.

had the skills and also the structural conditions to be able to exploit the margins and use equivocation 'in the service of virtue', as his aide, Conor Cruise O'Brien, put it.[44] In the more complex environment and challenges of the 1990s, this was no longer sustainable, and R2P steps into the breach to provide the necessary principled underpinnings.

3.5 Libya 2011

R2P thus channels selective moral indignation into collective policy remedies to prevent and stop atrocities. By its very nature including unpredictability, unintended consequences, and the risk to innocent civilians caught in the crossfire, warfare is inherently brutal; there is nothing humanitarian about the means. But, to be meaningful, the R2P spectrum of action must include military force as the option of last resort (conceptually, not sequentially). Both the potential mobilizing power and the limitations of R2P as a call to international arms were demonstrated in Libya in 2011. The Libyan experience also confirms that the debate on military interventions cannot avoid questions of regime legitimacy, state capacity, and state-building.

In poignant testament to its tragic origins and normative power, R2P was the discourse of choice in debating how best to respond to the Libya crisis in 2011, and the UNSC invoked R2P under the coercive chapter seven of the Charter for the first time.[45] The UNSC, Human Rights Council, Secretary-General Ban, and the Secretary-General's special advisers on genocide prevention and R2P, called on Libya to respect its R2P, human rights, and IHL obligations.[46] When their appeals were ignored, the UNSC passed Resolution 1970 on February 26, demanding an end to the violence in Libya, which 'may amount to crimes against humanity'; imposed sanctions; affirmed Libya's R2P obligations; and referred Gaddafi to the International Criminal Court.[47] When this failed to moderate Gaddafi's assaults on his people, UNSC Resolution 1973, adopted on March 17 by a 10-0-5 (China, Russia,

[44] Orford (n 33) 88.

[45] For a range of diverse opinions and perspectives on R2P and Libya, see e-International Relations (ed), *The Responsibility to Protect: Challenges and Opportunities in Light of the Libyan Intervention* (e-International Relations 2011) <http://www.e-ir.info/wp-content/uploads/R2P.pdf> accessed 25 November 2012.

[46] UNSC 'Press Statement on Libya' (22 February 2011) UN Doc SC/10180-AFR/2120; 'Ban strongly Condemns Qadhafi's Actions against Protesters, Calls for Punishment' (*UN News Centre*, 23 February 2011) <http://www.un.org/apps/news/story.asp?NewsID=37599> accessed 25 November 2012; 'Documents, Publications, Statements' (*Office of the Special Adviser on the Prevention of Genocide*) <http://www.un.org/en/preventgenocide/adviser/statements.shtml> accessed 25 November 2012.

[47] UNSC Res 1970 (26 February 2011) UN Doc S/RES/1970.

Brazil, Germany, India) vote, authorized the use of 'all necessary measures... to protect civilians and civilian populated areas'.[48] In the Balkans, it took NATO almost the full decade to intervene with air power in Kosovo in 1999. In Libya, it took just one month to mobilize a broad coalition, secure a UN mandate to protect civilians, establish and enforce no-kill zones, stop Gaddafi's advancing army, and prevent a massacre of the innocents in Benghazi.

Although Britain and France took the lead in mobilizing diplomatic support for military action to protect the rebels, the critical turning point was US backing. The key decision was made by President Barack Obama at a meeting with top officials on March 15.[49] The game-changer was the juxtaposition of R2P as a powerful new galvanizing norm; the defection of Libyan diplomats who joined the chorus of calls from the rebels for immediate action to protect civilians; and Arab, French, and British participation that provided political cover and international legitimacy.

3.6 Norm consolidation

By year's end, Gaddafi had been ousted, captured, and killed. The Libyan people's euphoria and NATO's relief over the successful military campaign tempered criticisms of the manner in which NATO over-interpreted UN authorization to protect civilians. Yet in early 2012, sporadic gun battles were still breaking out in Tripoli between rival militias, prompting Mustafa Abdul Jalil, the head of Libya's interim government, to warn of the danger of a descent into civil war.[50] There were inconsistencies in the muted international response to protests and uprisings in Bahrain and Saudi Arabia, where vital Western geopolitical and oil interests are directly engaged, and with the lack of equally forceful military action in Syria and Yemen. Western reticence in defending the dignity and rights of Palestinians under Israeli occupation has been especially damaging to claims to promote human rights and oppose humanitarian atrocities universally, instead of selectively.

[48] UNSC Res 1973 (17 March 2011) UN Doc S/Res/1973, Art 4.

[49] Helene Cooper and Steven Lee Myers, 'Obama Takes Hard Line with Libya after Shift by Clinton' *The New York Times* (Washington, 18 March 2011) <http://www.nytimes.com/2011/03/19/world/africa/19policy.html?pagewanted=all> accessed 21 November 2012.

[50] Kim Sengupta, 'Libya's Leader Warns of Civil War after Tripoli Gun Battles' *The Independent* (London, 5 January 2012) <http://www.independent.co.uk/news/world/africa/libyas-leader-warns-of-civil-war-after-tripoli-gun-battles-6285034.html>; Peter Beaumont, 'One Year On: Chaotic Libya Reveals the Perils of Humanitarian Intervention' *The Observer* (19 February 2012) <http://www.guardian.co.uk/commentisfree/2012/feb/19/peter-beaumont-libya-intervention-gaddafi> accessed 21 November 2012.

Despite the doubts, the alternative of standing idly on the sidelines yet again would have added to the shamefully long list of rejecting the collective responsibility to protect. Gaddafi would have prevailed and embarked on a methodical killing spree. The outcome was thus a triumph for R2P; it *is* possible for the international community, working through the authenticated, UN-centered structures and procedures of organized multilateralism, to deploy international forces to neutralize the military might of a thug and intervene between him and his victims.

But with the capture and killing of Gaddafi, hard questions, unasked so as not to complicate the push for victory, have come to the forefront. Who are the rebels? What do they stand for? For whom do they speak? How much popular support do they command? How committed are they to eschewing rule by terror? In insisting that Sharia would be the main reference point for the new Libya's legal framework, the National Transitional Council was telling its own people, the region, and the world, that it did not foresee being a mere puppet of the West. The obeisance to a moderate form of political Islam appeases Muslim pressures and buttresses domestic and regional legitimacy, by drawing on traditional and religious wellsprings of legitimacy, while signalling a deliberate distancing from the West.

In a January 18, 2012, speech to a conference to honour ICISS on the tenth anniversary of the R2P report, Ban noted that historically, the international community's 'chief failing…has been the reluctance to act in the face of serious threats', not too much intervention.[51] The price has been the loss of far too many lives and an erosion of UN credibility. In Ban's view, Libya in 2011 'demonstrated that human protection is a defining purpose of the United Nations'.[52] But, 'the execution of our collective responsibilities was not always perfect', and some innocent lives were lost in the name of R2P.[53] During the day-long discussions,[54] there was a striking depth of consensus in support of R2P principles among state representatives, UN officials, and other policy and civil society actors. There is a broadly shared understanding of the responsibilities. Yet, there was also deep disquiet among many participants, and outright distrust among some about how far UN authorization for the Libyan operation had been stretched.

[51] Ban Ki-moon, 'Address to Stanley Foundation Conference on the Responsibility to Protect' (*UN News Centre*, 18 January 2012) <http://www.un.org/apps/news/infocus/sgspeeches/statments_full.asp?statID=1433> accessed 25 November 2012.

[52] Ban, 'Address to Stanley Foundation Conference' (n 51).

[53] Ban, 'Address to Stanley Foundation Conference' (n 51).

[54] I was a participant in the event.

4. The Need for a Global Dialogue on R2P Implementation

Albeit qualified and incomplete, therefore, Libya marks an important milestone on the journey to tame atrocities that tyrants commit against their own people. But, inevitably, the first UN-authorized military intervention under R2P Pillar Three also showed flaws and imperfections in the machinery of implementation that will need to be addressed.

Carefully crafted both to authorize and delimit the scope of intervention, Resolution 1973 specified the purpose of military action as humanitarian protection and limited the means to that goal. It proscribed intervention in cases of civil war (any state has the right to use force to suppress armed uprisings), regime change, and foreign occupation of Libya. NATO ignored the restrictions to target Gaddafi directly in a transparent effort at regime change, spurned hints of any willingness on the part of the Gaddafi regime to negotiate a ceasefire, intervened in the internal civil war, and broke the UN's arms embargo by supplying weaponry to the rebels. NATO airstrikes greatly reduced, but did not totally eliminate, civilian casualties.[55] By the time Gaddafi was captured and killed, up to 30,000 civilians may have died in the war.[56] An independent report by a Middle Eastern human rights group concluded that all participants, including NATO, committed war crimes and human rights violations.[57]

If the 1973 restrictions had been respected, the civil war and the international intervention could well have been longer, more protracted, and messier, and could have prolonged the misery for everyone concerned. Thus, ignoring these restrictions may well have been justified, according to the logic of military necessity and efficiency. The US, British, and French leaders noted that, although the goal of military action was 'not to remove Qaddafi by force…it is impossible to imagine a future for Libya with Qaddafi in power'.[58] But the insistence by some NATO powers

[55] CJ Chivers and Eric Schmitt, 'In Strikes on Libya by NATO, An Unspoken Civilian Toll' *The New York Times* (Tripoli, 17 December 2011) <http://www.nytimes.com/2011/12/18/world/africa/scores-of-unintended-casualties-in-nato-war-in-libya.html?pagewanted=all> accessed 21 November 2012.

[56] Karin Laub, 'Libyan Estimate: At Least 30,000 Died in the War' *The Guardian* (Tripoli, 8 September 2011) <http://www.guardian.co.uk/world/feedarticle/9835879> accessed 21 November 2012.

[57] Rachel Shabi, 'Nato Accused of War Crimes in Libya' *The Independent* (19 January 2012) <http://www.independent.co.uk/news/world/africa/nato-accused-of-war-crimes-in-libya-6291566.html> accessed 21 November 2012.

[58] Barack Obama, David Cameron, and Nicolas Sarkozy, 'Libya's Pathway to Peace' *The New York Times* (14 April 2011) <http://www.nytimes.com/2011/04/15/opinion/15iht-edlibya15.html> accessed 21 November 2012.

that they fully adhered to the UN-authorized 'all necessary measures' to protect civilians and civilian-populated areas, is not credible.

4.1 A false north–south dichotomy

R2P is not and ought not to be a North–South issue. Many non-Western societies have a historical tradition of reciprocal rights and obligations that bind sovereigns and subjects. India's Emperor Ashoka (269–232 BC) proclaimed that 'this is my rule: government by the law, administration according to the law, gratification of my subjects under the law, and protection through the law'.[59] By contrast, the theory and practice of sovereignty is decidedly European in origin and flavor.

During the extensive 2001 ICISS outreach consultations in Asia, Africa, and Latin America, several reasons were expressed for the hesitations and doubts about 'humanitarian intervention'.[60] The word 'humanitarian' should never be associated with war. Although humanitarianism is good, interventionism is bad, and 'humanitarian intervention' is tantamount to marrying evil to good. In such a shotgun marriage, far from humanitarianism burnishing meddlesome interventions, interventionism will tarnish humanitarianism itself. The use of force for moral reasons is dangerous and counter-productive in its practical effects. On the one hand, it can encourage warring parties inside a country to be rigid and irresponsible in the hope of internationalizing the conflict.[61] On the other hand, it can facilitate interventions by those exploiting the cloak of legality for their own purposes. Both can provoke or prolong large-scale killings.

There is also an inherent conceptual incoherence. The individualistic conception of human rights in Western discourse is somehow transformed into collective rights (the protection of groups of people), at the same time as the collective rights of the entire nation are denied legitimacy. Moreover, critics said, the inconsistent practice, double standards, and sporadic nature of Western powers' interest in human rights protection, shows that noble principles are convenient cloaks for hegemonic interests.

With respect to the agency for lawful authorization, there was notable consensus around the world on the central role of the UN. There was also general agreement that interventions cannot become the pretext for imposing external political preferences with regard to regimes and political and economic systems. Consequently,

[59] Quoted in Stanley Wolpert, *A New History of India* (OUP 1977) 66–67.

[60] This is a very brief summary of Thakur, *The United Nations, Peace and Security* (n 27) ch 12 ('Developing Countries and the Eroding Nonintervention Norm'). See also Rama Mani and Thomas G Weiss (eds), *Responsibility to Protect: Cultural Perspectives in the Global South* (Routledge 2011).

[61] For a discussion of the moral hazard argument, see Belloni (n 37); Alan J Kuperman, 'The Moral Hazard of Humanitarian Intervention: Lessons from the Balkans' (2008) 52 *Int'l Studies Q* 49.

intervening forces must withdraw as soon as possible; considerations of political impartiality and neutrality between the domestic political contenders, as well as strict fidelity to IHL, must rigidly guide their actions while inside the target country; and, above all, they must respect and ensure the territorial integrity of the target state. It is important that interventions result from the explicit authority of a mandated multilateral organization and be linked to a political strategy that allows for a strategic engagement with the country subject to intervention.

After 2005, the most representative indication of developing country opinions came in the 23–28 July 2009, General Assembly debate on R2P, when about two-thirds of the speakers were from the global South.[62] Almost all reaffirmed the 2005 consensus, expressed opposition to any effort to reopen it, and insisted that its scope be restricted to the four crimes of genocide, crimes against humanity, war crimes, and ethnic cleansing. Most supported the Secretary-General's three pillar strategy. Several expressed reservations about selectivity and double standards in the implementation of R2P and criticism of past UNSC failures to act, with some urging voluntary self-restraint in the use of the veto when faced with atrocity crimes. Most affirmed that should other measures not be adequate, timely and decisive coercive action, including the use of force, is warranted to save lives.

4.2 Syria 2012

Syrians paid the price of NATO excesses in Libya.[63] Possible courses of action in Syria could not be contemplated without acknowledging that the crisis was also about relations with Iran, Russia, and China. Moreover, the caution required for a Western invasion of yet another Muslim country is deepened when the odds of success are low and the odds of unintended-cum-perverse consequences in attacking a more formidable enemy in a more volatile strategic environment, are good.

UN estimates put the number killed in Syria's yearlong crackdown on protestors at over five thousand by January 2012. The Arab and Western countries introduced draft UNSC resolutions in October 2011 and then again in February and July 2012, calling for an end to the flow of arms into Syria, the yielding of key powers of Syria's President Bashar al-Assad to a deputy, a government of national unity, and preparations for free presidential and parliamentary elections. In the UNSC debate on 4 October 2011, Russia explicitly said that the situation in Syria had to be considered

[62] For an examination of Southern perspectives on the subject since 2001, see Ramesh Thakur, *The Responsibility to Protect: Norms, Laws and the Use of Force in International Politics* (Routledge 2011) ch 10.

[63] See Joshua Foust, 'Syria and the Pernicious Consequences of our Libya Intervention' *The Atlantic* (6 February 2012) <http://www.theatlantic.com/international/archive/2012/02/syria-and-the-pernicious-consequences-of-our-libya-intervention/252631> accessed 21 November 2012.

in the light of the Libyan experience, where the UNSC mandate had been badly abused. China and Russia remained adamantly opposed to UNSC authorization of any international action without host state consent and cast a double veto on the draft UNSC resolutions on Syria.

Russian officials warned that such a resolution would put Syria on the path to civil war; that the UNSC was not in the business of imposing the parameters of an internal political settlement on member states and of dictating to them who should stay in power and who must go; that opposition groups, too, had to be condemned for perpetrating violence (the moral hazard argument) and be exhorted to engage constructively with the government;[64] and that the only solution to the Syrian crisis was through an inclusive, Syrian-led process to address the legitimate aspirations of the people, in an environment free of violence and human rights abuses. Analysts explained the Russian policy by pointing to Russian arms sales to Syria, the reopening of a Russian naval supply base at Tartus, fears of a loss of international credibility if an ally was abandoned under pressure from abroad, and a sense of frustration and humiliation at how Resolution 1973 in Libya was abused to effect regime change in Libya.[65] Moscow was firmly opposed to any UNSC resolution that could set in motion a sequence of events leading to a 1973-type authorization for outside military operations in Syria.

A Chinese ambassador explained that the February 2012 draft resolution would inflame, not calm, the situation; that it did not facilitate a political dialogue, nor address the distrust among the parties; and that, therefore, it amounted to a rash decision and not a sustainable solution that would bring peace and stability to Syria and the region.[66] While Ambassador Liu Xiaoming emphasized that China had used the veto a total of eight times in its forty-one years of membership on the UNSC,

[64] This ignored the November 2011 report of the UN Human Rights Council (HRC)-appointed independent commission of the significant asymmetry of responsibility for the violence in Syria, UNHRC 'Report of the Independent International Commission on the Syrian Arab Republic' (23 November 2011) UN Doc A/HRC/S-17/2/Add.1.

[65] Colum Lynch and Will Englund, 'Clinton, Diplomats Urge Russia to Allow Security Council Vote on Syria' *The Washington Post* (UN, 31 January 2012) <http://www.washingtonpost.com/world/national-security/clinton-other-diplomats-to-urge-russia-to-allow-security-council-vote-on-syria/2012/01/31/gIQA4axafQ_story.html> accessed 21 November 2012; Fyodor Lukyanov, 'Why Does Russia's Stance on Syria Baffle Everyone?' (*Russia in Global Affairs*, 23 February 2012) <http://eng.globalaffairs.ru/redcol/Why-Does-Russias-Stance-on-Syria-Baffle-Everyone-15478> accessed 21 November 2012.

[66] Liu Xiaoming, 'China Believes Syria Needs a Peaceful Solution' *The Guardian* (9 February 2012) <http://www.guardian.co.uk/commentisfree/2012/feb/09/china-syria-veto-un-resolution> accessed 21 November 2012. For support by an Indian analyst for the China-Russia suspicion that the draft resolution was a ruse to use human rights as the pretext for the real goal of regime change, see AG Noorani, 'Syria Needs Diplomacy, Not Intervention' (*The Hindu*, 7 February 2012) <http://www.thehindu.com/opinion/lead/article2866489.ece> accessed 21 November 2012.

a prominent Lebanese columnist noted that Washington had cast vetoes forty-two times since 1972 (roughly the same period) to shield Israel.[67]

The Arabs then introduced a resolution in the General Assembly where, it was passed by a 137-12 majority vote, with 17 abstentions, on 16 February 2012. The overwhelming margin of victory was an embarrassing measure of China's and Russia's isolation from world opinion.

4.3 Responsibility while protecting: bringing back legitimacy criteria

Still, the debate on how best to operationalize R2P requires a respectful conversation among proponents and skeptics over when, how, and by whom to execute the international responsibility to protect. The consensus on R2P in ICISS in 2001, and at the UN in and since 2005, resulted from a genuine dialogue within the Commission, during an extensive outreach and consultation exercise that ICISS undertook in 2001 with pan-regional interlocutors in every continent, and in successive rounds of intensive consultations across the UN membership since 2005. The global South's comfort level with R2P grew steadily as they studied the principle closely and recognized that all legitimate concerns had been incorporated. Had R2P merely repackaged the Western humanitarian warriors' wishes and brushed aside the sensitivities of the formerly colonized, it never would have gained the rapid uptake and traction that culminated in unanimous endorsement by world leaders in 2005. Ban's three reports sustained and consolidated a new global consensus on an inherently controversial and contentious subject. The leading NATO powers, instead of being disdainful and disrespectful of the critics—including Germany as well as Brazil, China, India, South Africa, and many others—of *how* R2P was implemented in Libya, should listen, acknowledge, and accommodate legitimate concerns.

This is desirable in principle. It is also required as a matter of pragmatism as the world order is rebalanced militarily, economically, geopolitically, and morally, with power and influence shifting from the North to the South. Gaps in expectation, communication, and accountability between those who mandated the operation and those who executed it, damaged the R2P consensus underpinning Resolution 1973. Brazil offered a paper on 'Responsibility while Protecting', with the potential to bring in some agreed-upon parameters on the conditions that will govern the use of UN-authorized R2P operations.[68] Its two key elements are the formulation of an agreed-upon set of

[67] Rami G Khouri, '42 Reasons to Dismiss Susan Rice's Rage' *The Daily Star* (11 February 2012) <http://www.dailystar.com.lb/Opinion/Columnist/2012/Feb-11/162875-42-reasons-to-dismiss-susan-rices-rage.ashx> accessed 21 November 2012.

[68] UNGA/UNSC 'Responsibility while Protecting: Elements for the Development and Promotion of a Concept' (11 November 2011) UN Doc A/66/551–S/2011/701.

criteria, or guidelines, to help the UNSC in the debate preceding the authorization of an R2P military intervention, and a monitoring or review mechanism to ensure that the Council has an oversight role over the operation during implementation.

As exemplified in the Brazilian initiative, the critics should engage with R2P and seek to improve the means and manner of implementing the norm. This way, the Southern players will become joint and responsible stakeholders in the emerging new world order. As long as the rising new powers remain more concerned with consolidating their national power aspirations than developing the norms and institutions of global governance,[69] they will remain incomplete powers, limited by their own narrow ambitions, with their material grasp longer than their normative reach. When the crunch came, the African Union (AU) prioritized state security over human security in Libya. The progressive agenda of promoting democracy, human rights, and good governance, as well as economic development, needs to be taken 'much more seriously within the AU system than has been the case thus far'.[70] This will have to include instruments for monitoring behaviour and promoting the compliance of member states. The reason this matters is that, following the Libya precedent, regional organizations may well acquire a critical 'gatekeeping role' in the global authorization of R2P-type operations.[71]

5. Conclusion

The human rights movement grew as an effort to curb arbitrary excesses by states against the liberties and rights of their own citizens. IHL emerged as an effort to place limits on the behaviour of belligerent forces during armed conflict. The convergence of the interests of human rights and humanitarian communities, with respect to protecting victims of atrocity crimes, is, from one point of view, a logical extension of their original impulses. From another point of view, it produces the paradox of humanitarianism—'an endless struggle to contain war in the name of civilization'[72]—encouraging, even demanding, the use of force.

[69] See Amitav Acharya, 'Can Asia Lead? Power Ambitions and Global Governance in the Twenty-first Century' (2011) 87 *Int'l Aff* 851.

[70] Solomon A Dersso, 'North Africa: Lessons from Uprisings for 2012 as the AU's Year of "Shared Values"' *Institute for Security Studies Weekly* (20 January 2012) 1.

[71] Alex J Bellamy and Paul D Williams, 'The New Politics of Protection? Côte d'Ivoire, Libya and the Responsibility to Protect' (2011) 87 *Int'l Aff* 825.

[72] Kennedy (n 41) 323.

> [The] transformation of human rights inverts the concept, from one premised on the protection of people from the violence of states to one justifying the application of violence by the world's most powerful states against weaker ones. With this transformation, human rights betrays its own premises and thus becomes its own travesty[.][73]

The template of robust 'humanitarian intervention' and foreign-led 'regime change', developed in Kosovo in 1999, proved too rusty for the task in Iraq in 2003. The Iraq War drove home the lesson that an appreciation of the limits of power, a concern for international institution-building, and sensitivity to the law of perverse consequences, must temper the sense of moral outrage that humanitarian atrocities provoke.[74]

The collision of different Charter norms that produced the heated and tense debates over 'humanitarian intervention' reflected a growing erosion of the sense of community among the different members of the family of nations. What values constitute a global society of states? How, and by whom, are the relative values of individual dignity and communitarian rights to be prioritized and enforced? These are questions that divide more than unite the 'international community' almost seven decades after the UN Charter seemingly settled them. As well as strongly held beliefs in contrary directions, states and peoples no longer share a common belief in the means and procedures by which to mediate and reconcile their differences.

This suggests that the response of states—whether individually, in groups, or collectively through the UN—will continue to be ad hoc and on a case-by-case basis, rather than principled and consistent.[75] Those with the capacity and engaged interests might be sufficiently motivated to mobilize external sentiment in support of interventions to protect victims of atrocities inside supposedly sovereign states. Acceptance of the responsibility to protect norm no more guarantees international intervention than its non-existence had foreclosed it as a tool of individual and collective statecraft. But, by shaping the calculation of a balance of interests,[76] the norm makes it modestly more, rather than less, likely that victims will not be callously abandoned.

Above all, the Libyan example shows that success in an R2P intervention is no more self-guaranteeing than in any other type of external intervention. Good intentions are not a magical formula by which to shape good outcomes in foreign lands. On the contrary, there is no humanitarian crisis so grave that an outside military

[73] Robert M Hayden, 'Biased Justice: "Humanrightism" and the International Criminal Tribunal for the Former Yugoslavia' in Raju GC Thomas (ed), *Yugoslavia Unraveled: Sovereignty, Self-determination, Intervention* (Lexington Books 2003) 280.

[74] See Ramesh Thakur and Waheguru Pal Singh Sidhu (eds), *The Iraq Crisis and World Order: Structural, Institutional and Normative Challenges* (United Nations UP 2006).

[75] See Lori Fisler Damrosch, 'The Inevitability of Selective Response? Principles to Guide Urgent International Action' in Schnabel and Thakur, in *Kosovo* (n 20) 405–19.

[76] See Ramesh Thakur, 'A Balance of Interests' in Andrew F Cooper, Jorge Heine, and Ramesh Thakur (eds), *The Oxford Handbook of Modern Diplomacy* (OUP 2013).

intervention cannot make it worse. Although no intervention will mean grave harm in some cases, fewer interventions may do less good, but will also do less harm. The guiding motto, therefore, should be: first do less harm.[77]

In the continuing evolution and development of R2P, both as a standard of state conduct and as a policy template to guide the international community's engagement with outbreaks of atrocities inside sovereign jurisdictions, the UNSC will take on the role of implementing R2P, while the General Assembly assumes the role of refining the concept and building political understanding and support for the norm. Both tasks will require partnerships among global, regional, and national governmental and NGO actors. It will also be necessary to convince non-state actors and armed groups that R2P applies to them, as well.

Further Reading

Bellamy AJ, *The Responsibility to Protect* (Polity 2009)

Evans G, *The Responsibility to Protect: Ending Mass Atrocities Once and For All* (Brookings Institution 2008)

Orford A, *International Authority and the Responsibility to Protect* (CUP 2011)

Thakur R, *The United Nations, Peace and Security: From Collective Security to the Responsibility to Protect* (CUP 2006)

—— *The Responsibility to Protect: Norms, Laws and the Use of Force in International Politics* (Routledge 2011)

Wheeler N, *Saving Strangers: Humanitarian Intervention in International Society* (OUP 2000)

Weiss TG, *Humanitarian Intervention: Ideas in Action* (Polity 2007)

[77] For similar arguments, see James Traub, 'Intervention in Syria Is Morally Justified—And Completely Impractical' *The New Republic* (10 February 2012) <http://www.tnr.com/article/world/100615/syria-symposium-intervention-arab-league> accessed 21 November 2012; Daniel Byman, 'Can We Help Syria without Making Things Worse?' *The Washington Post* (10 February 2012) <http://www.washingtonpost.com/opinions/can-we-help-syria-without-making-things-worse/2012/02/08/gIQAD6HJ4Q_story.html> accessed 21 November 2012; James Traub, 'The End of American Intervention' *The New York Times* (18 February 2012) <http://www.nytimes.com/2012/02/19/opinion/sunday/the-end-of-american-intervention.html?pagewanted=all> accessed 21 November 2012.

CHAPTER 35

TRADE LAW AND INVESTMENT LAW

SARAH JOSEPH

1. Introduction

INTERNATIONAL trade has long been a subject of international law. Indeed, the oldest surviving written treaty, concluded around 1259 BC between Egyptian pharaoh Rameses II and the Hittite King Hattuslii III, brought peace between the parties, in part by guaranteeing access for Egyptian traders to Hittite territories.[1] Absent such agreement, general international law respects a state's right to trade (or not to trade) with whomever it wishes. Global and regional treaties modify that right for most states. The General Agreement on Tariffs and Trade (GATT), first adopted in 1947, presaged current global treaties. The GATT was designed to address the protectionist policies that exacerbated the Great Depression, itself among the factors leading to the Second World War. The international human rights regime also burst onto the international law agenda as a response to the horrors of that war.

The modern international law of human rights and the protection of foreign investors both regulate the treatment of natural (and often legal) persons within a state's borders, a matter traditionally considered to be within the state's exclusive domestic jurisdiction. The earlier international law of diplomatic protection afforded some guarantees to foreigners, but did so indirectly as part of the obligations a host state

[1] A translation of this Peace Treaty can be found at <http://www.ancientworlds.net/aw/Article/797576> accessed 13 August 2012.

owed to a foreign person's state of nationality. Arguably, the law of diplomatic protection played its greatest role in protecting foreign traders and investors. That law generated customary international norms of non-discrimination, protected foreigners against denials of justice, and prohibited the expropriation of a foreigner's property without compensation.[2] These customary law guarantees are now key components of investment treaties, and they are also recognized as international human rights that extend to all persons.

The relationship between trade, investment, and human rights law is the subject of this chapter. After briefly introducing the key legal regimes in this section, the parts that follow assess the systemic relationship between the three regimes, followed by a discussion of the relevant legal relationships as reflected in the salient case law.

Human rights: The human rights law regimes include global United Nations (UN) treaties and regional treaties in Europe, the Americas, Africa, and the Arab world.

Trade: International trade law at the global level consists of the multilateral treaties concluded under the auspices of the World Trade Organization (WTO), the main focus of this chapter, supplemented by a growing multitude of regional agreements such as the North American Free Trade Agreement (NAFTA) and bilateral agreements.

The WTO agreements[3] were concluded in 1995 and bind the organization's 159 WTO members. The *raison d'être* of the WTO is to promote free trade by dictating the reduction and eventual removal of trading obstacles between states. The WTO's agreements impose obligations regarding trade in goods, trade in services, agricultural trade, and the regulation of non-tariff barriers to imports, such as quarantine measures and technical product requirements. They also protect intellectual property rights. The WTO agreements incorporate key GATT non-discrimination obligations, guaranteeing 'most favoured nation' (MFN) status and National Treatment. MFN status means all WTO members must treat the products and services of all other members equally, while National Treatment ensures that the products of a member are treated the same as locally produced 'like' goods, once they have legitimately entered another member's market.

The WTO has a strong dispute settlement mechanism. WTO panels or, in the case of appeals, the WTO's Appellate Body, decide unresolved disputes. The decisions of these bodies are binding, unless a consensus of WTO members rejects them. Such consensus is very unlikely, because a victorious member will rarely reject findings in its favor. If the unsuccessful litigating member fails to implement the final decision satisfactorily within a reasonable period of time, the WTO authorizes the prevailing party to impose retaliatory trade measures against that defaulting member.

[2] For a discussion of the law of diplomatic protection, see Chapter 10 in this *Handbook*.

[3] Marrakesh Agreement Establishing the World Trade Organization (WTO Agreement).

A member that fails to abide by adverse rulings of the dispute settlement bodies may therefore pay a significant commercial price.

Regional and bilateral trade treaties typically impose stronger reciprocal obligations on states parties. Such agreements represent a departure from the WTO's MFN guarantees, and are only permitted under WTO rules if they provide for extensive liberalization in respect of most of the parties' economies with regard to each other.[4]

Investment: Unlike international trade law, there is no overarching multilateral investment treaty. In 1998, proposals to conclude such a treaty within the Organisation for Economic Cooperation and Development (OECD) failed after civil society groups mounted a concerted global campaign in opposition.[5] Instead, investment treaties are generally bilateral, and occasionally regional, as in the case of the investment chapter of NAFTA.

Bilateral investment treaties (BITs) emerged in the post-war decolonization period as a means of protecting foreign investors, largely from capital-exporting developed states, from expropriation by developing states. Expropriation as an instrument of developing state policy had waned by the 1970s, yet political risks remained.[6] By the 1980s and 1990s, when neoliberal economic policies prevailed, BITs proliferated, even between developing states, and they came to be seen as a norm in governing international investment.[7] The number of BITs in existence skyrocketed to 2,495 by the end of 2005;[8] however, since the end of the twentieth century, there has been a downturn in the number of new investment treaties.

BITs are said to encourage foreign investment in a state,[9] though that assumption may be challengeable.[10] BITs act as 'bills of rights' for a state's investors when they operate in the territory of the other party. Substantive rights in BITs often guarantee against direct and indirect expropriation, non-discrimination in comparison with

[4] See GATT, Art XXIV; Sarah Joseph, *Blame It on the WTO: A Human Rights Critique* (OUP 2011) 281.

[5] See eg Peter T Muchlinski, 'The Rise and Fall of the Multilateral Agreement on Investment: Where Now?' (2000) 34 *Int'l Law* 1033.

[6] Michael S Minor, 'The Demise of Expropriation as an Instrument of LDC Policy 1980–1992' (1994) 25 *Journal of International Business Studies* 177.

[7] See Srividya Jandhyala, Witold J Henisz, and Edward D Mansfield, 'Three Waves of BITs: The Global Diffusion of Foreign Investment Policy' (2011) 55 *J Conflict Resol* 1047.

[8] See UN Conference on Trade and Development (UNCTAD), *World Investment Report 2006* (United Nations 2006) xix; UNCTAD, 'Latest Developments in Investor-state Dispute Settlement' (2010) 1 *International Investors Agreement Note* <http://unctad.org/en/Docs/webdiaeia20103_en.pdf> accessed 28 December 2012.

[9] See eg UNCTAD, *The Development Dimension of FDI: Policy and Rule-making Perspectives: Proceedings of the Expert Meeting Held in Geneva from 6 to 8 November 2002* (United Nations 2003) vii.

[10] See Mary Hallward-Driemeier, 'Do Bilateral Investment Treaties Attract FDI? Only a Bit...And They Could Bite' (2003) *World Bank Policy Research Paper* 3121 <http://www-wds.worldbank.org/external/default/WDSContentServer/WDSP/IB/2003/09/23/000094946_03091104060047/additional/105505322_20041117160010.pdf> accessed 18 November 2012.

local investors, and fair and equitable treatment; there is no particular model, however, and investment treaties materially differ in respect to the substantive obligations they contain.[11]

Significant procedural rights often supplement the substantive rights. Numerous BITs allow investors to bring their claims against governments directly to international arbitral tribunals, typically composed of experts in commercial law, and thus bypass local judicial systems. Such provisions reflect a lack of trust in the many legal systems where the judiciary lacks real independence. Awards can entail the payment of considerable compensation and other measures of redress, often amounting to hundreds of millions of dollars.[12] States are legally obliged to abide by arbitral awards. Failure to comply will likely attract economic and political pressure from the bilateral party to the BIT and will jeopardize a state's reputation with regard to foreign investors generally. Therefore, as with trade regimes, enforcement mechanisms under some investment treaties are very strong.

2. Trade, Investment, and Economic, Social, and Cultural Rights

2.1 General observations

International trade and investment are key aspects of economic globalization, which is said to increase net wealth in the world; foreign investment provides jobs, tax revenue, the transfer of technology and skills, foreign currency reserves, local business for subcontractors, and local competition to the benefit of consumers. Increases in wealth provide further resources which should improve the capacity of states to meet their obligations with respect to progressive implementation of economic, social, and cultural rights.

Free trade and investment can facilitate the access of individuals to important products and services that facilitate their enjoyment of economic, social, and cultural rights. For example, in 2002 Oxfam International noted that some African countries imposed a very high tariff on mosquito nets, a measure that surely cost

[11] Susan Karamanian, 'Human Rights Dimensions of Investment Law' in Erika de Wet and Jure Vidmar (eds), *Hierarchy in International Law: The Place of Human Rights* (OUP 2012) 243.

[12] Ursula Kriebaum, 'Is the European Court of Human Rights an Alternative to Investor-State Arbitration?' in Pierre-Marie Dupuy, Francesco Francioni, and Ernst-Ulrich Petersmann (eds), *Human Rights in International Investment Law and Arbitration* (OUP 2009) 244.

lives by increasing the exposure of the poor to malaria, arguably in breach of the right to health in the International Covenant on Economic, Social, and Cultural Rights (ICESCR), and even the right to life in the International Covenant on Civil and Political Rights (ICCPR).[13]

David Ricardo's nineteenth century theory of comparative advantage, which the WTO calls 'arguably the single most powerful insight into economics', supports the economic advantages of liberalized trade regimes, which all international trade regimes promote.[14] The theory holds that states, by concentrating on producing what they are best suited to produce, generate efficiency and lessen opportunity costs. If all states follow this practice and remove barriers to imports and exports, greater economic efficiency at both the domestic and global levels will be generated. Consumers will be able to access goods at the best prices while industries will be forced to innovate and become more efficient, in order to survive in the globally competitive marketplace. Ultimately, the theory holds that global free trade will generate greater global wealth, a goal that is congruent with human rights law.

Ricardo's theory is based on a perfect market. Yet numerous distortions pervade global markets. Barriers to free trade that persist, despite the efforts of the WTO and like regional bodies, include intellectual property protections (which many free trade arrangements mandate, as discussed below), the marketing power of major brands, anti-competitive practices, and large volumes of intra-corporate trade (whereby a multinational corporation will source components from affiliates, regardless of lower prices from others).[15] In 2003, Professor Joel R Paul estimated that no more than 25 per cent of the world's exports were traded in a perfect market, but the real figure was 'probably significantly less'.[16] It is doubtful that that figure has increased dramatically in the last decade. Therefore, it is fair to say that the accuracy of Ricardo's theory has not been truly tested.

Nevertheless, there is little doubt that trade obstacles can produce harm to overall welfare and also to specific human rights. For example, the World Bank reported that US and European cotton subsidies depressed world cotton prices by 71 per cent between 2001 and 2002, with devastating effects for the incomes of cotton growers in Africa and central Asia,[17] and therefore their rights to work and to a livelihood.[18] It is increasingly argued that states have human rights obligations toward

[13] Oxfam International, *Rigged Rules and Double Standards: Trade, Globalisation, and the Fight against Poverty* (Oxfam 2002) 62.

[14] WTO, 'Understanding the WTO: Basics: The Case for Open Trade' (2013) <http://www.wto.org/english/thewto_e/whatis_e/tif_e/fact3_e.htm> accessed 4 January 2013.

[15] Joel R Paul, 'Do International Trade Institutions Contribute to Economic Growth and Development?' (2003) 44 *Va J Int'l L* 285, 292–96.

[16] Paul (n 15) 298.

[17] World Bank, *World Development Report 2006: Equity and Development* (World Bank 2005) 212.

[18] In 2003, the 'C4' countries of Western Africa (Benin, Burkina Faso, Chad, and Mali), some of the poorest countries in the world, reported to the WTO that US subsidies caused direct and indirect

people in other countries.[19] Hence, the potential generation of human rights harms by protectionist measures indicates that, in principle, some limitation on the regulatory power of the state to restrict free trade is welcome from a human rights point of view.

The WTO regime still permits significant protectionism. As its rules stand, they favour the interests of developed states over poorer developing states.[20] WTO Director General Pascal Lamy has conceded the existence of this systemic bias,[21] even though it is counterintuitive for an organization ostensibly designed to combat poverty. With current rules tilted against poorer states, the WTO is not achieving optimal outcomes in promoting the right to development and alleviating poverty. At worst, unbalanced WTO rules could hamper development and exacerbate poverty in the poorest states, thereby prejudicing the realization of the right to development and other economic, social, and cultural rights. In this respect, economists Joseph Stiglitz and Andrew Charlton reported in 2005 that, by some estimates, forty-eight of the least developed countries have suffered annual economic losses of close to USD 600 million since they began implementing WTO agreements,[22] losses that no doubt reduced those states' capacities to ensure economic, social, and cultural rights.

Imbalances of power and technological expertise between the developed and developing states exacerbated the normative bias at the time the WTO agreements were negotiated. This imbalance has continued during negotiations for further liberalisation in new agreements. Certainly, the assertive positions of emerging economies, such as China, India, and Brazil, in current negotiations are one reason why they have stalled. Meanwhile, the bias continues, although it must be noted that it is less pronounced within the WTO than in the negotiation and outcomes of bilateral and regional treaties.[23]

A more fundamental issue, however, is whether trade liberalisation generally assists states in alleviating poverty and promoting and protecting economic, social,

losses of USD 1 billion a year. WTO Committee on Agriculture 'Poverty Reduction: Sectoral Initiative in Favour of Cotton' (16 May 2003) WTO Doc TN/AG/Gen.4.

[19] See Maastricht Principles on Extraterritorial Obligations in the area of Economic, Social and Cultural Rights, a set of principles adopted by international experts in 2010. 'Maastricht Principles on Extraterritorial Obligations in the area of Economic, Social and Cultural Rights' <http://209.240.139.114/wp-content/uploads/2012/03/Maastricht+ETO+Principles+-+Final+Version.pdf> accessed 30 May 2013.

[20] See eg the discussion of the Agreement on Agriculture below.

[21] Pascal Lamy, 'It's Time for a New "Geneva Consensus" on Making Trade Work for Development' (Emile Noel Lecture New York University Law School, New York, 30 October 2006) <http://www.wto.org/english/news_e/sppl_e/sppl45_e.htm> accessed 19 September 2010.

[22] Joseph E Stiglitz and Andrew Charlton, *Fair Trade for All: How Trade Can Promote Development* (OUP 2005) 47.

[23] See generally Ken Shadlen, 'Resources, Rules and International Political Economy: The Politics of Development in the WTO' in Sarah Joseph, David Kinley, and Jeff Waincymer (eds), *The World Trade Organisation and Human Rights: Interdisciplinary Perspectives* (Edward Elgar 2009).

and cultural rights. Over time, the strategy may well be beneficial, but swift liberalisation, as pushed in bilateral and regional treaties and in current WTO negotiations, may not be favourable for human rights. Loss of tariff revenue, for example, creates a significant hole in the budgets of developing states, which is difficult to replace because tariffs are relatively simple to collect and administer compared to internal taxes.[24] Furthermore, liberalisation undoubtedly generates detrimental social consequences for those in uncompetitive industries; developing states lack adequate social safety nets to cope with those consequences. While comparative advantage theory dictates that efficiency gains will ensue from the transfer of the means of production from inefficient industries to efficient ones,[25] Stiglitz and Charlton have argued that 'trade liberalization is not required to "free up" [the vast labour reserves in developing states] for use in new industries'.[26] Removal of protection for existing industries instead may mean that underemployed people in inefficient industries move to 'zero-productivity unemployment'.[27]

More generally, liberalization may trap a developing state in primary production and low cost, unskilled manufacturing, where it has a current comparative advantage, but which is disadvantageous in the long term. Cambridge University economist Ha-Joon Chang argues that liberalization is 'absolutely right' for states that are willing to accept their 'current levels of technology as given', but it is not appropriate where states wish to 'acquire more advanced technologies' and develop their economies.[28] A gradual sequenced approach to liberalization in developing states, incorporating the development of appropriate institutional capacities and dynamic niche industries, is preferable to the reduced policy space entailed in rapid and potentially premature liberalization.[29] Therefore, it is possible that liberalised trade, as promoted by international trade laws, in fact hinders the capacity of states to engage in the progressive development of economic, social, and cultural rights.

2.2 The chilling impact of trade and investment law

A systemic issue which arises with regard to the interaction of human rights law and trade law is the extent to which the latter rules may have a 'chilling effect' on the

[24] The International Monetary Fund has estimated that, between 1980 and 2005, developing States recovered less than 30 per cent of lost tariff revenue through other means. Thomas Baunsgaard and Michael Keen, 'Trade Revenue and (or?) Trade Liberalisation' (2005) *IMF Working Paper* 05/112 <http://www.imf.org/external/pubs/ft/wp/2005/wp05112.pdf> accessed 18 November 2012.

[25] Martin Wolf, *Why Globalisation Works* (2nd edn, Yale UP 2005) 81.

[26] Stiglitz and Charlton (n 22) 6. [27] Stiglitz and Charlton (n 22) 26.

[28] Ha-Joon Chang, *Bad Samaritans: The Myth of Free Trade and the Secret History of Capitalism* (Bloomsbury Press 2008) 47.

[29] See Dani Rodrik, 'How to Save Globalisation from its Cheerleaders' (2007) 1(2) *J Int'l Trade and Diplomacy* 1.

will of states to implement their human rights obligations. In respect to the right to health, for example, a state may wish to ban or prevent the importation of toxic products that harm consumer health. Article XX of GATT and the similar Article XIV of the General Agreement on Trade in Services (GATS), two of the WTO treaties, allow a state to adopt measures necessary to protect morals and public health. The exceptions have traditionally been interpreted narrowly and technically, however, to the point that a state may hesitate to rely on them in regulating imports to support human rights. In the few relevant cases decided thus far, discussed in Section 5, social measures have rarely survived WTO challenges intact.

WTO obligations traditionally have targeted protectionism, but some WTO rules suggest a more broad-based 'freedom to trade', divorced from notions of discrimination, which poses a much greater threat to the regulatory capacities of a state.[30] This shrinkage of policy space could limit the ability of a state to regulate in respect to essential services and utilities, thereby failing to meet core human rights obligations, such as the provision of safe drinking water and sanitation.[31]

The investment regime replicates the chilling impact. BIT rights are very broad and vague, and investors often claim them to escape regulatory changes that are likely to diminish future profits. For example, 'umbrella' clauses may provide international legal protection for contractual conditions, and 'stabilization clauses' may freeze a regulatory environment for the life of a contract, which can be very long for large-scale infrastructure or resources projects. Such protection poses a significant deterrent to the adoption of state regulation, which may have an impact on business profits, even if the changes are supportive of the fulfilment of human rights such as environmental or health regulations. Furthermore, unlike Article XX of GATT, some BITs do not explicitly permit regulations in areas of public interest.

Unpredictability in the investment arbitration regime, where there is no overarching appellate system, exacerbates the 'chilling' problem.[32] Decisions are inconsistent, for example, on the meaning of 'expropriation' or on the existence and scope of public interest regulation exceptions.[33] Furthermore, the arbitral system suffers from a lack of transparency; proceedings are often held in secret.[34] As the pool of arbitrators is quite small, the potential for conflicts of interest arises; a person may be involved in one case as counsel and in another as an arbitrator deciding similar legal issues.[35]

[30] David M Driesen, 'What is Free Trade? The Real Issue Lurking behind the Trade and Environment Debate' (2001) 41 *Va J Int'l L* 279.

[31] See Andrew Lang, 'The GATS and Regulatory Autonomy: A Case Study of Social Regulation of the Water Industry' (2004) 7 *J Intl Econ L* 801.

[32] However, courts may review arbitral awards in proceedings regarding enforcement of the award. See James D Fry, 'International Human Rights Law in Investment Arbitration: Evidence of International Law's Unity' (2007–08) 18 *Duke J Comp & Int'l L* 77, 118–19.

[33] For example, compare *Lauder v Czech Republic*, para 200 with *CME Czech Republic BV v Czech Republic*, paras 591, 604, coming to opposite conclusions on whether the Czech Republic's impugned actions were expropriations. See Fry (n 32) 83–84.

[34] Fry (n 32) 115–17.

[35] Fry (n 32) 115.

BIT enforcement via arbitration did not become commonplace until the 1990s; developing states were likely unaware of the consequential nature of BITs they signed during the prior three decades.[36] Now, states are increasingly alarmed at the regulatory costs of BITs, which may explain the decline in the number of new BITs in the 2000s.

3. Impact of WTO Rules on Specific Economic, Social, and Cultural Rights

This section discusses two of the many potential areas of concern regarding WTO rules and economic, social, and cultural rights: (1) intellectual property and the right to health, and (2) free trade and the right to food. Other issues worth mentioning include the impact of free trade (and foreign investment) on labour rights and the feared impact of the General Agreement on Trade in Services on the right to water.[37]

3.1 TRIPS and the right to health

Under the Agreement on Trade Related Aspects of Intellectual Property (TRIPS), WTO Members are required to protect intellectual property (IP) rights, such as copyright, patents, and trademarks. The least developed countries (LDCs) do not have to fully comply with TRIPS until 2021, nor do they have to protect patented pharmaceutical products until 2016.[38]

IP rights are justified by the rewards they deliver to creators, innovators, inventors and authors, and the consequent incentives they deliver to research and development. The TRIPS erection of barriers to trade in the form of temporary monopoly rights may seem anomalous within the WTO. However, proponents claim IP protection indirectly boosts trade, because foreign investment and technology transfer is promoted when investors are confident that host states will protect their valuable IP rights.[39]

[36] See eg Lauge N Skovgaard Poulsen and Emma Aisbett, 'When the Claim Hits: Bounded Rationality and Bilateral Investment Treaties' (2011) *Crawford School Research Paper* 5, 10–11.

[37] See generally, Lang (n 31) 801.

[38] The 2021 deadline was extended from 2013 in June 2013. It is likely the pharmaceutical deadline will follow suit.

[39] See Shanker A Singham, 'Competition Policy and the Stimulation of Innovation: TRIPS and the Interface Between Competition and Patent Protection in the Pharmaceutical Industry' (2000) 26 *Brook J Int'l L* 363, 375–85.

IP protection should also promote local innovation within a state by protecting investments in research and development against pirates and copycats.[40]

Human rights law protects some IP rights, as well, either specifically or as a form of property. Article 15(1)(c) of the ICESCR recognizes the right of everyone 'to benefit from the protection of the moral and material interests resulting from any scientific, literary or artistic production of which he is the author'. The Committee on Economic Social and Cultural Rights elaborated upon Article 15(1)(c) in its General Comment No 17.[41] The Committee distinguished Article 15(1)(c) rights from IP rights by noting that the latter were 'of a temporary nature' and could be 'revoked, licensed or assigned to someone else', whereas human rights were 'timeless expressions of fundamental entitlements of the human person'.[42] The right in Article 15(1)(c) protects 'the personal link between authors and their creations and between peoples, communities, or other groups and their collective cultural heritage, as well as their basic material interests which are necessary to enable authors to enjoy an adequate standard of living'.[43] In contrast, IP rights 'primarily protect business and corporate interests and investments'.[44] In that respect, the Committee underlined that Article 15(1)(c) rights vest only in human beings, rather than corporations.[45] Furthermore, the Committee anticipates that a variety of regimes could satisfy Article 15(1)(c),[46] an approach quite different from the 'one size fits all' TRIPS regime.

The most prominent human rights concern regarding TRIPS[47] is its alleged negative impact on the ability of poor people to access life-saving medicines, because compulsory patent protection for pharmaceutical products raises the prices of those products. Implementation of TRIPS may thus prejudice the right to health in ICESCR Article 12, especially in developing states that lack the resources to provide patented drugs via public health budgets. Proponents argue that IP protection for life-saving drugs is necessary in order to promote the research and development of those drugs. However, it seems unlikely that the relaxation of patents in developing

[40] However, it has been argued that this rationale for TRIPS effectively put 'the policy cart before the empirical horse'. Daniel J Gervais, 'TRIPS 3.0: Policy Calibration and Innovation Displacement' in Chantal Thomas and Joel P Trachtman (eds), *Developing Countries in the WTO Legal System* (OUP 2009) 370.

[41] Committee on Economic, Social and Cultural Rights 'General Comment No 17: The Right of Everyone to Benefit from the Protection of the Moral and Material Interests Resulting from Any Scientific, Literary or Artistic Production of Which He or She Is the Author' (12 January 2006) UN Doc E/C.12/GC/17.

[42] 'General Comment No 17' (n 41) para 2.

[43] 'General Comment No 17' (n 41) para 2.

[44] 'General Comment No 17' (n 41) para 2.

[45] 'General Comment No 17' (n 41) para 7.

[46] 'General Comment No 17' (n 41) paras 16, 47.

[47] Other concerns include its impact on the right to food (see Joseph, *Blame it on the WTO* (n 4) 207–10), the impact of global copyright rules on the right to education (see eg 3D, 'The Philippines: Impact of Copyright Rules on Access to Education' *3D* (July 2009)), and the way TRIPS notions of IP marginalize indigenous concepts of traditional knowledge and innovation (see eg Megan Davis, 'International Trade, the World Trade Organisation, and the Human Rights of Indigenous Peoples' (2006) 8 *Balayi* 1, 5).

states, particularly in the poorest of them, would lead to a significant reduction in the profits needed for pharmaceutical research.[48] Indeed, pharmaceutical innovation was hardly lacking prior to the advent of TRIPS. While there are dangers that cheap drugs from the developing world could undermine patent protection by making their way to developed country markets, those countries may take legal measures to guard against that phenomenon.

Exceptions to TRIPS exist, but in the absence of relevant WTO case law, it is uncertain whether the exceptions are flexible enough to ensure human rights. TRIPS allows states to invoke countervailing rights only as exceptions to the TRIPS regime, as a shield in defending against a failure to fully implement TRIPS, not as a sword to challenge the implementation of TRIPS. It thereby elevates IP rights over potentially conflicting human rights.

The issue regarding access to drugs was partially redressed when the WTO Members adopted the Doha Declaration on the TRIPS Agreement and Public Health in December 2001, followed by a waiver in 2003 that facilitates the export of inexpensive drugs to very poor states.[49] However, the rules for utilization of that waiver are cumbersome and administratively onerous.[50]

In his 2009 Report to the UN Human Rights Council, the Special Rapporteur on the Right to Health, Anand Grover, wrote extensively on TRIPS and the right of access to medicines.[51] Grover's report implies that TRIPS obligations do not conflict with the right of access to medicines, even though he concludes that TRIPS has 'had an adverse impact on prices and availability of medicines'.[52] He urges developing states to utilize all available TRIPS flexibilities, as needed, in order to ensure access to medicines domestically. In Grover's view, their common failure to do so, which economic and diplomatic pressure from richer states or international financial institutions often prompts, amounts to a violation of the right to health.

The TRIPS regime provides weaker IP protection than the 'TRIPS-plus' regimes that are commonly adopted within regional or bilateral trade treaties. The TRIPS-plus provisions of US bilateral agreements arguably contravene the spirit of cooperation

[48] The World Bank's 2006 '*World Development Report*' cited a 2004 study in which it was postulated that the profits from a twenty-year patent extension in the developing world would equal a two-week extension in the developed world. World Bank, *World Development Report 2006* (n 17) 214, citing Jean O Lanjouw and William Jack, 'Trading Up: How Much Should Poor Countries Pay to Support Pharmaceutical Innovation?' (2004) 4(3) *Center for Global Development* 1, 6.

[49] WTO, *Implementation of Paragraph 6 of the Doha Declaration on the TRIPS Agreement and Public Health* (30 August 2003) WTO Doc WT/L/540.

[50] Ellen FM 't Hoen, 'The Global Politics of Pharmaceutical Monopoly Power: Drug Patents, Access, Innovation and the Application of the WTO Doha Declaration on TRIPS and Public Health' (AMB 2009) 35–38.

[51] HRC 'Report of the Special Rapporteur on the Right of Everyone to the Enjoyment of the Highest Attainable Standard of Physical and Mental Health, Anand Grover' (31 March 2009) UN Doc A/HRC/11/12.

[52] HRC, 'Report of Anand Grover' (n 51) para 94.

that the Doha Declaration and waiver engender within the WTO.[53] Moreover, if TRIPS-plus commitments bind a WTO member state, it may have to guarantee equivalent rights to traders from all other WTO states, because TRIPS contains no exception to MFN with regard to bilateral and regional free trade deals.[54]

3.2 Free trade and the right to food

Only a small percentage of food, estimated at 15 per cent of food grown, is actually traded across borders,[55] and yet 'international trade and investment requirements dictate food and agricultural policies'.[56] There are serious concerns about the compatibility of the free trade regime with the enjoyment of the right to food, recognized, for example, in ICESCR Article 11. First, the bias of WTO rules against developing nations, mentioned above in Section 2.1, is manifest in the content and structure of the WTO's Agreement on Agriculture (AoA). Many developing states have a comparative advantage in agricultural products, but the AoA allows significant protectionism to their detriment.[57] The AoA does not combat 'tariff escalation', that is the escalation of tariffs imposed on processed agricultural goods compared to raw goods, for example. Such tariff schemes, which developed states commonly impose, stunt the growth of more sophisticated and lucrative agricultural industries in source countries.[58] This and other forms of continuing protectionism in developed country markets have harmed development prospects in poor countries. Particularly egregious examples of protectionism include Europe's sugar markets[59] and US cotton markets (as mentioned above). Therefore, it is unsurprising that some of the most prominent demands of developing states in the current round of WTO negotiations are for further agricultural liberalization.

Real concerns exist, however, about the appropriateness of liberalized trade for agricultural products.[60] Trade literature emphasizes that free markets will divert to those

[53] Jean-Frédéric Morin, 'Tripping up TRIPS Debates IP and Health in Bilateral Agreements' (2006) 1 *IJIPM* 37, 51.

[54] Frederick M Abbott and Jerome H Reichmann, 'The Doha Round's Public Health Legacy: Strategies for the Production and Diffusion of Patented Medicines under the Amended TRIPS Provisions' (2007) 10 *J Intl Econ L* 921, 963–64.

[55] Olivier De Schutter, *International Trade in Agriculture and the Right to Food* (Friedrich Ebert Stiftung 2009) 43.

[56] Carin Smaller and Sophia Murphy, *Bridging the Divide: A Human Rights Vision for Global Food Trade* (Institute of Agriculture and Trade Policy 2008) 8.

[57] The machinations of the AoA are extremely complicated. They are summarized in Joseph, *Blame it on the WTO* (n 4) 185–90.

[58] See Oxfam International (n 13) 102–103.

[59] Wouter Vandenhole, 'Third State Obligations under the ICESCR: A Case Study of EU Sugar Policy' (2007) 76 *Nord J Intl L* 73.

[60] The following is adapted from Joseph, *Blame it on the WTO* (n 4) 194–204.

who sell for less, but markets also divert to those willing to pay more.[61] For example, more of the finite amounts of arable land are being used to cultivate and feed livestock for meat to satisfy the more expensive tastes of a growing middle class in Asia than to grow staple foods for the poor and the hungry.[62] In the wake of the World Food Crisis in 2008, former US President Bill Clinton, who presided over the US's final negotiation of and ratification of the WTO Agreements, admitted that the world 'blew it' by treating food as if it were an ordinary commodity.[63] In fact, international agricultural markets suffer from a number of flaws that can exacerbate hunger and prejudice enjoyment of the right to food, given that 50 per cent of the world's hungry are in fact small agricultural producers.[64]

Agricultural commodities markets have generally delivered poor and erratic returns to producers over the last three decades.[65] A number of factors cause these markets to defy the orthodox economic theories regarding supply and demand.[66] It is difficult to tailor supply to demand, due to the vagaries of climatic conditions and the fact that it is not easy to simply 'move land into and out of production'[67] to suit market conditions. Poorer farmers cannot stockpile produce to wait for more advantageous market conditions because it is expensive to store food.[68] Low prices mean that many farmers cannot make a decent living. Price hikes are too unpredictable for those farmers to take advantage of, and they then suffer as consumers with sudden rises in food prices. The many poor States that are net food importers cannot afford sudden price rises.

Large-scale single-crop farms owned by multinational agribusiness companies dominate global agricultural trade.[69] Indeed, many commodities markets are dominated by only a few agribusiness multinationals, including coffee, cocoa,

[61] De Schutter (n 55) 10–11.

[62] Sophia Murphy, 'Concentrated Market Power and Agricultural Trade' (August 2006) EcoFair Trade Dialogue Discussion Paper No 1, 27 <http://www.iatp.org/files/451_2_89014.pdf> accessed 4 January 2013.

[63] 'Bill Clinton: "We Blew It" on Global Food: Ex-President Tells UN World Erred in Treating Food as a Commodity Instead of a Vital Right' *CBS News* (23 October 2008) <http://www.cbsnews.com/stories/2008/10/23/world/main4542268.shtml> accessed 22 September 2010.

[64] UN Millennium Project, *Halving Hunger: It Can Be Done, Summary of the Report of the Task Force on Hunger* (The Earth Institute 2005) 4–6 <http://www.unmillenniumproject.org/documents/HTF-SumVers_FINAL.pdf> accessed 19 August 2012.

[65] UNGA 'Report of the Special Rapporteur on the Right to Food, Olivier De Schutter' (21 October 2008) UN Doc A/63/278, para 18.

[66] See also UNGA 'Report of the Special Rapporteur on the Right to Food' (n 65) para 21; Wolf (n 25) 206.

[67] Sophia Murphy, 'WTO Agreement on Agriculture: Suitable Model for a Global Food System?' (2002) 7(8) *Foreign Policy in Focus* 3, 3.

[68] Murphy, 'Concentrated Market Power' (n 62) 5.

[69] Christine Breining-Kaufman, 'The Right to Food and Trade in Agriculture' in Thomas Cottier, Joost Pauwelyn, and Elizabeth Bürgi (eds), *Human Rights and International Trade* (OUP 2005) 368; Wolf (n 25) 206.

confectionary, and tea.[70] To some extent, the growth of global supply chains benefits smaller farmers by connecting them to global markets.[71] However, cartelization within these supply chains has created severe power imbalances between producers and buyers, allowing the latter to exercise effective monopsony power to drive down prices paid to producers.[72] Farmers now receive only a tiny proportion of the value of the final product, which increasingly reflects inputs by and the profits of others, such as wholesalers, processers, retailers (particularly supermarkets), and the providers of necessary inputs like fertilizers, machinery, and commercial genetically modified seeds. Markets in many of these areas are also unhealthily concentrated.

Measures to combat private monopolies are 'conspicuously absent' from the WTO.[73] The focus of (failed) WTO discussions was on promoting foreign competition against local firms in domestic markets, rather than on curbing the power of multinational corporations in global markets,[74] yet trade is hardly free in the absence of free competition. There is a danger that agricultural liberalization, without the opening up of competition in the sector, simply replaces 'border protections with cartels'.[75]

The dominant agribusiness corporations are 'more likely to be concerned with profitable trade than with local-level food security'.[76] Export orientation in agriculture has prompted switches from subsistence products to non-food cash crops, such as coffee, cocoa, and tobacco.[77] The diversion of resources from food can weaken local food security and transform a country into a net food importing country, with all of the vulnerabilities associated with that status.

Finally, the theory of comparative advantage encourages specialization rather than diversity in agricultural outputs. However, specialization can magnify losses if a crop should fail or plummet in price,[78] while monocultures can generate a loss of biological diversity and ecological resilience.[79]

[70] World Bank, *World Development Report 2008: Agriculture for Development* (World Bank 2007) 135–36.

[71] De Schutter (n 55) 30.

[72] United Nations Development Programme (UNDP), *Human Development Report 2005: International Cooperation at a Crossroads: Aid, Trade and Security in an Unequal World* (UNDP 2005) 142–43.

[73] UNDP (n 72) 139.

[74] Stiglitz and Charlton (n 22) 85.

[75] Murphy, 'Concentrated Market Power' (n 62) 29.

[76] Caroline Dommen, 'Raising Human Rights Concerns in the World Trade Organization: Actors, Processes and Possible Strategies' (2002) 24 *Hum Rts Q* 1, 34.

[77] United Nations Human Settlements Programme, *Global Report on Human Settlements 2003: The Challenge of Slums* (UN Habitat 2003) 41.

[78] Dommen (n 76) 40.

[79] International Assessment of Agricultural Knowledge, Science and Technology for Development (IAASTD), *Agriculture at the Crossroads: Synthesis Report* (IAASTD 2009) 10. The IAASTD is an intergovernmental entity that the World Bank and FAO created. The cited report was compiled over the course of three years, by 400 experts, including a wide range of scientists and development specialists.

The above problems conspire to leave vast numbers of small farmers extremely vulnerable in the world economy. Economists might advise many of them to move into more efficient industry sectors, but modern mechanized agribusiness cannot employ them all, and their skills are not easily adaptable to urban or non-agricultural industries. Cultural barriers seriously hinder the ability of the many poor rural women to simply 'move' to new areas and jobs. Further, extensive reduction in smallholders will only exacerbate some of the problems discussed above regarding the lack of competition in markets and overemphasis on cash crops and specialization. Finally, the assertion that smallholders should give up their land and independence arguably treats them as economic units rather than as human beings with human rights.

Agricultural activities are commercial activities, but they are also truly multifunctional, serving purposes beyond the production of commodities. They promote human welfare (nutrition, livelihoods, sustaining rural communities), traditional cultural practices (eg hunting, gathering, food rituals), and the provision of environmental and ecological services.[80] While the AoA acknowledges 'non-trade' concerns in some of its provisions, such as food security and environmental protection, overall it 'clearly fit under a programme of trade liberalization in agricultural products'.[81] In contrast, many experts, including from economic fields, argue that new agricultural management systems must be devised so as to serve these multifunctional purposes.[82]

4. The Benefits of Free Trade and Investment for Civil and Political Rights

Just as free trade and investment can facilitate the introduction of products and services that boost economic, social, and cultural rights, they can also facilitate the introduction of products and services that boost civil and political rights. For example, the use of social media, involving access to the internet and social media sites (services), mobile phones, and computers (products) in the Arab Spring facilitated the overthrow of long-standing dictatorships in Tunisia and Egypt in early 2011.[83]

[80] IAASTD, *Agriculture at the Crossroads: Synthesis Report* (n 79) World Bank, *World Development Report 2008* (n 70) 2.

[81] HRC, 'Background Document Prepared by the UN Special Rapporteur on the Right to Food, Mr Olivier de Schutter' (March 2009) UN Doc A/HRC/10/005/Add.2, 7.

[82] IAASTD, *Agriculture at the Crossroads: Synthesis Report* (n 79) 50.

[83] See Dubai School of Government, 'Civil Movements: The Impact of Facebook and Twitter' (2011) 1(2) *Arab Social Media Report*; Philip N Howard and others, 'Opening Closed Regimes: What

In this regard, it is intriguing to question China's internet censorship as a breach of WTO rules, as well as a violation of the right to freedom of expression.[84] China censors internet access via its 'Great Firewall', which blocks or slows foreign internet sites. The First Amendment Coalition, a non-government organization, claims that the firewall is an illegal barrier to trade, as it 'degrades the performance of websites based outside the country',[85] which seems to impair foreign competition via the internet in China's huge market. Indeed, it was reported that Google rapidly lost market share in China after moving its operations outside the firewall to Hong Kong early in 2010.[86]

Other Chinese regulations might also simultaneously harm human rights and WTO law, such as those which limit Wi-Fi capabilities and downloadable applications for mobile phones and computers in order to preserve the government's ability to spy on its population. Such practices breach the human right to privacy[87] and detract from political rights by allowing China to identify, track, and even suppress dissidents. These regulations also have a detrimental impact on trade. The Apple iPhone was released in the Chinese market, without its Wi-Fi capabilities, two years after its global launch, while new software must be installed in computers before they can be shipped to China.[88] Again, it is plausible that such measures breach WTO rules,[89] so WTO law could prove to be an ally of those who seek greater internet freedom in China. Should a state instigate a relevant complaint, however, the key issue in any resultant dispute resolution proceedings would not be human rights, but the technical issues of the scope of China's WTO obligations and the extent to which China's actions impair foreign trade.[90]

Was the Role of Social Media during the Arab Spring?' (2011) *Working Paper 2011.1* <http://pitpi.org/wp-content/uploads/2013/02/2011_Howard-Duffy-Freelon-Hussain-Mari-Mazaid_pITPI.pdf> accessed 30 May 2013.

[84] Article 19 of the Universal Declaration of Human Rights (UDHR) recognizes freedom of expression. Although China is not a party to any treaty that guarantees freedom of expression, the right may be protected under customary international law. In any event, the UDHR serves as a measure of the human rights obligations of UN Member States pursuant to the UN Charter. See also Joseph (n 4) 137–40.

[85] Peter Scheer, 'Obama Should Back up Google with More than Rhetoric: The US Should Challenge China's "Firewall" before the WTO' *The Huffington Post* (19 January 2010) <http://www.firstamendmentcoalition.org/2010/01/obama-should-back-up-google-with-more-than-rhetoric-the-us-should-challenge-chinas-firewall-before-the-wto> accessed 7 January 2013.

[86] See eg 'Google Losing Market Share in China' *The Boston Globe* (Hong Kong, 23 April 2010) <http://www.boston.com/business/technology/articles/2010/04/23/google_losing_market_share_in_china> accessed 7 January 2013.

[87] UDHR Art 12 recognizes the right to privacy.

[88] See Fredrik Erixon and Hosuk Lee-Makiyama, 'Chinese Censorship Equals Protectionism: Freedom of Speech Violations Aside, Beijing May Also Be Violating Its WTO Obligations' *The Wall Street Journal* (6 January 2010) <http://online.wsj.com/article/SB10001424052748704842604574641620942668590.html> accessed 7 January 2013.

[89] Brian Hindley and Hosuk Lee-Makiyama, 'Protectionism Online: Internet Censorship and International Trade Law' (2009) *ECIPE Working Paper* 12/2009, 8.

[90] See generally Tim Wu, 'The World Trade Law of Censorship and Internet Filtering' (3 May 2006) 10 <http://papers.ssrn.com/sol3/papers.cfm?abstract_id=882459> accessed 4 January 2013.

More generally, WTO Director-General Pascal Lamy has stated that global trade rules, along with international human rights law, are 'a rampart against totalitarianism'.[91] Indeed, it is commonly argued that economic openness promotes political openness[92] in the following ways. Economic openness can promote economic growth, which helps to create new economic elites, who can challenge the authority of dictatorial government power, creating further space for civil society. It leads to the creation of a middle class, which is more educated and which eventually demands greater political and social freedom.[93] Finally, foreign investors influence states positively by demanding adherence to the rule of law, as arbitrary decision-making intolerably threatens their investments.[94]

These theories are backed up by evidence; democracy and civil and political freedoms tend to flourish in richer, developed states, which generally have more liberal trade and investment regimes, more than in poorer developing countries, which generally have more restrictive regimes.[95]

The respected economics journalist Martin Wolf has posited that economic freedoms and the promotion of a flourishing private sector help to ensure the separation of wealth and power. If the public political sector dominates economic decisions, they dominate economic power: '[p]ower becomes the only route to wealth.'[96] Political elites are then inevitably tempted to utilize oppressive means to maintain their power as 'loss of power threatens a loss of livelihood'.[97] Growing economies are also important for the maintenance of democracy and human rights, as they prevent 'zero sum' societies, in which one person's gain necessarily results in another person's loss, which help to foster authoritarianism.[98]

Contrary examples exist, however. Singapore has long had an open economy, yet has only slowly increased its observance of civil and political freedoms. Similarly, economic reforms in China have not been matched by significant improvements in civil and political rights.[99] Furthermore, as noted, other developing states have experienced poor economic performance, rather than growth, as a result of eliminating trade barriers.

[91] Pascal Lamy, 'Towards Shared Responsibility and Greater Coherence: Human Rights, Trade and Macroeconomic Policy' (The Colloquium on Human Rights in the Global Economy, Geneva, 13 January 2010) <http://www.wto.org/english/news_e/sppl_e/sppl146_e.htm> accessed 20 September 2010.

[92] See Paul (n 15) 337–38. See also Joseph (n 4) 84–87.

[93] See Frank Garcia, 'The Global Market and Human Rights: Trading away the Human Rights Principle' (1999) 7 *Brook J Int'l L* 51, 59; Jagdish Bhagwati, *Free Trade Today* (Princeton UP 2002) 43–44.

[94] See eg World Bank, *World Development Report 2002: Building Institutions for Markets* (World Bank 2002) <http://www.worldbank.org/wdr/2001/fulltext/fulltext2002.htm> accessed 20 September 2010.

[95] See Daniel T Griswold, 'Trading Tyranny for Freedom: How Open Markets Till the Soil for Democracy' (2004) *Trade Policy Analysis* 26, 4–12 <http://www.freetrade.org/node/37> accessed 20 September 2010.

[96] Wolf (n 25) 30. [97] Wolf (n 25) 30. [98] Wolf (n 25) 30. [99] Gervais (n 40) 393.

Furthermore, the spread of marketization across the world has accompanied greater global inequality.[100] Trade and investment policies do not mandate any form of domestic wealth distribution. The benefits of economic growth might flow to only a small elite. When gaps between elites and the poor grow, there is a more pronounced divergence in their interests, leading to the possible generation of rules and institutions that favour the latter over the former.[101] Greater inequality may therefore lead to greater marginalization and intolerance of the poor.

In 2000, Professor Amy Chua questioned the assumption that the twin trajectories of free trade and democracy in the developed world will recur in the developing world. First, she noted that the development of democracy and free trade regimes in industrialized states was slow; universal suffrage and economic liberalization evolved over centuries. In contrast, the comparable economic transitions in developing states have been remarkably swift, and they have not allowed time for the development of economic safety nets for those who lose as a result of economic liberalization, legal protection for minorities, or the development of aspirational pro-market ideologies amongst a population.[102] In such circumstances, the impoverished majority may be very hostile to the inequalities free markets create, at least until a substantial middle class emerges, so democratization and marketization may pull in different directions for a time.

5. Human Rights Protections for Traders and Investors

Individual traders and investors have human rights. The right to a fair trial provides for due process in domestic legal proceedings, which is clearly important, for example, in resolving contractual disputes. The right of non-discrimination applies to protect against arbitrary and discriminatory treatment on the basis of foreign nationality. The right to privacy provides protection for business records.[103]

[100] See statistics cited in Joseph, *Blame it on the WTO* (n 4) 166–67. See also World Bank, *World Development Report 2006* (n 17).

[101] Thomas Pogge, 'Growth and Inequality: Understanding Recent Trends and Political Choices' (Winter 2008) 55(1) *Dissent* 66.

[102] See generally Amy Chua, 'The Paradox of Free Market Democracy: Rethinking Development Policy' (2000) 41 *Harv Int'l LJ* 287.

[103] See eg *Société Colas Est and Others v France*. cf *Claude-Reyes v Chile*, discussed below (n 167).

The right to property is of course relevant to IP and other property that investors and traders hold. Universal Declaration of Human Rights (UDHR) Article 17 recognizes property rights. Although neither of the two Covenants transposed this provision,[104] global human rights law does not leave property completely unprotected.[105]

Regional human rights treaties guarantee property rights. Article 1 of the First Protocol to the European Convention on Human Rights (ECHR) states:

> Every natural or legal person is entitled to the peaceful enjoyment of his possessions. No one shall be deprived of his possessions except in the public interest and subject to the conditions provided for by law and by the general principles of international law.
>
> The preceding provisions shall not, however, in any way impair the right of a State to enforce such laws as it deems necessary to control the use of property in accordance with the general interest or to secure the payment of taxes or other contributions or penalties.

The European Court of Human Rights (ECtHR) has adopted a very broad interpretation of 'possessions', including rights of ownership, as well as the pecuniary rights 'arising from shares, patents, arbitration award, established entitlement to a pension, [and] entitlement to a rent'.[106] A legitimate expectation to a proprietary right also counts as a possession,[107] as does 'enterprise', that is 'a mass of rights, interests, and relations destined to a determined purpose and organized as an economic unit by an entrepreneur' comprising 'interests and relations, such as clientele, good will, and business secrets, as well as potential sources of income'.[108]

The right guarantees the peaceful enjoyment of property. Interferences by the state are allowed if they are prescribed by law, proportionate (that is, necessary in a democratic society), and executed in the public interest.[109] Article 1(1) also prohibits deprivation of property (eg expropriation), except in the public interest. Even though the provision makes no mention of compensation, the European Court has found that the requirement of proportionality demands that some compensation be paid for most interferences with property, except in the most extraordinary of circumstances.[110] The state is given broad, but not unlimited, discretion to control the uses of property in the general interest.

Unlike some other human rights systems, the ECHR allows legal persons, such as corporations, to allege that they have been victims of human rights violations.

[104] This was largely due to the opposition of Eastern bloc countries during the drafting of the Covenants from 1948 to 1966.

[105] See eg *Simunek et al v Czech Republic*; *Adam v Czech Republic* (the Human Rights Committee found that the Czech Republic's restitution laws discriminated arbitrarily on the basis of nationality with regard to property rights, in breach of Art 26 of the ICCPR).

[106] Aida Grgić, Zvonimir Mataga, Matija Longar, and Ana Vilfan, *The Right to Property under the European Convention on Human Rights: A Guide to the Implementation of the European Convention on Human Rights and Its Protocols* (Council of Europe 2007) 7.

[107] Grgić and others (n 106) 7.

[108] Grgić and others (n 106) 8.

[109] Grgić and others (n 106) 12.

[110] Such a circumstance, needing to reconcile property laws and rights in the wake of German reunification, arose in *Jahn et al v Germany*.

A number of cases have concerned fact situations 'typical for investment arbitration'.[111] For example, in *Sovtransavto Holding v Ukraine*, the Court found a breach of the right to a fair hearing. The breach had resulted in a reduction in the applicant's Russian company's shareholding in, and the subsequent loss of, control over a particular company.[112] *Bimer SA v Moldova* concerned a Moldovan law that forced the closure of the applicant company's duty free business.

There are important differences between ECHR and BIT law. First, the investor's nationality is irrelevant under the ECHR, while the nationality of the investor is crucial under a BIT.[113] Second, under BITs, shareholders are generally recognized as having separate claims to the company in which they hold shares. Under the ECHR, shareholders are not recognized as having separate claims to the company, unless, for some reason, the company is unable to pursue the claim itself, or the claimants actually carry on business through the company so their rights are directly affected.[114]

The most important differences probably arise with regard to the consequences of an established interference with property. If expropriation is found under a BIT, full market price compensation must normally be paid, regardless of the reason for the expropriation.[115] In contrast, the ECtHR will distinguish between justified and unjustified expropriations. If an expropriation is justified, the affected person may well receive less compensation than the fair market value, or even no compensation in exceptional circumstances.[116] Nonetheless, the 'general principles of international law' to which the second sentence of Article 1 refers, dictate that a foreigner receives full compensation in the case of expropriation.[117] No difference between foreigners and nationals arises regarding the amount of compensation payable with regard to less drastic interferences with property.[118] Notably, the amounts the European Court awards in property cases are generally far less than those of arbitral tribunals. The highest sums the Court has awarded were around €24 million in two cases in 1994 involving Greece.[119] European Court proceedings are also much cheaper than arbitral processes, as there are no court fees.[120]

In the Americas, Article 21 of the American Convention on Human Rights (ACHR) similarly guarantees a right to property, stating:

1. Everyone has the right to the use and enjoyment of his property. The law may subordinate such use and enjoyment to the interest of society.

[111] Kriebaum (n 12) 219. [112] Grgić and others (n 106) 10. [113] Kriebaum (n 12) 220–22.

[114] Kriebaum (n 12) 222–28. See *Agrotexim and Others v Greece*.

[115] Kriebaum (n 12) 239. The reason for the alleged expropriation may, however, be relevant in deciding if an expropriation has in fact taken place.

[116] Kriebaum (n 12) 241–42.

[117] Kriebaum (n 12) 241. The European Court has never had a case involving the expropriation of a foreigner's property.

[118] Kriebaum (n 12) 242–43. [119] Kriebaum (n 12) 244. [120] Kriebaum (n 12) 244.

2. No one shall be deprived of his property except upon payment of just compensation, for reasons of public utility or social interest, and in the cases and according to the forms established by law.

The American Court has not decided any case in which Article 21 was the sole right at issue. *Ivcher-Bronstein v Peru*[121] concerned an investor's property rights, but also the rights to a nationality, to due process, and to free speech. Mr Bronstein was deprived of his Peruvian nationality after his media company had investigated government corruption. As a consequence, his majority shareholder rights in the company were suspended, and he lost his leadership position in the company, because only a Peruvian national could hold such positions under local law. The suspension was found to breach Article 21, as it obstructed his use of his property without compensation or due process, and without any apparent public interest justification.[122] The Court, unusually in its jurisprudence, ordered the local courts to determine the appropriate amount of compensation for the violation. Ultimately, a domestic arbitral tribunal awarded USD 6.2 million to Mr Bronstein.[123] This reluctance by the Court to itself determine damages in cases of economic damage[124] has been criticized as a failure to fulfil its role in international law.[125]

Unlike the European system, the Inter-American complaints procedure is not open for companies to seek remedies for violations of their 'human' rights. In fact, the Charter of the Organization of American States is unique among the treaties creating international organizations, in demanding that corporations obey the law of each host country, including the treaties to which the state is a party. This provision arguably could make them subject to the human rights and humanitarian law obligations contained in agreements to which the host state is party.[126]

As to the contrary practice of the European system, Anna Grear has argued that '[i]t would be meaningless to disconnect the Convention's democratic model from core values of a capitalist system',[127] which may explain the European Court's divergent approach on the issue of corporate human rights. Indeed, it is worth noting that Europe is a region where strong economic and human rights legal systems have emerged side by side over many decades, the former under the auspices of the European Communities (later the European Union (EU)) and the latter under the auspices of the Council of Europe. The Charter of Fundamental Rights of the

[121] *Ivcher-Bronstein v Peru*. See also Karamanian (n 11) 252.

[122] Karamanian (n 11) 252.

[123] Pedro Nikken, 'Balancing of Human Rights and Investment Law in the Inter-American System of Human Rights' in Dupuy, Francioni, and Petersmann (n 12) 252.

[124] See also *Cesti-Hurtado v Peru*, para 46.

[125] Nikken (n 123) 253.

[126] Charter of the Organization of American States, Art 37.

[127] Anna Grear, 'Challenging Corporate "Humanity": Legal Disembodiment, Embodiment and Human Rights' (2007) 7 *HRL Rev* 511, 535, quoting Marius Emberland, *The Human Rights of Companies: Exploring the Structure of ECHR Protection* (OUP 2006) 42.

European Union now binds EU members, and the EU is negotiating to become a party to the ECHR.

6. Hierarchies, Divergence, and Harmonization

The Vienna Convention on the Law of Treaties (VCLT) provides, in Article 31(3)(c), that treaties should be interpreted with an assumption that states parties do not mean to contradict other international legal obligations. Therefore, WTO dispute settlement bodies should endeavour to interpret the WTO Agreements, if possible, so as to conform to the parties' human rights obligations, investment tribunals should interpret BITs in conformity with human rights, and human rights bodies should do the same in the reciprocal situations. Another relevant provision, VCLT Article 53 provides that in the case of conflict between two international laws, peremptory or *jus cogens* norms will prevail over other norms.[128]

Apart from the rules of treaty interpretation, states declared the primacy of their human rights obligations in Article 1 of the Vienna Declaration and Programme of Action of 1993.[129] While this suggests that in theory, a human rights norm should prevail over international economic norms as a matter of international law,[130] it must be acknowledged that state practice does not usually bear out the alleged primacy of international human rights law.[131]

When two conflicting international norms are equal in value, as may be the case with some and even most human rights norms when compared to trade and investment treaty norms, the available tools for resolving these conflicts in international law are unhelpful. The more specific law will prevail over the more general law, while a later treaty will prevail over an earlier treaty. However, those principles do not apply when the two areas of law are not concerned with the same subject matter.[132]

[128] For a discussion of peremptory norms, see Chapter 24 in this *Handbook*.

[129] This Declaration was concluded after a major world conference on human rights in Vienna in 1993.

[130] See Adam McBeth, 'Human Rights in Economic Globalisation' in Sarah Joseph and Adam McBeth (eds), *Research Handbook on International Human Rights Law* (Edward Elgar 2010) 144–46. See also Pascal Lamy, 'The WTO in the Archipelago of Global Governance' (Institute of International Studies, Geneva, 14 March 2006) <http://www.wto.org/english/news_e/sppl_e/sppl20_e.htm> accessed 19 September 2010.

[131] Dinah Shelton, 'Normative Hierarchy in International Law' (2006) 100 *AJIL* 291, 294.

[132] See International Law Commission, 'Fragmentation of International Law: Difficulties Arising from the Diversification and Expansion of International Law: Report of the Study Group of the International Law Commission' (13 April 2006) UN Doc A/CN.4/L.682, paras 56–87, 116–18.

The next part discusses how WTO and investment bodies have addressed human rights norms and human rights bodies' reverse consideration of trade and investment law, providing examples of arguable conflict between the norms in case law.

6.1 WTO jurisprudence

No WTO case has directly concerned human rights, although several panel decisions have concerned challenges to environmental and health measures: a European ban on hormone-injected beef, a European ban on genetically modified organisms, a US ban on the import of Indonesian clove cigarettes, a Brazilian ban on retreaded tyres, and a European ban on asbestos products from Canada. Among these cases, WTO panels found only the ban on asbestos to be completely compatible with WTO rules. The overwhelming percentage of negative findings in these decisions regarding the compatibility of challenged social measures with WTO rules may reinforce the chilling effect of WTO law discussed in Section 2.2.

Article 3(2) of the WTO's Understanding on Rules and Procedures Governing the Settlement of Disputes[133] specifies that the WTO Agreements will be interpreted 'in accordance with [the] customary rules of interpretation', which are enshrined in the VCLT, including Article 31(3)(c). Customary international law is relevant to the application of WTO norms,[134] so, where possible, the Appellate Body and Panels should construe a WTO provision in conformity with those human rights protected by customary law.[135] Nonetheless, customary law will not displace inconsistent WTO norms, unless the norm is found to be *jus cogens*.[136]

The WTO Appellate Body in *US: Import Prohibition of Certain Shrimp and Shrimp Products* stated that Panels could take non-WTO treaties into account in interpreting WTO agreements, even if the parties in the case were not all parties to those treaties.[137] It did not refer to Article 31(3)(c) of the Vienna Convention, so that form of interpretation may be discretionary rather than mandatory. Indeed, in *European Communities: Measures Affecting the Approval and Marketing of Biotech Products*, a WTO panel decided that panels may choose to take a treaty into account in interpreting WTO law, but they did not *have to* do so unless all WTO Members were

[133] WTO Agreement, Annex 2 (Understanding on Rules and Procedures Governing the Settlement of Disputes).

[134] WTO, *Korea—Measures Affecting Government Procurement—Panel Report* (1 May 2000) WT/DS163/R, para 7.96; Peter Van den Bossche, *The Law and Policy of the World Trade Organization: Text, Cases and Materials* (CUP 2005) 57.

[135] Adam McBeth, *International Economic Actors and Human Rights* (Routledge 2010) 110–12.

[136] See eg WTO, *European Communities: Measures Concerning Meat and Meat Products—Report of the Appellate Body* (16 January 1998) WT/DS26/AB/R and WT/DS48/AB/R, paras 120–25 (Report of the Appellate Body).

[137] WTO, *US: Import Prohibition of Certain Shrimp and Shrimp Products—Report of the Appellate Body* (12 October 1998) WT/DS58/AB/R, paras 126–134.

party to the particular treaty.[138] Such unanimous membership of another treaty is virtually impossible, as the WTO permits the membership of certain non-states, such as Hong Kong and Chinese Taipei, which cannot ratify most other treaties. Less strict variations on this first option are for the relevant human rights treaty to bind all state members of the WTO, or for all state members to have either ratified or signed the treaty. The *Biotech* Panel approach indicates that non-trade rules may be relegated to a minor role, or may even have no role, in the determination of a dispute, regardless of the dispute's non-trade impact.[139]

In sum, it seems likely that the WTO's dispute settlement bodies would hold that WTO obligations prevailed over human rights obligations in the case of conflicts that could not be resolved by interpretation, except in the rare instance that the human right at issue was found to be a *jus cogens* obligation.[140]

6.2 Investment jurisprudence

Investment tribunals have referred to human rights norms on a number of occasions to inform their interpretation of the substantive BIT rights of investors,[141] such as guarantees against expropriation and denial of justice.[142] They have also referred to human rights law precedents in making decisions regarding procedural issues.[143] However, the use of human rights is haphazard and inconsistent, which is to be expected in an arbitral system that lacks an overarching appellate system and where the arbitrators' expertise in human rights law varies widely.

There have been a number of investment cases where the investor's claims were argued to clash with third party human rights. In *Glamis Gold v United States*, a Canadian company claimed that California's mining regulations diminished the value of its mining investment, in breach of the US's NAFTA obligations in respect of Canadian investors. The Quechuan Indian nation filed an amicus brief against the Glamis claim,[144] claiming that the regulations served to preserve their minority

[138] WTO, *European Communities: Measures Affecting the Approval and Marketing of Biotech Products—Reports of the Panel* (29 September 2006) WT/DS291/R, WT/DS292/R, and WT/DS/293/R, para 7.68.

[139] The International Law Commission criticized *Biotech* at 'Fragmentation of International Law' (n 132) para 471.

[140] See generally, Gabrielle Marceau, 'WTO Dispute Settlement and Human Rights' (2002) 13 *EJIL* 753, 756, 791–95; James Harrison, *The Human Rights Impact of the World Trade Organisation* (Hart 2007) 191.

[141] See generally Fry (n 32) 82–96.

[142] See also Karamanian (n 11) 248–49.

[143] Fry (n 32) 96–99.

[144] See Non-Party Submission, *Glamis Gold Ltd v United States*, Submission of the Quechua Nation, Application for Leave to File a Non-party Submission and Submission of the Quechan Indian Nation 8 <http://www.state.gov/documents/organization/52531.pdf> accessed 4 January 2013. Amicus briefs may be submitted to tribunals, though the tribunals do not have to accept them or take them into consideration when making decisions.

rights under Article 27 of the ICCPR, to which the US is a party. In the result, the arbitral tribunal found it unnecessary to make any ruling on the human rights issues, as Glamis's claim failed for other reasons.[145]

In *Foresti et al v South Africa*, Italian mining companies challenged the South African Black Economic Empowerment Laws, which had been adopted after the demise of the apartheid regime to redress the historic economic disadvantage of non-whites. The mining companies argued that the empowerment laws rendered their mining rights less valuable and amounted to expropriation, as well as breaches of requirements of 'fair and equitable treatment'.[146] In *Aguas del Tunari v Bolivia* a multinational consortium challenged the cancellation of a contract to run water utilities in the Bolivian city of Cochabamba. Critics claimed that the consortium's overly high prices had limited access to water, which led to civil unrest. Cancellation of the contract arguably enhanced the right of access to water in Cochabamba.[147]

The companies in *Foresti* and *Aguas del Tunari* discontinued their claims after significant civil society outrage appeared. Coupled with the decision in *Glamis Gold*, perhaps one may surmise that the perceived bark of investment law is worse than its actual bite. However, the doctrine of precedent does not operate within international investment law, so future cases may have different, less favourable outcomes for human rights. Furthermore, the costs for a state to defend arbitral challenges are considerable. South Africa's aborted defence in the *Foresti* proceedings cost €5 million, of which the claimants only paid €400,000.[148] The chilling impact of investment law upon a state's willingness to implement its human rights obligations remains apparent.

Investors brought a series of cases against Argentina in the wake of its adoption of emergency measures (including currency devaluation) to combat its economic crisis at the end of the 1990s. In *Suez v Argentina*, Argentina claimed that the need to protect human rights, namely the health and well-being of its people, justified its actions. It also claimed that its actions, in relation to water and sewage investments, were necessary to secure the right to water. The tribunal rejected the arguments, finding that Argentina could comply with its human rights obligations without breaching the relevant BIT.[149] The decision-makers thus concluded that the relevant norms did not in fact conflict. It is not clear that a human rights body would come to the same conclusion. The expertise on the two types of tribunal is very different.[150]

[145] See *Glamis Gold Ltd v United States* (Award) 22. See also Karamanian (n 11) 263.

[146] *Foresti et al v South Africa*, para 47.

[147] See 'Bechtel Bows to Bolivia' (2006) 27 *Multinational Monitor* 4.

[148] Luke Eric Peterson, 'South Africa Mining Arbitration Ends with a Whimper, as Terms of Discontinuance Are Set down in Award' (*IA Reporter*, 5 August 2010) <http://www.iareporter.com/articles/20100818_6> accessed 4 January 2013.

[149] Karamanian (n 11) 264.

[150] Fry (n 32) 111–12.

6.3 Human rights jurisprudence

Human rights bodies have been unhesitating in asserting the primacy of their area of law over other areas of law, a primacy that the UN treaty and intergovernmental human rights bodies have repeatedly proclaimed.[151] For example, the Committee on Economic Social and Cultural Rights has said that states must take their ICESCR obligations into account when entering into treaties or joining international organizations,[152] a view that presumably extends to a state joining the WTO or ratifying a BIT.

In *Sawhoyamaza Indigenous Community v Paraguay*[153] before the Inter-American Court, an indigenous community claimed rights over ancestral lands whose title was held by long-standing private owners. Paraguay argued that any requirement to return the lands would force it to breach guarantees against expropriation in a BIT with Germany. The Court responded that the BIT obligations had to be harmonized with ACHR obligations; the latter were not altered by the former. In any case, the Court interpreted the BIT as in fact allowing for expropriation in similar terms to that allowed under the ACHR.[154] It is uncertain whether an arbitral tribunal would come to the same conclusion.

Apart from conflicts of human rights with trade and investment law, in *Laing v Australia* the UN Human Rights Committee (HRC) indicated that the Hague Convention on the Civil Aspects of International Child Abduction of 1980 did not diminish the scope of ICCPR obligations. Similarly, it has not accepted arguments that a state's ICCPR obligations are modified by bilateral instruments concerning, respectively, the withdrawal of Soviet troops from a country[155] or cooperation in criminal matters.[156] In contrast, the HRC majority in the 2010 decision in *Sechremelis v Greece* implied (in some opaque reasoning) that the customary rules of state immunity constituted a justifiable limitation to the relevant ICCPR right (the right to a fair trial).

Of all of the international human rights bodies, the European Court of Human Rights has probably been the most consistently deferential to other areas of international law. For example, it has construed the ECHR in accordance with the rules of state immunity in *McElhinney v Ireland* and *Al-Adsani v UK*, and rules of jurisdiction and responsibility in *Bankovic v Belgium and others*[157] and *Behrami and Seramati v France, Germany and Norway.*

[151] See eg Committee on Economic Social and Cultural Rights (CESCR), 'Globalization and Its Impact on the Enjoyment of Economic, Social and Cultural Rights' (11 May 1998) UN Doc E/1999/22-E/C.12/1998/26, para 5.

[152] See eg CESCR 'General Comment No 12: The Right to Adequate Food (Art 11)' (12 May 1999) UN Doc E/C.12/1999/5, para 19.

[153] *Sawhoyamaza Indigenous Community v Paraguay*, para 140.

[154] Karamanian (n 11) 255. [155] *Borzov v Estonia.* [156] *Maksudov et al v Kyrgyzstan.*

[157] See International Law Commission, 'Fragmentation of International Law' (n 132) paras 161–64.

There are numerous UN cases where persons whose interests are in apparent conflict with those of an investor (albeit not necessarily a foreign investor) have claimed human rights. For example, numerous claims by indigenous people to minority rights under Article 27 of the ICCPR have concerned allegations that development projects (eg logging, mining) have unduly interfered with certain natural environments (eg forests) and harmed their traditional economic and cultural activities (eg reindeer herding, grazing). In most of these cases, the claimants have lost, as the HRC has found that while the industrial projects may have interfered with minority rights, the interference was not unreasonable or disproportionate.[158] On very few occasions, the impacts of the industrial developments have been so extensive as to breach Article 27.[159]

In *Hopu and Bessert v France*, the complainants claimed that a hotel development in Tahiti breached their rights to family life, as the construction would destroy the graves of their ancestors. The HRC agreed and found that the hotel project would breach the claimants' rights to respect for family life under Article 17 of the ICCPR.[160] The HRC recommended the provision of an 'effective and enforceable remedy' without specifying whether the project had to be cancelled.[161]

In *Haraldsson and Sveinsson v Iceland*, the HRC found a breach of the ICCPR's non-discrimination provisions entailed in the conferral of excessive property rights (in the form of fishing licenses and entitlements) upon vested commercial fishing interests, to the detriment of other commercial fishermen. The HRC recommended a review of Iceland's fishing management systems, indicating that Iceland was expected to reduce the existing property rights of certain commercial fishing enterprises.

The Inter-American Court has dealt with similar cases of indigenous rights, and claimants have generally been more successful, either because of the ACHR's explicit property right or because of the development of jurisprudence on the special duties owed to indigenous peoples. The Court has held that natural resources within traditional indigenous lands, which are needed for the continued survival of a tribe's culture and development, fall within Article 21. Such rights are not absolute. Development projects may take place on such land, so long as certain safeguards are observed. For example, indigenous peoples must receive prior information, must participate in the framing of the project, and must obtain some reasonable benefit from it; and there should be an independent environmental and social assessment of the project.[162] The IACtHR commonly orders restitution of land to indigenous

[158] See eg *Länsman et al v Finland* (26 October 1994); *Länsman et al v Finland* (30 October 1996).

[159] See eg *Poma Poma v Peru*.

[160] See *Hopu v France*. Therefore, the HRC majority found that long-dead ancestors could count as family for the purposes of Art 17. France has entered a reservation to Art 27, which precluded consideration of that provision in the case.

[161] *Hopu* (n 160) para 13.

[162] *Saramaka People v Suriname*, para 129; Karamanian (n 11) 254–55.

peoples, where possible, as the remedy for violation of their property (and other) rights.[163] Restitution is awarded because it is recognized that indigenous property rights have a social and cultural 'non-fungible' value that cannot be reduced to mere economic compensation.[164] In contrast, through the payment of fair monetary compensation, the state can meaningfully compensate any consequent expropriation of private property rights necessitated by the restitution of indigenous property rights.[165] Nevertheless, this approach does effectively mean that indigenous rights prevail over countervailing private property rights, which might sometimes include investor rights.[166]

Claude-Reyes v Chile concerned a claim before the American Court by Chilean citizens seeking information about a controversial planned deforestation project. Chile's Foreign Investment Committee had refused the request for information in order to safeguard the confidential business records of the company involved, arguably under its right to privacy. The American Court established a broad right of access to government-held information in Article 13 of the ACHR (as part of the freedom of expression) and found that such a right applied here, given the clear 'public interest' in the information of foreign investment in forestry exploitation.[167] Clearly, investor interests (including, arguably, its human rights, if one believes that companies have human rights) in this case gave way to countervailing human rights.[168]

6.4 Conclusion on jurisprudence

The relevant dispute settlement bodies have tended to interpret, or at least to claim that they interpret, their respective areas of law in congruity with other areas of international law. The outlier is the field of human rights, whose monitoring bodies have tended to enthusiastically embrace the notion of the primacy of human rights law.

The possibility of future conflicts cannot be discounted.[169] In such cases, the relevant dispute settlement bodies are likely to uphold the norms in their own system.[170] Therefore, a state could be subjected to conflicting obligations. In such instance, there is a danger of a de facto hierarchy developing, with trade and investment rules prevailing over human rights rules, due to the stronger enforcement systems

[163] Nikken (n 123) 262–63.

[164] Nikken (n 123) 262. It is recognized that restitution is sometimes impossible, in which case alternative lands might be granted, and/or compensation guided 'primarily by the meaning of the land for' the Indigenous claimants. *Yakye Axa Indigenous Community v Paraguay*, para 149.

[165] *Yakye Axa* (n 164) para 146.

[166] Nikken (n 123) 264–65.

[167] *Claude-Reyes* (n 103) paras 88–91.

[168] Karamanian (n 11) 256–57.

[169] See eg the discussion of a current arbitral dispute between Chevron and Ecuador in Sarah Joseph, 'Protracted Lawfare: The Tale of Chevron Texaco in the Amazon' (2012) 3 *JHRE* 70, 81–84.

[170] Marceau (n 140) 797; Karamanian (n 11) 238.

under the WTO and BITs, compared to the global human rights system.[171] Pascal Lamy has acknowledged this imbalance in the international system.[172] The disproportionate strength of the trade and investment regimes, compared to the human rights regime, can lead to prioritization of the former norms if they conflict with human rights norms, or to regulatory chill as states may fail to adopt measures to protect human rights because they fear that such measures might breach trade and investment law.

7. Conclusion

The WTO's outgoing Director General, Pascal Lamy, proclaimed in early 2010 that trade rules, including WTO rules, are based on the same values as human rights: 'individual freedom and responsibility, non-discrimination, rule of law, and welfare through peaceful cooperation among individuals'.[173] All of those values can probably be applied to the international investment law regime as well. They also fundamentally accord with the promotion of human rights principles.

Certainly, all three systems are concerned with the promotion of human agency and human flourishing. Trade and investment law promote free economic activity, while human rights promote freedom and capacities more generally. As noted above, there are certainly synergies between the relevant economic law regimes and economic social and cultural rights, as well as civil and political rights.

However, one must not be complacent in presuming the compatibility of international economic legal regimes with human rights law. Those regimes essentially promote the rights of a privileged few, namely foreign traders and investors,[174] which may lead to the inevitable prioritization of their rights when they clash with, or otherwise detract from, the human rights of others. Such a prioritization is unfortunate if it adds to the already great capacity for powerful entities to override the interests of the powerless and marginalized.

[171] Margot Salomon, *Global Responsibility for Human Rights: World Poverty and the Development of International Law* (OUP 2007) 155.

[172] Pascal Lamy, 'The Place and Role of the WTO (WTO Law) in the International Legal Order' (Address before the European Society of International Law, Paris, 19 May 2006) <http://www.wto.org/english/news_e/sppl_e/sppl26_e.htm> accessed 19 September 2010.

[173] Lamy, 'Towards Shared Responsibility' (n 91).

[174] See eg Jose E Alvarez, 'Critical Theory and the North American Free Trade Agreement's Chapter Eleven' (1997) 28 *U Miami Inter-Am L Rev* 303, 307–309.

Further Reading

Dupuy PM, Francioni F, and Petersmann EU (eds), *Human Rights in International Investment Law and Arbitration* (OUP 2009)

Harrison J, *The Human Rights Impact of the World Trade Organisation* (Hart 2007)

Joseph S, *Blame it on the WTO: A Human Rights Critique* (OUP 2011)

——, Kinley D, and Waincymer J (eds), *The World Trade Organisation and Human Rights: Interdisciplinary Perspectives* (Edward Elgar 2009)

Lang A, *World Trade Law after Neoliberalism: Reimagining the Global Economic Order* (OUP 2011)

Report of the United Nations High Commissioner for Human Rights, 'Human Rights, Trade and Investment' (2 July 2003) UN Doc E/CN.4/Sub.2/2003/9

Stiglitz JE and Charlton A, *Fair Trade for All* (OUP 2005)

PART VII

ASSESSMENTS

CHAPTER 36

CREATING AND APPLYING HUMAN RIGHTS INDICATORS

FRANCISCO LÓPEZ-BERMÚDEZ*

1. Introduction

Is it possible to identify those countries that have the worst record of human rights violations? Has each country improved its respect for human rights during the new millennium? Answers to these questions might emerge from the use of data, statistics or indicators, because even though human rights are normative in nature, they are linked to and often rely on facts and data. This chapter aims to analyse the creation and application of human rights indicators within the United Nations (UN). Section one builds a conceptual framework meant to reinforce awareness

* The author wishes to thank Andrea Villarreal and Courtney Hillebrecht for useful suggestions on an early draft of this article. He also wishes to acknowledge with gratitude the generous support and helpful observations of Ana Lucía Córdova Cazar in the preparation and revision of this chapter, as well as the infinite patience and intelligent comments of the editor of this *Handbook*, Professor Dinah Shelton.

that all measurements are artificial human creations that have been socially constructed.[1] This section recalls that during the foundational normative development of human rights, influential actors like the International Monetary Fund (IMF), World Bank (WB), and prominent statisticians developed economic, statistical, social, and development regimes which have strongly influenced the narrative of human rights indicators. Section two of the chapter focuses on the work of the UN Charter-based and treaty-based human rights bodies which are concerned with economic, social and cultural rights (ESC rights). Since the 1980s,[2] the discussion of the topic of human rights indicators by these UN bodies has taken place in the context of global debates and reiterated faith in measurements and indicators surrounding the topic of development. The creation of the Millennium Development Goals (MDGs) by the IMF, WB, OECD, and UN technocrats at the beginning of the millennium consolidated this target-setting philosophy and the indicators' narrative. The final section of the chapter examines the application of human rights indicators with a focus on theoretical and practical proposals, including 'illustrative indicators', developed by the Office of the High Commissioner of Human Rights (OHCHR).

As a starting point, it seems clear that human rights bodies understand the concept of human rights indicators in ways that are both inconsistent and heterogeneous, an unsurprising observation if one acknowledges that international actors other than human rights bodies themselves initiated the narrative on the topic. Indeed, human rights bodies have largely accepted the discourse of human development[3] and MDGs as a way to contribute to the debate over human rights indicators. It remains to be determined whether human rights theory and practice can fertilize the development discourse or, on the contrary, whether human rights law and practice will become blurred in the development framework. In either scenario, the state is the dominant actor in the human rights arena and in the theory and practice of measurement and indicators.

[1] For an introduction to social construction and its multiple roots, see the collection of articles contained in part I of Mary M Gergen and Kenneth Gergen (eds), *Social Construction: A Reader* (Sage 2003). See also the classic works of Peter L Berger and Thomas Luckman, *The Social Construction of Reality: A Treatise in the Sociology of Knowledge* (Doubleday 1966), and John R Searle, *The Construction of Social Reality* (Free Press 1995).

[2] In addition to the UN human rights bodies discussed herein, specialized agencies, such as the ILO, regional organizations, academics, universities, scientific communities, donors, non-governmental organizations, and even transnational business entities have been active on the issue of indicators. Further readings on the topic are listed at the end of the chapter.

[3] For a discussion of the similarities and differences between human development and human rights, see UN Development Programme, *Human Development Report 2000* (OUP 2000).

2. A Conceptual and Historical Framework of Human Rights Indicators

Those who refer to the topic of 'human rights indicators' use words like data, statistics, indicators, and indexes.[4] It is therefore important to define these words to have an understanding of the concept of human rights indicators.

In a narrow sense, 'statistics' refer to a collection of numerical data (information) that measures something. More broadly, statistics is a science or discipline that develops and applies methods to collect, organize, analyse, interpret, and report quantitative information. Two methods are widely used in statistics. The simpler one, descriptive statistics, provides a single descriptive value for a set of scores, and is commonly displayed in graphs and tables that measure a central tendency, such as mean (the average) and the median. The second method, inferential statistics, acknowledges the difficulty of studying entire populations, and instead makes generalizations about the population from studying samples of those populations.[5]

An indicator, in its most general understanding, is something that serves to indicate or signal the state of something. A more scientific understanding of the term is that it is a specific measure of a concept. Thus, the process of building an indicator includes: (a) identifying a concept; (b) specifying the concept by developing a definition of it; (c) operationalizing the definition, by identifying the dimensions and sub-dimensions of such concept; and (d) evaluating the validity[6] and reliability[7] of the created indicators. Indicators may be objective or subjective.

What, then, is a human rights indicator? An easy answer is that it is a measure of a human right, but this straightforward answer leads immediately into contentious territory, requiring a determination of the catalogue of human rights and content of the human right in question. The determination provided by each author or institution on this matter will then lead to a focus on measuring that subjective understanding of that particular right. Thus, for example, an author's belief that the right to work is not a human right will lead that person to exclude the topic from measurement efforts. And even if others accept that it is a human right, each of

[4] Index refers to a summary measure when a set of individual scores are combined.

[5] For a basic introductory text in statistics, see Gudmund R Iversen and Mary Gergen, *Statistics: The Conceptual Approach* (Springer 1997). For a dictionary and glossary of statistical terms see: Yadolah Dodge (ed), *The Oxford Dictionary of Statistical Terms* (OUP 2006); Organisation for Economic Co-operation and Development, 'Glossary of Statistical Terms' <http://stats.oecd.org/glossary/index.htm> accessed 18 February 2013.

[6] Validity refers to the idea of whether the indicator measures what it is supposed to be measuring.

[7] Reliability refers to the idea of consistency among measurements.

them is likely to have different views on the definition, scope and elements of the right. Any measurements they undertake regarding the right to work will therefore differ. In sum, the conceptualization of human rights entails a substantial question of definition, which is at the core of the human rights indicators' debate. Further, this conceptualization is part of the process of dialogue about universal values, and, in consequence, it has a high political content. Measures, then, are not 'givens' but are human creations which need to be put to social scrutiny. Knowing who, how, when and with what purpose these indicators were created can help to place them in context and assess their usefulness.

Developing human rights indicators thus requires an understanding of human rights. At the universal level, the UN Charter (1945) contains important references to human rights, but has no catalogue or definition of the term.[8] As a result, the first era of human rights history became one of normative development, in the context of the East-West political and ideological disputes that characterized the Cold War.[9] The adoption of the so-called International Bill of Rights[10] contributed to the construction of a minimal consensus of what constitutes human rights. However, international human rights treaties lack specificity, in part due to their nature (constitutional rights are also often stated in broad, ambiguous terms) and in part due to the need to achieve agreement in a heterogenous world. The task of identifying the precise scope and content of human rights became a dialectic process influenced by deep political,[11] religious and cultural[12] debates. In their most obvious forms, these disagreements are reflected in drafting delays, non-ratification, reservations attached to treaties,[13] and even their denunciation.[14] Challenges have also surfaced in response to the pronouncements of

[8] See Thomas Buergenthal, Dinah Shelton, and David Stewart, *International Human Rights in a Nutshell* (4th edn, West 2009).

[9] See David P Forsythe, *Human Rights in International Relations* (3rd edn, CUP 2012).

[10] Consisting of the Universal Declaration of Human Rights (UDHR), adopted in 1948; and the International Covenant on Civil and Political Rights (ICCPR) and the International Covenant on Economic, Social and Cultural Rights (ICESCR), both adopted in 1966.

[11] Such as whether economic, social, and cultural rights qualify as rights. This debate not only led to the division of the UDHR into two separate covenants, but lingered throughout the Cold War and to the present day.

[12] The idea of 'traditional values' has been a recurring part of the human rights debate and re-emerged strongly in 2012. See: Human Rights Council, 'Promoting Human Rights and Fundamental Freedoms through a Better Understanding of Traditional Values of Humankind: Best Practices' (21 September 2012) UN Doc A/HRC/21/L.2.

[13] For instance, the Committee on the Elimination of Discrimination against Women (CEDAW) has stated that: 'The Committee has noted with alarm the number of States parties which have entered reservations to the whole or part of article 16, especially when a reservation has also been entered to article 2, claiming that compliance may conflict with a commonly held vision of the family based, inter alia, on cultural or religious beliefs or on the country's economic or political status.' CEDAW Committee, 'General Recommendation No 21: Equality in Marriage and Family Relations' (1994) UN Doc A/49/38, para 41.

[14] For a regional example regarding the denunciation of the American Convention on Human Rights, see the case of Venezuela. OAS, 'IACHR Regrets Decision of Venezuela to Denounce the

the judicial and quasi-judicial human rights bodies created by the treaties, questioning these bodies' interpretations, concluding observations and general comments.

Notably, throughout the period of standard-setting, the interested actors paid little or no attention to human rights indicators. Other influential international actors, however, especially the international financial institutions and high-ranking statisticians, developed regimes of economic and social statistics and indicators that later had a decisive influence on the creation and application of human rights indicators.

3. Creating Human Rights Indicators

After the First World War, concern for statistical matters emerged within the League of Nations and other international institutions, especially the International Labor Organization (ILO). Such concern paved the way for the first discussions within the United Nations regarding this topic, in which the political divisions of the time were evident.[15]

The creation of a new interstate body, the United Nations Statistical Commission (UNStC) in 1947 initiated the construction of a universal statistical regime, which contributed to the creation and dissemination of statistical standards, despite sometimes tense exchanges with powerful institutions, including the World Bank and the IMF. During the first stage, which coincided with the foundational period of human rights, the UNStC worked to create and standardize macroeconomic statistics, resulting in its flagship work: the System of National Accounts (SNA). In this document, first published in 1953 and revised and expanded in 1968, one of the indicators most widely used (and criticized) stood out: the Gross Domestic Product (GDP).

Once the UNStC initiated its system, some entrepreneurs began advocating the idea of building a 'System of Social and Demographic Statistics' (SSDS). As Ward explains, various groups expressed opposition: 'The objections were primarily political but had also to do with the heavy practical burden imposed by the data

American Convention on Human Rights' (12 September 2012) Press Release No 117/12 <http://www.oas.org/en/iachr/media_center/PReleases/2012/117.asp> accessed 19 February 2013. Note that the UN Human Rights Committee has concluded that the ICCPR is incapable of denunciation in light of the law of treaties.

[15] Michael Ward, 'Aspects of "Quantifying the World: UN Ideas and Statistics"' (2005) Forum for Development Studies No 1-2005, 185 <http://www.unhistory.org/reviews/FDS_Ward.pdf> accessed 19 February 2013.

needs of the system. Thus the statisticians themselves opposed its introduction, particularly because it came so close on the heels of the new SNA.'[16] There was also an important political dimension: 'There was quite intense opposition from several 'independent' and often politically insecure sovereign states to the introduction of measures that might allow outsiders to make assessments of human rights progress and social achievement.'[17] Despite these concerns, the United Nations Statistical Office (UNSO) initiated modest work on social statistics in the 1970s. It was not until mid-1980s,[18] however, that the idea of measuring 'levels of living'[19] found a warmer welcome in the United Nations in the framework of debates about the need to have a broader understanding of 'development,' one that would go beyond measuring GDP. In those debates, the World Bank played a key role, especially when it decided to publish its *World Development Indicators*, a document that had been restricted to internal distribution since it was written in 1960.[20]

By the beginning of the 1990s, the broader concept of human development had penetrated other institutions, as reflected in the first UNDP Human Development Report (HDR).[21] This document offered a simple Human Development Index (HDI), presented as a counterweight to the widely used Gross National Product (GNP) index.[22] The impact of the HDI was significantly reduced, however, by the timing of its appearance, for it coincided with the emergence of the so-called Washington Consensus, an agenda of the IMF and WB that advocated economic stabilization, liberalization, and privatization, in the aftermath of the fall of the Berlin Wall in 1989. Within such framework, the United Nations convened several world conferences during this period which became forums to promote a target-setting philosophy and, to a lesser extent, for the emergence of social statistics and indicators. In 1996 the United

[16] Ward (n 15) 207. [17] Ward (n 15) 207.

[18] The resolutions of the UN General Assembly on this topic can be found in UN Research Institute for Social Development (UNRISD), 'Qualitative Indicators and Development Data: Current Concerns and Priorities' (UNRISD 1991) 2.

[19] Terminology utilized in the discussions included references to social development, basic needs, and human development, all of which reflected interest in measuring the consumption of food and levels of education, housing, clothing, healthcare, and social services. See UNRISD (n 18) 2–3.

[20] See World Bank, 'World Development Indicators' <http://data.worldbank.org/data-catalog/world-development-indicators> accessed 19 February 2013. The World Development Indicators were published as an Annex to the WB's World Development Report, which it first published in 1978. These indicators were mainly macroeconomic statistics with few social indicators. World Bank, *World Development Report 1978* (WB 1978) 73.

[21] In brief, the report placed human beings and their needs at the centre of the development process. See UNDP, *Human Development Report 1990* (OUP 1990).

[22] As one of the HDI's fathers (Amartya Sen) explained: 'Even though I had been very opposed to having one simple Human Development Index, I ended up gladly helping [Mahbub ul Haq] to develop it, since he persuaded me that there was no way of replacing the GNP unless we had another similarly simple index. But this index will be better in the sense that it will focus on human lives, and not just on commodities.' Quoted in Richard Jolly, Louis Emmerij, and Thomas G Weiss, *The Power of UN Ideas: Lessons from the First 60 Years* (UN 2005) 31.

Nations created an Expert Group which suggested the idea of a Minimum National Social Data Set (MNSDS) made up of fifteen indicators.[23] The fifteen items suggested were: (a) Population estimates by sex, age and, where appropriate and feasible, ethnic group; (b) Life expectancy at birth, by sex; (c) Infant mortality, by sex; (d) Child mortality, by sex; (e) Maternal mortality; (f) Percentage of infants weighing less than 2,500 g at birth, by sex; (g) Average number of years of schooling completed, by sex, and where possible by income class; (h) GDP per capita; (i) Household income per capita (level and distribution); (j) Monetary value of the basket of food needed for minimum nutritional requirements; (k) Unemployment rate, by sex; (l) Employment-population ratio, by sex, and by formal and informal sector where appropriate; (m) Access to safe water; (n) Access to sanitation; (o) Number of people per room, excluding kitchen and bathroom. Significantly, the Expert Group in their work[24] made no reference to the 1993 United Nations World Conference on Human Rights held in Vienna.[25] This omission in itself indicates the difficulty encountered by those engaged in human rights work when it comes to engaging in cross-disciplinary activities.

In sum, by the time human rights bodies ventured into the territory of human right indicators at the end of the 1980s and the beginning of the 1990s, diverse influential actors had already created and promoted social and development statistics and indicators.[26] Within that framework, and considering the fact that the international treaties do not refer to indicators,[27] some human rights actors viewed the use of existing indicators as a good option.[28] Others, however, requested the creation of new indicators that were linked directly to human rights. This latter option presented a great challenge in the human rights arena due to its lack of economic resources and specialists in social science. As a result, the treatment of statistical terms and indicators within human rights bodies has been inconsistent.

[23] UN Economic and Social Council, 'Report of the Expert Group on the Statistical Implications of Recent Major United Nations Conferences' (24 January 1996) UN Doc E/CN.3/AC.1/1996/R.4.

[24] Ward, however, notes that: 'The main work on social indicators, however, was hived off early on to a quasi-independent wing of the UN in Geneva, the UN Research Institute on Social Development (UNRISD). This was a body whose programme was independently approved and supervised by a board chaired, initially, by Jan Tinbergen. Not surprisingly, its programme had a strong analytical research emphasis and rather less empirical application.' Ward (n 15) 208.

[25] See Vienna Declaration and Programme of Action (12 July 1993) UN Doc A/CONF. 157/23.

[26] The Report that the Special Rapporteur on the Realization of ESC rights prepared captured a detailed collection of several initiatives on statistics and indicators in the UN system, extant until that time. See Commission on Human Rights, 'Realization of Economic, Social and Cultural Rights: Progress Report Prepared by Mr Danilo Türk, Special Rapporteur' (6 July 1990) UN Doc E/CN.4/Sub.2/1990/19.

[27] The 2006 Convention on the Rights of Persons with Disabilities is the first to include an article related specifically to statistics and data collection, but not indicators: Art 31.

[28] For instance, Thomas Jabine and Richard Claude went as far as to say that, 'Insomuch as the statistical description of human rights already is well established in areas on environmental quality, food, health, education, and employment, the challenge now arises to improve statistical description addressing personal security and political rights.' Thomas B Jabine and Richard P Claude, 'Exploring Human Rights Issues with Statistics' in Thomas B Jabine and Richard P Claude (eds), *Human Rights and Statistics: Getting the Record Straight* (U Pennsylvania Press 1992) 12.

Individuals and groups working in the field of economic, social and cultural rights were among those first and most interested in the creation and use of indicators.[29] This mood was reflected in the Limburg Principles,[30] a declaration adopted by an academic conference convened to contribute scholarly reflections to the recently created Committee on ESC rights (CESCR).[31] By the end of the 1980s some human rights bodies began to show interest in using statistics in their work. The CESCR in its General Comment regarding periodic reporting by states parties (1989),[32] generated seminal ideas on the topic, pointing out that one of the objectives of periodic reporting is to ensure that each state party will monitor the actual situation with respect to each of the rights in the Covenant. The General Comment emphasized the need to present disaggregated national statistics to reveal disparities between regions and groups. Recognizing that the process of gathering this information is expensive, it recommended that states in need should request international cooperation. The General Comment also introduced the idea that states need to identify 'national or other more specific benchmarks as an indication of progress'.[33]

The following year, the CESCR dealt more generally with the nature of states parties' obligations in General Comment No 3.[34] In it, the Committee emphasized the monitoring issues it had outlined in its previous General Comment. It reiterated that the obligations of states, including the obligation to monitor the extent of the realization of ESC rights, remain even where the available resources are scarce.

[29] Actors from other areas have also been interested in human rights statistics and indicators. For instance, CEDAW and other UN bodies, such as the UN Statistical Commission, have shown interest in developing statistics and indicators for women's issues. Whether those bodies coincide in the meaning of (women's) human rights indicators is questionable. See Commission on Human Rights, 'Preliminary Report Submitted by the Special Rapporteur on Violence against Women, Its Causes and Consequences, Ms Radhika Coomaraswamy, in Accordance with Commission on Human Rights Resolution 1994/45' (22 November 1994) UN Doc E/CN.4/1995/42; Human Rights Council 'Report of the Special Rapporteur on Violence against Women, Its Causes and Consequences, Yakin Ertürk: Indicators on Violence against Women and State Response' (29 January 2008) UN Doc A/HRC/7/6. See also World Bank, *World Development Report 2012: Gender Equality and Development* (World Bank 2012).

[30] See 'Limburg Principles on the Implementation of the Covenant on Economic, Social and Cultural Rights' (1987) 9 *Hum Rts Q* 124.

[31] Established under Economic and Social Council (ECOSOC), Resolution 1985/17 (28 May 1985) to carry out the monitoring functions assigned to ECOSOC in Part IV of the Covenant.

[32] See Committee on Economic, Social and Cultural Rights (CESCR), 'General Comment No 1: Reporting by States Parties' (24 February 1989) UN Doc E/1989/22.

[33] CESCR, 'General Comment No 1' (n 32) para 3 ('The Committee is aware that this process of monitoring and gathering information is a potentially time-consuming and costly one and that international assistance and cooperation, as provided for in article 2, paragraph 1 and articles 22 and 23 of the Covenant, may well be required in order to enable some States parties to fulfill the relevant obligations').

[34] CESCR, 'General Comment No 3: The Nature of States Parties Obligations (Art 2, para 1 of the Covenant)' (14 December 1990) UN Doc E/1991/23.

Although calling for statistical information, the Committee did not use the term 'indicator' in either of the two General Comments.

Over the next few years, the idea of human rights indicators gained momentum. The Special Rapporteur on the Realization of Economic, Social and Cultural Rights[35] prepared a study that included the use of the term indicator and expressed conviction that the systematic use of indicators will contribute to the realization of the ESC rights. Beyond sharing the basic objective previously identified by the CESCR, he articulated two important new ideas. The first was that indicators can contribute to the conceptualization of vaguely-worded treaty rights,[36] helping to identify the scope of the rights. Second, he referred to the importance of using indicators in making comparisons between states, ie creating rankings.[37] Several states reacted with hostility to the use of any comparisons or to the 'punitive use of indicators'.[38] Several such rankings, not free of controversy as they were based on qualitative judgments, had been put forward by NGOs such as Freedom House.[39] On its part, the UNDP had published the Human Freedom Index[40] in its 1991 HDR, and included the Political Freedom Index in the 1992 HDR.[41]

On its part, the Vienna Declaration and Programme of Action in 1993 included the idea that indicators might be useful to realizing ESC rights. The Declaration's paragraph 98—drafted in a neutral and somewhat hesitant manner to avoid any controversy—stated that: 'To strengthen the enjoyment of economic, social and cultural

[35] Commission on Human Rights, 'The New International Economic Order and the Promotion of Human Rights: Realization of Economic, Social and Cultural Rights' (6 July 1990) UN Doc E/CN.4/Sub.2/1990/19.

[36] Commission on Human Rights, 'Realization of ESC Rights' (n 35) para 7.

[37] In fact, he emphasized that indicators 'can provide yardsticks whereby countries can compare their own progress with that of other countries, especially countries at the same level of socio-economic development'. Commission on Human Rights, 'Realization of ESC Rights' (n 35) para 7.

[38] Report of the Satellite Meeting of the World Conference on Human Rights, convened on the basis of the recommendation of the Special Rapporteur on the Realization of ESC Rights: 'Many felt uncomfortable...in particular...ranking and rating...which some of the international agencies had started to do in their publications.' UNGA, 'Seminar on Appropriate Indicators to Measure Achievements in the Progressive Realization of Economic, Social and Cultural Rights' (20 April 1993) UN Doc A/CONF.157/PC/73.

[39] Freedom House, considered by some as a conservative organization, publishes two controversial indexes: *Freedom in the World*, a comparative assessment of political rights and civil liberties (published annually since 1972), and *Freedom of the Press*, an assessment of threats to media independence (published since 1980).

[40] This index was derived from the *World Human Rights Guide*, a work from the American political scientist Charles Humana.

[41] In its Human Development Report 2000, the UNDP explained its decision to no longer include such indexes. Specifically, both were based on qualitative judgments, not quantifiable empirical data. UNDP, *Human Development Report 2000* (n 3) 91. For an academic critical appraisal of measures based on qualitative judgments, see Kenneth A Bollen, 'Political Rights and Political Liberties in Nations: An Evaluation of Human Rights Measures, 1950 to 1984' in Jabine and Claude (n 28).

rights, additional approaches should be examined, such as a system of indicators to measure progress in the realization of the rights set forth in the International Covenant on Economic, Social and Cultural Rights...'[42]

The term indicator thus became part of the vocabulary used by human rights bodies. In 1999 the CESCR echoed its prior General Comments, in its General Comment No 13 on the right to education,[43] noting that states parties must monitor education and that educational data should be disaggregated by the prohibited grounds of discrimination. In further specifying the legal obligations of the states, the CESCR stated that that, at a minimum, the state party is required to adopt and implement a national educational strategy that 'should include mechanisms, such as indicators and benchmarks on the right to education, by which progress can be closely monitored'.[44]

The next General Comment, No 14 on the right to health,[45] contained further elaboration of the core obligations of states involving the development of health indicators and benchmarks:

> To adopt and implement a national public health strategy and plan of action, on the basis of epidemiological evidence, addressing the health concerns of the whole population; the strategy and plan of action shall be devised, and periodically reviewed, on the basis of a participatory and transparent process; they shall include methods, such as right to health indicators and benchmarks, by which progress can be closely monitored; the process by which the strategy and plan of action are devised, as well as their content, shall give particular attention to all vulnerable or marginalized groups.[46]

Moreover, the Committee considered that 'the failure to monitor the realization of the right to health at the national level, for example by identifying right to health indicators and benchmarks'[47] could constitute a violation of the obligation to fulfil the right to health. The Committee drafted an entire chapter on right to health indicators and benchmarks, in which it introduced the idea that the Committee should carry out a scoping process with states during the periodic reporting procedure, and, to go along with its idea of seeking international cooperation, recommended that states take guidance on appropriate right to health indicators from WHO and UNICEF. In particular, states should seek technical assistance from WHO in order to formulate and implement their right to health

[42] Vienna Declaration and Programme of Action (n 25).

[43] CESCR, 'General Comment No 13: The Right to Education (Art 13)' (8 December 1999) UN Doc E/C.12/1999/10.

[44] CESCR, 'General Comment No 13' (n 43) para 52.

[45] CESCR, 'General Comment No 14: The Right to the Highest Attainable Standard of Health (Art 12)' (11 August 2000) UN Doc E/C.12/2000/4.

[46] CESCR, 'General Comment No 14' (n 45) para 43(f).

[47] CESCR, 'General Comment No 14' (n 45) para 52.

national strategies; and 'when preparing their reports, states parties should utilize the extensive information and advisory services of WHO with regard to data collection, disaggregation, and the development of right to health indicators and benchmarks'.[48] As it can be seen, the Committee showed great interest in using and relying on the work of international organizations in the realization of its mission and in the use of indicators.

Outside the human rights bodies, by 1996 the OECD had determined to establish some 'international development goals'.[49] The organization therefore created a set of development objectives that could be measured and monitored over time, based on the results of the UN Conferences during the 1990s. Thus, the beginning of the new millennium saw consolidation of the target-setting philosophy incubated in the UN conferences and meetings of the 1990s. In 2000 the UN General Assembly meeting of heads of state and government adopted the United Nations Millennium Declaration,[50] in which the participants committed themselves to end extreme poverty and to make the 'right to development' a reality for everyone.[51] In that framework, they set a series of targets, some of them time-bounded.[52] With the 1996 OECD document and the UN Millennium Declaration at hand, technocrats representing the IMF, OECD and the WB together with members of the United Nations Secretariat merged the documents and created the Millennium Development Goals (MDGs), as well as the even more important and tangible corresponding indicators to measure these goals.[53] No developing country participated in the latter process. In sum, the technocrats created the narrative and the tools to measure this new creation.

[48] CESCR, 'General Comment No 14' (n 45) para 58.

[49] Development Assistance Committee, 'Shaping the 21st Century: The Contribution of Development Co-operation' (May 1996) <http://www.oecd.org/dac/2508761.pdf> accessed 19 February 2013.

[50] UN Millennium Declaration (18 September 2000) UN Doc A/RES/55/2.

[51] See UN Millennium Declaration, ch III: 'Development and Poverty Eradication'.

[52] UN Millennium Declaration, para 11. The UN Millennium Declaration included the language of 'good governance', as well, para 13. It also included a chapter titled 'Human rights, democracy and good governance', that lacked time-bounded goals. A well-known tool of this good governance doctrine was the Worldwide Governance Indicators, which the WB began publishing in 1996, and which became one of the most important engines for indicators worldwide. See World Bank Group, 'The Worldwide Governance Indicators (WGI) Project' (*Worldwide Governance Indicators*) <http://info.worldbank.org/governance/wgi/index.asp> accessed 19 February 2013. For a criticism of governance indicators, see Christine Arndt and Charles Oman, *Uses and Abuses of Governance Indicators* (OECD 2006).

[53] See UNGA, 'Road Map towards the Implementation of the United Nations Millennium Declaration' (6 September 2001) UN Doc A/56/326.

4. Applying Human Rights Indicators

The creation of the MDGs can also be seen as the consolidating moment of the international community's faith in measurement, including the use of targets and indicators. The 2000 HDR reflected this faith among human rights actors: 'Statistical indicators are a powerful tool in the struggle for human rights. They make it possible for people and organizations... to identify important actors and hold them accountable for their actions. That is why developing and using indicators for human rights has become a cutting-edge area of advocacy.'[54] As the UN created new Rapporteurships in the area of ESC rights, not surprisingly, the Rapporteurs took indicators as one of their main study topics. The Special Rapporteur on the right to education[55] presented a preliminary report in 1999, where she looked at the work on education within the United Nations system and concluded that conceptualization was at the core of all the problems. As a result, she expressed interest in creating a common language with the help of different actors within the system, with the objective of developing indicators for the realization of the right to education.[56] Thus, despite the Rapporteur's criticisms of the statistics and indicators available at the time,[57] she strongly favoured their use.

Another UN Special Rapporteur, on the right to health, analysed in his preliminary report[58] the three analytical frameworks which until then had been developed to deepen the understanding of ESC rights.[59] One of the three frameworks referred to the use of indicators and benchmarks, following the CESCR's General Comment No 14,[60] which specified that the states are responsible for selecting appropriate

[54] UNDP, *Human Development Report 2000* (n 3) 89.

[55] Commission on Human Rights, 'Preliminary Report of the Special Rapporteur on the Right to Education, Ms Katarina Tomasevski, Submitted in accordance with Commission on Human Rights Resolution 1998/33' (13 January 1999) UN Doc E/CN.4/1999/49.

[56] Commission on Human Rights, 'Preliminary Report of Special Rapporteur Tomasevski' (n 55) paras 10, 12.

[57] Commission on Human Rights, 'Preliminary Report of Special Rapporteur Tomasevski' (n 55) para 31.

[58] Commission on Human Rights, 'The Right of Everyone to the Enjoyment of the Highest Attainable Standard of Physical and Mental Health: Report of the Special Rapporteur, Paul Hunt, Submitted in Accordance with Commission Resolution 2002/31' (13 February 2003) UN Doc E/CN.4/2003/58.

[59] The first two *frameworks* to which the Rapporteur referred: (a) were moving along with the ideas expressed in the CESCR General Comment No 14—the Available, Accessible, Acceptable, and Quality framework; and (b) alongside with CESCR, the CEDAW Committee, and the Sub-Commission on the Promotion and Protection of Human Rights, presented the three types of obligations that human rights impose on states: to respect, protect, and fulfil. See Commission on Human Rights, 'Report of the Special Rapporteur, Paul Hunt' (n 58) paras 34, 35.

[60] Commission on Human Rights, 'Report of the Special Rapporteur, Paul Hunt' (n 58) para 36.

right to health indicators that will help them to monitor the different dimensions of the right to health. The Rapporteur's following Report[61] included a chapter on Right to Health Indicators, specifically mentioning the influence of a workshop on right to health indicators organized by the WHO and the UNDP HDR 2000. There, the Rapporteur on the right to health introduced two ideas that strongly influenced later literature on the subject of human rights indicators. First, he differentiated between a health indicator and a right-to-health indicator, stating that 'what tends to distinguish a right to health indicator from a health indicator is less its substance than (i) its explicit derivation from specific right to health norms; and (ii) the purpose to which it is put, namely right to health monitoring with a view to holding duty-bearers to account'.[62] Second, while acknowledging the absence of a 'commonly agreed and consistent way of categorizing and labeling different types of health indicators',[63] he proposed (influenced by the WHO) to adopt three categories of right-to-health indicators: structural, process, and outcome indicators.[64] For him, structural indicators measure whether key structures, systems and mechanisms that are considered necessary for the realization of a given right exist. Process indicators measure the extent to which necessary activities for the realization of a given right are carried out, measuring the effort, not the results. Outcome indicators measure the results of a given policy; they reflect many interrelated processes that taken together shape an outcome. Although he discussed the three categories, the Rapporteur failed to use them when identifying specific right-to-health indicators. Equally important, by using this developmental language and, in particular, the use of the terms 'process' and 'outcome', the Rapporteur embraces the possibility of there being a cause and an effect, an idea whose rigorousness can readily be called into question.

In sum, even though the Rapporteur said that not too much should be expected from right to health indicators, his report demonstrated a belief that such indicators may help monitor and measure the progressive realization of the right to health.

Another Rapporteur who placed indicators and monitoring tools in the context of the MDGs was the Rapporteur on adequate housing.[65] In a chapter of his 2003 report he focused on 'developing rights-sensitive indicators and monitoring tools', expressing his faith in the use of monitoring tools in an emphatic manner: 'Elaboration

[61] Commission on Human Rights, 'Interim Report of the Special Rapporteur of the Commission on Human Rights on the Right of Everyone to Enjoy the Highest Attainable Standard of Physical and Mental Health, Mr Paul Hunt' (10 October 2003) UN Doc A/58/427.

[62] Commission on Human Rights, 'Interim Report of Paul Hunt' (n 61) para 10.

[63] Commission on Human Rights, 'Interim Report of Paul Hunt' (n 61) para 14.

[64] Commission on Human Rights, 'Interim Report of Paul Hunt' (n 61) para 15. He also reported having coordinated with the CESCR on this terminology, para 16.

[65] Commission on Human Rights, 'Report of the Special Rapporteur on Adequate Housing as a Component of the Right to an Adequate Standard of Living, and on the Right to Non-Discrimination, Miloon Kothari, Submitted in Accordance with Commission Resolution 2002/21' (3 March 2003) UN Doc E/CN.4/2003/5.

of an operational framework for the realization of the right to adequate housing is inextricably linked to the issue of developing indicators and methods for monitoring and measuring the development process from a rights perspective. The need for such indicators and monitoring tools has become more pertinent with the emergence of the MDGs.'[66] Accordingly, he showed interest in flexibility to select contextually relevant indicators. This Rapporteur, like the Rapporteur on the right to health, presented three types of indicators that according to his criteria should be considered: input, process, and, output indicators.[67] At the end of his Report, he encouraged states and international organizations, such as the OHCHR, United Nations Human Settlements Programme (UN-Habitat), UNIFEM and UNICEF to undertake further work on developing rights-based indicators and monitoring tools.[68] In doing so, he recognized the different initiatives to quantify various aspects of housing, being developed as a result of the discussion on MDGs.

Subsequently, UN-HABITAT in close collaboration with the United Nations Statistic Division and the Cities Alliances convened an expert group meeting on Urban Indicators[69] in which the OHCHR and the Special Rapporteur participated. In April 2002, UN-HABITAT and the OHCHR launched a joint initiative, the United Nations Housing Rights Programme (UNHRP), to assist states with the implementation of the Habitat Agenda and the realization of the right to adequate housing. UNHRP then became an active promoter of the idea of using indicators, in alliance with the Rapporteur. Thereafter, the UNHRP convened an Experts Group in Geneva in November 2003 to discuss the development of a set of internationally applicable housing rights indicators. The meeting agreed with UNHRP that the creation of a Housing Rights Composite Index would be a complicated endeavor, both from a methodological and from a political perspective. The meeting thus agreed that 'the focus of the Expert Group Meeting be placed on the creation on a manageable set of indicators for monitoring progress towards the realization of the right to adequate housing'. The meeting also agreed to identify those indicators for which information was already being collected, or which could otherwise be easily collected by the UN. At the end, the meeting developed fifteen indicators.

By December 2006 the OHCHR organized another expert consultation to discuss housing rights indicators. Building upon all the prior work, the Rapporteur

[66] Commission on Human Rights, 'Report of Miloon Kothari' (n 65) para 51.

[67] Commission on Human Rights, 'Report of Miloon Kothari' (n 65) para 57.

[68] The Rapporteur specifically mentions the work that the Habitat International Coalition Housing and Land Rights Network, with which he cooperated, carried out: the Housing and Rights Monitoring Tool Kit. This initiative aimed to identify and design indicators for monitoring the realization of the right to adequate housing, based on fourteen elements relevant to the human right to housing, arising from international norms. Commission on Human Rights, 'Report of Miloon Kothari' (n 65) paras 60, 61.

[69] UN-Habitat, 'Expert Group Meeting on Urban Indicators: Secure Tenure, Slums and Global Sample of Cities' (28–30 October 2002) <http://www.citiesalliance.org/sites/citiesalliance.org/files/expert-group-meeting-urban-indicators[1].pdf> accessed 19 February 2013.

in his 2007 report[70] considered that it was time to endorse an 'illustrative list of indicators' for monitoring the right to adequate housing. He thus focused on identifying 'from the available data, to the extent feasible, illustrative indicators that as a starting point translate the narrative on the legal standard of the right... into a specific number of characteristic attributes that facilitate the identification of indicators for monitoring the implementation of the right'.[71] The Rapporteur therefore identified four essential elements to adequate housing: habitability, accessibility to services, housing affordability, and security of tenure, and built a framework based on structural, process, and, outcome indicators. Clearly, the Rapporteur was highly influenced by the work of other actors.

For his part, the Special Rapporteur on the right to food, recalling CESCR General Comment No 12, in his preliminary Report[72] put forward the idea that states should develop indicators and benchmarks to allow verification of progress in respect to the right to food at the country level. Referring to the 1996 Rome Declaration on Food Security and World Food Summit Plan of Action, the Rapporteur called for the adoption by states of an international code of conduct on the right to food, a code to be taken as a voluntary guideline. To that effect, the Rapporteur suggested that the International Code of Conduct on the Human Right to Adequate Food drafted by some non-governmental organizations in 1997 be further developed by FAO and the OHCHR. Maintaining this line of thinking, in his 2003 Report[73] he included a chapter on International Guidelines on the Right to Food, referring to voluntary guidelines that had been started under the auspices of FAO, and asking that the guidelines repeat the existing authoritative interpretation of the right to food contained in the CESCR General Comment No 12, and that they include benchmarks and indicators, as well as national monitoring mechanisms among the basic elements. The FAO Council adopted this voluntary document[74] including a chapter on 'monitoring, indicators and benchmarks' in November 2004. The section related to monitoring clearly takes some of its language from texts concerning governance and development, including the use of terms such as 'monitoring and

[70] Human Rights Council, 'Report of the Special Rapporteur on Adequate Housing as a Component of the Right to an Adequate Standard of Living, Miloon Kothari' (5 February 2007) UN Doc A/HRC/4/18.

[71] Human Rights Council, 'Report of Miloon Kothari' (n 71) para 9.

[72] UNGA, 'Preliminary Report of the Special Rapporteur of the Commission on Human Rights on the Right to Food, Jean Ziegler' (23 July 2001) UN Doc A/56/210.

[73] Commission on Human Rights, 'Report Submitted by the Special Rapporteur on the Right to Food, Jean Ziegler, in Accordance with Commission on Human Rights Resolution 2002/25' (10 January 2003) UN Doc E/CN.4/2003/54.

[74] Food and Agriculture Organization (FAO) of the United Nations, 'Voluntary Guidelines to Support the Progressive Realization of the Right to Adequate Food in the Context of National Food Security' (FAO Council 2004) <http://www.fao.org/docrep/meeting/009/y9825e/y9825e00.htm> accessed 19 February 2013.

evaluation' and 'impact assessment'.[75] It is also noteworthy that the guidelines mention the use of process, impact, and outcome indicators, reflecting trust in the indicators already in use by the FAO and its information system. In sum, most of the developments on the topic of human rights indicators that occurred in the context of the UN Special Procedures were highly influenced by international institutions.[76]

The groundswell in favour of indicators forced the OHCHR to start a modest unit on the topic in 2000, despite the constant lack of resources that hampers its work generally.[77] The OHCHR became even more involved in the subject after a meeting of the chairpersons of the human rights treaty bodies in 2005. They passed a resolution called 'Statistical information related to human rights' where they duly noted the assistance received from the secretariat in analysing statistical information related to human rights presented in the state parties' reports, and 'requested the secretariat to pursue this work further and prepare a background paper for the next inter-committee meeting on the possible uses of indicators'.[78] The OHCHR organized two experts' consultations in order to fulfil this task, and in 2006 presented a Report[79] setting forth an outline of a conceptual and methodological framework for developing indicators for monitoring compliance by states parties with international human rights treaties.

The document adopted many of the ideas developed by the human rights bodies up to that time. Thus, the OHCHR report used a formulation similar to that of the Rapporteur on the Right to Health, describing human rights indicators as: 'specific information on the state of an event, activity or an outcome that can be related to human rights norms and standards; that address and reflect the human rights concerns and principles; and that are used to assess and monitor promotion and protection of human rights'.[80] The OHCHR immediately added that although there could be some indicators that are uniquely human rights indicators, 'there could be a large number of other indicators such as socio-economic statistics (eg UNDP's

[75] 'Voluntary Guidelines' (n 74) 17.1, 17.2 in particular.

[76] For a discussion of special procedures, see Chapter 25 in this *Handbook*.

[77] The then UN High Commissioner, Mary Robinson, sent a very positive message about human rights and statistics to the Montreaux Conference on Statistics, Development and Human Rights in September 2000. She stated that 'The subject of your work here . . . is nothing less than a quest for a science of human dignity. When the target is human suffering, and the cause human rights, mere rhetoric is not adequate to the task in hand. What are needed are solid methodologies, careful techniques, and effective mechanisms to get the job done'. Claire Naval, Sylvie Walter, and Raul Suarez de Miguel (eds), 'Measuring Human Rights and Democratic Governance: Experiences and Lessons from Metagora' (2008) 9 *OECD Journal of Development* 3, 41.

[78] OHCHR, 'Seventeenth Meeting of Chairpersons of the Human Rights Treaty Bodies' (Geneva, 23–24 June 2005) <http://www2.ohchr.org/english/bodies/icm-mc/docs/MC17-ICM4.pdf> accessed 19 February 2013.

[79] International Human Rights Instruments, 'Report on Indicators for Monitoring Compliance with International Human Rights Instruments' (11 May 2006) UN Doc HRI/MC/2006/7.

[80] International Human Rights Instruments, 2006 'Report on Indicators' (n 79) para 7.

human development indicators) that could meet (at least implicitly) all the definitional requirements of a human rights indicator'. 'In all these cases', the OHCHR added, 'to the extent that such indicators relate to the human rights standards and are used for human rights assessment, it would be helpful to consider them as human rights indicators'.[81] The OHCHR also adopted the idea of relying on structural, process, and outcome indicators. The document concluded by presenting four illustrative sets of indicators, some of which were related to the MDGs and that had been developed previously by the Rapporteurs. They concerned the right to life, the right to judicial review of detention, the right to adequate food, and the right to health. The inter-committee meeting of treaty bodies asked the OHCHR to undertake validation of the document, develop a further list of indicators, and submit a report on this work.

After various consultations and almost two years of work, the OHCHR produced an updated document,[82] whose title has a slight but significant variation from the previous document in omitting the word compliance. Specifying the reasons for adopting the framework of structural, process, and outcome indicators, the OHCHR engaged the development discourse by emphasizing that these categories of indicators have been widely used in the development policy context and 'are likely to be more familiar to policy makers/implementers and development/human rights practitioners who are, in some sense, the main focus of this work. In fact, the use of structural, process, and outcome indicators in promoting and monitoring the implementation of human rights will help demystify the notion of human rights and take the human rights discourse beyond the confines of legal and justice sector discussions, but also facilitate the mainstreaming of human rights standards and principles in policy making and development implementation'.[83] The document also tried to relate the use of these indicators to the recognized framework of state obligations to 'respect, protect, and fulfil' rights.

Another salient feature of this OHCHR document is its effort to present a common approach to economic, social and cultural, and civil and political rights; it, however, completely left aside the idea of building a common list of indicators and a global measure for cross-country comparisons. In its place and using ambiguous language,[84] the

[81] International Human Rights Instruments, 2006 'Report on Indicator' (n 79) para 7.

[82] International Human Rights Instruments, 'Report on Indicators for Promoting and Monitoring the Implementation of Human Rights' (6 June 2008) UN Doc HRI/MC/2008/3.

[83] International Human Rights Instruments, 2008 'Report on Indicator' (n 82) para 9.

[84] 'The contextual relevance of indicators is a key consideration in the acceptability and use of indicators among potential users. Countries and regions within countries differ in terms of their level of development and realization of human rights. These differences are reflected in the nature of institutions, the policies and the priorities of the State. Therefore, it may not be possible to have a set of universal indicators to assess the realization of human rights. Having said that, it is also true that certain human rights indicators, for example those capturing realization of some civil and political rights, may well be relevant across all countries and their regions, whereas others that capture realization of economic or social rights, such as the rights to health or adequate housing, may have to be customized

document advocates using contextually relevant indicators, and so it presents twelve 'illustrative indicators' along with the corresponding meta-data sheets.[85] Regarding the sources and data-generating mechanisms, it leans toward considering the state as the data-generator and, specifically, toward relying on official statistical systems using administrative records and statistical surveys.[86]

The inter-committee meeting of the treaty bodies endorsed the conceptual and methodological framework and called for the development of resource materials and tools to help disseminate and operationalize the framework. In 2008, the treaty bodies approved the Compilation of Guidelines on the Form and Content of Reports for submission to States Parties to the International Human Rights Treaties.[87] The document suggests that states create institutional structures for the preparation of their reports, which should develop an efficient system for the collection of all statistical and other data relevant to the implementation of human rights from ministries and government statistical offices. It also suggests that states can benefit from technical assistance from the OHCHR, the Division for the Advancement of Women, and other relevant UN agencies.[88] The document mentions that statistical data should be disaggregated by sex, age, and population groups and that the sources be included; additionally, it suggests that data be collected during a period of at least five years in order to be able to do comparisons over time. It also says that the Report must consist of two sections, each one considered an integral part of the state's reports. The first section, called common core document, 'should present general factual and statistical information relevant to assisting the committees in understanding the political, legal, social, economic and cultural context in which human rights are implemented in the State concerned'.[89] This information should be contained in Appendix 3, called Indicators for Assessing the Implementation of Human Rights, which is the only part of the document that mentions the term 'indicator'. Among the different categories of 'indicators' that it mentions

to be of relevance in different countries. But even in the latter case, it would be relevant to monitor the minimum core content of the rights universally. Thus, in designing a set of human rights indicators, like any other set of indicators, there is a need to strike a balance between universally relevant indicators and contextually specific indicators, as both kinds of indicators are needed.' International Human Rights Instruments, 2008 'Report on Indicator' (n 82) para 16.

[85] The lists of indicators are: the right to life; the right to liberty and security of person; the right to participate in public affairs; the right not to be subjected to torture or cruel, inhuman, or degrading treatment or punishment; the right to the enjoyment of the highest attainable standard of physical and mental health; the right to adequate food; the right to adequate housing; the right to education; the right to freedom of opinion and expression; the right to a fair trial; the right to social security; the right to work; the right to non-discrimination and equality; and violence against women.

[86] Although tangentially, events-based data on human rights violations were also mentioned. See International Human Rights Instruments, 2008 'Report on Indicator' (n 82) para 13.

[87] International Human Rights Instruments, 'Compilation of Guidelines on the Form and Content of Reports to Be Submitted by States Parties to the International Human Rights Treaties' (28 May 2008) UN Doc HRI/GEN/2/Rev.5.

[88] International Human Rights Instruments, 'Compilation of Guidelines' (n 87) paras 13–15.

[89] International Human Rights Instruments, 'Compilation of Guidelines' (n 87) para 32.

are: demographic indicators; social, economic, and cultural indicators; indicators on the political system; indicators on crime and the administration of justice. Specifically, they request a diverse list of data and statistics and indicators which are widely used for other purposes including the GDP and the Gini coefficient.[90]

The second part of the Report is the treaty-specific document that should include all information related to states' implementation of the rights contained in each specific treaty, including the information requested by the relevant committee in its treaty-specific guidelines. The CESCR approved the guidelines in 2008,[91] and introduced the idea that states should use the document prepared by the OHCHR as a reference. More specifically, the guidelines mention that the treaty-specific document should indicate: 'Any mechanisms in place to monitor progress towards the full realization of the Covenant rights, including identification of indicators and related national benchmarks in relation to each Covenant right, in addition to the information provided under appendix 3 of the harmonized guidelines and taking into account the framework and tables of illustrative indicators outlined by the Office of the United Nations High Commissioner for Human Rights (OHCHR) (HRI/MC/2008/3).'[92] A similar idea is expressed in the Guidelines for the treaty-specific document adopted by the Human Rights Committee en 2010.[93] It is clear thus, that the Committees embraced the entire narrative constructed by the human rights bodies up to that point, relying on well-known statistics that were developed for other purposes and by other actors. Further, they accepted the state as the institution selecting and generating the data. Whether this framework can be used to monitor compliance with the treaties in practice has yet to be seen. Another issue for long-term evaluation is whether the generation and review of indicators promotes compliance and improvement of human rights throughout the world.

[90] The Gini coefficient tries to measure economic inequality in a given country by looking at the dispersion of its income per capita.

[91] CESCR, 'Guidelines on Treaty-Specific Documents to Be Submitted by States Parties under Articles 16 and 17 of the International Covenant on Economic, Social and Cultural Rights' (24 March 2009) UN Doc E/C.12/2008/2. This document replaced the previous guidelines. See CESCR, 'Revised General Guidelines Regarding the Form and Contents of Reports to Be Submitted by States Parties under Articles 16 and 17 of the International Covenant on Economic, Social and Cultural Rights' (17 June 1991) UN Doc E/C.12/1991/1.

[92] CESCR, 'Guidelines on Treaty-Specific Documents' (n 91) 4.

[93] Human Rights Committee, 'Guidelines for the Treaty-Specific Document to Be Submitted by States Parties under Article 40 of the International Covenant on Civil and Political Rights' (22 November 2010) UN Doc CCPR/C/2009/1. This document replaced the previous guidelines adopted at the seventieth session of the Committee. See Human Rights Committee, 'Consolidated Guidelines for State Reports under the International Covenant on Civil and Political Rights' (26 February 2001) UN Doc CCPR/C/66/GUI/Rev.2; International Human Rights Instruments, 'Compilation of Guidelines on the Form and Content of Reports to Be Submitted by States Parties to the International Human Rights Treaties' (3 June 2009) UN Doc HRI/GEN/2/Rev.6, ch III.

5. Conclusion

The analysis of 'human rights indicators' presented above illustrates why measures in general, and indicators in particular are not givens but human creations that have been socially constructed. In this context one can understand the inconsistent and heterogeneous use of human rights indicators by the UN human rights bodies. The lengthy debates on development that coincided with human rights standard-setting helped to instil faith in human rights' measurement and indicators, faith that was consolidated at the beginning of the new millennium. The creation of the MDGs contributed to ensure acceptance by human rights bodies of a particular indicators' narrative. Several ideas now seem fully solidified within human rights bodies.[94] First, as a result of the resistance states have shown towards comparison and nation rankings, human rights bodies have abandoned such purpose. Second, given their lack of resources and expertise, along with the decisive influence of powerful international actors, human rights bodies have resigned themselves to using indicators that have been created for other settings. Third, the idea that states should be the ones to select and produce those indicators and statistics nationwide has gained strength. In sum, the preponderance of the state within the human rights arena is mirrored in the creation and use of human rights indicators. In that framework, whether human rights theory and practice may fertilize the development literature, or whether human rights will become blurred within the theory and practice of development remains a question to be answered. More importantly, human rights indicators need to be put to the test of social scrutiny; their usefulness can only be evaluated if their users know who, how, when, and with what purpose they were created.

Further Reading

Asher J, Banks D, and Scheuren FJ (eds), *Statistical Methods for Human Rights* (Springer 2008)

Böhning WR, *Labour Rights in Crisis: Measuring the Achievement of Human Rights in the World of Work* (Palgrave 2006)

Jabine TB and Claude R (eds), *Human Rights and Statistics: Getting the Record Straight* (U Pennsylvania Press 1992)

Landman T and Carvalho E, *Measuring Human Rights* (Routledge 2010)

Naval C, Walter S, and Suarez de Miguel R (eds), 'Measuring Human Rights and Democratic Governance: Experiences and Lessons from Metagora' (2008) 9 *OECD Journal of Development* 3

[94] See also Ann Janette Rosga and Margaret L Satterthwaite, 'The Trust in Indicators: Measuring Human Rights' (2009) 27 *Berk J Intl L* 253; Sally Engle Merry, 'Measuring the World: Indicators, Human Rights, and Global Governance' (2011) 52 *Current Anthropology* S83.

CHAPTER 37

COMPLIANCE

GISELLA GORI

1. Introduction

THE international community has achieved impressive progress since the Second World War in re-thinking and strengthening its global and regional mechanisms for human rights protection. The adoption of universal instruments, such as the 1945 Charter of the United Nations and the 1948 Universal Declaration of Human Rights; and regional instruments, such as the European Convention for the Protection of Human Rights and Fundamental Freedoms, the American Convention on Human Rights, and the African Charter on Human and Peoples' Rights, has been coupled with the establishment of institutions and procedures aimed at enforcing the human rights and fundamental freedoms these instruments guarantee.

Against the expanding plethora of treaties, charters, and bodies, the central question remains: to what extent do states comply with their human rights obligations, including the judgments and recommendations of the different mechanisms, thereby guaranteeing their effectiveness? The effectiveness of international human rights monitoring may be measured by how well their decisions are enforced and the impact they have had—and they are having—on the individuals that are the subjects of their guarantees. In general, state compliance and the ensuing enforcement of judgments and recommendations will largely depend, on the one hand, on the nature of the monitoring body (ie whether it is a judicial or a non-judicial body), and on the other hand, on the type of follow-up which is exercised after the delivery of the decision or judgment. This chapter thus will broadly distinguish between judicial and non-judicial mechanisms, examining their effectiveness, commonalities, and differences. For practical purposes, it will mainly focus on the United

Nations (UN) in the context of non-judicial mechanisms and the Council of Europe and the Organization of American States (OAS) in the context of judicial mechanisms.

An underlying characteristic of all international mechanisms for human rights protection is the principle of subsidiarity,[1] which means that the protection and promotion of human rights should occur first and foremost at the national level. The principle of subsidiarity provides a conceptual tool through which to understand the dynamic between the role of states in human rights protection and the role of the international human rights protection mechanisms that states create at the global and regional levels. The latter are not replacements for the national systems, but are subsidiary to the states.

2. Non-Judicial Mechanisms: The UN Human Rights Bodies and Procedures

2.1 Preliminary considerations

The promotion and protection of human rights has become a major preoccupation of the UN. The Universal Declaration of Human Rights (UDHR) further develops the human rights provisions of the UN Charter. The UDHR is one of the first international documents to be based on the idea that rights are guaranteed to each human being. Although the UDHR was not adopted as a legally-binding treaty, it has created international human rights standards that various international treaties codify and that the constitutions and laws of many states incorporate.

Over the years, UN member states have concluded a network of human rights instruments and mechanisms to ensure the primacy of human rights and to confront human rights violations wherever they occur. All these mechanisms are of a non-judicial nature and can be divided into Charter-based and Treaty-based bodies. The former category includes the Human Rights Council, which replaced the Commission on Human Rights in 2006, and the Special Procedures. The latter category includes ten human rights treaty bodies,[2] which consist of independent experts. Nine of these treaty

[1] See Chapter 15 in this *Handbook*.

[2] The Human Rights Committee (International Covenant on Civil and Political Rights), Committee on Economic, Social and Cultural Rights (International Covenant on Economic, Social and Cultural Rights), Committee on the Elimination of Racial Discrimination (Convention on the Elimination of all Forms of Racial Discrimination), Committee on the Elimination of Discrimination against Women (Convention on the Elimination of Discrimination against Women), Committee against Torture (Convention against Torture and Other Cruel, Inhuman or Degrading Treatment or Punishment),

bodies monitor implementation of the core international human rights treaties, while the tenth treaty body, the Subcommittee on Prevention of Torture that was established under the Optional Protocol to the Convention against Torture, monitors places of detention in states parties to the Optional Protocol. The following discussion will focus on the Human Rights Council, briefly describing it and then exploring its effectiveness, giving some concrete examples.

2.2 The Human Rights Council

The Human Rights Council (HRCouncil) is an inter-governmental body within the UN system made up of forty-seven states responsible for strengthening the promotion and protection of human rights around the world. The UN General Assembly created the Council in 2006 with the main purpose of addressing situations of human rights violations and making recommendations relating to them.[3] It replaced the Commission on Human Rights, which had been facing increasing challenges to its work, with accusations of politicization and the application of double standards. The HRCouncil is one of the main UN bodies charged with human rights protection. The other two are the General Assembly Third Committee (the Social, Humanitarian and Cultural Affairs Committee) and the Office of the High Commissioner of Human Rights.[4] The work of the three bodies is closely inter-related. The functioning of the HRCouncil has been recently reviewed in order to improve its effectiveness, as described below.[5]

The fact that some countries whose human rights record is notably unsatisfactory were, or still are, members of the HRCouncil, raised criticism in many quarters about the real scope of the 2006 reform. However, the dynamism and impact of the HRCouncil has been improving in recent years, partly as an outcome of the United States' membership since 2010, and by reason of the peer pressure its members exercise towards 'undesired' candidatures.[6] Indeed, government officials sometimes concede publicly that criticism and recommendations from other governments carry more weight than the views of independent experts on treaty bodies.

Subcommittee on Prevention of Torture (Optional Protocol to the Convention against Torture), Committee on the Rights of the Child (Convention on The Rights of the Child), Committee on Migrant Workers (International Covenant on the Protection of the Rights of All Migrant Workers and Members of Their Families), Committee on the Rights of Persons with Disabilities (Convention on the Rights of Persons with Disabilities), Committee on Enforced Disappearance (International Convention for the Protection of All Persons from Enforced Disappearance).

[3] UNGA Res 60/251 (3 April 2006) UN Doc A/Res/60/251.

[4] The extensive human rights work of some of the UN Specialized Agencies is not included in this discussion.

[5] UNGA Res 65/281 (20 July 2011) UN Doc A/Res/65/281.

[6] As it was with the case with Iran in 2010.

The HRCouncil has at its disposal several procedures to monitor the respect and supervise the enforcement of international human rights standards by member states, ranging from the Universal Periodic Review (UPR) and the Collective Complaints Procedures, to the Special Procedures, Fact-Finding missions, and Commission of Inquiry. The 'Institution-Building Package', which the Council adopted in 2007,[7] defined further the organization of the UPR and the Complaints Procedure, which allows individuals and organizations to bring complaints about systematic human rights violations to the attention of the Council.

2.2.1 *Universal Periodic Review*

UPR is a mechanism aimed at reviewing the human rights records of all 194 UN member states once every four years. It provides an opportunity for each UN member state to review its own human rights record and display the actions it has taken to improve their protection. UPR is a peer-review mechanism in which Council members ask questions and make recommendations to reporting states. Innovative features of this unique monitoring system are: (i) universality and equal treatment among all member states, meaning that countries usually not under the spotlight for their human rights performance are being reviewed;[8] and (ii) interstate, interactive dialogue between the country under review and other UN member states. The review is based on the national report; other available reports from UN treaty-based mechanisms, including the Office of the High Commissioner for Human Rights' reports, special procedures, and independent human rights expert groups; and, finally, information that non-governmental organizations (NGOs) and national human rights institutions submit. The review concludes with a final report, which the HRCouncil plenary adopts, and which contains comments, questions, and recommendations, which the state under review can accept or reject. It is then up to the state concerned to implement the recommendations so as to show progress in time for the second round of review.

The first UPR cycle ran from 2008 to 2011; the second round began in May 2012. The HRCouncil launched a review of its own work with respect to UPR whilst the first round was ongoing and, in 2011, adopted two resolutions containing new modalities for its functioning.[9] Following suggestions by NGOs,[10] the review

[7] Human Rights Council, 'Review of the Work and Functioning of the Human Rights Council' (12 April 2011) UN Doc A/HRC/Res/16/21.

[8] Human Rights Watch, *Curing the Selectivity Syndrome: The 2011 Review of the Human Rights Council* (Human Rights Watch 2010) <http://www.hrw.org/sites/default/files/reports/hrc0610webwcover.pdf> accessed 15 January 2013.

[9] Human Rights Council, 'Follow-Up to the Human Rights Council Resolution 16/21 with Regard to the Universal Periodic Review' (19 July 2011) UN Doc A/HRC/DEC/17/119, on the follow-up to Human Rights Council, 'Review of the Work and Functioning of the Human Rights Council' (12 April 2011) UN Doc A/HRC/RES/16/21, with regard to the Universal Periodic Review.

[10] See, in particular, UPR Info, 'Analytical Assessment of the Universal Periodic Review: 2008–2010' (UPR-info.org 2010). UPR-info.org is a non-profit NGO aimed at promoting and strengthening the UPR.

extended the length of the cycle (four-and-a-half years), set the number of states reviewed at each session to fourteen, and increased the length of the interactive dialogue to 3.5 hours (seventy minutes for the state under review and 140 minutes for the other states). Moreover, it was decided that the review should focus in particular on implementation of the accepted recommendations and improvement of human rights in the reviewed state. To this end, each government's report should highlight the measures it has taken to implement the previous accepted recommendations and any other progress that has occurred in the meantime. Member states are also invited to provide a written answer to all the recommendations received. National human rights institutions and NGOs are also invited to focus on implementation.

According to NGOs' assessments carried out during the first cycle,[11] positive elements of UPR were, inter alia, (i) a 100 per cent rate of state participation, compared to the sporadic and often-delayed compliance with reporting obligations under human rights treaties; (ii) the high responsiveness of states in the interactive dialogue; (iii) the encompassing material scope of the procedure which extend to all human rights; and (iv) the catalytic role of UPR for implementing HRCouncil coordination and mainstreaming with regard to human rights monitoring in the UN context.

Although UPR represents a comprehensive and potentially objective mechanism, the many years elapsing between two reviews (four-and-a-half), and the fact that it is ultimately a state-driven process, may cast a shadow on the relevance and timeliness of the information received and on the objectivity and impartiality of the process. Both issues, in the end, may hamper its effectiveness. The peer-review process relies on the good will of the member state in providing relevant information and undertaking the necessary steps to comply with the recommendations it receives. Moreover, the fact that a member state can reject recommendations also represents an intrinsic limit to the procedure, coupled with the fact that there is no *ex-ante* mechanism foreseen in the case of persistent non-cooperation by a member state. Finally, NGOs should probably be provided with a broader role in the procedure, in order to counterbalance member states' submissions and monitor the effective implementation of the recommendations.

The second round began only in 2012, and thus a full-fledged assessment of the functioning of the UPR is not yet feasible. It is clear that the second round will be pivotal in measuring the impact of the UPR and the degree to which member states are complying with, or taking measures in view of complying with, the recommendations. This is why the HRCouncil's own review, as well as other assessments, have emphasized having the second round focus on the implementation of the recommendation. This should avoid the second cycle becoming just a repetition of the

[11] See eg UPR Info (n 10).

first one. Some participants, including the EU, are actively engaged in trying to achieve this goal.

2.2.2 *Complaint procedure*

In the context of the 2007 'Institution-Building Package', the Human Rights Council modified the former '1503' complaint procedure[12] to address consistent patterns of gross and reliably-attested violations of human rights and fundamental freedoms occurring in any part of the world and under any circumstances.[13] The procedure advances through two distinct working groups—the Working Group on Communications[14] and the Working Group on Situations[15]—which are given the mandate to examine the communications received and to bring to the attention of the Council the cases it consider serious violations.

The UN mechanism may be compared to the Collective Complaints Procedure that the Council of Europe instituted to ensure an additional mechanism for the enforcement of the revised European Social Charter (1994). The UN mechanism provides—at least in theory—access not just to victims, but also to other individuals or groups (including NGOs) with direct and reliable knowledge of gross human rights violations. Thus, it guarantees stakeholders an opportunity to have their voice heard. Moreover, the procedure is to be victim-oriented and shall be conducted in a timely manner. It applies to all countries, whether or not they are Parties to any given human rights treaty. The ability to name the offending countries provides this

[12] Named after the resolution of the Economic and Social Council that first created the procedure in 1970.

[13] Human Rights Council, 'Resolution 5/1: Institution-Building of the United Nations Human Rights Council' (18 June 2007) reprinted in Human Rights Council 'Report of the Human Rights Council' (2007) UN Doc A/62/53.

[14] The Human Rights Council Advisory Committee designated the Working Group on Communications from among its members, for a period of three years (mandate renewable once). It consists of five independent and highly qualified experts and is geographically representative of the five regional groups. The Working Group meets twice a year for a period of five working days to assess the admissibility and the merits of a communication, including whether the communication alone or in combination with other communications, appears to reveal a consistent pattern of gross and reliably attested violations of human rights and fundamental freedoms. All admissible communications and recommendations thereon are transmitted to the Working Group on Situations.

[15] Five members that the regional groups appoint from among the states member of the Council for the period of one year (mandate renewable once) comprise the Working Group on Situations. It meets twice a year for a period of five working days in order to examine the communications the Working Group on Communications transfers to it, including the replies of states thereon and information on the situations which the Council is already apprised of under the complaint procedure. The Working Group on Situations, on the basis of the information and recommendations that the Working Group on Communications provides, presents the Council with a report on consistent patterns of gross and reliably attested violations of human rights and fundamental freedoms and makes recommendations to the Council on what course of action to take.

procedure with the ability to exercise a subtle, yet powerful, pressure on governments to repair the violations and correct the situation.

On the negative side, the confidential nature of the mechanism, with a view to enhancing cooperation with the state concerned, offsets some of the positive features. It does not enable direct relief to victims; it can be lodged only after the exhaustion of all domestic remedies; it may be lengthy; and the confidential nature, while securing protection for victims, often plays to the advantage of the country concerned. It should be noted, too, that the two working groups do not seem to be presenting any cases to the Council under the complaint procedure. This prevents any further assessment of the effectiveness of this mechanism.

2.2.3 *Special procedures, fact-finding missions, and Commission of Inquiry*

The UN Special Procedures are meant to address country specific or thematic situations consisting of serious violations of human rights in which member states do not respect their human rights commitments. Special Procedures are resolution-mandated and may consist of an individual expert, a so-called Special Rapporteur or Independent Expert, or a group of Independent Experts. They may be country-specific or thematic. Mandate holders carry out country visits to investigate particular human rights situations upon acceptance by the country designated. Some countries have issued 'standing invitations', which allow the visits of any mandate holders. Under the institution-building process, the special procedures were thoroughly reviewed, following which all of the thematic mandates were extended and new ones established, while most of the country mandates were renewed. Among the novelties, measures were taken to allow all stakeholders to bring issues related to working-methods in order to increase the effectiveness of the Special Procedures and the cooperation by states, as well as self-regulation of the system and of the individual mandates.

The HRCouncil can also adopt country-specific resolutions, requesting the Office of the High Commissioner for Human Rights to dispatch Fact-Finding missions to investigate alleged gross human rights violations. Should the violations be confirmed, a Commission of Inquiry or a Special Rapporteur may be established, depending on the gravity of the country-specific situation.

The day-to-day work of the HRCouncil is clearly influenced both by international events and by politics. In particular, the membership of the Council may influence substantially its decision-making process and the outcomes of its sessions. The HRCouncil's swift engagement on Syria in 2011 is emblematic of its re-vamped role, in particular in the aftermath of the Arab Spring, and of the dynamic interaction between the Geneva-based body and the UN Security Council in New York. By mid-2012, the HRCouncil had adopted five resolutions and organized four Special Sessions on Syria. At the first special session, convened on 29 April 2011, as a result of US initiative, the HRCouncil adopted resolution S-16/1,[16] which contained a forceful statement condemning unequivocally the Syrian government's use of force to deny its population their universal human rights, including the freedoms of expression and assembly. The statement was coupled with the decision to establish a Fact-Finding mission that the Office of the High Commissioner for Human Rights would lead to ensure that the international community remained actively engaged in the human rights crisis in Syria. At the second special session, held at the end of August 2011, the HRCouncil examined the report of the High Commissioner's Fact-Finding Mission, which found a pattern of human rights violations in Syria that may amount to crimes against humanity. In light of the mission's finding and the growing international concern at the deteriorating human rights situation in the country, in particular the increasingly violent crack-down on peaceful protests by security forces, the HRCouncil decided to establish an independent Commission of Inquiry (COI).[17] HRC resolution S-18/1,[18] adopted at the third special session on 2 December 2011, again strongly condemned the Syrian authorities' continued, widespread, systematic, and gross violations of human rights and fundamental freedoms and decided to appoint a Special Rapporteur on the situation of human rights in the Syrian Arab Republic to monitor the situation of human rights in this country, as well as to monitor the implementation of the COI recommendations to the authorities, once the mandate of the COI ended. At the regular session of March 2012, the HRCouncil decided to extend the mandate of the COI.[19] Another special session was held on 1 June 2012 and a further resolution adopted at that time.[20]

As the actions above show, the HRC was swiftly and heavily involved in the Syrian crisis. However, the impact of the Council's actions must be analysed in conjunction with the role of the UN Security Council (UNSC), on the one hand, and the level of cooperation from the targeted member state, on the other. The contraposition between a majority of states in favour of a stronger international action coupled with sanctions, and a minority opposing international intervention, hampered action in the UNSC. The latter, among them China and Russia, argued for respecting the rights of sovereign nations and against the 'misuse' of country investigations whereby the alleged protection of human lives becomes a pretext for foreign intervention. For its part, Syria strongly resisted engaging in a dialogue and

[16] HRCouncil, 'The Current Human Rights Situation in the Syrian Arab Republic in the Context of Recent Events' (29 April 2011) UN Doc A/HRC/RES/S-16/1.

[17] HRCouncil, 'The Human Rights Situation in the Syrian Arab Republic' (23 August 2011) UN Doc A/HRC/RES/S-17/1.

[18] HRCouncil, 'Report of the Independent Commission of Inquiry on the Syrian Arab Republic' (23 November 2011) UN Doc A/HRC/S-17/2/Add.1.

[19] HRCouncil, 'Situation of Human Rights in the Syrian Arab Republic' (10 April 2012) UN Doc A/HRC/Res/19/22.

[20] HRCouncil, 'The Deteriorating Situation of Human Rights in the Syrian Arab Republic, and the Recent Killings in El-Houleh' (1 June 2012) UN Doc A/HRC/Res/S-19/1. China, Cuba, and Russia voted against the resolution after Russia called for the vote.

hindered access by the COI. Only with the adoption of UNSC Res 2043/2012[21] did the Syrian government finally give a UN observer mission access, while restricting its monitoring. Nonetheless, the 'preparatory work' the HRCouncil carried out established a substantial body of evidence that the Syrian military and security forces had committed gross human rights violations after March 2011, and paved the way for reaching a consensus in the UNSC over the six-point peace plan of the Joint Special Envoy of the UN and the Arab League of States for Syria, and the establishment of the UN Supervision Mission in Syria to monitor the cessation of violence and to support the implementation of a peace plan.

3. Regional Judicial Mechanisms—Effectiveness of the European and the Inter-American systems

At the regional level, various groups of countries, in the context of regional international organizations, have developed human rights legal instruments that provide additional protection to individuals' rights and freedoms, in parallel to those of the UN.[22] The Council of Europe (CoE) was founded in 1949, with the primary aim of creating a common democratic and legal area throughout the European continent that would ensure respect for human rights, democracy, and the rule of law. The European Convention on Human Rights (ECHR)[23] remains probably the most advanced human rights protection mechanism in the world.

The Organization of American States was founded in 1948 by member states to achieve 'an order of peace and justice, to promote their solidarity, to strengthen their collaboration, and to defend their sovereignty, their territorial integrity, and their independence'.[24] The Organization follows a four-pronged approach to implement its essential purposes, based on its main pillars: democracy, human rights, security, and development. The two main institutions of the inter-American human rights system are the Inter-American Commission (IACHR) and the Inter-American Court of Human Rights (IACtHR). The American Declaration of the Rights and Duties of Man, adopted in Bogotá, Colombia, in April 1948, provides the overall framework of the inter-American system. The 1969 American Convention on Human Rights, which entered into force in 1978, defines the human rights which the ratifying states

[21] UNSC Res 2043 (21 April 2012) UN Doc S/Res/2043 (adopted unanimously).

[22] See Chapter 28 in this *Handbook* for a discussion of regional systems.

[23] All forty-seven CoE member states are parties to the ECHR.

[24] Charter of the Organization of American States, Art 1.

have agreed to respect and ensure, and establishes the Inter-American Court of Human Rights. Twenty-five countries have ratified the Convention.[25]

Other regional organizations also have placed the protection and promotion of human rights at the centre of their missions. The African Union (AU), successor to the Organization of African Unity, includes among its aims, 'to promote and protect human and peoples' rights in accordance with the African Charter on Human and Peoples' Rights [entered into force in 1986] and other relevant human rights instruments'.[26] The African Commission on Human and Peoples' Rights, set up in 1987, is in charge of the oversight and interpretation of the Charter. In line with the other regional systems, a subsequent 1998 Protocol created the African Court on Human and Peoples' Rights, which became effective as from 2005.

The following sections will focus primarily on the European and the Inter-American systems.

3.1. The CoE's human rights protection mechanism

The ECHR was the first CoE treaty to protect human rights, as well as the first international human rights treaty with a judicial enforcement mechanism.[27] The ECHR deals mainly with civil and political rights, which are found in Articles 1–18. Articles 19–51 set forth the working mechanisms of the European Court of Human Rights (ECtHR), while Protocols 1, 4, 6, 7, and 12 provide for additional rights. The right of individual complaint (Article 25) obliges the states to accept the Court as having the authority to rule on cases alleging individual human rights violations. On 1 November 1998, Protocol 11 came into force creating a new and permanent ECtHR.[28]

[25] Argentina, Barbados, Brazil, Bolivia, Chile, Colombia, Costa Rica, Dominica, the Dominican Republic, Ecuador, El Salvador, Grenada, Guatemala, Haiti, Honduras, Jamaica, Mexico, Nicaragua, Panama, Paraguay, Peru, Suriname, Trinidad and Tobago, Uruguay, and Venezuela. The United States has not ratified it yet.

[26] Constitutive Act of the African Union, Art 3(h).

[27] The ECHR was signed in Rome on November 4, 1950, and entered into force on 3 September 1953. Only member states of the CoE can become a party to the ECHR. There is an abundant literature on the subject. See eg DJ Harris and others, *Law of the European Convention on Human Rights* (2nd edn, OUP 2009).

[28] Protocol No 11 to the Convention for the Protection of Human Rights and Fundamental Freedoms, Restructuring the Control Machinery Established Thereby. Similarly to the more recently established systems, the original structure of the European mechanism for handling cases provided for a two-tier system, which included the European Commission of Human Rights as well as the Court itself. The dichotomy between the two institutions initially worked well, since the Court dealt with a relatively small caseload. However, the caseload facing the court grew dramatically, and the states parties felt the need to create a new, single, and permanent Court, which was eventually created through the entry into force of Protocol 11.

The Court accepts applications alleging human rights violations from individuals as well as from states. In order for the Court to accept an application, an applicant must have exhausted all domestic legal remedies available to him. The Court's hearings are normally public. All judgments are binding under international law and may be delivered orally in court or in writing. Once the Court finds a violation, states are obliged to prevent similar violations from occurring in the future. 'Just satisfaction' can be awarded to victims, including compensation that the state found in violation of the Convention pays. The ECtHR may also issue interim measures under its Rule 39 and has the power to give advisory opinions—a little-used function that Articles 47 to 49 of the Convention now govern.

In order to understand the scope and challenge of the execution of the ECtHR judgments, it is worth briefly examining the workload facing the Court.[29] A few numbers indicate why any comparison with other international human rights tribunals is impracticable. Since the reform of the ECHR system and the creation of a single Court on 1 November 1998, there has been a considerable increase in the Court's caseload, as well as in its output. On 1 January 2012, approximately 151,600 applications were pending before the Court. In 2011, the ECtHR delivered 1,157 judgments. Though the Court was created in 1959, it delivered more than 91 per cent of its judgments (about 14,000) between 1998 and 2011. The increase in output is clearly one of the main reasons for the respective increase in the docket of cases pending execution.

Since 2000, the CoE has been engaged in an effort to reform the Convention system in order to ensure its long-term effectiveness, based along three main axes developed at the Ministerial Conference in Rome in 2009:[30] efficiency of procedures, domestic implementation of the Convention, and execution of the Court's judgments. These have been developed through the adoption of Protocol 14 and the work of High-Level Conferences. Protocol 14 creates new judicial formations for simple cases, adds a new admissibility criterion (the existence of 'significant disadvantage'), and introduces a nine-year, non-renewable term of office for judges.[31] Three

[29] For more details, see the ECtHR, *Annual Report 2011* (Registry of the European Court of Human Rights 2012).

[30] See ECtHR, *50 Years of the Court* <http://www.echr.coe.int/ECHR/EN/Header/The+Court/Events+at+the+Court/50+years+of+the+Court> accessed 27 January 2013.

[31] Protocol No 14 to the Convention for the Protection of Human Rights and Fundamental Freedoms, Amending the Control System of the Convention, Art 12. In order to provide the Court with more flexibility on how to handle incoming cases, Protocol 14 completed the existing admissibility criteria, ie the exhaustion of domestic remedies and a six-month time-limit, with the additional criterion known as the 'significant disadvantage'. This means that the Court may assess whether it is necessary to go into the merits of the case to ensure 'the respect of human rights' when it considers that the applicant has not suffered a 'significant disadvantage', or to eventually declare the application inadmissible. However, the Court will not be able to reject a case on this ground if there is no judicial remedy in the country concerned, in order to ensure that even the applicants with only minor complaints are not left without any remedy.

High-Level Conferences dedicated to shaping the future of the Court sought further changes to ensure the viability of the Convention system through the adoption of declarations and action plans.[32] These documents stress the primary responsibility of the states parties to implement the Convention at the national level by taking effective measures to prevent human rights violations from occurring (in line with the subsidiarity principle) and to redress such violations through domestic remedies. The documents also deal with such issues as filtering mechanisms;[33] measures to dissuade clearly inadmissible applications, without preventing the Court from examining well-founded applications; how to deal with repetitive applications; the need to maintain high quality in the selection of ECtHR judges; and, finally, measures to strengthen the transparency and efficiency of the execution mechanism. The Court has progressively put in place many of these measures, which are now playing their part in improving the effectiveness of this human rights mechanism.[34]

In 2011, the number of judgments decreased to 1,157 (from 1,499 in 2010), for a total of 52,188 applications decided. This can be ascribed to the reforms and a more dynamic use of the tools available to the Court. Data show that there has been a clear-cut increase in the number of applications ending in a decision that a single judge treats (46,900—twice as many as in 2010); in the number of inadmissibility decisions (about 50,000—30 per cent more than in 2010); and in the number of friendly settlements or unilateral declaration when there is well-established case law (1,500—25 per cent more than in 2010). When dealing with repetitive cases, which continue to be a source of concern,[35] the Court is currently concentrating its efforts on 'leading cases' and often adjourns the other applications, until it has reached a decision on the leading case, which would then guide the other decisions in similar cases. In 2011, about 2,100 applications were set aside as part of this procedure (a 300 per cent increase in comparison to 2010). Finally, it is also worth noting that in recent years, the ECtHR has concentrated its efforts on examining complex cases and, when they raise similar legal questions, on considering them jointly, using one such case as a 'pilot judgment' and freezing the others. Thus, although the number of judgments the ECtHR delivers each year is not increasing as rapidly as in the past, the Court has in practice examined more applications.

[32] Interlaken Declaration and Action Plan (2010); Izmir Declaration on the Future of the European Court of Human Rights and Follow Up Plan (2011); Brighton Declaration (April 2012). For the texts, see ECtHR, *Reform of the Court* <http://www.echr.coe.int/ECHR/EN/Header/The+Court/Reform+of+the+Court/Conferences> accessed 27 January 2013.

[33] A Filtering Section has been created within the Registry of the ECtHR, bringing together filtering teams working on applications made against the five states that account for the most new cases. The purpose of this change was to bring a degree of centralization to the process, streamlining procedures and improving working methods. The results have been positive, so the Filtering Section's remit may be extended to more states.

[34] A thorough analysis of all these reforms goes beyond the scope of this chapter.

[35] In his inaugural speech for judiciary year 2012, the President of the Court expressed concern with regard to the 33,000 repetitive cases pending before the Court.

The reform process has focused also on the execution of judgments, and some of the new working methods help to streamline the work of the Committee of Ministers when it is enforcing the Court's judgments. One notable pattern that may influence how the Committee of Ministers ensures better compliance and a more effective system is the country of origin of the applications. More than half of the 2011 applications were lodged against one of the following four countries: Russia, Turkey, Italy, or Romania. In 2011, more than a third of the judgments the Court delivered concerned seven of the CoE's forty-seven member states: Turkey (174), Russia (133), Ukraine (105), Greece (73), Poland (71), Romania (68), and Bulgaria (62). All together, they represent about 59 per cent of the Court's output. When examining the supervision process, the following section will take these elements into account in assessing its effectiveness.

3.1.1 *Committee of Ministers' Monitoring of the Execution of Judgments*

Monitoring and ensuring the execution of the judgments of the ECtHR is done through one of the most advanced treaty-based systems in the field of human rights.[36] Two basic provisions govern it: Article 46 of the ECHR, which provides for the supervision of ECtHR judgments, and Article 39 of the ECHR, which provides for the supervision of the terms of friendly settlements. Under Article 46 of the ECHR, the Committee of Ministers (CM) of the CoE is the main body entrusted with the task of monitoring the states parties' implementation of the Court's judgments. For this purpose, the Department for the Execution of Judgments of the European Court of Human Rights (part of the Council of Europe's Secretariat) prepares the work of the CM, which meets at the level of Ministries' Deputies.

As mentioned previously, Protocol 14's entry into force and, in particular, the process the process the high-level conferences aimed at ensuring the long-term efficiency of the Convention mechanism set in motion, have adopted innovations in the execution process.[37] The Interlaken Declaration of 2010 stressed that 'full, effective and rapid execution of the final judgments of the Court' is an indispensable component of the system, and the Action Plan called on the CM to strengthen its supervision and review its working-methods.[38] The Committee of Ministers later that year reiterated its goal to

[36] See the annual Activity Reports on the supervision of the execution of the judgments of the Court for further details. The 2011 editions are now available at ECtHR, *Directorates-General ('DGs') and Services Annual Activity Reports 2011*<http://ec.europa.eu/atwork/synthesis/aar/index_en.htm> accessed 27 January 2013.

[37] See ECtHR, *Annual Report 2011* (n 29). The reflection on the challenges facing the ECtHR started even before, with the 2000 Rome Conference. However, this reflection has become even more evident since 2010.

[38] Interlaken Declaration.

improve the efficiency and transparency of the CM's actions, and it highlighted the connection between the execution of judgments and the credibility of the ECHR system.[39] To follow-up on its commitment, the CM adopted new working methods for the supervision process starting from January 2011. The new modalities build upon the previously-adopted working methods of the CM and its Rules of Procedures,[40] modifying them in order to make the supervision process more effective and transparent.[41]

The core element of the execution of the ECtHR judgments is that states parties undertake 'to abide by the final judgment of the Court in any case to which they are parties'.[42] The CM's Rules of Procedure[43] summarize the meaning of this phrase, which Protocol 14 has not changed; and it has received considerable additional precision through the practice of states and the CM, as well as in the case law of the ECtHR. The state party must take two types of measures: (i) individual measures, which concern only the applicant(s); and (ii) general measures, which extend beyond the specific situation.

When adopting individual measures, the state party is under the obligation to erase the consequences the applicant(s) suffered because of the violations the Court established so as to achieve, as far as possible, *restitutio in integrum*.[44] This means that, to the extent possible, the individual situation of the applicant must be redressed to restore his or her pre-violation condition. Individual measures may consist of a 'just satisfaction', that is a sum of money the Court awards to the applicant under Article 41. However, monetary compensation is not always sufficient to redress the violation and put the applicant in the situation he/she was before the violation. Other measures may thus be necessary to remedy the violation, such as the re-opening of unfair criminal proceedings, the enforcement of a non-enforced domestic judgment, or the revocation of a deportation order (required because of

[39] CM, Follow-up to the High Level Conference on the Future of the European Court of Human Rights (120th Session, Interlaken, 11 May 2010) art 8: 'prompt and effective execution of the judgments and decisions delivered by the Court is essential for the credibility and effectiveness of the Convention system and a determining factor in reducing the pressure on the Court.'

[40] Working methods of the CM (2004); Rules of Procedure of the ACP-EC Council of Ministers [2006] OJ L285/47. The currently-applicable Rules of Procedure were adopted on 10 May 2006 at the 964th meeting of the Ministries' Deputies. Following Protocol 14's entry into force, they became fully applicable.

[41] See Department for the Execution of Judgments of the European Court of Human Rights, 'Supervision of the Execution of Judgments and Decisions of the European Court of Human Rights: Implementation of the Interlaken Action Plan' (6 September 2010) CM/Inf/DH(2010)37; Department for the Execution of Judgments of the European Court of Human Rights, 'Supervision of the Execution of the Judgments and Decisions of the European Court of Human Rights: Implementation of the Interlaken Action Plan: Outstanding Issues Concerning the Practical Modalities of Implementation of the New Twin Track Supervision System' (7 December 2010) CM/Inf/DH(2010)45final, which explain the reform in depth.

[42] ECHR, Art 46(1). [43] See Rule 6.2

[44] See Loukis G Loucaides, *Reparation for Violations of Human Rights under the European Convention and Restitutio in Integrum* [2008] EHRLR 182.

the real risk that the applicant may be subject to ill-treatment, including torture). Moreover, the CM has explicitly stated that 'adequate possibilities of re-examination of the case, including reopening of proceedings, in instances where the Court has found a violation of the Convention' represent an individual measure capable of achieving *restitutio in integrum*.[45]

The obligation on a state party to prevent violations similar to those the Court finds or to put an end to continuing violations generally necessitates the adoption of general measures. These may consist of legislative (including constitutional) or regulatory changes, practical measures (such as refurbishing a prison or increasing the number of judges), or the setting-up of specific remedies to deal with both existing and future potential violations. For example, as far as lengthy judicial proceedings are concerned, measures may involve reforming the procedural codes, simplifying the proceedings, reducing the judicial workload, or increasing the use of alternative dispute resolution procedures. General measures establishing domestic remedies are particularly relevant in respect to repetitive cases, as they may re-centre the burden of redressing the violation at the national level. The domestic remedy can also be seen as the first step towards the eradication of the violation through legislative reforms, which may take time to be elaborated and implemented. The creation of the remedy may prove successful and bring a series of cases to a close, as in the so-called Broniowski group of cases.[46] However, on occasion the remedy is insufficient, because it does not fully address the violation in question, thereby failing to prevent new cases from reaching the Court and, thereafter, the CM. The group of cases related to the length of proceedings in Italy is such an example. The Court examined the so-called 'Pinto law' Italian authorities introduced to address procedural delays in the judicial system after it did not stop the inflow of cases; it found that the law did not address in a sustained manner the violations previously found.[47] In other cases, such as *Burdov v Russia (No 2)*,[48] which concerned the non-enforcement of domestic judicial decisions in Russia, the Court assessed the remedy introduced and found it effective, helping to strike other cases from the roll. *Burdov No 2* is not a closed case, however, but has been joined to another group (*Timofeyev*),[49] because the authorities are expected to adopt further general measures in order fully to address the issue of non-execution of judicial decisions.

[45] CM, 'Recommendation on the Re-Examination or Reopening of Certain Cases at Domestic Level Following Judgments of the European Court of Human Rights' (19 January 2000) Rec No R(2000)2, Art 2.

[46] *Broniowski v Poland*. The group of cases linked to *Broniowski* concerned the lack of a mechanism for compensating for property that was abandoned as a result of boundary changes in the aftermath of the Second World War.

[47] See the *Mostacciuolo* (Pinto) group, composed of 133 cases concerning the insufficient amount of compensation and the delays in its payment, for excessively lengthy proceedings. *Mostacciuolo v Italy*.

[48] *Burdov v Russia (No 2)*.

[49] CM, 'Interim Resolution: Burdov No 2 against the Russian Federation' (4 May 2009) CM/ResDH(2011)293.

Protocol 14 has affected this issue in three main respects. First, it extends the CM's supervision to all friendly settlements (the CM previously supervised only the settlements contained in judgments, ie adopted after an admissibility decision had been rendered). Second, the CM is granted a new power to ask the ECtHR for an interpretation of a judgment to assist it in its task of supervising the execution of judgments, and particularly in determining what measures may be necessary to comply with a judgment. Finally, the CM, in exceptional circumstances, may now refer cases of non-execution of a judgment by a state party to the ECtHR. This means that when the CM considers that a state party is not complying with a judgment, it can request that the Court intervene and assess whether the State has failed to fulfil its obligation.

The main novelty of the new modalities for supervising compliance with judgments, which the CM introduced at the end of 2012, consists in streamlining the process and bolstering further the principle of subsidiarity. New rules introduce the so-called 'twin-track' supervision system, drawing a distinction between 'enhanced' and 'standard' supervision. The criteria to submit a case to 'enhanced' supervision are those that Rule No 4 already provided: priority for cases requiring urgent individual measures, pilot judgments, judgments otherwise disclosing major structural/complex problems, and interstate cases. With respect to both types of cases, the state authorities are in charge of preparing action plans and action reports.[50] These documents explain the measures planned or taken to remedy the violation the Court found. However, as regards 'standard supervision' cases, the CM's role is rather formal; it takes note of the reports and leaves the Department of Execution in charge of following the process. Its role is more developed under 'enhanced supervision', because the CM examines such cases at each meeting[51] and may take stock of the situation, express concern, encourage further progress, or suggest additional measures, generally in an Interim Resolution. Statements of the Chair and press releases can also be used to increase pressure on the state to comply. Finally, just satisfaction, the payment of which has in the past been revealed to be rather cumbersome and time-consuming,[52] has also been simplified. It is the responsibility of the applicants to communicate any difficulty they may encounter with the payment within the two months following publication on the Department of Execution's website of the information that state authorities receive concerning the payment. Otherwise, the issue of payment will be considered closed.

[50] See Department for the Execution of Judgments of the ECtHR, 'Action Plans—Action Reports: Definitions and Objectives' (3 June 2009) CM/Inf/DH(2009)29Rev.

[51] Under the new modalities, as well, the cases under 'standard supervision' are on the CM's agenda at every meeting, but they are not the object of specific examination.

[52] See Department for the Execution of Judgments of the ECtHR, 'Monitoring of the Payment of Sums Awarded by Way of Just Satisfaction: An Overview of the Committee of Ministers' Present Practice' (15 January 2009) CM/Inf/DH(2008)7.

Each case or group of cases needs a final resolution to be formally closed and exit the supervision process. Once again, the main responsibility lies with governments, which shall submit a report wherein they explain all the measures taken to implement the judgments. Both the CM and the other states assess this report, and a final resolution it is eventually follows it when the assessment is positive.

3.1.2 *Effectiveness*

Evaluating member states' compliance with ECtHR judgments implies the need to assess the effectiveness of the execution process. A good starting point is, again, numbers, though they may not tell the whole story. Being directly proportional to the output of the Court's workload, the docket of cases pending execution has dramatically increased since 1998, growing from 1,435 that year to 10,689 in 2011, and the number of cases pending execution for more than five years also increased.[53] This picture is modified, however, by the fact that, in 2011, for the first time, the number of new cases decreased by some 6 per cent (1,606 as compared to 1,710 in 2010), including the number of repetitive cases. Notably, the number of cases that a final resolution has closed increased for the third year in a row, going from 239 in 2009 to 816 in 2011, thereby reducing the backlog.

This encouraging evolution may be ascribed to various factors, some of which, already mentioned, relate to the changes introduced in the working methods of both the Court and the Committee of Ministers. As regards the new execution modalities, the CM was required to provide a first assessment of the reforms at the end of 2011, and it confirmed that they had contributed to improving the effectiveness of the supervisory process.[54] The combined use of pilot judgments and the emphasis on domestic remedies are also promising elements. The pilot judgment procedure is a means of dealing with large groups of identical cases that derive from the same underlying, and usually complex, problem. Repetitive cases represent a significant proportion of the Court's workload and therefore contribute to the congestion in the Court's processes. At the same time, the synergy that the use of 'pilot judgments' has created among the Court, the CM, and national authorities also contributes to resolving issues with structural problems and repetitive cases.[55] Progress in these cases may be (and is) achieved by freezing the other cases, by the Court providing

[53] See ECtHR, *Annual Report 2011* (n 29). The data are based on that which is contained in an internal data base of the Department for the Execution of Judgments of the European Court of Human Rights.

[54] CM, 'Annotated Agenda and Decisions Adopted' (6 December 2011) CM/Del/Dec(2011)1128, item 'b'.

[55] See *Burdov No 2* (n 48), which reads: 'the Court may adopt a pilot-judgment procedure allowing it to clearly identify in a judgment the existence of structural problems underlying the violations and to indicate specific measures or actions to be taken by the respondent state to remedy them', para 126. 'Another important aim of the pilot-judgment procedure is to induce the respondent state to resolve

indications about the kinds of measures necessary, and by national authorities working on domestic remedies, while adopting wider and deeper reforms to deal with the structural problems. Interim resolutions, recommendations, and bilateral activities (by the CM and the Department of the Execution) support the whole supervision process. According to the CM 2011 Annual Report, the priority the CM puts on these cases, coupled with the responsiveness of national authorities and their compliance with the time limit the Court imposed, has led to progress in many of the pending pilot judgments,

Among the other elements that may improve compliance, are the direct effect accorded to the judgments of the ECtHR with increasing frequency (facilitating the provision of adequate individual redress), the development of domestic law and practices to prevent similar violations, and the increasing emphasis the CM has put on domestic remedies, as Recommendations (2004)6 and (2010)3[56] underscore. The increased systematization of the interaction between the CM and national authorities, for example, by encouraging the establishment of a 'coordinator—individual or body—of execution of judgments at the national level', as Recommendation (2008)2 provides,[57] is another such tool. Finally, as underlined above, many problematic cases relate mainly to a limited number of countries. In order to deal with them more in depth than during the CM meetings, cooperation activities (such as round-tables, training, or legal expertise) have been organized with some of these countries (eg Albania, Poland, Turkey). The Human Rights Trust Fund, which the Council of Europe, the Council of Europe Development Bank, and Norway, with contributions from Germany, the Netherlands, Finland, Switzerland, and the United Kingdom established in 2008, is used to support these kinds of activities.[58]

Notwithstanding the improvements, however, the compliance process continues to present challenges which must be addressed in order to ensure the long-term viability of the system. One of the first of such challenges concerns the relationships between the CM and the states parties. The binding nature of the judgments of the ECtHR and the CM's role in supervising the full execution of those judgments by the states, are the keys to the success and the uniqueness of the ECHR system. That said, the implementation process may be legally, and at times politically, complex. There can be several domestic institutions involved with different

large numbers of individual cases arising from the same structural problem at the domestic level, thus implementing the principle of subsidiarity which underpins the Convention system', para 127.

56 CM, 'Recommendation to Member States on the Improvement of Domestic Remedies' (12 May 2004) Rec(2004/6); CM, 'Recommendation to Member States on Effective Remedies for Excessive Length of Proceedings' (24 February 2010) CM/Rec(2010)3.

57 CM, 'Recommendation to Member States on Efficient Domestic Capacity for Rapid Execution of Judgments of the European Court of Human Rights' (6 February 2008) CM/Rec(2008)2.

58 For example, the project concerns Freedom of expression and media in Turkey and lasts two year (2011–13). For additional information, see CoE, *Human Rights Trust Fund (HRTF): Providing Support to the Implementation of the European Convention on Human Rights at the National Level*

legal competences; political pressures or other interests often present obstacles that need to be overcome in order to speedily and effectively implement Court judgments. Moreover, the supervision process is ultimately carried out by a 'political' body where the peer pressure applies. This political peer review may lead to situations in which the states party may bend towards a more or less affirmative stance, according to different underlying dynamics, thereby affecting the effectiveness of the process. It becomes therefore absolutely crucial that member states with systemic problems giving rise to repetitive applications assume their own responsibility and give full meaning to the principle of subsidiarity, by implementing all the necessary measures to resolve the root causes of the violation. The additional supervisory role that the Parliamentary Assembly of the CoE (PACE) plays, although the Convention itself does not provide for it, is useful to reinforce the pressure on member states, through their own parliamentarians who are also members of PACE.[59] To this purpose, PACE has produced several reports analysing the most worrying delays in complying with the Court's judgments, thereby putting additional pressure on the member states concerned.[60]

A second challenge concerns the 'trilateral' relationship between the Court, the CM, and national authorities, as regards the extent to which execution measures are detailed in the judgment first and in the supervision work carried out by the CM via the Department of Execution thereafter. A tension lies at the bottom of this relationship between, on the one hand, the level of detail that the Court and the CM sometimes provide in identifying the necessary measures, and, on the other hand, the principle of subsidiarity which would imply the need to leave this task to the national authorities. The Izmir Declaration underlined this tension as regards the CM role, when it invited the CM to apply fully the principle of subsidiarity and highlighted the requirement that the CM carry out supervision only on the basis of a legal analysis of the Court's judgment.[61] The introduction of National Action Plans and Reports partly addresses this tension, since it puts the burden of identifying the measures and providing a time-frame for their enforcement on the national

<http://www.coe.int/t/DGHL/Monitoring/Execution/Themes/HRTF/Intro_HRTF_en.asp> accessed 27 January 2013.

[59] The Parliamentary Assembly of the Council of Europe (PACE) is composed of members of the national Parliaments of the forty-seven member states. They meet four times a year to discuss topical issues and to ask European governments to take initiative and report back.

[60] See the thorough analysis of Andrew Drzemczewski, 'The Parliamentary Assembly's Involvement in the Supervision of the Judgments of the Strasbourg Court' (2010) 28 *NQHR* 164. For the last report by PACE, see the Christos Pourgourides, Committee on Legal Affairs and Human Rights, 'Implementation of Judgments of the European Court of Human Rights' (20 December 2010) Doc No 12455, highlighting some of the key areas where progress in some states parties' execution of ECtHR judgments is needed.

[61] Point H.3 of the Follow-up Plan attached to the Izmir Declaration: 'Recalls the special role given to the Committee of Ministers in exercising its supervisory function under the Convention and

authorities. The publicity given to these documents on the Department of Execution website should put additional pressure on the authorities to comply.

Finally, a third challenge facing the ECHR system relates to the EU's accession to the ECHR. The accession constitutes a major step in the development of human rights in Europe, because it will submit the EU's legal system to independent external control. It will also close gaps in legal protection by giving European citizens the same protection vis-à-vis acts of the EU as they presently enjoy from those of the member states. Discussed since the late 1970s, the accession became a legal obligation under Article 6(7) of the Treaty of Lisbon, which entered into force on 1 December 2009.[62] After intense negotiations, draft legal instruments for the accession have now been transmitted to the CM of the CoE, with further negotiations ongoing. After PACE and the two European Courts[63] have all given their opinions on the final draft instrument, they require that the CM adopt it. Since the EU will accede to the ECHR only once the accession agreement has entered into force, and since the accession agreement requires that all states parties to the ECHR (as well as the EU itself) ratify it, the final result is still far from being achieved. As regards the supervision process, accession will introduce an additional layer of complexity, since modalities will have to be determined to ensure the participation of the EU (on an equal footing with member states), when judgments concerning the EU institutions are examined in the CM. This is particularly relevant because the EU is not a member of the Council of Europe and, as such, does not have any voting rights in the CM.

3.2 The Inter-American system

The European structure was the source of inspiration for the Inter-American system, but today it is structurally different.[64] The Inter-American system, composed of a Commission (IACHR) and a Court (IACtHR), reflects what the situation in Europe was like before Protocol 11 and the creation of the single court. The modalities of the enforcement of the judgments also differ broadly, as well as the distribution of the workload.

underlines the requirement to carry out its supervision only on the basis of a legal analysis of the Court's judgments.'

[62] Article 59(2) of the ECHR provides for the legal basis for accession of the EU: 'the European Union may accede to this Convention.'

[63] See the thorough analysis of Drzemczewski (n 60); Pourgourides (n 60), highlighting some of the key areas where progress in some states parties' execution of ECtHR judgments is needed.

[64] See Andrew James Sirel, 'Improving Compliance with Judgments of the Inter-American Court of Human Rights: Lessons Learned from Europe' (LLM Dissertation Paper, University of Essex School of Law 2010); Darren Hawkins and Wade Jacobi, 'Partial compliance: a comparison of the European

3.2.1 *The IACHR*

The IACHR is a quasi-judicial body entrusted with the mission of promoting human rights in the American hemisphere and with monitoring compliance with the main human rights instruments that the OAS adopted: the American Declaration of the Rights and Duties of Men and the American Convention on Human Rights. Seven members who serve in a personal capacity compose the IACHR. The IACHR organizes its work around three main functions: examining individual petitions, monitoring the human rights situation in the member states through on-site visits and country reports, and focusing on priority thematic areas through reports and the establishment of Special Rapporteurs. The Commission has progressively recognized increasing powers; in 1961, it began to carry out on-site visits to observe the human rights situation in a country or to investigate specific instances. In 1965, it was expressly authorized to examine complaints or petitions concerning specific human rights violations. When, subsequently, the Court was created, the Commission was entitled to submit cases against states accepting the Court's jurisdiction and required to appear in Court during litigation. The IACHR also issues precautionary measures and may request the Inter-American Court to order the adoption of 'provisional measures' in cases of extreme gravity and urgency, to prevent irreparable harm to persons, even if the Commission has not yet referred the case to the Court. Further, it may request advisory opinions from the Court, in accordance with the provisions of Article 64 of the American Convention.

In carrying out its mandate to promote and protect human rights, the Commission performs the core of its work through the petition system. The IACHR receives petitions from individuals and groups alleging violations of the rights protected by the Inter-American instruments. For each case, it can make a report and reach a determination on the merits. If it finds a violation, it transmits recommendations to the state concerned on how to remedy the violation.[65] When States fail to implement the recommendations, the Commission may transmit the case to the Court (if the state has accepted the Court's jurisdiction), or it may publish the report. Since 2001, the Commission has submitted nearly all cases to the Court. This has clearly increased the Court's workload.

The IACHR receives—in comparative terms—a rather high number of petitions annually, especially considering that it is composed of only seven individuals, each serving part-time. In 2011, the IACHR received 1,658 complaints (1,598 in 2010) and accepted 25 per cent of them.[66] During 2011, the Commission adopted a total of 165 reports, which included sixty-seven cases found to be admissible, eleven reports on

and the Inter-American Courts for Human Rights' (Annual Meeting of the American Political Science Association, Boston, 18 August 2008).

[65] See Art 44 of the Rules of Procedure of the IACHR.

[66] See the IACHR, 'Annual Report of the Inter-American Commission on Human Rights: 2011' (30 December 2011) OEA/Ser.L/V/II.

petitions found to be inadmissible, eight reports on friendly settlements, fifty-four decisions to archive, and twenty-five reports on the merits. The case docket at the end of the year (admissibility and merits) included 1,645 cases. In 2010, the IACHR received 422 requests for provisional measures and granted fifty-seven of them. Finally, in 2011, it transmitted twenty-three cases to the IACtHR (sixteen in 2010).

Over 50 per cent of the complaints received in 2011 came from a limited number of countries (Columbia, Mexico, Peru, Argentina), presenting a similar feature to that which is found in the ECtHR. In both systems, only a few countries make up the majority of the cases in front of the protection mechanisms. This means in practice that improving the human rights situation in a handful of countries in both systems will make a significant difference in terms of workload for the respective mechanisms, not to mention avoiding the creation of future victims.

The IACHR supervises state compliance with its own recommendations and reports on this issue in its Annual Report, which is delivered to the OAS Permanent Council and General Assembly. The Commission may decide what the most appropriate measures are for monitoring the measures national authorities have taken, such as by requesting information or organizing hearings.[67] Recognizing that implementing the measures necessary to remedy the violations can be a lengthy process, the Commission draws a distinction between full,[68] partial, and pending compliance.[69] Partial compliance means that the state has partially observed the recommendations the IACHR has made, either by complying with only one or some of them or by failing to completely comply with all of them. Pending compliance indicates that the state either has taken no steps to comply with the recommendation or that it has explicitly indicated that it will not comply with the recommendations. Pending compliance also covers cases in which the state has not reported to the IACHR, or in which it has no information from other sources that would suggest compliance. Looking at numbers, the situation appears challenging; out of the 143 cases that have been decided and published in the last ten years, twenty-five show full compliance, thirty-one partial compliance, and eighty-seven are pending. The data seems to put into question the effectiveness of the Commission in ensuring compliance with its recommendations. Notably, compared to the European system, there is a lack of a separate supervisory body, available budget, and follow-up by OAS political bodies in pressuring for compliance; these considerations appear to have a particular relevance in this context and also hold with respect to the Inter-American Court.

[67] ACHR, Art 41; OAS, 'Statute of the Inter-American Commission on Human Rights' (1 October 1979) OEA/Ser.P/IX.0.2, art 18.

[68] Total compliance means that the state has fully complied with all the recommendations that the IACHR has made, having regard to the principles of effectiveness, and fully observed those recommendations, where the state has begun and satisfactorily completed the procedures for compliance.

[69] See IACHR, 'Annual Report 2011' (n 66).

3.2.2 *The IACtHR*

The IACtHR, the judicial body of the Inter-American system, is composed of seven judges and based in Costa Rica. Its functions are three-fold: (i) it deals with contentious cases; (ii) it can issue provisional measures; and (iii) it can issue advisory opinions on the interpretation of human rights treaties and domestic laws' compliance with them, under Article 64 of the American Convention on Human Rights. Advisory opinions are particularly useful in developing the interpretation of the human rights instruments and setting standards for the promotion and guarantee of human rights, without having to first wait for a violation to occur.

Article 63(1) of the American Convention on Human Rights provides that when the IACtHR finds a violation of a right or freedom that the Constitution protects, the Court shall rule that the injured party be ensured the enjoyment of the right or freedom that was violated. To this end, the IACtHR rules, if appropriate, that the consequences of the measure or situation that constituted the breach be remedied through reparations to the injured party, including through material (often pecuniary) compensation. Reparations may take different forms. Measures of restitution entail, to the maximum extent possible, the re-establishment of the situation existing before the violation occurred (*restitutio in integrum*, as in the European system). Such measures may include re-establishing the liberty of a person who was illegally detained or annulling a judicial, administrative, or police record. Measures of rehabilitation include providing the victims with the medical and psychological care they need free of charge. Measures of satisfaction are aimed at remedying the non-pecuniary damage, so as to soothe the suffering the violation caused; they can include symbolic reparations, such as a monument in memory of the victim,[70] a public apology to the memory of the victims,[71] or the publication and dissemination of the judgment. The measures for guaranteeing the non-repetition of violations entail legislative reform to prevent the same violations from occurring, in particular when the violations originated from structural problems; training for public officials; and other measures appropriate to the purpose. Finally, the obligation to guarantee the effective investigation of violations pertains both to individuals and to more general measures. This implies the removal of all the obstacles preventing the investigation, both *de jure* and *de facto*, as well as the introduction of measures aimed at expediting proceedings in general.

While at the beginning of its operations, the IACtHR mainly received requests for advisory opinions,[72] it is now primarily deciding contentious cases. The increase in the number of cases before the Court led this jurisdiction to reform its rules of procedure in order to speed up proceedings and also to give a greater role to victims and their representatives.[73] In 2011, twenty-three new cases were submitted to the

[70] *Myrna Mack Chang v Guatemala.* [71] *Plan de Sanchez Massacre v Guatemala.*

[72] The first judgment on the merits it delivered was *Velasquez-Rodriguez v Honduras.*

[73] IACtHR Rules of Procedure (2009).

Court, and it delivered eighteen judgments, four of which were interpretative judgments; issued thirty-two orders of compliance with judgments; and promulgated thirty-six orders on provisional measures.[74]

The supervision process of the Inter-American system differs from the European system. Three main distinctive features may be described: the competence of the Court to supervise the enforcement of its own judgments, the lack of a political dimension of enforcement, and the Court's apparent disconnection from the human rights reality of the supervised countries.

First, the IACtHR itself (not, as in Europe, a separate body) supervises compliance with its own judgments. According to Article 69 of its Rules of Procedure, the IACtHR is empowered to request information about a particular judgment's state of execution from the state party concerned. Observations are also requested from the IACHR and the victims or their representatives. Once it has gathered all the information, the IACtHR draws its own conclusion as to what measures the state party must take in order to comply with the judgment in a six-month period. If no progress is made, the IACtHR can summon the country concerned to a compliance hearing and ultimately bring the matter to the OAS Assembly to exercise—at least in theory—the necessary political influence for the judgment to be implemented.

In 2011, 124 cases were pending compliance, in addition to the new cases the Court was processing.[75] Given the complexity of the reparations the Court awards, the enforcement process is cumbersome and lengthy, and not all cases are at the same stage of compliance. While the symbolic reparations may carry an important public message, they may also take more time to be implemented. Other means, such as effective investigations, the prosecution and punishment of perpetrators, legal reforms, or other measures relating to systemic human rights violations, have the lowest level of compliance. This implies in practice that a very large majority of the judgments has not yet been complied with, casting a shadow over the effectiveness of the system as a whole. However, positive developments have also been registered. Freedom of expression, amongst others, may be cited as a field where national authorities accomplished progress as regards the enforcement of inter-American standards. Several of the IACtHR's rulings, coupled with the concurrent efforts of the IACHR and its Special Rapporteur for Freedom of Expression, have led to legislative changes providing for the decriminalization of certain forms of expression (Argentina,[76] Mexico, El Salvador, Panama, and Uruguay); the protection of journalists (Colombia); and access to information and transparency in the public

[74] IACtHR *Informe Annual: 2011* (IACtHR 2011).

[75] See IACtHR, *Informe Annual* (n 74) 13.

[76] *Kimel v Argentina* has prompted the change. For other examples, see IACHR, 'Reparations for the Violation of the Right to Freedom of Expression in the Inter-American System' (30 December 2011) OEA/Ser.L/V/II.

administration (Brazil and Chile).[77] Moreover, several supreme and constitutional courts (Brazil, Colombia, and Mexico), as well as lower jurisdictions, struck down existing legislation, because it was incompatible with the inter-American standards; they cited both the jurisprudence and reports from the Special Rapporteur to reach the conclusion.[78]

The supervision system, however, faces several challenges, both structural and political. First, the fact that the Court itself is charged with the execution of its own judgments implies that time and resources must be devoted to the process and, thereby, subtracted from the judicial function. The Court lacks both time and resources, because it is not a permanent body, and it receives inadequate funding from the OAS. Currently, its budgetary resources represent slightly more than 2 per cent of the total OAS budget[79]—not enough to cover the ever-increasing work-load. Given this situation, the IACtHR, like the IACHR, supplements its budget with financial contributions by member states,[80] observer countries, and international organizations.[81] Though some member states complain, because it dilutes their influence over the IACHR and the Court, the OAS has not increased the budgetary allocation for either institution.

A second feature of the supervision system is its mainly 'judicial' nature. While it is true that Article 69 provides for the OAS General Assembly to intervene in cases of clear non-compliance with a judgment, the OAS political bodies seldom speak out, and the process does not reach the level of sophistication of the CM's role in the European system. Therefore, the enforcement system lacks a political dimension that can be pivotal in putting peer pressure on the member states to comply with the judgments and recommendations. Independently from any consideration of whether the European model would be the right one to follow in the inter-American context (the issue of the lack resources would discourage this option), it is worth underscoring that the General Assembly is often the scene of efforts to undermine the entire system, rather than strengthen it, when the system's organs criticize members who violated human rights. The current attacks that Venezuela and Ecuador are leading against the Commission and the Court highlight tensions existing among certain states and the OAS human right system. In 2012, Venezuelan President Hugo Chávez announced his country's intention to withdraw from the IACHR, which he has always considered a puppet of the US. This withdrawal would be legally impossible without exiting the entire OAS. However, since 2002, Venezuela has not allowed IACHR officials to enter the country. Similar

77 In relation to cases *Claude Reyes v Chile* and *Gomes Lund v Brazil*.

78 See IACHR, 'Reparations for the Violation of the Right to Freedom of Expression' (n 76).

79 In 2011, the Court received about USD 2 million; the OAS budget was over USD 83 million.

80 Costa Rica, Ecuador, Mexico, and Chile contributed to the Court budget in 2011.

81 In 2011, the Spanish International Cooperation Agency for Development, Norway, the US Agency for International Development, and the EU provided funding.

tensions have occurred in the past: in 1999 Peru purported to withdraw from the Inter-American Court's contentious jurisdiction, although the Court held that this could not be done without denouncing the Convention, which Peru did not do. After the departure of Peru's President Alberto Fujimori, Peru resumed cooperation with the inter-American system. Trinidad and Tobago is the only state to have denounced the American Convention of Human Rights, which it did in 1998, due to its concern over contentious cases dealing with the death penalty.

Third and finally, the number of cases before the IACtHR is extremely limited. Although the number of petitions for which the Commission reaches a conclusion on the merits determines this number (over 1,000 complaints reach the IACHR per year, while slightly more than a hundred cases are submitted to the IACtHR), it may be considered to have an impact on the legitimacy of the Inter-American human rights system. However, this should be a nuanced conclusion in light of the fact that in the Inter-American system, compliance is one part of the whole system, due to the multifaceted role the IACHR retains. The latter, in fact, examines cases involving hundreds of victims, thereby addressing country-wide problems; raises and analyses serious violations in Chapter IV of its Annual Report; and routinely offers to engage the parties in friendly settlements. It follows that more limited cases reach the Court, but they are nonetheless addressed and monitored elsewhere.

4. Conclusions

Human rights mechanisms are like concentric circles. The larger one comprises the UN system. By the very nature of the UN and its very diverse and wide membership, the Charter and treaty-based mechanisms constitute a significant achievement, notwithstanding their shortcomings in terms of effectiveness. The smaller circles are the various regional arrangements; the closer the level of integration, the stronger the human rights mechanism will be. The reason why the European system appears the most far-reaching is probably to be found in its origin (post-Second World War Europe) and the vision of a group of enlightened European politicians who were aiming to prevent the devastations and horrors of three wars in a century from happening again.

The judicial mechanisms of human rights protection, such as the European and the Inter-American Courts, have many similarities, but also fundamental differences. Although a vast majority of the cases the ECtHR deals with conclude that there was a violation of Article 6 (the right to a fair trial), an increasing number of violations (more than 23 per cent) concern the right to life or the prohibition of torture and inhuman or degrading treatment (Articles 2 and 3 of the Convention). These latter types of cases are like those common to the Inter-American system throughout its history. Differences between the systems include the budget and staff, the number of applications/decisions, their modus of supervising the execution of judgments, and the technical support they have to make sure that human rights are implemented nationally. Ultimately, however, the European and American Human Rights protection mechanisms differ in one fundamental element: the ECtHR, contrary to the IACtHR, is by now *de facto* an integral part of the national judicial systems as a court of last resort, enshrined in them almost to the point of blurring the subsidiarity principle. While this is certainly to the credit of the ECtHR, such a deep 'intermingling' of the ECtHR with the national judicial system is perhaps one of the causes of it increasingly being overburdened with cases and, in turn, facing the greatest threat to the effectiveness of the system as a whole.

The effectiveness of the mechanisms in ensuring compliance with human rights standards remains pivotal to the legal order. Even if each mechanism is the result of its own historical development and institutional dynamic, it is possible to ensure the necessary cross-fertilization between them, so that they build on each other's successes, failures, and best practices, to advance the cause of human rights. From a purely legal perspective, it is undeniable that a judicial mechanism for human rights protection that provides the right to individual complaint and the binding nature of its judgments remains the best-performing system of all, in terms of ensuring the independence, impartiality, and transparency of both the findings and the execution. In the course of countries' negotiations, a judicial system subtracts the human rights protection mechanism from the intricate political web in which it may fall. The challenge for the judicial mechanism, however, will be to continue to be 'near' to the national judicial systems (so as to influence their jurisprudence), while at the same time not becoming embroiled in the national systems themselves (thus defeating the subsidiarity principle on which the mechanism rests). Another challenge for the European and the Inter-American systems alike will be the need for continual political willingness to support their work and accept their findings; this means, in practice, the timely and full execution of the judgments, proper human and financial resources, the selection of highly qualified judges, and the implementation of measures to prevent human rights violations from reaching the international courts in the first place.

Further Reading

General

Shelton D and Carozza P, *Regional Protection of Human Rights* (2nd edn, OUP 2013)

European System

Bates E and others, 'Supervision of the Execution of Judgments Delivered by the European Court of Human Rights' in Christou TA and Raymond JP (eds), *European Court of Human Rights: Remedies and Execution of Judgments* (British Institute of International & Comparative Law 2005) 49–106

—— *The Evolution of the European Convention on Human Rights: From Its Inception to the Creation of a Permanent Court of Human Rights* (OUP 2010)

Drzemczwski A and Gaughan J, 'Implementing Strasbourg Court Judgments: The Parliamentary Dimension' [2010] *European Ybk Hum Rts* 233

Harris DJ and others, *Law of the European Convention on Human Rights* (2nd edn, OUP 2009)

Lawson R, 'Guaranteeing the Authority and Effectiveness of the European Convention on Human Rights' (2008) PACE Working Document AS/Jur Report Doc No12811

Leach P, *Beyond the Bug River—A New Dawn for Redress before the European Court of Human Rights* (2005) 10(2) *EHRLR* 148

—— 'The Effectiveness of the Committee of Ministers in Supervising the Enforcement of Judgments of the European Court of Human Rights' [2006] *PL* 443

Inter-American system

Basch F and others, 'The Effectiveness of the Inter-American System of Human Rights Protection: A Quantitative Approach to Its Functioning and Compliance with Its Decisions' (2010) 7(12) *SUR–Int'l J Hum Rts* 9

Cavallaro J and Brewer SE, 'Re-Evaluating Regional Human Rights Litigation in the Twenty-First Century: The Case of the Inter-American Court' (2008) 102 *AJIL* 768

Faúndez Ledesma H, *The Inter-American System for the Protection of Human Rights: Institutional and Procedural Aspects* (3rd edn, Inter-American Institute of Human Rights 2008)

Pasqualucci JM, *The Practice and Procedure of the Inter-American Court of Human Rights* (CUP 2003)

CHAPTER 38

WHAT OUTCOMES FOR VICTIMS?

FIONA MCKAY

1. Introduction

It is often asserted that seeking justice and redress following human rights violations is done for the sake of the victims,[1] recalling the great suffering of those individuals and groups. Victims, it is said, must be placed at the centre of any efforts to redress human rights violations, because they are at the core of the human rights project. It is immediately apparent that seeking redress for the victims may be caught up with other, competing goals, such as preventing future violations, achieving peace and reconciliation, promoting rule of law and social and economic development. Striking the right balance between such different demands is immensely challenging, but these considerations must not interfere with the imperative to respond to the suffering of victims of violations.

In his study of 1993, Professor Theo Van Boven, then Special Rapporteur of the United Nations Sub-Commission on Prevention of Discrimination and Protection of Minorities, stated that more attention needed to be given to the perspective of the victim, which is often overlooked, and that reparation should respond to the needs

[1] The term 'victim' that this chapter uses is the term most commonly used in legal instruments and litigation, although some prefer the more positive term 'survivor' or other more neutral terms, such as 'affected person' or 'injured party', which carry fewer connotations of vulnerability and dependence.

and wishes of the victims.[2] Examination of the practice during the twenty years since Van Boven issued his call reveals a mixed picture. While important advances have been made in legal norms, and tremendous efforts made by institutions and civil society to enforce them, there remain significant challenges. Not all victims are able to access remedies, the outcomes not always to their satisfaction, and implementation may come late or not at all. Particularly problematic is the scarcity of examples of reparation being received by victims in the wake of large scale abuses in parts of the world where few avenues for redress exist.

Redress processes for victims of human rights violations cannot be seen only in terms of a sum of money they may take home at the end of the day, a state action in response to a complaint, or the opportunity to tell their story to a truth commission or court. The outcomes must be seen as encompassing the entire experience for the victim and the full impact of the process on him or her. It is not simply a question of whether *any* remedy or outcome is produced, but whether that remedy or outcome is the *right* one for the victim. It is also to be expected that even if reparation measures target the individual, they will have an impact at different levels, on the individual victim, community and state.[3] Indeed, the complex relationship between individual and group identities and rights is a complicating factor when it comes to reparation. Under international human rights law, remedies are largely framed as rights of individuals, but the development of notions of group rights, together with the fact that many violations are committed against groups, present challenges to this framework.

This chapter explores the outcomes of human rights law from the point of view of victims of human rights violations. The chapter begins by asking what makes an outcome satisfactory for victims. It then gives an overview of the remedies envisaged in human rights law and how satisfactorily these reflect the range of outcomes that may be desirable for victims, the outcomes that the institutions and mechanisms created to enforce the law are able to deliver in theory, and, most importantly, what they are actually delivering in practice. Finally, the chapter examines this body of law and practice in terms of how successfully it responds to victims' expectations, perceptions and desires or needs, with some reflections on what a truly victim-centred approach would look like and what more can be done to ensure satisfactory outcomes for victims.

[2] UN Commission on Human Rights, 'Study Concerning the Right to Restitution, Compensation and Rehabilitation for Victims of Gross Violations of Human Rights and Fundamental Freedoms: Final Report Submitted by Mr Theo van Boven, Special Rapporteur' (2 July 1993) UN Doc E/CN.4/Sub.2/1993/8, paras 133, 137.

[3] For instance, there is a considerable amount of literature on questions such as the impact of reparations on reconciliation and on development, as well as on collective reparation.

2. What Outcomes Are Desirable for Victims?

A report published in 2001 warned of the dangers involved in responding to human rights violations without taking sufficient account of the victims' perspectives: 'We suggest that without a fuller understanding of survivors' perceptions and without the necessary support structures in place we are in danger of encouraging people whose lives have been traumatized to exercise rights they are unclear about, through processes that they are not actively involved in and do not understand, which then produce outcomes that do not match their expectations.'[4] Assumptions are made too often about what is good for victims without actually checking what victims themselves want or need.

Research conducted into victims' perceptions following human rights violations,[5] including country specific studies[6] reveals disagreement over whether the process of seeking reparation can have a value to victims in itself. Those who assert that it does attribute this variously to giving victims a sense of task or mission or the sense that they are regaining control over their lives, the sense of being able to bring benefits for others, that telling their story has value, as being heard or contributing to an official record, helping channel feelings of retribution and desire for revenge, or simply aiding victims to heal and move on.[7] Hamber and Wilson put it succinctly: 'genuine reparation, and the process of healing, we assert, does not occur through the delivery of the object (for example, a pension, a monument and so on) but through the process that takes place around the object.'[8] Legal scholars report that civil plaintiffs before US courts who obtained multimillion dollar

[4] REDRESS, *Torture Survivors' Perceptions of Reparation: Preliminary Survey* (Redress Trust 2001) 9, <http://www.redress.org/downloads/publications/TSPR.pdf> accessed 18 February 2013.

[5] A survey of available literature at that time was made in the Redress study of 2001. REDRESS, *Torture Survivors' Perceptions* (n 4); studies reviewed covered, inter alia, the 'comfort women' that the Japanese Army held as sex slaves in the Second World War, internees in Northern Ireland, the International Criminal Tribunal for the Former Yugoslavia, the truth and reconciliation processes in South Africa, Holocaust survivors, and survivors of political repression in Chile and Argentina.

[6] Inter-American Institute of Human Rights (IIHR), *Comprehensive Attention to Victims of Torture in Cases under Litigation: Psychological Contributions* (IIHR 2009), a report of a four-year project by mental health professionals who offered support to victims during litigation before the Inter-American human rights system. They looked at how to ensure that litigation is a healing process for torture victims by reference to several countries in the Americas. Country-specific studies on victims' perceptions have also been conducted, inter alia, in the Democratic Republic of the Congo, Uganda, Timor Leste, Nepal, South Africa, Burundi, and Cambodia—both before and after the establishment of justice mechanisms.

[7] *Torture Survivors' Perceptions* (n 4) 26–32.

[8] Brandon Hamber and Richard A Wilson, 'Symbolic Closure through Memory, Reparation and Revenge in Post-Conflict Societies' (2002) 1 *J Hum Rts* 35.

judgments for damages against human rights violators for violations committed around the world have taken tremendous personal satisfaction from these lawsuits even although hardly a cent of the awards has ever been collected.[9] In contrast, others assert that it is harmful for victims to go through such processes, as it may lead to re-traumatization or make victims feel they are being treated with suspicion and skepticism, and run counter to psychological healing. There is at least a consensus any process of litigation or other claims procedure must be carefully handled and victims should be supported throughout the process by psychological support and counselling.[10]

A key finding agreed by all is that victims' perceptions vary from individual to individual according to age, gender, culture, socio-economic or political context and many other factors. Different victims will want different things, and even the same victims may want different things over time—for instance, it may be difficult to think about reparation while violations are still going on, or while urgent material needs are unmet, but reparations may become important later on.[11] The Redress study found that groups of victims who suffered from the same or similar violations are almost always divided as to what they see as desirable.[12] Some victims (mothers of the disappeared in Argentina, Asian 'comfort' women, for example) strongly objected to accepting compensation, perceiving it as an attempt to buy their silence and avoid acknowledging the wrongs committed, whereas for others, it is a fitting recognition to which they are entitled. For some, symbolic reparations are meaningful, others perceive them as useless. One team of psychologists concluded that in order to be considered satisfactory, a reparatory act must be considered intensely related to the personal characteristics of the victim and his/her context and beliefs;

[9] Beth Stephens and Michael Ratner, *International Human Rights Litigation in US Courts* (Transnational Publishers 1996) 234. The string of cases began with the landmark case of *Filartiga v Pena-Irala*, brought under the Alien Tort Claims Statute; other cases have been brought using the Torture Victim Protection Act.

[10] Brandon Hamber, 'Do Sleeping Dogs Lie? The Psychological Implications of the Truth and Reconciliation Commission in South Africa' (Centre for the Study of Violence and Reconciliation, Johannesburg, 26 July 1995) <http://www.brandonhamber.com/pubs_papers.htm> accessed 18 February 2013.

[11] For instance, two studies that the Centre for the Study of Violence and Reconciliation (CSVR) published in 1998 and 2000 on the findings of the Truth and Reconciliation Commission in South Africa found that whereas at the time of the first study, people thought about reparation in terms of their immediate needs, the passage of time, combined with treatment, led to a change in victims' attitudes. As a result, by the time of the second study, they were likely to see prosecutions as more important. Brandon Hamber and others, 'Survivors' Perceptions of the Truth and Reconciliation Commission and Suggestions for the Final Report' (*CSVR*) <http://www.csvr.org.za/index.php/publications/publications-by-date.html?start=370> accessed 18 February 2013; CSVR, 'Two Years after the TRC Final Report: A Khulumani View' (July 2000) CSVR (both cited in *Torture Survivors' Perceptions* (n 4) 45–46).

[12] *Torture Survivors' Perceptions* (n 4) 25, 39–47.

whether or not it will be an effective reparation, from a psychological point of view, will depend on the victim: 'What is truly important is not the reparation itself that justice offers, but what the mind can reconstruct with it.'[13]

The traditional goal of reparation under international law is to restore the situation prevailing before the violation. Some victims seek the return of something taken away from them in the course of the human rights violation, such as property,[14] or legal rights and entitlements.[15] However the harm produced in most cases involving human rights violations is effectively irreparable. Victims have to be satisfied with something else, which is necessarily symbolic 'in the sense that what is lost is replaced by something that represents it'.[16] The goal is reparation that can legitimately aim to relieve suffering, alleviate the consequences of the wrongful acts and pursue societal goals such as deterrence, promoting reconciliation and goals specific to a particular case.[17]

The following list some of the elements put forward as desired by victims: financial compensation for different kinds of harm;[18] the opportunity to give testimony or speak the truth in settings such as truth commissions, said to contribute to psychological rehabilitation;[19]creation of an official and/or public record, acknowledgement of responsibility, recognition and apology. All are said to have the considerable capacity to reduce victims' suffering.[20] In some contexts investigation and punishment of those

[13] 'Reparations: A Judicial and Symbolic Act' in *Comprehensive Attention* (n 6) 274–75.

[14] Residents of Cyprus have brought several cases before the European Court of Human Rights in respect of their property in Northern Cyprus. In *Loizidou v Turkey*, lodged in 1989, the applicant claimed that the respondent State was under a duty to permit her to exercise her right to access her property.

[15] As part of the reparations programs put in place in Chile for human rights violations during the military dictatorship of 1973 to 1990, victims campaigned for measures for returning exiles and political prisoners, and the politically-dismissed for measures aimed at restoring benefits and entitlements. Elizabeth Lira, 'The Reparations Policy for Human Rights Violations in Chile' in Pablo de Greiff (ed), *The Handbook of Reparations* (OUP 2006).

[16] 'Reparations: A Judicial and Symbolic Act' (n 13) 274.

[17] The purposes of reparation, in addition to obliging the person responsible to repair the harm, as set out in *Decision Establishing the Principles and Procedures to Be Applied in Reparations*, para 179, *Prosecutor v Lubanga Dyilo*.

[18] The fact that compensation is so often requested may have much to do with the remedies that are available for victims to pursue and may not reflect what victims actually want. In the case of *Loizidou* (n 14), the remedy the Court awarded on finding a violation of Article 1 of Protocol No 1 of the Convention was compensation, not restitution of the property.

[19] Hamber (n 10). Nevertheless, Hamber and Wilson warn against an over-simplistic idea that 'revealing is healing'. Others challenge the assertion that truth necessarily heals or leads to reconciliation and critically examine the limitations of criminal trials in meaningfully contributing to reconciliation. See eg Erin Daly and Jeremy Sarkin, *Reconciliation in Divided Societies: Finding Common Ground* (U Pennsylvania Press 2006).

[20] Marcie Mersky and Naomi Roht-Arriaza, 'Guatemala' in Due Process of Law Foundation, *Victims Unsilenced: The Inter-American Human Rights System and Transitional Justice in Latin America* (Due Process of Law Foundation 2007) 26. Also 'Reparations: A Judicial and Symbolic Act' (n 13) 280.

responsible is considered very important for victims, in others, less so.[21] Some assert that many victims are concerned to ensure that their case brings about change to benefit others and affect society at large, affirming its values. A number of studies indicate that what matters most to victims is to relieve their immediate problems of security, poverty and livelihood. Identification by victims of human rights abuses with a group having broader national or other aspirations, such as the Kurds or the Palestinians adds another element to their understanding of a satisfactory remedy.

A key finding is that victims are interested in process as well as result. Thus, it is not only the final outcome of efforts to seek remedies that matters to victims, but also *how* that outcome is achieved. Research in the field of criminal justice and victimology has shown that how Courts proceed, and how they treat victims, is important to victims' sense of justice.[22] Victims of crime want to be treated with dignity and respect, to be notified about important developments and be informed about their rights and to receive support and protection; they are more likely to perceive proceedings as fair if they are given a voice.[23] Although such studies were conducted largely in national criminal justice systems in developed countries, other studies following the Truth and Reconciliation process in South Africa and the trials of the International Criminal Tribunal for the Former Yugoslavia suggest that concerns with procedural justice are broadly felt.[24]

In light of this complex picture of the great variety in what victims want and need, the law needs to create a framework that will enable human rights institutions and governments to do the right thing for victims. The next section looks at the law governing reparations and redress for human rights violations and the extent to which there is a convergence between what victims are entitled to expect under the law, on the one hand, and their wishes and needs, on the other.

[21] Psychologists assert that impunity can be devastating for the victim; it can exacerbate and perpetuate suffering and delay healing. Various reports are cited in support. *Torture Survivors' Perceptions* (n 4) 27; 'Reparations: A Judicial and Symbolic Act' (n 13) 280. Justice opens the possibility of mourning, helps the victim to recover his/her dignity, and directs his/her personal energy towards matters such as the construction of a new project of life.

[22] The literature refers to this as procedural justice, the perceived fairness of decision-making proceedings, as opposed to distributive justice, which refers to outcomes. For instance, E Allan Lind and Tom R Tyler, *The Social Psychology of Procedural Justice* (Springer 1988).

[23] As a result of such findings, standard setting exercises have been conducted in Europe since the 1980s, the latest of which is a draft Directive of which the stated purpose is 'to ensure that all victims of crime receive appropriate protection and support and are able to participate in criminal proceedings and are recognized and treated in a respectful, sensitive and professional manner, without discrimination of any kind, in all contacts with any public authority, victim support or restorative justice service'. European Commission, 'Proposal for a Directive of the European Parliament and of the Council Establishing Minimum Standards on the Rights, Support and Protection of Victims of Crime' (18 May 2011) COM (2011)275.

[24] Sanja Kutnjak-Ivkovich and John Hagan, *Reclaiming Justice: The International Tribunal for the Former Yugoslavia and Local Courts* (OUP 2011).

3. Outcomes for Victims in Human Rights Law and Practice

3.1 What outcomes for victims are envisaged in human rights law?

The starting point for identifying the remedial framework for human rights violations is general international law. In the 1928 *Chorzów Factory* case, the Permanent Court of International Justice declared that a breach of international law leads to an obligation to make full reparation; such reparation must, as far as possible, wipe out all the consequences of the illegal act and restore the situation that would have existed if the wrongful act had not been committed, and where this is not possible, provide compensation.[25] This basic framework for dealing with the consequences of breaches of international law was confirmed by the International Law Commission (ILC) in its Articles on State Responsibility finalized in 2001. The ILC states that '(f)ull reparation for the injury caused by the internationally wrongful act shall take the form of restitution, compensation or satisfaction', or a combination of those.[26] Although the ILC Articles are written in the context of interstate relations, the Commentary notes that they are without prejudice to obligations the state may owe to other actors.

With the development of international human rights norms, the language of rights is applied to this remedial framework. The major human rights instruments declare the right of victims to an effective remedy and reparation for the violation of their human rights.[27] Some human rights instruments specify that victims are entitled to compensation and/or other forms of reparation, though they tend not to define in detail what victims are entitled to receive, and there is no standard wording.[28] Most instruments impose these obligations on states. Individuals, and in some instances other entities such as corporations, may also have criminal or civil responsibility.[29]

25 *Factory at Chorzów (Germany v Poland)* (Jurisdiction) 21; *Factory at Chorzów (Germany v Poland)* (Merits) 29.

26 ILC, 'Draft Articles on Responsibility of States for Internationally Wrongful Acts' (2001) UN Doc A/56/10. Article 37 defines 'satisfaction' as 'an acknowledgement of the breach, an expression of regret, a formal apology or another appropriate modality'.

27 For example, Universal Declaration of Human Rights (UDHR), Art 8; International Covenant on Civil and Political Rights (ICCPR), Art 2(3).

28 ICCPR, Art 9(5) ('compensation'); International Convention on the Elimination of All Forms of Racial Discrimination, Art 6 ('just and adequate reparation or satisfaction'); Convention on the Rights of the Child, Art 39 ('physical and psychological recovery and social reintegration'); Convention against Torture and Other Cruel, Inhuman or Degrading Treatment or Punishment, Art 14 ('adequate compensation, including the means for as full rehabilitation as possible').

29 As regards individual criminal responsibility, Art 75 of the Rome Statute of the International Criminal Court provides that persons the ICC finds guilty may be ordered to make reparations to the

Explicit enunciation of a right to redress for groups has come with the emergence of the concept of group rights, such as the rights of minorities and indigenous peoples and the right to self-determination.[30]

Three important instruments focus specifically on the rights of victims to remedies and reparation. One is the Declaration of Basic Principles of Justice for Victims of Crime and Abuse of Power, developed under the auspices of the United Nations Commission on Crime Prevention and Criminal Justice. The text elaborates on the notion of who could be considered a 'victim', and affirms that a person should be considered a victim regardless of whether a perpetrator is identified or convicted.[31] The Declaration called for access to justice and fair treatment for victims, including the need for judicial and administrative processes to respond to the needs of victims by keeping them informed, allowing their views and concerns to be presented, providing them with proper assistance throughout proceedings and minimizing inconvenience to them, protecting their privacy and safety, and avoiding unnecessary delay.[32] The forms of reparation set forth are restitution, compensation and 'assistance', the last defined in paragraph 14 as 'the necessary material, medical, psychological and social assistance through governmental, voluntary, community-based and indigenous means'.[33]

More broadly, the UN Basic Principles and Guidelines on the Right to a Remedy and Reparation for Victims of Gross Violations of International Human Rights Law and Serious Violations of International Humanitarian Law (hereinafter the 'Principles and Guidelines on Reparation' or simply the 'Principles')[34] details the rights of victims of human rights violations to remedy and reparation. The text, finally adopted by the UN General Assembly in 2005 after a fifteen year contentious process, [35] is a wide ranging, in some respects victim-centred, compendium of the most important legal principles on the matter.

victims. On the potential for liability of corporations, see Menno Kamminga and Saman Zia-Zarifi, *Liability of Multinational Corporations under International Law* (Kluwer Law 2000).

[30] UN Declaration on the Rights of Indigenous Peoples, Art 8(2), states that States shall provide effective mechanisms for redress for a list of five actions, including dispossession of their lands and population transfer. Article 28 establishes a right to redress, including restitution—or, when this is not possible, compensation for traditional lands that are confiscated, taken, occupied, used, or damaged without their consent.

[31] UNGA, 'Declaration of Basic Principle of Justice for Victims of Crime and Abuse of Power' (29 November 1985) UN Doc A/Res/40/34, annex Arts 1, 2.

[32] Articles 4–6.

[33] Articles 8–17 (Restitution, compensation, and assistance).

[34] UNGA, 'Basic Principles and Guidelines on the Right to a Remedy and Reparation for Victims of Gross Violations of International Human Rights Law and Serious Violations of International Humanitarian Law' (21 March 2007) UN Doc A/Res/60/147.

[35] In 1989, the Sub-Commission on Prevention of Discrimination and Protection of Minorities, a body of the United Nations Commission on Human Rights, appointed Professor Theo van Boven to the post of Special Rapporteur tasked to undertake a study concerning the right to restitution, compensation, and rehabilitation for victims of gross violations of human rights and fundamental freedoms, with a view to exploring the possibility of developing basic principles and guidelines on the issue: Res 1989/13 (31 August 1989).

The Principles brought together for the first time the relevant standards governing the right to a remedy, including access to justice, and substantive reparation for the most serious violations. Even if states did not set out to establish new standards, and if in some respects the standards do not go as far as they might, the Principles filled a gap, created a point of reference and helped focus attention on implementation of the right to a remedy and reparation, and the need to consider the perspective and needs of victims. Since their adoption, the Principles have influenced the drafting of other instruments, including the Convention on Enforced Disappearances and the Rome Statute of the International Criminal Court.[36]

The main obligations of states are recalled: to provide 'fair, effective and prompt access to justice', and to make available 'adequate, effective, prompt and appropriate remedies, including reparation'. Such access to justice should be available 'irrespective of who may ultimately be the bearer of responsibility for the violation'.[37] Victims are defined in Principle 8 as 'persons who individually or collectively suffer harm, including physical or mental injury, emotional suffering, economic loss or substantial impairment of their fundamental rights' as a result of violations, and may include 'immediate family or dependants of the direct victim and persons who have suffered harm in intervening to assist victims in distress or to prevent victimization'.

The Principles include several provisions designed to take into account the vulnerability of victims and ensure they are treated with respect: measures should be taken 'to ensure their safety, physical and psychological well-being and privacy'; victims who have suffered violence or trauma should benefit from 'special consideration and care to avoid his or her re-traumatization'; information about available remedies should be disseminated; measures taken to ensure that victims are not inconvenienced; and proper assistance provided to victims going through proceedings.[38] Acknowledging that human rights violations can be suffered by groups of victims and not just individually, the Principles provide that states 'should endeavor' to allow groups of victims, and not just individuals, to present claims for reparation.[39] Although the last mentioned is not a strong exhortation, the provision at least highlights this important issue.

As regards the forms of reparation, the Principles adopt the international law framework: restitution, compensation, satisfaction and guarantees of non-repetition, setting forth what constitutes full and effective reparation in respect of each heading.[40] Rehabilitation is included as an additional category in its own right, rather than as a sub-category of compensation, in recognition of its significance for

[36] International Convention for the Protection of All Persons from Enforced Disappearances, in particular Arts 24.4, 24.5; Rome Statute, Art 75.

[37] Principles 2(b), 2(c), 3(c).

[38] Principles 10, 12, 24.

[39] Principle 13.

[40] Principles 18–23.

victims. Principle 21 specifies that this should include 'medical and psychological care as well as legal and social services'.[41]

The Principles reflect a certain caution on the part of states as regards the extent of their obligations under international law to provide a remedy and reparations.[42] A significant weakness in terms of its usefulness as a framework for all human rights violations is the fact that, notwithstanding a reference to the right to a remedy and reparation for all violations, the scope of the instrument is limited to the most serious ('gross') violations.[43] States were also cautious about acknowledging responsibility for acts that cannot be attributed to them, and about any responsibility for historic claims. Nevertheless, the Principles provide that states should 'endeavour' to establish national programmes for reparation in the event that those liable are unable or unwilling to provide reparation.[44]

A third important legal instrument is the updated set of principles to combat impunity.[45] These principles are bolder than the Principles and Guidelines on Reparations, affirming the right to reparation for *all* violations, asserting the victims' right to know the truth about the circumstances in which violations took place, and the duty to preserve memory including preservation of archives and other evidence concerning violations. They also emphasize the need to involve victims at every stage; where states establish truth commissions, there should be broad public consultations to receive the views of victims. Remedies and reparations should be available, and 'victims and other sectors of civil society should play a meaningful role in the design and implementation of such programs'.

Along similar lines, in the *Lubanga* case, the first decision of the ICC on reparations, the Trial Chamber set out principles on reparations, including a number of principles aimed at maximizing the meaning and the impact of the reparation measures that would be implemented, not only as regards the direct victims (who in this case are

[41] The first human rights treaty to specifically include rehabilitation as a form of reparation was the UN Convention against Torture and Other Cruel, Inhuman and Degrading Treatment or Punishment of 1984, which provides that States Party shall ensure victims of torture obtain redress 'and has an enforceable right to fair and adequate compensation, including the means for as full rehabilitation as possible', Art 14. For a full discussion of the relevant law and practice, see REDRESS, *Rehabilitation as a Form of Reparation under International Law* (Redress Trust 2009).

[42] Some states were particularly concerned with distinguishing violations that amount to international crimes with particular legal consequences, such as the duty to provide for universal jurisdiction (Principle 5) and the non-applicability of statutes of limitations (Principles 6–7).

[43] Principle 26 provides that '(I)t is understood that the present Principles and Guidelines are without prejudice to the right to a remedy and reparation for victims of all violations of international human rights law and international humanitarian law'.

[44] Principles 16, 17.

[45] Commission on Human Rights, 'Report of the Independent Expert to Update the Set of Principles to Combat Impunity' (8 February 2005) UN Doc E/CN.4/2005/102.

former child soldiers and their immediate family members), but also vis-à-vis their communities.[46]

It can be concluded from this review that the framework for remedies and reparation established in international human rights law is broadly compatible with the various types of process and outcomes that might be considered desirable by victims, identified in Section 2 above. That is, while further developments in the legal framework may be desirable,[47] the current framework seems capable of taking into account the various outcomes that may be relevant for victims.

Four broad categories of potential outcomes are useful to evaluate the extent to which these norms are implemented and the outcomes they are delivering for victims in practice:

(1) Individual remedies: measures targeted specifically at individual victims of human rights violations or groups of victims, and aimed at restoring the situation before the violation took place and/or providing relief and redress to the direct or indirect victim(s).[48]
(2) Justice and other measures of satisfaction: measures aimed at delivering justice regarding the specific violation and to the victim(s) affected, such as truth telling, official acknowledgement, investigation and punishment of those responsible.
(3) Measures of non-repetition: measures aimed at prevention of future violations and bringing about systemic change, such as legal reform, training of relevant officials, raising awareness, reforming institutions etc.
(4) Procedural justice: processes for achieving the above measures that treat the victim with dignity and respect, ensure equal and effective access to justice, allow special consideration for those who may have suffered trauma, and ensure that they have access to relevant information and assistance. These requirements are reflected in principles 10 to 12 and 24 of the Principles and Guidelines on Reparation.

[46] *Lubanga* (n 17) paras 213–216, 237–241. The Trial Chamber suggested, for instance, that the Court should reflect the importance of reintegrating child soldiers, in order to end the successive cycles of violence, and should consider measures such as educational campaigns designed to improve the position of victims and reduce stigmatization, raise awareness of the issue of child soldiers, issue certificates to victims acknowledging the harm experienced, and generally publicize the Court's judgment.

[47] The main concerns that victims consistently raise, especially in the developing world, are economic and social rights. The legal basis of the right to truth and the duty to consult victims, which the principles to combat impunity set out, could also be strengthened.

[48] These remedies fall under the categories of monetary or other economic compensation, restitution, and rehabilitation in the Principles and Guidelines on Reparation.

3.2. What outcomes do the human rights institutions and mechanisms actually deliver?

Things have considerably advanced from the time when individuals were not considered to be subjects of international law and had to rely on their states to represent their interests. Now victims and sometimes groups of victims are regarded as actors rather than passive observers, entitled to directly claim remedies on their own behalf. When remedies at the national level are unavailing, there may be recourse to avenues at the international level, including trans-national remedies in another state (universal jurisdiction). The explosion in remedies for violations of international human rights norms at national, regional and international levels, the ever growing plethora of institutions set up to monitor, protect and remedy human rights violations, have been well described and assessed. These extraordinary developments in human rights law and practice carry with them the promise to deliver much to victims, but it is necessary to examine the actual results.

In exploring what the various human rights mechanisms can offer to victims, it is useful to begin by examining what states intended when they were established. The preambles to some of the major regional and international human rights conventions do not shed much light beyond statements of general aspirations to promote, protect and implement the rights contained in the relevant convention,[49] and in some cases to provide avenues to enable individuals to seek (rather undefined measures of) redress. Instruments establishing national mechanisms in the wake of large scale abuses, on the other hand, tend to set out more specific objectives. For instance, one of the stated purposes of the Act establishing the Truth and Reconciliation Commission in South Africa was 'affording victims an opportunity to relate the violations they suffered; the taking of measures aimed at the granting of reparation to, and the rehabilitation and the restoration of the human and civil dignity of, victims of violations of human rights'.[50] The draft bill to implement reparation measures for human rights violations during the regime of Augusto Pinochet in Chile stated that: 'Reparations should be a process aiming towards the recognition of the facts in accordance with the truth, the

[49] The preamble to the International Covenant on Economic, Social and Cultural Rights recognizes that 'the ideal of free human beings enjoying freedom from fear and want can only be achieved if conditions are created whereby everyone may enjoy his economic, social and cultural rights, as well as his civil and political rights'. The European Convention on Human Rights' preamble indicates that the Convention aims at 'securing the universal and effective recognition and observance' of the rights contained within it, resolves to take 'first steps for the collective enforcement of certain of the rights stated in the Universal Declaration'. The preamble to the American Convention on Human Rights reaffirms an intention 'to consolidate in this hemisphere, within the framework of democratic institutions, a system of personal liberty and social justice based on respect for the essential rights of man'. The African Convention on Human and Peoples' Rights preamble recalls the duty of African States to promote and protect human and peoples' rights and freedoms.

[50] Promotion of National Unity and Reconciliation Act 34 of 1995, as amended by s 19 of Act 87 of 1995 <http://www.justice.gov.za/legislation/acts/1995-034.pdf> accessed 19 February 2013.

moral dignifying of the victims, and the achievement of a better quality of life for the families most directly affected.[51] Notably in recent years the language of victims' right to reparation and the need for transitional justice mechanisms has entered the lexicon of international diplomacy.[52]

Very often, then, the mechanisms set up to allow victims to seek justice or reparations are vague about what victims may receive at the end of the day. Mechanisms at national level tend to be more specific than international mechanisms as regards powers to award different remedies. The Constitution of India, for instance, having set out a list of fundamental freedoms to be protected, provides for the right to petition the Supreme Court in order to enforce these rights, and gives the Supreme Court the power to 'issue directions or orders or writs...whatever may be appropriate, for the enforcement of any of the rights conferred'.[53] International instruments, by contrast, give little direction as to how to repair human rights violations and what those responsible, whether states or individuals, should be directed to do in specific cases. Each mechanism is left considerable discretion both to orient the objectives to be achieved by the measures it decides upon, and to define the content of those measures. The result, not surprisingly, is a rather inconsistent picture.

The types of decision or order that human rights institutions are able or willing to issue, based on the powers they actually have, naturally heavily influence the outcomes for victims. Some bodies are limited to issuing non-binding findings or recommendations,[54] others have the power to deliver compensation, whether through administrative procedures (such as national reparations schemes) or judicial decisions or judgments directed at states, non-state actors or individuals, including awards of reparation delivered in a context of criminal or civil proceedings.

A summary of the main types of remedies delivered to victims under various mechanisms is given below.[55]

[51] Lira (n 15) 58.

[52] For example, UNSC Security Council Resolution 1593, referring the situation in Darfur to the International Criminal Court, which emphasizes the need to promote healing and reconciliation and encourages the creation of institutions, such as truth and/or reconciliation commissions. UNSC Res 1593 (31 March 2005) UN Doc S/Res/1593. The Agreement on Accountability and Reconciliation, signed between the Lords Resistance Army and the government of Uganda on 29 June 2007 and never implemented, provides for collective and individual reparations for the victims, as 'right of access to relevant information about their experiences and to remember and commemorate past events affecting them'. Art 9.

[53] Article 32(1), 32(2).

[54] For example, country and thematic mechanisms falling under the auspices of the United Nations Human Rights Council, such as the Special Rapporteurs on Extrajudicial, Summary, or Arbitrary Executions; the Special Rapporteurs on Torture and on the Situation of Human Rights and Fundamental Freedoms of Indigenous People; and the Working Groups on Enforced or Involuntary Disappearances and on Arbitrary Detention.

[55] This section does not aim to give a comprehensive survey of remedies and reparation; this is very ably done in other works, notably Dinah Shelton, *Remedies in International Human Rights Law* (2nd edn, OUP 2005). The aim is, rather, to give a sense of the types of outcomes that victims can expect from different human rights mechanisms.

3.2.1 *Individual remedies (compensation, restitution, and rehabilitation)*

Compensation is easily the most common form of reparation recommended or ordered, and the most commonly delivered to victims in practice. In national justice systems, compensation is a universal remedy awarded by courts in criminal and/or civil actions.[56] Many countries establish specific avenues for petitioning for remedies for human rights violations, particularly where rights are entrenched in constitutions or bills of rights.[57] However there are often significant obstacles, whether procedural or substantive, to actions for human rights violations, including immunities, limitation periods and costs. National courts also commonly have the power to order restitution (for instance, for breach of contract) or acts of rehabilitation. Some national judiciaries have been particularly proactive and inventive in ordering remedies in public interest cases brought to enforce fundamental constitutional rights; for instance, Commonwealth courts have consistently awarded damages even though their remedial powers are typically framed only very generally.[58]

Reparations programmes established in the aftermath of large scale abuses of human rights benefit large numbers of victims, typically administering compensation for individuals who have suffered from identified categories of violation. The most ambitious schemes have been those instituted by Germany for victims of Nazi crimes, and others were instituted in response to the brutality of the dictatorships during the last decades of the twentieth century (Chile, Argentina, Peru) and more recently, Colombia. Others have been either less ambitious or less successful (Haiti, El Salvador, South Africa). Several mass claims programmes have also been set up with international involvement, including several to deal with property claims as a fall-out of the conflicts in the Balkans, and the United Nations Compensation Commission to compensate victims of the 1990-1991 Gulf War.[59] These programmes

[56] Dinah Shelton found surprisingly little difference in substantive types of compensation for injury between various legal systems, despite variation in procedural rules. She found that they typically include compensation for medical expenses, loss of earnings, loss of or injury to property, pain and suffering, funeral expenses and loss of services of a deceased or injured person. Shelton, *Remedies* (n 55) 35.

[57] Michael Anderson and Matthew Happold point out that all fifty-four of the Commonwealth states have written constitutions with explicit Bills of Rights (in fifty-two cases), or specific statutes that reflect, to varying degrees, the substance of international human rights law. Michael Anderson and Mathew Happold, *Constitutional Human Rights in the Commonwealth* (British Institute of International and Comparative Law 2003) xii.

[58] Jeremy McBride, 'Commonwealth Practice on Compensation for Rights Violations' in Anderson and Happold (n 57) 176. The first decision in which this was established was the Privy Council in *Maharaj v Attorney General of Trinidad and Tobago (No 2)*. Exemplary damages have also been awarded for breaches of constitutionally-protected fundamental rights by Commonwealth courts.

[59] In the Palestinian context, a UN General Assembly Resolution created a UN Conciliation Commission. UNGA Res 194 (11 December 1948) UN Doc A/Res/194. It worked in the 1950s to assess property claims, on the basis of the resolution, which had established a right of return for the Palestinian refugees or compensation for those choosing not to return (para 11(1)). Its findings were

were empowered to provide monetary compensation or restitution to claimants able to demonstrate their entitlement.[60] While not strictly human rights bodies, they often deal with suffering and loss in situations where violations of international human rights or humanitarian law have occurred. These bodies are a useful model for human rights violation and have efficiently paid many millions of dollars in compensation.

The regional and international human rights bodies also commonly recommend or order individual reparations. A team of researchers surveyed and analysed a total of 462 remedies (recommendations, orders, agreements through friendly settlements) adopted in 92 final decisions of the Inter-American Commission and Court of Human Rights between 2001 and 2006 (the SUR study).[61] They found that by far the most common remedies ordered—61 per cent of the total remedies—were compensation, symbolic reparation and restitution of rights. Indeed, the Inter-American system has been the most advanced of all the institutions adjudicating individual cases in its jurisprudence on restitution, compensation and rehabilitation. The Court has interpreted its power under Article 63 to award compensation for material losses resulting from the violation (loss of earnings and consequential damages such as costs incurred in searching for victims who have disappeared) as well as moral harm (subjective elements such as emotional distress, pain and suffering) determined on the basis of equity, and legal costs and expenses.[62] The Court issues detailed reparations judgments and has introduced several innovations in its decisions on compensation. In one case in dealing with lost earnings and future income, it tentatively introduced the notion that a violation of human rights had disrupted the 'life plan' of the victim.[63] On moral damages, the Court has been willing to make presumptions that suffering will occur, even in the absence of evidence being presented, based on factors such as a close family relationship and the seriousness of the violation. The Court has also been willing to award compensation collectively to indigenous communities, recognizing that violations can be directed at a community as a whole and not just to individuals.[64] In addition to compensation, the Inter-American Court has also awarded measures of restitution and rehabilitation,

never implemented. Palestinians who lost property have to wait for an overall political settlement before individual rights will be addressed.

[60] For a full description of eleven mass claims processes, see Howard Holtzmann and Edda Kristjansdottir, *International Mass Claims Processes: Legal and Practical Processes* (OUP 2007).

[61] Fernando Basch and others, 'The Effectiveness of the Inter-American System of Human Rights Protection: A Quantitative Approach to its Functioning and Compliance with Its Decisions' (2010) 7 *SUR International Journal on Human Rights* 9.

[62] For a detailed analysis of the Court's practice and jurisprudence as regards reparations, see Arturo Carrillo, 'Justice in Context: The Relevance of Inter-American Human Rights Law and Practice to Repairing the Past' in de Greiff (n 15); Shelton, *Remedies* (n 55).

[63] The Court raised this notion in *Loayza Tamayo v Peru*. The ICC, in its first decision on reparations, noted that this concept may be relevant to reparations at the ICC. *Lubanga* (n 17) fn 418.

[64] *Mayagna Community (SUMO) Awas Tingni v Nicaragua*, where Nicaragua had allowed contractors to exploit natural resources without taking into account the indigenous community's legitimate

emphasizing in its decisions the importance of medical and psychological care for victims to assist them in overcoming their trauma.[65] The ICC, in its first decision on reparations, cited extensively the case law of the Inter-American Court on compensation and rehabilitation.

The other regional human rights bodies have been disappointing when it comes to compensation, and there is little to say about their contribution. Dinah Shelton, in her seminal work on remedies for human rights violations, observes that none of the human rights bodies have taken the opportunity to develop coherent and consistent theory and practice regarding damages.[66] The European Court of Human Rights has shown little interest in responding to the specific needs of victims. Whether or not detailed claims are argued on the basis of specific losses or harm (frequently they are), the Court disposes of 'just satisfaction' in a couple of lines, simply ordering a lump sum by way of pecuniary and/or non-pecuniary damages, typically declaring that it has decided 'on an equitable basis', and rarely giving reasons for the amounts determined.[67] Nevertheless, the Court does regularly order damages to be paid and there is a relatively high degree of compliance with its reparations decisions. The African Commission on Human and Peoples' Rights has not developed a consistent approach to remedies either. Open Society Justice Initiative (OSI) compiled a study of the European, Inter-American and African human rights courts and the United Nations Human Rights Committee, published in 2010.[68] According to the OSI study, the African Commission has recommended compensation in around 15 per cent of its cases, rarely specifying the amount. It remains to be seen whether the African Court will take a different approach.

The UN treaty bodies tend not to be very specific in the remedies they recommend, but where they find that a violation has taken place, consistently state that the state party must provide an effective remedy to the victim, and sometimes call

claims to the land. The Court held that the state should pay an amount in works or services for the benefit of the community as a whole.

[65] For example *Barrios Altos v Peru*, in which the State agreed to provide the victims of an attack by a military intelligence squad with free access to a range of social and health services for life.

[66] Shelton, *Remedies* (n 55) 467.

[67] To take one of many examples by way of illustration, in the case of *Kaya v Turkey*, where a violation of Article 3 was found, the applicant had claimed €30,000 in non-pecuniary damages for ill-treatment in police custody. In applying Art 41 of the Convention, the Court simply stated that 'the applicant must have suffered pain and distress which cannot be compensated for solely by the Court's finding of a violation. Having regard to the nature of the violation found and ruling on an equitable basis, it awards the applicant €9,750 in respect of non-pecuniary damage', para 51. In response to detailed claims for pecuniary damages, the Court typically says it 'does not discern any causal link between the violations found and the pecuniary damage alleged' or 'cannot speculate' about the claims made. Eg *Khrabrova v Russia*. Where no damages are claimed, the Court will not order them.

[68] Open Society Justice Initiative, *From Judgment to Justice: Implementing International and Regional Human Rights Decisions* (Open Society Foundations 2010) <http://www.opensocietyfoundations.org/sites/default/files/from-judgment-to-justice-20101122.pdf> accessed 19 February 2013.

for compensation.[69] As part of the reporting mechanism, several of the UN treaty bodies, including the UN Committee against Torture and the Committee on the Elimination of all Forms of Discrimination Against Women, regularly encourage states to set up specialized rehabilitation services and other programmes of support and assistance for victims.

Of the international criminal tribunals, only the International Criminal Court and the Extraordinary Criminal Chamber for Cambodia (ECCC) may award reparations to victims if they convict an accused of crimes.[70] In its first decision on reparations, in the *Lubanga* case, the ICC cited international human rights law in defining principles relating to restitution, compensation and rehabilitation. The victims in the case are largely former child soldiers, and the Trial Chamber included, in its definition of what might be covered by rehabilitative measures, steps to facilitate their reintegration into society, address the shame that child victims might feel, avoid stigmatization, and take symbolic measures that might contribute to the process of rehabilitation such as commemorations and tributes.[71]

Few judgments to date include remedies for groups as such, although the Inter-American Court of Human Rights makes such awards consistently in respect of indigenous land claims, following its seminal decision in respect of an indigenous community in Nicaragua.[72] The ICC is empowered to award reparation on a collective basis, but it is not yet clear whether that will involve awards to collective victims as such.[73]

In general, in the absence of any international standards on levels of damages awards, unless there are applicable scales determining damages in a particular case (such as where relevant national law might apply), human rights litigation will almost always be a lottery from the point of view of level of awards.[74] Even the Inter-American Court of Human Rights, in so many ways the pioneer on reparations, lacks consistency in its own awards. The levels of awards made by courts in many human rights cases are so high that it would simply not be feasible for states to pay them to every victim. These vagaries of litigation are understandably bewildering for victims. It is clearly possible to develop more objective ways of determining damages awards and making them predicable and objective, as is shown in

[69] Shelton, *Remedies* (n 55) 184.

[70] Rome Statute, Art 75. A decision on reparations principles has been issued in the Court's first case, the *Lubanga* case, but it is currently on appeal and has not been implemented yet. The ECCC only has the power to order collective and moral reparations to civil parties. ECCC, 'Internal Rules and Regulations' <http://www.eccc.gov.kh/sites/default/files/legal-documents/ECCC%20Internal%20Rules%20(Rev.8)%20English.pdf> accessed 10 February 2013.

[71] *Lubanga* (n 17) 232–36.

[72] *Awas Tingni* (n 64).

[73] ICC, 'Rules of Procedure and Evidence' (9 September 2002) UN Doc PCNICC/2000/1/Add.1, Rule 97(1).

[74] Compare the multimillion dollar awards in the US for international human rights cases to the nominal sums that the European Court of Human Rights awards.

constitutional litigation or criminal and civil proceedings at national level, including for emotional suffering and other difficult to measure heads of damage.

3.2.2 *Justice and other measures of satisfaction*

In national attempts to deal with the past in the wake of large scale violations, the question of impunity has been highly contentious. In Latin America following the dictatorships of the 1970s and 1980s, victims insistently called for those responsible to be brought to justice, for amnesties to be set aside and for formal acknowledgement of state responsibility for the violations. The Inter-American Court of Human Rights' landmark and highly influential decision in 1988 in the case of *Velasquez-Rodriguez* established the duty to prevent, investigate and punish human rights violations in addition to compensating the victims.[75] While regional and international human rights bodies recommend or order such measures on a regular basis, usually upon request of the victims, it has often proved difficult for states emerging from repression or conflict to bring to justice those responsible for past crimes.[76] The SUR study on the Inter-American system found that of the total remedies ordered during the period of the study, only 15 per cent related to investigation and punishment and those orders had by far the lowest level of compliance (only 10 per cent total compliance, and 13 per cent partial compliance).[77] The African Commission on Human and Peoples' Rights almost never, in its recommendations, includes the investigation and punishment of those responsible.[78]

The European Court of Human Rights regularly affirms the duty to investigate and punish, but generally holds it will not indicate which measures are required to execute a judgment. Even in right to life cases, the Court generally declines to indicate that a government should hold a new investigation, based on the general principle that the state is free to choose the means by which it will discharge its obligation to abide by the judgment of the Court. Only more recently, since it adopted a new procedure for dealing with repetitive cases, and taking great pains to stress the exceptional circumstances that led it to do so, has the Court in rare cases indicated that the state should open a new investigation.[79] The United Nations treaty bodies such as the Human Rights Committee often highlight the need for such measures, particularly investigations to establish the facts and bring to justice those responsible,[80] however, with the important limitation that they do not have the power to issue binding orders.

[75] *Velasquez-Rodriguez v Honduras.*

[76] This debate was particularly acute in South Africa and Chile.

[77] Basch and others (n 61) 18.

[78] Open Society Justice Initiative, *From Judgment to Justice* (n 68) 103.

[79] *Abuyeva and Others v Russia*, a case involving an attack on a village in the context of Russian military operations in Chechnya. To justify making an exception, the Court referred to the fact that the government had disregarded the findings of a previous judgment, as well as availability of large amounts of data as a result of the investigation of the case by the Court.

[80] Shelton, *Remedies* (n 55) 184.

The Inter-American Court has also recognized a wide range of other measures aimed at providing satisfaction to victims, including public disclosure of the truth, official statements acknowledging responsibility of the state, identification of the remains of the disappeared and symbolic measures such as monuments. Quite a number of truth commissions (or commissions of inquiry) have been established following periods of transition from conflict or political oppression. They are sometimes viewed as an alternative to or even as a means of avoiding bringing to justice those responsible for violations.[81] In some instances they have triggered prosecutions, acknowledgements and apologies, as well as establishing a record of events.[82] In Sierra Leone, prosecutions took place in parallel with the truth commission. They are considered further below.

3.2.3 *Measures of non-repetition*

Fewer institutions have powers to recommend or order such remedies, and overall they are the least often enforced of all the types of remedies in practice. At national level, specific bodies such as national human rights commissions may have powers to make recommendations for changes to legislation and other measures targeted at avoiding repetition of human rights violations. Using public law remedies, the courts in some countries have been able to order the relevant authorities to amend practices. The Indian Supreme Court has been particularly assertive. For instance, when dealing with a constitutional rights case involving a death in custody, it attempted to tackle the problem in a wider way by setting out eleven 'requirements' and ordering that they be issued to every police station and followed in all cases of arrest and detention.[83]

Among the regional and international human rights bodies, the UN Human Rights Committee regularly recommends law reform, and frequently calls upon states to take steps to ensure similar violations do not occur in the future.[84] The European Court of Human Rights did not have a strong record on ordering

[81] For a full description and analysis of truth commissions established up to 2002, see Priscilla B Hayner, *Unspeakable Truths: Facing the Challenge of Truth Commissions* (Routledge 2002).

[82] For instance, in Argentina, when the National Commission on the Disappeared concluded its work it, handed its files to prosecutors, enabling them to mount prosecutions against some of the most senior members of the prior regime. In Uganda and Haiti, however, similar handovers did not lead to significant efforts at prosecution. See Hayner (n 81) ch 7.

[83] *DK Basu v State of West Bengal*. While the Court did not have the power to order the government to enact legislation, this decision did lead to the Law Commission of India recommending the incorporation of the eleven requirements into law. Amnesty International reported that steps were taken to make the requirements known to local officials, even though significant problems with implementation remained. Amnesty International, *Combating Torture—A Manual for Action* (Amnesty International Publications 2003). See also the cases of *Ramamurthy v State of Karnataka* and *Sunil Batra v Delhi Administration*, in which the Supreme Court attempted to tackle prison reform. See generally Fiona McKay, 'Freedom from Torture' in Anderson and Happold (n 57).

[84] Shelton, *Remedies* (n 55) 184–85.

measures of non-repetition until recently. As noted, the Court from its early cases chose to interpret its powers to order reparation narrowly, declining to deal with systemic underlying causes of violations. More recently, however, faced with the reality of thousands of identical petitions deriving from the same underlying problem ('repetitive cases') that have clogged the system, the Court introduced a new Pilot Judgment Procedure in 2004. This procedure enables the Court to select one or more cases for priority treatment, and in doing so, 'will seek to achieve a solution that extends beyond the particular case or cases so as to cover all similar cases raising the same issue', including identifying the 'dysfunction' that is the root of the violation, giving clear indications to the Government as to how it can deal with it, and 'bring about the creation of a domestic remedy capable of dealing with similar cases ... or ... the settlement of all such cases pending before the Court'. According to the OSI study, the African Commission on Human and Peoples' Rights has recommended some type of legal reform in around 20 per cent of its cases.

Notwithstanding, while states usually implement just satisfaction awards (damages), they are often less willing to implement measures to prevent repetition of the violation, such as amending legislation or practices. States pay up, but don't change the underlying practice; it has to be recognized that doing so may require legislation or even constitutional amendment that can be a prolonged process and politically difficult to achieve. According to the SUR study, of the total remedies ordered by the Inter-American human rights system during the study period, 22 per cent could be described as preventive measures (training public officials, raising social awareness, introducing legal reforms, creating or reforming institutions).[85] Interestingly, levels of compliance with these types of remedies were relatively high in the Inter-American system: remedies requiring the training of public officials had a 42 per cent compliance rate. On the other hand, remedies agreed upon in the framework of processes of friendly settlements almost never included measures of legal reform.[86] The Inter-American Court has also made some important pronouncements including in the Barrios Altos case, that applying amnesty laws to gross human rights violations contravened international human rights norms.

3.2.4 *Procedural justice*

Given the importance to victims of procedural justice, including being treated with dignity and respect, being kept informed, receiving support and protection and having their voices heard, it is important to consider the record of human rights institutions in this respect. The more victims are informed and participate in the process, the more they are likely to find the outcome satisfying, even if it is unfavourable.

[85] Shelton, *Remedies* (n 55) 14. The remaining two per cent related to the protection of victims and witnesses or 'others'.

[86] Shelton, *Remedies* (n 55) 17.

In Europe, significant political will has been generated to improve the treatment of victims in criminal justice systems. Extensive standard-setting exercises have been carried out, even if implementation in European states remains patchy.[87]

International human rights mechanisms have improved significantly over time in their general friendliness and openness to victims. Most of the regional and international human rights mechanisms have prepared user-friendly information to assist applicants.[88] Some truth commissions and international mass claims processes instituted public information campaigns to make potential claimants aware of their programmes and how to access them. Legal aid is available for indigent applicants in the Inter-American and European Courts of Human Rights and for victims wishing to participate in international criminal proceedings, where they are permitted to do so.[89]

The UN human rights bodies present particular challenges for victims, because of the confusing proliferation and fragmentation of bodies. Non-governmental organizations have published and distributed various manuals on how to navigate the international human rights mechanisms. Nonetheless, serious criticisms are warranted of system that establishes so many different specialized treaty bodies, each dealing with a specific right or affected group and following differing procedures set out under the respective human rights convention, forcing applicants to choose between them. It is also notable that most UN treaty bodies afford no hearing to victims presenting cases but instead decide the matter solely on the written record. Some assert that this situation undermines the overall understanding of human rights as well as the individual's ability to claim them.[90] States also may undermine the system by focusing the different mechanisms on reporting and verifying individual facts, making them lose sight of the overall picture and allowing violations to take place making the apparent increase in accountability deceptive. Others argue that the proliferation of avenues is healthy and necessary.[91]

87 See European Commission, 'Proposal for a Directive' (n 23).

88 For example, the Inter-American Commission on Human Rights has prepared instructions for filling in the form for filing an individual petition. Inter-American Commission on Human Rights, 'Form for Filing Petitions Alleging Human Rights Violations' <https://www.cidh.oas.org/cidh_apps/instructions.asp?gc_language=E> accessed 19 February 2013. Similar guidance is available in relation to the different UN mechanisms.

89 Rules of the Inter-American Commission on Human Rights on the Legal Assistance Fund of the Inter-American Human Rights System (entered into force 1 March 2011) rules 100–105; Rules of Court of the European Court of Human Rights (1 May 2012) rule 90.5; ICC, 'Rules of Procedure and Evidence' (n 73).

90 Alexandra R Harrington, *Delayed Devotion: The Rise of Individual Complaint Mechanisms within International Human Rights Treaties* (29 July 2011) Albany Law School Research Paper No 17 of 2011–2012, 30.

91 For a contrary view, see Mireille GE Bijnsdorp, 'The Strength of the Optional Protocol to the United Nations Women's Convention' (2000) 18 *NQHR* 329, 346; Daniel Albahary, 'International Human Rights and Global Governance: The End of National Sovereignty and the Emergence of a Suzerain World Polity?' (2010) 18 *Mich St J Int'l L* 511, 514–15 (both cited in Harrington (n 90)).

The reality is that it remains very difficult for many victims to access legal mechanisms for enforcing human rights without assistance. Even in developed countries, ignorance of legal rights, lack of available funding or legal assistance and lack of confidence can make access to remedies rather random, and particularly challenging for groups such as women, the disabled, migrants, and immigrants. For this reason, programmes have been established by non-governmental organizations to assist applicants to access the various human rights mechanisms, both the international and the national ones. The SUR study of remedies awarded by the Inter-American system showed that 80 per cent of petitions were brought by national and/or international non-governmental organizations and ombudsman offices, whereas only 20 per cent were brought by individual petitioners.[92] Unfortunately, such programmes are not available everywhere.

Assistance is required not only to enable victims with the technical legal aspects of accessing remedies. General support and accompaniment through the process can make the difference between a victim feeling empowered and transformed by the process, or feeling disappointed and frustrated.[93] Innovative projects have been initiated in the Inter-American human rights system and some truth commissions to engage psychologists alongside lawyers to support victims through the legal process. A team of health professionals engaged in such a project in the Inter-American system concluded that there is a need to help lawyers to understand the importance of providing psychological support to victims, to accompany the victim regarding their emotions and experiences, establish comforting human contact, assistance in mourning, control fears, build bridges with lawyers and generally provide a framework of safety and trust.[94]

Victims' attitudes towards human rights processes are greatly influenced by their relations with the persons with whom they have the most contact in that context, including lawyers, officials and NGOs. These relationships are crucial and persons dealing with victims should have appropriate training. Lawyers have to be able to find a way to engage with victims in order to be able to explain the relevant proceedings, take their instructions and represent their interests properly. Lawyers may not come across such challenges in their normal caseload. A set of best practice guidelines for lawyers dealing with victims of domestic violence and sexual assault issued by the American Bar Association warns: 'Each victim experiences and processes the trauma of abuse differently; some victims display outward signs of distress while others display no signs of trauma at all. Some victims may present as excessively

[92] Basch and others (n 61) 26.

[93] Adopting an interdisciplinary approach towards legal strategy can maximize the chances of the remedy being satisfactory for the victim and capturing the 'extraordinary symbolic potential of the reparatory act'. Mental IIHR, 'Reparations: A Judicial and Symbolic Act' (n 13) 308.

[94] Pilar Raffo, 'Psychological Support and Therapy' in IIHR, *Comprehensive Attention to Victims of Torture* (n 6) 50.

hostile or difficult or, in contrast, be surprisingly flat in their affect. Aggressive or emotional over-reactions and emotional numbness (sometimes with accompanying high-risk behaviours) are normal responses to both isolated and ongoing assaults and should not be taken as indicators of instability or lack of credibility of the victim.'[95] Lawyers representing victims of human rights violations need to know how to deal with such behaviours and to call on professional counselling and support when necessary, and seek at the very least, assistance from individuals who are trained to respond appropriately.

NGOs are equally important, often being the ones with the most constant contact with victims. International standards require state action to enable victims to receive support and assistance, but in practice, it is often left to the non-governmental organizations to provide support to victims through whatever process they follow. In North America and Europe, victim support programmes can be highly professionalized. Elsewhere, NGOs may not always be best equipped to attend to the needs of victims effectively. Given the central importance of such groups around the world in ensuring remedies for victims, more needs to be done to support human rights organizations on the front line to ensure they are equipped with the tools to manage their interactions with victims appropriately. While some organizations develop guidelines for their interactions with victims,[96] this is by no means common, and this is an area where more best practice guidelines and training could be beneficial.

3.3 Vehicles for delivering reparation to victims

Results do not necessarily come from one measure in isolation. It is common for simultaneous action to be taken by different actors on many fronts when human rights violations occur, including seeking local remedies, reporting to UN treaty mechanisms and bringing individual complaints to international bodies. Timing can be important: while violations are still going on, it may be difficult to obtain anything other than individual remedies (while publicizing the fact that violations are going on), whereas after a transition, other options for broader benefits may emerge, such as reparations programmes and truth commissions.

The relative merits of individualized over other processes for responding to human rights violations are much debated. There are many reasons why it is not

[95] American Bar Association Commission on Domestic Violence, *Best Practices for Lawyers Assisting Pro Se Victims of Domestic Violence, Sexual Assault, and Stalking with Civil Protection Cases* (American Bar Association 2006) 21.

[96] Some NGOs have guidelines on how to conduct interviews with victims. See eg Human Rights Watch, 'Our Research Methodology' <http://www.hrw.org/node/75141> accessed 19 February 2013. See, in particular, the section on 'How we conduct interviews with victims/witnesses'.

in victims' interests to rely on individual remedies through judicialized proceedings unless they have to. Legal obstacles such as immunities, general lack of political will and delay, or simple lack of resources or capacity to implement, all may impede the process, with the result that the promised results do not materialize, or arrive extremely late. The UN treaty bodies are overwhelmed by the volume of work accompanying the growth of the treaty body system and have significant backlogs.[97] Enforcement and length of proceedings are huge problems. State compliance with decisions is disappointing. The SUR study on the Inter-American human rights system found non-compliance with respect to 50 per cent of the remedies.[98] The highest level of compliance was with remedies demanding some type of individual reparation (47 per cent total compliance, 13 per cent partial compliance), and remedies agreed upon through a process of friendly settlement were the most likely of all to secure compliance (54 per cent total compliance). The study showed that the *average* duration of proceedings, from receipt of the petition to resolution, was seven years and four months.[99] The OSI report also found serious problems of compliance with the UN Human Rights Committee's decisions.[100] Both the European Court of Human Rights and the African Commission on Human and Peoples' Rights have in recent years improved their follow up and enforcement of judgments, which can be expected to improve compliance.[101]

The adversarial nature of many legal proceedings can be painful for victims. Another frustration for victims can be the selectiveness of many legal processes. In human rights courts, victims may have to argue for widening the scope of those who benefit from reparations awards. In international criminal courts, there has been

[97] Of the nine treaty bodies with a reporting procedure, statistics relating to eight of them, as of May 2011, showed that 263 reports were pending consideration, while 459 communications submitted under the individual complaints procedures were pending consideration. UNGA, 'Measures to Improve Further the Effectiveness, Harmonization and Reform of the Treaty Body System' (7 September 2011) UN Doc A/66/344, para 11. Of the individual complaints, 333 were pending before the Human Rights Committee, which is only able to dispose of an average of ninety cases per year.

[98] Basch and others (n 61) 18.

[99] In 88 per cent of cases, the proceedings took four years or more. Basch and others (n 61) 26.

[100] Based on the 2009 annual report of the Office of the High Commission for Human Rights Petitions Section, of the 546 cases in which the Human Rights Committee found violations, only sixty-seven cases had received a 'satisfactory' response, while the Committee Against Torture fared better, with an almost 50 per cent compliance rate with its decisions. Open Society Justice Initiative, *From Judgment to Justice* (n 68) 27.

[101] In the case of the ECHR, Protocol 14 expands the powers of the Committee of Ministers to seek interpretive rulings from the Court, if the meaning of a judgment is unclear, and to bring proceedings in cases of non-compliance. Changes to the Rules of Procedure in 2006 also require states to submit implementation plans and the Committee of Ministers to review the implementation of judgments at regular intervals. For the African Commission, rule changes in 2010 provide a comprehensive follow-up process for its recommendations, as well as a process for referring cases to the new Court in cases of non-implementation.

considerable frustration about the determination of which victims are included or excluded as participants in proceedings. In the ECCC's first case, a number of victims were first accepted civil parties at the pre-trial stage, then rejected at the trial stage. At the International Criminal Court, the Prosecutor's policy to limit charges brought to a few representational incidents means it is likely that only victims of selected incidents are entitled to participate in the proceedings or receive reparation.[102]

Despite this catalogue of drawbacks, individual complaints mechanisms of various kinds have proved to be very effective. Remedies such as habeas corpus and writ of *amparo*, and interim measures have provided important relief. Cases have prevented application of the death penalty or corporal punishment. Individual litigants, as some of the examples in this chapter show, can create important legal precedents, raise awareness and galvanize action to address violations.[103] It should not be forgotten that taking proactive steps in their own names to enforce rights can be important to victims' sense of regaining control, and the opportunity to drive a process can be important to some.

In cases of large scale abuses, alternatives such as administrative compensation schemes, friendly settlement procedures and other non-contentious mechanisms can be effective in providing remedies to many more victims, and are also less stressful for victims. Mass claims programmes have introduced methodologies and techniques designed to facilitate the processing of large numbers of claims expeditiously, while responding to the difficulties that victims often face in producing proof and allowing for alternative means of verification.[104] For instance, they have introduced lower evidentiary standards, reliance on presumptions, statistical sampling and standardized verification and valuation. In some instances techniques put

[102] In the case of *Prosecutor v Bemba Gombo*, for instance, the charges include pillage. In communities that claimed to have suffered as a result of attacks from the armed group in question, those who had goods or personal belongings pillaged were found to be within the scope of the case, for the purpose of being accepted to participate in the proceedings, while their neighbours whose homes were burned to the ground, but without first having their belongings pillaged, were excluded. In the *Lubanga* case, when it came to establishing principles for reparations, the question arose whether reparation would be limited to those victims who had participated in the proceedings or applied for reparations. The Trial Chamber decided not to limit reparations to those victims who only represented a relatively small proportion of victims, but to open it up to other victims. However, reparations would still be limited to victims linked to the case. *Lubanga* (n 17) para 187.

[103] For instance, the series of cases brought to the European Court of Human Rights against Turkey is thought to have helped bring about changes in state policy towards the Kurds. The impact of individual cases will depend on the wider context and what the obstacles are in each particular circumstance—whether it is lack of political will, economic resources, or capacity.

[104] See Holtzmann and Kristjansdottir (n 60) ss 5.02 and 5.06, in particular. The UN Compensation Commission on Iraq, which had to process 2.6 million claims in eight years, was a pioneer in developing these new methodologies and techniques.

in place allow individual claimants to avoid having to present evidence.[105] However establishing such mechanisms requires political will and action, often at the international as well as the national level.

Large scale violations also highlight possible tension between individual and group rights, and raises the question of whether it would be more appropriate to apply a different remedial framework and allow claims to be made by groups in certain cases. In cases of violations against persons who identify themselves as members of a minority (whether cultural, ethnic, national or other) or indigenous group, for instance, where the violation is clearly targeted against a group as such and symptomatic of wider abuses, it may not make sense to address the problem through cases brought by individuals. Some courts, such as the Indian courts responding to fundamental constitutional rights petitions, have issued orders that aim to have a wider reach even when the original petitioner is an individual. The European Court of Human Rights has moved in a similar direction with its pilot judgment process. In general, however, courts or other remedial processes only rarely accept group claims,[106] often in favour of collectives such as institutions. The International Criminal Court now can recognize as victims institutions such as schools, hospitals or religious or cultural organizations that have suffered harm as a result of crimes.

Transitional justice mechanisms are often criticized for not satisfying everybody. Criminal courts are not a forum for victims to tell their stories, but truth commissions have the opposite problem. While they allow victims to tell their stories and sometimes to receive formal acknowledgement, they may provide no, or at best only minimal, measures to investigate and punish. Moreover, their record at delivering reparation is poor. While advocates for appropriate transitional justice mechanisms call for the full range of responses, there is rarely the political will or resources to make it happen.

It is not possible to conclude, based on the above picture, that particular types of responses to human rights violations are always more effective or successful than others from the victims' point of view. A lot depends on what sort of process is put in place around the particular response, and how the victim is treated in that process.

[105] For instance, the Commission for Real Property Claims of Displaced Persons and Refugees in Bosnia and Herzegovina was able to gather evidence itself from official records, so that claimants did not.

[106] See the discussion on the Inter-American Court of Human Rights' more recent and limited willingness to recognize group rights of indigenous groups in this chapter. The UN Compensation Commission on Iraq allows claims by governments and international organizations, including for damage to the environment ('category F' claims) and by corporations.

4. Are Victims Getting the Right Outcomes: What is a Victim-Centred Approach?

There are increasing calls to put victims at the centre of all steps taken in the aftermath of human rights violations, whether individual complaints, truth commissions, reparations programmes, criminal proceedings, or other. There is a sense that if this is not done, any measure taken will have failed in a fundamental aspect. On the individual level, victims will be left unsatisfied by what is done to repair violations, even if decisions are taken with the best of intentions. At the societal level, reparation measures will be less likely to achieve important goals such as reconciliation. A comprehensive and generally accepted view on what a victim centred approach actually means, however, and how things should be done differently appears to be lacking. Policy makers need clear instructions.

There would appear to be four different junctures at which a victim centred approach could be considered:

(a) Choice of measures to be taken: in the wake of large scale violations of human rights, in practice those most affected are rarely consulted meaningfully on decisions on which measures should be taken. Standard transitional justice models are helpful as guidelines, but the UN Commission on Human Rights has recalled the necessity for 'a comprehensive process of national consultation, particularly with those affected by human rights violations, in contributing to a holistic transitional justice strategy that takes into account the particular circumstances of every situation and in conformity with international human rights standards'.[107] Indeed, drawing particularly on human rights approaches to development, the Office of the High Commissioner for Human Rights (OHCHR) asserts that national consultations are required under international human rights law.[108] The same principle of consultation holds good for those advising individual victims on seeking remedies, when determining which avenue of redress would be most appropriate for the particular victim. The rationale is that if measures chosen do not accord with what the victims consider important, they will be less effective.

[107] Commission on Human Rights, 'Human Rights and Transitional Justice' (20 April 2005) UN Doc E/CN.4/Res/2005/70.

[108] OHCHR, *Rule-of-Law Tools for Post-Conflict States: National Consultations on Transitional Justice* (UN 2009).

(b) Design of measures: for measures to achieve their objective, victims must have input into the design of specific measures. Consultations were held in Peru and Chile, for example, on the form of reparations that should be implemented in the respective national programmes. The Inter-American Court of Human Rights has experimented with involving psychologists and other experts, and seeking victims' views in designing reparations awards, on the basis this is more likely to bring about results which will provide satisfaction to the victims. One commentator has called for a more participatory model involving negotiation with victims and mediation between stakeholders.[109]

(c) Implementation: during the process, whether judicial proceedings, national programme, or other process, a victim-centred approach would involve provision of regular information to victims, and their continuing participation.

(d) Evaluation: quantitative and qualitative surveys and other evaluations conducted after measures have been taken to redress human rights violations are important to enable adjustments to be made or simply to serve as lessons for the future.[110] Studies of truth commissions and victim participation in criminal proceedings in Timor-Leste, South Africa, Nepal, and Cambodia revealed where processes failed to match victims' expectations.[111]

In determining how victims should be given a central role at each of these junctures, nothing should be presumed, as victims' views will vary from case to case and will need to be identified. There will often be many people claiming to speak on behalf of victims. The Office of the High Commissioner for Human Rights has published a handbook on national consultation that provides guidance on different methods of holding consultations with examples of good practices.[112] Expertise in quantitative and qualitative population based surveys exists and has been applied in a number of places including Kosovo, the DRC and Northern Uganda.[113] The ICC

[109] Thomas Antkowiak, 'Remedial Approaches to Human Rights Violations: The Inter-American Court of Human Rights and Beyond' (2008) 46 *Colum J Transnat'l L* 45.

[110] Surveys of victim attitudes in the International Criminal Tribunal for the Former Yugoslavia, ECCC, and ICC could be used to improve the way those courts deal with subsequent cases.

[111] A survey to evaluate victims' satisfaction with the *Duch* trial in the Extraordinary Chambers of the Courts of Cambodia (known as the ECCC or the Khmer Rouge tribunal) found that, generally, the civil parties in the case viewed the experience of participating positively, although they did not describe a healing effect and felt some disappointment at the outcome of the trial. See Phuong Pham and others, 'Victim Participation and the Trial of Duch at the Extraordinary Chambers in the Courts of Cambodia' (2011) 3 *Journal of Human Rights Practice* 264. Surveys of victims following transitional justice processes in Timor-Leste and South Africa revealed that these processes were also disappointing for victims. For instance, in Timor-Leste the victims said that economic support, dealing with the missing and the dead, and symbolic measures, were more important to them than prosecutions. In South Africa, by contrast, there was dissatisfaction with the lack of accountability.

[112] OHCHR, *Rule-of-Law Tools* (n 108).

[113] The Human Rights Center of the University of California, Berkeley, together with others, conducted population-based surveys addressing questions on attitudes toward peace and justice, including preferences as regards reparations.

Trial Chamber in the *Lubanga* case set out a five-step process including appointment of experts, consultation with local communities, public debates to explain the reparations principles and address victims' expectations, and collection of proposals, before any decisions on reparation could be made.[114]

Consultations will often reveal divergent views among victims. This is to be expected as a normal part of the process, and, whether it arises in the course of collective applications to judicial bodies, national consultations in the wake of mass violations or otherwise, will need to be discussed and addressed.

A victim-centred approach would also be one that gives priority to the needs and concerns of victims over other concerns, wherever possible. It is clear that the law cannot be guided solely by the expressed wishes of the victims. There may be other policy imperatives or wider interests that trump them. For instance, individual victims' desires for revenge may conflict with wider society's views of what is desirable. Debates around what constitutes appropriate punishment (death penalty, corporal punishment) is one area where such conflicts might arise. Another is competition for scarce resources: in the aftermath of conflict or large scale violations of human rights, post-war Germany and the oil reserves of Iraq following its invasion of Kuwait proved capable of meeting massive compensation awards without being considered to unduly hamper their countries' development. Governments in South Africa and Chile, in contrast, felt constrained to limit compensation schemes to ensure their countries' development. Studies that have been done of victims' views show that social grievances, economic support, basic needs and security are consistently a high priority for victims, whereas transitional justice arrangements commonly do not address these.[115] For instance, a survey of a representative sample of 160 families of people disappeared in Nepal found that those victims emphasized the need for truth about the disappeared and economic support to meet basic needs, while criminal justice was not a priority.[116] A practical problem may be that what victims want may simply be impossible. Some rights, social and economic rights, for instance are inherently more difficult to implement than others and can present huge challenges.

One lesson that should have been learnt is the vital importance of careful and responsible management of communications with victims, taking into account their vulnerability and intense emotional engagement. This is as important when dealing with an individual in a specific case as when dealing with large numbers of victims about a national reparations programme or justice exercise. There are too many examples where victims have felt hugely let down, at least partially due

[114] *Lubanga* (n 17) para 282.

[115] Studies in the DRC, Timor-Leste, and Nepal, for example.

[116] Simon Robins, 'Towards Victim-Centered Transitional Justice: Understanding the Needs of Families of the Disappeared in Post-Conflict Nepal' (2011) 5 *International Journal of Transitional Justice* 75.

to poor communication or inadequate decision making. In Cambodia's ECCC, for instance, victims in the *Duch* case were led to believe that they might receive reparations, which ultimately could not be delivered.[117] There is no avoiding the need to deliver news that victims do not wish to hear on occasions. In societies where there are not sufficient resources for reparations, difficult decisions have to be taken about whether to use precious resources for general development or for reparations. Courts will take decisions that victims do not like, but this is a good example of why it is essential to have participation and consultation from the earliest stages, including awareness raising about the full range of options, the relevant constraints and the goals to be pursued.

A related crucial matter in many impoverished societies is to make sure that any measures taken to recognize and redress victims of past violations are actually understood and perceived by victims as being intended as reparation. How a particular measure is presented has a lot to do with providing meaning, in reparatory terms.[118] The ICC's Trust Fund for Victims, for instance, has to take care in how it explains its assistance projects for victims of ICC crimes, or it risks being viewed as just another humanitarian agency operating in Africa. Given that so many victims' studies show that economic and social issues figure prominently in the demands and expectations of victims following large scale human rights abuses, and those violations are often linked to access to resources issues, it becomes increasingly difficult to ignore economic and social justice questions when thinking about reparations.

Debate has emerged fairly recently on whether or not policy makers should be prepared to consider local forms of justice if they are the most meaningful for the victims. While this is a controversial topic, recent attention has been paid to the value of local practices of memorialization and commemoration and customary or traditional forms of justice and reconciliation. Some argue that these can be more meaningful for victims or are at least a pragmatic solution.[119]

Societies may also have to engage with complex societal issues. What if the interests of individual victims differ from those of their broader community? What if some victims want to seek remedies that are counter to the broader political goals of their (national, political, ethnic) group? What if there is a clash between some

[117] Pham and others (n 111).

[118] The work of Pablo de Greiff and others on reparation and development provides some very helpful thinking. For example Pablo de Greiff and Roger Duthie (eds), *Transitional Justice and Development: Making Connections* (International Center for Transitional Justice 2009).

[119] See eg Lia Kent, 'Local Memory Practices in East Timor: Disrupting Transitional Justice Narratives' (2011) 5 *International Journal of Transitional Justice* 434. The *gacaca* courts in Rwanda caused debates between the purists, such as some human rights organizations that criticize them for not conforming to international fair trial standards, and others who argue that these courts are the best that can be done in the circumstances or that they have a positive value. The ICC's intervention in Uganda in 2004 triggered lively debates on the relevance or lack thereof of local cleaning and accountability rituals, such as *mato oput*, as alternative methods of justice.

victims who do not want to return to the situation before the violation took place but want reparation to bring about transformation to a better future? These questions have been raised particularly in the context of women.[120] In its first decision on reparation, the ICC judges endorsed the need to take such issues into consideration, stating that 'reparations need to address any underlying injustice and in their implementation the Court should avoid replicating discriminatory practices or structures that predated the commission of the crimes'.[121] This decision reflects the increasing attention being given to such issues and provides a welcome indication that they are not being shirked.

Taking a victim-centred approach need not always mean that victims are the main drivers in every process. In criminal proceedings, the main focus must be on determining guilt or innocence. This does not mean that victims' voices cannot be heard, as indeed is the case in some national and international criminal proceedings, but their views and concerns are held within prescribed limits. Even so, permitting victims to be active participants in some of the international criminal tribunals has opened up a debate about the extent to which this represents a shift in international criminal law away from a purely punitive goal towards a goal that is more reparative and victim-centred.[122] The role of civil party or 'participant' afforded to victims in some international criminal tribunals, following civil law models more or less closely, gives victims the opportunity to convey their views and concerns during the pre-trial and trial proceedings through a legal representative and, if a conviction results from the trial, claim reparations. While there is fairly limited experience to date, tribunal watchers are asking how meaningful can this be when the main business of the Court is determining guilt or innocence, when the role of each victim is diluted by sharing a lawyer with hundreds or in some cases thousands of other victims, and when (in the case of the ICC and the Special Tribunal for Lebanon) the Court's proceedings take place far away in another continent.[123] Nevertheless, those courts that have adopted such an approach have embarked on a path that has an impact on its work in general. This significance was remarked on by one

[120] Colleen Duggan and others, 'Reparations for Sexual and Reproductive Violence: Prospects for Achieving Gender Justice in Guatemala and Peru' (2008) 2 *International Journal of Transitional Justice* 192. See also Ruth Rubio-Marín (ed), *What Happened to the Women? Gender and Reparations for Human Rights Violations* (Social Science Research Council 2006).

[121] *Lubanga* (n 17) para 192.

[122] In *Lubanga* (n 17) para 177, the Chamber noted that the Rome Statute 'reflects a growing recognition in international criminal law that there is a need to go beyond the notion of punitive justice, towards a solution which is more inclusive, encourages participation and recognizes the need to provide effective remedies for victims'.

[123] Two new studies address this debate: T Markus Funk, *Victims' Rights and Advocacy at the International Criminal Court* (OUP 2010); Godfrey Musila, *Rethinking International Criminal Law: Restorative Justice and the Rights of Victims in the International Criminal Court* (LAP Lambert Academic Publishing 2010).

Chamber of the ICC which stated that: 'The reparation scheme provided for in the Statute is not only one of the Statute's unique features. It is also a key feature. In the Chamber's opinion, the success of the Court is, to some extent, linked to the success of its reparation system.'[124]

There is an ever increasing volume of literature on transitional justice, much of it scrutinizing how satisfactory different measures are, or are not, for victims. Because reparative justice can only aim to reduce the consequences of victimization and not to undo the human rights violation itself, this is in some ways an impossible task. No reparation will entirely remove the harm done, so the goal in most instances can only be symbolic, to alleviate the suffering and not to erase it entirely. This is one reason why it is vital to engage an inter-disciplinary mixture of specialists to evaluate the impact of different measures and recommend best practices and courses of action.[125]

Another important policy debate that arises in designing remedies for human rights violations is how to strike the right balance between providing relief for victims of past violations, and preventing similar violations in the future. Some processes are clearly more geared towards relieving the effects of violations on victims. Others, such as judgments of the European Court of Human Rights, aim to bring about change but do not pay much attention to individual victims, while others simply do not have the power to do so (UN human rights bodies). A few, like the Inter-American human rights system and some transitional justice mechanisms try to do both. When considering the outcomes for victims of attempts to redress human rights violations, many questions arise about what goals should be pursued—individual or collective relief for victims, reconciliation in society, retribution, longer term improvement in human rights. It is easy to forget the individual victim in focusing on bringing about wider change. One important reason for paying attention to this is the fact that, as many studies have shown, the way all efforts to address human rights violations are perceived by victims will have an impact on the effectiveness of those efforts. Experiences to date show that there are many ways to ensure satisfactory outcomes for victims, even with a focus on other goals.

5. Conclusions

Putting right a wrong that has been done has always been one of the basic tenets of international law and the desire to do something to alleviate the suffering of victims

[124] *Corrigendum of the Decision on the Prosecutor's Application for a Warrant of Arrest*, para 150.

[125] In the *Lubanga* decision, the Chamber recommended the appointment of a multidisciplinary team of experts, including experts on the local context and specialists in child and gender issues. *Lubanga* (n 17) paras 263–264.

has been a huge impetus in the development of human rights law. The massive violations that took place during the Second World War, particularly the Holocaust, are often cited as the major trigger for the development of human rights law and institutions. Since then, there have been extraordinary achievements in developing legal norms and institutions designed to promote and protect human rights, including the procedural and substantive remedies that victims of those violations are entitled to expect.

At the outset, this chapter posited that the measure of success is not so much whether the mechanisms established to promote and protect human rights are in fact producing outcomes for victims at all, but crucially, to what degree those outcomes resolve in some way the situation for the victims and are seen by them as satisfactory. The review undertaken shows that while efforts to redress human rights violations have produced a considerable volume of legal instruments, reports, recommendations, decisions, and programmes, and a lot has been achieved in terms of standard-setting, what victims have actually received at the end of the day is less impressive. There are some significant issues that need to be addressed. To make victims' right to reparation effective, the elaboration of a convention based on the Principles and Guidelines on reparation would be a constructive step. The outcomes for victims are patchy: more results are seen in some countries and regions than others. This chapter has provided more examples from Latin America and Europe, fewer from Africa and Asia. The fact remains that many victims of human rights violations are not able to access any avenue of redress, and this is especially the case in the aftermath of large scale violations arising from conflict.

We now know a lot about what victims say themselves about what they want when human rights violations occur, and what is beneficial for them. Surveys and studies by psychologists and others have explored the expectations and perceptions of victims of human rights violations and sought to identify what outcomes will help them to heal, move on with their lives and achieve reconciliation, as well as to assess what impact the models adopted so far have had. Political, social, economic and cultural factors may all come into play in shaping victims' perceptions, in addition to the experience of the violation itself. A key message emerging from recent scholarship on transitional justice and reconciliation is the warning that there are no easy options, and no 'one size fits all' solutions in such circumstances. Victims want a complex mix of things that cannot be presumed in advance, so efforts must be made to establish it in each instance. While it is important to take action to prevent future violations and reconcile societies, the need remains to provide relief to victims who have already suffered violations.

What also emerges is the importance of procedural justice and victim-centred approaches; going through various reparations processes can be positive and empowering, but it is important to ensure that victims are properly supported through the process and can have a voice. Human rights law needs to be demystified and humanized, support structures created and procedures made less stressful for victims. More can be done to develop and make available best practice guidelines and training of people who interact with victims in the course of reparative measures including lawyers, officials and NGOs, as well as in areas such as consultation and participatory processes. The interplay between group rights and remedies could usefully be further explored and clarified.

Finally, to put victims at the centre and do more to give them what they want and need, requires paying more attention not only to achieving *more* remedies for victims, but the *right* ones. If this is not done, there should be no pretence that it is for the sake of the victims.

Further Reading

Commission on Human Rights, 'Report of the Independent Expert to Update the Set of Principles to Combat Impunity' (8 February 2005) UN Doc E/CN.4/2005/102

de Greiff P (ed), *The Handbook of Reparations* (OUP 2006)

European Commission, 'Proposal for a Directive of the European Parliament and of the Council Establishing Minimum Standards on the Rights, Support and Protection of Victims of Crime' (18 May 2011) COM (2011)275

Holtzmann HM and Kristjánsdóttir E, *International Mass Claims Processes: Legal and Practical Processes* (OUP 2007)

IIHR, *Comprehensive Attention to Victims of Torture in Cases under Litigation: Psychological Contributions* (IIHR 2009)

Office of the UN High Commissioner for Human Rights, *Rule-of-Law Tools for Post-Conflict States: National Consultations on Transitional Justice* (UN 2009)

Open Society Justice Initiative, *From Judgment to Justice: Implementing International and Regional Human Rights Decisions* (Open Society Foundations 2010)

REDRESS, *Torture Survivors' Perceptions of Reparation: Preliminary Survey* (Redress Trust 2001)

Shelton D, *Remedies in International Human Rights Law* (2nd edn, OUP 2005)

UNGA, 'Declaration of Basic Principles of Justice for Victims of Crime and Abuse of Power' (29 November 1985) UN Doc A/Res/40/34

——, 'Basic Principles and Guidelines on the Right to a Remedy and Reparation for Victims of Gross Violations of International Human Rights Law and Serious Violations of International Humanitarian Law' (21 March 2006) UN Doc A/Res/60/147

CHAPTER 39

HUMAN RIGHTS MAKE A DIFFERENCE: LESSONS FROM LATIN AMERICA

JUAN E MÉNDEZ

CATHERINE CONE

1. Introduction

In a broad sense, the struggle for human dignity, which is the essence of human rights, has no beginning or end. In Latin America, as in other parts of the world, examples of such struggles—with victories and defeats—go back at least to the day on which Christopher Columbus 'discovered' the continent for the Europeans. More recently, the 'democratic spring' of the last quarter century has not resulted in full observance of human rights for all. Nevertheless, there is no gainsaying that today human rights occupy a central place in all Latin American republics, both as an engine of progressive change and as a civil society agenda to improve the quality of institutional performance. Latin American communities have adopted the language of international human rights, perhaps more so than in other regions of the world, to advance the construction of more just and free societies with accountable governments.

As will become clear from this chapter, the change is more profound than the adoption of language; it reflects recognition and acceptance of the normative framework of international law about how governments treat their populations. The change has come about through a gradual process of incorporating those norms into the domestic legal systems, with an increasing tendency to give them effect through local courts. Equally importantly, it defines a segment of civil society that is willing and able to use the human rights canon to establish and nurture links with international networks and to shape national policy through increasingly sophisticated means and methods.

The 1960s brought a trend of replacing legitimate though ineffective governments with military dictatorships, installed through *coups d'état* and intent on remaining in power more or less indefinitely. By the mid-1970s, most countries were led by military dictatorships or by nominally civilian regimes with strong and unaccountable armed forces. These governments were authoritarian, intolerant on issues of 'public morals', and harsh in imposing social discipline, especially when it came to trade unions and street demonstrations. They opened markets to foreign capital and imposed local conditions attractive to multinational enterprises. They suppressed freedom of expression, sometimes grotesquely imposing prior censorship and telling citizens what they could read or watch. Most importantly, when acting in the broadly-defined name of 'national security' against those they considered subversive, they embarked on programmes of systematic violations of the most fundamental human rights. At levels and with a scope previously unknown, they inaugurated widespread and systematic use of torture, political assassination, attacks on civilian populations, and forced disappearances. Political repression was officially, though clandestinely, carried out by ignoring the rule of law. The 1964 coup in Brazil, which lasted until 1985, was both the earliest and the longest-lasting of these regimes, and also the most emblematic of these features.[1]

By the late 1960s and early 1970s, the regimes were confronted with highly organized and lethal armed insurgencies. Whether the authorities became criminally repressive in response to the subversive threat, or whether the insurgent violence originated in resistance to the military regimes, is a question that has multiple answers across the continent. It is clear, however, that the insurgent threat and violence were countered with unlawful and tragically criminal means that went far beyond any reasonable or lawful acts for purposes of law enforcement. As Argentine dictator Jorge Rafael Videla famously said in 1976, for these regimes, 'subversives' were not only the armed guerrillas, but included lawyers who defended the guerrillas, priests who preached ideas contrary to the regime's view of 'Christian and Western' values, academics who taught proscribed ideas, grass-roots union leaders,

[1] Naturally, the region had previously known military coups and decades-long combinations of weak civilian governments with strong military institutions. However, the era inaugurated with the Brazilian coup of 1964 is distinct in its combination of a refusal to recognize democratic principles, its authoritarianism, and its ruthlessness in repression of dissent.

students, and others.[2] In countries, including Guatemala, El Salvador, Nicaragua, Colombia, and Peru, where counter-insurgency battles were fought in rural areas, patterns of repression included massacres of indigenous and *campesino* communities, forced displacement, and refugee flows. The numbers of the disappeared, the murdered, the tortured, the banned, and the exiled far exceeded any reasonable estimates of the strength of the armed insurgent movements, even at their highest.

The decision to ignore constitutional and other legal safeguards was adopted at the outset of each coup, but the breakdown occurred gradually. To differing extents, each military regime kept up the appearance of legality for the consumption of supporters at home and abroad. Given this facade, human rights defenders at first attempted to use domestic remedies and to denounce abuses through the national media, at considerable risk to themselves, their families, and institutions. These human rights defenders and the organizations they formed invoked constitutional and statutory norms, as well as domestic legal traditions, seldom mentioning 'human rights'. This marked preference for domestic protections remained apparent, even as their effectiveness in curbing abuse was visibly diminishing. International mechanisms were not frequently used, in part because the perceived urgency of each situation called for more immediate action than international procedures could deliver; in addition, international organizations at that time had not yet developed the practices and mechanisms that may more effectively address those challenges today. In fact, the increasing effectiveness of the human rights machinery of international law is a direct response to the demands for protection that victims and their defenders made as the space for democratic efforts within each nation shrunk.

By the late 1970s and early 1980s, the room left for the defence of fundamental freedoms was so narrow that the recourse to international protection became inevitable. By then, sizable exile populations could be found in various countries, and they were in a position to act, including by raising awareness about the true nature of the military dictatorships and the tragic dimensions of the mass atrocities they committed. As a result, the international human rights movement began to pay much greater attention to events in Latin America; inter-governmental organs, especially the Inter-American Commission on Human Rights (IACHR), began to issue increasingly effective reports and take other initiatives in regards to the widespread human rights violations.[3] In turn, Latin American societies became aware of the international obligations of their governments and that international law could provide a measure of protection of citizens' rights, overriding the hitherto absolute conceptions of sovereignty and non-interference in internal affairs.

[2] See generally Alberto Bolívar, 'Latin America's Terrorist and Insurgent Groups' (May 2006) Foreign Policy Research Institute, <http://www.fpri.org/pubs/200605.bolivar.latinamericaterrorism.pdf> accessed 14 October 2012.

[3] See also Section 4 in this chapter: The Role of Civil Society.

2. The Nature of the Violations

Latin American human rights defenders had to struggle with new patterns and categories of human rights violations, precisely because the regimes sought to achieve 'national security' objectives without having to respect the rule of law. The phenomenon of 'disappearances' spread rapidly. It was used extensively, and perhaps originally, in Guatemala. The Junta that governed Argentina from 1976 to 1983 chose forced disappearances as its principal counter-insurgency tactic and coined the term 'dirty war' as an attempted justification for its actions, asserting their equivalence to the enemy's tactics. Juntas in Chile, Brazil, Honduras, and Peru also systematically engaged in disappearances; Uruguay did so in a more focused way and subordinate to other tactics, like torture. In Mexico, it appeared intermittently.

Human rights leaders struggled to make sense of a practice that was based on the authorities' denial of any information about the fate and whereabouts of the detainee, even of the fact of detention. The aim was not only 'plausible deniability', but also to instil fear and uncertainty among the direct victim's next of kin. Courts went through the motions of reviewing ineffective writs of habeas corpus. For the benefit of domestic and international public opinion, authorities would say that the *desaparecidos* had simply fled or gone underground and that the complaints made were part of a campaign to discredit the state, orchestrated by the subversive organizations. Some regimes played on Cold War divisions to buttress their assertions of politically motivated charges against them.

It was imperative to come up with evidence of a pattern. Human rights defenders did so by painstakingly accumulating the bits of evidence in each case, including testimony of relatives, documentation about administrative and judicial initiatives, and, eventually, testimonies of the rare survivors of the practice. Over time, Latin American human rights organizations reconstructed the phenomenon of disappearances and showed the existence of clandestine detention and torture centres, the complicity of most judges (though there were some brave exceptions), the 'pact of silence' among military and police officers, and the explicit and implicit orders from above that explained the total impunity that accompanied disappearances. As described in more detail in Part 4, human rights non-governmental organizations (NGOs) were able to disclose this tragic practice to the outside world and to agree on its main features.

Eventually, the evidence influenced the international community. In 1982, the then UN Commission of Human Rights established the still-functioning Working Group on Disappearances to come up with effective strategies to curb the practice. At the regional level, in addition to heart-breaking chapters in its country reports on Chile and Argentina, the Inter-American Commission on Human Rights had made several urgent calls to the Organization of American States (OAS) General

Assembly to express concern about disappearances as a global assault on human rights principles by the mid-1980s. At the request of the OAS, the IACHR drafted an Inter-American Convention on Forced Disappearance of Persons, approved in 1994, which entered into force with unusual speed in 1996. A United Nations Convention on the same matter entered into force in 2009.[4]

The work of domestic and international human rights organizations on disappearances found lasting recognition in jurisprudence, including the landmark 1988 judgment of the Inter-American Court of Human Rights in the case of *Angel Manfredo Velasquez-Rodriguez v Honduras*. The Court ascertained that disappearances constitute a crime against humanity and, consequently, that the state has an obligation to investigate, prosecute, and punish the perpetrators; to disclose the truth to the relatives and society about the fate and whereabouts of each *desaparecido*; to offer reparations to the families; and to reform the public institutions that were used in this fashion, to ensure non-repetition. UN experts later adopted similar principles.[5]

Dictatorships, especially in the Southern Cone, also engaged widely in prolonged arbitrary detention without trial, claiming a legal basis for it in the 'states of emergency' they declared in order to fight subversion. Indeed, human rights instruments consider the right to personal liberty as a 'derogable' one that can be lawfully suspended, if necessary, during a duly established emergency. Civil society organizations sought to ensure that this power was not exercised in an arbitrary manner, but most courts of the period showed excessive deference to the executive branches and refused to look beyond a boiler-plate explanation of the reasons given to hold someone indefinitely without trial. From the international community, human rights activists obtained important pronouncements that effectively put the burden on the state to show, for each person, a reasonable relationship between the detention and the basis for the state of emergency, in which the longer the period of detention is, the higher the burden on the state. Courts are obligated to apply this 'control of reasonableness' as a matter of both domestic and international law. This approach is now well established in Latin America.

Disappearances and arbitrary arrests declined in the 1980s and 1990s, in part because of the efforts of the human rights movement. Other forms of human rights abuses continued. Latin American human rights advocates had to contend with the use of military courts to try civilians and the use of special 'faceless' courts in Peru and Colombia. The exercise of military jurisdiction impeded the serious investigation of the crimes state agents committed, revealed in the reports and decisions

[4] International Convention for the Protection of All Persons from Enforced Disappearance.

[5] See UN Commission on Human Rights (UNCHR) 'Report by Special Rapporteur Theo van Brown' (2 July 1993) UN Doc E/CN.4/Sub.2/1993/8; UNCHR 'Report by Special Rapporteur Louis Joinet' (2 October 1997) UN Doc E/CN.4/Sub.2/1997/20/Rev.1; UNCHR 'Report by Special Rapporteur Cherif Bassiouni' (18 January 2000) UN Doc E/CN.4/2000/62; UNCHR 'Report by Independent Expert Diane Orentlicher' (8 February 2005) UN Doc E/CN.4/2005/102/Add.1.

of the Inter-American Commission and Court. The international standards that emerged from the regional bodies have been largely implemented in domestic settings.[6]

Extra-judicial killings were prevalent throughout the period. Perhaps the best known examples are the murders of Archbishop Oscar Romero in El Salvador in 1980 and of six Jesuit priests, their landlady, and her teen-age daughter in 1992. More recently, the murder of Bishop Juan Gerardi in Guatemala in 1998, two days after he released a ground-breaking report on violence by the Army against indigenous communities, showed that political murder persists after the recovery of democracy and the end of armed conflict.[7] Such examples exist in every country, targeting religious leaders, popular artists, journalists, politicians, and other human rights defenders. The regimes have paid some price in the loss of legitimacy internally, as well as abroad, even though the authors of such crimes retain near total impunity.

In countries where the armed conflict was mostly rural, the massacre of large numbers of the civilian population was another terrifying phenomenon, all the more tragic because its victims were mostly anonymous *campesinos* or indigenous persons from among the most underprivileged and neglected segments of the population. Within these communities, a disproportionate number of massacre victims were women and children. Latin American NGOs faced difficult campaigns, given the problems of access to the territory and the dangers associated with fact-finding therein. They eventually won important judicial victories that have also served to publicize these tragic episodes.[8] A different but related phenomenon is the use of violence by 'private armies' to settle disputes over land between large landowners and landless peasants or indigenous people—a problem that has been a recurring challenge to the human rights movements in Brazil, Guatemala, and recently, Paraguay.

Throughout these periods of repression, the use of torture has been rampant, especially as a means to obtain confessions or to gather intelligence. Massacres in the countryside and extra-judicial killings also have been accompanied by unspeakable physical and mental cruelty. The possibility of torturing without scrutiny is at the heart of the practice of disappearances. All countries conducting counter-insurgency campaigns used torture in varying degrees. The Uruguayan

[6] *Loayza Tamayo Case*; *Castillo Petruzzi et al v Peru*; *Barrios Altos v Peru*; *Almonacid-Arellano et al v Chile*, para 114.

[7] Francisco Goldman, *The Art of Political Murder: Who Killed the Bishop?* (Grove Press 2008).

[8] *Cayara v Peru*; *Plan de Sánchez Massacre v Guatemala*; *Mapiripán Massacre v Colombia*; *La Rochela Massacre v Colombia*. Perhaps the most emblematic of these massacres is the murder of dozens of elderly, women, and children in the village of El Mozote in El Salvador in 1981 by a US-trained elite battalion of the Salvadoran Army. See Pedro Linger Gasiglia, *El Mozote: La Masacre 25 Años Después* (P Linger Gasiglia 2007). On 10 December 2012 the Inter-American Court of Human Rights ruled against El Salvador on the *El Mozote* case.

dictatorship used torture and appalling conditions of detention as its principal tactics to destroy subversive organizations and instil fear in the population.

In response to the pervasive use of torture, and at the insistence of Latin American NGOs, the region produced an Inter-American convention against torture in 1987.[9] In the new democratic setting, there has been some progress in instituting procedural safeguards to prevent torture during interrogation, as well as inspection mechanisms in detention centres. Ombudsman offices (*defensores del pueblo* or *defensores penitenciarios*) have conducted effective, though largely unheralded, efforts to protect inmates from mistreatment and hold perpetrators accountable. Civil society organizations in some countries have put an emphasis on prison conditions, battling against public opinion that is often unconcerned with the treatment of convicted or accused criminals.

Unfortunately, the use of torture has not disappeared with the advent of democracy. Abusive means and tactics may be less brutal and less frequent against common crime suspects than against political enemies, but torture continues to be the principal means to investigate crime in Latin America, and efforts to curb it by prosecuting cases have been few and far between. In addition, Latin American detention facilities, especially in Venezuela, Brazil, Mexico, and Honduras, are so abject that their very existence constitutes cruel, inhuman, and degrading treatment and, in many cases, torture as well.

3. Innovations in Law from the Transitions in Latin America

3.1 Applying international humanitarian law

As Latin America began emerging from conflict and transitioning to democracy, the international legal framework of human rights, humanitarian law, and refugee law, took on even greater importance. Domestic human rights organizations, most notably the *Oficina de Tutela Legal del Arzobispado* in El Salvador, researched and reported on abuses, seeking to force all sides to the internal conflict to respect humanitarian concerns. Colombia broke new ground in applying international humanitarian law to its conflict, and to this end ratified Protocol II to the Geneva Conventions. In neighbouring Peru, human rights organizations applied international humanitarian law not only to state actors, but also to insurgents, in the

[9] Inter-American Convention to Prevent and Punish Torture.

aftermath of the Alberto Fujimori regime. Peru's official Truth and Reconciliation Commission (*Comisión de la Verdad y Reconciliación* (CVR)) enthusiastically supported the efforts of the human rights community in this respect.

Collectively, the region's human rights movement further recognized and embraced international humanitarian law by adopting international mechanisms—specifically the Geneva Conventions of 1949 and its Additional Protocols of 1977, and more recently the Rome Statute for an International Criminal Court (ICC). Newly democratic Latin American countries participated actively in the discussions leading to the creation of the ICC and have widely ratified that treaty. The incorporation of these agreements, designed to afford international protection to the human person during war and peace, means that most Latin American courts can now exercise jurisdiction over crimes against humanity and war crimes.

In a parallel effort, in the 1980s international NGOs like Americas Watch (now Human Rights Watch) joined their counterparts in domestic civil societies and pioneered the systematic application of the laws of war to domestic conflicts, first in Central America and then worldwide. The IACHR instituted a momentous change of course when it addressed these complaints through the lens of international humanitarian law, as well as international human rights law. In *Abella v Argentina*,[10] the Commission addressed whether international humanitarian law should apply to a series of claims arising from a single episode of armed conflict between members of the *Movimiento Todos por la Patria* (MTP) and the Argentine military. The conflict took place when an armed group sought to overtake the La Tablada military base, allegedly to prevent a military coup against the democratic regime.[11] The Commission found that in order to evaluate the merits of the MTP members' claims, it first had to determine the nature of the conflict, specifically, whether it could be characterized 'merely [as] an example of an "internal disturbance or tensions" or whether it constituted a non-international or internal armed conflict within the meaning of Article 3 common to the four 1949 Geneva conventions ("Common Article 3")'.[12] If the conflict amounted to a mere internal disturbance, then the case would be governed by domestic law and relevant rules of international human rights law.[13]

[10] See *Abella v Argentina*, paras 146–190.

[11] *Abella* (n 10) paras 147–148.

[12] See *Abella* (n 10) para 147 (explaining that because the legal rules governing these two types of conflicts differ, the Commission had to first answer the question of what kind of conflict was at play, in order to then apply the relevant source of law). See also Geneva Convention for the Amelioration of the Condition of the Wounded and Sick in Armed Forces, Art 3 (Common Art 3) (providing protections of international humanitarian law to conflicts not of an international character).

[13] See *Abella* (n 10) para 152 (describing how even though Common Art 3 applies to armed strife between the state's armed forces and insurgents, this does not require 'large-scale and generalized hostilities or a situation comparable to a civil war').

The Commission found that the conflict involved hostilities between governmental armed forces and organized armed insurgents and could not be characterized as a mere internal disturbance.[14] Given this conclusion about the nature of the hostilities, international humanitarian law should govern[15] for reasons the Commission explained:

> [N]one of these human rights instrument was designed to regulate...situations [involving warfare] and, thus, they contain no rules governing the means and methods of warfare. In contrast, international humanitarian law generally does not apply in peacetime, and its fundamental purpose is to place restraints on the conduct of warfare in order to diminish the effects of hostilities. It is understandable therefore that...humanitarian law generally afford[s] victims of armed conflicts greater or more specific protections than do the more generally phrased guarantees in the American Convention and other human rights instruments. It is, moreover, during situations of internal armed conflict that these two branches of international law most converge and reinforce each other.[16]

The Commission found that it could properly address questions of humanitarian law in part because the Convention requires the Commission to give legal effect to the instrument providing for the most favourable protection of rights and freedoms.[17] The Commission indicated that by not specifically defining or distinguishing civilians from combatants and other military targets, and by not prescribing the instances where a civilian could lawfully be attacked, the American Convention failed to provide the highest level of protection to civilians.[18] Instead, the law of armed conflict should apply to the claims before the Commission as *lex specialis*.[19] Lastly, because Article 27(1) of the American Convention prevents the state from adopting derogation measures that would violate its other international law obligations, the state's obligations would necessarily also apply during situations of armed

[14] *Abella* (n 10) paras 152–156 (pointing to the following factors as relevant to its determination regarding the nature of the conflict: (1) the concerted nature of the MTP members' hostile acts; (2) the armed forces' direct involvement; and (3) the sustained nature and correspondingly high (as compared to internal disturbances) level of violence).

[15] *Abella* (n 10) paras 156–170.

[16] See *Abella* (n 10) paras 158–160 (delineating how in these instances international human rights law should reinforce and converge with international humanitarian law but cede to international humanitarian law where it provides greater individual protections).

[17] *Abella* (n 10) paras 164–165.

[18] See *Abella* (n 10) para 161 (explaining how not applying international humanitarian law would otherwise require the Commission to decline to exercise jurisdiction on cases involving attacks by the state that lead to great civilian loss of life—an absurd result, in light of the Convention's object and purpose).

[19] See *Abella* (n 10) paras 165–166 (relating how Protocol II's higher standard of protection apply, except where the Protocol might not incorporate provisions of an international human rights instrument that offer greater individual protection). See also Antonio Cassese, *International Law* (2nd edn, OUP 2005) 393–94 (defining *lex specialis* as a principle of law requiring a special law to prevail over a general law).

conflict and would thus require the state to not derogate from its obligations under international humanitarian law.[20]

The Commission made an equally unprecedented decision when it applied the laws of war not only to the state's armed forces, but also to subversives.[21] In *Abella,* the Commission found that the MTP attackers had engaged in hostilities against Argentina's military and that these actions were sufficient to trigger international humanitarian law obligations on all parties involved.[22] Thus, 'the provisions of the Geneva Conventions of 12 August 1949...must be fully applied in all circumstances...without any adverse distinction based on the nature or origin of the armed conflict or on the causes espoused by or attributed to the Parties of the Conflict'.[23] Consequently, in *Abella*, Common Article 3's mandatory provisions expressly bound both the MTP attackers and the Argentine armed forces, such that both parties had the same duties under international humanitarian law.[24]

3.2 Discrediting amnesty laws

Countries in Latin America wrestled not only with what body of law to apply to perpetrators of past crimes, but also with whether to apply sanctions to them. Following the fall of authoritarian regimes across Latin America, the question became how best to repair the torn 'fabric of society' left behind by legacies of abuse.[25] For many years following the fall of autocratic governments, the passage of amnesty laws gave safe harbor to those who had participated in human rights abuses.[26] Chile, Argentina, and Peru, for example, passed broad amnesty laws, while Brazil, Uruguay, Argentina, El Salvador, Nicaragua, and Guatemala passed laws that similarly allowed for violators to take cover and for impunity to take root.

Chile's Supreme Court set the tone for impunity in the early years of the democracy by choosing to uphold a military tribunal's application of the Amnesty Law as

[20] See *Abella* (n 10) paras 168–170 (noting how temporary derogation is appropriate only if the rights in question are subject to suspension under certain genuine emergency circumstances).

[21] See *Abella* (n 10) paras 172–189 (deciding to apply international humanitarian law to the insurgents who attacked the La Tablada base and Argentine military, while determining that Common Art 3's protections did not cover the insurgent attackers, because though civilians, once they initiated hostilities against the base, the civilians consequently lost the privilege of any civilian protections).

[22] See *Abella* (n 10) paras 172–173.

[23] Protocol Additional to the Geneva Conventions of 12 August 1949, and Relating to the Protection of Victims of International Armed Conflicts. See also *Abella* (n 10) para 173.

[24] *Abella* (n 10) para 174.

[25] Garth Meintjes and Juan E Méndez, 'Reconciling Amnesties with Universal Jurisdiction' (2000) 2 *Int'l L Forum du Droit Int'l* 76, 76 (explaining the wide gamut of measures various states transitioning from conflict contemplated, ranging from complete impunity to vigorous attempts to bring about truth and justice).

[26] See Meintjes and Méndez (n 25) 76 (describing the original tendency of many states to choose extreme clemency and oblivion under the guise of reconciliation through amnesty laws).

constitutional.[27] Specifically, the Chilean Supreme Court held that the constitution's amnesty provisions trumped the duty of the state to investigate, as required under Chile's criminal codes.[28] The decision also elevated the Amnesty Law above other constitutional norms relating to the state's duty to respect and promote rights guaranteed under domestic and international law, as well as norms providing for the judicial authority to make determinations of criminal culpability.[29] Consequently, the Court's interpretation of the effect of the Amnesty Law effectively made any kind of redress, including civil compensation, 'not only illusory but juridically impossible'.[30] The Chilean Supreme Court did eventually strike down Pinochet's self-amnesty law in a series of later cases that upheld the victim's right to a remedy and the state's duty to investigate and prosecute.[31]

In Brazil, the government had enacted a similar blanket amnesty intended to allow opponents of the military to be released or to return from exile, but it was also applied to perpetrators of human rights abuses within the military and police forces.[32] The issue eventually reached the Inter-American Court of Human Rights in *Gomes Lund et al v Brazil*,[33] where the Court clearly held that the state had an obligation, in cases of enforced disappearances, to investigate without delay and to do so in a serious, impartial, and effective manner. The Court found that to be effective, the 'state must establish the appropriate normative framework to develop the investigation.... [It] must guarantee that no normative or other type of obstacles prevent the investigation of said acts'.[34]

The Inter-American Court invalidated the Brazilian amnesty law because the Court recognized that the amnesty law had served as a *de jure* obstacle to the state's ability to fulfil effectively its obligation to investigate and prosecute, where appropriate.[35] Moreover, allowing the amnesty law to trump the state's duty would effectively prevent the investigation of serious human rights violations, leading to the perpetuation of impunity, the defencelessness of victims, and the inability of

[27] Marny A Requa, 'A Human Rights Triumph? Dictatorship-Era Crimes and the Chilean Supreme Court' (2012) 12 *HRL Rev* 79, 83. See also *Iván Sergio Insunza Bascuñán*, Corte Suprema de Justicia [Supreme Court], Case No 27.640 (24 August 1990).

[28] *Iván Sergio Insunza Bascuñán* (n 27) paras 22–23.

[29] See *Iván Sergio Insunza Bascuñán* (n 27) paras 22–23 (finding that the state could legitimately declare an amnesty as a valid exercise of its legislative power to suspend declarations of criminality).

[30] Requa (n 27) 84 (referencing *Garay Hermosilla et al v Chile*, para 9). See also *Almonacid-Arellano* (n 6) paras 105–114 (requiring the state to remove the self-amnesty law—even while acknowledging that the Supreme Court had not applied it recently—and to remove, as well, similar obstacles, like pardons, statutes of limitations, and *res judicata* of military decisions, because these obstacles precluded realizing any meaningful accountability efforts).

[31] *Miguel Ángel Sandoval*; *Diana Frida Arón Svigilsky*; *Villa Grimaldi (Re Pinochet)*; *Manuel Tomás Rojas Fuentes*.

[32] *Gomes Lund et al v Brazil*, para 2.

[33] *Gomes Lund* (n 32) para 108. *Manuel Cepeda Vargas v Colombia*, paras 117–119.

[34] *Gomes Lund* (n 32) para 109.

[35] *Gomes Lund* (n 32) para 173.

the next of kin to know the truth.[36] Meanwhile, in Argentina, Raúl Alfonsín, the first democratically elected president following the country's military dictatorship, faced pressure from middle-ranking military officers to put an end to prosecutions. The military faction, known as the *carapintadas*, engaged in four uprisings, each more violent and costly in human lives than the preceding one.[37] In response to this pressure, Alfonsín's majority in Congress put in place laws amounting to amnesty, and the next President, Carlos Menem, issued blanket pardons to complete the cycle of impunity. The Supreme Court upheld these measures at the time, but in 2001 Federal Judge Gabriel Cavallo ruled that the laws were unconstitutional and violated Argentina's obligations under international law by effectively nullifying Argentina's obligation to bring to justice those responsible for crimes against humanity.[38] In unprecedented and historic moves, the Federal Court of Appeals and Supreme Court of Argentina also declared the laws to be unconstitutional, thus moving Argentina from an era of impunity to one of justice and accountability.[39]

Thus, both on the domestic and international levels, the courts and legal systems of Latin America eventually condemned impunity and imposed accountability for the most serious crimes against human rights. 'Some newly democratic governments attempted to settle the[ir] accounts rather than leave them as permanent wounds in the fabric of society.'[40] A powerful shift had occurred in terms of how to assess and reckon with the past, cemented by a string of state-led prosecutions and the recognition of the state's responsibility in prior atrocities.

4. The Role of Civil Society

During the dictatorial period, civil society in Latin America played an instrumental role in informing international organs of the situation and raising awareness of instances of mass violations. In the early days of the transition to democracy, they broke ground domestically and internationally by insisting on accountability and urging debates about the ethical, political, and legal dimensions of impunity.

[36] *Gomes Lund* (n 32) para 173.

[37] Juan E Méndez, *Truth and Partial Justice in Argentina: An Update*' (Human Rights Watch 1991) 73.

[38] See Rebecca Lichtenfeld, 'Accountability in Argentina: 20 Years Later, Transitional Justice Maintains Momentum' (August 2005) *International Center for Transitional Justice (ICTJ)* 5, <http://ictj.org/sites/default/files/ICTJ-Argentina-Accountability-Case-2005-English.pdf> accessed 15 October 2012 (establishing that international law obligations and treaty obligations trump domestic laws in Argentina).

[39] Lichtenfeld (n 38) 6.

[40] Meintjes and Méndez (n 25) 77.

To varying degrees, they succeeded in transferring this agenda to the larger societies and to the political arena. From the start they reached out to the international community and to the organs of human rights protection. In Argentina, following the end of the military coup in 1983, civil society organizations organized efforts to move the human rights agenda forward on various fronts and by way of varying strategies. As the country's truth commission, the National Commission on the Disappeared, reported the near 9,000 deaths and disappearances that had taken place in Argentina from 1975–83, family members of the disappeared created new human rights organizations to overcome the 'failed solitary searches for their loved ones'.[41] The *Madres de Plaza de Mayo* [Mothers of the Plaza de Mayo], for example, chose to critically watch the government and focus on public platforms to generate awareness, utilizing public spaces such as the Plaza de Mayo.[42] Other groups, like the Center for Legal and Social Studies (CELS) and the Permanent Assembly for Human Rights, instead chose to challenge the legality of the government's actions through testimonies and judicial presentations.

Argentina's civil society was able to leverage critical support and generate awareness by collaborating with international non-governmental organizations like Amnesty International and regional institutions such as the IACHR.[43] In drafting its groundbreaking report investigating the human rights situation in Argentina in 1979, the IACHR Commissioners had relied heavily on both human rights activists and the hundreds of victims and family members who provided testimony for inclusion in the report.[44] It was the work of the Argentine civil society sector—with leaders like Emilio Mignone, the founder of CELS—that led the IACHR to recommend that the government of Argentina 'initiate the corresponding investigations, to bring to trial and to punish, with the full force of the law, those responsible'[45]—a daring move for the time. Lastly, human rights advocates complemented their calls for justice and accountability with initiatives aimed at memorializing and commemorating the many victims of the dictatorship and preserving documents, as well as creating historical archives.[46] Through these efforts, civil society sought not only to advance justice, but also to prevent any tendency to let the painful past fall into oblivion.

[41] Kathryn Sikkink, *The Justice Cascade: How Human Rights Prosecutions Are Changing World Politics* (Norton 2011) 62–63.

[42] Lichtenfeld (n 38) 6.

[43] Sikkink (n 41) 65, 68.

[44] Sikkink (n 41) 65–66.

[45] Sikkink (n 41) 66–67. See also IACHR, 'Report on the Situation of Human Rights in Argentina' (11 April 1980) OEA/Ser.L/V/II.49 Doc 19 corr 1. Sikkink also describes how Uruguay, to a great extent, followed in Argentina's footsteps when its citizens and human rights groups organized a campaign that was able to gather a half-million signatures in order to force a popular referendum on an immunity law, even though the referendum yielded more votes in favour of granting the military immunity from prosecution. Sikkink (n 41) 80.

[46] Lichtenfeld (n 38) 6.

Similarly, in Chile, a group of human rights lawyers, armed forces representatives, the Minister of Defense, and members of the church and civil society, gathered to discuss how to approach the legacy of human rights abuses committed during the prior military regime, including the issue of enforced disappearances. The human rights discussion table became known as '*Mesa de Diálogo*',[47] and its efforts were notable insofar as they produced a signed declaration recognizing the grave human rights violations committed under the military government.[48] 'After 27 years of complete denial on the part of the armed forces, in particular the army, that they had been responsible for human rights violations, an acknowledgement of the deaths of 200 people who had been arrested was made.'[49]

Civil society groups in Latin America also emerged around particular identity politics, like gender, ethnicity, and indigenous culture. Women, not only in Argentina and Chile but also El Salvador and Guatemala, formed groups to publicly demand the truth regarding the status and condition of their disappeared loved ones.[50] Women activists also helped develop civic participation, most notably through their willingness to serve in state and local agencies, often with the end goal of improving the status of women in the wake of conflict.[51] Meanwhile, Maya communities in Mexico and Central America advocated for a pluralist approach to national development, an approach that embraced 'the coexistence and mutual enrichment of culturally diverse peoples within a single state and respect of internationally recognized human and cultural rights'.[52] More than just manifesting an ethnic identity, many Maya movements emerged as the voice of resistance against military-led and military-controlled transitions to civilian rule.[53]

Communities in the Andean region undertook similar efforts to heighten discourse on cultural pluralism and to confront authoritarian rule. In Bolivia, for example, the Revolutionary Movement Tupaj Katari used radio and literacy programmes not only to articulate political grievances, but also to increase indigenous rights, eventually leading to significant advances like the Bolivian ratification of ILO Convention No 169 on the rights of indigenous peoples.[54] In Ecuador, indigenous political movements

[47] Amnesty International, 'Chile: Testament to Suffering and Courage: The Long Quest for Justice and Truth' (10 December 2001) AI-Index AMR 22/014/2001 (Chile Report) 7–8.

[48] Chile Report (n 47) 8. [49] Chile Report (n 47) 8.

[50] Marc Belanger, 'Democratization, Civil Society, and Latin American Social Movements' in Rachel A May and Andrew K Milton (eds), *(Un)civil Societies: Human Rights and Democratic Transitions in Eastern Europe and Latin America* (Lexington Books 2005) 66–69.

[51] Belanger (n 50) 67–69.

[52] Belanger (n 50) 71–72. See also Demetrio Rodríguez Guaján, 'Maya Culture and the Politics of Development' in Edward Fischer and R McKenna Brown (eds), *Mayan Cultural Activism in Guatemala* (U Texas Press 1996) 83.

[53] Belanger (n 50) 72 (referencing Ethnic Communities We Are All Equal (CERJ), the National Coordinating Committee of Guatemalan Widows (CONAVIGUA), and the Council of Displaced Guatemalans (CONDEG)).

[54] This significant process of empowerment of indigenous people also led to the popular election of Evo Morales as president of the country—the first indigenous leader to achieve such electoral success

advocated for land rights and eventually for stronger cultural rights and autonomy, including through bringing cases to the Inter-American system. Overall, the civil society sector in Latin America carved out a significant role for itself in the region's human rights discourse, combating any efforts to further systematically repress human rights and raising awareness of how prior regimes had trampled on the human rights of the region's inhabitants.

5. Effects of the Transitions

The period of transition in Latin America brought with it a movement toward accountability, but it also created some dilemmas of its own, in the form of inadequate protection for and violations of the rights of indigenous peoples, a predominant rule of violence to settle disputes over land in rural areas, constant police brutality in urban areas, and a lack of judicial capacity to provide for due process and fair trials. A contemporary scholar describes a regional paradox—namely that despite the democratic advances made by human rights and civil society organizations, traces of the old political and administrative culture remain.[55] The rigidly Presidential structure of government, a fragile system of checks and balances, very low institutional credibility, corruption, and a lack of public accountability, have facilitated the entrenchment of the elites. All of these factors contributed to make for a rough transitional phase, particularly when set against 'a background of deep socio-economic gaps and continuing poverty'.[56]

The spread of criminal and social violence, particularly in Guatemala, the Southern Cone, and Brazil, led the public increasingly to question the character and ability of emerging democracies to govern effectively and to protect the citizenry, thus leading to growing doubt about the democratic system of government and some nostalgia for the days of autocratic 'order'.[57] Colombia has operated under a rule of violence that continues even under democracy, but the political system has thus far stood by its democratic principles and attempted to improve the democratic capacities of the society and the public administration. Perhaps the most damaging

in Latin America. In 2005, Morales won with 53 per cent of the vote. See Santiago Anria, 'Bolivia's MAS: Between Party and Movement' in Maxwell A Cameron and Eric Hershberg (eds), *Latin America's Left Turn: Politics, Policies and Trajectories of Change* (Lynne Rienner 2010).

[55] Luis Roniger, 'Representative Democracy and Effective Institutions: Democratic Practice in Contemporary Latin America' in Carlos H Waisman and Raanan Rein (eds), *Spanish and Latin American Transitions to Democracy* (Sussex Academic Press 2005) 133.

[56] Roniger (n 55) 133. [57] Roniger (n 55) 134–35.

effect of such violence is a public perception of the social system 'as influenced by sheer power, reinforcing the predictions of violence and fuelling a vicious circle of "self-fulfilling prophecy" which ensconces fear in the public space and disarticulates social solidarity, tilting the odds toward force and violence'.[58]

The public's loss of confidence in the social system is greatly influenced by unreformed security forces, especially the police, who often employ force and brutality when attempting to maintain law and order. In Guatemala, for example, pursuant to the Peace Agreements calling for a civilian peace force to further stability and increase the people's sense of safety, the government created the National Civil Police (PNC) Force in 1997. However, the IACHR reported that it was the PNC itself that 'has become the main instigator of the most serious violations of priority human rights'.[59] Moreover, the IACHR noted how the police often used excessive force and abused their power by not respecting the principles of necessity and proportionality.[60]

Similarly, in Brazil, in the wake of the 1994 elections that brought Fernando Henrique Cardoso to power, Human Rights Watch reported that Brazilian police began using excessive force in their overweening efforts to reduce heavy crime rates in major urban centres.[61] In Rio de Janeiro, police were rewarded for demonstrating 'bravery' that often translated to bonuses and promotions for officers who killed criminal suspects, regardless of the circumstances.[62] The extreme and unwarranted police tactics eventually reached such levels that cities like São Paulo, Belo Horizonte, and Olinda-Recife implemented efforts to combat these excesses.[63]

Transitions also brought challenges in the realm of the administration of justice. In Guatemala, the vast majority of the population could not access speedy and effective justice during the transition to peace, mainly because of the nationwide lack of capacity, which included a shortage of judges and inadequate infrastructure and training of members of judicial agencies.[64] Parallel problems arose in Colombia, where the IACHR highlighted the inability of Colombian justice to afford the guarantees of due process and full exercise of human rights,[65] all of which were

[58] Roniger (n 55) 135.

[59] See IACHR, *Justice and Social Inclusion: The Challenges of Democracy in Guatemala* (OAS 2003) (*Justice and Social Inclusion*) para 105.

[60] *Justice and Social Inclusion* (n 59) para 108.

[61] James Cavallaro and Anne Manuel, 'Police Brutality in Urban Brazil' (Human Rights Watch 1997) 17.

[62] Cavallaro and Manuel (n 61) 34.

[63] See Cavallaro and Manuel (n 61) (describing the efforts that cities undertook, including: programmes that removed officers who had been involved in killings from the line of duty and provided them with psychological counselling, newly created complaint offices, special divisions to prosecute human rights violations, and witness protection programmes).

[64] See *Justice and Social Inclusion* (n 59) paras 57–63.

[65] IACHR, 'Second Report on the Situation of Human Rights in Colombia' (1 January 1993) OEA/Ser.L/V/II.84 Doc 39 rev 14 (Second Report on the Situation of Human Rights in Colombia) ch IV.

aggravated by judicial proceedings that proceeded in secret and under the influence of military justice.[66] In neighbouring Ecuador, the IACHR also found serious problems, like an overwhelmed and underfunded judiciary and a lack of impartial and independent administration of justice, due to factors including corruption and impermanence in judicial positions. The result impaired the individual's ability to exercise his right to an effective judicial remedy, in contravention of Article 25 of the American Convention.[67]

In sum, the historic move towards peace and relative democracy did not come without significant, though not insurmountable, problems like the plight of indigenous peoples, the ongoing cycle of violence and police brutality, and the lack of judicial capacity. These problems were accompanied, however, by hyperawareness of the acute nature of the setbacks, eventually leading to a new chapter and approach to how to tackle further evolution in the post-transition period. Even today, a tendency toward authoritarianism remains in some elected governments, with elected leaders accumulating power and eroding the quality of institutional checks and balances. Serious threats to some human rights, notably freedom of expression, but also, in some cases, the right to life, the right to physical integrity, and the right to a remedy, are the result. This has been the greatest challenge recently to the organs of the Inter-American system, in particular,[68] and to human rights law and monitoring bodies, in general. President Hugo Chávez announced in April 2012 that Venezuela would 'find ways' to withdraw from the jurisdiction of the IACHR and of the Inter-American Court. That August, Venezuela formally announced that it would denounce the American Convention on Human Rights, although the jurisdiction of both organs would remain in effect for a full year after the deposit of the denunciation instrument. Drastic and unprecedented as a denunciation of a human rights treaty would be, Venezuela would still be subject to the jurisdiction of the Commission, because the latter is a 'principal organ' of the OAS and is part of its Charter.

[66] Second Report on the Situation of Human Rights in Colombia (n 65) ch IV.

[67] IACHR, 'Report on the Situation of Human Rights in Ecuador' (24 April 1997) OEA/Ser.L/V/II.96 Doc 10 rev 1, ch III.

[68] In 2011 and early 2012, Ecuador led a concerted effort to force changes in the way the Inter-American Commission does its work, especially in regards to precautionary measures, the discussion of comprehensive country situations in its annual report to the General Assembly, and the independence of the Commission's Special Rapporteur on Freedom of Expression. See the Permanent Council of the OAS, 'Report of the Special Working Group to Reflect on the Workings of the Inter-American Commission on Human Rights with a View to Strengthening the Inter-American Human Rights System for Consideration by the Permanent Council' (13 December 2011) OEA/Ser.G GT/SIDH-13/11 rev 2; OAS Press Release, 'OAS Permanent Council Approved the Report of the Working Group to Strengthening the Inter-American Human Rights System' (25 January 2012) E-018/12 <http://www.oas.org/en/media_center/press_release.asp?sCodigo=E-018/12> accessed 18 October 2012.

6. Mechanisms of Change

6.1 Transitional justice prosecutions

In determining how to address the wounds authoritarian regimes caused to Latin American societies, sectors of these societies expressed the need to judge those responsible for the violation of human rights, notably from the perspective of the afflicted. The idea that justice must be tied to the right of the victim was one that only gradually emerged and today continues to coalesce when states implement measures like prosecutions, truth commissions, reparations, institutional reform, and memorialization. International law helped provide the framework by placing an affirmative obligation on states to investigate and prosecute those who, under color of state law, had violated fundamental human rights and thus created a class of victims entitled to redress.[69] The discussion on how to deal with legacies of abuse thus came together around two debates: first, how to move forward, which necessarily involved discussing the effects of any measures, such as investigations, prosecution, and reparations; and second, what was required of the states under international law following a period of systemic human rights abuse.[70]

In formulating an answer to the question of how to move the society forward through a transition, states could not escape the need to examine the extent to which international law required them to provide some element of redress to victims. The states had a host of obligations under ratified human rights agreements that required compliance.[71] Although the treaties and conventions set forth baseline requirements and rights, neither the rights of the victims nor the state obligations were fully detailed or effectuated until the various monitoring bodies interpreted them.[72] When they did so, the monitoring bodies held the states perpetrating

[69] See Naomi Roht-Arriaza, 'Introduction' in Naomi Roht-Arriaza (ed), *Impunity and Human Rights in International Law and Practice* (OUP 1995) 3.

[70] Roht-Arriaza (n 69) 5.

[71] Roht-Arriaza (n 69) 6. See International Covenant on Civil and Political Rights, Arts 2, 4, 26 (providing for a right to an effective remedy for violations under Art 2). See also American Convention on Human Rights, Art 25 (requiring states to uphold the 'rights and freedoms recognized' in the Convention, including the right to judicial protection); Universal Declaration of Human Rights, preamble.

[72] See Cassese (n 19) 183 (positing how the decisions of judicial bodies interpreting treaties, although secondary law, carry great weight, because they interpret treaties that are primary or 'hard law'). See also M Cherif Bassiouni, 'International Recognition of Victims' Rights' (2006) 6 *HRL Rev* 203, 226 (discussing how the Inter-American Court of Human Rights, among other international bodies, required Latin American states to investigate and bring perpetrators to justice in cases of serious violations of physical integrity, as part of the Court's interpretation of a common general provision found in international human rights law instruments obliging states parties to respect or secure the rights embodied in the instrument).

violations to be required to provide justice, truth, reparations, and institutional reform, as a guarantee of non-repetition in efforts to address and redress such gross violations.[73] This panoply of measures, which Latin American states began implementing in their attempts to comply with international law obligations, became known as tools of transitional justice.

The most significant components of the accountability spectrum to emerge were criminal prosecution of all those responsible, including high and low level offenders; maintaining legitimacy by conducting prosecutions within the standards of fair trials and due process; overcoming legal and *de facto* obstacles; and living up to the obligation to extradite or prosecute.[74] Prosecutions faced many obstacles in Latin America, from amnesty laws to pressures from the military and their allies, to the ruling elite's desire to sweep the abuses under the rug for the purpose of some ill-defined 'national reconciliation'. To their credit, victims' groups and their allies in civil society confronted these obstacles and eventually prevailed, albeit with varying degrees of success. Although by now it has been three or four decades since the abuses happened, the power of the idea that some crimes simply cannot go unpunished (bolstered by the jurisprudence of the Inter-American system) has resulted in a remarkable wave of prosecutions and trials, especially in the Southern Cone, Guatemala, and Peru.

In Argentina, the efforts to put such accountability into action became manifest in the country's 1985 trial of the military Juntas. For the first time, the human rights demands and discourses that human rights organizations launched took root in a tangible form, aimed both at deterring future violations and punishing those who had committed grave human rights abuses.[75] The Argentine trials took on a landmark quality, with the prosecutors having no previous roadmap to follow. The trials set a precedent for the region by using domestic criminal law, rather than international human rights law, in order to avoid accusations of retroactive application of the law.[76] The trials focused on the highest-level offenders first (specifically, 700 cases for which the prosecution felt there was sufficient underlying evidence), produced a vast historical record, and led to the convictions of five of the nine leaders of the Juntas, including General Videla and Admiral Massera. Perhaps most

[73] Bassiouni (n 72) 226.

[74] See José Zalaquett, 'Confronting Human Rights Violations Committed by Former Governments: Applicable Principles and Political Constraints' (1990) 13 *Hamline L Rev* 623, 630, 643.

[75] See Sikkink (n 41) 70–71. See also Jaime Malamud-Goti, 'Punishing Human Rights Abuses in Fledgling Democracies: The Case of Argentina' in Roht-Arriaza (n 69) 165 (arguing that the approach taken by the Argentine trials regarding punishment failed to fully meet the 'victim-centred' theory of punishment associated with goal-oriented retributivists who attach to punishment 'the function of restoring… [the] lost trust' of victims because some of the tried did not play a very active role in the abuses, while many who did went unpunished).

[76] Malamud-Goti (n 75) 165.

importantly, the trials reiterated that no one could be subjected to torture or summary execution.

In later efforts spanning the first decade of the new millennium, the courts have declared pseudo-amnesty laws and pardons unconstitutional, and mega-cases have been successfully prosecuted throughout the territory. General Videla and some other notorious criminals, like Generals Bussi, Menendez, Riveros, and Diaz Bessone, received life sentences. Twenty persons have been acquitted.[77] This last figure is very significant; the vast majority of the population and all the major political parties support the trials, not only because of the need to see justice done for the atrocities of the 'dirty war' era, but also because the trials observe the most stringent demands of due process and fair trial guarantees.

Accountability efforts in Chile developed in three phases: the first phase (1990–97), discussed above, allowed for traces of authoritarianism to continue by upholding amnesty; the second phase (1998) shifted from impunity to accountability, calling for investigations under domestic law and attempting to adhere to international law, while not expressly overruling the amnesty law; and the third era (1999–2007), when Chile deliberately departed from the amnesty law and established a commitment to protect human rights through domestic law, recognizing that the state's international law obligations were superior to domestic law in the country's legal framework.[78] From low expectations of justice for past atrocities, the country went through a steady upward trend, arguably accelerated by the impact of General Pinochet's arrest in London in 1998, pursuant to an arrest warrant that a Spanish court issued. When Pinochet died, he was no longer a revered leader. He had been stripped of his immunity as a senator-for-life and was facing prosecution. By July 2008, 256 high- and mid-ranking officers had been convicted, and 482 others were facing prosecution.[79]

In Uruguay, the courts found ways to breach the seemingly formidable impunity wall created by the *Ley de Caducidad de la Pretensión Punitiva del Estado* (Law of Expiration),[80] Uruguay's version of an amnesty law, enacted in 1986 and twice retained by referenda.[81] Some cases were brought for civil damages and later for criminal prosecution, with the Supreme Court twice declaring the law unconstitutional. Civilian leaders of the regime, like President Juan María Bordaberry and Foreign Minister Juan Carlos Blanco, were prosecuted and convicted, because the amnesty law only covered military and police officials. Some cases were excluded

[77] Horacio Verbitsky, 'Preguntas sin Respuesta' *Página 12* (6 May 2012) <http://www.pagina12.com.ar/diario/elpais/1-193425-2012-05-06.html> accessed 16 October 2012.

[78] Requa (n 27) 83–90. See also nn 27–31 and accompanying text.

[79] Human Rights Watch, 'Chile: Country Summary' (Human Rights Watch January 2009) <http://www.hrw.org/sites/default/files/related_material/chile.pdf>.

[80] No 15.848 of 22 December 1986.

[81] Robert K Goldman and Cynthia Brown, *'Challenging Impunity: The Ley de Caducidad and the Referendum Campaign in Uruguay'* (Human Rights Watch 1989).

from the amnesty under the presidencies of Tabare Vázquez (2005–10) and José Mujica (2010–present), because the law allowed the Executive branch to do so. As a result, around thirty cases of human rights violations under the dictatorship were successfully tried or under trial in Uruguay as of 2010.[82] In response to the *Gelman* decision by the Inter-American Court, in 2011 the Congress passed a law to 'interpret' the *Ley de Caducidad* and, in effect, to authorize the prosecution of military and police figures protected by the impunity legislation. In February 2013, the Supreme Court ruled some aspects of the 'interpretative law' unconstitutional, significantly affirming that even the nature of crimes against humanity of the deeds would not overcome the application of the statute of limitation in favour of the accused. As of mid-2013, the status of the struggle against impunity for the crimes of the military dictatorship remains undefined.

In Brazil, prosecutors tried to break through the amnesty laws in several notorious cases, like the disappearance of around sixty insurgents captured by the Army in the case known as *Guerrilha do Araguaia*, for which the Inter-American Court had demanded an investigation, prosecution, and punishment in *Gomes Lund v Brazil*. As of May 2012, those initiatives had faced the obstacle of the amnesty law, which the Supreme Court has upheld, even despite the Inter-American Court ruling. Nevertheless, a military officer known to have participated in those abductions and subsequent disappearances has been arraigned.

Peru marked a very significant victory over impunity in 2010, when a criminal law panel of the Supreme Court convicted former President Alberto Fujimori and sentenced him to twenty-six years in prison. Fujimori was found guilty as the 'actor behind the scenes' in two notorious cases of murder and disappearance: *Barrios Altos* and *La Cantuta*[83]—both of which the Inter-American Commission and Court of Human Rights had analysed. Peru's accountability efforts are notable, not only for prosecuting a former head of state, but also for bringing charges against and prosecuting former members of the guerilla forces, most notably the Shining Path, through a specialized terrorism court.[84] Despite severe political obstacles, several other human rights cases have been criminally prosecuted since the fall of the Fujimori regime in 2000; the Supreme Court has confirmed seven convictions and three acquittals, and in 2010 some thirty cases were underway.[85]

[82] Martin Prats, 'Uruguay' in Fundación para el Debido Proceso Legal, *Las Víctimas y la Justicia Transicional: ¿Están Cumpliendo Los Estados Latinoamericanos con los Estándares Internacionales?* (Fundación para el Debido Proceso Legal 2010).

[83] *La Cantuta v Peru*.

[84] See generally Luis E Francia Sánchez, 'Criminal Trial of Terrorist Organizations' in Lisa Magarrell and Leonardo Filippini (eds), *The Legacy of Truth: Criminal Justice in the Peruvian Transition* (ICTJ 2006) 29–56.

[85] Carlos Rivera Paz, 'Perú' in Fundación para el Debido Proceso Legal (n 82).

In Colombia, efforts at accountability began under the Justice and Peace Law (Law 975) of 2005.[86] The law was designed to exchange the reduced sentences of demobilized paramilitaries bearing the highest responsibility for grave crimes committed in the course of the internal armed conflict, for the beneficiary's 'contribution to the attainment of national peace, collaboration with the justice system [including a full confession exposing the truth of the events], reparation for the victims, and adequate re-socialization'.[87] Very few trials have gone forward, and those most responsible for the commission of systematic and grave international crimes have not yet been investigated or punished.[88]

By early 2012, even in Guatemala, a place where impunity has had a long reign, a court had indicted a former dictator—Efraín Ríos Montt, indicted for committing genocide against Mayan Indian communities during the scorched earth campaigns conducted under his *de facto* presidency in the early 1980s. Rios Montt was tried in April of 2013, convicted of genocide against the Ixil community of Mayan Indians and sentenced to eighty years in prison. In May 2013 the Constitutional Court vacated the decision and ordered a retrial of certain aspects.

6.2 Truth reports

Truth-telling efforts require an organized and systematic process, especially where secrecy or denial has surrounded violations. Expert Priscilla Hayner proposed a set of core principles that truth-telling efforts should meet: (1) implementation, as the product of a national choice based on a broad consultative process; (2) coordination with other transitional justice mechanisms, as part of a comprehensive transitional justice strategy; (3) response to unique, country-specific needs; (4) the foundation of genuine political will and operational independence; and (5) reliance on international support.[89]

In Peru, truth-telling efforts made great strides through the implementation of the CVR. The CVR made particular inroads by conducting public hearings where victims were heard. The CVR comprehensively covered and investigated violations that state actors and insurgents committed.[90] Most recently, Brazil established a truth commission to provide 'a legal framework to open governmental records' and

[86] Diario Oficial No 45.980 of 25 July 2005 (Ley 975). Text in Spanish of Law 975 is available at <http://cja.org/downloads/Ley 975 de 2005>.

[87] Ley 975 (n 86) Art 1.

[88] 'Background: Demobilization, Justice and Peace Law, and Other Initiatives' (*ICTJ*) <http://ictj.org/our-work/regions-and-countries/colombia> accessed 15 October 2012.

[89] Suggestions adopted by the United Nations. See Office of the United Nations High Commissioner for Human Rights, 'Rule-of-Law Tools for Post-Conflict States: Truth Commissions' (2006) UN Doc HR/PUB/06/1, 5–6.

[90] See generally Gloria Cano and Karim Ninasquipe, 'The Role of Civil Society in Demanding and Promoting Justice' in Magarrell and Filippini (n 84) 42–43.

make it possible for the country to 'start to break the wall of silence that forbids Brazilians from knowing their own history' while furthering human rights advocacy efforts overall.[91]

6.3 Reparations

In regard to reparations, there is little guidance on *quantum* or mode of reparation, but at a minimum, state programmes are required to universally cover victims and provide for simple, accessible procedures. Therefore, in general, an administrative scheme is preferable to judicial determinations. The Inter-American Court of Human Rights has always ordered the payment of reparations when it has found a violation of a right under the American Convention on Human Rights, and states have generally complied with this part of the Court's orders. The Commission routinely recommends the payment of reparations in accordance with domestic law. In the 1990s, Brazil offered reparations to the families of the disappeared in the events known as *Guerrilha do Araguaia*, but there has been no comprehensive plan to compensate all victims of the military dictatorship thus far. Uruguay has paid the reparations that the domestic courts have ordered in a number of successful lawsuits. In the case of Peru, the Fujimori regime paid reparations to the families of victims in one case. Argentina and Chile have created comprehensive administrative schemes that cover the victims of both dictatorships and that feature a simple, straightforward administrative process and fairly generous monetary settlements for the beneficiaries. Peru and Colombia are developing such programmes as of 2012.

6.4 Institutional reform

Efforts related to institutional reform should assert civilian, democratic supervision over the state institutions through which violations were committed (police, armed forces, prosecutors, and courts, in some cases). Moreover, the state should emphasize vetting officials to disqualify those who have abused their power and to provide for mechanisms of control and supervision ('horizontal accountability'), and human rights education.[92] In this area, the efforts have been less systematic,

[91] Eduardo Gonzalez, 'Brazil Shatters its Wall of Silence' (*ICTJ*, 6 December 2011) <http://ictj.org/news/brazil-shatters-its-wall-silence-past> accessed 15 October 2012.

[92] See United Nations High Commissioner for Human Rights, 'Rule-of-Law Tools for Post-Conflict States: Vetting: An Operational Framework' (2006) UN Doc HR/PUB/06/5, 4 (noting other institutional reform measures, including: 'the creation of oversight, complaint and disciplinary procedures; the reform or establishment of legal frameworks; the development or revision of ethical guidelines and codes of conduct; changing symbols that are associated with abusive practices; and the provision of adequate salaries, equipment and infrastructure'). See also Roger Duthie, 'Introduction' in Alexander

and yet, after decades of democracy and the rule of law, the military establishments are now very different. El Salvador conducted an important vetting exercise in the mid-1990s, as part of the peace agreements that, under UN sponsorship, put an end to the armed conflict. A special commission of Salvadoran notables, asked to look at the behaviour of the top ranks of the military during the war, produced a report recommending the dismissal of more than one hundred high-ranking, active duty officers. Although the report caused considerable turmoil, the government implemented the recommendations. The Salvadoran Armed Forces continue to be professionalized and subordinate to civilian authority.

The same can be said of the armed forces in all three Southern Cone countries. By a combination of reduced military spending, forced retirement of some elements and refusal to promote others, participation in international peace-keeping missions, and reform of education and training programmes, the military establishments no longer threaten democracy. Domestic laws have been amended so that military forces are not allowed to participate in internal security operations. Pending, however, are effective means of transforming and reforming police bodies, despite some encouraging efforts that were ultimately frustrated by political interventions.

7. Conclusion: Human Rights and the Quality of Democracy

Latin America is experiencing a long spell of governments emanating from popular vote in unquestionably fair elections. As noted above, the temptations of authoritarianism are far from over, as some elected leaders accumulate power and weaken institutions of control in what the late Guillermo O'Donnell, quoting Max Weber, has called 'delegative democracy' and 'sultanistic' exercises of power.[93] This is undoubtedly a serious challenge for the quality of democracy and for the effective exercise of human rights, because without independent judiciaries, human rights are fragile. In addition, authoritarian regimes tend to suppress freedom of expression in a variety of ways, although for now, at least, independent and opposition media is alive in every country.

Meyer-Rieckh and Pablo de Greiff (eds), *Justice as Prevention: Vetting Public Employees in Transitional Societies* (Social Sciences Research Council 2007) 17.

[93] Guillermo O'Donnell, 'Delegative Democracy' (1994) 5 *Journal of Democracy* 55, 59; Guillermo O'Donnell, 'Horizontal Accountability in New Democracies' (1998) 9 *Journal of Democracy* 112, 117.

Throughout the region, the culture of human rights permeates publicly and puts some brakes on the undemocratic tendencies of powerful elites. Human rights has become the language of the most influential and well-functioning independent organizations of civil society. Latin Americans organize themselves in a multitude of institutions with a broad variety of mandates, and they find ways of using judicial, legislative, administrative, and public policy mechanisms to promote their agendas. They have also become proficient in using the media and social networks to disseminate those agendas and to gather support.

Magistrates and prosecutors have become more attuned to finding ways to implement human rights, including economic, social, and cultural rights, by applying constitutional and international law standards. Advocates have successfully applied their principles to advance protection of rights through judicial decisions, as well as through legislative measures.

Even if a causal relationship is difficult to prove, it seems evident that the stability of democracy in Latin America has a lot to do with the fact that both large majorities of the population and the parties with a truly democratic vocation have embraced human rights. With the invaluable assistance of the regional organs of protection, Latin Americans are making a strong contribution to the development of international law everywhere, and to the consolidation of democracy and the rule of law in their own countries.

Further Reading

Cameron MA and Hershberg E (eds), *Latin America's Left Turn: Politics, Policies and Trajectories of Change* (Lynne Rienner 2010)

Lichtenfeld R, 'Accountability in Argentina: 20 Years Later, Transitional Justice Maintains Momentum' (August 2005) International Center for Transitional Justice <http://ictj.org/sites/default/files/ICTJ-Argentina-Accountability-Case-2005-English.pdf> accessed 15 October 2012

Méndez JE, O'Donnell G, and Pinheiro PS (eds), *The Un-Rule of Law & the Underprivileged in Latin America* (University of Notre Dame Press 1999)

Méndez JE with Wentworth M, *Taking a Stand: The Evolution of Human Rights* (Palgrave MacMillan 2011)

Roht-Arriaza N (ed), *Impunity and Human Rights in International Law and Practice* (OUP 1995)

Sikkink K, *The Justice Cascade: How Human Rights Prosecutions Are Changing World Politics* (Norton 2011)

Weschler L, *A Miracle, A Universe: Settling Accounts with Torturers* (University of Chicago Press 1990)

Index

Lightning Source UK Ltd.
Milton Keynes UK
UKOW05f1001210815
257298UK00001B/1/P

9 780198 748298